CRIMINAL
Investigation

TENTH EDITION

Brief Contents

SECTION 5 / OTHER CHALLENGES TO THE CRIMINAL INVESTIGATOR 506

APPENDIXES 675

Contents

CHAPTER 3

Writing Effective Reports   70

CHAPTER 4

Searches   94

CHAPTER 5
Forensics/Physical Evidence   122

CHAPTER 6
Obtaining Information and Intelligence   178

CHAPTER 7
Identifying and Arresting Suspects 212

SECTION 3 INVESTIGATING VIOLENT CRIMES 254

CHAPTER 8
Death Investigations 258

CHAPTER 9
Assault, Domestic Violence, Stalking and Elder Abuse
300

CHAPTER 10
Sex Offenses   324

CHAPTER 11
Crimes against Children   350

CHAPTER 12

SECTION 4 | INVESTIGATING CRIMES AGAINST PROPERTY 406

CHAPTER 13

CHAPTER 18
A Dual Threat: Drug-Related Crime
and Organized Crime   546

CHAPTER 21
Preparing for and Presenting Cases in Court   652

APPENDIXES   675

Preface

Welcome to *Criminal Investigation*, Tenth Edition. Designed to be one of the most practical, hands-on, reliable textbooks you will ever read, *Criminal Investigation* presents the procedures, techniques and applications of private and public investigation. The book seamlessly integrates coverage of modern investigative tools alongside discussion of established investigation procedures and techniques. The Tenth Edition features updated, enhanced coverage of such important topics as terrorism and homeland security, cybercrime, forensics and physical evidence, federal law enforcement investigations, report writing, crimes against children, investigative photography and sketching, preparing and presenting cases in court, identity theft, white-collar crime and much more.

Forensics and crime-scene investigation are increasingly popular components of criminal investigation courses today and are correspondingly emphasized in this text, which features complete coverage of digital fingerprinting, DNA evidence and databases, ballistics, body-fluid collection and examination, contamination of evidence, new technologies, exhibiting evidence in court and new technologies that are changing the way crime scenes are documented through photography, sketching and so on.

Opportunities in investigations have altered since the terrorist attacks of September 11, 2001. New careers have opened up in federal law enforcement, and interest in working with federal agencies has grown among job seekers. This new edition increases its focus on federal investigations. It also delves more deeply into the fight against terrorism and the ways in which law enforcement—whether federal, state or local—must be involved and must work collaboratively with other agencies to be effective.

Criminal Investigation can serve as an overview of the entire field or as a solid foundation for specialized coursework. Although the content of each chapter could easily be expanded into an entire book or course, this text provides the basic concepts of each area of investigation and will prove to be an invaluable reference long after students move on from the classroom.

ORGANIZATION OF THE TEXT

In Section 1, the student is introduced to the broad field of criminal investigation; to the elements of an effective, efficient investigation; and to the equipment, technology and procedures that facilitate investigation (Chapter 1). Important court cases and decisions are cited and explained throughout the text.

Section 2 is designed to acquaint readers with various investigative responsibilities: documenting the scene by note taking, photographing and sketching (Chapter 2); writing reports (Chapter 3); searching crime scenes and suspects (Chapter 4); identifying and collecting physical evidence for forensic examination (Chapter 5); obtaining information and intelligence (Chapter 6); and identifying and arresting suspects (Chapter 7).

Sections 3, 4 and 5 illustrate how these responsibilities are carried out in specific types of investigations. Section 3 discusses the basics in investigating violent crimes: death investigations (Chapter 8); assault, domestic violence, stalking and elder abuse (Chapter 9); sex offenses (Chapter 10); crimes against children (Chapter 11); and robbery (Chapter 12). Section 4 discusses crimes against property: burglary (Chapter 13); larceny/theft, fraud and white-collar crime (Chapter 14); motor vehicle theft (Chapter 15); and arson, bombs and explosives (Chapter 16). Section 5 discusses other investigative challenges: computer crimes and their evolution into cybercrimes (Chapter 17); the dual threats of drug-related crime and organized crime (Chapter 18); the illegal activities of gangs and other dangerous groups, such as hate groups and cults (Chapter 19); terrorism and homeland security (Chapter 20); and the culmination of investigations: preparing for and presenting cases in court (Chapter 21).

NEW TO THIS EDITION

The Tenth Edition of *Criminal Investigation* has been completely updated with more than 190 new references, most of which were published between 2008 and 2011. Through the use of color, we capture the details of technical photographs and other instructional images, which facilitates more complete student understanding of the material. A truly exhaustive revision, the Tenth Edition features the following chapter-by-chapter enhancements:

■ *Chapter 1: Criminal Investigation: An Overview*— This chapter has added to the history of criminal investigation, expanded Table 1.1 (Major Advances in Criminal Investigation), added a new Table 1.2 (A Brief Summary of the Investigative Process), added to the discussion on setting up a crime scene perimeter, added how community corrections personnel and social services may help investigators and updated the statistics regarding victimization and the caseload of forensic crime labs.

■ *Chapter 2: Documenting the Crime Scene: Note Taking, Photographing and Sketching*—Updated and expanded the discussion on digital photography, deleted content about film and added a new Technology Innovation.

■ *Chapter 3: Writing Effective Reports*—This chapter has expanded the section on digital report writing and citizen online reporting, added the term *disposition* and included a new Technology Innovation.

■ *Chapter 4: Searches*—Six new court decisions dealing with searches are discussed: consent to search (*United States v. Matlock*, 1974; *Wright v. United States*, 1938; *Illinois v. Rodriguez*, 1990), exigent circumstances and warrantless searches (*Michigan v. Fisher*, 2009), vehicle searches (*Arizona v. Gant*, 2009) and warrantless search/seizure of trash located within the cartilage (*United States v. Segura-Baltazar*, 2006). The discussion of consent to search has been expanded slightly and a new term has been added: *nightcapped warrant*.

■ *Chapter 5: Forensics/Physical Evidence*—We restructured the section on "Protecting, Storing and Managing Evidence"; added the FBI's new Advanced Fingerprint Identification Technology (AFIT) system, as part of their new Next Generation Identification (NGI) initiative; added a new discussion on using DNA to solve property crimes; updated the DNA analysis section to include current data and statistics, as well as the DNA Fingerprint Act of 2005; created a new table on collecting DNA evidence; added to the discussions of firearms/ammunition evidence and collecting

evidence involving weapons of mass destruction; provided new information on collecting shoe/tire impressions in snow; expanded the discussion of digital evidence (although most new content will follow in Chapter 17); and added a new Technology Innovation.

■ *Chapter 6: Obtaining Information and Intelligence*— This chapter includes new content about conducting neighborhood canvasses; defines four new terms: *closed-ended question, open-ended question, leading question,* and *dying declaration*; and covers five new court cases related to *Miranda*—no exact wording is required to satisfy *Miranda* (*Florida v. Powell*, 2010); interrogating after *Miranda* (*Maryland v. Shatzer*, 2010; *United States v. Banks*, 2003; *Burket v. Angelone*, 2000; *Dormire v. Wilkinson*, 2001).

■ *Chapter 7: Identifying and Arresting Suspects*—New content on the use of backscatter X-ray devices in surveillance; new case (*United States v. Garcia*, 2007) in discussion on GPS devices used in surveillance; new linear use-of-force continuum; updated material on CEDs/TASERs; expanded coverage of the PIT maneuver as an alternate use of force technique; and new Technology Innovations, including acoustic surveillance.

■ *Chapter 8: Death Investigations*—All crime statistics have been updated to the most recently available (2009 FBI UCR data); added two new terms: *clearance rate,* and *postmortem artifact*; added new content on posing versus staging and the challenges of staged homicide scenes; updated the content on excited delirium; added post-traumatic stress disorder (PTSD) as contributor to officer suicide; new content on how skeletal remains can be analyzed to aid in identification; new information on cold cases; and many new photos.

■ *Chapter 9: Assault, Domestic Violence, Stalking and Elder Abuse*—This chapter, with crucial information for future law enforcement professionals who continue to be called on to respond to domestic and family violence calls, includes new statistics on domestic violence and elder abuse expanded content on intimate partner violence and weapons used, a new table on "Evidence Obtained in Intimate Partner Violence Cases in 16 Large Counties, by Charge Type," and an updated and expanded discussion on stalking, including challenges to investigation.

■ *Chapter 10: Sex Offenses*—This chapter includes new statistics and content on sex trafficking victims and suspects; updated rape statistics; new material on the Violence Against Women Act (VAWA); and an explanation of the distinction between forcible rape, drug- or alcohol-facilitated rape and incapacitated rape.

- *Chapter 11: Crimes against Children*—This chapter includes updated statistics on child abuse and neglect; new content regarding evidence to seek in investigating child sexual abuse; updated content and statistics on SIDS investigations; a new term, *sexting*; and a new table comparing two child molester typologies (FBI). Some of the lists that were aimed more at parents and caregivers than at criminal investigators were deleted.

- *Chapter 12: Robbery*—This chapter includes updated crime statistics on robbery and new content on carjacking. Robbery identification figures were deleted.

- *Chapter 13: Burglary*—This chapter includes updated statistics on burglary.

- *Chapter 14: Larceny/Theft, Fraud and White-Collar Crime*—All crime statistics have been updated. New content was added regarding organized retail crime (ORC) and cargo theft.

- *Chapter 15: Motor Vehicle Theft*—This chapter includes updated statistics on the most common stolen vehicles and the most commonly cloned vehicles.

- *Chapter 16: Arson, Bombs and Explosives*—The chapter contains updated statistics on arson as well as a better defined classification of fires, including definitions provided by the National Fire Protection Association pursuant to Code 921 (national guidelines for fire and explosion investigations). The chapter also has expanded content on insurance loss investigators and who to interview during the preliminary fire investigation.

- *Chapter 17: Computer Crime*—The latest techniques for investigating cybercrime are addressed in this chapter, along with key information on new crimes and criminal strategies online. In addition to updated statistics, new terminology (*dynamic IP address, phishing, script kiddie, skimming, static IP address*) and results from the most recent electronic crimes surveys, the chapter has new content about prosecuting computer crimes and the Computer Fraud and Abuse Act of 1986 as well as a new table listing types of digital evidence to look for when investigating specific crimes.

- *Chapter 18: A Dual Threat: Drug-Related Crime and Organized Crime*—This chapter includes updated crime statistics, new material on the harmful cutting agent used in cocaine production, new content on K2/"spice," a synthetic form of marijuana, and a new term, *body packing*. Also, the table on the meth production process was omitted and replaced with a list of things an investigator should do when processing a meth lab.

- *Chapter 19: Criminal Activities of Gangs and Other Dangerous Groups*—This chapter has incorporated new statistics regarding gangs and hate crimes as well as changed the term *swarming* to *flash mob*; restructured and tightened up the section on "types of gangs" and deleted many types as terms; reduced the coverage given to general descriptive content of gangs and placed more emphasis on the law enforcement response to gangs and investigating gang activity; added a Technology Innovations box in the graffiti discussion; and updated strategies used to address gangs and the gang problem.

- *Chapter 20: Terrorism and Homeland Security*—Terrorism and homeland security are increasingly hot topics for law enforcement, and this chapter has been thoroughly updated, including the most recently available statistics and survey results regarding terrorism. There is also a slight reduction on descriptive content of some terrorist groups to allow room to add content on the investigative response to terrorism.

- *Chapter 21: Preparing for and Presenting Cases in Court*—This key chapter has been reviewed to be sure it helps prepare future investigators to defend their cases in a court of law.

HOW TO USE THIS TEXT

Criminal Investigation is a carefully structured learning experience. The more actively you participate in it, the more you will learn. You will learn and remember more if you first familiarize yourself with the total scope of the subject. Read and think about the table of contents, which provides an outline of the many facets of criminal investigation.

Then follow these steps for *quadruple-strength learning* as you study each chapter.

1. Read the objectives at the beginning of the chapter. These are stated as *Do You Know?* questions and are designed to help you assess your current knowledge of the subject of each question. Consider any preconceptions you may hold. Also, look at the key terms in the *Can You Define?* section, and watch for them when they are used.

2. Read the chapter while underlining, highlighting or taking notes—whatever is your preferred study method. Pay special attention to all highlighted information or words that appear in boldface type. The former represent the answers to the chapter-opening *Do You Know?* questions, and

the latter comprise the key terms identified in the chapter-opening *Can You Define?* section.

3. When you have finished reading the chapter, read the Summary—your third exposure to the chapter's key information. Then return to the beginning of the chapter and quiz yourself. Can you answer the *Do You Know?* questions? Can you define the key terms?

4. Finally, in Sections 3, 4 and 5, complete the Application exercises at the end of each chapter. These exercises ask you to apply the chapter concepts in actual or hypothetical cases. Then read the Discussion Questions and be prepared to contribute to a class discussion of the ideas presented in the chapter.

By following these steps, you will learn more information, understand it more fully and remember it longer.

Note: The material selected to highlight using the quadruple-strength learning instructional design includes only the chapter's key concepts. Although this information is certainly important in that it provides a structural foundation for understanding the topic(s) discussed, you cannot simply glance over the *Do You Know?* highlighted boxes and summaries and expect to master the chapter. You are also responsible for reading and understanding the material that surrounds these boxed features.

EXPLORING FURTHER

The text also provides an opportunity for you to apply what you have learned or to go into specific areas in greater depth through discussions and Internet assignments. Explore each of these areas as directed by the text or by your instructor. Be prepared to share your findings with the class. Good learning!

ANCILLARIES

Book-Specific Supplement for Students

CourseMate — Criminal Justice CourseMate is available for *Criminal Investigation*, 10th edition. This CourseMate includes:

■ An interactive eBook, with highlighting, note taking and search capabilities

■ Interactive learning tools including:

- Quizzes

- Flashcards
- Videos
- Study Guide (including numerous exercises and self-tests)
- Case Studies
- and more!

To learn more about this resource and access free demo CourseMate resources, go to **www.cengagebrain.com**, and search by this book's ISBN (9781133018926). To access CourseMate materials that you have purchased, go to login.cengagebrain.com, enter your access code, and create an account or log into your existing account.

Book-Specific Supplements for Instructors

Instructor's Resource Manual with Test Bank — This manual offers you learning objectives, key terms, lecture outlines, discussion questions, active learning suggestions, supplemental lecture ideas, student activities and projects and additional resources for instructors. Also included is a test bank of more than 1,200 questions in multiple-choice, true/false, fill-in-the-blank and essay formats, along with a full answer key. ISBN: 9781133018933.

PowerLecture — This one-stop lecture and class preparation tool makes it easy for you to assemble, edit and present custom lectures for your course using Microsoft® PowerPoint®. PowerLecture™ includes lesson plans, real-world resources, text-specific lecture outlines, art from the text and more. The DVD-ROM also contains ExamView® computerized testing, which allows you to create tests in minutes using items from the test bank in electronic format. ISBN: 9781133018995.

CourseMate with Engagement Tracker — Criminal Justice CourseMate is available for *Criminal Investigation*, 10th edition.

The instructor version of CourseMate includes Engagement Tracker, a first-of-its-kind tool that monitors student engagement in the course. Instructors also have full access to the interactive eBook and other student CourseMate resources.

To access this CourseMate with Engagement Tracker, go to login.cengage.com, sign in with your SSO (single sign-on) login, and add this title to your bookshelf. (Note: Engagement Tracker monitors students who have purchased access to CourseMate.)

Companion Web Site — The Instructor Companion Web site to accompany *Criminal Investigation*, 10th Edition, features PowerPoint® lecture slides, the instructor's resource manual and test banks in ExamView®, Blackboard and rich text format. ISBN: 9781133438830.

WebTutor™ Advantage Plus on Blackboard® with eBook — Jumpstart your online course with customizable, rich, text-specific content—all easily and immediately accessible within your existing learning management system. Simply load a WebTutor™ cartridge into your course management system and add, edit, reorganize or delete content—quizzes, learning objectives, flashcards, Web links, games, exercises and more—as you see fit. Plus, use your book's test bank and your own gradebook to make assessment easier than ever. Whether you want to Web-enable your class or put an entire course online, WebTutor delivers. Visit www.cengage.com/webtutor to learn more. ISBN: 9781133018971.

Discipline-Wide Supplements Related to This Text

The following supplements, referenced in this text but not produced specifically for this text, are available to qualified adopters. Instructors, please consult your Cengage Learning sales representative for details.

ONLINE Database **Gale's Custom Journals Database for Emergency Services and Criminal Justice** — *Criminal Investigation*, 10th edition, contains exercises referencing Gale's Custom Journals Database for Emergency Services and Criminal Justice, available for bundling with criminal justice titles. Containing customized portions of the Gale Journals Database (which is known for its accurate and authoritative reference content), this Custom Journals Database provides a 24/7 library reference of the latest information and research in this topic area. Learners who desire additional resources and research beyond the scope of their textbook will find this to be a useful tool.

Instructors, talk to your Cengage Learning sales representative to find out about adding the database to your adoption of this textbook. Students, talk to your instructors to find out whether you have access to this database.

Features of the Gale Custom Journals Database include:

- Material drawn from magazines, academic journals, books, news and multimedia.
- Digital access allowing easy-to-use, powerful search capabilities, creating a great reference tool.

- Current articles to help students prepare for their careers by way of industry journal information.
- Additional tools such as citation tools, downloads and even translation features. ISBN: 978-1-4354-8232-6

 Crime and Evidence in Action CD-ROM — Criminal Justice CourseMate for *Criminal Investigation*, 10th edition, includes exercises based on this engaging simulation that provides an interactive discovery of criminal investigations. This CD-ROM, which is available for purchase separately from the text, features three in-depth crime-scene scenario cases that will allow students to analyze crime-scene evidence and then make decisions that will affect the outcome of the case. Each case allows the student to take on various roles—from scene investigation (including forensics) to arrest, the trial, incarceration and even parole of the convicted felon. Students are encouraged to make choices as the case unfolds and conduct interactive investigative research in a simulated setting. ISBN: 9780534615314.

Additional Discipline-Wide Supplements

The following supplements can also help augment your course. Instructors, please consult your Cengage Learning sales representative for details.

Careers in Criminal Justice Web Site — The Careers in Criminal Justice Web site offers extensive career profiling information and self-assessment testing designed to help students investigate and focus on the criminal justice career choices that are right for them. This resource-rich Web site includes over 70 Career Profiles and more than 25 video interviews with links and tools to assist students in finding a professional position. It also features a career Rolodex, interest assessments and a career planner with sample résumés, letters, interview questions and more. View a demo at academic.cengage.com/criminaljustice/careers. ISBN: 9780495595236 (Instant Access Code)/9780495595229 (Printed Access Card)

Crime Scenes 2.0: An Interactive Criminal Justice CD-ROM — This simulation CD-ROM uses six scenarios of various crimes (juvenile murder, prostitution assault, arresting force/DUI, search and seizure, embezzlement/white-collar crime and incarceration classification/parole) to illustrate all of the stages of the criminal justice system. The student is able to make choices about the outcomes of the simulation at various decision points in each scenario, thus illustrating the consequences of each choice. The scenarios utilize video, court room drawings and numerous forms to build the evidence of each case. This CD-ROM can be used to introduce new material, as a reviewing device, to spark class discussions or as a basis for group research projects. And students can use this exciting and game-like CD-ROM to explore on their own. ISBN: 9780534568313.

Careers in Criminal Justice and Related Fields: From Internship to Promotion, Sixth Edition

— (J. Scott Harr and Kären M. Hess) This supplemental book helps students develop a job-search strategy through résumés, cover letters and interview techniques. It also provides students with extensive information on various criminal justice professions, including job descriptions, job salary suggestions and contact information. ISBN: 9780495600329.

Wadsworth's Guide to Careers in Criminal Justice, Third Edition

— (Carol Mathews, Century College) This handy, concise booklet provides a brief introduction to the exciting and diverse career choices in the criminal justice field. Students learn about opportunities in law enforcement, courts and corrections—and how to get those jobs. ISBN: 9780495130383.

InfoTrac® College Edition Student Guide for Criminal Justice

— This 24-page booklet provides detailed user guides for students that illustrate how to use the InfoTrac® College Edition database. Special features include login help, a complete search tips cheat-sheet and a topic list of suggested keyword search terms for criminal justice. ISBN: 9780534247195.

Acknowledgments

We would first like to acknowledge Wayne W. Bennett, LLB (d. 2004), a graduate of the FBI National Police Academy and lead author on the first few editions of *Criminal Investigation*, a text originally based on his 45 years of experience in law enforcement and investigation. He was the director of public safety for the Edina (Minnesota) Police Department as well as chief of police of Boulder City, Nevada. Bennett taught various aspects of criminal investigation for more than 30 years and was coauthor of *Management and Supervision in Law Enforcement* (4th edition).

Second, we must acknowledge Kären Matison Hess, PhD (d. 2010), the author who first developed this text with Bennett and carried it through eight very successful revisions, earning it the Text and Academic Authors Association's McGuffey Longevity Award in 2010. Dr. Hess was an instructor at Normandale Community College (Bloomington, MN) who crafted a line of enduring, practical textbooks in the fields of law enforcement and criminal justice that include *Criminal Procedure; Corrections in the Twenty-First Century: A Practical Approach; Introduction to Law Enforcement and Criminal Justice* (9th edition); *Introduction to Private Security* (5th edition); *Juvenile Justice* (5th edition); *Management and Supervision in Law Enforcement* (4th edition); *Community Policing: Partnerships for Problem Solving* (5th edition); *Police Operations* (4th edition); and *Careers in Criminal Justice: From Internship to Promotion* (6th edition). She was a member of the Academy of Criminal Justice Sciences (ACJS), the American Association of University Women (AAUW), the American Society for Industrial Security (ASIS), the International Association of Chiefs of Police (IACP), the International Law Enforcement Educators and Trainers Association (ILEETA), the Justice Research and Statistics Association (JRSA), the Police Executive Research Forum (PERF) and the Textbook and Academic Author's Association (TAA). In 2006, Dr. Hess was honored by the University of Minnesota College of Education and Human Development at the school's 100-year anniversary as one of 100 alumni who have made a significant contribution to education and human development. Without her tireless dedication to authorship and the education of criminal justice students, this text—and the many others she developed—would not have the 30-year track record of success that it does. Her passion and commitment will forever be an inspiration to us.

A number of professionals from academia and the field have reviewed the previous editions of *Criminal Investigation* and provided valuable suggestions, and we thank them all: Joel J. Allen, Western Illinois University; Thomas Allen, University of South Dakota; Captain Frank Anzelmi, Pennsylvania State Police; Greg Arnold, Manatee Community College; John Ballard, Rochester Institute of Technology; Robert Barthol, Chabot College; Alison McKenney Brown, Wichita State University; Jeffrey Bumgarner, Minnesota State University; Joseph Bunce, Montgomery College; William Castleberry, University of Tennessee at Martin; Walt Copley, Metropolitan State College of Denver; Edward Creekmore, Northland Community College; Elmer Criswell, Harrisburg Area Community College; Tom Cuda, Bunker Hill Community College; Stanley Cunningham, Western Illinois University; Andrew Dantschich, St. Petersburg Junior College; Chris DeLay, University of Louisiana at Lafayette; Everett Doolittle, Metropolitan State University; Wayne Dunning, Wichita State University; Cass Gaska, Henry Ford Community College; Bruce Gordon, University of Cincinnati; Edmund Grosskopf, Indiana State University; Robert E. Grubb, Jr., Marshall University; Keith Haley, University of Cincinnati; George Henthorn, Central Missouri State University; Robert Hewitt, Edison Community College; John Hicks, Hocking Technical College; Ron Holt, Mercer University; Robert R. Ives, Rock Valley College; George Keefer, Southern Illinois University at Carbondale; Charles Thomas Kelly, Jr., Northwestern State University; Richard Kurek, Erie Community College North; Robert A. Lorinskas,

Southern Illinois University at Carbondale; Stan Malm, University of Maryland; Richard Mangan, Florida Atlantic University; Jane E. McClellan; Gayle Mericle, Western Illinois University; Michael Meyer, University of North Dakota; Jane Kravits Munley, Luzerne County Community College; Robert Neville, College of the Siskiyous; James F. Newman, Rio Hondo Community College; Thomas O'Connor, North Carolina Wesleyan College; William L. Pelkey, Eastern Kentucky University; Russ J. Pomrenke, Gwinnett Technical College; Ronald A. Pricom, New Mexico State University; Charles Quarles, University of Mississippi; Walter F. Ruger, Nassau Community College; Shelley Shaffer, Keiser University; Jo Ann Short, Northern Virginia Community College, Annandale; Joseph R. Terrill, Hartford Community College; Charles A. Tracy, Portland State University; Bob Walker, Trinity Valley Community College; and Richard Weber, Jamestown Community College.

We are also very grateful to the following reviewers for their constructive criticism and suggestions, which contributed significantly to this Tenth Edition: Kimberly Blackmon, Axia College of UOP, RETS College Online, and Central FL College Online; Thomas Drerup, Clark State Community College; James Lauria, Pittsburgh Technical Institute; Todd Lough, Western Illinois University; James Scariot, Heald College; and Jason Waller, Tyler Junior College.

We greatly appreciate the input of these reviewers. Sole responsibility for all content, however, is our own.

The authors also wish to thank the following individuals for adding valuable insight to the discussions concerning their respective areas of expertise: Jeffrey Liroff, Ray Fernandez, Timothy Kennedy and Captain Tommy Bibb for their contributions on cargo theft investigations; Richard Scott for his review of and input concerning computer crime and cyber crime investigations; and retired investigator Richard Gautsch for his careful review of the manuscript and for lending his exceptional personal experiences for inclusion in the text.

Additional special thanks go to Shelley Esposito and Anne Orgren, our editor and product manager, respectively, at Delmar; Sara Dovre Wudali, production editor at Buuji, Inc.; Robin Gold, our copyeditor; and Terri Wright, photo researcher.

Finally, thank you to our families and colleagues for their continuing support and encouragement throughout the development of *Criminal Investigation*, Tenth Edition.

About the Authors

Christine Hess Orthmann, M.S., has been writing and researching in various aspects of criminal justice for more than 20 years. She is a coauthor of numerous Cengage books, including *Community Policing: Partnerships for Problem Solving* (6th edition), *Corrections for the Twenty-First Century*, *Constitutional Law and the Criminal Justice System* (5th edition), *Introduction to Law Enforcement and Criminal Justice* (10th edition), *Management and Supervision in Law Enforcement* (6th edition) and *Police Operations* (5th edition), as well as a major contributor to *Introduction to Private Security* (5th edition), *Juvenile Justice* (5th edition) and *Careers in Criminal Justice and Related Fields: From Internship to Promotion* (6th edition). She is a member of the Academy of Criminal Justice Sciences (ACJS), the American Society of Criminology (ASC), the Text and Academic Authors Association (TAA) and the National Criminal Justice Honor Society (Alpha Phi Sigma) and is a reserve officer with the Rosemount (Minnesota) Police Department. Orthmann has a Master of Science Degree in criminal justice from the University of Cincinnati.

Kären Matison Hess, Ph.D., wrote extensively in the field of law enforcement and criminal justice. She was a member of the English department at Normandale Community College as well as the president of the Institute for Professional Development. Hess held a Ph.D. in instructional design from the University of Minnesota. Other texts Dr. Hess coauthored are *Criminal Procedure*; *Corrections in the Twenty-First Century: A Practical Approach*; *Introduction to Law Enforcement and Criminal Justice* (9th edition); *Introduction to Private Security* (5th edition); *Juvenile Justice* (5th edition); *Management and Supervision in Law Enforcement* (4th edition); *Community Policing: Partnerships for Problem Solving* (5th edition); *Police Operations* (4th edition); and *Careers in Criminal Justice: From Internship to Promotion* (6th edition).

Dr. Hess was a member of the Academy of Criminal Justice Sciences (ACJS), the American Association of University Women (AAUW), the American Society for Industrial Security (ASIS), the International Association of Chiefs of Police (IACP), the International Law Enforcement Educators and Trainers Association (ILEETA), the Justice Research and Statistics Association (JRSA), the National Council of Teachers of English (NCTE), the Police Executive Research Forum (PERF) and the Textbook and Academic Author's Association (TAA), of which she was a Fellow and also a member of the TAA Foundation Board of Directors.

About the Contributor

Sergeant Henry Lim Cho holds an M.A. in Human Services with an emphasis on Criminal Justice Leadership from Concordia University–St. Paul, Minnesota. He has worked in the field of criminal justice for more than 12 years, having held positions in private security, as a community service officer, police officer and detective. He currently holds the rank of Sergeant with the Rosemount (Minnesota) Police Department. Sgt. Cho has experience as a use-of-force instructor and a crime scene investigator. His professional memberships include the Minnesota Police and Peace Officer's Association, International Association of Identification—Minnesota Chapter, Minnesota Sex Crimes Investigator Association, High Technology Crime Investigation Association, National White Collar Crime Center and Fraternal Order of Police. Sgt. Cho has been published in the *Minnesota Police Journal*, appeared as a profile contributor in *Introduction to Law Enforcement and Criminal Justice* (9th edition) and is a contributor to *Police Operations* (5th edition) and *Introduction to Law Enforcement and Criminal Justice* (10th edition).

SECTION 1
INTRODUCTION

1 | Criminal Investigation: An Overview

Welcome to criminal investigation. What are you in for? Here's a glimpse . . .

New to law enforcement, Officer Richard Gautsch found himself standing over the bullet-ridden corpse of a 15-year-old gas station attendant. The boy had been robbed, kidnapped and brutally executed, all for the 48 bucks in his pocket, and Gautsch's view of the world was forever changed. The 24-year-old detective (the youngest in Minnesota) had had little time to transition from life as a college jock to the violent world of murder investigations. And although naïve and inexperienced, he played a lead role in the pursuit, arrest and conviction of the two murder suspects.

During the next five years with a suburban metro police department, Gautsch worked a variety of major cases throughout the metropolitan area, including numerous undercover assignments. His youthful appearance quickly landed him in the middle of a major angel dust investigation, and it didn't take long for him to realize that the glitz and glamour of *Miami Vice* was pure fiction. Detective Gautsch

unexpectedly found himself in a car with two dealers, his informant and a lit pipe full of the pungent chemical. As the pipe was being passed around, the dealers demanded to know why Gautsch wasn't inhaling. The informant (who was inhaling deeply) asked the same question. With no weapon or backup, Gautsch suddenly felt a sensation he'd never seen portrayed by the heroes of those one-hour cop shows—fear and the urge to flee. After a sprint to safety, Gautsch wondered if he'd chosen the right career.

As the young detective gained experience, he learned that successful investigations rely on communication skills and attention to tedious tasks. Searching filthy attics and sifting through the rotting contents of a dumpster are more common than are excitement and intrigue. Investigators' abilities to interview and to write reports are far more important than how accurately they shoot or how fast they can drive.

Gautsch was promoted to detective supervisor and placed in charge of the Investigation Unit. That same year, he investigated the murder of a young police officer answering

a burglary call. The case was his most difficult—the officer was one of his best friends.

Five years later, Gautsch pinned on his captain's bars, his command expanding to include the Investigative Unit and a special multijurisdictional undercover task force. In 1988, he led a highly publicized murder investigation that stunned the entire community. After an argument with her boyfriend, a young mother was brutally stabbed to death in her apartment. The evidence against the boyfriend was so overwhelming that no one doubted his guilt, yet he remained uncharged. The community was outraged. Gautsch and his detectives doggedly pursued the suspect for three years, only to learn they had the wrong guy.

This thumbnail sketch of one detective's career offers a glimpse into the world of the criminal investigator. Criminal investigation is a complex, sophisticated field, each aspect of which could constitute a book. This text includes the most basic aspects of criminal investigation. Section 1 presents an overview of criminal investigation and general guidelines to follow or adapt in specific circumstances, as well as basic considerations in the preliminary investigation, the most critical phase in the majority of investigations.

Investigators must be thoroughly familiar with crimes and their elements, modus operandi (MO) information, the major goals of investigation, the basic functions of investigating officers and the investigators' relationships with other individuals and agencies.

Investigators do not operate in a vacuum but must relate to constitutional safeguards. They must also understand how case law determines the parameters within which they perform the investigative process. How these constitutional safeguards and case law specifically affect investigations is emphasized throughout the text.

CHAPTER 1

Criminal Investigation: An Overview

© Mario Tama/Getty Images

Outline

Can You Define?

civil liability
community policing
crime
crime mapping
criminal intent
criminal investigation
criminalist
criminalistics
criminal statute
culturally adroit
data mining
deductive reasoning
elements of the crime
exculpatory evidence
felony
forensic science
hot spots
inductive reasoning
intuition
investigate
leads
Locard's principle of exchange
misdemeanor
modus operandi (MO)
ordinance
res gestae statements

Do You Know?

- What criminal investigation is?
- What the major goals of criminal investigation are?
- What basic functions investigators perform?
- What do effective investigators do?
- What characteristics are important in investigators?
- Who usually arrives at a crime scene first?
- What should be done initially?
- What to do if a suspect is still at a crime scene? Has recently fled the scene?
- How the crime scene and evidence are protected and for how long?
- What responsibilities are included in the preliminary investigation?
- What the meaning and importance of *res gestae* statements are?
- How to determine whether a crime has been committed?
- Who is responsible for solving crimes?
- With whom investigators must relate?
- How to avoid civil lawsuits?

On April 19, 1995, Trooper Charlie Hanger of the Oklahoma Highway Patrol was traveling north on Interstate 35 when he saw a 1977 Mercury Marquis with no license plate. Hanger pulled the car over, and the only occupant, a white male, got out. While Hanger was questioning the driver about the license plate, the trooper noticed a bulge in the man's clothing. When asked, the man admitted he had a gun and was arrested. The driver—Timothy McVeigh—was later found responsible for the bombing of a federal building in Oklahoma City that killed 168 people and left hundreds injured. Some would say that the arrest was just plain luck. However, experience and alertness often play important roles.

An observant police officer can initiate an important criminal investigation, sometimes without realizing it at first. Criminal investigation combines art and science and requires extraordinary preparation and training. And in today's high-tech society, where information flows faster than ever and citizens expect results more quickly, investigators need to step up their technology and teamwork skills—they need an edge. The International Association of Chiefs of Police (IACP) declares,

> It's a new world and the role of the detective has changed dramatically. In the old world, shoe leather was the detective's primary tool. Luck and persistence were cornerstones of success. The key to managing a detective bureau was motivating the investigators.
>
> Now, in the information age, where technology advances daily, shoe leather is still important—as are luck and persistence—but aggressive detectives and their supervisors are constantly looking for a new edge. That edge might be a new method or approach to criminal investigations, or it may be the result of taking advantage of new developments in the forensic and management sciences. ("Recognizing Innovation," 2003, p.140)

Because no two crimes are identical, even if committed by the same person, each investigation is unique. The great range of variables in individual crimes makes it impossible to establish fixed rules for conducting an investigation. Nevertheless, some general guidelines help to ensure a thorough, effective investigation. Investigators modify and adapt these guidelines to fit each case.

Investigators need not have superhuman reasoning ability. They must, however, proceed in an orderly, systematic way, gathering facts to analyze and evaluate. This chapter introduces decisions to be made and the actions to be taken. Subsequent chapters explain each step of the preliminary investigation more fully.

A BRIEF HISTORY OF CRIMINAL INVESTIGATION

Contemporary criminal investigation owes its genesis to several notable individuals and events, the first significant one being the 1748 appointment of Henry Fielding as Magistrate of England's Bow Street. In 1750, as a response to widespread crime and disorder throughout his jurisdiction, Fielding formed the Bow Street Runners, which became the first paid detective unit.

Another noteworthy individual in the evolution of criminal investigation was Eugène François Vidocq, a former criminal turned crime fighter who is considered the father of modern criminology. In 1811 Vidocq organized a plain-clothed civilian detective unit called the Brigade de la Sûreté (Security Brigade), and in 1812, when the police realized the value of this unit, it was officially converted to the National Police Force, with Vidocq appointed head of the unit.

In 1833 Vidocq created Le Bureau des Renseignements (Office of Information), which combined private police and private investigation into what is considered the first private detective agency. Interestingly, most of the agents were ex-criminals. As head of the unit, Vidocq is often recognized as the first private detective in history. Vidocq is credited with introducing undercover

Henry Fielding (1707–1754)

Henry Fielding (1707–1754) engraved by Samuel Freeman (1773–1857) (engraving) (b&w photo), Hogarth, William (1697–1764) (after)/Private Collection/The Bridgeman Art Library

François Eugène Vidocq (1775–1857)

François Eugène Vidocq (1775–1857) (litho) (b&w photo), French School (19th century)/Bibliothèque Nationale, Paris, France/The Bridgeman Art Library

work, ballistics and criminology. He made the first plaster shoe cast impressions and created indelible ink and unalterable bond paper. The exclusive Vidocq Society—a fraternal organization whose members are both law enforcement professionals and nonprofessionals and meet monthly in a social setting to evaluate and discuss unsolved crimes, often homicides, officially brought to them by other law enforcement agencies—is named after him.

Also around this time, in 1842, England's Scotland Yard created an investigative branch.

Meanwhile, in the United States, the first municipal detective divisions were beginning to take shape. Allan Pinkerton, who immigrated from Scotland to the United States in 1842, played a significant historical role in modern police investigations. He was appointed the first detective in Chicago in 1849 and was a cofounder of the Northwestern police agency, which later became the Pinkerton National Detective Agency, whose symbol was a watchful eye and whose motto was, "We never sleep." Pinkerton's agents were the forerunners for the U.S. Secret Service, and his agency was employed at the federal level for many famous cases including protecting Abraham Lincoln in his presidency. Pinkerton developed several investigative techniques still used today in law enforcement that include stings and undercover work, as well as the surveillance methods of shadowing and following targets or suspects. He was also known for working on a centralized database of criminal identification records that is now maintained by the Federal Bureau of Investigation (FBI).

Investigative units also began cropping up in other police agencies after Chicago's lead, with Detroit establishing a detective bureau in 1866, followed by New York in 1882 and Cincinnati in 1886.

The use of biometrics and identification systems in criminal investigation began in 1882, when French police officer Alphonse Bertillon, now considered the father of personal identification, unveiled a system known as anthropometry, in which offenders were identified by their unique physical measurements, as well as personality characteristics and individual markings, such as tattoos and scars. In 1884, Bertillon used his technique to identify 241 multiple offenders, demonstrating that the Bertillon system could successfully distinguish first-time offenders from recidivists. The system was quickly adopted by American and British police forces.

Bertillon also standardized the criminal mug shot, advocated that crime scene pictures be taken before the scene was disturbed in any way and developed "metric photography" to reconstruct the dimensions of a particular space and the placement of objects in it. Other forensics techniques credited to Bertillon include forensic document examination, ballistics, the use of molding compounds to

President Abraham Lincoln (C), flanked by Major Allan Pinkerton (L) of the Pinkerton National Detective Agency and General John A. McClernand (R), visits the Union camp at Sharpsburg, Maryland in October 1862, a few weeks after the Battle of Antietam. Lincoln visited the camp in an attempt to persuade General George McClellan to take his army on the attack.
© Bettmann/CORBIS

preserve footprints and use of the dynamometer to determine the degree of force used in breaking and entering.

The field of criminalistics and forensics began taking shape in 1910, when Edmund Locard, a French criminologist, set forth his "exchange principle" stating that a criminal always removes something from a crime scene or leaves incriminating evidence behind. Under police leaders such as August Vollmer and J. Edgar Hoover, law enforcement and investigators in the United States began adopting Locard's exchange principle in 1932.

August "Gus" Vollmer, known as the father of modern policing, pioneered the movement to professionalize police by started the first school in which officers could learn the laws of evidence. In 1905 he was elected town marshal of Berkeley, California, and in 1909 he became its first police chief. However, before officially becoming the chief, Vollmer was bringing innovation to criminal investigation. In 1907 he became the first American officer to implement the use of blood, fiber and soil analysis in criminal investigations. In 1920 he was the first chief to have his department use the lie detector, an instrument developed by the University of California during a criminal investigation.

These early developments, as shown in Table 1.1, set the stage for a rapidly evolving field of criminal investigation in the United States. But what, exactly, *is* criminal investigation?

CRIMINAL INVESTIGATION DEFINITIONS

An investigation is a patient, step-by-step inquiry or observation, a careful examination, a recording of evidence or a legal inquiry. The word **investigate** is derived from the Latin word *vestigare*, meaning to track or trace, a derivation easily related to police investigation.

> A **criminal investigation** is the process of discovering, collecting, preparing, identifying and presenting evidence to determine what happened and who is responsible.

Criminal investigation is a reconstructive process that uses **deductive reasoning**, a logical process in which a conclusion follows from specific facts. Based on specific pieces of evidence, investigators establish proof that a suspect is guilty of an offense. For example, finding the suspect's watch at the scene of a burglary is one piece of evidence that supports the premise that the suspect was at the scene. An issue that might arise is whether the watch could have been planted there. Investigators need to anticipate what issues might arise and what evidence is needed to support the prosecutor's case. All issues in dispute must be supported by evidence. The more evidence an investigation yields, the stronger the proof of guilt. Equally important, however, is evidence establishing innocence.

OTHER TERMS DEFINED

Criminalistics refers to specialists trained in recording, identifying and interpreting the *minutiae* (minute details) of physical evidence. A **criminalist** (aka crime scene technician, examiner or investigator) searches for, collects and preserves physical evidence in investigations of crime and suspected criminals. Criminalistics is a branch of **forensic science**, which is a broader field encompassing the application of science to the law: "Forensic science involves applying scientific processes to solve legal problems, most notably within the context of the criminal justice system" (Fantino, 2007, p.26). Thus, forensic science covers a wide array of disciplines, including pathology, entomology, odontology, anthropology, photography, serology, toxicology and on and on.

TABLE 1.1 Major Advances in Criminal Investigation

1750	First paid detective unit forms in England—Fielding's Bow Street Runners.
1833	First private detective agency formed in France by Vidocq.
1849	Pinkerton becomes first American detective (in Chicago). Other municipalities across the country soon establish detective positions.
1868	DNA discovered.
1882	Alphonse Bertillon uses anthropometrics as a means of identification.
1893	First major book on investigation, *Criminal Investigation* by Austrian Hans Gross, published.
1896	Edward Henry developed a fingerprinting system, which was adopted throughout England in 1900.
1909	Dr. Karl Landsteiner discovered the different human blood types and classified them into the A, B, AB and O groups.
1910	Dr. Edmond Locard set forth his "exchange principle."
1913	Professor Victor Balthazard published his classic article on firearms identification.
1920s	Calvin Goddard raised firearms identification to a science and perfected the bullet comparison microscope.
1923	August Vollmer established the first full forensic laboratory, in Los Angeles.
Early 1950s	James Watson and Francis Crick identified the structure of DNA.
1967	FBI creates the National Crime Information Center (NCIC), which has been called the lifeline of law enforcement. A collective database that includes stolen items, identity of terrorists, missing persons and so forth, the system runs 24 hours a day, 365 days a year and is a resource used by all American as well as international law enforcement.
1970s	FBI implements the Behavioral Science Unit, more commonly known as "criminal profiling." This criminal investigation technique seeks to understand the psychological characteristics of an individual as a way to predict future crimes as well as narrow down a profile of a likely suspect in a case.
1979	Herman Goldstein's *Problem-Oriented Policing* published.
1985	Alec Jeffreys discovered the parts of the DNA structure that were unique in each person, making positive identification possible.
1986	First use of DNA typing in a criminal case, in England: DNA was used to clear a suspect in a murder. (A detective in the East Midlands read of the case and sought Jeffreys's help in solving the vicious murder and rape of two British schoolgirls. The police held a prime suspect in the case, a kitchen porter at an insane asylum who had confessed to one of the murders. They brought Jeffreys semen samples from the murder scenes and a blood sample from the suspect. Jeffreys confirmed that the same person committed both crimes, but it was not the suspect the police held. On November 21, 1986, the kitchen porter became the first person in the world to have his innocence proven by DNA testing.)
1988	First use of DNA typing in a criminal case, in the United States, in which a criminal was identified by DNA (*Florida v. Tommy Lee Andrews, 1988*). (Lifecodes Corporation [Stamford, CT] performed the tests in the first case in the United States in which a criminal was identified by DNA. The trial of accused rapist Tommy Lee Andrews began in Orlando, Florida, on November 3, 1987. A scientist from Lifecodes and an MIT biologist testified that semen from the victim matched Andrews's DNA and that Andrews's print would be found in only 1 in 10 billion individuals. On November 6, 1987, the jury returned a guilty verdict, and Andrews was subsequently sentenced to 22 years in prison.)
1994	CompStat developed in New York.
1998	FBI launches the Combined DNA Index System (CODIS), a database that stores DNA profiles submitted by law enforcement and private laboratories and is used to identify criminal suspects.
1999	FBI launches the Integrated Automated Fingerprint Identification System (IAFIS), a database that retains fingerprints taken from law enforcement and is used to identify suspects.
2011	FBI launches Next Generation Identification (NGI), a system upgrade to replace IAFIS that integrates a fingerprint database and incorporates other biometric identification methods, such as voice, facial recognition, iris recognition, fingerprint, palm print and more.

The first determination in a criminal investigation is whether a crime has, in fact, been committed. Does the evidence support a specific offense? A legal arrest cannot be made for an act that is not defined by statute or ordinance as a crime. Although everyone has a notion of what crime is, investigators must have a very precise understanding of what it means. Specific definitions of such terms as *crime, felony, misdemeanor, criminal statute* and *ordinance* are found in case law:

- A **crime** is an act in violation of penal law and an offense against the state. The broader use of the term includes both felonies and misdemeanors. A crime is a violation of a public right or law. It is an act or omission forbidden by law and punishable by a fine, imprisonment or even death. This contrasts with torts, or private harms.

- A **felony** is a serious crime, graver than a misdemeanor; it is generally punishable by death or imprisonment of more than one year in a penitentiary.

- A **misdemeanor** is a crime or offense that is less serious than a felony and is punishable by a fine or imprisonment of as long as one year in an institution other than a penitentiary.

- A **criminal statute** is a legislative act relating to a crime and its punishment.

- An **ordinance** is an act of the legislative body of a municipality or county relating to all the rules governing the municipality or county, including misdemeanors.

Crimes and their penalties are established and defined by state and federal statutes and local ordinances. An act that is not declared a crime by statute or ordinance is not a chargeable offense, no matter how wrong it may seem. Designated crimes and their punishments change as society's attitudes change. In the past, for example, behavior associated with alcoholism was considered criminal, but today many states regard alcoholism as an illness. However, driving while intoxicated is now considered a much more serious offense than it was previously. Conversely, our society has designated as crimes certain acts, such as computer fraud, that were unknown in earlier times.

Crimes fall into two general categories—felonies and misdemeanors—depending on the severity of an act and its recommended punishment. The more serious society considers a crime, the more severe the penalty. Investigations involve both types of crimes. Misdemeanors are sometimes further subdivided into gross and petty misdemeanors, based on the value of the property involved.

Because definitions of crimes and their penalties vary considerably depending on whether they occur at the municipal, county, state or federal level, investigators must be familiar with their area's criminal statutes and ordinances. For example, in some states, such as Michigan, shoplifting is a felony. Otherwise, in most states, the value of the shoplifted property determines whether the crime is a misdemeanor or a felony.

Statutes and ordinances list specific conditions, called the **elements of the crime**, that must occur for an act to be called a specific kind of crime. For example, a state statute might define burglary as occurring when (1) an accused enters a building (2) without the consent of the rightful owner (3) with the intent to commit a crime. An investigation must prove each element, even if the suspect has confessed. Many crimes have as an element **criminal intent**, that is, purposely performing an unlawful act or knowing an act to be illegal. Sections 3 and 4 of this text discuss the elements of major crimes. Knowing these elements is essential to gathering evidence to prove a crime has been committed.

In addition to proving a crime has been committed, investigators must determine who committed it. Investigation is often aided by knowing how criminals usually operate, that is, their **modus operandi**, or **MO**. For example, it was relatively easy to recognize the "work" of Jack the Ripper or the Washington DC–area snipers. The peculiarities of each crime scene may be entered into an MO file and matched with characteristics of known perpetrators of previous crimes. However, investigators must always be vigilant for the potential for "copycat" offenders.

MO information can provide clues in numerous cases. For example, if several burglaries are committed between 11 A.M. and 1 P.M. in one area of a community and all involve broken glass in a door, one may infer that the same individual committed the crimes. The probability of the burglaries being unrelated is low. One may further assume that the burglar would not commit armed robbery or other crimes unless surprised while committing a burglary.

Such assumptions are *not certainties*, however. Some criminals commit several types of crimes and may change the type according to need, opportunity, inability to repeat certain types of crimes or greater sophistication. For example, a narcotics user may commit larceny, burglary or robbery to obtain money for drugs. A burglar may switch from targeting residences to engaging in shoplifting or may first steal checks and a check writer and then turn to forgery to cash the checks. Suspects should never be eliminated simply because their known MO does not fit the crime being investigated.

GOALS OF CRIMINAL INVESTIGATIONS

The goal of criminal investigation would seem to be to solve cases, to discover "whodunit." In reality, the *goals* of criminal investigation are not quite so simple. To discover the truth and hold offenders to account, criminal investigation has several important goals.

The goals of criminal investigation are to
- Determine whether a crime has been committed.
- Legally obtain information and evidence to identify the responsible person.
- Arrest the suspect.
- Recover stolen property.
- Present the best possible case to the prosecutor.

While committing crimes, people may make mistakes. They almost always leave some type of evidence. They may overlook tangible evidence such as a jacket, pen, purse, piece of paper or card that connects them with a crime scene. Such evidence may be left for any number of reasons: carelessness, panic, underestimation of police capabilities, emotional or mental instability or the influence of drugs or alcohol. More often, however, criminals leave *trace evidence*, less visible evidence such as fingerprints, small particles of glass or dirt, a faint footprint, body hairs or clothing fibers.

Investigators search for evidence using methods discussed fully in Chapter 4. Sometimes, however, little or no evidence exists. Thus, not all crimes are solvable. For example, a theft committed by a transient who enters a house through an open door, takes food (larceny), eats it and then leaves the area unseen is a crime not likely to be solved. A burglary committed by a person wearing gloves and whose footprints are washed away by a hard rain before police arrive will be more difficult to solve than if it had not rained. Often fingerprints are found but cannot be matched with any prints on file. Many cases have insufficient evidence, no witnesses and no informants to provide leads.

Investigators learn to recognize when a case is unsolvable, but only after all **leads** (avenues bearing clues or potential sources of information relevant to solving the crime) have been exhausted. An FBI agent once remarked, "Any average person with training can pursue 'hot' leads. It is the investigator who can develop leads when the trail grows cold who is the superior investigator." A successful investigation is one in which

- A logical sequence is followed.
- All physical evidence is legally obtained.
- All witnesses are effectively interviewed.
- All suspects are legally and effectively interrogated.
- All leads are thoroughly developed.
- All details of the case are accurately and completely recorded and reported.

Investigators systematically seek evidence to identify the individual who committed a crime, locate the individual and obtain sufficient evidence to prove in court that the suspect is guilty beyond a reasonable doubt. Procedures to accomplish these goals are the focus of the remainder of this text. However, determining the truth is more important than obtaining a conviction or closing a case.

BASIC FUNCTIONS OF INVESTIGATORS

Successful investigation involves a balance between scientific knowledge acquired by study and experience and the skills acquired by the artful application of learned techniques. Police portrayals in mystery stories and on radio and television seldom depict police investigations accurately.

Police investigations involve great attention to detail, an exceptionally suspicious nature at the appropriate time, considerable training in the classroom and the field, an unusual ability to obtain information from diverse types of personalities under adverse circumstances and endless patience and perseverance.

Investigators perform the following functions:
- Provide emergency assistance
- Secure the crime scene
- Photograph, videotape and sketch
- Take notes and write reports
- Search for, obtain and process physical evidence
- Obtain information from witnesses and suspects
- Identify suspects
- Conduct raids, surveillances, stakeouts and undercover assignments
- Testify in court

Most of these basic functions are discussed in Section 2. What is important at this point is to realize the complexity of and interrelationships among the various functions performed by investigators and the skills they must develop.

Although criminal investigation has become increasingly scientific over the past two centuries, investigators are frequently required to practice the "art" of investigation, that is, to rely on skill acquired by experience, study and observation rather than on scientific principles. Investigators must develop the ability to see relationships between and among apparently unrelated facts and to question the apparently unquestionable.

CHARACTERISTICS OF AN EFFECTIVE INVESTIGATOR

A good investigator is knowledgeable, creative, patient and persistent. Regardless of title, pay or rank, investigative officers are more effective when they possess specific intellectual, psychological and physical characteristics.

Intellectual Characteristics

Investigators must absorb training and apply it to their work. They must know the elements of the crime, understand and be able to apply investigative techniques and be able to work with many different types of people. Exceptional intelligence is not a requisite trait of an effective investigator; objectivity, logic and common sense are more important.

Effective investigators obtain and retain information, apply technical knowledge, and remain open-minded, objective and logical. They are also **culturally adroit**, that is, skilled in interacting across gender, ethnic, generational, social and political group lines.

Investigators meet and talk with people from all walks of life—blue-collar workers and professionals, males and females, adults and juveniles—and must adjust their approach to each. In addition, each crime scene must be absorbed and recalled, sometimes months or years later. Thus, accurate, complete and well-organized reports and records are essential.

Investigators also develop knowledge of and skill in investigative techniques such as interviewing and interrogating, photographing and sketching, searching, note taking and numerous other areas discussed in Section 2. Such knowledge and skill is acquired through continuous training and experience, including academic classroom experiences, personal experiences, street learning and learning from others in the field.

The abilities to obtain and retain information and to use investigative techniques effectively are worth little without the ability to reason through a case. The mental process involved in investigation is extremely complex.

Popular television series such as CSI have brought the role of the criminal investigator into the public eye, perhaps leading to unrealistic expectations of how quickly or easily most cases can be solved.
© Eric Liebowitz/CBS Photo Archive via Getty Images

Logic is indispensable and often involves reverse thinking, that is, working the case backward. Why did an event happen? When? How? Who is culpable? Investigators must examine all possible cause-and-effect relations, find links and draw conclusions—but only after they thoroughly explore all alternatives.

Decision making is continual and, to be effective, must be based on facts. When investigators review information and evidence, they concentrate on what is known (facts), rather than on what is only probable (inferences), and they eliminate personal opinions as much as possible. With sufficient facts, investigators can make valid inferences, from which they can logically draw definite conclusions.

A *fact* is an action, an event, a circumstance or an actual thing done. In contrast, an *inference* is a process of reasoning by which a fact may be deduced (deductive reasoning). An *opinion* is a personal belief. For example, an investigator called to the scene of a shooting finds a dead man with a revolver in his hand (fact) and a suicide note on the table (fact). The officer might infer that the man committed suicide. He or she might also hold the opinion that people who commit suicide are cowards. This opinion is irrelevant to the investigation. The inference, however, is critical. If the officer formulates a theory about the death based on suicide and sets out to prove the theory correct, much information and evidence may be ignored. This is known as **inductive reasoning**, going from the generalization and establishing it by gathering specific facts. (Recall that criminal investigation is a reconstructive process that uses deductive reasoning.) Often both types of reasoning are required in an investigation.

Although investigators must draw inferences and form theories, they must also remain open-minded and willing to consider alternatives. Effective investigators guard against the tendency to become sold on a suspect or theory early in an investigation because such a mindset creates an investigative myopia or shortsightedness, fostering the subconscious shaping of evidence or interpreting information to support their premature theory. Preconceived ideas hinder good investigation; objectivity is essential. Whenever an inference is drawn, its validity should be tested by examining the facts on which it is based.

The investigator seeks the truth, not simply proof of the suspect's guilt. Article 10 of the *Canons of Police Ethics* (International Association of Chiefs of Police) states,

> The law enforcement officer shall be concerned equally in the prosecution of the wrongdoer and the defense of the innocent. He shall ascertain what constitutes evidence and shall present such evidence impartially and without malice. In so doing, he will ignore social, political and all other distinctions among the persons involved, strengthening the tradition of the reliability and integrity of an officer's word.
>
> The law enforcement officer shall take special pains to increase his perception and skill of observation, mindful that in many situations his is the sole impartial testimony to the facts of a case. (IACP, 1957)

Psychological Characteristics

Certain psychological characteristics are indispensable to effective investigation.

> **Effective investigators are emotionally well balanced, detached, inquisitive, suspecting, discerning, self-disciplined and persevering.**

Investigation is highly stressful and involves many decisions. Therefore, it requires emotional stability. Overly defensive or overly sensitive officers may fall victim to stress. Investigators must also absorb abuse and at the same time show kindness and empathy. Further, they must remain detached and uninvolved; otherwise, the problems of those with whom they are in contact will decrease their objectivity. Personal involvement with individuals associated with an investigation hinders the investigation and poses a direct threat to the investigator's emotional well-being.

Although remaining detached and objective, effective investigators are intimately involved with every aspect of the case. They do not accept things at face value; rather, they question what they hear and see. They use their knowledge of human nature to determine the truth of what is said. People often lie or tell half-truths, but this does not necessarily mean they are criminals. With experience, investigators develop a sense for who is telling the truth, who has important information and who is acting suspiciously. The ability to distinguish the ordinary from the extraordinary and the normal from the suspicious is a hallmark of an effective investigator.

In addition, investigators must be self-disciplined and able to organize their time. Closely related to self-discipline is the willingness to persevere, to "stick with it" as long as is reasonable. Investigation often involves hours, days or months of waiting and watching, of performing tedious, boring assignments that may or may not yield information or evidence helpful to the case. Thus, patience and perseverance are often the key to successful investigation. And although perseverance is desirable, it should not be confused with a stubborn refusal to admit a case is not likely to be solved.

Investigators often experience cases in which facts, reason and logic seem to lead nowhere. Yet, just when the case is about to be closed, an obscure newspaper item, an anonymous phone tip, an overheard remark at a social function or even a series of events having no apparent connection with the case may provide leads for further investigation. Many cases are solved when investigators develop leads and pursue both relevant and seemingly irrelevant information. This is where the art of investigation supersedes the science of investigation.

Perseverance, coupled with inquisitiveness and intuition, is indispensable in difficult cases. Scores of experienced investigators attest to the value of **intuition**, a "sudden knowing" without conscious reasoning or apparent logic. Based on knowledge and experience, intuition is commonly referred to as *street sense*. It is the urge to proceed with no apparent valid reason, a "gut feeling" developed through experience.

Physical Characteristics

Age, height and weight, unless they are extreme, are not important characteristics for investigators. However, some physical characteristics are important.

> **Effective investigators are physically fit and have good vision and hearing.**

Good health and a high energy level are beneficial because the hours spent performing investigative duties can be long and demanding. In addition to being physically fit, investigators are aided by keen vision and hearing. Investigators may have to listen to words during sobbing, moans and hysteria; hear a very weak voice from a seriously wounded or dying person; listen to more than one person talking at a time; or conduct an interview while a plane is flying overhead, machinery is operating or heavy traffic is passing by.

AN OVERVIEW OF THE INVESTIGATIVE PROCESS

A criminal investigation is usually initiated following either the personal observation of a crime by a police officer or the receipt of information from a citizen. Such information is received at police headquarters or central dispatch by telephone, fax, e-mail, radio or direct report when a person steps up to make a complaint or report

a crime. A police dispatcher relays the information to a patrol officer by radio, phone or mobile computer in the officer's squad car, and the officer responds. However the incident becomes known to police, this awareness of or reporting of a crime sets the investigative wheels in motion and is the first stage in a criminal investigation. The various stages of the investigative process, as well as the personnel involved; the official reports generated; and the victim's, complainant's and suspect's roles, are described in Table 1.2.

THE PRELIMINARY INVESTIGATION: BASIC CONSIDERATIONS

Most preliminary investigations begin the same way, and the same basic procedures are followed regardless of whether the first officer at the scene is a patrol officer, an investigator or the chief of police.

The Initial Response

The first officer who responds, also known as the primary officer, is in charge until relieved by another officer. Department policy defines who is to respond as well as the duties of these individuals.

> **The initial response is usually by a patrol officer assigned to the area where a crime has occurred.**

The initial response is crucial to the success of an investigation. Although it is popularly believed that cases are won or lost in court, more cases actually are lost during the first hour of an investigation—the initial response period—than in court.

After notification, either through direct observation or departmental communications, the officer goes to the scene as rapidly and safely as circumstances permit. A crime-response survey conducted by the Law Enforcement Assistance Administration (LEAA) revealed that a response time of one minute or less is necessary to increase the probability of arrest at the scene. Most police departments, however, cannot assure their citizens of such a short response time, even for emergencies. To provide a one minute response time, police agencies would need much smaller patrol areas, much larger staffs, computer-dispatched vehicles and personnel and, thus, much larger budgets.

TABLE 1.2 A Brief Summary of the Investigative Process

Stage of Investigation	Police Role	Stage of Reports	Victim's/ Complainant's Role	Suspect's Role
Initial Report	Dispatched to call for service	Recording of initial call/report	Reports the incident, requests police response	Sometimes interferes with the call
Initial Investigation/ Police Contact	Arrive on scene and acquire information; may collect evidence	Incident reports and all applicable forms	Provides interviews and information about the incident and suspect; may provide evidence	Provides interviews and information about the incident; may provide evidence
Incident Review	Determine if further investigation is required after a review of the case	Police supervisor reviews the case for approval	Sometimes informed of case status	None
Follow-Up Investigations	Gather remaining information and evidence required for the case	Additional reports, additional interviews and evidence	Verifies and confirms information	Additional interviews and interrogations if cooperative and warranted
Case Preparation and Approval	Review the reports, coordinate the case with prosecution	Ready to submit for formal charging or court processing	None	None
Prosecution and Charging of Crime	Be available for court and testimony	Prosecution and court reports	Be available for court and testimony	In custody or present for court; if not present, have legal representation
Conclusion	Clear reports, release or purge evidence; close case with a disposition	File all complete reports into records	Retrieve any property used as evidence in the case	None

Source: Henry Cho, Cho Research & Consulting, LLC, Copyright 2011.

The initial response is a crucial stage in an investigation. The responding officer should obtain as much information from dispatch as possible before arriving on the scene.
© Henry Cho

It is important to arrive at a crime scene rapidly because

- The suspect may still be at or near the scene.
- Injured persons may need emergency care.
- Witnesses may still be at the scene.
- A dying person may have a confession or other pertinent information to give.
- Weather conditions may change or destroy evidence.
- The integrity of the crime scene and evidence must be preserved.

The responding officers proceed to the scene as quickly as safety allows. Officers who injure themselves or someone else on the way to a call may create more serious problems than exist at the crime scene. They may, in fact, open themselves, their department and even their city to civil and criminal liability.

The seriousness of a crime and whether it is in progress are important factors in driving speed and the rapidity of response. The use of emergency lights and siren may depend on the information furnished or may be dictated by department policy. A siren speeds arrival, but it also prompts the criminal to flee the scene. On the other hand, in a violent crime against a person, a siren alerts the offender but may prevent further violence. Sometimes the victim, to avoid attracting attention, requests that no sirens and red lights be used. Some agencies and states, however, have policies or laws that require a responding officer to use both lights and siren together. Officers must know the specific laws governing their jurisdiction and whether they are allowed discretion in using lights and siren.

The route taken is also an important consideration. Officers should know which streets are under construction in their areas and avoid them. They must also choose between the fastest route and the route the suspect might use to leave the scene. When approaching a scene, officers should observe people leaving the scene and make mental notes of their descriptions. If two officers are in the patrol vehicle, one may write descriptions of people and vehicles observed leaving the scene. Many officers use in-squad video or digital recorders for such observations, permitting a single officer to record information while proceeding to the scene.

While driving to the scene, officers formulate a plan of action based on the type of crime and its location. An immediate response may be crucial because, even if no immediate arrest is made, the amount of information that can be obtained is directly related to the speed of response.

Initial information is often the most important and accurate. Many departments are developing necessary guidelines for rapid responses, replacing the assumption that all calls for service should be responded to as rapidly as possible.

Many departments have found that sending several vehicles to a crime scene may not be the most effective approach. Instead, they implement a "bull's-eye," or target, approach, dispatching only a few vehicles directly to the crime scene (the bull's-eye). Other units are sent to observe traffic at major intersections radiating away from the crime scene in an attempt to intercept fleeing suspects. Success depends on broadcasting the suspects' descriptions rapidly and getting to the major intersections quickly. In many cases, such a response is more effective in catching the suspects than focusing all resources directly on the crime scene itself.

The Point of Arrival

When the first officers arrive, the scene may be either utter chaos or deserted. Regardless of the situation, the officers must take charge immediately and form a plan for proceeding based on the information they have at hand, which might not be much. The actions the first responders take at a crime scene can determine the value of the evidence for investigators and prosecutors.

People at a crime scene may be excited, apprehensive or perplexed. They may be cooperative or uncooperative, confused or lucid. Therefore, officers must be flexible and understanding. Discretion and good judgment are essential because the greatest potential for solving the case lies with those present at the scene, even though many details of the crime may not be known at this stage. More decisions are made in less time at the point of arrival than at any other stage in the investigation, and this is when officers obtain most leads for subsequent action.

Setting Priorities

Circumstances at the scene often dictate what is done first.

The priorities are
- Handle emergencies first.
- Secure the scene.
- Investigate.

The following guidelines can be adapted to fit specific circumstances.

Handling Emergency Situations

Sometimes emergencies dictate procedure. An emergency may include a dangerous suspect at or near the scene or a gravely injured person. For example, if you arrive at a crime scene and the suspect begins to shoot at you, apprehending the suspect obviously becomes your first priority.

In other instances, a person may be so seriously injured that without immediate aid, death is probable. Such an emergency takes precedence over all other procedures, unless officer safety or other public safety concerns preclude it. Then the scene must be secured before an officer administers aid.

Good judgment and the number of available officers dictate what should occur first if more than one emergency exists. Sometimes the decision is difficult. For example, if a victim is drowning, a suspect is running away and only one officer is at the scene, the officer must make a split-second decision. Usually, saving life takes precedence. However, if the officer can do nothing to save the victim, the best alternative is to pursue the suspect. Apprehending the suspect may save other victims.

Responding to emergency situations causes the adrenaline to flow. At the same time, officers must plan their approach and remain extremely vigilant regarding the inherent danger associated with in-progress crimes. Officers should also attempt to think like the suspect. They should decide which escape routes are probable and block them. Available information about the situation helps officers decide whether using lights and siren is advantageous to them or to the suspect. Officers should think about what they would do if they were the suspect and were cornered at the crime scene. If it is daytime, officers may be visible and the suspect not. If it is nighttime, officers may be able to take advantage of a darker area for their approach.

Flexibility is essential. The situation must be carefully assessed because each incident is different and requires different approaches and techniques. Officers should be cognizant that more than one suspect may be present. They should check their equipment on the way to the scene and provide the dispatcher with all pertinent information. Maintaining some physical distance can facilitate observation and give officers time to make decisions that will enhance their safety.

A Suspect at or near the Scene.

If a call is made rapidly enough and officers can respond quickly, they may observe the crime in progress and arrest the suspect at the scene.

> Any suspect at the scene should be detained, questioned and then released or arrested, depending on circumstances.

Departmental policy determines whether the first officer at the scene thoroughly interrogates a suspect. Before any in-custody interrogation, an officer must read the *Miranda* warning to the suspect (a legality discussed

in Chapter 6). Even if the policy is that officers do not interrogate suspects, officers often use discretion. For example, they may have to take a dying declaration or a suspect's spontaneous confession. If this occurs, a statement is taken immediately because the suspect may refuse, or be unable, to cooperate later. A more formal interrogation and written confession can be obtained later at the police department.

The suspect is removed from the scene as soon as possible to minimize the destruction of evidence and to facilitate questioning. The sooner suspects are removed, the less they can observe of the crime scene and possible evidence against them.

If the Suspect Has Recently Fled.

If the suspect has just left the scene, immediate action is required. If the information is provided early enough, other units en route to the scene may make an arrest.

> If a suspect has recently left the scene, officers obtain descriptions of the suspect, any vehicles, direction of travel and any items taken. The information is dispatched to headquarters immediately.

As soon as practical, officers obtain more detailed information about the suspect's possible whereabouts, friends, descriptions of stolen items and other relevant information regarding past criminal records and MOs.

If a Person Is Seriously Injured.

Emergency first aid to victims, witnesses and suspects is often a top priority of arriving officers. Officers should call for medical assistance and then do whatever possible until help arrives. They should observe and record the injured person's condition. When medical help arrives, officers should assist and instruct medical personnel during the care and removal of those injured to diminish the risk of contaminating the scene and losing evidence.

If a person is injured so severely that he or she must be removed from the scene, attending medical personnel should be instructed to listen to any statements or utterances the victim makes and to save all clothing for evidence. If the injured person is a suspect, a police officer almost always accompanies the suspect to the hospital. The humanitarian priority of administering first aid may have to become second priority if a dangerous suspect is still at or near the scene because others may be injured or killed.

If a Dead Body Is at the Scene.

A body at the crime scene may immediately become the center of attention, and even a suspect may be overlooked. If the victim is obviously dead, the body should be left just as it was found but it and its surroundings protected. Identifying the body is not an immediate concern. Preserving the scene is more important because it may later yield clues about the dead person's identity, the cause of death and the individual responsible, as discussed in Chapter 8.

Protecting the Crime Scene

Securing the crime scene is a major responsibility of the first officers to arrive. Everything of a nonemergency nature is delayed until the scene is protected. The critical importance of securing the crime scene is better understood when one considers **Locard's principle of exchange**, a basic forensic theory that objects that come in contact with each other always transfer material, however minute, to each other. This evidence can easily be lost if the crime scene goes unprotected. At outdoor scenes, weather conditions such as heat, wind, rain, snow or sleet can alter or destroy physical evidence. In addition, people may accidentally or intentionally disturb the scene. Additions to the scene can be as disconcerting to later investigation as the removal of evidence is.

Officers should explain to bystanders that protecting the crime scene is critical and that the public must be excluded. Bystanders should be treated courteously but firmly. A delicate part of public relations is dealing with the family of someone who has been killed. Officers should explain what they are doing and why and help family members understand that certain steps must be taken to discover what happened and who is responsible.

Crime scene protection can be as simple as locking a door to a room or building, or it can involve roping off a large area outdoors. Within a room, chairs or boxes can be used to cordon off an area. Many officers carry rope in their vehicle for this purpose and attach a sign that says, "CRIME SCENE—DO NOT ENTER."

Officers setting up a crime scene perimeter should allow a wide enough area where they are confident most of the evidence will be, keeping in mind that a crime scene can always be made smaller; however, expanding it often proves more difficult. *Only* those officers directly involved in processing the crime scene should be allowed inside the crime scene perimeter. A buffer area should then be established around the crime scene area, where other officers and administrators, or other public officials, can be. Outside of that the buffer area is where the public and media may be allowed.

Sometimes other officers arriving at the scene can cause problems by ignoring posted warnings and barriers. *Ironically, police officers with no assigned responsibilities at a scene are often the worst offenders.* Arriving officers and everyone present at the scene should be told what has happened and what they need to do. Other officers can be asked to help preserve the scene, interview witnesses or search for evidence. Officers not involved in processing the scene must be made aware that if they enter the actual crime scene they must complete a full report, a step that serves the dual purposes of maintaining the integrity of the scene and deterring unnecessary intruders.

A guard should be stationed to maintain security. If all officers are busy with emergency matters, a citizen may be asked to help protect the area temporarily. In such cases, the citizen's name, address and phone number should be recorded. The citizen should be given specific instructions and minimal duties. The citizen's main duty is to protect the crime scene by barring entrance and to keep passersby moving along. He or she should not let any person into the area except police who identify themselves with a badge. The citizen should be relieved from guard duty as soon as possible and thanked for the assistance.

All necessary measures to secure the crime scene must be taken—including locking, roping, barricading and guarding—until the preliminary investigation is completed.

Evidence should be protected from destruction or alteration from the elements by being covered until photographing and measuring can be done. Sometimes investigators must move evidence before they can examine it. For example, a vehicle covered with snow, dust or other materials can be moved into a garage. In one case, a car used in a kidnapping was found four days later in a parking lot. Snow that had fallen since the kidnapping covered the car. To process the car's exterior for fingerprints, investigators took the car to a garage to let the snow melt and the surface dry. Evidence is discussed in depth in Chapter 5.

Conducting the Preliminary Investigation

After all emergency matters have been handled and the crime scene has been secured, the actual preliminary investigation can begin. This includes several steps whose order depends on the specific crime and the types of evidence and witnesses available. Appendix A contains a detailed checklist of steps to be taken by first responders at a crime scene.

> **Responsibilities during the preliminary investigation include**
> - Questioning victims, witnesses and suspects.
> - Conducting a neighborhood canvass.
> - Measuring, photographing, videotaping and sketching the scene.
> - Searching for evidence.
> - Identifying, collecting, examining and processing physical evidence.
> - Recording all statements and observations in notes.

Each of these procedures is explained in Section 2. At this point, what is important is the total picture, the overview. In simple cases, one officer may perform all these procedures; in complex cases, responsibilities may be divided among several officers. Everything that occurs at a crime scene is recorded with photographs, videotape, sketches and complete, accurate notes. This record is the basis of future reports and for future investigation and prosecution of the case.

Information may be volunteered by victims, witnesses or suspects at or very near to the time of the criminal actions. Unplanned statements about what happened by people present are called *res gestae* ("things done") statements.

> ***Res gestae* statements** are spontaneous statements made at the time of a crime concerning and closely related to actions involved in the crime. They are often considered more truthful than later, planned responses.

Res gestae statements are generally an exception to the hearsay rule because they are usually very closely related to facts and are therefore admissible in court. *Res gestae* statements should be recorded in the field notes, and the person making the statements should sign or initial them so there is no question of misunderstanding or of the person later denying having made the statement.

In addition to receiving and recording voluntary statements by victims and witnesses, investigators must go looking for information by conducting a neighborhood canvass as discussed in Chapter 6.

Determining Whether a Crime Has Been Committed and When.

As soon as possible during the preliminary investigation, it is necessary to determine whether a crime has, in fact, been committed.

> **Determining whether a crime has been committed** involves knowing the elements of each major offense and the evidence that supports the offenses and ascertaining whether that evidence is present. Officers also try to determine when the event occurred.

Individual elements of various offenses are discussed in Sections 3 and 4.

Officers should observe the condition of the scene and talk to the complainant as soon as possible. After discussing the offense with the victim or complainant, the officers should determine whether a specific crime has been committed. It is common for crime victims to misclassify what has occurred. For example, they may report a burglary as a robbery. In addition, state statutes differ in their definitions of the elements of certain crimes. For example, in some states, entering a motor vehicle with intent to steal is larceny. In other states, it is burglary. Determining when the event occurred is critical for checking alibis and reconstructing the MO.

If no crime has been committed—for example, the matter is a civil rather than a criminal situation—the victim should be told how to obtain assistance.

Field Tests.

Investigators often want to know whether evidence discovered is what they think it is—for example, a bloodstain or an illegal substance. Field-test kits help in this determination. Field tests save investigators' time by identifying evidence that may have little chance of yielding positive results in the laboratory, and field tests are less expensive than full lab examinations. However, they are used on only a small number of specific items of evidence located at crime scenes. If a field test is affirmative, the evidence is submitted to a laboratory for a more detailed, expert examination whose results can then be presented in court.

Investigators can use field tests to develop and lift fingerprints; discover flammable substances through vapor and fluid examination; detect drugs, explosive substances on hands or clothing, imprints of firearms on hands or bullet-hole residue; and conduct many other tests. Local, state and federal police laboratories can furnish information on currently available field-test kits and may provide training in their use.

Establishing a Command Center. In complex cases involving many officers, a command center may be set up where information about the crime is gathered and reviewed. This center receives summaries of communications, police reports, autopsy results, laboratory reports, results of interviews, updates on discovered evidence and tips. Personnel at the center keep files of news releases and news articles and prepare an orderly, chronological progress report of the case for police command, staff and field personnel. If the investigation becomes lengthy, the command center can be moved to police headquarters.

Dealing with the News Media. A close, almost symbiotic relationship exists between the police and the news media. They depend upon each other. Thus, it is important that the media and the police understand and respect each other's roles and responsibilities.

At any major crime scene or during any major criminal investigation, the media will be seeking all the human interest stories they can find. The media serve the public's right to know within legal and reasonable standards, a right protected by the First Amendment. The public is always hungry for news about crime. The police, on the other hand, are responsible for upholding the Sixth and Fourteenth Amendment guarantees of the right to a fair trial, the protection of a suspect's rights and an individual's right to privacy. This often necessitates confidentiality. Further, making some information public could impair or even destroy many investigations. On the other hand, the police rely on the media to disseminate news about wanted

suspects or to seek witnesses from the community. Many cases are solved because of information from citizens.

In their quest for information, the media may target victims and witnesses. In some instances, victims are taken by surprise when the media shows up and safeguards have not yet been put in place to protect the victims' identities. And in some cases, victims or witnesses inadvertently reveal information that is being withheld from the media by law enforcement, as the police attempt to preserve the integrity of an investigation. A tool used by some police departments to protect both the privacy of victims and witnesses and the integrity of an investigation is a card telling these citizens how to deal with the media (Figure 1.1). The back of the card lists telephone numbers for the public information office and the victim services section.

Some departments use public information officers (PIOs) to interface with the media. Other departments assign the highest-ranking officer at the time of an incident or use written information releases. Still others allow virtually any officer involved in a case to address the media.

Media access to police information is neither comprehensive nor absolute. In general, the media have no right to enter any area to which the public does not have access, and all rules at cordoned-off crime scenes are as applicable to the media as they are to the general public. On the other hand, police may not construct a "cocoon" of secrecy. Neither should regard the other as the enemy.

Despite the need for cooperation, complaints from both sides are prevalent. Reporters complain that police withhold information and are uncooperative. The police

Providing an appropriate response to media questions can help an investigation, whereas poorly planned responses may actually hinder progress on a case.

© Tom Carter/Alamy

FIGURE 1.1
Media advisory for crime victims and witnesses.
Source: Used by permission of the Fairfax County Police Department.

complain that reporters interfere with cases and often sensationalize.

Most members of the media understand the restrictions at a crime scene and cooperate. It is necessary to exercise firmness with those who do not follow instructions and even to exclude them if they jeopardize the investigation. Only facts—not opinions—should be given to reporters. The name of someone who has been killed should be given only after a careful identity check and notification of relatives. No information on the cause of death should be released; the medical examiner determines this. Likewise, no legal opinions about the specific crime or the perpetrator should be released. If officers do not know certain information, they can simply state that they do not know. The phrase "no comment" should be avoided because it implies you are hiding something. The benefit of a healthy relationship with the media is clear: "A good rapport with the media fosters a positive relationship with the general public. If you have a good partnership with the media, you generally have a good relationship with the public, because that's how the public gets information" (Garrett, 2007, p.24).

Suggestions for dealing with the media include these: confirm the situation and verify information before giving any statement; position yourself with a provision for an easy exit; give a brief initial statement (5–10 seconds) with no questions answered and indicate police concern for the safety of those involved; establish your intent to return with additional information and set the time for the return (Paris, 2007).

Additional advice for dealing with television reporters involves presenting a positive image, including marked patrol cars in the background and uniformed personnel actively engaged in the crime scene. Negative views to be avoided include body bags, yellow crime scene tape, hysterical victims and relatives, identifying or referencing items such as addresses, evidence that needs to be kept confidential and officers just standing around (Donlon-Cotton, 2007).

Officers who are not identified or trained as media liaisons should defer questions to a supervisor or speak with their supervisor prior to providing any information to the media. There might be facts or circumstances an officer is unaware of that may compromise the investigation or violate the data privacy act.

A Final Consideration about Initiating Investigations

Although an investigations section may handle complex cases and those extending beyond the ability of patrol, patrol officers should handle a case from beginning to end whenever possible, including presenting it to the prosecutor, even if it means taking a case beyond the end of the shift (Stockton, 2006, p.12). Important benefits of this follow-through include:

1. Patrol officers' effectiveness and expertise increase significantly.
2. Initial effort increases because officers know who's working on the follow-up.
3. Follow-up is timelier, resulting in more reliable witness interviews.
4. Job satisfaction increases.
5. When patrol officers know how to conduct an investigation, a department has investigators working around the clock.

Whether patrol officers or detectives investigate a case, crime scene investigators become involved in many instances.

CRIME SCENE INVESTIGATORS

A crime scene investigator (CSI) is a specialist in organized scientific collection and processing of evidence. A CSI develops, processes and packages all physical evidence found at the crime scene and transports it to the lab for forensic

Photographers watch as investigators collect evidence at a mass gravesite. The media have no right to enter any area to which the public does not have access. However, the police may not construct a cocoon of secrecy around a case either.

© AP Images/Staton R. Winter

evaluation; attends and documents autopsies; and writes reports and testifies in court about the evidence.

Although some law enforcement agencies hire civilians to handle crime scene processing and forensics and to work closely with investigators, it is more common that the CSI is a licensed peace officer with specialized training who is part of an investigative unit.

The public has become familiar with how CSIs operate through the popular television series *CSI: Crime Scene Investigation*, which first aired on CBS in October 2000 and has attracted millions of viewers. Hollywood's depiction of CSI, however, has created a glamorized, impractical image of this field in the public's mind: "In today's world of TV and movie drama, every case is solved, a conclusion always reached and the 'smoking gun' consistently found, most times with very little effort. . . . The 'CSI' culture also includes costumes, sets and vehicles the real CSI teams don't even dream of" (Mertens, 2006, p.52). Fantino (2007, p.26) calls this the *CSI effect*, where "unrealistic portrayals of the science have translated to equally unrealistic expectations from not only

the public but also other professions that operate within the justice system who now apparently believe in magic."

The challenges of the CSI effect for investigators and forensic experts alike are being brought to life in America's courtrooms: "Popular forensic drama television shows have resulted in a phenomenon which is impacting criminal investigations and driving jury verdicts across America. People who end up on a jury know, or think that they know, a great deal about forensic science and the kind of science necessary to solve crimes. Prosecutors say juries expect scientific evidence in every case, even though the majority of criminal cases do not call for such evidence" (Dutelle, 2006, p.113).

This blurring of reality and fiction (the CSI effect) was the topic of a study published in the *National Institute of Justice Journal* (Shelton, 2008), in which 1,000 jurors were surveyed about their expectations regarding forensic evidence before their participation in the trial process:

- 46 percent expected to see some kind of scientific evidence in *every* criminal case.

- 22 percent expected to see DNA evidence in *every* criminal case.

- 36 percent expected to see fingerprint evidence in *every* criminal case.

- 32 percent expected to see ballistic or other firearms laboratory evidence in *every* criminal case (Shelton, 2008, p.3).

The survey found that for all categories of evidence, CSI viewers had higher expectations for scientific evidence than did nonviewers. However, "Potential jurors' increased expectations of scientific evidence did *not* translate into a demand for this type of evidence as a prerequisite for finding someone guilty." Says Shelton (2008, p.5), "There was scant evidence in our survey results that CSI viewers were either more or less likely to acquit defendants without scientific evidence."

THE FOLLOW-UP INVESTIGATION

Preliminary investigations that satisfy all the investigative criteria do not necessarily yield enough information to prosecute a case. Despite a thorough preliminary investigation, many cases require a follow-up investigation. A need for a follow-up investigation does not necessarily reflect poorly on those who conducted the preliminary investigation. Often factors exist that are beyond the officers' control. For example, weather can destroy evidence before officers arrive at a scene, witnesses can be uncooperative and evidence may be weak or nonexistent, even after a very thorough preliminary investigation. Other times, new information or evidence may come to light at a later time and require some follow up.

The follow-up phase builds on what was learned during the preliminary investigation and can be conducted by the officers who responded to the original call or, most often, by detectives or investigators, depending on the seriousness and complexity of the crime and the size of the department. If investigators take over a case begun by patrol officers, coordination is essential.

Investigative leads that may need to be pursued include checking the victim's background, talking to informants, determining who would benefit from the crime and who had sufficient knowledge to plan the crime, tracing weapons and stolen property and searching MO, mug shot and fingerprint files. Figure 1.2 provides an example of an investigative lead sheet that might be used in the

Investigative Lead Sheet

Case number _____ Lead number _____

Priority level: ☐ Low   ☐ Medium   ☐ High

Subject _____   Informant _____

Name _____   Name _____

Address _____   Address _____

Race _____ DOB _____ Sex _____   Home telephone _____

Height ___ Weight ___ Eyes ___ Hair ___   Other telephone _____

Identifying features _____   How informant knows subject _____

Employed _____ Occupation _____

Telephone numbers   Home _____   Work _____

Vehicle make _____ Year _____ Model _____ Color _____ Condition _____ Tag _____

Associates _____

ID confirmed ☐ Yes   ☐ No   How? _____

Details of lead _____
_____

Lead received by _____   Date/Time _____

Lead # assigned _____

Lead status ☐ Good lead   ☐ Questionable lead   ☐ Suspicious informant   ☐ Insufficient information

Lead assigned to _____   Date/Time _____

Findings _____
_____

☐ Open lead   ☐ Additional investigation required   ☐ Subject has weak alibi
            ☐ Could not locate subject   ☐ Other
☐ Closed lead   ☐ Unfounded   ☐ Subject has alibi   ☐ Cleared by evidence   ☐ Other

Other lead number references _____

Report completed ☐ Yes   ☐ No   Report# _____

Investigative supervisor _____   Date _____

Lead-room supervisor _____   Date _____

FIGURE 1.2
Investigative Lead Sheet.

Source: Stephen E. Steidel, Ed. *Missing and Abducted Children: A Law-Enforcement Guide to Case Investigation and Program Management*, Third Edition. Washington, DC: National Center for Missing and Exploited Children, 2006.

follow up. Specific follow-up procedures for the major offenses are discussed in Sections 3, 4 and 5.

COMPUTER-AIDED INVESTIGATION

Computers have significantly affected police operations. The role of computers in law enforcement and criminal investigation has evolved from being a useful aid (a nice thing to have) to being an essential tool (a *must* have) (Chapter 17 discusses Computer Crime Investigations).

One of the biggest advances in using computer technology came in 1994 when William Bratton implemented the CompStat (Computerized Statistics, aka Compare Statistics) program in New York. From the beginning CompStat was hailed as an innovative managerial paradigm in policing, an information-driven strategy that stressed accountability at all levels of the police hierarchy. To achieve the goal of enhancing quality of life through reduced levels of crime, CompStat was built around four basic principles: (1) accurate and timely intelligence, (2) rapid deployment of resources, (3) effective tactics, and (4) relentless follow-up and assessment (Jang et al., 2010).

Computers also can help investigators efficiently access existing information such as fingerprint records and DNA tests, record new information and store it compactly for instant transmission anywhere, analyze the information for patterns (mapping), link crimes and criminals, manipulate digital representations to enhance the images and recreate and visually track a series of events. Computers are also increasingly being used for electronic document management, allowing investigators to scan evidence captured from paper and attach audio and video clips to the case file. Furthermore, software is available to help investigators develop an analytical time line and manage the scheduling of tasks related to the investigation, such as follow-up interviews and evidence handling and analysis.

The ability to share data across jurisdictional lines is one of the most valuable benefits computers provide to investigators. In addition, the Internet has become an invaluable tool to criminal investigators. And although some agencies have yet to realize the full potential of Internet access, many others are already capitalizing on the multiple benefits of being online. The Internet offers hundreds of thousands of Web sites to aid informed investigators.

Crime Analysis, Mapping and Geographical Information Systems

Using crime mapping, spreadsheet software and advanced data analysis, crime analysis units have become integral partners in today's policing. Before the computer revolution, the traditional crime map consisted of a large representation of a jurisdiction glued onto a bulletin board with colored pins stuck into it. These maps suffered many limitations—they lost previous crime patterns when they were updated, could not be manipulated or queried and were difficult to read when several types of crimes represented by different colored pins were mixed together.

In addition to pushpin maps, investigators routinely used link charts to keep track of the people and places involved in a case, connecting index cards and photos with a maze of strings as relationships became established and details of an investigation emerged. The cumbersome pin maps and link charts have since given way to computerized crime maps and crime analysis programs. **Crime mapping** changes the focus from the criminal to the location of crimes—the **hot spots** where most crimes occur (Figure 1.3).

According to the National Institute of Justice ("NIJ Crime Mapping Resources," 2007), "The ability to visualize how crime is distributed across the landscape (i.e., crime mapping) gives analysts and policymakers a graphic representation of crime and its related issues. Simple maps help law enforcement leaders direct patrols to areas where they are most needed. Complex maps help policymakers and investigators observe trends and respond more intelligently to changing issues. For example, detectives may use maps to understand the hunting patterns of serial criminals, determine where these offenders might live and identify their next likely target."

Geographic information systems (GIS) and geographic profiling are other powerful tools for investigators: "Today the majority of law enforcement agencies use some degree of Geographic Information Systems/mapping technology to locate callers and provide first responders with critical information before arriving on the scene. . . . In recent years GIS has evolved to provide significantly more information to improve safety and answer important questions during an emergency" (Wandrei, 2007, p.61).

GIS has moved beyond its traditional uses into the next trend in mapping technology—location intelligence: "Location intelligence solutions consist of a combination of software, data and expert services that help organizations leverage spatial capabilities without the need for a GIS expert" (Donahue, 2007, p.32). Location intelligence includes automatic vehicle location (AVL) and global positioning systems (GPS). Three ways to implement AVL/GPS technology are (1) to place a unit inside or on a police vehicle, (2) to install a unit into a laptop computer or (3) to equip the officer's portable radio with a built-in GPS transceiver (Brewer, 2007). Any of these applications enhance officer safety and increase the efficiency of frontline police.

Geographic profiling is yet another advancement in mapping and is based on the theory that all people, spatial analysis techniques and have proved more difficult to develop and implement thus far. The improvement of technology and the corresponding expansion of information now accessible to investigators have created a new set of challenges.

Data Mining

Although information is, indeed, the cornerstone of investigation, the plethora of information being generated can easily overwhelm an investigator. To be effective, investigators must know how to sift through the mountains of available information to find the data that pertain to their case, a process known as **data mining**. For example, data mining applied in a homicide case might allow investigators to more quickly develop a possible motive and thus expedite the identification of a suspect or help narrow the field of possible suspects.

PROBLEM-ORIENTED POLICING

Problem-oriented policing (POP) can be defined as "a departmental-wide strategy aimed at solving persistent community problems. Police identify, analyze and respond to the underlying circumstances that create incidents" (Eck and Spelman, 1987). Goldstein (2001) explains problem-oriented policing as,

> an approach to policing in which discrete pieces of police business (each consisting of a cluster of similar incidents, whether crime or acts of disorder, that the police are expected to handle) are subject to microscopic examination (drawing on the especially honed skills of crime analysts and the accumulated experience of operating field personnel) in hopes that what is freshly learned about each problem will lead to discovering a new and more effective strategy for dealing with it. Problem-oriented policing places a high value on new responses that are preventive in nature, that are not dependent on the use of the criminal justice system and that engage other public agencies, the community and the private sector when their involvement has the potential for significantly contributing to the reduction of the problem. Problem-oriented policing carries a commitment to implementing the new strategy, rigorously evaluating its effectiveness and, subsequently, reporting the results in ways that will benefit other police agencies and that will ultimately contribute to building a body of knowledge that supports the further professionalization of the police.

Data collected during criminal investigations can be extremely valuable to the problem-oriented policing

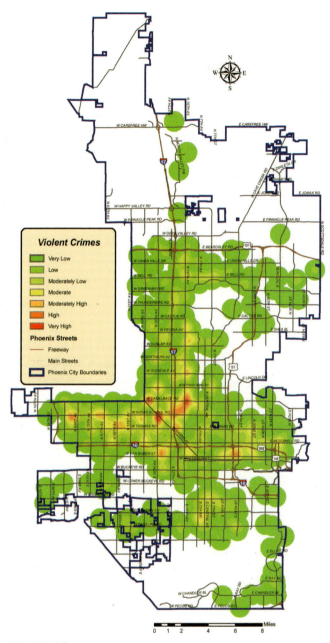

FIGURE 1.3

Computerized crime analysis programs have changed the focus of crime mapping from the criminal to the location of crimes—the hot spots where most crimes occur. This map shows several hot spots in Phoenix, Arizona, where gang activity occurs more often.

Source: Reprinted by permission of the Phoenix Police Department.

including criminals, have a pattern to their lives. This pattern involves, among other things, a limited geographical area that encompasses the bulk of a person's daily activities. According to the "least effort" principle of human behavior, people travel only as far as necessary to accomplish their goals, so the most likely area for a crime is where an offender's desire for anonymity intersects with the offender's desire to stay within his or her comfort zone.

In addition to location, computer programs can help investigators uncover patterns in the timing of criminal events. Unfortunately, time analysis methods have lagged behind that many departments are adopting. Investigators can analyze data to determine groups of problems rather than isolated incidents. Once specific underlying problems are identified, departments can seek alternative approaches to reduce or eliminate the incidence of particular crimes.

The subject of problem-solving policing is beyond the scope of this text, but problem-oriented strategies can be used in criminal investigations in many ways. One way is to expand collaborations by having investigators work more effectively with patrol officers and with other law enforcement agencies. Another way is to improve the quality of information in existing data systems, especially MO files. The likelihood that an offender in a new case has been arrested previously (and should be in the MO file) is greater than often thought. Although criminal investigations are, by nature, reactive, combining problem-oriented strategies with traditional investigative techniques can help investigators improve their ability to solve crimes and help them be proactive in preventing crime.

INVESTIGATIVE PRODUCTIVITY

Productivity has been of interest in the police field for some time. Major opposition to a focus on productivity in police work may arise because of alleged "quota systems" in issuing traffic citations. Productivity involves considerably more than issuing citations, however. Nearly all jobs have some standard of productivity, even though the job may not involve a production line.

A screening process to eliminate criminal investigations with low potential for being solved can often increase productivity. Many police departments screen investigations with a form that asks specific questions. If the answers to these questions are negative, the department either gives the case low priority for assignment or does not assign it at all.

Criminal investigation personnel have traditionally been evaluated by the number and type of cases assigned to them, the number of cases they bring to a successful conclusion and the number of arrests they make and the amount of property they recover. The evaluations should also assess how well the officers use investigative resources and how well they perform overall within the department and in the community.

An advantage of continuous evaluation of productivity is that updating case status is possible at any time. Such information is useful for investigating and for developing budgets, making additional case assignments,

identifying MO similarities among cases and responding to public inquiries.

THE INVESTIGATIVE FUNCTION: THE RESPONSIBILITY OF ALL POLICE PERSONNEL

Early police organizations were one-unit/one-purpose departments with everyone performing generalized functions. However, over time, departments perceived a need for specialization because of

■ The need to know about criminals and their MOs.

■ The amount of training necessary for learning and developing investigative techniques.

■ The frequency with which investigators had to leave their assigned shifts and areas during an investigation.

■ Patrol forces' heavy workloads.

■ A general administrative philosophy that supported specialization as a means of increasing efficiency and therefore solving more crimes.

In larger police departments, specialization developed first in investigative functions before it did in other areas such as traffic, crime prevention, juveniles and community relations. In departments with specialized investigative units, the investigative and patrol functions often experienced difficulty separating their respective duties. Duties often overlapped, decreasing efficient coordination.

Many of these difficulties have been overcome, but many others remain. Regardless of whether departments have specialists or generalists, their goal is the same: solving crimes.

 The ultimate responsibility for solving crimes lies with all police personnel. It must be a cooperative, coordinated departmental effort.

All levels of police administration and operations contribute to successful investigations. Administrative decisions affect the selection and assignment of personnel as well as the policies regulating their performance.

In most larger departments, the investigative division remains a separate unit under its own command and supervisory personnel. The officer in charge reports directly to the chief of police or a chief of operations. Department policy specifies the roles of and the relationships among the administrative, uniformed patrol and investigative divisions. When these roles are clearly defined, the department can better achieve its common goals, with the investigative division fulfilling its assigned responsibilities in coordination with all other departments.

Today, however, researchers are studying the extent to which specialization should remain, its effectiveness, the number of personnel that should be assigned to specialized investigative functions and the selection and training required for such specialization. Several specific factors appear to support the training of all officers to perform investigative duties:

- Increasing competition for tax monies
- Possession of highly sophisticated equipment by some criminals
- More criminals using multiple MOs
- "Withdrawal syndrome" within the general public (i.e., the desire to remain uninvolved necessitates specialized training in interviewing techniques)
- Overwhelming workload of cases assigned to investigative personnel
- More intelligent, better-educated police recruits
- More police training available

In addition, most police officers' daily activities are investigative, even though the matters they investigate may not involve crimes. Therefore, the trend is for a few specialists to direct an investigation and for all officers to assume a more active role in investigating crimes. This role gives patrol officers more responsibility when responding to a call to proceed

to a crime scene. It also enables them to conduct as much of the follow-up investigation as their shift and assigned areas of patrol permit. The importance of the patrol officer's investigative role cannot be overemphasized.

Traditionally, uniformed patrol has been considered the backbone of the police department and has been responsible for the initial response to a crime. Because they are the first to arrive, patrol officers are in an ideal position to do more than conduct the preliminary investigation. Experiments have shown that initial investigations by patrol officers can be as effective as those conducted by specialists. This is partly because the officers deal with the entire case.

This new challenge for patrol officers—involvement in the entire investigative process—creates interest in crime prevention as well as investigation. In addition, giving patrol officers increased responsibility for investigating crimes frees detectives to concentrate on offenses that require detailed investigations as well as on cases that require them to leave the community to conduct special interviews or to pursue leads. The result is better investigation by the patrol officer of the more frequent, less severe crimes.

INTERRELATIONSHIPS WITH OTHERS—COMMUNITY POLICING

Investigators do not work in a vacuum but rely heavily on assistance from numerous other individuals and agencies. Investigators can benefit greatly from the trend

Successful investigations often depend on information provided by victims and witnesses. These statements are typically taken by the officer first responding to the crime scene.
© Michael Newman/PhotoEdit

toward departments adopting a **community policing** philosophy. In 1829 in England, Sir Robert Peel stated, "The police are the public and the public are the police." Scholars have pointed to this philosophy as the modern-day roots of community policing. Miller et al. (2011, p. xix) note, "Community policing... is a philosophy, a belief that working together, the police and the community can accomplish what neither can accomplish alone. The synergy that results from community policing can be powerful. It is like the power of a finely tuned athletic team, with each member contributing to the total effort." According to the Community Oriented Policing Services (COPS) Office,

> Community policing is a philosophy that promotes organizational strategies, which support the systematic use of partnerships and problem solving techniques, to proactively address the immediate conditions that give rise to public safety issues, such as crime, social disorder and fear of crime.... Community policing is often misunderstood as a program or set of programs.... Although programs may be incorporated as part of a broader strategic community policing plan, these programs are not community policing. Rather, community policing is an overarching philosophy that informs all aspects of police business. ("Community Policing Defined," 2008, p.1)

> Using a community policing orientation, investigators interrelate with uniformed patrol officers; dispatchers; the prosecutor's staff; the defense counsel; community corrections personnel; social services; physicians, the coroner or medical examiner; laboratories; and citizens, including witnesses and victims.

Uniformed Patrol

Patrol officers are a vital part of the investigative process because they are usually the first to arrive at a crime scene. What patrol officers do or fail to do at the scene greatly influences the outcome of an investigation. The patrol officer, as the person daily in the field, is closest to potential crime and has probably developed contacts who can provide information.

A potential pitfall is lack of direct, personal communication between uniformed and investigative personnel, which can result in attitudinal differences and divisiveness. Communication problems can be substantially reduced by using a simple checklist describing the current investigative status of any cases jointly involving patrol and investigators.

Patrol officers want to know what happens to the cases they begin. Officers who have been informed of the status of "their" cases report a feeling of work satisfaction not previously realized, increased rapport with investigative personnel and a greater desire to make good initial reports on future cases.

Dispatchers

In most cases, a police dispatcher is the initial contact between a citizen and a police agency. Most citizens call a police agency only a few times during their lives, and their permanent impression of the police may hinge on this contact and the citizens' perceptions of the police agency's subsequent actions.

In addition, the information obtained by the dispatcher is often critical to the officer, the victim, other citizens and the success of the investigation. The accuracy of the information dispatched to the field officer or investigator may determine the success or failure of the case. The responding officer needs to know the exact nature and location of the incident. A direct radio, computer or phone line should be cleared until the officer arrives at the scene. All pertinent descriptions and information should be dispatched directly to the responding officer.

As with working relationships with the media, the relationship between the police and dispatchers is not always positive: "There is no better example of a 'love-hate relationship' than the daily interaction between street cops and dispatchers. When things are going well, we love each other; when they're not, tempers flare, attitudes take a nosedive and we temporarily hate each other" (Brantner Smith, 2007). One reason for the discord is that dispatchers spend their shifts responding to crisis after crisis and rarely get to hear the outcome. Officers should be sensitive to this situation (Brantner Smith, 2007). Dispatchers constantly deal with rage, fear and helplessness but must diffuse these elevated emotions while enhancing the caller's functionality and ability to answer questions or receive instructions (Bumpas, 2006, p.20). Dispatchers are sometimes the lifeline for victims requiring assistance and the officers responding to a crime. Good working relationships with these individuals can go a long way in effectively responding to a crime scene.

Prosecutor's Staff

Another group of individuals with whom good working relationships are a necessity are prosecutors. Cooperation between investigators and the prosecutor's staff depends on the personalities involved, the time available, a recognition that it is in everyone's best interest to work together and an acceptance of everyone's investigative roles and responsibilities. Given sufficient time and a willingness to work together, better investigations and prosecutions result. When investigators have concluded an investigation, they should seek the advice of the prosecutor's office. At this point, the case may be prosecuted, new leads may be developed or the case may be dropped, with both the investigator and the prosecutor's office agreeing that it would be inefficient to pursue it further.

The prosecutor's staff can give legal advice on statements, confessions, evidence, the search and necessary legal papers and may provide new perspectives on the facts in the case. The prosecutor's office can review investigative reports and evidence that relates to the elements of the offense, advise whether the proof is sufficient to proceed and assist in further case preparation. The role of the prosecutor in investigations is discussed further in Chapter 21.

Defense Counsel

Our legal system is based on the adversary system: the accuser against the accused. Although both sides seek the same goal—determining truth and obtaining justice—the adversarial nature of the system requires that contacts between the defense counsel and investigators occur only on the advice of the prosecutor's office. Inquiries from the defense counsel should be referred to the prosecutor's office. If the court orders specific documents to be provided to the defense counsel, investigators must surrender the material, but they should seek the advice of the prosecution staff before releasing any documents or information. The role of the defense counsel is also discussed in greater depth in Chapter 21.

Community Corrections Personnel

Investigators may find it beneficial to have good working rapport with community corrections personnel because, often, people who are suspected of crimes have had prior run-ins with the law and may be on parole or probation for a previous crime. Actually, "The number of times a prisoner has been arrested in the past is a good predictor of whether that prisoner will continue to commit crimes after being released" (Langan and Levin, 2002, p.10). According to the most current data available, of the nearly 300,000 prisoners released from 15 states during 1994, more than two thirds (67.5%) were *rearrested* for a new offense (almost exclusively a felony or serious misdemeanor) within three years of their release (Langan and Levin, 2002). Nearly half of those released (46.9%) were *reconvicted* for a new crime. In 2009, nine percent of parolees were re-incarcerated for a new criminal offense (Glaze and Bonczar, 2010). Probation and parole officers may be good sources of information for officers who suspect a repeat offender may be involved in their case.

Social Services

Social services, especially for investigators who specialize or work on family, domestic and children crimes, can be valuable partners in helping elicit relevant information from suspects and victims. Investigators will often conduct child-victim interviews in tandem with trained social service personnel.

Physicians, Coroners and Medical Examiners

If a victim at a crime scene is obviously injured and a doctor is called to the scene, saving lives takes precedence over all aspects of the investigation. However, the physician is there for emergency treatment, not to protect the crime scene, so investigators must take every possible precaution to protect the scene during the treatment of the victim.

Physicians and medical personnel should be directed to the victim by the route through the crime scene that is least destructive of evidence. They should be asked to listen carefully to anything the victim says and to hold all clothing as evidence for the police.

The coroner or medical examiner is called if the victim has died. Coroners and medical examiners have the authority to investigate deaths to determine whether they were natural, accidental or the result of a criminal act. They can also provide information about the time of death and the type of weapon that might have caused it.

About 2,000 medical examiners and coroners' (ME/C) offices provided death investigation services across the United States in 2004 (Hickman et al., 2007, p.1). These officers are responsible for the medicolegal investigation of deaths. They may conduct death scene investigations, perform autopsies and determine the cause and manner of death when a person has died as a result of violence, under suspicious circumstances, without a physician in attendance or for other reasons. In a typical year, ME/C offices handle about 4,400 unidentified human decedents, of which about 1,000 remain unidentified longer than one year. Nearly one million human death cases were referred to ME/C offices in 2004, of which about 500,000 were accepted. Depending on the individual case, investigators and the ME/C may work as a team, with an investigator present at the autopsy. The ME/C may obtain samples of hair, clothing, fibers, blood and body organs or fluids as needed for later laboratory examination.

Forensic Crime Laboratories

Many criminal investigations involve the processing of physical evidence through a forensic crime lab. All law enforcement agencies now have access to highly sophisticated criminalistic examinations through local, state, federal and private laboratories.

The state crime laboratory is usually located either in the state's largest city or in the state capital and can be used by all police agencies of the state. The FBI Laboratory in Washington, DC, is also available to all federal, state and local law enforcement agencies, with personnel available to provide forensic examinations, technical support, expert witness testimony and training.

The National Institute of Justice (*Increasing Efficiency in Crime Laboratories*, 2008, p.1) reports, "Television has given forensic science great public visibility, but provides viewers with the mistaken notion that crime laboratories provide results quickly. In truth, most crime laboratories have large case backlogs." A census of publicly funded crime laboratories revealed that, in 2005, the nation's forensic crime labs received evidence from an estimated 2.7 million criminal investigations, with requests for services including DNA analysis, latent fingerprint examination, fiber and hair examination, firearms and toolmark analysis and controlled substance identification (Durose, 2008). Any evidence not processed within 30 days was classified as "backlogged," and approximately 359,000 cases nationwide were backlogged at year-end 2005, a 24 percent increase from the backlogged caseload of 287,000 at year-end 2002 (Durose, 2008).

Citizens

Investigators are only as good as their sources of information. They seldom solve crimes without citizen assistance. In fact, citizens frequently provide the most important information in a case. Witnesses to a crime should be contacted immediately to minimize their time involved and inconvenience. Information about the general progress of the case should be relayed to those who have assisted. This will maintain their interest and increase their desire to cooperate at another time.

Citizens can help or hinder an investigation. Frequently, citizens who have been arrested in the past have information about crimes and the people who commit them. The manner and attitude with which such citizens are contacted will increase or decrease their cooperation with the police, as discussed in Chapter 6.

Witnesses

Witnesses are often the key to solving crimes. They can provide eyewitness accounts, or they can provide leads that would be otherwise unavailable. However, such testimony is often unreliable, with the results of one study estimating that as many as 75 percent of the defendants eventually exonerated through the use of DNA evidence were wrongly convicted in the first place because of erroneous eyewitness testimony (Sonenshein and Nilon, 2010). Several states have passed legislation to create tougher standards for identifying suspects by witnesses, which is often considered one of the most problematic aspects of an investigation. Despite criticism and controversy regarding the value of eyewitness testimony, judges and juries accord significant weight to eyewitness evidence.

Key witnesses should be kept informed of the progress of the case and of their role in the prosecution, if any. If they are to be called to testify in court, their testimony should be reviewed with them, and they should be given assurances that their participation is important in achieving justice. Police officers must be aware of the problem of witness intimidation, which can also be directed at victims of crime.

Victims

Almost every crime has a victim. According to the National Crime Victimization Survey (NCVS), U.S. residents age 12 or older experienced an estimated 20 million violent and property victimizations in 2009, the lowest overall victimization levels recorded since the NCVS began in 1973 (Truman and Rand, 2010). Jordan et al. (2007, p.44) contend, "The law enforcement community has historically focused on the apprehension and prosecution of perpetrators, and although state laws define the rights and redress of victims of crime—such as the right to be treated with fairness, dignity and respect; to be informed and present throughout the entire criminal justice process; to be reasonably protected from the accused; and to be entitled to seek restitution—these individuals are very often neglected in the criminal justice system."

Even so-called victimless crimes often have innocent victims who are not directly involved in a specific incident. The victim is often the reporting person (complainant) and often has the most valuable information. Yet, in many instances, the victim receives the least attention and assistance.

Police should keep victims informed of investigative progress unless releasing the information would jeopardize prosecuting the case or unless the information is confidential. The federal Victimization Bill provides matching-fund assistance to states for victims of some crimes. Numerous states also have victimization funds that can be used for funeral or other expenses according to predetermined criteria. Police agencies should maintain a list of federal, state and local agencies; foundations; and support groups that provide assistance to victims. Police should tell victims how to contact community support groups. For example, most communities have support groups for victims of sexual offenses—if not locally, then at the county or state level.

In larger departments, psychological response teams are available. In smaller agencies, a chaplains' corps or clergy from the community may assist with death notifications and the immediate needs of victims.

Investigating officers should also give victims information on future crime prevention techniques and temporary safety precautions. They should help victims understand any court procedures that involve them. Officers should tell victims whether local counseling services are available and whether there is a safe place they can stay if this is an immediate concern.

Unfortunately, although millions of people in the United States are victimized every year, only a small percentage of these victims and family members obtain the services they need to manage the stress that develops when falling victim to crime (Oetinger, 2007, p.40).

MAJOR-CASE TASK FORCES

Shrinking police budgets and the complications of modern-day crime have resulted in task forces becoming necessary for many crimes involving drugs, gangs and terrorism. Combined federal, state and local task forces now exist for these and other crimes. In addition, "Task forces are critical when addressing multi-jurisdictional needs, investigating major cases impacting several agencies or when combating regional crime problems" (Boetig and Mattocks, 2007, p.51).

A *multidisciplinary* approach to case investigation uses specialists in various fields from within a particular jurisdiction. A *multijurisdictional* investigation, in contrast, uses personnel from different police agencies. Many metropolitan areas consist of 20 or more municipalities surrounding a core city. In a number of metropolitan areas, multijurisdictional major-case squads or metro crime teams have been formed, drawing the most talented investigative personnel from all jurisdictions. In addition, the services of federal, state or county police agency personnel may be used.

Many agencies are developing special investigation units, focusing resources and training efforts on specific local crime problems. Other areas commonly investigated by special units include drug trafficking and gaming enforcement. In some major cases—for example, homicides involving multijurisdictional problems, serial killers, police officer killings or multiple sex offenses—it is advisable to form a major-case task force from the jurisdictions that have vested interests in the case. All evidence from the

joint case is normally sent to the same laboratory to maintain continuity and consistency. Murphy et al. (2004, p.13) observe, "Local law enforcement have long been scrutinized for how they handle large-scale, complex criminal investigations—often those involving serial, spree or mass murderers or violence against national leaders or celebrities. Many of these notorious crimes were investigated within a task force structure, involving multiple agencies, jurisdiction or levels of government. These crimes shared a number of characteristics that called for complicated, demanding investigations that challenged the agencies tasked with solving them in unprecedented ways."

In examining the lessons learned from the Washington, DC sniper investigation, Murphy et al. (2004) were able to identify some critical aspects of a successful investigation, including thorough planning and preparation, advanced role definition and delineation of responsibilities, efficient information management and a focus on effective communication.

On the federal level, the Violent Criminal Apprehension Program (VICAP) has been created within the FBI to study and coordinate investigation of crimes of interstate and national interest: "VICAP's mission is to facilitate cooperation, communication and coordination among law enforcement agencies and provide support in their efforts to investigate, identify, track, apprehend and prosecute violent serial offenders" (Murphy et al., 2004, p.41).

LAW ENFORCEMENT RESOURCES

Investigators also have available several resources at the federal level as well as at the global level.

Federal Law Enforcement Resources

Federal law enforcement agencies can provide numerous resources to aid local and state agencies involved in high-profile investigations. Federal agencies may have forensic experts that a local or state law enforcement agency does not employ in-house. The Bureau of Alcohol, Tobacco, Firearms and Explosives (ATF), FBI and Secret Service are available for such forensic expertise. Specialized response units, such as the FBI's Critical Incident Response Group (CIRG), the Rapid Deployment Logistics Unit (RDLU) and the Hostage Rescue Team (HRT) are also accessible to local and state law enforcement. In addition, the National Center for the Analysis of Violent Crime (NCAVC) Behavioral Analysis Unit (BAU) provides behavioral-based investigative and operational support: "BAU . . . provides assistance to law enforcement through 'criminal investigative analysis,' a process of reviewing crimes from behavioral and investigative perspectives. BAU staff—commonly called profilers—assess the criminal act, interpret offender behavior and/or interact with the victim for the purposes of providing crime analysis, investigative suggestions, profiles of unknown offenders, threat analysis, critical incident analysis, interview strategies, major case management, search warrant assistance, prosecution and trial strategies and expert testimony" (Murphy et al., 2004, p.41).

Other federal resources available to investigators will be discussed throughout the remainder of the text.

Interpol

INTERPOL, whose correct full name is the International Criminal Police Organization (ICPO), has participated in disseminating information related to stolen or seized property since 1947. Information maintained in the INTERPOL computerized database is available to law enforcement agencies worldwide.

AVOIDING CIVIL LIABILITY

Before concluding this overview of criminal investigation, it is worth briefly considering what can happen if investigators step outside their legal boundaries during an investigation. Some might think the worst-case scenario is that the suspect walks, but that would be only part of the bad news. The other part: The investigator finds that the shoe is on the other foot, as he or she has now become the defendant in a civil liability suit.

Civil liability refers to a person's degree of risk of being sued. Officers must face the unfortunate reality that being sued goes with wearing the uniform: "In the past few years, police litigation has skyrocketed in terms of both the number of lawsuits and the amount of money needed to defend these lawsuits (and to pay out large verdicts when they occur)" (Ramirez, 2006, p.52). Many aspects of police work (e.g., use of force, high-speed pursuits) leave officers and their departments vulnerable to possible lawsuits. Searches and arrests have the potential for lawsuits, as do failures to investigate or arrest.

Most civil lawsuits brought against law enforcement officers are based on Statute 42 of the U.S. Code, Section 1983, also called the Civil Rights Act. This act, passed in 1871, was designed to prevent the abuse of constitutional rights by officers who "under color of state law" denied defendants those rights and states, "Every person who, under color of any statute, ordinance, regulation,

custom, or usage, of any State or Territory, subjects, or causes to be subjected any citizen of the United States or other person within the jurisdiction thereof to the deprivation of any rights, privileges, or immunities secured by the Constitution and laws, shall be liable to the party injured in an action at law, suit in equity, or other proper proceeding for redress."

Basically, Section 1983 states that anyone who acts under the authority of law and who violates another person's constitutional rights can be sued. Of particular relevance to criminal investigations are those constitutional protections involving searches and seizures, interrogations and custody situations.

Operations manuals and training are critically important in protecting departments against lawsuits (Cotton and Donlan-Cotton, 2007). Such manuals provide guidelines within which officers and investigators should operate. Manuals should be updated as case law changes and as new technologies become available.

Hess and Orthmann (2012, p.449) observe, "Investigative procedure is [one] area of police work commonly brought up in lawsuits. Almost every investigation gives officers discretion to decide what evidence should be included in prosecutor reports and warrant applications, and what evidence should be omitted." If investigators withhold **exculpatory evidence**, which is evidence favorable to the accused, the courts have deemed this to be a violation of a defendant's due process rights: "Leaving out exculpatory evidence may lead to liability for false arrest, malicious prosecution and illegal search and seizure claims. To support such liability claims, a plaintiff must show that the affiant knowingly and deliberately, or with reckless disregard for the truth, omitted facts that are material or necessary to a finding of probable cause [*Franks v. Delaware*, 1978]."

One of the best ways to avoid lawsuits or to defend yourself if sued is to keep complete, accurate records of all official actions you take. Hess and Orthmann (2011, p.510) offer suggestions to avoid lawsuits.

Protection against lawsuits includes
- Effective policies and procedures clearly communicated to all.
- Thorough and continuous training.
- Proper supervision and discipline.
- Accurate, thorough police reports.

Means (2007, p.33) offers another suggestion for avoiding lawsuits: "Nothing whatsoever reduces legal problems and liability risks in law enforcement like good interpersonal communication skills. We all know officers who can go in a biker bar, make an arrest and leave with a friend. Other officers could start a fight in a Quaker Friends meeting." Means notes, "Dealing with people can be complex and demanding, especially in law enforcement. But there are straightforward, guiding principles that, when applied, sharply improve odds of success and reduce both physical and legal risks." These interpersonal communication techniques are discussed in Chapter 6.

Summary

A criminal investigation is the process of discovering, collecting, preparing, identifying and presenting evidence to determine what happened and who is responsible. The goals of police investigation vary from department to department, but most investigations aim to

- Determine whether a crime has been committed.
- Legally obtain sufficient information and evidence to identify the responsible person.
- Arrest the suspect.
- Recover stolen property.
- Present the best possible case to the prosecutor.

Among the numerous functions performed by investigators are those of providing emergency assistance; securing the crime scene; photographing, videotaping and sketching; taking notes and writing reports; searching for, obtaining and processing physical evidence; obtaining information from witnesses and suspects; identifying suspects; conducting raids, surveillances, stakeouts and undercover assignments; and testifying in court.

All investigators—whether patrol officers or detectives—are more effective when they possess certain intellectual, psychological and physical characteristics. Effective investigators obtain and retain information, apply technical knowledge and remain open-minded, objective and logical. They are also culturally adroit, that is, skilled in interacting across gender, ethnic, generational, social and political group lines. They are emotionally well balanced, detached, inquisitive, suspecting, discerning, self-disciplined and persevering. Further, they are physically fit and have good vision and hearing.

The first officer to arrive at a crime scene is usually a patrol officer assigned to the area. In any preliminary investigation, it is critical to establish priorities. Emergencies are handled first, next the crime scene is secured and finally the investigation can begin. Any suspect at the scene should be detained, questioned and then either released or arrested, depending on circumstances. If a suspect has recently left the scene, officers obtain descriptions of the suspect, any vehicles, direction of travel and any items taken. The information is dispatched to headquarters immediately.

After emergencies are dealt with, the first and most important function is to protect the crime scene and evidence. All necessary measures to secure the crime scene should be taken—including locking, roping, barricading and guarding—until the preliminary investigation is completed.

Once the scene is secured, the preliminary investigation is conducted, which includes questioning victims, witnesses and suspects; conducting a neighborhood canvass; measuring, photographing, videotaping and sketching the scene; searching for evidence; identifying, collecting, examining and processing physical evidence; and recording all statements and observations in notes. *Res gestae* statements are spontaneous statements made at the time of a crime, concerning and closely related to actions involved in the crime. They are often considered more truthful than later, planned responses.

As soon as possible, officers should determine whether a crime has been committed by knowing the elements of each major offense and the evidence that supports the offenses and then ascertaining whether that evidence is present. Officers should also try to determine when the event occurred.

Even in police departments that have highly specialized investigation departments, the ultimate responsibility for solving crimes lies with all police personnel. It must be a cooperative, coordinated departmental effort. Cooperation and coordination of efforts are also required outside the police department. Investigators must interrelate with uniformed patrol officers; dispatchers; the prosecutor's staff; the defense counsel; community corrections personnel; social services; physicians, the coroner or medical examiner; laboratories; and citizens, including witnesses and victims. Criminal investigation is, indeed, a mutual effort.

Protection against lawsuits includes (1) effective policies and procedures clearly communicated to all, (2) thorough and continuous training, (3) proper supervision and discipline and (4) accurate, thorough police reports.

Checklist

Preliminary Investigation

- Was a log kept of all actions taken by officers?
- Were all emergencies attended to first? (First aid, detaining suspects, broadcasting information regarding suspects)
- Was the crime scene secured and the evidence protected?
- Were photographs or videotapes taken?
- Were measurements and sketches made?
- Was all evidence preserved?
- Were witnesses interviewed as soon as possible and statements taken?
- How was the complaint received?
- What were the date and time it was received?
- What was the initial message received? (State the offense and location.)
- Where was the message received?
- Who was present at the time?
- Were any suspicious persons or vehicles observed while en route to the scene?
- What time did officers arrive at the scene?
- How light or dark was it?
- What were the weather conditions? Temperature?
- Were there other notable crime-scene conditions?
- How did officers first enter the scene? Describe in detail the exact position of doors or windows—open, closed, locked, glass broken, ajar, pried or smashed. Were the lights on or off? Shades up or down?
- Was the heating or air conditioning on or off? Was a television, radio or stereo on?
- Were dead or injured persons at the scene?
- What injuries to persons were observed? Was first aid administered?
- What type of crime was committed?
- Was the time the crime occurred estimated?
- Who was the first contact at the scene? (Name, address, telephone number)
- Who was the victim? (Name, address, telephone number) Was the victim able to give an account of the crime?
- What witnesses were at the scene? (Names, addresses, telephone numbers)
- Were unusual noises heard—shots, cars, screams, loud language, prying or breaking noises?
- Had clocks stopped?
- Were animals at the scene?
- Was an exact description of the suspect obtained? (Physical description, jewelry worn, unusual voice or body odors; unusual marks, wounds, scratches, scars; nicknames used; clothing; cigarettes or cigars smoked; weapon used or carried; direction of leaving the scene)
- Was a vehicle involved? Make, model, color, direction, unusual marks?
- Were items taken from the scene? Exact description?
- What was done to protect the crime scene physically?
- What officers were present during the preliminary investigation?
- Were specialists called to assist? Who?
- Was the coroner or medical examiner notified?
- What evidence was discovered at the scene? How was it collected, identified, preserved? Were field tests used?

Discussion Questions

1. What are the benefits of having police investigators who specialize in a certain area? What are the drawbacks? Do you support specialization or generalization?
2. Of all the suggested characteristics required for an effective investigator, which three are the most critical? Are these qualifications more stringent than those required for a patrol officer?
3. What is the role of the victim in investigating crime?
4. What misconceptions regarding investigation are conveyed by television shows and movies?
5. What do you believe is the most important goal of a criminal investigation?
6. What major factors must responding officers consider while proceeding to a crime scene?
7. How important is response time to the investigation of a crime? How is the importance affected by the type of crime?
8. What determines who is in charge at a crime scene? What authority does this officer have?
9. Controversy exists over which emergency takes precedence: an armed suspect at or near the scene or a severely injured person. Which do you think should take priority? Why?
10. What balance should be maintained between freedom of the media to obtain information during a crime investigation and the right to privacy of the individuals involved?

Media Explorations

 Internet

Complete one of the following assignments and be prepared to share your findings with the class.

■ Go to the Web site of the National Institute of Justice (NIJ) and find "Mapping Crime: Principle and Practice." Outline the chapters in this research guide. Then select one chapter and outline it in detail.

■ Go to the Web site of the Bureau of Justice Statistics and summarize what the site says about crimes reported and not reported to the police.

■ Go to the Mapping and Analysis for Public Safety Web site at U.S. Department of Justice's main site or to the National Center for Geographic Information and Analysis (NCGIA) and summarize the information you feel is important and informative for you and the rest of the class.

ONLINE Database **Gale Criminal Justice Database Assignments**

The following assignments require access to Gale's Custom Journals Database for Emergency Services and Criminal Justice. Check with your instructor if you have questions about this.

■ Find the article, "Crime Analysis Reporting & Mapping for Small Agencies: A Low Cost and Simplified Approach," on the Gale Emergency Services Database. Read and outline the article. Be prepared to discuss your outline with the class.

■ Find the article, "Preserving Police History: Benefits for the Present and the Future," on the Gale Emergency Services Database. Read the article and summarize what it says about police history.

■ Find the article, "Preliminary Crime Statistics for 2009," on the Gale Emergency Services Database. Summarize what the article says about crime statistics for 2009. Do any of the trends surprise you? Be prepared to discuss your thoughts with the class.

References

Boetig, Brian Parsi, and Mattocks, Mike. "Selecting Personnel for Multi-Agency Task Forces." *Law and Order*, December 2007, pp.51–54.

Brantner Smith, Betsy. "The 'Love/Hate' Relationship between Cops and Their Dispatchers." *Police One*, July 2007. Accessed March 17, 2011. http://www.policeone.com/police-products/communications/dispatch/articles/1271472-The-love-hate-relationship-between-cops-and-their-dispatchers/

Brewer, Brad. "AVL/GPS for Front Line Policing." *Law and Order*, November 2007, pp.46–54.

Bumpas, Sandy. "Permission to Be Human." *9-1-1 Magazine*, July 2006, pp.20–43.

"Community Policing Defined." *Community Policing Dispatch*, January 2008, p.1.

Cotton, Mark, and Donlon-Cotton, Cara. "Operations Manuals, Training and Liability." *Tactical Response*, November–December 2007, pp.18–20.

Donahue, Greg. "Intelligent GIS." *9-1-1 Magazine*, May 2007, pp.32–35, 62.

Donlon-Cotton, Cara. "Positive Scene Presentations." *Law and Order*, March 2007, pp.74–76.

Durose, Matthew R. *Census of Publicly Funded Forensic Crime Laboratories, 2005*. Washington, DC: Bureau of Justice Statistics, July 2008. (NCJ 222181)

Dutelle, Aric. "The CSI Effect and Your Department." *Law and Order*, May 2006, pp.113–114.

Eck, John E., and Spelman, William. *Problem-Solving: Problem-Oriented Policing in Newport News*. Washington, DC: The Police Executive Research Forum, 1987.

Fantino, Julian. "Forensic Science: A Fundamental Perspective." *The Police Chief*, November 2007, pp.26–28.

Garrett, Ronnie. "Taming the Beast: How to Keep News-Hungry Media Fed." *Law Enforcement Technology*, October 2007, pp.22–32.

Glaze, Lauren E., and Bonczar, Thomas P. *Probation and Parole in the United States, 2009*. Washington, DC: Bureau of Justice Statistics, December 2010. (NCJ 231674)

Goldstein, Herman. "What Is POP?" Center for Problem Oriented Policing, 2001. Accessed September 3, 2008. http://www.popcenter.org/about/?p=whatiscpop

Hess, Kären M., and Orthmann, Christine H. *Police Operations*, 5th ed. Clifton Park, NJ: Delmar, Cengage Learning, 2011.

Hess, Kären M., and Orthmann, Christine H. *Introduction to Law Enforcement and Criminal Justice*, 10th ed. Clifton Park, NJ: Delmar, Cengage Learning, 2012.

Hickman, Matthew J.; Hughes, Kristen A.; Strom, Kevin J.; and Ropero-Miller, Jeri D. *Medical Examiners and Coroners' Offices, 2004*. Washington, DC: Bureau of Justice Statistics Special Report, June 2007. (NCJ 216756)

Increasing Efficiency in Crime Laboratories. Washington, DC: National Institute of Justice, January 2008.

International Association of Chiefs of Police. *The Canons of Police Ethics*. Alexandria, VA: IACP, 1957.

Jang, Hyunseok; Hoover, Larry T.; and Joo, Hee-Jong. "An Evaluation of CompStat's Effect on Crime: The Fort Worth Experience." *Police Quarterly*, December 2010, pp.387–412.

Jordan, Suzanne; Romashkan, Irina; and Werner, Serena. "Launching a National Strategy for Enhancing Response to Victims." *The Police Chief*, October 2007, pp.44–50.

Langan, Patrick A., and Levin, David J. *Recidivism of Prisoners Released in 1994*. Washington, DC: Bureau of Justice Statistics, June 2002. (NCJ 193427)

Means, Randy. "The Greatest Liability Reduction Tool." *Law and Order*, December 2007, pp.33–34.

Mertens, Jennifer. "The Smoking Gun." *Law Enforcement Technology*, March 2006, pp.52–61.

Miller, Linda S.; Hess, Kären M.; and Orthmann, Christine H. *The Police in the Community: Partnerships for Problem Solving*, 6th ed. Belmont, CA: Wadsworth Publishing Company, 2011.

Murphy, Gerard R.; Wexler, Chuck; Davies, Heather J.; and Plotkin, Martha. *Managing a Multijurisdictional Case: Identifying the Lessons Learned from the Sniper Investigation.* Washington, DC: Police Executive Research Forum, October 2004.

"NIJ Crime Mapping Resources." *Justice Resource Update*, Vol.1, No.1, 2007, pp.1–2.

Oetinger, Thomas. "Providing Better Service to Victims of Crime." *The Police Chief*, October 2007, pp.40–43.

Paris, Chris. "Lights, Camera, Action." *Law Officer Magazine*, March 2007, pp.50–55.

Ramirez, Eugene P. "Limiting SWAT Liability." *Police*, August 2006, pp.52–57.

"Recognizing Innovation in the Art and Science of Criminal Investigations." *The Police Chief*, April 2003, p.140.

Shelton, Donald E. "The 'CSI Effect': Does It Really Exist?" *NIJ Journal*, March 2008, pp.1–8. (NCJ 221500)

Sonenshein, David A., and Nilon, Robin. "Eyewitness Errors and Wrongful Convictions: Let's Give Science a Chance." *Oregon Law Review*, Vol.89, No.1, 2010, pp.263–304.

Stockton, Dale. "Patrol Investigators." *Law Officer Magazine*, September 2006, p.12.

Truman, Jennifer L., and Rand, Michael R. *Criminal Victimization, 2009.* Washington, DC: Bureau of Justice Statistics Bulletin, October 2010. (NCJ 231327)

Wandrei, Greg. "Instant Access to Vital Information: The Role of GIS." *Law Enforcement Technology*, November 2007, pp.56–61.

Cases Cited

Florida v. Tommy Lee Andrews, 533 So. 2d 841 (Fla. Dist. Ct. App., 1988)

Franks v. Delaware, 438 U.S. 154, 165–166 (1978)

SECTION 2
BASIC INVESTIGATIVE RESPONSIBILITIES

As Berg[1] points out, "Police can learn a few lessons from legendary basketball coach John Wooden," who believed that constantly practicing, mastering and executing the basics were the keys to a team's success. Berg contends,

> Officers, detectives and sergeants should constantly evaluate their fundamentals. Are reported crimes being thoroughly investigated or merely reported? Are neighborhoods being canvassed for that one witness who may give us the little piece of information we need to identify the suspect? Have we searched thoroughly for evidence, including fingerprints, and have we protected evidence and gathered it in an expert manner? Are we completing well written reports that contain all of the information that will make a subsequent follow-up successful? Are we doing a comprehensive job investigating at a crime scene or do we always expect the experts and the specialists to "figure it out"?

Essentially, how well do our frontline patrol investigators, detectives and sergeants execute the fundamentals of high-quality police work at the scene of a crime? As Coach Wooden taught us so many years ago, you don't get to cut the net down after the final game if you don't understand the most basic fundamentals of the game and perform them consistently well. So it is with frontline police work.

The basic investigative techniques introduced in Chapter 1 are central to the successful resolution of a crime. Investigators must be skilled in documenting the crime scene and any continuing investigation, including taking notes and photographs or videotaping and sketching (Chapter 2) and then casting this information into an effective report (Chapter 3). Investigators must also be skilled in searching (Chapter 4); obtaining and processing physical evidence (Chapter 5); obtaining information through interviews and interrogation (Chapter 6); and identifying and arresting suspects and conducting raids, surveillances, stakeouts and undercover assignments (Chapter 7).

Although these techniques are discussed separately, they actually overlap and often occur simultaneously. For example, note taking occurs at almost every phase of the

---

[1] Gregory R. Berg. "Crime Scene Investigations—Time to Get Back to the Basics." *Law Enforcement News,* March 31, 1999, p.8.

© 2013 istockphoto.com

© 2013 istockphoto.com

investigation, as does obtaining information. Further, the techniques require modification to suit specific crimes, as discussed in Sections 3, 4 and 5. Nonetheless, investigation of specific crimes must proceed from a base of significant responsibilities applicable to most investigations. This section provides that base.

CHAPTER 2

Documenting the Crime Scene: Note Taking, Photographing and Sketching

© Scott Olson/Getty Images

Outline

Can You Define?

backing

baseline method

compass-point method

competent photograph

cross-projection sketch

finished scale drawing

forensic photogrammetry

immersive imaging

laser-beam photography

legend

macrophotography

marker

material photograph

megapixel

microphotography

mug shots

overlapping

Pictometry®

pixel

PPI

rectangular-coordinate method

relevant photograph

resolution

rogues' gallery

rough sketch

scale

sketch

trap photography

triangulation

ultraviolet-light photography

 Do You Know?

Documentation is vital throughout an investigation. Most people who go into law enforcement are amazed at the amount of paperwork and writing that is required—as much as 70 percent of an investigator's job is consumed by these functions. In addition, photography plays an important role in documenting evidence and presenting cases in court. Some larger departments have a photographic unit. Other departments rely on their investigators to perform this function. Often both photographs and sketches must accompany written notes to provide a clear picture of the crime scene.

- Why notes are important in an investigation?
- When to take notes?
- What to record in investigative notes?
- What the characteristics of effective notes are?
- Where to file notes if they are retained?
- What purposes are served by crime scene photography?
- What the advantages and disadvantages of using photography and videography are?
- What the minimum photographic equipment for an investigator is?
- What to photograph at a crime scene and in what sequence?
- What errors in technique to avoid?
- What types of photography are used in criminal investigations?
- What basic rules of evidence photographs must adhere to?
- What purposes are served by the crime scene sketch?
- What should be sketched?
- What materials are needed to make a rough sketch?
- What steps to take in making a rough sketch?
- How plotting methods are used in sketches?
- When a sketch or a scale drawing is admissible in court?

FIELD NOTES: THE BASICS

Note taking is not unique to the police profession. News reporters take notes to prepare stories; physicians record information furnished by patients to follow the progress of a case; lawyers and judges take notes to assist in interviewing witnesses and making decisions; students take notes in class and as they read. Quite simply, notes are brief records of what is seen or heard.

 Investigative notes are a permanent written record of the facts of a case to be used in further investigation, in writing reports and in prosecuting the case.

Note taking and report writing are often regarded as unpleasant, boring tasks. Yet no duty is more important, as many officers have found, much to their embarrassment, when they did not take notes or took incomplete notes. Detailed notes can make or break a case. For example, when a defense attorney challenges in court the reliability or validity of various breath or blood measurements of alcohol content, the case often hinges on the thoroughness of an officer's written report. Accurate notes aid later recall and are used for preparing sketches and reports. Notes are important throughout an entire investigation.

 Start taking notes as soon as possible after receiving a call to respond and continue recording information as it is received throughout the investigation.

When to Take Notes

Sometimes it is physically impossible to take notes immediately—for example, while driving a vehicle or in complete darkness. At other times, taking notes immediately could hinder obtaining information if it intimidates a witness or suspect. Whether to take out a notebook immediately in the presence of a person being questioned is a matter of personal insight and experience.

When people are excited, want to get their name in the newspaper or want to get your attention, you can usually record information immediately. Most people are willing to give information if you are friendly and courteous and you explain the importance of the information. In such cases, no delay in taking notes is required.

On the other hand, reluctant witnesses and suspects may not talk if you record what they say. In such cases, obtain the information first and record it later. You must sense when it is best to delay writing notes.

Often, rookie officers are so focused on taking good notes that they fail to do well on building rapport with suspects, victims and witnesses, which can lead to a failed interview. Note taking is supposed to benefit the investigation, but how information is obtained—whether the officers establishes good rapport or not—can greatly influence investigative success. Specific methods of obtaining information from willing and unwilling people are discussed in Chapter 6.

If someone gives you an exact wording of what was said by a person committing a crime, have the witness initial that portion of your notes after reading it to help ensure its accuracy. If possible, have people who give you

Witnesses are important sources of information regarding crimes committed in their community.
© Kayte Deioma/PhotoEdit

information take time to write a statement in their own handwriting. This avoids the possibility that they may later claim that they did not make the statement or were misunderstood or misquoted.

What to Record

Enter general information first: the time and date of the call, location and arrival time at the scene. Police departments using centrally dispatched message centers may automatically record date, time and case numbers. Even if this is done, make written notes of this initial information because digital records may not be kept for extended periods or may become unusable. The computerized records and notes corroborate each other.

 Record all information that helps answer the questions Who? What? Where? When? How? and Why?

As you take notes, ask yourself specific questions such as these:

■ When: did the incident happen? was it discovered? was it reported? did the police arrive on the scene? were suspects arrested?

■ Where: did the incident happen? was evidence found? stored? do victims, witnesses and suspects live? do suspects tend to spend a lot of time? were suspects arrested?

■ Who: are suspects? accomplices? Complete descriptions include gender, race, coloring, age, height, weight, hair (color, style, condition), eyes (color, size, glasses), nose (size, shape), ears (close to head or protruding), distinctive features (birthmarks, tattoos, scars, beard), clothing, voice (high or low, accent) and other distinctive characteristics such as walk.

■ Who: were the victims? associates? was talked to? were witnesses? are children of those involved? saw or heard something of importance? discovered the crime? reported the incident? made the complaint? investigated the incident? worked on the case? marked and received evidence? was notified? had a motive?

■ What: type of crime was committed? are the elements of the crime? was the amount of damage or value of the property involved? happened (narrative of the actions of suspects, victims and witnesses; combines information included under "How")? evidence was found? preventive measures had been taken (safes, locks, alarms, etc.)? knowledge, skill or strength was needed to commit the crime? are possible motives?

was said? did the police officers do? further information is needed? further action is needed?

■ How: was the crime discovered? does this crime relate to other crimes? did the crime occur? was evidence found? was information obtained?

■ Why: was the crime committed (was there intent? consent? motive?)? was certain property stolen? was a particular time selected?

Make notes that describe the physical scene, including general weather and lighting conditions. Witnesses may testify to observations that would have been impossible given the existing weather or lighting. Accurate notes on such conditions will refute false or incorrect testimony.

Record everything you observe in the overall scene: all services rendered, including first aid, description of the injured, location of wounds, who transported the victim and how, including ambulance and hospital information. If, at a later time, you wish to obtain medical records for sustained injuries related to the case, such hospital information will be useful. Record complete and accurate information regarding all photographs taken at the scene. As the search is conducted, record the location and description of evidence and its preservation. Record information to identify the type of crime and what was said and by whom. Include the name, address and phone number of every person present at the scene and all witnesses.

The amount of notes taken depends on the type of offense, the conditions of the case, your attitude and ability and the number of other officers assigned to the case. Make sure you take enough notes to completely describe what you observe and do during an investigation. This will provide a solid foundation for a detailed report and for court testimony. If in doubt about whether to include a specific detail, record it. As noted in the Federal Bureau of Investigation (FBI)'s *Handbook of Forensic Services* (2007, p.178): "Nothing is insignificant to record if it catches one's attention." Take notes about everything you do in an official investigative capacity. Record all facts, regardless of where they may lead. Information establishing a suspect's innocence is as important as that establishing guilt:

Very few cases are of the open-and-shut variety. In most cases, there will be some evidence pointing to the suspect's guilt ("inculpatory") and other evidence that appears inconsistent with the suspect's guilt ("exculpatory"). For example, two witnesses might identify the suspect as the perpetrator of the crime, while a third insists that the suspect is not the one; a victim might make a positive ID of a suspected robber who nevertheless has an alibi based on a time clock at his job. When such evidentiary conflicts exist, the general rule is that *all* of the evidence, both inculpatory and exculpatory, should be reported to the prosecutor for evaluation. (Rutledge, 2007, p.68)

This begins with including such information in the notes about a case.

Do *not* jot down information unrelated to the investigation—for example, the phone number of a friend, an idea for a poem or a doodle. If the defense attorney, judge or jury sees your notes, such irrelevant material will reflect poorly on your professionalism.

Where to Record Notes

Use a notebook to record all facts observed and learned during an investigation. Despite the availability of sophisticated recorders and computers, the notebook remains one of the simplest, most economical and most basic investigative tools. Notes taken on scraps of paper, on the backs of envelopes or on napkins are apt to be lost, and they reflect poorly on an officer's professionalism.

Divide the notebook into sections for easy reference. One section might contain frequently used telephone numbers. Another section might contain frequently needed addresses. This information can be a permanent part of the notebook. Identify the notebook with your name, address and telephone number, as well as the address and telephone number of your police department.

Opinions vary about whether it is better to use a loose-leaf notebook or separate spiral-bound notebooks for each case. The decision to use a loose-leaf or spiral-bound notebook is sometimes a matter of department policy. If you use a loose-leaf notebook, you can easily add paper for each case you are working on as the need arises, and you can keep it well organized. Most investigators favor the loose-leaf notebook because of its flexibility in arranging notes for reports and for testifying in court. However, use of a loose-leaf notebook opens the opportunity for challenge from the defense attorney that the officer has fabricated the notes, adding or deleting relevant pages. This can be countered by numbering each page, followed by the date and case number or by using a separate spiral notebook for each case.

Disadvantages of the latter approach are that the spiral notebook is often only partially used and therefore can be wasteful and may be bulky for storage. Further, if other notes are kept in the same notebook, they also will be subject to the scrutiny of the defense. A final disadvantage is that if you need a blank sheet of paper for some reason, you should not take it from a spiral notebook because most of these notebooks indicate on the cover how many pages they contain. The defense can only conjecture about loose-leaf pages that might have been removed, but missing pages from a spiral notebook can be construed as evidence that something has been removed.

In addition to the notebook, always carry pens and pencils. Use a pen for most notes because ink is permanent. You may want to use pencil for rough sketches that require minor corrections as you sketch.

How to Take Notes

Note taking is an acquired skill. Time does not permit a verbatim transcript. Learn to select key facts and record them in abbreviated form. Do not include words such as *a, and* and *the* in your notes. Omit all other unnecessary words. For example, if a witness said, "I arrived here after having lunch at Harry's Cafe, a delightful little place over on the west side, at about 1:30, and I found my boss had been shot," you would record, "Witness arrived scene 1:30 (after lunch at Harry's Cafe) to find boss shot." You would not know at the time if the fact that she had lunch at Harry's Cafe was important, but it might be, so you would include it.

Whenever possible, use standard abbreviations such as *mph, DWI, Ave.* Do *not,* however, devise your own shorthand. For example, if you wrote, "Body removed by A. K.," the initials *A. K.* would be meaningless to others. If you become ill, injured or deceased, others must be able to read and understand your notes. This is necessary to further the investigation, even though some question regarding admissibility in court may arise.

Some police departments use digital recorders extensively because of the definite advantage of recording exactly what was stated with no danger of misinterpreting, slanting or misquoting. However, digital recorders do not replace the notebook. Despite their advantages, they also have serious disadvantages. The most serious is that they can malfunction and fail to record valuable information. Weak batteries or background noise can also distort the information recorded. In addition, transcribing recordings is time consuming, expensive and subject to error. Finally, the recordings themselves, not the transcription, are the original evidence and thus must be retained and filed.

CHARACTERISTICS OF EFFECTIVE NOTES

Effective notes are complete and describe the scene and the events well enough to enable a prosecutor, judge or jury to visualize them.

> Effective notes are complete, factual, accurate, specific, legible, clear, arranged in chronological order and well organized.

The basic purpose of notes is to record the *facts* of a case. Recall the discussion of the importance of objectivity in an investigation. Use this same objectivity in note taking. For example, you might include in your notes the *fact* that a suspect reached inside his jacket and your *inference* that he was reaching for a gun. Your *opinion* on the merits of gun-control laws, however, has no place in your notes. If you have a specific reason for including an opinion, clearly label the statement as an opinion. Normally, however, restrict your notes to the facts you observe and learn and the inferences you draw. If, for example, you see a person you consider to be nervous and you make a note to that effect ("The man appeared nervous"), you are recording an inference. If, on the other hand, you record specific observations such as, "The man kept looking over his shoulder, checking his watch and wiping perspiration from his forehead," then you are recording facts on which you based your inference. These facts help support the inference that the man was nervous, as you may not remember six months or a year later why you thought that the man was nervous.

Record facts accurately. An inaccurately recorded name can result in the loss of a witness or suspect. Inaccurate measurements can lead to wrong conclusions. Have people spell their names for you. Repeat spellings and numbers for verification. Recheck measurements. If you make an error, cross it out, make the correction and initial it. Do *not* erase. Whether intentional or accidental, erasures raise credibility questions.

Be as specific as possible. Rather than writing *tall, fast* or *far*, write *6′8″, 80 mph* or *50 feet*. Little agreement may exist on what is tall, fast or far.

Notes are usually taken rapidly, increasing the chance of errors. Take enough time to write legibly and clearly. Legibility and clarity are not synonymous. *Legibility* refers to the distinctness of your letters and numbers and is especially important when recording names, addresses, telephone numbers, license numbers, distances and other specific facts. *Clarity*, on the other hand, refers to the distinctness of your statements. For example, lack of clarity is seen in a note that states, "When victim saw suspect he pulled gun." *Who* pulled the gun: the victim or the suspect? The same lack of clarity is seen in the statements "When suspect turned quickly I fired" (Did the suspect turn quickly, or did the officer fire quickly?) and "When the suspect came out of the house, I hit him with

the spotlight." Make certain your notes are clear and can be interpreted only one way.

Effective notes are also arranged in chronological order and well organized. Make entries from each case on separate pages and number the pages. Keep the pages for each case together and record the case number on each page.

FILING NOTES

Some officers destroy all their field notes after they have written their reports, contending that notes simply duplicate what is in the report and may in fact contain information no longer pertinent when the report is written. Some police departments also have this as a policy. Be aware, however, that the defense attorney may ask for an officer's notes regarding an investigation, with the strategic intent to imply that, in cases where officers have discarded their notes, the investigators may be trying to withhold or hide crucial facts or evidence to make the prosecution's case stronger. Thus, it is important to consider a method of saving and filing field notes in preparation for this defensive tactic. One common response to this potential challenge is for investigators to digitally record everything along with taking their field notes, helping to avoid any issues later if the field notes have been discarded.

If department policy is to keep the notes, place them in a location and under a filing system that makes them available months or even years later. Department policy usually determines where and how notes are filed.

> If notes are retained, file them in a secure location readily accessible to investigators.

Store notes in an official police department case file or any secure location where they are available on short demand. Some departments file notes with the original file in the official records department. Others permit an officer to keep the original notes and file only the report made from the notes. Wherever notes are filed, they must be secure.

No one filing system is best. Notes may be filed alphabetically by the victim's name, by case number or in chronological order. As long as the system is logical, the notes will be retrievable. Appeals have been granted as long as 20 years after convictions, with the defendant being granted a new trial. Because of this, many officers retain their notes indefinitely.

ADMISSIBILITY OF NOTES IN COURT

The use of notes in court is probably their most important legal application. They can help discredit a suspect's or a defense witness's testimony; support evidence already given by a prosecution witness, strengthening that testimony; and defend against false allegations by the suspect or defense witnesses. Notes give you an advantage because others rarely make written notes and, therefore, must testify from memory.

All officers who are present at the scene while the notes are being taken and who witness the writing and initial the notes at that time may use the notes during courtroom testimony. If you anticipate the need to have other investigators testify from a specific set of notes, be sure they do in fact witness the original note taking at the crime scene and provide their initials on the original notes. The admissibility of notes in court is presented in greater detail in the final chapter of this text.

In addition to accurate notes, photographs and video recordings provide vital and necessary means of documenting a crime scene.

INVESTIGATIVE PHOTOGRAPHY: AN OVERVIEW

A picture is, indeed, worth a thousand words, and investigative photographs and videos are essential to proper crime scene documentation. The basic purpose of crime scene photography is to record the scene permanently. Photos and video taken immediately, using proper techniques to reproduce the entire crime scene, provide a factual record of high evidentiary value. The time that elapses between the commission of a crime and when a suspect in that crime is brought to trial can stretch into months or years, with the condition of the crime scene and physical evidence deteriorating along the way. Photos and videos preserve the scene. Do not touch or move any evidence until pictures and video have been taken of the general area and all evidence.

 Photographs and video recordings reproduce the crime scene in detail for presentation to the prosecution, defense, witnesses, judge and jury in court and are used in investigating, prosecuting and police training.

Although investigators take most crime scene photographs, they may also be acquired from commercial or amateur photographers, attorneys, news media personnel or the coroner's staff. For example, in an arson case at a church, photographs came from three outside sources. The pastor hired a photographer to take pictures for historical purposes and to assess damage, an insurance company photographer took pictures, and a television news crew had taken live in-progress footage. These pictures, along with those taken by police personnel, provided an excellent record of the fire in-progress, its point of origin and the resulting damage.

Video is now well established as an investigative tool. Lightweight, handheld video recorders are easy to use at a crime scene and provide a high-quality digital format of crime scene images. Video can also be taken of witness testimony, depositions, evidence, lineups and even trials.

Advantages and Disadvantages of Photographs

One advantage of photographs is that they can be taken immediately, an important factor in bad weather or when many people are present. For example, a picture of a footprint in the dirt outside a window broken during a burglary can be important if it rains before a casting can be made. The same is true when the large number of people present might alter the scene.

Another obvious advantage of crime scene photographs is that they accurately represent the crime scene in court. The effect of pictures on a jury cannot be overestimated. Photographs are highly effective visual aids that corroborate the facts presented.

 Advantages of photographs: They can be taken immediately, accurately represent the crime scene and evidence, create interest and increase attention to testimony.

Benefits of digital photography are numerous: the images are quickly adaptable as e-mail attachments; most digital cameras record technical information about each photograph, such as the date and time and specific camera settings, in a text file associated with the image; the issue of image degradation, a common problem with film, is avoided; and the physical space required to file and store a large number of photographs is greatly reduced.

Although photographs of a crime scene accurately represent what was present, they include everything at the scene, both relevant and irrelevant. So much detail may distract viewers of photographs. Another drawback is that some cameras may lack the capability to pick up small nuances or discrete evidence, such as finger print outlines.

> Disadvantages of photographs: They are not selective, do not show actual distances and may be distorted and damaged by mechanical errors in shooting or processing.

Despite these disadvantages, photography is a valuable investigative technique, and photographic quality continues to improve as technology advances. Even the inexpensive point-and-shoot cameras currently available can often provide better quality images than could the more expensive, cumbersome cameras commonly used a decade ago.

The introduction of digital video technology into crime scene investigation has allowed investigators to compensate for some of the shortcomings of still photography.

Advantages and Disadvantages of Video

A video or DVD, played before a jury, can bring a crime scene to life and offers some distinct advantages over photographs, such as showing distance and including audio capability. Furthermore, a slow pan of a crime scene is more likely than is a series of photographs to capture all evidence, including that in the periphery of view, which might seem rather inconsequential at the time.

> Advantages of videos: They accurately represent the crime scene and evidence, are able to show distance more clearly than photos and have sound capability to more fully document what is being seen.

As part of the *CSI effect*, juries now expect to see video of a crime scene. Regrettably, many agencies, whether because of lack of funding or prioritization, fail to provide adequate training to those tasked with videotaping a crime scene, assuming that if officers are able to tape their cousin's wedding or their daughter's soccer game, they should be able to handle a camcorder in any venue.

The negative consequences of poor video can damage a case. Some common mistakes made by untrained crime scene videographers include shooting without planning ahead, not shooting enough, shooting too much (resulting in a boring presentation), poor focusing, overusing the zoom feature, making jerky camera movements, including unintentional audio and failing to use a tripod.

The use of digital technology is becoming commonplace in criminal investigations. Digital cameras allow instant verification of a photo's quality, and most automatically stamp the date and time of the image capture on an attached text file.
© Ruslan Ivantsov/Shutterstock

Proper training can help eliminate most, if not all, of these common videotaping errors and increase the video's documentation value.

> Disadvantages of videos: Many people mistakenly believe that no training in videotaping is necessary, which leads to poor video quality and a diminished value in the video's documentation of the crime scene.

A vast array of modern equipment has greatly enhanced the investigative usefulness of photography and videography.

BASIC PHOTOGRAPHIC EQUIPMENT

Previous editions of this text discussed both film and digital photography. Indeed, film photography was, for more than a century, a fundamental technique in criminal investigation. The first time photographic evidence was used in a criminal case was in 1874 (*Udderzook v. Commonwealth*), and color photography gained prominence during the 1960s (Dutelle, 2010). Digital photography entered the scene during the 1990s, and by the mid-1990s, many criminal justice agencies had begun using this technology. Early digital equipment lacked the high-resolution capability found in film cameras used at the time—a capability necessary for identification, examination and courtroom purposes—but advances in technology have since elevated digital image resolution to levels that match or exceed that available from film photography. Thus, by year-end 2009, all 50 state crime laboratories had officially converted from film to digital technology: "Processing film is now a thing of the past, as is submitting film as photographic evidence" (Dutelle, 2010, p.60). Therefore, this section on photographic equipment no longer presents information on film photography.

Crime scene photography uses both common and special-function cameras and equipment, depending on the crime investigated and the investigator's preferences.

> At a minimum, have available and be skilled in operating a Polaroid-type instant-print camera, a point-and-shoot camera, a digital single-lens reflex (DSLR) camera, a fingerprint camera and video equipment.

Investigators commonly have individual preferences about the equipment to use in a given situation, and agencies are well advised to purchase a variety of photographic equipment for different applications: "A garden-variety traffic accident investigation doesn't require a lot of photographic horsepower.... This is mostly point-and-shoot work, and the main concern is whether there's enough power in the camera's strobe to illuminate the scene at night. But if the same officer's next call is to take a report and document the injuries of a domestic violence victim at the hospital, that point-and-shoot camera may not be up to the task" (Dees, 2008, p.68).

Instant-print cameras such as those made by Polaroid and Impulse provide pictures at low cost per image. Instant-print photography, which is now in digital format, provides immediate confirmation of the quality and accuracy of the picture at a time when it is possible to take another shot. The cameras are simple to operate, which lessens the need for training. Every officer on the force can use an instant-print camera. These cameras have good optics, resolution and color and can document small evidence such as bullet holes. The greatest advantage, however, is that the photographer can tell immediately whether the photo is good.

Point-and-shoot cameras, which have a fixed lens, have become relatively inexpensive and are easy to use. These cameras automatically adjust the shutter speed, aperture control and other settings, lessening the likelihood of poor image quality resulting from operator error. Some models are ruggedized to be water-, shock- and temperature-resistant; although they cost more, they do not need to be replaced as often (Dees, 2008). Because this type of equipment is adequate for so many routine investigations, a large number of departments have purchased point-and-shoot cameras to place in every patrol car. These cameras provide instant feedback regarding a photo's quality, allowing the officer to verify whether the shot contains what it was intended to capture, that the lighting is sufficient and that the image is not blurry.

Digital single-lens reflex (DSLR) cameras offer significantly higher image quality and resolution than do point-and-shoots but are more difficult to use properly and are generally, sometimes considerably, more expensive. The benefit is that, with accessories, they can be adapted to take better photos in more challenging situations. A zoom or telephoto lens can capture details from far away, if it is not possible to physically reach the location of piece of evidence. DSLR cameras are also superior to point-and-shoots for taking photos at close range. And with wide-angle lenses, an officer is able to better document evidence in close quarters, such as bathrooms, vehicle interiors and other small spaces (Dees, 2008).

Fingerprint cameras are specially constructed to take pictures of fingerprints without distortion. They provide their own light through four bulbs, one in each corner. Removing a bulb from any corner provides slanted lighting to show fingerprint ridge detail. According to the *Handbook of Forensic Services* (2007, p.82), a tripod and cable release should be used when photographing latent prints. This camera can also photograph trace evidence such as bloodstains and tool marks.

Video cameras are used to record alleged bribery, payoffs and narcotics buys. Permanently installed units frequently photograph crimes actually being committed, such as bank robberies or shoplifting. Videotaping crime scenes is now common. The cameras have become much less expensive, much more portable and much easier to operate. They have the advantage of immediacy and eliminate a middle processing step in the chain of evidence. In addition, most can operate in quite limited light.

Camcorders and video recording equipment have for some time been used for in-station recording of bookings and for testing of suspects in driving-while-intoxicated stops. Use of video cameras for crime scene investigations is now prevalent. Many police departments have purchased video equipment to record crime scenes and criminal acts such as vandalism, drug deals and thefts, increasing convictions.

Many police departments have mounted video cameras on their patrol vehicles' dashboards, an application that offers many benefits. *Specialized cameras* such as binocular cameras and trip cameras (cameras that set themselves off) are helpful in surveillance.

A Maryland State Police Officer shows a video screen that is connected to a live video feed in state police cars to record traffic stops and other violations. Recordings from such equipment can be used in court and for training purposes as well.

© AP Images/The Daily Times, Megan Raymond

Accessories, depending on the camera(s) used, include an exposure meter, flash attachments and flood lamps and high-intensity spotlights. Lighting equipment can also assist in illuminating the scene as officers search for minute evidence. Lenses and filters are available for different purposes. Normal lenses are best for evidence, but sometimes special lenses are needed. For example, a telephoto lens can capture a distant subject, whereas a wide-angle lens can cover an entire room in a single frame. Various filters can eliminate certain colors from a photograph. Lens care products and a soft bristled lens airbrush and lens cloth are also a necessity.

Storage of photographic equipment is a concern, and cameras should be protected from contact with other items commonly used in criminal investigation. Dees (2008, p.68) cautions, "One agency I know of went to considerable trouble and expense to make fitted cases for all of their crime scene investigation gear so officers could check it out of the station at the beginning of the watch and throw it in the trunk until needed. None of the gear ever got broken, but the cameras didn't work well once they had been coated inside and out with fingerprint powder."

Selection of a camera and accessories is determined by budget, local needs and investigator preference. Sometimes investigators can borrow equipment from local schools or community organizations or share it with other agencies. In some communities, citizens lend special-purpose equipment to the police department.

A major advance is the ability of computer software to stitch together digital photos of 180 degrees or more to create one 360-degree photo—a panoramic view of a

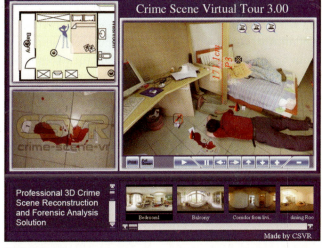

FIGURE 2.1

The Crime Scene Virtual Tour software program allows investigators to recreate the crime scene and to piece together better the events that occurred. These programs may also be presented during trial to help a jury visualize the crime scene.

© Crime Scene Virtual Tour

crime scene that is interactive, allowing viewers, including jury members, to walk through it as though they were there (Figure 2.1). This type of 360-degree photographic view is called **immersive imaging**. Crime Scene Virtual Tour (CSVT) software lets jurors virtually step into a crime scene. The software allows the scene to be viewed from any angle with zoom, pan, tilt and rotate features. If a witness claims to have been standing at a certain place, an investigator can virtually go there to view that perspective.

TRAINING IN AND USING INVESTIGATIVE PHOTOGRAPHY

Investigators can master most photographic equipment by reading the accompanying manuals and practicing. Some equipment, however, requires special training. Photographic training includes instruction in operating all available photographic equipment; shooting techniques; anticipated problems; and identifying, filing and maintaining continuity of photographic evidence. Learn the nomenclature and operation of your available photographic equipment. Sometimes camera and equipment manufacturers or outlets provide such training.

Professional commercial photographers in the community can sometimes assist in training or serve as consultants. They can provide information on photographic techniques and special problems such as lighting, close-ups, exposures and use of filters. Training programs also include instructions on identifying and filing photographs and on establishing and maintaining the continuity of the chain of evidence.

As with other types of crime scene processing techniques, proper training in the use of digital equipment is essential. Digital technology brings with it a new language and application skill set for investigators to learn. Although an in-depth discussion of digital technology, capabilities and applications is beyond the scope of this text, a few examples should make clear the critical need for investigators to be thoroughly trained in using digital equipment.

One of the most basic terms used when discussing digital photography is **resolution**, which refers to the fineness of image detail captured with a camera, displayed on a monitor or printed on paper. High resolution produces a sharp image; low resolution, a blurrier image. Resolution is commonly quantified by pixels. A **pixel** is the smallest unit of a digital image, generally a dot within the image (just as traditional newsprint photos are made up of tiny dots); one **megapixel** is about a million dots. The more dots, the larger the image can be made without losing resolution quality. Digital cameras or other capture devices range in resolution from two megapixels to 24 megapixels. However, resolution of computer monitors and printers, referred to as *output devices*, are given in pixels per inch, or **PPI**. Both types of resolution must be factored in when taking digital photographs because both affect the final size and quality of the image. An image photographed with a high-resolution camera (the capture device), if printed on a low-resolution printer (the output device), will not show fine detail clearly. A low-resolution image, if enlarged too much, will also lose quality.

An understanding of resolution is critical for investigators who use digital cameras to document a crime scene because resolution affects every aspect of digital imaging. Improper choice of equipment or incorrect settings on it will produce low-quality results, which may have damaging consequences in the courtroom.

The importance of understanding resolution, and the plethora of other digital terms and concepts too detailed to explore here, is brought into focus when one considers evidentiary standards and requirements surrounding this technology. For example, an investigator photographing latent prints at a crime scene must know that the FBI's Integrated Automated Fingerprint Identification System (AFIS) requires a latent print to be photographed with a minimum resolution of 1,000 PPI (Dutelle, 2010). In effect, for digital images to have value in the courtroom, investigators must thoroughly understand their equipment and apply the technology properly. (Admissibility of photographs is examined shortly.)

What to Photograph or Videotape

The *Handbook of Forensic Services* (2007, p.179) recommends photographing the crime scene as soon as possible and photographing the most fragile areas of the crime scene first. Take sufficient photographs or video to reconstruct the entire scene. This usually requires a series of shots, notably of the entrance point, the crime commission area and the exit point. If possible, show the entire crime scene in a pictorial sequence. This helps relate the crime to other crimes.

Move the camera to cover the entire crime scene area, but plan a sequence of shots that least disturb the scene. The initial photographs showing the entire crime scene should use a technique called **overlapping**. Photograph the scene clockwise and take the first picture with a specific object on the right. For the second photo, make sure that the same object is on the left side of the photograph. Continue in this way until you have covered the entire scene.

First, photograph the general area, then specific areas and finally specific objects of evidence. Take exterior shots first because they are the most subject to alteration by weather and security violations.

This progression of shots or video will reconstruct the commission of a crime:

1. Take *long-range* shots of the locality, points of ingress and egress, normal entry to the property and

buildings, exterior of the buildings and grounds and street signs or other identifiable structures that will establish location.

2. Take *medium-range* shots of the immediate crime scene and the location of objects of evidence within the area or room.

3. Take *close-range* shots of specific evidence such as hairs, fibers, footprints and bloodstains. The entire surface of some objects may be photographed to show all the evidence; for example, a table surface may contain bloodstains, fingerprints, hairs and fibers.

Zoom lenses allow close shots without disturbing the crime scene, and close-ups are possible with macro lenses. Such close-range shots usually should include a marker, sometimes called a *scale*. A **marker** is anything used in a photograph to show accurate or relative size. It is usually a ruler, but it can be some other object of a known size, such as a pen or pencil. An important point: Using a marker introduces something foreign to the crime scene. The same is true of chalk marks drawn around a body or placed on walls to illustrate bullet direction. Therefore, first take a picture of the scene or object without the marker, then add the marker and take a second photograph.

Different crimes require different types of photographs. In arson cases, photograph the point of origin and any incendiary devices. In burglaries, photograph the points of entry and exit, tool marks, fingerprints and other trace evidence. In assaults, photograph injuries. In homicides or suicides, photograph the deceased, including pictures of the clothing worn; take a full-length picture showing height, position of the body and all extremities and evidence near the body. Photograph injured parts of the body to show the location and extent of injuries or petechiae and any postmortem lividity (discussed in Chapter 8).

Photogrammetry can be used at most crime scenes. **Forensic photogrammetry** is the technique of extrapolating three-dimensional (3-D) measurements from two-dimensional photographs. Photogrammetry can also automatically orient photographs taken from awkward angles and can correct for camera misalignment. Furthermore, this technique can cut in half the amount of time investigators spend performing on-site mapping of a crime scene. The major advantage is that images can be recorded quickly, reducing time spent at the crime scene.

Errors to Avoid

To obtain effective photographs and videos, be familiar with your equipment and check it before you use it. Unfamiliarity and lack of practice with photographic equipment increases the chance of error.

If something has been moved, do *not* put it back. It is legally impossible to return an object to its original position. To minimize distortion or misrepresentation, maintain proper perspective and attempt to show the objects in a crime scene in their relative size and position. Take pictures from eye level, the height from which people normally observe objects.

> Take photographs and videos before anything is disturbed. Avoid inaccuracies and distortions.

Checklists are important when it comes to crime scene photography and can help eliminate errors. A checklist for a DSLR camera might include such items as the following: Are the batteries in the camera? Is the memory media loaded? Is the camera on? Is the lens cap removed? Are there spare batteries and memory media readily available?

TYPES OF INVESTIGATIVE PHOTOGRAPHY

In addition to crime scene photography, certain other types of photography play vital roles in investigation.

> Types of investigative photography include crime scene, surveillance, aerial, night, laboratory, mug shot and lineup.

Surveillance Photography

Surveillance photography establishes the identity of a subject or records criminal behavior without the photographer's presence being known to the subject. The photographs or video can help identify a suspect's associates, destroy an alibi, plan a raid or develop a surveillance plan. Banks and stores frequently use surveillance cameras to help identify robbers and burglars. Numerous bank robbers have been identified through photographs taken by surveillance cameras installed in the bank. With a well-thought out plan, surveillance tapes can potentially be a "real force multiplier for law enforcement agencies of any size" (Kanable, 2008, p.30).

Photographs during a stakeout are usually taken with a DSLR camera with several telephoto lenses. Sometimes infrared capability is used. It may be necessary to use a van—preferably borrowed because it is best to use a vehicle only once for such purposes. An appliance repair van or any van that would commonly be seen in the area is desirable.

Concealing a camera can be a problem. You might use a bag, briefcase, suitcase or coat pocket with an opening. You can also conceal the camera by using rooftops or windows of buildings or vehicles in the area. A camera kept away from a vehicle window is rarely seen by people outside the vehicle. Keep the camera on and adjusted to the required light so you can take pictures instantly.

Surveillance photography is often called **trap photography** because the photos prove that an incident occurred and can help identify suspects and weapons. These photos corroborate witness testimony and identification. The fact that the photos exist often induces guilty pleas without court appearances, thus saving investigators' time.

Often the recordings from security cameras leave much to be desired. Problems such as poor lighting conditions, blurry images and low resolution can be overcome through use of professional video and audio forensic tools such as dTective and dVeloper, both available from Ocean Systems. Such video analysis, according to a national video forensics expert, is the "new DNA for law enforcement" (Heinecke, 2007, p.86).

The Department of Justice and the International Association of Chiefs of Police (IACP) have developed four

Technology Innovations

WHAT IS DVELOPER?

Many times crucial details are hidden in video because of poor lighting or improperly adjusted and maintained cameras and video equipment. When dealing with color video, details are often more prevalent in one color than another. With dVeloper, it's easy to isolate the video color space that holds the most valuable information. With the click of a mouse, dVeloper compensates for the poorly exposed video. By analyzing the entire video, or just a region of interest, dVeloper automatically adjusts brightness, contrast and gamma to bring out more detail.

dVeloper removes noise and video graininess through a time-lapse processing technique called *frame averaging*. When the target remains still for even a moment, video noise and other transient items like rain and snow are removed, revealing the details hidden beneath.

Source: http://www.oceansystems.com/dtective/dveloper_index.html

Regional Forensic Video Analysis Labs, located in Cincinnati, Ohio; Fort Worth, Texas; Raynham, Massachusetts; and Phoenix, Arizona. These labs are equipped with dTective, currently in use by 90 percent of all agencies with video analysis capabilities: "Just as DNA has CODIS and fingerprints have AFIS, now forensic video evidence will have the Regional Forensic Video Analysis Labs—a national database of criminals caught on tape" (Heinecke, 2007, p.87).

Enhanced surveillance capability can be provided by using robots: "Through the addition of cameras and microphones, as well as wireless communications, critical intelligence can be gathered without exposing officers" (Ashley, 2008, p.32).

Surveillance photography can also be a crime prevention and detection tool. For example, the Newark, New Jersey, Police Department has video cameras mounted in six different areas of the two-square-mile downtown area. An officer observes what is taking place in each area from a central location. Burglaries and street robberies have decreased, and the police have successfully presented the videos as evidence in court.

Aerial Photography

Investigators often use aerial photography to cover extensive areas. For example, it can be used following a bank robbery to show roads leading to and from the bank. Aerial photography is also useful when police know that a crime is going to be committed but not when. Aerial photography shows routes to the scene as well as how to block escape routes and avoid detours during pursuit and where to set up roadblocks. It is essential in locating dead-end streets—information that can be very important if a chase ensues. Aerial pictures can also help establish the location of a crime scene, especially in large rural areas or mountainous sectors. An unmanned aerial vehicle (UAV) might be used to provide aerial video in real time.

Geographical information systems (GIS) technology is now enhancing the aerial views of crimes scenes by providing background information about specific crime scenes, such as buildings and streets, to the investigator: "GIS used successfully with leading public safety software will continue to offer the speed and performance needed to respond when seconds matter" (Wandrei, 2007, p.56). Historically, many agencies have multiple and separate data silos within a local government (Wandrei, p.58). For example, the road commission maintains a schedule of road closures and ongoing road construction projects, and the fire department maintains much information about commercial buildings, including floor plans, alarm codes, evacuation routes and on-premise hazardous materials. Wandrei suggests such information can be invaluable to law enforcement: "A significant improvement in GIS technology now allows those silos of data to be shared with each other in near real time."

Aerial photographs are often available in commercial photographers' files, engineering offices or highway-planning agencies. The vast areas covered by highways and engineering projects usually require aerial mapping. Federal, state, county and municipal agencies also may have aerial photos. If none are available, a local photographer can be hired to provide them. Many larger departments and county sheriff's offices have helicopters that may be available.

Aerial photos can be enlarged or presented on slides to show the relationships of streets and roads. For example, in the John F. Kennedy assassination investigation, the entire area was photographed, including all points from which shots might have been fired. More recently, software based on aerial photography was used by multiple jurisdictions involved in the Washington, DC, sniper investigation.

A high-tech application of aerial photography involves **Pictometry**®, a unique, patented computer technology that integrates various aerial shots of a land-based artifact taken straight down (orthogonal) and from numerous angles (oblique). The result is a high-resolution 3-D image of the object, whether it be a landmark, a neighborhood, a bridge, a river, a house or any other structure or geological feature, which investigators may view from multiple perspectives with the simple click of a mouse (Figures 2.2A and 2.2B). The software also features extreme zooming capabilities, allowing investigators to rotate and zoom in on a particular structure.

Night Photography

Taking pictures at night presents special problems, particularly that of illuminating a scene. Adequate light can be obtained by increasing exposure time, using a photoflash for small areas and a flash series for larger areas or using floodlights. Floodlights also aid in locating evidence and decrease the chance of evidence being accidentally destroyed.

Investigators can make the camera see as the photographer sees through camera position, time exposure and supplemental lighting. State-of-the-art night-vision devices and cameras are dramatically better than earlier ones, with a range extending as far as a mile. Night-vision devices use image intensification and can be binoculars, weapon mounted, camera mounted or head mounted.

Laboratory Photography

Not all investigative photography is done in the field. Sometimes objects are photographed in a laboratory with special equipment that is too large, delicate or expensive to use in the field. For example, infrared film photographs can reveal the contents of unopened envelopes, bloodstains, alterations to documents, variations in types of ink and residue near where a bullet has passed through clothing. X-ray cameras can detect loaded dice.

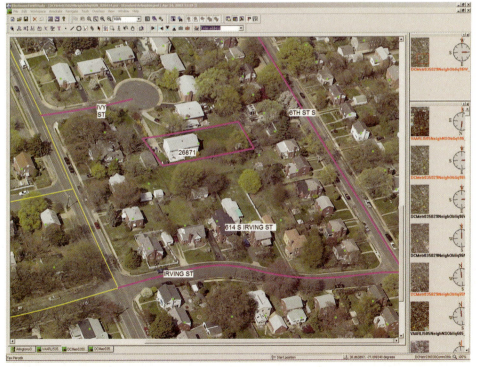

FIGURE 2.2A

Pictometry software with GIS overlays allows investigators to see as many as 12 different views of this geographic area.

Images courtesy of Pictometry International

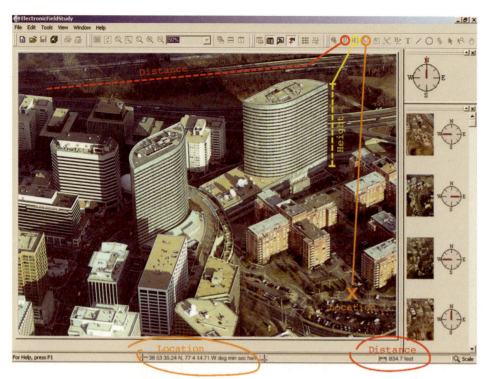

FIGURE 2.2B
This screen capture highlights some of the different functions available with Pictometry software, such as measuring distances and heights, and determining a precise geographic location with latitude/longitude coordinates.
© Will Smith/Pictometry

Microphotography takes pictures through a microscope and can help identify minute particles of evidence such as hairs or fibers. In contrast, **macrophotography** enlarges a subject. For example, a fingerprint or a tool mark can be greatly enlarged to show the details of ridges or striations.

Laser-beam photography can reveal evidence indiscernible to the naked eye. For example, it can reveal the outline of a footprint in a carpet, even though the fibers have returned to normal position.

Ultraviolet-light photography uses the low end of the color spectrum, which is invisible to human sight, to make visible impressions of bruises and injuries long after their actual occurrence. Bite marks, injuries caused by beatings, cigarette burns, neck strangulation marks and other impressions left from intentional injuries can be reproduced and used as evidence in criminal cases by scanning the presumed area of injury with a fluorescent or blue light. The damage impression left by the injury is then photographed. In addition, the type of weapon used in committing a crime can often be determined by examining its impression, developed by using ultraviolet light.

Mug Shots

Although investigators seldom take **mug shots** themselves, these photographs are often significant in criminal investigations. Mug shots originated in 19th-century France when Alphonse Bertillon developed a method of identification

that used an extensive system of measurements to describe people. The Bertillon identification system included a written description, the complete measurements of the person and a photograph. The pictures of people in police custody were kept in department files for identification and became known as *mug shots*. Gathered in files and displayed in groups, they were called a **rogues' gallery**.

Opinions differ regarding the preferred poses for mug shots. Some agencies believe the front and profile of the head are sufficient; others prefer full-length, stand-up pictures. No matter what the pose, mug shots should include the facial features and the clothing worn at the time of arrest, because a defendant's appearance may change between the time of arrest and trial. Mug shots can be filed by age, sex and height to make them more readily accessible for viewing. Mug shots can be carried in the field to identify suspicious persons or to show to crime victims to assist in identifying their attacker. Mug shots are also used for "wanted" circulars distributed to other police agencies and the public. The use of mug shots in suspect identification is discussed in Chapter 7.

Lineup Photographs

The computer's capacity to sort through a database of mug shots and bring up all the "hits" within specific categories can assist in generating photographic lineups. After entering characteristics of a known suspect, an officer can select 6 to 12 other "hits" to be used for presentation with the suspect's photo. In addition, videotapes or photographs of people included in lineups may be taken to establish the fairness of the lineup.

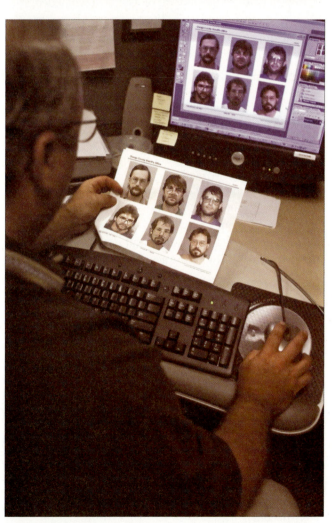

A video imaging system allows officers to sort a database using specific parameters—race, sex, hair color, height, age, distinguishing marks—any feature that can be visually described. The "hits" can then be used to assemble a photographic lineup.
© Joel Gordon

IDENTIFYING, FILING AND MAINTAINING SECURITY OF EVIDENCE

Photographs must be properly identified, filed and kept secure to be admissible as evidence.

Identifying

In the field notes, the photographs taken should be dated and numbered in sequence. Include the case number, type of offense and subject of the picture. To further identify the photograph with the crime scene and the subject, record the photographer's name, location and direction of the camera, lens type, approximate distance in feet to the subject, lighting, weather conditions and a brief description of the scene in the picture.

The photos should also be marked like any other evidence relating to the crime scene using a procedure called **backing**. This includes writing on the back of the photo your initials, the date the photo was taken, what the photo depicts and the direction of north.

Filing

File the images for easy reference. Pictures in the case file are available to others; therefore, it is usually best to put them in a special photograph file, cross-referenced by case number. For digital images, file them appropriately as evidence or within the department's internal secured hard drive, whatever department policy dictates.

Maintaining Security

Record the chain of custody of the photographs in the field notes or in a special file. Mark and identify the memory media as it is removed from the camera. Each time the media changes possession, record the name of the person accepting it.

ADMISSIBILITY OF PHOTOGRAPHS IN COURT

Photographs must be taken under certain conditions and must meet specific criteria to be admissible in court.

 Photographs must be material, relevant, competent, accurate, free of distortion and noninflammatory.

A **material photograph** relates to a specific case and subject. Material evidence is relevant and forms a substantive part of the case presented or has a legitimate and effective influence on the decision of the case. A **relevant photograph** helps explain testimony. A **competent photograph** accurately represents what it purports to represent, is properly identified and is properly placed in the chain of evidence and secured until court presentation.

Testimony reports the exact conditions under which the photographs were taken and the equipment used. Photographs must be accurate and free of distortion. If nothing has been removed from or added to the scene, the photograph will be accurate. Inaccuracies do not necessarily render the photograph inadmissible as evidence as long as they are fully explained and the court is not misled about what the picture represents.

Likewise, distortion will not necessarily disqualify a photograph as evidence if no attempt is made to misrepresent the photograph and if the distortion is adequately explained. For example, an amateur photographer may have taken the picture from an unusual camera height to produce a dramatic effect, not knowing the picture would later be useful as evidence in a criminal investigation.

Color distortion is a frequent objection. Because most objects have color, black-and-white photographs are technically distorted. Therefore, color photographs usually constitute better evidence. However, color can also be distorted by inadequate lighting or faulty processing. Nevertheless, the photograph can still be useful, especially if the object's shape is more important than its color.

Although color photographs are less distorted and are usually better evidence than black-and-white photographs, they have often been objected to as being inflammatory—for example, showing in gruesome, vivid color a badly beaten body. To be ruled inadmissible, color photographs must be judged by the court to be so inflammatory that they will unduly influence the jury. Sometimes taking both color and black-and-white pictures is advisable. The black-and-white pictures can be introduced as evidence; the color pictures can be used for investigatory purposes only.

The transition from film to digital photography, and the ready availability of software that modifies, enhances or otherwise alters digital images, has raised authenticity issues and concerns regarding such digital photographs' originality and integrity. However, "The legal requirements for the admissibility of digital images as evidence within court are the same as that for film images. The majority of legal challenges surrounding digital images have been concerned with processed images" (Dutelle, 2010, p.63). The FBI's Scientific Working Group on Imaging Technologies (SWGIT) has implemented a policy stating that altering or processing a digital image is legally acceptable within forensic applications provided the following criteria are met:

- "The original image is preserved;
- The processing steps are logged when they include techniques other than those used in a traditional photographic darkroom;
- The end result is presented as an enhanced image, which may be reproduced by the logged steps to the original image" (Dutelle, 2010, p.63).

To overcome defense challenges that a digital image was altered or otherwise tampered with, investigators must rigorously maintain the chain of custody and use techniques that safeguard the authenticity of their photographs. Several software programs have been developed that "watermark" or authenticate the original image, either at the point of capture (within the camera) or as it is downloaded from the camera to a computer. The programs then store the original image in a secure location and write-protect it, making it impossible to alter the original, yet still allowing copies to be manipulated for investigative purposes.

CRIME SCENE SKETCHES: AN OVERVIEW

In addition to admissible photographs and videotapes, investigators usually must prepare a crime scene sketch. An investigator's scene sketch can be more descriptive than hundreds of words and is often an extremely important investigative aid. The crime scene **sketch**

- Portrays the physical facts accurately.
- Relates to the sequence of events at the scene.
- Establishes the precise location and relationship of objects and evidence at the scene.
- Helps create a mental picture of the scene for those not present.
- Is a permanent record of the scene.
- Is usually admissible in court.

 A crime scene sketch assists in (1) interviewing and interrogating people, (2) preparing the investigative report and (3) presenting the case in court.

The sketch supplements photographs, notes, plaster casts and other investigative techniques. Artistic ability is helpful but not essential in making crime scene sketches.

Still, many police officers avoid making sketches. To overcome this hesitance, practice by drawing familiar scenes such as your home, office or police station. Use graph paper to make sketching easier.

The most common types of sketches are those drawn at the crime scene, called *rough sketches*, and those completed later by an investigator or a drafter, called *scale* (or *finished*) *drawings*. Both describe the crime scene pictorially and show the precise location of objects and evidence.

THE ROUGH SKETCH

A **rough sketch** is the first pencil-drawn outline of a scene and the location of objects and evidence within this outline. It is not usually drawn to scale, although distances are measured and entered in the appropriate locations.

> Sketch all serious crime and crash scenes after photographs are taken and before anything is moved. Sketch the entire scene, the objects and the evidence.

It is better to include too much rather than too little, but do not include irrelevant objects that clutter and confuse the sketch.

The area to be sketched depends on the crime scene. If it involves a large area, make a sketch of nearby streets, vegetation and entrance and exit paths. If the scene is inside a house or apartment building, show the scene's location in relation to the larger structure. If the scene involves only a single room, sketch only the immediate crime scene, including an outline of the room, objects and the evidence within it.

Do not overlook the possible availability of architectural drawings of the house or building. These are often on file with local engineering, assessing or building departments or with the architect who drew the original plans.

Sketching Materials

Materials needed for rough sketches should be assembled and placed in their own kit or in the crime scene investigation kit.

> Materials for the rough sketch include paper, pencil, long steel measuring tape, carpenter-type ruler, straightedge, clipboard, compass, protractor and thumbtacks.

Paper of any type will do, but plain white or graph paper is best. No lines interfere if you use plain white. On the other hand, graph paper provides distance ratios and allows for more accurate depictions of the relationships between objects and evidence at the scene. When sketching, use a hard lead pencil to avoid smudges. Keep two or three pencils on hand.

Use a 50- to 150-foot steel measuring tape for measuring long distances. Steel is preferable because it does not stretch and therefore is more accurate than cloth tape. Use a carpenter-type ruler to take short and close-quarter measurements and a straightedge to draw straight lines. A clipboard will give a firm, level drawing surface.

Use a compass to determine true north, especially in areas and buildings laid out in other than true directions. Use a protractor to find the proper angles when determining coordinates.

Thumbtacks are helpful to hold down one end of the tape when you measure. You can also use them to fasten paper to a drawing surface if no clipboard is available.

STEPS IN SKETCHING THE CRIME SCENE

Once photographs have been taken and other priority steps in the preliminary investigation performed, you can begin sketching the crime scene. First, make an overall judgment of the scene. Remember not to move, remove, touch or pick up anything until it has been photographed, located on the rough sketch and described in detail in your notes. Then handle objects only in accordance with the techniques for preserving evidence.

> To sketch a crime scene:
> ■ Observe and plan.
> ■ Measure distances and outline the area.
> ■ Plot objects and evidence within the outline.
> ■ Take notes and record details.
> ■ Identify the sketch with a legend and a scale.
> ■ Reassess the sketch.

Step One: Observe and Plan

Before starting to sketch, observe the scene as many times as you need to feel comfortable with it. Take in the entire scene mentally so you can recall it later. Plan in advance how to proceed in an organized way to avoid destruction of evidence. Ask yourself, "What is relevant to the crime? What should be included in the sketch?"

The size of the area determines how many sketches you make. For example, part of the crime may have taken place indoors and another part outdoors a considerable distance away. To include the entire area would make the scale too small. Therefore, make two sketches.

The overview also helps you determine where to start sketching and measuring. If the scene is a room, stand in the doorway and start the sketch there. Then continue clockwise or counterclockwise. The photographs, sketch and search are all made in the same direction. Usually it does not matter which direction is selected, but try to use the one that is least disturbing to evidence.

Step Two: Measure Distances and Outline the Area

All measurements must be accurate. Do not estimate distances or use paces or shoe length measurement. Use conventional units of measurements such as inches, feet or yards. Do not move any objects while measuring.

If another officer is helping you take measurements, reverse the ends of the tape so you both can observe the actual distance on the tape. Legally, it is *hearsay* for officers to testify to what they did not actually observe. If a third officer is taking notes, that officer can testify to only the measurements given to him or her unless he or she actually saw the tape measurement. However, all officers may testify from the same notes if they review and initial them as they are made.

Do not measure from movable objects. Use *fixed locations* such as walls, trees, telephone poles, building corners, curbs and so on. Measure from wall to wall, not baseboard to baseboard.

Once the outside measurements have been made, sketch the outline, maintaining some distance ratio. Use the longest measurement first and orient the sketch paper to this distance, positioning the sketch so *north is toward the top of the paper*. Place the outside limits in the sketch using dimension lines such as this:

Determine the **scale** by taking the longest measurement at the scene and dividing it by the longest measurement of the paper used for sketching. For example, if your paper is 10 inches and the longest measurement at the scene is 100 feet, let 1 inch equal 10 feet. Use the largest, simplest scale possible. Table 2.1 presents suggested scales for sketches.

Graph paper makes it easier to draw to scale. Each square can equal 1 square foot or 1 square inch, depending

TABLE 2.1 Suggested Scales for Sketches	
Indoor Areas	**Outdoor Areas**
1/2" = 1' (small rooms)	1/2" = 10' (large buildings and grounds)
1/4" = 1' (large rooms)	1/8" = 10'0 (large land areas)
1/8" = 1' (very large rooms)	

© Cengage Learning, 2013

Accuracy is vital when making crime scene measurements. Here, police measure the distance between spent handgun casings at an outdoor crime scene.
© AP/World Wide Photos

on the size of the scene. The outline sketch of an outdoor scene might look like Figure 2.3, whereas the outline sketch of a room might look like Figure 2.4.

Figure 2.4 also includes locations and measurements of doors and windows. On the sketch, record these measurements and indicate whether the doors open in or out. To measure windows, use the width and height of the actual window opening; do not include the window frame.

Sketch the location of physical objects within the perimeter. Use approximate shapes for large objects and symbols for small ones. Place items of evidence in the sketch at the same time you place objects. Use numbers to designate objects and letters to designate evidence. Include such items as bullet entry or exit points, body, hair, gun, fibers, bloodstains and so on. Use exact measurements to show the location of evidence within the room and in relation to all other objects.

Opinions differ about whether to include the location of evidence in this sketch. If evidence is placed within the sketch, some courts have withheld introduction of the sketch until the evidence has been approved. If the evidence is placed only in the finished scale drawing, the sketch can be introduced and used by witnesses to corroborate their testimony.

While sketching, check measurements frequently. Make corrections if needed, but make no changes after leaving the scene. Measurements may or may not be placed in the sketch itself, depending on how many objects are located in the available space. Measurements can be placed in your notes and later entered in the scale drawing.

Many software products allow laser measurements to be coupled with digital photographs of an area to create a virtual scene that, such as those generated by Pictometry, can be rotated and zoomed in on.

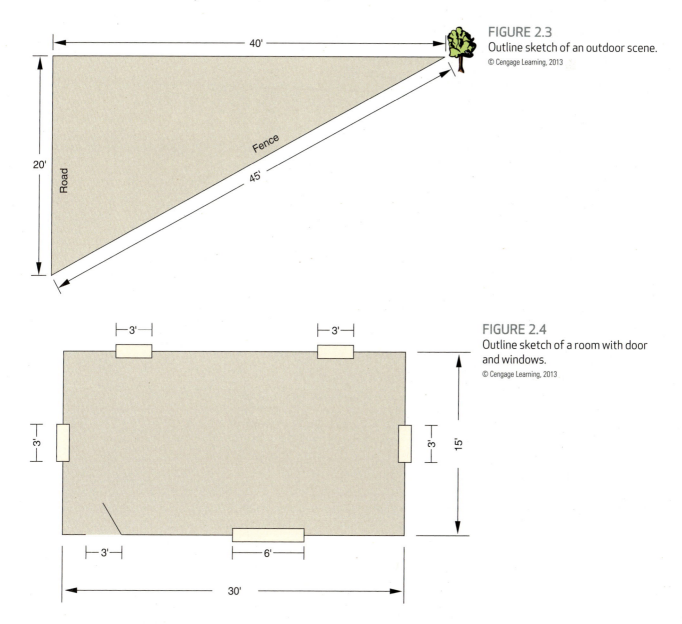

FIGURE 2.3
Outline sketch of an outdoor scene.
© Cengage Learning, 2013

FIGURE 2.4
Outline sketch of a room with door and windows.
© Cengage Learning, 2013

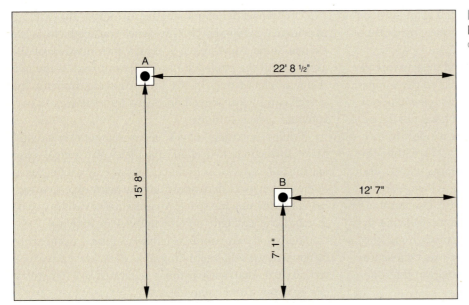

FIGURE 2.5
Rectangular-coordinate method.
© Cengage Learning, 2013

Step Three: Plot Objects and Evidence

> Plotting methods are used to locate objects and evidence on the sketch. These methods include the use of rectangular coordinates, a baseline, triangulation and compass points. A cross-projection sketch shows the floor and walls in the same plane.

To plot objects and evidence accurately, determine fixed points from which to measure.

Rectangular-Coordinate Method. The rectangular-coordinate method is a common way to locate objects and evidence in a room. The **rectangular-coordinate method** uses two adjacent walls as fixed points from which distances are measured at right angles. Locate objects by measuring from one wall at right angles and then from the adjacent wall at right angles. This method is restricted to square or rectangular areas (Figure 2.5).

Baseline Method. Another way to measure by coordinates is to run a baseline from one fixed point to another. The **baseline method** establishes a straight line from one fixed point to another, from which measurements are taken at right angles. Take measurements along either side of the baseline to a point at right angles to the object to be located. An indoor baseline method sketch might look like Figure 2.6 or Figure 2.7. Outdoors, it might look like Figure 2.8.

Sometimes the distance between two locations is important. For example, the distance from the normal route to a door might be very important if evidence is found in

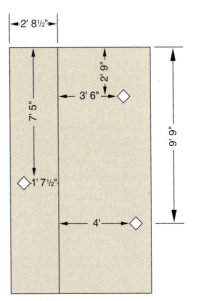

FIGURE 2.6
Center baseline method.
© Cengage Learning, 2013

a room. The 34-foot measurement in Figure 2.8 illustrates this need in an outdoor setting.

Triangulation Method. Triangulation is commonly used in outdoor scenes but can also be used indoors. **Triangulation** uses straight-line measures from two fixed objects to the evidence to create a triangle with the evidence in the angle formed by the two straight lines. The degree of the angle formed at the location of the object or evidence can then be measured with a protractor. The angle can be any degree, in contrast to the rectangular-coordinate and baseline methods, in which the angle is always a right angle (90 degrees). Triangulation is illustrated in Figure 2.9.

Always select the best fixed points possible, with emphasis on their permanence. Fixed points may be closet doors, electrical outlets, door jambs or corners of a structure. It is sometimes impossible to get to the corners of a room for accurate measurements because of obstacles.

Compass-Point Method. The **compass-point method** uses a protractor to measure the angle formed by two lines. In Figure 2.10, for example, Object *A* is

located 10'7" from origin *C* and at an angle of 59 degrees from the vertical line through point *C*. Object *B* is 16'7" from origin *C* at an angle of 47 degrees from the vertical.

Cross-Projection Method. For some interior crime scenes, it is useful to show the relationship between evidence on the floors and the walls. This can be done by sketching the room as though the viewer is straight above it, looking down. In effect, the room is flattened out much like a box cut down at the four corners and opened flat. A **cross-projection sketch** presents the floor and walls as though they were one surface. Objects of evidence on both the floor and the walls can be measured to show their relationship on a single plane, as shown in Figure 2.11.

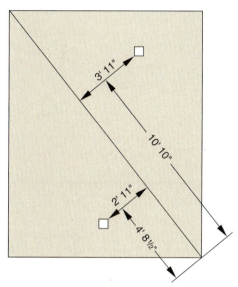

FIGURE 2.7
Diagonal baseline method.
© Cengage Learning, 2013

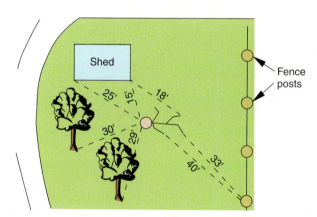

FIGURE 2.9
Triangulation method.
© Cengage Learning, 2013

FIGURE 2.8
Outdoor baseline method.
© Cengage Learning, 2013

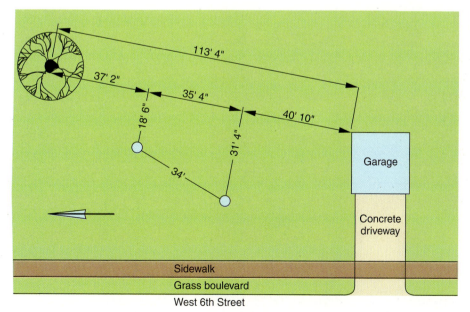

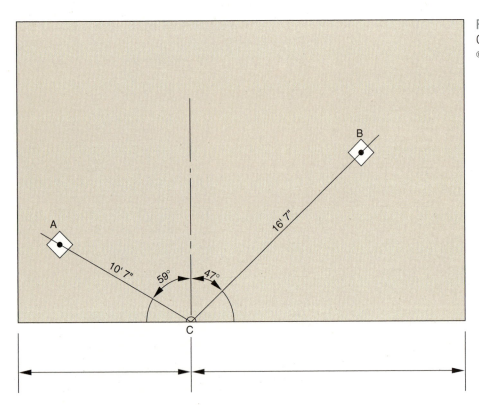

FIGURE 2.10
Compass-point method.
© Cengage Learning, 2013

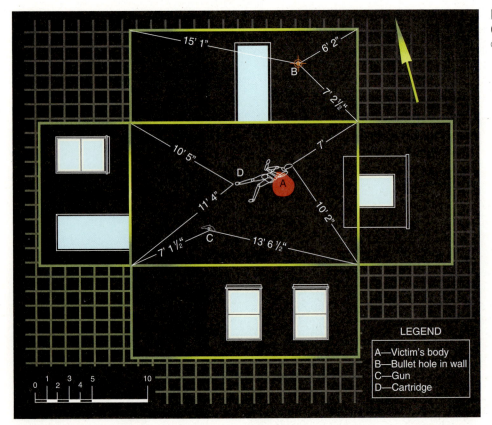

FIGURE 2.11
Cross-projection sketch
© Cengage Learning, 2013

LEGEND
A—Victim's body
B—Bullet hole in wall
C—Gun
D—Cartridge

Step Four: Take Notes and Record Details

After you have completed your sketch, take careful notes regarding all relevant factors associated with the scene that are not sketchable, such as lighting conditions, colors and people present.

Step Five: Identify the Scene

Prepare a **legend** containing the case number, type of crime, name of the victim or complainant, location, date, time, investigator, anyone assisting, scale of the sketch, direction of north and name of the person making the sketch (see Figure 2.12).

Step Six: Reassess the Sketch

Before leaving the scene, make sure you have recorded everything you need on the sketch. Make sure nothing has been overlooked or incorrectly diagrammed. Once you have left, nothing should be added to the sketch. Compare the scene with the sketch. Are all measurements included? Have all relevant notations been made? Have you missed anything? Figure 2.12 is a completed rough sketch of a crime scene.

FILE THE SKETCH

Place the rough sketch in a secure file. It is a permanent record for all future investigations of the crime. It may be used later to question witnesses or suspects and is the foundation for the finished scale drawing. The better the rough sketch is, the better the finished drawing will be.

Keep the rough sketch in its original form even after the scale drawing is completed because it may be needed for testifying. Otherwise, the defense may claim that changes were made in preparing the scale drawings.

THE FINISHED SCALE DRAWING

Given a well-drawn rough sketch, the finished scale drawing can be completed. The **finished scale drawing** is done in ink on a good grade of paper and is drawn to

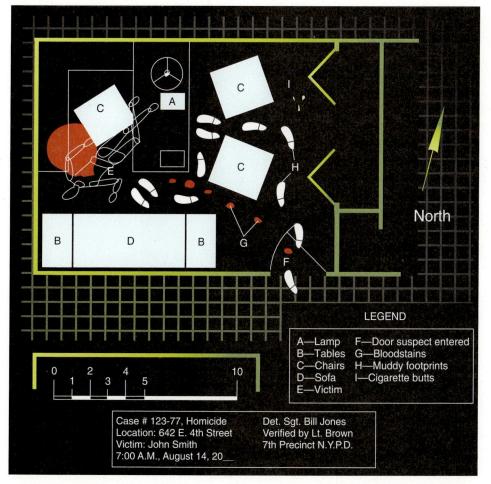

FIGURE 2.12
Completed crime scene sketch.
© Cengage Learning, 2013

North

0 2 4 10
  1 3 5

LEGEND

A—Lamp   F—Door suspect entered
B—Tables   G—Bloodstains
C—Chairs   H—Muddy footprints
D—Sofa   I—Cigarette butts
E—Victim

Case # 123-77, Homicide   Det. Sgt. Bill Jones
Location: 642 E. 4th Street   Verified by Lt. Brown
Victim: John Smith   7th Precinct N.Y.P.D.
7:00 A.M., August 14, 20___

scale, using exact measurements. The materials used for making scale drawings are listed in Table 2.2.

The artistic refinements of the scale drawing do not permit it to be made at the crime scene. Instead, the scale drawing is made at the police station by the investigator or by a drafter. If anyone other than the investigator prepares the finished scale drawing, the investigator must review it carefully and sign it along with the drafter.

The finished drawing can be simple or complex, but it must represent the actual distances, objects and evidence contained in the rough sketch. Color designations and plastic overlays to illustrate other phases of the investigation are often added. The drawing can be duplicated for other investigators and distributed to the prosecuting attorney. It is usually placed on white mounting board for display in court. A finished scale drawing is illustrated in Figure 2.13.

TABLE 2.2 Materials for Making Scale Drawings	
Materials	**Uses**
Drawing kit	Contains tools for finer drawing
Triangular scale rule	Accurate scaling
Templates (assorted shapes, sizes)	Curves, oddly shaped objects
Indelible ink	For permanency of finished drawing
Drafting table	Ease, perfection in drawing
T-square	Accurate, straight lines, right angles
Drafting paper	Higher-quality absorption of inks, better display
Colors	Show areas of comparison

© Cengage Learning, 2013

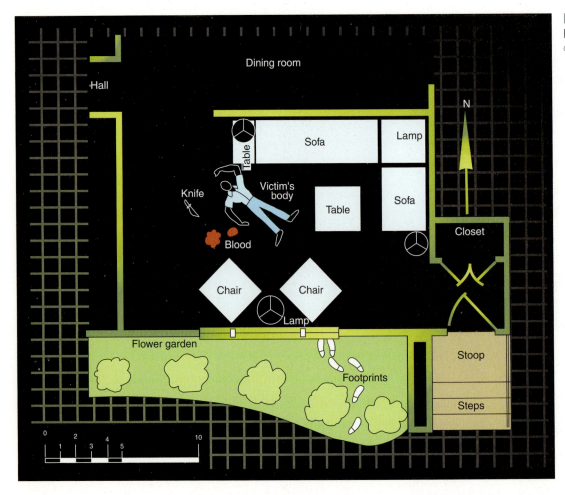

FIGURE 2.13
Finished scale drawing.
© Cengage Learning, 2013

COMPUTER-ASSISTED DRAWING

As evidenced throughout this entire chapter, computer technology has enhanced many of the processes and procedures involved in crime scene documentation. In the fourth edition of this text (1990), computer-aided design (CAD) was highlighted as a technological advance, a cutting-edge tool for criminal investigators. Back then, cumbersome, confusing and complicated CAD software made it challenging for even the most computer-savvy investigators to fully implement this technology. However, drawing software for investigators has improved significantly, and today a plethora of user-friendly CAD programs are available: Crime Zone, Quick Scene, DeltaSphere-3000, iWitness, Linear Systems, MapScenes, ScenePD, Smart-Draw, SmartRoads, Panoscan, Vista FX, HawkEye, VS Investigator Suite—and the list is sure to grow.

Benefits of CAD programs, alternately called computer-assisted drafting programs, include their accuracy, repeatability and simplicity. In addition, the diagram files can be inserted into other documents, including final crime reports. Figure 2.14 compares a typical hand-drawn diagram with one drawn with a CAD software program.

Crime Zone, a popular forensic diagramming application, is easy to use and can create diagrams with great precision and attention to detail, giving the drawing greater credibility in court. Crime Zone's 3-D graphics have been used to diagram the trajectory of bullets, to document the scene of a carjacking and to help a jury visualize the locations of witnesses, victims and suspects at the scene of a shooting (Figure 2.15).

The Vista FX drawing program, like many software packages, contains several versions, each with features geared toward different applications (Figure 2.16). For example, crash reconstruction programs would likely include a linear momentum analysis feature, calculators for deriving acceleration and deceleration rates and pre-drawn symbols of intersections and other driving- and road-related icons. In contrast, a crime scene investigation edition of the same general CAD package might offer a bloodstain-pattern analysis feature, ballistics data and pre-drawn symbols of bodies or various weapons.

The MapScenes software package has more than 7,000 pre-drawn shapes and symbols, and can generate 3-D animation computer movies like those shown on *CSI*. A 3-D crime scene is illustrated in Figure 2.17.

Technology Innovations

In addition to the old-fashioned tape measure, today's diagramming tools include survey equipment, global position systems (GPS), scanners and lasers—equipment that can run from hundreds of dollars to hundreds of thousands of dollars (Brown, 2009, p.63):

Laser Technology, Inc.... offers a device an officer can operate as a speed enforcement tool and, when responding to a crash scene, also use (with some additional tools) to map the scene three dimensionally. Using the LTI laser with an angle encoder and data collector is a one-cop operation utilizing the same technology found in other survey equipment.

The benefits of such a system include portability, versatility and accuracy. (You may be able to carry it on a police motorcycle.) The drawbacks to such a system include range and nighttime use on large crash scenes.

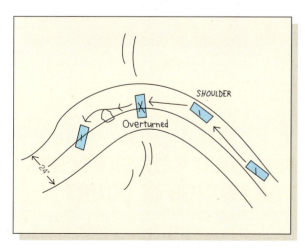

Typical hand-drawn diagram

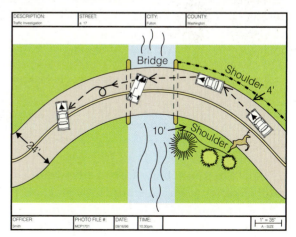

Courtroom-quality diagrams drawn
with the Crime Zone diagramming software

FIGURE 2.14

Comparison of a hand-drawn and computer-generated crime scene "sketch."

Source: Reprinted by permission of the CAD Zone, Inc.

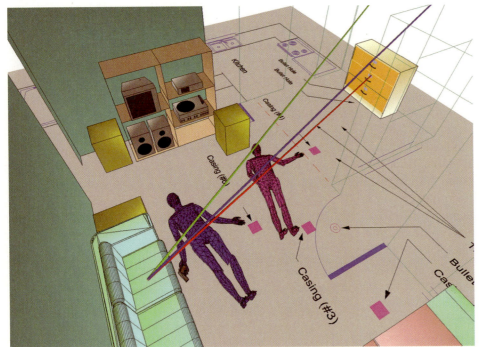

FIGURE 2.15
This is a 3-D recreation of a homicide shooting, showing in detail the bullet trajectories and the final resting positions of the fatalities. The diagram contains both solid and "see-through" walls to display a more correct perspective. The diagram was created with The Crime Zone diagramming software, available from the CAD Zone, Inc.
Source: Image created by CAD Zone, Inc.

FIGURE 2.16
A screen capture of the Vista FX CAD program in use. Officers can enter measurements and ballistic data to create a recreation of a crime scene and then manipulate the images to view the scene from various angles.

Source: Created by VS Visual Statement, Inc., using Vista FX software

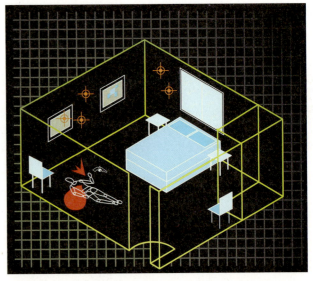

Homicide

FIGURE 2.17
3-D crime scene.

Source: Reprinted by permission of The CAD Zone, Inc.

Speed and portability are two other features investigators look for when selecting a CAD program. Portable data collection and drawing units save investigators time by rapidly generating accurate, scaled diagrams at crime scenes, thus reducing time spent measuring and diagramming and allowing more time to actually investigate.

ADMISSIBILITY OF SKETCHES AND DRAWINGS IN COURT

As with all other evidence, the investigator must be prepared to testify about the information contained in the sketch, the conditions under which it was made and the process used to construct it.

An *admissible sketch* is drawn or personally witnessed by an investigator and accurately portrays a crime scene.

A scale drawing also is admissible if the investigating officer drew it or approved it after it was drawn and if it accurately represents the rough sketch. The rough sketch must remain available as evidence.

Well-prepared sketches and drawings help judges, juries, witnesses and other people visualize crime scenes. The responsibilities of an investigator in court are the focus of Chapter 21.

Summary

Investigative notes and reports are critical parts of a criminal investigation. Notes are a permanent written record of the facts of a case to be used in further investigation, in writing reports and in prosecuting the case. Start taking notes as soon as possible after receiving a call to respond and continue recording information as it is received throughout the investigation.

Record all relevant information concerning the crime, the crime scene and the investigation, including information that helps answer the questions Who? What? Where? When? How? and Why? Effective notes are complete, factual, accurate, specific, legible, clear, arranged in chronological order and well organized. If notes are retained, file them in a secure location readily accessible to investigators.

Photography, one of the first investigative techniques to be used at a crime scene, helps establish that a crime was committed and helps trace the occurrence of the crime. Photographs and video recordings reproduce the crime scene in detail for presentation to the prosecution, defense, witnesses, judge and jury in court and are used in investigating, prosecuting and police training.

Photography has become increasingly important in criminal investigation because it can immediately preserve evidence, accurately represent the crime scene and evidence, create interest and increase attention to testimony. However, photographs also have disadvantages: they are not selective, do not show actual distances and may be distorted and damaged by mechanical errors in shooting or processing.

Videos are now well established as an investigative tool. Videos accurately represent the crime scene and evidence, are able to show distance more clearly than do photos, and have sound capability to more fully document what is being seen. The disadvantages of videos, however, center around the mistaken belief that no training in videotaping is necessary, which leads to poor video quality and a diminished value in the video's documentation of the crime scene. At a minimum, have available and be skilled in operating a Polaroid-type instant-print camera, a

point-and-shoot camera, a digital single-lens reflex (DSLR) camera, a fingerprint camera and video equipment.

Take photographs and video of the entire crime scene before anything is disturbed, and avoid inaccuracies and distortions. First, photograph the general area, then specific areas and finally specific objects of evidence. Take exterior shots first because they are the most subject to alteration by weather and security violations. Categories of investigative photography include crime scene, surveillance, aerial, night, laboratory, mug shot and lineup.

After photographs are taken, they must be properly identified, filed and kept secure to be admissible as evidence. In addition, rules of evidence dictate that photographs be material, relevant, competent, accurate, free of distortion and noninflammatory.

In addition to photographs, crime scene sketches are often used. A crime scene sketch assists in (1) interviewing and interrogating people, (2) preparing the investigative report and (3) presenting the case in court.

Sketch all serious crime and crash scenes after photographs are taken and before anything is moved. Sketch the entire scene, the objects and the evidence. Materials needed for making the rough sketch include paper, pencil, long steel measuring tape, carpenter-type ruler, straightedge, clipboard, compass, protractor and thumbtacks. The steps involved in sketching include (1) observing and planning, (2) measuring distances and outlining the general area, (3) plotting objects and evidence within the outline, (4) taking notes and recording details, (5) identifying the sketch with a legend and a scale and (6) reassessing the sketch.

Plotting methods are used to locate objects and evidence on the sketch. These methods include the use of rectangular-coordinates, a baseline, triangulation and a compass-point. A cross-projection sketch shows the floor and walls in the same plane. An *admissible sketch* is drawn or personally witnessed by an investigator and accurately portrays a crime scene. A scale drawing also is admissible if the investigating officer drew it or approved it after it was drawn and if it accurately represents the rough sketch. The rough sketch must remain available as evidence.

Checklists

Note Taking

- Is my notebook readily available?

- Does it contain an adequate supply of blank paper?

- Is it logically organized?

- Have I recorded all relevant information legibly?

- Have I identified each page of notes with case number and page number?

- Have I included sketches and diagrams where appropriate?

- Have I filed the notes securely?

Police Photography

- Have I photographed the entire scene and specific objects before moving anything?

- Have I included markers where needed to indicate size of evidence?

- Have I recorded equipment and techniques used, lighting conditions and so on in my notes?

- Have I checked for other sources of available photographs?

- Do the photographs taken at the crime scene depict the scene as I saw it?

- Do they show the exact appearance and condition of the scene as it appeared on my arrival?

- Have exterior pictures been taken to show entrances to the scene and the outside appearance of the crime scene?

- Have close-up shots been taken of the entry and exit points?

- Were aerial photos taken of the crime scene to show routes into and out of the scene area?

- Were interior pictures taken showing the entire layout of the facility in which the crime occurred?

- Do the photographs show the criminal act itself? For example, in a burglary, do the pictures show pry marks on the door, a broken window or shattered glass on the ground or floor?

- Were detailed pictures taken of how the crime was committed? The tools with which it was committed? Any weapon used?

- Do photographs show the victim? Injuries? Were wounds, scratches, bruises or other marks recorded in color as soon as possible after the commission of the crime? A day or two later as well?

- Were pictures taken of the deceased at the scene, including exact position, clothing worn, wounds?

- Were pictures taken at the autopsy?

- Do photographs show the property attacked?

- Were detailed pictures taken of all items of evidence before they were collected, showing exact condition and position at the scene?

- Was anything moved before the picture was taken? (If so, was it recorded in your notes?)

- Were photographs true and accurate representations of relevant material?

- Are laboratory photos available for scientific tests conducted?

- Were photographs taken of the suspect to show appearance and condition at the time of the crime, including close-ups of clothing worn?

- Were all pictures used for identifying suspects placed in special envelopes for later court testimony?

- If a lineup was conducted, were pictures taken of the lineup to show the people selected and their appearance in relation to each other?

- If a motor vehicle was involved, were detailed pictures taken of the vehicle's exterior and interior, color, license plate and any damaged areas?

- What types of photographs are available? Moving pictures, black-and-white, color, videos?

- Are there crime-in-progress pictures from on-the-scene cameras such as bank surveillance cameras or were pictures taken by media photographers?

- Have photographs been suitably mounted for presentation in court?

- Have all relevant notes been recorded in the notebook?

Sketches

- Is my sketching kit readily available?

- Is the kit completely equipped?

- Have I formed a plan for making the sketch?

- Have I selected the simplest, largest scale?

- Have I sketched the outline of the room or area first?

- Have I used the appropriate plotting method to locate objects and evidence?

- Have I then added objects and evidence, including measurements?

- Have I recorded in my notes information that cannot be sketched?

- Have I prepared a legend for the sketch that includes identifying information, the scale and the direction of north?

- Have I reassessed the sketch and compared it with the scene?

- Have I kept the sketch secure?

- Have I prepared or had someone else prepare a finished scale drawing if needed?

Discussion Questions

1. Do you agree that note taking is a skill? Is this skill something all police officers must possess to do their jobs properly?

2. What is the *most* important use of notes?

3. Compare and contrast the benefits and drawbacks of retaining and filing field notes.

4. Do you think notes should be retained or destroyed after a report has been written?

5. Have you ever found yourself in a position where you realized that you did not take sufficient notes? Explain.

6. When should notes be taken? Not taken?

7. In what types of crimes are photographs likely to be important to the investigation?

8. How are investigative photographs developed and filed in your police department?

9. What basic sketching materials would you want in an investigative kit?

10. By which plotting method could you best locate your precise position in your surroundings at this moment?

Media Explorations

 ### Internet

Go to the Web sites of Kodak, Canon and Fuji Film and take notes comparing and contrasting the cameras available from the three companies.

ONLINE Database Gale Criminal Justice Database Assignments

The following assignments require access to Gale's Custom Journals Database for Emergency Services and Criminal Justice. Check with your instructor if you have questions about this.

- Find the article, "Say Goodbye to Film: After 136 Years, Digital Tech Takes Over," on the Gale Emergency Services Database. Read and summarize the article and highlight the benefits and drawbacks of this transition.

- Find the article, "Painting with Light: Capturing the Night Time Accident or Crime Scene with Photography," on the Gale Emergency Services Database. Read this article and be prepared to discuss the techniques in class.

- Find the article, "The Admissibility of Digital Photographs in Criminal Cases," on the Gale Emergency Services Database. Read the article and identify why the admissibility of digital photographs might be an issue when used in criminal cases, compared with using film-based photographs.

References

Ashley, Steve. "High-Tech Tin Soldiers." *Police*, March 2008, pp.32–37.

Brown, Weston. "Crash & Crime Diagramming: A Look at the Latest Tech Tools." *Law Officer Magazine*, January 2009, pp.60–63.

Dees, Tim. "Digital Cameras: 6 Questions to Ask Before You Buy." *Law Officer Magazine*, July 2008, pp.68–71.

Dutelle, Aric. "Say Goodbye to Film: After 136 Years, Digital Tech Takes Over." *Law Enforcement Technology*, June 2010, pp.60–66.

Handbook of Forensic Services. Kim Waggoner, editor. Washington, DC: Federal Bureau of Investigations, 2007. http://www.fbi.gov/about-us/lab/handbook-of-forensic-services-pdf

Heinecke, Jeannine. "Criminals Caught on Tape." *Law Enforcement Technology*, April 2007, pp.86–91.

Kanable, Rebecca. "Setting Up Surveillance Downtown." *Law Enforcement Technology*, February 2008, pp.30–39.

Rutledge, Devallis. "Full Disclosure." *Police*, December 2007, pp.68–71.

Wandrei, Greg. "Instant Access to Vital Information: The Role of GIS." *Law Enforcement Technology*, November 2007, pp.56–61.

Case Cited

Udderzook v. Commonwealth, 76 Pa 340 (1874)

CHAPTER 3
Writing Effective Reports

© dmac/Alamy

Outline

One of the most important skills investigators must develop is report writing. The remainder of this volume discusses in detail how evidence is located and processed; how witnesses, victims, suspects and others are questioned; and how specific cases are investigated. Report writing is included here because the report captures the essentials of an investigation.

Do You Know?

- Why reports are important to an investigation?
- How reports are used?
- Who reads your reports?
- What common problems occur in many police reports?
- Which is more important: content or form?
- What the characteristics of effective investigative reports are?
- How to differentiate between facts, inferences and opinions?
- Why your reports should be well written?

THE IMPORTANCE OF REPORTS

Orlando W. Wilson and Roy C. McLaren wrote *Police Administration* more than 30 years ago, but their words ring as true today as they did then: "Almost everything that a police officer does must be reduced to writing. What is written is often the determining factor in whether a suspect is arrested in the first place and, if he is arrested, whether he is convicted and sentenced. The contents of written reports, in fact, often have great bearing in life-and-death situations. To say that officers need to be proficient in report writing is an understatement."

Another reason report-writing skills are so important is that as much as 20 percent of frontline officers' time is spent writing reports (Brewer, 2007, p.36).

The importance of well-written reports becomes obvious when you realize that your reports are *used*, not simply filed away. If investigative reports were not required for efficient law enforcement, you would not have to write them.

> Reports are permanent written records of important facts of a case to be used in the future and are a crucial and necessary cog in the wheel of justice.

Well-written reports further the cause of justice and reflect positively on your education, your competence and your professionalism. In fact: "Your reputation and that of your department often rest on your written words" (Arp, 2007, p.100).

Figure 3.1 shows the typical path of an investigative report. The number of times the report loops between the supervisor and the officer, or between the prosecutor and the officer, depends on how carefully (or carelessly) the officer constructs the report to begin with.

Most law enforcement officers submit their reports for prosecution with concern about the outcome but without much thought about the wheels they've started in motion. This is understandable, for they've done their jobs and many more cases wait to be investigated. But what happens

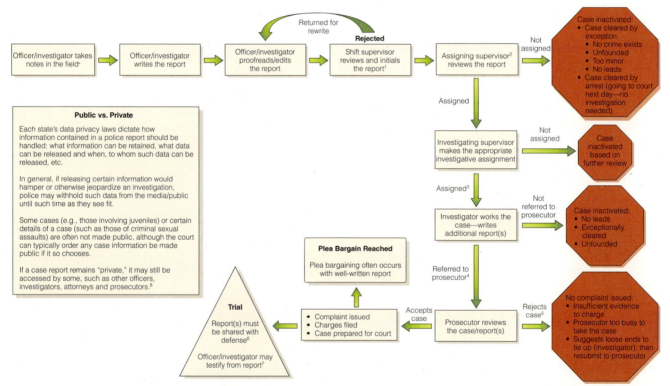

[1] Often the report is simply handwritten by the officer, given to the shift supervisor for a cursory review/initialing, and then sent off for transcription before going to an assigning supervisor.
[2] Assigning supervisor is typically of higher rank (lieutenant, captain, etc.).
[3] In smaller departments, the case may go to a generalized investigator. In larger departments, several investigative units may exist (homicide, arson, motor vehicle theft, etc.).
[4] Case can proceed to prosecutor with or without an arrest having been made.
[5] A rejection does not necessarily mean the case is not prosecutable at a later date. It means only that a complaint is not issued at that time.
[6] Who has access to the report(s) at trial varies by state. For example, in Minnesota, the judge and jury do not automatically receive the report(s).
[7] The report itself is not evidence, but any testimony the officer/investigator provides based on the content of a report becomes part of the trial record (testimonial evidence).
[8] Check with your state's data privacy law. Laws vary from state to state regarding what can be retained, what must be released and when information must be released. Consideration must also be given to whether or not release of information would hamper any ongoing investigations.

FIGURE 3.1

Typical path of an investigative report. Note: Because this process varies from department to department, this flowchart illustrates a generalized oversimplification of one way an investigative report might travel from origination to final disposition.

when they haven't really done their jobs? When their reports are distorted or incomplete (as many are) because of poor writing? The results cost the taxpayers in wasted personnel hours, and they breed disaster in the courtroom, if the case even makes it that far. Poor police report writing can jeopardize effective criminal prosecution.

The little things in a report can have major consequences for the **disposition** of a case, or how the case is disposed of, referred, closed (inactive), open (active), dismissed, pending further information and so on. Consider this all-too-common example: in one criminal case, the reporting officer, using the passive voice, wrote, "The weapon was found in the bushes where the suspect had thrown it." He did not clarify this statement elsewhere in his report. Expectedly, the prosecuting attorney subpoenaed the reporting officer to testify at the preliminary hearing. Unfortunately, the reporting officer's testimony revealed that his partner, not he, had observed the suspect's action and had retrieved the weapon. The partner was unavailable to testify on short notice. Without her testimony, the necessary elements of the crime could not be established, and the case was dismissed, having to be refiled. The personnel hours expended at the time of the dismissal—by witnesses, secretaries, clerks, attorneys and the judge—were virtually wasted because the whole process had to be repeated. The reporting officer could have avoided the problem at the onset through use of the active voice, which would have provided clarification. Sadly, this basic writing error is not an isolated example; it, and others like it, slip into the system daily, where they are often caught by defense attorneys who meticulously comb through reports, looking to exploit such defects. Such report writing errors result in delays in the judicial process and the depletion of dwindling budgets.

To better understand how to write effective reports, consider first how they may be used.

USES OF REPORTS

Reports are permanent records of all important facts in a case. They are a stockpile of information to be drawn on by all individuals on a law enforcement team. They are an aid to individual law enforcement officers and investigators, supervisors, administrators, the courts, other governmental agencies, reporters and private individuals. Further, a department's efficiency is directly related to the quality of its reports and reporting procedures.

Consider the case of an officer called to the scene of a hit-and-run. The initial accident report will be used to continue the investigation of the offense. If the offender is apprehended, the report will be used by the prosecuting attorneys in preparing the case, by the responding police officer when testifying in court, by the judge in determining the facts of the case and by the jury if a trial results. The report might also be used by the department in determining where dangerous intersections exist and in making future plans. Additionally, an officer's supervisor could use the report to evaluate the investigating officer's performance. If the officer failed to conduct a thorough investigation, this lack of thoroughness would show in the report.

Retrieving and recording information are essential steps in constructing a sound report. Improved technology in squad cars allows officers to take notes in the field and look up relevant information, thereby increasing the accuracy and effectiveness of their reports.
© Henry Cho

Reports are used to

- Examine the past.
- Provide a documented record of incidents.
- Keep other police officers informed.
- Continue investigations.
- Prepare court cases.
- Provide the courts with relevant facts.
- Coordinate law enforcement activities.
- Plan for future law enforcement services.
- Evaluate individual officer and department performance.
- Refresh a witness's memory about what he or she said occurred.
- Refresh the investigating officer's memory during the trial.
- Compile statistics on crime in a given jurisdiction.
- Provide information to insurance investigators.

Reports are critical in examining police performance and investigating potentially illegal police practices such as racial profiling. Many departments have begun voluntarily augmenting their traffic stop reports in an effort to shed light on allegations of racial profiling. Although some agencies are embracing the initiative as a way to seize control of their traffic data and build confidence in the fairness of their policing, other departments are opting out of the program, claiming that the more extensive reports add to their already excessive paperwork load. Critics of the program believe officers might be dissuaded from making legitimate traffic stops because of the undue amount of paperwork these will generate.

The various uses of reports make it obvious that they will be read by many different people for many different reasons. These people make up your audience.

THE AUDIENCE

What you write may be read by other officers, your supervisor, lawyers, judges, jurors, social workers, city officials, insurance adjusters and investigators, civil rights groups, citizens and the media—people from different backgrounds and fields who have varying degrees of familiarity with legal terms and police jargon. Certainly, most of your audience will not have been present at the crime scene. Therefore, you must communicate clearly to these numerous readers *what* happened, *when* and *how*.

Reports are read by

- Other officers.
- Supervisors.
- Attorneys and judges.
- Jurors.
- Social workers.
- City officials.
- Insurance adjusters and investigators.
- Civil rights groups.
- Citizens.
- Media.

You should neither talk down to your audience nor try to make your report appear "more professional" by using bureaucratic, complicated language. Keep your reports straightforward and reader friendly, focusing on the need to *express* the facts of the case rather than on trying to *impress* the audience with your expansive vocabulary. Writing to impress rather than to express is a common problem with many investigative reports.

COMMON PROBLEMS WITH MANY POLICE REPORTS

Writing effective investigation reports is a skill that must be learned and practiced just as any other skill necessary in police work, such as firearms use, self-defense techniques and interview methods. Unfortunately, some departments have yet to develop a full appreciation of the benefits of well-written reports. In these agencies, reports are viewed as tedious time wasters that keep investigators from more significant tasks. Field training officers encourage new recruits to take report shortcuts,

Among the common problems in police reports are

- Confusing or unclear sentences.
- Conclusions, assumptions and opinions.
- Extreme wordiness and overuse of police jargon and abbreviations.
- Missing or incomplete information.
- Misspelled words and grammatical or mechanical errors.
- Referring to "above" information.

while administrators look the other way, happy to avoid the overtime that can occur with thorough, accurate, complex reports. Amid such an environment, effective report writing skills are neither taught nor recognized as important and problems in the department's police reports abound.

Having briefly looked at the "don'ts" of report writing, the discussion now turns to the "dos" and how to craft a well-written report.

THE WELL-WRITTEN REPORT: FROM START TO FINISH

Report writing is a skill that takes time and practice to develop. It is *not* a talent—you are not expected to write entertaining literary masterpieces, full of insight and originality. Instead, to write an effective report, you must organize your notes and adhere to some basic standards of written English regarding content and form.

Organizing Information

A cornerstone of good report writing is organization. Good reports do not just happen. The writer plans in advance in what order the information should be written. Too many officers simply sit down and start writing without giving any thought to how the report should flow, which results in more time spent rewriting and revising later. To use your time most efficiently, first make an informal outline. Next, list what you want to include under each heading in the outline. Review your notes and number each statement to match a heading in your outline. For example, if Section III.C of the outline is headed "Description of Suspect #2," write *III.C* in the margin wherever Suspect #2 is described in your notes. List the facts of the investigation in **chronological order**, beginning with the response to the call and concluding with the end of the investigation. If the report is long (more than four pages), use headings to guide the reader—for example, "Initial Response," "Crime-Scene Conditions," "Photographs Taken," "Evidence," "Witnesses," "Suspects" and so on. After you complete the outline and determine where each note fits, you are ready to begin writing.

Structuring the Narrative

Usually the **narrative**, the "story" of the case in chronological order, is structured as follows:

1. The opening paragraph of a police report states the time, date, type of incident and how you became involved.

2. The next paragraph contains what you were told by the victim or witness. For each person talked to, use a separate paragraph.

3. Next record what you did based on the information you received.

4. The final paragraph states the disposition of the case.

Steps 2 and 3 may be repeated several times in a report on a case where you talk to several witnesses and victims.

A Brief Look at Law Enforcement Report Forms. Although this chapter focuses on writing narrative reports, many departments use box-style law enforcement report forms for certain offenses and incidents. Law enforcement report forms vary greatly in format, and the example shown in Figure 3.2 is only one type of forms in use.

Hess and Orthmann (2008, p.iv) state, "Report forms … contain boxes or separate category sections, e.g., property loss section, for placement of descriptive information, addresses and phone numbers of those involved. It is unnecessary to repeat this information in the narrative *unless it is needed for clarity* because it tends to interrupt the flow of words and clutter the narrative." In contrast, narrative reports that do *not* use the box-style format include descriptive information, addresses and phone numbers within the body of the narrative.

Read the following excerpt from a narrative report, noting the underlined descriptive information.

> I talked to the victim, Betty Jones, <u>355 Rose St., Albany, New York, phone 555-9002.</u> Jones told me that her diamond ring was taken during the burglary. The ring was a <u>2-carat diamond stone, platinum setting, with the initials B.A.J. inside the band, valued at $11,500.00.</u>

If these data were, instead, to be formatted into a box-style report, the underlined descriptive information, address and phone number would be deleted from the narrative *unless that information was needed for clarity*, as shown in the following excerpt:

> The victim, Betty Jones, told me that her diamond ring was taken during the burglary.

Characteristics of Effective Reports: Content and Form

In addition to a well-structured narrative, an effective report exhibits several other characteristics, which generally fall into one of two areas: **content**, or *what* is said, and **form**, or *how* it is written.

Test City
Disposition: Cleared by Arrest

INCIDENT

Case Number: 11001234
Title: Domestic Assault

Charges/Offenses: 609.2242.4, 609.78.2

Needs Follow-up: No **Investigation Needed:** No **Investigation Complete:** Yes **Citation Issued:** No **CAD #:**

Gang Related: No **Incident Type:** Other **How Initiated:** Dispatch

OFFICER INFORMATION

Name	Agency	Badge	Type
Billy Bob Testman	Test City	978675	Primary

EVENT DATES

Reported	On Scene	Cleared
2011-05-02 11:16	2011-05-02 11:16	2011-05-02 11:16

INCIDENT DETAILS

Address: 1234 American Boulevard; Test City, MN 55100 US

Location Type: RESIDENCE/HOME

Location Description:

Start Date: 2011-05-02 11:17 **End Date:** 2011-05-02 11:17

SYNOPSIS

On 04/30/11 at 0055 hours I and Officer Jones responded to 1223 American Blvd. in regards to a Domestic Assault. Upon arrival I observed the suspect John Jacob Johnson, DOB-01/01/80 physically assaultinag his wife Mary Margaret Johnson, DOB-01/02/80.John was arrested without further incident and transported to jail. See Report.

Parties Involved

PERSON 001

Role(s): Suspect, Arrested

Last: Johnson	**First:** John	**Middle:** Jacob	**Suffix:**
Date of Birth: 1980-01-01	**Age:** 31	**Is Juvenile:** No	

Sex: Male	**Height:** 6-0	**Weight:** 200 lbs	**Hair:** Bald	**Eyes:** Brown
Race: Unknown	**Ethnicity:** Unknown	**Build:** Large	**Complexion:** Ruddy	

EMPLOYMENT INFORMATION

Name: Buy Things, Inc. **Type:** RETAIL
Occupation: Sales **Shift:**

CHARGES/ORDINANCES

Type: Statute **Chapter:** 609 **Section:** 2242 **Subdivision:** 4 **Citation #:**
UOC: 1302B **Level:** Felony **Enh. Factor:** Previous Convictions
Description: Domestic Assault-Felony, two prior convictions with the same victim.

- -

Type: Statute **Chapter:** 609 **Section:** 78 **Subdivision:** 2 **Citation #:**
UOC: 5399 **Level:** Gross Misdemeanor **Enh. Factor:** Domestic

Test City (MN0190000)	Page 1 of 2	Creation: Mary B Cerkvenik 2011-05-02 11:36:00

Incident Report

(continued)

FIGURE 3.2

An example of a law enforcement report form.

Source: Henry L. Cho, Cho Research & Consulting, LLC.

Test City

Disposition: Cleared by Arrest

INCIDENT

Case Number: 11001234

Title: Domestic Assault

Description: Emergency Telephone Calls/CommunicInterfere with 911 Call

PERSON 002

Role(s): Reporting Person, Victim

Last: Johnson	**First:** Mary	**Middle:** Margaret	**Suffix:**
Date of Birth: 1980-01-02	**Age:** 31	**Is Juvenile:** No	
Cell Phone: (555) 888-1111		**Description:**	

Sex: Female	**Height:** 5	**Weight:** 100 lbs	**Hair:** Black	**Eyes:** Brown
Race: Unknown	**Ethnicity:** Unknown	**Build:** Small	**Complexion:** Fair	

EMPLOYMENT INFORMATION

Name: Flotech, Inc.   **Type:** Technology

Occupation: Software Engineer   **Shift:**

Vehicles Involved

VEHICLE 001

Role(s): Involved

Associated with: John Jacob Johnson (Owner), Mary Margaret Johnson (Owner)

Regular Passenger Automobile Plates	**Number:** 5589L	**Authority:** MINNESOTA	**Tab:** 144478 ()
Make: Chevrolet	**Model:** Malibu	**Year:** 2001	**Style:** Sedan
Primary Color: Blue	**Secondary Color:**	**VIN:** 145J45K719OPU77	
Odometer Reading: 85000	**Estimated Value:** 3000	**Keys Location:**	
Doors Locked: No	**Ignition Locked:** No	**Trunk Locked:** No	

PROPERTY INFORMATION

ID: 392   **Associated with:** Mary Margaret Johnson (Owner)

Description: Personal Data Device

Quantity: 1	**Unit Price:** 300	**Value:** 300.00	**Seized:** Yes	**Forfeiture:** No
Brand Name: Blueberry	**Model:** P45	**Code:**	**Color:** black	
Serial Number: 7844KK855Y2E		**Owner Applied Number:**		

NARRATIVE

DOCUMENT APPROVAL HISTORY

Created By: Mary B Cerkvenik   **On:** 2011-05-02 11:36:00

(right margin, vertical text): 11001234

(right margin, vertical text): Incident Report

FIGURE 3.2
(*continued*)

> The effective report writer attends to both content and form because they are equally important in a well-written report.

The *content* of an effective report is factual, accurate, objective and complete. The *form* of a well-written report is concise, clear, grammatically and mechanically correct and written in Standard English. An effective report is also organized into paragraphs and written in the past tense, using the first person and active voice. Finally, a well-written report is audience-focused, legible and submitted on time. Table 3.1 illustrates the differences between content and form as they relate to investigative reports.

> An effective report is factual, accurate, objective, complete, concise, clear, grammatically and mechanically correct, written in Standard English, organized into paragraphs and written in the past tense; uses the first person and active voice; and is audience-focused and legible, leaving the reader with a positive impression of the writer's competence. A well-written report is also submitted on time.

Facts, opinions and inferences were introduced in Chapter 1. Investigators *must* differentiate between these three types of statements: "The ability of investigators to explain both verbally and in writing how inferences (e.g., clues, evidence, etc.) lead them to draw logical and reasonable conclusions (e.g., probable cause, facts, etc.) remains a critical skill in investigative work" (Jetmore, 2007, p.22).

Factual. The basic purpose of any investigation report is to record the facts. A *fact* is a statement that can be

TABLE 3.1 Investigative Reports: Content and Form Compared

Content—*what* is said	Form—*how* it is said
The elements of the crime	Word choice
Descriptions of suspects, victims, etc.	Sentence and paragraph length
Evidence collected	Spelling
Actions of victim, witnesses, suspects	Punctuation
Observations: weather, road conditions, smells, sounds, oddities, etc.	Grammar
	Mechanics

© Cengage Learning 2013

proven. (It may be proven false, but it is still classified as a factual statement.) The truthfulness or accuracy of facts will be discussed shortly. First, consider how to clearly distinguish between these three basic types of statements.

Fact:	A statement that can be proven.
Example:	The man has a bulge in his black leather jacket pocket.
Inference:	A conclusion based on reasoning.
Example:	The man is probably carrying a gun.
Opinion:	A personal belief.
Example:	Black leather jackets are cool.

A well-written report is factual. It does *not* contain opinions. You can discuss and debate facts and inferences logically and reasonably and come to some agreement about them. An *opinion,* however, reflects personal beliefs, on which there is seldom agreement. For example, how do you resolve the differences between two people arguing about whether pie tastes better than cake? You can't. It's simply a matter of personal preference.

Inferences (conclusions) can prove valuable in a report, provided they are based on sufficient evidence. Sometimes it is hard to distinguish between facts and inferences. One way to tell them apart is to ask the question, "Can the statement be simply proven true or false, or do I need other facts to make it reasonable?" For example, if you wanted to verify the statement, "The driver of the truck was drunk," you would need to supply several facts to support your inference. One such fact might be that he had a blood alcohol content higher than 0.10. Other facts might include your observations, such as his slurred speech, his red and watery eyes, five empty beer cans behind the driver's seat and the strong odor of an alcoholic beverage on the driver's breath.

An *inference* is not really true or false; it is sound or unsound (believable or not believable). And the only way to make an inference sound (believable) is to provide facts to support it. One way to ensure that your inference is clearly an inference, instead of a fact, would be to use the word *apparently* or *appeared* (e.g., "The driver appeared to be under the influence of alcohol.").

Inferences are also referred to as **conclusionary language**. Avoid conclusionary language by *showing,* not *telling.* For example, do not write, "The man *could not* walk a straight line." You do not know what another person can or cannot do. A more factual way to report this would be, "The man *did* not walk a straight line." Even better would be, "The man stepped 18 inches to the right of the line twice and 12 inches to the left of the line three times." Consider this account by Rutledge (2000, pp.110–111):

> I once got into a drunk driving trial where, according to the arresting officer, the defendant had "repeatedly refused" to take a chemical test. The defendant was named Sanchez, and at trial he insisted, through a court interpreter, that he neither spoke nor understood any English. His defense that he couldn't possibly refuse an English-language request when he couldn't even understand it sold well with the jury, especially after the officer had to admit that he didn't recall exactly how or in what specific words the defendant had "refused" a test. The cop couldn't live with his conclusionary report. Neither could I. The defendant lived with it very comfortably, and he owed his acquittal directly to the same officer who had arrested him. Ironic?

> We would have been much better off if the cop had never used the conclusionary word "refused," but had instead married the defendant to his own words! The report could have helped the prosecution, instead of the defense, if it had been written like this:

> *After I explained the need to take a chemical test, Sanchez said, in Spanish-accented English, "Screw you, cop….I ain't taking no test, man. Why don't you take it yourself?" I told him he had to take a test or his license would be suspended. He said, "I don't need no license to drive, man. I know lots of people drive without a license. You ain't scared me, man, and I ain't taking no stupid test. I'll beat this thing."*

> See the difference? Not a single conclusion or interpretation. The reader gets to "hear" the same things the writer heard. The officer could have lived with something like that—the defendant couldn't.

The following conclusionary statements can also jeopardize the effectiveness and value of investigative reports:

- "They *denied* any involvement in the crime."
- "She *confessed* to seven more arsons."
- "He *admitted* breaking into the warehouse."
- "He *consented* to a search of the trunk."
- "She *waived* her rights per Miranda."

Table 3.2 presents alternatives to conclusionary words and phrases that will make reports more factual and, thus, more effective and valuable.

Conclusionary language may also lead to inaccuracies in your report.

Accurate. To be useful, facts must be accurate. An effective report accurately records the correct time and date, correct names of all persons involved, correct phone numbers and addresses and exact descriptions of the crime scene, property, vehicles and suspects involved. Have people spell their names. Repeat spellings and numbers for verification. Recheck measurements. Be sure of the accuracy of your facts. An inaccurately recorded license number may result in losing a witness or suspect. Inaccurate measurement or recording of the distance and location of skid marks, bullet holes or bodies may lead to wrong conclusions.

To be accurate, you must be specific. For example, it is better to say, "The car was traveling in excess of 90 mph" than to say, "The car was traveling fast." It is more accurate to describe a suspect as "approximately 6-foot-6″" than to describe him as "tall."

You must have the facts in the case correct. If your report says four men were involved in a robbery but in reality, three men and a woman were involved, your report would be inaccurate. If you are unsure of the gender of the

TABLE 3.2 Avoiding Conclusionary Language			
You Can't Live with These	**So Use**	**You Can't Live with These**	**So Use**
Indicated, refused, admitted, confessed, denied, consented, identified, waived, profanity, threatening, obscene, evasive, deceptive	A verbatim or approximate quotation of what was said	Angry, upset, nervous, excited, happy, unhappy, intentional, accidental, heard, saw, knew, thought	The source of your conclusions (when you're attributing them to someone else)
Assaulted, attacked, accosted, confrontation, escalated, struggle ensued, resisted, battered, intimidated, bullied, forced	A factual account of who did what	Matching the description, suspicious, furtive, strange, abnormal, typical, uncooperative, belligerent, combative, obnoxious, abusive, exigent	The reasons for your belief that these apply

Source: From RUTLEDGE, *The New Police Report Manual*, 1E. © 2000 Cengage Learning.

individuals involved in an incident, identify them as "people," "suspects," "witnesses," or whatever the case may be. If your facts come from the statement of a witness rather than from your own observation, say so in your report.

Phrases such as "He saw what happened" or "He heard what happened" are conclusionary and may lead to inaccuracies in your report. People can be looking directly at something and not see it, either because they are simply not paying attention or because they have terrible vision. The same is true of hearing. Again, you do not know what another person sees or hears. Your report should say, "He *said* he saw what happened" or "He looked directly at the man committing the crime."

Another common conclusionary statement found in police reports is, "The check was signed by John Doe." Unless you saw John Doe sign the check, the correct (accurate) statement would be, "The check was signed John Doe." The little two-letter word *by* can create tremendous problems for you on the witness stand.

Vague, imprecise words have no place in police reports. The following words and phrases should *not* be used because they are not specific: *a few, several, many, frequently, often.* Finally, instead of writing *contacted*, be specific by using *telephoned, visited, e-mailed* or whatever particular mode of communication was involved.

Another common mistake often found in police reports is using the phrase *the PC for the stop*, referring to *probable cause*: "It should be clear that PC is not needed for a stop—only for an arrest. All the Fourth Amendment requires for a stop (detention) is reasonable suspicion" (Rutledge, 2008, p.66). Police officers who write about "the PC for the stop" feed the confusion of legal standards that may already be cloudy to some prosecutors, the defense attorneys and trial judges.

Objective. You have seen that reports must be factual. It is possible, however, to include only factual statements in a report and still not be objective. Being **objective** means being non-opinionated, fair and impartial. Lack of objectivity can result from either of two things: poor word choice or omission of facts.

Word choice is an often overlooked—yet very important—aspect of report writing. Consider, for example, the difference in effect achieved by these three sentences:

The woman cried.

The woman wept.

The woman blubbered.

Although you want to be specific, you must also be aware of the effect of the words you use. Words that have little emotional effect, for example, *cried*, are called **denotative** words. The denotative meaning of a word is its

objective meaning. In contrast, words that do have an emotional effect are called **connotative** words, for example, *wept, blubbered.* The connotative meaning of a word comprises its positive or negative overtones. In the three earlier sentences, only the first sentence is truly objective. The second sentence makes the reader feel sympathetic toward the woman. The third makes the reader unsympathetic.

Likewise, derogatory, biased terms referring to a person's race, ethnicity, religion or sexual preference have no place in police reports. A defense attorney will certainly capitalize on words with emotional overtones and attempt to show bias. Even the use of *claimed* rather than *stated* can be used to advantage by a defense attorney, who might suggest that the officer's use of *claimed* implies the officer did not believe the statement.

Also, use the correct word. Do not confuse words that are similar, or you can be made to appear ridiculous. For example, this sentence in an officer's report would probably cast suspicion on the officer's intelligence: "During our training we spent four hours learning to resemble a firearm and the remainder of the time learning defective driving."

Keep to the facts. Include all facts, even those that may appear to be damaging to your case. Objectivity is attained by including both sides of the account. **Slanting**, that is, including only one side of a story or only facts that tend to prove or support the officer's theory, can also make a report nonobjective. A good report includes both sides of an incident when possible. Even when facts tend to go against your theory about what happened, you are obligated to include them. Omitting important facts is *not* objective. Recall the previous discussion of the importance of including both inculpatory and exculpatory statements in reports: "There are significant legal and ethical reasons why police officers should include all known material statements and evidence in reports submitted to the prosecutor. Due process disclosure of exculpatory evidence must be determined and made by the prosecutor, and 'tainted' evidence may still be fully admissible, or useful for limited purposes. Full reporting helps avoid civil liability, reversals of convictions, and miscarriage of justice" (Rutledge, 2007, p.71).

Complete. Information kept in the reporting officer's head is of no value to anyone else involved in the case. Scarry (2007, p.68) points out, "What officers write in their report stays with them forever." Therefore, she recommends, "Every report should reflect the basic details of the event, and the important details must be included. Why? Simply put, in today's litigious society, police officers and their agencies are easy targets for civil lawsuits, particularly officers involved in a shooting or other incident ending in death or great bodily harm." She (p.69) contends, "If it's not documented in the police report, a savvy attorney representing the suspect will always argue that it never happened." Scarry (p.71) concludes, "When it comes to writing police reports, officers should always strive to document all injuries they receive during any incident, even if it's a minor injury; record any unusual statements germane to the event; and explain why the officers took certain actions, particularly with respect to the need to use force (p.71)."

An effective report contains answers to at least six basic questions: Who? What? When? Where? How? and Why? The *who, what, when* and *where* questions should be answered by factual statements. The *how* and *why* statements may require inferences. When this is the case, clearly label the statements as inferences. This is especially true when answering the question of cause. To avoid slanting the report, record all possible causes no matter how implausible they may seem at the time.

If a form is used for your reports, all applicable blanks at the top of the form should be filled in. Certain agencies require a slash mark, the abbreviation NA (not applicable) or the abbreviation UNK (unknown) to be placed in any box that does not contain information.

Each specific type of crime requires different information. Sections 3, 4 and 5 discuss specific offenses and contain checklists outlining information that should be included in your report.

Concise.
Being **concise** means making every word count without leaving out important facts. Avoid wordiness; length alone does not ensure quality. Some reports can be written in half a page; others require 12 or even 20 pages. No specific length can be prescribed, but strive to include all relevant information in as few words as possible.

You can reduce wordiness in two basic ways: (1) leave out unnecessary information and (2) use as few words as possible to record the necessary facts. For example, do not write, "The car was blue in color"; write "The car was blue." A phrase such as "information that is of a confidential nature" should be recognized as a wordy way of saying "confidential information."

Do not make the mistake of equating conciseness with brevity. Being brief is not the same as being concise. For example, compare

Brief	She drove a car.
Concise	She drove a maroon 1992 Chevrolet Caprice.
Wordy	She drove a car that was a 1992 Chevrolet Caprice and was maroon in color.

Avoiding wordiness does not mean eliminating details; it means eliminating empty words and phrases.

Consider these examples of how to make wordy phrases more concise:

Wordy	Concise
made a note of the fact that	noted
square in shape	square
in the amount of	for
despite the fact that	although
for the purpose of determining	to determine

Table 3.3 lists more natural-sounding alternatives for wordy, artificial phrases.

Clear.
An investigation report should have only one interpretation. Two people should be able to read the report and come up with the same word-picture and understanding of the events. Make certain your sentences can be read only one way. For example, consider the following unclear sentences:

- When completely plastered, officers who volunteer will paint the locker room.
- Miami police kill a man with a machete.
- Three cars were reported stolen by the Los Angeles police yesterday.
- Police begin campaign to run down jaywalkers.
- Squad helps dog bite victim.

Rewrite such sentences so that only one interpretation is possible. For example, the first sentence in the previous list might read, "Officers who volunteer will paint the locker room after it is completely plastered." The third sentence might read, "According to the Los Angeles police, three cars were reported stolen yesterday."

Follow these guidelines to make your reports clearer:

- *Use specific, concrete facts and details.* Compare the following statements and determine which is clearer:
  1. The car sped away and turned the corner.
  2. The gold 1996 Cadillac Fleetwood pulled away from the curb, accelerated to approximately 65 mph and then turned off First Street onto Brooklyn Boulevard.

  The second statement is clearer because it contains concrete facts and details.

- *Keep descriptive words and phrases as close as possible to the words they describe.* Compare the following statements and determine which is clearer.
  1. He replaced the gun into the holster which he had just fired.

TABLE 3.3 Artificial-Sounding vs. Natural-Sounding Words and Phrases

Artificial	Natural	Artificial	Natural
initiated commenced inaugurated originated	began	altercation mutual combat physical confrontation exchange of physical blows	fight
presently currently at the present at the present time at this time	now	in reference to reference in regard to regarding on the subject of	about
due to the fact that considering that as a result of the fact that in view of the fact that in light of the fact that	because, since	visually perceived visually noticed observed viewed	saw
made an effort made an attempt endeavored attempted	tried	related stated verbalized articulated	said
maintained surveillance over kept under observation visually monitored	watched	informed advised indicated communicated verbally	told
at this point at this time at which time at which point in time	then	6' in height 2' in width 3' in length 8" in depth	6' tall/high 2' wide 3' long 8" deep
as of this date as of this time as of the present time	yet	telephonically contacted reached via landline contacted by telephone	phoned
alighted from exited dismounted	got out	verbal altercation verbal dispute verbal confrontation	argument
requested inquired queried	asked	prior to previous to in advance of	before
in order to with the intention of with the objective to	to	for the reason that in order that	so

Source: From RUTLEDGE, *The New Police Report Manual*, 1E. © 2000 Cengage Learning.

2. He replaced the gun, which he had just fired, into the holster.

The second statement is clearer because the phrase "which he had just fired" is placed close to the word it modifies (*gun*).

■ *Use diagrams and sketches when a description is complex.* This is especially true in reports of crashes, homicides and burglaries. The diagrams do not have to be artistic masterpieces. They should, however, be in approximate proportion and should help the reader follow the narrative portion of the report. As noted in Chapter 2, several software programs for computer-assisted diagrams are now readily available.

■ *Do not use uncommon abbreviations.* Some abbreviations (such as *Mr., Dr., Ave., St., Feb., Aug., NY, CA*) are so commonly used that they require no explanation. Other abbreviations, however, are commonly used only in law enforcement. Do not use these in your reports because not all readers will understand them. Confusion can result if two people have different interpretations of an abbreviation. For example, what does S.O.B. mean to you? To most people it has a negative meaning. But for people in the health field, it means "short of breath." Consider the following example as information that can be written in your notes but should *not* appear, as such, in a report: Unk/W/F/, nfd, driving Fd/4DRed, nfd.

Instead, write out, "I saw an unknown white female (no further description available) driving a red Ford 4-door (no further description available)." Use only abbreviations common to everyone.

■ *Use short sentences, well organized into short paragraphs.* Short sentences are easier to read. Likewise, paragraphs should be relatively short, usually 5 to 10 sentences. Each question to be answered in the report should have its own paragraph. The report should be organized logically. Most commonly, it begins with *when* and *where* and then tells *who* and *what*. The *what* should be in chronological order—that is, going from beginning to end without skipping back and forth.

Grammatically and Mechanically Correct.
If you were to *hear* the words, "Your chances of being promoted are good if you can write effective reports," you would probably feel differently than if you were to *read* the same words written like this: "yur chances of bein promottid are gud if you kin rite afectiv riports." The **mechanics**—spelling, capitalization and punctuation—involved in translating ideas and spoken words into written words are important. Mistakes in spelling, punctuation, capitalization and grammar give the impression that the writer is careless, uneducated or stupid—maybe all three!

Arp (2007, p.101) contends, "Spelling is the most important part of writing. Even if the structure of your paragraph leaves a little to be desired, if you spell everything correctly, the reader will have some forgiveness. But not if your spelling is bad!" He points out that many officers make the mistake of using words that are too complicated: "A good rule to follow is that if you can't spell it, don't use it."

Use a dictionary and a grammar book if in doubt about how to write something. The dictionary can tell you how to spell a word and whether it should be capitalized and how it should be abbreviated. To make spelling less difficult, consider using a *speller/divider*. These little reference books contain thousands of the most commonly used words, showing their spelling and how they are divided. The reader is not distracted by definitions, information on the history of the word, synonyms and so on. The most important advantage is that one speller/divider page has as many words on it as 15 to 20 dictionary pages.

Use caution when relying on grammar- and spell-checker programs to find mistakes in computerized documents. For example, if an investigator wrote that a victim of an assault was unable to be interviewed because "she had lapsed into a *comma*," or that a suspect had been restrained because "he was acting *erotically*," when what the writer meant to say was "coma" and "erratically," respectively, the reader might question the investigator's intelligence or attention to detail.

Written in Standard English.
People often disagree about what Standard English is. And the standards for spoken and written English differ. For example, if you were to *say*, "I'm gonna go walkin' in the mornin'," it would probably sound all right. People often drop the final "g" when they speak. In writing, however, this is not acceptable.

Just as there are rules for spelling, capitalization and punctuation, there are rules for *what* words are used *when*. For example, it is standard to say "he doesn't" rather than "he don't," "I don't have any" rather than "I ain't got none," and "he and I are partners" rather than "him and me are partners."

Your experience with English will often tell you what is standard and what is not—especially if you have lived in surroundings in which Standard English is used. If you speak Standard English, you will probably also write in Standard English. But that is not always true.

Paragraphs.
As discussed earlier, in structuring the narrative and making your report clear, effective writers use paragraphs to guide the reader. Keep the paragraphs

short (usually 100 words or less). Skip a line to indicate the beginning of a new paragraph. Discuss only one subject in each paragraph. Start a new paragraph when you change speakers, locations, time or ideas—for example, when you go from observations to descriptions to statements.

Paragraphs are reader friendly, guiding the reader through your report. Most paragraphs should be 5 to 6 sentences, although they may be a single sentence or as many as 10 or 15 sentences on occasion.

Past Tense. Write in the **past tense** throughout the report. Past-tense writing uses verbs that show that events have already occurred. Your report contains what *was* true at the time you took your notes. Use of present tense can cause tremendous problems later. For example, suppose you wrote, "John Doe *lives* at 100 South Street and *works* for Ace Trucking Company." One year later, you find yourself on the witness stand with a defense attorney asking you, "Now, Officer, your report says that John Doe lives at 100 South Street. Is that correct?" You may not know, and you would have to say so. The next question: "Now, Officer, your report says John Doe works for Ace Trucking Company. Is *that* correct?" Again, you may be uncertain and be forced into an "I don't know" response. Use of the past tense in your report avoids this problem.

First Person. Use the first person to refer to yourself. **First person** in English uses the words *I, me, my, we, us* and *our*. The sentence "*I* responded to the call" is written in the first person. This contrasts with "*This officer* responded to the call," which uses the third person. Whether you remember your English classes and discussions of first-, second- and third-person singular and plural is irrelevant. Simply remember to refer to yourself as *I* rather than as *this officer*.

Active Voice. A sentence may be either active or passive. This is an easy distinction to make if you think about what the words *active* and *passive* mean. (Forget about the term *voice*; it is a technical grammatical term you do not need to understand to write well.) In the **active voice** the subject of the sentence performs the actions—for example, "I wrote the report." This contrasts with the *passive* voice, in which the subject does nothing—for example: "The report was written by me." The report did not do anything. The problem with the passive voice is that often the *by* is left off—for example: "The report was written." Later, no one knows who did the writing. Passive voice results in a "whodunit" that can have serious consequences in court.

Statements are usually clearer in the active voice. Although most sentences should be in the active

voice, a *passive* sentence is acceptable in the following situations:

1. If the doer of the action is unknown, unimportant or obvious.

   EXAMPLE: "The gun had been fired three times." We don't know who fired it. This is better than "Someone had fired the gun three times."

   EXAMPLE: "The woman has been arrested four times." Who arrested her each time is not important.

   EXAMPLE: "Felix Umburger was paroled in April." *Who* is obviously the parole board.

2. When you want to call special attention to the receiver of the action rather than the doer.

   EXAMPLE: Officer Morris was promoted after the examination.

   You want to call attention to Officer Morris, rather than to the person who promoted him.

3. When it would be unfair or embarrassing to be mentioned by name.

   EXAMPLE: The program was postponed because the wrong film was sent.

   BETTER THAN: The program was postponed because Sergeant Fairchild sent the wrong film.

   EXAMPLE: Insufficient evidence was gathered at the crime scene.

   BETTER THAN: Investigator Hanks gathered insufficient evidence at the crime scene.

Audience-Focused. Always consider who your audience is. Recall the diversity of possible readers of police reports. Given these varied backgrounds and individuals with limited familiarity with law enforcement terminology, the necessity for audience-focused reports becomes obvious. By keeping in mind this diverse audience, you will construct a reader-friendly report.

One way to be reader friendly is to be certain that the narrative portion of your report can stand alone. That calls for eliminating such phrases as *the above*. A reader-friendly report does not begin like this: "On the above date at the above time, I responded to the above address to investigate a burglary in progress."

Using such phrases presents two problems. First, if readers take time to look "above" to find the information, their train of thought is broken. It is difficult to find where to resume reading, and time is wasted. Second, if readers do *not* take time to look "above," important information is not conveyed, and it is very likely the reader, perhaps subconsciously, will be wondering what would have been found "above." If information is important enough to refer to in your report, include it in the narrative. Do not take the lazy approach and ask your reader to search for the information "above."

Another way to write a reader-friendly report is to avoid police lingo and other bureaucratic language and use plain English rather than "Cop Speak." One of the most common mistakes officers make is failing to prepare their report so that civilian jurors or review board members ("most of whom get their law enforcement expertise from watching *Law and Order* or *NYPD Blue* re-runs") can clearly understand why the officers had to do what they did (Grossi, 2008, p.31). Consider this example provided by Robinson (2006, p.30):

> "Officer, would you read the marked section from your report?"
>
> "I attempted to apply an escort hold to the subject, but I noted resistive tension in his arm, so I applied pain compliance instead. The subject actively resisted, so I administered a focused knee strike to the lower abdominal area, and decentralized the subject."
>
> "In other words, Officer, you tried to grab my client's arm, and when he pulled away, you twisted his wrist, and then kicked him in the groin and threw him down on the pavement, is that about it?"
>
> "Well, I wouldn't put it in quite those words."
>
> "No, officer, I imagine you wouldn't. No further questions."

Robinson explains that the defense attorney made the jury think the officer tried to hide his use of force behind a smoke screen of clinical language and that he did so to minimize brutality. According to Robinson, law enforcement trainers use such jargon to make communication *within* the profession more concise and efficient. When it comes to this clinical-sounding terminology for use of force, they use it for two additional reasons: (1) to enable precise description and (2) to differentiate between trained techniques and "street-fighting." Robinson explains, "As litigation has driven improvements in use-of-force training, it has also promoted a push for precision in describing what actually happens during a fight. A term like 'focused strike' rather than 'punch' affords more accuracy in distinguishing, for example, a blow with a closed fist from a 'diffuse strike' with an open hand.... Being able to refer to those trained techniques in reporting a use of force makes it easier to show the officer's use of force was objectively reasonable under the circumstances, a requirement under *Graham v. Connor*" (p.32).

Robinson (2006, p.32) does not suggest that officers abandon clinical-type describing but rather should describe their actions in everyday language: "For example, instead of saying, 'I decentralized the subject,' have the officer describe exactly what push-down technique was used to take Mr. Jones to the ground. 'I pulled him toward me and stabilized his forehead against my upper chest, by locking my arms around the back of his head and neck. Then I stepped back, and used my hands to direct him to the ground, while also verbally commanding him to get down.'"

Robinson (2006, p.32) concludes, "If officers learn to articulate their use of force in specific, everyday language, the reasonableness will become more apparent. A good report can make an excessive-force lawsuit less likely to be filed in the first place, and if it does go to court, less likely to be successful."

Legible and On Time. It does little good to learn to write well if no one can read it or if the report is turned in after it was needed. Ideally, reports should be typed, and in today's computer-driven world, most reports are generated this way. Sometimes, however, this is not practical or possible. In fact, a poorly typed report is often as difficult to read as an illegible one.

If you do not type your reports, and if you know that you have poor handwriting, you may want to print your reports by hand. A key factor in legibility is speed, and most officers need to slow their writing speed (Arp, 2007). A report that cannot be read is of little use to anyone. Whether your reports are typed, written or printed, make certain that others can read them easily and that they are submitted on time.

RECORDING AND DICTATING REPORTS

Recording or dictating reports is common in some departments, and the demand for transcription services and software is increasing across the country (Lesney et al., 2008). Many departments are moving toward digital report recording because it is more efficient and less costly than the old-fashioned method of tape recording. Reports that need quick attention may be red-tagged, and records personnel type all red-tagged cases first.

Recording or dictating reports shifts the bulk of writing time to the records division. Even with recording or dictating, however, officers must still take final responsibility for what is contained in the report. Do not assume that what you think you spoke into a dictation machine is what will end up on paper. Following are some humorous illustrations of how some dictated sentences can be misinterpreted:

- He called for a toe truck.
- Smith was arrested for a mister meaner.
- Jones was a drug attic.
- The victim was over rot.
- Johnson died of a harder tack.

COMPUTERIZED REPORT WRITING

How many times have you heard, "Great job. Now do it again"? This demoralizing phrase can deflate an officer who has gone to great lengths to ensure an accurate, complete report. Yet police officers often encounter this "do it again" hurdle when they write a report. Report writing is filled with redundancies—turning handwritten notes into typed reports, sometimes filling out numerous forms along the way, all involving the same basic information garnered from the initial note-taking event. Each transfer of data takes time from an investigator and introduces an opportunity for error—a transposed number or two, a misspelled name, a detail that gets overlooked and never makes it to the final report.

Computers have made significant contributions to efficiency in report writing. The hardware available for word processing has become smaller and faster. It is easier to use and much more portable. Most of today's officers use vehicle-mounted computers or portable laptops. Software has also kept pace, with software developments allowing faster, more efficient report writing (Jetmore, 2008, p.27). In addition to sophisticated spell- and grammar-checker programs (to be used with the caveats noted earlier in "Grammatically and Mechanically Correct"), other programs have been developed to help in the actual preparation of police reports: "Software selection is specific to each agency and their particular requirements, based on that agency's roles and responsibilities" (Brewer, 2007, p.38). For example, an agency with a large marine section should have the ability to query a boat's hull identification number (HID) on the software's query mask (Brewer). Pen-based computers, which involve use of a special "pen" to write on the computer screen, have also made report writing easier.

One advance is computer-assisted report entry (CARE). This live-entry system centers around a CARE operator who leads officers through preformatted screens and questions, allowing them to complete reports in minutes. The CARE system has reduced report-writing times and improved the quality, accuracy and timeliness of police reports. In addition, Uniform Crime Reporting information is automatically aggregated.

Digital report writing software, such as that offered by Digital FTO and Presynct, can greatly streamline the handling of data and workflow management. It is important to use "open" software programs and networks, which are nonproprietary and interface with myriad systems already in use. This technology also enables departments to file Uniform Crime Reports (UCR) and National Incident-Based Reporting System (NIBRS) data electronically.

Although computerized report writing has greatly increased officers' efficiency, it cannot correct sloppy data entry. Officers are responsible for the accuracy and clarity of the data. The accuracy and clarity of a report are often deciding factors in whether a case is prosecuted. Preparing for and presenting cases in court are discussed in Chapter 21.

An unavoidable and critical part of law enforcement is documenting actions taken during a shift. Here police officers in San Antonio, Texas, complete their arrest reports at the City Detention facility.
© Bob Daemmrich/The Image Works

Technology Innovations

As agencies look for ways to "do more with less," paperless reporting is becoming increasingly popular: "Paperless... reporting offers measurable (dollar) savings in staff time, office supplies and postage. Paperless gets the information where it needs to be in the shortest amount of time. Paperless protects privacy when it needs to be preserved. Paperless enables data sharing and facilitates individual agency control over what is shared and with whom" (Graham, 2009).

One such technology innovation is *Presynct_DictaTrans* for field-based reporting:

Presynct_DictaTrans is a secure Web-based application for paperless management of the incident and investigative reporting processes from creation to archive. *Presynct_DictaTrans* uses digital versions of existing forms so there is minimal training or behavior change required on the part of the users.

Presynct_DictaTrans combines voice and text in one application that integrates with proprietary records management systems or operates as a stand-alone document management system.

Confidentiality is enhanced by doing away with paper drafts, lost or broken tapes and misplaced tape recorders. Turnaround time from incident to data sharing no longer takes days or weeks.... [but] is measured in minutes. Dictated reports are typed by data entry staff, leaving officer time and resources more effectively utilized in the field. Authors can also type their own reports and skip the dictation and data entry step. Transcription can be securely outsourced without losing control and management of the workflow.

Encrypted voice recordings are created in *Presynct_DictaTrans* with digital handheld recorders, computer workstations or telephones. The recorded dictation is immediately available for typing or automatic speech recognition (ASR). *Presynct_DictaTrans* electronically routes reports for author review and editing. Immediately on approval, reports are automatically routed by *Presynct_DictaTrans* for supervisor approval or rejection with comments. Workflow routing is configurable to five levels. Finalized reports are archived in a searchable database, and incident data is exported to the RMS.

Source: http://www.presynct.com/solutions/ps_dicta-trans.html

EVALUATING YOUR REPORT

Once you have written your report, evaluate it. Do not simply add the final period, staple the pages together and turn it in. Reread it. Proofread it to look for mistakes in spelling, punctuation and capitalization.

Also make certain it says what you want it to and contains no content or composition errors. Ask yourself if the report is factual, accurate, objective, complete, concise, clear, grammatically and mechanically correct, written in Standard English, organized into paragraphs, written in the past tense, uses the first person and active voice and is audience-focused and legible. For larger reports, ask a colleague whose writing you admire to read your report. It is very difficult to proofread your own writing.

Table 3.4 provides an evaluation checklist for investigative reports.

TABLE 3.4 Evaluation Checklist for Reports
Is the Report:
Factual?
Accurate?
Objective?
Complete?
Chronological?
Concise?
Clear?
Mechanically correct?
Grammatically correct?
Written in Standard English?
Organized into paragraphs?
Does the Report Use:
First person?
Active voice?
Past tense?
Are the Sentences Mechanically Correct in:
Spelling?
Capitalization?
Punctuation?
Abbreviations?
Is the Report Audience-Focused and Legible?
Does the Report Allow the Reader to Visualize What Happened?

Source: Adapted from Kären M. Hess and Christine Hess Orthmann. *For the Record: Report Writing in Law Enforcement*, 6th ed. Rosemount, MN: Innovative Systems-Publishers, Inc., 2008, p.208. Used with permission.

CITIZEN ONLINE REPORT WRITING

Allowing citizens to file crime reports online has the potential to increase caseload processing efficiency, increase patrol office effectiveness and ease reporting delays for those jurisdictions suffering from staffing shortages or unmanageable caseloads (Cartwright, 2008). Such reporting is used only for discovery crimes, not involvement crimes, and is most appropriate for property crimes where no suspect information is available. For example, the San Francisco Police Department allows citizens to file online police reports for lost property, theft, vandalism and graffiti, vehicle tampering, vehicle burglary and harassing phone calls (Gitmed, 2007, p.127). Special applications can also be used, such as allowing private security guards to file shoplifting reports online (Cartwright, 2008).

In accessing the local department's Web site and pulling up the page with the crime report form, citizens are able to complete an online report with such required fields as name, address, type of incident or loss experienced, and so on. Before the citizen can submit the report, a warning appears stating the penalties for filing a false report. Gitmed (2007, p.124) notes, "Trying to obtain police reports from tourists, who would rather get back to their vacations than deal with filing a report, and trying to obtain a copy of these reports for insurance purposes can be a logistical nightmare."

Benefits of citizen online reporting include a reduction in time and resources spent responding to and writing reports for minor incidents that often lack a suspect and are usually filed only for insurance purposes (Cartwright, 2008). These systems often allow the police department to e-mail a copy of the report, once approved by the agency, back to the citizen for easier, more timely submission to their insurance company. Furthermore, such systems often meet Americans with Disabilities Act (ADA) requirements and can receive reports in multiple languages, features that help agencies overcome communication barriers and better serve segments of the population that have traditionally been less likely to report crime and victimization (Cartwright, 2008).

Once submitted, the report can be retrieved and proofed by a records clerk in the police department, who determines whether the report is valid and assigns a case number to those meeting the predetermined criteria. Some systems allow the report to be directly downloaded into the department's records management system.

THE FINAL REPORT

The culmination of the preceding steps is the final, or prosecution, report, containing all essential information for bringing a case to trial. The final report will be examined more closely in Chapter 21, as part of preparing a case for court.

A FINAL NOTE ON THE IMPORTANCE OF WELL-WRITTEN REPORTS

Given the many uses of reports and the number of individuals who rely on them, the importance of reports should now be clear. What is key here is to make these necessary documents as well written as possible, thus maximizing the benefits they can provide. A report written well the first time means less time spent rewriting it. A well-written report also keeps everyone involved in the case current and clear about the facts, which can lead to higher prosecution rates, more plea bargains, fewer trials and an easing of caseloads on the court system. A well-written report can also save an investigator from spending an inordinate amount of time on the witness stand attempting to explain any omissions, errors or points of confusion found in poorly written reports. All these benefits ultimately save the department time and expense. Jetmore (2008, p.26) stresses,

> Although great strides have been made in the forensic and scientific aspects of investigation, most would agree criminal investigation is still an art in which skills are enhanced through a combination of experience, training and the ability to apply investigative techniques to complex situations. Attention to detail, perseverance and common sense prove critical.
>
> It's not just skillful investigation that brings the bad guy to justice, however. It's the investigator's ability to prepare a report that will withstand minute scrutiny by judges, prosecutors, defense counsel, citizens and the media. The report's ability to hold up under scrutiny may determine whether the guilty go free or justice is rendered to the victim. Why? Because in a democracy, the police are rightly constrained by a legal framework that not only presumes innocence, but places strict legal limitations on every police contact, detainment, arrest and search of its citizens. Every police report must jump over the substantial hurdle of the exclusionary rule—which states that illegally obtained evidence can't be used against a defendant in a criminal trial—by explaining in detail how and under

what conditions a person's pre-existing individual rights were provided during the investigative process.

Swobodzinski (2007, p.47) notes, "Your investigative report may be the one pivotal piece of documentation that makes a difference in the prosecution of a murderer or a serial rapist. You certainly don't want it to be the weakest link in the investigation and provide a gap for an offender to get away with their crimes."

In today's litigious society, where anyone can sue anyone else for practically anything, law enforcement is not immune to becoming the target of a lawsuit. For this reason, well-written reports can reduce legal liability for both the officer and the department by clearly documenting the actions taken throughout the investigation. Jetmore (2008, p.29) points out, "Writing a good investigative report proves difficult without significant knowledge of the legal concepts inherent to the profession. The tools of our trade include exceptional knowledge of basic principles relative to local, state and federal law. These include knowledge of what constitutes a crime; probable cause; arrest, search and seizure; the exclusionary rule; the various U.S. Supreme Court decisions we deal with on a daily basis (e.g., *Miranda v. Arizona*); and departmental policy and procedures."

A final benefit of well-written reports is to the writer, in that they can greatly enhance an officer's career by reflecting positively on the investigator's education, competence and professionalism.

A well-written report helps the criminal justice system operate more efficiently and effectively, saves the department time and expense, reduces liability for the department and the officer and reflects positively on the investigator who wrote it.

Figures 3.3 and 3.4 (provided, along with the accompanying narrative, by Detective Richard Gautsch) are examples of a poorly written and a well-written report, respectively.

FIGURE 3.3
Example of a bad police report.
Source: Courtesy of Detective Richard Gautsch. Reprinted with permission.

Report of Officer Iam Clueless

This officer was working the middle shift to cover for Officer Johnson who had called in sick. While on routine patrol in the north shopping center at the above listed time I responded with lights and siren in accordance with our policy to a report of a robbery at Helen's Liquor Store. The perp had been arrested by officer Andrews driving northbound several blocks from the scene. When this officer arrived at the above listed address their were two men standing near the front door. The clerk was frightened bad and nearly out of control as he walked back into the store. He said he'd been ripped off by a man wearing orange colored coveralls, a blue baseball cap about 40 years old, 6', with big ears weighing about 200 pounds who pushed him against the wall and grabbed money from the till and a gun had been fired as he exited the front door. No one was hurt and this officer decided not to request an ambulance. The other witness followed us into the store and was obviously drunk and also adorned in coveralls orange in color and two sizes too big, which made him look sloppy. This witness proceeded to the main door and a piece was pointed out a short distance from the sidewalk where the perp must have thrown it. The clerk indicated that he new the guy and that there regular customers. This officer asked the clerk if he could make a positive identification of the party and he acknowledged in the affirmative. I new Officer Andrews was 10–12 with one and I asked him his ETA. He said he was waiting for a CSO to stand by for the hook, but there always late and we needed a new system for tows. He snapped your just gonna have to wait, I'll get there ASAP. He said he thought we were close enough in time to do a one on one showup and this officer concurred. When I first arrived at the scene, this officer was of the opinion that the man in the orange colored coveralls was acting strange and may have been thinking about booking on me. I contemplated cuffing him, but the PC was a little weak. I engaged the party in further conversation to ascertain weather he'd offer additional incriminating evidence or make a damaging utterance. Having recently attended training in the latest Miranda rulings, this officers surmised he was within his rights to converse with the subject since he wasn't in custody and he hadn't lawyered up. As I asked him questions, he became defensive and moved in a suspicious manner. It became evident that he had drug and alcohol problems and this officer made the decision to render the firearm safe and secure it in the trunk of my squad. On the arrival of Officer Andrews, the clerk shouted out the door that their brothers and of course he can identify him. Officer Andrews then rolled up and lowered his window. The clerk went hysterical and screamed that he owed him a hundred bucks. Both witnesses positively identified the suspect sitting in the back seat with a sour look. Officer Andrews gave the clerk back a hundred dollars and transported the suspect who was wearing orange colored coveralls and a blue hat to the PD for booking. He identified the defendant as Bart Jennings, 5-11-65. The suspect confessed in front of us and totally exonerated his brother. The clerk calmed down and asked when he'd get the gun back. I said that was up to the detectives and cleared the scene at 5624 Forest Street. This officer identified the witnesses as Stanley Jennings and Thomas Benson. See above for addresses and DOB's. END OF REPORT

Report of Officer Gotta Clue

On 10-20-04 at 1900 hours, I was dispatched to Helen's Liquor Store (5624 Forest Street) regarding a robbery. I arrived at 1905 and saw the victim, Thomas Benson, and a witness, Stanley Jennings, standing outside the front door. Both men identified themselves with Minnesota driver's licenses. I followed Benson into the store.

Benson paced and his hands trembled as he spoke. He told me that at 1845 hours a customer pushed him against the wall, grabbed about $100 from the cash register, and ran from the store. The robber dropped a handgun outside the door as he left, and it fired. Benson described the man as white, about 40 years old, 6 feet tall, 200 pounds, with big ears. He wore orange coveralls and a blue baseball hat. Benson said he knew the man and could identify him.

As I spoke with Benson, S. Jennings came into the store and stood by the front door. He was wearing orange coveralls, swayed from side to side, and repeatedly moved his hands in and out of his pockets. His eyes were red and watery, and I smelled the odor of an alcoholic beverage on his breath. S. Jennings opened the door and pointed at a Colt 38 caliber revolver in the grass about 6 feet west of the sidewalk.

After marking the location of the revolver with an evidence tag, I placed the gun in the trunk of my squad for safety reasons.

At 1910 hours Officer Andrews contacted me by radio. He had detained Bart Jennings (5-11-65) several blocks north of Helen's Liquor Store. Andrews brought B. Jennings back to the liquor store at 1925 hours. B. Jennings was wearing orange coveralls, a blue baseball cap, and had big ears. He stayed in the back seat of the squad. (Please see Officer Andrews' arrest report.)

Benson ran toward the squad and shouted, "That's him, that's the creep. He owes me 100 bucks." He also told me that Stanley and Bart Jennings were brothers.

S. Jennings leaned against the front door of the store and said, "Yup, that's him."

B. Jennings shifted forward in his seat and stated, "I done it, but I didn't use no gun. It just fell out of my pocket. And Stan didn't know I was going to do it."

Officer Andrews transported B. Jennings to the Police Department. I told Benson and S. Jennings that a detective would contact them. I logged the gun into evidence.

Case referred to Investigations.

FIGURE 3.4
Example of a good police report.
Source: Courtesy of Detective Richard Gautsch. Reprinted with permission.

Summary

Reports are permanent written records of important facts of a case to be used in the future and are crucial and necessary cogs in the wheel of justice.

Reports are used to examine the past, provide a documented record of incidents, keep other police officers informed, continue investigations, prepare court cases, provide the courts with relevant facts, coordinate law enforcement activities, plan for future law enforcement services, evaluate individual officer and department performance, refresh a witness's memory about what he or she said occurred, refresh the investigating officer's memory during the trial, compile statistics on crime in a given jurisdiction and provide information to insurance investigators. Reports are read by other officers, supervisors, attorneys and judges, jurors, social workers, city officials, insurance adjusters and investigators, civil rights groups, citizens and media.

Among the common problems in police reports are

■ Confusing or unclear sentences.

■ Conclusions, assumptions and opinions.

■ Extreme wordiness and overuse of police jargon and abbreviations.

■ Missing or incomplete information.

■ Misspelled words and grammatical or mechanical errors.

■ Referring to "above" information.

The effective report writer attends to both content and form because they are equally important in a well-written report. An effective report is factual, accurate, objective, complete, concise, clear, grammatically and mechanically correct, written in Standard English, organized into paragraphs and written in the past tense; uses the first person and active voice; and is audience-focused and legible, leaving the reader with a positive impression of the writer's competence. A well-written report is also submitted on time.

A fact is a statement that can be proven, an inference is a conclusion based on reasoning and an opinion is a personal belief.

A well-written report helps the criminal justice system operate more efficiently and effectively, saves the department time and expense, reduces liability for the department and the officer and reflects positively on the investigator who wrote it.

Checklist

Report Writing

- Have I made a rough outline and organized my notes?
- Have I included all relevant information?
- Have I included headings?
- Have I proofread the paper to spot content and composition errors?
- Have I submitted all required reports on time?
- Have both negative and positive information been submitted to the prosecuting attorney?

Discussion Questions

1. What is the *most* important use of reports?
2. Do you think notes should be retained or destroyed after a report has been written?
3. How important are reports for prosecution of a case?
4. Is time a factor in the quality of reports?
5. Can the content and form of a report actually be separated?
6. What gives you the most difficulty in writing reports?
7. What are your strengths in report writing?
8. Are you familiar with any report-writing software? If so, what is your opinion of the program(s)?
9. What are the advantages and disadvantages of having citizens use online reporting?
10. How do you feel about having to submit both positive and negative information to the prosecuting attorney?

Media Explorations

Internet

Search for *report writing in law enforcement*. Find one article relevant to writing offense reports, outline it and share your outline with the class.

ONLINE Database Gale Criminal Justice Database Assignments

The following assignments require access to Gale's Custom Journals Database for Emergency Services and Criminal Justice. Check with your instructor if you have questions about this.

- Find the article "Getting it Write Right: Convictions Require Good Report Writing" on the Gale Emergency Services Database. Read and summarize the points made in the article identifying the importance of good report writing.
- Find the article "Reducing Redundancy in Report Writing" on the Gale Emergency Services Database. Read and outline it, and be prepared to discuss this topic in class.
- Find the article "Officer Safety in the Mobile Office" on the Gale Emergency Services Database. Be prepared to discuss the "Omaha Experience" that is outlined in this article and identify the effects it can have on police report writing.

References

Arp, Don, Jr. "Effective Written Reports." *Law and Order*, April 2007, pp.100–102.

Brewer, Brad. "ABCs of Mobile Reporting." *Law and Order*, November 2007, pp.36–44.

Cartwright, Andrew. "Beyond the Paper Chase." *Law Enforcement Technology*, November 2008, pp.58–62.

Gitmed, William. "Citizens Reporting Crimes Online." *The Police Chief*, August 2007, pp.124–131.

Graham, Evelyn J. "Paperless Incident Reporting with Minimum Pain and Maximum Benefit." *PoliceOne.com*, September 22, 2009. Accessed April 5, 2011. http://www.policeone.com/police-technology/articles/1912600-Paperless-Incident-Reporting-with-Minimum-Pain-and-Maximum-Benefit/.

Grossi, Dave. "Tactics for Survival Writing." *Law Officer Magazine*, October 2008, pp.30–33.

Hess, Kären M., and Orthmann, Christine Hess. *For the Record: Report Writing in Law Enforcement*, 6th ed. Rosemount, MN: Innovative Systems-Publishers, 2008.

Jetmore, Larry F. "Hone Your Investigative Skills." *Law Officer Magazine*, September 2007, pp.22–23.

Jetmore, Larry F. "Investigative Report Writing." *Law Officer Magazine*, February 2008, pp.26–30.

Lesney, Terry; Rose, Michael; and Aspland, Michael. "Transcription Outsourcing: A Rapidly Emerging Trend in Law Enforcement." *The Police Chief*, June 2008, pp.76–80.

Robinson, Patricia A. "What You Say Is What They Write: Everybody Teaches Report Writing." *The Law Enforcement Trainer*, January/February 2006, pp.30–32.

Rutledge, Devallis. *The New Police Report Manual*, 2nd ed. Belmont, CA: Wadsworth Publishing Company, 2000.

Rutledge, Devallis. "Full Disclosure." *Police*, December 2007, pp.68–71.

Rutledge, Devallis. "Unmixing Mixed-Up Concepts." *Police*, January 2008, pp.66–67.

Scarry, Laura L. "Report Writing." *Law Officer Magazine*, February 2007, pp.68–71.

Swobodzinski, Kimberle. "The Crime Scene Report." *Law Officer Magazine*, February 2007, pp.47–49.

Wilson, Orlando W., and McLaren, Roy C. *Police Administration*, 4th ed. New York: McGraw-Hill, 1977.

Cases Cited

Graham v. Connor, 490 U.S. 386 (1989)

Miranda v. Arizona, 384 U.S. 436 (1966)

CHAPTER 4
Searches

© Mario Villafuerte/Getty Images

Outline

Can You Define?

anticipatory warrant
Buie sweep
Carroll decision
Chimel decision
circle search
curtilage
"elephant-in-a-matchbox" doctrine
exclusionary rule
exigent circumstances
frisk
"fruit-of-the-poisonous-tree" doctrine
good-faith doctrine
immediate control
inevitable-discovery doctrine

lane-search pattern
nightcapped warrant
no-knock warrant
particularity requirement
patdown
plain feel/touch evidence
plain-view evidence
probable cause
protective sweep
strip-search pattern
Terry stop
totality-of-the-circumstances test
true scene
uncontaminated scene
zone

Do You Know?

- Which constitutional amendment restricts investigative searches?
- What is required for an effective search?
- What basic restriction is placed on all searches?
- What the exclusionary rule is and how it affects investigators?
- What the preconditions and limitations of a legal search are?
- When a warrantless search is justified?
- What precedents are established by the *Weeks, Mapp, Terry, Chimel, Carroll* and *Chambers* decisions?
- What a successful crime scene search accomplishes?
- What is included in organizing a crime scene search?
- What physical evidence is?
- What search patterns are used in exterior searches? Interior searches?
- Whether evidence left in plain view may be lawfully seized and is admissible in court?
- How to search a vehicle, a suspect and a dead body?
- How dogs can be used in searches?

To search is to go over or look through a house or other building, a person or a vehicle to find contraband or illicit or stolen property or some evidence of guilt to be used in prosecuting a criminal action or offense. In *United States v. Jacobsen* (1984) the Supreme Court defined a search as "a governmental infringement of a legitimate expectation of privacy." Rutledge (2008, p.28) explains, "In situations where it would be unreasonable for a person to expect privacy, there is no 'search' to justify, so no warrant is needed."

Investigators make many kinds of searches. They search crime scenes, suspects, dead bodies, vehicles, hotel rooms, apartments, homes and offices. Searching is a vital task in most criminal investigations because through searching, evidence of crime and against criminals is obtained. Equally vital, however, is an investigator's understanding of the laws relating to searches. Every search must be firmly based on an understanding of the restrictions under which police officers must operate.

LEGAL SEARCHES AND THE FOURTH AMENDMENT

An understanding of the Fourth Amendment to the U.S. Constitution and its relevance for searches and seizures is critical for any investigator. The Fourth Amendment states, "The right of the people to be secure in their persons, houses, papers, and effects, against unreasonable searches and seizures, shall not be violated, and no warrants shall issue, but upon probable cause, supported by oath or affirmation, and particularly describing the place to be searched, and the persons or things to be seized."

> The Fourth Amendment to the U.S. Constitution forbids unreasonable searches and seizures.

The Fourth Amendment strikes a balance between individual liberties and the rights of society. It is an outgrowth of the desire of the founders of the United States to eliminate the offensive British practices that existed before the Revolutionary War, such as forcing the colonists to provide British soldiers housing and indiscriminately searching the homes of those suspected of disloyalty to the king. The Fourth Amendment meant to ensure that the new government would respect its citizens' dignity and privacy: "The critical distinction to be made at this point is that the only 'privacy' that counts is that privacy that society is willing to accept as reasonable as interpreted by the courts. The determination of reasonableness depends on the balance between the public interest and the individual's right to be left alone from arbitrary interferences from law enforcement" (Ivy and Orput, 2007, p.8).

The courts are bound by rules and can admit evidence only if it is obtained constitutionally. Thus, the legality of a search must always be kept in mind during an investigation.

> To conduct an effective search, know the legal requirements for searching, the items being searched for and the elements of the crime being investigated; be organized, systematic and thorough.

BASIC LIMITATION ON SEARCHES

All searches have one limitation.

> The most important limitation on any search is that the scope must be narrow. General searches are unconstitutional.

Laws regulating how and when searches may be legally conducted are numerous and complex. It is critical, however, that officers responsible for criminal investigations know these laws and operate within them. The penalty for not doing so is extreme—no evidence obtained during an illegal search will be allowed at a trial, as established by the exclusionary rule.

THE EXCLUSIONARY RULE

Through the exclusionary rule, the courts enforce the prohibition against unreasonable searches set forth in the Fourth Amendment. In the early 1900s the federal courts declared that they would require evidence to be obtained in compliance with the constitutional standards set forth in the Fourth Amendment.

> The **exclusionary rule** established that courts may not accept evidence obtained by unreasonable search and seizure, regardless of its relevance to a case. *Weeks v. United States* (1914) made the rule applicable at the federal level; *Mapp v. Ohio* (1961) made it applicable to *all* courts.

The exclusionary rule affects illegally seized evidence as well as evidence obtained as a result of the illegally seized evidence, referred to as *fruit of the poisonous tree*. The **"fruit-of-the-poisonous-tree" doctrine** established that evidence obtained as a result of an earlier illegality must be excluded from trial. The exclusionary rule may seem to favor criminals at the expense of law enforcement, but this was not the Court's intent. The Court recognized that important exceptions to this rule might occur. Two of the most important exceptions are the inevitable-discovery doctrine and the good-faith doctrine.

The Inevitable Discovery Exception

In *Nix v. Williams* (1984) a defendant's right to counsel under the Sixth Amendment was violated, resulting in his making incriminating statements and leading the police to the body of his murder victim. Searchers who had been conducting an extensive, systematic search of the area then terminated their search. If the search had continued, the search party would inevitably have discovered the victim's body. The **inevitable-discovery doctrine** established that if illegally obtained evidence would in all likelihood eventually have been discovered legally, it may be used.

The intent of the exclusionary rule, the Court said, was to deter police from violating citizens' constitutional rights. In the majority opinion, Chief Justice Warren E. Burger wrote, "Exclusion of physical evidence that would inevitably have been discovered adds nothing to either the integrity or fairness of a criminal trial."

The Good Faith Exception

In *United States v. Leon* (1984) police in Burbank, California, were investigating a drug-trafficking operation and, following up on a tip from an unreliable informant, applied for and were issued an apparently valid search warrant. Their searches revealed large quantities of drugs and other evidence at various locations. The defendants challenged the sufficiency of the warrant and moved to suppress the evidence seized on the basis of the search warrant. The district court held that the affidavit was insufficient to establish probable cause because of the informant's unreliability. The U.S. Court of Appeals affirmed the district court's action. Then the U.S. Supreme Court reviewed whether the exclusionary rule should be modified to allow the admission of evidence seized in *reasonably good faith*. The Court noted that the exclusionary rule is a *judicially created remedy* intended to serve as a deterrent rather than a guaranteed constitutional right. The **good-faith doctrine** established that illegally obtained evidence may be admissible if the police were truly not aware they were violating a suspect's Fourth Amendment rights.

Scarry (2007a, p.76) notes, "Courts know police officers can and will make reasonable mistakes. It's simply the nature of the job." Rutledge (2007a, p.71) contends, "Objectively reasonable good faith may prevent suppression and liability in these kinds of cases: search warrants, misidentification, invalid statutes, arrest warrants and consent."

JUSTIFICATION FOR REASONABLE SEARCHES

The courts have adopted guidelines to assure law enforcement personnel that if they adhere to certain rules, their searches or seizures will be reasonable, and thus legal.

A search can be justified and therefore considered legal if any of the following conditions are met:
- A search warrant has been issued.
- Consent is given.
- An officer stops a suspicious person and believes the person may be armed.
- The search is incidental to a lawful arrest.
- An emergency exists.

If any *one* of these *preconditions* exists, a search will be considered "reasonable" and therefore legal. However, states can impose further restrictions on police powers within their boundaries.

Search with a Warrant

Technically—according to the Fourth Amendment—all searches are to be conducted under the authority of a warrant. In 1948, the Supreme Court ruled in *Johnson v. United States* that without exigent circumstances, searches are presumptively unconstitutional if not authorized by a search warrant.

To obtain a valid search warrant, officers must appear before a judge and establish probable cause to believe that the location contains evidence of a crime and specifically describe that evidence. **Probable cause** is more than reasonable suspicion. Probable cause to search requires that a combination of facts makes it more likely than not that items sought are where the police believe them to be. Probable cause is what would lead a person of "reasonable caution" to believe that something connected with a crime is on the premises or person to be searched: "Probable cause is a commonsense, non-technical conception that deals with the factual and practical considerations of everyday life on which reasonable and prudent men, not legal technicians, act" (Scarry, 2007b, p.59).

Jetmore (2007b, p.28) explains probable cause as "less than proof, but more than suspicion that a crime is being, has been or will be committed. Thus, probable cause requires a higher standard than reasonable suspicion, but less than the proof beyond a reasonable doubt required for a conviction in court." A partial list of guilt-laden or other facts to build probable cause includes flight, furtive movements, hiding, an attempt to destroy evidence, resistance to officers, evasive answers, unreasonable explanations, contraband or weapons in plain view, a criminal record, police training and experience, unusual or suspicious behavior and information from citizens (Jetmore, 2007b). The more of these conditions that exist, the stronger the probable cause.

When officers use information from civilians on search warrant applications, they should state whether the civilian is an informant or citizen giving information as a civic duty.

Using Informants.
The Supreme Court has established requirements for using informants in establishing probable cause. In *Aguilar v. Texas* (1964) the Court adopted a two-pronged test: (1) is the informant reliable/credible? and (2) is the information believable? This two-pronged approach was upheld in *Spinelli v. United States* (1969) when the Court ruled that the affidavit of the Federal Bureau of Investigation (FBI) for a warrant was insufficient to establish probable cause because there was not enough information to adequately assess the informant's reliability.

The Court abandoned this two-pronged approach in *Illinois v. Gates* (1983), where the Court ruled that probable cause is a practical concept that should not be weighed by scholars using tests, such as the *Aguilar-Spinelli* two-pronged test. Rather, the test for probable cause under the Fourth Amendment should be a **totality-of-the-circumstances test**. This is a principle upon which a number of legal assessments are made; it refers to the sum total of factors leading a reasonable person to a course of action. However, federal courts are still guided by the two-pronged *Aguilar-Spinelli* test, and several states adhere to this more stringent requirement for establishing probable cause.

Other Requirements.
In addition to establishing probable cause for a search, the warrant must contain the reasons for requesting it, the names of the people presenting affidavits, what specifically is being sought and the signature of the judge issuing it. The warrant must be based on facts and sworn to by the officer requesting the warrant. An address and description of the location must be given—for example, "100 S. Main Street," "the ABC Liquor Store," or "1234 Forest Drive, a private home." Figure 4.1 is an example of a search warrant. For an example of the complete search warrant application, log in to cengagebrain.com and access the CourseMate that accompanies this text.

A search warrant can be issued to search for and seize:

■ Stolen or embezzled property.

■ Property designed or intended for use in committing a crime.

■ Property that indicates a crime has been committed or a particular person has committed a crime.

In *Groh v. Ramirez* (2004) the Supreme Court sent a message to law enforcement on the importance of paying attention to detail. In this case, police obtained a warrant to search a residence. Although the application and affidavit described the items to be seized, the warrant did *not* contain such a description as required by the Fourth Amendment. The section that was to contain a list of *items* to be seized instead described the *place* to be searched. A judge reviewed and signed the warrant, which was then executed. The officer was sued for an alleged Fourth Amendment violation. The lower court agreed that a constitutional violation occurred and that any reasonable officer would have concluded that the warrant was invalid. The U.S. Supreme Court agreed: "It is incumbent upon the officer executing a search warrant to ensure the search is lawfully authorized and lawfully conducted."

Once a warrant is obtained, it should be executed promptly. In many states, the warrant is good for a set number of days (for example, 7 or 10 days) and is to be executed during daytime hours, typically between 6 A.M. and 9 P.M. unless endorsed otherwise. A **nightcapped warrant** authorizes a search or arrest at any time, day or night. Nightcapped warrants can generally be served when a suspect is in any public area regardless of time. The court determines the legitimacy of a nightcapped warrant based on considerations such as safety of the public and those executing the warrants, or the prevention of the loss, destruction or removal of evidence.

Usually the officer serving the warrant knocks on the particular door, states the purpose of the search and gives a copy of the warrant to the person who has answered the knock. If officers attempting to serve a search warrant are not admitted by occupants following a knock-notice announcement, forcible entry may be made, but unnecessary damage to the structure may make the entry unreasonable: "Destruction of property in the course of a search may violate the Fourth Amendment, even though the entry itself is lawful (*United States v. Ramirez*)" (Rutledge, 2007d, p.78). The "knock-and-announce" rule is based on English common law and ensures the right to privacy in one's home.

The Knock-and-Announce Rule.
The knock-and-announce rule requires officers serving a search warrant to knock, announce themselves and wait a "reasonable length of time" before attempting entry.

FIGURE 4.1
An example of a
search warrant.
© Cengage Learning, 2013

Warrant 1-1t

SEARCH WARRANT

STATE OF MINNESOTA, COUNTY OF ANYCITY   DISTRICT COURT

TO: **DETECTIVE C.Y. LIM**, (A) PEACE OFFICER(S) OF THE STATE OF MINNESOTA.

WHEREAS, **C.Y. LIM** has this day on oath, made application to the said Court applying for issuance of a
search warrant to search the following described Property,:

- **An AMD hard drive removed from a Hewlitt Packard Laptop Computer found in
  the possession of John Jacob Smith, date of birth January 1, 1980, bearing serial
  number 7864532, which is currently located at the Anycity Police Department, 1234
  American Blvd. in the City of Anycity, Anycity County, Minnesota.**

located in the City of Anycity, County of Anycity STATE OF MINNESOTA for the following described
property and things:

**All data contained on the hard drive to include all documents, files and images that
depict child pornography.**

**All data contained on the hard drive to include all documents and files that show
ownership of Hewlitt Packard Laptop Computer.**

WHEREAS, the application and supporting affidavit of C.Y. Lim was/were duly presented and read by the
Court, and being fully advised in the premises.

NOW, THEREFORE, the Court finds that probable cause exists for the issuance of a search warrant upon the
following grounds:

1. The property above-described was used as means of committing a crime.
**2. The property above-described constitutes evidence which tends to show a crime has been committed, or
tends to show that a particular person has committed a crime.**

The Court further finds that probable cause exists to believe that the above-described property and things are
within the property.

NOW, THEREFORE, YOU, DETECTIVE C.Y. LIM AND ALL OTHER OFFICERS ACTING UNDER
YOUR DIRECTION AND CONTROL, THE PEACE OFFICER(S) AFORESAID, ARE HEREBY
COMMANDED TO DELIVER THE HEREINBEFORE DESCRIBED COMPUTER HARD DRIVES(S)
TO THE ANYCITY POLICE DEPARTMENT AT ANYCITY, MINNESOTA, FOR EXAMINATION,
AND THEREAFTER, RETURN TO AFFIANT TO RETAIN THE COMPUTER HARD DRIVE(S) IN
CUSTODY SUBJECT TO COURT ORDER AND ACCORDING TO LAW.

BY THE COURT:

Dated: April 31 2011   _____

JUDGE OF DISTRICT COURT

COPIES TO: COURT • PROS. ATTY • PEACE OFFICER • PREMISES/PERSON

In *Wilson v. Arkansas* (1995) the Court made this centuries-old rule a constitutional mandate: "The underlying command of the Fourth Amendment is always that searches and seizures be reasonable, and that the common-law requirement that officers announce their identity and purpose before entering a house forms a part of the Fourth Amendment inquiry into the reasonableness of the officers' entry."

The knock-and-announce rule is intended (1) to protect citizens' right to privacy, (2) to reduce risk of possible violence to police and residence occupants and (3) to prevent needless destruction of private property. "Most officers find it judicious to know and announce their presence and intentions. 'Surprise' entries can lead to misunderstanding on the suspect's part, creating situations that can escalate into unnecessary violence" (Geoghegan, 2007, p.99).

The courts have recognized that in some instances safe and effective law enforcement requires certain exceptions be made to the knock-and-announce rule. A **no-knock warrant** may be issued if evidence may be easily destroyed or if there is advance knowledge of explosives or other specific danger to an officer (*Richards v. Wisconsin*, 1997)—for example, if a suspect has a prior history of being armed, combative or resistant to arrest.

In a unanimous ruling in *United States v. Banks* (2003), the Supreme Court upheld the forced entry into a suspected drug dealer's apartment 15 to 20 seconds after police knocked and announced themselves. This ruling strengthened police powers in cases where loss of evidence or physical danger were crucial factors and provides guidance to law enforcement officers and entry teams on how long they need to wait before forcing entry into a residence.

Then in 2006 the Supreme Court ruled 5–4 in *Hudson v. Michigan* that the Constitution does not require the government to forfeit evidence gathered through illegal "no knock" searches while executing a search warrant, stating, "Suppression of evidence has always been our last resort, not our first impulse. The exclusionary rule generates substantial social costs which sometimes include setting the guilty free and the dangerous at large." Writing for the Court's five-member conservative majority, Justice Samuel Alito said police blunders should not result in a "get-out-of-jail-free card" for defendants. The Court also referred to alternative remedies to police errors, such as internal discipline or civil lawsuits. Such alternatives, which allow the evidence to be admitted but sanction the officer, mirror the procedure used in the British system (del Carmen, 2010). Hilton (2007, p.38) cautions, "Some police departments have interpreted the Supreme Court's recent *Hudson v. Michigan* ruling as a license to execute warrants without knocking, announcing and waiting a reasonable amount of time for a resident to answer the door before entering. That interpretation is both wrong and dangerous. Failure to adhere to the requirements of the knock-and-announce rule can result in terrible tragedy and extremely expensive litigation."

Video recording of knock-notice announcement and entry provides evidence of compliance with the rule as well as the amount of time officers waited before entry.

> A search conducted with a warrant must be limited to the specific area and specific items named in the warrant, in accordance with the **particularity requirement** (*Stanford v. Texas*, 1965).

During a search conducted with a warrant, items not specified in the warrant may be seized if they are similar to the items described, if they are related to the particular crime described, if they are contraband or if such unrelated, unspecified evidence is in plain view.

Anticipatory Search Warrants. In *United States v. Grubbs* (2006) the Supreme Court approved use of an anticipatory search warrant. The Court defined an **anticipatory warrant** as one "based upon an affidavit showing probable cause that at some future time (but not presently) certain evidence of crime will be located at a specified place." The Court noted that, in a sense, all search warrants are anticipatory. Anticipatory warrants are constitutional if a proper showing is made that contraband or evidence will likely be found at the target location at a given time or when a specific triggering event occurs. The Court ruled that where a triggering condition was specified in the search warrant application or affidavit, the failure to include that triggering condition in the warrant did not undermine the warrant's validity.

Search with Consent

Officers can conduct a search without a warrant under certain circumstances, one of which occurs when consent to search is given. Searching without a warrant is allowed if consent is given by the actual property owner or, as set forth in *United States v. Matlock* (1974), by a person in charge of that property. In *Matlock* the Supreme Court held that if a third party has common authority over the premises of items to be searched, this individual could provide government officials with a valid consent. Examples of relationships where third-party consent may be valid include:

- Parent/Child—A parent who owns a property can generally give consent to search the room and other belongings of a child living on those premises. However, if the child uses a given area of the premises exclusively, has sectioned it off, has furnished it with his or her own furniture, pays rent or has otherwise established an expectation of privacy, the parent may not consent to a search of that area occupied by the child.

- Employer/Employee—In general, an employer may consent to a search of any part of the employer's premises used by an employee (e.g., employees' lockers can be searched with the employer's consent). Recent court cases have held that the contents of electronic devices owned by the employer (computers, cell phones, etc.) are *not* shielded by employees' right to privacy.

- Host/Guest—The host, owner or primary occupant of the premises may consent to a search of the area in which a guest is staying. Any evidence found would be admissible against the guest.

- Spouses—If two people, such as husband and wife, have equal rights to occupy and use premises, either may give consent to a search.

If more than one person owns or occupies a building, only one need give permission. Thus if two people share an apartment, all that is required is the consent from one of them (*Wright v. United States*, 1938). However, consent may be given for only those areas commonly used, not private space of one or the other. Even spouses do not have totality in area of consent if one area is considered to be off-limits to one party.

If the police believe the person giving consent has authority, they may act on this belief, even though it later turns out the person did not have authority (*Illinois v. Rodriguez*, 1990). Examples of instances when individuals *cannot* give valid consent to search include:

■ Landlord/Tenant—A landlord, even though the legal owner, does not have authority to give consent to a search of a tenant's premises or a seizure of the tenant's property. Only the tenant may offer consent. This situation includes children (tenants) living at home but paying rent to their parent (landlords).

■ Hotel Employee/Hotel Guest—The Supreme Court extended the principles governing a landlord's consent to a search of tenant's premises to include consent searches of hotel and motel rooms allowed by hotel/motel employees. In these searches, only the hotel guest can give consent.

As with a search warrant, searches conducted with consent have limitations.

> Consent to search must be voluntary, and the search must be limited to the area for which consent is given.

The consent must not be in response to an officer's claim of lawful authority or phrased as a command or threat. It must be a genuine request for permission to search. A genuine affirmative reply must also be given; a simple nodding of the head or opening of a door is not sufficient. Silence is *not* consent. The Supreme Court ruled in *Schneckloth v. Bustamonte* (1973) that it would use the totality-of-the-circumstances test to determine whether the consent was voluntary. This includes the characteristics of the subject, the environment (location, number of people and officers present and time of day), the subject's actions or statements and the officer's actions or statements. Scarry (2007b, p.57) recommends, "It's good practice when asking for a consent to search that officers actually ask for the consent as opposed to stating they would like to conduct a search. Additionally, it's good practice to get an affirmative answer before conducting a search and even better practice to obtain a written consent to search." Even when police have an alternative justification for a search, such as a warrant, they may ask for consent to establish "another layer of validation" for their actions. And they may ask for this consent even if the subject is in custody,

is in handcuffs or has been stopped for a traffic violation and is not free to go (Means and McDonald, 2010a, p.12).

Officers should thoroughly document everything they say and do when asking for consent and while conducting the search. Some officers use a prepared consent form to be signed by the person giving consent. If consent is given, the person granting it must be legally competent to do so. Further, the person may revoke the consent at any time during the search. If this occurs, officers are obligated to discontinue the search.

A form of consent with which officers should be familiar is the *consent once removed* exception to the search warrant requirement. Under this exception, officers can make a warrantless entry to arrest a suspect if consent to enter was given earlier to an undercover officer or informant.

In *Georgia v. Randolph* (2006) the Supreme Court addressed the issue of what happens when one occupant grants permission to search a private premise and another one withholds consent. In this case, Scott Randolph's estranged wife, Janet, gave police consent to search the marital residence for items of her husband's drug use after Randolph, who was also present, had unequivocally refused to give consent. The police went ahead and searched, finding evidence of cocaine possession, and Scott Randolph was indicted. The trial court denied his motion to suppress the evidence as products of a warrantless search unauthorized by consent. The Georgia Court of Appeals, however, reversed. In affirming, the state supreme court held that consent given by one occupant is invalid in the face of the refusal of another physically present occupant. In a 5–3 opinion, the court stated, "If any party who is present and has authority to object to the search does object to the search, the police may not conduct the search on the authority of that party who gave consent."

Patdown or Frisk during a "Stop"

Another exception to the warrant requirement is a stop and frisk situation. Two situations require police officers to stop and question individuals: (1) to investigate suspicious circumstances and (2) to identify someone who looks like a suspect named in an arrest warrant or whose description has been broadcast in an all-points bulletin (APB).

The procedures for stopping and questioning suspects are regulated by the same justifications and limitations associated with lawful searches and seizures. If it is suspected that a person stopped for questioning may be armed, the officer is justified in conducting a through-the-clothes patdown for weapons. If the officer feels an object that may be a weapon, the officer may seize it.

The prime requisite for stopping, questioning and possibly frisking someone is *reasonable suspicion*, a lesser standard than probable cause but equally difficult to define. A stop and a frisk are two separate actions, and each must be separately justified: "Stops and frisks, though usually factually related, are two separate matters legally. Just because a stop is permissible doesn't mean a frisk is permissible. In fact, in most stops, a non-consensual frisk would not be permitted because of the absence of reasonable suspicion of the presence of weapons" (Means, 2008, p.23). The landmark decision in *Terry v. Ohio* (1968) established police officers' right to **patdown** or **frisk** a person they have stopped to question if they believe the person might be armed and dangerous.

> The *Terry* decision established that a patdown or frisk is a "protective search for weapons" and as such must be "confined to a scope reasonably designed to discover guns, knives, clubs and other hidden instruments for the assault of a police officer or others."

The Court warned that a patdown or frisk is "a serious intrusion upon the sanctity of the person which may inflict great indignity and arouse strong resentment, and it is not to be undertaken lightly." The "search" in a frisk is sometimes referred to as a *safety* search. Officers should know the limits of their authority to protect themselves—physically and legally—so that they never are forced to choose between being safe and being sued (Rutledge, 2007b, p.36).

Terry has been further expanded in other cases. *Adams v. Williams* (1972) established that officers may stop and question individuals based on information received from informants. *United States v. Hensley* (1985) established that police officers may stop and question suspects when they believe they recognize them from "wanted" flyers issued by another police department.

Stop-and-frisk has been validated on the basis of furtive movements; inappropriate attire; carrying suspicious objects such as a television or a pillowcase; vague, non-specific answers to routine questions; refusal to identify oneself; and appearing to be out of place. As established in *Alabama v. White* (1990), such a stop-and-frisk can also be made based on an anonymous tip, provided the tip predicts future activities the officer can corroborate, making it reasonable to think the informant has reliable knowledge about the suspect. However, in *Florida v. J. L.* (2000), the Court held that police could not stop and frisk someone based solely on an anonymous tip.

Usually during a ***Terry* stop**, law enforcement officers ask those they detain to identify themselves. *Hiibel v. Sixth Judicial District Court of Nevada, Humboldt County* (2004) ruled that state statutes requiring individuals to identify themselves as part of an investigative stop are constitutional and do not violate the Fourth or Fifth Amendments. However, the *Hiibel* ruling applies only if a state law requires people to provide their names to law enforcement officers.

In *United States v. Drayton* (2002) the Supreme Court ruled that law enforcement officers do not need to advise bus passengers of their right not to cooperate during a consensual bus interdiction. Vehicle stops as well as checkpoints for various purposes are discussed shortly.

The Court has also ruled (*Illinois v. McArthur*, 2001) that officers may detain residents outside their homes until a search warrant can be obtained if necessary.

Search Incident to Arrest

Every lawful arrest is accompanied by a search of the arrested person to protect the arresting officers and others and to prevent destruction of evidence. Any weapon or dangerous substance or evidence discovered in the search may be seized. Limitations on a search incidental to arrest are found in *Chimel v. California* (1969).

When officers have reasonable suspicion to believe someone they have stopped to question may be armed and dangerous, they are legally justified in frisking that person for weapons, as established by the *Terry* decision.

© Joel Gordon

The ***Chimel*** **decision** established that a search incidental to a lawful arrest must be made simultaneously with the arrest and must be confined to the area within the suspect's immediate control.

A person's **immediate control** encompasses the area within the person's reach. The Court noted that using an arrest to justify a thorough search would give police the power to conduct "general searches," which were declared unconstitutional nearly 200 years ago.

If law enforcement officers take luggage or other personal property into their exclusive control and there is no longer any danger that the arrestee might gain access to the property to seize a weapon or destroy evidence, a search of that property is no longer an incident of the arrest and a search warrant should be obtained.

Maryland v. Buie (1990) expanded the area of a premises search following a lawful arrest to ensure officers' safety. In this case, the Supreme Court added authority for the police to search areas immediately adjoining the place of arrest. Such a **protective sweep**, or ***Buie sweep***, is justified when reasonable suspicion exists that another person might be present who poses a danger to the arresting officers. The search must be confined to areas where a person might be hiding.

New York v. Belton (1981) established that the vehicle of a person who has been arrested can be searched without a warrant: "When a policeman has made a lawful custodial arrest of the occupant of an automobile, he may, as a contemporaneous incident of that arrest, search the passenger compartment of that automobile. It follows from this conclusion that the police may also examine the contents of any containers found within the passenger compartment, for if the passenger compartment is within reach of the arrestee, so also will containers in it be within his reach."

Jetmore (2007a, p.31) cautions, "Individual state statutes and/or department policies and procedures may further limit the scope of a search incidental to arrest. Officers should understand their individual state statutes and department policies."

Search in an Emergency Situation

In situations where police officers believe there is probable cause but have no time to secure a warrant—for example, if shots are being fired or a person is screaming—they may act on their own discretion. Imminent danger to public safety and medical emergencies are situations also classified as exigencies.

A warrantless search in the absence of a lawful arrest or consent is justified only in emergencies or **exigent circumstances** where probable cause exists and the search must be conducted immediately (*New York v. Quarles,* 1984).

Most courts recognize three conditions that must be met to support a warrantless entry under the exigent circumstances exception:

1. Officers must believe a real emergency exists requiring immediate action to protect or preserve life or to prevent serious injury.
2. The entry or search must not be motivated primarily to find evidence.
3. The emergency and the area entered or searched must have a connection.

In *Mincey v. Arizona* (1978) the Supreme Court stated that the Fourth Amendment does not require police officers to delay a search during an investigation if to do so would gravely endanger their lives or the lives of others. Once the danger has been eliminated, however, any further search should be conducted only after obtaining a search warrant.

In *Brigham City, Utah v. Stuart* (2006) the Supreme Court ruled that "law enforcement officers may enter a home without a warrant to render emergency assistance to an injured occupant or to protect an occupant from imminent injury," as occurred in this case, when officers entered a private home to stop a fight in progress and ended up making an arrest (Means and McDonald, 2010b). The defendant argued that his conduct was not serious enough to justify the officers' intrusion into the home, and that evidence observed by officers should be suppressed as fruit of an illegal entry. The Supreme Court, however, disagreed and held the entry reasonable, noting "the role of a peace officer includes preventing violence and restoring order, not simply rendering first aid to casualties." The Court also stated, "Because the Fourth Amendment's ultimate touchstone is 'reasonableness,' the warrant requirement is subject to certain exceptions." Citing entry onto private property to fight a fire, or to engage in "hot pursuit" of a fleeing suspect, the Court held, "Thus the 'exigencies of the situation' may make the needs of law enforcement so compelling that a warrantless search is objectively reasonable under the Fourth Amendment."

In *Michigan v. Fisher* (2009) the Court further clarified when officers may enter a home under the exigent circumstances to the warrant requirement by specifically identifying the *emergency aid requirement*: "The 'emergency aid exception' does not depend on the officers' subjective intent of the seriousness of the crime they are investigating." Rather, what matters is whether officers have "an objectively reasonable basis for believing that someone needs medical assistance or is in danger. 'Iron-clad proof' of a serious or life-threatening injury is not required to trigger the emergency aid exception" (Means and McDonald, 2010b, p.20). This exception extends to suicidal persons and allows officers to make an immediate, warrantless entry to protect a person from him or herself (Rutledge, 2010).

Warrantless Searches of Vehicles

A vehicle stop is a seizure within the meaning of the Fourth Amendment and, therefore, must generally be supported by reasonable suspicion of wrongdoing. Officers can often search vehicles after a lawful traffic stop because "one has a lesser expectation of privacy in a motor vehicle as its function is transportation and it seldom serves as one's residence or the repository of personal effects" (Scarry, 2008, p.62). This is also known as the automobile exception. Warrantless searches are often justified because of a vehicle's mobility, that is, the vehicle can be easily moved. The precedent for a warrantless search of an automobile was established in *Carroll v. United States* (1925).

The ***Carroll* decision** established that automobiles may be searched without a warrant if (1) there is probable cause for the search and (2) the vehicle would be gone before a search warrant could be obtained.

After stopping a moving vehicle, if officers have probable cause, they may search the vehicle and any closed containers in it. If probable cause does not exist, officers may be able to obtain voluntary consent to search the vehicle, including any closed containers (*Florida v. Jimeno*, 1991). The driver must be competent to give such consent, and silence is not consent. If at any time the driver rescinds consent, the search must cease.

Officers must also know their state's laws regarding full searches of vehicles pursuant to issuing a traffic citation, which may often seem contradictory. Although several states have statutes that authorize searches of vehicles following the issuance of a traffic citation, the policy in most states is to allow searches only after a driver has been arrested and is in custody. In *Knowles v. Iowa* (1998) the Supreme Court ruled that when an officer issues a citation instead of making an arrest, a full search of the driver's car violates the Fourth Amendment.

Pretext Stops.

Scarry (2007c, p.82) notes, "Ulterior motive for a valid traffic stop does not violate the Fourth Amendment." The so-called *pretext* stop is overridden by an officer's probable cause to believe the motorist is, or is about to be, engaged in criminal activity. In other words: "Probable cause trumps pretext" (Scarry, p.82). Scarry (p.86) says, "State vehicle codes are written to provide law enforcement officers ample opportunity to establish probable cause to initiate a traffic stop when an individual is suspected of having committed, or about to commit, a crime other than the infraction of the vehicle code. They are invaluable tools."

Searches of Passengers in a Stopped Vehicle.

According to Rutledge (2007f, p.70), "Passengers' rights during vehicle stops often differ from those of drivers." He (p.71) further notes, "All passengers in private vehicles are detained at a stop. Passengers may be ordered out and kept from leaving. Passengers may be arrested for joint possession of contraband. And passengers' property and the vehicle may be searched incident to their arrest (passenger compartment), or with probable cause (any hiding place)."

However, the Court has also ruled in *Wyoming v. Houghton* (1999) that an officer may search an automobile passenger's belongings simply because the officer suspects the driver has done something wrong. This "passenger property exception" ruling was intended to prevent drivers from claiming that illegal drugs or other contraband belonged to passengers, rather than themselves.

In *Brendlin v. California* (2007) the Supreme Court reaffirmed what officers already knew—that they must have a reasonable suspicion of criminal activity to stop a vehicle. "If officers have no lawful basis for a traffic stop, *Brendlin* makes clear that anyone in the car—the driver or its passengers—may challenge the stop's constitutionality" (Scarry, 2007d, p.64).

Searches of Vehicles Incident to and Contemporaneous with Lawful Arrests.

Previous editions of this text cited *New York v. Belton* (1981) as the landmark case regarding warrantless searches incident to and contemporaneous with a lawful arrest. The Supreme Court defined a bright-line rule in *Belton*: "Once an officer determines that there is probable cause to make an arrest, it is reasonable to allow officers to ensure their safety and to preserve evidence by searching the entire passenger compartment." However, *Belton* has since been limited by *Arizona v. Gant* (2009), in which the Supreme Court reduced law enforcement's authority to search the passenger compartment of a vehicle incident to arrest: "The *Gant* decision changes the landscape dramatically with regard to an officer's authority to conduct a warrantless search of a vehicle incident to arrest as a matter of routine. In short, the bright-line rule allowing automatic searches of vehicles incident to the arrest of an occupant has been narrowed to allow such a search only if the officer has a reasonable belief that the arrestee can gain access to the vehicle or that evidence of the crime of arrest will be found in the vehicle" (Judge, 2009, p.12). It is important to understand that although *Gant* restricts searches incident to arrest, it has no impact on the other warrant exceptions, such as consent, exigent circumstances and the motor vehicle exception (Myers, 2011).

In *Thornton v. United States* (2004) the Supreme Court ruled that police can search the passenger compartment of a vehicle incident to arrest when the arrestee was approached after recently occupying that vehicle.

Vehicle Searches at Roadblocks and Checkpoints.

A quarter-century ago, in *United States v. Martinez-Fuerte* (1976), the Supreme Court ruled that checkpoints at the country's borders were constitutional because they served a national interest and that this interest outweighed the checkpoint's minimal intrusion on driver privacy. A border search can be made without probable cause, without a warrant and without any articulable suspicion. The only limitation on a border search is the Fourth Amendment requirement that it be conducted reasonably. The *functional equivalent doctrine* establishes that routine border searches are constitutional at places other than actual borders where travelers frequently enter or leave the country, including international airports.

Three years later in *Brown v. Texas* (1979), the Supreme Court created a *balancing test* (an evaluation of interests and factors) to determine the constitutionality of roadblocks. The *Brown* balancing test requires that courts evaluating the lawfulness of roadblocks consider three factors:

1. The gravity of the public concerns served by establishing the roadblock
2. The degree to which the roadblock is likely to succeed in serving the public interest
3. The severity with which the roadblock interferes with individual liberty

Michigan v. Sitz (1990) established that *sobriety checkpoints* to combat drunken driving were reasonable under the *Brown* balancing test if they met certain guidelines. However, the Court ruled in *City of Indianapolis v. Edmond* (2000) that checkpoints for *drugs* are unconstitutional: "We cannot sanction stops justified only by the generalized and ever-present possibility that interrogation and inspection may reveal that any given motorist has committed some crime." Thus, vehicle checkpoints for general crime control are constitutionally unreasonable.

In *Illinois v. Lidster* (2004) the Court upheld the constitutionality of *informational checkpoints*. Justice Stephen Breyer explained, "The stop's primary law enforcement purpose was not to determine whether a vehicle's occupants were committing a crime, but to ask vehicle occupants, as members of the public, for their help in providing information about a crime in all likelihood committed by others. The police expected the information elicited to help them apprehend, not the vehicle's occupants, but other individuals."

This ruling was a victory for law enforcement. Another victory for law enforcement came in 2004 in *United States v. Flores-Montano*, in which the Supreme Court unanimously overturned a decision by a circuit court of appeals, ruling that privacy interests do not apply to vehicles crossing the border. Chief Justice William Rehnquist wrote, "Complex balancing tests to determine what is a 'routine' search of a vehicle . . . have no place in border searches of vehicles. The government's interest in preventing the entry of unwanted persons and effects is at its zenith at the international border. Time and again, we have stated that searches made at the border . . . are reasonable simply by virtue of the fact that they occur at the border."

Inventory Searches.

Unlike a search incidental to an arrest, a vehicle search need not be made immediately.

 Chambers v. Maroney (1970) established that a vehicle may be taken to headquarters to be searched.

When police take custody of a vehicle (or other property), the courts have upheld their right to inventory such property for specific reasons:

- *To protect the owner's property*. This obligation may be legal or moral, but the courts have supported the police's responsibility to protect property taken into custody from unauthorized interference.

- *To protect the police from disputes and claims that the property was stolen or damaged*. Proper inventory at the time of custody provides an accurate record of the property's condition at the time it was seized.

- *To protect the police and the public from danger*. Custody of an automobile or a person subjects the police to conditions that require searching the person or the vehicle for objects such as bombs, chemicals, razor blades, weapons and so on that may harm the officers or the premises where the vehicle or person is taken.

- *To determine the owner's identity*. Identifying the owner may be associated with identifying the person under arrest, or it may help the police know to whom the property should be released.

The courts have held that each of these factors outweighs the privacy interests of property and therefore justifies an inventory search. The search must be reasonable. To be correct in the inventory procedure, the police must show legal seizure and make an inventory according to approved procedures.

Although inventory and search are technically two different processes, in practice they may take place simultaneously. If property found during such an inventory is evidence of a crime, it is admissible in court. It is advisable, however, where a vehicle is no longer mobile or is in police custody, to obtain a search warrant so as not to jeopardize an otherwise perfectly valid case.

Although the major cases governing warrantless searches of a vehicle have just been discussed, others may be encountered during an investigation. Table 4.1 summarizes the relevant court rulings related to vehicle searches.

TABLE 4.1 Summary of Major Court Rulings Regarding Vehicle Searches

Case Decision	Holding
Carroll v. United States (1925)	Automobiles may be searched without a warrant if (1) there is probable cause for the search and (2) the vehicle would be gone before a search warrant could be obtained.
Chambers v. Maroney (1970)	A vehicle may be taken to headquarters to be searched.
South Dakota v. Opperman (1976)	Warrantless routine inventory searches of automobiles impounded or otherwise in lawful police custody, pursuant to standard police procedures, are reasonable and not prohibited by the Fourth Amendment.
United States v. Ross (1982)	A search may be made when probable cause exists to believe that contraband or evidence is within the vehicle. This includes the trunk or closed containers in the vehicle.
Texas v. Brown (1983)	Contraband or evidence in plain view may be confiscated. Two conditions must exist: (1) the officer must be legally present and (2) there must be probable cause to believe that the object in plain view is contraband or the instrumentality of a crime.
Florida v. Wells (1990)	The contents of a lawfully impounded vehicle may be inventoried for purposes of property accountability, public safety and protection against later claims of damage or loss of property.
Florida v. Jimeno (1991)	A warrantless search may be made when consent is obtained from the owner or person in possession of the vehicle. The entire vehicle may be searched, including closed containers, unless the consenter has expressed limitation.
United States v. Ibarra (1991)	If there is no statutory authority to impound, the vehicle cannot be taken into custody legally; therefore, an inventory search under these circumstances would be inadmissible.
United States v. Bowhay (1993)	Because a department policy required officers to search everything, the officers had no discretion. Therefore, the presence of an investigative motive did not prohibit the inventory search.
Knowles v. Iowa (1998)	When an officer issues a citation instead of making an arrest, a full search of the driver's car violates the Fourth Amendment.
Wyoming v. Houghton (1999)	An officer may search an automobile passenger's belongings simply because the officer suspects the driver has done something wrong. This "passenger property exception" ruling was intended to prevent drivers from claiming that illegal drugs or other contraband belonged to passengers, rather than themselves.
Thornton v. United States (2004)	Police can search the passenger compartment of a vehicle incident to arrest when the arrestee was approached after recently occupying that vehicle.
Brendlin v. California (2007)	Officers must have a reasonable suspicion of criminal activity to stop a vehicle. If officers have no lawful basis for a traffic stop, anyone in the car—the driver or its passengers—may challenge the stop's constitutionality.
Arizona v. Gant (2009)	This case narrowed the previously allowed automatic searches of vehicles incident to the arrest of an occupant (*New York v. Belton,* 1981) to permit such a search only if the officer has a reasonable belief that the arrestee can gain access to the vehicle or that evidence of the crime of arrest will be found in the vehicle.

Having looked at the legal restrictions on searching, now consider the searches themselves, beginning with the search of a crime scene.

THE CRIME SCENE SEARCH

A basic function of investigators is to conduct a thorough, legal search at the scene of a crime. Even though not initially visible, evidence in some form is present at most crime scenes. Although each crime scene is unique, certain general guidelines apply. The goal of any search during an investigation, at the crime scene or elsewhere, is to discover evidence that helps

- Establish that a crime *was* committed and *what* the specific crime was.
- Establish *when* the crime was committed.
- Identify *who* committed the crime.
- Explain *how* the crime was committed.
- Suggest *why* the crime was committed.

> A successful crime scene search locates, identifies and preserves all evidence present.

Evidence found at a scene assists in re-creating a crime in much the same way that bricks, properly placed, result in constructing a building. A meticulous, properly conducted search usually results in the discovery of evidence. The security measures taken by the first officer at the scene determine whether evidence is discovered intact or after it has been altered or destroyed. During a search, do not change or contaminate physical evidence in any way, or it will be declared inadmissible. Maintain the chain of custody of evidence from the initial discovery to the time of the trial as discussed in the next chapter.

Organizing the Crime Scene Search

After emergencies have been attended to, the scene has been secured, witnesses have been located and separated for interviewing, and photographing and sketching have been completed, a search plan must be formulated. Also, a search headquarters needs to be established away from the scene to prevent destruction of evidence.

> Organizing a search includes dividing the duties, selecting a search pattern, assigning personnel and equipment and giving instructions.

Proper organization results in a thorough search with no accidental destruction of evidence. However, even the best-organized search may not yield evidence. Evidence may have been destroyed before the search or removed by the criminal. In a few rare instances, evidence is simply nonexistent.

In a single-investigator search, one officer conducts the physical search and describes, identifies and preserves the evidence found. If two or more officers conduct the search, the highest-ranking officer on the scene usually assumes command. In accordance with department policy, the officer in charge assigns personnel based on their training. For example, if one officer has specialized training in photography, another in sketching and a third in fingerprinting, they are assigned to their respective specialties. Someone is assigned to each function required in the search. Often two officers are assigned to take measurements to ensure accuracy. These same two officers can collect, identify and preserve evidence as it is found. Evidence should never be removed from the scene without the search leader's permission.

The search leader also determines the number of personnel needed, the type of search best suited for the area and the items most likely to be found. Personnel are assigned according to the selected search pattern. Search party members are given all known details of the crime and instructed on the type of evidence to seek and the members' specific responsibilities.

The search leader also determines whether anyone other than the person who committed the crime has entered the scene. If so, the person is asked to explain in detail any contacts with the scene that might have contaminated evidence. If no one has entered the scene between the time the crime was committed and when the police arrived, and if the scene was immediately secured, the scene is considered to be a **true**, or **uncontaminated, scene**; that is, no evidence has been introduced into it or taken from it except by the person who committed the crime.

Physical Evidence

Physical evidence ranges in size from very large objects to minute substances. Understanding what types of evidence can be found at various types of crime scenes is important to the search. Not everything found at a scene is evidence.

> Knowing what to search for is indispensable to an effective crime scene search. *Physical evidence* is anything material and relevant to the crime being investigated.

The elements of the crime help determine what will be useful as evidence. For example, a burglary requires an illegal entry; therefore, tool marks and broken glass in a door or window are evidence that help prove burglary.

A wooden stake with a long rope is driven into the ground at the center of the area to be searched. Knots are tied in the rope at selected regular intervals. The searcher circles around the stake in the area delineated by the first knot, searching the area within the first circle. When this area is completed, the searcher moves to the second knot and repeats the procedure. The search is continued in ever-widening circles until the entire area is covered.

Zone- or Sector-Search Pattern.
In the **zone** or sector search, an area is divided into equal squares on a map of the area and each square is numbered. Search personnel are assigned to specific squares (Figure 4.6).

Interior Searches

Most searches are interior searches. The foregoing exterior search patterns can be adapted to an interior crime scene. Of prime concern is to search thoroughly without destroying evidence.

> Interior searches go from the general to the specific, usually in a circular pattern, covering all surfaces of a search area. The floor should be searched first.

In making an interior search, look closely at all room surfaces, including the floor, ceiling, walls and all objects on the floor and walls. Evidence can be found on any surface.

The floor usually produces the most evidence, followed by doors and windows. Although the ceiling is often missed in a search, it too can contain evidence such as stains or bullet holes. It can even contain such unlikely evidence as footprints. Footprints were found on the ceiling by an alert officer during a bank burglary investigation. Paperhangers had left wallpaper on the bank's floor during the night and had hung it on the ceiling early the next morning before the burglary was discovered. During the night, one burglar had stepped on the wallpaper,

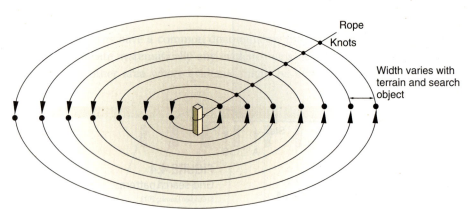

FIGURE 4.5
Circle-search pattern.
© Cengage Learning 2013

Rope
Knots
Width varies with terrain and search object

FIGURE 4.6
Zone- or sector-search pattern.
© Cengage Learning 2013

A	B	C
A	B	C
A	B	C

leaving a footprint that was transferred in a faint outline to the ceiling.

An interior room search usually starts at the point of entry. The floor is searched first so no evidence is inadvertently destroyed during the remainder of the search. The lane- or zone-search patterns are adaptable to an interior floor search.

After the floor search, the walls—including doors and windows—and then the ceiling are searched, normally using a clockwise or counterclockwise pattern around the room. Because doors and windows are points of entry and exit, soil, fingerprints, glass fragments and other evidence are often found there. Walls may contain marks, bloodstains or trace evidence such as hairs or fibers.

After a room is searched in one direction, it is often searched in the opposite direction because lighting is different from different angles. The same general procedures are followed in searching closets, halls or other rooms off the main room. The search is coordinated, and the location of all evidence is communicated to members of the search team.

General Guidelines

The precise search pattern used is immaterial as long as the search is systematic and covers the entire area. Assigning two officers to search the same area greatly increases the probability of discovering evidence. Finding evidence is no reason to stop a search. Continue searching until the entire area is covered. Schonely (2007, p.60) notes, "Many officers search like it is a race and they are being timed to complete the task. These officers will miss many suspects over their careers. . . . Slowing down and being patient will allow your senses to work as you complete the search."

Plain-Sense Evidence

The limitations on searches are intended to protect the rights of all citizens and to ensure due process of law. They are not intended to hamper investigations, nor do they preclude the use of evidence that is not concealed and is accidentally found through any of the officer's senses. The most common type of plain-sense evidence is that seen by an officer.

Plain-View Evidence. Anywhere officers have a right to be, they have a right to see. The plain-view doctrine permits the warrantless seizure of contraband or evidence of a crime, as long as the officers are legally allowed to be where they are. This doctrine puts few constraints on officers and often yields very productive results.

> **Plain-view evidence**—unconcealed evidence seen by an officer engaged in a lawful activity—is admissible in court.

Although the Fourth Amendment prohibits unreasonable intrusions into a person's privacy, the precedent for plain-view evidence was established in *Katz v. United States* (1967) when the Supreme Court held, "The Fourth Amendment protects people, not *places*. What a person knowingly exposes to the public, even in his own home or office, is not a subject of Fourth Amendment protection. But what he seeks to preserve as private, even in an area accessible to the public, may be constitutionally protected." In both *Michigan v. Tyler* (1978) and *Mincey v. Arizona* (1978) the Court ruled that while officers are on the premises pursuing their legitimate emergency activities, any evidence in plain view may be seized.

Containers can be opened if their outward appearance reveals criminal contents, for example, a kit of burglar tools or a gun case (Rutledge, 2007c, p.71). By their nature, they do not support a reasonable expectation of privacy because their contents can be inferred from their appearance.

An officer cannot obtain a warrant and fail to mention a particular object and then use "plain view" to justify its seizure. If the officer is looking for it initially, it must be mentioned in the warrant. Plain-view evidence itself is not sufficient to justify a warrantless seizure of evidence; probable cause must also exist.

Officers may seize any contraband they discover during a legal search. In *Boyd v. United States* (1886) Justice Joseph Bradley stated, "The search for and seizure of stolen or forfeited goods or goods liable to duties and concealed to avoid payment thereof, are totally different things from a search or a seizure of a man's private books and papers. In one case the government is entitled to the property, and in the other it is not."

Plain Feel/Touch. The "plain feel/touch" exception is an extension of the plain-view exception. If a police officer lawfully pats down a suspect's outer clothing and feels an object that he *immediately* identifies as contraband—in other words, **plain feel/touch evidence**—a warrantless seizure is justified because there is no invasion of the suspect's privacy beyond that already authorized by the officer's search for weapons (*Minnesota v. Dickerson*, 1993).

Plain Smell. Evidence may also be seized if an officer relies on a sense other than sight or touch. For example, a customs officer who smells marijuana coming from a package has probable cause to make an arrest under a "plain-smell" rationale (*United States v. Lueck*, 1982). Rutledge (2007c, p.71) notes, "Some distinctive odors can be detected by officers (for example, the odor of gasoline in an arson investigation); some can be detected by trained dogs. Merely smelling the air surrounding a suspect, his vehicle or some container does not constitute a search. If the odor reveals the presence of seizable objects, they may be seized."

Plain Hearing. Officers or undercover agents can position themselves in accessible locations where they can overhear criminal conversation without any extraordinary listening devices (such as wiretaps or parabolic microphones). Anything overheard can be used as evidence.

OTHER TYPES OF INVESTIGATORY SEARCHES

In addition to crime scene searches, officers may search buildings, trash or garbage cans, vehicles, suspects and dead bodies as they investigate criminal offenses.

Building Searches

When executing a warrant to search a building, officers should first familiarize themselves with the location and the past record of the person living there. Check records for any previous police actions at that location. Decide on the least dangerous time of day for the suspect, the police and the neighborhood. For example, the time of day when children come home from school would not be a good time to execute a warrant.

All officers who will be executing the warrant should meet to discuss a plan of action, including which positions they are all responsible for and how they should each approach. All available resources should be accessed during this planning stage, such as Google maps or real estate information, to gain a thorough understanding of the targeted property's layout.

Do not treat the execution of a search warrant as routine. Plan for the worst-case scenario. Think *safety* first and last. Arrive safely. Turn off your vehicle's headlights, dome light and brake lights (often times squadcars have a cut out switch for this) as you approach the building, as well as anything that may illuminate your location, such as the mobile data terminal (MDT) computer screen inside the squad. Once outside the squadcar, stay away from other lights and use any available cover as you approach the building. Also consider radio volume, as the noise can notify suspects of police presence if radio volume is turned on high. Officers will often use ear microphones to keep radio noise minimized or will notify dispatch of entry times to avoid immediate welfare checks while positioning.

Before entering the building, secure the outside perimeter and as many exits as possible—at a minimum, the front and rear doors. If possible, call for a backup before entering and search with a partner. Use extreme caution in the "fatal funnel," that zone that exists through a doorway, where officers are most vulnerable to attack by a suspect. Move through the fatal funnel rapidly and then, once clear, slow down to perform the search operations. Once inside the structure, wait for your vision to adjust to interior light conditions.

Keep light and weapons away from your body. Go quickly through doors into dark areas. When moving around objects, take quick peeks before proceeding. Avoid windows. Use light and cover to your advantage. Know where you are at all times and how to get back to where you were. Look for exits. If the entire building is to be searched, use a systematic approach. Secure each area as it is searched.

Sometimes when police search a suspect's home under authority of a search warrant, several people may be present, perhaps outnumbering the officers on the scene, creating problems of safety and control. Guidelines for this situation were established in *Michigan v. Summers* (1981) when the Supreme Court stated, "We hold that a warrant to search for contraband founded on probable cause carries with it the limited authority to detain the occupants of the premises while a proper search is conducted." The Court did not say whether detained individuals could be handcuffed or for how long they could be detained.

Law enforcement officers may also require residents to remain outside their home until a search warrant can be obtained if the officers have probable cause to believe the home contains evidence of illegal activity (*Illinois v. McArthur*, 2001).

Officers should be aware of the ruling in *Kyllo v. United States* (2001), which held that thermal scanning of a private residence from outside the residence is a search under the Fourth Amendment and requires a search warrant. The *Kyllo* decision is a slight respite from government-sponsored surveillance.

Trash or Garbage Can Searches

Trash and garbage cans in alleys and on public sidewalks are often the depository for evidence of thefts, drug possession and even homicides. In *California v. Greenwood* (1988) the Supreme Court ruled that containers left on public property are open to search by police without a warrant. The Supreme Court ruled that such a search does not constitute a violation of the Fourth Amendment or a reasonable expectation of privacy: "It is common knowledge that plastic garbage bags left on a public street are readily accessible to animals, children, scavengers, snoops and other members of the public," and therefore "no reasonable expectation of privacy" is violated by such a search. Searches of trash may also extend to the local landfill.

Trash pulls can yield valuable incriminating evidence that investigators may use to obtain a search warrant of a home. However, a single trash pull is rarely sufficient to justify a legally valid search warrant. Furthermore, "When applying for a search warrant based on a trash pull, investigators must establish probable cause that two separate elements exist: (1) that a crime has been committed and (2) that relevant evidence is likely located at the place to be searched" (Sanchez and Rubin, 2010, p.12).

The most important factor in determining the legality of a warrantless trash inspection is the physical location of the retrieved trash. Police cannot trespass to gain access to the trash location, and, generally, the trash must not be located within the **curtilage**, which the Supreme Court has described as "the area to which extends the intimate activity associated with the sanctity of a man's home and the privacies of life." In other words, curtilage is that portion of a residence that is not open to the public. It is reserved for private owner or family use, and an expectation of privacy exists. This is in contrast to sidewalks and alleys that are used by the public. In *United States v. Dunn* (1987) the Court ruled, "We believe that curtilage questions should be resolved with particular reference to four factors: the proximity of the area claimed to be curtilage to the home, whether the area is included within an enclosure surrounding the home, the nature of the uses to which the area is put and the steps taken by the resident to protect the area from observation by people passing by."

Although trash or garbage containers within the curtilage of private property are generally considered off-limits to warrantless searches, the courts have allowed the warrantless seizure of trash from within the curtilage for very fact-specific instances (*United States v. Segura-Baltazar*, 2006); however, investigators are wise to consult with their agency's legal advisors or the local prosecutor before seizing trash from within a home's curtilage (Sanchez and Rubin, 2010).

Vehicle Searches

Cars, aircraft, boats, motorcycles, buses, trucks and vans can contain evidence of a crime. Again, the type of crime determines the area to be searched and the evidence to be sought. In a hit-and-run accident, the car's undercarriage can have hairs and fibers or the interior may reveal a hidden liquor bottle. In narcotics arrests, various types of drugs are often found in cars, planes and boats. An ordinary vehicle has hundreds of places to hide drugs. In some cases, vehicles may have specially constructed compartments.

As with other types of searches, a vehicle search must be systematic and thorough. Evidence is more likely to be found if two officers conduct the search.

> Remove occupants from the car. First, search the area around the vehicle and then the exterior. Finally, search the interior along one side from front to back and then return along the other side to the front.

Before entering a vehicle, search the area around it for evidence related to the crime. Next, examine the vehicle's exterior for fingerprints, dents, scratches or hairs and fibers. Examine the grill, front bumper, fender areas and license plates. Open the hood and check the numerous recesses of the motor, radiator, battery, battery case, engine block, clutch and starter housings, ventilating ducts, air filter, body frame and supports. Open the trunk and examine any clothing, rags, containers, tools, the spare-tire well and the trunk lid's interior.

Finally, search the vehicle's interior, following the same procedures used in searching a room. Vacuum the car before getting into it. Package collections from different areas of the car separately. Then systematically examine ashtrays, the glove compartment, areas under the seats and the window areas. Remove the seats and vacuum the floor. Hairs and fibers or traces of soil may be discovered that will connect a suspect with soil samples from the crime scene.

Use a flashlight and a mirror to examine the area behind the dashboard. Feeling by hand is not effective because of the numerous wires located there. Look for fingerprints in the obvious places: window and door handles, underside of the steering wheel, radio buttons, ashtrays, distributor cap, jack, rearview mirror, hood latches and seat adjustment levers.

Figure 4.7 illustrates the areas of vehicles that should be searched. The vehicle is divided into specific search areas to ensure order and thoroughness.

As in any other search, take precautions to prevent contaminating evidence. Be alert to what is an original part of the vehicle and what has been added. For example, compartments for concealing illegal drugs or other contraband are sometimes added. The systems and equipment

to exhume it for further examination. If the body is cremated, no further examination is possible.

Underwater Searches

Underwater searches might involve victim, aircraft, firearm or vehicle recovery. Underwater searches are affected by limited visibility, extreme water temperature, swift currents and hazardous materials. When a victim is located, the first concern is whether it is a crime scene or an accident scene. The normal body position of a drowning victim is face down and in a semi-fetal position. If a victim found underwater has straight limbs and closed fists, this indicates the person may have been killed on land and rigor mortis had set in before the body was submerged.

Metal detectors are needed in most underwater searches—particularly pulse induction metal detectors, which are known for their deep seeking capabilities. Advances in the technology have reduced power requirements, resulting in longer battery life and decreased weight.

USE OF DOGS IN A SEARCH

"Field deployable electronic sensors or instruments can't top dogs, which have been increasingly in demand since 9/11," says Kanable (2007, p.68). Canines are a valuable force multiplier for law enforcement and can be trained to detect drugs and other chemicals, explosive devices, weapons, accelerants and igniters (in arson investigations), money and cadavers. A keen sense of smell enables a dog to complete a building search in 10 minutes when it would otherwise take two or three officers an hour to conduct the same search. Dogs can track and capture suspects and are ideally suited to assist in searching large areas; areas with poor visibility, such as warehouses that may contain thousands of items; or any area with numerous hiding places. In addition, using dogs for such purposes lessens the physical risk to investigating officers.

> Dogs can be trained to locate suspects, narcotics, explosives, cadavers and more.

The use of dogs to sniff out narcotics has been widely publicized. Because narcotics can be concealed in so many different ways, using dogs to locate them has greatly assisted law enforcement officers. Attempts to mask drug odors from dogs trained to sniff out drugs are futile because dogs can smell more than one odor simultaneously.

In *Illinois v. Caballes* (2005) the Supreme Court confirmed that a dog sniff was not a search under the Fourth Amendment, a ruling that reinforced law enforcement's ability to identify drug traffickers and users by using police K-9s in walk-around searches of vehicles stopped for traffic offenses. If, however, use of a drug-sniffing canine prolongs a stop, the dog sniff may become an illegal search.

Dogs have also been trained to detect explosives both before and after detonation. Their ability to detect explosives before detonation lessens the officer's risk and can help prevent crimes. A study by the Law Enforcement Assistance Administration and the Federal Aviation Authority demonstrated that dogs can locate explosives twice as often as people can. In the case of detonated explosives, dogs have helped locate bomb fragments hidden under piles of debris and at considerable distances from the detonation point.

As agents of the police, dogs are subject to the same legal limitations on searches that officers are. Court rulings appear to highlight the benefits of using K-9s to build probable cause to seize and arrest. In *United States v. Place* (1983) the Supreme Court ruled that exposing luggage located in a public place to a police K-9 sniff was not a search within the meaning of the Fourth Amendment. In essence, such a ruling concedes that the use of dogs may lead to the same end via less intrusive means, thus sparing law enforcement other time-consuming steps required to effect a legal search.

K-9s have also been used to seek and detain suspects. Courts have ruled that using K-9s can enhance the safety of officers, bystanders and suspects and that K-9s might be considered as less-lethal alternatives to deadly force. Guidelines for deploying K-9s are found in *Graham v. Connor* (1989). Before deploying a K-9, a handler should consider the totality of the circumstances and the available information, including the severity of the crime, whether the suspect poses an immediate threat to the safety of officers or others and whether the suspect is actively resisting arrest or attempting to evade arrest by flight. Administrators and trainers should be familiar with case law pertaining to K-9s.

If a police department is not large enough to have or lacks sufficient need for a search dog and trained handler, learn where the nearest trained search dogs are and how they can be obtained if needed. Many major airports have dogs trained to locate explosives and may make these dogs available to police upon request.

Specially trained K-9s can be invaluable in searching for drugs or explosives. Here a U.S. Capitol Police dog team searches motorists passing near the U.S. Capitol in Washington, DC.
© Paul J. Richards/AFP/Getty Images

WARRANT CHECKLIST

Rutledge (2008, p.29) states, "For every entry and search not authorized by a recognized exception, a warrant is required." He summarizes the recognized exceptions from a somewhat different perspective. No search warrant is required in the following instances:

- No search (plain sense, open fields, abandoned property, private-party delivery, controlled delivery, exposed characteristics)

- Independent justification (consent, probation or parole, incident to arrest, officer safety, booking search, inventory)

- Exigent circumstances (rescue, protection of property, imminent destruction of evidence, fresh pursuit, escape prevention, public safety)

- Fleeing target (car, van, truck, RV, bus, boat, aircraft, etc.) with PC and lawful access

The courts have also identified several "special needs" exceptions that do not fit into other categories, such as school searches, searches of highly regulated businesses (such as firearms dealers, pawn shops and junkyards), employment and educational drug screening and the immediate search for "evanescent" evidence (such as blood-alcohol content) (Rutledge, 2007e, p.56).

A REMINDER

Jetmore (2007b, p.26) stresses, "Ability to skillfully document in writing facts and circumstances that lead to logical inferences and reasonable conclusions remains a professional requirement in criminal investigation. Excellent investigative work is negated and the guilty may walk free if the legal framework on which it was based can't be adequately explained." The Fourth Amendment requires that officers' actions be *reasonable*: "Clearly outline in your report every detail known to you at the time so that a subsequent reviewing authority has the full situation in mind when deciding whether your actions were reasonable given the totality of the circumstances" (Jetmore, p.30).

Summary

The Fourth Amendment to the Constitution forbids unreasonable searches and seizures. Therefore, investigators must know what constitutes a reasonable, legal search. To search effectively, know the legal requirements for searching, the items you are searching for and the elements of the crime. Be organized, systematic and thorough.

The most important limitation on any search is that the scope must be narrow; general searches are unconstitutional. If a search is *not* conducted legally, the evidence obtained is worthless. The exclusionary rule established that courts may not accept evidence obtained by unreasonable search and seizure, regardless of its relevance to a case. *Weeks v. United States* (1914) made the rule applicable at the federal level; *Mapp v. Ohio* (1961) made it applicable to all courts.

A search can be justified and therefore considered legal if any of the following conditions are met: (1) a search warrant has been issued, (2) consent is given, (3) an officer stops a suspicious person and believes the person may be armed, (4) the search is incidental to a lawful arrest or (5) an emergency exists. Each of these situations has limitations. A search conducted with a warrant must be limited to the area and items specified in the warrant, in accordance with the particularity requirement. A search conducted with consent requires that the consent be voluntary and that the search be limited to the area for which the consent was given. The search in a stop-and-frisk situation must be limited to a patdown for weapons. The *Terry* decision established that a patdown or frisk is a "protective search for weapons" and as such must be "confined to a scope reasonably designed to discover guns, knives, clubs, and other hidden instruments for the assault of a police officer or others." The *Chimel* decision established that a search incidental to a lawful arrest must be made simultaneously with the arrest and must be confined to the area within the suspect's immediate control. A warrantless search in the absence of a lawful arrest or consent is justified only in emergencies or exigent circumstances where probable cause exists and the search must be conducted immediately.

Vehicles may be searched without a warrant if there is probable cause and if the vehicle would be gone before a search warrant could be obtained (*Carroll*).

A successful crime scene search locates, identifies and preserves all evidence present. Organizing a search includes dividing the duties, selecting a search pattern, assigning personnel and equipment and giving instructions. Knowing what to search for is indispensable to an effective search. *Physical evidence* is anything material and relevant to the crime being investigated.

Search patterns have been developed that help ensure a thorough search. Exterior search patterns divide an area into lanes, strips, concentric circles or zones. Interior searches go from the general to the specific, usually in a circular pattern, covering all surfaces of a search area. The floor should be searched first. Plain-view evidence—unconcealed evidence seen by an officer engaged in a lawful activity—is admissible in court.

In addition to crime scenes, investigators frequently search vehicles, suspects and dead bodies. When searching a vehicle, remove the occupants from the car. First, search the area around the vehicle, then the vehicle's exterior. Finally, search the interior along one side from front to back and then return along the other side to the front. *Chambers v. Maroney* (1970) established that a vehicle may be taken to headquarters to be searched in certain circumstances.

When searching a suspect who has not been arrested, confine the search to a patdown for weapons (*Terry*). If the suspect has been arrested, conduct a complete body search for weapons and evidence. Always be on your guard. Search a dead body systematically and completely; include the immediate area around and under the body. Dogs can be trained to locate suspects, narcotics, explosives, cadavers and more.

Checklist

The Search

- Is the search legal?
- Was a pattern followed?
- Was all evidence photographed, recorded in the notes, identified and packaged properly?
- Was the search completed even if evidence was found early in the search?
- Were all suspects searched?
- Did more than one investigator search?
- Was plain-view evidence seized? If so, were the circumstances recorded?

Discussion Questions

1. Why do you suppose the Fourth Amendment was written?
2. What are the advantages of having several officers search a crime scene? What are the disadvantages?
3. What are the steps in obtaining a search warrant?
4. What procedure is best for searching a suspect?

5. Many court decisions regarding police involve the question of legal searches. What factors are considered in the legal search of a person, a private dwelling, abandoned property, a business building, a car or corporate offices?

6. What basic steps constitute a thorough search of a dwelling?

7. Should there be legal provisions for an officer to seize evidence without a warrant if the evidence may be destroyed or removed before a warrant can be obtained?

8. Under what circumstances are police authorized to conduct no-knock searches?

9. Imagine you are assigned to search a tavern at 10 A.M. for illegal gambling devices. Twenty patrons plus the bartender are in the tavern, but the owner is not present. How would you execute the search warrant?

10. Police officers frequently stop vehicles for traffic violations. Under the plain-view doctrine, what evidence may be taken during such a stop? May the officers search the vehicle? The driver? The occupants?

Media Explorations

 **Internet**

Select one assignment to complete.

1. Search the Internet for one of these key terms: *exclusionary rule, fruit-of-the-poisonous-tree doctrine, inevitable-discovery doctrine* or *plain-view evidence*. Select one article and outline it to share with the class.

2. Using Google, search for *Terry v. Ohio*. Select one article and outline it to share with the class.

3. Go to the FBI Web site to view the *Handbook of Forensic Services*. Outline the chapter on the crime scene search.

 Gale Criminal Justice Database Assignments

The following assignments require access to Gale's Custom Journals Database for Emergency Services and Criminal Justice. Check with your instructor if you have questions about this.

■ Find the article "The Inevitable Discovery Exception to the Exclusionary Rule" on the Gale Emergency Services Database. Read and be prepared to explain in detail the exclusionary rule as well as the inevitable discovery exception. Be ready to explain how they are related to each other.

■ Find the article "Stop and Frisk: The Power and the Obligation of the Police" on the Gale Emergency Services Database. Explain the court case *Terry v. Ohio* and its impact on searches and seizures. Share your findings with the class.

■ Find the article "Excluding Automobile Passengers from the Fourth Amendment Protection" on the Gale Emergency Services Database. Outline the article and be prepared to discuss in class how this is related to *Terry v. Ohio*.

References

del Carmen, Rolando V. *Criminal Procedure: Law and Practice*, 7th ed. Belmont, CA: Wadsworth Publishing Company, 2010.

Geoghegan, Susan. "*Hudson v. Michigan* and Forced Entry." *Tactical Response*, March–April 2007, pp.96–99.

Hilton, Alicia M. "Clearing Up Knock-and-Announce Confusion." *Police*, August 2007, pp.38–43.

Ivy, Peter, and Orput, Peter. "Defendants Must Demonstrate Standing before the Exclusionary Rule Applies." *Minnesota Police Chief*, Summer 2007, pp.8–11.

Jetmore, Larry F. "Searching without a Warrant." *Law Officer Magazine*, April 2007a, pp.26–31.

Jetmore, Larry F. "Understanding Probable Cause." *Law Officer Magazine*, March 2007b, pp.26–30.

Judge, Lisa A. "Bye-Bye Belton? Supreme Court Decision Shifts Authority for Vehicle Searches from Automatic to Manual." *The Police Chief*, June 2009, pp.12–13.

Kanable, Rebecca. "The Best from Man's Best Friend." *Law Enforcement Technology*, September 2007, pp.68–77.

Means, Randy. "Frisk Searches Are Not Automatic, Part I." *Law and Order*, March 2008, pp.23–24.

Means, Randy, and McDonald, Pam. "Myth of Custody and Consent." *Law and Order*, June 2010a, pp.12–14.

Means, Randy, and McDonald, Pam. "Warrantless Entry and the Emergency Aid Exception." *Law and Order*, February 2010b, pp.18–20.

Myers, Kenneth A. "Searches of Motor Vehicles Incident to Arrest in a Post-*Gant* World." *FBI Law Enforcement Bulletin*, April 2011, pp.24–32.

Rutledge, Devallis. "The 'Good Faith' Doctrine." *Police*, June 2007a, pp.70–71.

Rutledge, Devallis. "How to Justify Officer Safety Searches." *Police*, October 2007b, pp.36–40.

Rutledge, Devallis. "Plain Sense Seizure." *Police*, April 2007c, pp.70–71.

Rutledge, Devallis. "Reasonable Execution of Search Warrants." *Police*, August 2007d, pp.78–79.

Rutledge, Devallis. "Search Warrant Exceptions." *Police*, February 2007e, pp.54–56.

Rutledge, Devallis. "Seizing and Searching Passengers." *Police*, September 2007f, pp.70–71.

Rutledge, Devallis. "How to Tell When You Need a Search Warrant." *Police*, March 2008, pp.28–30.

Rutledge, Devallis. "The 'Emergency Aid Doctrine.'" *Police*, February 2010, pp.60–63.

Sanchez, Antonio J., and Rubin, James K. "The Use of Garbage to Establish Probably Cause for Granting Valid Search Warrants." *The Police Chief*, June 2010, pp.12–13.

Scarry, Laura L. "Oops, Wrong House." *Law Officer Magazine*, October 2007a, pp.76–78.

Scarry, Laura L. "Probable Cause to Search." *Law Officer Magazine*, November 2007b, pp.56–59.

Scarry, Laura L. "Probable Cause Trumps Pretext." *Law Officer Magazine*, August 2007c, pp.82–86.

Scarry, Laura L. "U.S. Supreme Court Clarifies Passengers' 4th Amendment Rights." *Law Officer Magazine*, September 2007d, pp.64–65.

Scarry, Laura L. "Vehicle Search—Get It Right." *Law Officer Magazine*, February 2008, pp.62–63.

Schonely, Jack H. "Tactical Search Techniques." *Police*, August 2007, pp.60–62.

Cases Cited

Adams v. Williams, 407 U.S. 143 (1972)

Aguilar v. Texas, 378 U.S. 108 (1964)

Alabama v. White, 496 U.S. 325 (1990)

Arizona v. Gant, 556 U.S. ____ (2009)

Boyd v. United States, 116 U.S. 616 (1886)

Brendlin v. California, 551 U.S. 249 (2007)

Brigham City, Utah v. Stuart, 547 U.S. 398 (2006)

Brown v. Texas, 443 U.S. 47 (1979)

California v. Greenwood, 486 U.S. 35 (1988)

Carroll v. United States, 267 U.S. 132 (1925)

Chambers v. Maroney, 399 U.S. 42 (1970)

Chimel v. California, 395 U.S. 752 (1969)

City of Indianapolis v. Edmond, 531 U.S. 32 (2000)

Florida v. Jimeno, 500 U.S. 248 (1991)

Florida v. J. L., 529 U.S. 266 (2000)

Florida v. Wells, 495 U.S. 1 (1990)

Georgia v. Randolph, 547 U.S. 103 (2006)

Graham v. Connor, 490 U.S. 386 (1989)

Groh v. Ramirez, 540 U.S. 551 (2004)

Hiibel v. Sixth Judicial District Court of Nevada, Humboldt County, 542 U.S. 177 (2004)

Hudson v. Michigan, 547 U.S. 586 (2006)

Illinois v. Caballes, 543 U.S. 405 (2005)

Illinois v. Gates, 462 U.S. 213 (1983)

Illinois v. Lidster, 540 U.S. 419 (2004)

Illinois v. McArthur, 531 U.S. 326 (2001)

Illinois v. Rodriguez, 497 U.S. 177 (1990)

Johnson v. United States, 333 U.S. 10 (1948)

Katz v. United States, 389 U.S. 347 (1967)

Knowles v. Iowa, 525 U.S. 113 (1998)

Kyllo v. United States, 533 U.S. 27 (2001)

Mapp v. Ohio, 367 U.S. 643 (1961)

Maryland v. Buie, 494 U.S. 325 (1990)

Michigan Department of State Police v. Sitz, 496 U.S. 444 (1990)

Michigan v. Fisher, 558 U.S. ____ (2009)

Michigan v. Summers, 452 U.S. 692 (1981)

Michigan v. Tyler, 436 U.S. 499 (1978)

Mincey v. Arizona, 437 U.S. 385 (1978)

Minnesota v. Dickerson, 508 U.S. 336 (1993)

New York v. Belton, 453 U.S. 454 (1981)

New York v. Quarles, 467 U.S. 649 (1984)

Nix v. Williams, 467 U.S. 431 (1984)

Richards v. Wisconsin, 520 U.S. 385 (1997)

Schneckloth v. Bustamonte, 412 U.S. 218 (1973)

South Dakota v. Opperman, 428 U.S. 364 (1976)

Spinelli v. United States, 393 U.S. 410 (1969)

Stanford v. Texas, 379 U.S. 476 (1965)

Terry v. Ohio, 392 U.S. 1 (1968)

Texas v. Brown, 460 U.S. 730 (1983)

Thornton v. United States, 541 U.S. 615 (2004)

United States v. Banks, 540 U.S. 31 (2003)

United States v. Bowhay, 992 F.2d 229 (9th cir. 1993)

United States v. Drayton, 536 U.S. 194 (2002)

United States v. Dunn, 480 U.S. 294 (1987)

United States v. Flores-Montano, 541 U.S. 149 (2004)

United States v. Grubbs, 547 U.S. 90 (2006)

United States v. Hensley, 469 U.S. 221 (1985)

United States v. Ibarra, 502 U.S. 1 (1991) (per curiam)

United States v. Jacobsen, 466 U.S. 109 (1984)

United States v. Leon, 468 U.S. 897 (1984)

United States v. Lueck, 678 F.2d 895, 903 (11th Cir. 1982)

United States v. Martinez-Fuerte, 428 U.S. 543 (1976)

United States v. Matlock, 415 U.S. 164 (1974)

United States v. Place, 462 U.S. 696 (1983)

United States v. Ramirez, 523 U.S. 65 (1998)

United States v. Ross, 456 U.S. 798 (1982)

United States v. Segura-Baltazar, 448 F. 3d 1281 (11th Cir., 2006)

Weeks v. United States, 232 U.S. 383 (1914)

Wilson v. Arkansas, 514 U.S. 927 (1995)

Wright v. United States, 302 U.S. 583 (1938)

Wyoming v. Houghton, 526 U.S. 295 (1999)

A Helpful Resource

The Web site for Canine Legal Updates and Opinions, hosted by Deputy Sheriff and Terry Fleck, an expert in canine legalities, is a helpful resource on case law pertaining to canines.

CHAPTER 5
Forensics/Physical Evidence

© Stephen Ferry/Liaison/Getty Images

Outline

Can You Define?

Advanced Fingerprint Information Technology (AFIT)
associative evidence
ballistics
best evidence
biometrics
bore
caliber
cast
chain of custody
chain of evidence
circumstantial evidence
class characteristics
competent evidence
contamination
corpus delicti
corpus delicti evidence
cross-contamination
Daubert standard
direct evidence
DNA
DNA profiling

elimination prints
evidence
forensic science
indirect evidence
individual characteristics
inkless fingerprint
integrity of evidence
latent fingerprints
material evidence
physical evidence
plastic fingerprints
prima facie evidence
probative evidence
proxy data
relevant evidence
rifling
standard of comparison
striations
tool mark
trace evidence
visible fingerprints
voiceprint

Do You Know?

- What is involved in processing physical evidence?
- How to determine what is evidence?
- What the common errors in collecting evidence are?
- How to identify evidence?
- What to record in your notes?
- How to package evidence?
- How to convey evidence to a department or a laboratory?
- How and where evidence is stored?
- How to ensure admissibility of physical evidence in court?
- How physical evidence is finally disposed of?
- What types of evidence are most commonly found in criminal investigations and how to collect, identify and package each?
- Where fingerprints can be found and how they should be preserved?
- What can and cannot be determined from fingerprints, DNA, bloodstains and hairs?
- What DNA profiling is?

(continued)

"The evolution of law enforcement has benefited greatly from the many extraordinary advances in the field of **forensic science**—the application of scientific processes to solve legal problems most notably within the context of the criminal justice system" (Fantino, 2007, p.26). Modern forensic science dates back to 1910 and the "exchange principle" set forth by French criminologist Dr. Edmond Locard. As explained in Chapter 1, *Locard's exchange principle* states that whenever two objects come in contact with each other (e.g., a criminal and an object or objects at a crime scene), there is always a transfer of information, however minute, between them. In other words, a criminal always removes something from the crime scene and leaves behind incriminating evidence. The remnants of this transfer are called

123

- How identifying blood and hair are useful?
- Where shoe and tire impressions can be found and how they should be preserved?
- How to preserve tools that might have been used in the crime, as well as the marks they made?
- What a tool mark should be compared with during forensic analysis?
- How to mark and care for weapons used in crimes?
- How to preserve such things as glass fragments, soil samples, safe insulation material, rope, tapes, liquids and documents?
- What evidence UV light can help discover?
- What evidence to collect in hit-and-run cases?
- What can be determined from human skeletal remains?

proxy data, the evidence analyzed by forensic scientists to uncover the relationships between people, places and objects.

A primary purpose of an investigation is to locate, identify and preserve **evidence**—data on which a judgment or conclusion may be based. Evidence is used for determining the facts in a case, for later laboratory examination and for direct presentation in court. **Best evidence**, in the legal sense, is the original evidence or highest available degree of proof that can be produced. Investigators should be cognizant throughout an investigation of the best-evidence rule, which stipulates that the original evidence is to be presented in court whenever possible. Other factors pertaining to admissibility of evidence will be discussed later in the chapter.

Students should also keep in mind that entire books have been written about the collection and analysis of the various types of evidence discussed in this chapter. Because of space constraints, this discussion will present merely an overview of the most common types of physical evidence investigators are likely to encounter and, where applicable, will refer the reader to other resources that provide a more detailed examination of specific types of evidence.

DEFINITIONS

Evidence is generally categorized as one of four types: testimonial, documentary, demonstrative or physical. *Testimonial evidence* is information obtained through interviewing and interrogating individuals about what they saw (eyewitness evidence), heard (hearsay evidence) or know (character evidence). Testimonial evidence is the subject of Chapter 6. *Documentary evidence* typically includes written material, audio recordings and videos. *Demonstrative evidence* includes mockups and scale models of objects or places related to the crime scene and helps juries visualize more clearly what they are unable to view personally. Occasionally, however, juries are taken to the crime scene if the judge deems it vital to the fair processing of the case, but this is expensive and time-consuming. Most commonly, investigators deal with physical evidence. **Physical evidence** is anything real—that is, which has substance—that helps establish the facts of a case. It can be seen, touched, smelled or tasted; is solid, semisolid or liquid; and can be large or tiny. It may be at an immediate crime scene or miles away; it may also be on a suspect or a victim.

Some evidence ties one crime to a similar crime or connects one suspect with another. Evidence can also provide new leads when a case appears to be unsolvable. Further, evidence corroborates statements from witnesses to or victims of a crime. Convictions are not achieved from statements, admissions or confessions alone. A crime must be proven by independent investigation and physical evidence.

For example, in a small western town, a 6-year-old girl and her parents told police the girl had been sexually molested. The girl told police that a man had taken her to the desert, had shown her some "naughty" pictures that he burned and had then molested her. Because it was difficult for the police to rely on the girl's statement, they needed physical evidence to corroborate her story. Fortunately, the girl remembered where the man had taken her and led the police there. They found remains of the burned pictures and confiscated them as evidence. The remains of one picture, showing the suspect with a naked young girl on his lap, were sufficient to identify him by the rings on his fingers. This physical evidence supporting the girl's testimony resulted in a charge of lewdness with a minor.

Physical evidence can be classified in different ways. One common classification is direct and indirect evidence. **Direct evidence** establishes proof of a fact without any other evidence. **Indirect evidence** merely *tends* to incriminate a person—for instance, a suspect's footprints found at the crime scene. Although the footprints do not directly prove the suspect committed the crime at issue, the prints do place the suspect at the scene of the crime. And if the suspect states that he or she was never at the scene, that statement will prove to be untrue based on the indirect evidence. This helps build a case against the suspect and contributes to convictions based on circumstantial evidence. Indirect evidence is also called **circumstantial evidence**, or evidence from which inferences are drawn. A popular myth is that circumstantial evidence will not stand alone without other facts to support it; however, indirect evidence combined with suspect interviews and testimonial evidence can often lead to convictions.

Extremely small items, such as hair or fibers, are a subset of direct evidence called **trace evidence**. Evidence established by law is called *prima facie* **evidence**. For example, 0.8 percent ethanol in the blood is direct or *prima facie* evidence of intoxication in some states. **Associative evidence** links a suspect with a crime. Associative evidence includes fingerprints, footprints, bloodstains, hairs and fibers.

Corpus delicti evidence establishes that a crime has been committed. Contrary to popular belief, the **corpus delicti** ("body of the crime") in a murder case is not the dead body but the fact that death resulted from a criminal act. Corpus delicti evidence supports the elements of the crime. Pry marks on an entry door are corpus delicti evidence in a burglary.

Probative evidence is vital to the investigation or prosecution of a case, tending to prove or actually proving guilt or innocence. Also of extreme importance to the investigator is *exculpatory evidence*, discussed in Chapter 1, which is physical evidence that clears one of blame—for example, having a blood type different from that of blood found at a murder scene.

Material evidence forms a substantive part of the case or has a legitimate and effective influence on the decision of the case. **Relevant evidence** applies to the matter in question. **Competent evidence** has been properly collected, identified, filed and continuously secured.

A forensic laboratory technician prepares a blood sample for DNA analysis.
© Sean O'Brien/CUSTOM MEDICAL STOCK PHOTO

David Coffman of the Florida Department of Law Enforcement shows how the agency's high-tech DNA database allows investigators to search for DNA matches.
© AP/Wide World Photos

To locate and properly process evidence at a crime scene, investigators must have the necessary tools and equipment.

INVESTIGATIVE EQUIPMENT

Frontline police personnel who conduct a preliminary investigation need specific equipment to accomplish their assigned tasks. Although not all crime scenes require all items of equipment, you cannot predict the nature of the next committed crime or the equipment you will need. Therefore, you should have available at all times a crime scene investigation kit containing basic equipment. Check the kit's equipment after each use, replacing items as required.

Investigations can be simple or complex and can reveal little or much physical evidence. Consequently, the equipment needs of each investigation are different. Table 5.1, alphabetized for easy reference, contains the investigative equipment most often used.

Although the list may seem extensive, numerous other items are also often used in investigations: bags, binoculars, blankets, brushes, bullhorns, cable, capsules, chains, checklists, chemicals, chisels, coat hangers (to hang up wet or bloodstained clothing), combs, cotton, cutters, directories, drug kits, eyedroppers, files, fingernail clippers, fixatives, flares or fuses, flood lamps, forceps, forms, gas masks, generators, gloves, glue, guns, hammers, hatchets, levels, lights, magnets, manuals, maps, matches, metal detectors, moulages (for making impressions or casts),

TABLE 5.1 Equipment for Processing Evidence

Item	Uses
Cameras and memory cards	To photograph scene and evidence
Chalk and chalk line	To mark off search areas; to outline bodies or objects removed from the scene
Compass*	To obtain directions for report orientation and searches
Containers	(Boxes, bags of all sizes and shapes; lightweight plastic or paper; telescoping or collapsible glass bottles and new paint containers) To contain all types of evidence
Crayon or magic marker	To mark evidence
Envelopes, all sizes	To collect evidence
Evidence markers, alphas and numerics	To label/identify evidence
Fingerprint kit	(Various developing powders, brushes, fingerprint camera, fingerprint cards, ink pads, spoons, iodine fumer tube, lifting tape) To develop latent fingerprints
First-aid kit	To treat injured persons at the crime scene
Flashlight and batteries	To search dark areas, such as tunnels, holes, wells, windowless rooms; to search for latent fingerprints
Knife	To cut ropes, string, stakes, etc.
Labels, all sizes	(Evidence labels; labels such as "do not touch," "do not open," "handle with care," "fragile") To label evidence and to provide directions
Magnifier	To locate fingerprints and minute evidence
Measuring tape, steel	To measure long distances
Mirror with collapsible handle	To look in out-of-the-way locations for evidence
Notebook*	To record information
Paper*	(Notebook, graph, scratch pads, wrapping) To take notes, sketch scene, wrap evidence
Pencils*	(At least two; sharpened) To make sketches
Pens*	(At least two; non-smudge type) To take notes, make sketches
Picks	(Door lock picks and ice picks) To use as thumbtacks; to hold one end of a rope or tape
Plaster	To make casts of tire treads and footprints
Pliers	To pry and twist; to obtain evidence
Protractor	To measure angles
Rope	(Fluorescent, lightweight, approximately 300 feet) To protect the crime scene

TABLE 5.1 (*continued*)

Item	Uses
Ruler, carpenter-type*	To measure short distances
Ruler, straightedge*	To measure small items/distances
Scissors	To cut tapes, reproduce size of objects in paper, cut first-aid gauze
Screwdrivers, standard and Phillips	To turn and pry
Scribe	To mark metal objects for evidence
Sketching supplies*	(Ruler, pencil, graph paper, etc.) To make sketches
Spatula	To dig; to stir
Sterile distilled water	To use with swabs
String	To tie objects and boxes containing evidence; to protect the crime scene; to mark off search areas
Swabs	For lifting DNA evidence
Tags	To attach to items of evidence
Templates	To aid in sketching
Tongue depressors, wooden	To stir; to add reinforcements to plaster casts; to make side forms for casting; to lift objects without touching them
Tubes, glass, with stoppers	To contain evidence
Tweezers	To pick up evidence without contamination
Wrecking bar	To pry open doors, windows, entryways or exits

*The use of these items has been discussed earlier in the text (see Chapter 2).

© Cengage Learning, 2013

nails, padlocks, pails, plastic sheets, punches, putty, rags, receipts, rubber, saws, scrapers, shovels, side cutters, solvent, sponges, sprays, stamps, syringes, tape, tape recorders, thermometers, tin snips, towels, transceivers (to communicate in large buildings, warehouses, apartment complexes or open areas), vacuums, wax, wire and wrenches. The blood-test kits, gun-residue kits and other field-test kits described in Chapter 1 are also used.

More specialized equipment for investigation includes night-vision goggles, metal detectors, electronic tracking systems, digital voice recorders, camcorders and much more, discussed throughout this section. Many departments are able to use forfeiture assets confiscated during drug busts and other law enforcement efforts to purchase specialized investigative equipment. Additional heavy-duty, less-portable types of equipment such as large pry bars or long ladders are frequently found on fire and rescue vehicles and can be used jointly by the police and fire departments.

Selecting Equipment

Survey the types of crimes and evidence most frequently found at crime scenes in your jurisdiction. Select equipment to process and preserve the evidence you are most likely to encounter. For example, because fingerprints are often found at crime scenes, fingerprint-processing equipment should

be included in the basic kit. However, you would probably not need to take a shovel along to investigate a rape.

After the basic equipment needs are identified, select specific equipment that is frequently needed, lightweight, compact, high quality, versatile and reasonably priced. For example, boxes should either nest or be collapsible. Containers should be lightweight and plastic. The lighter and smaller the equipment, the more items can be carried in the kit. Consider miniaturized electronic equipment rather than heavier, battery-operated items. Select equipment that accomplishes more than one function, such as a knife with many features or other multipurpose tools.

Equipment Containers

The equipment can be put into one container or divided into several containers, based on frequency of use. This is an administrative decision determined by each department's needs. Dividing equipment results in a compact, lightweight kit suitable for most crime scenes while ensuring availability of other equipment needed to investigate less common cases.

Carriers or containers come in all shapes, sizes, colors and designs. Briefcases, attaché cases and transparent plastic bags are convenient to use. Some commercially produced kits include basic equipment. However, many departments prefer to design their own kits, adapted to their specific needs. The container should look professional, and a list of its contents should be attached to the outside or inside the cover.

Transporting Equipment

Crime scene investigative equipment is transported in a police vehicle, an investigator's vehicle or a crime van. The equipment can be transported in the trunk of a car, or a vehicle can be modified to carry it. For example, special racks can be put in the trunk, or the rear seat can be removed and special racks installed. Investigators are advised, when storing equipment in a car trunk, to organize items laterally instead of longitudinally, for if the car is involved in a high-speed rear-end collision, equipment oriented front-to-back can puncture through the back seat of the car or rupture the fuel tank.

A mobile crime lab is usually a commercially customized van that provides compartments to hold equipment and countertops for processing evidence. However, a van cannot go directly to some crime scenes, so the equipment must be transported from the van in other containers. The most frequently used equipment should be in the most accessible locations in the vehicle. Substances that freeze or change consistency in temperature extremes should be protected.

All selected vehicles should be equipped with radio communication and be able to convey equipment to disaster scenes as well as crime scenes—to make them cost-effective. Cost-effectiveness can be further enhanced if the vehicles are available as command posts, for stakeouts and as personnel carriers.

Regardless of whether you work with a fully equipped mobile crime laboratory or a small, portable crime scene investigation kit, your knowledge and skills as an investigator are indispensable to a successful investigation. The most sophisticated, expensive investigative equipment available is only as effective as you are in using it.

Training in Equipment Use

The largest failure in gathering evidence is not the equipment available but lack of training in using it effectively. Each officer should understand the use and operation of each item of equipment in the kit. Expertise comes with training and experience. Periodic refresher sessions should be held to update personnel on new techniques, equipment and administrative decisions.

Once investigators have the proper equipment and are competent in using it, they are ready to begin finding and processing evidence. Before actually stepping into the crime scene to process evidence, however, it is vitally important that investigators protect the integrity of the scene to keep it from becoming contaminated.

CRIME SCENE INTEGRITY AND CONTAMINATION OF EVIDENCE

The value of evidence is directly affected by what happens to it immediately following the crime. Evidence in an unprotected crime scene will degrade, diminish or disappear over time unless collected and preserved. Recalling Locard's principle of exchange, the very act of collecting evidence, no matter how carefully done, will result in a post-crime transfer of material—**contamination**.

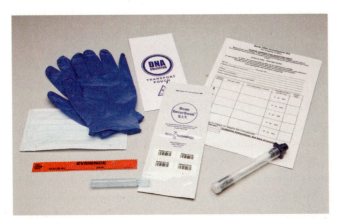
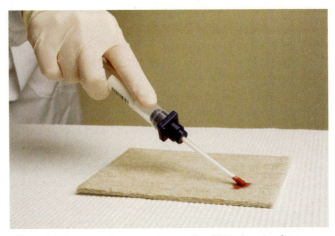

(Left image) The Bode SecurSwab Collection Kit allows investigators to collect, document and transport up to five DNA samples from a crime scene. The kit contains a SecurSwab SIT Collector, a DNA Collector Transport Pouch, a sterile water vial, a dust mask, a pair of gloves and a pre-printed envelope for documentation and transport to the lab. If additional samples are required, a sterile swab from a crime scene toolbox is used. (Right image) The Bode SecurSwab has been validated for sample collection on surfaces commonly found at crime scenes including aluminum, paper, cotton, ceramic, concrete, wood, glass, metal, and cardboard.

To minimize contamination of a crime scene and the evidence within, cordon off the area and keep all unnecessary people, including police officers, outside the scene perimeter. Law enforcement officers not assigned to the crime who walk through a scene out of curiosity can obliterate clues and add trace evidence.

Make sure that evidence does not lose its value—its integrity—because of a contaminated crime scene. **Integrity of evidence** refers to the requirement that any item introduced in court must be in the same condition as when it was found at the crime scene. This is documented by the **chain of evidence**, also called the **chain of custody**: documentation of what has happened to the evidence from the time it was discovered until it is needed in court, including every person who has had custody of the evidence and why.

The value of evidence may also be compromised by improper collection, handling or identification. Therefore, investigators' evidence processing skills are extremely important.

PROCESSING EVIDENCE: MAINTAINING THE CHAIN OF CUSTODY FROM DISCOVERY TO DISPOSAL

Simply collecting physical evidence is not enough. To be of value, the evidence must be legally seized and properly and legally processed. Of importance at this point is processing evidence correctly.

> Processing physical evidence correctly includes discovering or recognizing it; collecting, recording and identifying it; packaging, conveying and storing it; examining it; exhibiting it in court; and disposing of it when the case is closed.

Discovering or Recognizing Evidence

During a crime scene search, it is often difficult to determine immediately what is or might be evidence. Numerous objects are present, and not all are evidence.

> To determine what is evidence, first consider the apparent crime. Then look for any objects unrelated or foreign to the scene, unusual in location or number, damaged or broken or whose relation to other objects suggests a pattern that fits the crime.

Evidence at a crime scene must be properly identified, collected and preserved to be of value. Crime scene tape helps protect the area from contamination or the destruction or removal of evidence. Here, investigators walk between police lines in front of the wreckage of a tractor-trailer truck that burned after crashing into the southern entrance of the California State Capitol building the previous day. The driver of the truck was killed in the crash. Police officials believed the crash was intentional and treated the area as a crime scene.
© Reuters/CORBIS

Recall from Chapter 4 that evidence left out in the open, in plain view, that is immediately recognizable as relating to a crime, can be seized by officers engaged in a lawful activity. Also recall from Chapter 1 that investigators may discover exculpatory evidence, or that evidence favorable to the accused. According to the Brady Rule, which will be explored in greater depth in Chapter 21, law enforcement officers are required to gather all evidence that helps establish guilt *or* innocence. Officers must, however, be aware of the risks inherent in both over- and under-disclosure: "Over-disclosure could unnecessarily muddy the waters of the case and, in some cases, harm the reputation of a witness officer. Under-disclosure would deprive the original defendant of his constitutional right to a fair trial and could even lead to civil liability for law enforcement" (Means, 2008, p.12). Investigators must use common sense in deciding what is or might be evidence.

The importance of physical evidence depends on its ability to establish that a crime was committed and to show how, when and by whom. Logic and experience help investigators determine the relative value of physical evidence. Evidence in its original state is more valuable than altered or damaged evidence is.

Probabilities play a large role in determining the value of evidence. Fingerprints and DNA, for example, provide positive identification. In contrast, blood type does *not* provide positive identification, but it can help eliminate a person as a suspect.

An object's individuality is also important. For example, a heel mark's value is directly proportional to the number of its specific features—such as brand name, number of nails and individual wear patterns—that can be identified. Some objects have identification marks on them. Other evidence requires a *comparison* to be of value—a tire impression matching a tire, a bullet matching a specific revolver, a torn piece of clothing matching a shirt.

A **standard of comparison** is an object, measure or model with which evidence is compared to determine whether both came from the same source. Fingerprints are the most familiar example of evidence requiring a standard of comparison. A fingerprint found at a crime scene must be matched with a known print to be of value. Likewise, a piece of glass found in a suspect's coat pocket can be compared with glass collected from a window pane broken during a burglary.

Sometimes how an object fits with the surroundings determines whether it is likely to be evidence. For example, a man's handkerchief found in a women's locker room does not fit. The same handkerchief in a men's locker room is less likely to be evidence.

Sometimes, to detect evidence, the human eye needs assistance. Tools and techniques available to enhance evidence detection include forensic light sources and three-dimensional (3-D) technology.

Forensic light sources (FLSs), also called alternative light sources (ALSs), are becoming increasingly popular and easier to use. An FLS that works on the principle of ultraviolet fluorescence, infrared luminescence or laser light can make evidence visible that is not otherwise detectable to the naked eye, such as latent prints, body fluids and even altered signatures.

Ultraviolet (UV) light is the invisible energy at the violet end of the color spectrum that causes substances to emit visible light, commonly called *fluorescence*. Evidence that fluoresces, or glows, is easier to see—sometimes thousands of times easier. For some kinds of hard-to-see evidence—small amounts of semen, for instance, or fibers—an FLS is the only practical way to make the invisible visible. An inexpensive tool for investigators projects a filtered light beam onto evidence dusted with fluorescent powder, and a luminescent print appears immediately. A portable long-wave UV-light source can illuminate latent prints on several types of objects. Evidence is then exposed to superglue (cyanoacrylate), then stained or dusted. After this, it can be viewed under the UV light source.

Lasers can also assist in investigations by helping to detect evidence such as body fluids, fibers, fingerprints and various other materials containing chemicals that fluoresce under the high-energy beam of laser light (Geberth, 2010b). Thermal imaging is another common forensic light technique. In one case, a motorcyclist driving along a highway had shot a trucker. The crime scene was 1.5 miles long, and officers had 14 shell casings to locate. Using a thermal imager, they were able to recover all 14 casings.

The Law Enforcement Thermographers Association (LETA) has approved thermal imaging for search and rescue missions, fugitive searches, perimeter surveillance, vehicle pursuits, flight safety, marine and ground surveillance, structure profiles, disturbed surfaces and hidden compartments. Police often use thermal imaging to detect heat generated by indoor marijuana-growing operations. However, recall from Chapter 4 that the Supreme Court has ruled that using thermal imaging to view inside a residence is a search under the Fourth Amendment and requires a search warrant.

Technology Innovations

Spraggs (2008, p.39) describes the TracER forensic laser, which illuminates evidence details not easily seen by other means:

> TracER stands for Trace Evidence Recovery. This diode-based solid state laser provides a whopping 5 watts of power output in a completely self-contained portable light source. The TracER is marketed as weighing less than 50 pounds and costing under $50,000. At close to 50 pounds the TracER is certainly not light, but this weight includes its built-in DC (direct current) power supply and battery. . . . [T]he TracER is unique because it can be powered from a standard 110 volt AC outlet or it can run off its integrated battery for about 1.5 hours of continuous use. This means no more portable generators and extension cords in your remote crime scenes.
>
> Physically, the TracER is about the size of a large breadbox. It has a carrying handle on top and a 15-foot fiber optic cable that delivers the laser light. This cable terminates in a hand wand that allows the user to adjust the spread of the laser with an optical zoom, as well as control the light intensity. . . .
>
> The Coherent TracER is a unique forensic laser light source that offers cutting-edge technology with incredible power and portability. It's already in service with the FBI, the Bureau of Alcohol, Tobacco and Firearms, and the Border Patrol, as well as many smaller agencies throughout the United States, Canada and the United Kingdom.

Marking, Identifying and Collecting Evidence

Once evidence is discovered, place an evidence marker next to it (these come in alpha and numeric versions, and some have a ruler on them for scale); record the item on an evidence log, listing the marker (letter or number) placed by it for identification; and then photograph and sketch it before collecting or otherwise moving it. Mark, log, photograph and collect all objects that are or may be evidence, leaving the final decision regarding relevance to the prosecutor.

Collecting evidence requires judgment and care. Put liquids in bottles. Protect cartridges and spent bullets with cotton, and put them in small containers. Put other items in appropriate containers to preserve them for later packaging and transporting. The scene of a violent crime should be vacuumed with a machine that has a filter attachment. The vacuumed material can then be placed in an evidence bag and submitted to a crime laboratory.

Be sure to collect an adequate amount of the sample and to obtain standards of comparison, if necessary. Take extreme care to avoid **cross-contamination**, that is, allowing items of evidence to touch one another and thus exchange matter. When using the same tool for several tasks, be certain it is thoroughly cleaned after each use to prevent the transfer of material from one piece of evidence to another.

> Common errors in collecting evidence are (1) not collecting enough of the sample, (2) not obtaining standards of comparison and (3) not maintaining the integrity of the evidence.

To simplify testimony in court, one officer usually collects evidence and another officer takes notes on the location, description and condition of each item. The officer collecting evidence enters this information in personal notes or witnesses and initials the notes of the officer assigned to record information. All evidence is identified by the officer who collects it and by any other officer who takes initial custody of it.

> Mark or identify each item of evidence in a way that can be recognized later. Indicate the date and case number as well as your personal identifying mark or initials.

Make your marking easily recognizable and as small as possible—to reduce the possibility of destroying part of the evidence. Mark all evidence as it is collected or received. Do not alter, change or destroy evidence or reduce its value by the identification marking. Where and how to mark depends on the item. A pen is suitable for some objects. A stylus is used for those that require a more permanent mark that cannot be done with a pen, such as metal boxes, motor parts and furniture. Other objects can be tagged, labeled or placed in containers that are then marked and sealed.

> Record in your notes the date and time of collection, where the evidence was found and by whom, the case number, a description of the item and who took custody of it.

Forensic light sources help investigators find hard-to-see crime evidence. Here an examiner uses UV light and a special color filter to detect fingerprints and other traces of bodily fluids.
© imagebrokers.net/Photolibrary

Evidence descriptions can be entered into the computer and cross-referenced to current cases in the local jurisdiction and the surrounding area.

Packaging and Preserving Evidence

Careful packaging maintains the evidence in its original state, preventing damage or contamination. Do not mix, or cross-contaminate, evidence. Package each item separately, keeping in mind the specific requirements for that type of evidence. Some evidence is placed in sterile containers. Other types, such as firing-pin impressions or markings on a fatal bullet, are packed to prevent breakage or wrapped in cotton to prevent damage to individual characteristics. Hairs, fibers and other trace evidence are often placed in paper that is folded using a druggist fold so that the evidence cannot fall out.

> **Package each item separately in a durable container to maintain the integrity of evidence.**

Packaging is extremely important. An investigator should have both plastic and paper forms of packaging available so items can be packed properly based on what the evidence is. Although sometimes plastic bags are used, few departments use plastic because it does not "breathe" and hence may cause condensation to form. This can impede laboratory examination of the evidence. Many departments use new brown-paper grocery bags, especially for clothing. Although boxes may be better in some respects, they can be impractical to carry and difficult to find. You can usually find a supermarket open somewhere if you run out of bags. Be sure to provide a means of sealing whatever type of container is used to maintain the integrity of the evidence.

Preserve evidence on immovable items at the scene. Often some reproduction of the evidence is made. Fingerprints are developed, photographed, lifted and later compared. Tool marks are reproduced through photography, modeling clay, moulage, silicone and other impression-making materials. (These methods are acceptable in accordance with the best-evidence rule.) Specific requirements for the most frequently found evidence and best evidence are discussed later.

Submit movable items directly into evidence or send them to a laboratory for analysis. Sometimes an object is both evidence and a container of evidence. For example, a stolen radio found in a suspect's car is evidence of theft, and the fingerprints of a second suspect found on the radio are evidence that links that person to the theft.

Before packaging evidence for mailing to a laboratory, make sure it was legally obtained and has been properly identified and recorded in your notes. Submitting inadmissible evidence is costly and inefficient. Pack any bulky item in a sturdy box, seal the box with tape and mark it "evidence." If any latent evidence such as a fingerprint is on the surface of the object be sure to state this clearly (Figure 5.1).

Place a transmittal letter to the laboratory in an envelope attached to the outside of the box. This letter should contain the name of the suspect and the victim, if any; indicate what examinations are desired and which tests, if any, have already been done; and refer to any other pertinent correspondence or reports. Include a copy of the letter with the evidence, and mail the original separately. Retain a copy for your files. Figure 5.2 shows a sample letter.

Transporting Evidence

If the crime laboratory is nearby, an officer can deliver the evidence personally. However, even if the evidence is

> **Personal delivery, registered mail, insured parcel post, air express, FedEx and United Parcel Service (UPS) are legal ways to transport evidence. Always specify that the person receiving the evidence is to sign for it.**

personally delivered, include with it a written request on department letterhead or a department form.

How evidence should be transported depends on its size and type and the distance involved. Use the fastest method available. If the package is mailed, request a return receipt.

Protecting, Storing and Managing Evidence

Before, during and after its examination, evidence must be securely protected, properly stored and consistently managed. Securing, storing and tracking evidence is no small task because each article must be accounted for at all times.

A major crime scene investigation might generate more than 200 pieces of evidence. The amount of property that must be tracked and stored in metropolitan departments is typically 100,000 to 400,000 or more items. To account for so many items accurately and to maintain the chain of custody, each item must be categorized and described, including ownership (rightful, seized, found,

DNA/Biological Evidence

DNA and other forms of biological evidence should be collected and packaged dry using paper bags, envelopes and boxes. Avoid using plastic or containers that hold moisture to prevent decomposition of the sample.

Latent Prints

Latent cards and lift tape are packaged in sealed envelopes. Paperwork, photographs and information about where the prints were lifted should be included as well.

Controlled Substances/Narcotics

Items can vary in type and size: bongs, pipes, containers, cans, etc. Items can also include vegetation and organic substances. Nonorganic items should be packaged accordingly using bags or boxes to match their size. Items should be dry when packaged. Organic items should also be packaged using paper instead of plastic to avoid decomposition.

Ballistics/Tool Mark/Castings

Firearms should be packaged securely in an evidence gun box. Plastic zip ties should be used to secure the firearm in place. Firearms should only be packaged unloaded and with the safety on. Casings and loose ammunition should be packaged separately from the firearm.

Trace

There is a wide range of trace evidence. Depending on the evidence the proper packaging can differ. Trace evidence related to explosives is typically analyzed through the ATF and packaged using their specific guidelines. For residues use sterile absorbent materials such as swabs or gauzes. These items should be packaged in dry paper envelopes. Soil samples should be frozen or refrigerated, and collected in a plastic or glass container which should then be packaged in a Styrofoam container to maintain cold temperatures. Liquids should be packaged in glass vials and carefully secured and packaged in evidence boxes. Evidence related to arson that may have flammable chemicals should be packaged in appropriate containers such as lined metal cans.

Multimedia/Digital

Multimedia and digital evidence can include, but is not limited to, computer hard drives (external and internal), USB flash drives, various forms of memory cards, video game consoles with hard drives, cell phones, pad computers, digital cameras, etc. Evidence should be packaged securely in evidence boxes.

Sealing of Evidence

Proper sealing of evidence is imperative to prevent contamination and to maintain the integrity of the sample. Self-sealing evidence bags, evidence tape or heat sealing are all acceptable ways to seal evidence. Evidence tape must completely cover open seams and edges of the evidence bag. The sealer should initial or place another form of identification, such as a badge number, directly on or across the seal. If the evidence contains biohazardous material, a biohazard sticker should also be placed on the evidence.

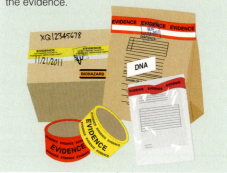

Evidence Submission

All chain of custody forms, related reports, invoices and other required forms should be completed and attached with the evidence. If the evidence is to be mailed, the evidence should be safely packaged in a box that will ensure protection. An invoice and other required paperwork should be attached to the outside of this packaging. If necessary, the package should also be identified using markers or stickers to notify the receiver of the type of evidence contained or if the evidence is hazardous. The package should then be wrapped to cover the invoice and package.

FIGURE 5.1

Evidence packaging.

© Cengage Learning, 2013

Print Form

001-EV
Authorization: DAS 05/03/2010
Page 1 of 3 Pages

**MINNESOTA BCA FORENSIC SCIENCE SERVICE
ANALYSIS REQUEST FORM**

Bureau of Criminal Apprehension
Forensic Science Laboratory
1430 Maryland Avenue East
St. Paul, MN 55106
651-793-2900
Email: bca.lab@state.mn.us

Bureau of Criminal Apprehension
Forensic Science Laboratory
3700 N. Norris Court NW
Bemidji, MN 56601
218-755-6600

Please provide the following information, as well as the Submitting Agency Report, so we can effectively and efficiently process your case. If submitting by mail or delivery service, please mail each case separately. Please type or print clearly.

Submitting Agency: Anycity Police Department

Agency Case Number: 11-0011

Investigating Officer Name/Phone: Detective Christine Y. Lim

Investigating Officer Email: CYLIM@ci.anycity.mn.us

Name of Person Submitting Evidence: Detective Christine Y. Lim

Type of Offense: Burglary

If Burglary: **Residential** ☒   **Commercial** ☐

Date of Offense: 04/01/2011

Is this a New Case?   Yes ☒   No ☐

If No: Additional Item(s) ☐   Resubmitted Item(s) ☐

If Additional/Resubmitted – BCA Lab #

Requested Analysis (please check):

Alcohol	☐	Questioned Documents	☐
Toxicology	☐	Arson	☐
Latent Prints	☒	Trace	☐
Firearms	☐	Drug Chemistry	☐
Nuclear DNA	☐	Mitochondrial DNA	☐

UNCONTROLLED COPY WHEN PRINTED
MN BCA Forensic Science Service

FIGURE 5.2
Bureau of Criminal Apprehension (a division of the Minnesota Department of Public Safety) evidence processing request.
Source: https://dps.mn.gov/divisions/bca/bca-divisions/forensic-science/Documents/Minnesota%20BCA%20Forensic%20Science%20Service%20Analysis%20Request%20Form.pdf

etc.). Its location should be documented, as should its disposition (returned, auctioned, burned, etc.).

All evidence received is recorded in a register, properly marked and put in an appropriate storage place. An evidence custodian checks each piece of evidence to ensure that all forms are properly completed and that the evidence is the same as described in the forms. Strict checkout procedures ensure that the evidence is always accounted for. Everyone who takes evidence signs for it, giving the date, time, place it is to be taken and purpose. When the evidence is returned, it is again signed for, dated and examined to ensure it is in the same condition as when taken. Any change in condition is noted and explained.

001-EV
Authorization: DAS 05/03/2010
Page 2 of 3 Pages

MINNESOTA BCA FORENSIC SCIENCE SERVICE
ANALYSIS REQUEST FORM - Continued

Drug Cases :

Possession ☐

Sale ☐

Search Warrant ☐

Manufacture ☐

For Marijuana Cases, Please Provide the Jury Court Date: _____
(Marijuana cases will not be accepted without a Jury Court Date)

Syringes are not accepted

Latent Print Cases:

Elimination Prints from All Principals	Yes	☒	No	☐
Major Case Prints (fingers/palms) for Crimes Against People	Yes	☒	No	☐
Is the Evidence Processed?	Yes	☐	No	☒

If Yes, what Type of Processing? _____

DNA Cases:

Known DNA Samples from All Principals	Yes	☐	No	☒

*EACH ITEM MUST BE **SEALED SEPARATELY**. INITIALS MUST BE ON SEALS.*

Principals Information

Victim(s) *(Last Name, First Name, Middle Name)*	Date of Birth *(MM/DD/YYYY)*	SID Number or N/A
Smith, Joseph Daniel	01/03/1980	N/A

FIGURE 5.2
(continued)

Package evidence properly to keep it in substantially the same condition in which it was found and store it securely. Document custody of the evidence at every stage.

Physical evidence is subject to chemical change, negligence, accident, intentional damage, theft and alteration during handling: "In many evidence rooms, car parts, bikes, lawn mowers, computers, backpacks, six-packs, suitcases and even tree limbs from nonviolent cases sit mixed in with delicate biological samples from the most

001-EV
Authorization: DAS 05/03/2010
Page 3 of 3 Pages

MINNESOTA BCA FORENSIC SCIENCE SERVICE
ANALYSIS REQUEST FORM - Continued

Suspect(s) *(Last Name, First Name, Middle Name)*	Date of Birth *(MM/DD/YYYY)*	SID Number or N/A
Unknown		

Elimination Principal(s) *(Last Name, First Name, Middle Name)*	Date of Birth *(MM/DD/YYYY)*	SID Number or N/A
Johnson, John Jacob	01/01/1980	N/A
Johnson, Mary Margaret	01/02/1980	N/A

Additional Information/Comments:

To Evidence Processing Personnel:

I would like to request that Anycity Police Department case File#11-0011, Burglary of a residence evidence items #1-3, which are the suspect's fingerprints that were lifted from the scene, be compared with the known prints of John Jacob Johnson DOB-01/01/80 item #1a, and Mary Margaret Johnson DOB-01/02/80 item #2a. Items #1-3 were submitted on 04/31/11.

Any questions, please contact me at 555-222-3333.

Thank You,

Detective Christine Y. Lim, Badge# 100
Anycity Police Department

UNCONTROLLED COPY WHEN PRINTED
MN BCA Forensic Science Service

FIGURE 5.2
(continued)

heinous rapes and murders. Piles accumulate in cramped and aging rooms often not built to store evidence" (Kiley, 2008, p.6). With proper storage, however, theft, loss, tampering, contamination and deterioration may be prevented. The storage area must be secure, well organized and free from pests, insects and excessive heat or moisture. A proper storage area has ample space and is climate controlled, typically kept at 65° to 75° F. Evidence is stored in vaults, property rooms, evidence rooms, evidence lockers, garages or morgues or under special conditions such as refrigeration. At a crime scene, an officer's vehicle trunk can provide temporary storage.

Some evidence requires more care than others. For example, explosives or biohazardous material may pose a danger to property room managers, require special training in handling and necessitate specialized facilities and features for safe storage. Electronic evidence, such as computers and digital storage media, must be kept away from strong magnets and other forces that may corrupt the data. Improperly sealed containers can allow liquid evidence to evaporate or moisture to enter; envelopes can split open; tags can fall off; writing on labels can become smudged, blurred or faded to the point of illegibility. Therefore, use extreme care whenever handling evidence, keeping it away from moisture, heat sources and any other factor that may degrade the integrity of the evidence.

Managing the growing mass of evidence is becoming increasingly challenging. Nationwide, law enforcement agencies are facing a growing need for more storage space to accommodate the seemingly exponential increase in the quantity of evidence they must store for longer periods, as scientific advances in DNA technology have caused many state legislatures to extend or eliminate their statutes of limitation.

Automated evidence storage can prevent many problems. Computer programs are available to help manage the property/evidence room. Many property control systems are using bar codes, which are extremely efficient and effective. At the time property is "booked," it is entered into a computer and given a bar code, which is affixed to the item. During any subsequent signing in or out of the property, the chain of custody is updated by scanning the item's evidence bar code into the log. Such a system provides an audit trail, helps with the inventory process and prints management and audit reports and disposition logs.

Handheld computers and portable printers capable of generating bar-coded labels are making the task of tagging and securing evidence more manageable. Bar codes can also help reduce the time investigators need to spend collecting and recording evidence at complicated crime scenes, such as homicides or major traffic crashes.

More advanced evidence tracking systems include software that can integrate both physical and electronic evidence, allowing the attachment of electronic images (e.g., digital crime scene photos and images of the physical evidence itself) to individual case files. If investigators need to access the evidence, they can pull up the electronic version online rather than having to check the physical evidence out of the system. These systems usually include a digital signature feature to track who has accessed the evidence (Mitchell, 2009).

The consequences of mishandling such property can range from public embarrassment to financial liability, criminal charges against the department and the inadmissibility of key evidence. All too often defendants are found not guilty because evidence in the chain of custody is not documented and cannot be determined. Furthermore, officers may be held civilly or even criminally liable if a case is thrown out because their negligence has compromised the chain of custody. Mismanaged evidence compromises the case at hand and can have negative impacts on other cases as well, if defense attorneys are able to show prior instances of poor evidence management (Schreiber, 2009).

Exhibiting Evidence in Court

Evidence is of little value to a criminal case if it is inadmissible in court. Therefore, adherence to a strict protocol is essential to ensure that evidence may be used during a trial.

> To ensure admissibility of evidence in court, be able to (1) identify the evidence as that found at the crime scene, (2) describe exactly where it was found, (3) establish its custody from discovery to the present and (4) voluntarily explain any changes that have occurred in the evidence.

Typically, the officer who will identify the evidence in court obtains it from the evidence custodian and delivers it to the prosecuting attorney, who takes it to the courtroom and introduces it at the proper time. The identifying officer uses the notes he or she made at the scene to lay the proper foundation for identifying the evidence.

In addition to the integrity of the evidence itself, consideration should be given to *how* evidence is presented in court. Evidence presented in a dirty, battered cardboard box creates a much different image than evidence presented in a clean, neatly labeled box. Simple details like this can make a difference in jury perception, which, right or wrong, influences the credibility of the prosecution's case.

Scientific evidence is commonly presented in court as part of either the prosecutor's or the defense's case and is frequently accompanied by expert testimony. When assessing the admissibility of expert opinions based on scientific evidence or knowledge, courts look to the rulings of the *Frye* and *Daubert* cases for guidance.

The opinion in *Frye v. United States* (1923) reads, in part, "Just when a scientific principle or discovery crosses the line between the experimental and demonstrable stages is difficult to define. Somewhere in this twilight zone the evidential force of the principle must be recognized, and while courts will go a long way in admitting expert testimony deduced from a well-recognized scientific principle or discovery, the thing from which the deduction is made must be *sufficiently established to have gained general acceptance in the particular field* in which it belongs" [emphasis added].

The merits of *Frye* faced much debate, and the *Frye* test was effectively displaced when the Supreme Court, in *Daubert v. Merrell Dow Pharmaceuticals* (1993), held that the Federal Rules of Evidence, not *Frye*, provide the standard for admitting expert scientific testimony. Within the rules is specifically R.702, which speaks directly to expert testimony: "If scientific, technical, or other specialized knowledge will assist the trier of fact to understand the evidence or to determine a fact in issue, a witness qualified as an expert by knowledge, skill, experience, training, or education, may testify thereto in the form of an opinion or otherwise."

In its opinion summary the Supreme Court stated, "'General acceptance' is not a necessary precondition to the admissibility of scientific evidence under the Federal Rules of Evidence, but the Rules—especially R.702—do assign to the trial judge the task of ensuring that an expert's testimony both rests on a reliable foundation and is relevant to the task at hand. Pertinent evidence based on scientifically valid principles will satisfy those demands." This requirement that an expert's testimony be both *reliable* and *relevant* is known as the two-pronged **Daubert standard**.

Final Disposition of Evidence

Evidence must be legally disposed of to prevent major storage problems as well as pilferage or unauthorized conversion to personal use. State statutes and city ordinances specify *how* to dispose of evidence, but most do not specify *when* this should occur. Therefore, departments typically go by the statute of limitations for the type of case when deciding how long to hold items of evidence before disposing of them. Every criminal offense has a statute of limitations except homicide, and these statutes vary from state to state.

In cases involving suspects, arrests, plea bargains or trials, evidence is held until the case is cleared, at which time personal property may be returned to the rightful owner. In cases in which prosecution is not anticipated, contraband items can be released at any

time. In misdemeanor cases where there are no suspects or arrests after one year, the property can generally be returned to the owner, sold or destroyed. Items of evidence may also be returned or otherwise disposed of because the cases have exceeded the statute of limitations. As a general rule, evidence for felony cases is held three to five years, and evidence in sexual assault cases is retained for five to six years. However, when an appeal occurs or is anticipated or the case is a homicide, evidence must be maintained indefinitely. "More mandates are being placed on evidence with DNA implications, which sometimes must be saved for as long as the case remains open, or must remain available to convicted individuals during the terms of his or her incarceration" (Schreiber, 2009, p. 11).

Furthermore, guidelines for disposing of evidence are changing because of advancing forensic technologies, which are allowing cases to be solved many years after the commission of a crime.

> After a case is closed, evidence is returned to the owner, auctioned or destroyed.

Evidence is either disposed of continuously, annually or on a special date. Departments using computerized evidence management programs can generate routine inventory reports that show the status of each case and whether the related evidence must be maintained or can be disposed of. Departments without such a system must manually review the status of items and then either return them as evidence to storage or dispose of them. Witnessed affidavits of disposal list all items sold, destroyed or returned. The affidavits include the date, type of disposition, location and names of all witnesses to the disposition.

An innovative approach to disposing of evidence that is no longer needed is the online auction: "PropertyRoom.com is an auction Web site created by retired police officers to take the burden of unclaimed property off of police departments' hands. And for many, the site saves them money and hassle in comparison to doing a local auction. . . . At the end of the auction, Property Room keeps half the proceeds from items that sell for less than $1,000. And if it sells for more than that, Property Room only keeps 25 percent from the sale. The company estimates that about 98 percent of everything it auctions, sells" (Whitehead, 2007, pp. 72–74).

Having explored the path evidence generally takes during the course of an investigation, the discussion now turns to the most common types of evidence encountered and how they are examined.

FREQUENTLY EXAMINED EVIDENCE

The laboratory analyzes evidence associated with the physical characteristics of suspects using biometrics. **Biometrics** is the statistical study of biological data and a means to positively identify an individual by measuring that person's unique physical or behavioral characteristics (Moradoff, 2010). Biometric identification technology ranges from fingerprints to techniques that recognize voices, hand geometry, facial characteristics and even blood vessels in the iris of an eye. Fingerprints and iris recognition are considered most reliable, followed by facial and hand, with voice the least reliable.

The lab also analyzes the class and individual characteristics of objects providing evidence. **Class characteristics** are the features that place an item into a specific category. For example, the size and shape of a tool mark may indicate that the tool used was a screwdriver rather than a pry bar. **Individual characteristics** are the features that distinguish one item from another of the same type. For example, chips and wear patterns in the blade of a screwdriver may leave marks that are distinguishable from those of any other screwdriver. Whether the examination is done in house or by a public or private forensic lab, quality can be enhanced by using a lab that is accredited: "Participating in a forensic science accreditation program is the best hope of obtaining an unbiased evaluation of the forensic science operation within a law enforcement agency. . . . The consequences of shoddy, incompetent, or presumed results can be momentous, including costs of lawsuits for innocent convictions or ruined careers" (Fitzpatrick and Ely, 2007, p. 50).

> Frequently examined physical evidence includes fingerprints; voiceprints; language; DNA; blood and other body fluids; scent; hairs and fibers; shoe and tire prints and impressions; bite marks; tools and tool marks; firearms and ammunition; glass; soils and minerals; safe insulation; rope, strings and tapes; drugs; weapons of mass destruction; documents; digital evidence; laundry and dry-cleaning marks; paint; skeletal remains; wood; and other types of evidence.

Fingerprints

"Since Francis Galton published his classic textbook *Finger Prints* in 1852 and Sir Edward Henry developed a system to classify fingerprints in 1897, it could be argued that the science of fingerprinting remains the single most important discovery in criminal justice. Only DNA rivals the fingerprint as an absolute method of proving a person's identification" (Jetmore, 2008, p.77).

At the end of each human finger, on the palm side, exists a unique arrangement of small lines called *friction ridges*, which provide just enough roughness to give fingers "traction" when holding or otherwise manipulating objects. Within these friction ridges lie sweat pores. When the sweat they produce mixes with body oils, dirt or other matter, that substance will rub off on any surface the finger touches, leaving behind a print if the surface is relatively smooth.

These prints are useful in criminal investigations because a person's friction-ridge patterns are formed before birth and remain the same throughout that person's life. The lines in the thumbprint raindrops made by a second grader in art class will be the same pattern the person's thumb will leave on the newspaper she reads every morning before going to work years later. Besides remaining consistent over time, prints are useful because they are unique—no two people have the same friction-ridge pattern. Therefore, through friction ridge analysis, a fingerprint can be a positive way to prove that a suspect was at a crime scene. The implications of finding identifiable prints at the scene vary with each case. For example, prints may not be important if the suspect had a legitimate reason for being there. Often, however, this is not the case.

Although many laypeople assume that identifiable fingerprints are almost always found at a crime scene, in many cases none are found. Even when they are, it is often difficult to locate the person who matches the prints. If a person's prints are not on file and there are no suspects, fingerprints are virtually worthless. Other times, however, fingerprints are the most important physical evidence in a case (Figure 5.3). Finding fingerprints at a crime scene requires training and experience. An excellent reference for more information on fingerprint identification is *The Fingerprint Sourcebook* (2011) by the Scientific Working Group on Friction Ridge Analysis, Study and Technology (SWGFAST).

Fingerprints are of various types:

- **Latent fingerprints** are impressions transferred to a surface, either by sweat on the ridges of the fingers or because the fingers carry residue of oil, dirt, blood or other substances. Latent prints are not readily seen but can be developed through powders or chemicals. They are normally left on nonporous surfaces.

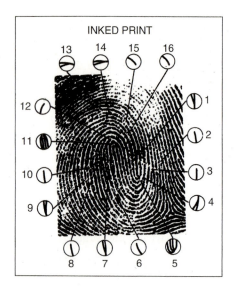

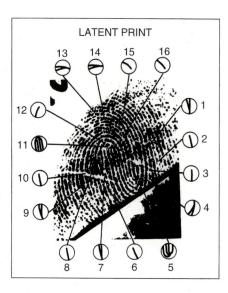

FIGURE 5.3

Three men checked into a motel at 11:00 P.M. Shortly after midnight, when a new desk clerk came on duty, the men went to the office and committed an armed robbery. Police investigating the scene went to the room occupied by the three men and found a latent fingerprint on an ashtray. The print was later matched to one of the suspects whose fingerprints were on file with the police department.

© Cengage Learning, 2013

■ **Visible fingerprints** are made when fingers are dirty or stained. They occur primarily on glossy or light-colored surfaces and can be dusted and lifted.

■ **Plastic fingerprints**, one form of visible print, are impressions left in soft substances such as putty, grease, tar, butter or soft soap. These prints are photographed, not dusted.

 Any hard, smooth, nonporous surface can contain latent fingerprints.

Nonporous surfaces include light switches; window frames and moldings; enameled surfaces of walls, doors and painted or varnished objects; wood; lamps; polished silver surfaces; and glass. Fingerprints often occur on documents, glass, metals, tools and weapons used in a crime as well as on any objects picked up or touched by a suspect or any other person. Objects such as firearms, tools, small metal objects, bottles, glassware, documents and other transportable items are submitted to a laboratory, where the prints are developed by experts.

Some porous materials also produce latent prints. For example, paper and cloth surfaces have developed excellent prints. Passing a flashlight at an oblique angle over a surface helps to locate possible prints. Latent prints have even been collected from human skin.

Technology Innovations

Researchers at the Los Alamos National Laboratory in New Mexico have developed a novel method of detecting fingerprints using X-rays that don't disturb the print in any way (Page, 2007b, pp.128–131):

The technique uses a process called microbeam X-ray fluorescence (MXRF), which rapidly reveals the elemental composition of a sample by irradiating it with a thin beam of X-rays without disturbing the sample.

So far the research is proof-of-concept only: to demonstrate the possibility of detecting fingerprint patterns using MXRF, whereby the fingerprint pattern is determined by detecting inorganic elements present in the print residue.

"Thus, we both detect the print pattern digitally and collect chemical information from the print as well," [Los Alamos chemist] Worley says.

Fingerprints contain detectable quantities of salts, such as sodium chloride and potassium chloride, excreted in sweat. The Los Alamos researchers have shown they could detect the sodium, potassium and chlorine from these salts. Since these salts are deposited along with the patterns present in a fingerprint, an image of the fingerprint can be visualized producing an elemental image for analysis.

Begin the search for fingerprints by determining the entry and exit points and the route through a crime scene. Look in the obvious places as well as less-obvious places such as the underside of toilet seats and the back of car rearview mirrors. Examine objects that appear to have been moved. Consider the nature of the crime and how it was probably committed. Prints found on large, immovable objects are processed at the scene by photographing or dusting with powder or chemicals.

Dusting Latent Fingerprints.
Fingerprint dusting powders are available in various colors and chemical compositions to provide maximum development and contrasts. When dusting for fingerprints, use a powder that contrasts in color to the surface.

> Do not powder a print unless it is necessary, and do not powder a visible print until after you photograph it.

Spraggs (2007, p.26) cautions, "The number one mistake officers make is over-processing the latent fingerprint. First rule: use less powder than you think you need." Another serious error, one that can negate the forensic integrity and evidentiary value of the print, is using a contaminated brush: "Although using fingerprint powder is quick and inexpensive, concerns have been raised recently concerning the possibility of contamination due to the transfer of DNA through the use of fingerprint brushes. . . . Crime scene examiners are being warned to be aware of this possibility" (Yamashita and French, 2011, p.14).

To dust for fingerprints, follow these steps:

1. Make sure the brush is clean. Roll the handle of the brush between your palms to separate the bristles.
2. Shake the powder can to loosen the powder. Apply the powder lightly to the print, following the contour lines of the ridges to bring out details.
3. Remove all excess powder.
4. Photograph.

Use a camel-hair brush for most surfaces. Use an aspirator for dusting ceilings and slanted or difficult areas. If in doubt about which powder or brush to use, test them on a similar area first.

Learn to use the various materials by watching an experienced investigator demonstrate the correct powders, brushes and techniques. Then practice placing latent prints on various surfaces and using different-colored powders to determine how well each adheres and how much color contrast it provides. Practice until you can recognize surfaces and select the appropriate powder.

When photographing developed latent prints, record the color of the powder used, the color of the surface and the location of the prints. Place your identification, date and case number on the back of the photograph and submit it to the crime laboratory. The laboratory will determine whether it is an identifiable print and whether it matches a known suspect or other people whose prints were submitted for elimination.

Lifting Prints.
To lift fingerprints, use a commercially prepared lifter that has both a black-and-white background and a wide transparent lift tape. Use black lifters for light powders and light lifters for black powders.

To lift prints on doorknobs or rounded surfaces, use transparent tape so you can see any spots where the tape is not sticking. Put the tape over the dusted print. Do not use too much pressure. Work out any bubbles that appear under the tape by applying extra pressure. When you have lifted the print, transfer it to a fingerprint card.

Common errors in lifting prints include removing too much or too little powder from the ridges, allowing bubbles to develop under the tape and failing to make two lifts when a second lift would be better than the first.

Chemical Development of Latent Fingerprints.
Although powders are used to develop latent fingerprints on many surfaces, they are not recommended for unpainted wood, paper, cardboard or other absorbent surfaces. Using powder on such surfaces will smudge any prints, destroying their value as evidence. For such surfaces, use a special chemical such as iodine, ninhydrin or silver nitrate.

Use gloves and a holding device to avoid contaminating the evidence by inadvertently adding your own fingerprints. The chemicals can all be applied to the same specimen because each reacts differently with various types of materials. However, if *all* are used, the order must be iodine first, then ninhydrin and finally silver nitrate.

In the *iodine method*, iodine crystals are placed in a fuming cabinet or a specially prepared fuming gun. The crystals are heated and vaporized, producing a violet fume that is absorbed by the oil in the fingerprints. The fingerprint ridges appear yellow-brown and must be photographed immediately because they fade quickly. Fuming cabinets and guns can be made or purchased from police supply houses.

A forensic investigator uses a fine brush to apply fingerprinting dust to a cup. The dust adheres to the oil of a fingerprint, revealing a distinctive ridged pattern that can be used to identify the person who held the cup, thereby linking that person to this crime scene.

© Mauro Fermariello/Science Photo Library/Photo Researchers, Inc.

The *ninhydrin method* develops amino acids. Ninhydrin (highly flammable) is available in spray cans or in a powder form from which a solution of the powder and acetone or ethyl alcohol is made. The evidence is then either sprayed or brushed with or dipped into the ninhydrin. Development of prints can be speeded up by applying heat from a fan, pressing iron or oven. At room temperature, prints develop in a minimum of two hours; with a pressing iron, they develop almost immediately. Ninhydrin-developed prints do not fade immediately, but they eventually lose contrast. Therefore, photograph them soon after development.

The *silver nitrate method* develops sodium chloride in the fingerprint ridges into silver chloride that appears as a red-brown print. Because silver nitrate destroys oils and amino acids, it must be used *after* the iodine and ninhydrin methods. Immerse the specimen in a solution of 3 to 10 percent silver nitrate and distilled water. Remove it immediately and hang it to dry. The prints can be developed more rapidly by applying light until they start to develop. They should be photographed immediately because they disappear after several hours.

Other Methods of Lifting Prints. Fingerprints may also be located and developed by using

Magnabrush techniques, laser technology, gelatin lifters and cyanoacrylate (superglue). Superglue fuming involves heating three or four drops of glue to generate fumes that adhere to fingerprints. The process can effectively develop prints on plastic, bank checks, counterfeit money, metal and skin. Portable lasers are used to find and highlight fingerprints. They can detect fingerprints on the skin of a murder victim and trace a gunshot path.

Investigators can also use gelatin lifters to lift dusted prints or dust marks (footprints) from a wide variety of surfaces. Used in Europe for decades, the lifters are flexible and easily cut to suit specific needs. They can lift dust prints from any smooth surface—from tile floors to cardboard boxes. The high contrast of the black lifters allows investigators to see dust prints not visible to the naked eye, and the lifted prints photograph extremely well. In addition, the lifters can pick up particle samples such as hair or paint chips. In the laboratory, tweezers or a scalpel can remove the samples from the lifter without damaging the sampled material.

Page (2007b, p.128) points out, "As most crime scene experts know, dusting for fingerprints can sometimes destroy parts of the prints, erasing potentially valuable forensic clues." In addition, conventional fingerprinting

RF Corbis/Photolibrary

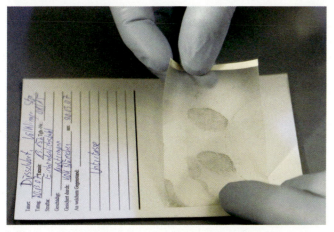

Lifting a print involves dusting powder onto a surface to reveal the print (top image) and then applying a lifter, typically a transparent adhesive tape, over the print. The next step is to transfer the lifted print on the tape to a print card (bottom image).

© Imagebroker.net/Photolibrary

methods may use liquids or vapors that might alter the prints.

Elimination Prints.
If fingerprint evidence is found, it is important to know whose prints "belong" at the scene. Prints of persons with reason to be at the scene are taken and used as **elimination prints**. For example, family members in a home where a crime has occurred or employees of a business that has been robbed should be fingerprinted so that their fingerprints at the scene can be eliminated from suspicion.

Inked Prints.
Most police departments have equipment for taking fingerprints. Standard procedure is to fingerprint all adults who have been arrested, either at the time of booking or at the time of release. These fingerprint records help ensure that the person arrested is identified correctly. Some departments have portable fingerprint kits in patrol vehicles that allow them to take inked prints and develop latent prints at crime scenes.

To take inked prints, start by rolling the right thumb and fingers in the order stated on the card. Then roll the left thumb and fingers in order. Use a complete roll—that is, go from one side to the other. Next, *press* the fingers and then the thumb of each hand on the spaces provided on the card. The card also has spaces for information about the person and the classification made by the fingerprint examiner. Learn to take inked fingerprints by having someone demonstrate.

Digital Fingerprinting.
Advances in computer technology are allowing digital fingerprinting to replace inked printing. Latent fingerprints are scanned and converted into an electronic image or **inkless fingerprint** that is stored in a database for rapid retrieval. In this method, a suspect's hand is placed onto a glass platen, where a laser optically scans the prints and transfers them onto a fingerprint card. Benefits of using optical live-scan devices include rapid, accurate acquisition of a print; simple storage; easy retrieval; and quick transmittal to other officers and agencies.

Stored fingerprint information includes the person's gender, date of birth, classification formula and each finger's ridge count. This automated fingerprint identification system (AFIS) technology maps fingerprints and creates a spatial geometry of the minutiae of the print, which is changed into a binary code for the computer's searching algorithm. When queried, the system selects the cards within the range limitations for the entered classification formula. The capability of registering thousands of details makes it possible for the computer to complete a search in minutes that would take days manually. The search success rate has been as high as 98 percent in some departments with files under one million. Once the computer search finds a hit, a fingerprint expert then visually compares the prints.

If no match is found in local or state files, prints are submitted to the Federal Bureau of Investigation (FBI) Identification Division for a further search. This division has on file fingerprints of arrested people as well as of nearly 100 million other people such as aliens and individuals in government services, including the military.

Given that approximately 35 to 40 percent of crime scenes have latent prints, AFIS has provided a tremendous advance in crime fighting, first proving its value when it was used to solve the "Night Stalker" serial killer case in 1985.

The FBI's automated fingerprint identification system provides five major services to local, state and federal law enforcement and criminal justice agencies:

■ Ten-print–based identification services (i.e., 10 rolled fingerprint impressions and 10 flat fingerprint impressions)

■ Latent fingerprint services

■ Subject search and criminal history services

■ Document and image services

■ Remote search services

One benefit of electronic fingerprinting systems is their increased speed and accuracy. Another major benefit of this technology is the ability to transmit the print image over telephone or cable lines from one AFIS system to another or to computerized criminal records centers. This feature also allows international sharing of databases to help capture criminals who move from one country to another.

In September 2006, the FBI and the Department of Homeland Security merged their fingerprint databases into what is called the Integrated Automated Fingerprint Identification System, known as IAFIS. The merger of databases containing millions of fingerprints taken from convicted criminals and illegal immigrants marks an unprecedented interagency effort to capture more terrorists and solve more crimes. A fingerprint entered into IAFIS led to Lee Boyd Malvo, one of the two suspects in the Washington, DC-area sniper case. Malvo had been previously arrested by the Immigration and Naturalization Service (INS).

In 2011 the FBI upgraded its AFIS to **Advanced Fingerprint Information Technology (AFIT)**, an integrated system that can also incorporate additional biometric data such as latent palmprints and facial recognition technology ("FBI Upgrades Fingerprint System, 2011). AFIT is part of the FBI's broader technology initiative called Next Generation Identification (NGI), which also includes an enhanced IAFIS repository. The new system reduces the time it takes to analyze fingerprints, from hours with AFIS to minutes with AFIT, and is more than 99 percent accurate, whereas the old system performed at a 92 percent accuracy rate.

Automated fingerprint systems are constantly being augmented with the introduction of new services and features and recently went mobile, allowing investigators in the field to take a live scan of a person's prints. The potential exists to adapt mobile fingerprint systems to quickly identify prints at crime scenes. The units will need to be modified to accommodate the scanning of crime scene prints, but this process could greatly reduce the important time frame of the first 24 hours after the commission of a crime, the period in which a suspect is most likely to be identified.

Despite the many benefits provided by automated fingerprint technology, these programs simply search the

Technology Innovations

Mobile fingerprint readers are an investigative tool growing in popularity and usage among police departments nationwide and are carried by homicide detectives, coroner staff, motorcycle and foot patrol officers and those patrolling on public transit buses or trains: "These devices . . . are designed to provide law enforcement professionals with the ability to gain a positive identification on a person who has either no government-issued identification or possesses one that officers believe is fraudulent or altered. The positive return in Los Angeles County includes a photograph, a name, and the latest arrest information" (Norton, 2009, p.34).

Extremely portable, the device chosen by the Los Angeles County Sheriff's Department weighs less than three ounces, is smaller than the average cell phone and can return a hit fairly quickly, often in less than two minutes. The impact of such fingerprint readers in Los Angeles County has been significant, and success stories continue to accrue. For example:

> [In 2008] a homicide detective reported that during an investigation of a murder in Palmdale, he had arrested two suspects and was actively searching for a third. After about three weeks, the detective got a call from an LAPD officer informing him that the third suspect was in custody. . . . [T]he LAPD officer had stopped the suspect for possible narcotics activity, and the suspect (who had changed his appearance dramatically) had given a false name. Using a fingerprint reader, the officer was able to take the suspect into custody after acquiring a positive identification and conducting a warrant check, all of which took only a few minutes. (Norton, 2009, p.39)

databases for possible matches. In the end, a human fingerprint examiner must determine the match. In addition: "The database contains the fingerprints of only a small percentage of the population. Moreover, to make a comparison, the latent print must be of sufficient quality to identify certain individual characteristics" (Bowen and Schneider, 2007).

Fingerprint Patterns, Analysis and Identification.

Once a print has been captured, whether chemically developed, rolled in ink or digitally scanned, the fingerprint patterns are analyzed for unique features that will, it is hoped, lead to identifying one individual. Fingerprint patterns are classified as *arched, looped* or *whorled*. Variations of these configurations result in the nine basic fingerprint patterns illustrated in Figure 5.4. Normally, 12 matchable characteristics on a single fingerprint are required for positive identification.

When using digital fingerprint images, the image quality becomes critical. As with rolled (inked) prints, smudges and distortions reduce the print's usefulness. Digital programs, if not up to standard, might also create artifacts or false minutiae in the image, which will impair an examiner's ability to analyze and match a print. Minimum standards have been established to ensure maximum usefulness of the prints they scan.

Usefulness of Fingerprints.

Fingerprints are extremely valuable in criminal investigations.

Fingerprints are *positive* evidence of a person's identity. They cannot, however, indicate a person's age, sex or race.

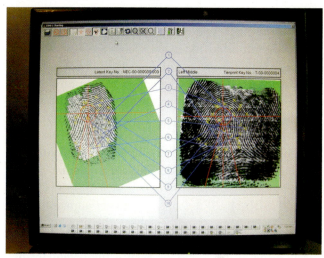

An automated fingerprint identification system compares fingerprints recovered at crime scenes with the millions of prints stored in its database. This technology enables large numbers of fingerprints to be analyzed more rapidly and accurately than did the traditional method of visual analysis conducted by a print technician. Here the software identifies specific minutiae (unique characteristic identifiers) shared by the evidence (latent) print and a particular individual's (suspect's) print.
© Joel Gordon

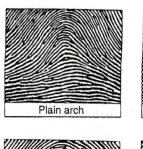
Plain arch

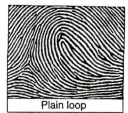
Tented arch

Plain loop

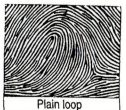
Plain loop

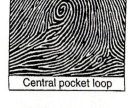
Whorl

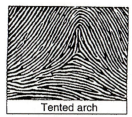
Central pocket loop

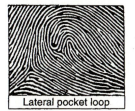
Lateral pocket loop

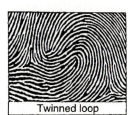
Twinned loop

Accidental

FIGURE 5.4
Nine basic fingerprint patterns.
Source: Courtesy of the FBI Law Enforcement Bulletin

Fingerprinting is increasingly being applied to homeland security efforts because fingerprints can be sent via communications systems across the country and around the globe and visually reproduced. Crime victims are identified by their prints to prove the corpus delicti. Courts, parole and probation officers and prosecutors use fingerprints to positively identify people with multiple criminal records.

Fingerprints also aid in noncriminal investigations by helping to identify victims of mass disasters, missing persons, amnesia victims and unconscious persons. Military agencies use fingerprints recorded at enlistment to identify those killed in combat. Hospitals use fingerprints or footprints to identify newborn babies. Furthermore, fingerprints are becoming widely used as identification for cashing checks and processing legal documents.

Admissibility in Court. To ensure admissibility in court, investigators should establish the probative value of the print; that is, either the defendant had claimed never being at the scene, or even if the defendant had legitimate access to the scene, he or she did not have legitimate access to the object on which the print was found, or the print was found on the instrumentality of the crime. Investigators should also ensure admissibility by the testimony of the investigator who lifted the latent print, by the level of expertise used by the fingerprint examiner and by the testimony of the file supervisor who maintained the print.

As with digital photography, digital fingerprinting has faced authenticity and admissibility challenges in court. Despite attempts to create tracking software, such as MoreHits, to overcome such challenges, thus far no tool has been designed that will offer a secure chain of custody for digital prints.

Other Types of Prints. Suspects may leave palmprints, footprints or even prints of lips, and these impressions can be photographed and developed just as fingerprints are. Palmprints contain many more friction-ridge landmarks than fingerprints have, thus giving print examiners more points of comparison when determining matches. Biometric databases are also beginning to store prints from the part of the hand called the *writer's edge*, the side of the hand, from the wrist up to the curled fifth, or "pinkie," finger that rests on the table or paper when someone is writing.

In one interesting case, a burglar shattered a restaurant's plate glass window. The police found no fingerprints around the window but did find footprints and a toe print on a piece of the broken glass. These were developed and lifted. Later, a 17-year-old was arrested for vagrancy. Learning that he often went barefoot, police also took his footprints and forwarded them to the FBI. They were identical to those on the plate glass window fragment. It was learned that the youth had taken off his shoes and put his socks on his hands to avoid leaving fingerprints at the crime scene. He was found guilty.

In another case, a string of peeping-Tom cases was solved because of three lip impressions left by the suspect on a windowpane. And in a case in Illinois, authorities matched lip prints on a piece of duct tape the suspect had held in his mouth while binding a victim.

Voiceprints

A **voiceprint** is a graphic record made by a sound spectrograph of the energy patterns emitted by speech. Like fingerprints, no two voiceprints are alike. Voiceprints can assist in identifying bomb hoaxers, obscene phone callers and others who use the phone illegally: "Valuable evidence often rests on an answering machine recording, cell phone message, 911 call tapes, etc. Most state crime laboratories and many private companies now perform audio forensic investigation" (Hanson, 2007, p.134). However, "As with all crime scene evidence, strict chain-of-custody rules and procedures must be adhered to. When a piece of audio evidence is found, it should be immediately placed in an evidence bag or appropriate container and shipped to the audio lab" (Hanson, p.137).

A voiceprint made during a phone call can be retained until a suspect is in custody. Then a sample of a suspect's voice can be taken and compared with the voiceprint evidence: "Spectrographic examinations compare an unknown recorded voice sample with a known verbatim voice exemplar produced on a similar transmission-and-recording device such as the telephone. Decisions regarding spectrographic voice comparisons are not conclusive. The results are for investigative guidance only" (Waggoner, 2007, pp.18–19).

As with many other investigative techniques, advances in forensic audio analysis are giving investigators higher-quality data despite efforts of those being surveilled to distort their voices or conceal them with high levels of background noise. Use of adaptive digital filters can remove background noise and enhance speech and data from tapes. This technology can also analyze sounds other than voices, thus converting annoying background noise into isolated, distinguishable sounds that give clues about where the calls are originating.

The use of voiceprints in criminal trials is controversial. In a number of cases, convictions obtained through voiceprints have been reversed because the voiceprints were not regarded as sufficiently reliable.

Language Analysis

An individual's communication, whether written or spoken, may provide clues about his or her gender, age, race or ethnicity or what part of the country (or world) the person grew up in or has spent recent time in. Language analysis may also provide insight into a person's educational level, political views and religious orientation, which may in turn provide further evidence regarding a criminal motive. One area of language analysis involves *psycholinguistics*, the study of the mental processes involved in comprehending, producing and acquiring language.

A useful and often overlooked type of evidence is the actual language used by victims, witnesses and suspects at the crime scene. Analysis of such "excited utterances" can reveal the speaker's state-of-mind and may be admitted into testimony even if the person does not testify. To qualify for this exception to the hearsay rule, the victim or witness must have seen an exciting or startling event and made the statement while still under the stress of the event. This is similar to *res gestae* statements discussed in Chapter 1. To capture this type of evidence, many officers and investigators carry lightweight digital voice recorders with date- and time-stamp features.

Human DNA Profiling

Human cells contain discrete packs of information known as chromosomes, which are made of DNA. **DNA**, or *deoxyribonucleic acid*, is an organic substance contained in a cell's nucleus. The DNA double-helix strand is composed of building blocks called *nucleotides*, which consist of a base molecule connected to a molecule of sugar and a molecule of phosphoric acid. The four bases are adenine (A), guanine (G), cytosine (C) and thymine (T), which link to each other to form a chain millions of nucleotides long. Within this DNA chain are areas of *conserved regions*, where the A-T-C-G pattern is the same for every human, and *variable regions*, where the nucleotide sequence is distinct and different for every person, thereby determining a person's individual characteristics. This unique genetic code can be used to create a genetic fingerprint to positively identify a person. Except for identical twins, no two individuals have the same DNA structure.

 DNA profiling uses material from which chromosomes are made to identify individuals positively.

DNA can tell investigators the sample donor's gender, ethnicity, eye color and hair color (Garrett, 2009c). DNA profiling can be done on cells from almost any part of the body and is used in paternity testing, immigration disputes, missing persons and unidentified-body cases and criminal and assailant identification. DNA analysis was used to identify many of the World Trade Center victims killed on September 11, 2001. DNA keeps its integrity in dried specimens for long periods and consequently can help resolve cold cases.

In the past, DNA evidence was usually collected only in violent crimes. In fact, the FBI laboratory does not accept cases involving property crimes such as theft, fraud, burglary and automobile theft unless the cases involve more than $100,000. Part of the reason is that an average DNA case costs approximately $2,000 in forensic science, analytical time and supplies. However, law enforcement agencies nationwide are beginning to recognize the value of using DNA technology to solve high-volume property crimes, such as burglary, despite the cost of such analysis (Wilson et al., 2010). "Property crime offenders have a high recidivism rate, and people who commit burglary often graduate to more serious offenses. Analysis of DNA evidence for property crime could ultimately reduce the incidence of more violent crimes in the future" (Geoghegan, 2009, p.50).

Several National Institute of Justice (NIJ) projects demonstrate that analyzing DNA from property crimes can be extraordinarily useful and can have major public safety benefits. For example, one study that compared burglary investigations using traditional methods, including fingerprint analysis, to burglary investigations that added DNA technology to traditional methods found, "When DNA was added to the investigations, suspects were identified more than 2½ times more frequently than when traditional investigative methods only were used. Arrest and prosecution rates were also doubled when DNA was added" (Johns and Rushing, 2009). The Denver (Colorado) DNA Burglary Project led to the arrest and conviction of more than 95 serial burglars and resulted in a 26 percent drop in the city's burglary rate, demonstrating that DNA evidence can keep repeat offenders off the streets and save communities money: "Cases built on DNA evidence had a 42% higher prosecution filing rate; an increase in prison time done by offenders apprehended through DNA evidence; and a total annual savings of more than $29 million" (Geoghegan, 2009, p.52).

Identifying, Collecting and Preserving DNA Evidence.
Considering the potential value of DNA evidence in a criminal case, investigators must understand and be trained in proper identification, collection and preservation procedures for this type of evidence. Table 5.2 lists possible items of crime scene evidence on which DNA might be located.

TABLE 5.2 **Identifying DNA Evidence**

Evidence	Possible Location of DNA on the Evidence	Source of DNA
Baseball bat	Handle, end	Sweat, skin, blood, tissue
Hat, bandanna or mask	Inside	Sweat, hair, dandruff
Eyeglasses	Nose or ear pieces, lens	Sweat, skin
Toothpick	Tips	Saliva
Tape or ligature	Inside/outside surface	Skin, sweat
Bottle, can or glass	Sides, mouthpiece	Saliva, sweat
"Through and through" bullet	Outside surface	Blood, tissue
Bite mark	Individual's skin or clothing	Saliva
Fingernail, partial fingernail	Scrapings	Blood, sweat, tissue
Used cigarette	Cigarette butt	Saliva

Source: U.S. Department of Justice, National Institute of Justice, National Commission on the Future of DNA Evidence, *What Every Law Enforcement Officer Should Know about DNA Evidence*, Washington, DC, 1999. (Old, but still used and available online.)

Laska (2007, p.40) points out, "DNA is a tool available to every officer. Collection is simple to conduct. The supplies are inexpensive. Processing time in the field is minimal. Standards are easily obtained. By recognizing contamination issues and the needs and status of the lab, a patrol officer can ensure samples are used to their highest potential." An example of the ease of collection is seen where a suspect agrees to provide a DNA sample and the officer performs a simple buccal swab of the suspect's mouth to obtain a saliva sample (Longa, 2008). Sterile, cotton-tipped applicator swabs, which are inexpensive, easily obtained and easy to carry and store, are used to collect four DNA samples by rubbing the inside surfaces of the cheeks thoroughly and then air-drying the swabs and placing them back into the original paper packaging or an envelope with sealed corners. Plastic containers should not be used, as they can retain moisture that may damage the integrity of the DNA sample (Waggoner, 2007, pp.96–97).

The NIJ offers guidelines to help investigators avoid contaminating DNA evidence (U.S. Department of Justice, 1999):

■ Wear gloves, and change them often.

■ Use disposable instruments or clean them thoroughly before and after handling each sample.

■ Avoid touching the area where you believe DNA may exist.

■ Avoid talking, sneezing and coughing over evidence.

■ Avoid touching your face, nose and mouth when collecting and packaging evidence.

■ Air-dry evidence thoroughly before packaging.

■ Put evidence into new paper bags or envelopes, not into plastic bags, and never use staples.

Guidelines for collecting and preserving DNA evidence are provided in Table 5.3.

Investigators should be aware that of the various forms of DNA evidence that may exist at a crime scene—blood, oral/saliva, worn (such as skin cells left on a hat brim or shirt collar) and touch—some types are more valuable than others when it comes to helping identify an offender: "Blood and saliva samples are significantly more likely to yield usable profiles when compared with samples consisting of cells from items that were touched or handled. . . . Whenever possible, evidence collectors would be well served to collect whole items rather than swab the evidence item for DNA, a practice that maximizes the probability of obtaining a DNA profile. For instance, items such as soda cans can be used to search for multiple types of DNA evidence (touch samples and cells left on the mouthpiece of the can) as well as for fingerprinting" (Roman et al., 2008, p.44)

In some cases, DNA analysis has been rendered worthless by the defense's successful attack on the methods used to collect and store the evidence on which DNA analysis was performed. For example, in the O. J. Simpson double-murder trial, jurors disregarded DNA matches after questions were raised about how blood samples were collected, preserved and examined.

DNA Testing. Because of the expense and time involved, three criteria must usually be met for a lab to accept DNA samples:

■ Sufficient material must be submitted.

■ Samples (exemplars) must be submitted from both the suspect and the victim.

■ The evidence must be probative.

TABLE 5.3 Collecting Evidence for DNA Analysis

DNA Collection and Analysis	DNA Sample Type	Collection Method	Proper Packaging and Storage of DNA Evidence	Investigation/ Disposition
Unknown or Questionable Samples	Any biological sample including liquid or dried blood, liquid or dried saliva, liquid or dried semen, on almost all surfaces; genital/ vaginal/cervical/ rectal/anal swabs; penile swabs, skin/tissue; fingernails; hair (head and pubic); skin cells on items such as cups, cigarettes, clothing; and liquid urine.	Liquid samples require about 3 drops; 1 cc or 1 ml. Swabbed samples require 2 swabs. Dried or stained samples must be about the size of a quarter or a dime. Other types are unpredictable because of variables such as age and concentration.	Wet samples should be dried if possible before collected to avoid bacterial contamination. If samples are collected wet, use items such as glass vials or plastic air-tight bags until the items can be brought to an area where they can be dried for a sample. Dried samples should be collected in paper bags and kept free of moisture. The evidence should be sealed and signed by the collector. Proper evidence chain of custody and forms should be completed as well.	DNA evidence should be submitted for forensic analysis to the responsible investigating agency. The results of the evidence dictate the follow-up of the investigation and whether or not the evidence needs to be kept or destroyed.
Unidentified Individual	Blood, buccal (oral) swabs, hairs, bone, teeth, fingernails, skin, muscle and tissue from internal organs.	Liquid samples require about 3 drops; 1 cc or 1 ml. Swabbed samples require 2 swabs. Dried or stained samples must be about the size of a quarter or a dime. Other types are unpredictable because of variables such as age and concentration.	Wet samples should be dried if possible before collected to avoid bacterial contamination. If samples are collected wet, use items such as glass vials or plastic air-tight bags until the items can be brought to an area where they can be dried for a sample. Dried samples should be collected in paper bags and kept free of moisture. The evidence should be sealed and signed by the collector. Proper evidence chain of custody and forms should be completed as well.	DNA evidence should be submitted for forensic analysis to the responsible investigating agency. The results of the evidence dictate the follow-up of the investigation and whether or not the evidence needs to be kept or destroyed.

(continued)

TABLE 5.3 *(continued)*

DNA Collection and Analysis	DNA Sample Type	Collection Method	Proper Packaging and Storage of DNA Evidence	Investigation/ Disposition
Known Sample/ Identified Individual	Blood, buccal (oral) swabs, hair (head and pubic).	Liquid samples require about 3 drops; 1 cc or 1 ml. Swabbed samples require 2 swabs.	Wet samples should be dried if possible before collected to avoid bacterial contamination. If samples are collected wet, use items such as glass vials or plastic airtight bags until the items can be brought to an area where they can be dried for a sample. Dried samples should be collected in paper bags and kept free of moisture. The evidence should be sealed and signed by the collector. Proper evidence chain of custody and forms should be completed as well.	DNA evidence should be submitted for forensic analysis to the responsible investigating agency. The results of the evidence dictate the follow-up of the investigation and whether or not the evidence needs to be kept or destroyed.
No Conventional Reference Sample	Soiled clothing with deposited biological fluids including woman's underwear, blood, saliva and semen stained items. Other clothing that has had contact with skin cell transfer such as a shirt collar, hat or waistband. Bedding with biological stains or skin cell transfer, fingernail clippings, hair, cigarettes, toothbrushes, razors, combs, discarded tissues, gum, used condoms, feminine products, teeth.	Liquid samples require about 3 drops; 1 cc or 1 ml. Swabbed samples require 2 swabs. Dried or stained samples must be about the size of a quarter or a dime.	Wet samples should be dried if possible before collected to avoid bacterial contamination. If samples are collected wet, use items such as glass vials or plastic airtight bags until the items can be brought to an area where they can be dried for a sample. Dried samples should be collected in paper bags and kept free of moisture. The evidence should be sealed and signed by the collector. Proper evidence chain of custody and forms should be completed as well.	These samples are considered when samples are taken from reluctant individuals or those that are unavailable. The same investigation and disposition should be executed.

TABLE 5.3 *(continued)*

DNA Collection and Analysis	DNA Sample Type	Collection Method	Proper Packaging and Storage of DNA Evidence	Investigation/ Disposition
Known Transfused Sample	Liquid blood or stains on materials such as clothing or bedding. Oral, genital, rectal/anal swabs and other items listed above depending on the investigation.	Liquid samples require about 3 drops; 1 cc or 1 ml. Swabbed samples require 2 swabs. Dried or stained samples must be about the size of a quarter or a dime.	Wet samples should be dried if possible before collected to avoid bacterial contamination. If samples are collected wet, use items such as glass vials or plastic airtight bags until the items can be brought to an area where they can be dried for a sample. Dried samples should be collected in paper bags and kept free of moisture. The evidence should be sealed and signed by the collector. Proper evidence chain of custody and forms should be completed as well.	These samples are considered after a victim has received a transfusion shortly before a blood sample is provided (such as in a homicide). The DNA analysis may identify the presence of more than one DNA. Typically the predominant DNA type is the result, but a combination of other DNA samples might be required for definitive results. The same investigation and disposition should be executed.
Relatives for Testing	Buccal swab, blood, tissue. These samples are typically taken from relatives for DNA comparison of samples taken from another category.	Liquid samples require about 3 drops; 1 cc or 1 ml. Swabbed samples require 2 swabs.	Wet samples should be dried if possible before collected to avoid bacterial contamination. If samples are collected wet, use items such as glass vials or plastic airtight bags until the items can be brought to an area where they can be dried for a sample. Dried samples should be collected in paper bags and kept free of moisture. The evidence should be sealed and signed by the collector. Proper evidence chain of custody and forms should be completed as well.	These samples are considered in cases such as identifying a body of a missing person. A person inherits DNA from each parent. It is common and possible to use DNA collected from relatives as reference samples. This comparison can establish a biological relationship with the family of a victim. The same investigation and disposition should be executed.

(continued)

TABLE 5.3 (*continued*)

DNA Collection and Analysis	DNA Sample Type	Collection Method	Proper Packaging and Storage of DNA Evidence	Investigation/ Disposition
Paternity/ Maternity Testing	Aborted fetal tissue, buccal swab, blood, tissue.	This form of collection would be done by a medical doctor, forensic pathologist or private organization, not law enforcement.	These samples would be packaged and stored in a laboratory or medical facility.	These samples are considered to determine the paternity or maternity of a fetus or child. This might be evidence used in sexual assault cases and incest cases that are criminal. If it is criminal, the investigation and disposition should be executed as cited earlier.

Source: Henry L. Cho, Cho Research & Consulting, LLC (2011)

The FBI's *Handbook of Forensic Services* (Waggoner, 2007, p.34) explains the types of DNA used in DNA analysis:

There are two types of DNA used in forensic analyses. Nuclear DNA (nDNA) is the more discriminating of the two types and is typically analyzed in evidence containing blood, semen, saliva, body tissues and hairs that have tissue at their root ends. The power of nDNA testing done by the DNA Analysis Unit lies in its ability to potentially identify an individual as being the source of the DNA obtained from an evidence item in a reasonable degree of scientific certainty, as well as the definitive power of exclusion.

Mitochondrial DNA (mtDNA) is typically analyzed in evidence containing naturally shed hairs, hair fragments, bones and teeth. Typically, these items contain low concentrations of degraded DNA, making them unsuitable for nDNA examinations. The high sensitivity of mtDNA analysis allows scientists to obtain information from old items of evidence associated with cold cases, samples from mass disasters and small pieces of evidence containing little biological material.

Different methods of DNA analysis are available, but most crime labs' typing systems use the polymerase chain reaction (PCR), duplicating short segments of DNA. The short pieces of DNA that PCR targets are areas where the genetic code repeats, called short tandem repeats (STRs) (Geberth, 2010a). Each human chromosome contains hundreds of different types of STRs, with the number of repeats on each chromosome varying greatly among individuals. This variation creates a genetic uniqueness for every person that DNA analysts are able to profile.

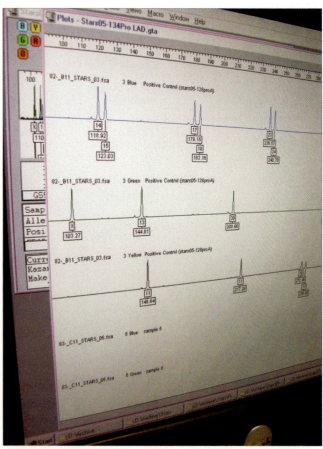

The polymerase chain reaction (PCR) technique known as the short tandem repeat (STR) DNA method. STRs are genetic markers that vary in size among individuals and are very discriminating for single-source samples, meaning they can be used to determine with 99.999% certainty that a specific DNA sample came from a particular individual.
© Joel Gordon

Before PCR, the dominant technique for DNA analysis was restriction fragment length polymorphism (RFLP, pronounced *riff-lip*). Although many labs still use this method, a significant shortcoming is that it requires a large amount of intact DNA, whereas PCR needs only a tiny amount of DNA, even if degraded.

Another extremely useful forensic DNA analysis method examines a genetic marker called a single nucleotide polymorphism (SNP, pronounced *snip*) (Figure 5.5). A SNP is a one-base difference in the DNA sequence between individuals. Advancements continue to be made in DNA testing. The National Institute of Standards and Technology has developed a quality assurance standards kit for DNA typing that laboratories can use to assess the accuracy of their DNA testing procedures within a narrow margin of error.

body. A new technique called Y-STR analysis is being used in such cases (Prime and Newman):

> The Y chromosome is a male-specific identifier, and typing techniques are now available that develop profiles specific to the male contributor of the DNA. The advantage of this test is in its high level of sensitivity; the test is able to generate a profile of a male perpetrator in the presence of DNA from a female contributor.
>
> A limitation of Y-STR analysis is that the DNA profile obtained will be identical for all males within the same paternal lineage (i.e., the father's profile will be the same as that of his son, whose profile will also match that of his grandfather on his father's side, and so on).

Technology Innovations

Prime and Newman (2007, p.34) note, "One of the difficulties associated with DNA analysis is that if a sample contains DNA from more than one individual (known as a mixed profile), the profiles cannot be easily separated, reducing the overall success of the testing." They give as a common example a mixed profile obtained in a sexual offense in which semen is recovered from a woman's

DNA Databases. In October 1998, under the authority of the DNA Identification Act of 1994, the FBI activated a database called the National DNA Index System (NDIS) in an effort to establish a national DNA index for law enforcement purposes. In 1990, the FBI Laboratory launched a pilot project called the Combined DNA Index System (CODIS), which blended forensic science and computer technology to help solve violent crimes. CODIS created a distributed database with three hierarchical tiers—local, state and national—enabling participating laboratories to exchange and compare DNA

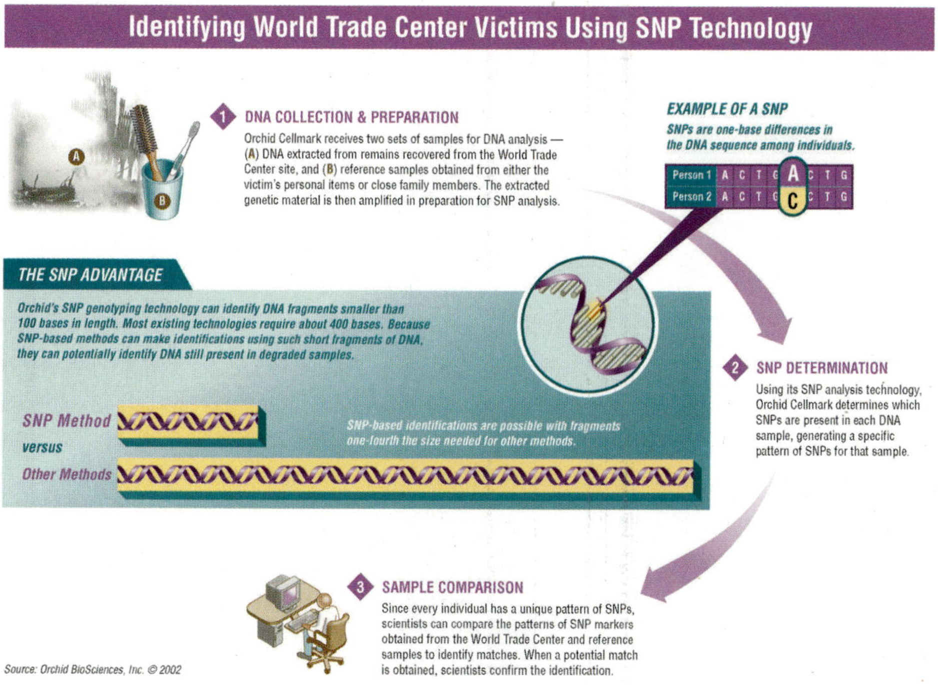

Identifying World Trade Center Victims Using SNP Technology

1 DNA COLLECTION & PREPARATION
Orchid Cellmark receives two sets of samples for DNA analysis — (A) DNA extracted from remains recovered from the World Trade Center site, and (B) reference samples obtained from either the victim's personal items or close family members. The extracted genetic material is then amplified in preparation for SNP analysis.

EXAMPLE OF A SNP
SNPs are one-base differences in the DNA sequence among individuals.

Person 1 A C T G A C T G
Person 2 A C T G C C T G

THE SNP ADVANTAGE
Orchid's SNP genotyping technology can identify DNA fragments smaller than 100 bases in length. Most existing technologies require about 400 bases. Because SNP-based methods can make identifications using such short fragments of DNA, they can potentially identify DNA still present in degraded samples.

SNP Method
versus
Other Methods

SNP-based identifications are possible with fragments one-fourth the size needed for other methods.

2 SNP DETERMINATION
Using its SNP analysis technology, Orchid Cellmark determines which SNPs are present in each DNA sample, generating a specific pattern of SNPs for that sample.

3 SAMPLE COMPARISON
Since every individual has a unique pattern of SNPs, scientists can compare the patterns of SNP markers obtained from the World Trade Center and reference samples to identify matches. When a potential match is obtained, scientists confirm the identification.

Source: Orchid BioSciences, Inc. © 2002

FIGURE 5.5
DNA profiling process.
Source: Courtesy of Orchid Cellmark Inc.

profiles electronically. DNA profiles are generated at the local level (LDIS) and then flow to the state (SDIS) and national (NDIS) levels. NDIS is at the top of the CODIS hierarchy. When CODIS was first implemented, it served 14 state and local laboratories. It has since grown to serve more than 180 public law enforcement laboratories across the United States and, internationally, more than 60 law enforcement laboratories in over 30 countries ("CODIS Brochure," 2011).

The CODIS database is organized into two indexes: the forensic and offender indexes. The *forensic index* contains DNA profiles from crime scene evidence where the offender's identity is unknown. The *offender index* contains DNA profiles of individuals convicted of sex offenses and other violent crimes. Investigators can submit biological evidence from a crime scene to CODIS and cross-check it against existing profiles, generating investigative leads and making links between crimes and offenders. As with IAFIS and fingerprint searches, all DNA hits identified by CODIS must be subsequently validated as a match by a qualified DNA analyst.

By March 2011 the NDIS forensic index contained 366,762 profiles, and the convicted offender index contained 9,535,059 profiles, an increase of more than 4 million offender profiles since year-end 2007 ("CODIS—NDIS Statistics," 2011). However, many more profiles could, and should, be added to CODIS if the enormous backlog of untested DNA evidence were addressed.

Backlog of DNA Awaiting Testing.
McGhee (2008) observes, "Throughout the country, DNA tests that could pave the way to jailing violent predators are routinely delayed, sometimes for years, because of staffing and funding constraints of crime labs and increasing numbers of convicts being tested." Although crime laboratories have made great strides to increase their capacity to process samples, they continue to accumulate a backlog because the demand for DNA analysis continues to outpace existing capacity: "A nationwide sample of more than 2,000 agencies found that in 2007, 14 percent of unsolved homicide cases (an estimated 3,975 cases) and 18 percent of unsolved rape cases (an estimated 27,595 cases) contained forensic evidence that was not submitted by law enforcement agencies to a crime laboratory for analysis" (Nelson, 2011, p.5). Nationally, the year-end backlog of offender DNA samples has increased steadily, from 657,166 in 2007, to 793,852 in 2008, to 952,393 in 2009 (Nelson, 2011, p.8).

Admissibility in Court.
Spagnoli (2007, p.42) asserts, "Today a DNA match is virtually undisputable in court. DNA can identify a criminal with near absolute certainty or exonerate innocent suspects." Ivy and Orput (2007, p.30), likewise, note, "Be it chromosomal DNA evidence from a cell's nucleus (PCR-STR DNA) or chromosomal evidence taken from a cell's cytoplasm outside the nucleus (mitochondrial DNA), DNA evidence has tremendous potential value for proving crimes beyond a reasonable doubt at trial."

According to Prime and Newman (2007, p.35), "Through partnerships between police and scientists, DNA analysis will continue to be regarded as the standard of excellence for the development of impartial, unbiased scientific evidence in the support of the justice system."

Preeminent forensic scientist Henry C. Lee examines a DNA profile. Such profiles are entered into state and national databases to help solve a variety of crimes.
© AP Images/Steve Miller

However, the potential for human error and contamination is a critical factor in determining DNA evidence's admissibility in court.

Exoneration of Incarcerated Individuals through DNA Evidence.
Moore (2007) states, "State lawmakers across the country are adopting broad changes in criminal justice procedures as a response to the exoneration of more than 200 convicts through the use of DNA evidence. . . . Nationwide, misidentification by witnesses led to wrongful convictions in 75 percent of the 207 instances in which prisoners have been exonerated over the last decade, according to the Innocence Project, a group in New York that investigates wrongful convictions."

In the first appeal from a finding of guilty, the Virginia State Supreme Court upheld the conviction and death sentence of Timothy Spencer in the rape and murder of two women, holding that DNA test results were reliable. Another man who served more than two decades in prison for the rape and murder of two children had his convictions thrown out after an advanced DNA test showed that a neighbor may have been responsible for the crimes (Gold, 2007).

Moral and Ethical Issues.
Prime and Newman (2007, p.34) note, "Some of the challenges for the future will test the balance between the needs of the law enforcement community and the public's interest in preserving its own civil liberties. Techniques are currently under development that will enable the prediction of some physical traits through DNA analysis, providing police with a potential genetic 'eyewitness.' In addition, databanks are being used to identify perpetrators through kinship relationships to relatives whose profiles may already be included in a DNA databank; this use of the technology is raising moral and ethical questions about such applications." For example, when police in Wichita, Kansas, were unable to obtain a DNA sample from Denis Rader to confirm he was the murderer known as BTK (Bind, Torture, Kill), they used instead Rader's daughter's DNA—left at a hospital after a doctor appointment—to make a familial match (Shapiro, 2007).

Another controversial development in the use of DNA evidence is the sampling of people not yet convicted of a crime but who have been arrested and are awaiting trial. Such pre-conviction DNA sampling is generally done at the same time fingerprints are taken and involves a simple buccal swab of an arrestee. As of April 2011, 24 states had passed laws requiring DNA collection from certain felony arrestees, and many other states were considering such legislation (DNA Saves, 2011). The DNA Fingerprint Act of 2005 requires that, effective January 1, 2009, a DNA sample be collected from any adult arrested for a federal crime. This Act also mandates the DNA collection from individuals detained under the authority of the United States who are not U.S. citizens or are not lawfully in the country (Berson, 2009, p.10). Federal law, however, requires states to expunge such DNA samples if an arrestee is found not guilty or is never prosecuted (Garrett, 2009b).

Several studies have demonstrated that collecting DNA upon arrest can save lives, money and time by identifying repeat offenders earlier, before they continue a protracted pattern of crime (Wallentine, 2010). A study by the Denver, Colorado, District Attorney's Office examined the criminal history of five defendants and concluded that DNA collection upon arrest of these prolific offenders would have prevented 3 murders, 18 sexual assaults, 1 attempted sexual assault, 7 kidnappings, 4 robberies, 3 felony assaults and 11 home invasions during the study period (Wallentine, 2010).

Blood and Other Body Fluids

Blood is frequently analyzed for DNA, but it and other body fluids such as semen and urine can also provide other valuable evidence to investigators. Blood assists in establishing that a violent crime was committed, in re-creating the movements of a suspect or victim and in eliminating suspects. Body fluids can be found on a suspect's or victim's clothing, on the floor or walls, on furniture and on other objects. Some body fluids, such as semen and saliva, may be difficult to detect but, given their natural fluorescent property, will become visible under a variety of FLSs.

Blood is important as evidence in crimes of violence. Heelprints of shoes in blood splashes may be identifiable apart from the blood analysis. It is important to test the stain or sample to determine whether it is, in fact, human blood. In addition, because blood is so highly visible and recognizable, those who commit violent crimes usually attempt to remove blood from items. A number of reagents—including luminol, tetramethyl benzedrine and phenolphthalein—can identify blood at a crime scene, and because crime laboratories are swamped with evidence to examine, such preliminary on-scene testing is important.

Luminol, for example, is an easy-to-apply water-based solution sprayed from a pump bottle over an area where blood traces are suspected. Luminol causes blood to fluoresce a pale blue color and can detect blood that has been diluted as much as 10,000 times. Another benefit to using luminol is that it does not harm DNA in blood, thus allowing the blood to be collected for further analysis. However, luminol can give false positive reactions and is only a presumptive positive test for blood. Luminol also reacts with bleach products and some metals or strong

Investigators use luminol to look for the possible presence of blood at a crime scene. Even if blood has been cleaned up, enough can remain that when the chemicals in luminol come into contact with the hemoglobin in the blood traces, a light-producing chemical reaction takes place. Investigators using luminol will try to make the crime scene as dark as possible so that the glow of the reaction can illuminate patterns, footprints or possibly traces of blood in unsuspected places. This crime-scene investigator is wearing specialized gear recommended when luminol is used.
© Spencer Grant/PhotoEdit

oxidizing agents. Consequently, if a surface was cleaned with bleach, it might react when sprayed with luminol.

Bloodstains and spatter patterns are useful evidence because they are characteristics of certain physical forces and can help investigators determine how a criminal event played out. With a sufficient quantity of bloodstain evidence at a crime scene, investigators can determine the location of people or objects at a crime scene; the movement of people or objects within the scene; areas of origin of bloodshed; type(s) of weapon(s) used and force levels involved; the minimum number of blows, shots or events; and whether the suspect may have been injured. Furthermore, blood-spatter patterns can help to determine a suspect's truthfulness. In many cases, suspects have claimed a death was accidental, but the location and angle of blood-spatter patterns refuted their statements.

Some blood evidence is easier to interpret than others: "Bloodstain pattern analysis can range from the simple to the complex. The trails of blood in a crime scene or cast-off blood patterns are reasonably straightforward and understandable. Determining areas of convergence and origin employing string methods or trigonometric methodologies are more complex and call for a trained specialist" (Geberth, 2007, p.38).

As a general rule, the greater the amount of force applied to the source, the smaller the drops will be. In other words, as the force increases, the drop size decreases. Force levels are broken into three categories. The low velocity level produces drops of blood. Medium velocity spatter produces bloodstains 4 mm to 6 mm in diameter or larger. High velocity force produces a mist or spray-type pattern. Investigators or technicians must accurately measure, record and photograph blood spatters at a crime

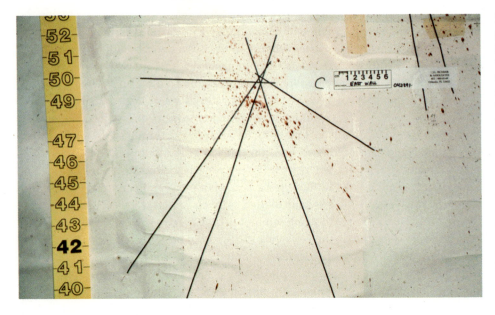

Blood pattern analysis can help investigators determine where the blood originated; the distance from there to where the blood came to rest; the type and direction of impact creating the bloodstains; the type of object producing them; and the position of the victim and the assailant during and after the bloodshed. Generally, the smaller the size of the blood spatters, the greater the energy used to create them. This blood spatter was the result of a beating and is an example of a medium-velocity event. The various measurements made by the investigators show the technique of examining the pattern to determine the area of convergence before calculating the area of origin.
Source: Lakewood Police Department Crime Lab

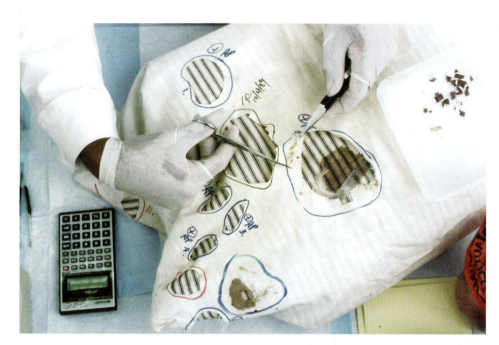

A laboratory technician recovers samples from a bloodstained pillow found at a crime scene. These samples can be used for DNA testing against blood drawn from a suspect. Good conservation of samples is the only condition required for DNA tests to be reliable, even after a long time.

© Stephen Ferry/Liaison/Getty Images

scene to allow proper interpretation of the spatter data by expert bloodstain analysts.

Bloodstain pattern software has been a mainstay of criminal forensic analysis for several decades and has made bloodstain analysis faster, easier and more accurate. Some programs can calculate bloodstain measurements for point of origin, letting investigators know, for example, where a gunshot victim stood. Computer software is also available that takes bloodstain pattern data and converts them into a 3-D model of the crime scene, helping investigators reconstruct specific spatial and sequential events that occurred before and during the act of bloodshed.

Collect *liquid* blood with an eyedropper and put it in a test tube. Write the subject's name and other pertinent information on medical tape applied to the outside. Send by air express, priority mail or registered mail. Scrape *dry* blood flakes into a pillbox or envelope, identified in the same way. Mark bloodstained clothing with a string tag or directly on the clothing. If the bloodstain is moist, air-dry the clothing or use an evidence drying chamber before packing.

> Blood can be identified as animal or human and is most useful in eliminating suspects. Age and race cannot be determined from blood samples, but DNA analysis can provide positive identification.

In some cases, blood, without DNA analysis having been performed on it, can help to infer race—for example, sickle-shaped red blood cells occur primarily in African Americans.

Scent

A type of evidence that does not receive much attention is scent evidence. Every person has a unique scent, which cannot be masked or eliminated, not even by the most potent perfume. A person's scent profile is the combination of sweat, oils and gases his or her body produces. These smells, along with the skin cells everybody constantly sheds, are detectable to specially trained scent-discriminating dogs. Scents can also be categorized as primary and secondary. For example, in a child abduction case, a dog was given a shirt of the missing girl as the scent article and tracked this primary scent to the location of her body in a field. At this point, the investigators held off going to her body right away to allow the dog to refocus on the secondary scent of the abductor. However, if officers, search volunteers, parents or any other person comes in contact with the victim, the scene becomes scent-contaminated and a valuable opportunity to track the perpetrator's secondary scent is lost.

Scent evidence can also be collected by placing a sterile gauze pad on another item of evidence. A Scent Transfer Unit uses a vacuum system to trap the scent on the gauze. If no scent article is available, the unit can be put in a closed room to vacuum the air for five minutes to try to capture a scent. These scent pads can be presented to a tracking dog or placed in a freezer for preservation.

Hairs and Fibers

Hairs and fibers are often difficult to locate without a careful search and strong lighting. FLSs are commonly used to locate hair and fiber evidence in carpets and bedding or on other surfaces. They are valuable evidence because they can place a suspect at a crime scene, especially in violent crimes in which interchange of hairs and fibers is likely to occur. The suspect can also take hairs and fibers from the scene.

Place hairs and fibers found at the crime scene in paper, using a druggist fold, or in a small box. Seal all edges and openings, and identify on the outside. If hairs and fibers are found on an object small enough to send to a laboratory, leave them on the object. Hairs and fibers often adhere to blood, flesh or other materials. If the hairs are visible but are not adhering firmly to the object, record their location in your notes. Then place them in a pillbox or glass vial to send to a laboratory. Do not use plastic.

If you suspect that hairs are on an object, carefully wrap the object and send it intact to a laboratory. Attempt to obtain 25 to 50 full hairs from the appropriate part of the suspect's body for comparison, using a forceps or comb. Document the hair and fiber evidence using special filters, light sources and photomicrographs to reproduce the specimens in black and white or color.

Examining Hair. A hair shaft has a *cuticle* on the outside consisting of overlapping scales that always point toward the tip, a *cortex* consisting of elongated cells, and the *medulla*—the center of the hair—consisting of variably shaped cells. Variations in these structures make comparisons and identifications possible.

A micrograph of a hair sample showing a recent cut. This cross section lets investigators view the three basic layers of a hair shaft: the cuticle, the outer layer of protective scales; the cortex, a second, thicker layer that provides strength to the hair shaft and determines the color and texture of hair; and the medulla, a third, inner layer that is present only in thick, large hairs.

© Clouds Hill Imaging Ltd./Corbis

> Microscopic examination determines whether hair is animal or human. Many characteristics can be determined from human hair: the part of the body it came from; whether it was bleached or dyed, freshly cut, pulled out or burned; and whether there is blood or semen on it. Race, sex and age cannot be determined.

As with blood samples, it is extremely difficult to state that a hair came from a certain person, but it can usually be determined that a hair did *not* come from a certain person. Hair evidence is important because it does not deteriorate and is commonly left at a crime scene without a subject's knowledge. Laboratory examination does not destroy hair evidence as it does many other types of evidence. Hair evidence may be subjected to microscopic examination to determine type (e.g., facial or pubic), to biological examination to determine blood-type group and to toxicological examination to determine the presence of drugs or poisons. Secondary ion mass spectrometry (SIMS) chemicals can distinguish trace hair samples using consumer chemicals as identifiers. Chemicals in hair conditioning products produce distinct chemical signatures, allowing the identification of hair samples. Although chemical colorants and other products commonly applied to hair can thwart microscopic analysis, SIMS is not affected by such substances and can capitalize on their presence to improve identification.

Examining Fibers. Fibers fall into four general groups: mineral, vegetable, animal and synthetic. Mineral fibers most frequently submitted are glass and asbestos. Vegetable fibers include cotton, jute, manila, kapok, hemp and many others. Animal fibers are primarily wool and silk. Synthetics include rayons, polyesters, nylons and others. Each fiber has individual characteristics that can be analyzed chemically.

Fibers are actually more distinguishable than hairs are. Fiber examination can determine a fiber's thickness, the number of fibers per strand and other characteristics that help identify clothing. Fibers can be tested for origin and color. Although often overlooked, fibers are the most frequently located microscopic evidence. They are often found in assaults, homicides and rapes, where personal contact results in an exchange of clothing fibers. Fibers can be found under a suspect's or victim's fingernails. Burglaries can yield fibers at narrow entrance or exit points where clothing becomes snagged. Hit-and-run accidents often yield fibers adhering to vehicles' door handles, grilles, fenders or undercarriages.

Advances in FLSs used to examine evidence have been particularly beneficial in the area of fiber evidence, where often only a strand or two is found.

Shoe and Tire Prints and Impressions

Shoe and tire prints and impressions are common evidence at crime scenes and, if collected, recorded and analyzed properly, can yield valuable investigative data. Shoe footprints, in addition to providing unique wear patterns that can be compared with a suspect's shoes, can indicate whether a person was walking or running, was carrying something heavy or was unfamiliar with the area or unsure of the terrain. Tire marks, which also commonly have unique wear patterns, can show the approximate speed and direction of travel and the manufacturer and year the tires were made. In the July 1999 slaying of a Yosemite Park naturalist, the killer left behind footprints and the distinctive tracks of his vehicle, which had a different brand of tire on every wheel.

If two-dimensional shoe or tire prints are found on paper, cardboard or other surface, photograph them and then submit the originals for laboratory examination. Use latent fingerprint lifters to lift shoe and tire tread impressions from smooth surfaces. Photograph with and without a marker before lifting the impression. Never attempt to fit your shoe into or on top of the suspect's shoe print to determine size. This can destroy the shoe print and contaminate the evidence.

Regarding two-dimensional tire prints, unless the actual impression occurs on material small enough to be submitted to the lab, the only way to collect the evidence is to photograph the length of the impression with a long scale adjacent to it.

Shoes and boots can leave distinctive impressions that can be traced to an individual's personal possessions. Manufacturers can provide photographs of their specific lines of shoes and boots that can be compared with photographs taken at the scene.

© County of Westchester, New York. Used with Permission.

A relatively new technique in preserving shoe impression evidence involves a device called an electrostatic dust print lifter (EDPL). EDPL is used on dry-origin shoe impressions, which involve the transfer of dry residue on a shoe tread to another dry surface, such as a carpet or seat cushion. These impressions are very fragile and among the most difficult to locate. The lift must then be photographed before it can be analyzed, as the lift itself is extremely fragile.

Three-dimensional shoe and tire impressions should be photographed and then cast. When photographing shoe impressions in snow, mud, sand or other substrate, it is imperative to use the proper scale in the proper plane, meaning the ruler should be level with the bottom of the impression, not placed next to the impression on the top of the snow or soil surface: "Footwear examiners require 1:1, or life-sized, photographs of the impression to conduct a comparison with the known shoe. The distortion created by the placement of the scale above the impression may make this task very difficult, if not impossible" (Adair, 2009, p.18). Also, when placing the scale next to and level with the bottom of the impression, take care not to allow snow or soil to fall into the impression.

> **After photographing, cast shoe or tire tread impressions found in dirt, sand or snow.**

To **cast** is to make an impression. The word also refers to the impression that results. Some departments use plaster, whereas others prefer dental casting material because of its strength and durability and because it needs no reinforcement. Premeasured-mix kits are also available. The steps in making a plaster cast of a soil impression are these:

1. Build a retaining frame around the impression about two inches from its edges.

2. Coat the impression with five or six layers of alcohol and shellac or inexpensive hairspray, allowing each coat to dry before applying the next. Apply talcum powder to the last layer so the spray can easily be removed from the cast.

3. Rapidly mix the plaster following directions on the box.

4. Pour the plaster into the impression, using a spatula to cushion its fall and guide it into all areas of the impression. Fill the impression halfway.

5. Add wire or gauze to reinforce the impression.

6. Pour in more plaster until it overflows to the retaining frame.

7. Before the cast hardens, use a pencil or other pointed instrument to incise your initials, the case number and the date on the back of the impression.

8. After the cast hardens, remove it and the retaining frame. Do not wash the cast; the laboratory does this.

9. Carefully wrap the cast in protective material to avoid breakage, and place it in a strong box to ship to the laboratory.

Investigators must be aware that the typical techniques used to cast in soil or sand may actually damage impressions in snow. Making a "dry cast" of an impression in snow requires particular attention to the moisture content of the casting material (too wet will collapse the fragile snow impressions) and allowing time for the dental stone powder to cool after mixing it with water, as this material heats up during the curing process. Pouring the casting material into the impression too soon will melt impression details (Adair, 2009). Once the cast is cured (the colder the temperature, the longer it takes to cure), lift it gently, place it in a safe storage container with the impression side up, and allow it to dry completely (usually about 24 hours) before packaging it to send to the laboratory.

The laboratory compares the cast with manufacturers' shoe and tire tread files. Several databases are available to help in the identification of shoe and tire prints. Crimeshoe.com is an inexpensive online resource containing details of more than 25,000 shoes and is continuously updated every season with new models of sport, work and casual footwear. SoleMate is another footwear database containing information—manufacturer, date of market release, an image or offset print of the sole and pictorial images of the uppers—for more than 24,000 sport, work and casual shoes. SoleMate is sold on DVD and updated and distributed to subscribers every 3 months. Similarly, TreadMate is a reference collection containing details of more than 8,500 vehicle tires.

Bite Marks

Bite mark identification is based on the "supposed" individuality of teeth and is legally admissible in court, having endured a number of legal challenges (Page, 2007a). Bites may occur during commission of a violent crime, inflicted by either the victim or the perpetrator, and the marks left behind can be collected as evidence. Bite marks may also be found in partially eaten food or other objects that had been placed inside a person's mouth. If the impression is visible, photograph it and then swab the bite area for saliva, blood residue, DNA and microorganisms. Then cast it in the same way as shoe and tire tread impressions. Dental impression material is again preferred because of its fine texture.

A forensic latent impressions examiner compares the shoe cast from a crime scene with a possible match.
© AP Images/The Livingston Enterprise, Ryan Sones

If a bite mark is too shallow to cast, photograph it and then "lift" it by placing tape over it and then transferring the tape to plastic to see the outline of the mark. FLSs help locate bite marks that are not visible. Again, once illuminated, photograph the bite marks.

Investigators may need to enlist the services of a forensic odontologist to examine tooth-related evidence (Jetmore, 2007).

Tools and Tool Marks

Common tools such as hammers and screwdrivers are often used in crimes and cause little suspicion if found in someone's possession. Such tools are often found in a suspect's vehicle, on the person or at the residence. If a tool is found at a crime scene, determine whether it belongs to the property owner. Broken tool pieces may be found at a crime scene, on a suspect or on a suspect's property.

Identify each suspect tool with a string tag, wrap it separately and pack it in a strong box for transport to the laboratory.

A **tool mark** is an impression left by a tool on a surface. For example, a screwdriver forced between a window and a sill may leave a mark the same depth and width as the screwdriver. The resiliency of the surface may cause explainable differences in mark dimensions and tool dimensions. If the screwdriver has a chipped head or other imperfections, it will leave impressions for later comparison. Tool marks are often found in burglaries, auto thefts and larcenies in which objects are forced open.

A tool mark provides leads to the size and type of tool that made it. Examining a suspect tool determines, within limits, whether it could have made the mark in question. Even if you find a suspect tool, it is not always possible to match it to the tool mark, especially if the tool was damaged when the mark was made. However, residue from the forced surface may adhere to the tool, making a comparison possible.

Do not attempt to fit a suspected tool into a mark to see if it matches. This disturbs the mark, as well as any paint or other trace evidence on the suspect tool, making the tool inadmissible as evidence.

 Photograph tool marks and then either cast them or send the object on which they appear to a laboratory.

First, take mid-range photographs documenting the location of the tool or tool mark within the general crime scene. Then take close-ups first without and then with a marker to show actual size and detail.

After photographing tool marks, cast them. Casting of tool marks presents special problems because tool marks often are not on a horizontal surface. In such cases, construct a platform or bridge around the mark by taping tin or other pliable material to the surface. Plaster of Paris, plasticine and waxes do not provide the detail necessary for tool striation marks. Better results are obtained from moulage, silicone and other thermosetting materials.

Tool marks are easy to compare if a suspect tool has not been altered or damaged since it made the mark. If the tool is found, send it to the laboratory for several comparison standards.

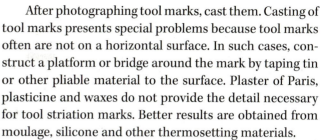 A tool mark is compared with a standard-of-comparison impression rather than with the tool itself.

The material used for the standard is as close as possible to the original material. Ideally, a portion of the original material is used.

The tool mark found at the scene and the standard of comparison are placed under a microscope to make the striation marks appear as light and dark lines. The lines are then adjusted to see whether they match. Variations of approximately 10 degrees in angle are permissible. Roughly 60 percent of the lines should match in the comparison.

A specific mark may be similar to or found in the same relative location as tool marks found at other crimes. Evidence of the way a tool is applied—the angle, amount of pressure and general use—can tie one crime to another. A tool mark also makes it easier to look for a specific type of tool. Possession of, or fingerprints on, such a tool can implicate a suspect.

Tool mark comparison. A cold chisel and a magnified image of the tip of the chisel, showing the imperfections along the working surface. These imperfections are unique to this specific tool. Marks made with this chisel on a test surface can be compared with marks left at a crime scene. If found to be a reasonable match, such evidence can link the person in possession of the tool to the crime.

Courtesy Ventura County Sheriff's Department Forensic Sciences Laboratory

This photomicrograph is a comparison of striated tool marks created using a lateral scraping motion with the tip of a cold chisel. The random imperfections present on the tip of the chisel create a unique, reproducible, three-dimensional contour pattern. The striated tool marks were made in sheet lead. Because the striations made in the test environment line up consistently with those found at the crime scene, this image depicts a positive identification.

Courtesy Ventura County Sheriff's Department Forensic Sciences Laboratory

Firearms and Ammunition

Many violent crimes are committed with a firearm: a revolver, a pistol, a rifle or a shotgun. Each firearm imparts a distinctive fingerprint, or ballistic signature, to every bullet and casing fired through it, which provides useful evidence to investigators. The broad definition of **ballistics** is that it is the study of the dynamics of projectiles, from propulsion through flight to impact; a narrower definition is that it is the study of the functioning of firearms.

The **bore** refers to the inside portion of a weapon's barrel, which is surrounded by raised ridges called *lands* and recessed areas called *grooves*. These lands and grooves comprise the **rifling**, the spiral pattern cut down the entire length of the firearm barrel that grips and spins the bullet as it passes through the bore, providing greater projectile control and accuracy (Figure 5.6). **Caliber** refers to the diameter of the bore as measured between lands, as well as the size of bullet intended for use with a specific weapon. As the bullet rotates through the barrel, it receives highly individualized and characteristic **striations**, or scratches, from the rifling, which provide valuable comparison evidence on recovered bullets. A fired bullet is marked only by the barrel, but a fired cartridge case is marked by several parts of the weapon when it is loaded, fired and extracted.

When collecting a firearm found at a crime scene, do NOT put an object inside the barrel to pick it up. The object may scratch the inside of the barrel, affecting a ballistics test. Include the firearm make, caliber, model, type, serial number and finish, along with any unusual characteristics in your notes.

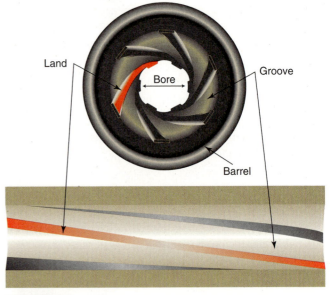

Land
Bore
Groove
Barrel

FIGURE 5.6
Features of a rifled firearm's barrel.
© Cengage Learning, 2013

Examine weapons for latent fingerprints. Photograph weapons and then identify them with string tags. Unload firearms and record their serial numbers on the string tags and in your notes. Label the packing container "Firearms." Identify bullets on the base, cartridges on the outside of the case near the bullet end and cartridge cases on the inside near the open end. Put ammunition in cotton or soft paper and ship to a laboratory. Never send live ammunition through the mail; use a common carrier instead.

A plethora of physical evidence can be obtained from gun-related crimes, including the actual firearms and spent bullets, shell casings, slugs and shot pellets, as well as the fingerprints and DNA often located on these items. Ballistic evidence can help solve a crime even when the weapon is not recovered (Spraggs, 2010).

Gunpowder tests, shot pattern tests and functional tests of a weapon can be made and compared. Defects in weapons acquired through use or neglect often permit positive identification. The rifling of a gun barrel, the gun's ejection and extraction mechanisms and markings made by these mechanisms can also be compared. Class characteristics of a bullet caused by the firearm's barrel can help identify the weapon used. These class characteristics include the number of lands and grooves in the firearm's barrel and their height, width and depth.

Gunshot residue (GSR) is another type of evidence investigators may seek in crimes involving firearms. Whenever a firearm is discharged, the gunpowder and primer combine to form a gaseous cloud or residue, sometimes referred to as a *plume*, that can reach as far as five feet from the weapon. This residue may settle on the hands, sleeves, face and other parts of the shooter, as well as any other object or person within the residue fallout radius. Through various techniques, this residue may be detected and used as evidence.

Laboratory examination of GSR under a scanning electron microscope (SEM) is still considered a reliable analysis method, although enhancements in technology have been necessary to better detect, classify and report on new types of lead-free ammunition (Geberth, 2010c). GSR can be collected by applying adhesive tape to a person's hands or clothing; a technician then runs the sample through an analyzer to locate and identify specific residue particles and their composition.

Shooter identification kits are also available for conducting GSR tests in the field. These kits allow officers to quickly test multiple suspects and may be used by investigators in distinguishing between a suicide and a homicide, with the absence of GSR on a victim indicating homicide and an abundance of GSR suggesting suicide.

As with fingerprints and DNA, a national database of ballistic information has helped investigators link firearms with offenders. Before 2002, the Bureau of Alcohol, Tobacco, Firearms and Explosives (ATF), with the Integrated Ballistics Identification System (IBIS) (originally called

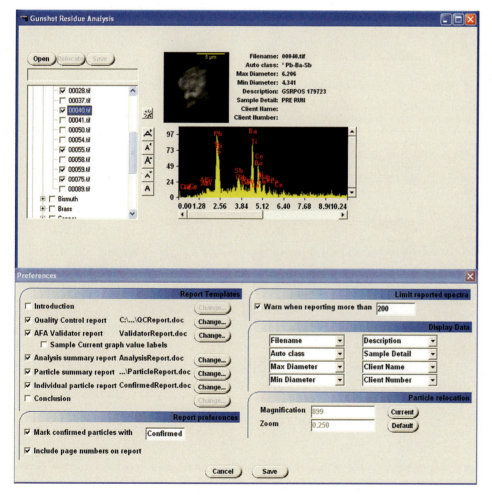

Software allows the automatic analysis of gunshot residue (GSR). This screen capture shows the results of GSR analysis with a scanning electron microscope (SEM, top image) and an X-ray beam (bottom image with spikes). Particles of interest can be isolated and relocated for further analysis.

Courtesy Aspex Corporation

"CeaseFire"), and the FBI, with DrugFire, each collected ballistic data but kept their systems separate, because of incompatibility issues. Realizing the value in and need for a unified ballistic evidence system, the ATF created the National Integrated Ballistic Information Network (NIBIN), a grid that connects IBIS using departments across the country. NIBIN's database is continuously expanding and currently holds more than 1.5 million images of cartridge casings or bullets either recovered from crime scenes or generated from test fires into shoot tanks using recovered firearms (Cramer, 2009). Figure 5.7 illustrates how NIBIN uses ballistic signatures to help investigators solve crimes.

Glass

Glass can have great evidentiary value. Tiny pieces of glass can adhere to a suspect's shoes and clothing. Larger glass fragments are processed for fingerprints and can be fit back together to indicate the direction from which the glass was broken. The source of broken glass fragments also can often be determined.

> Label glass fragments using adhesive tape on each piece. Wrap each piece separately in cotton to avoid chipping, and place them in a strong box marked "Fragile" to send to the laboratory.

Microscopic, spectrographic and physical comparisons are made of the glass fragments. Microscopic examination of the edges of two pieces of glass can prove they were one piece at one time. Spectrographic analysis can determine the elements of the glass, even extremely small fragments. Submit for comparison pieces of glass at least the size of a half-dollar.

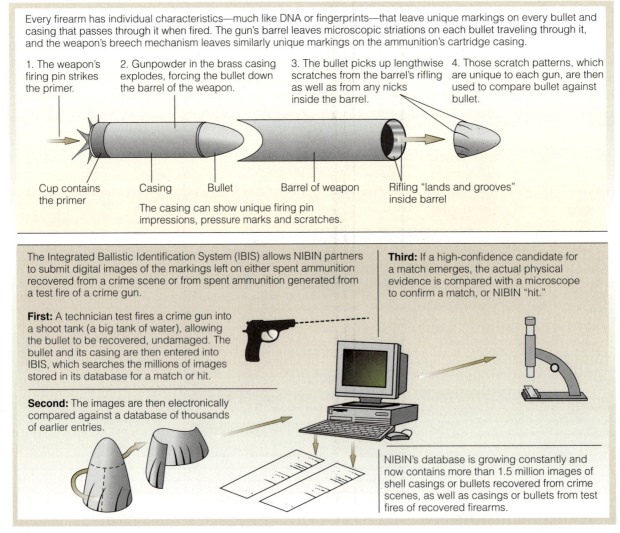

Every firearm has individual characteristics—much like DNA or fingerprints—that leave unique markings on every bullet and casing that passes through it when fired. The gun's barrel leaves microscopic striations on each bullet traveling through it, and the weapon's breech mechanism leaves similarly unique markings on the ammunition's cartridge casing.

1. The weapon's firing pin strikes the primer.

2. Gunpowder in the brass casing explodes, forcing the bullet down the barrel of the weapon.

3. The bullet picks up lengthwise scratches from the barrel's rifling as well as from any nicks inside the barrel.

4. Those scratch patterns, which are unique to each gun, are then used to compare bullet against bullet.

Cup contains the primer

Casing   Bullet

Barrel of weapon

Rifling "lands and grooves" inside barrel

The casing can show unique firing pin impressions, pressure marks and scratches.

The Integrated Ballistic Identification System (IBIS) allows NIBIN partners to submit digital images of the markings left on either spent ammunition recovered from a crime scene or from spent ammunition generated from a test fire of a crime gun.

First: A technician test fires a crime gun into a shoot tank (a big tank of water), allowing the bullet to be recovered, undamaged. The bullet and its casing are then entered into IBIS, which searches the millions of images stored in its database for a match or hit.

Second: The images are then electronically compared against a database of thousands of earlier entries.

Third: If a high-confidence candidate for a match emerges, the actual physical evidence is compared with a microscope to confirm a match, or NIBIN "hit."

NIBIN's database is growing constantly and now contains more than 1.5 million images of shell casings or bullets recovered from crime scenes, as well as casings or bullets from test fires of recovered firearms.

FIGURE 5.7
Bullets and casings.

Source: Adapted from Tom Cramer. "Nab'em with NIBIN: Ballistics Imaging Technology." *The Police Chief*, December 2009, pp.26–31. Copyright held by the International Association of Chiefs of Police, 515 North Washington Street, Alexandria, VA 22314 USA. Further reproduction without express written permission from IACP is strictly prohibited.

In general, high-velocity impacts are less likely to shatter glass than are low-velocity impacts. A bullet that does not shatter glass will generally leave a small, round entry hole and a larger, cone-shaped exit hole (Figure 5.8). The faster a bullet travels, the smaller the cracks and the tighter the entry point will be.

The sequence of bullets fired through a piece of glass can be determined from the pattern of cracks. The direction and angle of a bullet or bullets through glass can also be determined by assembling the fragments. When a bullet hits a glass surface, the glass bends, causing radial fractures on the side of the glass *opposite* the point of impact. These concentric rings indicate the bullet's direction.

This allows investigators to determine which side of a piece of glass has received an impact, because a blow causes the glass to compress on that side and to stretch on the opposite side. As the impact occurs, concentric fractures form around the point of impact and interconnect with radial cracks to form triangular pieces. The edge of each triangular piece has visible stress lines that reveal the direction of the blow. The lines on the side that was struck have almost parallel stress lines that tend to curve downward on the side of the glass opposite the blow (see Figure 5.9). Such an examination can establish whether a burglar broke out of or into a building.

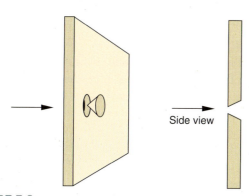

FIGURE 5.8
Bullet entry and exit holes.
© Cengage Learning, 2013

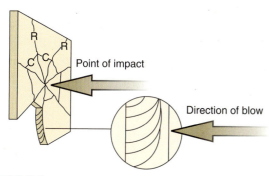

FIGURE 5.9
Glass cracks caused by blow.
© Cengage Learning, 2013

In addition to concentric and radial fractures, investigators should look for *Wallner lines*, also called ridges, which are rib-shaped marks with a wavelike pattern and are almost always concave in the direction from which the crack was propagating. In low-velocity impact fractures, the ridges or Wallner lines on radial cracks nearest the point of impact are at right angles to the side opposite, or to the rear, of the impact, a phenomenon referred to as the "4R Rule" (*R*idges on *r*adial cracks are at *r*ight angles to the *r*ear). However, tempered glass, laminated glass and small pieces of glass tightly held in a frame or window case do not reliably demonstrate the fracture patterns just described.

Because larger glass fragments can be matched by fitting the pieces together, a slight mark put on the side of the glass that was facing out helps to reconstruct stress lines. To protect glass as evidence, put sharp points in putty, modeling clay or some other soft substance.

The Glass Evidence Reference Database contains more than 700 glass samples from manufacturers, distributors and vehicle junkyards and is a useful resource for investigators (Bowen and Schneider, 2007). Although it cannot determine the source of an unknown piece of glass, the database can assess the relative frequency that two glass samples from different sources would have the same elemental profile.

Soils and Minerals

Forensic geologists examine soils and minerals—substances such as mud, cement, plaster, ceramics and insulation—found at a crime scene or on a victim, a suspect, clothing, vehicles or other items. This circumstantial evidence can place a suspect at a crime scene or destroy an alibi.

Although most soil evidence is found outdoors, suspects can bring soil into structures from the outside. Soils found inside a structure are most valuable if brought there on a suspect's shoes or clothing from his or her area of residence. Because soils found in the victim's residence may have been brought there by the victim or by other persons not suspected in the crime, collect elimination samples of soil from the area around the scene.

Put one pound of comparison soil into a container identified on the outside. Collect evidence soil the same way. Seal both containers to prevent loss, wrap them and send them to a laboratory.

Soils vary greatly in color, particle size, mineral content and chemical composition. Some comparisons are visual; others are made through laboratory analysis. Both differences and similarities have value because soils separated by only a few inches can be very different. Therefore, take sufficient samples (about one cup) directly from and around the suspected area at perhaps 5- to 100-foot intervals, depending on the scene. In addition, soil samples should only be packaged in glass vials or plastic locking bags, never envelopes.

If soil evidence is in or on a suspect's clothing, place the entire article with the soil intact in a paper bag and send it to the laboratory. If an object containing soil cannot be moved, use a spatula to scrape off or otherwise collect the soil. Then place the soil in a glass jar or plastic locking bag, properly marked and identified.

Chemical analysis of soil is expensive and not always satisfactory. Soil is generally examined by density, by X-ray diffraction (to determine mineral content) and by microscope.

Because varied species of plants grow in different sections of the country, examining dirt evidence that contains pollen and spores (palynology) is useful. This evidence can refute the alibi of a suspect who is arrested at a distance from a crime scene and denies having been there. Electron microscope detection of pollen and spores found at the crime scene and on the suspect's clothing or vehicle will refute the alibi.

Safe Insulation

Most safes are fire-resistant, sheet-steel boxes with thick insulation. If safes are pried, ripped, punched, drilled or blown open, the insulation breaks apart and falls or disseminates into the room. Burglars often carry some of this insulation in their clothing. People with safe insulation in or on their clothing must be considered suspects because few people normally come into contact with safe insulation. Tools used to open a safe can also have insulation on them, as may the floor of a vehicle in which the tools were placed after a burglary. Investigating burglary is the focus of Chapter 13.

> Put samples of safe insulation in paper containers identified on the outside.

Safe insulation can be compared with particles found on a suspect or on the tools or vehicle used during a crime. Comparison tests can show what type of safe the insulation came from and whether it is the same insulation found at other burglaries. Insulation is also found on paint chips from safes. Always take standards of comparison if safe insulation is found at a crime scene.

The FBI and other laboratories maintain files on safe insulations used by major safe companies. Home and building insulation materials are also on file. This information is available to all law enforcement agencies.

Ropes, Strings and Tapes

Ropes, twines, strings and tapes are frequently used in crimes and can provide leads in identifying and linking suspects with a crime.

> Put labeled rope, twine and string into a container. Put tapes on waxed paper or cellophane and then place them in a container.

A forensic scientist collects soil evidence from the sole of a shoe.
© Pablo Paul/Alamy

Laboratories have various comparison standards for ropes, twines and tapes. If a suspect sample matches a known sample, the laboratory can determine the manufacturer of the item and its most common uses. Cordage can be compared for composition, construction, color and diameter. Rope ends can be matched if they are frayed. Likewise, pieces of torn tape can be compared with a suspect roll of tape.

Fingerprints can occur on either side of a tape. The smooth side is developed by the normal powder method or by using cyanoacrylate (superglue) if the surface is extremely slick. The sticky-side prints will be visible and are either photographed or retained intact.

Drugs

Drug identification kits can be used to make a preliminary analysis of a suspicious substance, but a full analysis must be done at a laboratory. One valuable reference is Ident-A-Drug, which contains codes imprinted on tablets and capsules, information on color and shape, the national drug code and drug class (Bowen and Schneider, 2007). Another resource is PharmInfoNet, a free Internet database containing information on prescription drugs, including uses, marketing and availability and common side effects (Bowen and Schneider). If a drug is a prescription drug, verify the contents with the issuing pharmacist. Determine how much of the original prescription has been consumed.

> Put liquid drugs in a bottle and attach a label. Put powdered and solid drugs in a pillbox or powder box and identify them in the same way.

A device called the "Hound" helps investigators detect and identify drugs. This toolbox-sized sniffer can detect drug residue in concentrations so small that the skin oil left behind on a doorknob may trigger the device's alarm. It works by drawing several cubic feet of air through a filter and concentrating the compounds extracted into a smaller sample, which is then analyzed by an ion mobility spectrometer that is part of the device. A detailed discussion of evidence in drug investigations is contained in Chapter 18.

Weapons of Mass Destruction

As implied by its name, a weapon of mass destruction (WMD) is designed to produce substantial damage, disorder and disruption to people and infrastructures: "A weapon of mass destruction (WMD) is typically associated with nuclear and/or radiological, biological,

or chemical agents; however, it also may be an explosive" (Waggoner, 2007, p.144). These weapons have come to be known by a variety of acronyms, including CBRN (chemical, biological, radiological and nuclear) and CBRNE (chemical, biological, radiological, nuclear and explosive).

In our post–9/11 world, the entire law enforcement profession has a heightened awareness of terrorists and the tools they use to paralyze people, not only psychologically through fear, but also perhaps physically through chemical agents. Although the methods to analyze and fingerprint the source of these weapons are currently insufficient, technology continues to advance in an effort to help investigators detect such threats in the field. For example, a handheld laser spectroscopy device now available can analyze the chemical composition of a substance in the field within seconds. Thus, if an officer or investigator encounters a suspicious powder, such a device can reveal the chemical makeup of that powder with 95 percent certainty (Schultz, 2008).

The Centers for Disease Control and Prevention (CDC) have certified laboratories around the country to analyze hazardous materials, including suspected WMDs. The response protocol may vary from jurisdiction to jurisdiction, but the following is an example of how the FBI would respond to a report of a suspicious white powder discovered in a letter delivered through the mail ("FBI Casework: Suspicious Powders 101," 2004):

1. Specially trained FBI agents, local hazardous materials (hazmat) teams and other first responders are **dispatched to the scene.** One of the onsite agents **immediately contacts FBI Headquarters Counterterrorism**, which assembles a multi-agency team for threat assessment/response. The Headquarters team helps first responders address safety concerns, handle evidence properly, and develop an investigative plan.
2. The onsite team tests the material for radiation, volatile chemicals, pH and other characteristics; wraps it in an airtight overpack and sends it to the nearest CDC-certified lab for more testing.
   - If the field screen is negative, the team leaves the area.
   - If it's positive, (1) the local area is shut down and tested by hazmat teams in protective suits and (2) people who had any contact with the powder are identified, decontaminated, and possibly examined at a hospital as a precaution.
3. **If a threat letter has been found,** the CDC-certified lab makes sure it's not contaminated, then **sends it to the FBI Laboratory** in Quantico, Virginia, to test for clues like fingerprints, hair

samples, and—if the postage stamp/envelope has been licked—DNA. The letter's language and writing, which could provide important clues, are analyzed by the FBI Behavioral Science Unit.

4. Once lab tests determine definitively whether the powder is hazardous or not, the FBI works with the CDC and state and local health departments to **advise the public** whether the threat is real or a hoax.

5. The **evidence of the case is presented to the U.S. Attorney** to determine whether it should be prosecuted: If not, the case is closed. If so, a full investigation is begun. Even cases involving harmless substances, can, of course, be prosecuted because it's a violation of federal law even to threaten the use of a Weapon of Mass Destruction—including anthrax and other biological agents. The threat letters and substances collected during investigations are securely maintained as case evidence.

Investigating terrorism and other threats to homeland security is the focus of Chapter 20.

Documents

Typing, handwriting and printing can be examined. Typewriters and printers can be compared and paper identification attempted. Different types of writing instruments—pens, crayons and pencils—and various types of inks can also be compared. Indented writings, obliterated or altered writings, used carbon paper, burned or charred paper and shoeprint or tire tread impressions made on paper surfaces can all be examined in a laboratory. A document's age can also be determined.

 Do not touch documents with your bare hands. Place documents in a cellophane envelope and then in a manila envelope identified on the outside.

Standards of comparison are required for many document examinations. To obtain handwriting standards from a suspect, take samples until you believe he or she is writing normally. The suspect should not see the original document or copy. Tell the suspect what to write and remove each sample from sight after it is completed. Provide no instructions on spelling, punctuation or wording. Use the same size and type of paper and writing materials as the original. Obtain right-handed and left-handed samples as well as samples written at different speeds. Samples of undictated writings, such as letters, are also helpful as standards. In forgery cases, include the genuine signatures as well as the forged ones.

A useful resource for investigators is the Forensic Information System for Handwriting (FISH), which is maintained by the U.S. Secret Service. This database merges federal and Interpol databases of genuine and counterfeit identification documents, such as passports, driver's licenses and credit cards (Bowman and Schneider, 2007). Caution must be used in focusing solely on counterfeit documents, however, because in many cases criminals

Forensiclink.org is a secure social networking website for forensic professionals around the world to share information and connect with each other. The goal is to provide a safe forum to help advance the field of forensic investigations.

Courtesy www.forensiclink.org

are able to use legitimate documents in illegal ways. For example, the terrorists involved in the 9/11 attacks breached the U.S. border through fraudulently obtained—but genuine—U.S. travel documents. As a result of that discovery, the U.S. Department of State's Bureau of Diplomatic Security (DS) stepped up its overseas investigations of visa fraud, and these investigations resulted in revocation of 1,680 visas and 512 arrests in 2006 alone (Griffin, 2007, p.30).

To help identify and investigate other counterfeit or crime-related handwritten documents, the FBI maintains a national fraudulent check file, an anonymous letter file, a bank robbery note file, paper watermarks, safety paper and checkwriter standards. Also, as in other areas of evidence examination, computer programs have been developed to analyze handwriting.

People often type anonymous or threatening letters, believing that typewritten materials are not as traceable as handwritten ones. However, some courts have held that typewriting can be compared more accurately than handwriting and almost as accurately as fingerprints. To collect typewriting standards, remove the ribbon from the suspected typewriter and send the ribbon to a laboratory. Use a different ribbon to take each sample. Take samples using light, medium and heavy pressure. Submit one carbon-copy sample with the typewriter on stencil position. Do not send the typewriter to a laboratory, but hold it as evidence.

Given enough typing samples, it is often possible to determine the make and model of a machine. Typewriter standard files are available at the FBI laboratory. The information can greatly narrow the search for the actual machine. The most important comparison is between the suspect document and a specific typewriter.

As word processing replaces typewriters, the word-processing software program and the printer used become important evidence. Computer scanners and desktop publishing programs make producing fraudulent documents much easier. Collect as evidence the computer hard drive, printer, copier, scanner or whichever devices were used to generate the document.

Computer-related document evidence may be contained on tapes or disks, not readily discernible and highly susceptible to destruction. In addition to information on tapes and disks, evidence may take the form of data reports, programming or other printed materials based on information from computer files. Investigators who handle computer tapes and disks should avoid contact with the recording surfaces. They should never write on computer disk labels with a ballpoint pen or pencil and should never use paper clips on or rubber bands around computer disks. To do so may destroy the data

they contain. Computer tapes and disks taken as evidence should be stored vertically, at approximately 70°F, and away from bright light, dust and magnetic fields.

Photographs frequently are also valuable evidence, whether taken by an officer or by someone outside the department. Some researchers are focusing their efforts on techniques to enhance grainy, blurred or poorly contrasted photographs by digitally converting them and subjecting them to software programs. Photographic images of injuries on human skin can be enhanced using reflective and fluorescent UV imaging.

Recall that the best-evidence rule stipulates that the original evidence is to be presented whenever possible. For example, a photograph or photocopy of a forged check is not admissible in court; the check itself is required.

When submitting any document evidence to a laboratory, clearly indicate which documents are original and which are comparison standards. Also indicate whether latent fingerprints are requested. Although original documents are needed for laboratory examinations and court exhibits, copies can be used for file searches. A photograph is superior to a photocopy.

Digital Evidence

The digital revolution and preponderance of electronic devices pervading everyday life, such as cell phones, pagers, personal digital assistants (PDAs), computers, iPods, gaming systems and global positioning systems (GPSs), have generated a new class of evidence and requirements for handling it: "Technology touches nearly every crime today. Digital media seized in relation to an offense may include everything from computers, flash drives, cell phones, digital cameras and game units, all of which need forensic examination" (Garrett, 2009a, p.12). Because data and digital evidence can be located on anything a device sees as a "drive," a general suggestion is look at *anything* electronic found at the scene: "any kind of device, any kind of evidence" (Miller and Loving, 2009, p.38).

Learning about the suspects and their habits can help investigators zero in on particular devices: "The suspect's associates can often be counted on the reveal his or her habits, such as, 'He always has his thumb drive with him.' This can be especially crucial in cases of child pornography or intellectual property theft. Further, data recovered from devices such as in-vehicle GPS units and mobile phones can back up suspect patterns—or breaks in patterns" (Miller and Loving, 2009, p.44).

Much of the information available about digital evidence relates to cell phones: "Considering the pervasive nature of cell phones, and their ability to contain vast amounts of useful information and potentially powerful evidence, cell phone seizure devices are a critical component of the forensic examiner's toolkit" (Heinecke, 2007, p.62). All cell phones leave a trail: "Each time a cell phone is turned on, it sends a registration message, including the serial and phone numbers, to the closest cellular tower" (Puente, 2007). Cell phone records are often very useful in establishing an accurate timeline surrounding a criminal event (Spraggs, 2009). Furthermore, global positioning system chips built into cell phones allow authorities to track criminals as well as people in need of help.

The first part of collecting evidence from a cell phone is the actual handling of the device. Do not change the condition of the evidence. This is one of the most basic rules of digital evidence collection: if the device is off, leave it off; if it's on, leave it on. Investigators must also know their state's laws regarding electronic searches: "Many states make it possible for officers to search a subject's cell phone incident to arrest; some require a search warrant. To obtain carrier data, however, investigators almost always need a court order" (Miller, 2008, p.14).

Each cell phone carrier stores and maintains subscriber records, which include subscriber information such as name, address and birth date, as well as call-detail records containing data regarding incoming and outgoing phone numbers and the towers that transmitted these calls. Carriers have different lengths of time they hold onto records, ranging anywhere from six years to only a few days. Call-detail reports may be available for 45 days, whereas voicemail and text messages may be stored for a week or less (Miller, 2008). If a warrant cannot be obtained within that time, a preservation order letter should be submitted to the carrier specifically documenting which cellular records you need preserved (Reiber, 2007). The records will be pulled and maintained for 90 days from the date the carrier receives the request to give investigators time to obtain a warrant, unless investigators "refresh" the preservation request for an additional 90 days. For an example of a preservation request, log in to cengagebrain.com and access the CourseMate that accompanies this text.

Of course, in addition to cell phones, many more electronic devices exist that may hold critical digital evidence. As with any other type of evidence collection and examination, training is crucial: "To capably harvest digital evidence artifacts for criminal investigations, computer forensic training is an absolute requirement. Training ensures examiners not only understand the complex layout of data, the way the data is stored and how to recover it, but also how to articulate findings in court when called upon to do so" (Reiber, 2009).

About 100 colleges and universities now offer undergraduate and graduate courses in digital forensics, with a few offering majors (Whitcomb, 2007, p.42). Several publications are also available as resources to investigators, such as *The Journal of Digital Forensic Practice*, which debuted in 2007. The National Institute of Justice has published *Investigative Uses of Technology: Devices Tools and Techniques* (2007), which presents detailed information regarding digital evidence. The investigation of computer crimes is the focus of Chapter 17.

Laundry and Dry-Cleaning Marks

Many launderers and dry cleaners use specific marking systems. The Laundry and Dry Cleaning National Association has files on such marking systems. Many police laboratories also maintain a file of visible and invisible laundry marks used by local establishments. Military clothing is marked with the wearer's serial number, name and organization.

> Use UV light to detect invisible laundry marks. Submit the entire garment to a laboratory, identified with a string tag or a marking directly on the garment.

Laundry and dry-cleaning marks are used to identify the dead and injured in mass disasters such as airplane crashes, fires and floods and in other circumstances as well. For example, a dead baby was traced by a sheet's laundry marks. Clothing labels can also assist in locating the possible source of the clothing.

Paint

Paints are complex and are individual in color, composition, texture and layer composition: "The layer structure of a questioned paint sample can be compared with a known source from a suspect. The sequence, relative thickness, color, texture, number, and chemical composition of each of the layers can be compared" (Waggoner, 2007, p.101). Police laboratories and the FBI maintain files of standard automobile paints, which can help identify the year, make and color of a motor vehicle from a chip of paint left at the scene.

> In hit-and-run cases, collect paint samples from any area of the vehicle that had contact with the victim. Take paint samples down to the original metal to show the layer composition.

Use small boxes for submitting paint samples to the crime lab, putting samples from different parts of the vehicle in separate small boxes. If paint chips are on the clothing of the victim or suspect, send the entire article of clothing in a paper bag to the laboratory, properly labeled and identified.

Skeletal Remains

Laboratory examination can determine whether skeletal remains are animal or human.

> If adequate human skeletal remains are available, the sex, race, approximate age at death, approximate height and approximate time since death can be determined.

Dental comparisons and X-rays of old fractures are other important identifying features or individual characteristics.

Forensic anthropology uses standard scientific techniques developed by physical anthropologists and archaeologists to identify human skeletal remains as they relate to a criminal case. Ongoing research at the Body Farm in Knoxville, Tennessee, is helping scientists observe the decomposition process of the human body following death and how exposure to various environmental conditions affects this process. Death investigations are the focus of Chapter 8.

Wood

Wood comparisons are made from items on a suspect, in a vehicle or in or on clothing found at a crime scene. The origin is determined by the size or the fit of the fracture with an original piece of wood or by matching the sides

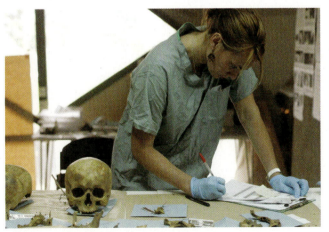

A forensic anthropologist examines a cranium exhumed from a mass grave. DNA samples from victims' remains are compared with the DNA samples taken from living family members in an effort to identify each victim.

© Marco Di Lauro/Getty Images

or ends of pieces of wood. The type of wood is determined from its cellular elements. When handling wood evidence, if it is found wet, keep it wet; if it is dry, keep it dry.

Other Types of Evidence

Prescription eyeglasses, broken buttons, glove prints and other personal evidence found at a crime scene can also be examined and compared. Investigators should learn to read "product DNA," the printed code that appears on nearly every manufactured, mass-produced item, because it can provide valuable leads. For example, the numbers on a candy bar wrapper can tell investigators when that candy bar was made, packaged, shipped and delivered and to what store. Other discarded items at a crime scene that may yield useful information include store and restaurant receipts, bank deposit slips, beverage containers, cigarette packages, membership and check-cashing cards, clothing manufacturer labels and laundry tags and footwear. If there is a problem processing any evidence, a laboratory can provide specific collecting and packaging instructions.

EVIDENCE HANDLING AND INFECTIOUS DISEASE

Throughout this chapter, you have looked at ways to collect evidence and keep it secure from contamination. As a final discussion in handling physical evidence, consider how to protect yourself from contamination. "One of the risks you face as a law enforcement officer is potential exposure to bloodborne pathogens such as the hepatitis B virus, the hepatitis C virus and the human immunodeficiency virus (HIV)" (*Bloodborne Pathogens*, no date, p.2). Investigators are likely to encounter crimes of violence involving the blood and other body fluids of people with infectious diseases. Police officers are likely to encounter these infectious body fluids during the search of crime scenes involving violence. Therefore, it is important to know the facts about these infectious agents.

AIDS is not spread through casual contact such as touching an infected person or sharing equipment. Nor is it spread through the air by coughing or sneezing. An important issue related to HIV/AIDS is a person's confidentiality rights concerning his or her HIV status, including disclosure of such information in police reports. Investigators should be familiar with their jurisdiction's basic medical information confidentiality laws as well as any other specific laws pertaining to HIV/AIDS.

Chances are less than one percent that an officer will contract the AIDS virus on the job. Tuberculosis (TB),

Investigators in hazmat suits are decontaminated between the Longworth and Rayburn House Office Buildings on Capital Hill in Washington, DC, on October 24, 2001. The buildings were being swept for anthrax.

© Reuters/William Philpott/CORBIS

meningitis and hepatitis pose greater threats. TB is transmitted through the air by coughing, hacking and wheezing. TB can also be transmitted through saliva, urine, blood and other body fluids. Meningitis, spread through the air, causes inflammation of the membranes that surround the brain. The hepatitis B virus, known today as HBV, is a blood-borne pathogen that can live outside the body longer than HIV can. HBV is found in human blood, urine, semen, cerebrospinal fluid, vaginal secretions and saliva. A safe, effective vaccine to prevent HBV is available.

Use precautions when collecting blood evidence and other body fluids. *Universal precautions*, which is the protocol used by medical health professionals, dictates that public safety officials treat every individual as if he or she is infected and take precautions to minimize risks. *Consider all body secretions as potential health hazards.* If body fluids are present at a crime scene, even if dried, wear latex gloves, goggles and a face mask. Secure evidence in glass, metal or plastic containers. Seal evidence bags with tape rather than staples. Do not allow hand-to-mouth or hand-to-face contact during collection. Do not eat, smoke, apply makeup or drink at crime scenes because these activities may transfer contaminated body fluids to you. When

finished, wash your hands thoroughly (20 to 30 seconds) with soap and water: "Hand washing ranks as the top protection against MRSA [methicillin-resistant *Staphylococcus aureus*] and other super bugs" (Garrett, 2008, p.51).

While processing the crime scene, constantly be alert for sharp objects, such as hypodermic needles and syringes. If practical, use disposable items where blood is present so the items can be incinerated. All nondisposable items, such as cameras, tools and notebooks, must be decontaminated using a bleach solution or rubbing alcohol. Even properly dried and packaged evidence is still potentially infectious. Therefore, place appropriate warnings on all items.

After processing, decontaminate the crime scene. If it is to be left for future decontamination, place biohazard warning signs and notify the cleaning team of possible contamination.

Further information on procedures for dealing with evidence with potential of transmitting an infectious disease can be obtained from the Centers for Disease Control and Prevention, Office of Health and Biosafety, 1600 Clifton Road N.E., Atlanta, GA 30333. 1-800-311-3435. http://www.cdc.gov.

Summary

Criminal investigations rely heavily on various types of evidence. To be of value, evidence must be legally and properly seized and processed. Processing physical evidence includes discovering or recognizing it; collecting, recording and identifying it; packaging, conveying and storing it; examining it; exhibiting it in court; and disposing of it when the case is closed.

To determine what is evidence, first consider the apparent crime. Then look for any objects unrelated or foreign to the scene, unusual in their location or number, damaged or broken or whose relation to other objects suggests a pattern that fits the crime.

Common errors in collecting evidence are (1) not collecting enough of the sample, (2) not obtaining standards of comparison and (3) not maintaining the integrity of the evidence.

Mark or identify each item of evidence in a way that can be recognized later. Indicate the date and case number as well as your personal identifying mark or initials. Record in your notes the date and time of collection, where the evidence was found and by whom, case number, description of the item and who took custody of it. Package each item separately in durable containers to maintain the integrity of evidence. Personal delivery, registered mail, insured parcel post, air express, FedEx and United Parcel Service (UPS) are legal ways to transport evidence. Always specify that the person who receives the evidence is to sign for it.

Package evidence properly to keep it in substantially the same condition in which it was found and store it securely. Document custody of the evidence at every stage. To ensure admissibility of the evidence in court, be able to (1) identify the evidence as that found at the crime scene, (2) describe exactly where it was found, (3) establish its custody from discovery to the present and (4) voluntarily explain any changes that have occurred in the evidence. After a case is closed, evidence is returned to the owner, auctioned or destroyed.

Frequently examined physical evidence includes fingerprints; voiceprints; language; DNA; blood and other body fluids (including blood); scent; hairs and fibers; shoe and tire prints and impressions; bite marks; tools and tool marks; firearms and ammunition; glass; soils and minerals; safe insulation; rope, strings and tapes; drugs; weapons of mass destruction; documents; digital evidence; laundry and dry-cleaning marks; paint; skeletal remains; wood; and many other types of evidence.

Know how to locate, develop, photograph, lift and submit fingerprints for classification by experts. Any hard, smooth, nonporous surface can contain latent fingerprints. Do not powder a print unless it is necessary; do not powder a visible print until after photographing it. Fingerprints are *positive* evidence of a person's identity. They cannot, however, indicate a person's age, sex or race.

DNA profiling uses material from which chromosomes are made to identify individuals positively. DNA can tell investigators the sample donor's gender, race, eye color and hair color. Blood can be identified as animal or human and is most useful in eliminating suspects. Age and race cannot be determined from blood samples, but DNA analysis can provide positive identification. Microscopic examination determines whether hair is animal or human. Many characteristics can be determined from human hair: the part of the body it came from; whether it was bleached or dyed, freshly cut, pulled out or burned; and whether there is blood or semen on it. Race, sex and age cannot be determined.

After photographing, cast shoe or tire tread impressions found in dirt, sand or snow. Identify each suspected tool with a string tag, wrap it separately and pack it in a strong box to send to a laboratory. Photograph tool marks and then either cast them or send the object on which they appear to a laboratory. A tool mark is compared with a standard-of-comparison impression rather than with the tool itself.

Examine weapons for latent fingerprints. Photograph weapons and then identify them with string tags. Unload firearms and record their serial numbers on string tags and in your notes. Label the packing container "Firearms." Identify bullets on the base, cartridges on the outside of the case near the bullet end and cartridge cases on the inside near the open end. Put ammunition in cotton or soft paper and ship to a laboratory. Never send live ammunition through the mail; use a common carrier instead.

Label glass fragments using adhesive tape on each piece. Wrap each piece separately in cotton to avoid chipping, and place them in a strong box marked "Fragile" to send to a laboratory. Put one pound of comparison soil into a container identified on the outside. Collect evidence soil the same way. Seal both containers to prevent loss, wrap them and send them to a laboratory.

Put samples of safe insulation in paper containers identified on the outside. Put labeled rope, twine and string in a container. Put tapes on waxed paper or cellophane and then place them in a container. Put liquid drugs in a bottle and attach a label. Put powdered and solid drugs in a pillbox or powder box and identify them in the same way.

Do not touch documents with your bare hands. Place documents in a cellophane envelope and then in a manila envelope identified on the outside. Use UV light to detect invisible laundry marks. Submit the entire garment to a laboratory, identified with a string tag or with a marking directly on the garment. In hit-and-run cases, collect paint samples from any area of the vehicle that had contact with the victim. Take paint samples down to the original metal to show the layer composition. If adequate human skeletal remains are available, the sex, race, approximate age at death, approximate height and approximate time since death can be determined.

Checklist

Physical Evidence

- Was all physical evidence photographed before anything was moved?
- Was the physical evidence located in the crime scene sketch?
- Were relevant facts recorded in your notebook?
- Was the evidence properly identified, including the date, case number, your initials or mark and a description of the evidence?
- Was the evidence properly packaged to avoid contamination or destruction?
- Were standards of comparison obtained if needed?
- Was the evidence sent in a way that kept it secure and provided a signed receipt, such as by registered mail?
- Was the evidence kept continuously secure until presented in court?

The following types of physical evidence are frequently found at a crime scene and should be searched for, depending on the type of crime committed:

- Blood
- Cigarettes, cigars and smoking materials
- Clothing and fragments
- Containers and boxes
- Dirt and dust particles
- Documents and papers
- Fibers, ropes and strings
- Fingernail scrapings
- Fingerprints, visible and latent
- Footprints
- Glass objects and fragments
- Greases, oils, salves and emulsions
- Hairs, human and animal
- Inorganic materials
- Insulation from safes, buildings and homes
- Metal objects and fragments
- Organic materials, plant and animal
- Paint and paint chips
- Palmprints
- Personal possessions
- Photographs
- Plastic impressions
- Soils
- Tires and tire tracks
- Tools and tool marks
- Weapons
- Wood chips or fragments

Discussion Questions

1. What kind of physical evidence would you expect to find at a burglary scene?
2. What kind of physical evidence would you expect to find at the scene of an armed robbery? Why does this differ from your response to Question 1?
3. What is *material, relevant* and *competent* evidence?
4. What legal rule requires the submission of original evidence, and when is this rule followed? When is it permissible to substitute evidence that is not original?
5. What general procedures would you follow in finding and collecting evidence at a crime scene?
6. Explain how you would mark for identification the following items of evidence: a broken window pane; a damaged bullet; dried blood scraped from a wood floor; a shotgun shell casing; a piece of clothing with semen stains.
7. How would you locate, preserve, lift and identify a latent fingerprint on a wall in a house? How would you have the print examined?
8. What two types of DNA evidence exist? What are the differences between the two?
9. *Continuity of evidence* is a legal term describing the chain of evidence necessary to make evidence legally admissible in court. Describe a chain of evidence from the time of discovery to introduction in court.

10. How does your police department dispose of evidence after it is no longer of value or has been released by the court?

Media Explorations

 Internet

Complete the following assignments, and be prepared to share your findings with the class.

■ Go to the FBI Web site to view the *Handbook of Forensic Services*. List the five sections of the handbook. Select one section and outline it.

■ Go to the U.S. Department of Justice's National Institute of Justice Web site and find the document *What Every Law Enforcement Officer Should Know about DNA Evidence*. Outline the most important information.

ONLINE Database **Gale Criminal Justice Database Assignments**

The following assignments require access to Gale's Custom Journals Database for Emergency Services and Criminal Justice. Check with your instructor if you have questions about this.

■ Find the article "Reducing the DNA Backlog: Florida Involves Local Law Enforcement to Prescreen Evidence" on the Gale Emergency Services Database. Read the article and outline it for in-class discussion.

■ Find the article "Beyond CODIS: The Changing Face of Forensic DNA Analysis" on the Gale Emergency Services Database. Be prepared to explain the details of CODIS and the benefits of the system with the class.

■ Find the article "Technology Speeds Up DNA Processing" on the Gale Emergency Services Database. Identify how technology has sped up DNA processing. Also, be prepared to discuss in class what you predict the future holds in terms of DNA evidence.

References

Adair, Tom. "Capturing Snow Impressions." *Law and Order*, November 2009, pp.14–20.

Berson, Sarah B. "Debating DNA Collection." *NIJ Journal*, No. 264, November 2009, pp.9–13.

Bloodborne Pathogens for Law Enforcement. Virginia Beach, VA: Coastal Training Technologies Corp., no date.

Bowen, Robin, and Schneider, Jessica. "Forensic Databases: Paint, Shoe Prints, and Beyond." *NIJ Journal*, October 2007.

"CODIS Brochure." Washington, DC: Federal Bureau of Investigation, 2011. http://www.fbi.gov/about-us/lab/codis/codis_brochure

"CODIS—NDIS Statistics." Washington, DC: Federal Bureau of Investigation, 2011. http://www.fbi.gov/about-us/lab/codis/ndis-statistics

Cramer, Tom. "Nab'em with NIBIN: Ballistics Imaging Technology." *The Police Chief*, December 2009, pp.26–31.

DNA Saves. Accessed April 27, 2011. http://dnasaves.org/dna_law.php

Fantino, Julian. "Forensic Science: A Fundamental Perspective." *The Police Chief*, November 2007, pp.26–28.

"FBI Casework: Suspicious Powders 101." Washington, DC: Federal Bureau of Investigation, April 20, 2004. http://www.fbi.gov/news/stories/2004/april/powders_042004

"FBI Upgrades Fingerprint System." *Homeland Security Newswire*, March 15, 2011. Accessed April 25, 2011. http://homelandsecuritynewswire.com/fbi-upgrades-fingerprint-system

Fitzpatrick, Frank, and Ely, Terence. "Ensuring the Quality of Forensic Service Providers through Accreditation." *The Police Chief*, November 2007, pp.50–53.

Garrett, Ronnie. "Super Bugs: Coming to a Department Near You." *Law Enforcement Technology*, March 2008, pp.46–51.

Garrett, Ronnie. "The Byte Stuff." *Law Enforcement Technology*, April 2009a, pp.10–16.

Garrett, Ronnie. "DNA Saves." *Law Enforcement Technology*, February 2009b, pp.28–37.

Garrett, Ronnie. "New DNA Testing Technique Pinpoints Hair, Eye and Skin Color." *Law Enforcement Technology*, July 2009c, pp.51–57.

Geberth, Vernon. "Blood Pattern Analysis." *Law and Order*, March 2007, pp.38–47.

Geberth, Vernon. "Amazing Advances in Forensic Science Part 1: DNA." *Law and Order*, June 2010a, pp.26–31.

Geberth, Vernon. "Amazing Advances in Forensic Science Part 2: Advances in Criminalistics." *Law and Order*, September 2010b, pp.72–75.

Geberth, Vernon. "Amazing Advances in Forensic Science Part 3: Firearms and Ballistics." *Law and Order*, October 2010c, pp.98–100.

Geoghegan, Susan. "Forensic DNA." *Law and Order*, June 2009, pp.49–53.

Gold, Jeffrey. "DNA Clears Man of Two Child Murders." *AOL News*, May 16, 2007.

Griffin, Richard J. "Operation Triple X: Hitting Hard at Illegal Document Trade." *The Police Chief*, October 2007, pp.30–36.

Hanson, Doug. "What You Say Can Hurt You." *Law Enforcement Technology*, October 2007, pp.134–140.

Heinecke, Jeannine. "An Evolution in Cell Forensics." *Law Enforcement Technology*, November 2007, pp.62–70.

Ivy, Peter, and Orput, Peter. "DNA Retention Policy: A Primer for Law Enforcement." *Minnesota Police Chief*, Spring 2007, pp.30–31.

Jetmore, Larry F. "The Truth's in the Teeth: Using Forensic Dentistry to Solve Crimes." *Law Officer Magazine*, July 2007, pp.22–25.

Jetmore, Larry F. "Dactyloscopy: The Science of Fingerprints." *Law Officer Magazine*, April 2008, pp.76–79.

Johns, Susan, and Rushing, Patricia. "Using DNA to Solve Property Crimes." *Community Policing Dispatch*, Vol.2, No. 12, December 2009. Accessed April 27, 2011. http://www .cops.usdoj.gov/html/dispatch/December_2009/dna.htm

Kiley, Bill. "Police Executives Need to Show Leadership on Evidence Storage and Security Issues." *Subject to Debate*, January 2008, pp.1, 6.

Laska, Paul R. "DNA: Technology the Street Cop Can Use." *Law Officer Magazine*, September 2007, pp.36–40.

Longa, Lyda. "In the Chain of Evidence, DNA the Strongest Link." *Daytona Beach News*, March 11, 2008.

McGhee, Tom. "Recent Cases Highlight the Database's Value and the Burden on U.S. Crime Labs." *The Denver Post*, February 4, 2008.

Means, Randy. "Brady Policy and Officer Credibility." *Law and Order*, February 2008, pp.12–14.

Miller, Christa. "The Other Side of Mobile Forensics." *Law Enforcement Technology*, July 2008, pp.10–18.

Miller, Christa, and Loving, Kipp. "The Crime Scene Evidence You're Ignoring." *Law Enforcement Technology*, October 2009, pp.36–45.

Mitchell, Billy. "Keeping Track: Four Common Pitfalls in Tracking and Storing Evidence." *Law Officer Magazine*, August 2009, pp.84–86.

Moore, Solomon. "Exoneration Using DNA Brings Change in Legal System." *The New York Times*, October 1, 2007.

Moradoff, Nissan. "Biometrics: Proliferation and Constraints to Emerging and New Technologies." *Security Journal*, Vol.23, No.4, October 2010, pp.276–298.

National Institute of Justice. *Investigative Uses of Technology: Devices, Tools, and Techniques*. Washington, DC: October 2007.

Nelson, Mark. *Making Sense of DNA Backlogs, 2010—Myths vs. Reality*. Washington, DC: U.S. Department of Justice, National Institute of Justice, February 2011. (NCJ 232197)

Norton, Leo M. "Who Goes There? Mobile Fingerprint Readers in Los Angeles County." *The Police Chief*, June 2009, pp.32–39.

Page, Douglas. "The Bite Stuff?" *Law Enforcement Technology*, February 2007a, pp.112–119.

Page, Douglas. "Fingerprinting Reforms at Hand." *Law Enforcement Technology*, October 2007b, pp.128–134.

Prime, Raymond J., and Newman, Jonathan. "The Impact of DNA on Policing: Past, Present, and Future." *The Police Chief*, November 2007, pp.30–35.

Puente, Mark. "Newest Crimefighting Tool: GPS Chips in Cell Phones." (Cleveland) *Plain Dealer Reporter*, July 31, 2007.

Reiber, Lee. "Using Cell Phone Records to Solve Crimes." *Law Officer Magazine*, June 2007, pp.40–41.

Reiber, Lee. "Going Mobile: Mobile Phone Forensics Requires a Considered Approach." *Law Officer Magazine*, June 2009, pp.28–29.

Roman, John K.; Reid, Shannon; Reid, Jay; Chalfin, Aaron; Adams, William; and Knight, Carly. *The DNA Field Experiment: Cost-Effectiveness Analysis of the Use of DNA in the Investigation of High-Volume Crimes*. Washington, DC: Urban Institute, Justice Policy Center, April 2008. (NCJ 222318). Accessed April 27, 2011. http://www.ncjrs.gov/ pdffiles1/nij/grants/222318.pdf

Schreiber, Sara. "How Clean Is Your (Evidence) House?" *Law Enforcement Technology*, November 2009, pp.8–13.

Schultz, Paul D. "The Future Is Here: Technology in Police Departments." *The Police Chief*, June 2008, pp.20–25.

Scientific Working Group on Friction Ridge Analysis, Study and Technology (SWGFAST), et al. *The Fingerprint Sourcebook*, Washington, DC: National Institution of Justice, March 2011. (NIJ Document 225320). http://www.nij.gov/ pubs-sum/225320.htm

Shapiro, Ari. "Police Use DNA to Track Suspects through Family." National Public Radio, December 14, 2007.

Spagnoli, Linda. "Beyond CODIS." *Law Enforcement Technology*, July 2007, pp.42–51.

Spraggs, David. "How to Lift Fingerprints." *Police*, February 2007, pp.24–26.

Spraggs, David. "Crime-Fighting Laser Beams." *Police*, February 2008, pp.38–41.

Spraggs, David. "Turn Their Gadgets against Them." *Police*, February 2009, pp.29–31.

Spraggs, David. Firearms Forensics." *Police*, February 2010, pp.43–45.

U.S. Department of Justice, National Institute of Justice, National Commission on the Future of DNA Evidence. *What Every Law Enforcement Officer Should Know about DNA Evidence*. Washington, DC, 1999.

Waggoner, Kim, editor. *Handbook of Forensic Services*. Quantico, VA: Federal Bureau of Investigation, 2007.

Wallentine, Ken. "Collection of DNA upon Arrest: Expanding Investigative Frontiers." *The Police Chief*, January 2010, pp.12–13.

Whitcomb, C. M. "The Evolution of Digital Evidence in Forensic Science Laboratories." *The Police Chief*, November 2007, pp.36–42.

Whitehead, Christy. "Online Auction: Property Room.Com" *Law and Order*, April 2007, pp.72–78.

Wilson, David B.; McClure, David; and Weisburd, David. "Does Forensic DNA Help to Solve Crime? The Benefit of Sophisticated Answers to Naïve Questions." *Journal of Contemporary Criminal Justice*, Vol.26, No.4, November 2010, pp.458–469.

Yamashita, Brian, and French, Mike. "Latent Print Development." Chapter 7 in *The Fingerprint Sourcebook*, by the Scientific Working Group on Friction Ridge Analysis,

Study and Technology (SWGFAST). Washington, DC: National Institute of Justice, March 2011. (NCJ 225320). http://www.ncjrs.gov/pdffiles1/nij/225327.pdf

Cases Cited

Daubert v. Merrell Dow Pharmaceuticals, Inc., 509 U.S. 579 (1993)

Frye v. United States, 54 App. D.C. 46, 293 F. 1013 (1923)

Additional Resource

Committee on Identifying the Needs of the Forensic Sciences Community and the National Research Council. *Strengthening Forensic Science in the United States: A Path Forward.* Washington, DC: The National Academies Press, August 2009. (NIJ Document 228091). http://www.ncjrs.gov/pdffiles1/nij/grants/228091.pdf

CHAPTER 6
Obtaining Information and Intelligence

© Jeff Greenberg/PhotoEdit

Outline

Can You Define?

admission
adoptive admission
beachheading
closed-ended question
cognitive interview
complainant
confession
custodial arrest
custodial interrogation
direct question
dying declaration
field interview
in custody
indirect question
informant
information age
interrogation

interview
leading question
Miranda warning
network
nonverbal communication
open-ended question
polygraph
public safety exception
rapport
sources-of-information file
statement
testimonial hearsay
third degree
waiver

Knowledge obtained through questioning and physical evidence is equally important. Physical evidence can provide a basis for questioning people about a crime, and questioning can provide leads for finding physical evidence. Although physical evidence is important by itself, supporting oral testimony adds considerable value when presented in court. Conversely, although a confession may appear conclusive, it cannot stand alone legally. It must be supported by physical evidence or other corroboration.

Do You Know?

- What sources of information are available to investigators?
- What a sources-of-information file is and what it contains?
- What the goal of interviewing and interrogation is?
- What the characteristics of an effective interviewer or interrogator are?
- How to improve communication?
- What the emotional barriers to communication are?
- What two requirements are needed to obtain information?
- What the difference between direct and indirect questions is and when to use each?
- What technique is likely to assist recall as well as uncover lies?
- When and in what order individuals are interviewed?
- What basic approaches to use in questioning reluctant interviewees?
- What the *Miranda* warning is and when to give it?
- What the two requirements of a place for conducting interrogations are?
- What techniques to use in an interrogation?
- What third-degree tactics are and what their place in interrogation is?
- What restrictions are placed on obtaining a confession?

(continued)

- What significance a confession has in an investigation?
- What to consider when questioning a juvenile?
- What a polygraph is and what its role in investigation and the acceptability of its results in court are?
- How to differentiate information from intelligence?

SOURCES OF INFORMATION

In addition to physical evidence, three primary sources of information are available.

> Important sources of information include (1) reports, records and databases, including those found on the Internet; (2) people who are not suspects in a crime but who know something about the crime or those involved; and (3) suspects in the crime.

Often these sources overlap. For example, information in a hotel's records may be supplemented by information supplied by the hotel manager or the doorkeeper.

Because so many informational sources exist in any given community, it is helpful to develop a sources-of-information file. Each time you locate someone who can provide important information on criminal activity in a community, make a card with information about this source or enter the information into a computer file. For example, if a hotel manager provides useful information, make a card with the manager's name, name of the hotel, address, telephone number, type of information provided and other relevant information. File the card under *hotel*.

> A **sources-of-information file** contains the name and location of people, organizations and records that may assist in a criminal investigation.

We have progressed from the agricultural age to the industrial age to the **information age**, a period in which knowledge and information are increasing exponentially, doubling every 2.5 years. Among the most important advances for law enforcement is the availability of computerized information. Such information has been in existence for several years but not in individual squad cars or easily accessible by the average officer on the beat.

Officers now receive information on stolen vehicles, individual arrest records and the like within minutes.

Reports, Records and Databases

Reports, records and databases at the local, state and federal level assist in criminal investigations.

Local Resources. An important information source is the records and reports of your police department, including all preliminary reports, follow-up investigative reports, offense and arrest records, modus operandi files, fingerprint files, missing persons reports, gun registrations and wanted bulletins. Closely examine a suspect's prior record and modus operandi. Examine all laboratory and coroner's reports associated with a case.

Also check records maintained by banks, loan and credit companies, delivery services, hospitals and clinics, hotels and motels, newspapers, telephone books, city directories, street cross-directories, utility providers, personnel departments, pawnbrokers, storage companies, schools and taxi companies. Each time you locate a source whose records are helpful, add it to your sources-of-information file.

Inventory Tracking Systems. Automatic inventory tracking systems can be helpful if businesses believe their inventory is shrinking or they are losing tools and other equipment. Such tracking systems automatically generate reports on inventory and can capture transaction activity by department or other classifications.

Caller ID. The telephone number from which a call is placed can be recorded by a caller ID service, even if the call is not answered. Caller ID also provides the date and time of the call and can store numbers in its memory when more than one call is received.

In some criminal investigations, evidence has been obtained from telephones enabled with caller ID. For example, a person who committed a burglary first called the business or home to see if anyone was there, and the number the burglar called from was recorded on the office or home telephone's caller ID, providing a valuable lead to police in identifying and locating the suspect. Caller ID can be helpful in cases involving telephone threats, kidnappings and the like.

Pen Registers. Pen registers are electronic devices that record all numbers dialed from specific phone lines. Title 18 of the U.S. Code defines a pen register as

> a device or process which records or decodes dialing, routing, addressing, or signaling information transmitted by an instrument or facility from which a wire or

electronic communication is transmitted, provided, however, that such information shall not include the contents of any communication, but such term does not include any device or process used by a provider or customer of a wire or electronic communication service for billing, or recording as an incident to billing, for communications services provided by such provider or any device or process used by a provider or customer of a wire communication service for cost accounting or other like purposes in the ordinary course of its business.

This expanded definition was set forth in the USA PATRIOT Act.

Dialed Number Recorders (DNR). A DNR can simultaneously monitor call activity on several lines and some have wiretapping capabilities. For each intercepted call, the DNR displays and prints a detailed call record. Once installed, the DNR is fully automatic and requires minimal attention.

State Resources.
Investigators also use information from the state police, the Department of Motor Vehicles, the Department of Corrections and the Parole Commission.

Federal Resources.
Federal resources include the U.S. Post Office; the Immigration and Naturalization Service; the Social Security Administration; the Federal Bureau of Investigation (FBI); the Bureau of Alcohol, Tobacco, Firearms and Explosives (ATF); and the Drug Enforcement Administration.

The FBI's National Crime Information Center (NCIC) contains online databases on wanted and missing persons; stolen guns, securities, articles, boats, license plates and vehicles; criminal histories; foreign fugitives and deported felons; gang and terrorist members; and persons subject to protection orders. The newest generation, NCIC 2000, includes mug shots (e.g., of sexual offenders and persons on probation or parole or incarcerated in federal prisons) and other personal identifying images, such as scars and tattoos; images of vehicles; an enhanced name search (of all derivatives of a name, e.g., Jeff, Geoff, Jeffrey); automated single-finger fingerprint matching; and information linking. These provide the ability to associate logically related records across NCIC files for the same criminal or the same crime. For example, an inquiry on a gun also could retrieve a wanted person or a stolen vehicle. The NCIC 2000 system is continuously being enhanced, with recent improvements including the addition of a separated file for violent gangs and terrorists, continued development of the dental repository database, faster search and response capability and the ability to add lost or stolen law enforcement credentials to the system.

The Internet

The Internet is an extremely valuable source of information. Fast-breaking cases, such as a kidnapping, can be aided by an investigator's ability to distribute photographs and important details efficiently and quickly.

Another resource is the Web site of the International Association of Chiefs of Police, http://www.theiacp.org. The FBI's Web site, http://www.fbi.gov, provides information about major investigations, wanted felons, various FBI programs and initiatives and ways to contact FBI agents regarding various crimes.

Victims, Complainants and Witnesses

In addition to reports and records, databases and other Internet resources, investigators obtain information from people associated with the investigation. Vast amounts of information come from people with direct or indirect knowledge of a crime. Although no one is legally required to provide information to the police except personal identification and accident information, citizens are responsible for cooperating with the police for their own and the community's best interests. Everyone is a potential crime victim and a potential source of information. Interview anyone other than a suspect who has information about a case. This includes victims, complainants and witnesses.

A victim is a person injured by a crime. Frequently the victim is also the complainant and a witness. Victims are emotionally involved and may be experiencing anger, rage and fear. Such personal involvement can cause them to exaggerate or distort what occurred. Victims may also make a **dying declaration**, a statement that can provide valuable information to investigators and usually qualifies as a hearsay exception, making it admissible as evidence.

A **complainant** is a person who requests that some action be taken. A complainant may also be the reporting party (RP), the individual who notified the police about a crime, but the RP is not always necessarily the complainant. For example, an overnight theft at a business might be discovered and called in to the police by the first employee who arrives in the morning, but the complainant might actually be the owner of the business. The complainant (or RP) is especially important in the initial stages of a case. Listen carefully to all details and determine the extent of the investigative problems involved: the type of crime, who committed it, what witnesses were present, the severity of any injuries and any leads. Thank the complainant for contributing to the investigation.

A witness is a person who saw a crime or some part of it being committed. Good eyewitnesses are often the best source of information in a criminal investigation. Record the information a witness gives, including any details that can identify and locate a suspect or place the suspect at the crime scene. Although not always reliable, eyewitnesses' testimony remains a vital asset in investigating and prosecuting cases.

Sometimes a diligent search is needed to find witnesses. They may not want to get involved, or they may withhold information or provide it for ulterior motives. Make every effort to locate all witnesses. Check with the victim's friends and associates. Make public appeals for information on radio, television and the Internet. An informational checkpoint might also be used, as described in Chapter 4. Check the entire crime scene area. Conduct a neighborhood canvass to determine whether anyone saw or heard anything when the crime occurred.

The Neighborhood Canvass.

Often the best way to solve a crime is to go door to door in the area around the crime scene. Nyberg (2006, p.36) says, "There's a sign mounted on the walls of our homicide office with wooden letters that read GOYAKOD. That's not some Russian obscenity. It's a piece of advice on how to close cases. We would sit sometimes during meetings about our current cases, brainstorming ideas to generate leads. More often than not, someone would nod, smile, and say GOYAKOD, which stands for 'Get off your ass and knock on doors.' If any one phrase exemplifies what good police work is, that's it."

Knocking on doors is essential in a major criminal investigation. The area canvass is one of the first tasks an investigator should have on his or her lead sheet: "A thoroughly conducted and documented neighborhood canvass can be the most important investigative tool in developing leads and solving cases, while a hastily conducted and poorly documented one can seriously hinder the timely and successful resolution of a case" (Boetig, 2010, p.66). Indeed, "Countless cases have been solved by a single item of information gleaned during a well-done area canvass" (Monheim, 2007, pp.48–49). Fundamentals of conducting a successful neighborhood canvass include (Boetig, 2010):

■ Identify one person to serve as canvass supervisor.

■ Establish geographic boundaries for the canvass, recognizing the perimeter can be expanded or contracted as needed.

■ Provide clear assignments and instructions to all canvass participants.

■ Ask for the names of everyone who lives at, works at, visits, delivers to or has access to the location.

■ Interview everyone separately.

■ Do not overlook or discount people who were not present at the time of the incident, as they may still be able to provide valuable information about local and neighborhood issues, past or recent suspicious activity, gossip and rumors and what is considered "normal" in the area.

■ Conduct a thorough, professional, well-documented canvass from start to finish, keeping in mind it is not a race.

Boetig (2010, p.67) stresses, "As the case develops, officers may not have another opportunity to speak to a certain person if he becomes a suspect and invokes certain constitutional rights. It is imperative for the first attempt to be done correctly."

The Knock and Talk.

Another technique to obtain information from others is the "knock and talk." As Scarry (2007, p.62) explains, "'Knock and talk' is a legitimate investigative technique that occurs at the home of a suspect or an individual with information about an investigation. A number of courts recognize that knock and talks are consensual encounters that do not violate the Fourth Amendment." In *United States v. Crapser* (2007), the Ninth District Court of Appeals set forth the general rule regarding knock-and-talk encounters that has become a firmly rooted notion in Fourth Amendment jurisprudence (Scarry, p.64): "Absent express orders from the person in possession against any possible trespass, there is no rule of private or public conduct which makes it illegal per se, or a condemned invasion of the person's right of privacy, for anyone openly and peaceably, at high noon, to walk up the steps and knock on the front door of any man's 'castle' with the honest intent of asking questions of the occupant thereof—whether the questioner be a pollster, a salesman, or an officer of the law." Scarry notes, "Police officers learn early on in their careers, they are permitted to briefly detain people as long as they can articulate the basis, or reasonable suspicion, for that detention."

A Caution.

Be aware that suspect and witness statements are not always reliable. A group of police officers attended a session on the reliability of witnesses' memory and were given a memory recall test. Every officer failed the test. Witnesses are often more confident in their knowledge of what happened than they are accurate. "What witnesses think they see is a function of what they expected to see, what they wanted to see and what they actually saw; the more ambiguous the last, the greater the influence of the first two factors" (Rossmo, 2009, p.55). Adding to the ambiguity is the fact that many people see only a part of the commission of a crime but testify as though they witnessed the entire event.

Informants

An **informant** is anyone who can provide information about a case but who is not a complainant, witness, victim or suspect. Informants may be interested citizens, individuals with criminal records, suspects with pending criminal records who are trying to work off cases against them and people who seek to make money by providing information and assistance.

Informants are frequently given code names, and only the investigator knows their identity. In some instances, however, informants may not remain anonymous, and their identity might have to be revealed. Be extremely careful in using such contacts. Never make promises or deals you cannot legally fulfill. Many jurisdictions have policies regarding the use of juveniles as informants, specifying a certain minimum age for informants or requiring police to first get permission from a court, parental or legal guardian.

Confidential Informants.

Of importance to investigators is the *confidential informant* or CI, described as "a person formally registered with and compensated by the department for supplying information or performing a service, such as a controlled purchase of drugs. Compensation may take the form of money and/or a reduced sentence for criminal behavior" (Jetmore, 2007a, p.22). Investigators' skill in recruiting, maintaining and motivating CIs to supply information can greatly enhance their effectiveness in solving cases: "There is still no substitute for gathering information from the street. A police officer's ability to develop a case by using sources of information from people engaged in criminal behavior or living on the fringes of society is the bread and butter of detective work" (Jetmore).

Feuer and Baker (2008) call CIs a detective's best friend: "They act as eyes and ears. They serve as secret tipsters. They take the police, by proxy, to the dangerous and privileged places where badges cannot go." CIs are usually recruited and managed in secret, making it hard to determine how many there are (Feuer and Baker). The FBI is said to maintain more than 15,000 secret informants; the Drug Enforcement Administration has about 4,000 at any one time.

Building trust is key in developing informants. A high level of trust in a CI can lead officers to regard that person "reliable." A reliable informant might be an individual with whom an officer has already worked successfully in the past. The status of being reliable might hold more weight with judges in cases where officers are seeking a search warrant based on information provided by an informant who has a record of being credible.

Establishing Reliability.

The following steps are recommended to help investigators achieve the totality of circumstances necessary to establish probable cause (Jetmore, 2007b, p.24):

1. Corroborate as much of the informant's information as possible.
2. Determine how, where, when and under what circumstances the informant obtained the information.
3. Explain (without citing specific cases and names) use of the informants' information in past criminal cases that led to arrests, convictions, seizures and so on.
4. Provide or reveal statements informants made.
5. Identify the informant if it's safe to do so.

Criteria for determining the reliability of informants' information were discussed in Chapter 4. The Court ruled in *Alabama v. White* (1990), "An anonymous tip can provide the foundation for reasonable suspicion when the tip predicts future activities that the officer is able to corroborate, which makes it reasonable to think that the informant has inside knowledge about the suspect."

Suspects

A suspect is a person considered to be directly or indirectly connected with a crime, either by overt act or by planning or directing it. Do not overlook the suspect as a chief source of information. An individual can become a suspect either through information provided by citizens or by his or her own actions. Any suspicious individuals should be questioned. Complete a field-interview card or create a field interview electronic document for any suspicious person you stop. This record places a person or vehicle in a specific place at a specific time and furnishes data for future investigative needs.

A person with a known modus operandi fitting a crime may be spotted at or near the crime scene. The person may be wanted for another crime or show an exaggerated concern for the police's presence, or the person may be in an illegal place at an illegal time—often the case with juveniles.

When questioning occurs spontaneously on the street (referred to as a **field interview**), it is especially advantageous to officers to question someone suspected of involvement in a crime right after the crime has occurred.

Sometimes direct questioning of suspects is not the best way to obtain information. In cases in which direct contact would tip off the person, it is often better to use undercover or surveillance officers or various types of listening devices, as discussed in Chapter 7.

Information is obtained continuously throughout an investigation. Some is volunteered, and some the police officer must really work for; some is useful and some worthless or even misleading. Most of an officer's time is spent meeting people and obtaining information from them, a process commonly referred to as either an *interview* or an *interrogation*.

An **interview** is questioning people who are not suspects in a crime but who know something about it or the people involved. An **interrogation** is questioning those suspected of direct or indirect involvement in a crime.

> The ultimate goal of interviewing and interrogating is to determine the truth—that is, to identify those responsible for a crime and to eliminate the innocent from suspicion.

Investigators must obtain all the facts supporting the truth, whether they indicate a person's guilt or innocence. The best information either proves the elements of the crime (the corpus delicti) or provides leads.

Characteristics of an Effective Interviewer/Interrogator

Many of the emotional and intellectual traits of an investigator (discussed in Chapter 1) are especially valuable in communicating with others. Presenting a favorable appearance and personality and establishing rapport are more important than physical attributes. Sometimes, however, it is an advantage to be of the same race or gender as the person being questioned. Under some circumstances, it is better not to wear a uniform. Sometimes a suit or jeans and a sweater are more appropriate.

> An effective interviewer/interrogator is adaptable and culturally adroit, self-controlled, patient, confident, optimistic, objective, sensitive to individual rights and knowledgeable about the elements of crimes.

■ *Adaptable and culturally adroit.* Your cultural and educational background and experience affect your ability to understand people from all walks of life, to meet them on their own level on varied subjects and to adapt to their personalities, backgrounds and lifestyles.

■ *Self-controlled and patient.* Use self-control and patience to motivate people to talk. Be understanding yet detached, waiting for responses while patiently leading the conversation and probing for facts. Remain professional, recognizing that some people you interview may feel hostile toward you.

■ *Confident and optimistic.* Do not assume that because the person you are questioning is a hardened criminal, has an attorney, is belligerent or is better educated than you that no opportunity exists to obtain information. Show that you are in command, that you already know many answers and that you want to corroborate what you know. If the conversation shifts away from the subject, steer the discussion back to the topic.

■ *Objective.* Maintain your perspective on what is sought, avoiding preconceived ideas about the case. Be aware of any personal prejudices that can interfere with your questioning.

■ *Sensitive to individual rights.* Maintain a balance between the rights of others and those of society. Naturally, suspects do not want to give information that conflicts with their self-interests or threatens their freedom. Moreover, many citizens want to stay out of other people's business. Use reason and patience to overcome this resistance to becoming involved.

■ *Knowledgeable of the elements of the crime.* Know what information you need to prove the elements of the crime you are investigating. Phrase questions to elicit information related to these elements.

Enhancing Communication

Successful questioning requires two-way communication between the investigator and the person being questioned. There are several ways to improve communication, whether in interviewing or interrogating.

> To improve communication: prepare in advance; obtain the information as soon after the incident as possible, but try to build some rapport before diving right into what you are looking for; be considerate and friendly; use a private setting; eliminate physical barriers; sit rather than stand; encourage conversation; ask simple questions one at a time; listen and observe.

Building trust with citizens, including children, is important for law enforcement. The ability to communicate with individuals from diverse populations—various ages, ethnicities, socioeconomic groups and so forth—is a critical skill for effective investigators.
© Myrleen Ferguson Cate/PhotoEdit

Emotional Barriers to Communication.

People often have reasons for not wanting to answer questions that police ask. Even though these reasons may have no logical basis, be aware of the common barriers to communication.

> Emotional barriers to communication include ingrained attitudes and prejudices, fear, anger or hostility and self-preservation.

One important barrier to communication between police and the public is the ingrained attitude that telling the truth to the police is wrong. The criminal element, those closely associated with crime and even the police commonly use such terms as *fink* and *snitch*, which imply that giving information to the police is wrong, unsavory or illegal.

Prejudices concerning a person's race, beliefs, religion, appearance, amount of education, economic status, sexual orientation or place of upbringing can be barriers to communication. You may encounter prejudice because you are a police officer or because of your race, gender or physical appearance. Equally important, prejudices you hold can interfere with your communicating with some people and therefore with your investigation.

Fear is another barrier to communication. Some witnesses fear that criminals will harm them or their family if they testify, or they fear the imposition on their time and the negative impact on their wages of having to go to court to testify.

People actually involved in a crime can be reluctant to talk for many reasons, the most important of which is self-preservation. Although suspects naturally do not want to implicate themselves, other factors may also cause them to not answer questions. Severe guilt feelings can preclude telling anyone about a crime. Fear of consequences can be so great that nothing will induce them to tell the truth. They may fear that if they are sent to prison they will be sexually assaulted or beaten, or they may fear that any accomplices they implicate will seek revenge.

Other Barriers to Communication.

As ethnic diversity increases and other languages proliferate, language barriers become an increasing challenge to law enforcement. Language barriers might be minimized or eliminated by seeking a mix of bilingual officers in hiring, training officers in conversational foreign languages and matching officers to appropriate beats and assignments.

One of the most common techniques used to help officers communicate with non-English-speaking people is the Point Talk Law Enforcement Translator, in which an officer locates the appropriate language either in a handbook or on a computer screen and then points to appropriate phrases to ask specific questions or elicit desired responses.

Additional barriers to communication exist with individuals who are hearing impaired, who have Alzheimer's disease or who are mentally retarded. It is highly recommended that officers learn sign language to help them communicate with the hearing impaired. This skill also allows officers to communicate silently among themselves when confronting suspects. In addition, it can be a universal means of recognition for undercover officers from different agencies or from large agencies where officers often do not know each other.

Effective Questioning Techniques

Most cases are solved through effective questioning techniques. Investigators use questions and repetition effectively and know how to question reluctant subjects. No matter which technique or combination of techniques you select, you should follow two key requirements:

> **Two basic requirements to obtain information are to listen and to observe.**

How people act during questioning can tell as much as or more than their words. An effective investigator must be able to read and react to body language and nonverbal cues. Signs of unusual nervousness, odd expressions, rapid breathing, visible perspiration or a highly agitated state are cause to question the person's truthfulness. Table 6.1 summarizes the guidelines for a successful questioning.

Types of Questions: Direct, Indirect, Closed-Ended, Open-Ended and Leading.

An important difference exists between direct and indirect questions. A **direct question** is to the point, allowing little possibility of misinterpretation—for example, "What time did you and your husband leave the restaurant?" In contrast, an **indirect question** is disguised. For example, a question such as, "How do you and your neighbor get along?," could elicit a variety of answers. Direct questions can be very useful in eliciting useful details. However, do not confuse a direct question with a **closed-ended question**, which requires only a "yes" or "no" or other short, simple answer. Closed-ended questions, such as "Do you get along well with your neighbor?" or "Did you go straight home after work?" should be avoided during interviews. In contrast, an **open-ended question** gives the victim, witness or suspect the opportunity to provide a much fuller response, allowing the investigator greater insight into the person's knowledge and feelings, for example, "What can you tell me about your relationship with your neighbor?" or "What did you do after work?" Open-ended questions often begin with "Why," "How" or "Tell me about." A **leading question** prompts or leads a person to a specific response and often implies an answer. For example, "How much did you drink before you went next door and assaulted your neighbor?" implies that the suspect had been drinking before the assault.

> **Ask direct questions and open-ended questions liberally. Asking leading questions can also be a useful interrogation technique. Use indirect questions and closed-ended questions sparingly.**

Knowing the elements of the crime you are investigating lets you select pertinent questions.

TABLE 6.1 Interview/Interrogation Guidelines

- Ask one question at a time and keep your responses simple and direct.
- Avoid questions that can be answered "yes" or "no"; a narrative account provides more information and may reveal inconsistencies in the person's story.
- Be positive in your approach, but let the person save face if necessary so that you may obtain further information.
- Give the person time to answer. Do not be uncomfortable with pauses in the interview. Often, guilty suspects are uncomfortable and feel a need to fill the silence because of their discomfort. This may cause them to provide more information that can be used against them throughout the interview or in later interviews.
- Listen to answers, but at the same time anticipate your next question.
- Watch your body language and tone of voice.
- Start the conversation on neutral territory.
- Digital recorders can be frightening. A technique commonly used is to tuck the recorder behind a portfolio or notepad. After a time, the interviewee often forgets that the recording device is there.
- React to what you hear.
- As you move into difficult territory, slow down.
- Don't rush to fill silences. Again, allow the witness's or suspect's words and actions a chance to expose themselves.
- Pose the toughest questions simply, directly and with confidence.
- No meltdowns. You must establish professional distance. Keep your role clear.

Repetition. Anyone who watches detective shows has heard victims or suspects complain, "I've already told my story to the police." This is true to life. Individuals *are* asked to tell and retell their version of what happened and for very good reasons. Someone who is lying will either provide very inconsistent stories or will tell a story *exactly* the same way each time, as if it is well rehearsed. A truthful story, however, will contain the same facts but be phrased differently each time it is retold. After a person has told you what happened, guide the discussion to some other aspect of the case. Later, come back to the topic and ask the person to repeat the story.

> **Repetition is an effective technique to obtain recall and to uncover lies.**

Often repeating what someone has told you helps the person provide additional information. Sometimes it also confuses the person being questioned, and if the original version was not true, another repetition will reveal this fact. If inconsistencies appear, go back over the information and attempt to account for them.

Recording and Videotaping Interviews and Interrogations.

Anand (2008, p.60) notes, "Tired of the debate over who said what, many agencies use new digital technology to record all interviews of suspects, victims and witnesses." Courts in Alaska and Minnesota have mandated recording all interrogations because of the exclusionary rule. Laws in other states vary as to whether suspects must consent to being recorded. Some agencies are videotaping interviews and confessions rather than simply recording them.

Tapes can benefit both the investigator and the person being interviewed or interrogated. For investigators, recordings provide a verbatim account directly from the source, verifying the accuracy of what the report says and alleviating any defense arguments about coercion, illegitimate handling of the suspect and lack of *Miranda* rights being read. Taping interviews and interrogations frees the investigator from having to scribble notes frantically, eyes down at their notepad, and lets them pay closer attention to the witness's or suspect's body language and nonverbal cues. Recordings also allow investigators the chance to review the conversation as often as needed. For those being interviewed or interrogating, the recordings ensure that detectives do not stray into third-degree tactics, take an unethical line of questioning or engage in any conduct that violates the rights of those being questioned.

Critics of mandatory recording policies voice concern that such techniques might deter confessions and cause some people to refuse to speak freely. Interestingly, a similar concern was voiced when *Miranda* was decided. Yet, people continue to volunteer information despite being given a *Miranda* warning.

THE INTERVIEW

Interviewing involves talking to people, questioning them, obtaining information and reading between the lines. The main sources of information at the crime scene are the complainant, the victim and witnesses. (These may be the same person.) Separate the witnesses and then obtain a complete account of the incident from each one.

> **Interview witnesses separately if possible. Interview the victim or complainant first, then eyewitnesses and then people who did not actually see the crime but who have relevant information.**

Finding, detaining and separating witnesses are high priorities. Witnesses who are not immediately detained can drift off into the crowd or decide not to become involved.

Obtain the information as rapidly as possible. Identify all witnesses and check their names and addresses against their identification. Ask witnesses not to speak to one another or to compare stories until they have written down in their own words what happened.

If there are many witnesses, discuss the incident briefly with each. Then establish a priority for obtaining statements based on the witnesses' availability and the importance of their information.

In most cases, interview complainants first because they can often provide enough information to determine whether a crime has been committed and, if so, what type of crime. If department policy requires it, have complainants read and initial or sign the information you record during the interview.

Anyone who saw what happened, how it happened or who made it happen is interviewed next. Such witnesses may be in a state of panic, frustration or anger. In the presence of such emotions, remain calm and detached, yet show empathy and understanding—a difficult feat. After interviewing witnesses, interview people who can furnish facts about what happened before or immediately after the crime or who have information about the suspect or the victim.

Not all people with relevant information are at the crime scene. Some people in the general area may have seen or heard something of value. Even people miles away from the scene may have information about the crime or the person committing it. Explain to such individuals why you are questioning them, check their identification and then proceed with your interview.

The main sources of immediate information away from the crime scene are neighbors, business associates, people in the general area such as motel and hotel personnel and longtime residents. Longer-term contacts may include informants, missing witnesses, friends and relatives. Appeals for public cooperation and reports from various agencies and organizations may also produce information. Record both positive and negative information. The fact that a witness did *not* see anyone enter a building may be as important as having seen someone.

Advance Planning

Many interviews, at least initial ones, are conducted in the field and allow no time for planning. If time permits, plan carefully for interviews. Review reports about the case before questioning people. Learn as much as possible about the person you are going to question before you begin the interview. Know which questions you need answers to, and have a plan of approach to the likely responses from those you are interviewing. This means anticipating how people may respond. A well-planned and prepared interview will mean greater success in obtaining information or getting a confession and prevents the need for a follow-up interview when an investigator has forgotten to ask something.

Selecting the Time and Place

Sometimes there is no time to decide when and where to conduct an interview. Arriving at a crime scene, you may be confronted with a victim or witness who immediately begins to supply pertinent information. Recall that these *res gestae* statements are extremely valuable. Therefore, record them as close to verbatim as possible.

After ensuring that the scene is safe and all emergencies, such as critical medical issues, have been handled, determine as soon as possible who the complainant is, where and how many witnesses exist and whether the suspect has been apprehended. If more than one officer is present, the officer in charge decides who will be questioned and assigns personnel to do it.

Immediate contact with people who have information about a crime improves the chances of obtaining information. Although emotions may be running high, witnesses are usually best able to recall details immediately after an incident. They are also less likely to embellish or exaggerate their stories because others present can be asked to verify the information. Moreover, witnesses can be separated so they will have no opportunity to compare information. Finally, the reluctance to give the police information is usually not so strong immediately after a crime. Given time to reflect, witnesses may fear that they will have to testify in court, that cooperation will take them away from work and cost them financially or that the criminal will retaliate.

Beginning the Interview

How an interview is started is extremely important. At this point, the interviewee and the interviewer size each other up. Mistakes in beginning the interview can establish insurmountable barriers. Make your initial contact friendly but professional. Begin by identifying yourself and showing your credentials. Then ask a general question about the person's knowledge of the crime.

Establishing Rapport

Rapport is probably the most critical factor in any interview. **Rapport** is an understanding between individuals created by genuine interest and concern. It requires empathy. *Empathy* means accurately perceiving and

Some interviews are conducted under difficult circumstances, when victims or witnesses have suffered trauma or are under duress. Obtaining statements from domestic violence victims can be particularly challenging. In such situations, what interview techniques should the investigator use so that useful information can be drawn out while remaining sensitive to the needs of the interviewee?

© Bob Daemmrich/PhotoEdit

responding to another person's thoughts and feelings. This differs from *sympathy*, which is an involuntary emotion of feeling sorry for another person.

People who are approached civilly may volunteer a surprising amount of useful information. Most people do not condone criminal behavior and will assist you. However, they often do not know what is important to a specific investigation. Provide every opportunity to establish rapport and to assist citizens in providing information.

Not everyone with information can provide it easily. People who are emotionally unstable or mentally deficient, have temporary loss of memory or fear the police often cannot or will not be forthcoming. With them, establishing rapport is critical. If a person is deaf or speaks a foreign language, arrange for an interpreter. If a person appears unwilling to talk, find out why.

Give reluctant witnesses confidence by demonstrating self-assurance. Give indifferent witnesses a sense of importance by explaining how the information will help a victim. Remind them that someday they may be victims themselves and would then want others to cooperate. Find a way to motivate every witness to talk with you and answer your questions.

Careful listening enhances rapport. Do not indicate verbally or nonverbally that you consider a matter trivial or unimportant; people will sense if you are merely going through the motions. Take a personal interest. Discuss their family, their work or their hobbies. Be empathetic and assure them that everything possible will be done but that you need their help.

Networking an Interview

Most people are familiar with the concept of a business or professional **network**—a body of personal contacts that can further one's career. In reality, networks can extend much farther than this.

Networks also establish relationships between people and their beliefs. Networks produce a context in which to understand a person. These networks may be social, ethnic, cultural, business, professional/occupational, religious or political. As American society becomes more diverse, officers will have to understand the networks in their jurisdictions.

Reluctant Interviewees

Most people who are reluctant to be questioned respond to one of two approaches: logical or emotional.

 Appeal to a reluctant interviewee's reason or emotions.

The *logical approach* is based on reason. Use logic to determine why the person refuses to cooperate. Explain the problems that result when people who know about a crime do not cooperate with investigators.

The *emotional approach* addresses such negative feelings as hate, anger, greed, revenge, pride and jealousy. You can increase these emotions or simply acknowledge them (e.g., "Anyone in your situation would respond the same way"). If such tactics do not work, warn the person of the serious consequences of withholding important information.

Whether to select a logical or an emotional approach depends on the person being interviewed, the type of investigation and your personal preference.

The Cognitive Interview

Interview style has important implications for how much information is received from subjects. The **cognitive interview** tries to get the interviewee to recall the scene mentally by using simple mnemonic techniques aimed at encouraging focused retrieval. These techniques include allowing interviewees to do most of the talking, asking open-ended questions, allowing ample time for answers, avoiding interruptions and encouraging the person to report all details, no matter how trivial.

The cognitive interview method calls for using a secluded, quiet place free of distractions and encouraging a subject to speak slowly. The interviewer first helps the interviewee *reconstruct the circumstances* by asking, "How did you feel . . .?" Have the interviewee describe the weather, the surroundings, objects, people and smells. Interviewees are encouraged to *report everything*, even if they think something is unimportant. They might also be asked to *relate the events in a different order* or to *change perspectives*. What would another person present have seen?

Among the drawbacks of this method are the amount of time it takes and the need for a controlled environment. Nonetheless, the cognitive interview is especially effective for obtaining information from victims and witnesses who have difficulty remembering an event.

Testimonial Hearsay

A recent development in interviewing individuals with knowledge of a crime has changed the timing of questioning in some situations, that is, those dealing with testimonial hearsay. **Testimonial hearsay** includes prior testimony as well as statements made as a result of police interrogation. Witness statements obtained through such "structured questioning" are inadmissible in a criminal trial unless the witness is unavailable to testify and was previously cross-examined by the defendant (*Crawford v. Washington*, 2004).

Police reports should differentiate between statements that resulted from structured questioning and those that did not. Officers should listen well, take good notes and make it clear in the notes and report that they did not direct or extract the specific information. If an interview yields substantial information related to a case, a statement should be obtained.

Statements

A **statement** is a legal narrative description of events related to a crime. It is a formal, detailed account. It begins with an introduction that gives the place, time, date and names of the people conducting and present at an interview. The name, address and age of the person questioned are stated before the main body of the statement. Figure 6.1 shows a sample statement.

The body of the statement is the person's account of the incident. A clause at the end states that the information was given voluntarily. The person making the statement reads each page, makes any needed corrections, initials each correction and then signs the statement.

Obtain statements in private, with no one other than police officers present, and allow no interruptions. However, other people will need to be called in to witness the signing of the statement.

Statements can be taken in several ways: prepared in longhand by the person interviewed, dictated to a typist in question-answer format or digitally recorded for later typing and signing.

A combination of questions and answers, with the answers in narrative form, is often the most effective format. However, a question and answer format is often challenged in court on grounds that questions guide and control the response. Another alternative is for you to write down the words of the person and have the person read and sign your notes. Also record the ending time.

Beginning and ending times may be of great value in court testimony.

Closing the Interview

End each interview by thanking the person for cooperating. If you have established good rapport with the interviewee, that person will probably cooperate with you later if needed.

THE INTERROGATION

Questioning suspects is usually more difficult than questioning witnesses or victims. Once identified and located, a person who *is* involved in a crime may make a statement, admission or confession that, corroborated with independent evidence, can produce a guilty plea or obtain a conviction.

Many of the procedures used in interviewing are also used in interrogating, but you should note some important differences in how you question suspects. One of the most critical is ensuring that you do not violate suspects' constitutional rights, so that the information you obtain

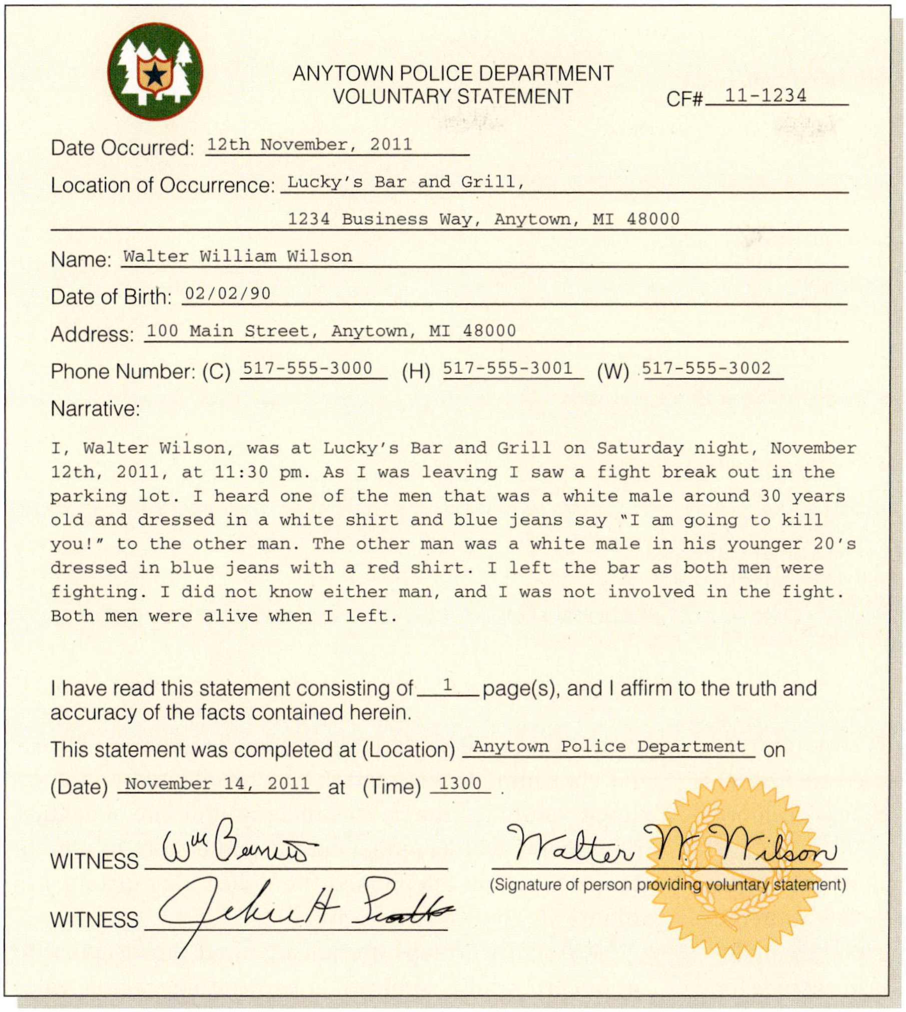

ANYTOWN POLICE DEPARTMENT
VOLUNTARY STATEMENT

CF# __11-1234__

Date Occurred: __12th November, 2011__

Location of Occurrence: __Lucky's Bar and Grill,__
__1234 Business Way, Anytown, MI 48000__

Name: __Walter William Wilson__

Date of Birth: __02/02/90__

Address: __100 Main Street, Anytown, MI 48000__

Phone Number: (C) __517-555-3000__ (H) __517-555-3001__ (W) __517-555-3002__

Narrative:

I, Walter Wilson, was at Lucky's Bar and Grill on Saturday night, November 12th, 2011, at 11:30 pm. As I was leaving I saw a fight break out in the parking lot. I heard one of the men that was a white male around 30 years old and dressed in a white shirt and blue jeans say "I am going to kill you!" to the other man. The other man was a white male in his younger 20's dressed in blue jeans with a red shirt. I left the bar as both men were fighting. I did not know either man, and I was not involved in the fight. Both men were alive when I left.

I have read this statement consisting of __1__ page(s), and I affirm to the truth and accuracy of the facts contained herein.

This statement was completed at (Location) __Anytown Police Department__ on

(Date) __November 14, 2011__ at (Time) __1300__.

WITNESS _____

WITNESS _____

_____
(Signature of person providing voluntary statement)

FIGURE 6.1
Sample voluntary statement.
Source: Drafted by Henry Cho, Cho Research & Consulting, LLC 2011

will be admissible in court. It is imperative that officers distinguish between questioning in a *Terry*-type stop/detention situation and a custodial situation requiring giving the *Miranda* warning.

The *Miranda* Warning

Before interrogating any suspect in custody, you must give the **Miranda warning**, as stipulated in *Miranda v. Arizona* (1966). In this decision, the Supreme Court ruled that suspects must be informed of their right to remain silent, to have an attorney present and to have a state-appointed attorney if they cannot afford private counsel. Suspects must also be warned that anything they say may be used against them in court. Many officers read suspects their rights from a card (Figure 6.2).

The *Miranda* warning informs suspects of their Fifth Amendment rights. Give the *Miranda* warning to every suspect you interrogate while in custody.

The Fifth Amendment states, "No person shall be compelled in any criminal case to be a witness against himself." The *Miranda* decision established that this right must be made known to suspects in custody before any questioning can occur.

Thousands of words have been written for and against this decision. The general interpretation and application of the *Miranda* decision is that once you have reasonable grounds to believe a person has committed a crime, that person's constitutional rights are in jeopardy unless the *Miranda* warning is given *before* any questioning.

Many court cases illustrate the gray area that exists in determining when to give the warning. The terms most often used to describe when it should be given are **in custody** or **custodial arrest**. *In custody* generally refers to a point at which an officer has decided a suspect is not free to leave, there has been considerable deprivation of liberty or the officer has arrested the suspect.

In *Oregon v. Mathiason* (1977), the Supreme Court defined **custodial interrogation** as questioning initiated by law enforcement officers after a person has been taken

FIGURE 6.2
Miranda warning.
© Cengage Learning, 2013

**Peace Officers
Constitutional Pre-Interrogation Requirements**

The following warnings must be given prior to questioning a person who is in custody or is deprived of his freedom of action in any significant way:

THE CONSTITUTION REQUIRES I INFORM YOU THAT:
1. YOU HAVE THE RIGHT TO REMAIN SILENT.
2. ANYTHING YOU SAY CAN AND WILL BE USED AGAINST YOU IN COURT.
3. YOU HAVE THE RIGHT TO TALK TO A LAWYER NOW AND HAVE HIM PRESENT NOW OR AT ANY TIME DURING QUESTIONING.
4. IF YOU CANNOT AFFORD A LAWYER, ONE WILL BE APPOINTED FOR YOU WITHOUT COST.

Waiver of Rights
The suspect may waive his rights, but the burden is on the officer to show the waiver is made voluntarily, knowingly and intelligently.
He must affirmatively respond to the following questions:
1. DO YOU UNDERSTAND EACH OF THESE RIGHTS I HAVE EXPLAINED TO YOU?
2. DO YOU WISH TO TALK TO US AT THIS TIME?

Election of Rights
A subject can avail himself of his rights at any time and interrogation must then cease. If a subject will not waive his rights or during questioning elects to assert his rights, no testimony of that fact may ever be used against him at trial.

into custody or otherwise significantly deprived of freedom. If a suspect chooses to remain silent, ask no further questions. If the suspect requests counsel, ask no more questions until counsel is present.

The *Miranda* custody standard is no different for juveniles. In *Yarborough v. Alvarado* (2004), the Supreme Court held that a trial court need not consider age in determining whether a "reasonable person" is in custody for *Miranda* purposes.

Another *Miranda*-related concern, the fruit-of-the-poisonous-tree doctrine (Chapter 4), makes inadmissible any evidence obtained through an earlier violation of the defendant's constitutional rights (*Wong Sun v. United States*, 1963). That same consequence does *not* follow from a failure to follow the *Miranda* procedures. If officers learn about contraband or evidence from a statement that does not comply with *Miranda*, the contraband or evidence need not be suppressed as "poisonous fruit" of the inadmissible statement (*United States v. Patane*, 2004).

The *Miranda* warning does not have to be given in the exact form described in *Miranda* (Rutledge, 2010). In fact, a Florida count found that law enforcement agencies had 89 different versions of the warning. In *Florida v. Powell* (2010), the U.S. Supreme Court held that no exact wording is required to satisfy *Miranda*, as long as the four components of the warning are conveyed.

When *Miranda* Does Not Apply. The *Miranda* warning has never applied to voluntary or unsolicited, spontaneous statements, admissions or confessions. Someone can approach a police officer and say, "I want to confess that I killed Mark Jones. I took a gun from my car and shot him." If this remark was unsolicited and completely voluntary, the police officer is under no obligation to interrupt the person giving the confession. In one instance, a person telephoned the police long-distance to voluntarily confess to a felony.

Miranda warnings are *not* required during identification procedures such as fingerprinting, taking voice or handwriting exemplars or conducting a lineup or sobriety tests. They are *not* required during routine booking questions, during brief on-the-scene questioning or during brief, investigatory questioning during a temporary detention such as a *Terry* stop. A *Miranda* warning is also *not* required during roadside questioning following a routine traffic stop or other minor violation for which custody is not ordinarily imposed. *Miranda* warnings are not required by probation officers questioning those on probation for whom they are responsible. Finally, a warning is *not* required during questioning by a private citizen who is not an agent of the government.

Waiving the Rights. A suspect can waive the rights granted by *Miranda* but must do so intelligently and knowingly. A **waiver**, that is a giving up of a right, is accompanied by a written or witnessed oral statement that the waiver was voluntary (Figure 6.3).

Silence, in itself, is *not* a waiver. The suspect must articulate a waiver of rights. Therefore, many officers read the *Miranda* warning aloud from a printed card and then have the suspect read and sign the card (see Figure 6.3). The date and time are also recorded. If no card

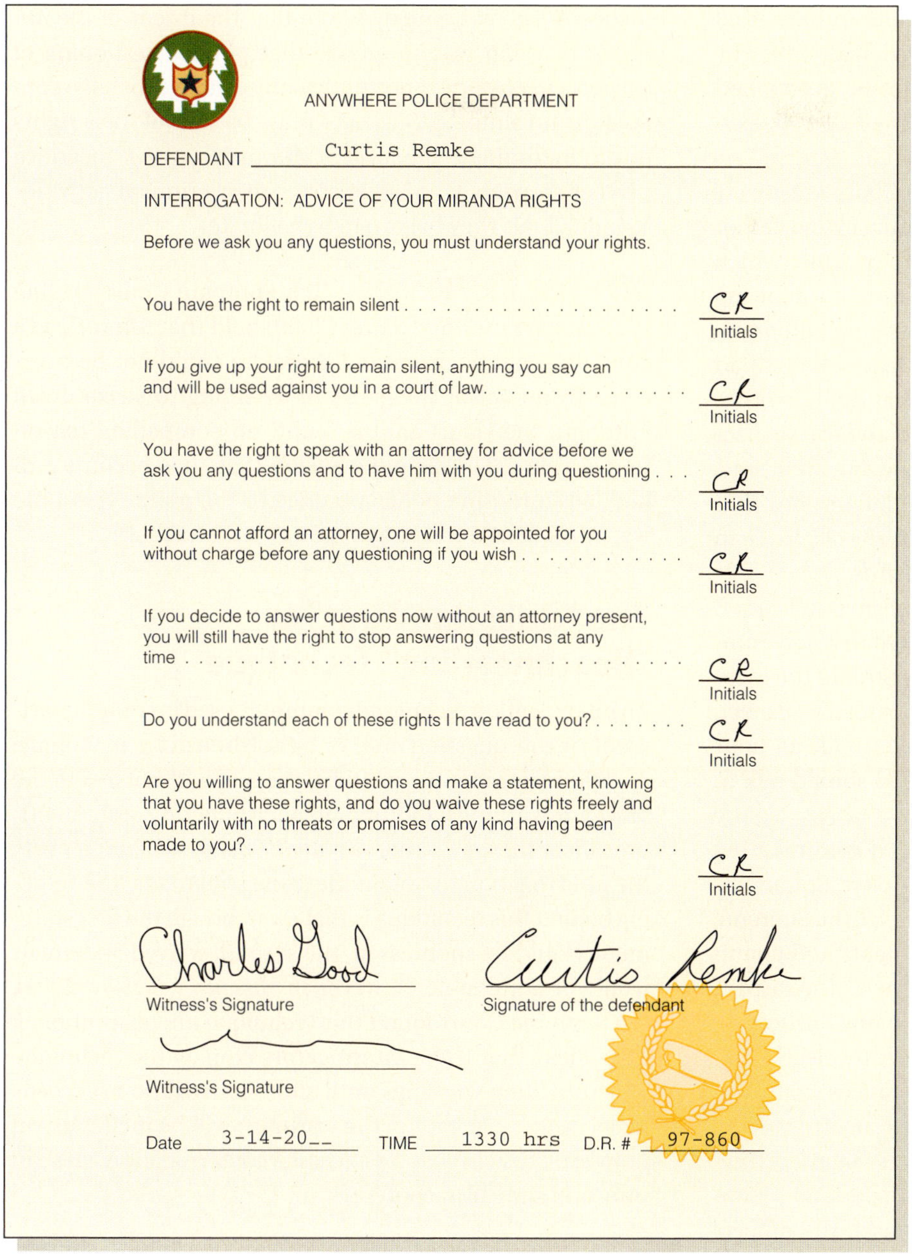

ANYWHERE POLICE DEPARTMENT

DEFENDANT Curtis Remke

INTERROGATION: ADVICE OF YOUR MIRANDA RIGHTS

Before we ask you any questions, you must understand your rights.

You have the right to remain silent . . . . CR Initials

If you give up your right to remain silent, anything you say can and will be used against you in a court of law. . . . . CR Initials

You have the right to speak with an attorney for advice before we ask you any questions and to have him with you during questioning . . . CR Initials

If you cannot afford an attorney, one will be appointed for you without charge before any questioning if you wish . . . . CR Initials

If you decide to answer questions now without an attorney present, you will still have the right to stop answering questions at any time . . . . CR Initials

Do you understand each of these rights I have read to you? . . . . CR Initials

Are you willing to answer questions and make a statement, knowing that you have these rights, and do you waive these rights freely and voluntarily with no threats or promises of any kind having been made to you? . . . . CR Initials

Charles Good
Witness's Signature

Curtis Remke
Signature of the defendant

Witness's Signature

Date 3-14-20__ TIME 1330 hrs D.R. # 97-860

FIGURE 6.3
Miranda waiver form.
© Cengage Learning, 2013

is available, a summary of the *Miranda* warning can be written, read and signed. Police have the legal burden of proving that the suspect did waive his or her rights. The suspect retains the right to stop answering questions at any point, even when he or she originally waived the right to remain silent.

Officers should not just state the suspect waived his rights; it is important they state which specific rights were waived (Rutledge, 2007a). The Fifth Amendment requires that suspects do not have to incriminate themselves; the Sixth Amendment requires that suspects be provided a lawyer. The Sixth Amendment right to counsel applies only to the specific crime for which the person has been indicted or arraigned. This situation often occurs when detectives are investigating a cold case and want to question suspects who are incarcerated on a different charge.

The Effects of *Miranda*. The *Miranda* warning does not prevent suspects from talking. It simply requires that suspects be advised of and fully understand their constitutional rights. The basic intent of the *Miranda* decision is to guarantee the rights of the accused. The practical effect is to ensure that confessions are obtained without duress or coercion, thereby removing any inferences that third-degree tactics were used.

Several Court decisions relate to the *Miranda* warning. In *Edwards v. Arizona* (1981), the Supreme Court held that after a suspect has been read his or her *Miranda* rights and then invokes the right to remain silent and to have legal counsel, the suspect cannot be re-approached, either by the same or different officers, and cannot be questioned further until a lawyer is made available. The *Edwards* decision, however, has since been modified under *Shatzer*.

In *Maryland v. Shatzer* (2010), the Court effectively set an expiration date on the right-to-counsel invocation by announcing a "14-day break-in-custody" rule, which changed *Miranda* protocol under *Edwards* by allowing police to reinitiate contact with a suspect who had previously asserted the right to counsel if at least 14 days had passed since the original invocation of that right. In other words, as long as two weeks have passed and the suspect has been out of *Miranda*, or police, custody for that time, having returned to his or her "normal" life, even if that "normal" life is as an inmate behind bars, the suspect can be re-approached without violating *Edwards*.

According to the *Davis* rule, as established in *Davis v. United States* (1994), police are not required to resolve ambiguous statements made by suspects regarding the invocation of the right to an attorney. In this case, the suspect, who had waived his *Miranda* rights, said about an hour and a half into the interrogation, "Maybe I should talk to a lawyer," but then said, "No, I don't want a lawyer," so the questioning continued, and Davis provided incriminating statements. Finding that the statements were not an unambiguous invocation of the right to counsel, the Supreme Court upheld admission of Davis's statements and unanimously affirmed his conviction and sentence: "The suspect must unambiguously request counsel. He must articulate his desire to have counsel present sufficiently clearly that a reasonable police officer in the circumstances would understand the statement to be a request for an attorney. . . . We decline to adopt a rule requiring officers to ask clarifying questions. If the suspect's statement is not an unambiguous or unequivocal request for counsel, the officers have no obligation to stop questioning him."

Examples of specific language that does not require questioning to stop are

- "I just don't think that I should say anything." (*Burket v. Angelone*, 2000)

- "I don't got nothing to say." (*United States v. Banks*, 2003)

- "Could I call my lawyer?" (*Dormire v. Wilkinson*, 2001)

In 1984 *Minnesota v. Murphy* established that probation officers do not need to give the *Miranda* warning, and *Berkemer v. McCarty* ruled that the *Miranda* warning is not required for traffic violations.

The Supreme Court ruled in *Illinois v. Perkins* (1990) that jailed suspects need not be told of their right to remain silent when they provide information to undercover agents.

Justice Anthony Kennedy wrote that the intent of the *Miranda* decision was to ensure that police questioning of suspects in custody is not sufficiently coercive to make confessions involuntary. Suspects must be told of their rights not to incriminate themselves. *Miranda* was *not* meant to protect suspects who boast about their criminal activities to individuals they believe to be cellmates.

Miranda Challenged. The Supreme Court's ruling in *Dickerson v. United States* (2000) held that *Miranda* is a constitutional decision and therefore could not be overruled by an act of Congress. In declining to strike down *Miranda*, the Court said it found no compelling reason to overrule a 34-year-old decision that "has become embedded in routine police practice to the point where the warnings have become part of our national culture."

The "Question First" or "Beachheading" Technique

An interrogation technique commonly used in some departments is the "question first," or **beachheading**, technique: An officer questions a custodial suspect without giving the *Miranda* warnings and obtains incriminating statements; the officer then gives the warning, gets a waiver and repeats the interrogation to obtain the same statement. The thinking behind this technique is that even though the first statement would be suppressed, the second, waived statement would be admissible. However, in *Missouri v. Seibert* (2004), the Supreme Court found this technique unconstitutional: "It is likely that if the interrogators employ the technique of withholding warnings until after interrogation succeeds in eliciting a confession, the warnings will be ineffective in preparing the suspect for successive interrogation, close in time and similar in content."

The Interplay of the Fourth and Fifth Amendments

Chapter 4 discussed how the Fourth Amendment restricts searches. This chapter discusses how the Fifth Amendment restricts confessions. Often the two amendments become intertwined, as seen in *New York v. Quarles* (1984), a case in which an exigent search resulted in a Fifth Amendment issue because of the statements elicited pursuant to the search. In *Quarles*, the Supreme Court ruled on the **public safety exception** to the *Miranda* warning requirement.

In 1980 two police officers were stopped by a young woman who told them she had been raped and gave them a description of her rapist, who, she stated, had just entered a nearby supermarket and was armed with a gun. The suspect, Benjamin Quarles, was located, and one officer ordered him to stop. Quarles ran, and the officer momentarily lost sight of him. When he was apprehended and frisked, he was wearing an empty shoulder holster. The officer asked Quarles where the gun was, and he nodded toward some cartons and said, "The gun is over there." The officer retrieved the gun, put Quarles under formal arrest and read him his rights. Quarles waived his rights to an attorney and answered questions.

At the trial, the court ruled pursuant to *Miranda* that the statement, "The gun is over there," and the subsequent discovery of the gun as a result of that statement were inadmissible. After reviewing the case, the Supreme Court ruled that the procedural safeguards that both deter a suspect from responding and increase the possibility of fewer convictions were deemed acceptable in *Miranda* to protect the Fifth Amendment privilege against self-incrimination. However, if *Miranda* warnings had deterred the response to the officer's question, the cost would have been more than just loss of evidence that might lead to a conviction. As long as the gun remained concealed in the store, it posed a danger to public safety.

The Court ruled that in this case the need to have the suspect talk (an exigent circumstance) took precedence over the requirement that the defendant be read his rights. The Court ruled that the material factor in applying this "public safety" exception is whether a public threat could possibly be removed by the suspect making a statement. In this case, the officer asked the question only to ensure his and the public's safety. He then gave the *Miranda* warning before continuing questioning.

The Fourth and Fifth Amendments also came into play in one case that was argued twice. The trials involved the same defendant (Robert Williams) but different prosecutors. In the first trial, *Brewer v. Williams* (1977), the issue revolved around information solicited from Williams without his being Mirandized. An arrest warrant was issued in Des Moines, Iowa, for Williams, an escapee from a mental institution wanted for murdering a little girl on Christmas Eve. Williams turned himself in to police in Davenport, Iowa. Des Moines police went to Davenport to transport Williams back to Des Moines, with all agreeing that Williams was not to be questioned on the way. However, one detective, knowing Williams was a psychiatric patient who possessed a strong religious faith, told Williams that he wanted him to think about where the little girl was buried. He could perhaps show them where the body was on the way back because it was sleeting and they might not be able to find it in the morning. The officer told Williams that the little girl who was snatched away on Christmas Eve needed a Christian burial (the Christian Burial Speech). Williams complied and showed the officers where he had buried the girl.

As Hess and Orthmann (2012, p.220) note, "Although the lower courts admitted Williams's damaging statements into evidence, the Supreme Court in *Brewer v. Williams* affirmed the court of appeals's decision that any statements made by Williams could not be admitted against him because the way they were elicited violated his constitutional rights to counsel." The Court granted Williams a new trial.

At the second trial, in *Nix v. Williams* (1984), the Court allowed the body of the little girl to be admitted into evidence because a search party had been approaching the location of the burial site and would have discovered the body without Williams' help. This case established the *inevitable-discovery doctrine* discussed in Chapter 4.

Right to Counsel under the Fifth and Sixth Amendments

The Supreme Court concluded in *Miranda* that custodial interrogation creates an inherently coercive environment that violates the Fifth Amendment protection against compelled self-incrimination by requiring that suspects be told of their right to an attorney. The Sixth Amendment right to counsel, however, does not hinge on the issue of custody. The right to counsel under the Sixth Amendment does not apply until proceedings against a suspect have begun.

Fellers v. United States (2004) illustrates the difference between these two rights. Officers went to John Fellers's home to discuss his involvement in methamphetamine distribution. They told him a grand jury had indicted him and four others and had a federal warrant for his arrest. The officers did not advise Fellers of his *Miranda* rights and asked him no questions, but Fellers told them he knew the four others and had used methamphetamine with them. The officers transported Fellers to jail and advised him of his rights, which he waived. At trial, Fellers filed a motion to suppress all his statements, claiming they were obtained in violation of his rights. The Supreme Court ruled in favor of Fellers, emphasizing that the Sixth Amendment right to counsel differs from the Fifth Amendment (*Miranda*) custodial-interrogation principle and applies even when the police do not question a defendant. The Court stated, "There is no question that the officers in this case deliberately elicited information from Fellers during the contact at his home."

Foreign Nationals, the Vienna Convention Treaty and Diplomatic Immunity

Partly because of concern that foreign nationals charged with crimes in the United States will not fully understand their rights within the complex U.S. legal system, the Vienna Convention Treaty, signed in 1963, gives foreign nationals the right to contact their consulate in the event of their detention or arrest. Another treaty signed in 1972 provides diplomatic immunity for certain individuals. Officers who want to interrogate a person claiming diplomatic immunity should request the diplomatic identification and check the reverse of the card. A general guideline is to treat foreign nationals and diplomats as you would want Americans to be treated under similar circumstances abroad.

Selecting the Time and Place

Like interviews, interrogations are conducted as soon as possible after a crime. Selecting the right place to question suspects is critical because they are usually reluctant to talk to police. Most interrogations are conducted at police headquarters. However, if a suspect refuses to come to the station and evidence is insufficient for an arrest, the interrogation may take place at the crime scene, in a squad car or at the suspect's home or place of work. If possible, suspects should be interrogated in an unfamiliar place, away from their friends and family.

> Conduct interrogations in a place that is private and free from interruptions.

Ideal conditions exist at the police station, where privacy and interruptions can be controlled. Visible movements or unusual noises distract a suspect undergoing questioning. Only the suspect, the suspect's attorney and the interrogators should be in the room. Having two officers conduct the interrogation helps deflect false allegations or other untrue claims by the suspect. Allow no telephone calls and no distracting noises; allow no one to enter the room. Under these conditions, communication is more readily established.

Opinions differ about how interrogation rooms should be furnished. An austere, sparsely furnished room is generally less distracting; pictures can reduce the effectiveness of questioning. Many interrogation rooms have only two chairs: one for the investigator and one for the suspect. Some include a small, bare table. Some officers feel it is better *not* to have a desk or table between the officer and the suspect because the desk serves as a psychological protection to the suspect. Without it, the suspect tends to feel much more uncomfortable and vulnerable. Keep all notebooks, pencils, pens and any objects of evidence to be used in the interrogation out of view, preferably in a drawer, until the appropriate time. A stark setting develops and maintains the suspect's

absolute attention and allows total concentration on the conversation.

Other investigators, however, contend that such a setting is not conducive to good rapport. It may remind suspects of jail, and a fear of going to jail may keep them from talking. Instead, some investigators prefer a normally furnished room or office for interrogations. Doctors, lawyers, insurance investigators and others have shown that a relaxed atmosphere encourages conversation. Even background music can reduce anxiety and dispel fear—major steps in getting subjects to talk.

Starting the Interrogation

Conducting the interrogation at the police station allows many options in timing and approach. A suspect can be brought to the interrogation room and left alone temporarily. Often the suspect has not yet met the investigator and is apprehensive about what the investigator is like, what will be asked and what will happen. Provide time for the anxiety to increase, just as a football team sometimes takes a time-out before the opposing team attempts a critical field goal.

As you enter the room, show that you are in command, but do not display arrogance. The suspect is in an unfamiliar environment, is alone, does not know you, has been waiting, is apprehensive and does not know what you will ask. At this point, select your interrogation technique, deciding whether to increase or decrease the suspect's anxiety. Some investigators accomplish their goals by friendliness, others by authoritarianism. Show your identification and introduce yourself to the suspect, state the purpose of the interrogation and then give the *Miranda* warning. Avoid violating the suspect's personal zone. Try to stay two to six feet away when questioning.

Do not become so wrapped up in yourself and your quest for information that you overlook body language or **nonverbal communication** that may indicate deception, anger or indifference. Research has shown that 10 percent of a message delivered is verbal and 90 percent is nonverbal. Officers who can correctly interpret what they see arm themselves with a powerful tool.

Deception, for example, may be indicated by looking down, rolling the eyes upward, placing the hands over the eyes or mouth or rubbing the hands around the mouth. Other possible indicators of deception include continual licking of the lips, twitching of the lips, intermittent coughs, rapid breathing, change in facial color, continuous swallowing, pulsating of the carotid artery in the neck, face flushing, tapping the fingers and avoiding eye contact. Excessive protestations of innocence should also be suspect, for example, "To be perfectly honest," or "I swear on my father's grave."

Establishing Rapport

As with interviewing, specific approaches during interrogating may either encourage cooperation or induce silence and noncooperation. The techniques for establishing rapport during an interview also apply in an interrogation. You may decide to instill the fear that there will be serious consequences if the suspect fails to cooperate. You may choose to appeal to the suspect's conscience, emphasizing the importance of getting out of the present situation and starting over with a clean slate. Try any approach that shows the person that cooperation is more desirable than having you find out about the crime another way.

It also helps to know why the crime was committed. Some crimes are committed out of uncontrollable passion, panic or fear without consideration of the consequences. Other crimes result from the demands of the moment; the presumed necessity of the crime appears to justify it. Some criminals' guilt becomes so overpowering that they turn themselves in to the police. Other criminals turn to drugs or alcohol or leave the area to start over somewhere else.

It takes skill to obtain information from those involved in crime, especially if they know the consequences can be severe. Suspects who understand there is no easy way out of a situation may become cooperative. At this point, offering alternatives may be successful. Because most people respond to hard evidence, show suspects the physical evidence against them. Acknowledge to the suspect that there is no completely agreeable solution, but point out that some alternatives may be more agreeable than others.

Make no promises, but remind the suspect that the court decides the sentence and is apt to be easier on those who cooperate. Also point out that family and friends are usually more understanding if people admit they are wrong and try to "go straight."

If the suspect will not provide the names of accomplices because they are friends, explain that such "friends" have put the suspect in the present predicament.

Approaches to Interrogation

As with interviews, interrogations can follow an emotional or a logical approach. An emotional approach is either empathetic or authoritarian. After talking with the suspect, select the approach that seems to offer the best chance for obtaining information. Rapport has been stressed previously.

Rationalization, projection and minimization are among techniques commonly used in interrogation.

> Interrogation techniques include inquiring directly or indirectly, forcing responses, deflating or inflating the ego, minimizing or maximizing the crime, projecting the blame, rationalizing and combining approaches.

Inquiring Indirectly or Directly. Indirect inquiry draws out information without mentioning the main subject. For example, an indirect approach may be phrased, "Have you ever been in the vicinity of Elm Street? Grove Street? the intersection of Elm and Grove?" In contrast, a direct question would be, "Did you break into the house on the corner of Elm and Grove Streets on December 16th?"

Forcing Responses. A forced response is elicited by asking a question that will implicate the suspect, regardless of the answer given. For example, the question "What time did you arrive at the house?" implies that the suspect *did* arrive at the house at some time. Answering the question with a time forces the suspect to admit having been there. Of course, the suspect may simply state, "I never arrived there," or may refuse to answer at all.

Deflating or Inflating the Ego. Belittling a suspect is often effective. For example, you may tell a suspect, "We know you couldn't be directly involved in the burglary because you aren't smart enough to pull off a job like that. We thought you might know who did, though." Question the suspect's skill in committing a crime known to be his specialty. Suggest that the suspect's reputation is suffering because his latest burglaries have been bungled. The suspect may attempt—out of pride—to prove that it was a professional job.

The same results can be obtained by *inflating* suspects' egos, praising the skill shown in pulling off the job. Suspects may want to take the credit and admit their role in the crime.

Minimizing or Maximizing the Crime. Concentrate your efforts on the crime itself, ignoring for the moment the person committing it. Instead of using the word *crime*, say "the thing that happened." Refer to stolen property as "the stuff that was taken." Do not use terms such as *robbery, homicide* or *arson*. Use other, less threatening terms. For example, asking the suspect "to tell the truth" is much less threatening than asking someone "to confess." Overstating the severity of an offense can be as effective as understating it. Mentioning that the amount of stolen money was $5,000 rather than the actual $500 puts the suspect on the spot. Is a partner holding out? Is the victim lying about the losses? Will the suspect be found guilty of a felony because of such lies? Making the offense more serious than it actually is can induce suspects to provide facts implicating them in lesser offenses.

Projecting the Blame. Projecting blame onto others is another effective way to get suspects talking. When suspects feel as if others are at fault, they may be more willing to share information that will ultimately incriminate them. This is often seen in rape cases where the officer suggests that the woman "was asking for it" by the way she was dressed.

Rationalizing. Rationalizing is another technique that shifts fault away from a suspect. Even though the suspect committed the act, there was a good reason to justify it. Skilled interrogators understand this psychology and convey empathy by saying they understand where the suspect is "coming from."

Combining Approaches. Having the suspect tell the story using different methods can reveal discrepancies. If an oral statement has been given, have the suspect put this information in writing and compare the two versions. Then give the story to two different investigators and have them compare the versions.

Using Persuasion during Interrogation

Sometimes investigators may obtain much better results using persuasive techniques: making sure the suspect is comfortable and has basic needs taken care of, such as being allowed to go to the restroom and to get a drink of water. Once the suspect has been made comfortable, begin by acknowledging that a problem exists but that before talking about it, the suspect needs to be informed of his rights. Then suggest that the suspect probably already knows all about these rights and ask the suspect to tell what he does know. Usually the suspect can paraphrase the *Miranda* warning, and you can then compliment him on his knowledge. This helps establish rapport. Next, encourage the suspect to tell his side of the story in detail, intervening only to give encouragement to continue talking. When the suspect has finished, review the account step by step.

Following this, begin a "virtual monologue about robbery" and how some people's desperate financial circumstances lead them into such a crime. The monologue describes how no one starts out planning a life of crime,

but some, like an addict, fall into a criminal pattern that leads either to getting shot and killed or to spending a lifetime in prison. End the monologue by emphasizing that the inevitable result of this pattern of crime is life in prison or death.

Next, suggest that the suspect can avoid this fate only by breaking this pattern and that the first step is to admit that it exists. Add that a person's life should not be judged by one mistake, nor should that person's life be wasted by a refusal to admit that mistake. Following this monologue, begin to talk about the suspect's accomplices and how they are still free, enjoying the fruits of the crime.

Finally, talk about the suspect's previous encounters with the criminal justice system and how fairly it has treated the suspect. In the past, the suspect has probably always claimed to be not guilty. Judges are likely to go easier on suspects who indicate remorse for what they

Technology Innovations

Phillips (2007, pp.112–117) describes virtual interrogation software that allows officers to fine tune their interrogation skills on or off duty.

Traditional role-playing scenarios are now becoming a thing of the past, thanks to sophisticated software technology allowing officers to train and practice interviewing techniques at their leisure. . . . SIMmersions's simulated people technology is very real, and is used by law enforcement agencies worldwide to help train professionals how to recognize the signs of deception, and to be a better interviewer. . . .

Using video and DVD capabilities, SIMmersion has created more than 20 life-like simulations of people in realistic settings. These "simulated" characters have realistic emotions, and a "simulated" brain that uses real-time interaction and logic to reflect the way people actually speak and respond to one another in real situations.

To keep the trainees' interest, they are scored like a video game with scores based on judgment to determine whether the suspect is being truthful or deceptive. Most of the scored points come from how rapport is developed and how accurately verbal and nonverbal clues are detected. Scores are tracked over time to measure and monitor how well the officer is improving. Scores are also visible to other officers, so it lends a competitive approach to learning.

have done. This cannot happen unless the suspect first admits the crime. Point out that intelligent people recognize when it is in their best interest to admit a mistake.

Investigative Questionnaires. An alternative to a face-to-face interrogation is the Crime Questionnaire, a document with 21 questions that test for truth and deception and can be used in conjunction with a polygraph or in situations where a polygraph cannot be used. Supporters of this method believe the questionnaire shows "considerable accuracy" in predicting guilt or innocence. Formal training, however, is required to interpret these questionnaires.

Ethics and the Use of Deception

Although law enforcement officers are expected to be honest, the Supreme Court has recognized that their duties may require limited officially sanctioned deception during a criminal investigation (Mount, 2007, p.10). Rutledge (2007b, p.59) contends, "Sometimes you have to resort to trickery to get confessions from suspects." Playing arrestees against each other can help elicit confessions: "For starters you may leave your arrestees cuffed in the cage in the back of your police car with a concealed tape recorder running in the front seat. If you walk away out of earshot, they may scramble to come up with a story" (Rutledge, 2008, p.61).

Several cases support officer use of deception. The Supreme Court stated in *Sorrells v. United States* (1932), "Criminal activity is such that stealth and strategy are necessary weapons in the arsenal of the police officer." In *United States v. Russell* (1973) the Court said, "Nor will the mere fact of deceit defeat a prosecution, for there are circumstances when the use of deceit is the only practicable law enforcement technique available." *United States ex rel. Caminito v. Murphy* (1955) held that it is permissible to tell suspects that they have been identified by witnesses even though that is untrue. *Moore v. Hopper* (1974) allowed telling suspects that material evidence, such as a firearm used to commit a crime, has been found, when it has not. *Frazier v. Cupp* (1969) held that it is permissible to tell suspects that an accomplice has already confessed, when this is untrue.

Interrogatory deception may include claiming to possess evidence that does not really exist, making promises, misrepresenting the seriousness of the offense, misrepresenting identity (for example, pretending to be a cellmate or a reporter) or using the "good cop/bad cop" routine. Actually creating or forging false evidence, however, is neither ethical nor legal.

Television and movies often depict the good-cop/bad-cop method of interrogation, portraying one officer as very hostile and another one as trying to protect a suspect from the hostile officer. Routines such as this could be considered illegal if carried to an extreme. Some interrogation techniques, even if not illegal, may be unethical. The use of deception in interrogation and the determination of ethical, professional behavior remain important issues.

Third-Degree Tactics

Considerable literature deals with the use of the third degree in police interrogations. It is not known how widely these methods are used and how much of what is claimed is exaggeration. **Third-degree** is the use of physical force; the threat of force; or other physical, mental or psychological abuse to induce a suspect to confess to a crime. Third-degree tactics, which are illegal, include striking or hitting a suspect, denying food or water or sleep for abnormal time periods, not allowing a suspect to go to the restroom, having a number of officers ask questions in shifts for prolonged periods and refusing normal privileges. Obtaining information by these methods is inexcusable.

> Third-degree tactics—physical force; threats of force; or other physical, mental or psychological abuse—are illegal. Any information so obtained, including confessions, is inadmissible in court.

The image of police brutality is difficult to offset when third-degree tactics are used. Such tactics create a loss of respect for the officer involved and for the entire department and the police profession.

Although physical force is not permitted, this does not rule out physical contact. Placing a hand on a shoulder or touching a suspect's hand can help to establish rapport. Looking directly at a suspect while talking and continuing to do so during the conversation is not using physical force, even though it usually makes the suspect extremely uncomfortable.

If you give a suspect all the privileges you yourself have within the interrogation context, there is no cause for a charge of third-degree tactics. Allow the suspect the same breaks for meals, rest and going to the restroom that you take. Law enforcement officers are obligated to protect both the public interest and individual rights. No situation excuses a deliberate violation of these rights.

Admissions and Confessions

When a suspect has become cooperative, you can increase the amount of conversation. Once rapport is established, listen for words indicating that the suspect is in some way connected with the crime, such as "I didn't do it, but I know who did." If the suspect is not implicated in the crime but has relevant information, attempt to obtain a statement. If the suspect is implicated, try to obtain an admission or confession. The format for obtaining admissions and confessions from suspects in criminal cases is fairly standard. However, state laws, rules and procedures for taking admissions and confessions vary, so you need to know the rules and requirements of your jurisdiction.

An **admission** contains some information concerning the elements of a crime but falls short of a full confession (Figure 6.4). A **confession** is information supporting the elements of a crime given by a person involved in committing it. It can be oral or written and must be voluntary and not given in response to threats, promises or rewards. It can be taken in question and answer form or in a narrative handwritten by the suspect or the interrogator (Figure 6.5).

A confession, oral or handwritten, must be given of the suspect's free will and not in response to fear, threats, promises or rewards.

The voluntary nature of the confession is essential. For example, Ernesto Miranda had an arrest record and was familiar with his rights; yet, his confession was ruled inadmissible because these rights had not been clearly stated to him. Although formal education is not required for making a confession, a suspect must be intelligent enough to understand fully everything stated.

In most states, oral confessions are admissible in court, but written confessions usually carry more weight. Put an oral confession into writing as soon as possible, even if the suspect refuses to sign it. Have the suspect repeat the confession in the presence of other witnesses to corroborate its content and voluntariness. In extremely important cases, the prosecutor often obtains the confession to ensure that it meets all legal requirements. Many departments are now videotaping statements and confessions.

After obtaining a confession, you may also go with the suspect to the crime scene and reenact the crime before witnesses. Take pictures or films of this reenactment. Go over the confession and the pictures with the suspect to verify their accuracy. (Such confessions and reenactments can also be used for police training.)

ANYTOWN POLICE DEPARTMENT
ADMISSION

CF# 11-1234

Date Occurred: 12th November, 2011

Location of Occurrence: Lucky's Bar and Grill,

1234 Business Way, Anytown, MI 48000

Name: Walter William Wilson

Date of Birth: 02/02/90

Address: 100 Main Street, Anytown, MI 48000

Phone Number: (C) 517-555-3000   (H) 517-555-3001   (W) 517-555-3002

Narrative:

I, Walter Wilson, was at Lucky's Bar and Grill on Saturday night, November 12th, 2011 at 11:30 pm. I met a friend there named John Jacobs and we ate dinner and had some drinks. While we were leaving the bar a guy came up to us and said he wanted to fight with us. He was a white guy around 30 years old wearing blue jeans and a white shirt. We got into a verbal argument because he was drunk and said he was going to kill us. We both left shortly after. The man was alive when we left the bar.

I have read this statement consisting of __1__ page(s), and I affirm to the truth and accuracy of the facts contained herein.

This statement was completed at (Location) Anytown Police Department on

(Date) November 14, 2011 at (Time) 1300 .

WITNESS _William Bennett_

WITNESS _John H. Scott_

Walter W. Wilson
(Signature of person providing voluntary statement)

FIGURE 6.4
Sample admission.
Source: Drafted by Henry Cho, Cho Research & Consulting, LLC 2011

ANYTOWN POLICE DEPARTMENT
CONFESSION   CF# 11-1234

Date Occurred: 12th November, 2011

Location of Occurrence: Lucky's Bar and Grill,

1234 Business Way, Anytown, MI 48000

Name: Walter William Wilson

Date of Birth: 02/02/90

Address: 100 Main Street, Anytown, MI 48000

Phone Number: (C) 517-555-3000 (H) 517-555-3001 (W) 517-555-3002

Narrative:

I, Walter Wilson, was at Lucky's Bar and Grill on Saturday night, November 12th, 2011 at 11:30 pm. I met a friend there named John Jacobs and we ate dinner and had some drinks. While we were leaving the bar a guy came up to us in the parking lot and said he wanted to fight with us. He was a white guy around 30 years old wearing blue jeans and a white shirt. We got into a verbal argument because he was drunk and he said he was going to kill us. I got angry at him because he was verbally threatening me and my friend as well as being belligerent. He then punched me in the face so I pulled out my pocket knife and stabbed him three times in the stomach with it. I think he was dead in the parking lot when we left.

I have read the ___1___ page(s) of this statement and the facts contained therein are true and correct.

This statement was completed at (Location) Anytown Police Department on

(Date) November 14, 2011 at (Time) 1300 .

WITNESS _W^m Bennett_

WITNESS _Jehue H Scott_

Walter M. Wilson
(Signature of person providing voluntary statement)

FIGURE 6.5
Sample confession.
Source: Drafted by Henry Cho, Cho Research & Consulting, LLC 2011

Even though a confession is highly desirable, it may not be true, it may later be denied or there may be claims that it was involuntary. Some research has found that the incidence of false confessions is higher than many believe and can be exacerbated by certain interrogation tactics, such as "the sympathetic detective with a limited time offer" (Davis et al., 2010). A letter from an inmate, incarcerated for a murder he pled guilty to but later claimed innocence for, sheds light on the reasons a suspect in jail awaiting trial might confess:

Jail can be hell. I was locked in a cell alone 23 hours a day. The other hour I was still alone, but able to take a shower, etc. The doors are solid steel. When it closes there is no more contact for another day. I used to dread the closing of that door. . . . Try and imagine sitting in a room the size of your bathroom with no window, not knowing when that door will open or what your family is doing outside it. Then picture that for a year.

They told me many times in many different ways how much better things would be if I cooperated with them. I don't know if I did it hoping things would get better or if I just didn't care. I do remember very clearly my feelings of being at the end of my rope. I would [have] sold my soul to the devil not to hear that door bang again, locking me in for another 23 hours with myself.

Your investigation will proceed in much the same way with or without a confession. However, a confession often provides additional leads. Although it cannot stand alone, it is an important part of the case.

 A confession is only one part of an investigation. Corroborate it with independent evidence.

According to the *Bruton* rule, which resulted from *Bruton v. United States* (1968), a defendant's Sixth Amendment right to confront and cross-examine witnesses

against him is violated if a confessing defendant's statement is used against a nonconfessing defendant at their joint trial (Rutledge, 2008, p.62). To avoid this situation, Rutledge (p.63) suggests that if two suspects have waived *Miranda* but only one has confessed, bring the two together and ask the confessor to repeat his confession implicating the other suspect. If the nonconfessing suspect does not deny the allegations made against him by the suspect who confessed, this can be considered an adoptive admission by the nonconfessor: "An **adoptive admission** occurs when someone else makes a statement in a person's presence and under circumstances where it would be logical to expect the person to make a denial if the statement falsely implicated him, but he does not deny the allegations" (p.63).

QUESTIONING CHILDREN AND JUVENILES

Special considerations exist when questioning children and juveniles. As in any interview, the first step is to build rapport. You might give the child a tour of the building and show him or her where the parent(s) will be waiting. Scoville (2007, p.32) notes, "Investigators face formidable challenges when interviewing child victims, especially in sex crime cases." He recommends establishing what words a child uses to refer to the private parts of the body. It is a good idea to have a specially trained investigator or social worker present to either assist or lead in the interview of youthful sex crime victims. The psychology of children can be entirely different than that of an adult, and the same techniques used on adults may not be effective on juveniles.

Investigators must obtain parental permission before questioning a juvenile, unless the situation warrants immediate questioning at the scene. Parents usually permit their juveniles to be questioned separately if the purpose is explained and you have valid reasons for doing so. Overprotective parents can distract and interfere with an interview or interrogation. Often, however, parents can assist if the youth is uncooperative. They can ask questions and bring pressures to bear that you cannot. They know and understand the child and can probably sense when the child is lying. Decide whether to question a juvenile in front of the parents or separately after you determine their attitudes when you explain to them the reasons for the inquiry.

Often juveniles will not feel comfortable being honest if their parents are present. If you sense this is the case, advise the parents and request to speak with the juvenile separately. Topics of inquiry that can hinder a juvenile interview, if parents are present, include drugs and sex.

> Obtain parental permission before questioning a youth. Do not use a youth as an informant unless the parents know the situation.

Your attitude toward youths will greatly influence how well you can communicate with them. Ask yourself whether you consider the youth a person who has a problem or a youth who *is* a problem.

Many juveniles put on airs in front of their friends. For example, in one case, a juvenile and some other youths were brought into a room for observation by witnesses. The suspect youth knew he was being watched and challenged his school principal by stating that he had a right to know who was looking at him and why. This 10-year-old boy wanted to impress his friends. A few days later, the boy's parents brought him to the police station at the officer's request. It took two questions to determine that the boy had set a fire that resulted in an $80,000 loss. After a third question, the youth admitted his guilt. Although he had acted like a big shot in front of his friends, his action weighed heavily on his conscience. The presence of the police and the knowledge that his parents were waiting in another room motivated him to cooperate.

Finally, juveniles may have definite opinions about the police. Some dislike adults in general and the police in particular. Like adults, however, most do not dislike the police and will cooperate with them. Put yourself in their shoes; learn their attitudes and the reasons for them. Time and patience are your greatest allies when questioning juveniles. Explain why you are questioning them, and you will probably gain their confidence.

Do not underrate young people's intelligence or cleverness. They are often excellent observers with good memories. Talk to them as you would to an adult. Praise them and impress upon them their importance to the investigation.

If a juvenile confesses to a crime, bring in the parents and have the youth repeat the confession to them. The parents will see that the information is voluntary and not the police's account of what happened. Parents often provide additional information once they know the truth. For example, they may be alerted to stolen items at home and report them.

EVALUATING AND CORROBORATING INFORMATION

Do not accept information obtained from interviews and interrogations at face value because often the information provided to the police is only partially truthful. Verify all information. You cannot know the motives of all those who provide information. Do not assume that all information, even though volunteered, is truthful. Corroborate or disprove statements made during questioning.

To cross-check a story, review the report and the details of the offense. Determine the past record, family status, hobbies and special interests of those questioned. If a person has a criminal record, determine his or her prior modus operandi. With such information, you can ask questions in a way that indicates you know what you are talking about and that deceptive answers will be uncovered.

A person who resorts to half-truths or lies usually ends up on the defensive and becomes entangled in deceit. Knowing the facts of a case allows you to neutralize deliberate lies. If discrepancies in statements occur, question the suspect again or use polygraph or psychological tests. Compare the replies of people questioned and assess whether they are consistent with the known facts. A person who is telling the truth can usually repeat the story the same way many times, although he or she may use different words and a different sequence in retelling it. Times and dates may be approximate, and the person may simply not be able to remember some things. In contrast, a person who is telling a fabricated story can usually repeat it word for word innumerable times. Dates and times are usually precise, and all details are remembered. However, it is difficult to repeat lies consistently; each one sounds better than the previous one, and the story becomes distorted with mistakes and exaggerations. To break a pat story, ask questions that require slightly different answers and that will alter memorized responses.

SCIENTIFIC AIDS TO OBTAINING AND EVALUATING INFORMATION

Many attempts have been made to determine the truth through scientific instruments. Even before instruments were developed, however, trials by ordeal and other tests relied on psychological and physiological principles.

For example, it was common knowledge for centuries that when a person was lying or nervous, visible or measurable physiological changes occurred in the body. These include dryness of the mouth, shaking or trembling, perspiration, increased heartbeat, faster pulse and rapid breathing. The ancient Chinese capitalized on the symptom of mouth dryness when they made a suspect chew rice. If the rice remained dry after being chewed, the suspect was assumed to be lying.

Science and technology have provided aids to help determine the reliability of information. Among them are the polygraph, the computerized voice stress analyzer (CVSA), hypnosis and truth serums.

The Polygraph and Voice Stress Tests

As implied by the name, a **polygraph** (literally, "many writings") records several measurements on a visible graph.

> The polygraph scientifically measures respiration and depth of breathing, as well as changes in the skin's electrical resistance, blood pressure and pulse rate.

The same factors measured by the polygraph may be visible to a trained observer through such signs as flushing of the face, licking the lips, slight pulsing of the neck arteries, beads of perspiration, rapid breathing and other signs of nervousness. A person does not actually have to respond verbally for a polygraph to work because the machine measures the mental and emotional responses regardless of whether the person answers questions.

Many law enforcement agencies use polygraphs in their investigations; however, the effectiveness of the polygraph has been questioned. Among polygraph supporters, opinions differ regarding its accuracy, which depends on the subject, the equipment and the operator's training and experience. In some cases, the machine may fail to detect lies because the subject has taken drugs, makes deliberate muscular contractions or has a psychopathic personality.

The subject must be physically, mentally and emotionally fit for the examination. The examination must be voluntary and completed under conditions conducive to cooperation. A clear, concise summary of the test results is furnished only to authorized personnel.

Despite advances in technology, improved training of polygraph operators and claims of 95 percent accuracy, polygraph results are not now accepted by the courts.

The Supreme Court has said, "There is simply no consensus that polygraph evidence is reliable. To this day, the scientific community remains extremely polarized about the reliability of polygraph techniques. . . . There is simply no way to know in a particular case whether a polygraph examiner's conclusion is accurate, because certain doubts and uncertainties plague even the best polygraph exams" (*United States v. Scheffer*, 1998). Some authorities claim that the results violate hearsay rules because it is impossible to cross-examine a machine.

> The polygraph is an instrument used to verify the truth, not a substitute for investigating and questioning. Although the results are not presently admissible in court, any confession obtained as a result of a polygraph test is admissible.

The polygraph is sometimes useful to develop leads, verify statements and cross-check information. Moreover, it provides the police with a psychological advantage that may lead to a confession. Such confessions are admissible in court even though the test results are not. Even in jurisdictions in which the polygraph is not admissible in court, prosecuting attorneys often give weight to the findings of a polygraph examination in deciding whether to prosecute a case.

The normal procedure for setting up a polygraph test is for the police agency to request in writing that a polygraph test be conducted. The examiner reviews the complete case, including any statements made by the subject before the test. A pretest interview with the subject covers the information to be included in the test, a review of the questions to be asked and an advisement of the suspect's constitutional rights.

The polygraph examiner will need some basic information before the test:

■ The case facts—the precise criminal offense involved, the complete case file and a summary of the evidence

■ Information about the subject—complete name; date of birth; physical, mental, emotional and psychological data, if known; and criminal history

The proper tests are then determined, and the questions prepared and reviewed with the subject. After the test is completed, the subject and the police are advised of the results in person or by letter. If the test indicates deception, an individual interrogation may follow. Any confessions that follow from such tests are almost universally accepted by the courts. The examiner's testimony is not conclusive evidence but rather opinion evidence regarding either guilt or innocence.

Computerized polygraphy eliminates most of the mechanical equipment, replacing it with a virtual graph on a computer monitor. The graph can be printed, if desired. In computerized polygraph systems, the software analyzes physiological changes and reports the probability that the person has answered the question truthfully.

The psychological stress evaluator (PSE), which measured stress in the micro-tremors of the human voice, was introduced in the 1970s. A more recent version of this technology is the computer voice stress analyzer (CVSA). Voice stress tests have not, however, undergone peer-reviewed, independent research to show that they have accuracy. Although law enforcement departments throughout the country have invested millions of dollars in voice stress analysis (VSA), a study by the National Institute of Justice (NIJ) found that two of the most popular VSA programs used by agencies nationwide are "no better than flipping a coin when it comes to detecting deception" (Damphouse, 2008, p.8).

Both the polygraph and the CVSA reduce investigative costs, focus on specific suspects, increase conviction rates (because many tests are followed by confessions) and eliminate suspects. Police agencies should not go on "fishing expeditions," however. Through normal investigative practices, the number of suspects should be narrowed to not more than two people before a polygraph examination or CVSA is used.

Hypnosis and Truth Serums

Like the polygraph, hypnosis and truth serums are supplementary tools to investigation. They are not used as shortcuts but rather in specific cases where the criteria

Detectives Steven Geckle (left), Paul Richard (center) and Al Everson (right) pose with a computer voice stress analyzer (CVSA) at the Upper Merion Township Police Department in King of Prussia, Pennsylvania. The computer, software and microphone are supposedly able to tell when an interview subject is lying through frequency modulations in the human voice.

© AP Images/Mark Stehle

for their use have been determined by thorough review. Cases that meet these criteria are normally crimes of violence or cases where loss of memory or ability to recall is involved and all other standard investigative efforts have been exhausted. Because of the restricted criteria, these techniques are used in a comparatively small number of cases.

Hypnosis.

Hypnosis psychically induces a trancelike condition in which the person loses consciousness but responds to a hypnotist's suggestions. Hypnosis is used with crime victims and witnesses to crimes, not with suspects. It should be used only after careful consultation with the person to be hypnotized and after a detailed review of the case as well as of the subject's mental, physical and emotional condition. Written consent from the subject and permission from the prosecutor's office should be obtained, and an attorney should be present.

A professional should carefully analyze the subject and the case before hypnosis is conducted. The actual act of hypnotism and interrogation should be performed only by a psychiatrist, psychologist or physician specifically trained in the techniques.

Courts have established guidelines for using testimony gained from hypnosis. The guidelines require that a trained professional perform it and that the professional be independent of, rather than responsible to, the prosecution. The number of people present should be restricted to the hypnotist and the coordinator from the police agency who has knowledge of the case and perhaps an artist who can draw a sketch based on any descriptions of suspects. And although forensic hypnosis has finally been accepted as a valuable crime-fighting tool, many states remain reluctant to allow testimony elicited from hypnosis into court.

The session should be videotaped, if possible. Questions should relate only to what the witness states under hypnosis. The witness should not be prompted or induced in any way.

Truth Serums.

Truth serums are fast-acting barbiturates of the type used to produce sleep at the approximate level of surgical anesthesia. Alcohol produces somewhat the same effects to a much lesser degree. The theory is that the drug removes a person's inhibitions so that he or she is more likely to tell the truth. In the past, scopolamine and hyascine were the most used drugs, but sodium amatol and sodium pentothal are more commonly used today.

Truth serums are not used extensively by the police because the accuracy of the information obtained with them is questionable. Truth serum is administered by a physician, preferably a psychiatrist, who remains to monitor the person's condition while the questions are asked. The drugs can cause serious side effects, so the subject must be monitored continually. Some patients also become violently excited. Moreover, individuals vary greatly in their response to truth serums. Some can withhold information even under the influence of a large dose of the serum.

The courts do not officially recognize truth serums or their reliability, nor do they admit the results as evidence.

USE OF PSYCHICS AND PROFILERS

Television shows have popularized the use of psychics and profilers in criminal investigations, and to many viewers, the incidents depicted are entirely believable. Although use of psychics in criminal investigations is controversial, some agencies are willing to consider any possible lead or source of information, including psychics.

Profilers are more commonly accepted. Profiling combines art and science, resting on the premise that careful analysis of the crime scene and the crime will yield clues about the type of person who would commit such a crime. Effective profiling relies on the profiler's ability to combine investigative experience, training in forensic and behavioral sciences and information about the characteristics of known offenders.

SHARING INFORMATION

In the beginning of this chapter, the vast amount of information available on the Internet was discussed. The Internet allows information related to criminal investigations to be shared across jurisdictional lines as never before. Since September 11, 2001, the sharing of information has become increasingly important as the United States focuses on homeland security: "The key to combating terrorism lies with the local police and the intelligence they can provide to federal authorities" (Hess and Orthmann, 2011, p.328). The role of police in the "war on terrorism" is discussed in Chapter 20.

"Substantial obstacles" that prevent police agencies from sharing information include competing local systems, incompatible data formats, issues of who controls the data, security questions, cost and training time and resources (Miller, 2008, p.54). To overcome the obstacle of incompatible data formats and enable federal, state and local justice and public safety agencies to exchange data information from all the department's investigative components—the Bureau of Alcohol, Tobacco, Firearms and Explosives; the Drug Enforcement Administration; the Federal Bureau of Investigation; the U.S. Marshals Service; and the Bureau of Prisons—with a single query.

Another initiative is the Law Enforcement National Data Exchange (N-DEx), developed by the Raytheon Corporation. This Internet-based information system, illustrated in Figure 6.6, will eventually link the more than 18,000 law enforcement agencies in the nation electronically: "The system is not limited to law enforcement information, but is truly a 'criminal justice' information system, which will eventually include probation and parole data as well as law enforcement incident and case reports" ("FBI Begins to Implement a System," 2008, pp.3–5). As of October 2011, the probation and parole extension of the system was still being developed, with the expectation that by year-end 2011, all components would be online and operational.

Although N-DEx is not an intelligence system, per se, and does not contain intelligence data, the information will be an extremely valuable resource to the intelligence community: "The vision of the N-DEx is clear: to share

Collaboration between law enforcement agencies is often required for the successful investigation of a crime. Here an ATF and an FBI agent look at a nail found outside of a nightclub that was bombed the previous night. The explosion injured five people. A second bomb was found by police and was detonated at the site.

© REUTERS/Tami Chappell

in a common, replicable format, the Global Justice XML Data Model (GJSCM) was developed. Over the past several years, GJSCM has become "the national, de facto data sharing standard" (Wagner, 2007, p.114). Other advances in technology have also enhanced data sharing efforts.

Haslip (2007, p.32) states, "The public rightly expects that criminal justice agencies and especially law enforcement agencies at all levels of government will cooperate and share information seamlessly." Many departments are already sharing information by contributing to the National Criminal Intelligence Sharing Plan (NCISP) developed by the International Association of Chiefs of Police and the U.S. Department of Justice after September 11, 2001 (Matney, 2007, p.28).

One such information sharing effort is the OneDOJ Initiative, a storefront for federal law enforcement information (Hitch, 2007, p.26). The OneDOJ Initiative allows state, local and tribal law enforcement partners to obtain

Technology Innovations

Siuru (2007, p.79) describes CrimeCog, an innovative information system technology:

Popular interactive Web sites such as MySpace.com and Wikipedia.org let anyone with Internet access add and retrieve information on the Web site. CrimeCog is a similar Internet-based information sharing and records management concept, but only for law enforcement and justice system use.

CrimeCog is powered by E*Justice™, . . . already used by large cities and counties across America. . . . CrimeCog's user-friendly Web browser can manage all types of police reports, court records, case histories and information about prisoners in jails and prisons. It even works with existing victim notification systems.

CrimeCog users enter data one time to share with other agencies, eliminating time-wasting and error-prone keying. It also allows a single service to handle all information about a crime from the first report through arrest, preliminary incarceration, prosecution, sentencing and parole.

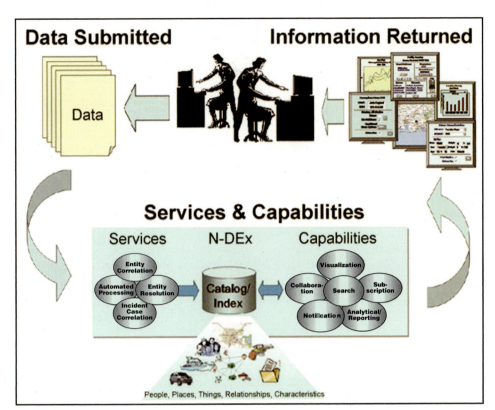

FIGURE 6.6
Flow of information in N-DEx.
Source: http//www.fbi.gov/about-us/cjis/n-dex/ndex_concept

complete, accurate, timely and useful information across jurisdictional boundaries and to provide new investigative tools that will enhance the ability of the United States to fight crime and terrorism" (Bush, 2008, p.12). N-DEx marks the first time in our nation's history that local, county, state and federal law enforcement information has been openly shared (Bush, 2008). O'Harrow and Nakashima (2008, p.A01) report, "Federal authorities hope N-DEx will become what one called a 'one-stop shop,' enabling federal law enforcement, counterterrorism and intelligence analysts to automatically examine the enormous caches of local and state records for the first time." Page (2007, p.98) quotes Paul Wormeli of the Integrated Justice Information Systems Institute, who is equally enthusiastic: "With respect to using technology to solve crimes, N-DEx is the biggest revolution in policing since NCIC was originally created."

INFORMATION VERSUS INTELLIGENCE

Information is simply data: "In order for information to be useful, there must be some value attached to it. . . . Information without connectivity to an intelligence problem is merely white noise that tends to overwhelm the analysts who are supposed to make sense of the fragmented bits and pieces of information that they are receiving" (Zimmerman, 2006, p.48).

 Information or data is not intelligence. Information plus analysis is intelligence.

Although law enforcement officers and agencies may be very skilled at collecting information, such data in isolation does not help generate the intelligence often required to solve complex cases: "Information has become so voluminous, those of us in law enforcement agencies may not be aware of what we already have. Simply put, we do not know what we know. Once we apply analytical skills to the relevant and credible information we collect, we create useful intelligence. Once disseminated, this intelligence can be used effectively for both tactical and strategic purposes" (Modafferi, 2007, p.28). An "Intelligence Toolbox" training program is offered through Michigan State University as a quick-start program to help state, local and tribal law enforcement agencies understand the intelligence process contained in the NCISP, which involves planning and direction (what to collect), collection, processing/collation, analysis, dissemination and feedback or reevaluation. This process is illustrated in Figure 6.7.

Fusion centers are another effective means by which to transform information into intelligence and have been a worthy avenue by which to implement elements of the NCISP. Advances such as these have paved the path to intelligence-led policing: "Leading police associations in the United States and the United Kingdom have advocated that law enforcement adopt an intelligence-led policing model (ILP). The model builds on community policing, problem solving and continuous improvement business models that have been adopted by police departments" (McGarrell et al., 2007, p.142). ILP is in the same situation community policing was 15 to 20 years ago, being endorsed by the key law enforcement professional organizations, but still a fairly nebulous concept (McGarrell et al., p.154).

FIGURE 6.7
The intelligence process.
Source: *Intelligence-Led Policing: The New Intelligence Architecture.* Washington, DC: Bureau of Justice Assistance, September 2005, p.6.

Summary

Most solved cases rely on both physical evidence and information obtained from a variety of sources. Important sources of information include (1) reports, records and databases, including those found on the Internet; (2) people who are not suspects in the crime but who know something about the crime or those involved; and (3) suspects in the crime. A sources-of-information file contains the name and location of people, organizations and records that may assist in a criminal investigation.

The ultimate goal of interviewing and interrogating is to determine the truth, that is, to identify those responsible for a crime and to eliminate the innocent from suspicion. An effective interviewer/interrogator is adaptable and culturally adroit, self-controlled, patient, confident, optimistic, objective, sensitive to individual rights and knowledgeable about the elements of crimes.

Regardless of whether you are interviewing or interrogating, there are several ways to improve communication: prepare in advance; obtain the information as soon after the incident as possible, but try to build a bit of rapport before diving right into what you are looking for; be considerate and friendly; use a private setting; eliminate physical barriers; sit rather than stand; encourage conversation; ask simple questions one at a time; listen and observe. Emotional barriers to communication include ingrained attitudes and prejudices, fear, anger or hostility and self-preservation.

Two basic requirements to obtain information are to listen and to observe. Ask direct questions and open-ended questions liberally. Asking leading questions can also be a useful interrogation technique. Use indirect questions and closed-ended questions sparingly. Repetition is an effective technique to obtain recall and to uncover lies.

Interview witnesses separately if possible. Interview the victim or complainant first, then eyewitnesses and then people who did not actually see the crime but who have relevant information. Appeal to a reluctant interviewee's reason or emotions.

Although many of the same principles apply to interrogating and interviewing, interrogating involves some special considerations. One important consideration is when to give the *Miranda* warning, which informs suspects of their Fifth Amendment rights and must be given to any suspect who is interrogated while in custody. It is also important to conduct interrogations in a place that is private and free from interruptions. Interrogation techniques include inquiring directly or indirectly, forcing responses, deflating or inflating the ego, minimizing or maximizing the crime, projecting the blame, rationalizing and combining approaches. Third-degree tactics—physical force; threats of force; or other physical, mental or psychological abuse—are illegal. Any information so obtained, including confessions, is inadmissible in court. Any confession, oral or handwritten, must be given of the suspect's free will and not in response to fear, threats, promises or rewards. A confession is only one part of the investigation. It must be corroborated with independent evidence.

Special considerations are also observed when questioning children and youths. Obtain parental permission before questioning a juvenile. Do not use a juvenile as an informant unless the parents know the situation.

In addition to skills in interviewing and interrogating, you can sometimes use scientific aids to obtain information and determine its truthfulness. The polygraph scientifically measures respiration and depth of breathing, as well as changes in the skin's electrical resistance, blood pressure and pulse rate. It is an instrument used to verify the truth, not a substitute for investigating and questioning. Although the results are not presently admissible in court, any confession obtained as a result of a polygraph test is admissible. Information or data is not intelligence. Information plus analysis is intelligence.

Checklist

Obtaining Information

■ Were the complainant, witnesses, victim and informants questioned?

■ Were all witnesses found?

■ Was all information recorded accurately?

■ Was the questioning conducted in an appropriate place? At an appropriate time?

■ Was the *Miranda* warning given to all suspects before questioning?

■ Were the type of offense and offender considered in selecting the interviewing or interrogating techniques?

■ Were answers obtained to the questions of who, what, where, when, why and how?

■ Were checks made of all available reports and records? The sources-of-information file? Field-identification cards? The National Crime Information Center? Other police agencies? Public and private agencies at the local, county, state and national levels?

■ Were confidential informants sought?

■ Was a request for public assistance or an offer of a reward published?

■ Is there a private number to call or a private post office box to write to that persons who have information about a crime can use?

■ Was a polygraph used to check the validity of information given?

■ Were all statements, admissions and confessions rechecked against other verbal statements and against existing physical evidence?

■ Were those providing information thanked for their help?

■ Were all statements, admissions and confessions properly and legally obtained? Recorded? Witnessed? Filed?

Discussion Questions

1. What do you consider to be the essential steps in developing information about a crime?

2. What advantages do you see in the concept of *interroview*? What disadvantages?

3. Emphasis is often placed on obtaining a confession, or at least an admission, from a suspect in a criminal inquiry. Under what conditions is a confession of greatest value? of no value?

4. The *Miranda* warning is now accepted by law enforcement agencies as a necessary requirement of interrogation under specific circumstances. What circumstances make it mandatory? What circumstances do not require its use?

5. Do you believe that use of the *Miranda* warning has increased or decreased the number of confessions obtained in criminal cases?

6. How could polygraph results be used in plea bargaining?

7. What categories are included in your police department's sources-of-information file?

8. Should informants be protected by law from having to testify in court about information they have furnished police? What are the effects on investigative procedures and the frequency of cases cleared if informants are not protected?

9. Criminals or others who give the police information about a crime that eventually leads to an arrest or a conviction are sometimes paid for the information. Is this a legitimate use of tax funds, or should private donations be used?

10. Do you think that recording interviews and interrogations facilitates or hinders the law enforcement objective of obtaining admissions and confessions? Why?

Media Explorations

Internet

Using a search engine, enter the key words *police interrogation*. Select an article of interest and outline it.

Go to the following Web sites and outline the differences between the polygraph and voice stress machines:

- http://www.polygraphplace.com
- http://www.voicestress.com

 ## Gale Criminal Justice Database Assignments

The following assignments require access to Gale's Custom Journals Database for Emergency Services and Criminal Justice. Check with your instructor if you have questions about this.

- Find the article "Understanding Interrogation" on the Gale Emergency Services Database. Read the article and identify why understanding police interrogations can be problematic. What other issues that are not pointed out in this article can be problematic?

- Find the article "The Truth Surrounding Lie Detection Technology: A New Contender Takes on the Polygraph" on the Gale Emergency Services Database. Read this article and be prepared to discuss it in class. Also be prepared to discuss if you think that law enforcement officers should be subjected to polygraphs before being employed. Find out if your state mandates a polygraph test to become a law enforcement officer.

- Find the article "Intentional Violations of *Miranda*: A Strategy for Liability" on the Gale Emergency Services Database. Read this article and be prepared to discuss in class why this can be a strategy as well as a liability. Come up with a scenario that may occur in real life where this strategy might be more beneficial than it would be a drawback.

References

Anand, Radhika. "Trends in Recording Police Interviews." *Law Enforcement Technology*, February 2008, pp.60–65.

Boetig, Brian. "Fundamentals of a Successful Neighborhood Canvass." *Law and Order*, June 2010, pp.66–70.

Bush, Thomas E, III. "N-DEx: A National System for Local Information Sharing." *The Police Chief*, February 2008, p.12.

Damphouse, Kelly R. "Voice Stress Analysis: Only 15 Percent of Lies about Drug Use Detected in Field Test." *NIJ Journal*, March 2008, pp.8–13. (NCJ 221500)

Davis, Deborah; Leo, Richard A.; and Follette, William C. "Selling Confession: Setting the Stage with the 'Sympathetic Detective with a Limited-Time Offer.'" *Journal of Contemporary Criminal Justice*, Vol.26, No.4, September 2010, pp.441–457.

"FBI Begins to Implement a System for Interstate Exchange of Data." *Criminal Justice Newsletter*, March 17, 2008, pp.3–5.

Feuer, Alan, and Baker, Al. "Officers' Arrests Put Spotlight on Police Use of Informants." *The New York Times*, January 27, 2008.

Haslip, Michael. "Interagency Information Sharing: The National Information Exchange Model." *The Police Chief*, April 2007, pp.32–37.

Hess, Kären M., and Orthmann, Christine H. *Police Operations*, 5th ed. Clifton Park, NY: Delmar Publishing Company, 2011.

Hess, Kären M., and Orthmann, Christine H. *Constitutional Law and the Criminal Justice System*, 5th ed. Belmont, CA: Wadsworth Publishing Company, 2012.

Hitch, Vance. "OneDOJ: The Storefront for Federal Law Enforcement Information." *The Police Chief*, April 2007, pp.26–31.

Jetmore, Larry F. "Confidential Informants: Tips for Recruiting, Paying and Reliability." *Law Officer Magazine*, October 2007a, pp.22–25.

Jetmore, Larry F. "Establishing Informant Reliability." *Law Officer Magazine*, November 2007b, pp.24–26.

Matney, Matthew. "Information Sharing." *Law Officer Magazine*, May 2007, pp.28–30.

McGarrell, Edmund F.; Freilich, Joshua D.; and Chermak, Steven. "Intelligence-Led Policing as a Framework for Responding to Terrorism." *Journal of Contemporary Criminal Justice*, May 2007, pp.142–158.

Miller, Eric. "It's All about Information." *Law Officer Magazine*, January 2008, pp.52–58.

Modafferi, Peter A. "The World Is Flat: The 21st-Century Reality to Law Enforcement." *The Police Chief*, May 2007, pp.26–31.

Monheim, Tony. "The Forgotten Area Canvass." *Law and Order*, March 2007, pp.48–54.

Mount, David C. "Strategic Deception Revisited: The Use of Fabricated Documents during Interrogation—Permissible Ploy or Prohibited Practice?" *The Police Chief*, June 2007, pp.10–11.

Nielsen, Eugene. "Microsoft OneNote 2010 for Investigators." *Law and Order*, October 2010, p.104.

Nyberg, Remesh. "Going Door to Door." *Police*, July 2006, pp.36–40.

O'Harrow, Robert, Jr., and Nakashima, Ellen. "National Dragnet Is a Click Away." *Washington Post*, March 6, 2008, p.A01.

Page, Douglas. "Ending Law Enforcement's Long Winter of Disconnect?" *Law Enforcement Technology*, July 2007, pp.98–105.

Phillips, Amanda. "Virtual Interrogation Software 'Fine Tunes' Skills on or off Duty." *Law Enforcement Technology*, August 2007, pp.112–117.

Rossmo, D. Kim. "Failures in Criminal Investigation." *The Police Chief*, October 2009, pp.54–66.

Rutledge, Devallis. "Cold Case Interrogations." *Police*, March 2007a, pp.70–72.

Rutledge, Devallis. "The Lawful Use of Deception." *Police*, January 2007b, pp.59–61.

Rutledge, Devallis. "The *Bruton* Rule." *Police*, March 2008, pp.61–63.

Rutledge, Devallis. "*Miranda* Wording." *Police*, April 2010, pp.60–61.

Scarry, Laura L. "Knock and Talk." *Law Officer Magazine*, April 2007, pp.62–66.

Scoville, Dean. "How to Interview a Child." *Police*, June 2007, pp.32–34.

Siuru, Bill. "CrimeCog Information System Technology." *Law and Order*, April 2007, pp.79–81.

Wagner, Winfield. "Eliminating the Information Exchange Bottleneck." *Law Enforcement Technology*, May 2007, pp.114–123.

Zimmerman, John K. "Operationalizing Intelligence Led Policing." *9-1-1 Magazine*, August 2006, pp.48–52, 70.

Cases Cited

Alabama v. White, 496 U.S. 325 (1990)

Berkemer v. McCarty, 468 U.S. 420 (1984)

Brewer v. Williams, 430 U.S. 387 (1977)

Bruton v. United States, 391 U.S. 123 (1968)

Burket v. Angelone, 208 F.3d 172 (4th Cir. 2000)

Crawford v. Washington, 541 U.S. 36 (2004)

Davis v. United States, 512 U.S. 452 (1994)

Dickerson v. United States, 530 U.S. 428 (2000)

Dormire v. Wilkinson, 249 F.3d. 801 (8th Cir. 2001)

Edwards v. Arizona, 451 U.S. 477 (1981)

Fellers v. United States, 540 U.S. 519 (2004)

Florida v. Powell, 559 U.S. ___ (2010)

Frazier v. Cupp, 394 U.S. 731 (1969)

Illinois v. Perkins, 496 U.S. 292 (1990)

Maryland v. Shatzer, 559 U.S. ___ (2010)

Minnesota v. Murphy, 465 U.S. 420 (1984)

Miranda v. Arizona, 384 U.S. 436 (1966)

Missouri v. Seibert, 542 U.S. 600 (2004)

Moore v. Hopper, 389 F. Supp. 931 (M.D. Ga. 1974)

New York v. Quarles, 467 U.S. 649 (1984)

Nix v. Williams, 467 U.S. 431 (1984)

Oregon v. Mathiason, 429 U.S. 492 (1977)

Sorrells v. United States, 287 U.S. 435 (1932)

United States v. Banks, 540 U.S. 31 (2003)

United States ex rel. Caminito v. Murphy, 222 F.2d 698 (2nd Cir. 1955)

United States v. Crapser, 472 F.3d 1141 (9th Cir. 2007)

United States v. Patane, 542 U.S. 630 (2004)

United States v. Russell, 411 U.S. 423 (1973)

United States v. Scheffer, 523 U.S. 303 (1998)

Wong Sun v. United States, 371 U.S. 471 (1963)

Yarborough v. Alvarado, 541 U.S. 652 (2004)

CHAPTER 7
Identifying and Arresting Suspects

© A. Ramey/PhotoEdit

Outline

Can You Define?

arrest

bugging

close tail

cover

criminal profiling

de facto arrest

entrapment

excessive force

field identification

fixed surveillance

force

geographic profiling

loose tail

open tail

plant

pretextual traffic stops

psychological profiling

racial profiling

raid

reasonable force

rough tail

show-up identification

solvability factors

stakeout

subject

surveillance

surveillant

tail

tight tail

undercover

wiretapping

Do You Know?

- What field identification or show-up identification is and when it is used?
- What rights a suspect has during field (show-up) identification and what case established these rights?
- How a suspect is developed?
- How to help witnesses describe a suspect or a vehicle?
- When mug shots are used?
- What the four basic means of identifying a suspect are?
- What photographic identification requires and when it is used?
- What a lineup requires and when it is used?
- What rights suspects have regarding participation in a lineup and which cases established these rights?
- Whether it is advisable to have the same person make both a photographic and lineup identification?
- When surveillance is used? What its objectives are?
- What the types of surveillance are?
- When wiretapping is legal and what the precedent case is?
- What the objectives of undercover assignments are? What precautions you should take?
- What the objectives of a raid are?

(continued)

The classic question in detective stories is "Whodunit?" This question is also critical in criminal investigations. In some cases, the suspect is obvious. However, in most cases, there is no suspect initially. Although many crimes are witnessed, victims and witnesses may not recognize or be able to describe the suspect. Further, many crimes are not witnessed.

Factors crucial to resolving criminal investigations are called **solvability factors**. These are factors you should consider when deciding whether to investigate a crime. Among the most important are the existence of one or more witnesses and whether a suspect can be named or at least described and located.

Even if a suspect is known or has confessed, you must prove the elements of the crime and establish evidence connecting the suspect with the criminal act.

Do You Know? *(continued)*

■ When raids are legal?

■ What precautions should be taken when conducting a raid?

■ When a lawful arrest can be made?

■ When probable cause must exist for believing that a suspect has committed a crime?

■ What constitutes an arrest?

■ In what areas officers leave themselves open to civil liability when making an arrest?

■ How much force is justified when making an arrest?

Some cases require that suspects be developed, located, identified and then arrested. Others begin with an arrest and proceed to identification. No set sequence exists. Regardless of whether an arrest begins or ends an investigation, the arrest must be legal.

IDENTIFYING SUSPECTS AT THE SCENE

If a suspect is at the scene, you can use the person's driver's license, mobile identification technology or field or show-up identification.

Identification by Driver's License

Technology has advanced by leaps and bounds since the first driver's license was issued more than 100 years ago. As an unfortunate consequence, today's driver's licenses and their rightful owners have fallen victim to theft, forgery and counterfeiting. According to multiple reports, all 19 of the September 11, 2001, hijackers had used valid driver's licenses to pass through airport security. By some accounts, these 19 men held as many as 63 driver's licenses between them.

In an effort to make driver's licenses more secure, Congress passed the REAL ID Act of 2005, requiring states to take new steps to verify the identity of applicants before issuing driver's licenses and other ID cards. Originally scheduled to take effect in 2008, overwhelming resistance from the states has led to two extensions, with the current effective date set for 2013. In the meantime, bills continue to be introduced into Congress aimed at amending or repealing REAL ID. The most recent bill, called PASS ID, seeks to eliminate many of the more difficult or excessive standards contained in the REAL ID Act, such as the obligation to verify birth certificates with the issuing department, while still requiring states to meet certain basic federal standards. The future of such laws remains uncertain.

Asking to see a suspect's driver's license is routine. However, often suspects do not carry identification or, if they do, it may be fake. Investigators need to determine whether licenses are legitimate as well as whether they belong to those using them. One aid in determining authenticity of driver's licenses is the *Drivers License Guide*, which contains information and graphics of more than 200 driver's licenses, as well as other documents commonly used for identification. Keep a current copy of this publication on hand.

Mobile Identification Technology

An important advance in law enforcement is the ability to receive information about suspects through officers' laptop or in-car computers. The amount of time it takes to identify a suspect is directly correlated with the length of time it takes to solve a crime.

Biometric Identification

Biometrics was introduced in Chapter 5 as a way to positively identify an individual. Common physiological or behavioral characteristics measured in biometric analysis include fingerprints, palm vein patterns, facial geometry, iris and retina patterns, voice or speech prints and handwriting: "Most of these features are well established and are genetically determined, and all are distinctive for each person" (Hanson, 2007, p.84).

Facial recognition is being used in many states to compare a photograph of someone applying for a replacement or renewal license with prior images to be sure the applicant is the same person. Such a system could improve the millions of manual ID verifications performed daily. Applications of face recognition in law enforcement include searching large databases for the "bad guys," the most wanted or suspects (the most common application); verifying travelers at border crossings; checking people against blacklists, such as shoplifters; performing remote

Technology Innovations

Reality Mobile's Reality Vision is software that broadcasts video and images from connected officers in its system to decision makers at headquarters and to law enforcement team members instantly (Kozlowski, 2007, pp.126–127):

> Reality Vision transmits an officer's live video to headquarters and then back out to other team members in the field. Acting as an intelligence gathering tool, the software allows law enforcement to handle issues they previously were unable to. The potential for in-field identification arose through the use of integrated technologies, such as facial recognition software, that would analyze the transmitted still image or video for suspects. If the software identified a suspect, law enforcement would then be able to take appropriate action based on more informed decisions. . . .
> Reality Mobile's Reality Vision provides decision makers the information to return the knowledge back to first responders in the field, saving time and manpower in the field and on the street.

surveillance; and analyzing collected surveillance video (Falk, 2007, p.37). Several challenges to facial recognition software include negative perceptions, tight budgets, image collection limitations and the fact that, unlike fingerprints, the face is always changing (Langerman, 2008, p.64). Nonetheless, "Facial recognition technology has come a long way. Experts and designers believe it must become a mainstay of biometrics and law enforcement. The ability to identify a subject by face in the field is critical when a suspect refuses to cooperate or is dangerous" (Langerman, p.67).

Field Identification or Show-Up Identification

If a suspect is apprehended while committing a crime, you can have witnesses identify the suspect. The same is generally true if the suspect is apprehended at or near the crime scene.

Field identification or **show-up identification** is on-the-scene identification of a suspect by a victim of or witness to a crime. Field identification must be made within a short time after the crime was committed.

The critical element in field identification is *time.* Identification must occur very soon after the crime was committed (usually 15–20 minutes). Some experts, however, suggest that if a suspect has been temporarily detained, the show-up may occur as long as two hours after the crime was committed. If the suspect has fled but is apprehended within minutes, you can either return the suspect to the scene or take the witness to where the suspect was apprehended. It is usually preferable to take the witness to the suspect than to return the suspect to the crime scene.

Whether the identification is made at or away from the scene, the victim or witness must identify the suspect as soon after the crime as possible so that details are still clear. However, a reasonable basis must exist for believing that immediate identification is required before using field identification.

United States v. Ash, Jr. (1973) established that a suspect does not have the right to have counsel present at a field identification.

Read suspects the *Miranda* warning before questioning them. Suspects may refuse to answer questions and may demand a lawyer before any questioning occurs, but they do not have the right to have a lawyer present before field identification is made. Suspects may not even know such identification is occurring. Victims or witnesses may be positioned so they can see the suspect but the suspect cannot see them.

Field identifications have been attacked on the basis that the victim or witness is too emotionally upset at the time to make an accurate identification, but such objections are seldom upheld. Mistaken identification is less likely if the person committing the crime is apprehended at the scene and is identified immediately. Have the victim or witnesses put their positive identification in writing and sign and date it and then have it witnessed.

An integrated biometric identification system (IBIS) shrinks this time factor and solves a problem continually faced by police—the need to obtain positive identification and information on suspects at a crime scene or during a traffic stop. An IBIS is a comprehensive data system that allows field officers to capture and analyze forensic-quality fingerprints, palmprints and facial and iris images on a handheld device. The images can be transmitted to the FBI's Advanced Fingerprint Information Technology (AFIT) system and the National Crime Information Center (NCIC). If a match is found, the system returns the individual's name and date of birth directly to the remote data terminal (RDT). The system also can query existing criminal history and warrant files and provide information within minutes.

DEVELOPING SUSPECTS

If a suspect is not at the scene and not apprehended nearby, you must develop a suspect.

Suspects are developed through several means:
- Information provided by victims, witnesses and other persons likely to know about the crime or the suspect
- Physical evidence left at the crime scene
- Psychological profiling
- Information in police files
- Information in the files of other agencies
- Informants

Many sources are sometimes needed to develop a suspect. Most of these sources were introduced in the preceding chapter. At other times, the victim or witnesses provide the required information. Then your task is to corroborate the identification through associative evidence such as fingerprints or DNA analysis, shoe prints, personal belongings and other such evidence left at the scene as described in Chapter 5. Police agencies also have automated fingerprint identification systems and computerized imaging systems to assist in identifying suspects.

Victims and Witnesses

Developing a suspect is much easier if the victim or witnesses can describe and identify the person who committed the crime. Witnesses may not have observed the actual crime but may have seen a vehicle leaving the scene and can describe it and its occupants. Obtain a complete description of the suspect(s) and any vehicles involved.

Help witnesses describe suspects and vehicles by asking very specific questions and using an identification diagram.

Rather than simply asking a witness to describe a suspect, ask specific questions about each item in Table 7.1. Also obtain information about how the suspect left the scene—on foot or in a vehicle. If in a vehicle, obtain a complete description of it. Identifying the car may lead to identifying the suspect.

Victims can provide information about who has a motive for the crime, who has the knowledge required to commit it and who is not a likely suspect. For example, in

TABLE 7.1 Key Items in Suspect Identification
Gender
Height
Weight
Build—stout, average, slim; stooped, square-shouldered
Age
Race
Face—long, round, square; fat, thin; pimples, acne, scars
Complexion—flushed, sallow; pale, fair, dark
Hair—color; thick, thin, partly bald, completely bald; straight, curly, wavy; long, short
Forehead—high, low; sloping, straight, bulging
Eyebrows—bushy, thin, average
Eyes—color; close together or wide-set; large, small; glasses or sunglasses
Nose—small, large; broad, narrow; crooked, straight; long, short
Ears—small, large; close to head or protruding; pierced
Mustache—color; short, long; thick, thin; pointed ends
Mouth—large, small; drooping, upturned
Lips—thick, thin
Teeth—missing, broken, prominent, gold, conspicuous dental work
Beard—color; straight, rounded; bushy, thin; long, short
Chin—square, round, broad; long, narrow; double, sagging
Neck—long, short; thick, thin
Distinctive marks—scars, moles, amputations, tattoos, birthmarks
Peculiarities—peculiar walk or talk, twitch, stutter, foreign accent, distinctive voice or dialect
Clothing—shabby or well dressed, monograms, association with an occupation or hobby, general description
Weapon (if any)—specific type, how carried, how displayed and when
Jewelry—any obvious rings, bracelets, necklaces, earrings, watches

© Cengage Learning, 2013

an "inside" burglary, the employer may be able to provide important information about which employees may or may not be suspects.

Eyewitness identification is highly fallible because of factors such as poor visibility, brief duration, distance and faulty memory (Rossmo, 2009). Because of such problems with witness identification, victim or eyewitness identification of a suspect should be corroborated by as much physical and circumstantial evidence as possible.

Mug Shots

If the victim or witness does not know the suspect but saw him or her clearly, mug shots may be used.

> Have victims and witnesses view mug shots if you believe a suspect has a police record.

This procedure, frequently depicted in television detective shows, is very time-consuming and is of value only if the suspect has a police record and has been photographed. Using facial recognition to scan the face of a suspect against a database of thousands of mug shots of known criminals helps officers pare down a list of suspects or solve a case.

The Integrated Law Enforcement Face-Identification System (ILEFIS) deploys a three-dimensional system to match images from surveillance or still photographs to existing mug shots with a high degree of accuracy.

Composite Drawings and Sketches

If witnesses can provide adequate information, a composite image can be made of the person who committed the crime. Composite drawings are most commonly used to draw human faces or full bodies, but they can also be used for any inanimate object described by a witness—for example, vehicles, unusual marks or symbols, tattoos or clothing.

Composite sketches can also be created using a computerized identification kit such as Identi-Kit®, although some training is required to use them. Identi-Kit Version 6.0 (released in 2005) is a computerized version of the original Identi-Kit, developed in the late 1950s. The process starts with a police officer asking a series of initial questions, which creates a general likeness of a suspect based on a victim's or witness's description. After creating a general composite, officers can fine-tune the image of the criminal. Figure 7.1 illustrates how Identi-Kit helps develop suspects. Other software such as CompuSketch or Visatex is also becoming more popular for drafting computer-generated composites.

Modus Operandi Information

A series of crimes often creates a recognizable modus operandi (MO). For instance, a forger may use the same or a very similar name on each forgery, or a burglar may take the same type of property. If a series of burglaries occurs at the same time of day, this may be the suspect's time away from a regular job. Such MOs furnish important investigative leads.

Check the details of a specific crime against your department's MO files. If no similar MO is listed, a new criminal may be starting activity in your area, or this may be the only crime the suspect intends to commit. In such cases, the suspect must be developed through sources other than MO information, such as information contained in a psychological or criminal profile.

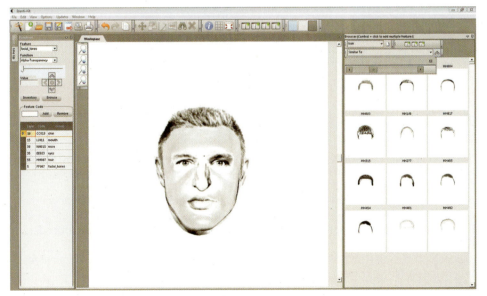

FIGURE 7.1
Computerized composite sketch applications, such as Identi-Kit®, help investigators work with victims and witnesses to generate more accurate images of suspects.
Source: © Identi-Kit Solutions, www.identikit.net

Psychological or Criminal Profiling and Geographic Profiling

One method of suspect identification is **psychological** or **criminal profiling**, which attempts to identify an individual's mental, emotional and psychological characteristics. Profiles are developed primarily for violent acts such as homicides, sadistic crimes, sex crimes, arson without apparent motive and crimes of serial or ritual sequence. The profile provides investigators with corroborative information about a known suspect or possible leads to an unknown suspect.

The psychological profile is determined by examining all data and evidence from a specific crime scene, including but not limited to crime scene photographs, detailed photos of bodily injuries to victims, photos of any mutilation evidence, information related to the condition of the victim's clothing or absence thereof, information regarding whether the crime scene was altered or unaltered, photos of the area beyond the immediate crime scene, available maps of the area, the medical examiner's report and opinion and any other relevant information concerning the crime, particularly abnormalities such as multiple slashings, disembowelment or dismembering of the body. Specific information is then categorized to produce predictive information regarding the suspect's likely age, sex, race, weight and height; physical, mental and psychological condition; area of residence; whether known to the victim; whether the suspect has a criminal record; and other details.

The psychological profile produced by experts in criminal behavior analysis can provide excellent leads for investigators. Investigators who desire such assistance may provide a complete crime report to the local office of the FBI, Domestic Cooperative Services. If the report is accepted, it is then forwarded to the FBI Behavioral Science Unit.

In one criminal investigation, the FBI's Behavioral Science Unit advised a police department that the serial rapist they were seeking was probably a 25- to 35-year-old, divorced or separated White male, with a high school education who worked as a laborer, lived in the area of the rapes and engaged in voyeurism. Based on this information, the agency developed a list of 40 suspects with these characteristics. Using other information in the profile, they narrowed their investigation to one suspect and focused on him. Within a week, they had enough information to arrest him.

William Tafoya of the FBI developed a psychological profile of the Unabomber that many rejected. However, after the arrest of Theodore Kaczynski, Tafoya's assessment was observed to be much more accurate than many in the FBI had believed.

Psychological profiling is most often used in crimes against people in which a motive is unknown. The profile seeks to disclose a possible motive. Continued use of the technique has shown that the more information the police furnish the FBI, the greater the possibility of obtaining accurate leads. Reporting the unusual is extremely important. Psychological profiling can help both eliminate and develop suspects, thereby saving investigative time.

Geographic profiling can also be helpful in identifying suspects who commit multiple crimes (serial criminals).

 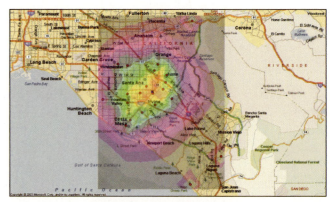

In December 2003, the city of Garden Grove, California, began experiencing a series of armed robberies involving several suspects. The robberies consisted of one to three offenders robbing liquor stores and motel desk clerks at gunpoint. All offenders were wearing masks. The offenders would often commit two or three robberies a night in a spree.

A geographic profile was initially done for this case in late December and was updated in January. At that point, the total had reached 32 robberies. The area of the crimes covered 546 square miles. There were now 11 police jurisdictions with crimes in the series.

The offenders were captured in early February 2004 after the suspects had completed 45 robberies. It was found that all offenders were staying at one of the motels they had previously robbed.

The peak profile area shown by the geographic profile was 8 square miles. The location of the motel (the offender's anchor point for the series) was in the top one percent of the updated profile (32 crimes), a highly accurate result.

Geographic profiling is based on the fact that everyone has a pattern to their lives, particularly in relation to the geographical areas they frequent. The serial criminal operates within a comfort zone—near to where he or she lives but far enough away to remain anonymous and still feel comfortable because he or she knows the area. However, "Creation of a geographic profile requires a lot of data gathering, refining and sorting before the case can be sent to an appropriate analyst who will generate the profile. It is not likely that it will become a routine practice because of its labor-intensive nature. In fact, it compares well with psychological profiling for the same

reasons. But when you have a major case and you're out of investigative leads, the effectiveness of these two tools can be the difference between capturing the bad guy and having him continue to prey on the citizens you serve" (Dees, 2008, p.71).

Despite its usefulness, profiling is not infallible. Investigators should not rely solely on a profile without supporting evidence. For example, in the Atlanta Olympic bombing case of 1996, the profile resulted in the arrest of the security guard, who was later cleared. In addition, the legitimate use of profiling is sometimes confused with racial profiling.

Racial Profiling

Welch (2007, p.276) reports, "The racial stereotyping of criminals has been an enduring and unfortunate feature of American culture. However, following the civil right movement, the linkage between Blacks and crime was galvanized. The stereotyping of Blacks as criminals is so pervasive throughout society that 'criminal predator' is used as a euphemism for 'young Black males.'" **Racial profiling** occurs when an officer singles out and focuses on an individual as a suspect based solely on that person's race, excluding legitimate factors such as behavior.

It is important to distinguish between *profiling* (legitimate) as a policing technique and the politically charged term *racial profiling* (not legitimate). Some have suggested replacing *racial profiling* with the term *biased-based policing* to emphasize this distinction: "Bias-based policing is an issue that police departments all across the country are addressing. Considering that bias-based policing undermines relationships between the police and the public, a considerable amount of research has been conducted to uncover and prevent the occurrence of bias-based policing. . . . This research found that 21 percent of survey respondents believed that bias-based policing is presently practiced by officers in their department, and 25.9 percent believed that bias-based policing is practiced by officers in other departments" (Ioimo et al., 2007, p.270).

Another viable alternative to racial profiling is "building a case." For example, airport security personnel are taught to watch for certain traits—young, African American male paying for a ticket in cash, no luggage, nervousness and so on—to profile possible drug dealers and are frequently criticized for such profiling. The more recent war on terror has led to heightened scrutiny of the behavior of Middle Easterners: "In the aftermath of September 11, Arab Americans have a greater fear of racial profiling and immigration enforcement than of falling victim to hate crimes, according to a national study financed by the Justice Department. . . . Arab Americans

Technology Innovations

Corbley (2008, pp.96–101) notes that geographic information systems (GIS) combined with global positioning systems (GPS) photomapping can be an excellent tool in helping investigators spatially piece together clues and evidence that are spread out over a relatively large area. In certain types of offenses, such as abductions, high-speed chases, assaults or rapes, the crime scene itself may be quite expansive, with evidence such as blood, bullet casings, tire treads or footprints, weapons and other items scattered across many yards or even miles. The pattern of evidence dispersal can enable a forensics expert to reconstruct how a scene unfolded. The GPS photomapping software uses photos taken by crime scene investigators and automatically maps the photos according to GPS location. The images are further stamped with coordinates, including the time and date of collection. The software then geo-references the photos according to their locations on a GIS base map, denoting each piece of evidence with an icon on the digital map, thus created a spatially accurate map of evidence locations.

In one example, investigators used this technology to help solve a 20-year-old case in which a man went missing during a boating excursion on Lake Powell in Utah and was presumed to have drowned. When human remains were found two decades later along the lakeshore, investigators used GPS photomapping to cross reference the location with where the man had been initially reported missing 20 years ago. But it was still unclear whether the victim had drowned by accident or by foul play. Investigators looked for answers at the site. The map of evidence suggested the body had simply been broken apart by waves and possibly coyotes over the years. The coroner found no evidence of foul play.

reported an increasing sense of victimization, suspicion of government and law enforcement, and concerns about protecting their civil liberties" (Elliot, 2006).

The *perception* of racial profiling may be bolstered by discussions of **pretextual traffic stops**, that is, stopping vehicles when the officer's intent (pretext) was not the real reason for the stop. For example, an officer may stop someone for a traffic violation when he really suspects that the person has drugs in the car, but he does not have reasonable suspicion to make the stop for drug possession. In *Whren v. United States* (1996), the Supreme Court affirmed that officers could stop vehicles to allay any suspicions even though they have no evidence of criminal behavior. The legality of the stop will be gauged by its objective reasonableness, as discussed in Chapter 6.

The courts *have* ruled that race can be one factor among others to use in developing suspects. In *United States v. Weaver* (1992), a Drug Enforcement Administration (DEA) agent stopped and questioned Arthur Weaver at a Kansas City airport "because he was 'roughly dressed,' young, Black, and on a direct flight from Los Angeles, a source city for drugs." Weaver was carrying illicit drugs but challenged the legality of the arrest. The Eighth Circuit Court of Appeals upheld the officer's conduct:

> Facts are not to be ignored simply because they may be unpleasant—and the unpleasant fact in this case is that the [DEA agent] had knowledge, based upon his own experience and upon the intelligence reports he had received from Los Angeles authorities, that young, male members of the African-American Los Angeles gangs were flooding the Kansas City area with cocaine. To that extent then, race, when coupled with the other factors [the agent] relied upon, was a factor in the decision to approach and ultimately detain [the suspect]. We wish it were otherwise, but we take the facts as they are presented to us, not as we would wish them to be.

Shortly after September 11, 2001, the Supreme Court refused to hear the only remaining case previously docketed concerning an equal protection claim in a case where police officers stopped persons based primarily on racial or ethnic descriptions. In *Brown v. City of Oneonta* (2001), a court of appeals for the Second Circuit held that where law enforcement officials have a description of a suspect that consists only of the suspect's race and gender, and lacking evidence of discriminatory intent, they can act on that description without violating the equal protection clause of the Fourteenth Amendment. Subjecting officers to equal-protection scrutiny when they detain or arrest could hamper police work. Officers who fear personal liability from equal-protection violations might fail to act when they are expected to. If police effectiveness is hobbled by special racial rules, inner-city residents would be harmed the most.

Tracking

Sometimes knowledge of tracking is helpful in developing suspects. Forensic tracking is the science of locating, retaining and interpreting footprint and tire tread impressions to solve criminal cases. Unfortunately tracking is becoming somewhat of a lost art: "'What we don't look for, we don't find' is a cliché that seems to apply to tracks. Footprints are truly 'the missed evidence' in many jurisdictions" (Hanratty, 2007, p.50).

Footprints can provide valuable clues. The length of stride and depth of impression of footprints can help determine the size or height of the person and whether the person was carrying a heavy load. To determine an individual's height from shoeprint length, "Measure the shoeprint length in inches and divide by two to get the height in feet. For example, a shoeprint that measures 12 inches in length will indicate a person six feet tall. This is a rough estimate for use at the scene to rule in or rule out possible suspects" (Hanratty, 2007, p.47).

Tire prints can also provide information to investigators. For example, transfer of sticky soils is a good way to determine vehicle direction. Wet sand, mud or clay will initially stick to tires. As the vehicle continues moving, this material will fall off the tires in the direction the vehicle is headed. If the tracks shine in grass, they are headed away from you. Tire tracks coming toward you will show faintly as an off color to the surrounding grass (Lee, 2007, pp.28–34).

Tracking skill can be developed for impressions other than footprints and can provide many investigative leads. People hiding in outside areas may leave foot, knee, hand, heel or body impressions. Broken tree branches provide evidence of when the branch was broken—the lighter the color of the break, the more recent it is. Recent overturning of a stone may be indicated by the dirt or by the moist side being on top.

Other Identification Aids

Visual aids such as newspaper photos or video and news films disseminated to the public may provide rapid identification of suspects. Yearbooks have also proved to be valuable in developing suspects.

If a suspect or victim is deceased and the identity is unknown, dental and orthopedic records may help. Facial reconstruction is also used in many areas to identify unknown victims or suspects if sufficient skull and facial parts are available.

Information in Police Files and Files of Other Agencies

Police records on solved crimes and on suspects involved in certain types of crimes often suggest leads. For example, in the "Son of Sam" case in New York City, one lead was provided by a woman who saw an illegally parked car that fit the description of the car reported as being used in the crimes. Police then checked all parking tickets issued on that date for that time and location. This, combined with other information, eventually led to the suspect.

Police files contain considerable information about people who have committed or are suspected of committing crimes. The files contain such information as their physical characteristics, date of birth, age, race, general build, kind of clothing usually worn, height, weight, hair color and style, facial features, unusual marks, scars, tattoos, deformities, abnormalities, alcohol or drug use, MO and other information.

Field-interview cards that patrol officers file when they stop people under suspicious circumstances can also provide leads. An officer may not know of an actual crime committed at the time of a stop but may later learn that a business or residence in the area of the stop was burglarized at about the same time. Descriptions of vehicles in a high-crime area that do not fit the neighborhood also help to identify suspects. Chapter 6 discussed sources of information ranging from the local to the federal level, as well as the use of informants.

LOCATING SUSPECTS

Many information sources used to develop a suspect can also help locate the suspect. If the suspect is local and frequents public places, the victim may see the suspect and call the police. In one instance, a rape victim saw the alleged rapist in a shopping center and remembered that she had seen him there just before her rape occurred. The investigator accompanied the victim to the shopping center for several evenings until the victim saw the suspect and identified him.

Telephoning other investigative agencies, inquiring around the neighborhood of the suspect's last known address or checking the address on a prison release form, questioning relatives and checking with utility companies and numerous other contacts can help locate suspects.

IDENTIFYING SUSPECTS

Several techniques are available to identify suspects.

> Suspects can be identified through field or show-up identification, mug shots, photographic identification or lineups.

Field identification and mug shots have been discussed previously.

Photographic Identification

Often the victim or witnesses get a good look at the suspect and can make a positive identification.

> Use photographic identification when you have a good idea of who committed a crime but the suspect is not in custody or when a fair lineup cannot be conducted. Tell witnesses they need not identify anyone from the photographs.

Photographs can be obtained through surveillance or from files. Select pictures of at least five people of comparable race, height, weight and general appearance. The photographs can be kept separate or mounted on a composite board. Write a number or code on the back of each photograph to identify the individual, but do not include any other information, especially that the person has a criminal record. Tell witnesses that they need not identify anyone from among the photographs and that it is as important to eliminate innocent people from suspicion as it is to identify the guilty.

> A suspect does not have the right to a lawyer if a photographic lineup is used (*United States v. Ash, Jr.*, 1973).

Many departments use a "six pack" photo display of mug shots, DMV license pictures or other photos of the suspect and five other individuals. Some investigators prefer to use larger, separate photos of each individual instead of presenting a grouping of smaller photos all together, the logic being that larger individual pictures provide less confusion when witnesses are viewing lineups because they can just focus on each picture individually. If there are several witnesses, have each one view a separate set of pictures independently—preferably in a different room if other witnesses are viewing the photographs at the same time. If witnesses recognize a photograph, have them indicate this by placing their initials and the date on the *front* of the photograph. Then have them initial and date the *back* of each remaining photograph. This procedure establishes the fairness of the identification.

Some departments use a sequential approach by showing witnesses one photograph at a time. Such a sequential showing allows a witness to decide about each photo before looking at the next, reducing the tendency to compare photos.

It is unwise to show a single photograph to a victim or witness to obtain identification. Such identification is almost always inadmissible as evidence because it allows a chance of mistaken identity and improperly suggests to the witness that the single person shown is the suspect sought. The Supreme Court decision in *Manson v. Brathwaite* (1977), however, did approve the showing of a single picture in specific circumstances. In this case, the witness who used a single photograph to positively identify suspect Manson as the man from whom he had purchased heroin was, in fact, Jimmy Glover, a specially trained, assigned and experienced undercover narcotics officer. Manson argued that the showing of a single photograph to Glover was "impermissibly suggestive," and in most cases, the courts would likely agree. However, the Supreme Court, in their analysis, weighed the following facts of this case:

- *The opportunity to view*—unlike many witnesses who view a crime from a distance or from behind some type of barrier, Glover stood face to face with the suspect.

- *The degree of attention*—Glover was not a casual or passing observer, as is so often the case with eyewitness identification, but rather was a trained police officer on duty.

- *The accuracy of the description*—Glover's description of the narcotics seller, given to a fellow officer within minutes after the transaction, was accurate enough to allow the other officer, who was familiar with many local drug dealers, to pull a photograph of the suspect from the police department's records division.

- *The witness's level of certainty*—Glover, in response to a question whether the photograph was that of the person from whom he made the purchase, testified: "There is no question whatsoever."

- *The time between the crime and the confrontation*—Glover's description of his vendor was given to the other officer within minutes of the crime. The photographic identification took place only two days later.

There was not the passage of weeks or months between the crime and the viewing of the photograph, as is often the case with witness identification and during which time the witness's memory of specific identifying details may deteriorate.

The facts of this case highlight the high level of scrutiny with which the courts assess witness identification. The vast majority of the witnesses that investigators deal with will not be highly trained and experienced officers; therefore, it is essential that investigators not compromise the identification process by improperly showing only a single photograph to a witness.

After identification is made, review with the witness the conditions under which the suspect was seen, including lighting at the time and distance from the suspect. Also ask witnesses just how confident they are in their identification. Record their statements and the conditions of the identification and have the witnesses sign the documents.

Lineup Identification

Lineup identification is commonly used when the suspect is in custody and there were witnesses to the crime: "At its most basic level, a police lineup involves placing a suspect among people not suspected of committing the crime (fillers) and asking the eyewitness if he or she can identify the perpetrator" (Schuster, 2007, p.3). Police have adopted lineup procedures to ensure accurate, fair identifications and to meet the standards established by Supreme Court decisions. Basically, a lineup has the same requirements as photographic identification.

> Use lineup identification when the suspect is in custody. Use at least five individuals of comparable race, height, weight, age and general appearance. Ask all to perform the same actions or speak the same words. Instruct those viewing the lineup that they need not make an identification.

Lineups may have from 5 to 10 people. The suspect must not be of a different race, exceptionally taller or shorter, have longer or shorter hair or be dressed very differently from the others in the lineup. The suspect must not be handcuffed unless everyone in the lineup is handcuffed. Nor may the suspect be asked to step forward, turn a certain direction or speak certain words unless everyone in the lineup is asked to do the same.

Recent studies on lineup structure and implementation have led to questions and disagreements. The person conducting the lineup typically knows who the suspect is,

This lineup, in which alleged rapist Ronald Cotton appears, shows seven individuals of comparable race, height, weight, age and general appearance in accordance with lineup standards set by the U.S. Supreme Court. A rape victim incorrectly identified Cotton from this lineup as the man who had sexually assaulted her. Cotton spent ten years behind bars for a crime he didn't commit, before the real rapist was identified and held accountable. In a later interview, following Cotton's exoneration, the victim recalled the lineup and identification process and stated, "I was certain, but I was wrong."

Courtesy Burlington Police Department, North Carolina

and some evidence exists that this person might, either purposefully or inadvertently, give the witness verbal or nonverbal cues to the suspect's identity. For example, the lineup administrator might say, "Take your time," in effect, leading the witness away from a filler. To compensate for this tendency, some have recommended using a *double-blind* lineup, where neither the administrator nor witness knows the suspect's identity (Gaertner and Harrington, 2009).

As with photographic identification, lineups may be simultaneous or sequential. In the traditional simultaneous lineup, the witness views all potential perpetrators at the same time, or six photographs at once, and selects the suspect from the fillers. In contrast, during a sequential lineup, the witness views only one person at a time and must make a decision on each one—*yes,* this is the perpetrator, or *no,* this is not the right person—before moving on to the next one. Some studies have shown that with simultaneous lineups, there is a tendency for the witness to compare one member with the others and make relative judgments, thereby selecting, through the process of elimination, the person who looks most like the perpetrator. The conclusion of these studies is that sequential lineups yield more accurate eyewitness identification. However, other studies have found that sequential lineups actually increase the risk of false identification (Mecklenburg et al., 2008). Despite the conflicting research, many departments have adopted the sequential double-blind lineup protocol.

If the suspect refuses to participate in the lineup or a lineup cannot be conducted for some reason, simply

Technology Innovations

Amidst growing research indicating that the blind, or double-blind, lineup protocol enhances the accuracy of eyewitness identification, efforts have begun to create a virtual officer who "walks," or rather "talks," a witness through a lineup and responds to simple voice commands. Brent Daugherty, a graduate student at the University of North Carolina at Charlotte, has developed "Officer Garcia," a virtual human computer program designed to conduct photo lineups according to established guidelines (Cutler et al., 2009, pp.293–294):

The virtual officer is a three-dimensional representation of a human, modeled to portray a plain-clothes detective, who converses by identifying keywords from the witness's speech and responding appropriately in a speech-synthesized voice. . . . The virtual officer . . . uses verbal and nonverbal cues in addition to normal communication protocols such as turn-taking, feedback, and repair mechanisms to communicate effectively with eyewitnesses. We created Officer Garcia using an iterative process for improvement that included consultation with other computer scientists, psychologists, and law enforcement officers.

photograph the suspect and each individual in the lineup separately and use photographic identification.

> Suspects may refuse to participate in a lineup, but such refusals can be used against them in court (*Schmerber v. California*, 1966). Suspects have a Sixth Amendment right to have an attorney present during a lineup.

In *United States v. Wade* (1967), a robber forced a cashier and a bank official to place money in a pillowcase. The robber had a piece of tape on each side of his face. After obtaining the money, he left the bank and drove away with an accomplice who had been waiting outside in a car.

In March 1965 an indictment was returned against Wade and an accomplice for the bank robbery. He was arrested on April 2, 1965. Approximately two weeks later, an FBI agent put Wade in a lineup to be observed by two bank employees. Wade's counsel was not notified of the lineup. Each person in the lineup had strips of tape similar to those worn by the bank robber, and each was requested to say words allegedly spoken at the robbery. Both bank employees picked Wade out of the lineup as being the robber, and both employees again identified Wade in the courtroom.

The defense objected that the bank employees' courtroom identifications should be stricken because the original lineup had been conducted without the presence of Wade's counsel. The motion was denied, and Wade was found guilty. Counsel held that this violated his Fifth Amendment right against self-incrimination and his Sixth Amendment right to counsel being present at the lineup.

The *Wade* decision ruled, "Prior to having a suspect participate in a lineup, the officer must advise the suspect of his constitutional right to have his lawyer present during the lineup." Recall that this right to a lawyer does not apply to field identification or photographic identification. The Court held that a suspect has the right to have counsel present at the lineup because a lineup is held for identification by eyewitnesses and may involve vagaries leading to mistaken identification. The Court cited the many cases of mistaken identification and the improper manner in which the suspect may have been presented. The Court commented that neither the lineup nor anything that Wade was required to do in the lineup violated his privilege against self-incrimination.

The Court stated in *Schmerber v. California* (1966) that protection against self-incrimination involved disclosure of knowledge by the suspect. Both state and federal courts have held that compulsion to submit to photographs, fingerprinting, measurements, blood analysis or samples of writing and speaking is not self-incrimination under the Fifth Amendment.

The ruling in *Gilbert v. California* (1967), a companion case to *Wade*, also held that ID evidence from a lineup conducted without counsel, after indictment and arraignment, was inadmissible at trial. This requirement of providing counsel to a suspect in a lineup that occurs after indictment or arraignment is known as the "Wade-Gilbert Rule." If suspects waive their right to counsel, get the waiver in writing. A waiver such as the one in Figure 7.2 can be used.

> Avoid having the same person make both photographic and lineup identification. If you do so, do not conduct both within a short time.

If suspects choose to have a lawyer, they may either select their own or ask you to obtain one. The lawyer may confer with the suspect in private before the lineup and may talk with witnesses observing the lineup, but witnesses are not obligated to talk with the lawyer. Witnesses may wear face covers to avoid recognition by the suspect. Usually the lineup room ensures viewers' anonymity.

Give witnesses clear instructions before the lineup. Tell them they need not identify anyone in the lineup and that they are not to confer with any other witnesses viewing the lineup. Tape record or videotape the proceedings and take a color photograph of the lineup to nullify any allegations by the defense counsel of unfair procedure. The form in Figure 7.3 provides additional evidence of the fairness and reliability of a lineup identification.

SURVEILLANCE, UNDERCOVER ASSIGNMENTS AND RAIDS: THE LAST RESORT

"Follow that car!" "I think we're being tailed!" "I lost him!" "My cover's blown!" "We've been made!" "It's a raid!" Police officers, criminals and the public are very aware of investigative practices such as observing suspects or their houses or apartments, tailing suspects, staking out locations and conducting raids. Television shows and movies, however, usually depict the glamorous, dangerous sides of this facet of investigation. They seldom show the long hours of preparation or the days—even weeks—of tedious watchfulness frequently required.

> Surveillance, undercover assignments and raids are used only when normal methods of continuing the investigation fail to produce results.

WAIVER OF RIGHT TO LEGAL COUNSEL AT LINEUP

Your Rights Are: The police are requesting you to personally appear in a lineup. There will be a number of other persons similiar in physical characteristics with you. The purpose of the lineup is to permit witnesses to observe all persons in the lineup, to make an identification. You may be asked to perform certain actions such as speaking, walking or moving in a certain manner or to put on articles of clothing. You must appear in the lineup, but you have a right to have legal cousel of your choice present. If you do not have an attorney, one can be appointed for you by the court, and the lineup will not be held until your legal counsel is present. An attorney can help you defend against an identification made by witnesses at the lineup.

You have the right to waive legal counsel being present at the lineup.

WAIVER

I have read, or have had read to me, this statement of my rights and I understand these rights. I am willing to participate in a lineup in the absence of legal counsel. I fully understand and give my consent to what I am being asked to do. No promises or threats have been made to me, and no pressure of coercion has been used against me. I understand that I must appear in the lineup, but this consent is to the waiver of legal counsel being present at the lineup.

Signed _____   Place _____

Witness _____   Date _____

Witness _____   Time _____

FIGURE 7.2
Sample waiver.
© Cengage Learning, 2013

These techniques are expensive and potentially dangerous and are not routinely used.

SURVEILLANCE

The covert, discreet observation of people or places is called **surveillance** ("to watch over").

> The objective of surveillance is to obtain information about people, their associates and their activities that may help solve a criminal case or to protect witnesses.

Surveillance can aid an investigation in many ways:

- Gain information required for building a criminal complaint
- Determine an informant's loyalty
- Verify a witness's statement about a crime
- Gain information required for obtaining and executing a search or arrest warrant, such as who lives at a property, how many people are there, what the layout of the property is and so forth
- Gain information necessary for interrogating a suspect
- Identify a suspect's associates
- Observe members of terrorist organizations
- Find a person wanted for a crime
- Observe criminal activities in progress
- Make a legal arrest
- Apprehend a criminal in the act of committing a crime
- Prevent a crime
- Recover stolen property
- Protect witnesses

Because surveillance is a time-consuming, expensive operation that can raise questions of invasion of privacy,

POLICE REPORT OF LINEUP

Boulder City Police

Police Department

Name of suspect __John Vance__   Birth date __2-14-1964__

Address __1424 Colten Street, Boulder City__

Case Number __6432__   Complainant or victim __Thelma Crump__

Name of legal counsel __John Simmons__ Present: Yes _X_ No ____

Was waiver signed: Yes _X_ No ____

Place of lineup __Las Vegas, Nevada, Police Dept.__

Date of lineup __5-12-20__ __   Time of lineup __1640__

Names of persons in lineup (left to right, facing the lineup)

Name	Height	Weight	Birth date	Other
1. Charles Upright	5-11	184	4-10-1966	
2. Gary Starrick	5-10	178	2-14-1965	
3. Jerry Stilter	5-11	190	10-11-1967	
4. Ralph Barrett	5-10	185	12-24-1968	
5. John Vance	5-10	183	2-14-1964	
6. Christian Dolph	5-11	190	6-12-1964	
7.				
8.				
9.				
10.				

Subject identified by witness: Number __5__ Name __John Vance__

Recording taken of lineup: Yes _X_ No___ Photos taken of lineup: Yes _X_ No___

Persons present at lineup __Thelma Crump   Alfred Nener__

__John Simmons   Emmanuel Sorstick__

Person conducting lineup __Sgt. Lloyd Brenner, LVPD__

FIGURE 7.3
Police report of lineup.
© Cengage Learning, 2013

first exhaust all alternatives. Balance the rights of the individual against the need for public safety.

The Surveillant

The **surveillant** is the plainclothes investigator who makes the observation. Surveillants must be prepared for tedium. No other assignment requires as much patience and perseverance while demanding alertness and readiness to respond instantly. Surveillants must display ingenuity in devising a cover for the operation. Lack of resourcefulness in providing adequate answers at a moment's notice can jeopardize the entire case. The most successful surveillants do not attract attention but blend into the general populace.

Multiple surveillants may also compose a surveillance team (ST). An effective ST requires everyone to be "on the same page," which calls for communication and briefings.

The Subject

The **subject** is who or what is being observed. It can be a person, place, property, vehicle, group of people, organization or object. People under surveillance are usually suspects in a crime or their associates. Surveillance of places generally involves a location where a crime is expected to be committed; the residence of a known criminal; a place suspected of harboring criminal activities such as illegal drug transactions, gambling, prostitution or purchase of stolen goods or fencing operations; or the suspected headquarters of a terrorist organization.

Types of Surveillance

The type of surveillance used depends on the subject and the objective of the surveillance. In general, surveillance is either stationary or moving.

> The types of surveillance include stationary (fixed, plant or stakeout) and moving (tight or close, loose, rough, on foot or by vehicle).

Stationary Surveillance. Stationary, or **fixed surveillance**, also called a **plant** or **stakeout**, is used when you know or suspect that a person is at or will come to a known location, when you suspect that stolen goods are to be dropped or when informants have told you that a crime is going to be committed. Such assignments are comparatively short. An outside surveillance simplifies planning. The observation may be from a car, van or truck or by posting an officer in an inconspicuous place with a view of the location. A "dummy" van or a borrowed business van and a disguise as a painter, carpenter or service technician are often used. Take photographs and notes throughout the surveillance.

In longer surveillances, it is often necessary to photograph people who frequent a specific location, such as a store suspected of being a cover for a bookmaking operation or a hotel or motel that allows prostitution or gambling. If the subject of surveillance is a place rather than a person, obtain a copy of the building plan and personally visit the building in advance if possible. Know all entrances and exits, especially rear doors and fire escapes. To properly record what is observed, use closed-circuit camera equipment, movie or video cameras, binoculars with a camera attached, telephoto lenses or infrared equipment for night viewing and photographing.

Lengthy fixed surveillance is often conducted from a room with an unobstructed view of the location, such as an apartment opposite the location being watched. Naturally, the surveillant must not be noticed entering the observation post.

Whether the stationary surveillance is short or long, have adequate communications such as radio, horn signals or hand signals. Use simple hand signals such as pulling up the collar, buttoning the shirt, pulling down the brim on a hat, tying a shoelace, running the hand through the hair or checking a wristwatch. If you use radio communications, find out whether the subject might be monitoring police radio frequencies and, if likely, establish a code.

Select the surveillance team to fit the case and area, and have enough surveillants to cover the assignment. Scout the area in person or by studying maps. Sketch the immediate area to determine possible ways the subject could avoid observation or apprehension. Be aware of alleys, abnormal street conditions, one-way streets, barricades, parking ramps and all other details. This is especially critical when the objective of the surveillance is to apprehend people committing a crime. In such cases, all members of the stakeout must know the signal for action and their specific assignments.

Moving Surveillance. The subjects of moving surveillance are almost always people. The surveillant may be referred to as a **tail**. The first step in planning such a surveillance is to obtain as much information about the subject as you can. View photographs and, if possible, personally observe the subjects. Memorize their physical descriptions and form a mental image of them. Concentrate on their appearance from behind, as this is the view you normally have while tailing them. Although subjects may alter their physical appearance, this usually presents no problem. The major problem is to keep subjects under constant surveillance for the desired time. Know the subjects' habits, where they are likely to go and whether they walk or drive. If they drive, find out what kind of vehicle(s) they use. Also find out who their associates are and whether they are likely to suspect that they are being observed.

Other problems of moving surveillance are losing the subject and having the subject recognize you as a surveillant. Sometimes it is not important if the subject knows of the surveillance. This is often true of material witnesses the police are protecting. It is also true of organized crime figures, who know they are under constant surveillance and expect this. In such instances, a **rough tail** or **open tail** is used. You need not take extraordinary means to remain undetected. The major problem of a rough tail is that it is liable to the charge of police harassment or invasion of privacy.

At other times, it is more important to remain undetected than to keep the subject under constant observation. In such cases, a **loose tail** is used. Maintain a safe distance one or two vehicles behind the subject and "hand off" the subject to another officer after taking one turn. If the subject is lost during surveillance, you can usually relocate the subject and resume the surveillance. A loose tail is often used when you need general information about the subject's activities or associates.

Often, however, it is extremely important not to lose the subject, and a very **close (tight) tail** is maintained. On a crowded street, this means staying within a few steps of the subject; on a less crowded street, it means keeping the subject in sight. A close tail is most commonly used when you know the subject is going to commit a crime, when you must know the subject's exact habits or when knowledge of the subject's activities is important to another critical operation.

When tailing a subject on foot, you can use numerous delaying tactics. You can cross to the other side of the street, talk to a person standing nearby, increase your distance from the subject, read a magazine or newspaper, buy a soda, tinker with the engine in your car, tie your shoe, look in windows or in parked cars or stall in any other way.

If the subject turns a corner, do not follow closely. When you do turn the corner, if you find the subject waiting in a doorway, pass by without paying attention. Then try to resume the tail by guessing the subject's next move. This is often possible when you have advance information on the subject's habits.

If the subject enters a restaurant, you can either enter and take a seat on the side of the room opposite from the subject, making sure you are near the door so you can see the subject leave or you can wait outside. If a subject enters a building that has numerous exits, follow at a safe distance, noticing all potential exits. If the subject takes an elevator, wait at the first floor until the subject returns, noticing the floors at which the elevator stops. If there is a stairway near the elevator, stand near the door so you can hear if the subject has gotten off the elevator and taken the stairs. Such stairs are seldom used, and when someone is going up or down, his or her footsteps echo and can easily be heard.

When tailing a subject on the street, do not hesitate to pass the subject and enter a store yourself. The less obvious you are, the more successful you will be. Use the glass in doors and storefront windows to see behind you.

Subjects who suspect they are being followed use many tricks. They may turn corners suddenly and stand in a nearby doorway, go into a store and duck into a restroom, enter a dressing room, hide behind objects or suddenly jump on a bus or into a taxi. They may do such things to determine *whether* they are being followed or to lose someone they *know* is following them. *It is usually better to lose subjects than to alert them to your presence or to allow them to identify you.*

Surveillants often believe they have been recognized when in fact they have not. However, if you are certain the subject knows you are following, stop the surveillance, but do not return to the police department right away because the subject may decide to tail *you.*

If it is critical not to lose the subject, use more than one surveillant, preferably three. Surveillant A keeps a very close tail immediately behind the subject. Surveillant B follows behind Surveillant A and the subject. Surveillant C observes from across the street parallel with the other two. If the subject turns the corner, Surveillant A continues in the previous direction for a while, and Surveillant B or Surveillant C picks up the tail. Surveillant A then takes the position previously held by the surveillant who picked up the close tail.

When tailing by vehicle, have descriptions of all vehicles the subject drives or rides in. The subject's vehicle can be marked in advance by an electronic device or beeper monitored by a receiver in your car, or you can place the beeper in an object the subject will be carrying. A small amount of fluorescent paint can be applied to the rear bumper of the vehicle to make it easily identifiable day or night.

Your own vehicle should be inconspicuous. Obtain unregistered ("dead") plates for it from the motor vehicle authorities and change them frequently, or change your vehicle daily, perhaps using rental cars. Changing the number of occupants tends to confuse a suspicious subject. If surveillance is to be primarily at night, install a multiple contact switch to allow you to turn off one of your headlights at will.

Like subjects being tailed on foot, subjects being tailed by vehicle often use tricks to determine whether they are being tailed or to lose an identified tail. They may turn in the middle of the block, go through a red light, suddenly pull into a parking space, change traffic lanes rapidly, go down alleys or go the wrong way down a one-way street. In such cases, if temporarily losing the subject causes no problem, stop the surveillance.

If it is critical not to lose the subject, use more than one vehicle for the surveillance. The ideal system uses four vehicles. Vehicle A drives ahead of the subject and observes through the rearview mirror. (This vehicle is not used if only three vehicles are available). Vehicle B follows right behind the subject. Vehicles C and D follow on left and right parallel streets to pick up the tail if the subject turns in either direction.

Avoiding Detection

Criminals are often suspicious of stakeouts or of being followed and may send someone to scout the area to see whether anybody has staked out their residence or their vehicle. This person may stand on the corner near the residence or drive around the block several times to see if everything is clear. Criminals often watch the windows or roofs of buildings across the street for movements. When they leave their residences, they may have an accomplice trail behind to see if anyone is following. Anticipate and plan for such activities: "Counter surveillance is the practice of avoiding surveillance or, at the very least, of making surveillance difficult. Half the battle for law enforcement officers is realizing that they are actually being watched, as opposed to being the watchers" (Donlon-Cotton, 2007, p.75). Sometimes a counter-counter-surveillance is used if personnel are available.

Not every surveillance is successful. In some instances, the subject is lost or the surveillant is recognized, despite the best efforts to avoid either. Like any other investigative technique, failure results from unforeseen circumstances such as vehicle malfunction, illness of the surveillant, unexpected absence of the subject because of illness or emergency, abnormal weather conditions or terrain and other factors beyond control. Usually, however, information and evidence obtained through surveillance are well worth the time and effort invested.

Surveillance Equipment

Surveillance equipment includes binoculars, telescopes, night-vision equipment, video systems, body wires, costumes and disguises. Surveillance systems have become extremely sophisticated. One system, for example, conceals a periscope in what looks like a standard air vent in the roof of a van. The periscope rotates 360 degrees and is undetectable. Remote motion detectors activate the system to videotape the area under surveillance.

GPS technology is also being used in surveillance operations. In *United States v. Knotts* (1983), the Court ruled that installing and monitoring a bird dog tracking device in a public location did not violate a suspect's rights.

Aerial Surveillance

Aerial surveillance may provide information about areas inaccessible to foot or vehicle surveillance. Communication between air surveillance and ground vehicles facilitates the operational movement in and around the target area. The aerial pilot should either be a police officer or be carefully selected by the police. The pilot should be familiar with the landmarks of the area because many such surveillances involve moving suspect vehicles.

Photographs taken from navigable air space, usually 1,000 feet, do not violate privacy regulations. In one aerial surveillance, officers viewed a partially covered greenhouse within the residential curtilage from a helicopter 400 feet above the greenhouse. The greenhouse, which contained marijuana plants, was located 10 to 20 feet behind the residence, a mobile home. A wire fence surrounded the entire property, and "Do Not Enter" signs were posted. Nonetheless, *Florida v. Riley* (1989) approved the warrantless aerial surveillance, noting that there should be no reasonable expectation of privacy from the skies above.

Visual/Video Surveillance

Video images are often used as evidence in high-profile criminal investigations, with thousands of lesser crimes caught on video each year: "Criminal acts are increasingly captured on analog video tape and in digital formats from closed-circuit television systems, cell phone cameras and other forms of security and surveillance equipment. The video is generally available to law enforcement officers, originating from banks, malls, schools, parking lots, office complexes, retail establishments, service stations, hotels, and restaurants" (Pincince, 2007, p.105). For example, the black-and-white video image of Timothy McVeigh's Ryder truck within a block of the Alfred P. Murrah Federal Building placed the suspected vehicle at the scene.

High-crime areas, such as locations commonly used for illegal drug sales, are increasingly being monitored by 24-hour surveillance cameras mounted on utility poles, buildings and other strategic vantage points (Dees, 2009). These cameras may have hardwired or wireless connections back to a viewing and recording station. Although there may or may not be someone actively supervising the output on the receiving end, the activity is recorded and can be accessed if an incident is reported. Many visual surveillance systems have night-vision or telephoto lenses, time-and-date generators and printers that produce black-and-white or color photographic copies on site.

Although many cameras are overtly placed, sometimes officers want to conduct covert surveillance, disguising video systems in a variety of ways, such as in clocks, picture frames, exit signs and domes. Such systems can record drug buys, money laundering, shoplifting and bank robberies and are usually admissible in court. Remote network video cameras are available that can send video via commercial cellular telephone networks.

A classic closed-circuit television infrared security camera.
© gualtiero boffi/Shutterstock

Automated license plate recognition (ALPR) technology can be used passively to record, with a time and location stamp, every license plate that passes in front of the camera: "This data can be analyzed later to establish or confirm alibis and place suspect vehicles in the area of the crime, even though the crime was unknown at the time the record was made" (Dees, 2010, p.31). Facial recognition software can be used in a similar fashion (Romanelli, 2009).

Although a warrant is generally required to use surveillance, the courts have allowed law enforcement to protect certain investigative techniques, to protect information regarding sensitive equipment or to protect surveillance locations. The courts have allowed warrantless surveillance if revealing the technique may endanger law enforcement officers' lives or the lives of those who allow their property to be used in such activity, or when the owners of property may no longer allow their property to be used for surveillance if the technique is revealed. The courts have also allowed warrantless surveillance if once a technique is revealed it will be of no further value to law enforcement or if revealing the technique might show criminals how to use the technique.

Another surveillance technology that raises privacy concerns with potential Fourth Amendment implications is backscatter X-ray devices. Such technology can help officers "see" inside closed containers, such as packages, suitcases and vehicles, and can help detect contraband (illegal drugs, weapons), stowaways and illegal immigrants, explosives and other dangerous or prohibited items (Kozlowski, 2009).

Grant Fredericks, a national video forensics expert says, "Video analysis is the new DNA for law enforcement. It is the next generation of investigation. Every police department in the country will have to have the ability to process video, just like they have police cars and officers have guns" (Heinecke, 2007, p.86). To this end, the Department of Justice and the International Association of Chiefs of Police have developed three Regional Forensic Video Analysis Labs, located in Cincinnati, Ohio; Fort Worth, Texas; and Raynham, Massachusetts: "Just as DNA has CODIS and fingerprints have AFIS, now forensic video evidence will have the Regional Forensic Video Analysis Labs—a national database of criminals caught on tape" (Heinecke, 2007, p.89). Visual or video surveillance is often used in conjunction with audio or electronic surveillance.

Technology Innovations

Miles (2007, pp.20–23) describes a potentially life-saving innovation—through-the-wall (TWS) surveillance:

TWS technology helps officers to determine if someone is in a room before putting themselves in harm's way and to save lives by using motion and images to differentiate between a hostage and a hostage taker. It can also detect motion through floors and rubble following a building structure failure and, therefore, help in the search for survivors. It allows users to conduct room-to-room searches for suspected terrorists, map the interior of buildings, and find military combatants and weapons caches—all through an interior or exterior building wall. Certain TWS technologies do not even need to be placed against a wall and can be used to perform standoff searches, for example, from a vehicle into a building. . . .

Current TWS technology is limited in what it can do. Metal in walls and metal-backed insulation can block the ability to see into a room, and most TWS technologies provide a lower resolution image compared to video images. . . .

TWS technology raises significant privacy issues. Does it violate a person's Fourth Amendment right against unreasonable search and seizure? In some situations, this technology would constitute an unreasonable search of a home unless a warrant with probable cause had been issued. The primary exception would be in emergency or exigent conditions. There is a significant body of case law that describes such conditions.

Audio or Electronic Surveillance

In special instances, electronic devices are used in surveillance. Such electronic surveillance techniques include wiring a person who is going to be talking with a subject or entering a suspicious business establishment, "**bugging**" a subject's room or vehicle or **wiretapping** a telephone.

The most common forms of lawfully authorized electronic surveillance available to law enforcement are pen registers, trap-and-trace devices and content interceptions. Pen registers and trap-and-trace devices record dialing and signaling information used in processing and routing telephone communication, such as the signals that identify the dialed numbers of outgoing calls or the originating numbers of incoming calls.

Electronic surveillance and wiretapping are considered forms of search and are therefore permitted only with probable cause and a court order (*Katz v. United States*, 1967).

In *Katz v. United States*, the Supreme Court considered an appeal by Charles Katz, who had been convicted in California of violating gambling laws. Investigators had observed Katz for several days as he made telephone calls from a particular phone booth at the same time each day. Suspecting he was placing horse-racing bets, the investigators attached an electronic listening/recording device to the telephone booth and recorded Katz's illegal activities. The evidence was used in convicting Katz. The Supreme Court reversed the California decision, saying, "The Fourth Amendment protects people, not places. . . . Wherever a man may be, he is entitled to know that he will remain free from unreasonable searches and seizures." The investigators did have probable cause, but they erred in not presenting their information to a judge and obtaining prior approval for their actions.

The importance of electronic surveillance is recognized in the introduction to Title III of the Omnibus Crime Control and Safe Streets Act of 1968, which authorized court-ordered electronic surveillance of organized crime figures. The U.S. Congress stated, "Organized criminals make extensive use of wire and oral communications in their criminal activities. The interception of such communications to obtain evidence of the commission of crimes or to prevent their commission is an indispensable aid to law enforcement and the administration of justice."

Title III does not prohibit surreptitiously recording telephone conversations if one party consents. To avoid wiretaps, suspects often use "drop phones," prepaid cell phones that are disposed of regularly. Prepaid phone cards serve the same purpose and can be easily purchased in many places without a person's having to produce identification.

Federal and state laws allow electronic surveillance (eavesdropping), provided it is authorized by a federal or state judge and specified procedures are followed. Advertisements in police magazines describe state-of-the-art surveillance systems that make undercover work more efficient and effective. Laser technology can direct a beam at the glass in a window with another beam modulated by sonic vibrations inside the room, bouncing the sound back to a receiver so officers can hear what is being said. Eavesdropping with "bugs" is now easier than ever. Criminals are using high-tech electronic countermeasures to detect such devices in a room before they hold a meeting or conversation there.

The courts have upheld the right of officers to tape conversations that occur inside their squad cars. In the case of *United States v. McKinnon* (1993), two suspects were stopped for a traffic violation and asked to sit in the

Technology Innovations

Acoustic surveillance systems, such as gunshot location technology, are gaining popularity and help law enforcement respond more quickly to life-threatening emergencies by detecting and locating incidents in real time. For example, the SpotShotter Gunshot Location System® (GLS), which was used by only five cities in 2004, had been deployed in 45 jurisdictions by mid-2009 and had helped police render life-preserving assistance more than 220 times since 2005, with 57 incidents occurring within the first six months of 2009 (Beldock, 2009). In addition to such emergency response benefits, the SpotShotter GLS technology has proven valuable in shooting investigations and prosecutions:

Because the SpotShotter GLS records incidents audio time-stamped with GPS (atomic clock) time from all reporting sensors, and because it detects and separately locates each individual round fired, SpotShotter data can provide evidence that helps put criminals away for a long time. . . .

Take, for example, a homicide committed by two gang members in South Los Angeles, CA. The SpotShotter GLS located the incident in real time, but the victim managed to stagger away from the scene and died sufficiently far away that responding officers did not see him when they responded to the scene.

The sole eyewitness was murdered prior to trial. The prosecution wished to prove that the assailants fired their weapons almost simultaneously, and therefore that they were both guilty of first degree murder. Without the now-deceased witness, that was a tall order. "The SpotShotter GLS was able to show that two different weapons were being fired, as well as the sequence in which those weapons, Weapon A and Weapon B, were fired," said Los Angeles County Sheriff's Detective Ty Labbe.

"It was also able to show distance, which put Shooter A and Shooter B where the witness said they were standing in relation to the victim. These distance measurements corroborated the location where the physical evidence (shell casings) was located by investigators, giving us evidence to recreate the crime scene and further corroborating the testimony of the lone witness to the murder."

The evidence did the trick. . . . Both defendants were convicted of first-degree murder (Beldock, 2009, pp.49–50).

patrol car while the officer conducted a consent search in the vehicle for drugs. While in the patrol car, the suspects made incriminating statements that were recorded without their knowledge. Although one defendant argued that the recording violated his right to privacy, the court disagreed, stating, "No reasonable expectation of privacy exists in the back seat of a patrol car."

The courts have also held that no expectation of privacy exists in prison cells or in interrogation rooms.

Surveillance and the Constitution

Throughout the discussion on surveillance, of most importance is the balance between acting without violating suspects' constitutional rights and the need for law enforcement to do its job of protecting society. The Court's desire to maintain this balance was seen in *Kyllo v. United States* (2001), introduced in Chapter 4. In this case, the Court held that thermal imaging of a house was a search and required a warrant. Use of a GPS device to monitor a vehicle's travel activity is not a search and does not intrude on a person's reasonable expectation of privacy, according to the Seventh Circuit Court in *United States v. Garcia* (2007), which held that the tracking device did not provide officers with any information they could not have acquired through conventional surveillance techniques. Furthermore, use of ALPR technology is not a search and requires no warrant: "An ALPR is essentially a cop with a good eye and really fast note-taking skills. It doesn't capture anything a patrol officer couldn't see with his or her own eyes" (Dees, 2010, p.32). X-ray devices, however, are a different matter and, like thermal imaging, require a warrant if they are to be used in a search capacity.

UNDERCOVER ASSIGNMENTS

The non-uniformed or plainclothes investigator is in a good position to observe illegal activities and obtain evidence. For example, a male plainclothes officer may appear to accept the solicitations of a prostitute, or any plainclothes police officer may attempt to buy stolen goods or drugs or to place illegal bets. Many such activities require little more than simply "not smelling like the law." Unlike other forms of surveillance in which a prime objective is not to be observed, **undercover** (UC) surveillants make personal contact with the subject using an assumed identity, or **cover**.

The objective of an undercover assignment may be to gain a person's confidence or to infiltrate an organization or group by using an assumed identity and to thereby obtain information or evidence connecting the subject with criminal activity.

Undercover assignments can be designed to

■ Obtain evidence for prosecution.
■ Obtain leads into criminal activities.
■ Check the reliability of witnesses or informants.

An undercover narcotics investigator makes a drug buy. "Looking the part" is essential to a successful undercover operation.
© Michael Newman/PhotoEdit

■ Gain information about premises for use in later conducting a raid or an arrest.

■ Check the security of a person in a highly sensitive position.

■ Obtain information on or evidence against subversive groups.

Some UC assignments are relatively simple and are referred to as *ruses*. The two general types of ruses are (1) deception as to identity—for example, posing as a drug dealer or prostitute and (2) deception as to purpose—for example, pretending to investigate a different person.

Many undercover assignments are more elaborate. Such UC assignments are frequently made when criminal activity is greatly suspected or even known but no legal evidence of it exists. Such assignments can be extremely dangerous and require careful planning and preparation.

The undercover agent selected must fit the assignment. Age, sex, race, general appearance, language facility, health, energy level, emotional stability and intelligence are all important selection considerations. Undercover agents must be good actors—able to assume their roles totally. They must be intelligent and able to deal with any problems that arise, make quick decisions, improvise plans and actions and work with the person or within the group or organization without arousing suspicion.

A good cover is essential. Rookies are often used because they are not yet known and because they have not been in law enforcement long enough to acquire expressions or mannerisms that hardened criminals recognize as "the law."

In addition to devising a good cover, the undercover agent learns everything possible about the subject, regardless of whether it is a person or an organization. If you are going to be working undercover, make plans for communicating with headquarters. Make telephone calls from public pay phones, or mail letters to a fictitious friend's post office box. Have a plan for communicating emergency messages, and know what to do if the authorities move in on the subject when you are there. Have a plan for leaving the subject when you have acquired the desired information or evidence.

Because you might be arrested if the subject is arrested, learn ahead of time whether you are to "blow your cover" or submit to arrest. In some instances, outside sources may interfere with the lawful arrest, posing great danger for an undercover agent whose identity has become known during the arrest. When the assignment is successfully completed, give the subject a plausible explanation for leaving because it may be necessary to reestablish the undercover contact later.

It is often better to use undercover agents than informants because the testimony of a reliable, trained investigator is less subject to a defense attorney's attack than is that of an informant.

The legality of placing an undercover officer in a high school to investigate student drug use was decided in *Gordon v. Warren Consolidated Board of Education* (1983). High school officials had put an undercover officer into classes. The claimants alleged deprivation of their civil rights, but the federal district court dismissed the case for failure to state a cause of action. On appeal, the Supreme Court affirmed the prior judgment, stating that the presence of the undercover officer did not constitute any more than a "chilling" effect on the First Amendment right because it did not disrupt classroom activities or education and had no tangible effect on inhibiting expression of particular views in the classroom.

Undercover officers posing as prison inmates can acquire key information from other inmates suspected of other crimes. They may also operate undercover online.

Grossi (2009, pp.24–28) offers several suggestions to consider when working undercover:

■ Adopt credible aliases. Keep your real first name and date of birth.

■ Whether you're going to "carry" or not may be a matter of personal preference or an issue your agency addresses.

■ Choose your "garb" based on your assignment. The primary objective is to fit in with your target group.

■ Avoid the draw of the street, which can be overwhelming and even addicting.

■ Although many UC operations require you to appear alone, always have backup within eye or earshot, either via wire or through direct visual contact.

■ Remember who you are. Nothing is worth compromising your integrity as a police officer.

It is vital that undercover investigators keep accurate notes during their investigation, yet they must not allow the subject to be aware of such documentation.

Precautions for undercover agents:

■ Write no notes the subject can read.

■ Carry no identification other than the cover ID.

■ Ensure that any communication with headquarters is covert.

■ Do not suggest, plan, initiate or participate in criminal activity.

The final precaution warrants particular notice because regardless of how well planned and executed an undercover operation is, if the suspect can prove the criminal action for which they were arrested resulted from a suggestion made by the undercover officer, the entire case may be jeopardized by a charge of entrapment.

Entrapment

The Supreme Court has defined **entrapment** in *Sorrells v. United States* (1932) as "the conception and planning of an offense by an officer, and his procurement of its commission by one who would not have perpetrated it except for the trickery, persuasion or fraud of the officer." *Sorrells* also explained the need for trickery in obtaining evidence: "Society is at war with the criminal classes, and the courts have uniformly held that in waging this warfare the forces of prevention and detection may use traps, decoys and deception to obtain evidence of the commission of a crime." *Sorrells* concludes, "The fact that government agents merely afford opportunities or facilities for the commission of the offense does not constitute entrapment."

These Court rulings still stand. In *Sherman v. United States* (1958), the Court explained, "Entrapment occurs only when the criminal conduct was 'the product of the creative activity' of law enforcement officials. To determine whether entrapment has been established, a line must be drawn between the trap for the unwary innocent and the trap for the unwary criminal."

Sting Operations

Sting operations target specific crimes such as fencing and stolen property, drug dealing, sales of alcohol and tobacco to minors, prostitution, car theft, fraud and corruption and child pornography (Newman, 2007). Because of the wide variety of illegal activity targeted by stings and the need to employ different techniques depending on the sting's immediate or long-term purposes, it is difficult to formulate a simple yet precise definition of a sting operation. "However, with some exceptions, all sting operations contain four basic elements:

1. An opportunity or enticement to commit a crime, either created or exploited by police.
2. A targeted likely offender or group of offenders for a particular crime type.
3. An undercover or hidden police officer or surrogate or some form of deception.
4. A 'gotcha' climax when the operation ends with arrests." (Newman, 2007, p.3)

Benefits of sting operations include the facilitation of investigation and increased arrests, enhanced public relations and police image, enhanced police presence, improved collaboration between police and prosecutors, provision of an impressive conviction record, the possibility of success without convictions or arrests and the necessary partnering with community and business organizations that improves community relations by recovering stolen property (Newman, 2007).

Stings also have their downside, including not reducing or preventing recurring crime problems, being expensive, being deemed unethical by some and raising privacy and entrapment issues.

RAIDS

A police **raid** is a planned, organized operation based on the element of surprise. Consider all other alternatives before executing a raid.

> The objectives of a raid are to recover stolen property, seize evidence or arrest a suspect.

Sometimes all three objectives are accomplished in a single raid. The first consideration is whether there are alternatives to a raid. A second consideration is the legality of the raid.

> A raid must be the result of a hot pursuit or be under the authority of a no-knock arrest or search warrant.

If you are in hot pursuit of a known felon and have no time to plan a raid, make sure enough personnel and weapons are available to reduce danger. Call for backup before starting the raid. If time permits, however, careful planning and preparation will enhance the likely success of the raid.

Planning, organizing and executing a raid are somewhat similar to undertaking a small military attack on a specific target. Without careful planning, the results can be disastrous, as illustrated in the 1993 federal raid on the compound of the Branch Davidian cult in Waco, Texas, in which 80 cult members were killed.

Planning a Raid

Begin planning a raid by gathering information on the premises to be raided, including the exact address and points of entry and exit for both the raiding party and the suspect. Obtain a picture or sketch of the building and study the room arrangement. Additional location information might be obtained from aerial photographs, surveillance photos, walking the neighborhood and the city planning department. Does the location have surveillance? Animals? Dogs are often used both as a means of notifying the suspects of trespassers and as weapons.

Consider whether there will be other people or the possibility of other people in or at the location. Will these people include other possible suspects, associates, innocent bystanders, juveniles and so forth?

If time permits, also consider the surrounding area. Is it in a neighborhood with families? Schools, parks and so on? Do people need to be evacuated or notified?

Next, study the suspect's background. What crimes has the suspect committed? What difficulties were encountered in making past arrests? Is the suspect a narcotics addict? An alcoholic? Likely to be armed? If so, what type of weapon is the suspect likely to wield?

Obtain the appropriate warrants. Most raids are planned and result from an arrest warrant. In such cases, the subject is usually living under circumstances that necessitate a raid to make an arrest. In addition, if the raid is conducted to obtain evidence or property, obtain an exact description of the property sought, its likely location on the premises and a legal search warrant. Specify that you require a no-knock warrant to conduct the raid and perhaps a nighttime warrant to enhance the element of surprise.

Throughout the entire planning process, keep the raid plan as simple as possible. Because the subject may be extremely dangerous, intend to use adequate firepower and personnel. Determine the required weapons and equipment. Plan for enough personnel to minimize violence, overcome opposition through superiority of forces and prevent the suspect's escape or destruction of evidence. Also anticipate that the suspect may have installed surreptitious surveillance devices or booby-trapped the premises to thwart intruders. Make sure all entrances and exits will be covered and that a communication system is established. Decide how to transport the raiding party to the scene and how to take the suspect or evidence and property away. Determine who will be in command during the raid.

Remember that other people may be in the vicinity of the raid. If possible, evacuate everyone from the area of the raid without making the suspect suspicious. It is not always possible to do this without losing the element of surprise vital to the success of the raid.

Executing a Raid

Surprise, shock and speed are essential elements in a raid: "You want to surprise your adversary, shock them so they can't really react to you, and capitalize on it by attacking with speed" (Hamilton, 2007, p.42).

A raid should occur only after a careful briefing of all members of the raiding party. Each participant must know the objective, who the suspect is or what evidence or property is sought and the exact plan of the raid itself. Give each participant proper equipment such as body armor, weapons, radios, whistles, megaphones and signal lights. Give each participant a specific assignment, and answer all questions about the raid before leaving the briefing. The raid commander directs the raid, giving the signal to begin and coordinating all assignments.

Decisions about the initial entry and control phase of a raid must be made rapidly, because control is usually established within the first 15 to 30 seconds of a successful raid. No two raids are executed in precisely the same manner. The immediate circumstances and events dictate what decisions and actions are made.

Handguns are still the most versatile weapon during a raid, but shotguns and other assault-type weapons are useful in the perimeter operations and to control arrested individuals. If guard animals are known to be inside the raid area, provide for their control. Special equipment such as sledgehammers or rams may help in breaking down fortified entrances. An ambulance should be on standby, or raid personnel should at least know the fastest route to the nearest hospital.

Because raids are highly visible, the public and the news media often take interest. Therefore, raids are likely to be the object of community praise or criticism. They are also often vital to successfully prosecuting a case.

Precautions in conducting raids:
- Ensure that the raid is legal.
- Plan carefully.
- Assign adequate personnel and equipment.
- Thoroughly brief every member of the raiding party.
- Be aware of the possibility of surreptitious surveillance devices or booby traps at the raid site.

SWAT Teams

Many police agencies have developed tactical squads, sometimes called special weapons and tactics (SWAT) teams, to execute raids. These units, also called paramilitary police units (PPUs), are thoroughly trained to search areas for criminals, handle sniper incidents and hostage situations, execute arrest and search warrants and apprehend militants who have barricaded themselves inside a building or other location.

SWAT was born on August 1, 1966, in Austin, Texas, when Charles Whitman went on a 96-minute shooting spree from the top of a tower at the University of Texas, killing 15 people and wounding 31 before two Austin police officers were able to climb the tower and stop him: "Since then, police departments across the country have constructed SWAT units, and these teams have successfully stopped many felons and saved many lives" (Polan, 2008, p.36).

In the 1990s, two seemingly contradictory models of policing emerged: community-oriented policing (COP) and SWAT teams. COP is a philosophy that stresses community partnerships and proactive problem solving, in contrast to the militaristic, reactive approach used by SWAT teams to deal with high-risk situations. Such teams generally adhere to the approach used by General Colin Powell of being the "meanest dog in town." According to the Powell doctrine, force should be used sparingly, but if used, it should be used decisively. In most jurisdictions, both approaches are needed depending on specific circumstances, with community policing being the predominant approach, but with SWAT teams at the ready for emergency situations and to execute well-planned operations such as raids. A successful raid usually results in arrests.

LEGAL ARRESTS

Once a suspect has been located and identified, the next step is generally an arrest. Police powers to arrest (or search) are restricted by the Fourth Amendment, which forbids unreasonable searches or seizures without probable cause. Just as state laws define and establish the elements of crimes, they also define arrest and establish who may make an arrest, for what offenses and when. Most state laws define an **arrest** in general terms as "the taking of a person into custody in the manner authorized by law for the purpose of presenting that person before a magistrate to answer for the commission of a crime." An arrest may be made by a police officer or a private citizen. It may be made with or without a warrant, although a warrant is generally preferred because this places the burden of proving that the arrest was illegal on the defense.

Police officers are authorized to make an arrest

- For any crime committed in their presence.
- For a felony (or for a misdemeanor in some states) not committed in their presence if they have probable cause to believe the person committed the crime.
- Under the authority of an arrest warrant.

Most arrests are for misdemeanors such as disorderly conduct, drunkenness, traffic violations, minor larceny, minor drug offenses, simple assaults, nuisances and other offenses of lesser severity. In most states, the police officer must *see* such offenses to make an arrest without a warrant. In *Atwater v. Lago Vista* (2001), the Supreme Court allowed personally observed probable cause to permit

A police SWAT team storms a building during a raid. Surprise, swiftness and sufficient personnel are required for a successful raid.
© AP Images

CERTIFICATE AND DECLARATION OF ARREST BY PRIVATE PERSON AND DELIVERY OF PERSON SO ARRESTED TO PEACE OFFICER

DATE __5-3-20__ __

TIME __1440__

PLACE __Boulder City__
__1115 Bolt St.__

I, __Joyce Mayberry__ , hereby declare and certify that I have arrested

(NAME) __John Mayberry__

(ADDRESS) __1115 Bolt St. Boulder City, Nevada__

for the following reasons: _____

__John arrived home about fifteen minutes ago and we had__

__an argument about his drinking and spending all the__

__money. He struck me twice on the side of my face and__

__twice in the stomach. He told me that next time he__

__would kill me.__

and I do hereby request and demand that you __Officer James McGraw__ ,
a peace officer, take and conduct this person whom I have arrested to the nearest magistrate to be dealt with according to law; and if no magistrate can be contacted before tomorrow morning, then to conduct this person to jail for safekeeping until the required appearance can be arranged before such magistrate, at which time I shall be present, and I will then and there sign, under oath, the appropriate complaint against this person for the offense which this person has committed and for which I made this arrest; and I will then and there, or thereafter as soon as this criminal action or cause can be heard, testify under oath of and concerning the facts and circumstances involved herein. I will save said officer harmless from any and all claim for damage of any kind, nature and description arising out of his acts at my direction.

Signature of private person
making this arrest ___*Joyce S Mayberry*___

Peace Officer Witnesses to this statement

___*James McGraw*___

___*C S Steiner*___

FIGURE 7.4
Certificate of citizen's arrest.
© Cengage Learning, 2013

an arrest and custodial detention for a minor misdemeanor. In other words, warrantless arrests for nonjailable offenses such as failing to wear a seatbelt were held to be constitutional. *Atwater* authorized police to arrest drivers of vehicles for violations punishable by only a monetary fine, widening police authority in traffic-related stops.

In many states, an arrest may also be made by a "private person" who witnesses a misdemeanor and then turns the suspect over to law enforcement authorities. Figure 7.4 shows a sample citizen's arrest form.

If you have probable cause to believe a suspect has committed a felony and there is no time to obtain an arrest warrant, you can make an arrest without the warrant. Facts gathered *after* the arrest to justify probable cause are *not* legally admissible as evidence of probable cause.

They can, however, strengthen the case if probable cause was established *before* the arrest.

> Probable cause for believing the suspect committed a crime must be established *before* a lawful arrest can be made.

An arrest for a felony or gross misdemeanor can usually be made any time if there is an arrest warrant or if the arresting officer witnessed the crime. An arrest may be made only in the daytime if it is by warrant, unless a magistrate has endorsed the warrant with a written statement that the arrest may be made at night. This is commonly referred to as a *nightcap provision*. Nightcapped warrants were discussed in Chapter 4.

Officers are allowed to break an inner or outer door to make an arrest after identifying themselves, stating the purpose for entry and demanding admittance. This is often necessary when officers are in plainclothes and hence not recognized as police. The courts have approved no-knock entries in cases in which the evidence would be immediately destroyed if police announced their intention to enter. Officers may break a window or door to leave a building if they are illegally detained inside. They may break a door or window to arrest a suspect who has escaped from custody. Finally, officers may break an automobile window if a suspect rolls up the windows and locks the doors to prevent an arrest. You should give proper notification of the reason for the arrest and the intent to break the window if the suspect does not voluntarily comply.

You can accomplish the physical act of arrest by taking hold of or controlling the person and stating, "You are under arrest for . . .". In most jurisdictions the arresting officer's authority must be stated, and the suspect must be told for what offense the arrest is being made. In some cases the apparent reason for the arrest turns out to be incorrect, with a different charge being brought. In *Devenpeck v. Alford* (2004), the Supreme Court ruled that an arrest is not rendered unlawful even if an arresting officer's probable cause for making it is not the same criminal offense for which the known facts provided probable cause. The Court held that although it is a "good police practice" to inform a person of the reason for his arrest at the time he is taken into custody, the Court has "never held that to be constitutionally required."

Arresting a suspect requires that the *Miranda* warning be given before any questioning can occur. An arrest also starts the clock on the time limits within which a judge must review the case, usually within 48 hours (*County of Riverside v. McLaughlin*, 1991). Officers who postpone an arrest can conduct additional investigation before starting the *McLaughlin* clock and can bolster their probable cause for arrest as well.

In some departments, it is common practice to take a suspect who is not under arrest to the department for questioning. If bringing someone in for questioning appears to be an arrest without probable cause, even if the suspect is not told he's under arrest, and even if the officers do not personally consider him to be under arrest, the courts are likely to rule that the officers have, in effect, made an illegal **de facto arrest**. As a result, the courts will suppress any evidence so obtained. At minimum, the Supreme Court has ruled four times that if police take someone involuntarily to a police facility for investigation, this will be considered a de facto arrest. The first case was *Davis v. Mississippi* (1969), followed by *Dunaway v. New York* (1979), then *Hayes v. Florida* (1985) and more

recently by *Kaupp v. Texas* (2003). If you are going to question the suspect, read the *Miranda* warning first.

> If your intent is to make an arrest and you inform the suspect of this intent and then restrict the suspect's right to go free, you have made an arrest.

Officers may also pursue a fleeing suspect to make a *Terry*-type stop that could escalate into an arrest. In *Illinois v. Wardlow* (2000), the Supreme Court ruled that a person's sudden flight upon seeing a police officer can be used to establish reasonable suspicion for a *Terry* stop.

Sometimes a suspect will refuse to identify himself or herself. Pursuant to the Supreme Court's opinion in *Hiibel v. Sixth Judicial District Court of Nevada* (2004), a state law requiring a subject to disclose his or her name during a *Terry* stop does not violate the Fourth Amendment's ban on unreasonable search and seizure (Bray, 2007, p.10): "Obtaining a suspect's name in the course of a *Terry* stop serves important government interests. Knowledge of identity may inform an officer that a suspect is wanted for another offense or has a record of violence or mental disorder. On the other hand, knowing identity may help clear a suspect and allow the police to concentrate their efforts elsewhere."

If, during the *Terry* stop, an officer establishes probable cause to arrest, and if the suspect resists, the officer may use force, but if he does, he may leave himself open to civil liability.

Residential Entry after Outdoors Arrest

"Entry incident to outdoors arrest" is not on the list of lawful ways to get inside a residence (Rutledge, 2008, p.60). Three separate Supreme Court cases have held such entries to be unconstitutional. In *James v. Louisiana* (1965), the defendant was lawfully arrested and then driven to his home more than two blocks away. Without a warrant, consent or an emergency, the officers entered and searched Otis James's home, finding narcotics equipment and morphine. He was convicted, but on appeal, the Supreme Court held that the evidence was the result of an illegal entry and could not be used against him: "In the circumstances of this case, the search of the defendant's home cannot be regarded as incident to his arrest on a street corner more than two blocks away. A search can be 'incident to an arrest' only if it is substantially contemporaneous with the arrest and is confined to the immediate vicinity of the arrest" (Bray, 2007, p.11).

In *Shipley v. California* (1969), officers had staked out a suspect in an armed robbery and arrested him when he got out of his car in front of his home. They took him inside and searched his home, finding the stolen jewelry. In this case, the Court also reversed Shipley's conviction: "The Constitution has never been construed by this Court to allow the police in the absence of an emergency to arrest a person outside his home and then take him inside for the purpose of conducting a warrantless search."

In the third case, *Vale v. Louisiana* (1970), police conducting surveillance on Donald Vale's home saw him walk outside and sell drugs to people who drove up and honked. They arrested Vale on the front steps of his house and then entered and searched the residence. In this case, the Court held, "If a search of a house is to be upheld as incident to arrest, that arrest must take place inside the house. Our past decisions make clear that only in a few specifically established and well-delineated situations may a warrantless search of a dwelling withstand constitutional scrutiny. We decline to hold that an arrest on the street can provide its own exigent circumstance so as to justify a warrantless search of the arrestee's house."

Police do, however, have a right to maintain control over a suspect once he is arrested: "If the suspect is arrested outside his home and requests an opportunity to go back inside temporarily (such as to obtain bail money or ID, to get a jacket or tell his family of his predicament), he is giving police *implied consent* to accompany him inside. If officers then see contraband or evidence in plain view, they have a right to seize it" (Rutledge, 2008, p.61).

Arresting a Group of Companions

In *Maryland v. Pringle* (2003), an officer stopped a car for speeding. The three male occupants consented to a search of the vehicle, which turned up more than $700 of rolled-up cash and five bags of cocaine. All three denied any knowledge of the money and drugs, so the officer arrested all three, including Joseph Pringle. The Maryland state court held that absent specific facts establishing Pringle's control over the drugs, the officer's mere finding that it was in a car occupied by Pringle was insufficient to justify probable cause to arrest. On appeal, the Supreme Court reversed, concluding that the officer had sufficient probable cause to arrest Pringle based on the information known to him at the time of arrest.

Off-Duty Arrests

Every department needs a policy that allows off-duty officers to make arrests. A suggested policy for off-duty arrests requires officers to

■ Be within the legal jurisdiction of their agency.

■ Not be personally involved.

■ Perceive an immediate need for preventing a crime or arresting a suspect.

■ Possess the proper identification.

Unless all these conditions exist, officers should not make an arrest but should report the incident to their department for disposition.

AVOIDING CIVIL LIABILITY WHEN MAKING ARRESTS

Officers should be aware of the situations in which they may find themselves named in a lawsuit and should be aware of case law in these areas.

> Officers leave themselves open to lawsuits in several areas related to arrests, including false arrests, excessive force, shootings and wrongful death.

False Arrest

Police officers always face the possibility of false arrest. Some officers carry insurance to protect themselves against such lawsuits. Most are idle threats, however.

A false-arrest suit is a civil tort action that attempts to establish that an officer who claimed to have authority to make an arrest did not have probable cause at the time of arrest. The best protection is to be certain that probable cause to arrest does exist, to have an arrest warrant or to obtain a conviction in court.

Even when the defendant is found not guilty of the particular offense, a basis for a false-arrest suit is not automatically established. A court will consider the totality of the circumstances at the time of the arrest and will decide whether they would lead an ordinarily prudent person to perceive probable cause and take the same action.

Police officers should know what the statute of limitations, the time frame within which a claimant can file a civil rights lawsuit, is for a federal claim for false arrest in their state (Scarry, 2007a, p.138). For example, In New York, the statute of limitations for false arrest is 90 days, meaning if someone is wrongfully arrested, they have 90 days from the date of the arrest to file a notice of claim regarding their intent to take action. However, in *Wallace v. Kato* (2007), the Supreme Court ruled, in a 7–2 decision, that the correct starting point for a false-arrest claim, or when the clock starts ticking, is when a judge reviews the criminal charges against the defendants and binds them over for trial.

Police officers reduce the probability of valid false-arrest actions by understanding the laws they enforce, the elements of each offense and what probable cause is needed to prove each element. Police officers who honestly believe they have probable cause for an arrest can use the "good-faith" defense, as established in *Pierson v. Ray* (1967): "A policeman's lot is not so unhappy that he must choose between being charged with dereliction of duty if he does not arrest when he has probable cause, and being mulcted [penalized] in damages if he does. Although the matter is not entirely free from doubt, the same consideration would seem to require excusing him from liability for acting under a statute that he reasonably believed to be valid but that was later held unconstitutional on its face or as applied."

Use of Force

The most difficult lawsuits to handle are those dealing with use of force. Physical force is not a necessary part of an arrest; in fact, most arrests are made without physical force. A 2001 study conducted by the International Association of Chiefs of Police (IACP) on use of force found that force of any kind was used only at a rate of 3.61 incidents per 10,000 calls for service. However, "It is an unfortunate reality that law enforcement officers around the world are often required to resort to some form of force in order to enforce the law, protect the public, and guard their own safety as well as that of innocent bystanders. This is particularly true in the United States" (Ruecker, 2007, p.6). Slahor (2008, p.75) notes, "Currently, one in 30 U.S. police officers is being sued. For the past five years, 40 percent to 45 percent of those cases involved allegations of excessive use of force."

Determining the Amount of Force to Use. The amount of resistance to arrest varies, and this determines how much force is allowed as *reasonable*. When making an arrest, officers may legally use that level of force necessary to gain control of the person: "The basic rule concerning the use of force while making an arrest is that law enforcement personnel may use whatever force is necessary to make the arrest, but not excessive force" (Ferdico et al, 2009, p.333). "In a regularly lengthening series of decisions, federal courts have held that the Constitution does not require officers to use the least amount of force possible in a given situation. It requires only that the force used be 'reasonable'" (Means and Seidel, 2009, p.31). The circumstances include when the officer believes deadly force is necessary to prevent the death or serious bodily injury to another. The takeaway from these cases is not

that police cannot use force, but that it must be *reasonable* under the circumstances.

> When making an arrest, use only as much force as is reasonably necessary to overcome any resistance and gain compliance.

Deciding how much force to use in making an arrest requires logic and good judgment. However, in the heat of the moment, police officers may use more force than intended. Courts and juries have usually excused force that is not blatantly unreasonable, recognizing that many factors are involved in such split-second decisions.

Force used by police is defined as the amount of physical influence required to control a person's behavior under police authority. **Reasonable force** is the amount of force used by police measured by what a prudent individual would accept or use themselves in a similar situation. **Excessive force** means more than ordinary force, going above and beyond what is required to control the situation or behavior of an individual. Excessive force used by police can be criminal and may leave the enforcer and agency open to both civil liability and criminal charges. Excessive force *may*, however, be justified if there is no other way to control or take an individual into custody. For example, use of excessive force (such as striking with a nightstick) is justified only when exceptional resistance occurs and there is no other way to make the arrest.

Officers should be aware of research findings about when force is most likely to be used. For example, some research has found that officers were significantly more likely to use higher levels of force with suspects encountered in disadvantaged neighborhoods and neighborhoods with higher homicide rates. Other research suggest that disrespectful suspects are more likely to have their behavior reciprocated, and some researchers conclude that force is most likely to be used when suspects show signs of alcohol or drug intoxication or engage in hostile behavior. Officers should be aware of this finding and not take any disrespect shown to them too personally or be goaded into using more force than necessary.

Most police departments know of officers who tend to become involved in resistance or violent situations more frequently than others do. In some instances, these officers' approach seems to trigger resistance. However, in any situation that is *not* out of control when you arrive, give a friendly greeting and state who you are and your authority if you are not in uniform. Speak calmly and convey the impression that you are in control. Show your badge or identification and give your reason for the questioning. Ask for identification and listen to their side of the story. Then decide on the appropriate action: Warn, release, issue a citation or make an arrest.

Claims of Excessive Force.
The landmark case on use of force, *Graham v. Connor* (1989), set parameters on use of force, which stated, "Our Fourth Amendment jurisprudence has long recognized that the right to make an arrest or investigatory stop necessarily carries with it the right to use some degree of physical coercion or threat thereof to effect it." In *Graham*, the Court explained, "The reasonableness of a particular use of force must be judged from the perspective of a reasonable officer on the scene, rather than with the 20/20 vision of hindsight." *Graham* established five factors to evaluate alleged cases of excessive force:

- The severity of the crime
- Whether the suspect posed an immediate threat to the officer or others
- Whether the circumstances were tense, uncertain and rapidly evolving
- Whether the suspect was attempting to evade arrest by flight
- Whether the suspect was actively resisting arrest

Graham v. Connor further held that plaintiffs alleging excessive use of force need show only that the officer's actions were unreasonable under the standards of the Fourth Amendment.

In *Saucier v. Katz* (2001), the Supreme Court held, "The inquiry as to whether an arresting police officer is entitled to qualified immunity for the use of excessive force is distinct from the inquiry as to whether the use of force was objectively reasonable under Fourth Amendment excessive force analysis."

Use-of-Force Policies and Continuums.
The public is very aware of and sensitive to police use of force. The instantaneous decisions and actions by police officers at the scene are subject to long-term review by the public and the courts. Police departments must review their use-of-force policies to ensure that they are clear and in accordance with court decisions as well as effective in ensuring officer safety. Officers must know their department's policies regarding use of force as well as their department's use-of-force continuum. Not all departments have the same continuum. For instance, in some agencies the TASER may be accepted for use at a lower level on the continuum compared with other departments that may have it on the higher end of a spectrum. Further, uses of force in making arrests should be critiqued, and complaints of excessive force should be thoroughly reviewed.

Although voluntary compliance is the "best" arrest, there are always situations that are not peaceful and require officers to apply force. Force continuums were developed in the 1960s to train officers in proper use of force. During the past half-century, dozens of continuums have been developed, most of which are based on a suspect's degree of resistance and specify what level of force is appropriate in response. Traditionally, use-of-force continuums have been linear (Figure 7.5), going from no resistance or very minimal resistance by the subject to aggravated, life-threatening aggression, and with corresponding officer response progressing from officer presence and verbal commands all the way to—in the case of life-threatening resistance—deadly force.

Note that the least amount of force relies on communication skills: "Communication has become a lost art, and some officers have begun to rely more on technology than on talking" (Ruecker, 2007, p.6). Officers must develop the communication skills necessary to resolve conflicts, where possible, before force is necessary.

Critics of linear use-of-force continuums note that the continuums seem to imply that force events are predictable and escalate in an orderly fashion, when this is not reality. However, even if officers are taught that they can skip steps and go up and down on the continuum, linear continuums are sometimes explained in court as calling for such an orderly progression: "Because the use-of-force policies and linear continuum-type training models of many agencies require (or at least suggest) that the officer must use the least or minimum amount of force possible, they assist the plaintiff in his effort to prove that the 'greater' amount of force used by the officer was unreasonable . . . Policy and training demands for the minimum or the least force possible are *not* mandated by law, at least not by federal constitutional law" (Means, 2007, p.12). Furthermore, "In many use-of-force situations, several levels or types of force would all be reasonable. Also, in respect to certain pairs of response options, it is difficult if not impossible to be sure which option is the greater and which is the lesser" (Means, 2007, p.14). In an attempt to address this situation, some departments are shifting from linear to nonlinear models.

One such circular model is a force wheel, with the spokes in the wheel representing a specific type of force, as shown in Figure 7.6. This continuum avoids the implied stepwise progression of linear models, but such models otherwise provide little guidance to officers' force decisions.

One option on most force continuums is use of less-lethal weapons.

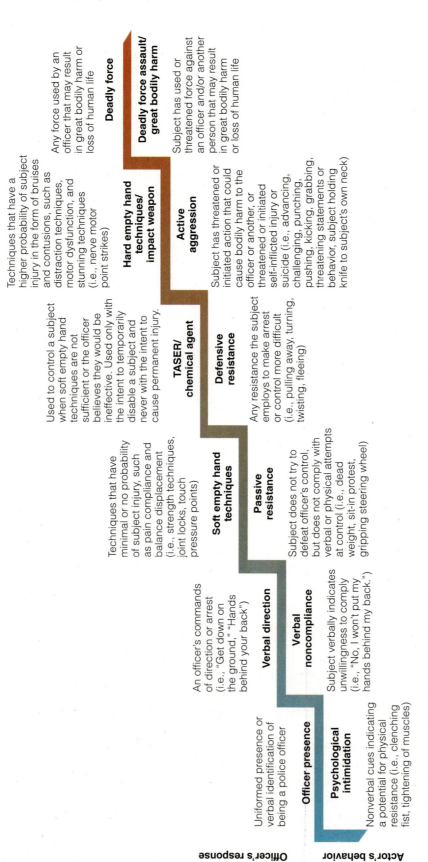

FIGURE 7.5

Linear use-of-force continuum.

Source: Owatonna (Minnesota) Police Department Use of Force Report

NOTE: Subject may enter the continuum at any level. Officer may enter at any level that represents a reasonable response to the perceived threat posed by the subject.

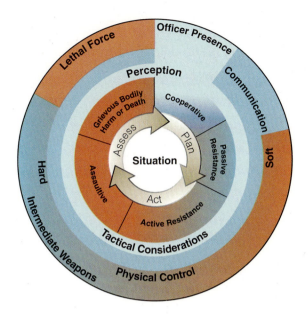

FIGURE 7.6
Circular use-of-force continuum of the Canadian Association of Chiefs of Police.

Source: From Joshua A. Ederheimer and Lorie A. Fridell. *Chief Concerns: Exploring the Challenge of Police Use of Force.* Washington, DC: Police Executive Research Forum, April 2005, p.50. Reprinted by permission.

Less-Lethal Weapons

Whether they are called *less-than-lethal, less-lethal* or *non-lethal weapons*, their intent is to avoid the use of deadly force. However, "Less-lethal does not imply never-lethal. Munitions fired from most less-lethal weapons can cause death if vital areas are struck: head, eyes, throat and possibly the upper abdomen" (Page, 2007, p.144).

Discussing the use of nonlethal use-of-force options during an arrest, Ashley (2007, p.72) notes, "That's what you use the most, and they remain the most likely to get you hurt and/or sued: There are dozens of non-lethal options out there, and probably hundreds of variations on each one. Generally, though, there are six basic options for controlling someone with non-lethal force/control. Your verbal/visual management of the scene, empty-hand control, restraints, aerosols, electronic control devices (ECDs) and impact weapons" (Ashley, p.72).

Restraints

The most commonly used restraint is handcuffs.

Handcuffs. Police officers are usually trained that the best way to transport a suspect under arrest is to place handcuffs on the person's wrists with the person's hands placed behind his or her back. Sometimes, when the handcuffs are removed, red marks, abrasions, bruising, numbness and other injuries can be seen. Several courts have addressed the issue of whether tight handcuffs can constitute excessive force under the Fourth Amendment,

but no general rule says handcuffs must be loose or at what level they become "too tight" (Scarry, 2007b, p.50). Ashley (2007, p.72) says, "Improper or sloppy use of handcuffs, and sometimes failure to use them at all, has probably gotten more officers hurt and killed than any other commonly used law enforcement tool." Departments typically train officers to double-lock the cuff to prevent the cuffs from getting increasingly tighter if a suspect struggles in them. Double-locking keeps a routine arrest from progressing into a medical call (and a lawsuit) caused by cuffs that have cut off circulation to a suspect's hands.

Aerosols. Ijames (2007, p.22) explains, "The two primary concepts of chemical munitions deployment are space deprivation and direct application. Space deprivation involves area contamination—as in outdoor riot situations—and enclosed space contamination—as in barricade resolution." Few officers will be directly involved with using tear gas. Most will be involved in direct applications, generally involving a close-range officer-suspect engagement via belt-carried aerosol spray, most commonly pepper spray, also called oleoresin capsicum (OC) spray (Ijames). Pepper spray has been used for about 20 years, and few officers go on duty without some type of OC product on their belt: "Pepper spray is very cost effective, generally safe, easy to train with and use, and effective about 81 percent of the time. As a result, pepper spray is considered by many to be the single most significant resistance-control and injury-reduction tool in law enforcement history" (Ijames, p.22).

Technology Innovations

Stradley (2007a, p.32) describes an innovative less-lethal weapon using OC spray—TigerLight:

The TigerLight provides officers with the ability to respond to an immediate threat with OC spray that is built into the tail of a flashlight tube. This makes the TigerLight a very effective less-lethal weapon. . . . TigerLight has been shown to achieve compliance in 95 percent of deployments.

TigerLight is more effective than belt-carried OC spray because it is already in the officer's hand at the point of the attack. The OC shot from the Tiger-Light is also a surprise to most subjects. This means the subject has no warning that the spray is on the way. He cannot hold his breath and cover or close his eyes in an attempt to defeat the pepper spray.

(continued)

Technology Innovations

(continued)

Stradley (2007b, p.45) also states,

> The TigerLight Non-Lethal Defense System is the most effective way to quickly deliver non-lethal force in the form of pepper spray that I've experienced. . . .
>
> Even during daylight hours, the light is blinding. When the light rotates out of the subject's face, he automatically looks right at where he believes I am. The subject doesn't prepare because he doesn't know the pepper is coming . . .
>
> The TigerLight is credited with achieving a 25 percent decrease in significant force being used. . . . This is an effective tool for taking aggressive, violent subjects into custody while reducing the likelihood of causing injury to them or risking injury to ourselves.

Impact Weapons. Impact munitions are "specially designed projectiles that are made to strike a subject's body causing nonlethal blunt trauma and incapacitation" (Young, 2007, p.26). For example, "The LAPD beanbag platform is capable of controlling combative subjects without causing serious injury and without compromising officer safety" (Hudson and Webb, 2007, p.51).

Technology Innovations

Munson (2007, pp.86–91) describes the PepperBall FlashLauncher:

> The PepperBall® FlashLauncher™ is a handheld projectile launcher with a built-in LED flashlight and laser aiming device, i.e., Flash(light) Launcher. The latest tool in PepperBall's non-lethal armory, the FlashLauncher is an option for a wide variety of law enforcement tasks: knife-wielding standoffs and similar contact weapon barricades, controlling uncooperative or combative suspects, crowd control and civil disorder, cell extraction, domestic violence and suicide-by-cop scenarios. Flash-Launcher appears to be an oddly shaped flashlight and is rather inconspicuous to the untrained eye.
>
> The FlashLauncher is a semi-auto launcher capable of firing five projectiles in 2 to 4 seconds. The FlashLauncher uses a standard 12-grain CO_2 cartridge, available at any sporting goods store.

> Once a CO_2 cartridge has been punctured, even if only one projectile has been fired, it must be replaced within a few hours.
>
> The FlashLauncher has one extremely valuable feature. The CO_2 cartridge is not punctured until the first shot. That means the device can be loaded and stored indefinitely without risk of a slow leak bleeding off pressure from the CO_2 cartridge.

Controlled Electronic Devices (CEDs). CEDs are also called ECDs. These handheld devices operate by causing neuron-muscular incapacitation (NMI) resulting in a subject's loss of motor function and, usually, consequent collapse to the ground (Guilbault, 2007b, p.42). More than 11,000 law enforcement agencies throughout the United States use CEDs (Bulman, 2011). Perhaps the best-known and most controversial less-lethal weapon is the TASER:

> The X26 TASER™ has taken American law enforcement by storm, with agencies reporting "full deployment" being added almost every day. Few things are as certain as the TASER getting the job done. Data reported from the field strongly suggests that it stops subjects in their tracks more frequently than any other incapacitation tool, including firearms.
>
> Also, the TASER works on people experiencing a "mind-body" disconnect, who are incapable of feeling pain and complying accordingly. This is especially important today, as officers deal with an ever-increasing number of self-medicated or highly intoxicated subjects and those with a mental illness. These issues can reduce or eliminate perception of pain—which not surprisingly—limits the officers' options in a resistance control world dominated with pain compliance techniques.
>
> Officers engaging such people often find their conventional efforts have little effect, which can be problematic to say the least. Thankfully, the TASER doesn't rely on pain compliance, which has greatly assisted officers facing law enforcement's most difficult challenges. (Ijames, 2008, p.22)

TASER International has developed a new Extended Range Electronic Projectile (XREP) that can be delivered with a 12-gauge shotgun (Williams, 2007, p.40). The XREP uses wireless technology to deliver an electro-muscular disruption (EMD) effect on a target at ranges beyond the handheld, hardwired TASERs. Another enhancement to the TASER X26 line is a camera accessory: "It records both black-and-white video and audio whenever the safety switch is flipped off. It works even in zero-light conditions. That means the TASER Cam™ is rolling whenever a TASER X26 is used. This will give law enforcement a tremendous advantage in the courtroom. Based on the in-car video experience, when video evidence is available, 96.2 percent of police officers are exonerated from misconduct allegations" (Rowe, 2007, p.35).

The Las Vegas Metropolitan Police Department (LVMPD) was involved in a TASER study with the hypothesis that the CED would reduce the number of officer-involved shootings, sparing officers the trauma of taking a life and increasing the community's trust in police (Ault et al., 2007, p.4). Results of the study indicated that officers armed with the CED were 75 percent less likely than were officers without the device to discharge a firearm. In addition, officers armed with CEDs were 90 percent less likely to deploy pepper spray. The study also found limited support for substituting CEDs for batons in situations where a suspect was openly aggressive toward the officers.

Researchers White and Ready (2007) studied the use of TASERs in 243 incidents involving primarily emotionally disturbed persons showing signs of violence at the time of arrest. Their study found that 85 percent of the suspects were incapacitated by use of the TASER and arrested without further incident. A more recent National Institute of Justice (NIJ)–funded study of injuries sustained during use-of-force events found that CED use substantially decreased injury rates for both officers and offenders (Bulman, 2011). Such use-of-force statistics have led many to consider the TASER to be the best less-lethal weapon available to law enforcement: "The facts are the TASER has the fastest effectiveness, fastest subject recovery time, lowest rate of officer injury, lowest rate of subject injury and the least liability to the department of the force options" (Sanow, 2007, p.6).

Despite claims of its effectiveness, the TASER remains a controversial tool. Headlines implicating the use of a TASER in deaths cause concern among citizens: "The public believes that TASERs kill, and something must be done to change their minds. . . . Almost every TASER death has involved a cocaine overdose, but that's never the headline" (Griffith, 2007, p.12).

One way to overcome public opposition is to have effective policies for the use of ECDs that address such issues as using ECDs on high-risk individuals, limiting the number of applications, placement of ECDs on the force continuum, medical evaluations after exposure and the like (Staton, 2008, p.93). Recognizing this need, Cronin and Ederheimer (2006), with the collective efforts of the Police Executive Research Forum and the Department of Justice, developed *Conducted Energy Devices: Standards for Consistency and Guidance: The Creation of National CED Policy and Training Guidelines*, an invaluable resource for those wanting to learn more about CEDs.

Other Less-Lethal Options. Capture nets have been an alternative for subduing combative suspects for decades. A modern version is the Super Talon™ net gun:

> The net deploys at 22 feet per second. Of course, it slows down as it spreads out and as it travels down range. The minimum range at which the Super Talon may be fired at a subject is 15 feet due to net spread. The ideal deployment range is between 20 and 30 feet.
>
> In the best case, the use of the net gun protects the officer from direct physical contact with the violent offender until the suspect is ensnared and at least partially subdued. Unique among less-lethal options, the net gun allows the capture of two, or even three, closely spaced suspects. (Munson, 2008, p.88)

Technology Innovations

Another innovation finding its way into law enforcement is acoustic technology (Borrello, 2007, p.50):

Acoustical weapon technology is basically the development of a directional system that can deliver a focused pulse of sound at such a high decibel (dB) level that it becomes intolerable for the target to bear. An air raid siren blasts sound at about 130 dB. The human threshold of pain is about 140 dB, which is considered the danger level for one's hearing. Sound weapons can send focused and sustained sound down range in excess of 146 dB, which is nearly the auditory equivalent to the roar of a jet turbine.

Ashley (2007, p.75) cautions, "Beware of an over-reliance on technology. Your weapons are useful tools, but never forget they can fail, and probably eventually will. When that time comes, be ready to react with another control option. And remember: What gets you sued is also what gets you hurt."

Always keep in mind that use of less-lethal alternatives is not required when use of deadly force is justified: "The old saying, 'Never bring a knife to a gunfight' applies just as well for a TASER. It is not a replacement for a gun. . . . Drawing a TASER when you need your duty weapon can be a fatal mistake" (Guilbault, 2007a, p.40).

Use of Deadly Force

From 2003 to 2006, 47 states and the District of Columbia reported 2002 arrest-related deaths. Of these, 1,095 were individuals killed by law enforcement (Mumola, 2007, p.1).

Police officers carry guns and are trained in using them. They also have department policy on deadly force as a guide. Unfortunately, the point of last resort may be immediate because many police situations rapidly deteriorate to the point of deadly force decision making. When such situations occur, they must be viewed from the perspectives of both the department's policies and the individual's situation.

Department policies on deadly force should be reviewed periodically in the light of the most recent Supreme Court decisions. Policies must be restrictive enough to limit unreasonable use of deadly force but not so restrictive that they fail to protect the lives of officers and members of the community.

Use of a deadly weapon is carefully defined by state laws and department policy. Such policies usually permit use of a gun or other weapon only in self-defense or if others are endangered by the suspect. Some policies also permit use of a deadly weapon to arrest a felony suspect, to prevent an escape or to recapture a felon when all other means have failed. Warning shots are not usually recommended because they can ricochet, harming others.

The landmark case on use of deadly force is the Supreme Court ruling in *Tennessee v. Garner* (1985), where the Court ruled, "It is not better that all felony suspects die than that they escape. Where the suspect poses no immediate threat to others, the harm resulting from failing to apprehend him does not justify the use of deadly force to do so. It is no doubt unfortunate when a suspect who is in sight escapes, but the fact that the police arrive a little late or are a little slower afoot does not always justify killing the suspect."

In this case, the Court banned law enforcement officers from shooting to kill fleeing felons unless an imminent danger to life exists. This ruling invalidated laws in almost half the states that allowed police officers to use deadly force to prevent the escape of a suspected felon. In this case, police shot and killed an unarmed 15-year-old boy who had stolen $10 and some jewelry from an unoccupied house. The Court ruled, "A police officer may not seize an unarmed, nondangerous suspect by shooting him dead."

The *Garner* decision did not take away police officers' right to use deadly force. The Court acknowledged legitimate situations in which deadly force is acceptable and necessary: "Where the officer has probable cause to believe that the suspect poses a threat of serious physical harm, either to the officer or to others, it is not constitutionally unreasonable to prevent escape by using deadly force. Thus, if the suspect threatened the officer with a weapon or there is probable cause to believe that he had committed a crime involving the infliction or threatened infliction of serious physical harm, deadly force may be used if necessary to prevent escape and if—where feasible—some warning has been given." In some deadly force incidents, officers have had suspects attempt to grab the officers' sidearms to use against them.

The "21-foot rule" in using deadly force states that a knife-wielding attacker could be as far away as 21 feet and still stab the officer before he could effectively fire his handgun (Irwin, 2007, p.82). Irwin quotes research by Lewinski and Fackler of the Force Science Research Center showing that officer reaction times are significantly longer than commonly believed:

> The Force Science Research Center has shown that it takes the average officer about half a second to perceive a threat and approximately another half second to decide what to do about it. All of this has to happen before the officer begins his or her draw stroke. What this means is that with the threat closing at 7 feet per half second, we are closer to a 35-foot rule.
>
> And it is extremely difficult to smoothly draw and accurately fire when under a life-threatening attack. So that means that we had better add another 10 feet to allow for the attacker to keep coming if we miss center mass or even if we hit him, even mortally wound him, but he doesn't go down.
>
> It's now the 45-foot rule. (Irwin, 2007, p.83)

Everyone understands that force should be used as a last resort, and whether to use deadly force is a major and difficult decision for police officers. When it should be used is generally defined in state statutes, but in any case of use of deadly force, the suspect must be threatening the life of an officer or another person.

"Ramming" in Pursuit as Use of Force. The intentional collision of a law enforcement officer's vehicle with another—ramming— constitutes a Fourth Amendment seizure and requires objective reasonableness at the time of the seizure (Risher, 2007, p.10). Ramming is viewed as deadly force by the courts. This issue was addressed in *Scott v. Harris* (2007), a case that resulted when Victor Harris ignored the blue lights and siren of Deputy Timothy Scott, who was trying to stop Harris for speeding. Harris led officers on a six-minute, 10-mile chase at speeds exceeding 85 miles per hour on mostly two-lane roads. The Eleventh Circuit Court ruled that the facts and circumstances did not justify use of deadly force, focusing on Harris's "crime" as speeding. When the case reached the Supreme Court, it focused on the "relative culpability" in balancing the nature and quality of the intrusion against the importance of the government interest.

The Court concluded that the motoring public in the area was innocent; Harris, however, was culpable because he, by initiating the chase, had placed himself and others in danger.

The case is significant in several respects: "First, the Court is willing to consider raw evidence (in this case, the recording of the chase) rather than reserving the factual determinations for the jury in a case where the objective recording eliminates any genuine issue of material facts. In addition, the Fourth Amendment does not require officers to abandon a pursuit when the pursued drives so recklessly as to endanger others" (Risher, 2007, p.11). As shown in *Harris*, the court will consider two questions:

1. Whether a law enforcement officer's conduct is objectively reasonable under the Fourth Amendment when the officer makes a split-second decision to terminate a high-speed pursuit by bumping the fleeing suspect's vehicle with his push bumper because the suspect has demonstrated that he would continue to drive in a reckless and dangerous manner that put the lives of innocent persons at a serious risk of death.

2. Whether at the time of the incident the law was clearly established such that no court had ruled the Fourth Amendment is violated when a law enforcement officer used deadly force to protect the lives of innocent persons from the risk of dangerous and reckless vehicular flight.

An alternative to ramming that is not necessarily viewed as use of deadly force is the Precision Immobilization Technique, more commonly known as the PIT maneuver. PIT is a driving technique that trains police officers to end a pursuit quickly using tactics such as hitting the suspect vehicle at a specific location at slower speeds, which throws the suspect vehicle into a tailspin and brings it to a stop. Proper execution of the PIT maneuver requires specialized training and certification that not all police officers have completed. The goal of this method is to terminate a pursuit safely.

In-Custody Death: Excited Delirium. When a person suddenly dies in police custody, it is often called *excited delirium*. This is not a medical diagnosis but, rather, a set of behaviors making up the conditions (Sullivan, 2007). Kulbarsh (2007) notes, "There is no medical or psychiatric diagnosis of excited delirium. The International Association of Chiefs of Police has not acknowledged the syndrome, either. It is the subject's behavior that indicates the syndrome. However, annually, excited delirium is increasingly determined to be the cause of in-custody deaths."

Sullivan (2007) quotes Deborah Mash, a professor of neurology at the University of Miami: "Someone who's disproportionately large, extremely agitated, threatening violence, talking incoherently, tearing off clothes, and it takes four or five officers to get the attention of that individual and bring him out of harm's way—that's excited delirium." Other signs and symptoms that might indicate excited delirium include elevated body temperature, paranoia, constant motion, inappropriate and often violent behavior and feats of incredible strength (Ho, 2007, p.28). Officers recognizing such symptoms should immediately call for help. Because of the potential for lawsuits in such cases, it is imperative that officers know how to investigate such deaths immediately. Investigating in-custody deaths is discussed in Chapter 8.

Use of Force and the Mentally Ill. Dealing with people who are mentally ill or otherwise emotionally disturbed can present a use-of-force challenge. Use of less-lethal weapons may contain the situation or worsen it. Researchers Swartz and Lurigio (2007, p.581) studied the relationships among psychiatric disorders, substance use and arrests for violent, nonviolent and drug-related offenses and found that the statistical association between serious mental illness (SMI) and arrest across psychiatric diagnoses was substantially but only partially mediated by substance use. For nonviolent offenses and for drug-related offenses, the relationship between SMI and arrest was almost completely mediated by substance use, reduced to statistical nonsignificance: "These findings suggest that co-occurring substance use increases the chances a person with any SMI, not just schizophrenia, will be arrested for any offense, not just violent offenses, but that the magnitude of this relationship varies by offense type and, to a lesser extent, by disorder" (Swartz and Lurigio).

Currently, an estimated 3.5 million Americans suffer from some form of severe mental illness, and the police are frequently called on to respond to incidents involving individuals with mental health issues. Often these individuals have not been diagnosed and are not on proper medication, have stopped taking their prescribed medication or are under the influence of another behavior altering drug. Research suggests that police often see the mentally ill as more dangerous than other suspects are. In fact, those with mental illness are often unfairly portrayed as violent.

One method used in responding to calls involving emotionally disturbed individuals is the deployment of a crisis intervention team (CIT). The Memphis Police Department established training under the CIT model in 1998, stressing communication and de-escalation, and many departments across the country have since adopted the model. CIT officers are taught to recognize the various psychiatric syndromes, the biologic basis for severe mental illness, de-escalation of crisis situations, the law pertaining to the detention of the mentally ill and access to emergency and nonemergency mental health services (Tactical Response Team Staff, 2006, p.54). Some contend that this should be standard training for *all* police officers, not just a specialized group because it is not plausible that there will be a CIT-trained officer available in every situation that calls for one.

Suicide by Police. When individuals who are mentally ill force police officers into shooting them, the question often arises, Is this a case of suicide by cop? *Suicide by police* is a phenomenon in which someone intentionally acts so threateningly toward officers as to force them to fire, accomplishing the subject's ultimate goal of dying, albeit not by his or her own hand. Sometimes it seems very implausible that a person really wants to die in what appears to be a suicide-by-cop situation. Such instances have been presented as "death by indifference." When it seems that suicide by cop is not probable, investigators should consider the possibility of death by indifference by an offender apathetic to his or her own fate.

Often when a law enforcement officer uses deadly force, a lawsuit will almost certainly follow. That underscores the criticality of use-of-force reports.

Use-of-Force Reports

As has been stressed, thorough, accurate, well-written reports are critical to the investigator. Litigation has prompted a push for precision in describing exactly what happened during the incident in a use-of-force report. Language intended to convey precision and professionalism may sound like euphemisms to a jury, as though the officer is being evasive. Therefore, officers need to articulate their use of force in everyday language to show the reasonableness of their actions (Grossi, 2008). For example, rather than writing "I decentralized the subject," the officer might have written, "I used a push-in/pull-down technique to take Mr. Jones to the ground, while verbally commanding him to get down" (Robinson, 2006, p.32). Using such language can reduce the likelihood of excessive-force lawsuits being filed in the first place, and, if the case does go to court, such reports make the defense's case less likely to be successful: "We have a duty to teach officers to use force effectively so they can survive on the street. If we don't also teach them to report it effectively, they may not survive in court" (Robinson, 2006, p.32).

Summary

Developing, locating, identifying and arresting suspects are primary responsibilities of investigators.

Field identification or show-up identification is on-the-scene identification of a suspect by a victim of or witness to a crime. Field identification must be made within a short time after the crime was committed. *United States v. Ash, Jr.* (1973) established that a suspect does not have the right to have counsel present at a field identification.

If the suspect is not immediately identified, you must develop a suspect through information provided by victims, witnesses and other people likely to know about the crime or the suspect; physical evidence at the crime scene; psychological profiling; information in police files; information in other agencies' files; or informants. Help witnesses describe suspects and vehicles by asking very specific questions and using an identification diagram.

Suspects can be identified through field identification, mug shots, photographic identification or lineups. Use field identification when the suspect is arrested at or near the scene. Use mug-shot identification if you believe the suspect has a police record. Use photographic identification when you have a good idea who committed the crime but the suspect is not in custody, or when a fair lineup cannot be conducted. Tell witnesses they need not identify anyone from the photographs. A suspect does *not* have the right to a lawyer if a photographic lineup is used (*United States v. Ash, Jr.*, 1973).

Use lineup identification when the suspect is in custody. Use at least five people of comparable race, height, weight, age and general appearance. Ask all to perform the same actions or speak the same words. Instruct those viewing the lineup that they need not make an identification. Suspects may refuse to participate in a lineup, but such refusal may be used against them in court (*Schmerber v. California*, 1966). Suspects have a Sixth Amendment right to have an attorney present during a lineup. Avoid having the same person make both photographic and lineup identification. If you do so, do not conduct both within a short time.

Surveillance, undercover assignments and raids are used only when normal methods of continuing the investigation fail to produce results. The objective of surveillance is to obtain information about people, their associates and their activities that may help solve a criminal case or protect witnesses. The types of surveillance include stationary (fixed, plant or stakeout) and moving (tight or close, loose, rough, on foot or by vehicle). Electronic surveillance and wiretapping are considered forms of search and therefore are permitted only with probable cause and a court order (*Katz v. United States*, 1967).

The objective of an undercover assignment may be to gain a person's confidence or to infiltrate an organization or group by using an assumed identity and to thereby obtain information or evidence connecting the subject with criminal activity. Precautions for undercover agents are to write no notes the subject can read; carry no identification other than the cover ID; make sure any communication with headquarters is covert; and do not suggest, plan, initiate or participate in any criminal activity.

The objectives of a raid are to recover stolen property, seize evidence or arrest a suspect. To be legal, a raid must be the result of a hot pursuit or under authority of a no-knock arrest warrant or a search warrant. Precautions in conducting raids include ensuring that the raid is legal, planning carefully, assigning adequate personnel and equipment, thoroughly briefing every member of the raiding party and being aware of the possibility of surreptitious surveillance devices or booby traps at the raid site.

An arrest may occur at any point during an investigation. Police officers are authorized to make an arrest (1) for any crime committed in their presence, (2) for a felony (or for a misdemeanor in some states) not committed in their presence if they have probable cause to believe the person committed the crime or (3) under the authority of an arrest warrant. Probable cause for believing the suspect committed a crime must be established *before* a lawful arrest can be made.

If your intent is to make an arrest and you inform the suspect of this intent and then restrict the suspect's right to go free, you have made an arrest. Officers leave themselves open to lawsuits in several areas related to arrests, including false arrests, excessive force, shootings and wrongful death. When making an arrest, use only as much force as is necessary to overcome any resistance.

Checklists

Identifying and Arresting Suspects

- Was a suspect observed by police on arrival at the scene?
- Was a suspect arrested at the scene?
- Was anyone observed at the scene by any other person?

- Was a neighborhood check made to determine suspicious people, vehicles or noises?
- Was the complainant interviewed?
- Were statements taken from witnesses or people with information about the crime?
- Was a description of the suspect obtained?
- Was the description disseminated to other members of the local police force? To neighboring police departments?
- Was any associative evidence found at the scene or in the suspect's possession?
- Were informants checked?
- Were similar crimes committed in the area? In the community? In neighboring communities?
- Were field-identification cards checked to determine who was in the area?
- Were modus operandi files reviewed to determine who commits a similar type of crime? Are the suspects in or out of prison?
- Were traffic tickets checked to see whether any person or vehicle was in the area at the time of the crime? How does the vehicle or crime compare with the suspect vehicle or person?
- Have other agencies been checked?—Municipal? County? State? Federal?
- How was the person identified? Field identification? Mug shots? Photographic identification? Lineup identification? Was it legal?
- Was the arrest legal?

Surveillance

- Is there any alternative to surveillance?
- What information is needed from the surveillance?
- What type of surveillance is needed?
- Have equipment and personnel needs for the surveillance area been determined?
- Are the required equipment and personnel available?
- Are proper forms available for recording necessary information during the surveillance?
- Are all signals preestablished?

Undercover Assignments

- Is there any alternative to undercover work?
- What information is needed from the assignment?

- Is adequate information about the subject available?
- Have you established a good cover?
- How will you communicate with headquarters?
- What are you to do if you are arrested?
- Do you have an alternative plan if the initial plan fails?
- Do you have a plausible explanation for leaving once the assignment is completed?

Raids

- Is there any alternative to a raid?
- Have appropriate warrants been obtained?
- Have the objectives of the raid been clearly specified?
- Has a pre-surveillance of the raid location been conducted?
- Are adequate personnel and equipment available?
- Has a briefing been held?

Discussion Questions

1. Imagine that a burglary has occurred each of the last four nights in a 10-block residential area in a city of 200,000 people. How might an investigator start to determine who is committing these crimes? What sources of information and techniques can be used in developing a suspect?

2. Suppose you have obtained information concerning a suspect in a rape case. Two witnesses saw someone near the rape scene at about the time of the offense, and the victim was able to describe her assailant. How should identification be made?

3. How do cooperation of the public and of other police agencies each help in identifying and arresting suspects? Which is more important: public cooperation or the cooperation of other police agencies?

4. How are people selected for a lineup? How should a lineup be conducted according to legal requirements? What is done if the suspect refuses to participate?

5. What balance must be maintained between an individual's right to privacy and the public interest when using surveillance?

6. Under what conditions should a police raid be considered?

7. In what types of crimes would the use of an undercover agent be justified?

8. What type of "tail" would you use for each of the following: Checking the loyalty of an informant?

A suspected bank robber planning to "case" a bank? A burglar known to meet frequently with another burglar? Someone suspected of being an organized crime leader?

9. How much risk is involved in undercover assignments and raids? How can you minimize this risk?

10. When do outside agencies participate in surveillances, undercover assignments and raids?

Media Explorations

Internet

Select one of the following assignments to complete:

- Go to http://www.driverslicenseguide.com and outline the contents of the I.D. Checking Guide.
- Search for these key terms: *criminal profiling, psychological profiling* and *racial profiling*. Write a brief report defining each and explaining how they are alike and different.
- Search for one of the following key terms: *entrapment, undercover officer* or *wiretapping*. Select one article to outline and share with the class.
- Search for *Miranda v. Arizona*. Select and outline one of the articles to share with the class.

ONLINE Database Gale Criminal Justice Database Assignments

The following assignments require access to Gale's Custom Journals Database for Emergency Services and Criminal Justice. Check with your instructor if you have questions about this.

- Find the article "Civil Liability for Violations of *Miranda*: The Impact of *Chavez v. Martinez*" on the Gale Emergency Services Database. Read the article and outline the impact of this case to the *Miranda* warning and how it opens law enforcement officers to civil liability. Be prepared to discuss your findings in class.

- Find the article "Undercover Investigations and the Entrapment Defense" on the Gale Emergency Services Database. Read the article and be prepared to explain in class the entrapment defense that is often used in undercover investigations.

- Find the article "The Role of Race in Law Enforcement: Racial Profiling or Legitimate Use?" on the Gale Emergency Services Database. Read the article and write a brief report defining and explaining this topic.

- Find the article "I.D. Reference Guide" on the Gale Emergency Services Database. Read the article and then follow the Internet link at the end of the summary. Look over the contents of the guide and explain why this type of resource may be beneficial to law enforcement.

References

Ashley, Steve. "What Gets You Sued Gets You Hurt." *Law Officer Magazine*, February 2007, pp.72–75.

Ault, Michael; Sousa, William; and Ready, Justin. "How Reliable Are Your Policies and Training? Putting the CED to the Test." *Subject to Debate*, April 2007, pp.4, 6.

Beldock, James. "Acoustic Surveillance Systems." *Law and Order*, October 2009, pp.46–50.

Borrello, Andrew. "Acoustic Force Technology." *Tactical Response*, May–June 2007, pp.50–56.

Bray, Jeff. "Suspects Who Refuse to Identify Themselves." *The Police Chief*, April 2007, pp.10–11.

Bulman, Philip. "Police Use of Force: The Impact of Less-Lethal Weapons and Tactics." *NIJ Journal*, No.267, March 2011, pp.4–11. (NCJ 233281)

Corbley, Kevin. "GPS Photo-Mapping in Law Enforcement." *Law Enforcement Technology*, January 2008, pp.96–101.

Cronin, James M., and Ederheimer, Joshua A. *Conducted Energy Devices: Development of Standards for Consistency and Guidance.* Washington, DC: Police Executive Research Forum and the Department of Justice, November 2006.

Cutler, Brian L.; Daugherty, Brent; Babu, Sabarish; Hodges, Larry; and Van Wallendael, Lori. "Creating Blind Photoarrays Using Virtual Human Technology." *Police Quarterly*, Vol.12, No.3, September 2009, pp.289–300.

Dees, Tim. "Crime Mapping and Geographic Profiling." *Law Officer Magazine*, December 2008, pp.68–71.

Dees, Tim. "Unblinking Eyes." *Police*, December 2009, pp.42–45.

Dees, Tim. "An End to Stakeouts?" *Police*, December 2010, pp.30–32.

Donlon-Cotton, Cara. "Counter Surveillance: Someone Is Watching." *Law and Order*, May 2007, pp.72–75.

Elliott, Andrea. "After 9/11, Arab-Americans Fear Police Acts, Study Finds." *The New York Times*, June 12, 2006.

Falk, Kay. "Putting a Name to a Face." *Law Enforcement Technology*, July 2007, pp.32–40.

Ferdico, John N.; Fradella, Henry F.; and Totten, Christopher D. *Criminal Procedure for the Criminal Justice Professional*, 10th ed. Belmont, CA: Wadsworth/Cengage Learning, 2009.

Gaertner, Susan, and Harrington, John. "Successful Eyewitness Identification Reform: Ramsey County's Blind Sequential Lineup Protocol." *The Police Chief*, April 2009, pp.130–141.

Griffith, David. "Propaganda and Protests." *Police*, September 2007, p.12.

Grossi, Dave. "Tactics for Survival Writing." *Law Officer Magazine*, October 2008, pp.30–33.

Grossi, Dave. "Going Under." *Law Officer Magazine*, April 2009, pp.24–28.

Guilbault, Rick. "Never Bring a TASER to a Gunfight." *Police*, June 20007a, pp.40–46.

Guilbault, Rick. "The Tactical Use of TASERS." *Police*, December 2007b, pp.42–47.

Hamilton, Melanie. "Surprise, Shock, and Speed." *Police*, March 2007, pp.42–43.

Hanratty, Thomas. "Walking in Another's Shoes." *Law Enforcement Technology*, April 2007, pp.42–51.

Hanson, Doug. "Biometric Analysis Answers 'Who Are You?'" *Law and Order*, April 2007, pp.84–89.

Heinecke, Jeannine. "Criminals Caught on Tape." *Law Enforcement Technology*, April 2007, pp.86–91.

Ho, Jeffrey. "How to Respond to Excited Delirium." *Police*, July 2007, pp.28–30.

Hudson, Doreen, and Webb, Richard. "Less-Lethal Taken to a Higher Level." *Law Enforcement Technology*, May 2007, pp.48–54.

Ijames, Steve. "Less-Lethal Technologies, Part 2." *Tactical Response*, November–December 2007, pp.22–24.

Ijames, Steve. "Less-Lethal Technologies, Part 3." *Tactical Response*, January–February 2008, pp.22–24.

Ioimo, Ralph; Tears, Rachel S.; Meadows, Leslie A.; Becton, J. Bret; and Charles, Michael T. "The Police View of Bias-Based Policing." *Police Quarterly*, September 2007, pp.270–287.

Irwin, Bob. "Rethinking the 21-Foot Rule." *Police*, October 2007, pp.82–85.

Kozlowski, Jonathan. "Instantly There." *Law Enforcement Technology*, August 2007, pp.126–131.

Kozlowski, Jonathan. "Seeing Past the Hard Stuff." *Law Enforcement Technology*, September 2009, pp.68–73.

Kulbarsh, Pamela. "In-Custody Deaths: Excited Delirium." *Officer.com*, March 4, 2007.

Langerman, Andrew. "Facial Fiction Becoming Fact." *Law Enforcement Technology*, January 2008, pp.60–67.

Lee, Bob. "Cuttin' Sign: Ten Tips for Following the Tracks." *Law Officer Magazine*, October 2007, pp.28–34.

Means, Randy. "Least Force? Or Reasonable Force?" *Law and Order*, June 2007, pp.12–14.

Means, Randy, and Siedel, Greg. "Maintaining Proportionality and Managing Force Escalations." *Law and Order,* February 2009, pp.31–32.

Mecklenburg, Sheri H.; Larson, Mark R.; and Bailey, Patricia J. "Eyewitness Identification: What Chiefs Need to Know Now." *The Police Chief*, October 2008, pp.68–81.

Miles, Christopher A. "Through-the-Wall Surveillance: A New Technology for Saving Lives." *NIJ Journal*, October 2007, pp.20–25.

Mumola, Christopher J. *Arrest-Related Deaths in the United States, 2003–2005*. Washington, DC: Bureau of Justice Statistics Special Report, October 2007. (NCJ 219534)

Munson, Don. "PepperBall's FlashLauncher." *Law and Order*, October 2007, pp.86–91.

Munson, Don. "Super Talon Net Gun." *Law and Order*, March 2008, pp.86–92.

Newman, Graeme R. *Sting Operations*. Washington, DC: Office of Community Oriented Policing Services, 2007.

Page, Douglas. "France Brings a New Weapon to the Less-Lethal Field." *Law Enforcement Technology*, June 2007, pp.142–147.

Pincince, Dennis. "Forensics Technology: Key to Rhode Island Convictions." *Law and Order*, October 2007, pp.105–106.

Polan, Jim. "SWAT Training." *Law Officer Magazine*, February 2008, pp.36–38.

Risher, Julie. "U.S. Supreme Court Decides 'Ramming' Case: Force Was Reasonable under the Circumstances." *The Police Chief*, July 2007, pp.10–12.

Robinson, Patricia A. "What You Say Is What They Write: Everybody Teaches Report Writing." *The Law Enforcement Trainer*, January/February 2006, pp.30–32.

Romanelli, Tim. "Chicago's Surveillance Strategy." *Law and Order*, October 2009, pp.28–30.

Rossmo, D. Kim. "Failures in Criminal Investigation." *The Police Chief*, October 2009, pp.54–66.

Rowe, Aaron. "TASER Cam Lowers Liability." *Tactical Response*, May–June 2007, pp.34–38.

Ruecker, Ronald C. "Examining the Use of Force." *The Police Chief*, December 2007, p.6.

Rutledge, Devallis. "Residential Entry after Outdoor Arrest." *Police*, February 2008, pp.60–62.

Sanow. Ed. "Use-of-Force and Legal Strategies." *Law and Order*, September 2007, p.6.

Scarry, Laura L. "False-Arrest Claims." *Law Officer Magazine*, May 2007a, pp.138–139.

Scarry, Laura L. "Tight Handcuffs: A Fourth Amendment Violation?" *Law Officer Magazine*, December 2007b, pp.50–53.

Schuster, Beth. "Police Lineups: Making Eyewitness Identification More Reliable." *NIJ Journal*, October 2007, pp.2–9.

Slahor, Stephenie. "Tactical Operations Liability, Part 1." *Tactical Response*, May–August 2008, pp.74–78.

Staton, Jerry. "A TASER Policy That Works." *Law and Order*, March 2008, pp.93–97.

Stradley, Mike. "StealthFighter." *Police*, April 2007a, pp.32–34.

Stradley, Mike. "TigerLight Non-Lethal Defense System." *Tactical Response*, May–June 2007b, pp.44–49.

Sullivan, Laura. "Death by Excited Delirium: Diagnosis or Coverup?" National Public Radio, April 19, 2007.

Swartz, James, and Lurigio, Arthur J. "Serious Mental Illness and Arrest: The Generalized Mediating Effect of Substance Use." *Crime & Delinquency*, October 2007, pp.581–604.

Tactical Response Team Staff. "Crisis Intervention Team." *Tactical Response*, May–June 2006, pp.54–58.

Welch, Kelly. "Black Criminal Stereotypes and Racial Profiling." *Journal of Contemporary Criminal Justice*, August 2007, pp.276–288.

White, Michael D., and Ready, Justin. "The TASER as a Less Lethal Force Alternative: Findings on Use and Effectiveness in a Large Metropolitan Police Agency." *Police Quarterly*, October 2007, p.170.

Williams, Mick. "TASER Extended Range Projectile." *Tactical Response*, May–June 2007, pp.40–41.

Young, Dave. "How to Deploy Impact Munitions." *Police*, December 2007, pp.26–31.

Cases Cited

Atwater v. Lago Vista, 532 U.S. 318 (2001)

Brown v. City of Oneonta, 221 F.3d 329 (2d Cir. 2000), *cert denied* 534 U.S. 816 (2001)

County of Riverside v. McLaughlin, 500 U.S. 44 (1991)

Davis v. Mississippi, 394 U.S. 721 (1969)

Devenpeck v. Alford, 543 U.S. 146 (2004)

Dunaway v. New York, 442 U.S. 200 (1979)

Florida v. Riley, 488 U.S. 445 (1989)

Gilbert v. California, 388 U.S. 263 (1967)

Gordon v. Warren Consolidated Board of Education, 706 F.2d 778 (1983)

Graham v. Connor, 490 U.S. 386 (1989)

Hayes v. Florida, 470 U.S. 811 (1985)

Hiibel v. Sixth Judicial District Court of Nevada, Humboldt County, 542 U.S. 177 (2004)

Illinois v. Wardlow, 528 U.S. 119 (2000)

James v. Louisiana, 382 U.S. 36 (1965)

Katz v. United States, 389 U.S. 347 (1967)

Kaupp v. Texas, 538 U.S. 626 (2003)

Kyllo v. United States, 533 U.S. 27 (2001)

Manson v. Brathwaite, 432 U.S. 98 (1977)

Maryland v. Pringle, 540 U.S. 366 (2003)

Pierson v. Ray, 386 U.S. 547 (1967)

Saucier v. Katz, 533 U.S. 194 (2001)

Schmerber v. California, 384 U.S. 757 (1966)

Scott v. Harris, 550 U.S. 372 (2007)

Sherman v. United States, 356 U.S. 369 (1958)

Shipley v. California, 395 U.S. 818 (1969)

Sorrells v. United States, 287 U.S. 435 (1932)

Tennessee v. Garner, 471 U.S. 1 (1985)

United States v. Ash, Jr., 413 U.S. 300 (1973)

United States v. Garcia, 474 F.3d 994 (7th Cir. 2007)

United States v. Knotts, 460 U.S. 276 (1983)

United States v. McKinnon, 985 F.2d 525 (11th Cir. 1993)

United States v. Wade, 388 U.S. 218 (1967)

United States v. Weaver, 966 F.2d 391 (8th Cir. 1992)

Vale v. Louisiana, 399 U.S. 30 (1970)

Wallace v. Kato, 549 U.S. 384 (2007)

Whren v. United States, 517 U.S. 806 (1996)

SECTION 3
INVESTIGATING VIOLENT CRIMES

The Federal Bureau of Investigation's (FBI) Uniform Crime Reports (UCR) contains statistics on eight types of serious crimes, previously called Index offenses: murder, aggravated assault, forcible rape, robbery, burglary, larceny/theft, motor vehicle theft and arson. In years past, data were collected for each of these offenses and published in an annual UCR to serve as a national barometer of crime in the United States. However, as noted by the FBI ("UCR General FAQs," no date),

In June 2004, the CJIS [Criminal Justice Information System] Advisory Policy Board (APB) approved discontinuing the use of the Crime Index in the UCR Program and its publications and directed the FBI [to] publish a violent crime total and a property crime total. The Crime Index, first published in *Crime in the United States* in 1960, was the title used for a simple aggregation of the seven main offense classifications (Part I offenses) in the Summary reporting system. The Modified Crime Index was the number of Crime Index offenses plus arson.

For several years, the CJIS Division studied the appropriateness and usefulness of these indices and brought the matter before many advisory groups including the UCR Subcommittee of the CJIS APB, the Association of State UCR Programs, and a meeting of leading criminologists and sociologists hosted by the Bureau of Justice Statistics. In short, the Crime Index and the Modified Crime Index were not true indicators of the degrees of criminality because they were always driven upward by the offense with the highest number, typically larceny-theft. The sheer volume of those offenses overshadowed more serious but less frequently committed offenses, creating a bias against a jurisdiction with a high number of larceny-thefts but a low number of other serious crimes such as murder and forcible rape.

Thus, although previous editions of this text discussed crime statistics in the context of the Crime Index, this edition simply divides such data into two categories—violent crime and property crime. This section looks at violent crime; property crime is the focus of Section 4.

© 2012 istockphoto.com

© 2012 istockphoto.com

© 2012 istockphoto.com

According to the Uniform Crime Reports for 2009 ("Crime Clock Statistics," 2010), a violent crime occurred nationally every 23.9 seconds:

- 1 robbery every 1.3 minutes
- 1 aggravated assault every 39.1 seconds
- 1 forcible rape every 6.0 minutes
- 1 murder every 34.5 minutes

FBI data also indicate that an estimated 1,318,398 violent crimes were committed in the United States in 2009, representing a decrease of 5.3 percent from the 2008 estimate. The five-year trend (2009 compared with 2005) indicated that violent crime decreased 5.2 percent. For the 10-year period (2009 compared with 2000), violent crime fell 7.5 percent. As in previous years, aggravated assaults comprised the largest portion of violent crime in 2009 at 61.2 percent, followed by robbery (31.0 percent), forcible rape (6.7 percent) and murder (1.2 percent). According to *Crime in the United States, 2009* (2010), an estimated 429.4 violent crimes per 100,000 inhabitants occurred in 2009. Firearms were used in 67.1 percent of the nation's murders, in 42.6 percent of the robbery offenses and in 20.9 percent of the aggravated assaults. (Weapon data are not collected for forcible rape.)

Levels of crime have fluctuated over the past decade. The nationwide decrease in violent crime that began in 1994 ended in 2004, as the numbers began to trend upward again. The increase, however, proved to be short-lived, as violent crime in 2006 began declining again. Figure III.1 illustrates the shifting trends in violent crime. Caution must be used when interpreting such figures, however, as they do not include crime data for categories not included in the UCR program and thus under-represent the true extent of violent crime.

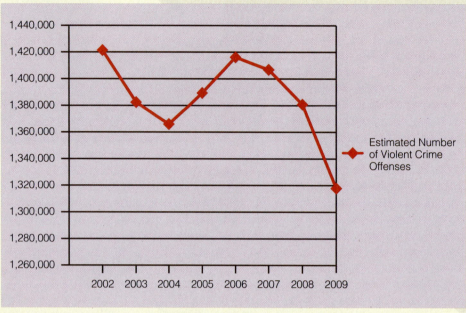

FIGURE III.1

Violent crime offense figure, nine-year trend, 2002–2009.

Source: Combined data from *Crime in the United States, 2006* and *Crime in the United States, 2009.* Individual year data points available at http://www.fbi.gov/about-us/cjis/ucr/ucr

Interestingly, homicides for law enforcement have been on an upward trend. In 2010, 61 law enforcement officers were killed in the line of duty by gunfire, an increase of 24 percent from 2009 (*Law Enforcement Fatalities Spike*, 2010). The trend of a high number of officers killed by gunfire in the line of duty continues to increase into 2011.

Another measure of crime is achieved through the National Crime Victimization Survey (NCVS), which tallied more than 4.3 million crimes of violence in 2009 (Truman and Rand, 2010). The overall violent crime rate was 17.1 victimizations per 1,000 persons age 12 or older. Note the difference between the findings of these two national measures of crime in the United States.

Investigating violent crimes is made more difficult by the emotionalism usually encountered not only from the victim but also from the public. Generally, however, investigating violent crimes results in more and better information and evidence than investigating crimes against property, discussed in Section 4.

Although states vary in what elements must be proven in a given crime, some common elements exist, as shown in Figure III.2.

In recent years, violent-crime investigations have been enhanced by the establishment of the Violent Crime Apprehension Program (VICAP) at the FBI National Police Academy in Quantico, Virginia: "VICAP is a national database on crimes of violence. VICAP's mission is to facilitate cooperation, communication and coordination between law enforcement agencies and provide support in their efforts to investigate, identify, track, apprehend, and prosecute violent serial offenders" (Cronin et al., 2007, p.139). Information considered viable is published in the *FBI Law Enforcement Bulletin*. If the case merits interagency cooperation, a major case investigation team of investigators from all involved agencies may be formed.

Viability is determined by specialists at VICAP who review the information submitted and compare it with information received from other departments about similar cases and their MOs. This is especially important in serial killings and other major violent crimes in which the suspects have moved to other areas and committed similar crimes.

The chapters in this section of the book discuss specific considerations in investigating deaths/murder (Chapter 8); assault, domestic violence, stalking and elder abuse (Chapter 9); sex offenses (Chapter 10); crimes against children (Chapter 11); and robbery (Chapter 12). In actuality, more than one offense can occur in a given case. For example, what begins as a robbery can progress to an assault,

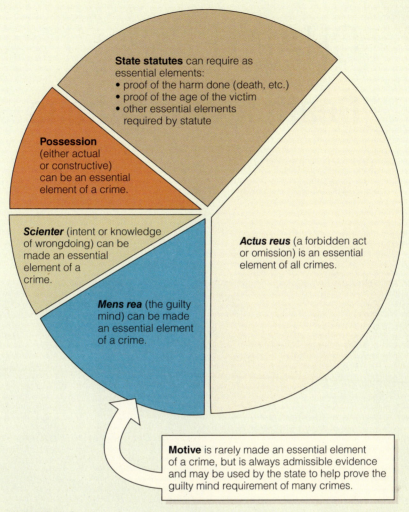

FIGURE III.2

Elements that may be essential to the proof of a crime.

Source: GARDNER/ANDERSON. *Criminal Law*, 9e, © Copyright 2006 Wadsworth, a part of Cengage Learning, Inc. Reproduced by permission. www.cengage.com/permissions.

then a forcible rape and finally a murder. Each offense must be proven separately.

References

"Crime Clock Statistics." In *Crime in the United States, 2009*. Washington, DC: Federal Bureau of Investigation, September 2010. Accessed May 19, 2011. http://www.fbi.gov/ucr/cius2009/about/crime_clock.html

Crime in the United States, 2009. Washington, DC: U.S. Department of Justice, Federal Bureau of Investigation, September 2010. Accessed May 19, 2011. http://www.fbi.gov/ucr/cius2009/index.html

Cronin, James M.; Murphy, Gerard R.; Spahr, Lisa L.; Toliver, Jessica I.; and Weger, Richard E. *Promoting Effective Homicide Investigations*. Washington, DC: Office of Community Oriented Policing and the Police Executive Research Forum, December 2007.

Law Enforcement Fatalities Spike Dangerously in 2010. Washington, DC: National Law Enforcement Officers Memorial Fund, Research Bulletin, 2010. Accessed May 19, 2011. http://www.nleomf.org/assets/pdfs/reports/2010_Law_Enforcement_Fatalities_Report.pdf

Truman, Jennifer L., and Rand, Michael R, *Criminal Victimization, 2009*. Washington, DC: Bureau of Justice Statistics Bulletin, October 2010. (NCJ 231327)

"UCR General FAQs." Washington, DC: Federal Bureau of Investigation, no date. Accessed May 19, 2011. http://www.fbi.gov/about-us/cjis/ucr/frequently-asked-questions/ucr_faqs

CHAPTER 8
Death Investigations

© Darren Hauck/Getty Images

Outline

Can You Define?

adipocere
algor mortis
asphyxiation
autoerotic asphyxiation
clearance rate
criminal homicide
criminal negligence
defense wounds
equivocal death
excusable homicide
expressive violence
first-degree murder
heat of passion
hesitation wounds
homicide
instrumental violence
involuntary manslaughter
justifiable homicide
livor mortis

lust murder
malicious intent
manslaughter
mass murder
mummification
murder
noncriminal homicide
postmortem artifact
postmortem lividity
premeditation
rigor mortis
second-degree murder
serial murder
suicide
suicide by police
third-degree murder
toxicology
voluntary manslaughter

Do You Know?

- What a basic requirement in a homicide investigation is?
- What the four categories of death are?
- How to define and classify homicide, murder and manslaughter?
- What degrees of murder are frequently specified?
- How excusable and justifiable homicide differ?
- What the significance of premeditation is?
- What special challenges a homicide investigation presents?
- What the first priority in a preliminary homicide investigation is?
- How to establish that death has occurred?
- What physical evidence is usually found in homicides?
- What information and evidence are obtained from a victim?
- How to identify an unknown homicide victim?
- What factors help in estimating the time of death?
- What effect water has on a dead body?
- What information is provided by the medical examiner or coroner?

(continued)

You arrive at the scene of a death in response to an emergency call and find the body of a 55-year-old white male crumpled at the bottom of a steep staircase—obviously dead. Did the victim trip and fall (accidental death)? Did he suffer a fatal heart attack at the top of the stairs and then fall (natural death)? Did he throw himself down the stairs to end some intense physical or mental suffering (suicide)? Or was he pushed (homicide)?

Only the fourth explanation involves a criminal action meriting an official police investigation. However, because the police must determine whether it actually was homicide, the other three possible explanations must be investigated.

A basic requirement in a homicide investigation is to establish whether death was caused by a criminal action.

- What the most frequent causes of unnatural death are and what indicates whether a death is a suicide or a homicide?
- Why determining a motive is important in homicide investigations?
- What similarities exist between school and workplace mass murders?
- How the conventional wisdom about homicide has changed in some departments?

Statistically, murder is the least significant of the violent crimes, with the FBI reporting 15,241 criminal homicides in the United States in 2009 (*Crime in the United States, 2009*), a decrease of 7.3 percent from 2008. However, deaths reported as accidents or suicides may actually have been murder, and vice versa. It may be necessary to determine whether a death was a murder made to appear as a suicide to eliminate further investigation or a suicide made to appear as an accident to collect life insurance.

Because homicides have received increasingly extensive media attention, it may appear as if this crime is occurring more frequently. However, it is actually declining. Males are most often the victims and the perpetrators in homicides, being 10 times more likely to commit murder than are females.

CLASSIFICATION OF DEATHS

The four categories of death are
- Natural
- Accidental: Noncriminal
- Suicide
- Homicide: Noncriminal or criminal

Natural Causes

Natural causes of death include heart attacks, strokes, fatal diseases, pneumonia, sudden crib deaths and old age. Frequently, a person who dies of natural causes has been under a physician's care, and a death from natural causes is easily established.

Sometimes, however, a death is made to look as though it resulted from natural causes. For example, drugs that simulate the effects of a heart attack may be used in a suicide or homicide.

Accidental Deaths

Among the causes of accidental death are falling; drowning; unintentionally taking too many pills or ingesting a poisonous substance; entanglement in industrial or farm machinery; or involvement in an automobile, boat, train, bus or plane crash. Some people advocate that certain accidental deaths be investigated as criminal homicide—for example, fatal crashes. A homicide investigation can routinely involve 30 officers. A fatal-crash clearance is usually completed by just one or two officers.

As with natural deaths, an apparently accidental death can actually be a suicide or a homicide. For example, a person can jump or be pushed from a roof or in front of a vehicle or can voluntarily or involuntarily take an overdose of pills. Or a person may engage in autoerotic asphyxiation to achieve sexual gratification but may accidentally kill himself or herself in the process.

Suicide

Suicide—the intentional taking of one's own life—can be committed by shooting, stabbing, poisoning, burning, asphyxiating or ingesting drugs or poisons. However, homicides are often made to look like suicides, and many suicides are made to look like accidents, usually for insurance purposes or to ease the family's suffering.

Although suicide is not a criminal offense, in most states it is a crime to *attempt* to commit suicide. This allows the state to take legal custody of such individuals for hospitalization or treatment. All states have a law or code that allows law enforcement officers and other qualified personnel to enforce a mandatory mental health hold for suicidal persons that require immediate evaluation for risk of being a danger to themselves or others.

It may also be a crime to help someone commit or attempt to commit suicide by either intentionally advising, encouraging or actually assisting the victim in the act. The topic of assisted suicide is extremely controversial. The Supreme Court has found that there is no constitutional "right to die" and has left this decision to each individual state. One high-profile figure in this controversy is Jack Kevorkian, "Dr. Death," a pathologist-turned-assisted-suicide-crusader who facilitated more than 130 suicides during the 1990s. After being tried multiple times on assisted suicide charges, Kevorkian was eventually tried for murder, found guilty and sent to prison in 1999. He was paroled in 2007 and died in June 2011.

Homicide

If another individual is the direct or indirect cause of the death, the death is classified as homicide.

> **Homicide** is the killing of one person by another.

Homicide includes the taking of life by another person or by an agency, such as a government. It is either criminal or noncriminal, that is, felonious or nonfelonious. **Criminal homicide** is subdivided into murder and manslaughter, both of which are further subdivided. **Noncriminal homicide** is subdivided into excusable and justifiable homicide.

> Classification of homicides:
> - Criminal (felonious)
>   - Murder (first, second or third degree)
>   - Manslaughter (voluntary or involuntary)
> - Noncriminal (nonfelonious)
>   - Excusable homicide
>   - Justifiable homicide

Thus, *murder* and *homicide* are not synonymous. All murders are homicides (and criminal), but not all homicides are murders (or criminal).

Criminal Homicide. The two classes of criminal homicide—murder and manslaughter—have several similarities but also important differences.

Murder, the killing of another human being with malice aforethought, is the most severe statutory crime, one of the few for which the penalty can be life imprisonment or death. (In some states, treason and ransom kidnapping carry a similarly severe penalty.) Some laws classify murder into first, second or third degrees. **First-degree murder** requires **premeditation** (advanced planning) and the intent to cause death. Some statutes include in this classification any death that results during the commission of or the attempt to commit a felony such as rape or robbery. **Second-degree murder** includes the intent to cause death, but not premeditation. An example is a violent argument that ends in one person spontaneously killing the other. **Third-degree murder** involves neither premeditation nor intent. It results from an act that is imminently dangerous to others and shows a disregard for human life, such as shooting into a room where people are likely to be present or playing a practical joke that may result in someone's death.

Manslaughter is the unlawful killing of another person with no prior malice. It may be voluntary or involuntary. **Voluntary manslaughter** is the intentional causing of the death of another person in the heat of passion, that is, because of words or acts that provide adequate provocation. For example, the law generally recognizes such acts as adultery, seduction of a child or rape of a close relative as outrageous enough to constitute adequate provocation. This provocation must result in intense passion that replaces reason and leads to the immediate act. The provocation, passion and fatal act must occur in rapid succession and be directly, sequentially related; that is, the provocation must cause the passion that causes the fatal act.

Involuntary manslaughter is accidental homicide that results from extreme (culpable) negligence. Examples of involuntary manslaughter include handling a firearm negligently; leaving poison where children may take it; and operating an automobile, boat or aircraft in a criminally negligent manner. Some states, such as California, have a third category of manslaughter: manslaughter with a motor vehicle.

Other acts that can be classified as involuntary manslaughter include shooting another person with a firearm or other dangerous weapon while mistakenly believing that person to be an animal; setting a spring gun, pitfall, deadfall, snare or other dangerous device designed to trap animals but capable of harming people; and negligently and intentionally allowing a known vicious animal to roam free.

■ Murder, the killing of another human with malice aforethought, is frequently classified as
- First degree—premeditated and intentional, or while committing or attempting to commit a felony
- Second degree—intentional but not premeditated
- Third degree—neither intentional nor premeditated, but the result of an imminently dangerous act

■ Manslaughter, the unlawful killing of another human with no prior malice, is classified as
- Voluntary—intentional homicide caused by intense passion resulting from adequate provocation
- Involuntary—unintentional homicide caused by criminal (culpable) negligence

Noncriminal Homicide. Although the term *homicide* is usually associated with crime, not all homicides are crimes.

Excusable homicide is the unintentional, truly accidental killing of another person. **Justifiable homicide** is killing another person under authorization of the law.

Excusable homicide results from an act that normally would not cause death or from an act committed with ordinary caution that, because of the *victim's* negligence, results in death, as when a person runs in front of a moving car.

Justifiable homicide includes killing in self-defense or in the defense of another person if the victim's actions and capability present imminent danger of serious injury or death. Killing an enemy during wartime is also classified as justifiable homicide. This classification further includes capital punishment, death caused by a public officer while carrying out a court order and deaths caused by police officers while attempting to prevent a dangerous felon's escape or to recapture a dangerous felon who has escaped or is resisting arrest. Officers need not risk their lives when faced with a shoot-or-be-shot situation.

ELEMENTS OF THE CRIME

Laws on criminal homicide vary significantly from state to state, but certain common elements are usually found in each, as summarized in Table 8.1. The degree eventually charged is decided by the prosecuting attorney based on the available evidence. For example, the only difference between first- and second-degree murder is the element of premeditation. If thorough investigation does not yield proof of premeditation, a charge of second-degree murder is made.

		Murder		Manslaughter	
Element to Be Proven	First Degree	Second Degree	Third Degree	Voluntary	Involuntary
Causing the death of another person	*	*	*	*	*
Premeditation	*				
Malicious intent	*	*			
Adequately provoked intent resulting from the heat of passion				*	
*While committing or attempting to commit a felony	*				
*While committing or attempting to commit a crime not a felony			*	*	
When forced or threatened				*	
Culpable negligence or depravity				*	
Negligence					*

TABLE 8.1 Degrees of Homicide

¹Indicates that starred elements other than causing the death of another person need not be proven.

© Cengage Learning, 2013

Causing the Death of Another Person

Usually the death of a person is not difficult to prove; a death certificate completed by a physician, coroner or medical examiner suffices. If a death certificate is not available, the investigator must locate witnesses to testify that they saw the body of the person allegedly killed by the suspect. When insufficient remains exist to identify the body positively, death is proven by circumstantial evidence such as examination by a qualified pathologist or by other experts and their expert testimony regarding dental work, bone structure and the like.

A more difficult portion of the element to prove is the cause of death. To show that the suspect's act caused the death, (1) prove the cause of death and (2) prove that the suspect, through direct action, inflicted injury sufficient to cause the death with some weapon or device. For example, if the cause of death was a fatal wound from a .22-caliber weapon, it is necessary to show that the suspect produced the cause of death. Did the suspect own such a weapon? Can witnesses testify that the suspect had such a weapon immediately before the fatal injury? Was the suspect seen actually committing the offense? Did the suspect admit the act by statement or confession?

Premeditation

Premeditation is the consideration, planning or preparation for an act, no matter how briefly, before committing it. Laws use such terms as *premeditated design to kill* or *malice aforethought*. Whatever the law's wording, it is necessary to prove some intention and plan to commit the crime before it was actually committed.

> Premeditation is the element of first-degree murder that sets it apart from all other classifications.

Were oral statements or threats made during a heated argument? Did the suspect buy or have a gun just before the crime was committed or travel a long distance to wait for the victim? Premeditation can be proved in many ways. Sometimes the time interval between thought and action is only a minute; other times, it may be hours, days, weeks, months or even years.

Determine at what time before the killing the suspect considered, planned, threatened or made some overt act to prepare to commit the murder. This may be established by statements from witnesses or from the victim before death, from evidence at the crime scene or through a review of the suspect's criminal history and past statements.

Intent to Effect the Death of Another Person

Intent is a required element of most categories of criminal homicide. Evidence must show that the crime was intentional, not accidental. **Malicious intent**, an element of first- and second-degree murder, implies ill will, wickedness or cruelty. How the act was committed shows the degree of intent. The type of weapon used, how and when it was acquired and how the suspect and victim came together help prove the intent as well as the act that caused the death.

Intent and *premeditation* are not the same. Premeditation is not a requirement of intent. Most crimes of passion involve intent but not premeditation or malicious intent.

This element—intent—also applies to a death caused to someone other than the intended victim. For example, in one case a woman intended to kill her husband by placing poison in a bottle of whiskey he kept under the seat of the family car. Unknowingly, the husband offered a drink from the bottle to a friend, who died as a result. The wife was charged with first-degree murder and convicted, even though the person who died was not her intended victim. It was a reasonable consequence of her act.

An explosive that was set for one person may detonate prematurely and kill someone else. A person shooting at an intended victim may miss and kill an innocent bystander. Both of these would constitute first-degree murder.

Adequately Provoked Intent Resulting from Heat of Passion

This element is the alternative to premeditation. It assumes that the act was committed when the suspect suddenly became extremely emotional, thus precluding premeditation. **Heat of passion** results from extremely volatile arguments between two people, from seeing a wife or family member raped, from a sudden discovery of adultery or from seeing a brutal assault being committed against a close friend or family member.

While Committing or Attempting to Commit a Felony

In some states, a charge of first-degree murder does not require that the murder was committed with premeditation if the victim died as a result of acts committed while the suspect was engaged in a felony such as rape, robbery or arson. Proof of the elements of the felony must be established.

While Committing or Attempting to Commit a Crime Not a Felony

If a death results from an act committed by a suspect engaged in a nonfelonious crime such as purse snatching or petty theft, it can be charged as either third-degree murder or voluntary manslaughter, depending on the state in which the offense occurs.

Culpable Negligence or Depravity

The act and the way it is committed establish this element. The act must be so dangerous that any prudent person would see death of a person as a possible consequence. A person causing a death while depraved and committing acts evident of such depravity is guilty of third-degree murder.

Negligence

A fine line separates this element from the preceding element. Some states make no distinction, classifying both in a separate category of **criminal negligence**. Where separate categories exist, this lesser degree of negligence involves creating a situation that results in an unreasonable risk of death or great bodily harm.

CHALLENGES IN INVESTIGATION

Police have an obligation to act on behalf of the deceased and their families. They are expected to conduct a professional investigation to identify, arrest and prosecute suspects. One apparent injustice in the criminal justice system is that to an outsider, it appears that the police are constantly trying to protect the rights of the perpetrator and pay slight attention to the rights of the deceased or the family.

Challenges in homicide investigations include pressure by the media and the public, the difficulty in establishing homicide rather than suicide or an accidental or natural death, identifying the victim and establishing the cause and time of death.

Homicides create high interest in the community, as evidenced by increased sales of newspapers and higher ratings for the news media. Indeed, the media have a special interest in police investigations of deaths—accidental or otherwise. Police officers who have dealt with the news media understand the important relationship between law enforcement and the media, as discussed in Chapter 1.

Police policies and guidelines should specify what information is to be released: the deceased's name, accused's name and general identifying information; any details regarding formal charges; and general facts about the investigation that are not harmful to the continuing investigation.

Do not pose the accused for photographs, and do not permit the accused to talk to the press. If investigators have details known only to them and the accused, that information must not be released. Exercising good sense, getting to know the reporters personally and refraining from giving off-the-record comments will prevent many problems. Reporters have a right to be at the scene, and cooperation is the best policy—within the policies and guidelines of the department.

From time to time, public outrage over particular crimes places increased pressure on the police to solve murders. A more serious problem is the difficulty of establishing that a crime has, in fact, been committed. Search warrants can be issued if proof of a crime exists; however, such proof may not be legally available without a warrant. In addition, many perpetrators attempt to make the crime scene look as if a robbery or burglary has taken place. It can also be difficult to determine whether the death was homicide or suicide.

EQUIVOCAL DEATH

Equivocal death investigations are situations that are open to interpretation. The case may present as homicide, suicide or accidental death. The facts may be intentionally vague or misleading as in staged crime scenes. A staged crime scene is one where a killer hopes to cover his or her tracks by making it look like the victim committed suicide, suffered a fatal accident or died of natural causes. Inexperienced investigators who jump to the hasty conclusion that a man found hanging in his garage or the dead woman in the bathtub with slit wrists must have committed suicide may be allowing a perpetrator to get away with murder.

A distinction exists between posing and staging. *Posing* refers to positioning of the body only, whereas *staging* refers to manipulation of the scene around the body in addition to posing of the body: "Any change in the crime scene which includes the manipulation of a victim's body is in fact staging" (Geberth, 2010b, p.30). Staging does not include actions taken by non-suspects upon discovering the victim, for example, when a husband discovers

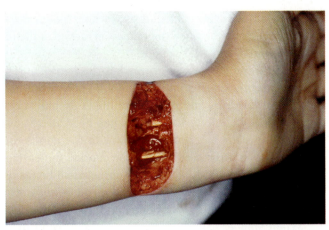

A slit wrist is often interpreted as a suicide indicator. Investigators should not automatically conclude that a person whose wrists are slit did, in fact, commit suicide.
© Dr. Lindsey Thomas

the naked body of his murdered wife and covers, dresses or moves the body before the police arrive in an effort to spare the victim further insult and embarrassment: "In death investigations, surviving family members and loved ones experience extreme emotional upset. Such persons may unintentionally do things in the crime scene out of shock or confusion. That is why it is important in the initial interviews that investigators learn from the survivors exactly what transpired and what actions were carried out prior to the arrival of the police" (Geberth, 2010b, p.29).

A critical piece of the investigation is assessing the victimology because it helps investigators develop and ascertain suspects, motives and risk factors: "Victimology is the collection and assessment of all significant information as it relates to the victim and his lifestyle. Personality, employment, education, friends, habits, hobbies, marital status, relationships, dating history, sexuality, reputation, criminal record, history of alcohol or drugs, physical condition and neighborhood of residence are all pieces of the mosaic that comprise victimology" (Geberth, 2008, p.83). What was the victim's state of mind in the days leading up to the death? Had the victim made long-term plans, such as having purchased plane tickets for a vacation, prepaid membership dues or begun a major house renovation project? Answers to these questions may not support an initial assessment of suicide. The prudent investigator approaches all equivocal death scenes as if they were homicides until forensic evaluation of evidence can point one way or the other—homicide or not.

Another equivocal death situation involves sudden, unexplained infant death (SUID), which is not to be confused with SIDS or sudden infant death syndrome. SIDS is the sudden death of a child under age one that remains unexplained even after a thorough investigation involving a complete autopsy, examination of the death scene and review of the infant's clinical history. It is a "diagnosis of exclusion," when all other possible causes of death (disease, illness, abuse, etc.) have been explored and ruled out. SUID is a pre-investigative term. A SUID case, after a thorough investigation, may be classified as SIDS (approximately 85 percent of cases) or will identify another cause of death, such as homicide. Investigating SUID is covered in Chapter 11.

Sudden in-custody deaths (SICD) present a tremendous challenge to investigators. These cases typically involve suspects who have been restrained for some time, during which they enter a state of medical crisis and die. Families of the deceased frequently file lawsuits claiming that police brutality caused the death, and the officers involved contend that the restrained person succumbed to some type of preexisting physical defect (weak heart, aneurysm, etc.) brought about by the subject's own state of agitation. Sometimes this state is referred to as *excited delirium*, as discussed in Chapter 7, and the deaths that result are often complex and multifactorial, with metabolic (e.g., low blood sugar), infectious (e.g., meningitis), psychological (e.g., underlying psychiatric illness), pharmacologic (e.g., cocaine or other stimulant abuse) or a combination of these factors constituting the primary and chronic risks (Peters, 2007). The four phases generally observed in a person experiencing excited delirium are (1) profuse sweating, which may indicate a high core body temperature; (2) delirium with agitation; (3) compromised breathing and respiratory arrest; and finally (4) cardiac arrest (Peters, 2007).

Because police are involved in the death, a thorough but objective investigation is critical:

> The investigator(s) should determine if the body is still at the scene. If so, information and photographs should be obtained and taken regarding the body's final position, location, clothing, etc. If possible, it should be determined if the person had been sweating. If it appears the person had been sweating, photographs should be taken of wet clothing, perspiration on the skin, hair, etc. to highlight and confirm the sweating.
>
> A core body temperature should be taken of the decedent, regardless of where (s)he is located. Asking for a core body temperature after the medical interventions have been completed is not an unreasonable request....
>
> Determine if the person was restrained prior to his or her death, and/or was restrained at the time of death. The type of restraint(s) used (e.g., metallic, plastic, nylon, specialty restraints, combinations) should be identified in the investigation report, and photographs taken of the restraint(s) applied to the person.

One specific area of photographic interest is the decedent's thumb(s). A person who is addicted to or uses crack cocaine on a regular basis will often use a disposable lighter to heat a crack pipe . . . several times a day which will many times cause a callous to be formed on the underside of their thumbs, known as "crack thumb." (Peters and Brave, 2006, pp.56–57)

A checklist for investigating sudden in-custody deaths is provided in Appendix C. As with SUID cases, in-custody deaths must be thoroughly investigated, beginning with a complete autopsy to determine whether a heart attack, stroke or other physical condition caused the death. Autopsies of people who displayed signs of excited delirium and had been restrained at the time of, or just prior to, death have shown myocardial contraction bands and other heart abnormalities, which can help investigators assess whether the death caused by restraint was secondary to some other primary, chronic medical condition (Otahbachi et al., 2010). Sometimes an equivocal death investigation reveals the cause to be suicide.

SUICIDE

Suicide often presents as a homicide. Investigators should keep in mind that more Americans die by suicide than by homicide. Often depression or schizophrenia is involved, and usually these people have made their intentions known to someone. Therefore, investigators should try to determine whether a suspected suicide victim was suffering from depression or schizophrenia or whether the victim had talked to anyone about committing suicide.

The reason for an apparent suicide must be determined. An act that appears to be too violent for suicide and is therefore a suspected homicide may actually be a natural death. Never exclude the possibility of death from natural causes in the initial phase of an investigation because of the presence of obvious marks of violence. The abnormal activity of a person suffering from an acutely painful attack can create the appearance of a struggle. The onset of more than 70 diseases can produce sudden death. People who experience such an attack may disarrange their clothing and sustain severe injury by falling. In one case, a man shot himself to relieve excruciating pain, and the autopsy showed that a ruptured aorta caused his death, not the gunshot. What appeared to be suicide was declared to be death by natural causes.

Check for weapons on or near the body, being aware that a weapon may be underneath the body and only noticeable after the body has been moved. In one case, investigators were called to a scene where a man had died from a gunshot wound to the head at close range. Seeing no weapon present, investigators began working the scene as a homicide. However, once the body was moved, a pistol was discovered beneath the body.

Learn whether the victim was left- or right-handed and see whether this fits with the method of committing suicide. Note lividity conditions and the body's location to determine how long the person has been dead and whether the body has been moved. Note the condition of rigor mortis. Are there "hesitation marks" indicating indecision before the final act? Do not assume that any blood on the victim is the victim's; it may be from a murderer. (These issues are discussed later in the chapter.)

When smaller-caliber weapons are fired, blood may not appear on the hands of the person firing the gun. In fact, in most suicide cases, blood does not appear on the hands. A test for gunshot residue (GSR), as explained in Chapter 5, will confirm whether the deceased fired the weapon. In more than 75 percent of suicide cases in which a gun is used, the gun is not found in the victim's hand but is near the body. If the victim is found clutching a weapon, ensure that the weapon in hand was the one used to cause the death. It might be that both the victim and an assailant were armed and that the death was not suicide. In a number of suicides, the victims have multiple wounds. If evidence surfaces after the initial investigation that proves a suicide was actually a homicide, the case should be reopened.

What appears to be a double suicide can also present problems. It may be a murder-suicide. Determine who died first or who inflicted the fatal wounds. Attempt to determine the motive. Search for a note. Look for signs of a violent struggle before death. Sometimes suicide is obvious, as when suspects kill themselves to avoid being captured by the police.

To gain a better understanding of the victim's frame of mind when the suicide occurred or to reveal that the act was perhaps not suicide at all, victimology is important. Investigators must study the personality traits, character and lifestyle of the victim, reconstructing as accurately as possible the days and hours preceding the victim's death. Were there any prior suicide attempts, a history of mental illness or recent traumatic incidents? Were there any recent changes or conflicts in the victim's personal relationships? Was the victim being treated for a medical condition? Were any prescription drugs found at the scene? What was the cause of death?

Although some suicides occur without any outward warning, most people who are contemplating suicide do display noticeable warning signs, including these:

■ Observable signs of serious depression:
  · Unrelenting low mood
  · Pessimism

- Hopelessness
- Desperation
- Anxiety, psychic pain and inner tension
- Withdrawal
- Sleep problems

■ Increased alcohol and/or other drug use

■ Recent impulsiveness and taking unnecessary risks

■ Threatening suicide or expressing a strong wish to die

■ Making a plan:
  - Giving away prized possessions
  - Sudden or impulsive purchase of a firearm
  - Obtaining other means of killing oneself such as poisons or medications

■ Unexpected rage or anger ("Warning Signs of Suicide," 2011)

When investigating suspected suicides, attempt to find a note or letter. However, lack of a note does not eliminate the possibility of suicide—a suicide note is left in only a fourth of the cases investigated. If you do find a note, have it compared with the deceased's handwriting.

Also look for videos or cassettes describing the actions taken. Examine any pads of paper near the body for the presence of indentation remaining from writing on sheets of paper torn from the pad and destroyed. Look for manuals on how to commit suicide. Check on prior arrangements with an undertaker or other evidence of putting one's affairs in order.

Preserve all evidence until the medical examiner or coroner's office rules whether the death is a suicide.

Suicide by Police

Suicide by police was introduced in Chapter 7 and refers to a situation in which a person decides he or she wants to die but does not want to pull the trigger. Such people may lack the constitution to take their own lives and take the option of forcing a police officer to do it for them; or they may view suicide as socially or religiously unacceptable but believe that if they are killed by police, the stigma of suicide will be averted and society may see them as victims. Some insurance policies will not pay if a person commits suicide, making suicide by cop an attractive option for those bent on killing themselves.

Often such cases involve a "man-with-a-gun" call. Arriving police are confronted with a person acting bizarrely and threatening to shoot himself or herself, a hostage or the responding officers. In many instances, the gun is not loaded, is a fake or is inoperative, but if it is pointed at the police, the police are forced to shoot. The actions of armed individuals who go out of their way to provoke a lethal response by police have led those in academia to refer to such suicide-by-cop incidents as "victim-precipitated."

When investigating a suspected case of suicide by cop, a critical element to determine is the probable motivation of the offender/victim. Suicide-by-cop offender profiles indicate that such subjects often have a poor self-image, feel a sense of guilt for harm they have caused, talk about death and express a desire to be with deceased loved ones, speak often of a higher being, are aggressively confrontational with police and possess an unloaded or nonfunctioning (toy) gun. Other issues that may potentially indicate suicidal motivations include

■ Financial concerns

■ Divorce or serious relationship issues

■ Loss of a job or retirement

■ Being investigated

■ Health problems

The presence of such factors may help officers identify potential suicide-by-cop cases. Investigators must evaluate the totality of physical evidence and behavioral indicators to accurately assess whether the incident is one of suicide by cop, as no single piece of evidence, action or behavior is usually sufficient to establish an offender's motivation.

Whatever the circumstances, a police officer who is forced to take a life may suffer emotionally. In some instances, officers who have taken a life end up taking their own.

Suicide of Police Officers

There is no question—police work is stressful. And it can take its toll in tragic ways. Although many consider police work to be a dangerous profession primarily because of the risk of encountering violent and armed individuals, more officers lose their lives to suicide than to homicide. Some data show that officers are three times more likely to die by their own hands as they are to be killed by criminals in the line of duty (Sanow, 2008). Grossi (2007, p.34) reports, "Some studies indicate police officers are eight times more likely to kill themselves than to die by felonious assault. Other experts report that police officers have a three times greater chance of taking their own life than to die in a job-related accident, and that they are twice as likely to commit suicide as other municipal workers. The National Police Suicide Foundation out of Pasadena, Maryland, reports that two to three times as many cops die by their hand than get killed on the job." Whichever study one chooses to reference, the fact remains that suicide rates for police—at least 18 per 100,000—are higher than for the general population (J. Ritter, 2007).

Contributing factors in police suicides, as with other victims of suicide, are alcohol, family issues and the breakup of relationships. Similar to the increased risk faced by military personnel who return to civilian life and succumb to suicide as a result of the traumatic experience of serving combat duty, police officers can suffer from post-traumatic stress disorder (PTSD) brought about by traumatic events they face on the job, such as seeing murdered children or other victims of brutal crimes, or being involved in a shooting. PTSD contributes to depression and various forms of addiction and can lead to suicide.

The public's image of the police, and indeed officers' image of themselves, is that of the strong protector of society. Yet police work forces officers to confront the dark side of human nature daily and may eventually cause officers to lose their faith in the goodness of humanity or in their abilities to make a positive impact on the lives of others. This sense of weakness and failure is so contradictory to the image of the police that some officers may simply see no other choice than to "take themselves out of the game."

About 97 percent of officer suicides involve their own duty weapon: "Officers have a special relationship with their gun. It is a source of control, of confidence and of comfort…. Although some critics argue the high rate of using a gun in a police-involved suicide is due to accessibility, others disagree saying, 'The weapon has a significance. It has an identity. It becomes someone who is trustworthy, reliable and someone with a solution'" (Perin, 2007, p.14).

When an officer commits suicide, the family—and sometimes the first officer on the scene—may attempt to make the death look accidental or like a homicide to avoid the stigma of suicide or to ensure that the family can collect the life insurance. Any officer's death requires a thorough investigation. As with suspected suicide-by-cop incidents, investigation into the officer's prior mental/emotional status (presence of depression, post-traumatic stress disorder), substance use or abuse, family situations (divorce, death of a spouse or child), financial status (large debts) and health (serious or chronic illness) provide critical insight into possible motivations for suicide. Being under an internal affairs investigation and facing the potential loss of one's identity as an officer is the most compelling reason for an officer to make a hasty decision to commit suicide.

Once forensic examination concludes that a death was caused by suicide, the investigation is over and the case closed. For those cases that are homicides, a thorough criminal investigation must be conducted.

PRELIMINARY INVESTIGATION OF HOMICIDE

"The homicide crime scene is, without a doubt, the most important crime scene to which a police officer or investigator will be called upon to respond," says Geberth (2006, p.140). He explains, "Because of the nature of the crime, death by violence or unnatural causes, the answer to what happened can be determined only after a careful and intelligent examination of the scene. The preliminary investigation conducted at the scene by the detectives will provide for the intelligent and effective retrieval of evidence paramount to the successful conclusion and prosecution of the case" (p.140).

The initial investigation of a homicide is basically the same as for any other crime, although it may require more flexibility, logic and perseverance. The primary goals of the investigation are (1) to establish whether a human death was caused by the criminal act or omission of another and (2) to determine who caused the death. *Promoting Effective Homicide Investigations* (Cronin et al., 2007) is a valuable resource for homicide investigators and covers clearance rates, managing homicide units, eyewitness identification, videotaping interrogations and cold case investigations.

The homicide case normally begins with a report of a missing person or the discovery of a body. The officer in the field seldom makes the initial discovery. The first notification is received by the police communications center or a dispatcher who records the date, time and exact wording used. Because the original call is sometimes made anonymously by a suspect, a voice recording is made for comparison with later suspects.

In *Flippo v. West Virginia* (1999), the Supreme Court held that police may make warrantless entries onto premises where they reasonably believe a person is in need of immediate aid or may make a prompt warrantless search of a homicide scene for other victims or a killer on the premises. However, the Court specifically rejected the idea that there is any general "murder scene exception" to the search warrant requirement of the Fourth Amendment. The situation qualifies as simply an exigent circumstance.

A study of 800 homicide cases ("Secrets of Success," 2000, p.1) found that investigators are more likely to clear a homicide if they arrive within 30 minutes of being notified, as compared with half an hour or longer. The researchers also found that following up on witness information made it more than twice as likely that a case would be solved and if that information proved valuable, more than 17 times as likely. Furthermore, the study (p.6) found, "The behavior of police at crime scenes plays a significant role, as well. Cases were less likely to be solved if the first officer at the scene failed to notify the homicide unit, medical examiner or crime lab. The chances of solving the case also fell if the first officer did not attempt to round up witnesses." As in any crime scene investigation, the first officer on the scene is extremely important.

As you enter the scene, it is important to introduce yourself, identify key personnel and assess the safety of the scene. The first priority is to make sure the scene is safe and to protect yourself, others and the victim from further danger posed by a suspect who might still be on scene and able to cause more harm. Then, the second priority is to render aid to the victim, making sure an ambulance is en route.

> After ensuring the safety of the scene, the priority is to give emergency aid to the victim if he or she is still alive or to determine that death has occurred.

If the suspect is still at the scene, priorities may differ slightly. An ideal outcome would be to take the suspects into custody and secure them after the victim has been attended to. However, if the suspect flees when you arrive, prioritize medical aid to the victim and others over pursuing the suspect. Normally, however, the suspect is not at the scene, and the victim is the first priority. If the victim is obviously dying, take a dying declaration. The live victim is taken to a hospital as rapidly as possible.

The first officer on the scene determines the path to the victim that will least disturb evidence and sets up the taped-off restricted crime scene area. If the victim is obviously dead, the body remains at the scene until the preliminary investigation is complete. It is then taken to the morgue by the medical examiner or coroner for postmortem examination or autopsy.

Following the assessment of the victim, investigators must document everything they can about the scene. This includes detaining and identifying everyone present, obtaining brief statements from each, maintaining control of the scene and everyone present, listing all officers present upon the investigator's arrival and throughout the investigation and recording the presence of all other personnel at the scene (medical personnel, coroner, family members). A death-scene checklist developed by the FBI can help ensure a thorough preliminary investigation. This checklist is reprinted in Appendix D.

Determining That Death Has Occurred

Medically, death is determined by the cessation of three vital functions: heartbeat, respiration and brain activity. The first two signs are observable.

> Signs of death include lack of breathing, lack of heartbeat, lack of flushing of the fingernail bed when pressure is applied to the nail and then released and failure of the eyelids to close after being gently lifted.

Cessation of respiration is generally the first visible sign of death. However, in cases such as barbiturate overdoses, breathing can be so shallow that it is undetectable. Therefore, always check for a heartbeat and pulse. Except in some drug overdoses and with certain types of blindness, failure of the pupils to dilate in reaction to light is also a sign of death.

If the victim appears to have died at the moment of the officer's arrival or dies in the officer's presence, the officer should attempt resuscitation with the standard cardiopulmonary resuscitation methods.

Securing and Documenting the Scene

As with any other criminal investigation, the homicide scene must be secured, photographed and sketched. Videotaping the crime scene can produce excellent results and is being done more frequently. All evidence must be obtained, identified and properly preserved. Physical evidence can be found on the body, at the scene or on the suspect.

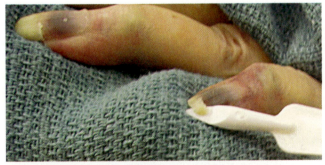

Broken nails on a homicide victim may indicate a violent struggle occurred during the commission of the crime. In such cases, the suspect's DNA may be found underneath the victim's fingernails.
© Dr. Lindsey Thomas

In violent homicides, the victim may grab the suspect's hair, shirt buttons or other parts of clothing or scratch and claw the suspect. A victim may leave injuries on the suspect, and traces of the suspect's flesh may be found under the victim's fingernails. Identify and preserve all belongings and evidence on or near the deceased. Carefully examine the location where the body was found even if it is not where death occurred.

 Physical evidence in a homicide includes a weapon, a body, blood, hairs and fibers.

Any of the various types of evidence discussed in Chapter 5 can be present at a homicide scene. Especially important are the body and the weapon.

Collecting and Moving the Body

After the entire scene and the evidence have been photographed and sketched, move the body carefully. Lift it a few inches off the surface and slide a sheet under it to catch any evidence that may fall while transporting the body to the vehicle. Itemize other possessions and send them along with the body to the morgue for later release to the family if they are not evidence. Although you may use a body bag, first wrap the body in a clean, white sheet. Evidence on the body that falls off is much easier to see on a sheet. The sheet also absorbs moisture.

The Focus of the Homicide Investigation

After priority matters are completed, the focus of the homicide investigation is to

■ Identify the victim.

■ Establish the time of death.

■ Establish the cause of and the method used to produce death.

■ Develop a suspect.

The preliminary investigation either accomplishes these things or provides leads that investigators can follow up.

A fact-finding capsule such as that shown in Figure 8.1 might guide homicide investigations.

Three important rules govern these investigative tactics:

■ *Specificity.* Explore all issues to obtain precise facts and enough details to make objective judgments and correlations.

■ *Element of surprise.* Keep witnesses from comparing stories and deny suspects time to cover their tracks or create alibis.

■ *Haste.* Accomplish all tasks quickly to gather and promptly develop facts.

Table 8.2 lists the investigative avenues to pursue.

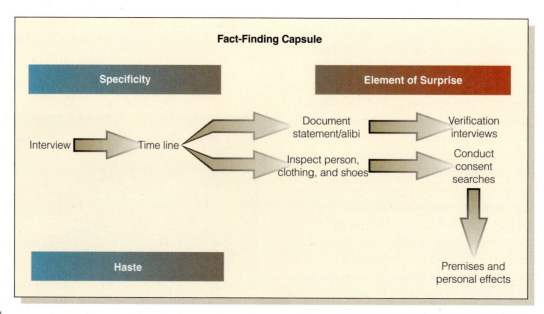

FIGURE 8.1
Fact-finding capsule.

Source: John B. Edwards. "Homicide Investigative Strategies." *FBI Law Enforcement Bulletin*, January 2005, p.12.

TABLE 8.2 Prompt Investigative Trilogy

Immediate		Pending
Specific Focus	**General Coverage**	**Informative**
Specific witnesses	Neighborhood canvass	Cell phone records
Specific evidence	Friends, family and associates (victimology)	Computer hard drives
Specific events	Coworkers	Other records
Specific facts	Victim/suspect time lines	Private papers

Source: John B. Edwards. "Homicide Investigative Strategies." *FBI Law Enforcement Bulletin*, January 2005, p.13.

THE HOMICIDE VICTIM

In most crimes, the victim provides verbal details of what occurred. In homicides, the victim may be able to provide such information if witnesses or the police are present before death occurs. However, the information usually comes from the crime scene, witnesses, physical and circumstantial evidence and the suspect.

Victims often know the persons who killed them, so information about the deceased can furnish leads to the suspect. Obtain the victim's name, address, age, sex, nationality and type and place of work. Also find out the names of family members, close friends and known enemies and learn about the victim's habits. Ask about any religious, political or business actions or remarks that might have enraged someone. Take the victim's fingerprints and determine whether any criminal history may lead to a suspect.

Interview personal contacts such as doctors, pastors or counselors to learn about the victim's physical and emotional condition, especially if it has not yet been determined whether the death was an accident, suicide or homicide. The person's medical background may provide information about an extremely painful or terminal disease that could motivate suicide. Inquire about the victim's mental stability. Most suicide victims attempt to avoid inflicting severe pain on themselves when they take their lives, but this is not always true. One woman cut off both her feet before fatally stabbing herself in the chest. Some people set themselves on fire to commit suicide.

A history of domestic violence can precede a homicide. Many batterers eventually kill their intimate partner (one out of six homicides is a partner homicide), and women who leave their batterers face a 75 percent greater risk of being killed by them than do women who stay. In some cases, batterers themselves become victims of homicide. Many of these homicides occurred despite restraining orders on the battering partner. In addition, four of five homicides by females are reported to be responses to domestic violence.

The victim's background provides information about whether the death was an accident, suicide or homicide. If a homicide, the background often provides leads to a suspect. Evidence on the victim's body can also provide important leads.

Discovering the Victim

In some cases, no body is present. It may have been burned, cut up beyond recognition or dissolved in a vat of acid. Some states allow the use of circumstantial evidence to prove the corpus delicti when no body can be found. In other cases, there is a body, but locating it is a challenge. It may have been weighted and sunk in a body of water or buried underground.

When searching for human remains, investigators can use technologies such as ground-penetrating radar, magnetometers, metal detectors and infrared thermography, which can distinguish between hidden new and old gravesites faster and more accurately than can other techniques. In addition, cadaver-search canines have proven effective: "Cadaver dogs are trained to locate and follow the scent of decomposing human flesh. Not a pretty thought, but their job is vital to both families of the victims, and to a justice system that ofttimes needs a body to prove a crime" (Mifflin, 2008). Dogs can be trained to detect human remains long after death, despite burial or attempted concealment. Trained dogs can distinguish between human remains, animal remains and a wide range of other odors that would normally be expected to distract them (Lowy and McAlhany, 2008). Their ability to distinguish between sources of similar biological odors enhances their use in human remains detection (HRD).

Identifying the Victim

Once a body is found, it must be identified.

> Homicide victims are identified by immediate family, relatives, friends or acquaintances; personal effects, fingerprints, DNA analysis and dental and skeletal studies; clothing and laundry marks; or through missing-persons files.

In many cases, identifying the deceased is no problem. The spouse, parents, a close friend or a relative makes the identification. If possible, have several people identify the body, because people under stress make mistakes. In a number of cases, a homicide victim has been identified only to turn up later alive. Although personal identification by viewing the deceased is ideal, corroborate it with other evidence. Personal effects found on the victim assist in identification. However, such personal effects may not necessarily belong to the deceased. Therefore, check them carefully.

If identification cannot be made by relatives or acquaintances or by personal effects, the most positive identification is by fingerprint or DNA analysis. Comparative fingerprints are not always available, however, and blood type does not provide a positive identification, although it can prove that a body is *not* a specific person.

Investigations involving unidentified human remains often require the involvement of experts from a variety of scientific fields, and the earlier they are brought into the case, the better the chances of resolving it. In addition to the medical examiner, the team should consist of a forensic anthropologist (to provide information on gender, height, race and age), a forensic odontologist (to provide an age range), a forensic osteologist (to determine if there is evidence of bone trauma) and a forensic entomologist (to provide information on the location and approximate time of death).

Identifying the mass fatalities resulting from the September 11, 2001, attacks presented the greatest forensic challenge in this country's history. A balance had to be struck between speed and accuracy: "To assist in this monumental effort, NIJ [National Institute of Justice] brought together a group of experts to advise and support New York City's Office of the Chief Medical Examiner during the identification effort. The Kinship and Data Analysis Panel (KADAP) made recommendations on forensic technologies, policies, and procedures to help identify victims who perished in the World Trade Center" (N. Ritter, 2007, p.20). The KADAP report, *Lessons Learned from 9/11: DNA Identification in Mass Fatality Incidents* (2006, p.1) states, "DNA analysis is the gold standard for identification of human remains from mass disasters. Particularly in the absence of traditional anthropological and other physical characteristics, forensic DNA typing allows for identification of any biological sample and the association of body parts, as long as sufficient DNA can be recovered from the samples. This is true even when the victim's remains are fragmented to inform DNA is degraded." The bulk of the report is aimed to inform technicians who perform such DNA analysis.

Cases involving unidentified human remains can be extremely challenging for criminal investigators, and these cases often intersect with missing person cases. Considering that an estimated 4,400 unidentified human remains cases are opened every year in the United States, with about 1,000 of these cases remaining unidentified after a year and going into "cold case" status, and with approximately 100,000 missing persons cases active on any given day, the need for a central repository for such case records became apparent (Pearsall and Weiss, 2009). In July 2007 the NIJ launched a program to help law enforcement agencies, medical examiners and others identify missing persons who have been murdered or have died of other causes. This program, the National Missing and Unidentified Persons (NamUs) Initiative, brings together two existing programs and their online, searchable databases: IdentifyUs.org, which contains data on unidentified human remains, and FindtheMissing.org, which provides information about missing persons.

For an unknown victim, record a complete description and take photographs if possible. Check these against missing-persons files. Circulate the description and photograph in the surrounding area. Check the victim's clothing for possible laundry marks or for labels that might indicate where the clothes were purchased. If there are leads to whom the victim might be, you can attempt identification by comparing dental charts and X-rays of prior fractures and by examining signs of prior surgical procedures, such as scars or other abnormalities.

If the body is badly decomposed, the bones provide a basis for estimating height, sex and approximate age as well as proof that the deceased was a human. Bone scans provide other leads because roughly 80 to 90 percent of skeletal remains reveal evidence of infection, arthritis or trauma (Steck-Flynn, 2008). Evidence of infection can help indicate which region of the world from which the person came and provide insight as to his or her general health at the time of death. Trauma to the bone can reveal whether an injury occurred before death or was a factor in the death: "Damaged or broken bones show signs of healing about a week after injury. If healing has begun or has already taken place, the injury did not occur at the time of death. A lack of healing indicates the injury occurred less than a week before the death, and unhealed fractures of the arms and wrists may be defense wounds" (Steck-Flynn, 2008, p.84.)

Bones often assist in identification of victims through comparison with health and dental records. If a victim's identity is unknown, bones can be used to create a facial model of what the victim may have looked like. Here, Trooper Sarah Foster, a Michigan State Police forensic artist, measures a three-dimensional facial reconstruction from an unidentified human skull at Richmond Post in Richmond, Michigan, in December, 2003. Foster didn't have formal art training when she joined the Michigan State Police three years earlier, but she has since used her artistic talents to help bolster the agency's investigative work.

© AP Images/Paul Sancya

In addition to identifying the victim, the homicide investigator must establish the time of death, typically with the help of the medical examiner or coroner.

ESTIMATING THE TIME OF DEATH (TOD)

In many homicides, there is a delay between the commission of the crime and the discovery of the body—sometimes only minutes, other times years. This period between death and corpse discovery is called the postmortem interval (PMI). Understanding the processes that occur in a body during the PMI can help investigators estimate a time of death. Research facilities, such as the Body Farm outside of Knoxville, Tennessee, are allowing forensic scientists to study and document these processes under various environmental conditions in an effort to help investigators more accurately determine the time of death. However, "Throughout the years, forensic scientists and pathologists have searched for a definitive method of determining time of death, but at present, there is no single reliable method…. Based on an appreciation of a large number of variables, an experienced pathologist can arrive at a reasonable estimation of time of death, usually placing it within a range of hours" (Geberth, 2007a, p.58).

The time of death relates directly to whether the suspect could have been at the scene and to the sequence of multiple deaths. It is also important to the victim's family in settling insurance claims and Social Security and pension payments.

Both the investigator and the medical examiner or coroner are responsible for estimating the time of death. Knowing how the professional examiner estimates time of death helps investigators to understand better what circumstances are important at the crime scene and alerts them to observe and record specific factors that aid in estimating the time of death, including environmental (or ambient) temperature. Some of these factors are available only to the first officers at the scene.

Without eyewitnesses, the time of death is seldom completely accurate. Normally, however, the time of the death—if it has occurred within the past four days—can be determined to within four hours, depending on the examiner's expertise and the factors available for examination. Figure 8.2 shows the timing of various body changes after death.

Factors that help in estimating the time of death are body temperature, rigor mortis, postmortem lividity (livor), eye appearance, stomach contents, stage of decomposition and evidence suggesting a change in the victim's normal routine.

Recent Death

A time of death that is less than one-half hour before examination is normally the easiest determination to make. The body is still warm; mucous membranes are still moist but drying; blood is still moist but drying; the pupils have begun to dilate; and in fair-skinned people, the skin is becoming pale. This characteristic of recent death becomes less discernable as skin pigmentation increases.

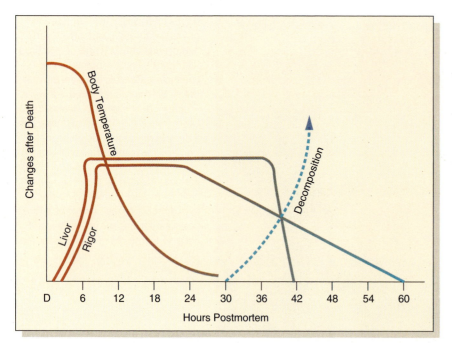

FIGURE 8.2
Timing of postmortem cooling, livor, rigor mortis and putrefactive changes.
Source: Irwin M. Sopher. "The Law Enforcement Officer and the Determination of the Time of Death." *FBI Law Enforcement Bulletin*, October 1973.

Death That Occurred One-Half Hour to Four Days Prior

Generally, if the death occurred within the past four days but more than one-half hour ago, the mucous membranes and any blood from the wounds are dry, there are skin blisters and skin slippage, the body is slightly pink, body temperature has dropped, rigor mortis and postmortem lividity are present and the pupils are restricted and cloudy.

Body Temperature. Though not an accurate measure of time of death, body temperature is helpful in conjunction with other factors. **Algor mortis** refers to the postmortem cooling process of the body and can be extremely helpful in homicide investigations. After death, the body tends to assume the temperature of its environment. Record the temperature of the surroundings and the amount of clothing on the body. Reach under the clothing to determine the body's warmth or coldness. Compare this with exposed parts of the body to determine whether the clothing is retaining body heat.

> Body temperature drops 2 to 3 degrees in the first hour after death and 1 to 1.5 degrees for each subsequent hour until 18 hours.

Some investigators use the formula of 1.5 degrees cooling per hour, assuming an internal temperature of 98.6° Fahrenheit and an environmental temperature of 70° to 75° Fahrenheit, with the rate of loss adjusted up and down depending on the actual environmental temperature and with the accuracy decreasing after 10 hours.

The formula would be $98.5 - T / 1.5 = N$, where T equals rectal temperature in degrees Fahrenheit and N is the number of hours since death.

These times vary in abnormally hot or cold environments. Also, body temperature drops more slowly in large or obese people, if a high fever was present before death, if humidity prevents evaporation or if strenuous physical activity occurred immediately before death.

Rigor Mortis. The body is limp after death until rigor mortis sets in. **Rigor mortis**, a Latin term that literally translates to "stiffness of death," is a stiffening of the joints of the body after death because of partial skeletal muscle contraction. Onset may occur anywhere from 10 minutes to several hours postmortem, depending on physical conditions concerning the body and the environment. Excitement, vigorous activity, heavy clothing and abnormally high temperatures increase the rapidity of rigor; cold slows it. Babies and the aged have little rigor.

Rigor mortis is first noticed in smaller muscles, such as those of the face, and spreads to larger muscle groups throughout the body, reaching maximum rigor between 12 and 24 hours. The body can remain rigid for approximately three days, until the muscles themselves begin to decompose, although rigor generally begins to diminish after 36 hours postmortem.

> Rigor mortis appears as a stiffening of muscles several hours after death, with maximum stiffness occurring 12 to 24 hours after death. Rigor then begins to disappear and is generally gone three days postmortem.

The degree of rigor mortis as an indicator of time of death is usually accurate to within four hours when used along with other factors, such as ambient temperature.

Postmortem Lividity. When the heart stops beating at death, the blood no longer circulates and gravity drains the blood to the body's lowest levels. This causes a dark blue or purple discoloration of the body called **postmortem lividity**, or **livor mortis**. Lividity is cherry red or a strong pink if death has been caused by carbon monoxide poisoning, and various other poisons give lividity other colors.

If a body is on its back, lividity appears in the lower portion of the back and legs. If facedown, it appears on the face, chest, stomach and legs. If the body is on its side, lividity appears on the side on which the body is resting and if the body is upright, it appears in the buttocks and lower legs.

> Postmortem lividity starts one-half to three hours after death and is congealed in the capillaries in four to five hours. Maximum lividity occurs within 10 to 12 hours.

Any part of the body pressing directly on a hard surface does not show lividity because the pressure of the body's weight prevents blood from entering the blood vessels in that area. If blood has been released from large wounds, very little if any lividity occurs.

Postmortem lividity and bruises appear similar, but they are easy to distinguish. When bruises are pressed with the thumb or fingers, they remain the same, whereas lividity turns white, or blanches, when pressure is applied. If the blood has already congealed, an incision reveals whether the blood is still in the vessels (lividity) or outside them (bruise). In addition, the color of a bruise varies, whereas the color of lividity is uniform.

> The location of lividity can indicate whether a body was moved after death.

Besides helping to establish time of death and sometimes the cause, lividity helps determine whether the body was moved after death occurred. Postmortem lividity in a body moved immediately after death would provide no clues. However, if the body was moved to a

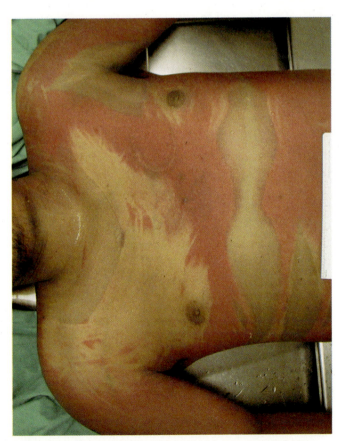

Postmortem lividity. When the heart stops beating at death, the blood no longer circulates and gravity drains the blood to the body's lowest levels. This results in a dark blue or purple discoloration. Areas of the body in hard contact with surfaces will often appear blanched because the pressure keeps blood from pooling there.
© Dr. Lindsey Thomas

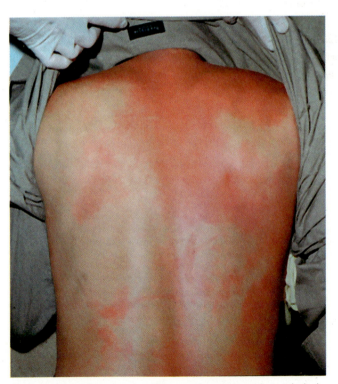

Carbon monoxide poisoning. When carbon monoxide is inhaled, it enters the bloodstream and displaces oxygen from the blood. Reddish lividity, as seen on the body in this photo, indicates carbon monoxide poisoning. This 35-year-old white male committed suicide by lying next to a running vehicle in a closed garage.
Source: Lakewood Police Department Crime Lab

different position after lividity had set in, lividity will occur in unlikely areas, indicating that the body was moved.

Examination of the Eyes.
The appearance of the eyes also assists in estimating the time of death. After death, eye muscle tone lessens and tends to disappear. The pupils tend to dilate.

> A partial restriction of the pupil occurs in about 7 hours. In 12 hours, the cornea appears cloudy.

The cornea clouds more rapidly if the eyes are open after death. During the medical examination, fluid can be withdrawn from the eyeball (or the spine) to determine the level of potassium, which tends to rise at a predictable rate after death.

Examination of Stomach Contents.
Although the stomach contents must be examined during the medical examination, the investigator can provide important information for the examiner: "It has been determined through extensive research that under ordinary circumstances, the stomach empties its contents four to six hours after a meal. If the stomach is found at autopsy to be filled with food and digestion of the contents not extensive, it is reasonable to assume that death followed shortly after the meal. If the stomach is entirely empty, death probably took place at least four to six hours after the last meal. If the small intestine is also empty, the probability is that death took place at least 12 or more hours after the last meal" (Geberth, 2007a, pp.62–63).

> Determine when and what the victim last ate. If any vomit is present, preserve it as evidence and submit it for examination.

Attempt to find out when the victim last ate. The medical examiner can often determine how long the victim lived after eating because digestion is a fairly constant process, measurable in hours. If the victim has vomited, the stomach is empty and will distort the estimate of time of death; therefore, report the presence of any vomit near the body. Preserve such vomit as evidence, as it may provide information on drugs or poisons related to the cause of death.

Many Days after Death

It is more difficult to estimate the ToD if death occurred several days before discovery of the body. The cadaver is bloated, lividity is darkened, the abdomen is greenish, blisters are filled with gas and a distinct odor is present.

The medical examiner makes a rough estimate of time of death based on the body's state of decomposition. Decomposition is first observed as an extended stomach and abdomen, the result of internal gases developing. In general, decomposition is increased by higher temperatures and decreased by lower temperatures.

If the body is in a hot, moist location, a soapy appearance called **adipocere** develops. This takes as long as three months to develop fully. Attacks by insects, bacteria, animals and birds also increase the decomposition rate.

Complete dehydration of all body tissues results in **mummification**. A cadaver left in an extremely dry, hot area will mummify in about a year and will remain in this condition for several years if undisturbed by animals or insects.

The presence on the body of insect eggs, their stage of development and the life cycle of the species, as well as various stages of vegetation on or near the body, also provide information about the time of death. A forensic entomologist (FE) can examine various types of insects to assist in estimating the time of death. Table 8.3 provides a checklist for investigators working a homicide where entomological evidence is found.

Examination of insects is especially helpful when death occurred more than a week before. Insects can detect newly dead body odors two miles away. Because particular insects work or rest during the day or the night, the types of insects at the scene provide clues as to the timing of the body's deterioration. Furthermore, it is possible to tie a suspect to the area in which a body is found by comparing evidence on the body with insect parts smashed on the suspect's windshield, grille or other vehicle parts. Rowe (2007, p.55) contends, "Forensic entomology is an exact science, supported by hard data from experiments." He notes that forensic entomologists can accurately estimate the postmortem interval and often additional information such as whether the body was moved and the location where the murder occurred. He also notes, "In some rare instances, insect evidence has been used to identify a murderer in even more spectacular ways. On one occasion, all but one part of a crushed grasshopper was found at a murder scene. The remaining piece of the puzzle, a fractured grasshopper leg, was located inside the pant cuff of the perpetrator. Yet another time, a body

TABLE 8.3 Checklist: Entomological Evidence at a Homicide Scene

Habitat

General—woods, a beach, a house, a roadside?
Vegetation—trees, grass, bush, shrubs?
Soil type—rocky, sandy, muddy?
Weather—at time of collection sunny, cloudy?
Temperature and possible humidity at time of collection?
Elevation and map coordinate of the death site?
Is the site in shade or direct sunlight?
Anything unusual, such as the possibility that the body may have been submerged in water at any time?

Remains

Presence, extent and type of clothing
Is the body buried or covered? If so, how deep and with what (soil, leaves, cloth)?
What is the cause of death, if known? In particular, is there blood at the scene?
Are any other body fluids present?
Are there any wounds? If so, what kind?
Are drugs likely to be involved? This may affect the decomposition rate.
What position is the body in?
What direction is the body facing?
What is the state of decomposition?
Is a maggot mass present? How many? This will affect the temperature of the body.
What is the temperature of the center of the maggot mass(es)?
Is there any other meat or carrion around that also might attract insects?
Is there a possibility that death did not occur at the present site?

Source: Jennifer Mertens. "It's a Bug Life." *Law Enforcement Technology,* November 2004, p.63. Reprinted by permission.

was found in one of the very few rural areas of Southern California where chiggers are known to attack humans. In this case, chigger bites found on the murderer greatly helped during court proceedings."

Effects of Water

Stevens (2007, p.110) cautions, "For too long the word 'drowning' has been synonymous with 'accident.'" An understanding of the drowning process will benefit the

Technology Innovations

Breakthroughs are being made in determining time of death, based on the progressive breakdown of biological compounds found in the human body (Geberth, 2010a, p.100):

Scientists have isolated 30 compounds specifically linked to decomposition in buried bodies.

Researchers from the University of Tennessee have identified these compounds which are uniquely human. This breakthrough will immediately be useful in creating chemicals to train cadaver dogs.

The future of forensics in recognizing the 30 human compounds of decomposition will be the development of hand-held devices, which will draw in the air with a pump to concentrate and analyze samples, which will provide an estimated time of death.

investigation by enabling detectives to recover evidence that might indicate foul play (Stevens, p.113). Bodies immersed in water for some time undergo changes that help investigators determine whether the drowning was accidental or a homicide. A body immersed in water may decompose rapidly, depending on the water temperature, salinity, mineral content and effects of fish and other marine life. Keep in mind that injuries observed on a body are not necessarily part of the cause of death. A **postmortem artifact** is an injury occurring after death from another source. An example would be fish nibbling on the skin of a drowning victim. The injuries can look as if they were related to the homicide but may actually have occurred from an outside source after death.

A dead body usually sinks in water and remains immersed for 8 to 10 days in warm water or two to three weeks in cold water. It then rises to the surface unless restricted. The outer skin loosens in five to six days, and the nails separate in two to three weeks.

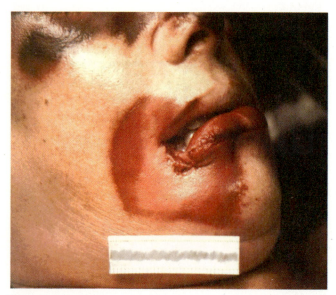

Postmortem artifact on a drowning victim. The damage to the flesh around the corner of the victim's lip and mouth occurred after death.

© Dr. Lindsey Thomas

Several factors can alert an investigator to whether a drowning is a suicide, an accident or a homicide (Stevens, 2007, p.117):

- **Body placement.** In a drowning, most victims curl up in a semi-fetal position.

- **Lividity and rigor mortis.** Lividity, position of rigor mortis and blanching of the body can show if the person was dead before entering the water.

- **The victim's eyes.** Drowning victims' eyes glisten for a short time when they are brought up but quickly dry out. If half the eye looks dry when examined immediately after being pulled from the water, the victim probably died on land.

The medical examination also determines whether the person was alive or dead at the time the body was immersed in water. This provides evidence to support homicide, suicide or accidental death.

As with insects found on bodies on land, diatoms and algal material can help forensic biologists determine the time of death for bodies found in water, as well as whether the person was drowned. Diatoms are tiny, single-celled aquatic organisms that live in both saltwater and freshwater environments. The composition of diatoms in one particular body of water or aquatic ecosystem is often unique and can be distinguished from other groups of diatoms from other locations. Thus, forensic biologists who collect diatoms from a suspect's shoes and match them to the population of diatoms existing in a pond where a murder victim was found can help investigators place that suspect at the crime scene.

Factors Suggesting a Change in the Victim's Routine

Check telephone calls made to and by the victim. Check dates on mail and newspapers and expiration dates on food in the refrigerator. Determine who normally provides services to the victim, such as dentists, doctors, barbers, hairdressers and clerks. Find out whether any appointments were not kept. Were any routines discontinued, such as playing cards or tennis, going to work on schedule or riding a particular bus? Was there food on the stove or the table? Was the stove on? Were the lights, television, radio or stereo on or off? Were pets fed? Were dirty dishes on the counters or in the sink? Was this normal for the victim? Was a fire burning in the fireplace? Was the damper left open? Determining all such facts helps estimate the ToD and can corroborate the estimate based on physical findings.

THE MEDICAL EXAMINATION OR AUTOPSY

After the preliminary investigation, the body is taken to the morgue for an autopsy, a term derived from the Greek *autopsia*, meaning "to see for oneself." Most large departments have medical examiners and forensic pathologists on staff or available as consultants for autopsies. The medical or forensic pathologist assists investigations by relating the evidence to the autopsy findings. The study of 800 homicides ("Secrets of Success," 2000, p.6) found that the presence of detectives at the postmortem examination nearly doubled the likelihood of a clearance.

The main purpose of the coroner's or medical examiner's (ME) office is to determine the cause and manner of death (Downs, 2007, p.44). If no unnatural cause is found, no crime exists. Much of the evidence that leads the examiner to conclude that the death was murder also provides corroborating evidence for investigating and prosecuting the case; therefore, pathologists and investigators work together closely.

Certain types of death must be investigated. These include all violent deaths, whether homicide, suicide or an accident; sudden deaths not caused by a recognizable disease; deaths under suspicious circumstances, including those of persons whose bodies will be cremated, dissected, buried at sea or otherwise made unavailable for further examination; deaths (other than from disease) of inmates in prisons or public institutions; deaths caused by disease that may constitute a public threat; and deaths resulting from hazardous employment.

Before an autopsy, the body is kept intact. An investigator present at the autopsy records the location, date, time, names of those attending and the name of the person

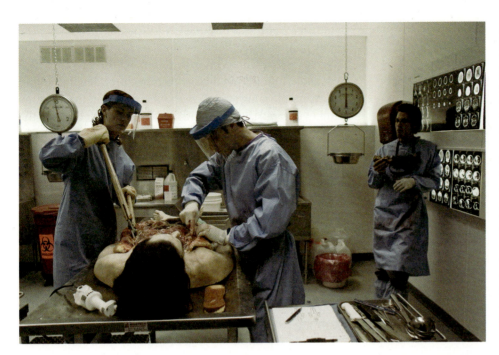

A medical examination or an autopsy provides legal evidence related to the cause and time of death and the presence of alcohol or drugs in the system of the deceased. The main job of the coroner's or medical examiner's office is to determine the cause of death. Much of the evidence that leads the examiner to conclude a death was murder also provides corroborating evidence for investigating and prosecuting the case; therefore, pathologists and investigators work together closely. Before an autopsy, the body condition is kept intact and is photographed in this state. In addition to being weighed and measured, the body is periodically photographed as each stage of the examination is completed.

© Photos 12/Alamy

who performs the autopsy. The body is weighed, measured and photographed before the autopsy begins and is then periodically photographed as each stage is completed. Facial features and any marks, cuts, wounds, bruises or unusual conditions are photographed close up. The deceased, including clothing, is completely described. The clothing is tagged, marked for identification and sent to the police laboratory for examination. Fingerprints are usually taken, even if the body has been personally identified.

> The medical examination provides legal evidence related to the cause and time of death and to the presence of drugs or alcohol.

After the autopsy is completed, the cause of death, if determined, is recorded. Deaths not recorded as natural, suicide or accidental are recorded as either undetermined or homicide. Before making a final determination, the medical examiner reads the police investigation reports to date. These reports indicate prior symptoms such as vomiting, a comatose state, partial paralysis, slow or rapid respiration, convulsions and various colorations.

During the investigation, report everything relating to the cause of death to the pathologist. Likewise, information discovered by the pathologist is conveyed to the investigative team.

All states have passed laws mandating that before any body is cremated, the coroner must approve the cremation. Although an autopsy is not typically done in most cases of death, the body is examined and X-rays are usually taken. This law is intended to decrease the likelihood of a murder going unnoticed.

Exhuming a Body for Medical Examination

It is not common to exhume a body. Usually this is done to determine whether the cause of death stated on the death certificate is valid. It may also be done if the body is suspected of having been buried to conceal the cause of death or if the identity of the body is in question.

Exhuming a body requires adherence to strict legal procedures to prevent later civil action by relatives. First, obtain permission from the principal relatives. If they do not grant it, it is necessary to obtain a court order to proceed. Arrange to have the coroner or medical examiner, a police representative, a gravedigger, a cemetery official and a family member present at the exhumation. Have the cemetery official or the person who placed the marker identify the grave. Photograph the general area, the specific grave with the marker and the coffin before exhumation.

Present at the lid opening at the morgue are the coroner, police, family, undertaker and pathologist. The body is then identified by the persons present if they knew the deceased, and the examination is conducted.

UNNATURAL CAUSES OF DEATH AND METHOD USED

As just discussed, in all cases of violent death, industrial or accidental death or suicide, the medical examiner determines the cause of death. A number of deaths involve circumstances that are investigated by police and the medical examiner, even though many are not criminal homicides.

> Among the most common causes of unnatural death are gunshot wounds; stabbing and cutting wounds; blows from blunt objects; asphyxia induced by choking, drowning, smothering, hanging, strangulation, gases or poisons; poisoning and drug overdose; burning; explosions, electrocution and lightning; drugs; and vehicles.

Table 8.4 indicates the probability of a specific cause of death being the result of an accident, suicide or homicide.

Gunshot Wounds

Most deaths caused by gunshot wounds result from discharges of handguns, rifles or shotguns. Knowing the type of weapon is important for making comparison tests and locating unknown weapons. The major cause of death from

TABLE 8.4 Cause of Death and the Likelihood It Resulted from Accident, Suicide or Homicide

Cause of Death	Accident	Suicide	Homicide
Gunshot wound	*	*	*
Stabbing and cutting wounds	Rare	*	*
Blow from blunt object			
Fall	*	*	*
Hit-and-run vehicle	*	*	*
Asphyxia			
Choking	*		
Drowning	*	*	*
Hanging	Autoerotic	*	Rare
Smothering	*		Rare
Strangulation	Autoerotic	Rare	*
Poisoning and overdose	*	*	*
Burning	*		
Explosion	*		
Electric shock	*	Rare	
Lightning	*		

gunshot wounds is internal hemorrhaging and shock. The size, number and velocity of the ammunition used and the type of weapon determine the effect on the body.

Shots fired from a large distance produce little or no powder tattooing or carbons on the skin around where the bullet entered the body, and it is difficult to determine the exact distance—even though the angle of trajectory can be determined from the bullet's path through the body. In the intermediate-distance range, tattooing appears on the clothing or the body when handguns are fired from as much as approximately 2 feet away. Powder tattooing results from both burned and unburned powder. By using test-firing pattern comparisons with the same weapon and ammunition, the actual firing distance can be determined. GSR evidence was discussed in Chapter 5.

If the muzzle of the weapon was in direct contact with the body, contact wounds will be evident. You may notice a muzzle impression on the skin and soot or powder fragments in the entrance area or around the wound. At the entry point, the hole is smaller than the bullet because the skin's elasticity closes the entry point slightly. Entrance wounds are normally round or oval with little bleeding. As the bullet passes through the skin, it leaves a gray to black abrasion collar around the edges of the entrance wound.

The exit wound is usually larger than the entrance wound, but this is not always the case. The exit wound also bleeds more profusely and has no abrasion collar. It is typically larger because gases build up in the body, especially from shots at close range, and tissues bunch up ahead of the bullet until reaching the outer skin. Elasticity then forces the skin outward until it breaks, permitting

The muzzle impression on the skin around the gunshot wound indicates the weapon was held in direct contact with the body. Gun powder residue on the victim's hand may support suicide, as would a wound occurring on the same side of the head as the victim's handedness (i.e., a right-handed victim would usually hold a gun to the right side of his or her own head).

the bullet and the gases to pass through. The exit wound is generally jagged and torn. The difference between entrance and exit wounds is observable.

Shotgun wounds are distinctly different because numerous pellets penetrate the body. At close range these leave a much larger hole than does a bullet, and at farther range, they produce a discernible pellet pattern. Both the entrance and exit wounds are larger than those produced by single bullets.

Shotgun-wound patterns and the appearance of entrance and exit wounds from handguns and rifles help determine the distance from which the gun was fired. Contact wounds (fired at point-blank range) cause a large entrance wound with smudging around the edges. The principal damage is caused by the blasting and flame of the powder. Smudging around a wound can be wiped off, but the tattooing pattern cannot be eliminated. If the gun is more than 18 inches from the body when fired, no tattooing or smudging occurs.

In addition, a bullet or pellets from any weapon produce a track through the body that follows the angle between the weapon and the victim at the time of firing. The bullet's path or angle helps determine the angle at which the weapon was fired and therefore the suspect's possible location at the time of firing. This angle also helps differentiate between suicide and murder.

When investigating gunshot deaths, determine whether the death was the result of the wound or from some other injury. Was the wound impossible for the victim to have produced? What is the approximate distance from which the weapon was fired? Were there one or more wounds? Examine the victim's hands to determine whether he or she fired the gun. What was the position of the body when found?

Gunshot wounds

- *Suicide indicators:*
  - Gun held against skin
  - Wound in mouth or in the right temple if victim is right-handed and the left temple if left-handed
  - Not shot through clothing, unless shot in the chest
  - Weapon present, especially if tightly held in hand
- *Homicide indicators:*
  - Gun fired from more than a few inches away
  - Angle or location that rules out self-infliction
  - Shot through clothing
  - No weapon present

Stabbing and Cutting Wounds

Stabbing and cutting wounds differ in shape, size and extent of external and internal bleeding. A knife is the most frequently used weapon. The weapon and wound can be different sizes, depending on the depth and severity of the wound and whether it is into or across the tissues and fibers.

Stab Wounds. Stab wounds are caused by thrusting actions. They vary in size in different areas of the body but are usually smaller than cutting wounds. A stab wound in a soft part of the body produces a larger hole than does one in the head or a bony area. Ice-pick wounds in a skull covered by a substantial amount of hair can easily be missed on initial examination.

The major damage in stab wounds is to internal tissues, followed by bleeding, primarily internal. The extent and rapidity of internal bleeding depends on the size of the blood vessels affected. In most cases, the cause of death is bleeding rather than damage to a vital organ. A stab wound can be deeper than the length of the weapon used because the force of the thrust on the softer tissues can compress the body's surface inward.

Even if a weapon is found, it can rarely be designated as the murder weapon unless part of it separates and remains in the body or it contains blood, tissue and fibers from the deceased.

Most stabbing deaths are homicides. In homicides, stab wounds can be single or multiple and can be in several areas of the body if the victim attempted self-defense. **Defense wounds**—cuts on the hands, arms and legs—result when the victim attempts to ward off the attacker.

Cutting Wounds. With cutting wounds, external bleeding is generally the cause of death. Cutting wounds are frequently the result of suicide. It is common in such cases to observe **hesitation wounds** in areas where the

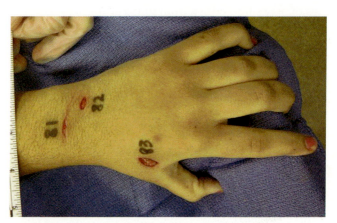

Defensive stab wounds on the hand of a homicide victim.
© Dr. Lindsey Thomas

main wound occurs. These less severe, superficial cutting marks are caused by attempts to build up enough nerve to make the fatal wound.

Suicidal cutting wounds are made at an angle related to the hand that held the weapon, generally in a downward direction because of the natural pull of the arm as it is brought across the body.

> **Stabbing and cutting wounds**
>
> ■ *Suicide indicators:*
> - Hesitation wounds
> - Wounds under clothing
> - Weapon present, especially if tightly clutched
> - Usually wounds at throat, wrists or ankles
> - Seldom disfigurement
> - Body not moved
>
> ■ *Homicide indicators:*
> - Defense wounds
> - Wounds through clothing
> - No weapon present
> - Usually injuries to vital organs
> - Disfigurement
> - Body moved

Blows from Blunt Objects

Fatal injuries can result from hands and feet and blows with various blunt objects, including hammers, clubs, heavy objects and rocks. It is often impossible to determine the specific type of weapon involved. The injuries can occur to any part of the body and can result in visible external bruises. The size of the bruise may not correspond to the size of the weapon because blood escapes into a larger area. Severe bruises are not often found in suicides.

In battered-child investigations, it has been found that death rarely results from a single blow or a single series of blows but, rather, from physical abuse over an extended period. An autopsy reveals prior broken bones or injuries. Death may also have been caused by starvation or other forms of neglect.

Falls can cause death or can be used to conceal the real cause of death. In some cases, the victim is taken to a staircase and pushed down after being severely beaten. Intoxication is often given as the reason for the fall, but this can easily be checked through blood tests.

Asphyxia

Asphyxiation results when the body tissues and the brain receive insufficient oxygen to support the red blood cells. An examination of blood cells shows this lack of

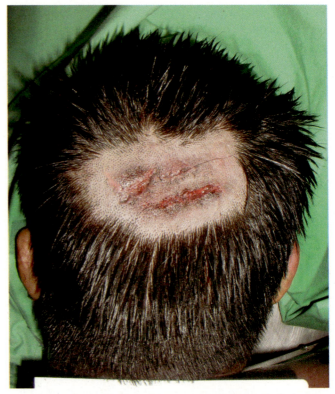

Lacerations caused by blunt force trauma on the head of a homicide victim.
© Dr. Lindsey Thomas

oxygen. Discoloration occurs in all dead bodies, but in asphyxia deaths, it is usually more pronounced and varied because of the lack of oxygen—especially in the blood vessels closest to the skin surface. It is most noticeable as a blue or purple color around the lips, fingernails and toenails. Although you need not know the varied coloration produced by different causes and chemicals, be certain to record precise descriptions of coloration that can be interpreted by the medical examiner and related to probable cause of death.

Asphyxia deaths result from many causes, including choking, drowning, smothering, hanging, strangulation, swallowing of certain chemicals, poisoning and overdosing on sleeping pills. Asphyxiation may also result from certain types of autoerotic behavior.

Choking. Foreign bodies in the throat cause choking, as do burial in grain or sand slides or rapid pneumonia in infants in cribs. Such deaths are almost always accidental.

Drowning. Most drownings are accidental. Homicide is rarely proven unless witnesses are present. If a dead body is placed in water to make it appear as though death was caused by drowning, a medical examination can determine whether the person was dead when immersed.

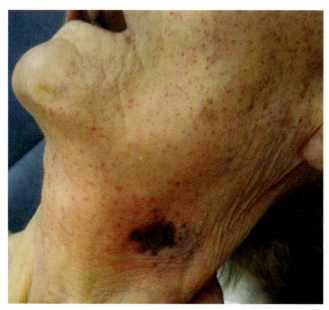

Petechiae—small spots or blotches caused by hemorrhaging—on the face or neck can be a sign of death by asphyxiation.
© Dr. Lindsey Thomas

If accidental or suicide, diatoms and algal material will be found in lungs. In a homicide, diatoms or algae may be found on the mouth or lips but not in the lungs. However, if the victim was killed by drowning, these organisms would be sucked into the lungs as the person struggled to escape and surface, similar to what happens to someone who accidentally drowns.

Smothering. Smothering is an uncommon means of homicide, despite many fictional depictions of this method. Intoxicated persons, the elderly and infants are most likely to be victims of smothering, usually by the hands or a pillow. Often, however, such deaths are accidental. For example, an infant weak from disease may turn over, face downward or become tangled in bedclothes and accidentally suffocate.

Hanging. Hangings are normally suicides, but homicides have been made to appear as suicides. Some hangings result from experimentation to achieve sexual satisfaction, as discussed later. In suicides, the pressure on the neck is usually generated by standing on a chair or stool and kicking the support away, jumping off or simply letting the body hang against the noose. (A body need not be completely suspended to result in death by hanging.) Although it is commonly thought that death results from a broken neck, it is usually the result of a broken trachea or a complete constriction of the air supply.

In hangings, the ligature marks start from the area of the neck below the chin and travel upward to the point just below the ears. The ligature marks form an inverted

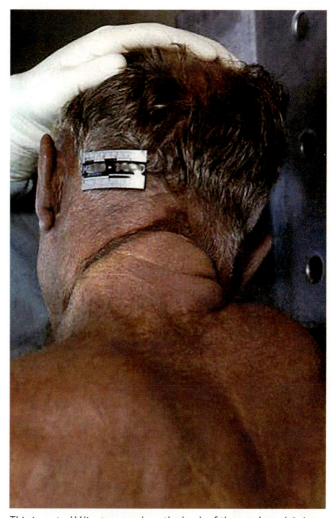

This inverted V ligature mark on the back of the man's neck is indicative of suicidal hanging.
© Dr. Lindsey Thomas

V across the back of the neck, which indicates the death was likely a suicide and not a homicide by strangulation, as strangulations do not typically leave an inverted V mark. Observe the condition and angle of these marks and save the entire rope, including the knot, as evidence.

Strangulation. Strangulation by rope, hands, wire or scarf produces the same effect as hanging. In both, the cause of death is total constriction of air. In contrast to hangings, however, the ligature marks caused by strangulation are normally evenly grooved and are horizontal around the neck. In cases of manual strangulation, marks often remain from the hand pressure.

In asphyxiation deaths, most cases of choking, drowning and smothering are accidental; most cases of hanging are suicides; most cases of strangulation are homicide.

Poisons, Chemicals and Overdoses of Sleeping Pills.
Asphyxiating chemicals, including ammonia and chloroform, can cause irritation severe enough to totally constrict the breathing passages. Ingestion of certain chemicals and drugs can also cause constriction and blockage of the airways. Examination of the air passages indicates paralysis.

Asphyxiation can occur by breathing carbon monoxide (CO), a method chosen by some to commit suicide. Accidental carbon monoxide poisoning can occur from improperly installed or malfunctioning gas appliances, such as furnaces, water heaters and clothes dryers. Using charcoal grills indoors or burning wood in an improperly vented fireplace can also lead to CO poisoning.

Autoerotic Asphyxiation.
In **autoerotic asphyxiation**, the victim has sought to intensify sexual gratification by placing a rope or other ligature around the neck and causing just enough constriction to create *hypoxia*, or a deficiency of oxygen in the bloodstream that results in semiconsciousness. Such experimentation may be successful a number of times, but then results in total unconsciousness rather than semiconsciousness. In such a case, the body goes limp in the noose, and the body's weight tightens the noose, causing death. Although not common, autoerotic asphyxiation should be recognized by police officers. In these instances, suicides are in fact tragic accidents that occurred during dangerous autoerotic acts. Such deaths are classified into three categories: suffocation, strangulation and chemical asphyxia—the most common of which is strangulation resulting from suspension of the body. In such cases, the body is usually touching the ground and the victim is often bound. Analysis will show, however, that the binding could have been done by the victim.

Indicators of accidental death during autoerotic practices include

- Nude or sexually exposed victim
- Evidence of solo sexual activity
- Mirrors placed to observe the ritual
- Evidence of masturbation and presence of such items as tissues or towels for cleanup
- Presence of sexual fantasy aids or sexually stimulating paraphernalia (vibrators, dildos, sex aids and pornographic magazines)
- Presence of bondage

In addition to asphyxiation, investigators should be aware of other types of autoerotic fatalities.

Other Types of Autoerotic Death
There is limited clinical or forensic information about other autoerotic fatalities, but in several documented cases, an act of risky solitary sexual behavior went further than anticipated, leading to accidental death. Such fatalities have involved electrocution, crushing, sepsis following perforation of the bowel and accidental self-impalement. Investigators should look for similar types of indicators as described under "Autoerotic Asphyxiation" earlier. Such accidental fatalities can easily be misinterpreted as suicide.

Poisoning
Poisoning, one of the oldest methods of murder, can occur from an overwhelming dose that causes immediate death or from small doses that accumulate over time and cause death. Poisons can be injected into the blood or muscles, inhaled as gases, absorbed through the skin surface, taken in foods or liquids or inserted into the rectum or vagina. Steck-Flynn (2007, p.118) contends, "The savvy detective familiarizes himself with the signs of accidental poisoning, signs of possible toxins and the forensic tests used to prove homicidal poisoning took place." She notes, "The terminally ill, mentally incapacitated, drug addicts, the elderly, and the very young are at highest risk of poisoning. The other high-risk group is the unwanted spouse or lover." Perpetrators of homicidal poisonings are often employed in the medical or caregiving fields (p.120).

Homicidal poisoning can be accomplished with any one of thousands of substances, but some are far more common that others. Among the most commonly used is arsenic, known as the King of Poisons and the Poison of Kings. Cyanide, also commonly used, is a favorite in mass homicides, suicides and politically motivated killings. Strychnine, given in large enough doses, produces "a dramatic and horrifying death with the victim's body frozen in mid-convulsion, eyes wide open" (Steck-Flynn, 2007, pp.121–124). Experts in **toxicology** (the study of poisons) can determine the type of poison, the amount ingested, the approximate time ingested and the effect on the body.

Investigators should ask several specific questions to help determine if a homicidal poisoning has occurred (Steck-Flynn, 2007, p.125):

- Was the death sudden?
- Has the caregiver been associated with other illnesses or death?
- Did the victim receive medical treatment and appear to recover, only to die later?
- Did the caregiver have access to restricted drugs or other chemicals?

■ Was the victim isolated by the caregiver? Did the caregiver position himself or herself to be the only one with access to the victim's food or medications?

■ Was there a history of infidelity of either the victim or spouse?

■ Is there a history of the deaths of more than one child?

If a child is poisoned by accidentally ingesting cleaning fluid, detergents, pills or other such substances, the parents are sometimes charged with manslaughter or negligent homicide.

An overdose death is not necessarily a suicide. It might have been accidental—a result of the person's not knowing when medication was last taken or being in a semi-stupor and taking more pills than intended. If a prescription bottle is found, determine from family members how many pills were in the bottle before the death. Check with the issuing pharmacist to determine whether it was a legal prescription, how many pills were prescribed and the date the prescription was last filled. Preserve all evidence until the coroner's office rules the death accidental or a suicide. Other important evidence includes the medicine cabinet's contents, any excretions or vomit at the scene and any food the victim recently ate.

Burning

Most deaths by burning are accidental. However, a death resulting from burns received in a fire caused by arson is classified as homicide. Moreover, people sometimes try to

A charred human arm, with a beer can still in hand. In this case, a victim was found lying on a couch, with his hand still wrapped around a beer can. An investigator would need to determine if the victim was so intoxicated that he did not wake when his house accidentally caught fire, or whether the victim had been killed prior to the fire and then the perpetrator staged the scene to look as if the victim had been drinking and smoking and had passed out, perhaps setting the house on fire with a cigarette. .
© Dr. Lindsey Thomas

disguise homicide by burning the victim's body. Even in the most destructive fires, however, considerable information is available from an autopsy because bones are not easily burned. Even in extreme heat, enough blood usually remains to enable a carbon monoxide analysis to determine whether the victim was alive at the time of the fire. In extremely hot fires, however, the heat may cause the skin to break open, and the resulting wounds may appear to be knife or other wounds inflicted by an assailant before the fire.

Explosions, Electrocution and Lightning

Explosives can cause death from the direct tearing force of the blast, from a shock wave or from the victim being blown off the top of a structure or against an object with enough force to cause death. Such deaths are usually accidental.

Electrocution paralyzes the heart muscle, causing rapid death. Nearly all electrocution deaths are accidental (except, of course, in capital punishment cases). High-voltage lines and lightning are the main causes. Lightning leaves linear stripes on the body, turns the skin blue and burns the skin, especially at the lightning bolt's entry and exit points.

> Poisoning deaths can be accidental, suicide or homicide. Most deaths caused by burning, explosions, electrocution and lightning are accidental, although burning is sometimes used in an attempt to disguise homicide.

Drugs

Many studies have documented the relationship between drugs and homicide and the prominent role drugs play in homicide events. The same techniques used in general death investigations also apply to drug-related death investigations. Look for evidence of alcohol use or consumption of drugs (pill bottles or paraphernalia). Alcohol mixed with certain drugs can pose a particularly lethal combination. Prescription drugs are the leading cause of drug-related deaths in the United States.

Different categories of drug-related homicides include deadly disputes involving individuals high on drugs (no organized drug or gang affiliation); deaths caused during the commission of economically motivated crimes, such as robbery, in the offender's effort to get money to buy drugs; and homicides associated with the systemic violence surrounding the drug business itself. This third category includes hits on traffickers, dealers or buyers (may be gang related); assassinations of law enforcement officers or others fighting drug trafficking; and the killing of innocent bystanders in drug-related disputes. The victim-offender relationship (VOR) requires an understanding of the difference between *expressive* and *instrumental* violence. **Expressive violence** is that stemming from hurt feelings, anger or rage, such as when the jealous lover stabs her ex-boyfriend while he's on a date with his new girlfriend. In these cases, the VOR is close and established. **Instrumental violence** is goal-directed predatory behavior used to exert control—for example, the carjacker who shoots his victim before stealing the vehicle. The VOR in events involving instrumental violence may or may not be close, with such events commonly occurring between strangers who have no preestablished relationship.

A prevalent theory regarding VOR and risk of instrumental versus expressive violence is that a close relationship (spouse/lover, family member, close personal friend) may protect a person from certain types of instrumental violence (e.g., robbery) because they have someone to watch out for them, but it may also make them more vulnerable to expressive violence.

Drug trafficking operations commonly cross jurisdictional boundaries, a factor that severely impedes the progress of an investigator working a drug trafficking homicide. To better address this challenge, some areas have developed a violent traffickers task force (VTTF). Investigating drug offenses is discussed in greater detail in Chapter 18.

Vehicles

According to the National Highway Traffic Safety Administration (NHTSA) (Subramanian, 2011), motor vehicle traffic crashes were the leading cause of death in 2007 for every age, from 3 through 5, 8, 9 and 11 through 33. Vehicular homicide can result from reckless driving, driving under the influence or other circumstances where a driver's failure to obey the rules of the road, either intentionally or negligently, leads to the death of another person. Aggressive driving and road rage can escalate to a case of vehicular homicide: in fact, the only difference between a vehicular homicide and other homicides is the use of a motor vehicle as a weapon rather than a gun or knife.

When a traffic crash results in a fatality, all vehicles involved must be thoroughly examined. Document the condition of the vehicles through photographs and written observations. Also of extreme importance are weather and road conditions at the time of the incident. An accident reconstruction expert must be brought in to help the investigator make sense of skid marks, impact dynamics and other factors present at the scene.

If the driver or drivers are still at the scene, obtain evidence for a toxicology examination to determine whether there were any drugs in the person's system at the time of the incident. Toxicology evidence is also necessary for the victim, even if that person wasn't driving a car, because his or her condition before the incident may have played a role.

If the case is one of hit-and-run, physical evidence left at the scene, such as paint, metal shavings, tire impressions and glass, can help link a suspect and a vehicle to the crime. Evidence to look for on the suspect's vehicle includes hairs, fibers, blood and other biological fluids from the victim. The vehicle may contain evidence of the impact. Evidence of fresh paint jobs or recent repairs warrants further investigation.

After the victim has been identified, the time of death has been estimated and the cause of and method used to produce death have been established, the homicide investigation turns to developing a suspect. Witnesses can be a vital source of information in this endeavor.

WITNESSES

In violent criminal deaths, struggles often create noise and attract the attention of neighbors or passersby. Witnesses may know and name a suspect, or they may have seen the suspect or vehicle. Often, however, there are no witnesses, and information must be sought from family members, neighbors and associates. Conducting a neighborhood canvass is a critical step in a thorough homicide investigation and was discussed in detail in Chapter 6.

Many jurisdictions have recognized the value of homicide hotlines and other venues for obtaining vital leads from citizens. For example, the St. Louis (Missouri) Regional Crime Commission has set up a Web site with a homicide victims page where people can provide anonymous tips regarding unsolved homicides (Figure 8.3).

SUSPECTS

If the suspect is arrested at the crime scene, follow the procedures described in Chapter 1. If the suspect is known but is not at the scene, immediately disseminate the description to other investigators, field officers and police agencies.

If the suspect is not known, identification becomes a priority. Often, several suspects are identified and eventually eliminated as information and evidence are obtained and the list is reduced to one or two prime suspects. In major cases, any number of suspects may be developed from information at the scene, from informants and from intelligence files.

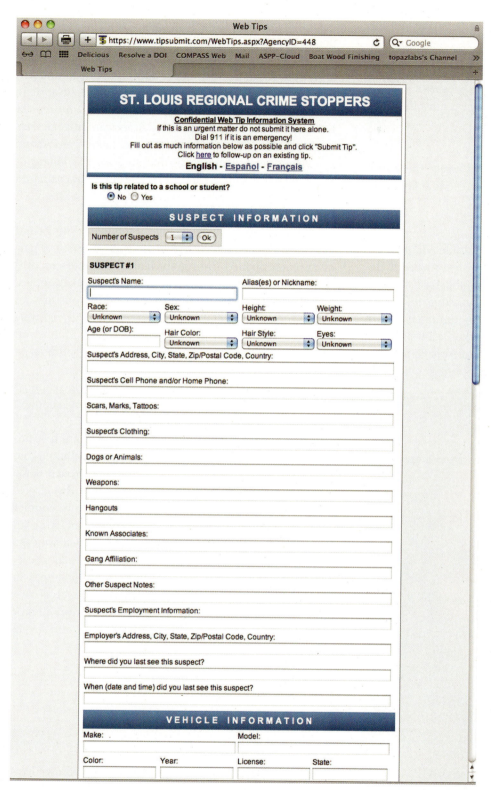

FIGURE 8.3
St. Louis (Missouri) Regional
Crime Stoppers Online
Homicide Tip Site
Source: © St. Louis Regional Crime Stoppers and © The
Crime Report

Discovering a motive is not a specific requirement in the investigation, but motive is so closely tied to intent and to developing a suspect that it should be determined. Homicides are committed for many reasons. Common types of criminal homicide include the anger killing, the love-triangle killing, the revenge or jealousy killing, killing for profit, random killing, murder-suicide, the sex-and-sadism killing and felony murder. Anger killings often begin as assaults. The possibility of killing for profit almost always exists. Thus, it is always critical to determine who would stand to profit from the victim's death.

> Determine the motive for a killing because it provides leads to suspects and strong circumstantial evidence against a suspect.

Some homicides are contracted or hired. This is frequently the case in murders of organized crime figures.

Mass Murderers

A **mass murder** occurs when multiple victims are killed in a single incident by one or a few suspects. Recent years have seen several highly publicized cases of mass familicides, particularly parents killing their children—the Fresno, California, man who murdered nine of his children; the Texas mom who methodically drowned her five kids. Without a doubt, the terrorist attacks of

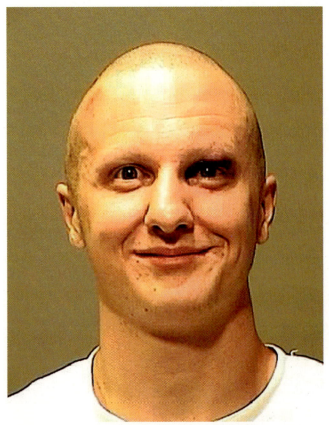

A January 8, 2011, file photo released by the Pima County Sheriff's Office shows Jared Loughner. Loughner is the suspect in a Tucson, Arizona, shooting rampage that killed six people, including a 9-year-old girl and a federal judge, and left 14 others injured, including U.S. Representative Gabrielle Giffords, who was the apparent target of the attack.
© AP Images/Pima County Sheriff's Dept. via The Arizona Republic, file

September 11, 2001, were the most horrific mass murder events ever witnessed by contemporary Americans in their homeland. The January 8, 2011, shooting outside a Tucson, Arizona, strip mall that left six dead and another 14 injured, including U.S. Representative Gabrielle Giffords, is the most recently publicized mass murder in the United States, and left many American citizens feeling like such an event could happen just about anywhere.

Felony-related mass murder, such as the killing of eyewitnesses during a robbery or a group of participants at a drug buy, increased during the last part of the 20th century.

The well-publicized episodes of school shootings and attacks at the workplace, in which a lone gunman or pair of gunmen opened fire on students, coworkers or others within a building or institution, are other examples. Frequently these killers unleash their murderous fury on total strangers. School shootings resulting in multiple deaths have occurred throughout the United States, and many of the shooters have, themselves, been youths who had attended the targeted school.

It is important to realize that school violence almost never occurs without warning, with most school shooters dropping hints about their intentions.

Workplace violence may also result in multiple homicides. As Hess and Orthmann (2011, p.265) note, "The perpetrators are frequently loners with poor social skills, often obsessed with violence and weapons. The targets include authority figures and peers who are in conflict with the perpetrators. The perpetrators often bring an arsenal of weapons and kill all who get in their way." As with school shootings, workplace violence may sometimes be anticipated by noting personality changes in the potential shooter as well as the occurrence of certain precipitating events, such as a missed promotion or a termination. Other triggers include divorce and severe financial troubles.

> Similarities between school and workplace murders include the perpetrators' profiles, the targets, the means and the motivation.

In many of these cases, the killers take their own lives at the end of the shooting rampage, leaving investigators to wonder about possible motives.

Serial Killers

Another type of murder suspect who also kills multiple victims is the serial killer. **Serial murder** is the killing of three or more separate victims, with a "cooling off" period between the killings. A number of serial killers in the United States have received national attention: Henry Lucas, who confessed to 188 murders in 24 states; Gary Ridgway, the Green River strangler, 48 murders over two decades; Theodore (Ted) Bundy, 40 murders; John Wayne Gacey, 33 murders; Jeffrey Dahmer, 16 murders; David Berkowitz, the "Son of Sam," 6 murders (he blinded one person, paralyzed another and wounded 7 others); and Aileen Wuornos, 7 murders. In 1997, Andrew Cunanan went on a cross-country murder spree of five men that culminated in the slaying of fashion designer Gianni Versace on the front steps of his Miami mansion and the suicide of Cunanan a week later. The Washington, DC, "Beltway snipers," John Allen Muhammad and Lee Boyd Malvo, terrorized the nation, particularly citizens along the Northeast coast, with their 21-day random shooting rampage that left 10 people dead and 3 wounded. And Dennis Rader was sentenced in August 2005 to 10 consecutive life terms for the 10 killings he confessed to as the BTK (Bind, Torture, Kill) serial killer.

Investigating a murder committed by a serial killer may initially seem the same as investigating any other homicide. As a case is investigated, however, and if no suspect can be developed, the investigator should consider reporting the crime to the FBI's National Center for the Analysis of Violent Crime (NCAVC) at Quantico, Virginia. NCAVC provides a profiling program as well as research and development, training and the Violent Criminal Apprehension Program (VICAP). Police departments investigating cases they believe involve serial murder can submit their cases to VICAP. Other cases with similar modus operandi submitted by other agencies are then compared, and information is furnished to the submitting agencies. As the Henry Lucas cases illustrate—where murders were committed in 24 states—VICAP is an important resource in investigating and prosecuting this type of killer. If VICAP determines that a serial murderer is probably involved, a multijurisdictional major crime investigation team may be assembled to handle the case.

In some cases, where media coverage leads to an avalanche of citizen tips to authorities, investigators find themselves overwhelmed by the flood of potentially useful, but more often useless, information.

Because of improved information sharing, interjurisdictional communication and media coverage, some homicide investigations that begin as single-incident investigations may now have the potential to develop into serial killing investigations. For example, Donald Blom, who confessed to abducting and murdering 19-year-old Katie Poirier in Minnesota, is now a possible suspect in several other unsolved disappearances and murders around the state and in neighboring states. Cary Stayner, a handyman convicted of the murder of a national park

tourist, is suspected of three other killings. Authorities speculate that if Stayner's last victim had not put up such a struggle, leaving behind a small but invaluable collection of physical evidence, Stayner's first three victims—and potentially more in the future—may have forever remained untraceable and unconnected to him.

DNA evidence obtained in any homicide can provide valuable leads for investigators, and the importance of such evidence is magnified greatly in serial killings, even if investigators are at first unaware of any links to other crimes. Police officers who understand the psychology underlying serial killings will be more effective in investigating the murders and in interviewing the murderers. Serial killers generally select strangers as their victims, although by the time the actual murder occurs, they may have become quite familiar with them.

Rader, the BTK serial killer, divulged in court how he selected victims as he played out his sexual fantasies. During his self-described "trolling phase," Rader would look for several potential victims, referring to them as "projects," and begin stalking them. Multiple projects were selected so if one didn't work out, he'd have some "backups." Over time, Rader explained, he'd start really honing in on one person to become *the* victim.

The acts of serial killers are typically considered in discussions of homicides, and, indeed, the very term used to describe this group of offenders focuses on the killing part of the crime. However, to the perpetrator, the actual homicide is more of an incidental event.

These killers are often quite intelligent and very much in touch with reality, which partially explains their success in eluding capture. When interviewing serial killers, any attempts to evoke sympathy for the victims or surviving relatives will probably be futile. Appeals to their ego, on the other hand, may succeed. It is also important not to display shock at the atrocities that may have been committed because this is often what serial murderers want.

The acts of serial murderers seem incomprehensible to "normal" people. For example, in 1991, the killing and mutilation of 16 young men and boys by Dahmer made national headlines. When police entered Dahmer's stench-filled apartment, they found body parts of 11 males—painted human skulls, severed heads and body parts in cold storage and torsos disintegrating in an acid-filled vat. Dahmer's murders can also be classified as lust murders.

Lust Murderers

A **lust murder** is a sex-related homicide involving a sadistic, deviant assault. In lust murder, the killer depersonalizes the victim, sexually mutilates the body and may displace body parts. Two types of lust murderers are often described—organized and disorganized. The *organized offender* is usually of above-average intelligence, methodical and cunning. He is socially skilled and tricks his victims into situations in which he can torture and then murder them. In contrast, the *disorganized offender* is usually of below-average intelligence, has no car and is a loner who acts on impulse.

Both the organized and the disorganized offenders usually murder victims from their own geographic area, and the murders involve fantasy, ritual, fetishes and symbolism. They also both usually leave some sort of physical evidence.

THE DECLINING CLEARANCE RATE

No other crime is measured as accurately and precisely as homicide. Homicides continue to receive the most attention by police because they are considered the most serious crime and are complex cases to investigate. Nonetheless, a significant proportion of these violent crimes go unsolved or without an arrest being made. The term used to define the quantity of cases removed from active investigation is the **clearance rate**, which is the ratio of crimes resolved to the number of crimes reported. *Cleared, closed* and *solved* are often used interchangeably. The FBI uses the term *cleared.*

A case can be cleared by arrest or by exceptional means. *Crime in the United States, 2009* explains, "In certain situations, elements beyond law enforcement's control prevent the agency from arresting and formally charging the offender. When this occurs, the agency can clear the offenses *exceptionally.*" To do so, law enforcement agencies must have identified the offender; garnered enough evidence to support an arrest, make a charge and turn over the offender to the court for prosecution; identified the offender's exact location so that the suspect could be taken into custody immediately; and encountered a circumstance outside the control of law enforcement that prohibits the officers from arresting, charging and prosecuting the offender. The FBI clarifies, "Examples of exceptional clearance include, but are not limited to, the death of the offender (e.g., suicide or justifiably killed by law enforcement or citizen); the victim's refusal to cooperate with the prosecution after the offender has been identified; or the denial of extradition because the offender committed a crime in another jurisdiction and is being prosecuted for that offense."

Although the national clearance rate for homicide is the highest of all the serious offenses, homicide clearances have declined dramatically over the past several decades, from a high of 94 percent in 1961 to a percentage in the low- to mid-60s (Regoeczi et al., 2008). According to *Crime in the United States, 2009*, 66.6 percent of murders were cleared by arrest or exceptional means in 2009. A critical factor in clearing homicides is time, as cases become harder to solve the longer it takes to make an arrest: "Detectives investigating homicides that are not cleared quickly run the risk of encountering offenders who have long fled the scene, witnesses who have forgotten key information or cannot be located again, and tainted physical evidence" (Regoeczi et al., 2008, p.143).

Cronin et al. (2007, p.2) report,

> Many practitioners attribute the declining clearance rates to several factors: an increase in stranger-to-stranger homicides, which are usually more difficult to solve than cases in which the perpetrator knows the victim; gang-related offenses that turn fatal; community and witness intimidation; and reductions in witness cooperation.
>
> Police departments also report that increasing numbers of "petty arguments" and incidents of "disrespect" lead to homicides.... Another factor is the reentry of prisoners [650,000 per year] into communities, which increases the number of persons prone to violence....
>
> Additionally, backlogs and heavy caseloads within crime labs and coroners' offices may reduce investigative effectiveness.
>
> Other factors include increases in illegal immigration from countries where residents fear and do not trust the local police; and the growth of "Thug Culture" and "Stop Snitchin'" campaigns.

Finally, higher standards of evidence needed to convict defendants and an expansion of the legal protections and rights afforded suspects have contributed to diminished clearance rates for homicide.

Aspects of the Offense Associated with Likelihood of Clearing a Case

Research indicates that several aspects of a homicide pertaining to the investigation are associated with the likelihood of clearing the case (Regoeczi et al., 2008, pp.145–146):

- ■ *Homicide circumstances.* Several studies report that felony-related homicides are more difficult to clear than are homicides resulting from other circumstances.

- ■ *Weapons.* Homicides committed with weapons that bring the offender and victim into contact with one another (such as a knife) increase the likelihood of closing the case.

■ *Location.* Among the more consistent findings concerning homicide clearance is the greater likelihood of clearance for cases occurring in residences.

Law Enforcement Actions Affecting Clearance

Research by University of Maryland Professor Charles Wellford and Police Executive Research Forum (PERF) Research Associate Jim Cronin focused on homicide clearance rates in 20 cities and found that high clearance rates were associated with several factors, including the initial response, actions of the detectives and other police actions (Cronin et al., 2007, pp.24–27).

The Initial Response. Variables associated with successfully clearing a homicide case during the initial response include:

■ The first officer on the scene immediately notifies the homicide unit, the medical examiner's office and the crime lab.

■ The first officer on the scene immediately secures the area and attempts to locate witnesses.

■ The detective assigned to the case arrives at the scene within 30 minutes of being notified.

Actions of the Detectives. Variables in the actions of the detectives that significantly affected whether a case was solved include:

■ Three or four detectives, instead of one or two, were assigned to the case.

■ The detectives took detailed notes describing the crime scene, including measurements.

■ Detectives followed up on all information provided by witnesses.

■ At least one detective assigned to the case attended the postmortem examination.

Other Police Actions. Variables in the "other police responses" category found to significantly increase the likelihood that a homicide is solved include:

■ A computer check using the local criminal justice information system was conducted on the suspect or on any guns found.

■ A witness interviewed at the crime scene provided valuable evidence such as information about circumstances of the death or the perpetrator's

motivation, an identification of the suspect or victim or the whereabouts of the suspect.

■ Witnesses, friends, acquaintances and neighbors of the victim were interviewed.

■ The medical examiner prepared a body chart of the victim, which was included in the case file.

■ The attending physician and medical personnel were interviewed.

■ Confidential informants provided information.

Many departments use a homicide case review solvability chart to determine which cases to focus on. Such tools can provide support for requesting additional resources. Appendix B shows an example of a solvability chart.

The 10 Most Common Errors in Death Investigations

Investigator error can have a substantial deleterious effect on homicide clearances. Geberth (2007b and 2008) lists the 10 most common errors in death investigations:

1. Improper response to the scene
2. Failure to protect the crime scene
3. Not handling suspicious deaths as homicides
4. Responding with a preconceived notion
5. Failure to take sufficient photos
6. Failure to manage the process (maintaining the chain of custody and proper documentation)
7. Failure to evaluate victimology
8. Failure to conduct an effective canvass
9. Failure to work as a team
10. Command interference or inappropriate action

Geberth (2007b, p.85) gives an example of an inappropriate response to a death:

Uniform officers respond to a call, "Man out the window." When they arrive, they observe a crowd gathered around a body in the alleyway of a tenement building. The officers determine that the man appears dead and call for an ambulance and detectives. They fail to establish any crime scene except where the body lies and they make no attempt to detain anyone or identify any witnesses.

Instead, they chase the crowd away and cordon off the body pending the arrival of the ambulance crew, which pronounces the victim dead. During this time a drunken man carrying a bottle persists on viewing the victim's body and states that he and the victim are roommates. The uniform officers threaten to arrest him if he doesn't go away.

When the detectives arrive, they ascertain from witnesses that the drunken man and the victim were in an altercation earlier in the evening in a fifth-floor apartment in the tenement. An assault had occurred and the drunken man threw his friend out the window, and his body ended up in the alleyway. None of these locations had been secured and the assailant had been chased away by the uniform officers.

Impact of Unsolved Homicides

Cronin et al. (2007, p.14) contend, "Unsolved homicides hamper the healing process for the family and friends of the victim, and have a significant effect on communities and all aspects of the criminal justice system.... Of course, the most important consequence of an unsolved homicide is that a killer remains free, able to commit additional murders or become a victim himself."

COLD CASES

Despite the relatively high clearance rate of homicides, nearly 40 percent go unsolved. At any given time, a large metropolitan jurisdiction may have thousands of cold homicide cases on its shelves: "The term 'cold case' means different things in different agencies. The definition depends on several factors. In particular, the number of cases and the number of employees available to investigate them will dictate a department's cold case definition" (Cronin et al., 2007, p.102).

Many departments have created cold case squads dedicated to handling these challenging cases. Although the mantra for fresh homicide investigations is typically "time is of the essence"—assuming that, if after 72 hours no suspect has been found, the case is unlikely to be solved—cold case squads use the passing of time to their advantage. Different squads use different criteria in deciding which cases to reinvestigate, but in general, the presence of well-preserved physical evidence and the ability to identify and locate original witnesses raise the priority level of a case. Other factors in deciding to reopen a case include whether a murder weapon was recovered, if fingerprints were found and collected and whether DNA analysis was ever requested (Schuster, 2008).

Phillips (2007, p.22) notes, "Typically, cold case investigations begin with a trip down memory lane and to the property storage room... retrieving every bit of evidence originally collected to allow for proper reexamination." Phillips also notes, "Dynamics in relationships are completely unscientific compared to DNA or AFIS, but knowing the dynamics between suspects and victims is

important, because it could change over the years" (p.24). Over time, witnesses who were once uncooperative, either feeling too threatened or intimidated to get involved or still in shock from what they saw, may no longer be afraid to talk to the police; people who had once had a relationship with the suspect but no longer do may decide to come forward with incriminating information.

In addition to getting information from witnesses, investigators may generate leads by having physical evidence reexamined. Advances in technology during the past decade, particularly DNA analysis techniques, are helping to crack once unsolvable cases. If fingerprint, DNA or other evidence in a cold homicide case had been previously examined but not entered into a national database, such as the Automated Fingerprint Information Technology (AFIT) system, the Combined DNA Index System (CODIS) or VICAP, that information should certainly be entered now. Besides national forensic evidence databases, cold case investigators have several other resources they should tap for help, including the media, the public and the inmate population.

Cold case investigators also need to work closely with prosecutors to ensure that their efforts will meet the requirements to get a case to court. Figure 8.4 is a checklist of the criteria used by the Kansas City (Missouri) Police Department in determining which cold case homicides to reopen. Appendix E provides the Las Vegas Metropolitan Police Department Cold Case Solvability Criteria.

Volunteer Cold Case Squads

Moore (2007, p.138) suggests, "Although departments can have their own cold case squads populated by active duty officers, why not shift those investigators to new cases and let the cases that linger in the evidence room in boxes covered with dust be handled by willing and knowledgeable volunteers?" She points out, "Your community may be the home of retirees from many different agencies. Why not tap into those resources?"

Treen (2007, pp.81–84) describes how when he retired from being a homicide detective he missed the work. So he teamed up with three other retirees, and they became known as the "Cold Case Cowboys." They simply didn't believe in dead ends. Together they solved numerous cold cases and, eventually, after various insurance issues were worked out, were sworn in as officers, issued badges and guns and given carte blanche to conduct full-blown investigations.

Benefits of a Cold Case Unit

Cronin et al. (2007, p.116) conclude, "The rewards associated with the development of a cold case unit are significant. Case clearance rates increase, guilty parties are

| Offense Number _____ |
| Victim _____ |
| Date of Crime _____ |

Evidence	Yes	Pt.	No	Unk	N/A
1. Fingerprints recovered?		2			
2. Prints checked through AFIS?		–			
3. Any prints AFIS quality?		3			
4. Prints available on possible suspect?		2			
5. Trace evidence recovered for DNA analysis?		4			
6. DNA analysis requested?		–			
7. DNA profile obtained from analysis?		3			
8. DNA sample obtained from suspects?		2			
9. Murder weapon recovered?		4			
10. Projectiles/casings recovered?		2			
11. Checked through NIBIN System?		–			
12. NIBIN identification made?		2			
13. Victim's property taken in crime?		2			
14. Stolen property entered in NCIC?		4			

Witness(es)	Yes	Pt.	No	Unk	N/A
15. Eyewitness(es) to the crime?		3			
16. Cooperative witness(es)?		2			
17. Hostile witness(es)?		1			
18. Good witness(es) developed in canvass?		2			

Suspect(s)	Yes	Pt.	No	Unk	N/A
19. Suspect(s) named by witness(es)?		4			
20. Does eyewitness(es) know suspect(s)?		2			
21. Suspect(s) developed in investigation?		2			
22. Can witness(es) identify suspect(s)?		2			
23. Is suspect(s) still in Kansas City?		2			

Total solvability points (50 possible)	

Detective _____   Date _____

FIGURE 8.4
Kansas City (Missouri) Police Department Cold Case Solvability Checklist
Source: Reprinted by permission of the Kansas City Police Department.

brought to justice, innocent parties are exonerated, victims' survivors get a measure of relief, and investigators benefit from the personal satisfaction associated with solving cold cases…. Regardless of how a cold case unit is organized, the resounding message from those with experience is that as long as it is staffed with passionate, patient, and experienced investigators, it will be a successful endeavor."

Cold cases are, without a doubt, one of the most challenging tasks a homicide investigator may face. Another difficult responsibility is that of making a death notification.

DEATH NOTIFICATION

Departments may use a police dispatcher, a police chaplain or an officer to perform death notifications, but such messages should be delivered by a two-person team. Generally, if the police chaplain or a pastor from the deceased's religious faith accompanies the officer, the chaplain or the pastor performs the initial notification and the officer fills in the details. If the relative is in another community or state or is out of the country, ask police of that jurisdiction to make the notification, using the telephone to make the actual notification only as a last resort.

Officers must be prepared for a wide range of emotional and physical reactions people may have upon hearing of a death. They may collapse or suffer another reaction that requires first aid. They may become aggressive or even violent and require physical restraint. Having two officers perform death notifications will afford better control of such reactions. Furthermore, if two or more survivors are to be notified at the same location, it may be advisable to do the notifications separately, particularly if one or more individuals will be asked to provide investigative information. Because some homicides are committed by the survivor receiving the notification, officers should be sure to observe and later record how the survivor reacted.

Page (2008, p.20) identifies "best practices" in death notifications: "Notification should be done in person, in pairs, in private, in plain language, and in time. Avoid words such as *passed on* or *expired*. And make notification before the family sees it on the news."

Finally, family members should be allowed to see the body, whether it is at the hospital or the morgue. Viewing a body at the scene may compromise the investigation.

Notifying the family of an officer who has been killed is even more difficult. Departments should develop a protocol for handling these notifications, including having officers fill out a questionnaire covering several points:

- Who should be notified after a line-of-duty death? Include address and relationship to officer.

- Are there any special circumstances to be aware of, such as a survivor's heart condition?

- Is there a clergy preference?

- Is there a family friend who can provide support?

STRATEGIES FOR REDUCING HOMICIDE

Traditionally, police have treated homicide as a crime relatively immune from police suppression efforts, a crime over which they had little control. Two trends are changing this reactive view. The first trend is crime analysis showing that homicide is greatest for young people in core, inner-city neighborhoods and is often related to drugs, guns and gangs. The second trend is the emergence of community policing and a problem-solving approach to crime. In this approach, homicide is viewed as part of a larger, more general problem—violence. Results of numerous studies of police departments across the country that have implemented community policing support the theory that greater community involvement and a shift in policing philosophy to one that emphasizes proactive problem solving can reduce overall levels of violence within a community.

> The conventional wisdom about homicide has changed in some departments from viewing it as a series of unconnected, uncontrollable episodes to seeing it as part of the larger, general problem of violence, which can be addressed proactively.

This change in perspective allows departments to be proactive rather than reactive and to develop strategies to reduce homicides in their jurisdictions. One strategy being used is CompStat, which uses computer software to perform statistical analysis of crime data and target geographic areas throughout the city that have high levels of violent crime. By focusing law resources and efforts on those areas, law enforcement is able to effect greater change and have a more positive impact. Other departments are implementing early intervention programs to keep small issues from growing into bigger, more violent events.

A CASE STUDY

Nyberg (2007, pp.38–41) presents the following case study: "The Moonberry Pond Murder" of James Mixon. James Mixon was a drunk who ran afoul of everyone he met. Ruth and Jason Brunson also didn't get along with regular society and slept in a tent with their 4-year-old daughter, Muffin. They had a deal with the state that they could camp on a slender peninsula of land that led to an antenna housing as long as they kept people from driving out to the little fenced structure. One day Mixon showed up, and they figured he was harmless so they let him stay. Muffin spent her time with her beloved kitten Moonberry. She also named all the critters around the campsite, including a young alligator she named "Tater the Gator."

One day a man looking for a place to dump some junk metal found Mixon's shirtless body in a small clearing, shot multiple times in the head. The Brunsons cooperated in turning over their Ruger .356 and providing fingerprints and handwriting samples. While detectives were interviewing Ruth Brunson, she was very cooperative, but when a detective asked, "Was there anything that caused you to decide he shouldn't stay?" she started to answer when Muffin interrupted with, "He was mean to Moonberry." At this, her mother exploded with "QUIET!" "You shut up when Mommy is talking," which was markedly different than the way she had treated Muffin before.

The investigators took the gun, the handwriting sample and the fingerprints and let the Brunsons go. Four days later, they got two calls and two hits. The bill of sale for a vehicle the Brunsons had purchased from Mixon was not in James Mixon's handwriting but, rather, close to Jason Brunson's. And the projectiles taken from Mixon's head matched the Ruger .357. Investigators called the Brunsons in and questioned them separately. Under pressure, the wife confessed. One detective assumed the husband was the killer, but it turned out to be the wife. This is sometimes referred to as "gender prejudice." What had happened is that Mixon had seized Muffin's beloved Moonberry and thrown the kitten into the pond where Tater devoured it.

Lessons learned by the Miami-Dade homicide unit:

- Work as a team—having two interviews going at the same time led to success.

- Avoid gender prejudice—women can kill, too.

- Stay attuned to subtle clues—Ruth's outburst at Muffin was a telltale clue.

Summary

Homicide investigations are challenging and frequently require all investigative techniques and skills. A basic requirement in a homicide investigation is to establish whether death was caused by a criminal action. The four basic categories of death are death by natural causes, accidental death, suicide and homicide. Although technically you are concerned only with homicide, you frequently do not know at the start of an investigation what type of death has occurred; therefore, any of the four types of death may require investigation.

Homicide—the killing of one person by another—is classified as criminal (felonious) or noncriminal (nonfelonious). Criminal homicide includes murder and manslaughter. Noncriminal homicide includes excusable homicide and justifiable homicide. Murder, the killing of another human with malice aforethought, is frequently classified into three degrees:

- First degree—premeditated and intentional, or while committing or attempting to commit a felony

- Second degree—intentional but not premeditated

- Third degree—neither intentional nor premeditated, but the result of an imminently dangerous act

Manslaughter, the killing of another human with no prior malice, is classified as

- Voluntary—intentional homicide caused by intense passion resulting from adequate provocation

- Involuntary—unintentional homicide caused by criminal (culpable) negligence

Excusable homicide is the unintentional, truly accidental killing of another person. Justifiable homicide is killing another person under authorization of the law. Premeditation is the essential element of first-degree murder that sets it apart from all other murder classifications.

Challenges in homicide investigations include pressure by the media and the public, difficulty in establishing homicide rather than suicide or an accidental or natural death, identifying the victim and establishing the cause and time of death.

After ensuring the safety of the scene, the priority in a preliminary homicide investigation is to give emergency aid to the victim if he or she is still alive or to determine that death has occurred—provided the suspect is not at the scene. Signs of death include lack of breathing, lack of heartbeat, lack of flushing of the fingernail bed when pressure is applied and then released and failure of the eyelids to close after being gently lifted.

Physical evidence in a homicide includes a weapon, a body, blood, hairs and fibers. The victim's background provides information about whether the death was an accident, suicide or homicide. If a homicide, the background often provides leads to a suspect. Evidence on the victim's body can also provide important leads. Homicide victims are identified by immediate family, relatives, friends or acquaintances; personal effects, fingerprints, DNA analysis and dental and skeletal studies; clothing and laundry marks; or through missing-persons files.

Factors that help in estimating the time of death are body temperature, rigor mortis, postmortem lividity (livor), eye appearance, stomach contents, stage of decomposition and evidence suggesting a change in the victim's normal routine. Body temperature drops 2 to 3 degrees in the first hour after death and 1 to 1.5 degrees for each subsequent hour until 18 hours. Rigor mortis appears as a stiffening of muscles several hours after death, with maximum stiffness occurring 12 to 24 hours after death. Rigor then begins to disappear and is generally gone three days postmortem. Postmortem lividity starts one-half to three hours after death and is congealed in the capillaries in four to five hours. Maximum lividity occurs within 10 to 12 hours. The location of lividity can indicate whether a body was moved after death. A partial constriction of the pupil occurs in about seven hours. In 12 hours, the cornea appears cloudy. Determine when and what the victim last ate. If any vomit is present, preserve it as evidence and submit it for examination. A dead body usually sinks in water and remains immersed for 8 to 10 days in warm water or 2 to 3 weeks in cold water. It then rises to the surface unless restricted. The outer skin loosens in five to six days, and the nails separate in two to three weeks.

The medical examiner provides legal evidence related to the cause and time of death and to the presence of alcohol or drugs.

Among the most common causes of unnatural death are gunshot wounds; stabbing and cutting wounds; blows from blunt objects; asphyxia induced by choking, drowning, smothering, hanging, strangulation, gases or poisons; poisoning and drug overdoses; burning; explosions, electrocution and lightning; drugs; and vehicles. In the case of a gunshot wound, suicide may be indicated if the wound shows gun contact against the skin; the wound is in the mouth or in the right temple if victim is right-handed and the left temple if left-handed; the shot did not go through clothing, unless the person was shot in the chest; or the weapon is present, especially if tightly held in hand. Homicide may be indicated if the gun was fired from more than a few inches away or from an angle or location that rules out self-infliction, if the victim was shot through clothing or if there is no weapon present.

Stabbing and cutting wounds may be the result of suicide if the body shows hesitation wounds; if the wounds appear under clothing or on the throat, wrists or ankles; if the weapon is present; if there is a lack of disfigurement; or if the body has not been moved. Defense wounds, wounds through clothing or to vital organs, the absence of a weapon, disfigurement and signs that the body has been moved indicate homicide. In asphyxiation deaths, most cases of choking, drowning and smothering are accidental; most cases of hanging are suicides; most cases of strangulation are homicides. Poisoning deaths can be accidental, suicide or homicide. Most deaths caused by burning, explosions, electrocution and lightning are accidental, although burning is sometimes used in an attempt to disguise homicide.

Determine a motive for the killing because it provides leads to a suspect and strong circumstantial evidence against a suspect. Similarities between school and workplace murders include the perpetrators' profiles, the targets, the means and the motivation.

The conventional wisdom about homicide has changed in some departments from viewing it as a series of unconnected, uncontrollable episodes to seeing it as part of the larger, general problem of violence, which can be addressed proactively.

Checklist

Homicide

- How were the police notified? By whom? Date? Time?
- Was the victim alive or dead when the police arrived?
- Was medical help provided?
- If the victim was hospitalized, who attended the victim at the hospital? Are reports available?
- Was there a dying declaration?
- What was the condition of the body? Rigor mortis? Postmortem lividity?
- How was the victim identified?
- Has the cause of death been determined?
- Was the medical examiner notified? Are the reports available?
- Was the evidence technician team notified?
- Was the crime scene protected?
- Were arrangements made to handle the news media?
- Are all the elements of the offense present?
- What types of evidence were found at the scene?
- How was the time of death estimated?
- Was the complainant interviewed? Witnesses? Suspects? Victim if alive when police arrived?

- What leads exist?
- Was a description of the suspect obtained? Was it disseminated?
- Was a search or arrest warrant necessary?
- Was all evidence properly collected, identified and preserved?
- Were photographs taken of the scene? Of the victim? Of the evidence?
- Were sketches or maps of the scene made?

Applications

A. Mary Jones, an 18-year-old high school girl, quarreled with her boyfriend, Thomas Smith. At 3 A.M. following the evening of their quarrel, Mary went to Tom's home to return his picture. Tom stated that after receiving the picture, he went to his room, went to sleep and awoke about 8 A.M. When he looked out his window, he saw Mary's car parked out front.

Looking into the car, he discovered Mary sitting erect behind the steering wheel, shot through the chest, a .22 revolver lying beside her on the front seat. She was dead—apparently a suicide. The revolver had been a gift to Mary from her father. Tom called the police to report the shooting.

Mary had been shot once. The bullet entered just below the right breast, traveled across the front of her body and lodged near her heart. The medical examiner theorized that she did not die immediately. When found, she was sitting upright in the car, her head tilted slightly backward, her right hand high on the steering wheel, her left hand hanging limp at her left side.

When questioned, Tom steadfastly denied any knowledge of the shooting. Mary's clothing, the bullet from her body and the gun were sent to the FBI laboratory for examination. An examination of her blouse where the bullet entered failed to reveal any powder residues. The bullet removed from her body was identified as having been fired from the gun found beside her body.

Questions

1. Is the shooting likely to be a suicide or a homicide? What facts support this?
2. How should the investigation proceed?

B. Ten-year-old Denise was playing in a school parking lot with her 9-year-old stepbrother, Jerry. A car pulled up to the curb next to the lot, and the man driving the car motioned for Denise and Jerry to come over. When the man asked where they lived, Denise described their house. The man then asked Denise to take him to the house, saying he would bring her right back to the lot afterward. Denise got into the car with the man, and they drove away. When they did not return after an hour, Jerry went into the school and told a teacher what had happened. Denise did not return home that evening. The next day the police received a report that a body had been found near a lover's lane. It was Denise, who had been stabbed to death with a pocketknife.

Questions

1. What steps should be taken immediately?
2. Where would you expect to find leads?
3. What evidence would you expect to find?
4. Specifically, how would you investigate this murder?

Discussion Questions

1. Questions remain regarding the assassination of President John F. Kennedy. Why is this murder so controversial? What special problems were involved in the investigation?
2. What special problems were encountered in investigating the shooting of Lee Harvey Oswald?
3. How many murders were committed in your community last year? In your state?
4. How do your state laws classify criminal homicide? What are the penalties for each classification? Are they appropriate? Are they more or less severe than in other states?
5. Are you for or against capital punishment for persons convicted of first-degree murder? Is execution of murderers a deterrent to crime? Is media publicity concerning such cases a deterrent to murder? Do television shows and movies showing criminal violence contribute to such crimes? Would gun-control laws deter murder?
6. When patrol officers are dispatched to a murder scene, what are their duties and responsibilities there?
7. An investigator is called to a murder scene by the patrol officer at the scene. What are the duties and responsibilities of the investigator? What activities can be performed jointly by the patrol officer and the investigator? Who is in charge?
8. The investigation of murder is considered the classic crime investigation. Are there factors that make this crime more difficult to investigate, or is it basically the same as any other criminal investigation?
9. What investigative procedures are required in homicides resulting from drowning? Gunshot? Electrocution? Stabbing? Hanging? Poisoning?
10. Mass deaths in Nazi concentration camps during World War II and in Guyana and Waco, Texas, involving religious cults introduce entirely new problems into homicide investigation. Who should be charged and with what degree of murder? What special problems are associated with such investigations?

Media Explorations

 **Internet**

Select one of the following assignments to complete.

■ Search for the key phrase *National Institute of Justice.* Click on "NCJRS" (National Criminal Justice Research Service). Click on "law enforcement." Click on "sort by Doc#." Search for one of the NCJ reference numbers from the list of References at the end of this chapter. Outline the selection to share with the class.

■ Go to the FBI Web site at www.fbi.gov. Click on "library and reference." Select "Uniform Crime Reports" and outline what the report says about homicides.

■ Select one of the following key terms: *homicide, homicide prevention, mass murder, serial murders, suicide.* Find one article relevant to homicide investigations to outline and share with the class.

■ Find and outline the article "Deadly Ambivalence" by Meredith Maran at http://archive.salon.com/news/feature/2001/03/06/misfit/index.html

 Gale Criminal Justice Database Assignments

The following assignments require access to Gale's Custom Journals Database for Emergency Services and Criminal Justice. Check with your instructor if you have questions about this.

■ Find the article "Resurrecting Cold Case Serial Homicide Investigations" on the Gale Emergency Services Database. Read the article and then research a similar cold case homicide investigation. Compare and contrast the differences in the investigations and be prepared to share your observations with the class.

■ Find the article "Implementing a Cold Case Homicide Unit: A Challenging Task" on the Gale Emergency Services Database. Read and identify the challenges with creating a cold case unit that are outlined in this article. Imagine that you are a police chief tasked with creating this unit. What are some steps you would take? Share and discuss your plan with the class.

■ Find the article "Body of Evidence: The Dead Man's Story" on the Gale Emergency Services Database. Read the article and explain the importance of forensic anthropology in death scene investigations. Be prepared to discuss it in class.

■ Find the article "Decreasing Urban Crime" on the Gale Emergency Services Database. Read the study on the City of Petersburg and violent crime. Identify the statistics and crime trends and identify whether the violent crime is increasing or decreasing. Also identify the factors that are causing either the increase or decrease for in class discussion.

References

Crime in the United States, 2009. Washington, DC: U.S. Department of Justice, Federal Bureau of Investigation, September 2010. Accessed May 19, 2011. http://www2.fbi .gov/ucr/cius2009/index.html

Cronin, James M.; Murphy, Gerard R.; Spahr, Lisa L.; Toliver, Jessica I.; and Weger, Richard E. *Promoting Effective Homicide Investigations*. Washington, DC: Office of Community Oriented Policing and the Police Executive Research Forum, December 2007.

Downs, J. C. Upshaw. "The Role of the Medical Examiner in Law Enforcement." *The Police Chief*, November 2007, pp.44–48.

Geberth, Vernon. "Preliminary Death Investigation." *Law and Order*, September 2006, pp.131–140.

Geberth, Vernon. "Estimating the Time of Death." *Law and Order*, March 2007a, pp.58–65.

Geberth, Vernon. "10 Most Common Errors in Death Investigations, Part 1." *Law and Order*, November 2007b, pp.84–89.

Geberth, Vernon. "10 Most Common Errors in Death Investigations, Part 2." *Law and Order*, January 2008, pp.81–84.

Geberth, Vernon. "Amazing Advances in Forensic Science, Part 3: Firearms and Ballistics." *Law and Order*, October 2010a, pp.98–100.

Geberth, Vernon. "Frequency of Body Posing in Homicides." *Law and Order*, February 2010b, pp.29–31.

Grossi, Dave. "Emotional Survival—Officer Suicide." *Law Officer Magazine*, April 2007, pp.34–36.

Hess, Kären M., and Orthmann, Christine H. *Police Operations: Theory and Practice*, 5th ed. Clifton Park, NY: Delmar, Cengage Learning, 2011.

Lessons Learned from 9/11: DNA Identification in Mass Fatality Incidents. Washington, DC: National Institute of Justice, September 2006. (NCJ 214781)

Lowy, Allen, and McAlhany, Pat. "Human Remains Detection 'Cadaver Dogs.'" Miami-Dade Police Department Canine Unit. Accessed May 1, 2008. http://www.crime-scene-investigator.net/cadaverdogs.html

Mifflin, Krista. *Cadaver Dogs*. About.com. Accessed May 1, 2008. http://dogs.about.com/cs/searchandrescue/a/cadaver_dogs.htm

Moore, Carole. "Cold Case Squads." *Law Enforcement Technology*, July 2007, p.138.

Nyberg, Ramesh. "The Moonberry Pond Murder." *Police*, January 2007, pp.38–41.

Otahbachi, Mohammad; Cevik, Cihan; Bagdure, Satish; and Nugent, Kenneth. "Excited Delirium, Restraints, and Unexpected Death: A Review of Pathogenesis." *American Journal of Forensic Medicine and Pathology*, Vol.31, No.2, June 2010, pp.107–112.

Page, Douglas. "Death Notification: Breaking the Bad News." *Law Enforcement Technology*, March 2008, pp.18–25.

Pearsall, Beth, and Weiss, Danielle. "Solving Missing Persons Cases." *NIJ Journal*, Issue No.264, November 2009, pp.4–8.

Perin, Michelle. "Police Suicide." *Law Enforcement Technology*, September 2007, pp.8–16.

Peters, John G., Jr. "Excited Delirium: What Every Chief Needs to Know." *Police and Security News*, Vol.23, No.5, September/October 2007. http://exciteddelirium.com/

Peters, John G., and Brave, Michael. "Sudden Death, 'Excited' Delirium, and Issues of Force." *Police and Security News*, September/October 2006, pp.55–61.

Phillips, Amanda. "Praying for a Breakthrough." *Law Enforcement Technology*, August 2007, pp.20–25.

Regoeczi, Wendy; Jarvis, John; and Riedel, Marc. "Clearing Murders: Is It about Time?" *Journal of Research in Crime and Delinquency*, May 2008, pp.142–162.

Ritter, John. "Suicide Rates Jolt Police Culture." *USA Today*, February 8, 2007.

Ritter, Nancy. "Identifying Remains: Lessons Learned from 9/11." *NIJ Journal*, January 2007, pp.20–26.

Rowe, Aaron. "Big Evidence." *Law and Order*, March 2007, pp.55–56.

Sanow, Ed. "Use CIT Two Ways." *Law and Order*, May 2008, p.6.

Schuster, Beth. "Cold Cases: Strategies Explored at NIJ Regional Trainings." *NIJ Journal*, Issue No.260, July 2008, pp.24–27. (NCJ 222904)

"Secrets of Success." *Law Enforcement News*, February 29, 2000, pp.1,6.

Steck-Flynn, Kathy. "Just a Pinch of Cyanide." *Law Enforcement Technology*, October 2007, pp.118–126.

Steck-Flynn, Kathy. "Hidden in Them Bones...." *Law Enforcement Technology*, October 2008, pp.78–84.

Stevens, Serita. "Investigating Water Deaths." *Law Enforcement Technology*, July 2007, pp.110–119.

Subramanian, Rajesh. *Motor Vehicle Traffic Crashes as a Leading Cause of Death in the United States, 2007.* Washington, DC: National Highway Traffic Safety Administration, National Center for Statistics and Analysis, March 2011. (DOT HS 811 443)

Treen, Joe. "Cold Case Cowboys" *AARP*, May & June 2007, pp.81–84,113.

"Warning Signs of Suicide." New York: American Foundation for Suicide Prevention, 2011. Accessed May 22, 2011. http://www.afsp.org/index.cfm?page_id=0519EC1A-D73A-8D90-7D2E9E2456182D66

Case Cited

Flippo v. West Virginia, 528 U.S. 11 (1999)

CHAPTER 9

Assault, Domestic Violence, Stalking and Elder Abuse

© Hambones/Alamy

Outline

Can You Define?

aggravated assault
assault
battery
cyberstalking
domestic violence
elder abuse
felonious assault
femicide
full faith and credit
indicator crimes
in loco parentis
simple assault
stake in conformity
stalking

Do You Know?

- What constitutes assault?
- How simple assault differs from aggravated assault?
- When force is legal?
- What the elements of simple assault, aggravated (felonious) assault and attempted assault are?
- What special challenges are posed in an assault investigation?
- How to prove the elements of both simple and aggravated assault?
- What evidence is likely to be at the scene of an assault?
- To aid in data collection, what offenses might be categorized as separate crimes?
- What constitutes domestic violence?
- What constitutes stalking?
- What constitutes elder abuse? How prevalent it is?

Two people have a violent argument and hurl insults at each other. A bouncer physically ejects a belligerent drunk from a bar; a mob enforcer breaks all the fingers of a man who is past due on a gambling debt. An angry wife hurls a frying pan, striking her husband in the back. A teacher slaps a disrespectful student. A group of teenagers mugs an old man. A jealous lover stabs a rival with a knife. Each of these scenarios has one thing in common—each is an assault.

Some assaults take place very publicly, often with victims and witnesses who are willing to press charges and testify in court. Others take place behind closed doors in the privacy of the home. Domestic violence, once viewed as a family matter, has become a priority in many departments, partly because such violence may end in homicide. Psychological assaults or stalking behaviors have become law enforcement concerns since 1990.

ASSAULT: AN OVERVIEW

The court has defined assault as "an intentional, unlawful act of injury to another by force, or force directed toward another person, under circumstances that create fear of imminent peril, coupled with an apparent ability to execute the attempt, if not prevented. The intention to harm is of the essence. Mere words, although provoking or insulting, are not sufficient" (*Naler v. State*, 1933).

> **Assault** is unlawfully threatening to harm another person, actually harming another person or attempting unsuccessfully to do so.

Assaults range from violent threats to brutal gangland beatings, from a shove to a stabbing. Many assaults arise from domestic conflicts, often during periods of heavy drinking by one or both parties. Some result from long-developing ill feelings that suddenly erupt into open violence. Some result from an argument such as a barroom dispute that ends in a brawl. Assaults often are connected with robberies.

In many states, the term *assault* formerly referred to threats of or attempts to cause bodily harm, whereas **battery** referred to the actual carrying out of such threats. Actual physical contact is not required for assault. The threat or fear of an assault along with ability to commit the act is sufficient.

In most revised state statutes, the term *assault* is synonymous with *battery*, or the two terms have been joined in a single crime termed *assault*. Some states, however, still have separate statutory offenses of assault and battery. Where one statute remains, battery includes the lesser crime of assault.

CLASSIFICATION

Assaults are classified as either simple or aggravated (felonious).

> **Simple assault** is intentionally causing another person to fear immediate bodily harm or death or intentionally inflicting or attempting to inflict bodily harm on the person. **Aggravated** or **felonious assault** is an unlawful attack by one person on another to inflict severe bodily injury.

Simple assault is usually a misdemeanor. It does not involve a deadly weapon, and the injuries sustained, if any, are neither severe nor permanent. Aggravated assault, on the other hand, is a felony. Nationally, it is the most frequently occurring of the serious violent crimes. Aggravated or felonious assault is sometimes further classified as assault with a deadly weapon or assault with intent to commit murder. National Crime Victimization Survey (NCVS) data indicates an overall victimization rate for violent crimes of 17.1 per 1,000 persons age 12 or older in 2009, a decline from the rate of 20.7 in 2006 (Truman and Rand, 2010). The rate was 11.3 for simple assault and 3.2 for aggravated assault. FBI data shows 806,843 aggravated assaults in 2009, at an estimated rate of 262.8 offenses per 100,000 inhabitants and a frequency of one aggravated assault every 39.1 seconds (*Crime in the United States, 2009*). The clearance rate for aggravated assault was 56.8 percent in 2009.

Officers Assaulted

The FBI reports that in 2009, 57,268 officers were assaulted while performing their duties, at a rate of 10.3 per 100 officers (*Law Enforcement Officers Killed and Assaulted*, 2009). The largest percentage (32.6) were assaulted responding to disturbance calls (family quarrels, bar fights, etc.); 12.7 percent were handling, transporting or maintaining custody of prisoners; and 9.6 percent were performing traffic stops.

Legal Force

Physical force may be used legally in certain instances.

> In specified instances, teachers, people operating public conveyances and law enforcement officers can legally use reasonable physical force.

Teachers have the authority of *in loco parentis* ("in the place of the parent") in many states and are allowed to use minimum force to maintain discipline, stop fights on school property or prevent destruction of school property. Bus drivers, train conductors, airplane pilots and ship captains have authority to use force to stop misconduct by passengers. Law enforcement officers may use as much force as needed to overcome resistance to a lawful arrest. Force used in self-defense is also justifiable.

ELEMENTS OF THE CRIME

The elements of the crime of assault are not as straightforward as with most other crimes and vary significantly from state to state.

Simple Assault

Most state statutes have common elements for simple assault.

> The elements of the crime of simple assault are
> - Intent to do bodily harm to another.
> - Present ability to commit the act.
> - Commission of an overt act toward carrying out the intention.

Intent to Do Bodily Harm to Another. Evidence of specific *intent* to commit bodily injury must be present. Injury that is caused accidentally is not assault. A suspect's words and actions or any injuries inflicted on a victim imply this intent. The injury must be to another person; injury to property or self-inflicted injury—no matter how serious—is not assault.

The bodily harm or injury in simple assault need not cause severe physical pain or disability. The degree of force necessary in simple assault ranges from a shove or a slap to slightly less than that required for the great bodily harm that distinguishes aggravated assault.

Present Ability to Commit the Act. The suspect must have been physically able to commit the act at the time. A suspect who hurled a knife at a victim who was obviously out of range would not have had the ability to hit the target.

Commission of an Overt Act. An overt act, more than a threat or gesture, must have been completed. If the suspect was in range to strike the victim, even if someone intervened, an assault can be proven. Intentionally pushing, shoving or physically preventing someone from entering or leaving property is often determined to be simple assault.

Aggravated Assault

Aggravated assault includes the three elements of simple assault plus an element relating to the severity of the attack. Aggravated assault is usually committed with a weapon or by some means likely to produce great bodily harm or death.

> An additional element of aggravated assault is that the intentionally inflicted bodily injury must have resulted in *one* of the following:
> - A high probability of death
> - Serious, permanent disfigurement
> - Permanent or protracted loss or impairment of the function of any body member or organ or other severe bodily harm

As with simple assault, the act must be intentional—not accidental.

High Probability of Death. An assault is considered aggravated if it is committed by any means so severe that a reasonable person feels it would result in a high probability of death. Examples include a blow sufficient to cause unconsciousness or coma, a gunshot or knife wound that causes heavy bleeding or burns inflicted over most of a person's body.

Serious, Permanent Disfigurement. Permanent disfigurement includes such things as losing an ear, eye or part of the nose, or permanent scarring of the face or other parts of the body that are normally visible. It cannot be a temporary injury that will eventually heal and not be evident.

Loss or Impairment of Body Members or Organs. Regardless of the body part affected, a charge of aggravated assault is supported by the loss or permanent impairment of body members or organs, or maiming. "Maiming signifies to cripple or mutilate in any way which deprives the use of any limb or member of the body, to seriously wound or disfigure or disable" (*Shackleford v. Commonwealth*, 1945).

Only one of these additional elements is needed to show aggravated assault, although two or all three are sometimes present. Some states do not require permanent or protracted injury or loss if the weapon used in the assault is a dangerous weapon that causes fear of immediate harm or death.

Attempted Assault

Attempted aggravated assault is also a crime in many states. If the suspect intended to assault someone but was prevented from doing so for some reason, it is still a punishable offense categorized as "unlawful attempt to commit assault."

> Attempted assault requires proof of intent along with some overt act toward committing the crime.

Intent or preparation is not enough to prove attempted assault. For example, a suspect must have done more than obtain a weapon or make a plan or even arrange to go to the scene. Rather, the suspect must actually have gone there and have had the weapon in possession when the effort was aborted.

A person who intends to rob a grocery store and whose gun accidentally discharges while the person is in the store has indeed committed an overt act. However, if the gun discharges while the person is driving to the store, there is no overt act to support an attempted assault charge. Likewise, if a potential rapist approaches a woman and has raised his arm to strike her when he is apprehended, an overt act toward an assault has been committed. But if the man is apprehended while still lurking behind a bush, reasonable doubt exists.

SPECIAL CHALLENGES IN INVESTIGATION

Sometimes it is difficult to know who started a fight. Both parties may claim the other person struck the first blow. In such cases, both may be charged with disturbing the peace or disorderly conduct, depending on the state and statute, until officers can obtain more information.

> Special challenges in assault investigations include distinguishing the victim from the suspect, determining whether the matter is civil or criminal and determining whether the act was intentional or accidental. Obtaining a complaint against a simple assault is also sometimes difficult. Moreover, such calls may be dangerous for responding officers.

It is also necessary to determine whether the altercation is a civil or a criminal matter. A person who accidentally injures someone is not guilty of a criminal offense but may be sued in civil court by the victim.

It is sometimes difficult, especially in cases of wife and child beating, to obtain a complaint from the victim. If it is simple assault, which is a misdemeanor, you must see the offense committed or obtain a complaint and arrest warrant or have the victim make a citizen's arrest. Some states, such as Pennsylvania, have given the same right of arrest for domestic assaults that exists for felony arrest—police can arrest without victim complaint and without actually witnessing the assault, as discussed later in the chapter.

Patrol officers usually make the first contact with the complainant or assault victim. Police on regular patrol sometimes observe an assault occurring. Usually, however, they are sent to the assault scene by the dispatcher. Assault calls are potentially dangerous for the police. According to the Federal Bureau of Investigation (FBI), more police officers are killed while investigating disturbance calls, such as family quarrels or bar fights, than in responding to robbery and burglary calls (*Law Enforcement*

Officers Killed and Assaulted, 2009). Officers may arrive at the point of most heated emotions and in the middle of a situation that stems from a deep-rooted problem entirely unknown to them. Their first act is to stop any assaultive action by disarming, separating or arresting the people involved. This reduces the possibility of further conflict.

Officers should be on their guard and not take sides in any dispute. If people are injured, first aid must be administered or emergency personnel summoned to the scene. The first officer on the scene should determine whether more help is needed and whether a description of the suspect must be broadcast.

In most assault cases, arriving police officers find that the assault has been completed. However, verbal abuse and considerable confusion may still exist. Interview the victim as soon as possible to obtain details about the

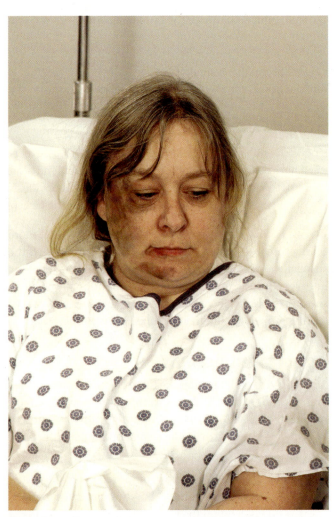

Some domestic assaults are severe enough to require hospitalization of the victim. Despite injuries, the assault victim is normally conscious and can provide critical information about the assailant and details about the severity of the attack. Battered spouses, however, are commonly reluctant to give investigators such details, either out of loyalty to their abuser or for fear of reprisal.

© Mark Burnett/Photo Researchers, Inc.

injury, the degree of pain, medical assistance rendered and other facts related to the severity of the attack. The extent and nature of the injury determines the degree of assault to be charged. Further facts supporting the severity of the attack are obtained by noting what treatment the victim requires and by talking to medical personnel.

The victim frequently knows who committed the assault, either by name or by an association that can be checked. Determine the reason for the assault. Find out what actions the victim and assailant took before, during and after the assault. If the victim of an aggravated assault is severely injured and indicates by words, gestures or appearance that death may be imminent, obtain a dying declaration.

If the suspect is at the scene, an arrest should be made if the situation warrants, or the victim may make a citizen's arrest. If the suspect is known but is not at the scene, the suspect's description should be broadcast and the investigation begun.

THE PRELIMINARY INVESTIGATION

At a minimum, an officer arriving on the scene of an assault should

- Have backup either with them or on the way until the scene is secure.
- Control and disarm those involved in the altercation.
- Provide medical aid to injured people.
- Separate suspects and victims.
- Protect the crime scene.
- Give the *Miranda* warning if applicable.
- Obtain preliminary statements.
- Photograph evidence.
- Collect and preserve evidence.
- Reconstruct the crime.

Proving the Elements of Assault

An assault that involves no dangerous weapon and results in no serious injury is a relatively minor crime. In contrast, aggravated assault is an extremely serious crime.

> To prove the elements of assault, establish the intent to cause injury, the severity of the injury inflicted and whether a dangerous weapon was used.

Establish intent by determining the events that led up to the assault. Record the suspect's exact words and actions, and take statements from the victim and any witnesses.

Establish the severity of the assault by taking photographs and describing all injuries in your notes. Describe the size, location, number, color, depth and amount of bleeding of any injuries. Some bruises do not become visible for several hours or even a day or two. Assault victims should be advised of this and told that additional photographs should be taken. Obtain an oral or written statement from a qualified medical person regarding the severity and permanence of the injuries and any impairment of bodily functioning. If injuries are severe enough to warrant hospitalization, attempt to obtain medical records documenting the injuries.

Determine the means of attack and the exact weapon used. Was it hands, fists, feet, a gun or a knife?

Evidence in Assault Investigations

Corroborate the victim's information with physical evidence.

> Physical evidence in an assault case includes photographs of injuries, clothing of the victim or suspect, weapons, broken objects, bloodstains, hairs, fibers and other signs of an altercation.

Two important pieces of evidence are photographs of injuries and the weapon used in the assault. If the hands, fists or feet were used, examine them for cuts and bruises and photograph any injuries. Obtain fingernail scrapings from both the victim and the suspect, but know first whether a warrant is required to seize DNA or other biological evidence from the suspect.

Take as evidence any weapons found at the scene. The victim's clothing may contain evidence such as bullet holes or tears made by a knife or other cutting instrument. Clothing may also contain biological evidence such as blood, saliva, semen, skin cells, etc.

If you suspect that alcohol or drug use may have contributed to the assault, arrange for the appropriate urine, blood and breath tests. Photograph and make notes regarding evidence that indicates the intensity of the assault—for example, overturned furniture, broken objects, torn-up sod and bent shrubs.

Reflective ultraviolet photography can allow investigators to document injuries on flesh as long as nine months after they have visibly healed. Reflective ultraviolet photography can reveal pattern injuries—that is, injuries that have a recognizable shape—including cigarette burns, whip or belt marks, bruising, contusions, abrasions, injury margins from immersion burns, bite marks and scratches.

> For data collection, special categories of assault are domestic violence, stalking and elder abuse.

INVESTIGATING DOMESTIC VIOLENCE

Officers may not understand that although it appears that the victim can change the circumstances, victims often do not believe they have this capability.

> **Domestic violence** is a pattern of behaviors involving physical, sexual, economic and emotional abuse, alone or in combination, often by an intimate partner and often to establish and maintain power and control over the other partner.

History of Domestic Violence: From Male Privilege to Criminal Act

Domestic violence has deep roots in the patriarchal systems the colonists brought with them when they settled in the New World. At the time, however, such violence was perceived not as a crime but as a man's duty, for he, as head of the family and the authority figure in the home, was expected to keep control over his wife and children and was allowed to use any means necessary to achieve order. In the case of *State v. Rhodes* (1868), the North Carolina Supreme Court ruled that although a husband had the right to whip his wife, if the switch was thicker than the thumb, it was considered abuse. This Rule of Thumb standard, adopted by most state courts across the nation during the colonial period, was derived from English common law and permitted men to use any instrument to physically enforce family obedience as long as the object was no larger than the thickness of the man's thumb.

The use of force was an acceptable male privilege, and domestic violence was considered a family matter to be handled privately. The police were rarely, if ever, summoned to intervene. But times have changed, and now law enforcement regards violence against a spouse or intimate partner as an offense appropriate for criminal justice intervention. During the 1970s and 1980s, police made arrests in only 7 to 15 percent of the intimate

partner violence cases to which they were called; however, by 2000, approximately 50 percent of domestic violence cases resulted in arrests (Hirschel, 2009). Despite the criminalization of such assaults, domestic violence remains a persistent problem for thousands of households across the country, partly because the abusive behavior is part of the family dynamic, tightly woven into the fabric of family relationships and passed from generation to generation through a cycle of violence.

The Cycle of Violence

Domestic violence is commonly thought of as occurring in a three-phase cycle: (1) the tension-building stage, (2) the acute battering episode and (3) the honeymoon. This cycle, which typically increases in both frequency and severity, is illustrated in Figure 9.1. This pattern of abuse often becomes a vicious intergenerational cycle because research has found that children who witness abuse or are abused themselves are more likely to abuse a spouse or child when they become adults. Crimes against children are the focus of Chapter 11.

Types of Assault and Weapons Used

The National Institute of Justice (NIJ) describes four main types of intimate partner violence (IPV; "Intimate Partner Violence," 2007):

Physical violence is the intentional use of physical force (e.g., shoving, choking, shaking, slapping, punching, burning, or use of a weapon, restraints, or one's size and strength against another person) with the potential for causing death, disability, injury, or physical harm.

Sexual violence can be divided into three categories: (1) the use of physical force to compel a person to engage in a sexual act unwillingly, whether or not the act is completed; (2) an attempted or completed sexual act involving a person who, because of illness, disability, or the influence of alcohol or other drugs, or because of intimidation or pressure is unable to understand the nature or condition of the act, decline participation, or communicate unwillingness to engage in the act; and (3) abusive sexual contact. [Sexual violence is the focus of Chapter 10.]

Threats of physical or sexual violence communicate the intent to cause death, disability, injury, or physical harm through the use of words, gestures, or weapons.

Psychological/emotional violence traumatizes the victim by acts, threats of acts, or coercive tactics (e.g., humiliating the victim, controlling what the

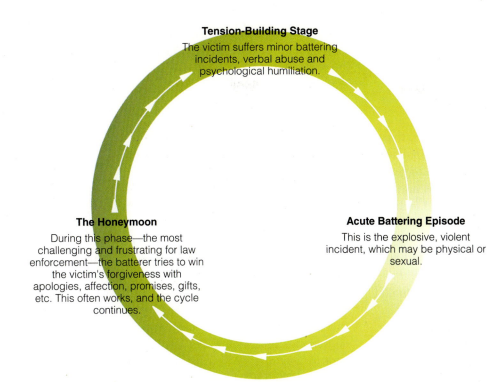

FIGURE 9.1
Three-phase cycle of violence.
Source: From Hess/Wrobleski. *Police Operations*, 5E. © 2011 Delmar Learning, a part of Cengage Learning, Inc. Reproduced by permission. www.cengage.com/permissions

victim can and cannot do, withholding information, isolating the victim from friends and family, denying access to money or other basic resources). In most cases, emotional violence has been preceded by acts of threats of physical or sexual violence.

Females are more likely than are males to use a weapon during an incident of IPV (Smith and Farole, 2009). Furthermore, women are twice as likely as men to use a knife or other sharp object and three times more likely than men to use a blunt object, such as a rock, during an IPV incident (Smith and Farole, 2009). Table 9.1 shows weapon use among defendants in IPV cases.

Prevalence of Domestic Violence and Its Victims

Domestic violence is found at all socioeconomic levels across all racial demographics. Domestic violence includes IPV as well as violence between family members. Intimate relationships involve current or former spouses, boyfriends or girlfriends, including same-sex relationships. Intimates are distinguished from other relatives (parent, child, sibling, grandparent, in-law, cousin), acquaintances (friend, coworker, neighbor, schoolmate, someone known) and strangers (anyone not previously known by the victim).

The Office for Victims of Crime (OVC) reports that one woman is victimized by an intimate partner every

TABLE 9.1 Weapon Use among Defendants in Intimate Partner Violence Cases

Weapon Use	All Cases
TOTAL	**100%**
Primary weapon defendant used during the incident	**26.0%**
Firearm	2.0%
Knife/sharp object	5.8%
Hard object/wall	5.7%
Blunt object	7.1%
Other weapon*	3.1%
Unknown weapon	2.3%
Defendant did not use a weapon**	**74.0%**

*Includes flammable items, ropes, telephone cords, belts and other items.

**Defendant may have used hands, fists or feet as a personal weapon.

Source: Data from BJS—Smith & Farole, 2009, p.3 Bureau of Justice Statistics.

52 seconds, one man is victimized every 3.5 minutes and one child is reported abused or neglected every 34.9 seconds ("Crime Clock," 2009). Data from the *National Crime Victimization Survey* indicates that 538,090 women and 117,210 men were affected by IPV during 2009 (Truman and Rand, 2010).

These figures, however, are an undercount because much of the domestic violence that occurs goes unreported. Domestic abuse in families from diverse ethnic or cultural backgrounds also commonly goes unreported. For example, female abuse victims of Asian descent are reluctant to notify the police because they do not want to bring shame on their family or community.

Fear is another reason such crimes go unreported. Many women do not report domestic assaults because of threats such as "I'll take the kids and you'll never see them again" or "I'll kill you if you call the police." In many instances the wife fails to report the abuse (and to leave the relationship) because she has no work skills and no independent income, because of the stigma and embarrassment associated with the offense or because she has one or more children to support. Some victims choose to stay with their batterers for fear that leaving would further enrage their partners.

Statistics document that many batterers eventually kill their intimate. One study found that in as many as 50 percent of domestic violence-related homicides, police had previously been called to respond to a domestic incident between the two parties (Kanable, 2010). In some instances, the male batterer becomes the victim of homicide. In such cases, the defense often attributes the murder to the "battered-woman syndrome," which is based on the concept of duress and results from a cycle of violence.

Women as Abusers. Although most abuse victims are women, women also perpetrate such violence. An estimated 12.5 percent of IPV cases, or one in eight, involve a female batterer and a male victim (Smith and Farole, 2009). Although it is common for battered women to feel shame at being victims of domestic abuse, the stigma for battered men is even greater. Many reports of husband abuse go unreported because these men anticipate an unsympathetic or incredulous reaction from responding officers. Indeed, the misperception persists that women who commit violence against men have been driven to it through years of victimization at the hands of these men (the battered-woman syndrome), and thus, the men "have it coming." However, officers responding to a domestic violence call must not assume the male is always the perpetrator and the female always the victim.

A study that examined whether women who assaulted their male partners were more likely to avoid arrest found that this was, indeed, the case (Felson and Pare, 2007, p.436). Another study examined the differences in how male and female batterers were treated by the criminal justice system and assessed four decision points: the decision to file charges (versus rejection for insufficient evidence); to file as a felony (versus a misdemeanor or probation violation); to dismiss for insufficient evidence (versus full prosecution); and to reduce felony charges to a misdemeanor or violation of parole.

The study found suspect gender to be statistically significant in all four outcomes, in favoring female over male suspects, suggesting that female intimate violence perpetrators are frequently viewed more as victims than as offenders (Kingsnorth and MacIntosh, 2007, p.461).

Same-Sex Domestic Violence. Traditionally the issue of gay and lesbian domestic violence was ignored and its extent undocumented. The fact that law enforcement once considered abuse within a heterosexual couple's relationship a private, personal matter makes understandable the lack of police concern regarding violence between homosexual partners. However, "The dynamics of same-sex domestic violence are similar to those of opposite-sex domestic violence in many respects" (Pattavina et al., 2007, p.5). The cause is cyclical, escalates over time and maintains a commonality in characteristics of batterers.

The rates of physical violence vary from 8 percent to 60 percent for lesbians and from 22 percent to 44 percent for gay men (Pattavina et al., 2007). Approximately 5 percent of all IPV cases involve an abuser and victim of the same gender (Smith and Farole, 2009). When the law enforcement response to domestic violence incidents involving heterosexual and same-sex couples is compared, the offenders receive similar treatment. However, same-sex victims rarely are afforded the same protection as heterosexuals are (Pattavina et al.).

When the Abuser Is a Police Officer. Knowing the seriousness of the crime and the damage it causes to victims and families does not make officers immune from committing domestic violence themselves. In fact, research suggests that domestic abuse may occur more often in police families than among the general public.

When the abuser is a police officer, special challenges exist. Few professions are characterized by the fierce loyalty to one's coworkers that prevails in law enforcement. This allegiance is put to the test when responding to a domestic violence call at an officer's home. In the past, responding officers would simply separate the parties and persuade the battered spouse to give the abuser time to cool off, explaining away the violence as the result of a stressful job and convincing the spouse that an arrest would only jeopardize the security of the entire family. Typically, no official report would be filed about the incident, and the abuse would be allowed to go on. Sometimes the abuse continues to escalate until the officer kills his spouse and then, commonly, himself. In many, if not most, of these cases, the officer's service weapon is used in the crime.

Spurred by research that showed how domestic abuse can evolve to domestic homicide, particularly when a firearm is available to the abuser, a federal law was passed in 1996 prohibiting anyone, including a police officer, who has been convicted of a qualifying misdemeanor domestic violence offense from owning or using a firearm or possessing ammunition. This law, known as the Lautenberg Act (18 U.S.C. § 922 (g)(9)), amended the Gun Control Act of 1968, which barred only those convicted of a felony offense from owning or using a firearm. This law also puts another wrinkle in the issue of police-involved domestic violence because an officer who is unable to carry a gun is unlikely to find or retain a job.

Predictors and Precipitators of Domestic Violence

Research has attempted to identify factors that predict or precipitate episodes of domestic violence, both for victimization and perpetration. As mentioned, one well-documented predictor of the likelihood of family abuse is a history of family violence: "Forty-six percent of intimate partner violence cases involved a defendant with a prior history of abuse toward the same victim, and 24 percent of victims of IPV had reported prior violence to police" (Smith and Farole, 2009, p.5). In many cases, victims have made prior reports not for domestic assault but for other crimes, which are referred to as **indicator crimes**. Indicator crimes are offenses that, in situations involving the same victim and suspect, can establish a pattern of events indicative of an abusive relationship. These crimes can range from harassing phone calls to hit-and-run.

Animal cruelty is another predictor of abusive or violent behavior. Results of numerous studies have demonstrated a link between animal abuse and domestic violence, with some research going beyond the surface correlation to explore deeper aspects of the abusive psyche. One study found that, of all the women seeking safety at a shelter who also had one or more pets at home, 71 percent reported that their partner had threatened, hurt or killed their companion animal (Ascione, 1998). Another study found that violent offenders sentenced to a maximum-security prison had a significantly higher rate of childhood cruelty toward pets and other animals than did nonviolent offenders (Merz-Perez et al., 2001).

Although not a predictor or precipitator of domestic violence, the presence of firearms can drastically change the complexion of domestic violence and make responding to such calls exponentially more dangerous for officers. Other risk factors for domestic violence include unemployment of the batterer and estrangement, where the victim has moved out of the previously shared residence.

A helpful Web site for both victims of domestic violence and those seeking to help them is www.enditnow.gov.

The Police Response

Response to such calls may be initiated by the dispatcher, who can save hours of legwork by exploring with the victim her frame of mind and that of the potential attacker. From that point on, responding officers' actions are critical.

The availability of computers in patrol vehicles and use of real-time response software enable a premises and individual records check as part of the preliminary investigation. This may include previous calls for service from the complainant's residence, complaints of illegal activities at this address, open warrants for involved parties and background information on the victim or alleged assailant. This information enhances the safety of the officers and helps them better assess the situation upon arrival at the scene.

Grossi (2007, p.28) asserts, "Most officers know the stats: domestic disputes are the most dangerous calls they respond to. And they're right. The latest statistics from the FBI Uniform Crime Reports again show the single largest category for officer assaults is response to domestic calls . . . . And most officers know why." Grossi explains what often happens when officers respond to domestic violence calls:

> The traditional domestic dynamic reveals that in any call involving family troubles, there are usually two principal players involved: the victim (usually the abused spouse) and the suspect (the abuser). As soon as you, the officer, arrive on the scene, the dynamic changes. A third element is now injected into the scenario: the rescuer. Of course, what most cops hope for is that you and your partner can get the principals separated, get things calmed down, arrest the abuser and in essence rescue the victim.
>
> However, what often happens is a change in dynamics and labels shift. The abuser now is seen as the victim, you are now viewed as the abuser and the only vacancy left—the rescuer slot—is filled by the abused spouse, who turns on you to "rescue" their abuser-spouse. The stage is set for a double-team assault. (p.28)

To avoid such a situation, Grossi (2007, p.28) recommends always responding with a backup or two. Further recommendations include separating people for the interviews, impounding all firearms at the scene if the laws and policies in your area permit and never dropping your guard just because you are dealing with a homosexual or lesbian couple (p.29).

Police officers must listen to the facts and determine who the offender is if the assault is not continuing when they arrive. Reduce the level of tension at the scene by separating and talking to the participants and being vigilant about the safety of the participants and any children present.

Evidence in Domestic Violence Cases. Gather evidence of the offense. If officers were dispatched to the scene because of a 911 call, preserve the 911 recording as evidence to be used at trial.

In any assault, one of the most important kinds of evidence is photographs of any injuries; however, some bruises do not become visible until well after the battering episode. Other evidence to obtain in IPV cases includes photographs of the scene, damaged clothing or other property, weapons used, prior police reports, medical reports, victim's statements, suspect's statements and statements from neighbors or other witnesses (see Table 9.2). Half of IPV events are witnessed by a third party, a majority of the witnesses were directly present to observe the violence and more than half of those direct eyewitnesses are children (Smith and Farole, 2009). Consequently, investigators working domestic violence cases need to be proficient in interviewing children. Statements of the crime can be particularly valuable:

> In many cases, victims can be compelled to testify in court. If the victim feigns memory loss, the written statement can be used either to refresh the victim's recollection of the event or as substantive evidence.

A statement from the abuser is equally valuable—*and officers should be aware that a lie can be as useful as the truth.* An abuser who concocts a statement to cover his crime is locked into that story if he has signed a written statement. . . .

In some cases, abusers later file charges against the victim in an effort to dissuade the victim from pursuing her case. Having a signed statement from the abuser is very helpful when the prosecutor is trying to decide which party is being truthful. (Hill, 2008, p.6)

The importance of the incident report should not be overlooked. The better the report, the better the chance of obtaining a conviction. Describe completely any injuries and the victim's physical condition. Some departments have a supplemental report form to document evidence in domestic violence cases.

Explain to the victim that an *order of protection* may be obtained from a court to help prevent future assaults, as discussed shortly. Many agencies also provide cards with a list of resources available to help victims of domestic violence.

To Arrest or Not? Basically, any evidence that would lead an officer to make an arrest in any other situation also applies to spousal situations. All states permit an arrest based on probable cause. Many states now mandate police to make an arrest in domestic violence incidents

TABLE 9.2 Evidence Obtained in Intimate Partner Violence Cases in 16 Large Counties, by Charge Type

Type of Evidence	All Cases	Percent of defendants charged with a	
		Felony	Misdemeanor
TOTAL	**100%**	**100%**	**100%**
Any evidence obtained	83.5	90.0	81.8
Physical evidence	67.9	74.9	66.3
Photos of victim/defendant	46.5	44.9	46.9
Tape of 911 call	25.9	30.4	24.9
Photos of scene	12.2	19.8	10.5
Weapon recovered	4.7	10.7	3.3
Medical records	3.4	10.4	1.8
Forensic evidence	3.3	9.8	1.8
Other evidence	8.3	11.3	7.7
Statement from witness	45.9	58.0	43.1
Statement from defendant	10.2	12.7	9.7
No evidence obtained	16.5	9.1	18.2

Note: Detail does not sum to total because more than one type of evidence was obtained in some cases.

Source: Data from BJS—Smith & Farole, 2009, p.5. Bureau of Justice Statistics.

if there is a protective or restraining order against the attacker, and some require an arrest even though no such order exists.

Many departments have a mandatory arrest policy for domestic abuse, requiring the officer to make an arrest if there is probable cause, even without a signed complaint by the victim. Some states have legislated that police must have and implement such a policy. This philosophy was largely the result of the Minneapolis Domestic Violence Experiment (MDVE) conducted by Sherman and Berk in the early 1980s, which concluded that arrest was a more effective deterrent to repeat offenses than was advising or sending the suspect away. This report, sometimes summarized as "arrest works best," helped create a nationwide pro-arrest sentiment in domestic violence situations. However, "It may be premature to conclude that arrest is always the best way for police to handle domestic violence, or that all suspects in such situations should be arrested. A number of factors suggest a cautious interpretation of the finding" (Sherman and Berk, 1984, pp.6–7).

Indeed, since that time, numerous other studies have found that alternatives to arrest may be better in specific circumstances, for example, when the batterer is employed and arrest would cause serious negative repercussions for the batterer as well as the family. In such instances, it is presumed the abuser has a higher stake in conformity and an alternative remedy can be more effective in breaking the abusive cycle. Sherman (1995, p.207) has asserted that arrest can backfire, and mandatory arrest laws can actually compound the domestic violence problem rather than alleviate it. Nonetheless, researchers continue to reexamine whether arrest is the best response to domestic violence:

> A series of fairly rigorous experiments in multiple jurisdictions finds that arrest deters repeat re-abuse, whether suspects are employed or not. In none of the sites was arrest associated with increased re-abuse among intimate partners. Another major study . . . found that whether police arrested the suspect or not, their involvement has a strong deterrent effect. . . .
>
> A Berkeley arrest study found similarly that actions taken by responding officers, including arrest, providing victims with information pamphlets, tracking down witness statements, and helping victims secure protective orders, all were associated with reduced re-abuse. By contrast, the highest re-abuse rates were found where responding officers left it to the victim to make a "citizen arrest," swearing out a complaint herself (Klein, 2008, p.16).

Officers should not base their decisions regarding arrest on their perception of the willingness of the victim or witnesses to testify. Furthermore, the victim need not sign a complaint.

Departments vary in their policies regarding mutual abuse. Some departments require the responding officer to determine who the primary physical aggressor was and then arrest that person, whereas other agencies have a dual arrest policy. Dual arrest policies, which gained use following passage of pro-arrest laws, allow officers to circumvent the primary aggressor assessment and arrest both parties when injuries to both sides are observed. Critics of dual arrest policies have argued that they result in more arrests than are necessary because officers find it easier to simply arrest both parties than try to determine who the primary aggressor was, even if only one party shows injury. A dual arrest policy does not preclude the single arrest of the primary aggressor only, if the officer is able to make that determination. Factors to consider in making this assessment include

- Prior domestic violence involving either person.

- The relative seriousness of the injuries inflicted upon each person involved.

- The potential for future injury.

- Whether one of the alleged batteries was committed in self-defense.

- Any other factor that helps the officer decide which person was the primary physical aggressor.

Specialized domestic violence units hold promise. Such a unit might consist of a detective who jointly works cases with a deputy sheriff in the county. Whenever a patrol officer takes a report, the domestic violence unit follows up to ensure proper procedures have been followed: "Cases involving domestic violence require a focused approach with a priority placed on the enforcement and prosecution of batterers, direct services and support of victims and community outreach. The utilization of dedicated and specialized units within police departments and prosecutors' offices has proven to be effective in a coordinated approach and seems best suited to dealing with the continuous cycle of domestic violence" (Bune, 2007, pp.12–13).

Police Nonresponse. One reason officers are criticized for not responding to domestic violence incidents is that they commonly receive calls from uninvolved third parties. For example, an apartment tenant calls to say the couple across the hall is shouting at each other and it sounds like things are being thrown and glass is breaking. When officers arrive, the couple may be embarrassed or angry because this is how they argue. They see no reason to involve the law and are irritated at the interference of neighbors and police. In other cases, a spouse may report a false domestic violence incident just to see the other party punished or the threat of punishment inflicted.

Several studies have examined whether the police response to domestic violence calls does receive a lower priority than other crime calls. The results generally show an increasingly high priority being placed on such calls.

Effectiveness of Various Interventions

Increasing numbers of departments throughout the United States are adopting a "zero-tolerance" approach to domestic violence, which appears to be highly successful. Although many departments view arrests as a critical part of a zero-tolerance stance, some researchers contend that it is not the arrest itself but what happens *after* the arrest that ultimately determines the effectiveness of the response.

In some jurisdictions, arrested batterers are processed through the justice system just as many other types of criminal offenders—jail, prosecution and, one hopes, conviction. In other jurisdictions, arrested abusers are required to participate in a batterer intervention program (BIP), a counseling and treatment alternative to sending these offenders to jail. The most common BIP used throughout the country is based on the Duluth Model, founded on the feminist theory that domestic violence is the result of a patriarchal ideology in which men are encouraged and expected to control their partners. The Duluth Model BIP seeks to enlighten abusive men by exploring their attitudes about control and teaching them strategies to better interact with their partners. Other BIPs are based on cognitive-behavioral modification to correct faulty thinking patterns, group practice models that seek to root out the multiple causes of battering and customize treatment to fit the offender's needs and group therapy BIPs that take the controversial position that spouses are equal participants in creating disturbances in relationships.

As with arrest research findings, results of studies that have examined the effectiveness of BIPs are mixed:

> Over the past two decades, a growing number of courts have come to rely on batterer programs as their mandate of choice, especially when the legal issues in a case preclude the imposition of jail [the case is classified as a misdemeanor]. Three of four

previously randomized trials produced largely negative results. The present study . . . randomly assigned misdemeanor domestic violence offenders in the Bronx, New York, to either a batterer program or not; and to either monthly or graduated judicial monitoring with the latter involving reduced court appearances in response to compliance and increased appearances in response to noncompliance. The study found that neither the batterer program nor either of the two monitoring schedules produced a reduction in official re-arrest rates for any offense, for domestic violence, or for domestic violence with the same victim. Similarly, one-year victim interviews indicated that neither program assignment nor monitoring schedule significantly affected victim reports of re-abuse. (Labriola et al., 2008, p.252)

Results of studies that have examined the effectiveness of BIPs suggest that perhaps the most significant factor in the rehabilitation of a batterer is the offender's **stake in conformity**, a constellation of variables that, in effect, comprise "what an offender has to lose," such as marital status, residential stability or employment.

Some jurisdictions have implemented intervention programs that draw on the cultural strengths of the community. In New Mexico, for example, domestic violence in Indian Country had become a significant problem, and the traditional route of incarceration was not having positive results. A sergeant with the local sheriff's department, himself a Navajo, suggested an intervention program built on a fundamental aspect of Native American communities—the clan and the wisdom of elders. The elders' knowledge and experience in resolving conflicts through peacemaking is what makes this unique intensive intervention program a success in Indian Country.

As important as intervention programs aimed at batterers are, of equal importance are efforts to help victims. It is fairly common for abuse victims who have filed a report and begun the process of pressing charges to change their minds and want to drop charges, whether out of guilt for having "turned" on their partner; out of worry that, because they are financially dependent on their abuser, conviction and imprisonment will lead to loss of income and medical insurance for the family; out of loyalty because they have patched things up with their abuser (the honeymoon phase has set in); or out of fear because the batterer threatens or tries to intimidate them into dropping the charges.

One option commonly suggested to victims of violent abuse is to obtain an order of protection, also called a restraining order.

Restraining Orders

Domestic violence victims themselves are taking a more active role in preventing recurring assaults by obtaining restraining orders, alternately called civil protective orders or orders for protection. These court-issued documents aim to restrict an alleged abuser's behavior to protect his intended victim. A provision of the Violence Against Women Act (VAWA) of 1994 assigns **full faith and credit** to valid orders of protection, meaning that an order issued anywhere in the country is legally binding and enforceable nationwide.

Restraining orders typically take several weeks to obtain, but if the victim is in immediate life-threatening danger, an emergency restraining order can generally be issued within 24 hours. A court hearing is usually conducted before a restraining order is issued, allowing a judge time to review the facts of the case provided by the victim on the request form and to hear from the abuser, if he appears at the hearing. If an order of protection is granted, it may contain a variety of conditions regarding the abuser's personal conduct, use of alcohol, child custody or visitation, child or spousal support, a stay-away order, a move-out order and a ban on the possession or use of firearms.

This final condition poses a problem for officers who have a restraining order filed against them, as they are prohibited from possessing a weapon even while on duty. Some restraining orders automatically expire after a specified time limit, unless renewed, but others are valid indefinitely unless a request is made for dismissal and a court grants such dismissal.

Although abuse victims are certainly encouraged to protect themselves, they cannot rely solely on a piece of paper for security. In fact, some studies have found that women who seek restraining orders are well aware of their potential ineffectiveness, and one study found that nearly 50 percent of IPV victims who obtain protective orders are stalked by their abusers (Hawkins, 2010).

Legislation

In addition to mandatory arrest laws, other laws address issues concerning convicted domestic abusers. One such statute already discussed is the Lautenberg Amendment to the Crime Control Bill of 1968, which prohibits individuals convicted of misdemeanor crimes involving domestic violence from owning or possessing a firearm. This retroactive statute is a problem for law enforcement officers, for if convicted of domestic violence, they will lose their jobs.

Despite the many laws devoted to reducing or eliminating domestic violence, criminal justice should not expect too much from such legislation.

Technology Innovations

Healy and Barrios (2007) describe a new Massachusetts law that requires an offender who violates a domestic order of protection to wear a global positioning system (GPS) monitoring device.

The GPS helps enforce the restraining order by preventing the batterer from entering "liberty zones," such as the battered partner's domicile and place of work, their children's schools, and the residences of extended family members. Probation agents will monitor offenders to ensure that they do not breach these zones. If they do, a record of a restraining order violation will be made, thus making stalking and further violent attacks more difficult. Further, police and the victim are automatically phoned if the offender breaches the battered partner's liberty zone, thus minimizing the victim's fears of an unexpected confrontation. . . .

The new law not only adapts technology that better protects victims, but it also represents a logical step toward changing the paradigm of responsibility for domestic violence—away from the victim to provide for her own safety by hiding, and onto the justice system to hold the offender accountable. By using GPS technology, we align accountability with criminal behavior and do more than simply apprise a battered partner of her options. The law utilizes modern technology to give teeth to a restraining order, making real progress toward returning liberty to battered partners and their children.

Avoiding Lawsuits

Failure to respond appropriately to domestic violence can result in serious financial liability to local governments. More and more, victims of domestic violence are suing local governments for failure to protect them. Perhaps the most well-known case is that of Tracy Thurman in Torrington, Connecticut. The police department was ordered to pay almost $1 million because they failed to protect Tracy from her husband, who had a history of battering her (*Thurman v. City of Torrington*, 1984).

To reduce lawsuits, departments should have a pro-arrest policy if officers have probable cause to believe a domestic assault has occurred. They should train officers in this pro-arrest policy and require them to document why an arrest has or has not been made.

INVESTIGATING STALKING

Closely related to investigating domestic violence cases is the challenge of investigating stalking cases. The National Institute of Justice ("Stalking," 2007) states,

> Like domestic violence, stalking is a crime of power and control. Stalking is conservatively defined as "a course of conduct directed at a specific person that involves repeated (two or more occasions) visual or physical proximity, nonconsensual communication, or verbal, written, or implied threats, or a combination thereof, that would cause a reasonable person fear." Stalking behaviors also may include persistent patterns of leaving or sending the victim unwanted items or damaging or threatening to damage the victim's property, defaming the victim's character, or harassing the victim via the Internet by posting personal information or spreading rumors about the victim.

> Although legal definitions vary among jurisdictions, **stalking** is generally defined as the willful or intentional commission of a series of acts that would cause a reasonable person to fear death or serious bodily injury and that, in fact, does place the victim in fear of death or serious bodily injury.

According to the National Center for Injury Prevention and Control and the Centers for Disease Control and Prevention (CDC), stalking affects 7 percent of women (1 in 14) and 2 percent of men (1 in 50) at some time in their lives (*Report to Congress*, n.d.). Data from the NCVS indicate that an estimated 3.4 million people age 18 and older are stalked every year (Baum et al., 2009). Many of these victims obtain protective orders, yet such orders are generally much less effective for stalking victims than for other types of victims (Hawkins, 2010).

Stalking is a crime in every state and the District of Columbia and at the federal level. Fifteen states classify stalking as a felony upon the first offense; 34 states classify it as a felony upon the second offense or when it involves aggravating factors such as possession of a deadly weapon, violation of a court order or condition of probation or parole (*Report to Congress*, n.d.). Additional aggravating factors include a victim younger than 16 or the same victim as in prior incidents ("Stalking Fact Sheet," 2008).

Stalking often leads to homicide. Statistics on **femicide**, the murder of a woman, reveal that the majority of femicide victims had been stalked by the person who killed them. One study found that 76 percent of women who were killed by their current or former intimate partner had been stalked by their killer within the year preceding the murder, and 85 percent of women who were victims of *attempted* murder by a current or former partner had also been victims of stalking by such partners in the 12 months leading up to the attempt (Garcia, 2010). More than half of these victims had reported the stalking to the police before they were murdered by their stalkers ("Stalking Fact Sheet," 2008).

Types of Stalking

Stalkers are typically categorized as a certain typology, usually based on the relationship between the stalker and the victim. One system of stalking typologies involves the three categories of intimate or former intimate, acquaintance and stranger stalking.

In *intimate or former intimate stalking*, the stalker and victim may be married or divorced, current or former cohabitants, serious or casual sexual partners or former sexual partners. This is the most common relationship involved in stalking cases. In *acquaintance stalking*, the stalker and victim know each other casually. They may be neighbors or coworkers. They might have even dated once or twice but were not sexual partners. In *stranger stalking*, the stalker and victim do not know each other at all.

The National Center for Victims of Crime (NCVC) presents a different set of typologies for stalkers, also including three varieties: the simple obsessional, the love obsessional and the erotomanic. *Simple obsessional* stalkers are the basic equivalent of the aforementioned intimate stalkers but also include acquaintance stalkers. These cases are the most common type and most often occur in the context of domestic violence. *Love obsessional* stalkers have no prior relationship with their victim but become fixated on that person, often a celebrity, believing they belong together. *Erotomanic* stalkers, the rarest of the three types, believe that their victim is in love with them.

Cyberstalking. The growth of e-mail and use of the Internet has resulted in cyberstalking, which, in previous editions of this text, was simply defined as preying on a victim via computer. However, the problem has grown in such scope and severity that more elaborate and specific definitions are now used. The Department of Justice defines **cyberstalking** as the repeated use of the Internet, e-mail or other digital electronic communications devices

Dawnette Knight reacts in court as a letter from Catherine Zeta-Jones is read Friday, July 8, 2005, in Los Angeles during Knight's sentencing for stalking the actress. Zeta-Jones, who almost suffered a nervous breakdown because of the vicious death threats, and her husband, Michael Douglas, testified that the 32-year-old Knight wrote more than a dozen letters describing how she was going to "slice [Zeta-Jones] up like meat on a bone and feed her to the dogs," so that when she finished with "this bitch/whore she will not be this pretty face actress." Knight's lawyer, Richard P. Herman (pictured at right), claimed his client simply had a "girlish crush" on Douglas, and was upset when she read in the tabloids that the actress was allegedly having an affair with one of her *Ocean's 12* costars. Knight was given three years in state prison.

© AP Images/Nick Ut

to stalk another person. Such technology is used to harass approximately one of every four stalking victims, which translates into roughly 1.2 million victims who have been stalked through use of some type of electronic device (Miller, 2009). Like other forms of stalking, cyberstalking can turn violent.

The perception of anonymity afforded by online activity is thought to be one reason cyberstalking is on the rise. Consequently, states have turned to legislation to address this problem.

Legislation and Department Policies

The first antistalking laws were passed in 1990 in California. Since 1999, all 50 states and the District of Columbia have enacted general antistalking laws, and 45 states have expanded their legislation to include cyberstalking offenses ("Cyberstalking Laws," 2008). Title 18, §875 of the U.S. Code makes it a federal offense to transmit, electronically or otherwise, any threatening communication in interstate or foreign commerce, with such acts punishable by fine, imprisonment for as long as five years or both.

Antistalking laws describe specific threatening conduct and hold the suspect responsible for proving that his or her actions were not intended to frighten or intimidate the victim. Most stalking laws require proof of a credible threat made by the perpetrator against the victim or the victim's family.

The NCVC has released model legislation to combat stalking by helping states update their laws to reflect changes in what is known about stalking and how stalkers operate ("Victims' Group Issues Model Code," 2007, p.1).

Although legislation makes stalking a specific crime and empowers law enforcement to combat the offense, a great deal of variation and subjectivity exists among the states' legal definitions of stalking. Many officers are unaware of antistalking legislation in their state. And many officers do not know about their own department's policy on stalking.

The Police Response

The traditional law enforcement response to stalkers has been to encourage victims to obtain court-issued restraining orders. Unfortunately, such orders are often ineffective, as demonstrated when one offender dramatically stabbed his wife to death and "knifed" the court order to her chest. Research has also found that women who are stalked after obtaining a restraining order have higher levels of fear of future harm and believed the orders were not as effective as they had anticipated. Furthermore, the stalking that occurred after the issuance of such protective orders was associated with more violence, "suggesting those who stalk are more violent and more resistant to court intervention" (Hawkins, 2010, p.6). Because of this proven ineffectiveness of restraining orders, the perceived inability of criminal justice to effectively handle stalkers and victims' fear of antagonizing and angering their stalkers, many stalking incidents go unreported.

Law enforcement faces a unique challenge in addressing and investigating stalking incidents because of the lack of clear definitions of stalking or of the elements constituting the offense. Other investigative challenges presented by stalking cases include these:

■ Stalking behaviors are complex and varied.

■ There is no standard psychological profile of stalkers to assist investigators.

■ When stalkers also commit domestic violence, investigations are likely to focus on the violence rather than the stalking.

■ Stalkers often cross state or tribal lines to monitor, harass or commit violence against victims.

■ Stalkers are not easily deterred.

■ Ensuring victim safety is difficult. (Velazques et al., 2009, p.31)

In general, victims should be encouraged to use answering machines to screen their calls and to document the threatening messages. All threatening electronic communications should be saved and a hard copy printed. Victims should obtain an unlisted phone number or a new e-mail address or change their user name if the harassment involves cyberstalking. In short, investigators should support victims in gathering evidence and in helping to keep themselves safe until the stalker can be stopped.

Investigators should conduct a technology risk assessment with the victim, asking such things as, "How many computers are in the house? Who has access? Which vehicles are equipped with GPS? How many cell phones do you use?" (Miller, 2009, p.58). In these types of investigations, time works against you because so much of the evidence is volatile and can disappear in a matter of weeks (Miller, 2009). And unlike detectives who track online child predators, "Investigators who deal with high-tech crimes are better served to get out in the field than to sit behind a computer. 'Our best tools these days are the search warrant and strong investigative techniques'" (Miller, 2009, p.59). Complications in investigating cyberstalking include the unwillingness of some Internet service providers (ISPs) to give law enforcement access to subscribers' records and the increased ability to communicate anonymously through Internet tools, such as remailers that strip identifying information from e-mail headers and erase transactional data from servers that would otherwise be used to trace a message's author.

One step an investigator should take is to assess the threat to determine the credibility and overall capability of the stalker to actually carry out his or her expressed intent to cause harm. Elements to consider include the target, the stalker's motivation, the stalker's ability to follow through on threats, the stalker's personal background and the victim-offender relationship.

Petrocelli (2007b, p.22) observes, "Stalking is truly a unique crime. It is not a single act, but rather several maybe disjointed acts that all have the same motive." Some of the acts reported to police during an investigation, such as receiving flowers, love notes and other gifts or unwanted items, are hardly associated with violent crimes, but if such seemingly "innocuous acts" disrupt a victim's life, it is a case of stalking (Petrocelli, 2007b). During stalking investigations, officers often learn that the crimes occurred at several locations across different jurisdictions, so joint efforts are often needed. Knowing what constitutes stalking in an officer's jurisdiction is crucial: "By definition stalking requires two or more incidents, so a good history is an important part of any investigation" (Petrocelli, 2007b, p.23).

Victim input is encouraged because the crime is partially defined by the victim's reaction. Victims must be instructed how to document, either in writing or with a video or audio recording, their emotional and physical reactions to each stalking act. This "stalking log" must include dates, times and locations, and should be recorded immediately: "A well-kept stalking log, supported by physical evidence (phone recordings, e-mails, etc.), will not only be strong evidence at a trial, but will empower the victim" because victims are no longer simply defenseless targets but are instead collectors of incriminating evidence, working toward their own justice (Petrocelli, 2007b, p.23).

Research findings support a strong connection between stalking and domestic violence. Evaluating the potential for violence is an important part of a stalking investigation because stalking behavior can, and in some cases does, elevate to homicide. The FBI's National Center for the Analysis of Violent Crime (NCAVC) is a valuable resource in helping stalking investigators assess an offender's potential for violence. The NCAVC stresses the need to consider a stalker's behavior in its totality by considering specific actions and other factors, including

■ Threats to kill.

■ Access to or recent acquisition of weapons.

■ Violations of protective orders.

■ Prior physical violence against the victim or others, including pets.

■ Substance abuse.

■ Location of violence (private vs. public setting).

■ Status of the victim-offender relationship.

■ Surveillance of the victim and "chance" meetings.

■ Mental illness.

■ Prior intimacy between victim and offender.

■ Fantasy—homicidal or suicidal ideation.

■ Obsessive jealousy.

■ Desperation.

■ Blaming the victim for personal problems.

■ Loss of power or control.

Officers should make a concerted effort to talk to the stalker, recording the conversation if possible. Officers must make it clear to the stalker that this behavior is a crime and the actions must cease or an arrest will be made. The conversation and the suspect's reaction should be in the official report (Petrocelli, 2007b, p.23).

INVESTIGATING ELDER ABUSE

A final area to examine in the investigation of assault and family violence is elder abuse. The U.S. Census Bureau projects that by 2025, nearly 62 million people will be older than age 65, and by 2040, that number will climb to 92 million. As the U.S. population ages, a growing concern in law enforcement is **elder abuse**, which the National Center on Elder Abuse (NCEA) defines as "intentional or neglectful acts by a caregiver or 'trusted' individual that lead to, or may lead to, harm of a vulnerable elder" ("Why Should I Care about Elder Abuse?," 2010).

Elder abuse is not a specific crime category in many states, which makes its frequency data difficult to obtain. Elder abuse is typically included in the assault, battery or murder category. Although incidents of burglaries, robberies, motor vehicle thefts, assaults, rapes and homicides of the elderly are relatively well documented in official reports, or at least at rates comparable to those documenting offenses against other age groups, cases of elder abuse typically involve the types of victimization that occur outside the spotlight focused on by the FBI, in the shadowy fringes of crime collection.

Types of Elder Abuse

The NCEA identifies the following types of elder abuse: physical abuse, neglect, emotional or psychological abuse, verbal abuse and threats, financial abuse and exploitation, sexual abuse and abandonment ("Why Should I Care about Elder Abuse?," 2010). In many states, self-neglect—a refusal or failure to provide oneself with adequate food, water, clothing, shelter, personal hygiene, medication (when indicated) and safety precautions—is also considered elder abuse ("Why Should I Care about Elder Abuse?," 2010). Three potential abusers of the elderly are family members, hired caregivers (in home or in a nursing home) and professional con artists.

> Elder abuse is the physical and emotional abuse, financial exploitation and general neglect of the elderly.

Financial abuse and exploitation of the elderly is an area of growing concern. Elderly financial abuse crimes generally fall into two categories: (1) fraud committed by strangers and (2) exploitation by relatives and caregivers (Johnson, 2004). Listed among the types of fraud commonly committed against the elderly by strangers are prize and sweepstakes scams, investment fraud, charitable contribution fraud, home and automobile repair scams, loan and mortgage fraud, bogus or unnecessary duplicates of health and life insurance policies, fraudulent funeral plans, false health remedies and "miracle cures," travel fraud, confidence games, telemarketing fraud, mail fraud and face-to-face contacts that give an offender a chance to steal from or otherwise scam the elderly victim, such as posing as a utility worker to gain access to the home to commit a robbery.

Even more unsettling than falling victim to a smooth-talking scam artist is the victimization endured at the hands of trusted family members or others with whom the victim has an ongoing relationship. This type of financial exploitation can occur when a relative or caregiver borrows money without repaying, withholds medical care or other services to conserve funds, sells the elder's possessions without permission, signs or cashes pension or Social Security checks without permission, misuses the elder's automated teller machine (ATM) or credit cards, forces the elder to sign over property or simply takes away the elder's money, property or valuables (Johnson, 2004). Other opportunities for exploitation occur with financial and legal arrangements such as joint bank accounts, deed or title transfers, powers of attorney and durable powers of attorney and living trusts and wills. Johnson (p.7) notes, "Distinguishing between an unwise, but legitimate, financial transaction and an exploitative transaction resulting from undue influence, duress, fraud, or lack of informed consent can be difficult. Suspicious transactions may be well intentioned but guided by poor advice. Generally, financial exploitation involves a pattern of behaviors, rather than single incidents."

Prevalence and Nature of Elder Abuse

The NCEA ("Elder Abuse Prevalence and Incidence," n.d.) reports, "According to the best available estimates, between 1 and 2 million Americans age 65 or older have been injured, exploited, or otherwise mistreated by someone on whom they depended for care or protection."

The OVC reports that one elderly person is victimized every 4.2 minutes ("Crime Clock," 2009). However, elder abuse has been called a "hidden" or "silent" crime because a large percentage of cases go unreported, with some research indicating fewer than 20 percent of cases of elder abuse are reported ("Why Should I Care about Elder Abuse?," 2010). Thus, determining the prevalence of elder abuse is a challenge because of the lack of data, a problem compounded by a reluctance to report the crime—similar to the situation with domestic assault. Some elderly individuals are physically incapable of providing information or may be suffering from conditions such as senility or Alzheimer's disease that might cause others not to believe their statements. In other cases, victims may fear further abuse or loss of the care of the only provider they have, or they may be embarrassed that their child could mistreat them. Persons of older generations and from other cultures often consider such abuse to be a private family matter, something that is not talked about and is certainly never reported to the police. Such cultural and generational attitudes present considerable challenges to those investigating these crimes.

 The extent of elder abuse is currently unknown.

Indicators of Elder Abuse

It cannot always be assumed that a broken bone in an elderly person or an unwise financial investment are the direct results of elder abuse or exploitation. Older people have weaker muscles and bones. They fall and bruise. They make bad choices on how to invest their money. But when these unfortunate events become a matter of routine, they may warrant further investigation.

Signs of Physical Abuse of the Elderly. Signs of physical abuse of the elderly that investigators should be aware of include

- Injury incompatible with the given explanation.
- Burns (possibly caused by cigarettes, acids or friction from ropes).
- Cuts, pinch marks, scratches, lacerations or puncture wounds.
- Bruises, welts or discolorations.
- Dehydration or other malnourishment without illness-related causes; unexplained loss of weight.
- Pallor, sunken eyes or cheeks.
- Eye injury.
- Soiled clothing or bedding.
- Lack of bandages on injuries or stitches where needed, or evidence of unset bone fractures.
- Injuries hidden under the breasts or on other areas of the body normally covered by clothing.
- Frequent use of the emergency room or clinic.

The American Medical Association (Aravanis, 1992) provided doctors with a series of questions to ask, which are equally applicable to law enforcement officers:

- Has anyone at home ever hurt you?
- Has anyone ever scolded or threatened you?
- Have you ever signed any documents that you didn't understand?
- Are you often alone?
- Are you afraid of anyone at home?
- Has anyone ever touched you without your consent?
- Has anyone ever made you do things you didn't want to?

Signs of Financial Abuse of the Elderly. Investigators looking into possible financial abuse and exploitation of the elderly should keep these indicators in mind (Johnson, 2004, pp.23–24):

- A recent acquaintance expresses an interest in finances, promises to provide care or ingratiates himself or herself with the elder.
- A relative or caregiver has no visible means of support and is overtly interested in the elder's financial affairs.
- A relative or caregiver expresses concern over the cost of caring for the elder, or is reluctant to spend money for needed medical treatment.
- The utility and other bills are not being paid.
- The elder's placement, care or possessions are inconsistent with the size of his or her estate.
- A relative or caregiver isolates the elder, makes excuses when friends or family call or visit and does not give the elder messages.
- A relative or caregiver gives implausible explanations about finances, and the elder is unaware of or unable to explain the arrangements made.
- Checking account and credit card statements are sent to a relative or caregiver and are not accessible to the elder.
- At the bank, the elder is accompanied by a relative or caregiver who refuses to let the elder speak for himself or herself, or the elder appears nervous or afraid of the person accompanying him or her.
- The elder is concerned or confused about "missing money."
- There are suspicious signatures on the elder's checks, or the elder signs checks and another party fills in the payee and amount sections.

■ There is an unusual amount of banking activity, particularly just after joint accounts are set up or someone new starts helping with the elder's finances.

■ A will, power of attorney or other legal document is drafted, but the elder does not understand its implications.

Risk Factors for Elder Abuse

The NCEA ("Risk Factors for Elder Abuse," 2007) lists several risk factors associated with elder abuse: domestic violence grown old; personal problems of the abuser, especially in the case of adult children; caregiver stress; personal characteristics of the elder (dementia, disruptive behaviors, problematic personality traits); and the cycle of violence. This last factor supports the theory that domestic violence is a learned problem-solving behavior transmitted from one generation to the next.

The Police Response

Controversy exists about the role of law enforcement in dealing with elder abuse, especially in identifying "hard-to-detect" cases. Some departments believe this is the responsibility of social services, rather than law enforcement. Other departments feel they are in an ideal position to learn from and to assist social services in dealing with cases of elder abuse. Albrecht (2008, p.45) suggests a number of investigative responses:

> Have patience with your victims. They are usually embarrassed, prideful, forgetful, scared and/or fearful their cooperation will make things worse.
>
> For physical abuse cases, take good photos during your first response and again several days later, if possible. If the victim is hospitalized, speak to the attending physicians about the type and severity of the injuries.
>
> For financial crimes, collect anything that looks like evidence, including credit cards and statements, ATM photos (which may be available from the bank for only 30 days), bank statements and annuity or investment account information.
>
> For neglect cases, it's better to document the scene by taking comprehensive video of the kitchen, bathrooms, bedrooms and other living areas.
>
> Make creative arrests to get those people out of the house. Run all suspects for warrants, criminal histories, probation and parole violations, gang membership, and DOJ [Department of Justice] hits.

Many of the same skills used in dealing with domestic violence and child abuse are applicable in an elder abuse investigation (Petrocelli, 2007a). Investigators should observe the general condition of the residence when arriving to investigate an elder abuse complaint. Once inside, investigators should carefully observe the general conditions and interview the alleged victim: "As with all interviews, nonverbal cues are as important as the content of the responses. Look for the following telltale cues: Is a suspected perpetrator hovering in the area, refusing to leave the senior alone to answer questions? Is the potential victim answering the questions by looking the officer in the eye and giving direct responses or is he or she averting eye contact and giving ambiguous answers?" (Petrocelli, 2007a, p.16).

One critical aspect of an investigation of physical elder abuse is to determine if bruising is the result of an accident or of abuse. Abuse indicators—known as forensic markers—can help distinguish between injuries caused by mistreatment and those that are the result of accidents, illnesses or aging (McNamee and Murphy, 2006). Researchers have found that accidental bruising occurs in predictable locations in older adults, with 90 percent of all bruises found on the extremities; accidental bruises are rarely, if ever, seen on the ears, neck, genitals, buttocks or soles of the feet (McNamee and Murphy).

NIJ-funded researchers also examined data from the deaths of elderly residents in long-term care facilities to identify potential markers of abuse. Although most investigations did not raise suspicions, the researchers identified four categories of markers that often led to referral to the attorney general for further investigation (McNamee and Murphy, 2006, p.19):

1. *Physical condition/quality of care.* Specific markers include documented but untreated injuries; undocumented injuries and factures; multiple, untreated, and/or undocumented pressure sores; medical orders not followed; poor oral care, poor hygiene, and lack of cleanliness of residents; malnourished residents who have no documentation for low weight; bruising in unusual locations; statements from family concerning adequacy of care; and observations about the level of care for residents with nonattentive family members.

2. *Facility characteristics.* Specific markers include unchanged linens; strong odors (urine, feces); trash cans that have not been emptied; food issues (unclean cafeteria); and documented problems in the past.

3. *Inconsistencies.* Specific markers include: inconsistencies between the medical records, statements made by staff members, and/or observations of investigators; inconsistencies in statements among

groups interviewed; and inconsistencies between the reported time of death and the condition of the body.

4. *Staff behaviors.* Specific markers include: staff members who follow an investigator too closely; lack of knowledge and/or concern about a resident; unintended or purposeful, verbal or nonverbal evasiveness; and a facility's unwillingness to release medical records.

Reducing Elder Abuse

Officers should advise their senior contacts to remain active in some type of community group (church, social, neighborhood) because social isolation is one of the greatest contributors to elder mistreatment. Officers should also make sure senior contacts know about the services and resource centers in their neighborhoods (Petrocelli, 2007a, p.17).

One approach to reducing elderly victimization is Triad, a cooperative effort of the International Association of Chiefs of Police (IACP), AARP (formerly the American Association of Retired Persons) and the National Sheriffs' Association (NSA). These three organizations are working together to design programs to reduce victimization of the elderly, assist those who have been victimized and generally enhance law enforcement services to older adults and the community at large. AARP is another resource to tap when trying to reduce the occurrence of elder abuse. The AARP Web site (www.aarp.org) posts numerous articles about how to protect against financial exploitation and what to do if nursing home or other caregiver problems exist, along with various other links to resources able to assist elderly victims.

Summary

Assault is unlawfully threatening to harm another person, actually harming another person or attempting unsuccessfully to do so. *Simple assault* is intentionally causing another to fear immediate bodily harm or death or intentionally inflicting or attempting to inflict bodily harm on the person. *Aggravated assault,* or *felonious assault,* is an unlawful attack by one person on another to inflict severe bodily injury. In specified instances, teachers, persons operating public conveyances and law enforcement officers use physical force legally.

The elements of the crime of simple assault are (1) intent to do bodily harm to another, (2) present ability to commit the act and (3) commission of an overt act toward carrying out the intent. An additional element in the crime of aggravated assault is that the intentionally inflicted bodily injury results in (1) a high probability of death; (2) serious, permanent disfigurement; or (3) permanent or protracted loss or impairment of the function of any body member or organ or other severe bodily harm. Attempted assault requires proof of intent and an overt act toward committing the crime.

Special challenges in investigating assaults include distinguishing the victim from the suspect, determining whether the matter is civil or criminal and determining whether the act was intentional or accidental. Obtaining a complaint against simple assault is also sometimes difficult. Moreover, such calls may be dangerous for responding officers.

To prove the elements of assault, establish the intent to cause injury, the severity of the injury inflicted and whether a dangerous weapon was used. Physical evidence in an assault case includes photographs of injuries, clothing of the victim or suspect, weapons, broken objects, bloodstains, hairs, fibers and other signs of an altercation.

For data collection, special categories of assault are domestic violence, stalking and elder abuse. Domestic violence is a pattern of behaviors involving physical, sexual, economic and emotional abuse, alone or in combination, often by an intimate partner and often to establish and maintain power and control over the other partner.

Although legal definitions vary among jurisdictions, *stalking* is generally defined as the willful or intentional commission of a series of acts that would cause a reasonable person to fear death or serious bodily injury and that, in fact, does place the victim in fear of death or serious bodily injury. *Elder abuse* is the physical and emotional abuse, financial exploitation and general neglect of the elderly. The extent of elder abuse is currently unknown.

Checklist

Assault

■ Is the assault legal or justifiable?

■ Are the elements of the crime of assault present?

■ Who committed the assault?

■ Is the suspect still at the scene?

■ Who signed the complaint? Who made the arrest?

- Has the victim made a written statement? Have witnesses done so?
- Are injuries visible?
- Have photographs been taken of injuries? In color?
- If injuries are not visible, has the victim received medical attention?
- If medical attention was received, has a report on the nature of the injuries been received? Did the victim grant permission?
- What words did the assailant use to show intent to do bodily harm?
- Was a dangerous weapon involved?
- Has a complete report been made?
- If the assault is severe enough to be aggravated assault, what injuries or weapons support such a charge?
- If the victim died as a result of the attack, was a dying declaration taken?
- Was it necessary and legal to make an arrest at the scene? Away from the scene?
- How was the suspect identified?

Application

Read the following and then answer the questions:

Mike was drinking beer with friends in a local park at about 9:00 P.M. It was dark. He knew Tom was at the other end of the park and that Tom had been seeing Mike's girlfriend, Suzy. Suzy was with Mike, trying to talk him out of doing anything to Tom. Mike said he was going to find Tom and "pound him into the ground. When I get through with him, they'll have to take him to the hospital."

Mike left the group and Suzy then, telling them to wait for him. Tom was found later that night two blocks from the park, lying unconscious on a boulevard next to the curb. His clothes were torn, and his left arm was cut. When he regained consciousness, he told police he was walking home from the park when someone jumped out from some bushes, grabbed him from behind, beat him with fists and then hit him over the head with something. He did not see his assailant.

Mike was arrested because a person at the park overheard his threats.

Questions

1. What is the probability that Mike committed the assault?
2. Did he have the intent? Did he have the present ability to commit the act?
3. Did he commit the act? Should he have been arrested?

Discussion Questions

1. A police officer is responding to an in-progress bank robbery. When she arrives, the perpetrator sees her and fires a shot toward the officer while attempting to flee on foot. The shot completely misses the officer, and the perpetrator is taken into custody with no injuries. Is this still considered assault? Explain why or why not.
2. Why does elder abuse and exploitation often go unnoticed and unreported?
3. Under what circumstances is a person justified in using force against another person? When is a police officer justified in using force?
4. You respond to a domestic call where Mrs. Jones and her husband, Mr. Jones, have been verbally arguing all day. You learn that as the day has gone on, the argument has been escalating; however, no physical contact has occurred. Mrs. Jones tells you that Mr. Jones has physically harmed her in the past and threatened to kill her. How would you deal with the incident? Is there an assault at this point?
5. What are your state's laws regarding domestic assault? Is there a mandate or standard for arrest even if the victim does not want to pursue charges?
6. Suppose a teacher is having a serious discipline problem with a 5-year-old student and sends the student to the principal's office. The principal spanks the student. Under the *in loco parentis* doctrine, is this action legal? Do you agree with this doctrine? Does your state have such a law?
7. Does a sniper firing on a crowd commit assault?
8. In what crimes is assault often an additional crime?
9. If two people become involved in a violent struggle that seriously injures one or both of them, and if both claim the other started the fight, what do you do?
10. Can police officers be sued for making verbal threats to a suspect?

Media Explorations

 ### Internet

Select one of the following assignments to complete.

- Search for the key phrase *National Institute of Justice*. Click on "NCJRS" (National Criminal Justice Research Service). Click on "law enforcement." Click on "sort by Doc#." Search for one of the NCJ reference numbers from list of References in this chapter. Outline the selection to share with the class.

- Go to the FBI Web site at www.fbi.gov. Click on "library and reference." Select "Uniform Crime Reports" and outline what the report says about assault.

- Select one of the following key terms: *assault, assault prevention, cyberstalking, domestic violence, elder abuse, stalking*. Find one article relevant to assault investigations to outline and share with the class.

ONLINE Database   Gale Criminal Justice Database Assignments

The following assignments require access to Gale's Custom Journals Database for Emergency Services and Criminal Justice. Check with your instructor if you have questions about this.

- Find the article "Prosecuting Cases without Victim Cooperation" on the Gale Emergency Services Database. Identify the evidence collections methods outlined in this article. Also write a brief paper on what makes domestic assault incidents so dangerous and challenging to law enforcement and be prepared to share your thoughts with the class.

- Find the article "Elder Abuse: A National Tragedy" on the Gale Emergency Services Database. Read the article and identify if elder abuse is a growing problem. Find a related case that is associated with elder physical abuse, neglect, sexual or financial exploitation and be prepared to discuss this case in class.

- Find the article "Cyber Stalking and Bullying: What Law Enforcement Needs to Know" on the Gale Emergency Services Database. Read the article and identify what cyber stalking and bullying are. Compare and contrast to traditional stalking and bullying, and identify why this method of stalking and bullying is creating a new set of challenges for law enforcement. Be prepared to discuss your thoughts with the class.

References

Albrecht, Leslie. "Elder Abuse Investigations." *Law Officer Magazine*, April 2008, pp.44–46.

Aravanis, S. C. *Diagnostic and Treatment Guidelines on Elder Abuse and Neglect.* Chicago: American Medical Association, 1992.

Ascione, Frank R. "Battered Women's Reports of Their Partners' and Their Children's Cruelty to Animals." *Journal of Emotional Abuse*, Vol.1, No.1, 1998, pp.119–133.

Baum, Katrina; Catalano, Shannan; Rand, Michael; and Rose, Kristina. *Stalking Victimization in the United States.* Washington, DC: Bureau of Justice Statistics Special Report, National Crime Victimization Survey, January 2009. (NCJ 224527)

Bune, Karen. "Specialized Units Make a Difference in Domestic Violence." *Justice Bulletin*, May/June 2007, pp.12–13.

"Crime Clock." Washington, DC: Office for Victims of Crime, 2009. Accessed May 29, 2011. http://ovc.ncjrs.gov/gallery/posters/pdfs/Crime_Clock.pdf

Crime in the United States, 2009. Washington, DC: U.S. Department of Justice, Federal Bureau of Investigation, September 2010. Accessed May 27, 2011. http://www2.fbi.gov/ucr/cius2009/index.html

"Cyberstalking Laws." Working to Halt Online Abuse. Accessed May 12, 2008. http://www.haltabuse.org/

"Elder Abuse." Washington, DC: National Institute of Justice, November 6, 2007.

"Elder Abuse Prevalence and Incidence." Fact Sheet. Washington, DC: National Center on Elder Abuse, no date.

Felson, Richard B., and Pare, Paul-Philippe. "Does the Criminal Justice System Treat Domestic Violence and Sexual Assault Offenders Leniently?" *Justice Quarterly*, September 2007, pp.435–459.

Garcia, Michelle M. "Voices from the Field: Stalking." *NIJ Journal*, No. 266, June 2010, pp.14–15.

Grossi, Dave. "Domestic Violence Calls: Protocol for a Positive Outcome." *Law Officer Magazine*, November 2007, pp.28–29.

Hawkins, Nikki. "Perspectives on Civil Protective Orders in Domestic Violence Cases: The Rural and Urban Divide." *NIJ Journal*, No. 266, June 2010, pp.4–8.

Healy, Kerry, and Barrios, Jarrett. "Technology against Violence." *The Boston Globe*, January 11, 2007.

Hill, Rodney. "Domestic Violence and the Reluctant Victim: Prosecuting without the Victim's Cooperation." *Subject to Debate*, March 2008, pp.3,6.

Hirschel, David. *Making Arrests in Domestic Violence Cases: What Police Should Know.* Washington, DC: National Institute of Justice, June 2009. (NCJ 225458)

"Intimate Partner Violence." Washington, DC: National Institute of Justice, October 24, 2007.

Johnson, Kelly Dedel. *Financial Crimes against the Elderly.* Washington, DC: Office of Community Oriented Policing Services, Problem-Oriented Guides for Police, Problem-Specific Guides Series, No. 20, August 4, 2004.

Kanable, Rebecca. "Learning to Read the Danger Signs." *Law Enforcement Technology*, March 2010, pp.8–14.

Kingsnorth, Rodney F., and MacIntosh, Randall C. "Intimate Partner Violence: The Role of Suspect Gender in Prosecutorial Decision-Making." *Justice Quarterly*, September 2007, pp.460–495.

Klein, Andrew R. "Practical Implications of Current Domestic Violence Research." Washington, DC: U.S. Department of Justice, unpublished report, April 2008. (NCJ 222319)

Labriola, Melissa; Rempel, Michael; and Davis, Robert C. "Do Batterer Programs Reduce Recidivism? Results from a Randomized Trial in the Bronx." *Justice Quarterly*, June 2008, pp.252–282.

Law Enforcement Officers Killed and Assaulted, 2009. Washington, DC: U.S. Department of Justice, Federal Bureau of Investigation, October 2010.

McNamee, Catherine C., and Murphy, Mary B. "Elder Abuse in the United States." *NIJ Journal*, November 2006, pp.16–21.

Merz-Perez, Linda; Heide, Kathleen M.; and Silverman, Ira J. "Childhood Cruelty to Animals and Subsequent Violence against Humans." *International Journal of Offender Therapy and Comparative Criminology*, Vol.45, No.5, October 2001, pp.556–573.

Miller, Christa. "High-Tech Stalking." *Law Enforcement Technology*, May 2009, pp.56–60.

Pattavina, April; Hirschel, David; Buzawa, Eve; Faggiani, Don; and Bentley, Helen. "A Comparison of the Police Response to Heterosexual versus Same-Sex Intimate Partner Violence." *Criminal Justice Research Reports*, September/October 2007, pp.5–6.

Petrocelli, Joseph. "Patrol Response to Elder Abuse." *Police*, February 2007a, pp.16–17.

Petrocelli, Joseph. "Patrol Response to Stalking." *Police*, August 2007b, pp.22–23.

Report to Congress on Stalking and Domestic Violence, 2005 through 2006. Washington, DC: U.S. Department of Justice, Office on Violence against Women, no date.

"Risk Factors for Elder Abuse." Washington, DC: National Center on Elder Abuse, August 21, 2007.

Sherman, Lawrence W. "Domestic Violence and Defiance Theory: Understanding Why Arrest Can Backfire." In *Australian Violence, Contemporary Perspectives II*, edited by Duncan Chappell and Sandra Egger, 1995, pp.207–220.

Sherman, Lawrence W., and Berk, Richard A. *The Minneapolis Domestic Violence Experiment*. Washington, DC: Police Foundation Reports, April 1984.

Smith, Erica L., and Farole, Donald J., Jr. *Profile of Intimate Partner Violence Cases in Large Urban Counties*. Washington, DC: Bureau of Justice Statistics, State Court Processing Statistics, October 2009. (NCJ 228193)

"Stalking." Washington, DC: National Institute of Justice, October 25, 2007.

"Stalking Fact Sheet." Stalking Resource Center. Accessed May 15, 2008. http://www.ncvc.org/src/AGP.Net/Components/DocumentViewer/Download.aspxnz?DocumentID=38733

Truman, Jennifer L., and Rand, Michael R. *Criminal Victimization, 2009*. Washington, DC: Bureau of Justice Statistics Bulletin, October 2010. (NCJ 231327)

Velazquez, Sonia E.; Garcia, Michelle; and Joyce, Elizabeth. "Mobilizing a Community Response to Stalking: The Philadelphia Story." *The Police Chief*, January 2009, pp.30–37.

"Victims' Group Issues Model Code to Improve Stalking Enforcement." *Criminal Justice Newsletter*, January 16, 2007, pp.1–2.

"Why Should I Care about Elder Abuse?" Washington, DC: National Center on Elder Abuse, March 3, 2010.

Cases Cited

Naler v. State, 25 Ala. App. 486 (1933)

Shackleford v. Commonwealth, 183 Va. 423, 426, 32 S.E. 2d 682 (1945)

State v. Rhodes, 61 N.C. 453 (1868)

Thurman v. City of Torrington, 595 F. Supp. 1521 (D. Conn. 1984)

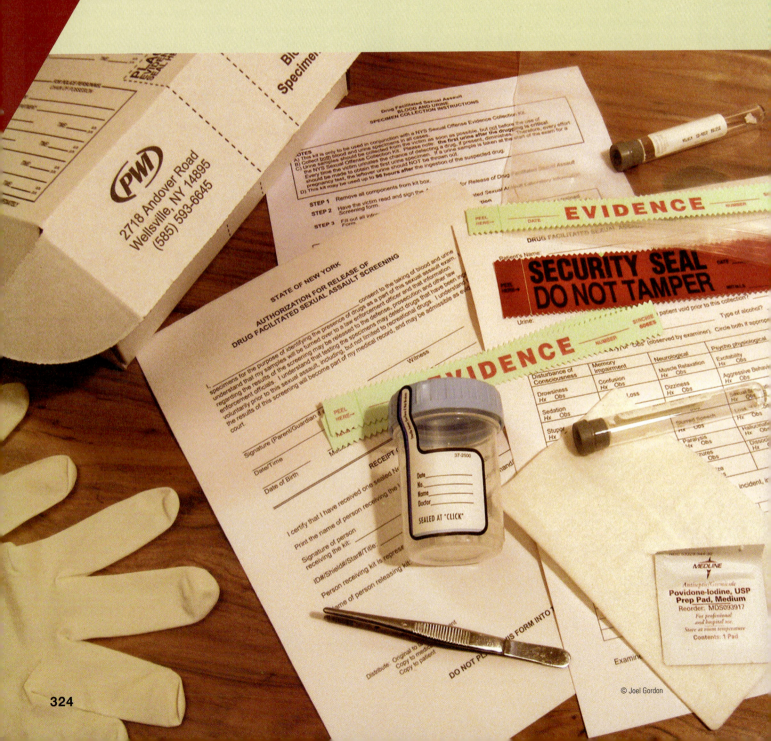

CHAPTER 10
Sex Offenses

© Joel Gordon

Outline

Can You Define?

bigamy

blind reporting

child molestation

cunnilingus

date rape

digital penetration

exhibitionists

fellatio

forcible rape

incest

indecent exposure

intimate parts

oral copulation

pedophile

penetration

prostitution

rape

Rohypnol

sadist

sadomasochistic abuse

sexual contact

sexual penetration

sexually explicit conduct

sodomy

statutory rape

voyeurism

Do You Know?

- What the key distinction between human trafficking and human smuggling is?
- How sex offenses are classified?
- How rape is defined and classified?
- What the elements of sexual assault are?
- What special challenges exist in investigating sex offenses?
- What modus operandi factors are important in investigating a sexual assault?
- What evidence is often obtained in sex offense investigations?
- What evidence to seek in date rape cases?
- What blind reporting is and what its advantages are?
- What agencies can assist in a sexual assault investigation?
- What is generally required to obtain a conviction in sexual assault cases?
- Whether recent laws have reduced or increased the penalties for sexual assault and why?
- Which three federal statutes form the basis for sex offender registries?

Physically attractive or unattractive people of any age—from very young children to senior citizens—may be victims of sexual assault. Sex offenses range from **voyeurism** (the peeping Tom) to rape and murder. Sex offenses can be difficult to investigate because the victim is often emotionally distraught. Moreover, investigating officers may be uncomfortable because they lack special training in interviewing sex offense victims or offenders.

Some sex offenders are emotionally disturbed and feel no remorse for their actions. For example, a 38-year-old man with a 20-year history of sex offenses admitted to a prison psychiatrist that even he could not remember how many rapes and sexual assaults he had committed. The suspect also talked freely about his sexual exploits with children and showed no emotion at all. A **pedophile**—a person who is sexually attracted to young children—can be extremely dangerous, as can a **sadist**, a person who derives sexual gratification from causing pain to others, often through mutilation.

Although some sex offenders are emotionally disturbed, the fact remains that most victims know their attacker and that most attacks occur not in dark alleys but in living rooms and bedrooms. "Most research supports the claim that sexual assault is common in physically abusive relationships" (Taylor and Gaskin-Laniyan, 2007). Before looking at specific sex offenses, consider three other crimes that are directly related to the major focus of this chapter—sexual assault.

INVESTIGATING OBSCENE TELEPHONE CALLS AND TEXTS

Obscene phone calls or text messages are not only harassing invasions of privacy but can also be stressful and frightening. Many people, including juveniles, are victims of obscene or harassing texting, which may include threats or obscene pictures. The threats have been reported as both intentional and random. Making obscene telephone calls is a crime. Recall that this is a frequent form of harassing stalking behavior. Police departments receive complaints of many types of harassment calls that are not of a sexual nature and have established procedures for investigating such calls. The same procedures apply to phone calls with sexual implications.

In most obscene phone calls, the callers want to remain anonymous, using the phone as a barrier between themselves and their victims. The callers receive sexual or psychological gratification from making contact with victims, even from a distance. Calls involving sexual connotations are threatening to the victims because they have no way of knowing the caller's true intent. Although such calls may be made randomly, the caller knows the victim in many cases.

If the victim wants to press charges, the first step is to make a police report. The next contact may be the phone company. The information section at the front of most phone directories provides information about what constitutes a violation of phone company regulations and the law and provides instructions about what to do if a person receives obscene or harassing calls (stay calm, do not respond and quietly hang up the phone; if the calls persist, call the phone company).

Caller ID may discourage obscene calls, although a caller may still be able to block his or her name, phone number or both. The police may use traps and traces if given a signed affidavit from the victim stating the facts related to the obscene calls. Police also have resources to identify service providers to a certain phone number, information that can be used to retrieve further suspect information. Phone numbers that are not assigned to certain individuals, such as pay-as-you-go phones, cannot necessarily be traced to a specific person. Furthermore, "phone spoofing," in which suspects cover or alter the source of their phone number information by using other existing ones, can provide even more challenges in locating a suspect in police investigations.

INVESTIGATING PROSTITUTION

Prostitution—soliciting sexual intercourse for pay—raises several concerns, including personal safety concerns, public health concerns and quality of life concerns (Jetmore, 2008). Prostitution contributes to the spread of venereal disease and HIV, and profits from it often go to organized crime. Of special concern to law enforcement officers is the practice of enticing very young girls into prostitution. Legislation—for example, the Mann Act—attempts to prevent such actions. Section 2423 of the Act prohibits "coercion or enticement of minor females and the taking of male or female persons across the state line for immoral purposes."

The National Institute of Justice's research on street prostitution reveals, "Many women enter prostitution as minors and use the income to support a drug habit or to stave off homelessness. Many suffered abuse as children. They have extremely high rates of on-the-job victimization—possibly the highest homicide rate of any group of women studied thus far—and a significant number of prostitute homicides remain unsolved" (Moses, 2006, p.22).

Moses (2006, p.23) provides the following profiles of single and serial murderers of prostitutes:

> Single and serial murderers, like their victims, appeared to resemble each other on the surface. They both shared violent criminal backgrounds, substance use histories, and lifestyle choices. The sample of perpetrators consisted of an equal proportion of African Americans and Caucasians who ranged in age from early to mid-30s.
>
> However, serial murderers differed from single murderers in three areas—sexual aggression, deviant sexual interests, and active sexual fantasies. Serial killers engaged more frequently in planning activities (such as bringing a victim to a preselected area, removing clothing from the victim's body, and so forth), ritualistic behaviors, body mutilation, and removal of body parts.

Moses suggests that such knowledge might help state and local law enforcement officers identify suspects and more efficiently and thoroughly investigate such homicides.

In some cases the women involved are sex slaves, another challenge facing law enforcement.

INVESTIGATING HUMAN TRAFFICKING

The Thirteenth Amendment to the U.S. Constitution, ratified in 1865, states, "Neither slavery nor involuntary servitude, except as a punishment for crime whereof the party shall have been duly convicted, shall exist within the United States, or any place subject to their jurisdiction." But it has yet to be abolished in this country. *The Crime of Human Trafficking* (2008, p.1) reports, "Human trafficking, commonly referred to as "modern day slavery," is a global phenomenon that involves obtaining or maintaining the labor or services of another through the use of force, fraud, or coercion in violation of an individual's human rights. Generating billions of dollars in profit each year, human trafficking is one of the world's fastest growing criminal activities, operating on the same scale as the illegal trade of guns and drugs. Fueled by global economic conditions and increased international mobility, the market for and trade of human beings continues to expand rapidly."

Human trafficking yields $9.5 billion a year in global profits, of which $3.5 billion is generated in the United States (Whiting, 2007). The U.S. State Department's *Trafficking in Persons Report* (2010, p.7) estimates that 12.3 million people are trafficked per year internationally, a figure that does not include those trafficked within their own countries. Globally, an estimated 80 percent of those trafficked are women and girls, and as many as half are minors.

The Trafficking Victims Protection Act (TVPA), signed into law in October 2000 and reauthorized in 2003, 2005 and 2008, was passed to (1) address the problem of trafficking in persons and (2) provide for protection and assistance for victims, prosecution of offenders and prevention efforts internationally. The TVPA defines human trafficking as, "The recruitment, harboring, transportation, provision or obtaining of a person for one of three purposes[1]:

■ Labor or services, through the use of force, fraud or coercion for the purposes of subjection to involuntary servitude, peonage, debt bondage or slavery.

■ A commercial sex act through the use of force, fraud or coercion.

■ Any commercial sex act, if the person is under 18 years of age, regardless of whether any form of coercion is involved."

Between January 2008 and June 2010 federally funded human trafficking task forces opened 2,515 suspected incidents for investigation, 82 percent of which were classified as suspected sex trafficking cases (Banks and Kyckelhahn, 2011). Eleven percent of the investigations involved suspected labor trafficking, and 7 percent were classified as "unknown trafficking type." Investigations confirmed and identified 460 sex trafficking victims and 63 labor trafficking victims, as well as 410 sex trafficking suspects and 78 labor trafficking suspects (see Tables 10.1 and 10.2). Note in Table 10.1 that more than half (53.9 percent) of the sex trafficking victims were age 17 or younger and nearly 94 percent were female.

Trafficking victims are often lured by the promise of better living conditions and good job opportunities, with adults and children being trafficked for commercial sex or forced labor: "Like domestic violence, sexual assault,

---

[1] Victims of Trafficking and Violence Protection Act of 2000. Pub. L. No. 106-386, 114 Stat. 1464.

TABLE 10.1 Victim Characteristics in Cases Confirmed to Be Human Trafficking by High Data Quality Task Forces, by Type of Trafficking

Victim characteristic	Total[a]	Sex trafficking	Labor trafficking
Sex			
Male	49	27	20
Female	477	432	43
Age			
17 or younger	257	248	6
18–24	159	142	17
25–34	68	46	22
35 or older	27	12	15
Unknown	16	12	3
Race/Hispanic origin			
White[b]	106	102	1
Black/African American[b]	167	161	6
Hispanic/Latino origin	129	95	34
Asian[b, c]	26	17	9
Other[b, d]	35	23	11
Unknown	63	61	2
Citizenship			
U.S. Citizen/U.S. National	346	345	1
Permanent U.S. resident[e]	6	6	0
Undocumented alien[f]	101	64	36
Qualified alien[e]	19	1	15
Temporary worker	2	0	2
Unknown	50	41	9
Number of victims identified	527	460	63

Note: Analysis restricted to cases opened and observed between January 2008 and June 2010 in high data quality task forces.

[a] Includes cases of unknown trafficking type.

[b] Excludes persons of Hispanic or Latino origin.

[c] Asian may include Native Hawaiian and other Pacific Islanders or persons of East Asian or Southeast Asian descent.

[d] Includes persons of two or more races.

[e] Permanent residents and qualified aliens are legal residents in the U.S., but do not have citizenship.

[f] Undocumented aliens reside in the U.S. illegally.

Source: From BJS: http://www.bjs.gov/content/pub/pdf/cshti0810.pdf, p.6, Table 5

stalking, and child and elder abuse, trafficking in persons is an underreported crime, and many cases go undiscovered" (Orchowsky et al., 2007, p.1). An additional challenge occurs when trafficking victims are unable to communicate in English: "Victims are often isolated, fear their captives, fear law enforcement and the legal system, and lack proper documentation. These factors often prevent them from cooperating with authorities' attempts to identify trafficking cases and assemble evidence against the traffickers" (Orchowsky et al., p.1).

Trafficking versus Smuggling

The Crime of Human Trafficking (2008, p.3) makes clear the key differences between the crimes of trafficking and smuggling:

> Smuggling occurs when someone is paid to assist another in the illegal crossing of borders. This relationship typically ends after the border has been crossed and the individual has paid the smuggler a fee for assistance. If the smuggler sells or "brokers" the

TABLE 10.2 Suspect Characteristics in Cases Opened between January 2008 and June 2010 and Confirmed to Be Human Trafficking by High Data Quality Task Forces, by Type of Trafficking

Suspect characteristic	Total[a]	Sex trafficking	Labor trafficking
Sex			
Male	368	314	54
Female	88	71	17
Unknown	32	25	7
Age			
17 or younger	11	10	1
18–24	147	145	2
25–34	114	105	9
35 or older	100	65	35
Unknown	116	85	31
Race/Hispanic origin			
White[b]	24	22	2
Black/African American[b]	224	219	5
Hispanic/Latino origin	119	89	30
Asian[b,c]	28	18	10
Other[b,d]	20	5	15
Unknown	73	57	16
Citizenship			
U.S. Citizen/U.S. National	276	269	7
Permanent U.S. resident[e]	12	2	10
Undocumented alien[f]	44	39	5
Qualified alien[e]	8	2	6
Unknown	148	98	50
Number of suspects identified	488	410	78

Note: Analysis restricted to cases opened and observed between January 2008 and June 2010 in high data quality task forces.

[a] Includes cases of unknown trafficking type.

[b] Excludes persons of Hispanic or Latino origin.

[c] Asian may include Native Hawaiian and other Pacific Islanders or persons of East Asian or Southeast Asian descent.

[d] Includes persons of two or more races.

[e] Permanent residents and qualified aliens are legal residents in the U.S., but do not have citizenship.

[f] Undocumented aliens reside in the U.S. illegally.

Source: BJS: http://www.bjs.gov/content/pub/pdf/cshti0810.pdf , p.6, Table 6

smuggled individual into a condition of servitude, or if the smuggled individual cannot pay the smuggler and is then forced to work that debt off, the crime has now turned from smuggling into human trafficking.

A person may choose and arrange to be smuggled into a country, but when a person is forced into a situation of exploitation where their freedom is taken away, they are then a victim of human trafficking. Central to

the distinction is the denial of the victim's liberty. An individual's willingness to be smuggled into another country does not minimize the victimization he or she may experience at the hands of a trafficker. . . .

Under U.S. law, once a person has been held in servitude, a person's status as a trafficking victim supersedes all other smuggling or immigration questions and affords them legal protection and social services.

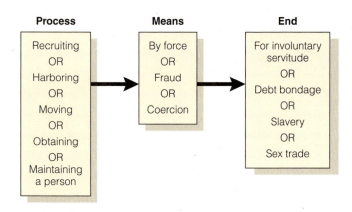

Process	Means	End
Recruiting OR Harboring OR Moving OR Obtaining OR Maintaining a person	By force OR Fraud OR Coercion	For involuntary servitude OR Debt bondage OR Slavery OR Sex trade

FIGURE 10.1
Three elements of trafficking.

Source: Reprinted from *The Crime of Human Trafficking: A Law Enforcement Guide to Identification and Investigation.* http://www.theiacp.org/documents/pdfs/rcd/completehtguide.pdf Copyright held by the International Association of Chiefs of Police, 515 North Washington Street, Alexandria, VA 22314 USA. Further reproduction without express written permission from IACP is strictly prohibited.

The key distinction between human trafficking and smuggling lies in the individual's freedom of choice.

Figure 10.1 illustrates three elements of trafficking.

Myths and Misconceptions of Human Trafficking

The Crime of Human Trafficking (2008, p.4) lists myths and misconceptions about human trafficking:

- The victim knew what he or she was getting into.
- The victim committed unlawful acts.
- The victim was paid for services.
- The victim had freedom of movement.
- There were opportunities to escape but the victim didn't.
- Trafficking involves the crossing of borders.
- U.S. citizens can't be trafficked.
- The trafficker's actions are culturally appropriate.
- It can't be trafficking when the trafficker and victim are related or married.

Challenges to Law Enforcement

"Trafficking involves movement from one place to another, often across international borders, leading to jurisdictional and investigatory difficulties for enforcement officials. Additional challenges lie in identification and later conviction of offenders because trafficking comprises multiple crimes instead of a singular event to prosecute. This, compounded with the low tendency of victims to report crimes, ensures difficult enforcement of laws" ("United Nations Releases Toolkit," 2006, p.5).

Identifying victims and perpetrators of human trafficking is a major challenge. Law enforcement professionals have to rely on their instincts to notice "red flags" that might indicate someone is a victim or perpetrator of trafficking. Officers should consider businesses in their community that might serve as fronts for trafficking. They should determine if building security is used to keep people out or to keep them in. What are the working conditions? Do workers have freedom of movement? Do they live and work in the same place? Do they owe a debt to their employers? Do the employers control their workers' immigration documents? Officers should also consider the appearance and mannerisms of the workers. Are there signs of trauma, fatigue, injuries or other evidence of poor care? Are individuals withdrawn, afraid to talk or is the communication censored? (*The Crime of Human Trafficking*, 2008, p.5).

It is difficult to get victims and witnesses who are in the country illegally to cooperate in investigations and prosecutions. A partial solution is now available: "Officers investigating human trafficking now have an option that can help overcome the fear and reluctance of victims and witnesses who are not in the United States legally. A new limited visa option, the T visa, now available under federal law, allows important witnesses or victims to remain in the United States to testify against human traffickers and their criminal enterprises" (Ramage, 2007, p.10).

CLASSIFICATION OF SEX OFFENSES

Sex crimes are sometimes classified according to whether they involve physical aggression and a victim—for example, rape—or are victimless acts between consenting adults, such as consensual sodomy. The former are most frequently reported to police and investigated. The latter are often simply offensive to others and are seldom reported or investigated.

Sex offenses include bigamy, child molestation, incest, indecent exposure, prostitution, sodomy and rape (*sexual assault*).

Bigamy is marrying another person when one or both parties are already married.

Child molestation is usually a felony and includes lewd and lascivious acts, indecent exposure, incest or statutory rape involving a child, male or female, under age 14. This is a difficult charge to prove because children frequently are not believed. Moreover, parents are often reluctant to bring charges in such cases. (This offense is discussed in depth in the next chapter.)

Incest is sexual intercourse between family members or close relatives, including children related by adoption.

Indecent exposure is revealing one's genitals to another person to such an extent as to shock the other's sense of decency. It is not necessary to prove intent. The offense is a misdemeanor, although repeated offenses can be charged as a felony in many states. Ordinarily, **exhibitionists**—those who expose themselves—are not dangerous but may become so if they are humiliated or abused.

Sodomy is any form of anal or oral copulation. Although commonly thought of as being performed by homosexual males, sodomy can occur between a male and female, between two females or between a human and an animal (bestiality). Oral or anal penetration must be proven. Both parties are guilty if the act is voluntary. When sodomy is a private act between consenting adults, it is difficult to obtain sufficient evidence for prosecution. In some states, sodomy between consenting adults is no longer a crime. Such acts between adults and juveniles remain crimes, however.

Rape—or sexual assault—is sexual intercourse with a person against his or her will. Rape is usually considered the most serious crime after murder and carries a heavy penalty in most states. It is now viewed as a violent assault rather than a type of deviance.

Terminology commonly used when investigating sex offenses includes:

- **Cunnilingus**—sexual activity involving oral contact with the female genitals.

- **Digital penetration**—the act of using fingers (digits) to penetrate or manipulate sexual organs that include the penis, vagina and anus.

- **Fellatio**—sexual activity involving oral contact with the male genitals.

- **Intimate parts**—usually refers to the primary genital areas, groin, inner thighs, buttocks and breasts.

- **Oral copulation**—the same as cunnilingus and fellatio; the act of joining the mouth of one person with the sex organ of another person.

- **Penetration**—any intrusion, however slight, of any part of a person's body or any object manipulated or inserted by a person into the genital or anal openings of another's body, including sexual intercourse in its ordinary meaning.

- **Sadomasochistic abuse**—fettering, binding or otherwise physically restraining; whipping; or torturing for sexual gratification.

- **Sexual contact**—includes any act committed without the complainant's consent for the suspect's sexual or aggressive satisfaction, such as touching the complainant's intimate parts, forcing another person to touch one's intimate parts or forcing another person to touch the complainant's intimate parts. In any of these cases, the body area may be clothed or unclothed.

- **Sexual penetration**—includes sexual intercourse, cunnilingus, fellatio, anal intercourse or any other intrusion, no matter how slight, into the victim's genital, oral or anal openings by the suspect's body or by an object. An emission of semen is not required. Any act of sexual penetration by the suspect without the affirmative, freely given permission of the victim to the specific act of penetration constitutes the crime of sexual assault.

- **Sexually explicit conduct**—any type of sexual intercourse between persons of the same or opposite sex, bestiality, sadomasochistic abuse, lewd exhibition or mutual masturbation.

RAPE/SEXUAL ASSAULT

Most states have substituted the term *sexual assault* for *rape*. In this chapter, the words *rape* and *sexual assault* are used synonymously and interchangeably. Although males report a significant number of rapes every year, women are by far the predominant victims. In view of that, this discussion assumes that the victim is usually female and the suspect male. Rape is often classified as either forcible or statutory.

Forcible rape is sexual intercourse against a person's will by the use or threat of force. **Statutory rape** is sexual intercourse with a minor, with or without consent.

A distinction is made in the research literature between forcible rape and two other kinds of rape: drug- or alcohol-facilitated rape and incapacitated rape (Kilpatrick et al., 2007). In a *drug-facilitated* or *alcohol-facilitated rape*, the perpetrator deliberately drugs the victim or tries to get the victim drunk and then commits the rape. An *incapacitated rape* occurs when the victim voluntarily uses drugs or consumes alcohol and then the perpetrator takes advantage of the victim's intoxicated state and inability to defend herself or deny consent to commit the rape. Either of these two types of sexual assault may also be called *date rape*, which is discussed shortly.

According to national studies, an estimated 18 to 20 million women and almost three million men have been forcibly raped at some time in their lives, and results from the National Violence Against Women Survey (NVAWS) suggest that more than 300,000 women and 93,000 men are raped every year in this country (Tjaden and Thoennes, 2006). An additional 2.6 million women have experienced drug-facilitated (0.6 million) or alcohol-facilitated (2.5 million) rape, and 3.1 million women have been victims of incapacitated rape (Fisher et al., 2008). Furthermore many of these victims are repeat victims, with the NVAWS estimating that women who had been raped during the previous 12 months experienced an average of three rapes during that time period. Yet, only a small percentage of these crimes—less than one in four—are captured in official statistics. According to the Uniform Crime Reports (UCR; *Crime in the United States*, 2010), an estimated 88,097 forcible rapes were reported to law enforcement in 2009, a 2.6 percent decrease from 2008. Compared with 2000 data, forcible rape declined 2.3 percent. The rate of forcible rapes in 2009 was estimated at 56.6 offenses per 100,000 female inhabitants. The clearance rate for forcible rape was 41.2 percent in 2009.

In most cases, the rapist was male, the victim knew the rapist, the rapes occurred in a private setting and the perpetrator did not have a weapon or threaten to harm or kill the victim. However, 38 percent of victims said they were slapped, hit, kicked, bitten, choked or otherwise "beaten up," and 13 percent said they feared that they or someone close to them would be harmed or killed. The NVAWS also notes that in nearly two-thirds of the rape incidents, the victim reported that the perpetrator had been using drugs, alcohol or both.

Results of large-scale national studies indicate that most sexual assault victims do not report the crime to police, and as many as 95 percent of such assaults go undocumented (Lonsway and Archambault (2010). A variety of reasons are given for the nonreporting of sex crimes, the most frequently cited being ambiguity about what illicit sexual conduct is, fear of reprisal from the offender and feelings of embarrassment and stigma.

Because researchers are hampered by insufficient data regarding the incidence and prevalence of intimate partner and sexual violence, both nationally and locally, the Centers for Disease Control and Prevention (CDC) initiated the development of the National Intimate Partner and Sexual Violence Survey (NISVS) program in 2006 to gather and disseminate information for each state about intimate partner violence, sexual violence and stalking.

Rape is underreported for a number of reasons. Many victims feel worthless or guilty afterward. Some fear the social stigma associated with rape. Others have a close relationship with their rapist and fear that a charge of rape would damage the relationship. Many victims appear to be intimidated by the criminal justice system in general or by the way the system appears to have dealt with rape cases in the past. Here, a policewoman takes oral evidence from a rape victim who is seated in the officer's squad car.
© Spencer Grant/PhotoEdit

The survey, originally slated to be conducted in 2010, was rescheduled for completion in November 2011 and, as this text goes to print, no results are yet available.

Elements of the Crime of Rape

Although rape is defined in various ways by state laws, certain elements of the offense are fairly universal.

The elements of the crime of rape or sexual assault commonly include
- An act of sexual intercourse
- with a person other than a spouse,
- committed without the victim's consent and
- against the victim's will and by force.

An Act of Sexual Intercourse.

The element of sexual intercourse does not require establishing that a complete sex act accompanied by ejaculation occurred. Any degree of penetration is sufficient to constitute sexual intercourse. An emission of semen is not required.

With a Person Other Than a Spouse.

This element now allows the possibility of a man being raped, either by a male or female. Some states, as noted, are revising their laws to include as rape forcible sex acts committed by an adult male against another male. Although most states require that the victim not be the man's wife, a husband can be charged with assault. Moreover, some states include as rape an act of forced sexual intercourse with a wife during a legal separation if the act fulfills the other requirements of rape. Other states are considering laws that would include as rape a husband's forced sexual intercourse accompanied by serious threats against a wife's life. New studies are shedding light on the sexual assault of women who want to leave, are in the process of leaving or who have left their marital or cohabiting partners (DeKeseredy, 2010). The prevalence of these rapes is calling into question whether this element—"with a person other than a spouse"—should be removed from the list of elements needed to prove a sexual assault.

Committed without the Consent of the Victim.

Consent given because of fear, panic, emotional disturbance, mental illness or retardation; while on drugs or unconscious; or by a child is *not* considered true consent.

Against the Victim's Will and by Force.

This element has traditionally been the most difficult to prove and the most subject to attack by the defense. Although laws require the victim to use the utmost resistance possible, such resistance can result in additional violence and even death. A person willing to rape is often willing to injure. Therefore, legislation in many states emphasizes the rapist's words, actions and intent rather than the victim's degree of resistance.

Police officers are often asked whether it is better for a victim to resist or to submit to a sexual attack. Does resistance increase the attacker's violence? It is a difficult question to answer because researchers have arrived at different conclusions. Some results indicate that resisting reduces the likelihood of continued assault; other results indicate that it makes the attacker more violent. Some people who have been sexually assaulted reported that they fought back only after they had already been harmed, which would appear to preclude that resisting caused increased violence. It has been found that people who have been attacked previously are more apt to resist.

One study pointed out that in no other crime are victims expected to resist or not to resist their assailants. Everyone has a right to defend himself or herself, but whether it is more harmful to the victim to choose to defend is not possible to state. This must be an individual decision. Some police departments do not give advice on this question because of the possibility of lawsuits.

More emphasis should be placed on the attacker's behavior than on that of the victim. Increasing the penalty where the attacker uses extreme violence may help reduce the severity of the attacks, although this is problematic because of the emotional status and possible mental instability of this type of criminal.

Challenges to Investigation

Sexual assaults are among the most difficult and challenging cases to investigate. Immediate reporting increases the changes of obtaining physical evidence. The initial call concerning a rape (or other sexual offense) is normally taken by the dispatcher, communications officer or complaint clerk. The person taking the call immediately dispatches a patrol unit because rape is a felony and because it is a crime in which the offender may be known or close to the scene. The person taking the call then tells the victim to wait for the police to arrive if she is at a safe location and not to alter her physical appearance or touch anything at the scene. The victim is asked whether she can identify or describe the suspect, whether she has sustained serious injuries and whether she needs immediate medical assistance. The victim should also be advised not to wash, shower or douche before having a medical exam. As with any violent crime, early response is critical in apprehending the suspect and in reducing the victim's anxiety.

> Special challenges to investigating rape include the sensitive nature of the offense, social attitudes and the victim's horror or embarrassment. A rape investigation requires great sensitivity.

THE POLICE RESPONSE

The first officers to arrive can make or break a rape case depending on how they approach the victim. All police officers should have special training in handling sexual assault victims. Whenever possible, an officer without such training should not be assigned to this kind of case.

As soon as you arrive at the scene, announce yourself clearly to allay fears the victim may have that the suspect is returning. Explain to the victim what is being done for her safety. If the rape has just occurred, if there are serious injuries or if it appears the victim is in shock, call for an ambulance.

Protect the crime scene and broadcast a description of the assailant, means and direction of flight and the time and exact location of the assault. Establish a command post away from the scene to divert attention from the address of the victim and to preserve the scene. Conduct the preliminary investigation as described in Chapter 1. At a minimum, officers on the scene should:

- Record their arrival time.
- Determine the victim's location and condition. Request an ambulance if needed. Obtain identification of the suspect if possible.
- Determine whether the suspect is at the scene.
- Protect the crime scene.
- Identify and separate witnesses. Obtain valid identification from them and then obtain preliminary statements.
- Initiate crime broadcast if applicable.

Information to Obtain

If a suspect is arrested at or near the scene, conduct a field identification. If much time has elapsed between the offense and the report, use other means of identification. If the victim knows the assailant, obtain the suspect's name, address, complete description and the nature of the relationship with victim. Then obtain arrest and search warrants. If the suspect is unknown to the victim, check modus operandi (MO) files and have the victim look at photo files on sex offenders.

> **MO factors important in investigating sex offenses include type of offense, words spoken, use of a weapon, actual method of attack, time of day, type of location and victim's age.**

These MO factors are manifested in the offender's behavior and should be asked about when interviewing victims, as discussed shortly.

The victim may be unable to describe the suspect because of stress or darkness or because the perpetrator wore a mask or other identity-concealing clothing. A time lapse before reporting the offense can occur because of the victim's embarrassment, confusion or shock or because the victim was taken to a remote area, giving the suspect time to escape.

Physical Evidence

Sometimes it is difficult to determine whether an assault or homicide is a sex-related crime. Evidence of sexual activity observable at the crime scene or on the victim's body includes torn or no clothing, seminal fluid on or near the body, genital bruising or injury and sexually suggestive positioning of the body.

> **Evidence in a rape case consists of stained or torn clothing; scratches, bruises or cuts; evidence of a struggle; and semen and bloodstains. Such evidence shows the amount of force that occurred, establishes that a sex act was performed and links the act with the suspect.**

Because such evidence deteriorates rapidly, obtain it as soon as possible. Some police departments have rape kits that contain the equipment needed to collect, label and preserve evidence.

Steck-Flynn (2007, p.66) describes how officers responding to a call of sexual assault should proceed:

> When responding to a sexual assault scene, the way the offender gained access to the victim is important in determining the scope of the crime scene. There also may be primary, secondary or multiple scenes.
>
> The first thing needed to preserve physical evidence is to secure the scene, ensuring the safety of the victim and witnesses. A log of all persons at the scene is important, including emergency personnel. They may be required to submit samples of hair, DNA, etc. at a later date to rule them in or out as a source of evidence at the scene. If something looks out of place, collect it, even if its connection to the crime or identification is unknown.
>
> In some cases emergency personnel may have arrived on the scene before the police. They may have noticed a vehicle or person of interest upon arrival. They may also have experienced transient evidence, such as odors, at the scene. . . .
>
> Medical personnel can be asked to help preserve evidence in several ways. First, if there are pools of liquid, such as blood, on the ground or floor, the stretcher can be carried around the material rather than wheeled. Wheel tracks through liquid or soil can contaminate the material.
>
> Any clothing removed from the victim can be placed in a clean paper evidence bag and sealed. . . .
>
> To maintain the chain of custody where evidence on the victim is concerned, whenever possible an officer should accompany the victim to the hospital.

Do not allow family members access to the scene, for even if they are not considered perpetrators of the crime, their presence may jeopardize the investigation by contaminating or destroying evidence.

Photograph all injuries to the victim, and take as evidence any torn or stained clothing. Examine the scene for other physical evidence such as fingerprints, footprints, a weapon, stains or personal objects the suspect may have left behind. Examine washcloths or towels the suspect may have used. Photograph any signs of a struggle such as broken objects, overturned furniture or, if outdoors, disturbed vegetation.

If the assault occurred outdoors, take soil and vegetation samples for comparison. If the assault occurred in a vehicle, vacuum the car seats and interior to obtain soil, hairs and other fibers. Examine the seats for blood and semen stains. DNA analysis has become increasingly important in sexual assault cases.

If a suspect is apprehended, photograph any injuries, marks or scratches on the suspect's body. Obtain blood and hair samples, and give the appropriate tests to determine whether the suspect is intoxicated or on drugs. Obtain any clothing or possessions of the suspect that might connect him with the rape. If necessary, obtain a warrant to search his vehicle, home or office. Such searches may reveal items associated with perversion or weapons of the type used in the assault.

Investigating Date Rape

A particularly difficult type of sexual assault is **date rape**, sometimes called acquaintance rape, in which the victim knows the suspect. Frequently drugs, including alcohol, are involved in such cases. According to the National Women's Health Center, "Because of the effects of these drugs, victims may be physically helpless, unable to refuse sex and can't remember what happened. The drugs often have no color, smell or taste and are easily added to flavored drinks without the victim's knowledge" ("Date Rape Drugs," n.d.). The center suggests that most experts prefer the term *drug-facilitated sexual assault.*

 Additional evidence in date rape cases may include the presence of alcohol, drugs or both in the victim's system.

The three most common date rape drugs are Rohypnol, gamma hydroxybutyric acid (GHB) and ketamine. **Rohypnol**, a Schedule IV drug under the Controlled Substances Act and illegal to manufacture, sell, possess or use in the United States, is the oldest drug used in this crime and is as much as 10 times more powerful than Valium and Halcion in producing a slowing of physical and mental responses, muscle reflexes and amnesia (DEA Drug Fact Sheets). Legal in other countries throughout Europe and in Mexico, and commonly prescribed to treat insomnia, it is manufactured in pill form and dissolves in liquids. As a safety feature, newly produced pills turn blue when added to liquids, but older pills, which are still available, have no color. According to the National Women's Health Information Center, Rohypnol can cause many problems: loss of memory concerning events that happened while under the influence of the drug, lower blood pressure, sleepiness, muscle relaxation or loss of muscle control, drunk feeling, nausea, problems talking, difficulty with motor movements, loss of consciousness, confusion, problems seeing, dizziness, confusion and stomach problems.

Another date rape drug is Ecstasy, or MDMA (3,4 methylenedioxymethamphetamine), a Schedule I drug under the Controlled Substances Act with no currently accepted medical use in the United States (DEA Drug Fact Sheets). Typically synthesized in clandestine labs, various forms of this drug include an odorless, colorless liquid, a white powder and a pill. Ecstasy is a stimulant with psychedelic effects that can last from four to six hours. It is usually taken orally in pill form. Its psychological effects include confusion, depression, anxiety, sleeplessness, drug craving and paranoia. Adverse physical effects include muscle tension, involuntary teeth clenching, nausea, blurred vision, feeling faint, tremors, rapid eye movement and sweating or chills.

Ketamine is a white powder that can cause hallucination, lost sense of time and identity, distorted perceptions of sight and sound, feeling out of control, impaired motor function, problems breathing, convulsions, vomiting, out-of-body experiences, memory problems, dream-like feeling, numbness and loss of coordination. Ketamine is classified as a Scheduled III non-narcotic drug under the Controlled Substances Act and is legal in the United States as an injectable, short-acting anesthetic commonly used by veterinarians (DEA Drug Fact Sheets). However, using it to facilitate sexual assault is clearly illegal, and assailants are often able to obtain the drug from diverted or stolen inventory from veterinary clinics or through smugglers bringing the drug in from Mexico (DEA Drug Fact Sheets).

Acknowledging the severe and dangerous nature of such drug-assisted sexual assaults, the Drug-Induced Rape Prevention and Punishment Act was signed in 1996, allowing courts to impose prison sentences of as long as 20 years on anyone who distributes a controlled substance, such as Rohypnol, to another person with the intent to commit a crime of violence, including rape. Given that the distribution of a controlled substance is already a federal crime, the act does not federalize any new conduct but does establish the basis for harsher penalties under federal law if the distribution facilitates a violent crime.

Officers investigating a sexual assault where the victim cannot give much information about the crime should suspect a date rape drug is involved. Therefore, in addition to following the usual protocol for investigating sexual assault, officers should inform emergency medical technicians and emergency room (ER) personnel that a date rape drug is suspected. Blood and urine tests may show the presence of a specific drug.

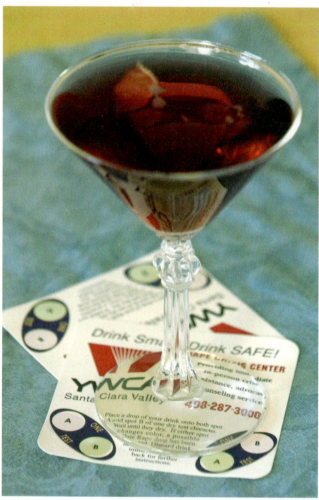

A cocktail sits atop a date rape drug detection coaster. The test spots in the corners of the coasters are supposed to turn dark blue in about 30 seconds if a splash of alcohol contains drugs often used to incapacitate victims. Colleges around the country are buying millions of coasters that test for "date-rape" drugs in drinks. But law enforcement experts say the coasters are ineffective and could lead to more assaults by creating a false sense of security. The coaster manufacturer, however, contends the 40-cent paper coasters are 95 percent accurate.

THE VICTIM'S MEDICAL EXAMINATION

Many rape victims choose not to go to the police immediately following their attack. Such victims, however, must be encouraged to seek prompt medical attention and to allow for the collection of evidence at a medical examination in case they later decide to proceed with an investigation. The medical examination can establish injuries, determine whether intercourse occurred and protect against venereal disease and pregnancy. Some hospitals provide drugs at the initial examination to lessen the possibility of pregnancy. Further examination for venereal disease is also conducted. A suspect apprehended at or near the scene also usually undergoes a medical examination.

Although each hospital has its own procedures, ER doctors and nurses are trained to observe and treat trauma; therefore, they can provide counseling and support services to the victim during this initial critical phase. Good examination-stage care promotes later cooperation from the victim.

Many hospitals have formed specially trained units of physicians and nurses to deal specifically with sexual assaults. These units may be on-call if an incident occurs and none of the team members are already on duty. One initiative that has been shown to enhance both the rape victim's recovery and the investigation's success, thereby increasing prosecution rates, is the Sexual Assault Nurse Examiners (SANE) program:

> SANE nurses receive a minimum of 40 hours of classroom training and 40 hours of clinical training. The training covers evidence collection, injury detection methods, chain-of-evidence requirements, ways to avoid re-traumatizing a victim during an examination and other topics. Most SANE teams use specialized equipment such as a colposcope, a lighted magnifying tool that can detect small cuts, bruises and other injuries. The colposcope is also equipped with a camera to document any injuries. . . . SANE teams are also available to testify in court as expert witnesses. (Bulman, 2009, pp.15,16)

The hospital or health care professional obtains medical-legal evidence that includes a detailed report of an examination of the victim for trauma, injuries and intercourse. The report contains precise descriptions of all bruises, scratches, cuts and other injuries; the examiner's findings and prescribed treatment; the victim's statements; documentation of the presence or absence of semen; documentation of the presence of drugs in the victim's system; the specific diagnosis of trauma; and any other specific medical facts concerning the victim's condition. The report should contain no conclusions about whether the woman was raped because this is a legal matter for the court to decide. However, in some states, hospitals are required by law to report suspected rape cases to the police.

Most hospitals have a sexual assault and vaginal kit in the examination room with the proper forms and tests for semen. Tests can be made of the vagina, anus or mouth, depending on the type of assault. After the examination, these kits are given to the police at the victim's request and sent to a crime laboratory for analysis.

The victim should be asked to sign a release form that authorizes the medical facility to provide police a copy of the examination record. Hospital reports may be introduced as evidence even if a police officer was not present during the examination. Also ask the hospital and the victim for the clothing the victim was wearing at the time of the assault if it was not obtained earlier.

The victim is reimbursed for medical examination costs in jurisdictions that have victim compensation laws. In other states, local or state health agencies may cover the costs. Before 2005, it was common practice to link victim reimbursement to an obligation for the victim to cooperate with the police investigation. In other words, if a victim declined to make a formal police report and press charges, they often were not reimbursed for the cost of the medical exam. In addition, much of the evidence from these exams was routinely disposed of after only a few months, making it nearly impossible for a victim to decide at a later date, once the raw horror of the attack had subsided, to go to the police and have the rape investigated. The reasoning behind this process was that medical exams were expensive to conduct and were considered another ordeal for the victim to endure, and if the victim was unwilling to report the crime or participate in the investigation, why make jurisdictions foot the bill and store evidence that would never be used to prosecute the offender? However,

> Imagine for a moment the trauma of being sexually assaulted. Immediately afterward, there is no time to make sense of what has happened, let alone figure out what to do about it. Many victims feel afraid, ashamed, and confused. They are probably not sure whom to tell. But regardless of whom they tell, they are likely to be confronted with the question of whether or not they will report the incident to police and press charges. . . .
>
> Unfortunately, this question is all too often framed as if it were an all-or-nothing, now-or-never decision. Victims often face intense pressure to

report their sexual assaults to police, frequently by well-meaning friends and family members as well as community responders. . . . Because of the intense pressure to make an immediate decision, their answer is usually "no." (Lonsway and Archambault, 2010, p.51)

The consequences of such scenarios playing out hundreds of thousands of times, year after year, have fostered a dire situation in which rape remains a seriously underreported and reoccurring crime: "Obviously, if the crime is not reported, no time-sensitive evidence is collected from the victim, suspect, or crime scene. No information is documented by law enforcement, so there is little or no opportunity to prosecute the crime. . . . No investigation occurs, and, as a result, perpetrators are free to offend again. Nothing changes for the next victim, so the cycle repeats" (Lonsway and Archambault, 2010, p.51).

The significance of this cycle is illustrated in a study of 1,882 men, with an average age of 26.5 years and demographically representative of the general male population in the United States (Lisak and Miller, 2002). In this sample of men, 120 (6.4 percent) admitted to engaging in acts that met the legal definition of rape against women they knew, yet none of them had had their offenses reported to law enforcement. Furthermore, nearly two-thirds (63.3 percent) of these men who had committed a sexual assault had done so more than once. In fact, this group was responsible for 439 rapes, which averages to nearly six rapes per undetected rapist. The percentage of sexual assaults committed by this small cohort of serial sex offenders (4 percent of the original sample group) was calculated to be 91 percent. A similar study of newly enlisted male military personnel found that 13 percent of the men had committed or attempted a rape and that 95 percent of the rapes involved serial rapists (McWhorter et al., 2009).

In an effort to diminish this cycle and hold more sex offenders accountable by increasing the victim report rate, a change was needed in how sexual assault victims were treated following their attack. In 2005 when the Violence Against Women Act (VAWA) of 1994 was reauthorized (it had also been reauthorized in 2003), it included a provision aimed at ensuring that all victims of sexual assault could receive a forensic medical exam at no cost, regardless of their decision to report the crime to the police or participate in the investigation (Lonsway and Archambault, 2010). This provision reduces pressure on rape victims to jump right into the criminal justice process immediately following their attack, yet encourages them to seek a prompt medical examination that not only addresses injuries sustained but allows the collection of crucial forensic evidence, should the victim later change her mind and decide to press charges. The change allows victims "time to rest, think, clean up, eat, drink, sleep, smoke, sober up, and do all the things they need to do to feel human again . . . [It offers victims] the opportunity to gather the information and support they need to make good, solid, well-educated decisions . . . In the meantime . . . law enforcement [can collect and properly store] any time-sensitive evidence to preserve the victim's option of reporting for later" (Lonsway and Archambault, 2010, p.52).

The take-away for investigators working sex offenses is that a softer response is often needed for victims of this crime compared with other crimes. For many rape victims, an aggressive response by law enforcement can backfire and damage the chances of bringing the perpetrator to justice. Many departments are implementing a reporting procedure for victims of sexual assault known as *blind reporting*.

BLIND REPORTING

Rape victims may feel foolish, hurt, ashamed, vulnerable and frightened. Furthermore, the prospect of reliving the entire experience by having the police ask detailed and personal questions is more than many victims can bear, particularly immediately after the incident. However, given time, victims may come to trust others enough to recount the attack, even hoping to prevent the same assailant from attacking others.

> **Blind reporting** allows sexual assault victims to retain their anonymity and confidentiality while sharing critical information with law enforcement. It also permits victims to gather legal information from law enforcement without having to commit immediately to an investigation.

Blind reporting procedures dovetail well with procedures for collecting crucial medical-legal evidence from sexual assault victims as set forth in VAWA 2005. The success of blind reporting hinges on whether trust can be established between the victim and the investigator. Six steps law enforcement agencies can take to develop an effective blind reporting system are

1. Establish and uphold a policy of victim confidentiality.
2. Allow victims to disclose as much or as little information as they wish.
3. Accept the information whenever victims might offer it—a delay of disclosure is not an indicator of the validity of the statement.

4. Develop procedures and forms to facilitate anonymous information from third parties (e.g., examiners).
5. Clarify options with victims for future contact— where, how and under what circumstances they may be contacted by the law enforcement agency.
6. Maintain blind reports in separate files from official complaints to prevent inappropriate use.

The legal acceptability of blind reporting varies from state to state, and even from county to county. In jurisdictions where prosecutors accept blind report records, such records become the "founding document" in the formal sexual assault investigation should the victim decide to file a complaint and proceed with a full investigation.

INTERVIEWING THE VICTIM

Rape is typically a horrifying, violent experience of violation to the victim. Reporting it to the police is frequently a courageous act because the victim knows that he or she will be forced to relive the experience through numerous retellings and that his or her word may be doubted. In addition, rape is humiliating and can involve numerous undesirable repercussions such as ostracism by friends and family, hospitalization, pregnancy, venereal disease and even AIDS. At the time of the interview, the rape victim may be hysterical or unusually calm. Remember: rape is a crime of aggression and hostility and is usually conducted violently. Attempt to establish rapport by using sympathetic body language and explaining the necessity for asking sensitive questions.

Attempt to reinforce the victim's emotional well-being, but also obtain the facts. The pressure and stress caused by rape can make victims uncooperative. Rape victims sometimes complain that investigative personnel question the complaint's validity even before hearing the facts, are rude and overly aggressive, fail to explain the procedures used in the investigation, ask highly personal questions too early in the interview or have or express unsympathetic or negative attitudes about the victim's personal appearance, clothing or actions, implying that the victim may be partly responsible for the crime.

Both uniformed and investigative personnel, male and female, can help the victim cooperate if they are understanding and supportive. Such an approach contributes to the victim's psychological well-being and helps obtain information and evidence required to apprehend and prosecute the offender. Some departments require that two investigators or a victim's advocate be present when a rape victim is interviewed. Some departments also have a specialized sexual assault investigative unit comprising specially trained investigators who focus on this type of crime. Despite the existence of such units, patrol officers are usually the first responding officer to an in-progress incident or assault that just occurred, and they must be cognizant of the special approach needed for these types of victimizations.

Although some police feel that professional medical personnel should obtain the personal details of a sexual attack, this is shirking responsibility. Deal with the victim's emotional and psychological needs completely while investigating the case and preserving evidence.

Whether the investigator's gender affects the victim's cooperation is debatable. Some believe that a female investigator should interview female victims, and male investigators should interview male victims. Insensitive actions by a male investigator may reinforce a female victim's image of male aggressiveness and result in refusal to answer questions. In fact, the mere involvement of a male officer, despite his every intention of helping the victim, may hinder the investigation if the victim has become so distrusting of men. Furthermore, if a male detective interviews a female victim, or a female detective interviews a male victim, one or both parties might be highly uncomfortable discussing the details of the assault and the victim's sexual history, which is an important part of the investigation.

However, how much victims cooperate usually depends less on the interviewer's gender than on his or her attitude, patience, understanding, competence and ability to establish rapport. Treat the victim with care, concern and understanding. Assume that the sexual assault is real unless facts ultimately prove otherwise.

The interview location is also important. The police station may be unsatisfactory. The victim's home may be ideal—if the rape did not occur there. Tell the victim you must ask questions about the incident and ask where he or she would be most comfortable talking about it. If the victim is hospitalized, consult with the medical staff about when you can question her or him.

No matter where the interview is conducted, do it privately. Although the victim should be allowed to have a relative or friend nearby to talk to, it is better to be alone with the victim when specific questions are asked. If the victim insists on having someone with her, discuss with this person the procedure to be followed. Explain that the person's presence is important to the victim for reassurance and security but that the person must allow the victim to talk freely and not interrupt.

The victim's family and friends can considerably influence whether the victim relates the entire story. A wide range of emotions can occur from mothers, fathers, husbands or other family members. They may be silent, hysterical or angry to the point that they have every intention of killing the perpetrator if they find him. Sometimes such anger is turned against the victim.

Make a complete report of the victim's appearance and behavior: presence of liquor or drugs; bruises, scratches or marks; manner of speech; emotional condition; appearance of clothes or hair; color of face; smeared makeup; torn clothes; and stains. Take photographs to supplement your notes.

The needed initial information includes the victim's name, age, home address, work address, telephone number(s) and any prior relationship with the offender, if the offender is known. At a *later* interview, investigators should obtain additional information about the victim, including:

- Children and their ages
- Educational level of victim
- Family, parents and the nature of the victim's relationship with them
- Fears
- Financial status, past and present
- Friends and enemies
- Hobbies
- Marital status
- Medical history, physical and mental
- Occupation, past and present
- Personal habits
- Physical description, including attire at the time of the incident
- Recent changes in lifestyle
- Recent court actions
- Reputation on the job and in the neighborhood
- Residence, past and present
- Social habits
- Use of alcohol and drugs

Obtain a detailed account of the crime, including the suspect's actions and statements, special characteristics or oddities and any unusual sexual behaviors. Determine exactly where and how the attack occurred, what happened before and after the attack and whether the victim can give any motive for the attack. Explain what you need to know and why, the procedures you will follow and how important the victim's cooperation is. Use open-ended questions such as, "Take your time and tell me exactly what happened."

Determine the exact details of resistance, even if not required by law. Was there any unconsciousness, paralysis or fainting? Was there penetration? Who did the victim first talk to after the assault? How soon was the report made, and if there was a delay, what was the reason?

Establish lack of consent. Obtain the names of any witnesses. Determine where the victim was before the attack and whether someone might have seen her and followed her. The suspect's description can then be used at that location to see whether anyone there can identify him. Obtain as much information as possible about the suspect: voice, mannerisms, clothing, actions and general appearance.

It is important to obtain as many details as possible even though they may appear insignificant at the time. How the initial contact was made; attempts at concealment; the suspect's voice, appearance and exact words; unusual behavior, including unusual sexual acts performed—all these can be helpful in identifying and prosecuting the offender.

Establishing the Behavioral Profile in Sex Offense Cases

Because rapists are generally recidivists (about 70 percent of them commit more than one rape), the details and MOs of offenses in another area of the same city or another community might be identical to the present case. For this reason, the usefulness of behavioral profiling becomes apparent, and interviews with victims should focus on the *offender's* behavior.

Several specific areas should be covered in the behavior-oriented interview of rape victims, embodied in three essential basic steps: (1) carefully interview the victim about the rapist's *behavior,* (2) analyze that behavior to ascertain the *motivation* underlying the assault and (3) compile a *profile* of the individual likely to have committed the crime.

The three types of rapist behavior of concern to investigators are physical (use of force), verbal and sexual. First, ascertain the method of approach. Three common approaches are the "con" approach, in which the offender is initially friendly, even charming, and dupes the victim; the "blitz" approach, in which the offender directly physically assaults the victim, frequently gagging, binding or blindfolding the victim; and the "surprise" approach, in which the offender hides in the back seat of a car, in shrubbery or behind a wall or waits until the victim is sleeping.

After determining the approach, you should determine how the perpetrator maintained control. Four common methods of control are (1) mere presence, (2) verbal threats, (3) display of a weapon and (4) use of physical force.

If the rapist used physical force, it is important to determine the amount of force because this gives insight into the offender's motivations. Four levels of physical force may be used: (1) *minimal,* perhaps slapping; (2) *moderate,* repeated hitting; (3) *excessive,* beating resulting in bruises and cuts; and (4) *brutal,* sadistic torture. This last type of offender is typically extremely profane, abusive and aggressive, and the victim may require hospitalization or die.

In addition to the offender's sexual behavior, investigators should inquire about the offender's verbal behavior. Themes in rapists' conversations include threats, orders, personal inquiries of the victim, personal revelations, obscene names, racial epithets and inquiries about the victim's sexual enjoyment. Also ask about the *victim's* verbal behavior. Did the offender demand that the victim say certain words or demand that she beg, plead, scream? Such demands also shed insight into the offender's motivation.

Specifically ask victims about any change in the offender's behavior, whether verbal, physical or sexual. Such changes can indicate weakness or fear if the offender lessens his efforts, or anger and hostility if he suddenly increases his efforts.

A further area of inquiry relates to the offender's experience level. Did he take actions to protect his identity, to destroy or remove evidence or to make certain he had an escape route? The novice rapist may take minimal or obvious actions to protect his identity—for example, wearing a ski mask and gloves, changing his voice tone, affecting an accent, ordering the victim not to look at him, or blindfolding and binding the victim. These are common precautions a person not knowledgeable about acid phosphatase tests of hair and fiber evidence would be expected to take. In contrast, the experienced rapist may walk through the residence or prepare an escape route, disable the phone, order the victim to shower or douche, bring bindings or gags, wear surgical gloves or take or force the victim to wash items the rapist touched or ejaculated on, such as bedding and the victim's clothing.

Also determine whether any items other than those of evidentiary value were taken by the offender. Of interest are items of value as well as items of a personal nature. It is important to determine whether items were taken and why. Again, such information may provide insight into the offender's motivation.

Ending the Victim Interview

End the interview with an explanation of available victim assistance programs, such as Sexual Offense Services (SOS). Arrange for relatives, friends or personnel from a rape crisis center to help the victim. If the victim refuses to be questioned, is incapable of answering questions because of shock or injuries or begins the interview but then breaks down emotionally, terminate the interview for the time being, but return later.

Explain to the victim what will happen next in the criminal justice system. Give the victim the case number and a phone number to call at the police department if any other details are remembered or if questions arise.

FOLLOW-UP INVESTIGATION

After the preliminary investigation, medical examination and initial interview are completed, conduct a follow-up investigation. Interview the victim again in two to five days to obtain further information and to compare the statements made after time has elapsed. Following that interview, determine whether the crime scene or evidence has been altered or contaminated and interview all possible witnesses to the offense.

Many prosecutors discourage conducting follow-up interviews with sexual assault victims, contending that the only thing these interviews accomplish is to provide the defense with inconsistent statements. Instead, these prosecutors argue, the victim should be interviewed by the on-the-scene officer and then formally interviewed by the investigator. Sexual assault investigators should be cognizant of this hazard of inconsistent statements and be familiar with the practices and preferences of prosecutors in their jurisdiction.

INTERVIEWING WITNESSES

Locate witnesses as soon as possible, and obtain their names, addresses and phone numbers. Canvass the neighborhood for possible witnesses. Even though witnesses may not have seen the incident, they may be able to describe the suspect or his vehicle. They may have heard screams or statements made by the victim or the offender.

Determine whether a relationship exists between the witness and the victim or offender. Determine exactly what the witness saw and heard. Did the witness see the victim before, during or after the assault? Did the witness see the victim with the suspect? How did the witness happen to be in the vicinity where the offense occurred? Interview acquaintances and individuals known to the victim because many victims know their rapists.

SEX OFFENDERS

Suspects fall into two general classifications: those who know the victim and those who are known sex offenders. In the first category are friends of the victim, people who have daily contact with the victim's relatives, those who make deliveries to the victim's residence or business and neighbors. In the second category are those on file in police records as having committed prior sex offenses. Known offenders with prior arrests are prime suspects because rehabilitation is often unsuccessful.

Some sexual assault offenders are sadistic and commit physical abuses in hostile, vicious manners that result in injury or even death. Others seek to control their victims through threats and physical strength but do not cause permanent physical injuries. Still others act out aggression and hatred in short attacks on women selected as random targets.

Sexual sadists become more sexually excited the more the victim suffers. The pleasure of complete domination over another person is the essence of the sadistic drive. Most sadists are cunning and deceitful and feel no remorse or compassion. They feel superior to society, especially the law. They often use pliers, electric cattle prods, whips, fire, bondage, amputation and objects inserted into the vagina. They may keep diaries, audiotapes, sexual devices and devices to torture victims, photographs of victims and other incriminating evidence—all items to be included in a search warrant.

Rapists are often categorized as motivated by either power or anger. Each category is further divided into two subcategories (Table 10.3). However, many rapists are opportunist sexual predators, and as one reviewer of this text noted, these predators "commit their acts not because of anger or power issues, but because they can. They want sex, and they are simply going to take it. Sometimes it's about evil people acting on their own hedonism against weaker individuals."

No personality or physical type can be automatically eliminated as a sex offender. Sex offenders include those who are married, have families and good jobs, are college educated and are active churchgoers.

The Significance of Fantasy in Sexual Assaults

Because fantasy is strongly associated with sexual assault, search warrant applications should include a list of the materials officers would expect to recover from an offender who indulged in sexual fantasies, such as sadistic pornography, drawings, videotapes, women's lingerie and clothing and fantasy stories featuring sexual sadism.

Sexual sadists may be obsessed with keeping trophies and recordings of the assaults. Therefore, any search warrant applications in such cases should include photographs, records, scripts, letters, diaries, audiotapes, videotapes and newspaper reports of the crimes as possible evidence to be seized (Geberth, 2008).

TABLE 10.3 Profiles of Rapists

	Power Rapists		Anger Rapists	
	Manhood Reassurance	**Manhood Assertion**	**Retaliatory/ Punishment**	**Excitation/Sadism**
Purpose	Confirm manhood to self	Express manhood to victim	Punish women for real or imagined wrongs	Obtain
Preassault behavior	Fantasizes about successful sexual relationships; plans attack	Seldom pre-planned; crime of opportunity	Spontaneous act in response to a significant stressor	Violent fantasies; careful planning
Victim selection	Observes (prowler, window peeker)	By chance	Spontaneous	Cruises
Victim characteristics	Same race; meek, nonassertive	Same age and race	Resembles female in his life	Same age and race
Location of approach	Inside victim's residence	Singles bars	Near his residence or job	Any location
Type of approach	Stealth; hand over mouth	Smooth talker; con	Blitz; immediate excessive use of force	Brandish a weapon
Weapon	Of opportunity (if used)	Of opportunity (if used)	Of opportunity (if used)	Of choice or planned
Time of day	Nighttime	Nighttime	Anytime	Anytime
Sexual acts	Normal	Self-satisfying; vaginal/penile intercourse; vaginal/anal intercourse; fellatio; spends long time	Violent, painful sex acts; degrading, humiliating acts; spends short time	Experimental sex; inserts objects into body cavities; spends long time
Sexual dysfunction	Erection problems; premature ejaculation	Retarded ejaculation	—	—
Other behaviors	Relatively nonviolent	Tears clothing off	Profanity; injury provoking; assaultive	Excessive, brutal force; bondage; torture; cuts clothing off; protects identity (mask, gloves); most likely to kill
Postassault behavior	Likely to apologize; takes personal items; keeps a diary	Likely to threaten; takes items as trophies; boasts of conquests	Leaves abruptly; may or may not threaten	Straightens scene; shows no remorse

Source: William C. Bradway. "Stages of a Sexual Assault." *Law and Order,* September 1990, pp.119–123. Reprinted by permission of the publisher.

TAKING A SUSPECT INTO CUSTODY AND INTERROGATION

If a suspect is apprehended at the scene, record any spontaneous statements made by the suspect and photograph him. If more than one suspect is present, separate them.

Do not allow communication among suspect, victim and witness. Remove the suspect from the scene as soon as possible.

When interrogating sex offenders, obtain as much information as possible, yet remain nonjudgmental. The suspect should be the last person interviewed. This allows the interviewer to have all information possible by the time of the suspect interview: facts about the victim, the type of offense and the location of the crime; statements from witnesses, neighbors and informants; and information about the suspect's background.

As in most interrogation situations, building rapport is the first step. Suggest to the suspect that you understand what he is going through. Ask about his family, his job and his interests. Assess the suspect's character. After rapport is established, ask the suspect to tell his side of the story from beginning to end and do not interrupt him. Show interest in what he is saying and keep him talking. The interrogator's approach should be one of "you tell me what happened and I will understand," even though that may not be the investigator's actual feelings.

The objective is to obtain the truth and the information necessary for proving guilt or innocence. To help accomplish this goal, attempt to gain the suspect's confidence. Many suspects feel they can justify their actions by putting some blame on the victim—for example, "She came on to me."

During the interrogation, remember that the seriousness of the charge to be brought will be based on the information you obtain. All elements of the charged offense must be proven, so keep the possible charges in mind and prepare questions to elicit supporting information.

COORDINATION WITH OTHER AGENCIES

A number of other agencies and individuals assist in handling rape cases.

> A rape case often involves cooperation with medical personnel, social workers, rape crisis center personnel and the news media.

The public and the news media can greatly influence the prosecution of a rape case. Medical and hospital personnel influence the victim's attitude and cooperation in obtaining facts for medical reports and the necessary evidence for use in court. Rape crisis centers can provide various kinds of support to victims and encourage them to sign a complaint.

PROSECUTION OF RAPE AND STATUTORY CHARGES

Few criminal cases are as difficult to prosecute as rape, at least under older laws. Despite changes in the law, it is virtually impossible to obtain a conviction on the victim's testimony alone.

> Conviction in sexual assault cases requires medical evidence, physical evidence such as torn clothing, evidence of injuries and a complaint reported reasonably close to the time of the assault.

Defendants usually want a jury trial because of present laws and attitudes regarding rape, and because the defendant is not required to testify. However, the victim must relate a very difficult ordeal and be subjected to cross-examination that can make *her* appear to be the one on trial.

Juries tend to be unsympathetic with a victim who was drinking heavily, hitchhiking or using drugs or who left a bar with a stranger or engaged in other socially "unacceptable" actions. Many newer laws make it very explicit that such conditions are not to be considered during the trial. Newer laws also state that the victim's testimony need not be corroborated and that testimony about the degree of resistance—although it may be admitted—is not required.

Moreover, testimony about the victim's previous sexual conduct is not admissible unless (1) the victim has had prior sexual relations with the defendant, (2) there is evidence of venereal disease or pregnancy resulting from the assault, (3) circumstances suggest that consent occurred within the calendar year or (4) the victim has not told the truth or has filed a false report.

Juries must not be instructed that a victim who consented to sexual intercourse with other persons would be likely to have consented with the defendant, that the victim's prior sexual conduct may be used to determine credibility or that the victim's testimony should be subjected to any greater test of credibility than in any other crime. Some have argued, however, that victims' characters are being judged even before a case has a chance to go to trial. These critics contend that victim characteristics and credibility issues frequently prevent sexual assault cases from ever reaching court by negatively affecting prosecutors' charging decisions in sexual assault cases.

> Many recent laws have reduced the penalties for sexual assault, which should lead to more convictions.

Former penalties were so severe that many juries hesitated to convict. More recent laws usually include both oral and anal sexual conduct, and many classify sexual offenses by degrees.

Some victims decide not to prosecute because of pressure from family or friends, fear of reprisal, shame, fear of going to court or emotional or mental disturbance.

Sometimes the prosecuting attorney refuses to take the case to court because the case is weak and thus has little chance of conviction. For example, there may not be enough physical evidence to corroborate the victim's complaint, the victim may be a known prostitute or a girlfriend of the rapist or she may be pregnant because of prior sexual relations with the assailant. At other times, the report is unfounded and unsubstantiated by the evidence.

False Reports

Women make false reports of sexual assault for a number of reasons, including getting revenge on lovers who have jilted them, covering up a pregnancy or getting attention. They may also file a false report as a way of defending against a lapse in judgment, a common scenario when a woman in a committed relationship goes out with friends, gets intoxicated and ends up having consensual sex with someone, only to realize the mistake at a later time. Such circumstances need to be ruled out when investigating a reported sexual assault. The credibility of rape reports is probably questioned more frequently than that of any other felony report. A polygraph can help determine the truth of the complainant's statements. If the evidence of a false report is overwhelming, include all the facts in your closeout report.

If the victim admits orally or in writing that her story was false, close the case. When the victim's credibility is in serious doubt because of contradictory evidence, the investigating officer's superior or the prosecutor can close the case.

CIVIL COMMITMENT OF SEX OFFENDERS AFTER SENTENCES SERVED

Because of the risk of recidivism by sex offenders following their release from jail or prison, many advocate legislation that allows the civil commitment of repeat sex offenders upon completion of their sentence. Sex offender civil commitment (SOCC) has been enacted in 16 states amid widespread controversy (Lucken and Bates, 2008, p.95). Such legislation acknowledges that although sex offenders may have paid a debt to society by spending time behind bars, often little if anything is accomplished during this incarceration to address and treat the disorders that lead offenders to commit sexual assault.

Although many contend that these acts violate offenders' civil rights, the Supreme Court has upheld the constitutionality of at least one state's civil commitment law. In *Kansas v. Hendricks* (1997), the Court upheld

Kansas's Sexually Violent Predator Act, which establishes procedures by which that state may civilly commit to a mental hospital people likely to commit predatory acts of sexual violence because of a mental abnormality or personality disorder.

However, in *Kansas v. Crane* (2002), the Supreme Court began refining its 1997 ruling in *Hendricks,* adding a new limitation on such civil commitments, saying that there must be "proof of [an offender's] serious difficulty in controlling [his] behavior."

SEX OFFENDER REGISTRY AND NOTIFICATION

With the realization that many convicted sex offenders have committed one or more such crimes before the current act for which they are serving time has come a flurry of legislation designed to notify the public of such predators living in their communities and to assist law enforcement in keeping track of these recidivism-prone individuals.

However, because of the highly mobile nature of today's society, it is increasingly difficult to monitor these offenders as they move from jurisdiction to jurisdiction, changing their names and appearances along the way. Nonetheless, state and national sex offender registries have proliferated in recent years, as mandated by law (Figure 10.2).

 The evolution of sex offender registries can be traced to a trilogy of federal statutes: the Jacob Wetterling Act, Megan's Law and the Pam Lychner Act.

The first act was named for 11-year-old Jacob Wetterling, who was abducted in October 1989 near his home in rural Minnesota and has never been found. The Jacob Wetterling Crimes against Children and Sexually Violent Offender Registration Act was enacted as part of President Bill Clinton's 1994 Crime Act. It required states to establish registration systems for convicted child molesters and other sexually violent offenders. States could release the information to the public, but they were not required to do so.

The second act was named for 7-year-old Megan Kanka, raped and murdered by a convicted sex offender who lived across the street from Megan's family with two other released sex offenders. Megan's Law, signed by President Clinton in 1996, amends the Jacob Wetterling Act in two ways: (1) it requires states to release any relevant

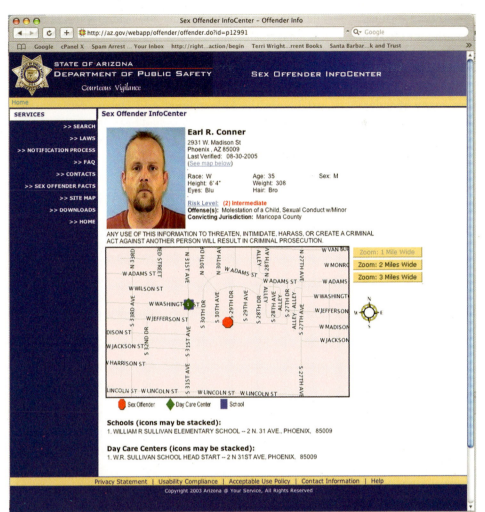

FIGURE 10.2
Sex offender registries vary from state to state, but most contain similar information. Many can be found on a state's Web site, such as this one taken from the Arizona Department of Public Safety. A disclaimer, shown above the map, is important to protect the offender's rights. Without such a disclaimer, the registry could be declared unconstitutional.

© State of Arizona, Department of Public Safety/Sex Offender info Center

information about registered sex offenders necessary to maintain and protect public safety and (2) it allows disclosure of information collected under a state registration program for any purpose permitted under the laws of the state.

The third law in the federal trilogy was named for a victims' rights advocate killed in a plane crash in July 1996. Officially called the Pam Lychner Sexual Offender Tracking and Identification Act, it directed the FBI to establish a national sex offender database. The permanent National Sex Offender Registry File is part of the FBI's National Crime Information Center (NCIC) and includes fingerprint and photo images of registered offenders.

The first sex offender registry was created in California in 1947, before it was legally required. By 1996, all states had enacted laws requiring sex offenders to register within their states to help law enforcement agencies manage offenders released from secure confinement. In California, failure to register as a sex offender is a felony, making punishment

more severe. If the previous sex crime itself was a felony, failure to register carries a mandated prison term.

In 2006 the Adam Walsh Child Protection and Safety Act was signed into law. Title I of the act was the Sex Offender Registration and Notification Act (SORNA), establishing comprehensive standards for sex offender registration and notification. As of July 1, 2006, all 50 states are included in the National Sex Offender Public Website (NSOPW), which incorporates real-time public data on sex offenders around the country, allowing citizens to view registries outside their own states. Sharing information on the more than 490,000 registered sex offenders in the United States is an effective prevention tool in tracking an individual from one area to another. The registry can be accessed at http://www.nsopw.gov.

Many arguments exist both for and against sex offender registries and notification laws. People who advocate sex offender registration and notification cite the significant number of sex offenders under community supervision, the fear of recidivism and the protection of children and their families. Critics contend that the registries violate the civil rights of offenders who have served their time and provide a false sense of security for the community because many sexual assaults are committed by first-time offenders who are, for obvious reasons, not identified on any registry. Furthermore, many offenders fail to register. The challenge is to balance the communities' rights to access public information with the protections provided to convicted offenders.

The three basic objections to notification laws center around punishment, privacy and due process issues. Some offenders claim that registering subjects them to additional punishment. The National Association of Criminal Defense Lawyers (NACDL) asserts, "It's a fiction to say that this is a civil matter when this is, in fact, an extension of the criminal punishment" (VanderHart, 2008). However, in April 1998 the Supreme Court rejected constitutional challenges that claimed that the laws' notification requirements represented an unconstitutional added punishment. Another concern of opponents is that notification will lead to harassment of offenders and increased acts of vigilantism. Sometimes the stigma placed on sex offenders is too great a burden to handle. A convicted child molester in Maine shot himself to death, saying in a tape-recorded message that he feared living in a world "with no forgiveness."

It appears that sex offender registration and notification have more supporters than opponents. Internet access is quickly revolutionizing the way the public keeps informed of the whereabouts of convicted sex offenders. In many jurisdictions, residents are now able to access a registry online, enter their zip codes and obtain information on sex offenders living in their area.

A case in point: the May 2005 kidnapping of 8-year-old Shasta Groene and her 9-year-old brother, Dylan, from their Idaho home by registered sex offender Joseph Edward Duncan III. The children's mother, older brother and the mother's boyfriend had been slain in their home just before the kidnappings, and Dylan's remains were later discovered after Shasta had been rescued and Duncan apprehended. At the time of the murders and kidnappings, Duncan was being sought for jumping bail on child molestation charges he faced in Minnesota and was listed as delinquent (missing) with both the North Dakota and Washington state sex offender registries.

In an effort to thwart those sex offenders who meet the legal criteria for required registration but fail to register, some jurisdictions are tracking such offenders through the use of global positioning systems (GPS) or other electronic monitoring devices. GPS has several key benefits, including the deterrent it provides against repeat offending and the higher level of protection offered to the public by ensuring a subject does not enter prescribed areas such as an elementary school or victim's neighborhood without enforcement agencies being immediately notified.

Another effort to track released sex offenders is to screen them against motor vehicle databases when they apply for or renew a driver's license. The National Center for Missing and Exploited Children says, "States should adopt policies that flag driver's-license and vehicle registration files of registered sex offenders as a means of keeping law enforcement authorities informed of address changes, vehicle information and personal data" ("Plan to Monitor Sex Offenders," 2008, p.6).

Summary

The key distinction between human trafficking and smuggling lies in the individual's freedom of choice. Sex offenses include bigamy, child molestation, incest, indecent exposure, prostitution, sodomy and rape (sexual assault). The most serious of these is rape—sexual intercourse with a person against the person's will. *Forcible rape* is sexual intercourse against a person's will by the use or threat of force. *Statutory rape* is sexual intercourse with a minor, with or without consent.

The elements of the crime of rape or sexual assault commonly include (1) an act of sexual intercourse, (2) with a person other than a spouse, (3) committed without the victim's consent, (4) against the victim's will and by force.

Special challenges in investigating rape include the sensitive nature of the offense, social attitudes and the victim's horror or embarrassment. A rape investigation requires great sensitivity.

MO factors important in investigating sex offenses include type of offense, words spoken, use of a weapon, actual method of attack, time of day, type of location and victim's age.

Evidence in a rape case consists of stained or torn clothing; scratches, bruises or cuts; evidence of a struggle; and semen and bloodstains. Such evidence shows the amount of force that occurred, establishes that a sex act was performed and links the act with the suspect. Additional evidence in date rape cases may include the presence of alcohol, drugs or both in the victim's system.

Many departments have implemented a procedure known as blind reporting, which allows sexual assault victims to retain their anonymity and confidentiality while sharing critical information with law enforcement. It also permits victims to gather legal information from law enforcement without having to commit immediately to an investigation.

A rape case often involves cooperation with medical personnel, social workers, rape crisis center personnel and the news media. Conviction in sexual assault cases requires medical evidence, physical evidence such as torn clothing, evidence of injuries and a complaint reported reasonably close to the time of the assault. Many recent laws have reduced the penalties for sexual assault, which should lead to more convictions.

The evolution of sex offender registries can be traced to a trilogy of federal statutes: the Jacob Wetterling Act, Megan's Law and the Pam Lychner Act.

Checklist

Sexual Assault

- What specific sex offense was committed?
- Are all the elements of the crime present?
- Who is the victim? Were there any injuries? Were they described and photographed?
- Were there any witnesses?
- Was the surrounding area canvassed to locate possible leads?
- Is there a suspect? A description of a suspect?
- Has there been a relationship between the suspect and the victim?
- What evidence was obtained at the scene?
- Was evidence submitted to the crime laboratory? Were reports received?
- Was the victim taken to the hospital for a medical examination?
- What evidence was obtained at the hospital? Is a medical report available?
- Was the victim interviewed? Will he or she sign a complaint?
- Was the victim reinterviewed two to five days after the assault?
- Was a background check made of the victim?
- Were other police agencies in the area notified and queried?

- Were field interrogation cards, MO files and other intelligence files checked?
- Have patrol divisions been checked for leads on cars or people in the area?
- Has a sexual assault or rape crisis center been contacted for help?

Application

Several young people in a car wave down a police car and tell the officers that screams are coming from the south end of a nearby park. At about the same time, the police dispatcher receives a call from a resident who says she hears screams and cries for help but cannot tell exactly what part of the park they are coming from. The officers talk to the juveniles, get their names and a description of the area and then head for the park without red lights and siren to avoid warning the attacker. Arriving at the south end of the park, the officers see a man running from some bushes. He is wearing a dark jacket and is bareheaded. One officer goes to find the victim; the other attempts to follow the fleeing man. At the scene, the officer observes a woman with torn clothing and a cut on the side of her head. She is unable to speak coherently, but she has obviously been assaulted. The juveniles have followed the squad car to the scene and crowd around the victim to offer help. The officer chasing the suspect has lost him and has returned to the scene. Both officers help the victim into the squad car and leave the scene with red lights and sirens, heading for the hospital. After leaving the victim at the hospital, they return to the scene. They find that branches are broken from some of the bushes. They also find an article of clothing from the victim and a switchblade knife on the ground. They secure the scene by posting several of the juveniles around the area until further help arrives.

Questions

1. Should red lights and siren have been used in going to the scene?
2. Was it correct for the officers to split up as they did?
3. Evaluate the effectiveness of the officers' actions after arriving at the scene.

Discussion Questions

1. What myths and prejudices have you heard about prosecuting rape cases? Are rape cases more difficult to prosecute than other crimes?
2. What are the penalties for rape in your state? Are these penalties adequate, or should they be more or less severe?

3. Past rape laws have required the utmost resistance by the victim. Present laws have reduced this requirement. Do you support this change?

4. What persons or agencies can assist the police in rape investigations? What functions or services can they provide? What resources are available in your community? In your state?

5. Should the rape victim be interviewed by male or female investigators?

6. Rape victims often complain about the attitudes of police and medical personnel during a rape investigation. Do you believe this is justified, or is it because of the victim's emotional stress?

7. A case in Oregon received wide publicity because a husband was charged with raping his wife during a temporary separation and was acquitted. Do you agree with this verdict? If so, are there circumstances under which such a charge should be supported?

8. What environment is best for interviewing the victim of a rape or sexual assault? How would you start the interview? How supportive of the victim would you be? What questions would you ask? Who would you allow to be present? How would you close the interview?

9. How vigorously should sex offenses such as sodomy, indecent exposure and prostitution be investigated? Should unnatural sexual acts between consenting adults be considered criminal acts?

10. Do you believe male victims of sexual assault have a more difficult time than women do when making a police report? Explain why or why not.

Media Explorations

Internet

Select one of the following assignments to complete.

■ Search for the key phrase *National Institute of Justice*. Click on "NCJRS" (National Criminal Justice Research Service). Click on "law enforcement." Click on "sort by Doc#." Search for one of the NCJ reference numbers from the Reference list from this chapter. Outline the selection to share with the class.

■ Go to the FBI Web site at www.fbi.gov. Click on "library and reference." Select "Uniform Crime Reports" and outline what the report says about sexual assault.

■ Select one of the following key terms: *blind reporting, date rape, prostitution, rape, sex crimes prevention, sexual assault, statutory rape*. Find one article relevant to

sexual assault investigations to outline and share with the class.

 Gale Criminal Justice Database Assignments

The following assignments require access to Gale's Custom Journals Database for Emergency Services and Criminal Justice. Check with your instructor if you have questions about this.

■ Find the article "Human Sex Trafficking" on the Gale Emergency Services Database. Read the article and outline why human sex trafficking continues to be a problem. Be prepared to discuss this topic in class.

■ Find the article "Barriers to Reporting Sexual Assault in Rural Areas" on the Gale Emergency Services Database. Identify reasons for the disparity in reports of sexual assaults in rural areas compared with urban areas. Be prepared to discuss possible solutions for this in class.

■ Find the article "A New Look At Sexual Violence" on the Gale Emergency Services Database. Read the article and write a brief synopsis of it.

References

Banks, Duren, and Kyckelhahn, Tracey. *Characteristics of Suspected Human Trafficking Incidents, 2008–2010.* Washington, DC: Bureau of Justice Statistics, Special Report, April 2011. (NCJ 233732)

Bulman, Philip. "Increasing Sexual Assault Prosecution Rates." *NIJ Journal*, November 2009, No.264, pp.14–17.

Crime in the United States, 2009. Washington, DC: U.S. Department of Justice, Federal Bureau of Investigation, September 2010. Accessed May 27, 2011. http://www2.fbi .gov/ucr/cius2009/index.html

The Crime of Human Trafficking: A Law Enforcement Guide to Identification and Investigation. Washington, DC: Office on Violence against Women and the International Association of Chiefs of Police, 2008.

"Date Rape Drugs." National Women's Health Information Center, no date.

DeKeseredy, Walter S. "Dangerous Exits in the Heartland: Separation/Divorce Sexual Assault in Rural America." *Criminal Justice Research Review*, July/August 2010, pp.100–103.

Drug Enforcement Administration (DEA). Drug Fact Sheets. http://www.justice.gov/dea/pubs/abuse/

Fisher, Bonnie S.; Daigle, Leah E.; and Cullen, Francis T. "Rape against Women: What Can Research Offer to Guide the Development of Prevention Programs and Risk Reduction Interventions?" *Journal of Contemporary Criminal Justice*, Vol.24, No.2, May 2008, pp.163–177.

Geberth, Vernon. "Fantasy Drawings Investigative Analysis." *Law and Order*, October 2008, pp.114–118.

Jetmore, Larry F. "The Oldest Profession: Investigating Street-Level Prostitution." *Law Officer Magazine*, October 2008, pp.92–96.

Kilpatrick, Dean G.; Resnick, Heidi S.; Ruggiero, Kenneth J.; Conoscenti, Lauren M.; and McCauley, Jenna. *Drug-Facilitated, Incapacitated, and Forcible Rape: A National Study. Final Report.* Washington, DC: National Institute of Justice, February 2007. (NCJ 219181)

Lisak, David, and Miller, Paul M. "Repeat Rape and Multiple Offending among Undetected Rapists." *Violence and Victims*, Vol.17, No.1, 2002, pp.73–84.

Lonsway, Kimberly A., and Archambault, Joanne. "The Earthquake in Sexual Assault Response: Police Leadership Can Increase Victim Reporting to Hold More Perpetrators Accountable." *The Police Chief*, September 2010, pp.50–56.

Lucken, Karol, and Bates, William. "Florida's Sexually Violent Predator Program: An Examination of Risk and Civil Commitment Eligibility." *Crime & Delinquency*, January 2008, pp.95–127.

McWhorter, Stephanie K.; Stander, Valerie A.; Merrill, Lex L.; Thomsen, Cynthia J.; and Milner, Joel S. "Reports of Rape Reperpetration by Newly Enlisted Male Navy Personnel." *Violence and Victims*, Vol.24, No.2, 2009, pp.204–218.

Moses, Marilyn C. "Understanding and Applying Research on Prostitution." *NIJ Journal*, November 2006, pp.22–25.

Orchowsky, Stan; Puryear, Veronica; and Iwama, Janice. "Federal and State Responses to Trafficking in Persons." *JRSA Forum*, March 2007, pp.1,6–7.

"Plan to Monitor Sex Offenders Poses Problems, Report Shows." *Criminal Justice Newsletter*, February 2008, pp.6–7.

Ramage, Michael. "New Visa Option May Fit Your Human Trafficking Witnesses and Victims to a T." *The Police Chief*, January 2007, pp.10–11.

Steck-Flynn, Kathy. "Being Smart about Sexual Assault." *Law Enforcement Technology*, January 2007, pp.64–72.

Taylor, Lauren R., and Gaskin-Laniyan, Nicole. "Sexual Assault in Abusive Relationships." *NIJ Journal*, January 2007, pp.12–14.

Tjaden, Patricia, and Thoennes, Nancy. *Extent, Nature, and Consequences of Rape Victimization: Findings from the National Violence against Women Survey.* Washington, DC, National Institute of Justice, January 2006. (NCJ 210346)

Trafficking in Persons Report, 10th ed. Washington, DC: U.S. Department of State, June 2010. Accessed June 1, 2011. http://www.state.gov/documents/organization/142979.pdf

"United Nations Releases Toolkit That Identifies Best Practices to Combat Human Trafficking." *NCJA Justice Bulletin*, October 2006, p.5.

VanderHart, Dirk. "States Mull Retroactive Sex-Offender Registries." *USA Today*, May 5, 2008.

Whiting, Brent. "Law Enforcement Learns to Battle Second Largest Crime: Human Trafficking." *Police One.com News*, November 2, 2007.

Cases Cited

Kansas v. Crane, 534 U.S. 407 (2002)
Kansas v. Hendricks, 521 U.S. 346 (1997)

CHAPTER 11
Crimes against Children

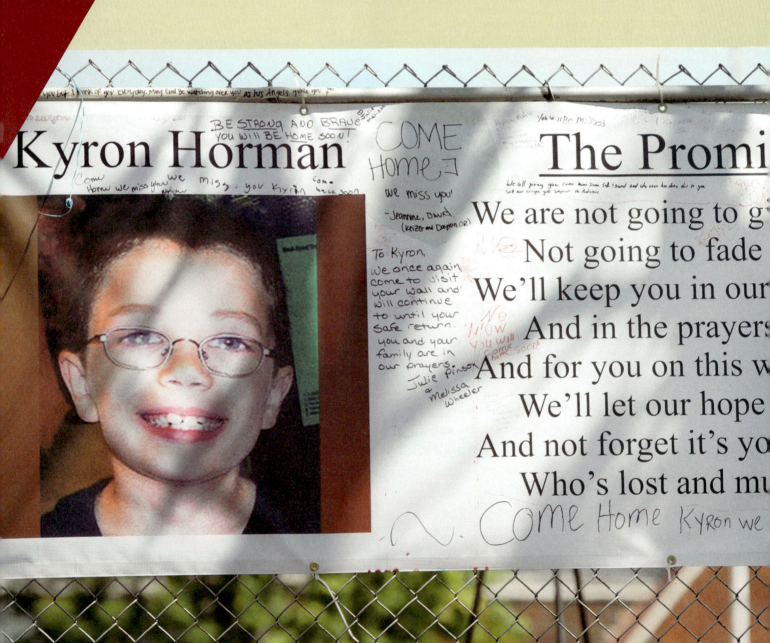

Outline

Can You Define?

chicken hawk

emotional abuse

exploitation

hebephile

kidnapping

lewdness

maltreatment

mandated reporters

minor

misoped

molestation

Munchausen syndrome

Munchausen by proxy syndrome (MBPS)

neglect

osteogenesis imperfecta (OI)

pedophile

physical abuse

sexting

sexual abuse

sexual exploitation

sexual seduction

sudden infant death syndrome (SIDS)

temporary custody without hearing

Do You Know?

- What crimes against children are frequently committed?
- What the four common types of maltreatment are?
- What the most common form of child maltreatment is and how serious it is?
- What has been identified as the biggest single cause of death of young children?
- What effects child abuse can have?
- Typically what three components are included in child abuse/neglect laws?
- What challenges are involved in investigating crimes against children?
- When a child should be taken into protective custody?
- What factors to consider in interviewing child victims?
- Whether children are generally truthful about abuse?
- Who usually reports crimes against children?
- What evidence is important in these cases?
- What things can indicate child neglect or abuse?
- What types of sex rings exist in the United States?
- How pedophiles typically react when discovered?
- What the Child Protection Act involves?
- What three law enforcement approaches are models to combat child sexual exploitation?
- What challenges a missing child report presents?
- What the most common type of child abduction is?
- What the AMBER Alert program is?
- How crimes against children can be prevented?

Throughout history, children have endured physical violence. Infants have been killed as a form of birth control, to avoid the dishonor of illegitimacy, as a means of power and as a method of disposing of retarded or deformed children. In ancient Greece, a child was the absolute property of the father. The father would raise the first son and expose subsequent children to the elements. Under Roman law, the father had the power of life and death (*patria potestas*) over his children and could kill, mutilate, sell or offer them as a sacrifice.

During the industrial, urban and machine age, the exploitation of child labor was common. Children of all ages worked 16 hours a day, usually with irons and chains on their ankles to keep them from running away. They were starved, beaten and dehumanized, and many died from exposure in the workplace, from occupational diseases or from suicide.

Karmen (2007, p.190) notes, "For centuries, parents were permitted to beat their children as they saw fit in the name of imposing discipline. Legal notions of progeny as the property of their parents, as well as religious and legal traditions (of 'honor thy father and mother' and 'spare the rod and spoil the child') legitimized parental violence toward youngsters as a necessary, even essential, technique of child rearing. Only if permanent injury or death resulted were adults in danger of being held responsible for going too far, a problem labeled cruelty to children."

Just as domestic violence used to be considered a family matter, so was mistreating children considered a family matter. Now both are considered crimes, and they must be thoroughly investigated. And like domestic violence, crimes against children are underreported. It is estimated that for every report of abuse the police and child protective services receive, there are 10 unreported cases.

Youths are also victims of the various other crimes that occur, but those crimes are usually investigated in the same ways as for adult victims, other than some changes in interviewing techniques, discussed later in this chapter.

Law enforcement agencies are charged with investigating all crimes, but their responsibility is especially great where crimes against children are involved. Children need the protection of the law to a greater degree than do other members of society because they are so vulnerable, especially if the offense is committed by one or both parents. Even after the offense is committed, the child may still be in danger of further victimization.

Crimes against children include maltreatment (neglect and abuse), sexual exploitation (pornography and prostitution), trafficking and abduction.

MALTREATMENT OF CHILDREN: NEGLECT AND ABUSE

Literally, **maltreatment** means to treat roughly or abuse. Maltreatment exists in many forms and along a continuum of severity and chronicity. Definitions of the various types of maltreatment vary from state to state and even locality to locality, but all are based on minimum standards set by federal law. The federal Child Abuse Prevention and Treatment Act (CAPTA) (42 U.S.C. §5106g), as amended by the Keeping Children and Families Safe Act of 2003, defines child abuse and neglect as

■ Any recent act or failure to act on the part of a parent or caretaker which results in death, serious harm, serious physical or emotional harm, sexual abuse or exploitation; or

■ An act or failure to act that presents an imminent risk of serious harm.

The four common types of maltreatment are neglect, physical abuse, emotional abuse and sexual abuse.

■ **Neglect** is the failure to meet a child's basic needs, including housing, food, clothing, education and access to medical care.

■ **Physical abuse** refers to beating, whipping, burning or otherwise inflicting physical harm upon a child. Child abuse has been identified as the biggest single cause of death of young children. One study found that between 3 and 4 million children have at some time been kicked, beaten or hit with a fist by their parents, and between 900,000 and 1.8 million have been assaulted with a knife or gun. In some tragic instances, the abuse results in death.

■ **Emotional abuse** refers to causing fear or feelings of unworthiness in children by such means as locking them in closets, ignoring them or constantly belittling them.

■ **Sexual abuse** includes sexually molesting a child, performing sexual acts with a child and statutory rape and seduction. Sexual assault victims may number in the millions, and perhaps some 90 percent of child molestations are not reported. The reason is unclear. Some cultures sanction sexual relationships between adults and children, but such acts are illegal in this country.

These forms of maltreatment may be found separately or in combination.

State statutes differ in their definitions of **minor**, with the most common specifying under the age of 16 or 18. When classifying crimes against children, several state statutes are applicable, including offenses of physical assault, sexual assault, incest, sexual seduction, indecent exposure, lewdness and molestation. Physical and emotional abuse are fairly straightforward. However, neglect and sexual abuse are not as clear-cut.

Neglect

Neglect is the most common form of child maltreatment and may be fatal.

Often the families from which neglected children come are poor and disorganized. They have no set routine for family activity. The children roam the streets at all hours. They are continually referred to juvenile court for loitering and curfew violations. The family unit is often fragmented by death, divorce or the incarceration or desertion of parents.

Broken homes—homes perhaps in which a single parent is struggling to survive and make ends meet, or those families otherwise mired in dysfunction, even if both parents are present—often deprive children of affection, recognition and a sense of belonging unless a strong parent can overcome these responses and provide direction. If a child's protective shield is shattered, the child may lose respect for moral and ethical standards. The broken or dysfunctional home, in and of itself, does not cause delinquency, but it can nullify or even destroy the resources youths need to

Two children play near their home and an open sewer. This poverty-stricken area in Tunica, Mississippi, is sometimes referred to as "Sugarditch."
© Jacques M. Chenet/CORBIS

handle emotional problems constructively. Children from such homes may suffer serious damage to their personalities. They may develop aggressive attitudes and strike out. They may think that punishment is better than no recognition. Even when marriages are intact, both parents often work. Consequently, many parents spend little time in the home interacting with or supervising their children.

Sexual Abuse

Sexual seduction means ordinary sexual intercourse, anal intercourse, cunnilingus or fellatio committed by a nonminor with a consenting minor. **Lewdness** means touching a minor to arouse, appeal to or gratify the perpetrator's sexual desires. The touching may be done by the perpetrator or by the minor under the perpetrator's direction. **Molestation** is a broader term, referring to any act motivated by unnatural or abnormal sexual interest in minors that would reasonably be expected to disturb, irritate or offend the victim. Molestation may or may not involve touching of the victim.

Legislatures in a number of states are attempting to broaden penalties to make them match the severity of the offense, especially if the victim is very young. There is also a concerted effort to expand the offenses to make genders equal, recognizing that victims and offenders may be male or female. The age of the offender as well as the type of crime are both considered. Illinois, for example, has consolidated nine sex offenses into four but provides for 24 combinations of charges.

In 2004 President George W. Bush signed the Unborn Victims of Violence Act, or Laci and Conner's Law. This law amended the U.S. Code and the Uniform Code of Military Justice to punish separately the harming of a child in utero. The punishment is the same as provided under federal law for conduct causing the injury to, or death of, the unborn child's mother, but the imposition of the death penalty is prohibited. This separate offense does not require proof that the person who committed the offense knew or should have known that the victim was pregnant or that the accused intended to harm the unborn child.

THE EXTENT OF THE PROBLEM

According to the Office for Victims of Crime ("Crime Clock," 2009), one child is reported abused or neglected every 34.9 seconds. The National Child Abuse and Neglect Data System (NCANDS) is a federally sponsored effort that collects and analyzes data on child abuse and neglect and prepares an annual report, *Child Maltreatment*, released each spring. According to the most recent report by the Children's Bureau

(*Child Maltreatment 2009*, 2010, p.viii): "During Federal fiscal year 2009, an estimated 3.3 million referrals, involving the alleged maltreatment of approximately 6.0 million children, were received by CPS [child protective services] agencies. Of these referrals, 61.9 percent were screened in for a response by CPS agencies." Of those cases screened for a CPS response, approximately 25 percent found that at least one child was a victim of abuse or neglect, which translates into more than 510,000 substantiated or indicated cases of *reported* child maltreatment in a single year. Bear in mind that many cases are undetected and unreported, and many cases involve more than one child victim.

In 2009, 60 percent of the child maltreatment reports came from "professional" sources, persons who encountered the alleged child victim as part of their occupations, such as child daycare providers and medical personnel, with the three largest percentage of report sources being teachers (16.5%), law enforcement and legal personnel (16.4%) and social services staff (11.4%) (*Child Maltreatment 2009*, 2010, p.ix). The remainder of the reports were submitted by "nonprofessional" sources, such as friends, neighbors, parents and relatives, clergy members, sports coaches, camp counselors and anonymous sources.

During 2006 an estimated 702,000 children were determined to be victims of abuse or neglect. Among the children confirmed as victims by CPS agencies in 2009 (*Child Maltreatment 2009*, 2010, p.ix):

▪ Victims in the age group of birth to 1 year had the highest rate of victimization at 20.6 per 1,000 children of the same age group in the national population.

▪ Victimization was split between the sexes with boys accounting for 48.2 percent and girls accounting for 51.1 percent. Less than 1 percent of victims had an unknown sex.

▪ Eighty-seven percent of victims were of three races or ethnicities— African American (22.3%), Hispanic (20.7%) and White (44.0%).

As in prior years, neglect was the most common form of child maltreatment (*Child Maltreatment 2009*, 2010, p.ix). CPS investigations determined that

▪ More than 75 percent (78.3%) of victims suffered neglect.

▪ More than 15 percent (17.8%) of the victims suffered physical abuse.

▪ Less than 10 percent (9.5%) of the victims suffered sexual abuse.

▪ Less than 10 percent (7.6%) of the victims suffered from emotional maltreatment.

Physical and sexual abuse, regardless of the age of the victim, are also classified as violent crimes.

CHILDREN AS VICTIMS OF VIOLENT CRIME

According to data from the National Survey of Children's Exposure to Violence (NatSCEV), more than 60 percent of children surveyed were exposed to violence during the previous year, either directly as victims or indirectly as witnesses (Finkelhor et al., 2009). Furthermore, the survey revealed that during the previous 12 months

- Nearly half of the children and adolescents (46.3 percent) had been assaulted at least once.

- More than 1 in 10 (10.2%) had been injured in an assault.

- 1 in 4 (24.6%) had been victims of robbery, vandalism or theft.

- 1 in 10 (10.2%) suffered maltreatment, including physical and emotional abuse, neglect or a family abduction.

- 1 in 16 (6.1%) had been sexually victimized.

- More than 1 in 4 (25.3%) had witnessed a violent act.

- Approximately 1 in 10 (9.8%) had observed one family member assault another.

The survey also revealed that nearly seven out of every eight children (86.6 percent) who reported being exposed to violence during their lifetime had also been exposed to violence within the past year, an indication that such children faced an ongoing, ever-present risk of violent victimization (Finkelhor et al., 2009, p.2). These violent crimes are investigated using the procedures described in the preceding chapters, but taking into consideration the age of the victims.

When the violence is severe enough, death can occur. Child fatalities are the most tragic consequence of maltreatment. During 2009

- An estimated 1,770 children died because of child abuse or neglect.

- The overall rate of child fatalities was 2.34 deaths per 100,000 children.

- Four-fifths (80.8%) of all child fatalities were younger than 4 years old.

- Boys had a slightly higher child fatality rate than girls at 2.36 boys per 100,000 boys in the population. Girls died of abuse and neglect at a rate of 2.12 per 100,000 girls in the population.

- One-third (35.8%) of child fatalities were attributed to neglect exclusively.

- One-third (36.7%) of child fatalities were caused by multiple maltreatment types (*Child Maltreatment 2009*, 2010, p.x).

> **Child abuse has been identified as the biggest single cause of death of young children.**

Child Abuse and Neglect Fatalities: Statistics and Interventions (2008), citing NCANDS statistics, reports that the rate of child abuse and neglect fatalities during the last several years has varied slightly, beginning with a rate of 1.95 per 100,000 in 2001, increasing to 1.98 in 2002, 2.00 in 2003 and 2.03 in 2004 and finally decreasing to 1.96 in 2005, the overall increase often attributed to improved reporting by some states.

However, many researchers and practitioners believe child fatalities are underreported, perhaps by 50 to 60 percent. Reasons include variation among reporting requirements and definitions of child abuse and neglect, variation in death investigative systems and in training for investigators, variation in state child fatality review processes and the amount of time it may take to establish the cause of death.

THE EFFECTS OF CHILD ABUSE AND NEGLECT

The effects of child abuse and neglect can be devastating.

> **Child abuse and neglect can result in serious and permanent physical, mental and emotional damage, as well as in future violent and criminal behavior.**

Physical damage may involve the brain, vital organs, eyes, ears, arms or legs. Severe abuse may also cause mental retardation, restricted language ability, restricted perceptual and motor-skill development, arrested physical development, blindness, deafness, loss of limbs or even death.

Emotional damage may include impaired self-concept as well as increased levels of aggression, anxiety and tendency toward self-destructiveness. These self-destructive tendencies can cause children to act out antisocial behavior in the family, the school and the community at large. Such self-destructiveness can also manifest itself in risky behavior that endangers youths' health and safety.

Research has examined the potential correlation between childhood maltreatment and the likelihood of criminality and arrest later in life, with some studies finding that offenders who were physically abused as children had higher rates of violent, property and total offending than did non-abused offenders (Teague et al., 2008). A literature review found that child abuse and neglect affected a significant proportion of children's lives, including being more aggressive, experiencing more internalizing behavior problems, having higher levels of impaired social functioning and having an increased risk of mental health problems, teenage pregnancy and alcohol and other drug abuse (Teague et al., 2008). A more recent study, however, concluded that physical abuse was *not* associated with future violent delinquency but that a history of sexual abuse and neglect was a significant predictor of violent delinquency (Yun et al., 2011).

Another likely effect of child abuse is that as an adult, the former victim frequently becomes a perpetrator of child abuse, thereby creating a vicious circle sometimes called the *intergenerational transmission of violence*. Research shows that a child's history of physical abuse predisposes that child to violence in later years. Victims of neglect are also likely to engage in later violent criminal behavior.

RISK FACTORS FOR CHILD MALTREATMENT

Parents or caretakers commit most emotional and physical child abuse. The causes of such abuse often center on a cycle of abuse passed from one generation to the next. Certain risk factors have been found to contribute to increased chance of child maltreatment, including

■ Children younger than 4 years of age

■ Special needs that may increase caregiver burden (e.g., disabilities, mental retardation, mental health issues and chronic physical illnesses)

■ Parents' lack of understanding of children's needs, child development and parenting skills

■ Parents' history of child maltreatment in family of origin

■ Substance abuse and/or mental health issues including depression in the family

■ Parental characteristics such as young age, low education, single parenthood, large number of dependent children and low income

■ Nonbiological, transient caregivers in the home (e.g., mother's male partner)

■ Parental thoughts and emotions that tend to support or justify maltreatment behaviors

■ Social isolation

■ Family disorganization, dissolution and violence, including intimate partner violence

■ Parenting stress, poor parent-child relationships and negative interactions

■ Community violence

■ Concentrated neighborhood disadvantage (e.g., high poverty and residential instability, high unemployment rates and high density of alcohol outlets) and poor social connections ("Child Maltreatment: Risk and Protective Factors," 2011).

Before looking at investigating cases of child maltreatment, consider the laws under which investigators must operate.

CHILD ABUSE AND NEGLECT LAWS

A complicating factor in investigating child abuse is the perceived ambiguity of what it is. Is spanking a child abuse? Belittling a child? Sending a child to bed without dinner? To address and reduce some of this ambiguity, laws regarding child abuse and neglect have been passed at both federal and state levels.

> Typically child abuse and neglect laws have three components: (1) criminal definitions and penalties, (2) a mandate to report suspected cases and (3) civil process for removing the child from the abusive or neglectful environment.

Federal Legislation

In 1974 the federal government passed CAPTA. It was amended in 1978 under PL 95–266 and again in 2003 as the Keeping Children and Families Safe Act (Pub. L. 108–36), as mentioned at the beginning of the chapter. The law states, in part, that any of the following elements constitutes a crime: "The physical or mental injury, sexual abuse or exploitation, negligent treatment, or maltreatment of a child under the age of 18, by a person who is responsible for the child's welfare under circumstances that indicate the child's health or welfare is harmed or threatened."

Nonetheless, federal courts have also ruled that parents are free to strike children because "the custody, care and nurture of the child resides first in the parents" (*Prince v. Massachusetts*, 1944). This fundamental right to "nurture" has been supplanted by the Supreme Court with the "care, custody and management" of one's child (*Santosky v. Kramer*, 1982). This shift from "nurture" to "management" could herald a return to older laws, such as the one expressed in *People v. Green* (1909): "The parent is the sole judge of the necessity for the exercise of disciplinary right and of the nature of the correction to be given." The court need only determine whether "the punishment inflicted went beyond the legitimate exercise of parental authority."

Current laws often protect parents, and convictions for child abuse are difficult to obtain because of circumstantial evidence, the lack of witnesses, the husband-wife privilege and the fact that an adult's testimony often is enough to establish reasonable doubt. All too often, the court determines punishment to be reasonable, never reexamining the age-old presumption that hitting children is permissible.

The courts' role is to decide when and to what degree physical punishment steps beyond "the legitimate exercise of parental authority" or what constitutes "excessive punishment." The courts always begin with the presumption that parents have a legal right to use force against their own children. In *Green*, 70 marks from a whipping was held to be excessive and unreasonable, even though the parent claimed he was not criminally liable because there was no permanent injury and he had acted in good faith. But the assumption remained that the parent had an unquestionable right "to administer such reasonable and timely punishment as may be necessary to correct growing faults in young children."

A determination of "reasonableness" was made in *Ingraham v. Wright* (1977) regarding the use of physical punishment of students by teachers, after one student was beaten by 20 strokes with a wooden paddle and another was beaten by 50 strokes. The Florida statute specified that the punishment was not to be "degrading or unduly severe."

CAPTA and the Keeping Children and Families Safe Act set forth a minimum definition of child abuse and neglect; identified the federal government's role in supporting research, evaluation, technical assistance and data collection activities; and provided federal funding to states in their efforts to prevent, assess, investigate and prosecute child maltreatment as well as treat those who perpetrate this crime.

In 2000 Congress passed the Child Abuse Prevention and Enforcement Act making more funds available for child abuse and neglect enforcement and prevention initiatives. In 2006 the Adam Walsh Child Protection and Safety Act was signed into law, aimed at tracking sex crime offenders and subjecting them to stiff, mandatory minimum sentences. The act is named for the 6-year-old son of John and Reve Walsh who was abducted and murdered in Florida in 1981 ("Adam Walsh Act Signed into Law," 2006, p.5). The act expands previous sex registry requirements, setting forth strict guidelines for states, territories and tribal nations to develop and maintain a jurisdiction-wide sex offender registry. Failure to comply with the guidelines can result in a reduction in the amount of federal funds received by a jurisdiction.

State Laws

Since the 1960s, every state has enacted child abuse and neglect laws. On the whole, states offer a bit more protection to children by statute than does the federal government. Legal definitions vary from state to state. California, for example, declares it illegal for anyone to willfully cause or permit any child to suffer or for any person to inflict unjustifiable physical or mental suffering on a child or to cause the child to "be placed in such situations that its person or health is endangered" (California Penal Codes, Sec. 273A).

Alaska defines abuse broadly: "The infliction, by other than accidental means, of physical harm upon the body of a child." Other state statutes are much less broad. For example, Maryland's statute states that a person is not guilty of child abuse if the defendant's intentions were good, but his or her judgment was bad. The defendant in *Worthen v. State* (1979) admitted he had punished his 2-year-old stepdaughter because she was throwing a temper tantrum, "but sought to explain as not having exceeded the bounds of parental propriety." The jury found him guilty of assault and battery for the multiple contusions about the girl's face, ribs, buttocks and legs, but the appellate court ordered a new trial because the trial court in its jury instructions had omitted the defense of good intentions and also the defense that the stepfather had not exceeded the bounds of parental authority. What is "reasonable" varies from state to state, from one judge or court to another and from jury to jury.

CASE PROCESSING

Most child abuse and neglect cases enter the child welfare system through CPS agencies (*Child Maltreatment 2009*, 2010). *Child protective services* generally refers to services provided by an agency authorized to act on behalf of a child when parents are unable or unwilling to do so. CPS may provide protective custody of a child outside the home or provide protective supervision of the child within the family unit at any point until a case is closed or dismissed. The specific options once a case enters formal court processing are the focus. Frequently a formal investigation is required.

CHALLENGES IN INVESTIGATING CHILD MALTREATMENT CASES

Many prosecutors, at all levels of the judiciary system, perceive crimes against children as among the most difficult to prosecute and for which to obtain convictions. Therefore, to most effectively prosecute the guilty and protect the innocent, officers interviewing child witnesses and victims should have specialized training themselves or should interview alongside a licensed professional with specialized training. Regardless of whether crimes against children are handled by generalists or specialists within the department, certain challenges are unique to these investigations.

> Challenges in investigating crimes against children include the need to protect the child from further harm, the possibility of parental involvement, the need to collaborate with other agencies, the difficulty of interviewing children and credibility concerns.

Protecting the Child

When child abuse is reported, investigators may initiate an investigation on their own, or they may investigate jointly with social services. Regardless of the source of the report, and regardless of whether the investigation is a single or joint effort, the primary responsibility of the investigator assigned to the case is the immediate protection of the child.

> If the possibility of present or continued danger to the child exists, the child must be removed into protective custody.

Under welfare regulations and codes, an officer may take a child into temporary custody without a warrant if there is an emergency or if the officer has reason to believe that leaving the child in the present situation would subject the child to further abuse or harm. **Temporary custody without hearing** usually means for 48 hours. Factors that would justify placing a child in protective custody include

- The child's age or physical or mental condition makes the child incapable of self-protection.

- The home's physical environment poses an immediate threat to the child.
- The child needs immediate medical or psychiatric care, and the parents refuse to obtain it.
- The parents cannot or will not provide for the child's basic needs.
- Maltreatment in the home could permanently damage the child physically or emotionally.
- The parents may abandon the child.

Consultation with local welfare authorities is sometimes needed before police officials ask the court for a hearing to remove a child from the parents' custody or for protective custody in an authorized facility. Because police rarely have such facilities, the child should be taken to the nearest welfare facility or to a foster home as soon as possible, as stipulated by the juvenile court. The parents or legal guardians of the child must be notified as soon as possible.

The Need to Involve Other Agencies: The Multidisciplinary Team Approach

Another challenge facing law enforcement is the need to collaborate with various social services, child welfare and health agencies to more effectively handle child abuse cases. Traditionally, law enforcement and social service agencies have worked fairly independently on child abuse cases, with each conducting its own separate interviews and investigations. Many police departments have seen no need to collaborate with social services unless their investigation determines a need to remove the child from parental custody. However, it is increasingly evident that this lack of communication and coordination among these agencies has led to numerous cases "falling through the cracks" of the disjointed system, sometimes with devastating results.

A multidisciplinary team (MDT) consists of professionals who work together to ensure an effective response to reports of child abuse and neglect. Coordinated responses can also minimize the likelihood of conflicts between agencies with different philosophies and mandates. Joint investigations often result in more victim corroborations and perpetrator confessions than do independent investigations. In addition, referral agencies provide support and assistance to families and victims experiencing child abuse or neglect. A collaborative, community-based approach to problems associated with children and youths should result in identifying, developing and implementing more effective, multiagency solutions.

Several national programs can assist in investigating abandoned or abducted children, such as the National Children Identification Program, which distributes fingerprint and DNA (cheek swab) collection kits to parents. This identifying information can be provided to law enforcement authorities if a child abduction occurs or a child runs away.

Other technological developments allow police to communicate more effectively with organizations such as the media in cases involving child abductions—cases where speed of information dissemination is critical.

Difficulty in Interviewing Children

When children are very young, a limited vocabulary can pose a severe challenge to investigators. Unfortunately, by the time children are old enough to possess the words or other skills needed to communicate and describe their abusive experiences, they have also developed the ability to feel such shame, embarrassment and fear over these events that they might resist talking about them.

Interviewing a child abuse victim takes special understanding, skill and practice. Children often have difficulty talking about abuse, and often they have been instructed not to tell anyone about it. They may have been threatened by the abuser, or they may have a close relationship with the abuser and not want anything bad to happen to that person. Keep in mind that you are a stranger to them and may be asking for information about someone they trust, such as a parent.

> When interviewing children, officers should consider the child's age, ability to describe what happened and the potential for retaliation by the suspect against a child who "tells."

Another difficulty in interviewing children is their short attention spans. Questions should be brief and understandable, a skill that often proves difficult and requires training and practice. Interviewers who are excellent with adults may not be so successful with children.

Investigators may consider inviting a social service professional to help conduct the interview because they often have more formal training and experience in interviewing children at their level and may therefore be better able to establish rapport. More specific guidelines for interviewing abused children are discussed in detail shortly.

Credibility Concerns

Assessing the credibility of people reporting child abuse is a constant challenge for investigators. As repulsive as society finds child abuse, particularly sexual abuse, investigators must exercise great care to protect the innocent and falsely accused. No other crime is so fraught with

stigma. Consequently, accusations of this type can be difficult to dispel even if false.

Because of the "loaded" nature of child sexual abuse allegations, parents who are divorcing may be tempted to use such claims as ammunition against their soon-to-be ex-spouse. For investigators, sorting through details of such allegations to determine their credibility can be extremely challenging. Occasionally, the credibility of the child victim is challenged. However, investigators must approach each case and each victim with an open mind.

> In most child abuse cases, children tell the truth to the best of their ability.

People who work with child abuse cases point out that children will frequently lie to get out of trouble, but they seldom lie to get into trouble. Although most child abuse reports are valid, investigators must use caution to weed out those cases reported by a habitual liar or by a child who is telling a story to offset other misdeeds he or she has committed. A child's motivation for lying may be revenge, efforts to avoid school or parental disapproval, efforts to cover up for other disapproved behavior or, in the case of sexual abuse, an attempt to explain a pregnancy or to obtain an abortion at state expense.

THE INITIAL REPORT

According to the NCANDS, of the 3.3 million referrals to CPS agencies in 2009, three-fifths were made by such professionals as educators, law enforcement and legal personnel, social services personnel, medical personnel, mental health personnel, child day care providers and foster care providers (*Child Maltreatment 2009*, 2010). Friends, neighbors and relatives submitted the rest of the reports.

> Most reports of child neglect or abuse are made by third parties such as teachers, physicians, neighbors, siblings or parents. Seldom does the victim report the offense.

In most states, certain individuals who work with or treat children are required by law to report cases of suspected neglect or abuse. These **mandated reporters** include teachers, school authorities, child care personnel, camp personnel, clergy, physicians, dentists, chiropractors, nurses, psychologists, medical assistants, attorneys and social workers. Such a report may be made to social services or CPS, the juvenile court or the local police or sheriff's department. It may be made verbally, but it should also be put in writing as soon as possible after the initial verbal report is made. Some states have special forms for child abuse cases. These forms are sent to a central location, thereby helping prevent child abusers from taking the child to different doctors or hospitals for treatment and thus avoiding the suspicion that would accompany multiple incidents involving the same child.

Child neglect and abuse reports should contain the name, age and address of the child victim; the name and address of the child's parents or others responsible for the child's care; the name and address of the person suspected of the abuse; the nature and extent of the neglect or abuse; and any evidence of this or previous neglect or abuse. These reports are confidential.

In most states, action must be taken on a report within a specified time, frequently three days. If, in the judgment of the person receiving the report, it is necessary to remove the child from present custody, this is discussed with the responsible agency, such as CPS or the juvenile court. If the situation is deemed life threatening, the police may temporarily remove the child. No matter who receives the report or whether the child must be removed from the situation, it is the responsibility of the law enforcement agency to investigate the charge.

THE POLICE RESPONSE

As noted, as with domestic violence, child abuse and neglect was traditionally viewed as a family matter—a social issue regulated by child protection agencies. It was not a crime. Currently, child abuse is viewed as a crime and within the jurisdiction of the criminal justice system. Therefore, it needs to be investigated by trained criminal investigators.

The investigator must talk with people who know the child and obtain background information about the child. For example, does the child have behavior problems? Is the child generally truthful?

If interviews are conducted with the parents, every attempt should be made to conduct the interviews in private. Explain why the interview is necessary. Be direct, honest, understanding and professional. Do not accuse, demand, give personal opinions about the situation, request information from the parents unrelated to the matter under discussion, make judgments, place blame or reveal the source of your information. If the parents are suspects, provide them the due process rights granted by the Fourth and Fifth Amendments, including the *Miranda* warning.

Interviewing Abused Children

Interviewing children requires special skills. Before the interview, obtain relevant background information from the parents or guardian and anyone else involved in the case, including caseworkers, counselors and physicians. Also review the incident report.

Often several interviews are necessary to get a complete statement without overwhelming the child. The initial interview should be brief, merely to establish the facts supporting probable cause, with a second interview later.

Generally, it is best to conduct the interview in private in the child's or a friend's home or in a small room at a hospital or the police station. An interview room in a police station can be converted into a friendly environment for youngsters with the addition of some simple toys or coloring books. If the interview is to take place at the child's home, it might be best not to wear a uniform, especially if the child thinks he or she is to blame. The uniform could be too intimidating and frighten the child into thinking that he or she is going to be arrested. Casual, comfortable clothes are usually best.

Regardless of whether the interview is conducted at the child's home or at the police station, it is usually not advisable to have a family member present—but if the child so desires, the wish should be respected. The family member should be seated out of the child's view to avoid influencing the interview. However, if a parent is suspected of being the offender, neither parent should be present. The investigator should record the time the interview begins and ends. Because taking written statements from children is difficult, it is sometimes better to videotape the interview. Videotapes may be used by other officers, prosecutors and the courts, which eliminates the need to re-question the victim.

When conducting an interview with a child, investigators must maintain rapport. The gender of the interviewer generally does not matter—the ability to elicit accurate information is the key quality. The interviewer should sit next to the child and speak in a friendly voice, without talking down to the child. It may help to play a game with the child or to get down on the floor at the child's level to get attention and to encourage the child to talk naturally. Allow the child freedom to do other things during the interview, such as moving around the room or playing with toys, but do not allow distractions from the outside. Learn about the child's abilities and interests by asking questions about everyday activities, such as school and household chores. Ask about the child's siblings, pets, friends and favorite games or television shows. It may help to share personal information when appropriate, such as about your own children or pets. Evaluate

This girl is being interviewed by a plain-clothes investigator in a child-friendly room. Achieving a comfortable rapport with the child is essential to getting that victim to open up and discuss the abuse. Doll play often helps the child relax and recount important details of the abuse event(s).
© Michael Newman/PhotoEdit

the child's cognitive level by asking if he or she can read, write, count or tell time. Does the child know his or her birth date? Can the child recount past events (yesterday, holidays)? Does the child know about various body parts and their functions? Assess the child's maturity level by asking about his or her responsibilities—making his or her own breakfast, walking the dog and so on. Does the child enjoy any privileges (staying home alone, going places on his or her own)?

Make the child feel comfortable, and keep in mind that questioning children is apt to be more of a sharing experience than a formal interview. Because young children have a short attention span, fact-finding interviews should last no more than 15 or 20 minutes. Questions should pertain to what happened, who did it, when it happened, where it happened and whether force, threats or enticements were involved. Ask simple, direct, open-ended questions. Avoid asking "why" questions, because they tend to sound accusatory. To alleviate the anxiety, fear or reluctance found in children who have been instructed or threatened not to tell by the offender (*especially* if a parent), try statements such as, "It's not bad to tell what happened," "You won't get in trouble," "You can help your dad/mom/friend by telling what happened," and "It wasn't your fault." Never threaten or try to force a reluctant child to talk because such pressure will likely lead a child to "clam up" and may cause further trauma.

To obtain the most thorough and accurate account of the abuse possible, investigators should be proficient in cognitive interview techniques, discussed in Chapter 6.

It is extremely important not to put words into a child's mouth. When the child answers your questions, be certain you understand the meaning of his or her words. A child may think "sex" is kissing or hugging or touching. If the child uses a word, learn what the word really means to the child to get to the truth and avoid later embarrassment in court.

In the case of sexual abuse of young children, it may be helpful to use drawings or anatomical dolls to assist the children in describing exactly what happened and the positions of the child and the abuser when the offense took place. Controversy exists, however, about whether such dolls help or hinder interview progress.

To assess the credibility and competence of children in sexual abuse cases, consider the following criteria, courtesy of the Sexual Assault Center, Seattle, Washington:

■ Does the child describe acts or experiences to which a child of his or her age would not normally have been exposed? The average child is not familiar with erection or ejaculation until adolescence.

■ Does the child describe circumstances and characteristics typical of a sexual assault situation? "He told me that it was our secret"; "He said I couldn't go out if I didn't do it"; "She told me it was sex education."

■ How and under what circumstances did the child tell? What were the child's exact words?

■ How many times has the child given the history, and how consistent is it regarding the basic facts of the assault (times, dates, circumstances, sequence of events, etc.)?

■ How much spontaneous information does the child provide? How much prompting is required?

■ Can the child define the difference between the truth and a lie? (This question is not actually very useful with young children because they learn these terms by rote and may not truly understand the concepts.)

During the interview, do not try to extract promises from the child regarding testifying in court, because an undue emphasis on a trial may frighten the child, causing nightmares and apprehension. Investigators should avoid asking leading questions, repeated interviews and confusing questions.

After the interview is completed, give the parents simple, straightforward information about what will happen next in the criminal justice system and approximately when, the likelihood of trial and so on. Enlist their cooperation. Let them know who to contact for status reports or in an emergency; express appreciation and understanding for the efforts they are making by reporting and following through on the process. Answer any questions the child or parents have.

A program called "Finding Words" trains officers in conducting child interviews and specifically teaches rapport, anatomy identification, touch inquiry, abuse scenarios and closure protocols (RATAC) (Stevens, 2008, pp.31–36). *Building rapport* is the critical first step in interviewing children. Sitting on the floor at eye-level with the child is one effective means to build rapport. Another way with younger children is to draw a picture of their face followed by family circles. Information can then be elicited about each face in the picture.

Anatomical identification then follows, using anatomically correct dolls to establish the names a child victim uses for various body parts. Investigators must be aware that children do not understand things as adults do.

Good touch, bad touch can be done with the dolls. Begin with the good touches: "Tell me about the touches you like. Show me where they are." Next, the child is asked, "Are there touches you do not like? Where are they?" Any yes or no answer should be followed with "Tell me about that."

The abuse scenario gives trainees a fictitious abuse report and asks them to construct a plan to interview the victim: "Law enforcement professionals are trained to avoid leading questions, but according to Finding Words, it's more important to avoid misleading or tag questions. For instance, asking, 'Your dad touched your butt, didn't he?' is both a statement and a question, leading the child to say things he might not mean" (Stevens, 2008, p.35).

The closure protocol for interviewing a child abuse victim calls for the investigator to be sensitive to the child's developmental age and reluctance to talk (Stevens, 2008).

Anatomical dolls are sometimes used to diagnose and treat sexual abuse victims. The dolls enable victims (generally children) to better express thoughts and actions by "acting out" their trauma. These adolescent dolls feature a male or female sex organ, breasts, ears, mouth, navel, jointed legs and individual fingers.
© Cynthia Harnest, www.teach-a-bodies.com

One final note: exact notes are critical in interviews of child sexual abuse victims because such cases are an exception to the hearsay rule, meaning an officer *may* testify in court about the victim's statements. Therefore, officers should be meticulous in recording all statements verbatim. The child may not be able to repeat the statements because of fear or anxiety. For this reason, as well as others mentioned earlier, interviews should be videotaped whenever possible.

Sample Protocol

The following excerpt from the Boulder City (Nevada) Police Department's protocol for investigating reports of sexual and physical abuse of children is typical.

It is the policy to *team* investigate all abuse allegations.

When a report comes in, a juvenile officer is immediately assigned all abuse cases. This officer is responsible for maintaining a 72-hour time frame. Contact is made as soon as possible.

The investigative process includes the following:

■ The investigator contacts Nevada Welfare, and together they contact the victim at a location where the victim can be interviewed briefly, and not in the presence of the alleged perpetrator of the crime.

■ During the initial interview the juvenile officer tries to determine if the report is a substantiated abuse, unsubstantiated or unfounded.

■ If the report is substantiated, the juvenile officer or Nevada State Welfare removes the child from the home and books the child into protective custody. If the juvenile officer and Nevada State Welfare investigator determine the child is not in danger of *any* abuse, the child can be allowed to remain in his/her home environment.

■ If the report is unsubstantiated, the child is left in the home.
■ If the report is unfounded, the reason for the false report is also investigated to identify other problems.
■ If the case is substantiated abuse, the victim is housed at Child Haven, and there is a detention hearing at 9:00 A.M. the following working day.

An in-depth interview is conducted with the victim by the juvenile officer and the Nevada State Welfare investigator. Several aids are used, depending on the child's age and mental abilities: structured and unstructured play therapy, picture drawings, and use of anatomical dolls.

The juvenile officer also contacts the accused person and interviews him/her about the specific allegations, makes a report or statement relevant to the interview, and makes these reports available to Nevada State Welfare and/or Clark County Juvenile Court. Nevada State Welfare is encouraged to attend these interviews, and a team approach is used during this phase of the investigation also.

The juvenile officer also interviews other people, including witnesses or victims—anyone who might have information about the case. The officer prepares an affidavit and presents the case to the district attorney's office to determine whether the case is suitable for prosecution. If so, a complaint is issued, and a warrant or summons is issued for the accused. Once a warrant is obtained, the investigating officer locates and arrests or causes the accused person to be arrested.

Investigators must know their own state laws, as well as federal statutes and the possibility of dual prosecution.

EVIDENCE

All the investigator's observations pertaining to the victim's physical and emotional condition must be recorded in detail.

> Evidence in child neglect or abuse cases includes the surroundings, the home conditions, clothing, bruises or other body injuries, the medical examination report and other observations.

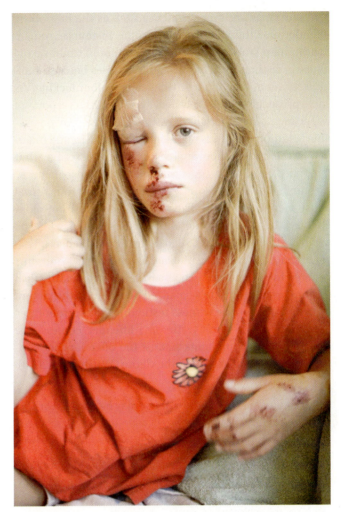

Injuries caused by abuse are best documented through photographs. Some of this girl's injuries will heal quite rapidly; thus, the severity of the battering will become less evident over time and must be captured as soon after the assault as possible. Note the scrapes and bruises on the girl's hand. Be sure to photograph all injuries.
© Hill Creek Pictures/Index Stock Imagery/Photolibrary

Photographs may be the best way to document child abuse and neglect where it is necessary to show injury to the child or the home environment conditions. Pictures should be taken immediately because children's injuries heal quickly and home conditions can be changed rapidly. Pictures in both color and black and white should be taken, showing bruises, burns, cuts or any injury requiring medical treatment. These photographs should be witnessed by people who can later testify about the location and extent of the injuries, including medical personnel who examined the child. Explain the need for the pictures to the child to avoid further fear or excitement. All procedures for photography at a crime scene (discussed in Chapter 2) should be followed.

Additional types of evidence that may be obtained in sexual assault cases include photographs, torn clothing, ropes or tapes and trace evidence such as the hair of the offender and the victim and, in some instances, semen. Researchers Walsh et al. (2010, p.438) note: "Child sexual abuse is distinct from other types of crimes because multiple forms of convincing evidence are often lacking. As such, prosecutors must rely heavily on children's reports of the crime…. Whether and how well children provide useable testimony depends on their understanding and memory of the abuse, their ability to verbally describe what happened, and their concerns about the consequences." Although disclosures and detailed testimony from sexual abuse victims are more likely to be obtained from older children than younger ones, other useful evidence may be available to investigators, such as medical evidence, physical or material evidence; unusual psychological symptoms suffered by the victim, such as severe nightmares; atypical or non-age appropriate sexualized behavior by the victim; eyewitness accounts; witness testimony that corroborates aspects of the victim's testimony; offender confessions; and additional complaints against the offender that support the actions disclosed by the victim (Walsh et al., 2010).

> Indicators of neglect or abuse may be physical or behavioral or both.

Caution: the lists of indicators in this section are not exhaustive; many other indicators exist. In addition, the presence of one or more of these indicators does not prove that neglect or abuse exists. All factors and conditions of each specific case must be considered before you make a decision.

Neglect Indicators

The *physical* indicators of child neglect may include frequent hunger, poor hygiene, inappropriate dress, consistent lack of supervision (especially in dangerous activities or for long periods), unattended physical problems or medical needs and abandonment. Such indicators often appear in families where the parents are drug addicts. The *behavioral* indicators may include begging, stealing (e.g., food), extending school days by arriving early or leaving late, constant fatigue, listlessness or falling asleep in school, poor performance in school, truancy, alcohol or drug abuse, aggressive behavior, delinquency and stating that no one is at home to care for them.

Emotional Abuse Indicators

Physical indicators of emotional abuse may include speech disorders, lags in physical development and general failure to thrive.

Behavioral indicators may include habit disorders such as sucking, biting and rocking back and forth and conduct disorders such as antisocial, destructive behavior; being physically or emotionally abusive toward others, including other children; and being persistently disruptive in social settings, including school. Other possible symptoms are sleep disorders, inhibitions in play, obsessions, compulsions, phobias, hypochondria, behavioral extremes and attempted suicide.

Physical Abuse Indicators

Physical indicators of physical abuse include unexplained bruises or welts, burns, fractures, lacerations and abrasions. These may be in various stages of healing. One obvious and important indicator of physical abuse is bruising.

Behavioral indicators include being wary of adults, being apprehensive when other children cry, extreme aggressiveness or extreme withdrawal, being frightened of parents and being afraid to go home.

Parental indicators may include contradictory explanations for a child's injury; attempts to conceal a child's injury or to protect the identity of the person responsible; routine use of harsh, unreasonable discipline inappropriate to the child's age or transgressions and poor impulse control.

Sexual Abuse Indicators

Physical indicators of sexual abuse include difficulty urinating and irritation, bruising or tearing around the genital or rectal areas. Venereal disease and pregnancy, especially in preteens, are also indicators.

Behavioral indicators of sexual abuse may include unwillingness to change clothes for or to participate in physical education classes; withdrawal, fantasy or infantile behavior; bizarre sexual behavior, sexual sophistication beyond the child's age or unusual behavior or knowledge of sex; poor peer relationships; delinquency or running away; and reports of being sexually assaulted.

Parental indicators may include jealousy and overprotectiveness of a child. Incest incidents are insidious, commonly beginning with the parent fondling and caressing the child between the ages of 3 and 6 months and then progressing over a long period, increasing in intensity of contact until the child is capable of full participation, usually between the ages of 8 and 10. A parent may hesitate to report a spouse who is sexually abusing their child for fear of destroying the marriage or for fear of retaliation. Intrafamily sex may be viewed as preferable to extramarital sex.

THE SUSPECT

A major concern in these types of cases involves the frequency with which children are abused by people they know. Although many parents stress to their children the importance of staying away from strangers, the sad truth is that most sexual abuse is committed by persons known to the child. Data from the Children's Bureau show that more than 80 percent of perpetrators of child abuse and neglect in 2009 were parents, another 6.3 percent were other relatives of the victim and 4.3 percent were unmarried partners of parents (*Child Maltreatment 2009*, 2010, p.70). Women comprised a larger percentage of all perpetrators (53.8 percent) than men (44.4 percent). Nearly three-fourths (73.2 percent) of all perpetrators were younger than age 39. The racial distribution of perpetrators was similar to the race of their victims.

People who have normal behavior patterns in all other areas of life may have very abnormal sexual behavior patterns. Child sexual abusers may commit only one offense in their lifetimes, or they may commit hundreds. Surveys indicate that 35 to 50 percent of offenders know their victims. Some studies indicate an even higher percentage. Therefore, the investigator of a child sexual crime may not be looking for an unknown suspect or stranger.

The Parent as Suspect

Sexual abuse of one or more children in a family is one of the most common child sexual abuse problems, but it is not often reported. Because of the difficulties in detecting it, it is the least known to the public. The harm to the child from continued, close sexual relationships with a family member may be accompanied by shame, fear or even guilt. Additional conflict may be created by admonitions of secrecy.

Although girls are more frequently victims, if a girl is sexually abused by a family member, a boy in the same family may also be a victim. Incest usually involves children under age 11 and becomes a repeated activity, escalating both in severity and frequency.

Courts have ruled that the spousal immunity rules do not apply to child sexual abuse cases. One spouse may be forced to testify against the other in court.

Investigators must be aware of unusual situations involving psychiatric or medical conditions that may lead to injuries in children and, consequently, cast suspicion on parents or caregivers as having been abusive.

Munchausen Syndrome and Munchausen by Proxy Syndrome. Munchausen syndrome

involves self-induced or self-inflicted injuries. If a child's injuries appear to be self-induced or self-inflicted, the child may be seeking attention or sympathy or may be avoiding something. Parents—usually the mother—may inflict injuries on their children for basically the same reasons. **Munchausen by proxy syndrome (MBPS)**, alternately called Munchausen syndrome by proxy (MSBP), is a form of child abuse in which a parent or adult caregiver deliberately provides false medical histories, manufactures evidence and causes medical distress in a child ("Munchausen Syndrome by Proxy," 2011). MBPS is usually done so the child will be treated by a physician and the abuser may gain the attention or sympathy of family, friends and others.

MBPS allegations frequently come from an anonymous source or a health care professional. An unknown percentage of the anonymous calls come from health care professionals concerned with liability issues. One of the most logical first steps is to contact the primary-care physician. Early contact should be made with a child care

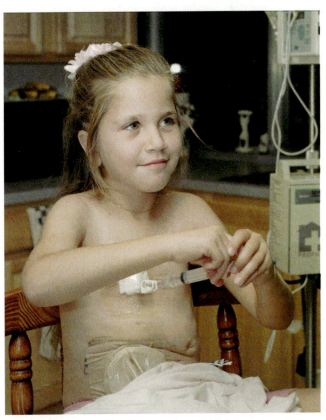

At her Coral Springs, Florida, home, Jennifer Bush applies medicine from a syringe as treatment for a rare disease. She has been hospitalized more than 200 times, undergone 40 operations and accumulated $3 million in medical expenses. Jennifer has been placed under state care and her mother jailed for allegedly causing her illnesses as a result of Munchausen by proxy syndrome, a rare form of child abuse in which an adult intentionally makes a child ill to get attention.

agency to coordinate issues regarding the child's safety when the investigation becomes known to the parent. MBPS should be considered as a possible motive in any questionable or unexplained death of a child.

Investigators assigned to work child abuse cases should investigate cases of MBPS as they do similar cases of abuse. In general, however, when confronted with possible cases of MBPS, investigators should

■ Review the victim's medical records.

■ Determine from contact with medical personnel the reporting parent's concerns and reactions to the child's medical treatment.

■ Compile a complete family history.

■ Interview family members, neighbors and babysitters.

■ Consider using video surveillance in the hospital.

■ Use a search warrant for the family's residence when collecting evidence.

Offenders often have a medical background or have been around the medical profession in some way.

Whereas MBPS is a disorder that clearly results in a form of child abuse, another disorder whose symptoms closely resemble child abuse and for which parents are often mistakenly accused of abuse, is osteogenesis imperfecta.

Osteogenesis Imperfecta. Osteogenesis imperfecta (OI), or brittle bone disease, is a genetic disorder characterized by bones that break easily, often from little or no apparent cause. However, child abuse may also result in broken bones. Consequently, improper diagnosis of OI can lead to the parents of children with the disease being wrongly accused of child abuse. The U.S. Osteogenesis Imperfecta Foundation (OIF) states, "A minor accident may result in a fracture; some fractures may occur while a child is being diapered, lifted, or dressed" (Child Abuse Issues," n.d.). The most routine child care activities, performed by the most careful and loving parents, can easily and spontaneously break the bones of a child with OI and, in some severe cases, the condition may be lethal. The OIF reports, "False accusations of child abuse may occur in families with children who have milder forms of OI and/or in whom OI has not previously been diagnosed. Types of fractures that are typically observed in both child abuse and OI include fractures in multiple stages of healing, rib fractures, spiral fractures and fractures for which there is no adequate explanation of trauma" ("Child Abuse Issues," n.d.).

During the 1940s, advances in diagnostic X-ray technology allowed physicians to detect patterns of healed fractures in their young patients. In 1946 Dr. John Caffey,

a pediatric radiologist, suggested that multiple fractures in the long bones of infants had "traumatic origin," perhaps willfully inflicted by parents. Two decades later, Dr. C. H. Kempe and his associates coined the phrase *battered child syndrome* based on clinical evidence of maltreatment: "In the typical case, the victim was younger than 3 years old and suffered traumatic injuries to the head and to limbs; and the caretakers claimed that the wounds were caused by an accident and not a beating" (Karmen, 2007, p.190). In 1964 individual states began enacting mandatory child abuse laws using Dr. Kempe's definition of a battered child, and by 1966 all 50 states had enacted such legislation.

The similarities between OI and child abuse symptoms can easily confuse investigators and anger parents wrongly accused of abuse. For example, in addition to displaying different types of fractures in various stages of healing, a child with OI often bruises easily. Furthermore, many children with OI are of shorter stature than average, a condition often mistaken as indicative of neglect (OIF). When these symptoms are detected, how do investigators determine whether the suspected abuse case is actually OI? First, a medical professional experienced in diagnosing OI should evaluate the child. Genetic counseling may also reveal a previously unrecognized family history of mild OI. Investigators should also look for inconsistencies between the explanation for the injury given by the child or parent and the diagnosis provided by the treating physicians and other medical personnel. Parents may also try to conceal child abuse by frequently changing doctors or hospitals, thus avoiding a buildup of incriminating records at any one office or facility. Keep in mind also that the presence of OI does not automatically preclude the existence of child abuse.

Sudden Infant Death Syndrome. Another tragic condition that takes the lives of young victims and for which parents may become suspected of child abuse is **sudden infant death syndrome (SIDS)**, briefly introduced in Chapter 8.

SIDS is a diagnosis by exclusion and is the most frequently determined cause of sudden unexplained infant death (SUID). "Investigation of a potential SIDS death should include a thorough death scene evaluation and a complete autopsy, with a radiographic skeletal survey and toxicology studies" (Adams et al., 2010, p.873). Because examination of the death scene is a critical factor in determining SIDS, officers responding to a call of an "infant not breathing" must observe several elements, including the infant's position when found, body temperature, presence or absence of rigor mortis, the condition of the crib and surrounding area, the presence of bedding and other objects in the crib, the type of bed or crib, any unusual or dangerous items in the room, any medications being given to the baby, room temperature, air quality, type of heating or cooling system used and the caregiver's response (Adams et al., 2009).

Officers may also observe certain bodily appearances in the victim that typically occur in SIDS cases resulting from the death process, including discoloration of the skin, frothy drainage from the mouth or nose and cooling rigor mortis that takes place quickly, usually in about 3 hours in infants. Recent studies by British and Australian researchers suggest two common bacteria might also play a role in SIDS, a discovery that may influence what additional tests are conducted during the autopsies of these young victims.

Table 11.1 compares the characteristic features of SIDS with child abuse, and Table 11.2 summarizes the characteristics of MBPS, OI and SIDS.

Investigating Child Fatalities.
Investigating the death of a child can be one of the most difficult tasks an investigator ever encounters. Tough questions must be asked to grieving parents or caregivers so the investigator may determine whether the fatality resulted from an unknown medical condition, an accident or a criminal act.

Many child fatalities are first reported as natural deaths or accidents (Walsh, 2005, p.25). The following checklists of potential witnesses and other information sources will assist investigators working a child fatality case (Walsh, pp.14, 18). Potential witnesses include

- Parents—including current and former stepparents and parents' significant others
- Siblings and other children
- Family members
- Caretakers—babysitters, child care employees
- Teachers—day care, preschool, school, church
- Neighbors—current and previous
- First responders—police and emergency medical technicians
- Emergency room personnel—physicians and nurses
- Medical providers who have seen the child previously, including school nurses
- Agency personnel—CPS, day care licensing, law enforcement personnel who have had prior contact with the family or child

TABLE 11.1 Comparison of Sudden Infant Death Syndrome (SIDS) and Child Abuse Characteristics

Characteristic/Feature	SIDS	Child Abuse/Neglect
Age typically affected	May occur from birth to 24 months but is most common from 2 to 4 months of age. Ninety percent of all cases occur by 6 months of age.	May occur at any time, but one-third of abused children are under 4 years old, and one-fifth of abused children are between 4 and 7 years of age. Children younger than 1 year old have the highest rate of victimization, with victimization rate generally decreasing with age.
External signs of injury?	Not usually	Yes—distinguishable and visible signs
Signs of malnourishment?	Not usually; appears well developed	Common
Do siblings show any symptoms?	Not usually; siblings appear normal and healthy	May show patterns of injuries
Parents' account of investigated event	Placed healthy baby to sleep in the crib and later found infant lifeless	May sound suspicious or may not account for all injuries to the child
Annual number of deaths in the United States	2,000–2,500 infants	1,500–1,000 children; more than 46% are infants (less than 1 year old)
Noteworthy trends	Number and rate of SIDS cases has dropped dramatically since 1992. SIDS tends to occur more often in winter months, peaking in January.	The number and rate of child fatalities has been increasing over the past 5 years.

Source: Adapted from Stephen M. Adams, Matthew W. Good and Gina M. Defranco. "Sudden Infant Death Syndrome." *American Family Physician*, Vol.79, No.10, May 15, 2009, pp.870–874.

"Sudden Infant Death Syndrome." Bethesda, MD: PubMed Health Online, Reviewed August 2, 2009. Accessed June 13, 2011. http://www.ncbi.nlm.nih.gov/pubmedhealth/PMH0002533/

Child Maltreatment 2009. Washington, DC: U.S. Department of Health and Human Services; Administration for Children and Families; Administration on Children, Youth and Families; Children's Bureau, 2010. Accessed June 11, 2011. http://www.acf.hhs.gov/programs/cb/stats_research/index.htm#can

TABLE 11.2 Comparison of the Characteristics of Munchausen by Proxy Syndrome (MBPS), Osteogenesis Imperfecta (OI) and Sudden Infant Death Syndrome (SIDS)

Characteristic/Feature	MBPS[a]	OI[b]	SIDS[c]
Age of child affected	Any age, although occurs more often in preschool-aged children	Any age	Typically occurs in newborn to 24 months but is most frequent from 2 to 4 months
Number of children who die every year in the United States due to it	Unknown	Unknown	2,000–2,500
External signs of injury (parent-inflicted)	Occasionally	Not usually	Not usually
Is it child abuse?	Yes	No	No

Source: [a] "Munchausen Syndrome by Proxy." Bethesda, MD: National Institutes of Health, MedlinePlus Medical Encyclopedia, Updated February 21, 2011. Accessed June 13, 2011. http://www.nlm.nih.gov/medlineplus/ency/article/001555.htm

[b] U.S. Osteogenesis Imperfecta Foundation: "Child Abuse Issues." Gaithersburg, MD: Osteogenesis Imperfecta Foundation, no date. Accessed June 13, 2011. http://www.oif.org/site/DocServer/_Child_Abuse__Child_Abuse_Issues.pdf?docID=7188 "Child Abuse or Osteogenesis Imperfecta?" Gaithersburg, MD: Osteogenesis Imperfecta Foundation, no date. Accessed June 13, 2011. http://www.oif.org/site/DocServer/_Child_Abuse__Child_Abuse_or_Ostegenesis_Imperfecta.pdf?docID=7189

[c] "Sudden Infant Death Syndrome." Bethesda, MD: PubMed Health Online, Reviewed August 2, 2009. Accessed June 13, 2011. http://www.ncbi.nlm.nih.gov/pubmedhealth/PMH0002533/

Other potential information sources include

■ CPS records—for the deceased child, siblings, other children that the child's caretakers have had contact with

■ Law enforcement records—criminal history, victim or suspect history, calls for service

■ Medical records for the deceased child and siblings—birth, prenatal care, pediatrician, medical, emergency room

■ 911 calls

■ Emergency medical services (EMS) reports

■ Telephone calls or other communications made or received by the suspect around the time of the child's death—including cell phones, pagers, e-mails, messages on answering machines

■ Autopsy results

If the child's family or suspect has previously lived in another community, check there for potential witnesses and other agency records that may document a history of abuse or neglect.

Walsh (2005, p.25) provides the following tips and reminders for investigators working possible child fatality cases:

■ An unreasonable delay in seeking medical attention is often a "red flag" that the child's injuries may have been caused by abuse.

■ 911 call records often contain important information about how a child's injuries were initially reported.

■ Treat cases involving severe injury as potential child fatalities because it is not uncommon for severely injured children to die days or weeks after the original injury.

■ Delayed deaths often involve more than one crime scene. Examine the place where the injury occurred,

the hospital where the child died and any private vehicle used to transport the child to the hospital.

■ There is no substitute for a timely, professional crime-scene search, including evidence collection, documentation and photo-documentation.

■ Coordinate and communicate with CPS investigators in child fatality cases. They have a legitimate role in the investigation and can often provide important information about the child and family involved.

Successful child fatality investigations hinge on three factors: effectively conducted, well-documented interviews of witnesses; thorough background checks on every witness and suspect involved in the case; and competent interrogation of the suspect(s) (Walsh, 2005, p.25). A final word of caution: do not automatically exclude children as potential suspects. Children have been known to inflict severe injuries on other children.

Sex Crimes by Other Children

Although seldom discussed, an increasing number of child sex crimes are being committed by other children. Many people think such crimes cannot occur because they often view children as not being sexually capable. Some child sex abusers were molested themselves. When investigators receive reports of children committing sex crimes against other children, they must not automatically dismiss them as fantasy and must thoroughly investigate all such reports.

The Nonparent Suspect

Perpetrators other than parents have included babysitters, camp counselors, school personnel, clergy and others. Habitual child sex abusers, whether they operate as loners or as part of a sex ring, have been classified into three types. First is the **misoped**, the person who hates children, has sex with them and then brutally murders them. The second type is the **hebephile**, a person who selects high school–age youths as his or her sex victims. The third and most common habitual child sex abuser is the **pedophile**, sometimes referred to as a **chicken hawk**, an adult who has either heterosexual or homosexual preferences for young boys or girls of a specific, limited age range. Although pedophiles are typically male, this is not always the case. Women are also involved in the sexual abuse of children.

THE PEDOPHILE

There is no specific demographic for a child predator, although statistically they are white males. Pedophiles come from all walks of life and range from professionals, to persons who are in a position of authority, to persons with an extensive criminal history.

Pedophilia is a sex offense in all states. Rarely deviating from the preferred age range, the pedophile is an expert in selecting and enticing young people. The pedophile frequently selects children who stand apart from other children, who are runaways or who crave attention and love. Although some pedophiles are child rapists, most rarely use force, relying instead on befriending the victims and gaining their confidence and friendship. Pedophiles may become involved in activities or programs that interest the type of victims they want to attract and that provide them with easy access to these children. Pedophiles may also use drugs or alcohol as a means of seduction, reducing the child's inhibitions.

The Federal Bureau of Investigation (FBI) Behavioral Science Services Unit identifies and categorizes two types of child predators based on their descriptive types. Table 11.3 describes these two typologies, known as *situational* and *preferential*.

TABLE 11.3 Child Molester Typologies

Child Molester Typologies	Victim Profile	Offender Profile-Methodology	Threat Level
Situational	The victim is often a relative, neighbor, friend or someone under the trusted care or authority of the offender. The victim might not have definite characteristics that attract the offender. The victim in this category may also only be a few years younger than the offender and perhaps becomes a victim in a social setting such as a party.	This offender can range from a one-time act to a long pattern of child sexual abuse. Typically this offender has a limited number of victims and may abuse out of opportunity. This offender may abuse children for other reasons than genuine sexual attraction.	There are fewer documented cases involving situational molesters because there are fewer victim-offender ratios. This is in addition to the less predictable behavior of this type of offender. The threat of offending and recidivism is lower than with the preferential molester.
Preferential	The victim is more likely unknown to the offender. The offender may meet the child at a random location that typically attracts children or through an online Internet forum. The child may have other issues in his or her life that the offender can exploit to gain trust. The victim is typically a specific gender or age range depending on what the offender is attracted to.	Often older, they look to "groom" a child and build a relationship. They have a definite sexual preference for children and are sexually attracted to them. A common form of building relationships can be through providing attention and tangible gifts. This type of offender is more apt to engage in highly predictable behavior and high-risk activities to locate and seduce victims. The preferential molester is more commonly identified as a pedophile.	Of the two types, the preferential is more dangerous. This is because those that fit under this category have a consistent need to fulfill their sexual desires and they will not stop pursuing them. Although statistically smaller in number than situational offenders, they have the potential to molest a larger number of victims.

Source: Table created by Henry Cho, Cho Research and Consulting, LLC

Pedophiles may obtain, collect and maintain photographs of the children with whom they are or have been involved. Many pedophiles maintain diaries of their sexual encounters with children. Pedophiles may collect books, magazines, newspapers and other writings on the subject of sexual activities with children. They may also collect addresses, phone numbers or lists of people who have similar sexual interests. Pedophiles also locate and attract victims through the computer, as discussed shortly. In addition, many pedophiles are members of sex rings.

Child Sexual Abuse Rings

Adults (at least 10 to 15 years older than the victims) are usually the dominant leaders, organizers and operators of sex rings. The adult leader selectively gathers young people together for sexual purposes. The involvement varies, with the longest periods occurring when prepubescent children are involved. Most cases involve male ringleaders, but some involve a female as well, usually a husband-wife pair.

Many ringleaders use their *occupation* as the major access route to the child victims. The adult has a legitimate role as an authority figure in the lives of the children selected for the ring or is able to survey vulnerable children through access to family records or history.

Sometimes rings are formed by an adult targeting a specific child, who then uses his or her associations and peer pressure to bring other children into the group. The initial child may be a relative or previously unknown. One common technique is to post a notice on a store bulletin board requesting girls to help with housework.

The adult's status in the neighborhood sometimes helps legitimize his or her presence with the children and their parents and permits unquestioned movement of young people into the offender's home. Such an offender often is well liked by his neighbors.

> Investigators should be aware of three types of sex rings: solo, transition and syndicated. Certain cults are also involved in the sexual abuse of children.

Solo Sex Rings. The organization of *solo sex rings* is primarily by the age of the child—for example, toddlers (ages 2 to 5), prepubescent (6 to 12) or pubescent (13 to 17). This type of offender prefers to have multiple children as sex objects, in contrast to the offender who seeks one child at a time.

Transition Sex Rings. Pedophiles have a strong need to communicate with others about their interest in children. In *transition sex rings*, experiences are exchanged, whereas in solo rings, the pedophile keeps his or her activities and photographs totally secret. In transition rings, photographs of children as well as sexual services may be traded and sold.

The trading of pornography appears to be the first move of the victim into the "possession" of other pedophiles. The photographs are traded, and victims may be tested by other offenders and eventually traded for their sexual services.

Syndicated Sex Rings. The third type of ring is the *syndicated sex ring*, a well-structured organization that recruits children, produces pornography, delivers direct sexual services and establishes an extensive network of customers. Syndicated rings have involved a Boy Scout troop, a boys' farm operated by a minister and a national boy prostitution ring.

Ritualistic Abuse by Satanic Cults

Cults are groups that use rituals or ceremonial acts to draw their members together into a certain belief system. When the rituals of a group involve crimes, including child sexual abuse, they become a problem for law enforcement. Crimes associated with cults are discussed in Chapter 19.

Victimology

People involved in intervening, investigating or prosecuting child pornography and sex ring cases must recognize that a bond often develops between the offender and the victims. Many victims find themselves willing to trade sex for attention, affection and other benefits.

Children and teens often make the perfect victims. They are often naïve and trusting. They often desire material things—things that perpetrators may promise in exchange for the child's participation in sex activities. Children are curious about sex. And teens are particularly at risk because they are more likely to engage in communication revolving around sex and relationships. Furthermore, children and teens are not generally viewed as credible witnesses or victims.

Pedophile ring operators are, by definition, skilled at gaining the continued cooperation and control of their victims through well-planned seduction. These operators are skilled at recognizing and then *temporarily* filling the emotional and physical needs of children. They know how to listen to children—an ability many parents lack. These operators are willing to spend all the time it takes to seduce a child.

This positive offender-victim bond must not be misinterpreted as consent, complicity or guilt. In one case, a prosecutor announced to television reporters that the victims were as guilty as—if not more guilty than—the offenders. Police investigators, in particular, must be sensitive to this problem.

Offender Reactions

When a child pornography and sex ring is discovered, certain reactions by the pedophile offenders are fairly predictable. The intensity of these reactions may depend on how much the offenders have to lose by their identification and conviction.

Usually a pedophile's first reaction to discovery is complete denial. The offenders may act shocked, surprised or even indignant about an allegation of sexual activity with children. This denial frequently is aided by their friends, neighbors, relatives and coworkers, who insist that such upstanding people could not have done what is alleged.

If the evidence rules out total denial, offenders may switch to a slightly different tactic, attempting to minimize what they have done in both quantity and quality. Pedophiles are often knowledgeable about the law and might admit to acts that are lesser offenses or misdemeanors.

Either as part of the effort to minimize or as a separate reaction, pedophiles typically attempt to justify their behavior. They might claim that they care for these children more than their parents do and that what the pedophiles do is beneficial to the children. They may claim to have been under tremendous stress, to have a drinking problem or not to have known how young a certain victim was. The efforts to justify their behavior often center on blaming the victim. Offenders may claim that they were seduced by the victims, that the victims initiated the sexual activity or that the victims were promiscuous or even prostitutes. When various reactions do not result in termination of the investigation or prosecution, pedophiles may claim to be sick and unable to control themselves.

> Pedophiles' reactions to being discovered usually begin with complete denial and then progress to minimizing the acts, justifying the acts and blaming the victims. If all else fails, they may claim to be sick.

Pedophiles are commonly involved in child pornography, either as a "hobby" or for commercial gain, although they are not the only individuals who participate in such child exploitation.

COMMERCIAL SEXUAL EXPLOITATION

Exploitation refers to taking unfair advantage of children or using them illegally. This includes using children in pornography and prostitution. At the federal level, child abuse statutes pertain mainly to exploitation, but they also set forth important definitions that apply to any type of child abuse. Public Law 95–225 (1978) defines **sexual exploitation** as follows: "Any person who employs, uses, persuades, induces, entices, or coerces any minor to engage or assist in engaging in any sexually explicit conduct for the purpose of producing any visual or print medium, knowing that such visual or print medium will be transported interstate or in foreign commerce or mailed, is guilty of sexual exploitation. Further, any parent or legal guardian who knowingly permits such conduct, having control and custody of the child, is also subject to prosecution."

Commercial sexual exploitation of children (CSEC) is "sexual abuse of a minor for economic gain. It involves physical abuse, pornography, prostitution, and the smuggling of children for unlawful purposes" (Albanese, 2007, p.1). The Justice Department reports that this type of crime is increasing at an alarming rate, with the number of federal cases nearly quadrupling between 1996 and 2006 ("Federal Child Exploitation Cases," 2008, p.6).

Pornography

According to the Child Protection Act of 1984, child pornography is highly developed into an organized, multimillion-dollar industry producing and distributing pornographic materials nationally, exploiting thousands of children, including runaways and homeless youths. The act states that such exploitation is harmful to the physiological, emotional and mental health of the individual and to society. Many states have passed similarly worded statutes and have increased penalties for sexual abuse and the production and distribution of child-pornographic materials.

> The Child Protection Act (1984) prohibits child pornography and greatly increases the penalties for adults who engage in it.

Although adult pornography has always been objectionable to many people, it has not resulted in the aggressive public and legislative action that child pornography has received. In 1977 Congress passed the Protection of Children against Sexual Exploitation Act. This and other federal and state laws have prohibited commercial and noncommercial distribution of pornographic materials and more recently have made it a violation of law to *possess* such materials.

The basis for these laws has been the acceptance of a relationship between child-pornographic materials and child sexual abuse offenders and offenses. In many cases, arrested pedophiles have had in their possession child-pornographic literature used to lower their selected victims' inhibitions. It is often necessary to obtain search warrants for the suspect's premises to obtain these materials. It is necessary in the investigation to gain as much evidence as possible, because the problems of child testimony in court are well established.

An emerging challenge in the area of child pornography is **sexting**, sending or posting a nude picture of oneself to another person through the Internet, using a cell phone to transmit the image. Often the persons taking and sending the photos of themselves are minors, and although the original transmission may be voluntary by the "victims," in the sense that they purposefully sent the images and intended the recipient to receive and view the photos, once an image is online, it is often passed along to other parties indiscriminately. The possession of such images, regardless of the device involved (computer, cell phone, etc.) and the age of the person in possession of the images, constitutes engagement in child pornography.

Internet Sex Crimes against Children

Advances in computer technology and the expansion of the Internet have created an entirely new global forum in which sex offenders can access potential victims, distribute or trade child pornography, network with other child abuse perpetrators, promote child sexual tourism and traffic children: "The Internet provides a child predator with access to children on a scale that makes the world his local playground. It is a medium through which digital images and movies documenting the most horrific crimes against children are distributed to a worldwide audience" (Geraghty, 2007, p.30). Law enforcement is aware of hundreds of thousands of people trafficking in child pornography on the Internet, and this exploding multibillion-dollar market must be continuously supplied with fresh content. This means thousands of new images are posted every week, involving the continued sexual assault and exploitation of children, with research indicating that the victims are getting younger and being exposed to increasingly brutal and sadistic abuse ("Internet Child Pornography Targeted," 2007).

All of the services the Internet provides—e-mail, the World Wide Web, instant messaging—can be used to facilitate crimes against children. Consider the following examples of how this occurs:

> A fourth-grade student was frequently pulled out of lunch by her teacher, who sexually abused her in the class coatroom and took explicit photographs to memorialize the moment. He demanded her silence by threatening to flunk her and post the pictures on the Internet if she told anyone. Another child, a prepubescent boy, was violently sexually assaulted for several years by a man who acted as his live-in babysitter. While the boy never disclosed his abuse to anyone, thousands of photographs depicting his horrific abuse were circulated around the globe. In another location, a man with no previous criminal record filmed himself sodomizing his 10-month-old granddaughter. He did not need to convince the child to keep the secret; in fact, he said he selected that particular victim because she was preverbal. (Collins, 2007, p.40)

Online technology has given rise to new terminology used in the investigation of crimes involving this medium. According to the National Center for Missing and Exploited Children (NCMEC), *online victimization* includes sexual solicitations or approaches, aggressive sexual solicitations, unwanted exposure to sexual materials or sexual harassment causing distress. *Sexual solicitation* refers to requests to engage in sexual activity, talk or information regardless of being wanted or unwanted by an adult to a child. *Aggressive sexual solicitation* includes requests and attempts by an offender for contact with the victim outside of the Internet through mail, gifts, phone or in person contact. *Unwanted exposure to sexual materials* refers to a child being exposed to unwanted sexual material of explicit photos or video of naked people performing sexual acts. A good example of this might be spam mail to pornographic links that children may receive in their e-mail inboxes.

Internet sex crimes against minors can be categorized in three mutually exclusive groups: (1) Internet crimes against identified victims involving Internet-related sexual assaults and other sex crimes, such as the production of child pornography committed against identified victims; (2) Internet solicitations unknowingly to undercover law enforcement officers posing as minors that involved no identified victims; and (3) the possession, distribution or trading of Internet child pornography by offenders who did not use the Internet to sexually exploit identified victims or unknowingly solicit undercover investigators. Figure 11.1 illustrates the categories.

Online predators use the Internet in many ways, and it has quickly become the preferred method for child

Three categories of Internet sex crimes against minors
Estimated 2,557 arrests in the year following July 1, 2000
(Range of estimate is 2,277 to 2,877)

Internet crimes against Identified victims (I-civ)	**Internet solicitations to undercover law enforcement (I-STULE)**	**Internet child pornography (I-CHP)**
39% of all arrests Estimated 998 arrests (Range is 898 to 1,098)	**25% of all arrests** Estimated 644 arrests (Range is 335 to 953)	**36% of all arrests** Estimated 935 arrests (Range is 827 to 1,042)
Crimes with identified victims, including production of child pornography	Undercover law enforcement investigators posed as minors; excludes crimes involving identified victims	Possession/distribution/trade of child pornography only; excludes crimes where child pornography was produced

Two categories of internet crimes against identified victims

Internet-initiated	**Family/Prior acquaintance**
20% of all arrests Estimated 508 arrests	**19% of all arrests** Estimated 490 arrests
Offender used the Internet to initiate a relationship with the victim	Offender was a family member or prior acquaintance of the victim

FIGURE 11.1

Categories of Internet sex crimes against minors. Note: the ranges for each estimate constitute margins of error, calculated separately for each estimate using a statistical formula based on the weighted number of cases in each category.

Source: Janis Wolak, Kimberly Mitchell and David Finkelhor. *Internet Sex Crimes against Minors: The Response of Law Enforcement*. Washington, DC: National Center for Missing and Exploited Children, November 2003. Reprinted by permission of The National Center for Missing and Exploited Children.

predators to use because of the ease of access to their prey and the anonymity and safety it affords in soliciting and grooming juveniles online. The grooming process often begins with an offender joining a chat room intended for children or teens and engaging his or her victims in dialogue. After the initial contact, the offender will build rapport and trust with the child victim. The offender usually likes to make the child victim feel important, and offenders often seek children with problems at home. Over time, the child's inhibitions become lowered, which eventually leads to some level of victimization.

Newsgroups are believed to be the largest single forum for child pornography on the Internet. Although hundreds of thousands of legitimate bulletin boards are used for common interest and posting discussion, predators often prefer to exploit such newsgroups because these forums are free and not policed or controlled, except by the Internet service provider (ISP), which has discretion on hosting them.

The challenge of controlling and investigating online sexual abuse of children is multifactorial and includes the decentralized structure of the Internet, immense volume of Internet activity, technological ability and expertise of offenders, jurisdictional uncertainties, differences and discrepancies in legislation between jurisdictions and a lack of monitoring and regulation of online activities. An additional challenge to investigators lies in the nontraditional skills often required to sift through the technical evidence involved in cybercrimes, including the need to identify the Internet Protocol (IP) address and where it is located. IP tracing technologies can provide valuable tools to identify the source of Internet communications. Helpful clues to the location of a suspect can be found by analyzing e-mail header information, which reveals the IP address of the system the e-mail came from. Once the IP address is obtained, investigators can easily identify the location with an IP tracing tool. Investigating cybercrime and other crimes that use the computer is the topic of Chapter 17.

Pedophiles lurk in cyberspace, waiting to lure unsuspecting children into ongoing online "friendships" and hoping to persuade the child to eventually meet them in person.
© L. Clarke/CORBIS

The Child Protection and Sexual Predator Punishment Act, passed in 1998, imposes tougher penalties for sex crimes against children, particularly those facilitated by the use of the Internet. The Act prohibits contacting a minor via the Internet to engage in illegal sexual activity and punishes those who knowingly send obscenity to children.

Several initiatives are aimed at protecting children in cyberspace. The Office of Juvenile Justice and Delinquency Prevention (OJJDP) of the U.S. Department of Justice funds the Internet Crimes against Children (ICAC) Task Force, which seeks to protect children online. This program helps state and local law enforcement agencies develop effective responses to online enticement and child pornography cases, including community education, forensic, investigative and victim service components. NCMEC has a congressionally mandated CyberTipline, a reporting mechanism for child sexual exploitation. It has handled more than 628,680 leads and serves as the national clearinghouse for child pornography cases across the country.

Project Safe Childhood (PSC) was designed and sponsored by the U.S. Department of Justice to empower federal, state and local law enforcement officers with tools needed to investigate cybercrimes against children. Forty-six federally funded ICAC task forces, consisting of more than 1,000 affiliated state and local organizations, have been created across the country since 1998 (McNulty, 2007, p.36). As a result of task force investigations, 7,328 arrests have been made in the past seven years. In addition, the FBI made 1,648 arrests in 2005 as part of its Innocent Images National Initiative.

Models to Combat Child Sexual Exploitation

Three law enforcement approaches have emerged as models to combat child sexual exploitation: special task forces, strike forces and law enforcement networks.

Special task forces are useful in jurisdictions with a steady load of child sexual exploitation cases. In addition to a steady caseload, the model includes a centralized location, a standing team of experts, specialized staffing, victim services and a multijurisdictional (federal, state, local) approach. In a *strike force* model, no core is dedicated exclusively to the problem. Rather, team members come together from individual agencies in response to a particular case. Under a *law enforcement network* model, law enforcement officers, prosecutors, victims' services providers, social service agents and others come together proactively to focus on education, recruitment, building resources and establishing personal contacts. This model has no dedicated resources and, over time, may evolve into a task force or strike force if needed.

Federal Agencies Working against Child Pornography

Several federal agencies are involved in combating child pornography. The FBI's Crimes against Children (CAC) unit provides quick, effective responses to all incidents of sexual exploitation of children.

The U.S. Customs Service targets the illegal importation and trafficking of child pornography and fights child sex tourism. The Customs CyberSmuggling Center (C3) is a front line of defense against smuggling over continental borders as well as through the Internet.

The U.S. Postal Inspection Service is responsible for investigating crimes involving the U.S. mails, including child pornography and child sexual abuse offenses. It is the lead agency in the federal government's efforts to eliminate the production and distribution of such material.

The Innocent Images National Initiative.
The Innocent Images National Initiative (IINI), part of the FBI's Cyber Crimes Program, is an "intelligence driven, proactive, multi-agency investigative initiative to combat the proliferation of child pornography/child sexual exploitation (CP/CSE) facilitated by an online computer" (*Innocent Images*, 2007). The program provides a coordinated FBI response to this nationwide problem by collating and analyzing information and images obtained from numerous sources, avoiding duplication of effort by all FBI field offices. Between fiscal years 1996 and 2007, this initiative accomplished the following:

- 20,134 cases opened (2,062 percent increase—from 113 in 1996 to 2,433 in 2007)

- 6,844 informations/indictments (1,003 percent increase—from 99 in 1996 to 1,092 in 2007)

- 9,469 arrests/locates/summons (2,501 percent increase—from 68 in 1996 to 1,023 in 2007)

- 6,863 convictions/pretrial diversions (1,404 percent increase—from 68 in 1996 to 1,023 in 2007)

IINI undercover operations are being conducted in several FBI field offices by task forces that combine the resources of the FBI with other federal, state and local law enforcement agencies. International investigations are coordinated through the FBI's Legal Attaché program as well as with the ICAC task forces, discussed next. FBI agents and task force officers go online undercover into predicated locations using fictitious screen names and engage in real-time chat or e-mail conversations to obtain evidence of criminal activity. Investigating specific online locations is initiated through a citizen complaint, a complaint by an ISP or a referral from a law enforcement agency.

Another approach to combating online sex crimes against children is to establish an ICAC task force.

Internet Crimes against Children Task Forces.
In September 1998 the OJJDP began a national program to counter the growing threat of offenders using the Internet to sexually exploit children by making 10 awards to state and local law enforcement agencies across the country.

CyberTipline.
The NCMEC CyberTipline (www.cybertipline.com) maintains a 24-hour-a-day number (1-800-843-5678) that receives leads in five basic areas: (1) possession, manufacture and distribution of child pornography; (2) online enticement of children for sexual acts; (3) child prostitution; (4) child sex tourism; and (5) child sexual molestation outside the family.

International Initiatives

In 1996 the First World Congress against Commercial Exploitation of Children convened in Stockholm, Sweden. This congress adopted a Declaration and Agenda for Action calling on states to, among other things:

- Accord high priority to action against the commercial exploitation of children and allocate adequate resources to the effort

- Promote stronger cooperation between states and all sectors of society and strengthen the role of families

- Criminalize the commercial sexual exploitation of children

- Condemn and penalize the offenders while ensuring that child victims are not penalized

- Review and revise laws, policies, programs and practices

- Enforce laws, policies and programs

INTERPOL has established a Standing Working Party (SWP) on Offenses against minors that seeks to improve international cooperation in preventing and combating child pornography and other forms of child sexual exploitation. The group meets twice a year to produce best-practices reports.

Prostitution of Juveniles

Yet another challenge for investigators involved in crimes against children is that of prostitution. "Child prostitution encompasses the exchange of sexual services for remuneration or other forms of consideration, including food, housing, drugs, or other commodities or intangibles such as approval or care. It is an age old and global problem that has existed for centuries" (*Child Prostitution*, 2008).

The prostitution of juveniles occurs in a variety of contexts. Both international rings and interstate crime operations traffic young girls to faraway places, promising them employment and money. Runaway and homeless youths are recruited by pimps or engage in "survival sex." Drug dealers get youths addicted and then force them to prostitute themselves to receive drugs or have a place to stay. Some parents have advertised and prostituted their children over the Internet. The big question becomes, Are these young prostitutes offenders or victims? Albanese (2007, p.8) urges,

> When child-victims of commercial sexual exploitation come to the attention of authorities, the public often regards them as teenage prostitutes, but this is not an accurate description. Rather, when a minor with few visible choices sells sex at the hands of an exploitive adult, it is generally a means of survival. The term "teenage prostitution" also overlooks the legal status of minors who have greater legal protections regarding sexual conduct because of their emotional and physical immaturity and the need to protect them from exploitative adults. Therefore, it is important that victims of child sexual exploitation are not mistaken for offenders.

Often the trafficking of children precedes their involvement in prostitution.

Trafficking of Children

Human trafficking often involves school-age children, particularly those not living with their parents, who are vulnerable to coerced labor exploitation, domestic servitude or commercial sexual exploitation. Sex traffickers target young children because they are vulnerable, gullible and in demand. The average age of entry into prostitution is 12 to 14 years of age (*Human Trafficking of Children*, 2007). Human trafficking was discussed in Chapter 10.

MISSING CHILDREN: RUNAWAY OR ABDUCTED?

Another major challenge facing law enforcement involves cases of missing children. The Missing Children's Act was passed in 1982 and the Missing Children's Assistance Act in 1984. The Missing Children's Assistance Act of 1984 defines a *missing child* as "Any individual, less than 18 years of age, whose whereabouts are unknown to such individual's legal custodian—if the circumstances surrounding the disappearance indicate that (the child) may possibly have been removed by another person from the control of his/her legal custodian without the custodian's consent; or the circumstances of the case strongly indicate that (the child) is likely to be abused or sexually exploited." This act requires the OJJDP to conduct periodic national incidence studies to determine the actual number of children reported missing.

NCMEC is a private, nonprofit organization established in 1984 to spearhead national efforts to locate and recover missing children and raise public awareness about ways to prevent child abduction, molestation and sexual exploitation. Since its inception, NCMEC has helped law

enforcement with more than 148,160 missing child cases, resulting in the recovery of more than 132,300 children. According to the NCMEC, an estimated 800,000 children are reported missing every year—more than 2,000 every day. As of December 31, 2010, the FBI's National Crime Information Center (NCIC) database contained 38,505 active juvenile missing person cases, accounting for 44.9 percent of all active missing persons records.

When children go missing, the question often asked is, Did they leave on their own accord (run away) or were they taken against their will (abducted)?

> A special challenge in cases where a child is reported missing is to determine whether the child has run away or been abducted.

Data from the *Juvenile Offenders and Victims: 2006 National Report* (2006) indicates

- Annually about 19 in 1,000 children younger than age 18 are missing from caretakers. Only a small fraction of missing children were abducted (about 10 in 100), most by family members (8 in 10). Runaway youth account for nearly half of all missing children (p.43).

- Teens ages 15 to 17 accounted for 68 percent of the estimated 1.7 million youths who were gone from their homes either because they had run away or because their caretakers threw them out. Fewer than 4 in 10 of all runaway/thrownaway youths are truly missing—their parents knew where they were staying. Most youths who ran away or were thrown out of their homes were gone less than a week (77 percent) (p.45).

Runaway Children

Many runaways are insecure, depressed, unhappy and impulsive with low self-esteem. Typical runaways report conflict with and alienation from parents, rejection and hostile control and lack of warmth, affection and parental support. Running away may compound their problems. Many runaways become streetwise and turn to drugs, crime, prostitution or other illegal activities.

For 21 percent of the 1.7 million runaway/thrownaway youths, their episode involved physical or sexual abuse at home before leaving or fear of such abuse upon their return (*Juvenile Offenders and Victims*, 2006, p.45). Other problems reported included parental drug or alcohol abuse, mental health problems within the family and domestic violence between the parents.

Considerations about whether youths are missing voluntarily include resources available to them to satisfy basic needs, such as food and shelter, access to money or credit cards, skills to obtain a job and access to a vehicle or public transportation. Another indicator that the absence is voluntary is that items such as clothing and treasured personal possessions are missing. Sometimes information can be obtained by examining the teenager's computer e-mails.

Sometimes a note is left confirming that the youth has indeed run away, but often there is no note. In other cases, evidence indicates that the child has not run away but, rather, has been abducted.

Abducted Children

Abducted children are often kidnapped. **Kidnapping** is taking someone away by force, often for ransom. Child kidnapping is especially traumatic for the parents and for those called upon to investigate. A highly publicized child kidnapping case in 1989 involved the abduction of 11-year-old Jacob Wetterling, who was taken at gunpoint from near his home in Minnesota by a masked man. No ransom was demanded, and despite national publicity and a nationwide search, Jacob remains missing.

Some child kidnappings are committed by a parent who has lost custody of the child in divorce proceedings. In such cases, ransom is not demanded. Rather, the parent committing the kidnapping may take on a new identity and move to another part of the country. Childless couples have also been known to kidnap babies or young children to raise as their own.

The most frequent type of child abduction is parental abduction.

In some cases, parents are simply poorly educated about the law, not knowing it to be a crime to abscond with their children. Other risk factors or warning signs of a possible parental abduction include prior threats of abduction or a history of hiding the child or withholding visitation; a parent's lack of emotional or financial ties to the area where the child is living; signs that a parent has liquidated assets, borrowed money or made maximum withdrawals of funds against credit cards; and various forms of mental illness in a parent.

Regardless of whether the investigator knows whether the child is a runaway or has been abducted, specific investigative steps should be taken.

Investigating a Missing Child Report

The NCMEC has put together *Missing and Abducted Children: A Law-Enforcement Guide to Case Investigation and Program Management* (edited by Steidel, 2006), which outlines a standard of practice for law enforcement officers handling missing-child cases, whether runaways, thrownaways, family or nonfamily abductions, or when the circumstances of the disappearance are unknown. The guide was authored by a team of professionals from local, state and federal agencies and describes—step-by-step with definitive checklists—the investigative process required for each of these types of cases and offers a wealth of resources to assist an investigator. The discussion that follows contains excerpts and highlights from this guide.

The first responder conducts the preliminary investigation. Interview the parent(s) or person who made the initial report, verify that the child is in fact missing and verify the child's custody status. Conduct a search to include all surrounding areas, including vehicles and other places of concealment, treating the area as a crime scene. Based on the circumstances of the child's disappearance, officers should consider using canine units, using forced entry into abandoned cars, sealing off any apartment complex where the child was last seen and considering use of search-and-rescue organizations, fire departments, military units and scout groups and other volunteers for a large-scale search (Steidel, 2006, p.44).

Officers should evaluate the contents and appearance of the child's room and determine whether any of the child's personal items are missing. Obtain photographs and videotapes of the missing child. Prepare reports. Enter the missing child into the NCIC Missing Persons File and report it to NCMEC. Interview other family members and friends and associates of the child and of the family to determine when each last saw the child and what he or she thinks happened to the child. Ensure that everyone at the scene is identified and interviewed separately.

As time permits, prepare and update bulletins for local law enforcement agencies, state missing children's clearinghouses, the FBI and other appropriate agencies. Also prepare a flyer or bulletin with the child's photograph and descriptive information and distribute it in appropriate geographic regions. Secure the child's latest medical and dental records. Establish a telephone hotline for tips and leads. Although the initial steps in the response are extensive, time-consuming and labor intensive, the preliminary investigation should be commenced as soon as possible after the original missing child report is received (Steidel, 2006, p.31).

If the preliminary investigation does not resolve the situation, a follow-up investigation must be conducted. Responsibilities of the investigative officer are many:

■ Obtain a briefing from the first responding officer and other on-scene personnel.

■ Verify all information developed during the preliminary investigation.

■ Obtain a brief, recent history of family dynamics.

- Correct and investigate the reasons for any conflicting information offered by witnesses and others submitting information.

- Develop an investigation plan for follow-up.

Runaways. If it is determined—either through a note or other evidence—that the child has run away, investigators (in addition to doing the investigative steps already described) should initially check agency records for recent contact with the child (arrests, other activities) (Steidel, 2006, p.111). Review school records and interview teachers, other school personnel and classmates and check the contents of the school locker.

Investigators should also consider several criteria to determine whether the runaway child is endangered (Steidel, 2006, p.117):

- Is the missing child younger than 13 years of age?

- Is the missing child believed to be out of the physical or geographic zone of safety for his or her age and developmental stage?

- Is the missing child mentally incapacitated?

- Is the missing child drug dependent—on a prescribed medication or an illegal substance—and is the dependency life-threatening?

- Was the missing child absent from home for more than 24 hours before being reported to police?

- Is the missing child believed to be in a life-threatening situation?

- Is the missing child believed to be in the company of adults who could endanger his or her welfare?

- Is the child's absence inconsistent with his or her established patterns of behavior and the deviation not readily explained?

- Are there other circumstances involved in the disappearance that would cause a reasonable person to conclude that the child should be considered at risk?

Any child who fits any of these criteria should be categorized as an endangered runaway, and efforts to locate the child should be immediately put into effect.

Abductions. For officers considering criminal charges against a parent who has abducted his or her child, several questions are pertinent (Steidel, 2006, p.97):

- Is there sufficient documentation to demonstrate parentage and the individual's right to physical custody or access?

- Can the suspect-parent actually be identified as the abductor?

- A vacation or change of address is not necessarily illegal. Can it be clearly established that the intent of the move was to unlawfully deny access to the complainant?

- If removal from the state is an element of the offense, can it be proven that the child has been physically taken across the state line?

- Can it be demonstrated that the suspect-parent is responsible for the removal?

- Have mitigating factors (such as domestic violence and abuse) been evaluated that, by statute, could undermine the filing of a charge?

- If an accomplice was involved, can it be proven that he or she had sufficient personal knowledge of the legal custody issues to form criminal intent?

- If the accomplice was the abductor, can the suspect-parent's complicity be demonstrated? How can he or she be directly implicated?

If the situation warrants, officers should use the federal Unlawful Flight to Avoid Prosecution (UFAP) statute (Steidel, 2006, p.98). Although UFAP warrants are not required for out-of-state arrests, they can be very helpful.

The investigation becomes exponentially more complicated when the suspect-parent leaves the country with the child: "As soon as it has been determined that a child may have been taken to a foreign country, the left-behind parent/guardian should immediately contact the U.S. Department of State … to discuss the filing of an application invoking [the] Hague Convention or actions to be taken under the International Parental Kidnapping Crime Act" (Steidel, 2006, p.103). The Hague Convention is an international treaty calling for the prompt return of an abducted child, usually to the country of his or her residence. Rapid action is necessary because after a child has been in another country for one year, the treaty is no longer binding. One helpful resource in such circumstances is *A Family Resource Guide on International Parental Kidnapping* (2007).

Because of the seriousness of missing child cases and the critical need for a prompt response, investigators are strongly advised to seek the assistance of national resources and specialized services. One such resource used in all 50 states is the AMBER Alert plan.

The AMBER Alert Plan

America's Missing: Broadcast Emergency Response (AMBER) Alert is a voluntary partnership between law enforcement and broadcasters to activate an urgent bulletin in the most serious child abduction cases. The AMBER Alert was created in the Dallas–Fort Worth region in 1996 in response to the death of 9-year-old Amber Hagerman, who was abducted while riding her bicycle in Arlington, Texas, and then brutally murdered. AMBER Alerts are emergency messages broadcast when a law enforcement agency determines that a child has been abducted and is in imminent danger. The broadcasts include information that could assist in the child's recovery, including a physical description of the child and abductor. All 50 states now have statewide AMBER Alert plans ("Department of Justice Marks 11th Anniversary," 2007, p.1). These alerts may be put on television and radio stations, electronic message systems on highways and other media. In most departments, the public information officer (PIO) is the communication cornerstone of this network and is the primary point of contact with the media.

> The National AMBER Alert Network Act of 2002 encouraged development of a nationwide alert system for abducted children. The Prosecutorial Remedies and Other Tools to end the Exploitation of Children Today (PROTECT) Act of 2003 provided $25 million to support state AMBER Alert plans.

According to AMBER Alert's home page, the program is a proven success and has helped rescue more than 540 children nationwide. The AMBER Alert system is being expanded to cell phone customers in Florida. Subscribers with phones capable of receiving text messages can register through their participating carriers' Web sites. The program is also being expanded to include tribal law enforcement agencies.

As AMBER Alert describes itself: "The goal of AMBER Alert is to recover abducted children before they meet physical harm. Statistics show that time itself is the enemy of an abducted child, because most children who are kidnapped and later found murdered die within the first three hours after being taken. AMBER Alert aims to turn that statistic around. Studies show that when ordinary citizens become the eyes and ears of law enforcement, precious lives can be saved" (*Bringing Abducted Children Home*, 2008).

A law enforcement agency can activate an AMBER Alert only if the circumstances surrounding a child's disappearance meet local or state criteria. The AMBER Alert criteria recommended by the U.S. Department of Justice are as follows:

1. Law enforcement officials must have a reasonable belief that an abduction of a child age 17 or younger has occurred.
2. Law enforcement officials must believe that the child is in imminent danger of serious bodily injury or death.
3. Enough descriptive information must exist about the victim and the abductor for law enforcement to issue an AMBER Alert.

4. The child's name and other critical data elements—including the child abduction (CA) and AMBER Alert (AA) flags—must have been entered into the NCIC system.

Law enforcement agencies should consider technologies to supplement the AMBER Alert program, such as e-mails to law enforcement agencies, a call to a cell phone, a fax blast, an Internet pop-up window or the A Child Is Missing system. Whatever system is used, however, it must be able to be implemented and accessed quickly, as time is of the essence in such cases. Remember: "When a child is going to be murdered during an abduction, 74 percent of the time, it happens within the first three hours" (Whitehead, 2008, p.85). Departments should consider establishing a child abduction response team.

A Child Abduction Response Team (CART)

Swager (2007, p.137) cites several reasons for having a CART: "Most abductions are short term and involve sexual assault; 44 percent of abducted children are killed in less than one hour of being abducted; 75 percent are killed within 3 hours of being abducted; 91 percent are killed within 24 hours of being abducted; 99 percent of those murdered are killed within 7 days of being abducted." Because of the time-sensitive nature of child abductions, the mission of a CART is to bring expert resources to child abduction cases quickly. Such a team typically consists of seasoned, experienced officers from around the region, each with a preplanned response related to that officer's field of expertise. Such teams might also include mounted patrol, all-terrain vehicles (ATVs), helicopters and K-9s—whatever resources are readily available.

Additional Resources Available

One valuable resource in missing children cases is the Missing and Exploited Children's Program. This program provides direct services through NCMEC, the Association of Missing and Exploited Children's Organizations (AMECO) and Health Opportunities for People Everywhere (Project HOPE). Services include the operation of a toll-free, 24-hour telephone hotline and a cyber-tipline to receive information about missing or exploited children, and the provision of mentoring and support programs for parents going through the trauma of having a missing child. The program also provides training and technical assistance to law enforcement, and it conducts research.

The Help Offering Parents Empowerment (Team HOPE) project, established in 1998, helps families of missing children handle the day-to-day issues of coping. Team

An AMBER Alert highway advisory sign engages the driving public as vital partners to law enforcement in the search for abducted children. Such advisories have met with considerable success in retrieving children alive.

© David R. Frazier/DanitaDelimont.com "Danita Delimont Photography"/Newscom

HOPE links victim-parents with experienced and trained parent volunteers who have gone through the experience of having a missing child. Because they speak from firsthand experience, these volunteers provide compassion, counsel and support in ways no other community agency can.

Having looked at the various incidents involving children as victims of crime, consider next their role in presenting a case in court. This discussion will be expanded in Chapter 21.

CHILDREN AS WITNESSES IN COURT

With the increase in criminal cases involving physical and sexual abuse of children, the problems associated with children providing testimony in court have increased proportionately. Court procedures and legal practices that benefit the child witness may not be balanced with the rights of the accused, and vice versa. To resolve some of these problems, the courts have changed a number of rules and procedures:

- Some courts give preference to these cases by placing them ahead of other cases on the docket.

- Some courts permit videotaping child interviews and then providing access to the tapes to numerous individuals to spare the child the added trauma of multiple interviews.

- Courts are limiting privileges for repeated medical and psychological examinations of children.

- To reduce the number of times the child must face the accused, the courts are allowing testimony concerning observations of the child by another person who is not a witness, allowing the child to remain in another room during the trial or using a videotape of the child's testimony as evidence.

- Some courts remove the accused from the courtroom during the child's testimony.

Many of these changes in rules and procedures are being challenged. Sixth Amendment issues arise concerning the right to confront witnesses. In *Coy v. Iowa* (1988), the Supreme Court ruled that a protective screen violated the Sixth Amendment, but Justice Sandra Day O'Connor opined that the *Coy* decision did not rule out using videotapes or closed-circuit television (CCTV). In *Maryland v. Craig* (1990), the Supreme Court carved out an exception to the Sixth Amendment by stating that alleged child abuse victims could testify by CCTV if the court was satisfied through testimony that face-to-face confrontation would traumatize the victim.

Despite some courts' stance that children should be made to testify in court as any other victim or witness, some studies have provided evidence that courtroom testimony is not always the best way to elicit accurate information from children. If children will be testifying in court, several courtroom preparation techniques might improve their testimony and place them more at ease, such as giving them a tour of the courtroom, making coloring or activity books depicting courtrooms and trials available or showing them videotapes about the court process.

PREVENTING CRIMES AGAINST CHILDREN

Child abusers can be of any race, age or occupation; they can be someone close or a complete stranger. Signs that a child may be at risk of victimization, particularly by online predators, include

- The child spends an inordinate amount of time online.
- The child minimizes a computer screen or turns the monitor off when a parent comes by.
- The child receives phone calls from unknown persons or gifts through the mail.
- The child experiences mood swings or behavioral changes.
- The child uses online accounts that belong to other people.
- The child hesitates or outright refuses to allow a parent to look at the contents of their cell phones or other digital hardware such as iPods, flash drives and so forth.

Often, children are unaware of the behaviors and activities they engage in that place them at risk. When given adequate information, children can avoid dangerous situations and better protect themselves against such predators.

> Crimes against children may be prevented by educating them about potential danger and by keeping the channels of communication open.

Digital technology is allowing police to become more effective in preventing and handling crimes against children. For example, some law enforcement departments are teaming up with schools and the community to create digital files of local children in a step toward discouraging child abduction. Such files contain digitized photographs, fingerprints and other personal information of area students and, because of their digital nature, can be dispatched within minutes to any law enforcement agency, business or other organization involved in the search for a missing child.

Technology Innovations

Mousetrap: Protecting America's Children from Online Predators is an interactive CD-ROM guide for parents, educators and children about the dangers online. Its three goals are to (1) educate adults on the basics of online activities, such as chat rooms and instant messaging, (2) raise awareness of adults on the tactics used by Internet predators and (3) provide adults with tools to prevent and detect possible exploitation. The program was developed by the Virginia Community Policing Institute and Blue Ridge Thunder, a group of cybercops who patrol the Internet for molesters and child pornographers.

Summary

Crimes against children include maltreatment (neglect and abuse), sexual exploitation (pornography and prostitution), trafficking and abduction. The four common types of maltreatment are neglect, physical abuse, emotional abuse and sexual abuse. Neglect is the most common form of child maltreatment and may be fatal. Child abuse has been identified as the biggest single cause of death of young children. Child abuse and neglect can result in serious and permanent physical, mental and emotional damage, as well as in future violent and criminal behavior.

Typically child abuse and neglect laws have three components: (1) criminal definitions and penalties, (2) a mandate to report suspected cases and (3) civil process for removing the child from the abusive or neglectful environment.

Challenges in investigating crimes against children include the need to protect the child from further harm, the possibility of parental involvement, the need to collaborate with other agencies, the difficulty of interviewing children and credibility concerns. If the possibility of present or continued danger to the child exists, the child must be removed into protective custody. When interviewing children, officers should consider the child's age, ability to describe what happened and the potential for retaliation by the suspect against a child who "tells." In most child abuse cases, children tell the truth to the best of their ability.

Most reports of child neglect or abuse are made by third parties such as teachers, physicians, neighbors, siblings or parents. Seldom does the victim report the offense.

Evidence in child neglect or abuse cases includes the surroundings, the home conditions, clothing, bruises or other body injuries, the medical examination report and other observations. Indicators of neglect or abuse may be physical or behavioral or both.

Investigators should be aware of three types of sex rings: solo, transition and syndicated. Certain cults are also involved in the sexual abuse of children.

Pedophiles' reactions to being discovered usually begin with complete denial and then progress to minimizing the acts, justifying the acts and blaming the victims. If all else fails, they may claim to be sick.

The Child Protection Act (1984) prohibits child pornography and greatly increases the penalties for adults who engage in it. Three law enforcement approaches have emerged as models to combat child sexual exploitation: special task forces, strike forces and law enforcement networks.

A special challenge in cases where a child is reported missing is to determine whether the child has run away or been abducted. The most frequent type of child abduction is parental abduction. The National AMBER Alert Network Act of 2002 encouraged development of a nationwide alert system for abducted children. The Prosecutorial Remedies and Other Tools to end the Exploitation of Children Today (PROTECT) Act of 2003 provided $25 million to support state AMBER Alert plans.

Crimes against children may be prevented by educating them about potential danger and by keeping the channels of communication open.

Checklist

Crimes against Children

- What statute has been violated, if any?
- What are the elements of the offense charged?
- Who initiated the crime?
- Are there witnesses to the offense?
- What evidence is needed to prove the elements of the offense charged?
- Is there physical evidence?
- Has physical evidence been submitted for laboratory examination?
- Who has been interviewed?
- Are written statements available?
- Would a polygraph be of any assistance in examining the victim? The suspect?
- Is there probable cause to obtain a search warrant?
- What items should you include in the search?

- Is the victim able to provide specific dates and times?
- Is the victim able to provide details of what happened?
- What physical and behavioral indicators are present in this case?
- Were photographs taken of the victim's injuries?
- Is the victim in danger of continued abuse?
- Is it necessary to remove the victim into protective custody?
- Has the local welfare agency been notified? Was there a joint investigation to avoid duplication of effort?
- Is there a file on known sexual offenders in the community?
- Is a child sexual abuse ring involved in the offense?
- Could the offense have been prevented? How?

Applications

A. A police officer receives an anonymous call reporting sexual abuse of a 10-year-old White female. The caller states that the abusers are the father and brother of the girl and provides all three names and their address. When the officer requests more details, the caller hangs up. You are assigned the case and initiate the investigation by contacting the alleged victim at school. She is reluctant to talk to you at first but eventually admits that both her father and brother have been having sex with her for almost a year. You then question the suspects and obtain written statements in which they admit the sexual abuse.

Questions

1. Should the investigation have been initiated on the basis of the anonymous caller?
2. What type of crime has been committed?
3. Was it appropriate to make the initial contact with the victim at her school?
4. Who should be present at the victim's initial interview?
5. What should be done with the victim after obtaining the facts?
6. What would be the basis for an affidavit for an arrest warrant?

B. A police officer receives an anonymous phone call stating that a child is being sexually assaulted at a specific address. The officer goes to the address—an apartment—and through an open door sees a child lying on the floor, apparently unconscious. The officer enters the apartment and, while checking the child for injuries, notices blood on the child's face and clothing. The child regains consciousness, and the officer asks, "Did your dad do this?" The child answers, "Yes." The officer then goes into another room and finds the father in bed, intoxicated. The officer rouses the father and places him under arrest.

Questions

1. Was the officer authorized to enter the apartment on the basis of the initial information?
2. Was the officer authorized to enter without a warrant?
3. Should the officer have asked whether the father had injured the child? If not, how should the question have been phrased?
4. Was an arrest of the father justified without a warrant?
5. What should be done with the victim?

C. A woman living in another state telephones the police department and identifies herself as the ex-wife of a man she believes is performing illegal sexual acts with the daughter of his present lover. The man resides in the police department's jurisdiction. The woman says the acts have been witnessed by her sons, who have been in the area visiting their father. The sons told her that the father goes into the bathroom and bedroom with his lover's 8-year-old daughter and closes the door. They also have seen the father making suggestive advances to the girl and taking her into the shower with him. The girl has told the woman's sons that the father does "naughty" things to her. The woman's sons are currently at home with her, but she is worried about the little girl.

Questions

1. Should an investigation be initiated based on this thirdhand information?
2. If the report is founded, what type of crime is being committed?
3. Who has jurisdiction to investigate?
4. What actions would be necessary in the non-initiating state?
5. Where should the initial contact with the alleged victim be made?

D. A reliable informant has told police that a man has been molesting children in his garage. Police establish a surveillance of the suspect and see him invite a juvenile into his car. They follow the car and see it pull into the driveway of the man's residence. The

man and the boy then go into the house. The officers follow and knock on the front door but receive no answer. They knock again and loudly state their purpose. Continuing to receive no answer, they enter the house through the unlocked front door, talk to the boy and based on what he says, arrest the suspect.

Questions

1. Did the officers violate the suspect's right to privacy and domestic security?
2. Does the emergency doctrine apply?
3. What should be done with the victim?
4. Was the arrest legal?

Note: In each of the preceding cases, the information is initially received not from the victim but from third parties. This is usually the case in child abuse offenses.

Discussion Questions

1. At what age does a child cease to be a minor in your state?
2. What is sexting, and why is it prevalent among juveniles?
3. What are some common physical and behavioral abuse indicators?
4. What evidence is commonly found in child sexual abuse cases?
5. What types of evidence are needed for establishing probable cause for a search warrant?
6. Who are suspects in child sexual abuse cases?
7. What are the types of sexual predators identified in this chapter? Do you think one type is worse or more dangerous than the other? Explain your reasoning.
8. What are some special difficulties in interviewing children? In having children testify in court?
9. What is being done in your community to prevent crimes against children?
10. Have any sex rings been exposed in your community? In your state?

Media Explorations

Internet

Select one of the following assignments to complete.

■ Search for the key phrase *National Institute of Justice.* Click on "NCJRS" (National Criminal Justice Research

Service). Click on "law enforcement." Click on "sort by Doc#." Search for one of the NCJ reference numbers from the list of References for this chapter. Outline the selection to share with the class.

■ Search for the acronym *OJJDP*. Select Office of Juvenile Justice Delinquency Prevention. Then click on "publications." Explore the publications available related to child abuse and neglect. Find one article to outline and share with the class.

■ Select one of the following key terms: *child abuse, child sexual abuse, hebephile, misoped, missing children, Munchausen by proxy syndrome, pedophile, sexual exploitation of children, sudden infant death syndrome.* Find one article relevant to crimes-against-children investigations to outline and share with the class.

ONLINE Database Gale Criminal Justice Database Assignments

The following assignments require access to Gale's Custom Journals Database for Emergency Services and Criminal Justice. Check with your instructor if you have questions about this.

■ Find the article "Interrogating Child Molesters" on the Gale Emergency Services Database. Read the article and identify the two categories of child molesters recognized by the FBI. Compare and contrast the differences and be prepared to discuss this in class.

■ Find the article "Sexting: Risky Actions and Overreactions" on the Gale Emergency Services Database. Read the article and write a one-page paper on sexting.

■ Find the article "The Best Kept Secret in Law Enforcement: A Look at the National Center for Missing and Exploited Children" on the Gale Emergency Services Database. Read and outline this article for in class discussion.

References

Adams, Stephen M.; Good, Matthew W.; and Defranco, Gina M. "Sudden Infant Death Syndrome." *American Family Physician*, Vol.79, No.10, May 15, 2009, pp.870–874.

"Adam Walsh Act Signed into Law." *The JRSA Forum*, December 2006, p.5.

Albanese, Jay. *Commercial Sexual Exploitation of Children: What Do We Know and What Do We Do about It?* Washington, DC: National Institute of Justice, December 2007.

Bringing Abducted Children Home. May 2008. Accessed May 25, 2008. http://www.ncjrs.gov/html/ojjdp/amberalert/000712

Child Abuse and Neglect Fatalities: Statistics and Interventions. Washington, DC: National Clearinghouse on Child Abuse and Neglect Information, 2008.

"Child Abuse Issues." Gaithersburg, MD: Osteogenesis Imperfecta Foundation, no date. Accessed June 13, 2011. http://www.oif.org/site/DocServer/_Child_Abuse__Child_Abuse_Issues.pdf?docID=7188

"Child Abuse or Osteogenesis Imperfecta?" Gaithersburg, MD: Osteogenesis Imperfecta Foundation, no date. Accessed June 13, 2011. http://www.oif.org/site/DocServer/_Child_Abuse__Child_Abuse_or_Ostegenesis_Imperfecta.pdf?docID=7189

"Child Maltreatment: Risk and Protective Factors." Atlanta, GA: Centers for Disease Control and Prevention, May 10, 2011. Accessed June 13, 2011. http://www.cdc.gov/ViolencePrevention/childmaltreatment/riskprotectivefactors.html

Child Maltreatment 2009. Washington, DC: U.S. Department of Health and Human Services; Administration for Children and Families; Administration on Children, Youth and Families; Children's Bureau, 2010. Accessed June 11, 2011. http://www.acf.hhs.gov/programs/cb/stats_research/index.htm#can

Child Prostitution. Web site. Summer 2008. Accessed May 28, 2008. http://gvnet.com/childprostitution/index.html

Collins, Michelle K. "Child Pornography: A Closer Look." *The Police Chief*, March 2007, pp.40–47.

"Crime Clock." Washington, DC: Office for Victims of Crime, 2009. Accessed May 29, 2011. http://ovc.ncjrs.gov/gallery/posters/pdfs/Crime_Clock.pdf

"Department of Justice Marks 11th Anniversary of AMBER Alert." *OJJDP News @ a Glance*, January/February 2007, p.1.

A Family Resource Guide on International Parental Kidnapping. Washington, DC: Office of Juvenile Justice and Delinquency Prevention, January 2007. (NCJ 215476)

"Federal Child Exploitation Cases Nearly Quadrupled in 10 Years." *Criminal Justice Newsletter*, January 2, 2008, pp.6–7.

Finkelhor, David; Turner, Heather; Ormrod, Richard; Hamby, Sherry; and Kracke, Kristen. *Children's Exposure to Violence: A Comprehensive National Survey*. Washington, DC: Office of Juvenile Justice and Delinquency Prevention, October 2009. (NCJ 227744)

Geraghty, Michael. "The Technical Aspects of Computer-Facilitated Crimes against Children." *The Police Chief*, March 2007, pp.30–33.

Human Trafficking of Children in the United States. Washington, DC: Office of Safe and Drug-Free Schools, August 6, 2007.

Innocent Images National Initiative: Online Child Pornography/Child Sexual Exploitation Investigations. Washington, DC: Federal Bureau of Investigation, 2007. Accessed September 30, 2008. http://www.fbi.gov/stats-services/publications/innocent-images-1

"Internet Child Pornography Targeted by Senate Measure." *Criminal Justice Newsletter*, July 2, 2007, p.7.

Juvenile Offenders and Victims: 2006 National Report. Washington, DC: Office of Juvenile Justice Delinquency Prevention, 2006.

Karmen, Andrew. *Crime Victims: An Introduction to Victimology*, 5th ed. Belmont, CA: Wadsworth Publishing Company, 2007.

McNulty, Paul J. "Project Safe Childhood." *The Police Chief*, March 2007, pp.36–39.

"Munchausen Syndrome by Proxy." Bethesda, MD: National Institutes of Health, MedlinePlus Medical Encyclopedia. Updated February 21, 2011. Accessed June 13, 2011. http://www.nlm.nih.gov/medlineplus/ency/article/001555.htm

Steidel, Stephen E., editor. *Missing and Abducted Children: A Law Enforcement Guide to Case Investigation and Program Management*, 3rd ed. Alexandria, VA: National Center for Missing and Exploited Children, May 2006.

Stevens, Serita. "Protecting the Children." *Law Enforcement Technology*, March 2008, pp.30–36.

"Sudden Infant Death Syndrome." Bethesda, MD: PubMed Health Online, Reviewed August 2, 2009. Accessed June 13, 2011. http://www.ncbi.nlm.nih.gov/pubmedhealth/PMH0002533/

Swager, Brent. "Tampa's Child Abduction Response Team." *Law and Order*, September 2007, pp.134–138.

Teague, Rosie; Mazerolle, Paul; Legosz, Margot; and Sanderson, Jennifer. "Linking Childhood Exposure to Physical Abuse and Adult Offending." *Justice Quarterly*, June 2008, pp.313–348.

Walsh, Bill. *Investigating Child Fatalities*. Washington, DC: Office of Juvenile Justice and Delinquency Prevention, August 2005.

Walsh, Wendy A.; Jones, Lisa M.; Cross, Theodore P.; and Lippert, Tonya. "Prosecuting Child Sexual Abuse: The Importance of Evidence Types." *Crime and Delinquency*, Vol.56, No.3, July 2010, pp.436–454.

Whitehead, Christy. "Responding to an Abducted Child." *Law and Order*, January 2008, pp.85–89.

Yun, Ilhong; Ball, Jeremy D.; and Lim, Hyeyoung. "Disentangling the Relationship between Child Maltreatment and Violent Delinquency: Using a Nationally Representative Sample." *Journal of Interpersonal Violence*, Vol.26, No.1, January 2011, pp.88–110.

Cases Cited

Coy v. Iowa, 487 U.S. 1012 (1988)
Ingraham v. Wright, 430 U.S. 651 (1977)
Maryland v. Craig, 497 U.S. 836 (1990)
People v. Green, 155 Mich. 524, 532, 119 N.W. 1087 (1909)
Prince v. Massachusetts, 321 U.S. 158 (1944)
Santosky v. Kramer, 455 U.S. 745 (1982)
Worthen v. State, 42 Md. App. 20, 399 A.2d 272 (1979)

CHAPTER 12
Robbery

© AP Images/Little Rock Police Department

Outline

Can You Define?

bait money

carjacking

dye pack

robbery

Stockholm syndrome

 Do You Know?

- How robbery is defined?
- How robberies are classified?
- What home invaders are?
- What carjacking is?
- In what types of robbery the FBI and state officials become involved?
- What the elements of the crime of robbery are?
- What factors to consider in responding to a robbery-in-progress call?
- What special challenges are posed by a robbery investigation?
- How to prove each element of robbery?
- What descriptive information is needed to identify suspects and vehicles?
- What modus operandi information to obtain in a robbery case?
- What physical evidence can link a suspect with a robbery?

R obbery has plagued the human race throughout history. During the 1930s, John Dillinger, America's number-one desperado, captured the attention of citizens and law enforcement officers alike. This notorious bank robber's tools of the trade were a Thompson submachine gun and a revolver. Although admired by many for his daring and cast as a folk hero, Dillinger gunned down 10 men. "Pretty Boy" Floyd began his criminal career by robbing a local post office of $350 in pennies. Like Dillinger, he also killed 10 people. Bonnie Parker and Clyde Barrow's murder and robbery spree through Missouri, Texas and Oklahoma is also legendary.

On February 28, 1997, two heavily armed men wearing full body armor robbed a branch of the Bank of America in North Hollywood, California, and, as they fled the building, were met by dozens of Los Angeles Police Department officers. The ensuing gun battle, which some likened to a war zone, lasted 44 minutes and ended with injuries to 11 officers and 7 civilians and the deaths of both suspects.

The preceding are vivid examples of the violent nature of many robberies. Robbery is one of the three most violent crimes against the person. Only homicide and rape are considered more traumatic to a victim. According to the FBI's Uniform Crime Reports (UCR), there were an estimated 408,217 robberies in the nation in 2009, an 8.0 percent decrease from the 2008 estimate (*Crime in the United States 2009*, 2010). Data from the National Crime Victimization Survey (NCVS) report a higher incidence of robberies—533,790 in 2009, at a rate of 2.1 per 1,000 households (Truman and Rand, 2010). Such differences underscore the need to recognize how crime data are gathered and to view such statistics with caution.

Robbery accounted for 31.0 percent of all violent crimes in 2009. The clearance rate for robbery was 28.2 percent in 2009 (*Crime in the United States 2009*, 2010). Other facts about robbery reported in *Crime in the United States 2009* include

- By location type, most robberies (42.8 percent) were committed on streets or highways (see Figure 12.1).
- The average dollar value of property stolen per robbery offense was

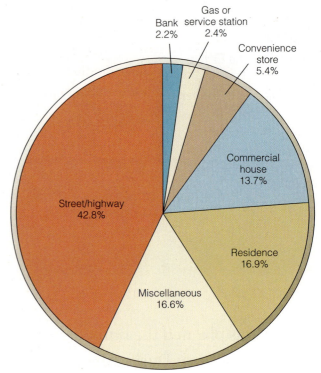

FIGURE 12.1
Robbery locations, percent distribution*, 2009.
* Due to rounding, the percentages may not add to 100.0.
Source: http://www2.fbi.gov/ucr/cius2009/offenses/violent_crime/robbery.html

$1,244. By location type, bank robbery had the highest average dollar value taken—$4,029 per offense.

- An estimated $508 million in losses were attributed to robberies during 2009.
- Firearms were used in 42.6 percent of robberies for which the UCR program received data.

This crime poses a definite hazard to law enforcement officers: "According to the FBI, the number-one reason why officers are killed and/or assaulted while off duty is intervening in or being the victim of a robbery or robbery attempt" (Rayburn, 2007, p.56).

ROBBERY: AN OVERVIEW

Robbery takes many forms, from the daring exploits of criminals such as Dillinger to purse snatching and muggings. Whatever the form, the potential for violence exists.

Robbery is the felonious taking of another's property, either directly from the person or in that person's presence, through force or intimidation.

To compel compliance from the victim, most robbers carry a weapon or other threatening item and make an *oral demand* for the desired money or property. The overt display of a weapon, or an indication by the robber that a weapon is concealed in a jacket pocket, usually keeps the victim from trying to fight off the robber. Therefore, little direct personal contact occurs between the robber and the victim, which reduces the probability of physical evidence remaining at the crime scene.

Some robbers present a *note* rather than speaking. The robber may or may not ask for the note to be returned. It is important evidence if left behind.

Despite the inherent danger to the victim during a robbery, most robberies do not result in personal injury, the theory being that the threat of force or the presence of a weapon reduces the likelihood of the victim resisting. Confronted with threatening statements, a threatening note or a visible weapon, most robbery victims obey the robber's demands. Sometimes, however, a violent physical act is performed against the victim early in the robbery, either by original intent or because of unexpected circumstances or resistance. Such cases involve additional charges of aggravated assault or, in the case of death, murder. Violence against the victim also occurs in muggings and purse snatchings in which the victim is struck with a weapon, club or the fists or is knocked down. Older people are often injured by the fall resulting from such violent acts. Any such violent contact increases the probability of hair, fibers, scratches or other evidence being found on the victim or the suspect. According to the UCR, the use of violence during robberies has increased during the past 10 years, but such violence is not nearly as frequent as the public might expect.

Hostages are held in some robberies and are used as collateral or protection by robbers. If materials are used to restrain hostages, such as rope or tape, such items may provide useful evidence to investigators. Presence of such items can also provide modus operandi (MO) information about the suspect and be used to link separate robberies to the same offender. Bank robberies and hostage situations are discussed later in this chapter.

Robbers use various ruses to get themselves into position for the crime. They may loiter, pose as salespeople or feign business, watching for an opportune moment to make their demands. Once the opportunity presents itself, robbers act quickly and decisively. Sometimes, however, their actions before the robbery give them away. One such case involved a robber who was captured by two FBI agents just as the teller was handing over the money. The robber was unaware that the FBI agents had been watching him since he'd entered the bank. His nervous actions had attracted their attention, even though they were in the bank on other business at the time.

Most robberies are committed by men. Robbers are usually serial criminals and may commit 15 to 25 robberies or more before being apprehended. People who commit robberies are often egotistical braggarts, prone to boasting of their crimes. Because of this, informants can provide excellent leads in robbery cases.

The most frequent victims of robberies are drug houses, liquor stores, fast-food establishments, jewelry stores, convenience stores, motels, gambling houses and private residences. The elderly are frequently robbery victims of purse snatchings and snatches of packages committed by amateurs or juveniles.

Consider several characteristics typical of robberies:

- They are committed by strangers rather than acquaintances.

- They are committed with the use of stolen cars, stolen motor-vehicle license plates or both.

- They are committed by two or more people working together.

- The offender lives within 100 miles of the robbery.

- Robberies committed by a lone perpetrator tend to involve lone victims and are apt to be crimes of opportunity (spur of the moment).

- Youths committing robberies tend to operate in groups and to use strong-arm tactics more frequently than do adults.

- Less physical evidence is normally found after robberies than in other violent crimes.

- They take much less time than other crimes.

- Middle-aged and older people tend to be the victims.

In confrontational robberies, regardless of the offender's weapon, victims who defend themselves in some way are less likely to lose property than are victims who take no actions. However, victims who defend themselves against armed offenders are more likely to be injured than are those who take no actions during the crime.

CLASSIFICATION

Robberies are classified into four categories, each committed by different types of people using different techniques.

> Robberies are classified as residential, commercial, street or vehicle driver.

Residential Robberies

Residential robberies include those that occur in hotel and motel rooms, garages, elevators and private homes. These robberies are less frequent than the other types but are dangerous and traumatic because they tend to involve entire families.

Entrance is frequently gained by knocking on the door and then forcing entrance when the occupant appears. Most residential robberies occur in the early evening when people are apt to be home. Victims are frequently bound and gagged or even tortured as the robber attempts to learn the location of valuables. In some cases, people are robbed because they arrive home to discover a burglary in progress. The burglar is thus "forced" to become a robber.

Hotel, motel, garage or elevator robberies are carried out rapidly and frequently involve injury. Information from employees that a person has a large amount of jewelry or money determines the victim for some robberies.

A type of residential robber challenging police departments across the country is the *home invader*. Home invaders usually target a resident, not a residence—often women, senior citizens or drug dealers.

> Home invaders are typically young Asian gang members who travel across the country robbing Asian families, especially Asian business owners.

Home invaders know that many Asian families distrust banks and keep large amounts of cash and jewelry in their homes. Home-invading robberies are increasing in rural areas.

Commercial Robberies

Convenience stores, loan companies, jewelry stores, liquor stores, gasoline or service stations and bars are especially susceptible to robbery. Drugstores are apt to be targets of robberies to obtain narcotics as well as cash. According to Chronister et al. (2009, p.36), "Robberies are the most frequent cause of work-related homicide, and one of the leading causes of violent injury among workers, especially in the retail industry.... Small retail businesses, many of them independently owned, have the highest risk for robbery and homicide."

Commercial robberies occur most frequently toward the end of the week between 6 P.M. and 4 A.M. Stores with poor visibility from the street and few employees on duty are the most likely targets. Many stores now keep only a limited amount of cash on hand during high-risk times. Stores also attempt to deter robbers by using surveillance cameras, alarm systems, guards and guard dogs.

Many commercial robberies are committed by individuals with criminal records; therefore, their MOs should be compared with those of past robberies. Because of the offenders' experience, commercial robberies are usually better planned than street or vehicle-driver robberies are.

Many robbers of convenience stores are on drugs or rob to pay for drugs, and the majority of convenience store robbers report being under the influence of an intoxicant when they committed their crime (Petrocelli, 2008b). Convenience stores that are robbed once are likely to be robbed again. In fact, about 8 percent of convenience stores account for more than 50 percent of these robberies. The Occupational Health and Safety Administration (OSHA) lists these recommendations for deterring workplace violence in late-night retail establishments:

- Keep the cash-register cash balance low.
- Provide good lighting outside and inside the store.
- Elevate the cash-register area so the clerk has better viewing ability and is in sight of passersby. (*Recommendations for Workplace Violence Prevention Programs*, 2009)

This resource also provides suggestions for post-incident response.

Street Robberies

Street robberies are most frequently committed on public streets and sidewalks and in alleys and parking lots, during the evening or nighttime and often in dimly lit areas. Most are committed with a weapon, but some are strong-arm robberies, in which physical force is the weapon. Both the victim and the robber are usually on foot.

Speed and surprise typify street robberies, which are often crimes of opportunity with little or no advance planning. Because such robberies happen so fast, the victim is often unable to identify the robber. Sometimes the victim is approached from behind and never sees the attacker. Because most street robberies yield little money, the robber often commits several robberies in one night.

In areas with large influxes of diverse groups of immigrants, especially undocumented ones, special problems occur. In Yonkers, New York, for example, numerous illegal immigrants from Mexico, Central America and South America are preyed upon by robbers. Because of their illegal status, few of these immigrants have Social Security numbers. Without these, they are unable to open bank accounts or be paid by check. Therefore, they tend to carry large amounts of cash, sometimes their entire savings. Compounding the problem of investigating such crimes are the language barrier, fear and mistrust of police, fear of deportation and lack of understanding of the justice system.

Vehicle-Driver Robberies

Drivers of taxis, buses, trucks, delivery and messenger vehicles, armored trucks and personal cars are frequent targets of robbers. In fact, taxi drivers are considered to have one of the most dangerous professions in the country (Petrocelli, 2007a). Taxi drivers are vulnerable because they are often alone while cruising for fares, work early mornings and late nights when fewer witnesses are likely to be present to assist or identify attackers, are dispatched to addresses in high-crime locations and may carry a lot of cash. Some taxi companies have taken preventive steps such as placing protective shields between the passenger and driver and reducing the amount of cash that drivers carry. Many cabs are now equipped with credit card scanners to further limit the amount of cash onboard. In an effort to reduce the amount of cash mass transit drivers possess, buses in many cities require passengers to have the exact change or to purchase tokens or passes at a central hub or satellite transit stations. Delivery vehicle drivers may be robbed of their merchandise as they arrive for a delivery, or the robbers may wait until after the delivery and take the cash.

Armored-car robberies are of special concern because they are usually well planned by professional, heavily armed robbers and involve large amounts of money. According to the FBI, in 2010 there were 48 armored carrier incidents with more than $12.6 million in loot taken, most in the form of cash. A little more than 12 percent of the loot was recovered (*Bank Crime Statistics*, 2011). A firearm was used in 39 of the 48 incidents, and acts of violence were reported in 21 of the 48 incidents, resulting in 18 injuries, one death of a guard and one person taken hostage. One approach to this problem is to develop an intelligence network between the police department and the armored-car industry.

Drivers of personal cars are often approached in parking lots or while stopped at red lights in less-traveled areas. These robberies are generally committed by teenagers. Drivers who pick up hitchhikers leave themselves open to robbery, to assault and to auto theft. Some robbers force people off roads or set up fake accidents or injuries to lure motorists into stopping. A combination of street and vehicle-driver robbery that has increased drastically over the past few years is carjacking.

Carjacking

Although not a "new" crime, carjacking had been included in the general category of "auto theft" before the 1990s and has since then been recognized as a growing threat. Carjackings often occur at gas stations, automatic teller machines (ATMs), car washes, parking lots, shopping

Sometimes a robber will stage an auto accident or other incident to gain access to a victim. Here, a man rear-ended a car stopped at a red light and used the incident as an excuse to approach the car and engage its occupants. Her guard down, the passenger allows the attacker to get close enough to carry out a brutal assault before taking her purse and other valuables. Occasionally, this tactic is used by carjackers to gain possession of their targeted vehicle.
© Eleanor Bentall/CORBIS

centers, convenience stores, restaurants, mass transit stations and intersections requiring drivers to come to a stop.

> **Carjacking**, a category of robbery, is the taking of a motor vehicle by force or threat of force. The FBI may investigate the crime.

The force may consist of use of a handgun, simulated handgun, club, machete, axe, knife or fists. The federal carjacking statute provides that a person possessing a firearm who takes a motor vehicle from the person or presence of another by force and violence or by intimidation shall (1) be imprisoned not more than 15 years; (2) if serious bodily injury results, be imprisoned not more than 25 years; and (3) if death results, be imprisoned for any number of years up to life.

Nearly every major city has experienced armed carjacking offenses in sufficiently substantial numbers that the UCR may soon be required to use carjacking as a designation rather than report these crimes without uniformity as armed robbery, auto theft or some other offense.

Carjackers use many ruses to engage a victim. Some stage accidents. Others wait for their victims at workplace parking lots or residential driveways. Carjackings have resulted in car thefts, injuries and deaths. Initially, the more expensive vehicles were involved, but this trend now covers all types of motor vehicles. The stolen vehicle is then used as in the conventional crime of vehicle theft: for resale, resale of parts, joyriding or use in committing another crime.

The motivation for carjacking is not clear because the vehicles are taken under so many different circumstances and for so many different reasons. One theory for the sudden increase is that the increased use of alarms and protective devices on vehicles, especially on more expensive ones, makes it more difficult to steal a vehicle by traditional means. Car operators are easy prey compared with convenience stores or other commercial establishments that may have surveillance cameras and other security measures in effect. Another theory suggests that status is involved: a criminal who carjacks a vehicle achieves higher status in the criminal subculture than does one who steals it in the conventional manner. And some police officers believe that the crime is becoming a fad among certain groups of young people as a way to enhance their image with their cohorts.

Carjackings have become a serious problem for police, who investigate them in the same way as other armed robberies. Publication of prevention techniques has become standard policy for police agencies in an effort to prevent property losses, injuries and deaths. Some agencies use decoys in an effort to apprehend carjackers. The U.S. Department of State ("Carjacking—Don't Be a Victim," 2002) provides this set of guidelines to those reporting a carjacking:

- Describe the event. What time of day did it occur? Where did it happen? How did it happen? Who was involved?

- Describe the attacker(s). Without staring, try to note height, weight, scars or other marks, hair and eye color, the presence of facial hair, build (slender, large) and complexion (dark, fair).

- Describe the attacker's vehicle. If possible, get the vehicle license number, color, make, model and year, as well as any marks (scratches, dents, damage) and personal decorations (stickers, colored wheels).

Crime scene investigators confer in the Bank of Texas parking lot where two gunmen attempted to rob an armored car in the south Oak Cliff section of Dallas. A gun battle ensued between the guards and the alleged robbers, wounding a guard, a suspect and a bank customer.
© AP Images/LM Otero

■ The golden rule for descriptions is to give only that information you absolutely remember. If you are not sure, don't guess!

In October 1992 Congress passed, and President George H. W. Bush signed, the Anti-Car Theft Act, making armed carjacking a federal offense. Under this law, automakers must engrave a 17-digit vehicle identification number on 24 parts of every new car.

In addition to knowing how robberies are generally classified, investigators must be familiar with the elements of the crime of robbery in their particular jurisdictions.

Bank Robbery

"Robbery in progress!" The call could mean a possible shootout or a hostage situation. Bank robbery is both a federal and a state offense. U.S. Code Title 18, Section 2113, defines the elements of the federal crime of bank robbery. This statute applies to robbery, burglary or larceny from any member bank of the Federal Reserve system, any bank insured by the Federal Deposit Insurance Corporation (FDIC), any bank organized and operated under the laws of the United States, any federal savings and loan association or any federal credit union.

> Bank robberies are within the jurisdictions of the FBI, the state and the community in which the crime occurred and are jointly investigated.

Most banks have surveillance cameras that might catch a robbery on tape. However, the video quality is often substandard and can be rendered useless by improper placement of equipment that places barriers between the offender and the camera or provides inadequate lighting (Petrocelli, 2008a).

Technology Innovations

Hudson (2007, p.115) describes how searchable video surveillance helps catch robbers.

While surveillance systems have traditionally just recorded and stored footage—requiring investigators to sift through hour after hour of real-time video to find the event or suspect—new products have incorporated analytical tools like facial recognition and advanced video searching capabilities. Using technology similar to what made millions of Internet pages searchable, these systems make thousands of hours of video from geographically distributed locations searchable in minutes. . . .

In an example of using searchable surveillance to investigate a crime, a bank robber produces a demand note. The robber, like 80 percent of all bank robbers, is low-key, preferring to blend in as a typical customer. The bank's cameras capture an image of his face. As soon as the bank's investigator is notified of the robbery, he can pull up the video remotely in seconds and e-mail it to the FBI and local law enforcement agency. He can query all branches for the same suspect and discover that the suspect has been casing another branch several times in a nearby town.

Because of the large sums of money involved, bank robberies are committed by rank amateurs as well as by habitual criminals. Amateurs are usually more dangerous because they are not as familiar with weapons and often are nervous and fearful. Weisel (2007, p.14) points out,

To a great extent, robbers can be classified as amateur or professional based on known characteristics of the robbery—the number of offenders, use of weapons and disguises, efforts to defeat security, timing of the robbery, target selection, and means of getaway.

Bank robberies by amateurs are less successful: nearly one-third of all bank robberies by unarmed solitary offenders fail. Takeover robberies—those involving multiple armed offenders—are less common but more lucrative: losses in takeover robberies are 10 times greater than average. . . .

Amateur bank robbers seek different targets from professionals and commit their offenses at different times. Solitary offenders tend to rob banks around midday, when branches are full of customers; professionals, on the other hand, prefer to operate when there are fewer customers, such as at opening time, which increases their control of the crime scene.

Table 12.1 summarizes the differences between the amateur and the professional bank robber.

Bank robbers often act alone inside the bank, but most have a getaway car with lookouts posted nearby. These individuals pose additional problems for the approaching police. The robbery car often has stolen plates or is itself stolen. Robbers use this "hot" car to leave the robbery scene and to transport them and their loot to a "cold" car left a distance from the robbery. Even if only one robber has been reported at the scene, an armed accomplice may be nearby.

The number of bank robberies has increased with the number of branch banks, many of which are housed in

TABLE 12.1 **Distinguishing Professional and Amateur Bank Robbers***

	Professional	**Amateur**
Offenders	Multiple offenders with division of labor Shows evidence of planning May be older Prior bank robbery convictions Travels further to rob banks	Solitary offender Drug or alcohol use likely No prior bank crime Lives near bank target
Violence	Aggressive takeover, with loud verbal demands Visible weapons, especially guns Intimidation, physical or verbal threats	Note passed to teller or simple verbal demand Waits in line No weapon
Defeat Security	Uses a disguise Disables or obscures surveillance cameras Demands that dye packs be left out, alarms not be activated or police not be called	
Robbery Success	Hits multiple teller windows Larger amounts stolen Lower percentage of money recovered More successful robberies Fewer cases directly cleared Longer time from offense to case clearance	Single teller window victimized Lower amounts stolen Higher percentage of money recovered More failed robberies Shorter time from offense to case clearance, including more same-day arrests Direct case clearance more likely
Robbery Timing	Targets banks when few customers are present, such as at opening time Targets banks early in the week	Targets banks when numerous customers are present, such as around midday Targets banks near closing or on Friday
Target Selection	Previous robbery Busy road near intersection Multidirectional traffic Corner locations, multiple vehicle exits	Previous robbery Heavy pedestrian traffic or adjacent to dense multifamily residences Parcels without barriers Parcels with egress obscured
Getaway	Via car	On foot or bicycle

* This table is not prescriptive because it generalizes about bank robberies. Some factors will not fit your local pattern, and there will be exceptions that fit no category.

The reader is encouraged to use the table as a starting point to separate and categorize local robberies.

Source: Deborah Lamm Weisel. *The Problem of Bank Robbery.* Washington, DC: Office of Community Oriented Policing Services, 2007.

storefront offices and outlying shopping centers, thus providing quick entrance to and exit from the robbery scene.

Adding clerks is not necessarily a deterrent because a person with a gun has the advantage regardless of the number of clerks. Adding bulletproof glass around the cashier may increase the incidence of hostage taking. This problem has been reduced in some banks by enclosing and securing the bank's administrative areas.

Other deterrents to bank robberies involve the use of bait money and dye packs, required by federal banking regulations for federally insured financial institutions. **Bait money** is U.S. currency with recorded serial numbers placed at each teller position. A **dye pack** is a bundle of currency containing a colored dye and tear gas.

Taken during a robbery, it is activated when the robber crosses an electromagnetic field at the facility's exit, releasing the brightly colored dye that stains the money and emits a cloud of colored smoke.

Robberies at ATMs

Robberies at ATMs are also of concern. Since their introduction in the United States during the late 1960s, ATMs have become a staple of the banking industry, facilitating billions of dollars in transactions every year (Petrocelli, 2007b, p.22). Brazen robbers wait nearby for people either on foot or in their vehicles to approach the ATM for a withdrawal. These types of robberies tend to occur after dark in poorly lit areas but can occur any time of the day. The most common ATM robbery pattern involves a lone, armed offender against a lone victim.

ELEMENTS OF THE CRIME: ROBBERY

Having looked at the various forms of robbery, consider now the elements that must be present and proven in any type of robbery. State statutes define *robbery* precisely. Although the general public tends to use the term *robbery* interchangeably with *burglary, larceny* and *theft*, the specific elements of robbery clearly distinguish it from these offenses. A businessman might say that his store was robbed when, in fact, it was burglarized. A woman may have money taken from her purse at work while she is busy waiting on customers and say that she was robbed when, legally, the crime was larceny. Such thefts are not robbery because the necessary elements are not present.

Some states have only one degree of robbery. Others have both simple and aggravated robbery. Still others have robbery in the first, second and third degree. However, in most state statutes common elements exist.

The elements of the crime of robbery are
- the wrongful taking of personal property,
- from the person or in the person's presence,
- against the person's will by force or threat of force.

Wrongful Taking of Personal Property

Various statutes use phrases such as *unlawful taking, felonious taking* and *knowing he is not entitled thereto*. Intent is an element of the crime in some, but not all, states. To take "wrongfully," the robber must have no legal right to the property. Moreover, property must be *personal property*, as distinguished from real property.

From the Person or in the Presence of the Person

In most cases, *in the presence of a person* means that the victim sees the robber take the property. This is not always the case, however, because the victim may be locked in a separate room. For example, robbers often take victims to a separate room such as a restroom or a bank vault while they search for the desired items or cash. Such actions do not remove the crime "from the presence of the person"

as long as the separation from the property is the direct result of force or threats of force used by the robber.

Against the Person's Will by Use of Force or Threat of Force

This essential element clearly separates robbery from burglary and larceny. As noted, most robberies are committed with a weapon or other dangerous device or by indicating that one is present. The force or threat is generally sufficient to deter resistance. It can be immediate or threatened in the future. It can be directed at the victim, the victim's family or a person who is with the victim.

RESPONDING TO A ROBBERY-IN-PROGRESS CALL

A robbery-in-progress call involves an all-units response, with units close to the scene going there directly while other units cover the area near the scene, looking for a possible getaway vehicle. Other cars go to checkpoints such as bridges, converging highways, freeway entry and exit ramps, dead-end streets and alleys.

Officers should observe all vehicles as they approach a robbery scene. Whether to use red lights and sirens depends on the information received from dispatch. It is often best to arrive quietly to prevent the taking of hostages. If shooting is occurring, using lights and siren may cause the robber to leave before police arrive.

Police response time can be reduced if the robbed business or residence has an alarm system connected to the police department or a private alarm agency. Silent alarms can provide an early response, and audible alarms sometimes prevent a robbery. The "lag-time"—that is, the elapsed time between the commission of a robbery and the time the police are notified—is usually much longer than the actual police response time.

When responding to a robbery-in-progress call,
- Proceed as rapidly as possible, but use extreme caution.
- Assume that the robber is at the scene, unless otherwise advised.
- Be prepared for gunfire.
- Look for and immobilize any getaway vehicle you discover.
- Avoid a hostage situation if possible.
- Make an immediate arrest if the suspect is at the scene.

Officers should guard against the dangers inherent in stereotyping when responding to robberies in progress. For example, an officer responding to a robbery alarm at a convenience store, expecting to see a young male running from the scene, sees a young female walking calmly from the store, and after she passes the officer (who is ignoring her), she shoots him in the back because she was the robber. (This scenario could apply to an elderly person, a disabled person or other assumed nonsuspect.)

Upon arrival at a robbery scene, attempt to locate any vehicle that the suspects might use, even if you have no description of it. It will probably be within a block of the crime scene, and its engine may be running. It generally has a person in it (the "wheelman," or lookout) waiting for the robber to return. If the vehicle is identified through prior information and is empty, immobilize it by removing the distributor cap or letting the air out of a tire. If a cohort is waiting in the car, arrest the person and then immobilize the vehicle.

If police could check every license plate within the containment circle to see whether it was on a stolen car, and then accumulate that information, they might identify serial robbers.

Technology Innovations

Automatic license plate recognition (ALPR) can be of great assistance in identifying a stolen vehicle that might be serving as a getaway car (Molnar, 2007, pp.20–23):

> While the technology may sound like something out of Star Wars, the reality is that automatic license plate recognition (ALPR) is already a reality in patrol cars across the country, and it's proving very effective in apprehending all types of criminals.
>
> According to PlateScan [a leader in ALPR], ALPR technology was developed in response to a number of high-profile terrorist attacks in the UK in the early 1990s. The system was designed to detect use of vehicle-borne improvised explosive devices before they reached their intended targets. . . . The result was a virtual ring of steel around cities like London, with many criminals detected and apprehended.
>
> As the system reads a license plate, it compares the plate to the database. If it makes a hit, it alerts the operator. . . .The addition of a separate color camera allows the capture of vehicle description, make, model, color, damage, unique characteristics, etc. to the database. In other words, you get the complete picture of the vehicle, not just the plate.

Decide whether to enter the robbery location immediately or to wait until sufficient personnel are in position. Department policy determines whether it is an immediate or a timed response. Too early an entry increases the chances of a hostage situation or of having to use weapons. The general rule is to avoid a confrontation if it will create a worse situation than the robbery itself.

If you arrive at the robbery scene and find a suspect there with the victim, surround the building and order the suspect to come out. Get other people in the area to leave because of possible gunfire. Know the operational limitations imposed by the number of officers and the amount of equipment available at the scene. Take advantage of vehicles and buildings in the area for cover.

Because the robber is committing a violent crime and is usually armed, expect that the robber may use a weapon against the police and that a hostage may be taken.

HOSTAGE SITUATIONS

Massock (2008, p. 66) explains, "Crisis negotiation is a complex discipline. Negotiating with an armed barricaded person holding hostages can be a prolonged and stressful event." The priorities in a hostage situation are to (1) preserve life, (2) apprehend the hostage taker and (3) recover or protect property. Accomplishing these priorities requires specialized training in hostage situations. It also requires that the media be dealt with effectively.

In general, direct assault should be considered only if there has already been a killing or if further negotiations would be useless. Hostage situations may last for less than an hour or for more than 40 hours; the average length is approximately 12 hours.

However, this approach may result in conflict within the department between special weapons and tactics (SWAT) teams and crisis negotiation teams (CNTs). SWAT teams are action oriented, whereas CNTs are communication oriented. Both types of team have a common goal but use a different approach. In reality, to successfully resolve a hostage situation, both teams must often work together. A successful hostage-incident outcome is not possible without a well-coordinated strategy.

Negotiators' biggest task is to convince subjects that no harm will come to them if they cooperate with the negotiation: "Are SWAT guys with big guns out there?" the subject may be very anxious to know. Assure the subject, "Sure, but they do what I tell them."

The need for negotiation is based on the principle that the main priority is to preserve life—that of the hostages or the hostage takers, as well as of police or innocent bystanders. SWAT teams or expert sharpshooters are often

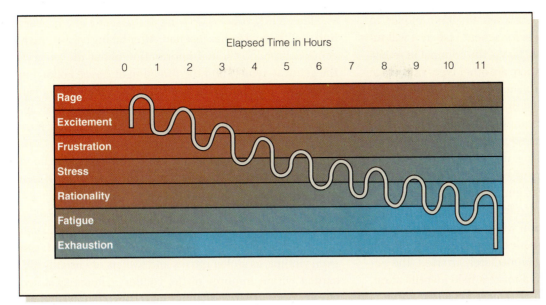

FIGURE 12.2
Timeline pattern for emotions of hostage takers during negotiations.
Source: Thomas Strentz. "The Cyclic Crisis Negotiations Time Line." *Law and Order*, March 1995, p.73. Reprinted by permission of the publisher.

at or near the scene but do not participate in negotiations and in some cases are not visible except as a last resort. Figure 12.2 illustrates the typical emotions hostage takers experience during negotiations.

Usually you do not need to rush into the scene immediately and proceed with direct contact. In a few cases, it may be better not to do anything, but to let the hostage taker resolve the situation. To its advantage, passage of time can

- Provide the opportunity for face-to-face contact with the hostage taker.
- Allow the negotiator to attempt to establish a trustful rapport.
- Permit mental, emotional and physical fatigue to operate against the hostage taker.
- Increase the hostage taker's needs for food, water, sleep and elimination.
- Increase the possibility of the hostage taker's reducing demands to reasonable compliance levels.
- Allow hostage-escape possibilities to occur.
- Provide for more rational thinking, in contrast to the emotionalism usually present during the initial stage of the crime.
- Lessen the hostage taker's anxiety and reduce his or her adrenalin flow, allowing more rational negotiations.
- Allow for important intelligence gathering concerning the hostage taker, hostages, layout, protection barriers and needed police reinforcement.

A disadvantage of the passage of time is that it could possibly foster the *Stockholm syndrome*, by which hostages begin to identify with their captors and sympathize with them. The **Stockholm syndrome** occurs when

hostages report that they have no ill feelings toward the hostage takers and, further, that they feared the police more than they feared their captors.

The negotiator should have street knowledge and experience with hostage incidents. Sometimes the first officers at the scene have established rapport with the hostage taker, and the negotiator only advises. In some cases, a trained clinical psychologist may be called to the scene, not as a negotiator but as a consultant regarding possible behavioral deviations of the hostage taker.

Face-to-face negotiations are ideal because they provide the best opportunity for gathering knowledge about and personally observing the hostage taker's reactions. Such contact should be undertaken only if circumstances indicate that the negotiator will not be in danger. An alternative is telephone contact, allowing for personal conversation and establishing rapport without the dangers of face-to-face contact. Use of a bullhorn is not the personal type of communication desired—nonetheless, it may be the only available method of communication.

Negotiable items may include food and drink (but not liquor, unless it is known that liquor would lessen the hostage taker's anxieties rather than increase them), money, media access and reduced penalties. Transportation is generally not negotiable because of the difficulty in monitoring and controlling the situation. Police departments should establish policies regarding hostage negotiations in advance. In general, nothing should be granted to a hostage taker unless something is received in return. Complicating the situation may be that the hostage taker is alcohol or drug impaired.

When criminals caught in the act of robbery take hostages, it is usually a spontaneous reaction to being cornered, and they know what to expect from the police. They generally desire media attention or want to escape safely from the crime scene. They may ask for more money to prove they are serious. Law enforcement response will invariably ensure safe apprehension of the criminal in return for release of the hostages. There are other types of hostage situations—for instance, involving terrorists, mentally disturbed persons, prisoners and the like—but the motives of the hostage taker and guidelines for action require handling consistent with the characteristics of those situations.

Most instances involving negotiations lend themselves to general guidelines but are also unique. Decisions have to be made based on the immediate factors involved. In the vast majority of cases, effectively handled negotiations can resolve the situation without injury or death.

If a robber emerges on request or is already outside the building, he or she should be immediately arrested. The victim and any witnesses should make a field identification, and then the suspect should be removed from the scene.

A wounded suspect presents an especially dangerous situation. Officers should be alert to the possibility that a suspect is feigning more serious injury than exists to draw them off guard and get them close enough to be shot. Suspects should be covered at all times and immobilized with handcuffs as soon as possible. If a suspect is seriously injured, an armed escort should accompany the robber in the ambulance and take a dying declaration if necessary. If the suspect is killed, the coroner or medical examiner is notified.

In a successfully resolved hostage situation, the robber is apprehended and the case is closed. In most robberies, however, an investigation is required.

THE PRELIMINARY INVESTIGATION AND SPECIAL CHALLENGES

As a violent crime, robbery introduces challenges that require special attention from the dispatcher, patrol officers, investigators and police administrators. Three major problems occur in dealing with robberies: (1) they are usually not reported until the offenders have left the scene, (2) the rapidity of the crime makes it difficult to obtain good descriptions or positive identification from victims and witnesses and (3) the items taken, usually currency, are difficult to identify.

> The lag time in reporting a robbery, the speed of its occurrence and the traumatizing effect on victims and witnesses and the nature of stolen items pose special challenges for investigators.

Frequently, officers arriving at the scene of a robbery find that the robber has just fled. After taking care of emergencies, broadcast initial information about the suspect, the getaway vehicle and the direction of travel. Follow-up vehicles dispatched to the general area of the robbery can then attempt to apprehend the escaping robbers. Early information helps determine how far the suspect may have traveled and the most likely escape routes.

Conduct an immediate canvass of the neighborhood because the suspect may be hiding in a parked car, in a gas station restroom or on the roof of a building. Check motels and hotels in the area. If another city is nearby, check the motels there. Look for discarded property such as the weapon, a wallet, money bag or other items taken from victims, as stolen purses and wallets are usually discarded within minutes of the robbery. However, stolen jewelry or cash usually cannot be recovered unless an arrest is made immediately after the crime.

Robbery usually leaves victims and witnesses feeling vulnerable and fearful, making it difficult for them to give accurate descriptions and details of what occurred. Be patient. Witnesses to a robbery suffer varying degrees of trauma even though they have not lost any property. They may have had to lie on the floor or been placed in a locked room or a bank vault, possibly fearing that the robber would return and kill them. Their ability to recall precise details is further impaired by the suddenness of the crime.

PROVING THE ELEMENTS OF THE OFFENSE

Know the *elements of robbery* in your jurisdiction so you can determine whether a robbery has in fact been committed. Each element must be proven separately. Proving only some of the elements is not sufficient.

Most state statutes have at least three elements for the crime of robbery.

Was Personal Property Wrongfully Taken?

Taking of property necessitates proving that it was carried away from the lawful owner or possessor to permanently deprive the owner of the property. Prove that the robber had no legal right to the property taken.

> Determine the legal owner of the property taken. Describe completely the property and its value.

Who is the legal owner? Take statements from the victim to show legal possession and control of the property before and during the robbery.

Was property taken or intended to be taken? Obtain a complete description of the property and its value, including marks, serial numbers, operation identification number (if available), color, size and any other identifying characteristics.

Obtain proof of what was lost and its value. In a bank robbery, the bank manager or auditor can give an accurate accounting of the money taken. In a store robbery, any responsible employee can help determine the loss. Cash-register receipts, sales receipts, quotations of retail and wholesale prices, reasonable estimates by people in the same business or the estimate of an independent appraiser can help determine the amount of the loss. In robberies of the person, the victim determines the loss. Some robbery victims claim to have lost more or less than was actually taken, thus complicating the case.

Was Property Taken from the Person or in the Person's Presence?

From the person or in the presence of the person necessitates proving that the property was under the victim's control before the robbery and was removed from the victim's control by the robber's direct actions.

> Record the exact words, gestures, motions or actions the robber used to gain control of the property.

Answer such questions as these: Where was the property before it was taken? Where was the victim?

Against the Person's Will by Force or the Threat of Force?

By force or the threat of force may be the most difficult element to establish. If the victim perceived a threat, it is real.

> Obtain a complete description of the robber's words, actions and any weapon used or threatened to be used.

If nothing was said, find out what gestures, motions or other actions compelled the victim to give up the property.

The force need not be directly against the robbery victim. For example, a woman may receive a call at work, telling her that her husband is a hostage and will be killed unless she brings money to a certain location, or the robber may grab a friend of the victim or a customer in a store and direct the victim to hand over money to protect the person being held from harm.

Record in your notes descriptions of any injuries to the victim or witnesses. Photograph the injuries, if possible, and have injured victims and witnesses examined by a doctor, emergency room personnel or ambulance paramedics.

THE COMPLETE INVESTIGATION

Most robberies are solved through prompt actions by the victim, witnesses and the police patrolling the immediate area or by police at checkpoints. In many cases, however, a robbery investigation takes weeks or even months. Begin your investigation with a follow-up canvass of the area in which the robbery occurred, seeking witnesses who may not have been identified immediately following the crime. Check car rental agencies if no vehicle was reported stolen. Check airports, bus and train stations and taxi companies for possible links.

Recheck all information and physical descriptions. Have a sketch of the suspect prepared and circulate it. Many robberies, particularly those of convenience stores, occur close to an offender's home, so ask the employees of these businesses if they are familiar with the offender or whether the robber seemed to be familiar with the layout of the store (Petrocelli, 2008b). Alert your informants to listen for word of the robbery. Check known "fences." Check MO files. Where applicable, check police field-interview/contact forms and communications records relating to recent citizen calls complaining about suspicious people or vehicles in the area of the robbery.

Prepare your report carefully and thoroughly and circulate it to any officers who may assist. Even if you do not apprehend your suspect, the suspect may be apprehended during a future robbery, and his or her MO and other evidence may implicate him or her in the robbery you investigated.

Identifying the Suspect

The various techniques used in suspect identification (discussed in Chapter 7) are relevant at this point.

> Obtain information about the suspect's general appearance, clothing, disguises, weapon and vehicle.

If the suspect is apprehended within a short time (20 minutes or so), he or she may be taken back to the scene for identification by the victim. Alternatively, the victim may be taken to where the suspect is being held. Several people should be in the area of the suspect to witness that the victim makes any identification without assistance from the police. Photo lineups may be used if no suspect is arrested at or near the scene of the crime. Photo lineups should include five other people in addition to the suspect. A person who has been arrested does not have the right to refuse to have a photo taken.

Eyewitness identification is affected by many factors: the distance between the witness and the suspect at the time of the robbery, the time of day and lighting conditions, the amount of violence involved, whether the witness had ever seen or knew the suspect and the time it took for the crime to be committed.

Disguises. To conceal their identities, many robbers use ski masks, nylon stockings pulled over their heads or paper sacks with eyeholes. Other disguises include wigs, dyed hair, sideburns, scarves, various types of false noses or ears and makeup to alter appearance. Gauze is sometimes used to distort the shape of the cheeks or mouth and tape is used to simulate cuts or to cover scars.

Clothing also can serve as a disguise. False heels and soles can increase height. Collars can be pulled up and hats pulled down: "Research indicates that many bank robbers prefer to strike on Friday afternoons in the winter when the extended hours intersect with the early winter darkness. The darkness and cold allow for 'natural disguises' such as hats, high collars, and scarves" (Petrocelli, 2008a, p.16). Various types of uniforms that fit in with the area of the robbery scene, such as delivery uniforms or work clothes, have also been used. Clothing and disguises may be discarded by the robber upon leaving the scene and are valuable evidence if recovered because they may provide DNA evidence.

Weapons. Pistols, revolvers and automatic weapons are frequently used in robberies. Sawed-off shotguns, rifles, air guns, various types of imitation guns, knives, razors and other cutting and stabbing instruments, explosives, tear gas and various acids have also been used. Such weapons and devices are often found on or near the suspect when arrested, but many are hidden in the vehicle used or are thrown away during the escape. Robbery victims are the most likely of all victims of violent crime to face an armed offender.

Vehicles. Most vehicles used in robberies are inconspicuous, popular makes that attract no attention and are stolen just before the robbery. Some robbers leave the scene on foot and then take buses or taxis or commandeer vehicles, sometimes at gunpoint.

Establishing the Modus Operandi

Even if the suspect is apprehended at the scene, the MO can help link the suspect with other robberies.

> Important MO information includes
> ■ Type of robbery
> ■ Time (day and hour)
> ■ Method of attack (real or threatened)
> ■ Weapon
> ■ Number of robbers
> ■ Voice and words
> ■ Vehicle used
> ■ Peculiarities
> ■ Object sought

Finding that an MO matches a previous robbery does not necessarily mean that the same robber committed the crime. For example, in one instance three masked gunmen robbed a midwestern bank of more than $45,000 and escaped in a stolen car. The MO matched a similar robbery in the same town a few weeks earlier in which $30,000 was obtained. The three gunmen were identified and arrested the next day, and more than $41,000 of the loot was recovered. One gunman told the FBI agent that he planned the robbery after reading about the successful bank robbery that three other masked gunmen had pulled off. The FBI agent smiled and informed the robber that the perpetrators had been arrested shortly after the robbery. Aghast, the copycat robber bemoaned the fact that he had seen no publicity on the arrest.

Physical Evidence

Physical evidence at a robbery scene is usually minimal. Sometimes, however, the robbery occurs where a surveillance camera is operating. The film can be processed immediately and used as evidence.

> Physical evidence that can connect a suspect with a robbery includes fingerprints, DNA, shoe prints, tire prints, restraining devices, discarded garments, fibers and hairs, a note and the stolen property.

Fingerprints may be found at the scene if the suspect handled any objects, on the holdup note if one was left behind, on the getaway car or on recovered property. They might also be found on pieces of tape used as restraints, which in themselves are valuable as evidence.

In one residential robbery, the criminal forced entrance into a home, bound and gagged the residents, stole several items of value and then left. As he backed up to turn his car around, he inadvertently left the impression of the vehicle's license plate clearly imprinted on a snow bank. He was apprehended within hours of the robbery.

Mapping Robbery

Because robbery is inherently serial, mapping it has proven successful. The Charlotte-Mecklenburg (North Carolina) Police Department used mapping to address an increase in robbery victimization among Charlotte's growing Hispanic population.

Officers used the Global Information Software (GIS) mapping capabilities in the department's Crime Analysis Unit to map all robbery incidents with Hispanic victims citywide. Overlaying the maps revealed a close correlation between Hispanic robbery incidents and areas of high concentrations of Hispanic residents. Mapping narrowed the problem to robberies of Hispanic victims in the apartment complexes where they lived. It then identified a particular complex, the Park Apartments, that was a hot spot for the robberies. This complex consisted of 51 buildings with approximately 2,000 residents. Hispanics constituted 49 percent of the complex population but 64 percent of its robbery victims. The analysis then identified a number of factors that increased the risk of robbery, including the fact that victims often carried large sums of money instead of using banks, that poor lighting and poor security made robberies easy to commit and that partly because of language barriers the police had done little community outreach.

In cooperation with complex managers, police officers addressed the identified physical factors. In addition to improving lighting, they restricted access to the apartment grounds and to the high-risk laundry area. An enforcement component with the department's robbery unit worked to arrest several suspects. Officers also built relationships with the residents to increase their willingness to report crime.

FALSE ROBBERY REPORTS

Investigators need to rule out the probability that a robbery report is false. Among the indicators of a false robbery report are

- An unusual delay in reporting the offense
- An amount of the loss not fitting the victim's apparent financial status
- A lack of correspondence with the physical evidence
- Improbable events
- An exceptionally detailed or exceptionally vague description of offender
- A lack of cooperation

Summary

Robbery is the felonious taking of another's property, either directly from the person or in that person's presence, through force or intimidation. Robberies are classified as residential, commercial, street or vehicle driver.

Home invaders are typically young Asian gang members who travel across the country robbing Asian families, especially Asian business owners. Another category of robbery is carjacking—the taking of a motor vehicle by force or threat of force. The FBI may investigate the crime.

Bank robberies are within the jurisdictions of the FBI, the state and the community in which the crime occurred and are jointly investigated. The elements of robbery are (1) the wrongful taking of personal property, (2) from the person or in the person's presence, (3) against the person's will by force or threat of force.

When responding to a robbery-in-progress call, proceed as rapidly as possible but use extreme caution. Assume that the robber is at the scene unless otherwise advised, and be prepared for gunfire. Look for and immobilize any getaway vehicle you discover. Avoid a hostage situation if possible, and make an immediate arrest if the suspect is at the scene. The lag time in reporting a robbery, the speed of its occurrence and the traumatizing effect on victims and witnesses and the nature of stolen items pose special challenges for investigators.

To prove that personal property was wrongfully taken, determine the legal owner of the property and describe the property and its value. To prove that it was taken from the person or in the person's presence, record the exact words, gestures, motions or actions the robber used to gain control of the property. To prove that the removal was against the victim's will by force or threat of force, obtain a complete description of the robber's words, actions and any weapon the robber used or threatened to be used. Obtain information about the suspect's general appearance, clothing, disguises, weapon and vehicle.

Important MO information includes type of robbery, time (day and hour), method of attack (real or threatened), weapon, number of robbers, voice and words, vehicle used, any peculiarities and object sought. Physical evidence at a robbery scene that can connect the suspect with a robbery includes fingerprints, DNA, shoe prints, tire prints, restraining devices, discarded garments, fibers and hairs, a note and the stolen property.

Checklist

Robbery

- Are maps and pictures on file of banks and other places that handle large amounts of cash? Are there plans for police response in the event that these facilities are robbed?
- Was the place that was robbed protected by an alarm? Was the alarm working?
- Was the place that was robbed protected by a surveillance camera? Was the camera working? Was the film immediately removed and processed?
- What procedure did police use in responding to the call? Did they enter directly? To avoid a hostage situation, did they wait until the robber had left?
- Did police interview separately everyone in the robbed place? Did they obtain written statements from each?
- Are all elements of the crime of robbery present?
- How was the robber dressed? Was a disguise used?
- What were the robber's exact words and actions?
- What type of weapon or threat did the robber use?
- Was anybody injured or killed?
- Was there a getaway car? Description? Direction of travel? A second person in the car?
- Was a general description of people and vehicles involved quickly broadcast to other police agencies?
- Did police secure and photograph the scene?
- What property was taken in the robbery? What was its value?
- Who is the legal owner?
- If a bank was robbed, were the FBI and state officials notified?
- If the suspect was arrested, how was identification made?
- If money or property was recovered, was it properly processed?

Application

Read the following account of an actual robbery investigation. As you read, list the steps the investigators took. Review the list and determine whether they took all necessary steps. (Adapted from a report by Captain Raymond J. Eagan, New Haven, Connecticut.)

On December 16, close to midnight, a woman looked in the window of the grocery store owned by Efimy Romanow at 187 Ashmun Street, New Haven, Connecticut, and saw Romanow lying behind the counter with the telephone receiver clutched in his right hand. Thinking Romanow was sick, the woman notified a neighbor, Thomas Kelly, who went to the store and then called an ambulance. Romanow was pronounced dead on arrival at the hospital.

Autopsy revealed he had been shot near the heart. The bullet was removed and turned over to detectives, who immediately began an investigation. Officers protected the crime scene and made a thorough search for possible prints and other evidence. They found a small amount of money in the cash register. At the hospital, $15.50 was found in Romanow's pockets, and $313 in bills was found in his right shoe. A thorough check of neighborhood homes was made without result. One report received was that two white men were seen leaving the store before Romanow's body was discovered.

About 7 A.M., December 17, Mrs. Marion Lang, who lived directly opposite the store but was not home when the officers first went there, was contacted. She stated that at about 11:10 P.M. she had heard loud talking in the street, including the remark, "Damn it, he is shot, let's get out of here." She had not looked out the window, so she was unable to describe the people she had heard talking.

The investigation continued without any tangible clues until 9:25 P.M., December 17, when a phone call was received from George M. Proctor, owner of a drugstore on a street parallel to Ashmun Street and one block away. He had just overheard a woman talking in the phone booth in his store say, "I will not stand for her taking my fellow away. I know who shot the storekeeper on Ashmun. It was Scotty and Almeda at 17 Dixwell." Mr. Proctor did not know the woman he had overheard.

Two detectives were assigned to this lead, and they began a search. A few hours later, they learned that Scotty and Almeda were in a room at 55 Dixwell Avenue. Arriving with several uniformed officers, they entered and found Francis Scott and Henry Almeda in bed with their clothes on. Both had previous records and were well known to the local police. The detectives took the two men to headquarters for questioning and then returned to the room. Their search revealed five .32 caliber bullets at the top of a window casing where plaster had been broken up.

They also received information that Scott and Almeda had earlier visited Julia Redmond, who had a room in the same house. They asked Ms. Redmond if Scott and Almeda had left anything there. She responded, "They put something under the mattress." Turning over the mattress, the detectives found a .32 caliber Harrington and Richardson revolver, serial number 430-087. Ms. Redmond said, "That belongs to Scott and Almeda."

The detectives returned to headquarters and searched the stolen gun files. They discovered that this gun had been reported stolen in a burglary at the home of Geoffrey Harrell, 46 Webster Street, in November. Both suspects were questioned during the night and denied any part in the shooting.

The questioning resumed on the morning of December 18 at 9:00 A.M. At 3:45 P.M. that day, Almeda broke and made a confession in which he involved Scott. Almeda's statement was read to Scott with Almeda present. When Almeda identified the confession and stated it was true, Scott also admitted his part in the shooting.

When Almeda was shown the .32 caliber H&R revolver, he identified it as the gun used in shooting Romanow. He explained that they had to shoot Romanow because he refused to give up his money and placed himself between them and the door. In order to get out, he shot Romanow. Both stated that they had no car and that no one else was involved.

A preliminary examination of the bullet taken from Romanow's body did not satisfy the detectives that the bullet had been fired from the gun in their possession, even though it had been identified by both Almeda and Scott as the one used.

A detective took the gun and bullet to the FBI Technical Laboratory in Washington, DC, where a ballistics comparison established that the gun furnished for examination was not the gun that fired the fatal bullet. A search of the Technical Laboratory files revealed that the gun matched a bullet furnished by the same department as evidence in a holdup of Levine's Liquor Store on December 1 of that year. One shot had been fired, striking a chair

and deflecting into a pile of rubbish in the rear of the store. Detectives had recovered the bullet after sifting through the rubbish.

When confronted with this information, Scott and Almeda admitted that they had committed this holdup and shooting while masked. They also admitted that they had stolen an automobile to use that night and that they had burglarized Harrell's home in November, when they took the gun.

The detectives conducted an extensive search for the gun used in killing Romanow. They cut a hole in the bottom of the flue leading from the room occupied by Scott and Almeda and even had the sewer department clean out 15 sewer catch basins in the area of the crime, but no weapon was discovered.

Both Almeda and Scott were indicted by the grand jury for first-degree murder. They were scheduled for trial February 13. The night before the trial was to begin, they told their lawyers that a third man had furnished the gun and driven the getaway car. In a conference with the state attorney and detectives, the lawyers identified the third man as William Sutton. Within half an hour, Sutton was apprehended and brought to the state attorney's office where, in the presence of Scott and Almeda, their statements were read to Sutton. He admitted participating in the crime.

This new turn in the case also revealed that the gun used in the killing was loaned to Sutton by John Foy. The morning after the shooting, Sutton brought the gun back to Foy and left it with him. A short time later Sutton returned and asked for the gun. He had decided he should get rid of it because it was hot. Sutton then took the cylinder from the gun while Foy broke the rest of it into small parts, which he threw in various places. Foy, who admitted he knew the gun was to be used in a holdup, was charged with conspiracy.

Sutton, Almeda and Scott pled guilty to second-degree murder and received life sentences in the Connecticut State Prison. Foy received a one-year jail sentence.

Questions

1. List the steps the investigators followed.
2. Did they omit any necessary steps?
3. What comparison evidence was helpful in the case?
4. How did law enforcement agencies cooperate?
5. What interrogation techniques did they use?
6. How important was citizen information?

Discussion Questions

1. In a robbery of a neighborhood grocery store, how important is citizen information? Should a neighborhood check be made if the incident occurred at 3 A.M.? How would you attempt to locate two witnesses who saw the robber enter the store if the owner does not know their names? How else could you develop information on the robber's description, vehicle and the like?

2. Imagine that you are a police officer responding to the scene of a bank robbery. Should you enter the bank immediately? Should you close the bank to business during the investigation? Can the drive-up window be used for business if it was not involved in the robbery? What should be done with the bank employees after the robbery? With customers in the bank at the time of the robbery? What agencies should work jointly on this type of crime?

3. How important is an immediate response to a robbery call? What vehicles should respond to the scene? To the area surrounding the scene? What types of locations near the scene are most advantageous to apprehending the suspect?

4. If a robber takes a hostage inside a building, what are immediate considerations? If the hostage situation is not resolved in the first 15 minutes, what must be considered? Should a police officer offer to take the hostage's place? What might you say to the robber to induce him or her to release the hostage? To surrender after releasing the hostage?

5. Why is a robbery in progress dangerous for the police? For the victim? What can the police do to reduce the potential danger while responding? To reduce the danger to the hostage?

6. Which takes priority: taking the robber at all risks (to remove him or her from the street and prevent future robberies) or ensuring the safety of the victim and witnesses?

7. What other crimes often occur along with a robbery?

8. What types of establishments are most susceptible to robbery? What types of establishments are most often robbed in your community?

9. What measures can a police department take to prevent robbery? What preventive measures does your department take?

10. What measures can citizens take to help prevent robberies? How can the police assist citizens in these measures?

Media Explorations

Internet

Select one of the following assignments to complete.

■ Go to the FBI Web site at www.fbi.gov. Click on "library and reference." Select "Uniform Crime Reports" and outline what the report says about robbery.

■ Select one of the following key terms: *bait money, dye pack, carjacking, robbery, robbery prevention, Stockholm syndrome*. Find one article relevant to robbery investigations to outline and share with the class.

Gale Criminal Justice Database Assignments

The following assignments require access to Gale's Custom Journals Database for Emergency Services and Criminal Justice. Check with your instructor if you have questions about this.

■ Find the article "Rifles On Patrol: The Rifle Has Returned To Front Duty In Law Enforcement Agencies Across The Nation And Is Now Standard Gear" on the Gale Emergency Services Database. Read the article and identify why rifles are an important weapon for law enforcement and the impact on fighting crimes such as robberies. Be prepared to discuss this in class.

■ Find the article "Suspects In Crisis: Crisis Negotiation Expert Says Negotiating With The Hostage-Taker Requires A Cool Head And Good Listening Skills" on the Gale Emergency Services Database. Read and outline this article for in-class discussion.

References

Bank Crime Statistics (BCS), Federally Insured Financial Institutions, January 1, 2010–December 31, 2010. Washington, DC: Federal Bureau of Investigation, March 16, 2011. Accessed June 15, 2011. http://www.fbi.gov/stats-services/publications/bank-crime-statistics-2010/bank-crime-statistics-2010

"Carjacking—Don't Be a Victim." Washington, DC: U S. Department of State, Bureau of Diplomatic Security, August 2002. Accessed June 20, 2011. http://www.state.gov/m/ds/rls/rpt/19782.htm

Chronister, Thomas; Casteel, Carri; Peek-Asa, Corinne; Hartley, Dan; Amandus, Harlan. "Robbery and Violence Prevention in Small Retail Businesses." *The Police Chief*, October 2009, pp.36–42.

Crime in the United States, 2009. Washington, DC: U.S. Department of Justice, Federal Bureau of Investigation,

September 2010. Accessed May 27, 2011. http://www2.fbi.
gov/ucr/cius2009/index.html

Hudson, James "Gator." "Searchable Video Surveillance Nabs
Fraudsters and Robbers." *Law Enforcement Technology*,
September 2007, pp.110–115.

Massock, Bill. "Negotiations for First Responders." *Tactical
Response*, May–June 2008, pp.66–69.

Molnar, J. P. "Automatic License Plate Recognition." *Law Officer
Magazine*, March 2007, pp.20–24.

Petrocelli, Joseph. "Crimes against Taxi Drivers." *Police*, July
2007a, pp.22–26.

Petrocelli, Joseph. "Crimes at ATMs." *Police*, September 2007b,
pp.22–24.

Petrocelli, Joseph. "Bank Robberies." *Police*, January 2008a,
pp.16–17.

Petrocelli, Joseph. "Convenience Store Robberies." *Police*,
August 2008b, pp.20–23.

Rayburn, Michael T. "Off-the-Clock Robbery Response." *Police*,
September 2007, pp.56–59.

*Recommendations for Workplace Violence Prevention Programs
in Late-Night Retail Establishments*. Washington, DC:
Occupational Health and Safety Administration, 2009.
(OSHA 3153-12R). Accessed October 24, 2011. http://www.
osha.gov/Publications/osha3153.pdf.

Truman, Jennifer L., and Rand, Michael R. *Criminal
Victimization, 2009*. Washington, DC: Bureau of Justice
Statistics, Bulletin, National Crime Victimization Survey,
October 2010. (NCJ 231327)

Weisel, Deborah Lamm. *The Problem of Bank Robbery*.
Washington, DC: Office of Community Oriented Policing
Services, 2007.

SECTION 4
INVESTIGATING CRIMES AGAINST PROPERTY

Most of the crimes discussed in this section do not involve the use of force or violence against people and therefore are often not considered as serious as assault, robbery, rape or murder. However, according to various official reports, crimes against property occur much more frequently than do crimes against persons. Federal Bureau of Investigation (FBI) statistics report an estimated 9,320,971 property crimes in the nation during 2009 (*Crime in the United States 2009*, 2010). The 2- and 5-year trends showed that the number of property crimes declined 4.6 percent from 2008 and 8.4 percent from 2005. (See Figure IV.1.)

The rate of property offenses in 2009 was 3,036.1 per 100,000 inhabitants. Two thirds (67.9%) of all property crimes were larceny/theft (the focus of Chapter 14). Property crimes accounted for an estimated $15.2 billion in losses in 2009.

FIGURE IV.1
Property Crime Offenses, 5-Year Trend, 2005–2009

Source: Crime in the United States 2009. Washington, DC: Federal Bureau of Investigation, September 2010. http://www2.fbi.gov/ucr/cius2009/offenses/property_crime/index.html

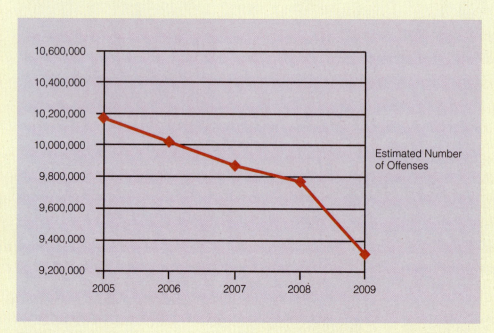

© 2013 istockphoto.com

© 2013 istockphoto.com

In 2009, according to the FBI, a crime against property occurred every 3.4 seconds in the United States:

- One larceny/theft every 5.0 seconds
- One burglary every 14.3 seconds
- One motor vehicle theft every 39.7 seconds

Figures from the National Crime Victimization Survey (NCVS) are much higher, showing 133,210 personal thefts and 15.6 million property crimes in 2009 (Truman and Rand, 2010). The property crime rate was 127.4 per 1,000 households. According to the NCVS, only about 40 percent of property crimes were reported to police in 2009.

Many property crimes are difficult to investigate because there is little evidence and there are usually no eyewitnesses. Physical evidence in property crimes is often similar to that found in violent crimes: fingerprints, footprints, tire impressions, hair, fibers, broken glass and personal objects left at the crime scene. Other important evidence in crimes against property includes tools, tool fragments, tool marks, safe insulation, disturbance of paint and evidence of forcible entry. Despite the possibility that touch DNA or other biological evidence may be left at the scene, unless it was a particularly severe crime resulting in significant monetary loss, such evidence will likely not be processed. For example, a rock suspected of being used to break a car window,

through which some personal items were stolen, may have fingerprints on it, but because the crime is minor and the time and cost required to process that evidence is excessive in relation to the severity of the offense, most agencies would chose to not process that evidence.

The modus operandi of a property crime often takes on added importance because there are no other significant leads. In addition, crimes against property tend to occur in series, so solving one crime may lead to solving an entire series of similar crimes.

The chapters in this section discuss specific considerations in investigating burglary (Chapter 13); larceny/theft, fraud and white-collar crime (Chapter 14); motor vehicle theft (Chapter 15); and arson, bombs and explosives (Chapter 16).

References

Crime in the United States 2009. Washington, DC: Federal Bureau of Investigation, Uniform Crime Reports, 2010.

Truman, Jennifer L., and Rand, Michael R, *Criminal Victimization, 2009*. Washington, DC: Bureau of Justice Statistics Bulletin, October 2010. (NCJ 231327)

CHAPTER 13
Burglary

Outline

Can You Define?

blowing a safe
burglary
burning a safe
chopping a safe
commercial burglary
crime prevention through environmental design (CPTED)
dragging a safe
fence
hit-and-run burglary
peeling a safe
presumptive evidence
pulling a safe
punching a safe
residential burglary
routine activity theory
safe
smash and grab
target hardening
vault
verified response policy

 Do You Know?

- What burglary is?
- What the basic difference between burglary and robbery is?
- What the two basic classifications of burglary are?
- What three elements are present in laws defining burglary?
- What additional elements can be included in burglary?
- What determines the severity of a burglary?
- What the elements of the crime of possession of burglary tools are?
- How to proceed to a burglary scene and what to do on arrival?
- What the most frequent means of entry to commit burglary is?
- How safes are broken into?
- What physical evidence is often found at a burglary scene?
- What modus operandi factors are important in burglary?
- Where to search for stolen property?
- What the elements of the offense of receiving stolen goods are?
- What measures may be taken to prevent burglary?

In a western city, police officers noticed what they believed was safe insulation on the steps of a cabin occupied by a known burglar. They obtained a warrant and searched the premises for evidence of a burglary. The substance found on the steps and some burglary tools found inside the home were mailed to a laboratory, where the substance was confirmed as safe insulation. The suspect was arrested and convicted of burglary. On appeal, the courts held that such knowledge by the officers was in effect an extension of the laboratory and was therefore probable cause even without the laboratory examination. The verification by the laboratory only strengthened the probable cause, and the charge of burglary was sustained.

The word *burglar* comes from the German words *burg,* meaning "house," and *laron,* meaning "thief"; thus the meaning "house thief." The Federal Bureau of Investigation's (FBI) Uniform Crime Reports (UCR) defines **burglary** as "the unlawful entry of a structure to commit a felony or theft, even though no force was used to gain entry." All such attempts also count as burglaries. The common-law definition of *burglary* (originating in 16th-century England) required that the breaking and entering be committed during the nighttime or "between sunset and sunrise." Many changes have been made in burglary statutes since that time, including eliminating the requirement that it occur at night.

> Burglary is the unlawful entry of a structure to commit a crime.

Burglary is reported by frequency and by the value of the property stolen and recovered. This is because many burglaries yield low losses, although a single burglary can yield a high loss. According to the FBI, an estimated 2,199,125 burglary offenses occurred throughout the nation during 2009, a decrease of 1.3 percent from 2008 (*Crime in the United States 2009*, 2010). Burglary offenses made up 23.6 percent of all property crimes reported in 2009. Of these, law enforcement cleared 12.5 percent by arrest or exceptional means (*Crime in the United States 2009*, 2010). Burglary offenses cost victims an estimated $4 billion in lost property, with the average dollar loss per burglary being $2,096. And although the number of burglaries in 2009 had increased by 7.2 percent from 2000, this crime has shown a general decline over the past three decades. Several reasons for the overall 30-year decline in burglaries include improvements in locks and burglar alarm technology, as well as the growing use of private security (Sullivan, 2008). An estimated one million private police and security guards work in residential communities. Since residents have started paying for private security, crime has dropped 70 percent.

The public regards burglary as a major crime problem. Many people fear arriving home or at work and confronting a burglar, a situation that can develop into an assault and robbery. Moreover, it is traumatic for people to realize they have been doubly victimized when someone has invaded the privacy of their home or business and stolen their possessions. Although the items taken may be covered by insurance, some may be irreplaceable because of their sentimental value.

BURGLARY VERSUS ROBBERY

A burglar seeks to avoid contact with people near the scene or on the premises.

> Burglary differs from robbery in that burglars are covert, seeking to remain unseen, whereas robbers confront their victims directly. Burglary is a crime against property; robbery is a crime against a person.

Most burglaries occur in unoccupied homes and businesses; therefore, few witnesses exist, and few alarms are given to provide advance notice to the police. The best chances of apprehending a burglar in the act are when a silent alarm is tripped, a surveillance camera records the crime, a witness hears or sees suspicious activities and reports them immediately to the police or alert patrol officers observe a burglary in progress. However, most burglaries are not solved at the crime scene but through subsequent investigation.

CLASSIFICATION

> Burglaries are classified as residential or commercial.

Residential Burglaries

A **residential burglary** occurs in buildings, structures or attachments that are used as or are suitable for dwellings, even though they may be unoccupied at the time of the burglary. Residential units include private homes, tenements, mobile homes, cabins, apartments, rooms within a house leased by a renter, houseboats used as dwellings and any other structure suitable for and used as a dwelling. Nearly three fourths of all burglaries are residential burglaries (72.6 percent in 2009 according to the FBI). Of these, nearly half took place during the day. The FBI's 2009 "Crime Clock" estimates that a home is burglarized every 14.3 seconds ("Crime Clock Statistics," 2010).

Residential burglaries are often committed by one or more juveniles or young adults who live in the same community. The targets are cash, items to convert to personal use or items to "fence" or sell, such as televisions, radios, computers, guns, jewelry, tools and other small household goods. Residential burglaries typically occur during weekdays when most people are away from their homes, either at work or at school.

Whereas the study of burglary and related crime rates has historically focused on the offender, new theories shift the focus toward the victims and particular times and places. For example, the **routine activity theory** proposes that crime results from the simultaneous existence of three elements: (1) the presence of likely or motivated offenders, (2) the presence of suitable targets and

(3) an absence of guardians to prevent the crime. This theory acknowledges the role, however indirect, of victims in their own victimization and suggests that certain locations may be more susceptible to burglary at certain times because of the routine absence of residents. Filbert (2008) suggests, "Routine activity theory and related theories point to crime opportunities as the principal cause of crime. Rather than concentrations of offenders or the absence of social controls, opportunity theories suggest that analysts should look for concentrations of crime targets." She gives as an example a suburban subdivision with dual-income families that have few people at home during weekdays. Because the property is unprotected, the neighborhood can become an area burglary hot spot.

Burglary at Single-Family House Construction Sites

Amateur opportunists and professional thieves alike take advantage of unprotected construction sites. With copper and other scrap metal prices on the rise, and a growing

Burglars often ransack rooms looking for valuables, making it difficult for the victim to know what is missing. Often there are no leads and, therefore, little hope of apprehending the burglar or recovering the stolen property.
© Digital Vision, Ltd./Super Stock

unemployment rate, construction sites have become an increasingly attractive target for burglars. The stolen metals are typically sold at junkyards and refineries. Until recently it was difficult for investigators to track stolen metals because the materials were often immediately melted down and there were few or no requirements for the seller to provide any identification or information. However, because of the rise in these types of crimes, businesses that buy these items have begun implementing higher standards of acceptance, including requiring the seller to provide positive identification and proof of where they obtained the products. Some states have now mandated these standards as law.

The primary responsibility for preventing such losses is with the builder. However, the police response might include enhancing natural surveillance and disrupting the stolen goods market. Responses that have met with limited success include patrolling construction sites, surveillance and "baiting" thieves and sting operations.

Commercial Burglaries

A **commercial burglary** is one that involves churches, schools, barns, public buildings, shops, offices, stores, factories, warehouses, stables, ships or railroad cars. Most commercial burglaries are committed in service stations, stores, schools, manufacturing plants, warehouses and office buildings. Burglars often specialize in one type of facility. Businesses located in out-of-the-way places are more susceptible to burglary because of a lack of police coverage and street lighting and because there are usually few witnesses to observe wrongdoing and notify the police. Businesses in high-poverty, rundown neighborhoods are also at high risk of burglary. In contrast to residential burglaries, most commercial burglaries take place afterhours, either at night (58.7 percent at night according to the FBI) or on weekends, whenever the establishment is closed.

Commercial burglaries are often committed by two or more people, depending on the type of premises, size, location and the planned burglary attack. Sometimes a lookout is used who acts like a drunk, works on a stalled car or walks an animal near the location. The building is "cased" in advance to learn about security devices, opening and closing times, employee habits, people in the neighborhood and the presence of a private security officer. Casing is also done by obtaining information from an employee or by posing as a worker, repairperson or salesperson to gain ostensibly legitimate entrance.

ELEMENTS OF THE CRIME: BURGLARY

Although burglary laws vary from state to state, statutes of all states include three key elements.

Elements of the crime of burglary include
- Entering a structure,
- without the consent of the person in possession,
- with the intent to commit a crime therein.

Entering a Structure

Paths of entry may be through an open door, window or transom; a ventilation shaft; a hole in a wall; or a tunnel. Means of entry can be by jimmying a door or window, reaching through an open door or window with a long stick or pole, using a celluloid strip to open a door lock, climbing a ladder or stairs outside a building, descending through a skylight, hiding in an entryway or breaking a window and taking items from the window display (called **smash and grab**). Entry also includes remaining in a store until after closing time and then committing a burglary.

Some state laws include vehicles, trailers and railroad cars as structures.

Without the Consent of the Person in Possession

To constitute burglary, the entry must be illegal and must be done without permission of a person having lawful authority, that is, the property owner, the legal agent of such person or the person in physical control of the property, such as a renter or part-owner.

Entering a *public* place is done with consent unless consent has been expressly withdrawn. The hours for legal entry usually are posted on public buildings; for example, "Open Weekdays 9 A.M. to 5 P.M." Entrance at any other time is without consent. If a specific individual is restricted from entering a public place during its open hours, that individual must be notified orally or in writing that consent has been withdrawn.

With Intent to Commit a Crime

Regardless of whether the burglary is planned well in advance or committed on the spur of the moment, intent must be shown. When the first two elements are present, the third is often presumed present; that is, if a person

Shoeprints indicate the burglar may have tried kicking the door to gain entry. In the end, the doorknob was broken off.
© 911 Pictures

enters a structure without the owner's consent, the presumption is that it is to commit a crime, usually larceny or a sex offense.

Additional Elements

Three additional elements are found in the laws of some states.

> Elements of burglary can also include breaking into the dwelling of another during the nighttime.

Breaking Into. Actual "breaking" is a matter of interpretation. Any force used during a burglary to enter or leave the structure, even if a door or window is partly opened or closed, constitutes breaking. Entrance through trick or ruse or through threats to or collusion with any person residing in the building is also considered breaking.

Breaking and entering is strong **presumptive evidence** that a crime is intended; that is, it provides a reasonable basis for belief. Some laws include such wording as this: "Every person who shall unlawfully break and enter a building or dwelling or other structure shall be deemed to have broken and entered or entered the same with intent to commit grand or petit larceny or a felony therein, unless such unlawful breaking and entering shall be explained by testimony satisfactory to the jury to have been made without criminal intent."

This, in effect, places the burden of proof on the defendant.

The Dwelling of Another. Some states still require that the structure broken into be a dwelling, that is, a structure suitable for sheltering people. This remnant from common law restricts burglary to residential burglaries.

During the Nighttime. Common law also specified that burglary occur under the cover of darkness, an element still retained in some state statutes. *Nighttime* is defined as the period from sunset to sunrise as specified by official weather charts.

ESTABLISHING THE SEVERITY OF THE BURGLARY

Most burglary laws increase the crime's severity if the burglar possesses a weapon or an explosive. Obtain the weapon and connect it with the burglar if possible. Check with the National Crime Information Center (NCIC). If the weapon is stolen, a separate felony charge of theft or illegal possession of a weapon can be made.

> A burglary's severity is determined by (a) the presence of dangerous devices in the burglar's possession or (b) the value of the property stolen.

If other crimes are committed along with the burglary or if the burglary is to commit another crime such as rape, the additional crime is separate and must be proven separately.

ELEMENTS OF THE CRIME: POSSESSION OF BURGLARY TOOLS

A companion crime to burglary is possession of burglary tools, an offense separate from burglary. The charge of possession of burglary tools can be made even if a burglary has not been committed if circumstances indicate that the tools were intended for use in a burglary.

> Elements of the crime of possessing burglary tools include
> - Possessing any device, explosive or other instrumentality,
> - with intent to use or permit its use to commit burglary.

Burglary tools include nitroglycerin or other explosives and any engine, machine, tool, implement, chemical or substance designed for the cutting or burning open of buildings or protective containers.

A person with a large number of automobile keys probably intends to use them to open varied makes and models of vehicle doors. Portable key cutters, codes and key blanks such as those used in hardware stores and key-making shops are also classified as burglary tools, as are *slam pullers,* devices that look like oversized screwdrivers and are inserted in car locks to force them open. A *bump key* is another burglary tool. *Lock bumping* is a lock picking technique used on standard pin tumbler locks in which the bump key (a generic key) is used along with another mechanism to apply force to open the lock. Lock bumping is an easy, quiet method used by thieves to commit burglaries and other crimes.

Many other tools used in burglaries are commonly obtained in hardware stores. These include pry bars, screwdrivers, bolt cutters, extension cords, pipe wrenches, channel locks and tire irons. Lock picks and tension wrenches, lever-type wrenches, warded pass keys, pick guns, cylinder drill jigs and various types of metal blades to open car doors can also be used as burglary tools.

Because many people, especially mechanics and carpenters, have tools that might be used in a burglary in their car or on their person, circumstances must clearly show intent to use or allow their use in committing a crime.

THE BURGLAR

The burglar is often portrayed as a masked person with a bag loaded with silverware and candlesticks over his shoulder. In reality, burglars fit no set image; they are of all sizes, ages, races and occupations. They are either amateurs or longtime professionals whose sole income is derived from burglaries. Most amateur burglars are between the ages of 15 and 25; most professionals are 25 to 55. The amateur is usually an unskilled, "infancy-level" burglar who steals radios, televisions, cash and other portable property and who learns through trial and error. In contrast, the professional burglar usually steals furs, jewelry and more valuable items and has been carefully trained by other professional burglars.

Even though amateurs gain experience in burglaries, they are apt to make a mistake eventually and be observed by the police while committing a burglary. If caught and sentenced to prison, amateur burglars gain the opportunity to learn more about the "trade" from the professionals while behind bars.

Professional burglars may have lookouts who are in communication through two-way radios. A getaway vehicle is usually close to the burglary site, and the lookout monitors police radio frequencies.

Although most burglars' motives are monetary or drug related, sometimes the excitement of committing burglary and evading detection is equally or more important. One burglar said it was a "thrill" not to know what was waiting for him and whether he would get away with the crime.

RESPONDING TO A BURGLARY CALL

On the way to the burglary scene, watch for anyone fleeing the area, suspicious-looking people still at the scene and suspicious automobiles. Do not use a siren on the way to the scene. Cut your flashing lights some distance from the scene, and do not use a spotlight or flashlight to determine the address. Park several doors away from the address of the call, turn the radio down and close car doors quietly. Approach the immediate area with low-tone conversation and avoid jangling keys or coins or flashing lights.

> Proceed to a burglary scene quietly. Be observant and cautious at the scene.

The first two officers arriving place themselves at diagonally opposed corners of the building. This places each out of the other's line of fire but in position to protect each other.

> Search the premises inside and outside for the burglar.

Use maximum cover and caution in going around corners. In a dark room, use a flashlight rather than room lights to prevent silhouettes. Hold the flashlight in front of you at a 45-degree angle. Have your gun drawn but not cocked.

Be alert for the possible presence of explosives at a burglary scene. If a bomb threat is connected with a burglary, notify the FBI. If explosives are actually detonated, notify the Bureau of Alcohol, Tobacco, Firearms and Explosives (ATF) Division of the Department of Homeland Security. To dispose of explosives at the scene or in the suspect's possession, call the bomb squad of the nearest large metropolitan area or the explosives ordnance unit of the closest military installation. If an explosion has already occurred at the burglary scene, intentionally or accidentally, it may leave behind potentially valuable evidence. Collecting and handling such evidence is discussed shortly.

False Burglar Alarms

False burglar alarms from personal residential and commercial security systems are a huge problem for law enforcement agencies. Data from the U.S. Justice Department indicates that 96 percent of all burglar alarm activations are false (Careless, 2007b, p.32). False alarms are typically caused by user error, although occasionally they occur because of faulty equipment.

The growing problem of false alarms has led many departments to implement policies on how to handle such nuisance calls. Some law enforcement agencies have implemented a **verified response policy**, meaning that they will not respond to a burglary alarm unless criminal activity is first confirmed through either an onsite security officer; verbal communication with a resident or employee onsite, either via the phone or through an intercom integrated into the security system; or some other method of electronic surveillance, such as closed-circuit television. An aggressive form of verified response is Enhanced Call Verification (ECV), which requires that a minimum of two phone calls be made from the alarm monitoring center, to assess whether user error activated the alarm. Only then will a law enforcement response be activated: "Those departments who have adopted verified response policies have seen their police dispatch rates drop an average of 72 percent, freeing officers' time for higher priority duties" (Careless, 2007b, p.34).

Another approach that departments are taking is to use an escalating series of fines and fees for police dispatch when the alarm turns out to be false. For chronic abusers, alarm response by police is suspended entirely. False alarms are a waste of time for responding officers, and, more important, they may cause officers to be caught off guard when a genuine alarm occurs.

THE PRELIMINARY INVESTIGATION

Although burglary is a very basic crime to investigate, many investigators cut corners or simply skip the necessary steps of a preliminary investigation because, with a national clearance rate of less than 13 percent, such cases are perceived as being high-time investments for low-result rewards. Yet, for this very reason, the preliminary investigation is of utmost importance.

If no suspect is found at the scene of a burglary, conduct the preliminary investigation as described in Chapter 1. Obtain detailed information about the type of structure burglarized, the means of entry, the time and date, the whereabouts of the owner, other persons recently on the premises, the property taken and the modus operandi (MO).

Determine who the occupants are and where they were at the time of the burglary. Were they on the premises? If not, when did they leave? Were the doors and windows locked? Who had keys? What visitors had recently been there? Obtain descriptions of salespeople, agents, service installers or maintenance workers on the premises recently. Was the burglar familiar with the premises? Could the location of the stolen items be known only to a person who worked on the premises; that is, was it an inside job?

Obtain a complete list of the property taken and an estimate of the value from the victim. Find out where the property was obtained and where it was stored. Where and when did the owner last see it? What type of property was *not* stolen?

Interview witnesses. In many burglaries, there is a connection between the victim and the suspect. The suspect may have recently performed work, made a delivery or attended a party in the home. Conduct a neighborhood canvass to see whether anyone saw anything and to alert neighbors.

Search for physical evidence, including latent fingerprints, items left on the premises by the burglar or tool marks on doors or windows. Without physical evidence, there is little chance of charging anyone. It is especially important to search for prints at the scene and to obtain elimination prints of those with normal access to it.

Check pawnshops where stolen items may have been left. Log articles with serial numbers into NCIC.

An important point to remember is that concern should be shown for the victim. Surveys indicate that victims' impressions of the police are related to how professionally investigators conduct the crime scene investigation. If officers are thorough, courteous, considerate, concerned and conscientious about keeping the victims informed of the progress of the investigation, victims generally express favorable opinions of the investigators. Solving the crime is the first priority for the police, but the victims' feelings must be considered as well. Victims may feel devastated, violated, angry or completely dejected. Investigators must keep these feelings in mind while conducting interviews with victims.

Preliminary Investigation of Residential Burglaries

The preliminary investigation of a residential burglary should include the following steps as a minimum:

- Contact the resident(s).
- Establish points and methods of entry and exit.
- Collect and preserve evidence.
- Determine the type and amount of loss, with complete descriptions.
- Describe the MO.
- Check for recent callers such as friends of children, salespeople and maintenance people.
- Canvass the neighborhood for witnesses, evidence, discarded stolen articles and so on.

Interviews of burglars have revealed that they prefer middle- to upper-class homes and corner homes that allow them to see people approaching from a maximum of directions. Burglars may knock on doors before entering to determine whether a dog is inside, and they may call in advance to see if anyone is home, although caller ID and the ability to "capture" the origin of an incoming phone call has deterred many burglars from using the latter technique.

When processing the crime scene in a residential burglary, process the exit as well as the entry area. When looking for fingerprints, check the inside of drawers that have been ransacked, smooth glass objects, papers strewn on the floor, countertops and clocks. The same procedures are followed if the burglary has occurred in a multiple-dwelling or a commercial-lodging establishment such as an apartment building or a hotel.

Preliminary Investigation of Commercial Burglaries

Preliminary investigation of a commercial burglary (of, for example, a market, shop, office, liquor store) should minimally include the following steps:

- Contact the owner.
- Protect the scene from intrusion by the owner, the public and others.
- Establish the point and method of entry and exit.
- Locate, collect and preserve possible evidence.
- Narrow the time frame of the crime.
- Determine the type and amount of loss.
- Determine who closed the establishment, who was present at the time of the crime and who had keys to the establishment.
- Describe the MO.
- Identify employees' friends, maintenance people and any possible disgruntled employees or customers.
- Rule out a faked or staged burglary for insurance purposes.

Fake Burglaries

Do not overlook the possibility of faked burglaries, especially in commercial burglaries where the owner appears to be in financial difficulty. Check the owner's financial status.

So-called combination safe jobs, in which the safe is opened by the combination without the use of external force, are usually the result of the combination being found on the premises, the safe being carelessly left open or improperly locked, a dishonest present or former employee using the combination or selling it to the burglar or the employer faking a burglary to cover a shortage of funds.

DETERMINING ENTRY INTO STRUCTURES

Burglary is a crime of opportunity and concealment. Entry is made in areas of a structure not normally observed, under the cover of darkness, in covered entryways, through

Burglars may smash display windows to reach valuables. Although many holes are made just big enough to reach an arm through, sometimes the hole is large enough for a person to crawl through. Some businesses place bars or grates over windows to prevent actual entry through a broken pane of glass.

© Prisma Bildagentur AG/Alamy

windows screened by shrubbery or trees or through ruse and trickery. Sometimes, however, the burglar breaks a shop window, removes some items on display and rapidly escapes by jumping into a nearby vehicle driven by an accomplice.

 Jimmying is the most common method of entry to commit burglary.

Almost every means imaginable has been used by burglars to gain entry, including tunneling; chopping holes in walls, floors and ceilings; and using fire escapes. Tool marks, disturbed paint, footprints and fingerprints, broken glass or forced locks help determine how the burglar gained entry.

Some burglars have keys made. For example, some people leave their car at a repair shop along with their full set of keys—an open invitation to make a duplicate house or office key. At other times, burglars hide inside a building until after closing. In such cases, they often leave behind evidence such as matches, cigarette butts or candy wrappers because their wait is often lengthy.

The **hit-and-run burglary**, also called "smash and grab," in which the burglar smashes a window to steal merchandise, is most frequently committed by younger, inexperienced burglars. Jewelry and furs are the most common targets.

In recent years, enterprising burglars have taken advantage of the prevalence of electric garage door openers.

Using "code grabbers," burglars can record and replicate the electronic signal emitted from an automatic garage door opener. When a person leaves the house and activates the garage door opener, the burglar is able to capture the signal from as far as several hundred yards away and reopen the door once the resident is safely out of sight. Some burglars are bold enough to back their own cars into the garage, load it up with stolen items and drive away, leaving no sign of forced entry. To combat the code-grabbing technique to gain entrance into homes, a device called a "code rotator" is available. Each time an automatic door opener is used, the internal code rotates to a new one, rendering a code grabber useless.

DETERMINING ENTRY INTO SAFES AND VAULTS

Safes are usually considered a good way to protect valuables, but most older safes provide little more than fire protection. Unless they are carried away or demolished by a burglar or lost in a fire, safes last many years; therefore, many old safes are still in use.

A **safe** is a semiportable strongbox with a combination lock. The size of the safe or lock does not necessarily correlate with its security. A **vault** is a stationary room of reinforced concrete, often steel lined, with a combination lock. Both safes and vaults are common targets of burglars.

Safes and vaults are entered illegally by punching, peeling, chopping, pulling or dragging, blowing and burning. Sometimes burglars simply haul the safes away.

In **punching**, the dial is sheared from the safe door by a downward blow with a sledge or by holding a chisel to the dial and using a sledge to knock it off, exposing the safe mechanism spindle. Sometimes a tire inner tube, or similar material, will be placed over the safe's dial to deaden the noise. Punching is most successful in attacking older-model fire-resistant safes and is less successful on newer models that have tapered spindles that will jam when someone attempts to punch them.

In **peeling**, the burglar drills a hole in a corner of the safe and then makes this hole successively larger by using other drills until the narrow end of a jimmy can be inserted in the hole to pry the door partially open. The burglar then uses the larger end of the jimmy to complete the job. Although slow, this method is less noisy than others.

In **chopping**, the burglar uses a sledge and chisels or a heavy chopping instrument, such as an axe, to chop a hole in the bottom of the safe large enough to remove the contents. This technique is also called a *rip* or *peel*, and all three terms are used to describe the opening by physical force of a hole, which is expanded until it is big enough to fit a hand inside the safe. A chop/rip/peel is commonly used on fire-resistant safes (sometimes after an unsuccessful punch).

In **pulling**, also called **dragging**, the burglar inserts a V plate over the dial, with the V in place behind the dial. The burglar then tightens the screw bolts one at a time until the dial and the spindle are pulled out. This method, the opposite of punching, works on many older safes but not on newer ones.

In **blowing**, the burglar drills a hole in the safe near the locking bar area or pushes cotton into an area of the safe door crack and puts nitroglycerin on the cotton. The burglar then places a primer cap against the cotton, tapes it in place and runs a wire to a protected area. Mattresses and blankets are often used to soften the blast. The burglar ignites the nitroglycerin, which blows the safe open. This dangerous, noisy method requires experience and is rarely used.

The process of **burning** often uses a "burning bar," a portable safecracking tool that burns a hole into the safe to gain entry. This hole may be burned near the safe's locking mechanism, or the safe may be tipped over and the hole burned through the bottom. An arc-air burning tool can punch a hole completely through a 1-inch steel plate in about 10 seconds.

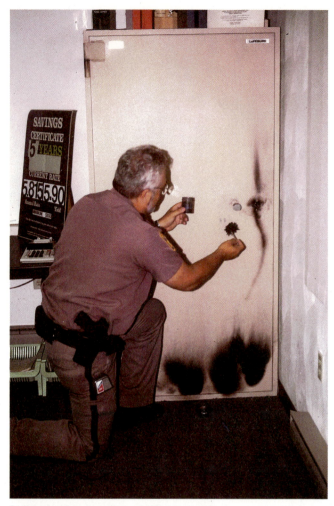

Safes are a frequent target of burglars.
© James Shaffer

Some burglars prefer a site of their own choosing at which to employ one or more of these methods. So, they steal the entire safe, haul it away in a truck and open it when they get there.

The preceding methods are used on older safes still found in many smaller stores. Often the safe can be entered in less than 15 minutes. Modern safes, however, do not have spindles and cannot be punched, peeled or pulled. Safes of newer steel alloys are highly resistant to burning and drilling.

OBTAINING PHYSICAL EVIDENCE

Most burglars are convicted on circumstantial evidence. Any physical evidence at the burglary scene is of utmost importance.

This bag contains stolen merchandise (wrist watches) as well as the tools used to illegally gain access to the merchandise.
© ImageState/Alamy

Physical evidence at a burglary scene includes fingerprints, footprints, tire prints, tools, tool marks, broken glass, paint chips, safe insulation, explosives residue and personal possessions.

The competent, professional burglar will wear gloves to avoid leaving fingerprints and palm prints. However, an offender's inexperience and haste could result in such prints being scattered throughout the crime scene. Therefore, process the scene for prints, particularly at the entry point.

Shoe impressions and footprints may be visible inside or outside the structure and should be cast following the guidelines in Chapter 5. Similarly, any tire impressions located around the burglary scene should be cast as possible evidence.

Tools and tool marks are especially important items of evidence. Pry bars, augers, picks and screwdrivers are commonly used to commit burglary. Locksmith tools can also be used and are illegal to possess unless one is a licensed locksmith. Burglars often have a "tool of choice"

to gain entry, and this same tool, used over and over at different crime scenes, will leave behind characteristic striation marks that can connect one burglary to another. Tools used to pry open a door or window always leave a mark behind (recall Locard's principle of exchange discussed in Chapter 1). If the frame is made of wood, striation marks may be visible and can be cast. Before casting an impression in wood, however, spray the surface with a silicone oil-based release agent to ensure that the silicone casting material, once cured, does not stick to the wood and pull out wood fibers when the cast is removed.

Be alert to the variety of containers used to carry burglary tools—handbags, suitcases, musical-instrument cases and packages that appear to contain merchandise. Tools can also be concealed under coats, inside pant legs or under car seats. Tools found on the premises are sometimes left there by the burglar to avoid being caught with burglary tools in possession and to thwart efforts to link multiple burglaries to one offender.

Broken glass and paint chips are common items of evidence at burglary scenes. An offender who smashes a window to gain entry to a building may unwittingly carry away tiny fragments of glass on his clothing or the soles of his shoes. Samples of glass or chipped paint collected at the scene can be matched to glass and paint fragments detected on the suspect, helping to establish his presence at the crime scene.

Evidence at the scene of a safe burglary may also include safe insulation. As with glass and paint fragments, the burglar often has some of this insulation on his or her clothing, either in pants, coat or jacket pockets or in the nail holes of shoes. Take comparison standards of safe insulation to be matched with particles found on the suspect, on tools the suspect used or in the vehicle used during the crime. In some cases, safe insulation can also be matched with a series of burglaries.

Sometimes explosives are encountered at a burglary scene. Use extreme caution in handling and preserving such evidence. If an explosion has already occurred at the burglary scene, intentionally or accidentally, identify and preserve fragments from the explosive device and send them to a crime laboratory.

DNA is also becoming important in burglary investigations. If a burglar gets cut breaking into a structure, he or she may leave blood behind that can be analyzed for DNA, perhaps linking the burglary to others. Touch or trace DNA can be obtained from surfaces at the scene, such as when a nervous and perspiring suspect presses his or her face against a window or a burglar with a cold sneezes on a counter. These types of actions, and the trace evidence they leave behind, are now receiving recognition among investigators and helping solve some difficult burglary cases.

Critics argue that DNA analysis is too expensive to use in an attempt to solve a burglary that, on average, involves a loss amount less than that of the analysis. However, the National Institute of Justice (NIJ) has advocated collecting DNA evidence in "minor" crime investigations as a way to yield major public safety benefits, noting the high recidivism rates of property crime offenders, that their crimes and violence often escalate and that many property crime cases go unsolved. Recall from Chapter 5 the study that showed how DNA analysis can more than double the identification rate of suspects, leading to a doubling of the arrest and prosecution rates of burglary suspects (Johns and Rushing, 2009). Another study found that DNA analysis helps identify serial burglars, the arrest of whom can significantly reduce an area's burglary rate by taking repeat offenders off the streets, thereby saving communities millions of dollars in investigative resources and lost personal property (Geoghegan, 2009).

Despite the potential benefits of DNA analysis, many forensic laboratories have backlogs extending several months, and much of the caseload involves higher priority evidence from violent crimes. Thus, processing such evidence from property crimes is currently impractical for many jurisdictions. If, however, the cost of such analysis is reduced in the future and the process becomes more simplified, more burglary investigations may rely on DNA evidence.

MODUS OPERANDI FACTORS

Effective MO files are essential in investigating burglaries because most burglars commit a series of burglaries. Look for patterns in the location, day of week, time of day, type of property stolen and method of entry and exit. The burglar may commit vandalism, ransack, write with lipstick on mirrors, take only cash or jewelry, drink liquor from the scene or eat from the refrigerator. Such peculiarities can tie several burglaries to one suspect.

> Important MO factors include the time, type of victim, type of premises, point and means of entry, type of property taken and any peculiarities of the offense.

Suspects often commit burglaries on only a certain day of the week, perhaps related to their day off from a regular job. The time of the burglary should be as accurate as possible, but when victims are gone on vacation, this is not easy to determine. Knowing the time also helps in checking alibis, interviewing witnesses and, in some states, determining the degree of the burglary.

Determine any peculiarities of the offense, including oddities of the suspect. What method of search was used? Was anything else done besides committing the burglary? Did the burglar telephone first to ensure that no one was home or pose as a delivery person? Did neighbors see such activities? Determine any trademarks of the burglar. Some burglars take such pride in their professionalism that they leave a calling card of some type to let the police know whose work it is.

Check the MO with local files. Talk to other officers, inquire at other agencies within a 100-mile radius and discuss the case at area investigation meetings. Other officers may have encountered a similar MO.

EFFECTIVE CASE MANAGEMENT

Because burglary is predominantly a serial crime, the serial burglar should be the primary target of the burglary unit. This requires effective case management, including an effective system for prioritizing cases. Profiling and mapping may be of considerable help.

Using the computer's search capabilities, information retrieval is fast and simple and investigations can proceed on information that in the past would have taken hundreds of hours to retrieve if indeed it could have been retrieved at all.

Effective case management also recognizes the mobility of burglars and makes assignments on the MO rather than on the geographic area—for example, burglaries involving forcible entry, daytime burglaries involving no force and nighttime residential burglaries. All information should be shared with the drug enforcement unit because many burglaries are drug related.

A new investigative management tool to help deal with the rise in narcotics and other prescription drug thefts from pharmacies is a national database called Rx Pattern Analysis Tracking Robberies and Other Losses (RxPATROL). According to the program's Web site RxPATROL, 2011), RxPATROL is "designed to collect, collate, analyze and disseminate pharmacy theft intelligence to law enforcement throughout the nation." Pharmacies provide data directly to RxPATROL in the aftermath of a theft involving controlled substances, including any video or still photos captured. An analyst at RxPATROL uses an incident analysis software platform to evaluate the data, identify trends and provide intelligence to the respective law enforcement agencies for action as they deem appropriate. Analysis provided by RxPATROL has helped several law enforcement agencies successfully apprehend and prosecute those involved in controlled substance pharmacy crime.

RECOVERING STOLEN PROPERTY

Stolen property is disposed of in several ways. Because many people are looking for a bargain, thieves can often sell the property on the streets, thus avoiding a record of the sale but also risking being reported to the police by someone who sees the transaction. Other common forums for disposing of stolen property include pawnshops and Internet auction sites, the latter being popular because the seller can remain anonymous.

In the case of property being sold to pawn shops or secondhand stores or left at a store on consignment for sale, most states and communities have statutes or ordinances requiring a permanent record of the transaction. The seller must be given a receipt describing the property purchased and the amount paid, with the seller's name and address. A copy of the transaction is often sent to the police department of the community listed as the seller's home address. If the property is identified as stolen, the police contact the shop owner and, upon proof that the property is stolen, can recover it. Shop records are open to police inspection at all times. Information in these records can lead to the arrest of the seller as the person who committed the burglary.

Informants can often locate stolen property because they usually know who is active in the area. Surveillance of pawnshops also is often productive. Circulate a list of the stolen property to all establishments that might deal in such merchandise in your own community and surrounding communities. If the property is extremely valuable, enter it into the FBI's NCIC files.

 Check with pawnshops, secondhand stores, flea markets, online auction sites and informants for leads in recovering stolen property.

As with so many other types of crimes and evidence, national database and tracking tools are being implemented to help law enforcement find and recover stolen goods.

When you recover stolen property, record the date on which the property was recovered, where it was recovered, who turned it in and the circumstances surrounding the recovery. List the names and addresses of anyone present at the time of recovery. Mark the property as evidence and take it into custody. In some states, it is legal to return the property as long as its identification is recorded and a photograph is taken. There is no reason the original property must be produced in court unless it was an instrument that caused death or serious injury.

Recovering stolen property and returning it to the rightful owner is aided by Operation Identification programs. In such programs, homeowners mark all easily stolen property with a personal identification number (PIN). The numbers are recorded and placed in a secure location.

Technology Innovations

Careless (2007a, pp.100–101) describes JustStolen.net, a Web site that can assist in the recovery of stolen property:

JustStolen.net is a Web site where people can register the name, model, serial number, photos and other details of their valued property. Should it be stolen, the victim can refer to this data when he files a police report. When police anywhere subsequently recover this property, all they have to do is log on to JustStolen.net's law enforcement database (which cannot be accessed by the public) and enter any of the property's description, name, model or serial number into the site's search engine. If this property has been reregistered in the system, either before or after the theft took place, JustStolen.net provides the officer with an e-mail link that can be used to alert the owner.

JustStolen.net is entirely free to the public and the police.

Would-be thieves should realize that Just Stolen.net has closed a major gap in law enforcement cases—linking stolen property and the culprits who commit home burglary and other property crimes to their rightful owners, so a successful prosecution can take place.

THE OFFENSE OF RECEIVING STOLEN GOODS

A go-between who receives stolen goods for resale is referred to as a **fence**.

> The elements of the offense of receiving stolen goods are
> - Receiving, buying or concealing stolen or illegally obtained goods,
> - knowing them to be stolen or otherwise illegally obtained.

Receiving stolen property for resale is a crime, as is concealing stolen property, even though not purchased. A burglar does not have to personally sell goods to a fence. An "innocent" third party can sell the property for the burglar, but it is still an offense if the buyer knows the property was stolen.

It is difficult to prove that a buyer knew the purchased goods were stolen. The property must be found in the receiver's possession and identified as the stolen property by the owner's testimony, marks, serial numbers or other positive identification. Knowing can then be proved by the very low price paid for the goods in comparison with the true value.

Usually evidence of the sale is provided through an informant who either made the sale or knows who did. The property may have been resold, and the person buying the item may be the informant who identifies the receiver of stolen goods. This person assists the police in making another sale or identifying property in the receiver's possession.

The receiver of stolen goods is often discovered when the person who stole the property is arrested and identifies the receiver. It is necessary to show that the receiver could not legitimately own the item unless he or she had bought it from a thief. Show that it was not purchased through a normal business transaction. The character of the person selling the property or any indication that the property was being concealed is evidence. Evidence that markings or serial numbers have been altered or removed indicates concealment and intent to deprive the rightful owner of the property. The seller can testify to conversations with the receiver about the property and the fact that it was stolen. The receiver's records may not show the transaction, which would be evidence of intent to conceal. The charge of receiving stolen goods can be used when possession of stolen items can be shown but there is not sufficient evidence to prove theft.

One indicator of fencing activity is an operation that makes merchandise available to retailers at extremely low wholesale prices provided they pay cash. Another possible indicator is a small local outlet that offers significant savings to customers, conducts a large volume of business over a short period and then closes suddenly. Sales from fenced goods amount to tens of billions of dollars annually.

Sting Operations

Many cities have established sting operations, in which the police legally establish a fencing operation. A suitable shop is set up as a front for the operation. Normally, secondhand stores, repair shops, salvage dealers, appliance dealers or pawnshops make good front operations. The store is stocked with items to support the type of business selected.

Word is spread through informants and the underworld that the business will "buy anything." Attractive prices are paid to get the business started. All transactions between the fence and the seller of stolen goods are recorded by closed-circuit television. The camera is usually focused on an area in which a calendar and clock are clearly visible to establish the date and time of each transaction. A parking lot surveillance camera shows the vehicle used to transport the property and its license number.

When an item is presented at the counter, the seller, the amount paid for the property and the buyer are recorded. The property is then dusted for fingerprints to further prove the seller's possession. The stolen goods are checked through normal police channels to determine where they were stolen.

The shop is run for two to three months and then discontinued. Arrest warrants are then issued for those implicated during the store's operation.

PREVENTING BURGLARY

Research shows that premises that are burglarized are likely to be burglarized again. The Electronic Security Association (ESA, 2011) states on its Web site (http://www.alarm.org): "Homes without security systems are about three times more likely to be broken into than homes with security systems. (Actual statistic ranges from 2.2 times to 3.1 times, depending on the value of the home.) Businesses without alarm systems are 4.5 times more likely to be burglarized than commercial locations with electronic security in place. Losses due to burglary average $400 less in residences with security systems than for a residence without security systems."

Officers who work with burglary victims can help them avoid future burglaries by conducting a security check of the premises and "hardening" the target. **Target hardening**, also called **crime prevention through environmental design (CPTED)**, involves altering physical characteristics of the property to make it less attractive to criminals. CPTED measures include removing dense shrubbery next to windows and doors because this provides concealment to burglars and increases the attractiveness of the target. High privacy fences around homes also give cover to people attempting to break in. Inadequate lighting increases the attractiveness of a property to burglars. Open garages and unlocked service doors from the home to the garage are other ways burglars gain entry.

Officers can also assist their jurisdiction in reducing burglaries by having input into building codes that would require adequate locks, lighting and other security measures to deter burglaries.

Measures that deter burglaries include

- Installing adequate locks, striker plates and doorframes.
- Installing adequate indoor and outdoor lighting.
- Providing clearly visible addresses.
- Eliminating bushes or other obstructions to windows.
- Securing any skylights or air vents larger than 96 square inches.
- Installing burglarproof sidelight window glass beside doors.
- Installing a burglar alarm and placing exterior signage to visibly indicate the presence of such an alarm.
- Keeping dogs on the premises.

Summary

Burglary is the unlawful entry of a structure to commit a crime. It differs from robbery in that burglars are covert, seeking to remain unseen, whereas robbers confront their victims directly. Burglary is a crime against property; robbery is a crime against a person.

Burglaries are classified as residential or commercial. The primary elements of the crime of burglary are (1) entering a structure (2) without the consent of the person in possession (3) with the intent to commit a crime therein. Elements of burglary can also include (1) breaking into (2) the dwelling of another (3) during the nighttime. A burglary's severity is determined by (a) the presence of dangerous devices in the burglar's possession or (b) the value of the stolen property. The elements of the crime of possessing burglary tools include (1) possessing any device, explosive or other instrumentality (2) with intent to use or permit its use to commit burglary.

When responding to a burglary call, proceed to the scene quietly. Be observant and cautious at the scene. Search the premises inside and outside for the burglar. Jimmying is the most common method of entry to commit burglary. Safes and vaults are entered illegally by punching, peeling, chopping, pulling or dragging, blowing and burning. Sometimes burglars simply haul the safes away.

Physical evidence at a burglary scene includes fingerprints, footprints, tire prints, tools, tool marks, broken glass, paint chips, safe insulation, explosives residue and personal possessions. Important MO factors include the time, the type of victim, type of premises, point and means of entry, type of property taken and any peculiarities of the offense.

Check with pawnshops, secondhand stores, flea markets, online auction sites and informants for leads in recovering stolen property.

The elements of the offense of receiving stolen goods are (1) receiving, buying or concealing stolen or illegally obtained goods (2) knowing them to be stolen or otherwise illegally obtained.

Measures to deter burglaries include installing adequate locks, striker plates and door frames; installing adequate indoor and outdoor lighting; providing clearly visible addresses; eliminating bushes or other obstructions to windows; securing any skylights or air vents larger than 96 square inches; installing burglar-proof sidelight window glass beside doors; installing a burglar alarm and pacing exterior signage to visibly indicate the presence of such an alarm; and keeping dogs on the premises.

Checklist

Burglary

- Was a thorough preliminary investigation conducted?
- What is the address and description of the structure burglarized?

- What time and date did the burglary occur?
- What means was used to enter? Was it forcible?
- Who is the rightful owner? Was consent given for the entry?
- What visitors had recently been on the premises?
- Was the burglar familiar with the premises?
- What was taken (complete description and value of each item)?
- Where was the property located, and when was it last seen by the owner?
- What was *not* taken?
- What pattern of search did the burglar use?
- What was the burglar's MO?
- What physical evidence was found at the scene?
- Did any witnesses see or hear anything suspicious at the time of the burglary?
- Does the owner have any idea who might have committed the burglary?
- Have the MO files been checked?
- Have neighboring communities been informed of the burglary?
- Have you checked with fences, pawnshop owners and secondhand stores for the stolen property? Have you circulated a list to the owners of such businesses?
- Might this be a fake burglary?

Application

Read this account of a criminal investigation and evaluate its effectiveness:

> In a California city, two janitors showing up for work were met at the door of the restaurant they were to clean by two armed men. One janitor was taken inside; the other escaped and notified the police. When the police arrived, both suspects were outside the building in different areas and claimed they knew nothing of a crime being committed. Inside, the one janitor was tied up in the kitchen, unharmed. The safe had been punched open. A substance believed to be safe insulation, along with paint chips, was found in the trouser cuffs and shoes of both suspects. Both janitors made a positive field identification of the two suspects. Laboratory analysis of the substance found in the suspects' clothing and shoes matched a comparison sample of the safe insulation, and the paint chips matched the top two layers of paint on the safe. The men were charged with burglary.

Questions

1. Was it legal to take the men into custody?
2. Was field identification appropriate?
3. Was it legal to submit the safe insulation and paint chips for laboratory analysis?
4. Was the charge correct?
5. What additional evidence should have been located and seized?

Discussion Questions

1. Many people think of *burglary* and *robbery* as interchangeable terms. What is the principal difference between these two offenses from an investigative viewpoint?
2. Describe the following methods of entering a safe: a pull job, a peel job, a chopping, blowing a safe, burning.
3. What types of evidence would you expect to find at the scene of a safe burglary? How would you collect and preserve it?
4. What are the elements of burglary in your state? What is the penalty?
5. How frequent is burglary in your community? In your state? Has burglary been increasing or decreasing in the past five years?
6. If you are investigating a burglary, which persons would you be most interested in talking to at the scene? Away from the scene?
7. What other crimes are often committed along with burglary?
8. Is it legal to "steal back" your own property if someone has stolen it from you?
9. If the object stolen in a burglary is valued less than $100, what level of crime would this be and why?
10. Is there a difference in the severity level of a burglary if it is committed on an occupied residence rather than an unoccupied one, such as a furnished rental property that currently has no tenants?

Media Explorations

 ### Internet

Select one of the following assignments to complete.

- Go to the FBI Web site at www.fbi.gov. Click on "library and reference." Select "Uniform Crime Reports" and outline what the report says about burglary.

■ Select one of the following key terms: *burglary, routine activity theory, smash and grab.* Find one article relevant to burglary investigations to outline and share with the class.

 Gale Criminal Justice Database Assignments

The following assignments require access to Gale's Custom Journals Database for Emergency Services and Criminal Justice. Check with your instructor if you have questions about this.

■ Find the article "An Ounce of Prevention" on the Gale Emergency Services Database. Read the article and identify how technology is used for burglary investigations. Be prepared to discuss this in class.

■ Find the article "The Routine Activity Theory: A Model for Addressing Specific Crime Issues" on the Gale Emergency Services Database. Identify how this theory is applicable to burglary investigations. Outline it and share with the class.

References

Careless, James. "JustStolen.net Helps Police Return Property." *Law and Order*, June 2007a, pp.100–101.

Careless, James. "Verified Alarm Solution to Staffing Problems." *Law and Order*, February 2007b, pp.32–34.

"Crime Clock Statistics." In *Crime in the United States, 2009*. Washington, DC: Federal Bureau of Investigation, September 2010. Accessed June 21, 2011. http://www2.fbi.gov/ucr/cius2009/about/crime_clock.html

Crime in the United States, 2009. Washington, DC: U.S. Department of Justice, Federal Bureau of Investigation, September 2010. Accessed May 27, 2011. http://www2.fbi.gov/ucr/cius2009/index.html

Electronic Security Association. "Security Systems Facts." 2011. Accessed June 24, 2011. http://www.alarm.org/HomeSafety/FactsandStats/SecuritySystemsFacts.aspx

Filbert, Katie. "Targeting Crime in Hot Spots and Hot Places." *Geography & Public Safety*, March 2008.

Geoghegan, Susan. "Forensic DNA." *Law and Order*, June 2009, pp.49–53.

Johns, Susan, and Rushing, Patricia. "Using DNA to Solve Property Crimes." *Community Policing Dispatch*, Vol.2, No.12, December 2009. Accessed April 27, 2011. http://www.cops.usdoj.gov/html/dispatch/December_2009/dna.htm

RxPATROL. "What's RxPATROL?" 2011. Accessed November 1, 2011. http://rxpatrol.org/aboutrxpatrol.aspx

Sullivan, Laura. "Burglaries on the Decline in the United States." National Public Radio, March 13, 2008.

CHAPTER 14
Larceny/Theft, Fraud and White-Collar Crime

© AP Images/Torsten Silz/dapd

Outline

Can You Define?

confidence game
corporate crime
cramming
economic crime
embezzlement
flaggers
floor-release limit
fluffing
forgery
fraud
goods
gouging
grand larceny
holder
identity theft
integration
jamming
larceny/theft
layering

leakage
long-con games
money laundering
parallel proceedings
petty larceny
placement
poaching
Ponzi scheme
property
property flipping
short-con games
shrinkage
slamming
sliding
smurfing
structuring
white-collar crime
zero floor release

Larceny/theft is one of the eight Index crimes reported in the Federal Bureau of Investigation's (FBI) Uniform Crime Reports (UCR). Although fraud, white-collar crime and environmental crime are not Index crimes, they are so closely related to larceny/theft that they are included in this chapter. Furthermore, they all have elements in common and are investigated in similar ways.

Some states eliminate the distinctions between larceny, fraud and white-collar crimes, combining them into the single crime of *theft*. However, because many states have separate offenses, this chapter discusses them separately. The distinction may be unimportant in your jurisdiction.

Reported larceny/thefts exceed the combined total of all other Index crimes. Data from the FBI indicate that two-thirds of all property crimes in 2009 were larceny/

Do You Know?

- How larceny differs from burglary and robbery?
- What the elements of larceny/theft are?
- What the two major categories of larceny are and how to determine them?
- What legally must be done with found property?
- What the common types of larceny are?
- Whether a shoplifter must leave the premises before being apprehended?
- When the FBI becomes involved in a larceny/theft investigation?
- What fraud is and how it differs from larceny/theft?
- What the common means of committing fraud are?
- What the common types of check fraud are?
- What the elements of the crime of larceny by debit or credit card are?
- What form of larceny/theft headed the FTC's top 10 consumer fraud complaints in 2006?
- What white-collar crime is and what offenses are often included in this crime category?
- What the nature of the FBI's two-pronged approach to investigating money laundering is?

(continued)

Do You Know? *(continued)*

- What the main problems in prosecuting environmental crime are?
- How the monetary loss value of certain thefts, frauds or other economic crimes influences which agency has jurisdiction over a criminal investigation?

thefts (*Crime in the United States, 2009*, 2010). An estimated 6.3 million thefts occurred nationwide, a 4.0 percent decrease from 2008 and a 9.2 percent decrease from 2000. The Office for Victims of Crime's "Crime Clock" (2009) reports that one home is victimized by theft every 4.8 seconds. The National Crime Victimization Survey (NCVS) reported 133,210 personal thefts (pickpocketing, purse snatching) in 2009, at a rate of 0.5 per 1,000 households, and 11,709,830 other thefts, at a rate of 95.7 per 1,000 households (Truman and Rand, 2010). The average value of property stolen was $864 per offense, for an estimated $5.5 billion in lost property in 2009. Nationwide, law enforcement cleared 21.5 percent of all reported larceny/thefts in 2009 (*Crime in the United States, 2009*, 2010).

Investigators may find themselves working a case with the FBI if the matter involves fraud, theft or embezzlement within or against the national or international financial community. The priority problem areas of this category of crime identified by the FBI's Financial Crimes Section (FCS) include corporate fraud, health care fraud, mortgage fraud, identity theft, insurance fraud and money laundering. One unit of the FCS, the Economic Crimes Unit, investigates significant frauds targeted against individuals, businesses and industries such as corporate fraud, securities and commodities fraud, telemarketing fraud, insurance fraud not related to health care, Ponzi schemes, advance fee schemes and pyramid schemes. A **Ponzi scheme**—named after Charles Ponzi, whose pyramid-type fraud scheme during the 1920s led to a major federal investigation—involves using capital from new investors to pay off earlier investors. This scheme requires an ever-expanding base of new investors to support the financial obligations to the existing "higher ups"—hence the pyramidal shape used to depict such structures.

Typically, there must be either interstate involvement or a loss exceeding a minimum financial threshold of $250,000 for federal investigators to take the case. Although these crimes may be investigated and prosecuted at the federal level, the victims typically call the local police first.

LARCENY/THEFT: AN OVERVIEW

Larceny/theft is the unlawful taking, carrying, leading or driving away of property from the possession of another. Larceny is committed through the cunning, skill and criminal design of the professional thief or as a crime of opportunity committed by the rank amateur. The FBI notes, "These crimes are characterized by deceit, concealment, or violation of trust, and are not dependent upon the application or threat of physical force or violence" (*2009 Financial Crimes Report*, 2009). The adage that "there is a little larceny in everyone" has considerable truth. Although some thefts result from revenge or spite, the motive for most larcenies is the same for the professional and the amateur thief—monetary gain: either actual cash or articles that can be converted to cash or personal use.

> Both larceny and burglary are crimes against property, but larceny, unlike burglary, does not involve illegally entering a structure. Larceny differs from robbery in that no force or threat of force is involved.

ELEMENTS OF THE CRIME: LARCENY/THEFT

The crime of larceny/theft takes many forms, but the basic elements of the offense are similar in the statutes of every state.

> The elements of the crime of larceny/theft are
> - The felonious stealing, taking, carrying, leading or driving away,
> - of another's personal goods or property,
> - valued above (grand) or below (petty) a specified amount,
> - with the intent to permanently deprive the owner of the property or goods.

Felonious Stealing, Taking, Carrying, Leading or Driving Away. This element requires an unlawful, wrongful or felonious removal of the property; that is, the property is removed by any manner of stealing. Taking items such as fuel and electricity is also included in this element. Withholding property is a form of larceny by a failure to ever return, or properly account for, the property or to deliver the property to the rightful owner when it is due. Failure to pay a debt is *not* larceny; civil remedies are sought for this type of conduct.

The Personal Goods or Property of Another. **Goods** or **property** refers to all forms of tangible property, real or personal. It includes valuable documents; electricity, gas, water and heat supplied by municipalities or public utility companies; and domestic animals such as cats, dogs and livestock. It also includes property in which the accused has a co-ownership, lien, pledge, bailment, lease or other subordinate interest. Larceny laws also cover cases in which the property of a partnership is converted to one partner's personal use adverse to the other partner's rights, except when the accused and the victim are husband and wife.

In the definition of larceny/theft, *another* refers to an individual, a government, a corporation or an organization. This element refers to the true owner or the one authorized to control the property. Care assignment, personal custody or some degree of legal control is evidence of possession. In numerous cases, ownership has been questioned. Ownership usually designates the true owner or the person who has superior rights at the time of the theft. The owner must support the charge of larceny; otherwise, there is no prosecution.

Of a Value Above or Below a Specified Amount. *Value* determines whether the offense is grand or petty larceny. *Value* refers to the market value at the time of the theft. Value is determined by replacement cost, legitimate market value, value listed in government property catalogs, fair market value or reasonable estimates.

If the property is restored to the owner, value means the cost-equivalent of the property's use or the damage it sustained, whichever is greater, during the time the owner was deprived of its possession. However, this cannot exceed the original value declared.

If several items are stolen in a single crime, the value of *all* items combined determines the value of the loss, even if the property belonged to more than one owner. Identical items stolen from different larceny locations are not combined but are treated as separate offenses.

With the Intent to Permanently Deprive the Owner of the Property or Goods. Intent either exists at the time the property was taken or is formed afterward. The person may have intended only to borrow the property but then decided to keep it permanently. Intent is usually the most difficult element to prove. Establish ownership through documents of purchase, statements describing how the property was possessed, the length of time of possession and details of the delegation of care and control to another by the true owner.

Because of its frequency, much police time is devoted to larceny, and individual merchants and private security forces are also involved. Millions of dollars in losses go unreported each month. Those that are reported are usually for collecting insurance rather than in the hope of recovering the property or clearing the case.

CLASSIFICATION OF LARCENY/THEFT

Most statutes have two major categories of larceny/theft based on the total value of the property stolen.

> The categories of larceny/theft are **grand larceny**, a felony; and **petty larceny**, a misdemeanor. Which category the crime falls under is based on the value of the property stolen.

In many states, the amount of theft that predicates grand larceny is $100 or more; any lesser amount is petty (petit) larceny. Check the laws in your jurisdiction for the dollar value that distinguishes petty and grand larceny. It is important to know whether the crime is a misdemeanor or a felony before proceeding with the investigation.

FOUND PROPERTY

Keeping or selling property lost by the owner is a form of theft.

> In most states, taking found property with the intent to keep or sell it is a crime.

Although the finder has possession of the property, it is not legal possession. Thieves apprehended with stolen property often claim to have found it—an invalid excuse. A reasonable effort must be made to find the owner of the property—for example, by making inquiries or advertising in a newspaper. The owner, if located, must pay the cost of such inquiries before the property is returned.

If the owner is not located after reasonable attempts are made to do so and after a time specified by law, the finder of the property can legally retain possession of it.

To help prevent theft, a security guard monitors the facilities of a California computer company using multi-image closed-circuit television sets.
© Bill Varie/CORBIS

THE PRELIMINARY INVESTIGATION

Investigating larceny/theft is similar to investigating a burglary, except that in a larceny/theft, even less physical evidence is available because no illegal or forcible entry occurred. Physical evidence might include empty cartons or containers, empty hangers, objects left at the scene, footprints and fingerprints.

Do not give the complainant or victim the impression that the investigation of the reported theft is unimportant. If there is little hope of recovering the property or finding the thief, inform the complainant of this, but only after you obtain all the facts.

TYPES OF LARCENY/THEFT

The UCR for 2009 indicates the relative frequency of each type of larceny (Figure 14.1). The growing problem of identity theft is discussed later in the chapter.

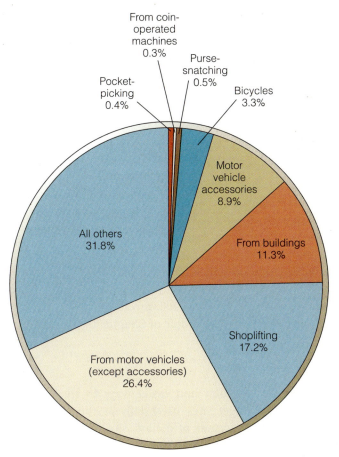

FIGURE 14.1
Relative frequency of different types of larceny/theft.

*Due to rounding, the percentages may not add to 100.0

Source: Crime in the United States, 2010 U.S. Department of Justice—Federal Bureau of Investigation September 2011. http://www.fbi.gov/about-us/cjis/ucr/crime-in-the-u.s/2010/crime-in-the-u.s.-2010/property-crime/larcenytheftmain

> Common types of larceny are pocket picking and purse snatching; bicycle theft; theft from motor vehicles; mail theft; retail shrinkage, including employee theft, shoplifting and organized retail crime; jewelry theft; art theft; numismatic theft, including coins, metals and paper money; agricultural theft; fish and wildlife theft; and cargo theft.

Pickpockets and Purse Snatchers

Pickpockets are difficult to apprehend because the victim must identify the thief. This proves challenging, if not impossible, unless the thief is observed by someone else or is caught in the act. The purse opener and purse snatcher are modern versions of the pickpocket. These thieves use force if necessary but generally rely instead on their skills of deviousness and stealth to avoid the use of force and evade identification. These types of thefts are sometimes called *distraction thefts* because of how the offender gains access to the victim's property. The two necessary elements of this crime are a distraction followed by an extraction, the actual theft. Lost wallets and purses, often the work of the pickpocket, are often not reported as thefts because the victims do not realize that theft has occurred.

Sporting events, New Year's Eve parties, parades, rock concerts, fairs and festivals, public transportation and commuter trains present ideal situations for the pickpocket, full of potential victims in tight, distracted crowds.

Behavior that may indicate a pickpocket at work is "looping," in which a suspect exits at one train or bus door and reboards at another. Another common tactic is for pickpockets to immerse themselves in a crowd getting onto a bus or train and take advantage of the jostling body contact that almost always occurs during a boarding rush. Watch for "passengers" who join the crowd rushing toward the vehicle doorway but then, at the last minute, fail to board.

Purse snatching may be a larceny/theft or a robbery depending on whether force is used. There are two distinct types of purse snatches. One type occurs when a victim is seated at a bus stop, outdoor restaurant, gambling casino or similar public place and sets a purse, bag or like item on the seat or floor next to her and a thief grabs the property and runs off with it. Because this act lacks the element of use of force, it qualifies as a larceny/theft. The other type occurs when a victim is clutching a bag or purse tightly, has a purse strap over her shoulder or has used some similar means of securing the property and force is used by the thief to seize it, qualifying the act as a robbery. As a general rule, investigators should determine whether the victim experienced any sensation of force being used because any force, no matter how slight, would satisfy the element of robbery. The statement of the victim on this point will be a critical factor for the prosecutor to determine whether to charge robbery or larceny/theft.

Obtain from the victim a description of what was stolen and its value. Ask if the victim recalls being jostled or distracted momentarily, and, if so, obtain complete details. Keep careful records of pickpockets and purse snatchers, as often they are caught.

Bicycle Theft

As bicycles have increased in popularity, so has bicycle theft. According to the Web site of the National Bike Registry (www.nationalbikeregistry.com), more than 1.5 million bicycles, worth an estimated $200 million, are stolen each year in the United States. Experienced thieves can steal a locked bike in less than 20 seconds. And although nearly 50 percent of all stolen bicycles are recovered every year by law enforcement, only 5 percent are returned to their owners because most bikes are unregistered.

Bicycles are most frequently stolen from schoolyards, college campuses, sidewalk parking racks, driveways and residential yards. Juveniles are responsible for most thefts, although some professional bike theft rings operate interstate, even exporting stolen bicycles out of the country. Stolen bikes are used for transportation; are sold on the street, at flea markets or to bike stores; and are disposed of through fences. On the street, the value of a stolen bicycle is approximately 5 to 10 percent of the bicycle's original retail value, with an inverse relationship between value and percentage worth on the street ("Crime and No Punishment," n.d.). In other words, less expensive bikes are resold for a higher percentage of their original price than are top-of-the-line bikes. In some bicycle thefts, the crime is grand larceny because of the high value of the stolen bike.

The professional thief, often using a van or covered truck, steals several expensive bikes at one time, takes them to a garage and repaints them or dismantles them for parts. Bicycles are easy to disguise by painting over or removing identification (ID) tags. Many are immediately disassembled and sold for parts and are easily taken from one location to another by simply riding them or placing them in a vehicle trunk, van or truck.

A single bike theft is best investigated by the patrol force. Determine the bicycle's value and have the owner sign a complaint. A juvenile apprehended for a single theft can be prosecuted, especially with a prior record of similar or other offenses. Restitution for damage and an informal probation are usually initiated. If multiple thefts have occurred, the offender usually goes to juvenile court. Adults are prosecuted by the same procedures used for other larcenies.

The investigative division compiles a list of bike complaints organized by make of bike, serial number and color. Bike thefts are also entered into the police computer system. Patrol officers are given a bike "hot sheet" similar to that for stolen vehicles and periodically check bike racks at parks, schools and business areas against this sheet.

Bikes are sometimes reported stolen to defraud insurance companies. Even if the bike is recovered, the owner has already collected its value, and there will seldom be a prosecution. Large numbers of thefts in a short time may indicate an interstate ring has moved into the community. These rings use covered trucks to transport bicycles from the area, making recovery almost impossible. However, when interstate or international bicycle theft rings attempt to dispose of their stolen inventory, their activity may become identifiable. For example, customs officials at a port in New Jersey have, at various times, noticed spikes in the number of shipments of both bicycles and bicycle parts ("Crime and No Punishment," n.d.).

Identification of bicycles is difficult because of failure to have a registration system or to use one that exists, the complex method of providing serial numbers and the fact that stolen bikes are often altered, dismantled, repainted and resold.

Theft from Motor Vehicles

"Theft from parked cars is one of the most common complaints received by police departments. Though largely unreported, these thefts still account for at least one-third of all larcenies reported to police. Thefts from cars usually involve a small amount of property value, but put a large strain on police resources. These thefts increase citizens' fear of crime and diminish the public confidence in their police" (Petrocelli, 2008b, p.18). Theft of motor vehicles themselves is the topic of Chapter 15.

Mail Theft

In the quest for new and easier ways to steal money, thieves may target sites used daily as repositories for hundreds of thousands of dollars, sites often left unsupervised for hours—mailboxes. On certain days of the month, with tremendous predictability, many households receive government assistance checks. Other mailboxes hold numerous applications for credit cards or the actual cards themselves.

Mailboxes are used to receive money as well as to submit payments. Millions of people leave their bills, accompanied by checks, for pickup in their mailboxes. Thieves known as **flaggers** go around neighborhoods targeting mailboxes with their flags up, searching for envelopes containing checks and other forms of payment. Thieves may also raid the large blue mailboxes used by people who may not trust leaving their own flag up. Thieves also steal mail from postal trucks, apartment mailbox panels, co-op mailing racks and neighborhood delivery and collection box units, looking for checks, credit card applications and bank account statements.

Once thieves have checks, they may call the bank posing as a legitimate business to confirm that the funds are available, or they may simply go ahead and alter the checks, assuming the checks will clear. The thieves protect the check signer's signature using a "liquid skin" coating and then use another solution to strip off the remaining ink, thus enabling them to rewrite the check payable to another source and for another amount.

Mail theft is a felony-level federal offense and is investigated by the U.S. Postal Service (USPS) Postal Inspectors. Postal Inspectors are federal law enforcement agents who investigate and enforce more than 200 federal postal-related laws. In 2010 USPS Postal Inspectors arrested more than 6,000 mail theft suspects ("Mail Theft," n.d.). The U.S. Postal Inspection Service also maintains a state-of-the-art National Forensic Laboratory in Dulles, Virginia, staffed by highly trained forensic scientists and technical specialists who play a key role in identifying, apprehending, prosecuting and convicting individuals responsible for postal-related criminal offenses.

Retail Shrinkage: Employee Theft, Shoplifting and Organized Retail Crime

Shrinkage refers to the unexplained or unauthorized loss of inventory, merchandise, cash or any other asset from a retail establishment due to employee theft, shoplifting, organized retail crime, administrative errors and vendor fraud. According to the *2009 National Retail Security Survey*, retail losses were $33.5 billion or 1.44 percent of sales, a decrease from the 1.51 percent reported in 2008 (Hollinger, 2010). The survey, in its 18th year, is a collaborative effort between the National Retail Federation (NRF) and the University of Florida.

According to the survey, most retail shrinkage—an estimated $14.4 billion—was caused by employee theft, representing almost half of the losses (43 percent). Shoplifting accounted for $11.7 billion of shrinkage, more than one-third of losses (35 percent). Other losses were from administrative errors ($4.9 billion and 14.5 percent of shrinkage) and vendor fraud ($1.3 billion and 3.8 percent of shrinkage). The survey also found that organized retail crime (ORC) was gaining more awareness within the retail industry.

A report from the Loss Prevention Research Council states that only 10 percent of retailers characterized their shrink as high when compared with their competitors. Another 66 percent said their shrinkage was average. In effect, the report says retailers inaccurately believe their shrink rate is better than that of their competitors (Daniels, 2007a, p.14).

Employee Theft. Although many assume that most of a retail company's shrinkage is the result of shoplifting, more thefts and losses from stores are internal, committed by employees. In a Spherion Workplace Snapshot survey, nearly one in five (19 percent) of workers admitted taking office supplies for personal use ("Nearly 20 Percent of Workers," 2007). Of those who admitted stealing office supplies, only 21 percent felt guilty or regretted doing so. The primary reason given for stealing office supplies was a need for them (41 percent). Nearly one-third (32 percent) said their manager told them they could do so, and 15 percent said the company would never miss the supplies.

One recommendation for reducing employee theft is to keep the more expensive items under security lock and to have frank discussions with employees regarding the problem. Employees who are aware of management's policy regarding employee theft are less likely to steal. Some companies attempt to eliminate potential employee thieves by informing job applicants that a drug test is required, even if it is not. This announcement alone may weed out applicants who have a drug habit and therefore are more prone to steal to support it.

Shoplifting. Shoplifting, also known as *boosting*, involves taking items from retail stores without paying for them. It is usually committed by potential customers in the store during normal business hours. Shoplifting does *not* include thefts from warehouses, factories or other retail outlets or thefts by employees.

Shoplifting has increased with modern merchandising techniques that display goods for sale, remove barriers between customers and merchandise and permit potential buyers to pick up and handle goods. Most items shoplifted are taken from the main floor, where it is easier to leave the store. Shoplifting is rising at many retail chains, and the prime cause is the sputtering economy: "Wages aren't keeping up with inflation, especially the price of food and energy" (Dugas, 2008). In the past, much of shoplifting was done to support a drug habit, but in the current economy, everyday items, such as groceries, are being stolen.

Security technology is being employed to limit losses caused by shoplifting. For example, electronic article surveillance (EAS) uses small security tags applied to high-theft merchandise that alert retailers when shoplifters try to take stolen items through electronic sensors at exit doors. Systems using radio frequency identification (RFID) are also becoming more popular among retailers.

Closed-circuit television (CCTV) has become a standard security tool to curb shoplifting and help in the apprehension and prosecution processes. Despite advancing technology, the apprehension rate for shoplifters remains extremely low compared with the total number of shoplifting offenses committed.

Most apprehensions are by private security forces working for department stores and shopping centers or by floorwalkers or supervisory personnel. Stores that detect and apprehend shoplifters often do not prosecute because it is relatively expensive when compared with the value of the item(s) shoplifted. Other reasons for not prosecuting are fear of facing a false arrest suit, the hope that a reprimand will cure the problem or the belief that notifying a juvenile shoplifter's parents will control the situation. Managers sometimes call the police for the chastening effect it will have on the shoplifter, but if the property is recovered, they often decline to sign a formal complaint.

If a charge is made by a merchant or merchant's employee, officers may arrest a suspected shoplifter without a warrant if reasonable cause exists for believing that the person has attempted or actually committed shoplifting. In some states store personnel themselves are encouraged to interview the suspect because they are not police officers and thus do not have to warn suspects of their rights.

Elements of Larceny by Shoplifting.

The elements of shoplifting are very similar to those required for general larceny:

■ Intentionally taking or carrying away, transferring, stealing, concealing or retaining possession of merchandise or altering the price of the merchandise,

■ without the consent of the merchant,

■ with intent to permanently deprive the merchant of possession or of the full purchase price.

> **Altering the price of an item is considered larceny. It is usually not required that the person leave the premises with the stolen item before apprehension.**

Early laws required that a shoplifter leave a store before an apprehension could be made. However, many laws have been changed to permit apprehension after the suspect has passed the last cashier's counter in the store for the particular level or department. The farther the suspect is from the normal place of payment, the greater the degree of intent shown to permanently deprive the merchant of the item. After being told why, the suspect may be detained for a reasonable time and then delivered to a police officer, parent or guardian.

In this photo taken from a surveillance videotape, a woman and her daughter (behind the counter) and her son (at left) are shown at a consignment store in New Hampshire. Police allege the woman used her children to help her steal more than $2,000 worth of jewelry from the store. The woman turned herself in after local police made the video public.

© AP Images/Consignment Gallery release via New Bedford, N.H. Police Dept.

Because intent is absent, it is not a crime for a person to walk out of a store after simply forgetting to pay for an item. This is a common problem for individuals who suffer from Alzheimer's disease and some other types of mental impairment. Such people may forget that they have picked up an item, may forget to pay for it or may honestly believe that they have paid for it when they have not. Such incidents require officers to exhibit patience and excellent communication skills in resolving the situation.

Because shoplifting can be either petty or grand larceny, a misdemeanor or a felony, the value of the property must be established. If the shoplifter is placed under arrest, the stolen item should be recovered and retained as evidence. Whether the individual is prosecuted depends on the individual's attitude, the policy of the store and the police department, the value of the property taken and how many of the legal requirements for prosecution are fulfilled. Evidence to support shoplifting or altering a price requires an eyewitness or proof that the item could not have been removed except by the person charged. The property must be carried away or removed but not necessarily to outside the store. The manager or clerk should identify the property and show proof of the store's ownership.

Proving the intent to permanently deprive is the most difficult problem in investigating shoplifting. This intent is shown by the shoplifter's actions from the time the item was stolen until the arrest was made. Stores are legally within their rights to recover items taken from a store if there is no proof of purchase. This does not mean the person is guilty of shoplifting. It may be impossible to prove intent to steal.

If a store manager wants to prosecute, review the store's reports to determine whether a crime has been committed. If it has, take the shoplifter to the police station and book and search him or her for additional property. The store personnel making the arrest must sign a complaint. Most shoplifters never reach the stage of arrest and release to the police. When it does occur, encourage store cooperation because good arrests by store personnel aid convictions and can deter shoplifting in the particular store.

Overcrowded courts have become a problem to retailers who want to prosecute for shoplifting. Prosecutors have difficulty obtaining convictions. Many states have passed statutes providing for civil fines instead of or in combination with criminal penalties. Retailers are dissatisfied with criminal prosecution because of the delays, low conviction rate and lack of restitution for the lost property. The civil approach permits the retailer to sue in small claims court, even in cases in which the offender is not convicted of a crime. Penalties under civil action range from $50 to $500, or in some cases actual damages plus five times the value.

In addition to contributing to the trade in and abuse of drugs, shoplifting has been recognized as a way for terrorist and organized crime groups to generate revenue.

Organized Retail Crime (ORC). The NRF defines ORC as "the theft/fraud activity conducted with the intent to convert illegally obtained merchandise, cargo, cash, or cash equivalent into financial gain (no personal use), where/when the following elements are present:

- Theft/fraud is multiples of items
- Theft/fraud is conducted
  - over multiple occurrences
  - and/or in multiple stores
  - and/or in multiple jurisdictions
  - by two or more persons, or an individual acting in dual roles (booster and fence)" (*2011 Organized Retail Crime Survey*, n.d., p.6).*

The NRF (*2011 Organized Retail Crime Survey*, n.d., p.6) adds,

> Groups, gangs and sometimes individuals are engaged in illegally obtaining retail merchandise through both theft and fraud in substantial quantities as part of a criminal enterprise. These crime rings generally consist of "boosters"—who methodically steal merchandise from retail stores or trailers (cargo theft)—and fence operators who convert the product to cash or drugs as part of the criminal enterprise. Sophisticated criminals have even found ways to switch UPC bar codes on merchandise so they ring up differently at checkout, commonly called "ticket switching." Others use stolen or cloned credit cards to obtain merchandise, tamper with retail equipment such as pin-pads or produce fictitious receipts to return products back to retail stores.

According to the *Organized Retail Crime Survey*, now in its seventh year, 94.5 percent of all retailers reported being victims of organized retail crime activity in 2011, an increase from the reported 89.5 percent victimization levels in 2010 (n.d., p.8). The FBI has estimated U.S. retailers lose $30 billion annually to ORC (Daniels, 2008a, p.13). Furthermore, "ORC is quickly becoming a bigger problem because of its scope and that it is often coupled with other criminal acts" (Daniels, 2008b, p.13). The NRF reports, "Law enforcement and industry experts believe members of organized retail crime groups are engaged in 'gateway' crimes, with connections to street gangs, drugs,

---

* Source: Reprinted by permission of the National Retail Federation.

weapons, immigration issues and even terrorist financing. On average, retailers believe that 41 percent of organized retail criminals are involved in gateway crimes, including drugs, weapons or gangs" (*2011 Organized Retail Crime Survey*, n.d., p.8).

ORC is a relatively low-risk, high-reward crime conducted by fairly sophisticated and skilled groups of criminals (Maestri, 2008). The thefts usually involve specific small, high-priced items that have a high resale value on the black market, such as baby formula, coffee, steaks, cigarettes, smoking cessation products, eyeglass frames, over-the-counter health products, razor blades, fragrances, batteries, electronic goods, printer ink cartridges, power tools and athletic apparel. Appendix A in the *2011 Organized Retail Crime Survey* (n.d., p.19) presents a list of highly targeted items.

Once an item is boosted, it can be converted into cash through one of three primary avenues (*2011 Organized Retail Crime Survey*, n.d., p.22):

- Fenced at a physical location (e.g., pawn shop, flea market) for roughly 30 percent of the original retail value.

- e-Fenced (listed and sold online through auction sites or other Web pages) for as much as 70 percent of retail value.

- Fraudulently refunded by returning the merchandise to a retail store for 100 percent of the retail value plus tax (if applicable).

A Web-based national database called the Law Enforcement Retail Partnership Network, or LERPnet, is a public-private partnership between the NRF, the Retail Industry Leaders Association and the FBI. Joseph LaRocca, vice president of loss prevention for NRF, contends that LERPnet puts the industry's "efforts in combating ORC into overdrive" (Daniels, 2007b, p.1). LERPnet will be used to analyze, track and prevent activities by these criminal networks. Retailers will pay $1,200 a year to participate, helping arm law enforcement with information from multiple stores to investigate illegal activity such as ORC, burglaries, robberies, counterfeiting and e-fencing (Daniels). Retailers already signed on to LERPnet include Albertson's, AutoZone, . . . Kohl's, JCPenney, Lego, Macy's, Mervyn's, Safeway, Saks Fifth Avenue, Tiffany & Company, Walmart and Williams-Sonoma (Friedrick, 2007, p.17).

Jewelry Theft

According to the FBI, the jewelry industry loses more than $100 million each year to jewelry and gem theft. Most often stolen by sophisticated professional thieves, jewelry is also the target of armed robbers and burglars.

Jewel thieves know the value of jewels, that they are extremely difficult to identify once removed from their settings and that the rewards are higher for the amount of risk involved than in other types of larceny. Thieves also have ready outlets for disposition.

Most jewelry thefts are from vehicles owned by jewelry salespeople, who typically carry thousands of dollars in jewels, and from private individuals known to be careless about the security of their jewelry. Jewel thieves also operate in stores, distracting the salesperson and then substituting a cheap facsimile for expensive jewelry. Jewel thieves tend to operate interstate and to use locally known fences. Thieves use many ingenious methods to steal and hide jewelry.

The Jeweler's Security Alliance (JSA) published an alert in July 2005 to inform retail jewelry shop owners of a new trend in jewel theft—burglars entering a store overnight via the roof with the intention of carrying out an armed robbery when employees arrive at work the next morning.

Because jewel thieves operate interstate, the FBI becomes involved. The local FBI office maintains files of known jewel thieves and their last known operations; their pictures, descriptions and modus operandi (MOs); and information about whether they are in or out of prison.

 Always inform the FBI of jewel thefts, even without immediate evidence of interstate operation.

Since 1992, the FBI's Jewelry and Gem (JAG) Program has helped local law enforcement investigators by providing a sophisticated and multijurisdictional response to these types of thefts ("Jewelry and Gem Program," n.d.). FBI jurisdiction is attained under several sections of Title 18 of the U.S. Code, two of which are Sections 2314 and 2315, known collectively as the Interstate Transportation of Stolen Property (ITSP). These two statutes "prohibit the transportation in interstate or foreign commerce of any goods of the value of $5,000 or more where the goods are known to have been stolen, converted or taken by fraud. These statutes also prohibit the receipt and sale of such known stolen goods." Mailing packages that contain illegally obtained jewels to another state also constitutes interstate operation.

Investigating jewelry theft is the same as for any other larceny. To obtain physical evidence, search the crime scene as you would in a burglary. Obtain the names of people in neighboring rooms at motels and hotels. Interview employees and other possible witnesses.

Review the victim's account of the theft. Obtain a complete description of the jewelry, the value of each item and the amount of insurance carried. Contact informants and have them be on the alert for information about the thieves and the location of the stolen items.

Art Theft

The FBI reports, "Art and cultural property crime—which includes theft, fraud, looting and trafficking across state and international lines—is a looming criminal enterprise with estimated losses running as high as $6 billion annually" ("Art Theft Program," n.d.). This offense usually comes to the attention of law enforcement through an art gallery's report of a burglary or theft. In other instances, art objects are recovered during the investigation of another crime, or the theft is reported by another police agency. The stolen objects are frequently held for a long time and are then sold or moved coast-to-coast or internationally for disposition.

Art theft is an international problem. To cope with the problems resulting from the interstate and international nature of these thefts, the FBI created the National Stolen Art File (NSAF) in 1979. Administered through the FBI's Criminal Investigative Division, Violent Crimes and Major Offenders Section, Major Theft/Transportation Crimes Unit, the NSAF provides a computerized index of stolen art and cultural property as reported to the FBI by law enforcement agencies throughout the United States and internationally. For an object to be eligible for entry into the NSAF, it must meet these criteria:

- The object must be of artistic or historical significance; this includes fine arts, decorative arts, antiquities, Asian art, Islamic art, ethnographic objects (Native American, African, Aboriginal), archaeological material, textiles, books and manuscripts, clocks and watches, coins, stamps, musical instruments and scientific instruments.

- The object must be valued at $2,000 or more, or less if associated with a major crime.

- The request must come through a law enforcement agency accompanied by a physical description of the object, a photograph of the object, if available, and a copy of any police reports or other information relevant to the investigation.

Thefts of valuable art should be reported to the FBI and to the International Criminal Police Organization (INTERPOL), which also has an international stolen art file.

Few police officers have training in identifying art, so they should conduct only the normal burglary, theft or fraud investigation. Then an authenticity check of the art object should be conducted by the FBI and national art dealers. People who own art objects rarely have adequate

descriptions or photos of each piece and the pieces rarely have identification numbers. Investigators should submit to the FBI all known information concerning the theft and a photograph of the art if available.

The FBI's specialized art crime team consists of eight agents working in major art markets around the country, including New York, Los Angeles and Philadelphia; two assistant U.S. attorneys; and several FBI analysts. The field agents are art savvy and can tell a Monet from a Manet; know the dealers, appraisers, collectors, curators and auction houses; are well versed in the art markets; and are knowledgeable about the unique laws that apply. Art theft cases the FBI has handled in recent years include

- January 2004: the return of a Civil War sword stolen from the U.S. Naval Academy Museum in 1931.

- March 2004: the arrest of a Manhattan art dealer and gallery owner, later convicted on federal mail fraud charges for an international art forgery operation that spanned nearly two decades.

- February 2005: the return of eight ancient stone seals looted from Iraq during the aftermath of Saddam Hussein's fall.

Numismatic Theft: Coins, Metals and Paper Money

Coin collections are typically stolen during commercial and residential burglaries. Obtain the exact description of the coins, the condition, any defects, scratches, dye breaks, how they were jacketed and any other identifying information. The condition of coins determines their value; a coin in mint condition may be worth twice the value of a coin in poor condition. Stolen coins may be taken from one coast to the other for disposition. Large coin shows are held throughout the year in larger cities, usually at convention centers or hotels. If interstate transportation is suspected, notify the FBI.

Metals such as gold, copper, silver and aluminum are valuable. Copper is obtained from electrical and telephone lines or from storage yards of these companies. Thieves have been known to cut down telephone lines and to strip electrical lines in remote areas. A weekly check of scrap yards may be advisable in some jurisdictions.

The increasing demand for copper and rising resale market prices have fueled copper thefts that cost industries across the country nearly $1 billion in 2006 and increased the cost of each new home by about $3,000 (Johnson, 2007). Copper thieves have posed as utility or construction workers, outfitted in hard hats and reflective vests as they strip spools of wire from light poles or construction sites. Thieves may also take advantage of natural disaster sites. For example, following Hurricane Katrina, an Energy Department inspection reported that the tons of scrap copper that should have been found throughout the wreckage of buildings and fallen power lines across Louisiana and other affected areas of the Gulf Coast had "simply vanished" (Johnson). Metal thefts have also involved copper and brass piping, aluminum siding and gutters, storm sewer grates and manhole covers. Investigators should check the area recycling centers and scrap yards and review their logs to see who is bringing in scrap metal (Kozlowski, 2008).

Agricultural Theft

In certain areas of the country, agricultural theft is an increasing problem that requires investigation. Agricultural theft rings are targeting a variety of items, including ginseng in Michigan, irrigation valves in Washington, anhydrous ammonia fertilizer in Minnesota and Ohio, Japanese radishes in Hawaii and nuts and citrus in California. Such crimes have also targeted timber, cactus, livestock, farm equipment and chemicals.

Timber Theft. The U.S. Forestry Service estimates $100 million in lumber is stolen annually through illegal logging. Tree "rustlers" harvest burls, the large gnarly root at the base of walnut trees. Burls can weigh as much as 2,000 pounds and are used to make fine woodwork. Tree "tippers" harvest the tips of pine trees to make into wreaths.

A timber theft crime scene will usually contain traceable evidence, such as tire tracks, stumps and other items the thief may have discarded or accidentally left behind. As part of a stolen timber investigation, investigators should know how the timber might be used. For example, Douglas fir is harvested for firewood, and cedar for shake shingles and fence posts. Investigators can then contact area mills and timber buyers to obtain information that might help them apprehend the thief.

Cactus. As communities have cropped up in the desert Southwest, the demand for landscape cactus has soared and poachers have found a lucrative business in stealing these prickly plants. The theft of cactus has become such a problem in some areas of Arizona, Texas and other Western states that special police units have been formed to crack down on the crime. Some jurisdictions, such as Lake Mead, Nevada, have gone as far as to implant computer ID chips in certain species of cactus to be able to track them if they go missing.

As with a timber theft, a cactus theft crime scene will likely contain tire tracks, shoe imprints and perhaps residue from tools and equipment used to harvest the plants.

Soil and sand samples from the crime scene may be linked to a particular vehicle used by the thieves or with transplanted cactuses at residences or commercial businesses.

Livestock. Just as in the days of the Wild West, cattle rustlers are still around, stealing millions of dollars worth of cattle annually and showing no signs of stopping. Most livestock is stolen from the open range and consequently may go undetected for weeks or even months. Cattle are usually stolen at night and are fairly easy to lure away because they are herd animals—once rustlers get one animal to come, the rest soon follow. Cattle rustlers are almost always armed because they often slaughter the animals on the spot, butcher them and load them into refrigerated trucks. Detectives may need the help of stock auctioneers, slaughterhouses, feedlot operators and livestock associations when investigating these crimes.

Evidence in such cases again includes shoe and tire impressions, soil samples, broken fences and perhaps forged bills of sale. Livestock branding, a practice dating back to 2700 BC, can also provide valuable evidence in cattle thefts. Brands, both hot irons and freeze brands, are unique identifying symbols placed on each animal of a specific ranch's herd. Brands are registered through a state's brand inspection office, which is generally under the jurisdiction of the state's department of agriculture. To the experienced livestock person, brands are a readable language, read from left to right, top to bottom and outside to inside (Figure 14.2). In addition to branding, cattle are also ear marked and wattle marked, commonly with a knife, according to branding protocol. These cuts are further means of identification.

Horse rustling is another problem, with more than 50,000 horses stolen annually. Like cattle, horses are herd animals and are fairly easy to steal once rustlers have lured one animal away. Sometimes after the desired horses are loaded onto a truck, the rustlers break down the fence and scatter the remaining horses. Owners may then think the horses broke out themselves, and those not recovered are simply lost. Most stolen horses are slaughtered, and the meat is sold in Europe and Japan. The United States is the world's leading exporter of horsemeat, which in many countries is considered better than our best steaks.

As with cattle, horses are branded, with various breeds being marked in specific locations. In addition, thoroughbreds have registration numbers tattooed under the upper lip.

Brand altering is a common method used by livestock thieves to disguise the stolen animals, although with well-chosen and well-designed brands, such alterations are very difficult to make appear original. To foil brand-altering rustlers, DNA analysis is now being used to identify stolen cattle.

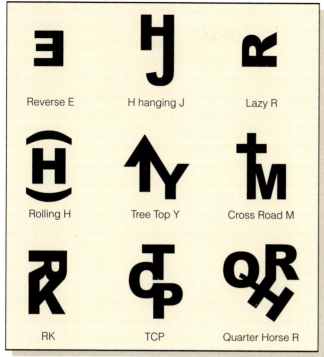

FIGURE 14.2
Cattle branding irons. Brands are composed of capital letters of the alphabet, numerals, pictures and characters such as slashes, circles, crosses and bars, with many combinations and adaptations. Letters can be used singly, joined or in combinations. They can be upright, lying down ("lazy") or reversed.

© Cengage Learning, 2013

Farm Equipment and Chemicals. Farm equipment and chemicals are also targets for thieves. Because of their expense, pesticides and herbicides are especially attractive. Farmers themselves may be the thieves, or they may buy their chemicals and equipment at unreasonably low prices from such thieves. Evidence of this crime may be uncovered by examining purchasing records.

Fish and Wildlife Theft

Poaching is illegally taking or possessing fish, game or other wildlife, including deer, elk, bear, pheasant, ducks, wild turkeys and grouse. This crime may be committed by the amateur—the usually law-abiding hunter who is faced with an unexpected opportunity to poach, such as coming across an animal not in season to hunt while hunting another animal that is in season—or the professional poacher, who, in contrast, sets out to hunt prey illegally, often as a "trophy hunter." Hunting-license verifications and vehicle stops to check limits are two means of detecting poachers.

Game wardens and conservation officers may help in investigating fish and wildlife theft. Wardens know the hunting and wildlife laws, and they may be familiar with many of the local hunters and poachers and with certain poachers' MOs. Wardens can also help gather evidence.

A powerful computerized database, Green Parrot, has about 3,300 images and textual data for some 7,000 animal and 15,000 plant species. This database should enable police and customs authorities worldwide to more effectively investigate wildlife theft.

Cargo Theft

Nearly everything we wear, eat and use at home or work has, at some point, been on the back of a truck. The amount of cargo crisscrossing our country is mind-boggling and critical to daily life. The increasing popularity of cargo theft is the result of two primary features: it is low risk (few thieves are apprehended, prosecuted or incarcerated), and it is extremely profitable. The FBI reports that cargo theft causes an estimated $30 billion in losses each year ("Inside Cargo Theft," 2010). The FBI notes an interesting fact about cargo theft: "It's usually a 'gateway' crime. In many instances, a cargo theft investigation will turn into a case involving organized crime, public corruption, health care fraud, insurance fraud, drug trafficking, money laundering, or possibly even terrorism" ("Inside Cargo Theft," 2010).

The illegal or unauthorized removal of cargo from the supply chain is called **leakage**, a concept similar to that of shrinkage. Cargo theft can occur from an 18-wheel trailer, a shipping container left on a dock or placed on a railway or in a warehouse. Although some cargo thieves will take whatever commodity crosses their path, many groups steal to order. Common commodities targeted include consumer electronics, designer clothing and fragrances, alcohol and tobacco (Kennedy, 2005).

A national survey of retailers found that almost half (49.6 percent) were victims of cargo theft during the previous 12 months (*2011 Organized Retail Crime Survey*, 2011). The majority of thefts (57.4 percent) occurred while the cargo was en route from the distribution center to the store, with the second most common point of leakage occurring between the manufacturer and the distribution center (39.7 percent). Other points of cargo theft occurred at the distribution center (22.1 percent), after items arrived at the store (17.6 percent) and when the merchandise was being shipped from one store to another (10.3 percent) (*2011 Organized Retail Crime Survey*, n.d.). *Note:* The percentages add to more than 100 because the same retailer may report cargo theft occurring at more than one point along the path from distribution center to store.

Methods used to steal cargo vary, and such crimes are generally extremely difficult to detect after they occur. In some cases, thieves break the locking mechanism off the back door of a trailer or container or drill out a rivet holding the door in place, empty the cargo and then shut the door again, sometimes taking the time to replace the rivet or otherwise visually disguise the theft so that nothing looks amiss to a passing security guard. Other times, the driver is hijacked en route. These "driver give-ups" typically happen close to major interstate corridors (Bibb, 2005).

A large portion of cargo theft occurs from commercial truck stops. Thieves know that truck drivers usually cannot offload their cargo over a weekend; thus, drivers who stop on a Friday evening are likely to drop their trailer and take only the tractor for transportation until Monday morning. During that time, the unsupervised trailer is extremely vulnerable to theft (Bibb, 2005). Other times, thieves wait at truck stops and, knowing that many drivers simply leave their truck running for the few minutes it takes them to grab some food or use a restroom, get in and drive the entire rig away.

Not uncommon are drivers who are part of the theft crew itself. For example, South American crews operating along the East Coast, primarily in New York and New Jersey, commit "leakage theft," where one member works as a truck driver, picks up a legitimate load from a marine terminal or distribution center and then diverts the cargo before delivery. The thieves enter the container or trailer, leaving the manifested seal intact, take out a portion of the load and then close the container. When the load is delivered, it appears to be short-shipped (Kennedy, 2005), that is, that the mistake was made by the shipper.

Although arresting thieves is still a goal, many agencies, including the FBI, are now focusing on finding the source—the organized crime (OC) groups and their front businesses. Approximately half of all domestic cargo thefts are the result of OC, and law enforcement is now using criminal statutes that target money laundering to shut down cargo theft. Kennedy (2005) notes the existence of certain nontraditional OC groups who engage in cargo theft. Cuban and South American (Ecuadorian, Peruvian, etc.) groups operate nationwide and are fairly sophisticated. These groups typically work in cells or crews of three or four, occasionally more, and lack the typical hierarchy found in more traditional OC groups, such as La Cosa Nostra. The MOs do not vary much by group, except for the Asian and street gangs in Southern California, which tend to be quite violent and will use guns to conduct armed hijackings.

Numerous challenges face cargo theft investigators, not the least of which is the lack of respect or seriousness historically given to the issue. Although this crime has traditionally been categorized in the UCR simply as theft, a provision in the law reauthorizing the USA PATRIOT Act may help overcome this challenge by designating a UCR code specifically for cargo theft and requiring the establishment of a national cargo theft database.

Another investigative challenge centers on the mobile nature of the crime. Numerous jurisdictions around the country, particularly those close to major seaports and cargo distribution hubs, have developed cargo theft task forces to increase their effectiveness in conducting investigations. The success of these units has demonstrated that the surveillance and investigative abilities of a multijurisdictional team surpass those of any single agency.

In the absence of a task force, experts recommend that an investigator work a cargo theft case backward, from the point of recovery to the initial loading of the product (Kennedy, 2005). Contact the container or trailer carrier for information on where the load should be. If the theft was from a refrigerated container, known as a *reefer*, collect the temperature chart as evidence. This chart will reveal a spike in temperature whenever the container was opened and will, presumably, indicate when the theft occurred (Kennedy).

Having looked at the various types of larceny/theft, consider next how the crimes can be proved.

PROVING THE ELEMENTS OF THE CRIME

To prove the felonious stealing, taking, carrying, leading or driving away of property, you must gather enough evidence to prove that the property is missing—not simply misplaced. Obtain proof of ownership through bills of sale or receipts or through evidence that the owner had custody or possession of or responsibility for the item. Determine the item's value by ascertaining its replacement cost or legitimate market value or by obtaining reasonable estimates. The owner can testify to the actual value if he or she is familiar with the specific item and its quality and condition at the time of the theft. People with business knowledge of similar items can help determine value. If certain items obviously exceed the petty larceny limitation, it is not necessary to know their exact value. Take statements from the owner regarding where the property was located and what security was provided. Also obtain evidence that the owner no longer possesses the property.

Intent to permanently deprive the owner of the property is shown by the suspect's selling, concealing, hiding or pawning the property or converting it to personal use. Intent is proven by a motive of revenge, possession under circumstances of concealment, denial of possession where possession is proven or flight from normal residence.

FRAUD

Fraud is a general term used for deceit, trickery and cheating as well as to describe the activity of individuals who pretend to be what they are not. Legally, however, fraud has a narrower meaning.

Fraud is an intentional deception to cause a person to give up property or some lawful right. It differs from theft in that fraud uses deceit rather than stealth to obtain goods illegally.

Advances in technology and, in particular, the proliferation of electronic commerce has given innovative criminals yet another way to commit fraud. Use of computers to commit fraud is discussed in Chapter 17.

Fraud victims are in a good position to provide information regarding suspects because they have had first-hand dealings with the suspects.

Fraud includes confidence games, real estate and mortgage fraud, insurance fraud, health care fraud, mass marketing fraud, mail fraud and fraud committed through counterfeiting or the use of checks or debit/credit cards. An increasingly serious and pervasive type of fraud is identity theft.

Because fraud often involves use of interstate communications devices (e.g., phones, computers), the mail system or financial and banking institutions, many, if not most, types of fraud fall under the jurisdiction of the FBI. However, if the value amount involved does not meet or exceed a minimum monetary threshold, the federal government may opt not to become involved in the case, leaving local jurisdictions to deal with many of these types of crimes.

Confidence Games

Confidence games have separated people from their money for centuries; in fact, con games were known as early as 100 BC. Changing times require changing techniques, but four basic elements are always present: (1) locating a mark from whom to obtain money, (2) selecting

the game, (3) conducting it and then (4) leaving the area as rapidly as possible.

A **confidence game** obtains money or property by a trick, device or swindle that takes advantage of a victim's trust in the swindler. The confidence game purports to offer a get-rich-quick scheme. The victim is sworn to secrecy and told that telling anyone could cause the deal to fall through or the profits to be divided among more people. The game may require the victim to do something dishonest or unethical, thus making the victim less apt to report the swindle to the police. It is often conducted away from the victim's hometown so the victim cannot obtain advice from friends.

A particular type of person is needed to make the con game work. Con artists develop cunning, guile and skills through their own systems of learning and education. They are taught by older people in the "trade," usually starting as the "number two" or "straight man." As they gain experience, they work their way up until they are the "number one" in a swindle of their own. Con artists understand human nature, are extremely convincing, lack conscience, have an uncanny ability to select the right victim and have no mercy for their victims, often extracting the life savings of elderly people.

Two basic approaches are used in con games: the short con and the long con. **Short-con games** take the victims for whatever money they have with them at the time of the action. For example, three-card monte, similar to the old shell game, entices victims to bet on whether they can select one card from among three. "Huge Duke" involves betting on a stacked poker hand, with the victim dealing the final hand. "The Wipe" involves tying money into a handkerchief for safekeeping and then switching it with one containing newspaper bits. **Long-con games** are usually for higher stakes. For example, in "The Wire," the original long-con game, the victim is enticed to bet on horse races, convinced through an elaborate telegraph office setup that the manager can beat the bookmaker by delaying the results of the race long enough to let the victim and other cohorts in the scheme make bets. After allowing the victim to win a few games at low stakes, the "big bet" is made in which the victim may lose thousands of dollars.

When investigating con-game fraud, obtain a complete description of the confidence artists and the type of fraud, trick or false pretense they used, as well as the exact amount of money involved.

Because the victim usually sees and talks with the con artists, it is often easy to identify them, but unless the police are notified quickly, the suspects will be gone from the area. Obtain descriptions of the perpetrators and their MO. Keep this information on file for future reference.

The FBI maintains a confidence artist file to assist in locating such suspects, as well as a general appearance file of con artists (even though photographs are not available). The FBI assists in investigating violations that occur on interstate conveyances such as planes, boats and trains. It also assists if there is evidence that radio, television or telegraph was used in committing the crime or if a money order was sent to a person in another state. If the swindle exceeds $5,000, the FBI has jurisdiction under the Interstate Transportation of Stolen Property Act. (Many con games exceed this amount.) Postal authorities may assist investigators in cases in which con artists use the mails to execute their crimes.

Most states include con games in statutes relating to larceny by trick and to obtaining money under false pretenses. Check the statutes in your jurisdiction for the specific elements that must be proven.

Online auction Websites are becoming used more frequently to perpetuate scams. In referring to Craigslist, a free online bazaar used by about 30 million people each month, Pulkkinen (2008) reports, "The site is increasingly a spot to court victims, sell sex and pass stolen goods." He defines the site as a "digital haven for hucksters." In addition, armed robbers are alleged to have used Craigslist to lure victims by posting ads online that offered discounted iPhones. When the victims showed up to purchase the phones, they were robbed at gunpoint. New York police arrested four men, ages 18 to 20, who were charged with conspiracy, robbery and possession of weapons.

Other scams that investigators may be summoned to examine include

- *Easy-credit scams.* Con artists target people who seek to repair damaged credit ratings by offering credit cards in exchange for advanced payments or deposits.

- *Bogus prize offers.* Mail or phone announcements proclaim, "You're a big winner!" The winner is instructed to wire money to cover taxes or fees to receive the "grand prize."

- *Phony home repairs.* Workers knock on a door and explain that they are finishing several jobs (roofing, siding, driveways) in the neighborhood. They have leftover material and can offer to fix anything at a great discount. They may take a deposit or the entire payment and never return to complete the job, or they may begin the work and then claim the job is more involved than they had thought and state they will need additional payment to finish the job.

- *Travel scams.* Victims are promised an exciting, free vacation in an exotic location but must first provide a credit card number for "verification."

- *Cyber-scams.* The Internet offers numerous sites to sell or trade merchandise, and con artists are taking advantage of this lucrative virtual swap shop to sell defective or nonexistent products.

Although it may be hard to believe that people would fall for some of these scams, con artists are extremely well versed and tend to target more typically vulnerable and trusting victims, such as the elderly.

Real Estate and Mortgage Fraud

In many areas of the country, real estate scams, such as phantom down payments and "flipping," are costing lenders and homebuyers tremendous amounts of money. The FBI states, "Mortgage fraud can be summarized as a form of bank robbery where the bank is not even aware it has been robbed until months or years later" (*2009 Financial Crimes Report*). According to the FBI, each mortgage fraud scheme uses "some type of material misstatement, misrepresentation, or omission relating to the property or potential borrower which is relied on by an underwriter or lender to fund, purchase or insure a loan" (*2009 Financial Crimes Report*, 2009). Common mortgage fraud schemes include equity skimming, illegal property flipping, air loans, foreclosure schemes, loan modification, builder bailouts, inflated appraisals, nominee loans/straw buyers and silent seconds.

Common equity skimming schemes involve use of corporate shell companies, corporate identity theft and use of bankruptcy/foreclosure to dupe homeowners and investors. In **property flipping**, the offender buys a property near its estimated market value, artificially inflates the property value through a false appraisal and then resells (flips) the property, often within days of the original purchase, for a greatly increased price. This process can be repeated several times with a single property through the help of the flipper's associates, ultimately leading to foreclosure by the victim lenders. Many deals rely on fraudulent appraisals inflating the property's value. Although flipping per se is not illegal, it often involves mortgage fraud, which is illegal.

Air loans involve a nonexistent property loan where there is usually no collateral. For example, a broker invents borrowers and properties, establishes accounts for payments and maintains custodial accounts for escrows. Foreclosure schemes involve perpetrators identifying homeowners at risk of foreclosure or already in foreclosure and misleading them into believing they can save their homes in exchange for a transfer of the deed and up-front fees. The perpetrator then either re-mortgages the property or pockets the fees.

Loan modification scams purport to help homeowners who are delinquent in their mortgage payments and on the verge of losing their home renegotiate the terms of their loan with the lender, but the scammers demand large up-front fees and either negotiate unfavorable terms or do not negotiate at all, with the result being the homeowners ultimately lose their homes. This scheme is similar to a foreclosure rescue scam. In a builder bailout, a builder who is facing severe losses resulting from rising inventory and declining demand for newly constructed homes finds "buyers" to obtain loans for the properties, who then allow the properties to go into foreclosure.

Inflated appraisals, as the name suggests, involve an appraiser acting in collusion with a borrower and providing a misleading appraisal report to the lender. Nominee loans or straw buyers conceal the identity of the borrower through use of a nominee who allows the borrower to use the nominee's name and credit history to apply for a loan. In the silent second, the buyer of a property borrows the down payment from the seller through the issuance of a nondisclosed second mortgage. The primary lender believes the borrower has invested his or her own money as the down payment, when in fact, it is borrowed.

Insurance Fraud

Insurance is one of the largest industries in the United States, comprising more than 7,000 companies collecting more than $1 trillion in annual premiums (*2009 Financial Crimes Report*, 2009). According to the FBI, insurance fraud (not including health care insurance) costs the average American family hundreds of dollars every year in the form of higher premiums and results in losses of up to $80 billion annually (*2009 Financial Crimes Report*).

The most prevalent type of insurance fraud involves premium diversion by insurance agents and brokers, where customers' payments are pocketed for personal gain instead of being sent to the policy underwriter. Scams run by unauthorized, unregistered and unlicensed agents are also common and involve collecting premiums for nonexistent policies. The scam lasts as long as customers have no claims. Once claims start to be filed, the fraudster closes up shop and relocates. These fraudulent operations take advantage of individuals who seek high-risk lines of insurance for which few legitimate providers exist.

Another type of insurance fraud involves worker's compensation, in which the con operator collects a premium without providing any legitimate protection against claims. This type of fraud can leave injured victims and families of deceased victims with little or no coverage to pay their medical bills.

Insurance companies are duty-bound to hold customer premiums secure until a claim is made. However, when the economy takes a downturn and finances become strained, some insurance executives fraudulently

dip into this premium pool to cover their own company's operating expenses. This illegal act leads to further illegal acts because accounting documents and financial statements must be doctored to cover up the misuse of customer premiums (*2009 Financial Crimes Report*, 2009).

The FBI has investigated and shut down several highly profitable insurance fraud schemes. For example, in fiscal year 2009, the agency investigated 152 insurance fraud cases, which led to 43 indictments/information, 22 arrests and the convictions of 42 insurance fraud criminals, as well as generated $22.9 million in restitution, $31.4 million in recoveries and $618,480 in seizures (*2009 Financial Crimes Report*, 2009).

Although the FBI has focused its efforts on higher priority white-collar crime matters, insurance fraud investigations continue to be addressed using liaison efforts in conjunction with other federal, state and local law enforcement. Insurance fraud investigations often require the collaborative efforts of the FBI, National Association of Insurance Commissioners (NAIC), International Association of Insurance Fraud Agencies (IAIFA), state fraud bureaus and state insurance regulators. In addition to traditional investigation methods, the FBI uses covert undercover investigations to apprehend fraudsters.

Health Care Fraud

As with insurance fraud, health care fraud adds billions of dollars each year to U.S. health care costs. Noting that Medicare and Medicaid are the most visible programs affected by such fraud, the FBI reports, "Estimates of fraudulent billings to health care programs, both public and private, are estimated between 3 and 10 percent of total health care expenditures. The fraud schemes are not specific to any general area, but are found throughout the entire country" (*2009 Financial Crimes Report*, 2009). The FBI expects health care fraud to continue rising as people live longer. One of the most serious trends observed involves the increased number of medical professionals willing to risk patient harm in their fraud schemes, which can include unnecessary surgeries, dilution of cancer and other lifesaving drugs and fraudulent lab tests.

Mass Marketing Fraud

The FBI states, "Mass marketing fraud is a general term for frauds that exploit mass-communication media, such as telemarketing, mass mailings, and the Internet" (*2009 Financial Crimes Report*). Although these fraud schemes take a variety of forms, they have in common use of false or deceptive representations to induce potential victims to make advance fee-type payments to fraud perpetrators.

One such fraud that has been around for decades is the Nigerian letter fraud, referred to as 4-1-9 Fraud by INTERPOL. Victims are contacted regarding substantial sums of money held in foreign accounts and are asked for their "assistance" in paying various fees to secure the funds transfer to the United States in exchange for a portion of the total proceeds. Alternatively, victims are asked to act as a U.S. agent in securing the release of such funds and are provided with counterfeit instruments that are to be cashed to pay any required fees, only to discover they must reimburse their financial institution for cashing a counterfeit instrument.

Telemarketing fraud and other types of fraud using the telephone have proliferated, and the victims are predominantly the elderly. In one such scam, a "representative" informs potential victims that they have won a sweepstakes prize and that the company needs their name, address and Social Security number to process the award. The company then uses the Social Security number for fraudulent purposes. Other scams simply involve informing the "winner," aka victim, that he or she must first pay a service fee or tax for their prize and that once the payment has been received, the prize will be shipped. Of course, it never is.

A federal and state crackdown against telemarketing scams that have bilked thousands of consumers, many of them elderly, out of tens of millions of dollars was dubbed "Operation Tele-PHONEY." Coordinated by the Federal Trade Commission (FTC), it was the largest such operation the FTC had ever coordinated. The sweep resulted in 180 cases, including new civil charges against 13 telemarketers that defrauded more than 500,000 consumers of $100 million (Rugaber, 2008).

Frauds involving cell phones and personal communication services (PCS) are growing problems. One prevalent form of high-tech fraud is cloning, or "grabbing." Individuals obtain legitimate account information by theft from an owner carrier or by on-the-air interception. The thief then programs the account number into a cell or PCS phone, creating a clone of the legitimate phone. Other telephone scams include:

- **Slamming** is the unauthorized switch of a long-distance carrier.

- **Cramming** involves billing consumers for unauthorized, misleading or deceptive charges, such as a personal 800 number, paging and voice mail. The vendor levies the charge against a phone number, and the phone company is required by law to pass the charges on to the customer. Because the amounts are typically quite small, many customers never even notice they have been scammed.

- **Gouging** refers to companies charging undisclosed fees when calls are made from pay phones or hotel rooms.

- **Sliding** occurs when an unauthorized carrier switches a specific call from the long-distance carrier.

- **Jamming** refers to setting up roadblocks to make it difficult to switch in-state long distance service.

- **Fluffing** occurs when rates are increased without notification.

Caller ID can both enhance and *hinder* fraud investigations. It can identify perpetrators of fraud, but it can also pose a danger to officers who work undercover. They may be exposed by having their phone numbers revealed to the criminals they call.

Mail Fraud

Mail fraud involves perpetuating scams through the mail—for example, bogus sweepstakes entries and notices. If mail fraud is suspected, police officers should contact the postal inspector through their local post office. Postal authorities can assist in investigating if the scheme uses the mails to obtain victims or to transport profits from crime.

Counterfeiting

Counterfeiting of money generally comes to the attention of the police through a retailer or a bank. The U.S. Secret Service publishes pamphlets on identifying counterfeit money. The most common denominations of counterfeit money are $10, $20 and $50. The paper of authentic bills has red and blue fibers embedded in it, and the bills have intaglio (incised) printing. The portrait is detailed and lifelike; the U.S. Treasury seal is clear and distinct on sawtooth points; the borders are clear and unbroken; and serial numbers are distinct, evenly spaced and the same color as the Treasury seal. INTERPOL's Counterfeits and Security Documents Branch (CSDB) has established programs that provide forensic support, operational assistance and technical databases to help federal and local investigators in counterfeit currency cases.

If a bill is suspect, give a receipt to the retailer or bank and turn the bill over to the nearest Secret Service office to determine its authenticity. Obtain details of how the bill came into the complainant's possession as well as an accurate description of the bill passer.

A felt-tip marker can instantly detect even the finest-quality counterfeit money with a single stroke. With the felt-tip marker, a dot or short line is made on

A counterfeit specialist with the U.S. Secret Service points out different styles of counterfeiting at the Secret Service's anti-counterfeiting lab in Washington, DC.
© AP Images/Lawrence Jackson

the suspected bill. If the "ink" remains gold, the bill is authentic. If the "ink" turns black, the bill needs scrutiny.

Counterfeit Identification Documents.

It is fairly easy for a perpetrator to make fake identification documents, a crime that can yield a large profit. Consider, for example, a Mexican man who entered the country illegally and quickly bought a fake green card and a Social Security card for $200. Within a few weeks, he had rented an apartment in Philadelphia and was running his own document fraud business, making about $3,000 to $5,000 a week, more than the average $2,000 to $3,000 needed to start such a business (Poulos, 2007, p.106).

Commercial Counterfeiting.

Currency is not the only item targeted for counterfeiting. Commercial counterfeiting includes trademark counterfeiting and copyright pirating. *Trademark counterfeiting* is the illegal production of cheap "knock-offs" of well-known pricier products, such as Rolex watches, Gucci handbags or Mont Blanc fountain pens. *Copyright pirating* is making—for trade or sale—unauthorized copies of copyrighted material, including print and sound media. In contrast to trademark counterfeiting, where products are sold far below the retail value of their legitimate counterparts, pirated music or movies impose much steeper prices on

the consumer. It is also a felony in most states to pirate sound recordings, and nearly every state has some type of law related to pirated recordings. Despite the illegalities of this business, the practice continues, particularly on the Internet, as discussed in Chapter 17.

Check Fraud

Losses from bad-check operations cannot be determined exactly because no single clearinghouse gathers statistics on this offense. Estimates range from $815 million to $5 to $10 billion annually.

Checks used to defraud include personal, business, counter, draft and universal checks, as well as money orders. Fraudulent checks are made to appear genuine in many ways. The check blank can be similar to the one normally used and difficult to detect. In fact, many fraudulent and forged checks are written on stolen check blanks. Handwriting is practiced to look authentic. Various stamps, check writers, date stamps and cancellation stamps are placed on the front and back of the check to give it a genuine appearance.

In some cases, the checks are not stolen but handed over willingly to thieves—for a price. The checking account owner benefits by being paid more money than is actually in the account, while the thief is allowed to cash checks or purchase merchandise for a few days before the bank is notified of the check "theft."

> Common types of check fraud are issuing insufficient-fund or worthless checks and committing forgery.

The *insufficient-* or *nonsufficient-fund check* falls into one of two categories: (1) accidental, in which people carelessly overdraw their checking account and are generally not prosecuted unless they do so habitually or (2) intentional, in which professionals open a checking account with a small deposit, planning to write checks well in excess of the amount deposited. This is intent to defraud—a prosecutable offense.

Most bad checks are not written with intent to defraud. They may have been mistakenly drawn against the wrong bank, the account balance may have been less than the writer thought, two or more people may have used the same account without knowing the actual balance or the bank may have made an error.

Issuing a worthless check occurs when the issuer does not intend the check to be paid. Proof of intent is shown if the issuer has no account or has insufficient funds or credit or both. A worthless check is normally prosecuted the same as one for insufficient funds. Obtain the check as well as statements from the person who accepted it, any other witnesses and bank representatives. Also obtain a signed complaint.

Forgery is signing someone else's name to a document with the intent to defraud. This includes actually signing the name and using a rubber stamp or a check writing machine. To prosecute, obtain the forged check or document, statements from the person whose name is forged, any witnesses to the transaction and the testimony of a handwriting expert if necessary. Blank checks are often obtained through burglaries or office thefts committed by professionals. The check is authentic and therefore easier to cash once the endorsement is forged.

It is also forgery to alter the amount on a check or to change the name of the payee. The person who initially draws the check must testify as to the authorized amount and payee. It is also forgery to change a name on a charge account slip.

Investigating bad or fraudulent checks requires precise details about the check and the entire transaction. The check itself is the main evidence. Carefully examine the front and back of the check and note peculiarities. Describe the check: type, firm name and whether it is personal, payroll, federal or state. Was it written in pencil or ink or typed? Were any special stamps used? Was anything altered: the payee, the date, the amount? Was the signature forged? Were there erasures or misspellings? Were local names and addresses used? Put the check in a protective polyethylene envelope or plastic container so it can also be processed for fingerprints.

Where was the check passed? Who took it? Were there other witnesses? If so, obtain their names and addresses. If currency was given, what were the denominations? Obtain an exact description of the check passer. Was the suspect known to the person taking the check? Had he or she ever done business with the store before? What identification was used: driver's license, Social Security card, bank identification card, credit card? Was the suspect alone? If with others, what did they look like? What approach was used? What words were spoken? If the check passer used a car, did anyone notice what it looked like or the license number?

Professional check passers who write several checks in a city in a short time and then move to another city or state often use the same technique. The FBI's National Fraudulent Check File helps identify such people and often shows a pattern of travel. The FBI maintains other files that assist in tracing bad-check writers. These include files on check-writer standards, watermarks, confidence operators, safety paper standards, rubber stamps, anonymous letters and typewriter standards.

Debit and Credit Card Fraud

A *debit card*, sometimes called a check card, refers to a card presented to a merchant exactly as a credit card would be, with the amount instantly credited before verification of the existence of funds is established. A *credit card* refers to any credit plate, charge plate, courtesy card or other identification card or device used to obtain a cash advance, a loan or credit or to purchase or lease property or services on the issuer's credit or that of the holder. The **holder** is the person to whom such a card is issued and who agrees to pay obligations arising from its use.

Use of debit and credit cards, referred to by the Department of Justice as *access devices*, has become a way of life in the United States. The cards have opened a new avenue for criminals to obtain goods and services by theft and fraud. Losses from debit and credit card fraud are in the billions annually, with U.S. businesses absorbing $3.2 billion in losses in 2007 from online credit card fraud alone, a figure that excludes fraudulent purchases made from retail stores (Petrocelli, 2008a, p.16). Despite such losses, these cards, like checks, reduce cash thefts from individuals and reduce the amount of cash-on-hand in places such as filling stations, as well as the amount of cash transferred to banks from businesses. Use of these cards also aids in identifying criminals who have the cards in their possession, more so than does cash, which is not as easily identifiable.

Because credit card fraud is often spread throughout several jurisdictions, many police departments place low priority on this type of offense. Further complicating this crime, many businesses accept credit card phone purchases. Fraudulent orders are placed, and if the victims do not review their bills, the fraud can go completely undetected: "The biggest problem that police face in dealing with this crime is that victims seldom report credit fraud. Most credit fraud is reported directly to the credit card companies, who in turn rarely hold the card member responsible for the losses" (Petrocelli, 2008a, p.16).

Most people involved in credit card fraud are also involved in other types of crimes. The credit cards are obtained principally by muggers, robbers, burglars, pickpockets, purse snatchers, thieves and prostitutes. They can also be obtained through fraudulent application or by manufacturing counterfeit cards.

Credit cards can be stolen by mailbox thieves who may have been tipped off by a postal employee, by someone at apartment boxes or by dishonest employees of the card manufacturer. Cards from the manufacturer are desirable because they are unsigned. Criminals can sign their holder's name in their own handwriting. These cards also provide more time for use before the theft is discovered. For the same reasons, these cards are more valuable for resale to other fraudulent users. To take maximum advantage without being detected, the criminal obtains the card by fraud, theft or reproduction, uses it for a short time and then disposes of it.

> The elements of the crime of larceny by debit or credit card include
>
> ■ **Possessing a credit card obtained by theft or fraud,**
> ■ **by which services or goods are obtained,**
> ■ **through unauthorized signing of the cardholder's name.**

To use another person's debit or credit card illegally, the criminal must either forge the cardholder's signature on sales slips or alter the signature on the card. The latter is made difficult by colored or symbol undertones that indicate when erasures and alterations are attempted.

The criminal must also operate under the floor-release limit to avoid having a clerk check the card's validity. The **floor-release limit** is the maximum dollar amount that may be paid with a charge card without getting authorization from the central office unless the business assumes liability for any loss. The limit is set by each company and is subject to change. It can be $50 or $100; in some gas stations, it is only $10. **Zero floor release** means that all credit card transactions must be checked. A suspicious merchant usually runs a check regardless of the amount of credit requested. Often, the criminal is asked for additional identification, which is difficult to produce unless other identification was also obtained in the theft.

Credit cards are attractive to criminals who operate interstate. Such criminals know that few companies will pay the witness fees for out-of-state prosecutions and that extradition is difficult to obtain unless the losses are great.

Many laws cover larceny or fraudulent use of credit cards. Possessing a forged credit card or one signed by a person other than the cardholder is the basis for a charge of possession of a forged instrument. Possessing two such cards is the basis for presuming intent to defraud. Illegally making or embossing a credit card or changing the expiration date or account number also subjects the person to a charge of intent to defraud. In most jurisdictions, it is not necessary to prove that the person possessing the card signed it. People who have machinery or devices to counterfeit or forge credit cards can be charged with possession of forgery devices.

It is larceny to fail to return a found credit card or to keep one sent by mistake if the finder or recipient uses the card. Airline tickets bought with a stolen or forged credit card are also stolen property. The degree of larceny, petty or grand, is determined by the ticket's value. It is also larceny to misrepresent credit information or identity to obtain a credit card. If a person sells his or her credit card to someone who uses it and the original cardholder then refuses to pay, the cardholder can be charged with larceny.

Some merchants and businesspeople commit credit card fraud themselves. For example, a merchant may direct an employee to make more than one authorized record of charge per sale and then forward the charges for payment or raise the amount on the credit card charge slip. This is larceny, with the degree determined by the difference between the actual charge and that forwarded for payment. It is also forgery because a document was altered. It is an attempt to commit larceny if such actions are not completed because of intervening circumstances, such as the cardholder becoming suspicious.

Most large credit card issuers assign personnel to work with local police in cases of credit card larceny. These people can be contacted for help or for information on the system used to manufacture and issue the cards.

When investigating credit card fraud, obtain samples of handwriting from sales slips signed by the suspect. If a card is obtained by false credit application, handwriting is available on the credit application form. If the card is used for a car rental, other information about the rented vehicle is available. Gas stations often record the state and license number of vehicles they service. Driver's licenses are used for identification. If a suspect is arrested, obtain a warrant to search the suspect's vehicle and residence for copies of sales slips or tickets obtained with the card, even though it has been discarded or sold.

Examine credit cards for alteration of the signature panel; the numbers or name can be shortened by using a razor blade to shave them off. New numbers can be entered to defeat the "hot card" list. Merchandise on sales slips found in the criminal's possession can provide further proof of illegal use. If the service obtained is a motel room, telephone calls can be traced to pinpoint accomplices. Clerks who handle the transactions often initial the sales slip, which enables the company or store to furnish the name of a witness.

As serious as credit card fraud is, it can have an even graver consequence—identity theft.

Identity Theft

A type of theft that can wreak enormous havoc on a person's credit and financial security is **identity theft**, the unauthorized use or attempted use of a credit card, existing accounts, misuse of personal information, or any combination of the preceding. On its Web site, the FTC defines identity theft as occurring "when someone uses your personally identifying information, like your name, Social Security number, or credit card number, without your permission, to commit fraud or other crimes" ("About Identity Theft," n.d.).

Identity theft, currently the fastest growing crime in the country, has become perhaps the defining crime of the information age (*Identity Theft*, n.d.). Approximately one in four people in the United States will fall victim to identity theft at some point in their lives (Barton and Higgins, 2008 p.14). During 2007, 7.9 million U.S. households (about 6.6 percent of all households in the country) learned that at least one member of the residence had been a victim of identity theft (Langton and Baum, 2010). By 2008 the number of identity theft victims in the United States had climbed to 9.9 million, an increase of 22 percent over the 2007 figure (Kanable, 2009).

Identity theft became a federal crime in the United States in 1998 with the passage of the Identity Theft and Assumption Deterrence Act. Before this act, no nationally accepted definition of *identity theft* existed, a factor that complicated the investigation and prosecution of these offenses. However, this act defines identity theft broadly, making it easier for prosecutors to conduct their cases. Most states have passed identity theft legislation, but the laws vary from state to state.

One difficulty in defining identity theft has been the considerable number of different crimes that it may involve, including check fraud, credit cards, check cards, immigration fraud, counterfeiting, forgery, terrorism using false or stolen identities, theft of various kinds (pickpocketing, robbery, burglary or mugging) and postal fraud. Each month, on average, the FTC enters 21,000 identity theft complaints into its Identity Theft Clearinghouse (Crane and Leach, 2007, p.18). In fact, identity theft topped the list of consumer complaints made to the FTC in 2006, totaling nearly $50 billion in losses (Spadanuta, 2007, p.18).

> **Identity theft tops the list of fraud-related complaints filed with the FTC.**

When President George W. Bush signed the Identity Theft Penalty Enhancement Act in 2004, he stressed, "The crime of identity theft undermines the basic trust on which our economy depends. When a person takes out an insurance policy, or makes an online purchase, or opens a savings account, he or she must have confidence that personal financial information will be protected and treated with care. Identity theft harms not only its direct

victims, but also many businesses and customers whose confidence is shaken. Like other forms of stealing, identity theft leaves the victim poor and feeling terribly violated."

Identity theft is especially prevalent on college campuses. Identity thieves know this and hang around campus post office boxes to gain access to applications and fill them in themselves. Complicating the problem is the fact that there are more than 200 valid forms of ID or driver's licenses issued in the United States.

Identity theft has proliferated as use of the Internet has grown. The FTC notes that thieves steal identities through dumpster diving, skimming (using a special storage device when processing a card), completing a change of address form to divert billing statements to another location, "old-fashioned" stealing and phishing ("About Identity Theft," n.d.). Phishing involves tricking consumers into replying to an e-mail or accessing a Web site that appears to be associated with a legitimate business but is actually a carefully concocted hoax intended to strip consumers of personal identifying information that can be used for criminal purposes, such as identity theft and fraud. A Gartner survey showed that phishing attacks escalated in 2007 with more than $3 billion lost to these attacks. Debit cards were the financial instruments targeted most often by fraudsters ("Gartner Survey Shows," 2007). Figure 14.3 shows the four types of identity theft, based on the combinations of commitment and motive.

The FBI says that identity theft went to a new level when one company tried to steal $23 million by pretending to be another company ("Corporate Takeover," 2007). The scam was made possible by a remarkable coincidence: two private security companies with nearly identical names. One, based in Michigan, was named Executive Outcome, Inc. (note the singular form of the word *Outcome*). The other, in South Africa, was named Executive Outcomes, Inc. (with a plural *Outcomes*). The crime began in late 2001 when a British debt collector called the Michigan-based company asking if they, Executive Outcome, wanted help collecting $23 million owed by the government of Sierra Leone for military equipment, security and training. The debt was legitimate but was actually owed to the other firm, Executive Outcomes, a half a world away. Seeing an opportunity to make some money off a confusing situation, two members of the American company set about forging documents to claim their interest in this debt. When the South African company found out what was happening, a legal skirmish followed, and the conflict turned malicious. A representative of the South African company called the police, and a special FBI agent assigned as a legal attaché in London took over the case. With a search warrant, they searched the American company and found evidence of forged documents. The

	Financial Gain	**Concealment**
High commitment (substantial planning)	*Organized:* A fraud ring systematically steals personal information and uses it to generate bank accounts, obtain credit cards, etc. *Individual:* The offender sets up a look-alike Internet Web site for a major company; spams consumers, luring them to the site by saying their account information is needed to clear up a serious problem; steals the personal/financial information the consumer provides; and uses it to commit identity theft.	*Organized:* Terrorists obtain false visas and passports to avoid being traced after committing terrorist acts. *Individual:* The offender assumes another's name to cover up past crimes and avoid capture over many years.
Low commitment (opportunistic)	An apartment manager uses personal information from rental applications to open credit card accounts.	The offender uses another's name and ID when stopped or arrested by police.

FIGURE 14.3

There are four types of identity theft, based on the combinations of commitment and motive. Any single case could reflect aspects of more than one type.

Source: Graeme R. Newman. *Identity Theft*. Washington, DC: Office of Community Oriented Policing Services, Problem-Oriented Guides for Police, Problem-Specific Guides Series No.25, July 26, 2004, p.15.

perpetrators both pled guilty to conspiracy, wire fraud and other charges and received prison time and paid $51,000 to the South African representative they threatened.

An effective police response to and investigation of identity theft will very likely require a multijurisdictional approach. The investigation begins with the victim reporting the theft to police per the provisions of the 2003 Fair and Accurate Credit Transactions Act (FACT Act). This federal law provides new rights and remedies to identity theft victims, but with a catch—the victim must first file a police report. Although this would appear to be common sense by the victim, the act was intended primarily to serve as an impetus to law enforcement in developing identity theft prevention and investigation policies and protocols. To comply with the FACT Act, agencies must now have personnel trained in completing identity theft crime reports; investigating identity theft crimes, including the collection of evidence; and preparing identity theft cases for possible prosecution. Once a victim has a police report proving that he or she has suffered a theft of identity, the lengthy, difficult process of repairing the victim's damaged credit becomes somewhat easier through use of certain privileges not available to other consumers, such as blocking fraudulent trade lines on credit reports and obtaining the suspect's credit application.

Databases that investigators should search include the Financial Crimes Database, which includes information on stolen U.S. mail as well as stolen and fraudulently used checks and credit, automated teller machine (ATM) and debit cards. The FTC's Identity Theft Data Clearinghouse is a national identity theft database containing more than 815,000 victim complaints, allowing investigators to search for information on identity theft victims and suspects across the country. Financial Crimes Enforcement Network (FinCEN) is another valuable resource for investigators because it links approximately three dozen independent databases in three main areas: law enforcement, finance and commerce. Yet another valuable database is the FBI's National Crime Information Center (NCIC) Identity Theft File, which became operational in April 2005 and is designed to aid both police officers and crime victims (Keenan and O'Neal, 2007, p.32).

With authorization from the victim, an investigator can get the victim's identity theft–related transaction records from creditors without first obtaining a subpoena, under the 2003 amendments to the Fair Credit Reporting Act, section 609(e).

In addition to victim interviews, investigators should also seek information from informants. Other possible sources of informants include peripheral players in the identity theft, such as store employees who sold to suspects they knew were using stolen identities.

Identity theft is unique in that it is a crime in itself and is an MO to commit other crimes. A challenge for investigators, therefore, may be deciding what offense to accuse a suspect of involvement in.

Investigators should recognize the tools of the identity thief's trade, including blank checks, laminating machines, laptop computers, typewriters, color scanners and copiers and skimming devices, through which a user can swipe a credit card and retrieve information from the card's magnetic strip. McQuiggin (2008, p.18) points out, "A surprising amount of information may be gleaned from forensic examination of recovered electronic devices. This is obvious

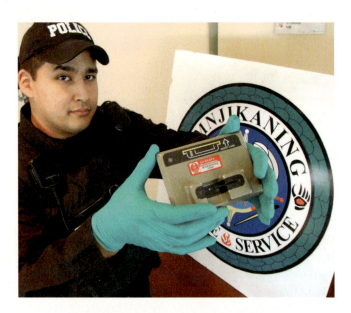

First Nation Mnjikaning Police Const. John Sahanatien displays a card skimmer, a device that houses a magnetic strip that copies account information, allowing criminals to steal personal information from a variety of types of credit and debit cards (top image). Courtesy Officer Jason Valdez and the Madera Tribune
Another much smaller hand-held card-skimming device, this one only the size of a pager (bottom image). These tiny devices can be easily concealed and carried, making it easy for a perpetrator to steal card information.
© Orillia Today, photographer Frank Matys

when seizing computers, cellular telephones, and similar devices…. What is not generally known, however, is that seized ATM skimmers, modified point-of-sale (POS) terminals, hidden cameras, and similar devices may also yield valuable forensic clues for investigators if the technical details of their construction are properly evaluated."

Because the average American possesses 20 IDs in various forms—credit cards, bank accounts, personal identification numbers (PINs), Social Security numbers, driver's licenses, username/password combinations—the key to stopping identity theft may be biometrics, which relies on unique biological properties to positively identify an individual. Biometric identifiers include fingerprints, voiceprints, retinal scans and facial recognition—IDs that are extremely difficult to steal or forge.

The Identity Theft and Assumption Deterrence Act allows prison sentences as long as 25 years for those convicted of the offense of identity theft and enables victims to seek restitution for identifiable losses and for expenses related to restoring their credit rating.

In May 2006 the President's Task Force on Identity Theft was established, cochaired by the attorney general and the chair of the FTC. The task force's mission is to provide a coordinated approach among government agencies to combat identity theft (*Identity Theft Is a Crime*, 2008). It is also beneficial for law enforcement to form partnerships with the FTC, the National White Collar Crime Commission (NW3C), the Postal Inspection Service, the Secret Service and the FBI (Berger, 2008, p.14).

A three-year "trial" partnership has been formed between Bank of America and the International Association of Chiefs of Police (IACP) (Green, 2007, p.14): "Four working groups composed of law enforcement leaders, bankers, prosecutors, and government officials have been busy developing resources for consumers, victims, the law enforcement community, and the banking industry…. The project's first accomplishment was the launch of a comprehensive Web site, www.idsafety.org. The site—a first for the banking industry and the law enforcement community—was named 'Best in Class' by the Interactive Media Awards, its highest award."

Just as identity theft can overlap with and include other crimes such as credit card fraud and counterfeiting, identity theft can also be classified as white-collar crime.

WHITE-COLLAR CRIME

White-collar crime, also called **economic** or **corporate crime**, involves illegal acts characterized by fraud, concealment or a violation of trust and does not depend on the actual or threatened use of physical force or violence. Many instances of larceny/theft and fraud can also be classified as white-collar crime. In some cases, perpetrators of white-collar crime do not "look like" criminals—they are often highly educated, socially accepted people who hold high-level positions of trust within a company. Because of such positions, high-level company executives are able to commit crimes involving millions of dollars.

White-collar crime makes headlines: the frauds and crooked accounting involved in the Enron and WorldCom bankruptcies, the scandals involving Tyco International and Adelphia Communications, and the ImClone stock debacle that sent the all-things-domestic guru Martha Stewart to prison for five months. With CEOs pocketing millions, even billions, of dollars, investors and pensioners lost everything. This is probably the ultimate white-collar crime, perhaps better termed *corporate terrorism*. The American Society of Industrial Security (ASIS) Standing Committee on White-Collar Crime has changed its name to the Economic Crime Committee.

Much white-collar crime is never reported because it involves top-level executives of organizations that do not want their reputations damaged. White-collar crimes may be committed by individuals against other individuals such as family members, lawyers, real estate agents, insurance agents and physicians. These crimes may be committed against organizations by insiders such as business partners, office managers, computer programmers and senior executives. White-collar crimes may also be committed by individuals with no relationship to the victim, such as corporate spies, forgers, counterfeiters, computer hackers and information pirates. Differences exist in how to define *white-collar crime* and what types of other crimes should fall within this classification.

White-collar or economic crime includes (1) securities and commodities fraud; (2) insurance fraud; (3) health care and medical fraud; (4) telemarketing fraud; (5) credit card and check fraud; (6) consumer fraud, illegal competition and deceptive practices; (7) bankruptcy fraud; (8) computer-related fraud; (9) bank fraud, embezzlement and pilferage; (10) bribes, kickbacks and payoffs; (11) money laundering; (12) election law violations; (13) corruption of public officials; (14) copyright violations; (15) computer crimes; (16) environmental crimes; and (17) receiving stolen property.

Although traditionally law enforcement and the general public have focused on street crimes rather than white-collar crime, two recent studies show that this is no longer the case. Piquero, Carmichael and Piquero (2008, p.306) report that two-thirds of their sample believed that the resources allocated to deal with white-collar crime should be at least as much as—if not more than—that which is spent on street crime. Unnever, Benson and Cullen (2008, p.163) also report that Americans generally favor getting tough on corporate illegality.

Investigate these crimes as you would any larceny or fraud case. Whether they are felonies or misdemeanors depends on the value involved.

White-collar crimes can be committed by any employee within a business or organization. However, low-level employees usually do not have the opportunity to steal large amounts from their employers. Most often, low-level employees' crimes consist of pilferage. Many

Bernard "Bernie" Madoff, seen leaving a hearing, is flanked by federal custody agents. In 2009 Madoff plead guilty to 11 federal felonies and admitted to orchestrating the largest Ponzi scheme in history, defrauding investors of tens of billions of dollars over a 20-year period. He was sentenced to 150 years in federal prison and forfeiture of more than $17 billion.

employees do not see taking office supplies or placing personal long-distance phone calls from a work phone as dishonest. However, they would not think of doing the same thing in a place where they did not work. Over time, the losses from pilferage are often much more than what a high-level employee might embezzle.

Few law enforcement agencies are equipped to investigate white-collar crime, encouraging such investigations to be conducted internally by in-house or contracted private investigators. The NW3C links criminal justice agencies across international borders and bridges the gap between local and state criminal justice agencies. This center provides assistance in preventing, investigating and prosecuting economic crime.

Corporate Fraud

Corporate fraud has gained national attention in recent years and is one of the highest priorities of the FBI's Financial Crimes Section. Despite all the media coverage and heightened scrutiny of business practices in corporations nationwide, the FBI anticipates no reduction in the number of such cases in the foreseeable future. FBI investigations show that corporate fraud involves such activities as falsification of financial information ("cooking the books"); self-dealing by corporate insiders, including insider trading and kickbacks; fraud in connection with an otherwise legitimately operated mutual or hedge fund; and obstruction of justice designed to conceal criminal conduct (*2009 Financial Crimes Report*, 2009). Many cases of corporate fraud involve securities and commodities.

The highly publicized Enron scandal involved numerous illegal practices committed over several years by high-ranking company executives who sought to hide Enron's growing debt and keep perceived stock market value high. The deception and fraud began to receive notice when, in October 2001, the company made public the fact that it was actually worth $1.2 billion less than previously reported. This announcement set off an investigation by the Securities and Exchange Commission (SEC), which uncovered a tangled conspiracy between Enron executives, investment banking partners and members of Enron's accounting firm to commit securities fraud, wire fraud, mail fraud, money laundering and insider trading.

Other notable corporate fraud cases have included WorldCom and ImClone, companies both charged with securities fraud and other illegal accounting practices. These types of corporate fraud are generally discovered during routine auditing procedures and are often jointly investigated by the SEC and the FBI. In the WorldCom case, the company and its executives have also been investigated by two congressional committees.

Money Laundering

Money laundering is converting illegally earned (dirty) cash to one or more alternative (clean) forms to conceal its illegal origin and true ownership. Drug traffickers and other racketeers who accumulate large cash inventories face serious risks of confiscation and punishment if considerable, unexplained cash hoards are discovered. For these criminals to fully benefit from their illicit activities, they must first convert those cash proceeds to an alternative medium—one that is both easier than cash to use in everyday commerce and avoids pointing, even indirectly, to the illegal activity that generated it.

Federal laws that drive the need for money laundering include the Bank Secrecy Act (BSA) of 1970, the first major piece of legislation to address the problem and require the reporting of certain cash transactions. Specific sections of this act include

- 31 U.S.C. § 5313: requires U.S. banks and other financial institutions to report cash transactions exceeding $10,000.

- 31 U.S.C. § 5324: prohibits intentionally dividing cash sums exceeding $10,000 into smaller amounts to evade detection by ducking in under the required reporting threshold.

Other federal laws pertaining to money laundering include

- 18 U.S.C. § 982: allows the seizure of all property or money associated with a money laundering scheme and the forfeiture of such assets to the federal government.

- 18 U.S.C. § 1951: the Hobbs Act; addresses government corruption and makes illegal the act of extortion, through the actual or threatened use of violence or fear, exercised by someone in a position of authority or official capacity, for the purpose of personal gain.

- 26 U.S.C. § 7201 and § 7206(1): prohibits the filing of a false federal income tax return or the commission of tax evasion through failure to report income.

- 26 U.S.C. § 60501: requires all entities (individuals or organizations) engaged in commerce to report all cash transactions exceeding $10,000.

- The Money Laundering Control Act of 1986.

■ The Anti-Drug Abuse Act of 1988.

■ The 2001 USA PATRIOT (Providing Appropriate Tools Required to Intercept and Obstruct Terrorism) Act, which created a new money laundering statute, 18 U.S.C. § 5316, to deal with bulk cash smuggling.

The basic process of laundering money begins with **placement** of the funds into the legitimate U.S. market. Common methods of placement include creating shell corporations or fake cash-intensive businesses and **smurfing**, more technically known as **structuring**, whereby large amounts of cash are broken into increments less than $10,000, to avoid federal reporting requirements, and deposited into various bank accounts.

The second step in the laundering process is **layering**, where the money is cleaned by moving it around through a series of elaborate transactions, often involving offshore bank accounts and international business companies (IBCs). These multiple, complex transactions aim to obscure the connection between the money and the criminal group and to continue until the organization feels confident the money is adequately clean.

The third and final step in the money laundering cycle is **integration**, where criminals repatriate their money through seemingly legitimate business transactions. For example, the launderer creates a bogus export company in a free trade zone and a bogus import company owned through an IBC in a different country. A trading relationship is established where the exporter sends nonexistent goods or goods invoiced at greatly inflated prices to the importer, who pays the exporter in cleaned money, thus completing the laundry cycle.

A variety of businesses are used in laundering money. The amount of money laundered through these types of businesses and financial institutions across the country has been estimated at hundreds of billions of dollars and, despite efforts to curb such criminal practices, many expect money laundering to continue to increase with both domestic and international enforcement challenges given the ever-expanding potential of the Internet.

As part of the Money Laundering and Financial Crimes Strategy Act of 1998, High Intensity Financial Crimes Areas (HIFCA) were designated to help focus law enforcement efforts in those parts of the country where money laundering and related financial crimes were most prevalent.

Investigating money laundering usually uses white-collar-crime investigative techniques such as financial auditing and accounting, undercover operations (perhaps through sting operations) and electronic surveillance.

The FBI's proactive, two-pronged approach to investigating money laundering includes

■ Prong 1: Investigating the underlying criminal activity. If there is no criminal activity, or specified unlawful activity that generates illicit proceeds, then there can be no money laundering.

■ Prong 2: A parallel financial investigation to uncover the financial infrastructure of the criminal organization. This involves following the money, discerning how it flows through an organization and what steps are taken to conceal, disguise or hide the proceeds (*2009 Financial Crimes Report*, 2009).

Investigators should routinely monitor the anti–money laundering initiatives of other countries. The Financial Action Task Force (FATF), of which the United States is a member, is an international assembly of 34 countries and territories, as well as two regional organizations, deemed to have strong anti–money laundering controls. Although FATF has no enforcement authority, its value lies in information sharing and promoting cooperation among nations. FATF's member-country Web sites are resources for information on current methods and trends in money laundering and the investigative techniques used to uncover them.

Investigators should carefully scrutinize the business activity of the suspected launderer, paying particular attention to such cash-intensive businesses as restaurants and bars, import/export companies and diamond and fine jewelry businesses. Furthermore, know your community and the surrounding area.

Embezzlement

Embezzlement is the fraudulent appropriation of property by a person to whom it has been entrusted. The property is then used by the embezzler or another person contrary to the terms of the trust. The owner retains title to the property during the trust period. The property so entrusted may be real or personal property. Even though the title remains with the owner, the embezzler usually has control through appointment as agent, servant, bailee or trustee. Because of the relationship between owner and embezzler, the embezzler has custody of the property. Most embezzlements involve employees. Most bank losses are from embezzlement, often involving large sums of money.

Businesses, industries and other financial institutions besides banks are also victims of embezzlement. Embezzlement includes committing petty theft over time; "kiting" accounts receivable, in which a check is written on an account that does not have enough funds to cover the check amount; overextending credit and cash returns; falsifying accounts payable records; and falsifying information put into computers—a highly sophisticated crime. (Computer-related crimes are discussed in Chapter 17.)

Bank embezzlements often start small and gradually increase. Surprisingly, many embezzlements are committed not for the embezzler's benefit but as provision of unauthorized credit extensions to customers. As the amount increases, the employee is afraid to make the error known to the employer and attempts to cover the losses. In other cases, the employee uses funds to start other businesses, fully intending to replace the borrowed funds, but the businesses often fail. Other motives for embezzlement are to cover gambling debts, to support a drug habit, to make home improvements, to meet heavy medical expenses or to get even with the employer for real or imagined grievances.

Embezzlement losses may be discovered by accident, by careful audit, by inspection of records or property, by the embezzler's abnormal behavior, by a sudden increase in the embezzler's standard of living or by the embezzler's disappearance from employment. Bank embezzlement is jointly investigated by the local police and the FBI. However, the prosecution rate is low because of adverse publicity for both the individual and the company. Often the employee has been trusted for many years, and sympathy overrules justice.

Because police training rarely includes accounting courses, investigating embezzlement cases often requires help from professional accountants. In embezzlement cases, prove fraudulent intent to convert property contrary to the terms of a trust by establishing how and when the property was converted, what the exact amount was and who did the converting. Establish that a financial loss did in fact occur. Determine the amount of the loss. Describe the property accurately if it is not money. Describe and prove the method of obtaining the property. Establish the nature of the trust. Seize all relevant books and financial records as evidence. It is necessary to determine the motive to prove fraudulent intent.

Environmental Crime

Our environment—air, land and water—has become a casualty in the battle among companies. Investigating environmental crime is a new area of specialization that mixes elements of law, public health and science. Environmental crime is considered within the larger realm of white-collar crime because the motive behind these offenses is almost always an economic one. And contrary to what many believe, environmental crime is not victimless—the victims are our children and our children's children. Environmental crime is far-reaching and pervasive, and its consequences are often hidden for years or even decades.

INTERPOL entered the fight against environmental crime in 1992 when its general assembly adopted a resolution authorizing the creation of the Environmental Crimes Committee, with an initial participation of approximately 40 countries from all regions of the world. INTERPOL states on its Web site,

> Environmental crime is any breach of a national or international environmental law or treaty that exists to ensure the conservation and sustainability of the world's environment, biodiversity, or natural resources. This type of crime includes but is not limited to illegal trade in wildlife, illegal logging or fishing, pollution of air, water and soil and theft of natural resources.
>
> Environmental crime has a major influence on the global economy and security. It is not restricted by borders and often involves criminals who engage in other crime types such as murder, corruption, fraud and theft. ("Environmental Crime," 2010)

The most common environmental crimes prosecuted in the United States involve illegal waste disposal or dumping. Hazardous wastes are the most frequently involved substances in such offenses. Other substances often involved include used tires and waste oil. Collecting and processing evidence in these cases often require special training and equipment. Many law enforcement officers lack the scientific background needed to put together an environmental pollution case or to deal safely with the illegal disposal of hazardous waste. Indeed, walking into a hazardous waste site without proper protective gear or skills for handling the material may be just as deadly as facing an armed robber in a dark alley.

Furthermore, most officers have little or no idea of the existence of the complex array of environmental control laws with all their exceptions, changes and omissions. For example, Congress and administrative agencies are continuously amending environmental laws and regulations to increase punishments for environmental criminal offenses, in many cases making them felonies rather than misdemeanors. Acts that have been amended to convert misdemeanor offenses into felonies include the

■ Comprehensive Environmental Response, Compensation and Liability Act (CERCLA), also called Superfund, of 1980.

■ Resource Conservation and Recovery Act (RCRA) of 1976.

■ Federal Water Pollution Control Act (FWPCA), also known as the Clean Water Act (CWA), of 1972.

■ Clean Air Act (CAA) of 1970.

In 1990 the Pollution Prosecution Act was enacted, making enforcement of environmental crimes a new concern for law enforcement. Violations of various environmental crime acts call for penalties of as much as $25,000 per day for noncompliance or imprisonment for as long as 10 years.

Signs of Possible Environmental Violations.

The Environmental Protection Agency (EPA) provides a list of some signs of possible environmental violations, including

- Containers or drums that appear to be abandoned, especially if they are corroded or leaking.

- Dead fish in streams or waterways, especially if the water appears to contain foreign substances (such as detergent, bleach or chemicals) or has a strange color.

- Dead animals alongside a riverbank or in a field.

- Discolored or stressed, dying plant life.

- Foul-smelling or oddly colored discharges onto the ground or into a stream or waterway.

- Visible sheen on the ground or in the water.

- Foul-smelling or strange-looking emissions into the air.

- Stains around drains, sinks, toilets or other wastewater outlets.

- Pipes or valves that appear to allow the bypass of wastewater treatment systems.

- Pipes or valves that would allow for discharge from a plant that appear hidden.

- Building demolition that may involve illegal removal of asbestos or other hazardous materials. ("Signs of Environmental Violations," 2011)

The EPA also recommends that investigators be aware of "odd activities" such as a truck dumping materials into a manhole or sewer drain or unloading drums at odd hours or in odd places. Also suspicious is a person burying drums on business or residential property. If any of the preceding is observed, law enforcement officers should investigate.

Investigating Possible Environmental Crimes.

Local law enforcement plays an important role in protecting the environment. Convictions and harsh penalties for crimes against the environment send a message to companies and individuals that local police actively monitor and enforce compliance with environmental laws (Johnson and Coy, 2007, p.24).

The main problems in investigating environmental crimes are understanding the numerous laws regarding what constitutes environmental crime, the fact that it is often considered a civil matter and collaborating with civil regulatory agencies.

Civil regulatory agencies are knowledgeable in these laws and have the resources to document evidence of a violation. For these reasons, in addition to the safety issues, many investigators find it beneficial to seek assistance from an environmental regulatory agency. Collaboration with specially equipped environmental labs, rather than crime labs, may also be necessary.

Some jurisdictions have designated specially trained law enforcement officers to investigate environmental crimes. Although many such officers are derisively being called "the garbage police," some agencies' sanitation police are gaining respect and recognition for their efforts in keeping the city clean and free of environmental wrongdoings. Massachusetts is one of several states that have created an environmental crimes strike force, an interagency law enforcement initiative that combines the technical, investigative and legal resources necessary to detect, investigate and prosecute environmental crimes.

Environmental hazards once common in industry, in America and abroad, include lead, asbestos and chlorofluorocarbons (CFCs)—all of which have become regulated under various environmental laws. For example, when Freon, a brand name the public generally equates with the broader class of CFCs, was shown to contribute to the global problem of ozone depletion, countries from around the world gathered to find a solution. Through an international agreement signed by more than 160 countries at the 1987 Montreal Convention, the United States agreed to completely phase out CFC production by the year 2000. However, as the FBI found, continued demand for CFCs and dwindling supplies created an enormous black market, second only to the black market for narcotics. The FBI ("Criminal Fraud," n.d.) notes, "To date, cooperative law enforcement efforts have resulted in the seizure of 1.5 million pounds of illegally imported CFCs with a 'street' value of $18 million."

Many of the problems associated with investigating environmental crime are similar to investigating other crimes that have become more prevalent in the 21st century. Definitions of environmental crimes vary from state to state. Statistics are not uniformly compiled. The suspects are often otherwise upstanding businesspeople who often do not feel they are committing crimes.

Premeditation or malice is not required to prove an environmental crime. All that must be proved is that an act that violated the law was done knowingly rather than by mistake. For example, the owner of a company makes a conscious decision to dump hazardous materials into a waterway or unload a truck full of construction and demolition debris, referred to by environmental investigators more simply as C&D debris, in a remote location off a desolate road under cover of darkness. Evidence of "knowing" may include tire tracks in remote locations and documented "after hours" activities, for it may be concluded that such "detours" are made to illegally dump and are not accidental.

As in any other crime, there must be a victim. Officers should determine who owns the property. Most judges do not like to see *State of X v. X* unless the state actually owns the property. In addition, officers should conduct a standard administrative interview, obtaining such information as name, date of birth, address and whatever information is routinely asked *before* giving the *Miranda* warning if an interrogation is to take place.

Of special concern in environmental crime investigations is the search warrant. Investigators must know what substances they may seek and how they should collect such samples to avoid becoming contaminated. Again, regulatory personnel may provide assistance.

Through criminal prosecution of environmental crimes, local prosecutors have a crucial function and can assume the role of protector of the public health. Often, such prosecution is most successful using **parallel proceedings**, that is, pursuing civil and criminal sanctions at the same time.

Trafficking in Wildlife and Organized Crime.

An often overlooked environmental crime is the international wildlife trade, estimated to be worth billions of dollars per year, including hundreds of millions of plant and animal specimens (Sellar, 2007, p.26). Investigating wildlife crime may result in apprehending organized crime rings: "There is ample evidence to show a strong link between organized crime and wildlife crime" (Sellar). The following list of indicators may reveal the involvement of organized crime in illicit wildlife trafficking: detailed planning, significant financial support, use or threat of violence, international management of shipments, sophisticated forgery and alteration of permits and certifications, well-armed participants with the latest weapons and the opportunity for massive profits (Sellar).

A FINAL NOTE ABOUT JURISDICTION

A recurring theme throughout this chapter has been the interjurisdictional nature of many types of theft and fraud. Sometimes a single crime will violate local, state and federal laws. Investigators must be aware that even though a crime may fall under federal jurisdiction, such as a theft of federally insured monies, that fact alone does not dictate whether another agency will assume responsibility for the investigation. Other factors, including the monetary value of the loss, will play a role in determining who is assigned the case. The amounts of these thresholds vary with the crime. For example, the monetary threshold for jewelry theft or con games is $5,000, whereas the threshold for art theft is $2,000. The monetary threshold for the crime of trafficking counterfeit or unauthorized credit cards is $1,000 over a one-year period. Some crimes have no monetary threshold that must be exceeded before the federal government gains jurisdiction. The FBI's Web site (http://www.fbi.gov/hq.htm) lists the FBI's national security and criminal priorities, many of which were covered in this chapter, and provides additional details on which cases the federal government is more likely to become involved with. Furthermore, although INTERPOL offers a variety of support services to police agencies across the globe, such as training, communication and database services, in many cases, this agency will not take an active role in investigations.

 Jurisdictional issues are a reality in many cases involving theft, fraud and other economic crimes. Investigators must be aware of monetary thresholds that must be surpassed for a case to elevate to a federal investigation.

Summary

Larceny/theft is the unlawful taking, carrying, leading or driving away of property from another's possession. Larceny is synonymous with theft. Both larceny and burglary are crimes against property, but larceny, unlike burglary, does not involve illegally entering a structure. Larceny differs from robbery in that no force or threat of force is involved.

The elements of the crime of larceny/theft are (1) the felonious stealing, taking, carrying, leading or driving away (2) of another's personal goods or property (3) valued above (grand) or below (petty) a specified amount (4) with the intent to permanently deprive the owner of the property or goods. The categories of larceny/theft are grand larceny, a felony; and petty larceny, a misdemeanor. Which category the crime falls under is based on the value of the property stolen. In most states, taking found property with the intent to keep or sell it is also a crime.

Common types of larceny are pocket picking and purse snatching; bicycle theft; theft from motor vehicles; mail theft; retail shrinkage, including employee theft, shoplifting and organized retail crime; jewelry theft; art theft; numismatic theft, including coins, metals and paper money; agricultural theft; fish and wildlife theft; and cargo theft.

When dealing with shoplifters, remember that altering the price of an item is considered larceny. It is not usually required that the person leave the premises with the stolen item before apprehension. Always inform the FBI of jewel thefts, even without immediate evidence of interstate operation.

Fraud is intentional deception to cause a person to give up property or some lawful right. It differs from theft in that fraud uses deceit rather than stealth to obtain goods illegally. Fraud includes confidence games, real estate and mortgage fraud, insurance fraud, health care fraud, mass marketing fraud, mail fraud and fraud committed through counterfeiting or the use of checks or debit/credit cards. An increasingly serious and pervasive type of fraud is identity theft. Common types of check fraud are issuing insufficient-fund or worthless checks and committing forgery.

Elements of the crime of larceny by debit and credit card include (1) possessing a credit card obtained by theft or fraud (2) by which services or goods are obtained (3) through unauthorized signing of the cardholder's name. Identity theft tops the list of fraud-related complaints filed with the FTC.

White-collar or economic crime includes (1) securities and commodities fraud; (2) insurance fraud; (3) health care and medical fraud; (4) telemarketing fraud; (5) credit card and check fraud; (6) consumer fraud, illegal competition and deceptive practices; (7) bankruptcy fraud; (8) computer-related fraud; (9) bank fraud, embezzlement and pilferage; (10) bribes, kickbacks and payoffs; (11) money laundering; (12) election law violations; (13) corruption of public officials; (14) copyright violations; (15) computer crimes; (16) environmental crimes; and (17) receiving stolen property. The FBI's proactive two-pronged approach to investigating money laundering includes (1) investigating the underlying criminal activity (in simple terms, if there is no criminal activity, or specified unlawful activity that generates illicit proceeds, then there can be no money laundering) and (2) a parallel financial investigation to uncover the financial infrastructure of the criminal organization. This involves following the money and discerning how it flows through an organization and what steps are taken to conceal, disguise or hide the proceeds.

The main problems in investigating environmental crimes are understanding the numerous laws regarding what constitutes environmental crime, the fact that it is often considered a civil matter and collaborating with civil regulatory agencies.

Jurisdictional issues are a reality in many cases involving theft, fraud and other economic crimes. Investigators must be aware of monetary thresholds that must be surpassed for a case to elevate to a federal investigation.

Checklist

Larceny

- What are the name, address and phone number of the complainant or the person reporting the crime?
- What are the name, address and phone number of the victim if different from the complainant?
- Has the victim made previous theft complaints? If so, obtain all details.
- What were the date and time the crime was reported and the date and time the crime was committed, if known?
- Who owns the property or has title to it or right of possession?
- Will the owner or person in control or possession sign the complaint?
- Who discovered the loss? Was this the logical person to discover it?
- Where was the item at the time of the theft? Was this the usual place for the item, or had it been recently transferred there?
- When was the item last seen?
- Has the area been searched to determine whether the property might have been misplaced?
- What security precautions had been taken? Were these normal?
- Exactly what property was taken? Obtain a complete description of each item, including number, color, size, serial numbers and other identifying marks.
- What was the value of the items? How was the value determined: estimated original price, replacement price or estimated market value?
- How easily could the items be sold? Are there likely markets or buyers?

- Were there any witnesses to the theft or people who might provide leads?
- Who had access to the property before and during the time of the theft?
- Who were absentee employees?
- Who are possible suspects and why? What might be the motive?

Application

A cash box was left on top of a desk at a university office. Some students had registered early that day, so there was about $600 in the box. The box was closed but not locked. The office manager went to lunch, leaving a college student in charge. The student took a phone call in the dean's office, and the box was out of her sight for about five minutes. Later she heard a noise in the hallway outside the office. She went out to see what had happened and discovered that a student had been accidentally pushed through a glass door across the hallway from the main office. She observed the scene in the hallway for about five minutes and then went back to the registration office, where she did not notice anything out of order.

After a half hour, the office manager returned from lunch and helped register two students at the front counter. When she went to the cash box to make change, she found that the $600 was missing. She immediately notified the administrator's office, and a controller was sent over to the registration office. The controller conducted a brief investigation and then notified the police. You are the investigator arriving at the registration office.

Questions

1. What procedure would you use upon arrival?
2. What steps would you take immediately?
3. What evidence is likely to be located?
4. What questions would you ask?
5. What is the probability of solving the case?

Discussion Questions

1. Larceny has been called the most underreported crime in the United States. What factors might account for failure to report larceny? Is there a way to determine how many larcenies actually occur when you consider shoplifting, bicycle thefts and minor thefts of property that victims may regard as having been simply lost or misplaced?
2. What are possible motives for committing a larceny such as bicycle theft? Shoplifting? Embezzlement?

Thefts from autos? Gasoline Thefts? Theft by check or credit card?

3. How can you protect yourself against identity theft? If it should occur, what would you expect the police to do?
4. How do petty and grand larceny differ in your state? Do the elements that must be proved for each of these crimes differ in your state?
5. A con artist has bilked a senior citizen in your community out of $2,000. The senior citizen has filed a complaint in hopes of having the money returned and the perpetrator arrested. What crime has been committed under your state laws, and what is the procedure for following up the complaint?
6. A man has been arrested for shoplifting and taken to the police station for booking. During the search for this offense, the police discover several credit cards that are not issued in the name of the person arrested. What offense is involved? Is there a separate offense from the original offense of shoplifting? Can the person be tried on both offenses? What procedure is necessary to prove the second charge?
7. Embezzlement is most frequently associated with white-collar crime. Has it been a problem in your community?
8. How do the following differ: stealing a suitcase (a) from the baggage claim area at an airport, (b) from an automobile and (c) from a retail store?
9. What type of crime is it to change the price of an item at a store with the intention of buying it at a lower price?
10. What can the police do to reduce the number of larcenies in a community? Does your community have an anti-shoplifting program? An anti–bike theft program? Do banks send literature to senior citizens concerning con games? What other measures have been initiated in your community? What additional measures may be taken?

Media Explorations

 ### Internet

Select one of the following assignments to complete.

- To learn more about identity theft, go to www.identitytheft.org, www.privacyrights.org or www.futurecrime.com. Write a brief report on what new information you learned about this crime.
- Go to the FBI Web site at www.fbi.gov. Click on "library and reference." Select "Uniform Crime Reports" and outline what the report says about larceny/theft.

■ Select one of the following key terms: *confidence games, cramming (phone), embezzlement, environmental crime, fraud, fraud prevention, identity theft, identity theft prevention, larceny/theft, larceny/theft prevention, poaching, shoplifting, white-collar crime, white-collar crime prevention.* Find one article relevant to larceny/theft, fraud, white-collar crime and environmental crime investigations to outline and share with the class.

 Gale Criminal Justice Database Assignments

The following assignments require access to Gale's Custom Journals Database for Emergency Services and Criminal Justice. Check with your instructor if you have questions about this.

■ Find the article "The Face of Identity Theft: Recognize It When You See It—And Help Your Community Identify It" on the Gale Emergency Services Database. Write a one-page paper on identity theft using information from this article.

■ Find the article "Digital Defense Begins at Home: Protecting the Internet's Digital Borders Begins with Protecting Local Citizens From Cyber Harm" on the Gale Emergency Services Database. Read the article and be prepared to discuss it in class.

■ Find the article "Swindles, Cons and Rip Offs: As White-Collar Crime Scams Escalate, Law Enforcement's Challenges Mount" on the Gale Emergency Services Database. Outline the article for an in-class discussion.

References

"About Identity Theft." Washington, DC: Federal Trade Commission, no date. Accessed July 6, 2011. http://www.ftc.gov/bcp/edu/microsites/idtheft/consumers/about-identity-theft.html

"Art Theft Program." Washington, DC: Federal Bureau of Investigation, no date. Accessed July 2, 2011. http://www.fbi.gov/about-us/investigate/vc_majorthefts/arttheft/arttheft

Barton, Liz, and Higgins, Dana. "Tips to Help Prevent Identity Theft during Tax Season." *The Police Chief*, March 2008, pp.14–15.

Berger, William. "It Can Happen to Anyone—Even Chiefs." *The Police Chief*, January 2008, pp.14–15.

Bibb, Thomas. Marion County [Florida] Sheriff's Office, Author interview, August 11, 2005.

"Corporate Takeover: A New Twist on Identity Theft." Washington, DC: Federal Bureau of Investigation, June 18, 2007.

Crane, Joanne, and Leach, Jennifer. "Identity Theft Victim Recovery Starts with Local Law Enforcement." *The Police Chief*, December 2007, pp.18–22.

"Criminal Fraud." Washington, DC: Federal Bureau of Investigation, no date. Accessed June 18, 2008. www.fbi.gov

"Crime and No Punishment." Washington, DC: National Bike Registry. Accessed July 2, 2011. http://www.nationalbike-registry.com/crime.html

"Crime Clock." Washington, DC: Office for Victims of Crime, 2009. Accessed May 29, 2011. http://ovc.ncjrs.gov/gallery/posters/pdfs/Crime_Clock.pdf

Crime in the United States, 2009. Washington, DC: U.S. Department of Justice, Federal Bureau of Investigation, September 2010. Accessed May 19, 2011. http://www2.fbi.gov/ucr/cius2009/index.html

Daniels, Rhianna. "Retailers Misperceive Own Shrink Rates." *Security Director News*, August 2007a, pp.14–15.

Daniels, Rhianna. "Retail's All-Star Team: On Deck." *Security Director News*, May 2007b, pp.1, 16.

Daniels, Rhianna. "ORC Not a Main Driver of Shrink." *Security Director News*, 2008a, pp.13–14.

Daniels, Rhianna. "RILA Addresses ORC, e-Fencing and Pushes Information Sharing." *Security Director News*, February 2008b, pp.13–14.

Dugas, Christine. "More Consumers, Workers Shoplift as Economy Slows." *USA Today*, June 19, 2008.

"Environmental Crime." INTERPOL Web site, Fact Sheet COM/FS/2010-11/PST03, 2010. Accessed November 1, 2011. http://www.interpol.int/Crime-areas/Environmental-crime/Resources

Friedrick, Joanne. "Retailers Are Counting on LERPnet to Combat Organized Theft, Fraud." *Security Director News*, June 2007, p.17.

"Gartner Survey Shows Phishing Attacks Escalated in 2007." Accessed June 12, 2008. http://www.gartner.com

Green, Ron. "The Partnership in Action." *The Police Chief*, November 2007, pp.14–15.

Hollinger, Richard. *2009 National Retail Security Survey.* National Retail Federation, 2010.

Identity Theft Is a Crime. Washington, DC: Resources from the Government, no date. Accessed June 15, 2008. http://www.idtheft.gov/

"Inside Cargo Theft: A Growing, Multi-Billion Dollar Problem." Washington, DC: Federal Bureau of Investigation, November 12, 2010. Accessed July 6, 2011. http://www.fbi.gov/news/stories/2010/november/cargo_111210/cargo_111210

"Jewelry and Gem Program." Washington, DC: Federal Bureau of Investigation, no date. Accessed June 14, 2008. http://www.fbi.gov/hq/cid/jag/jagpage.htm

Johnson, Aisha, and Coy, Heidi. "Police Protecting the Environment." *The Police Chief*, June 2007, pp.22–25.

Johnson, Kevin. "Copper Is Hot Loot and Quick Cash for Some Thieves." *USA Today*, October 29, 2007.

Kanable, Rebecca. "The Face of Identity Theft." *Law Enforcement Technology*, April 2009, pp.28–33.

Keenan, Vernon M., and O'Neal, Marshal. "The National Crime Information Center Identity Theft File." *The Police Chief*, May 2007, pp.32–34.

Kennedy, Tim. Former security expert for New York Harbor and Target Corp., Author interview, August 3–4, 2005.

Kozlowski, Jonathan. "Lifting Heavy Metal." *Law Enforcement Technology*, October 2008, pp.40–45.

Langton, Lynn, and Baum, Katrina. *Identity Theft Reported by Households, 2007—Statistical Tables*. Washington, DC: Bureau of Justice Statistics Bulletin, June 2010. (NCJ 230742)

Maestri, Nicole. "More Retailers Victims of Organized Crime: Survey." New York: Reuters, June 4, 2008.

"Mail Theft." Washington, DC: United States Postal Inspection Services, no date. Accessed July 2, 2011. https://postalinspectors.uspis.gov/investigations/MailFraud/fraudschemes/mailtheft/MailTheft.aspx

McQuiggin, Kevin. "A Forensic Approach to Effective Identity Theft Investigations." *The Police Chief*, April 2008, pp.18–20.

"Nearly 20 Percent of Workers Admit Taking Office Supplies for Personal Use." *Security Products Newsletter*, July 3, 2007.

Petrocelli, Joseph. "Fraudulent Credit Card Purchases." *Police*, April 2008a, pp.16–19.

Petrocelli, Joseph. "Theft from Cars." *Police*, February 2008b, pp.18–19.

Piquero, Nicole Leeper; Carmichael, Stephanie; and Piquero, Alex F. "Assessing the Perceived Seriousness of White-Collar and Street Crimes." *Crime & Delinquency*, April 2008, pp.291–312.

Poulos, Andrew, Jr. "Illegal ID's." *Law Enforcement Technology*, April 2007, pp.104–111.

Pulkkinen, Levi. "Free and Friendly Craigslist Has Its Dark Side." *Seattle Post-Intelligencer*, April 25, 2008.

Rugaber, Christopher S. "Federal, State Agencies Crack Down on Phone Scams." *Newsday.com*. May 20, 2008.

Sellar, John M. "International Illicit Trafficking in Wildlife." *The Police Chief*, June 2007, pp.26–32.

"Signs of Environmental Violations." Washington, DC: Environmental Protection Agency, June 8, 2011. Accessed July 6, 2011. http://www.epa.gov/oecaerth/criminal/investigations/signsofviolations2.html

Spadanuta, Laura. "Identity Theft Task Force." *Security Management*, August 2007, pp.18–20.

Truman, Jennifer L., and Rand, Michael R, *Criminal Victimization, 2009*. Washington, DC: Bureau of Justice Statistics Bulletin, October 2010. (NCJ 231327)

2011 Organized Retail Crime Survey. Washington, DC: National Retail Federation, no date. Accessed July 5, 2011. www.nrf.com/organizedretailcrime

2009 Financial Crimes Report. Washington, DC: Federal Bureau of Investigation, 2009. Accessed July 6, 2011. http://www.fbi.gov/stats-services/publications/financial-crimes-report-2009

Unnever, James D.; Benson, Michael L.; and Cullen, Francis T. "Public Support for Getting Tough on Corporate Crime." *Journal of Research in Crime and Delinquency*, May 2008, pp.163–190.

CHAPTER 15
Motor Vehicle Theft

Tracking software allows law enforcement to map the path of a stolen vehicle (active target). In this image, note the "trail" of green arrows indicating the direction of travel of an active target.

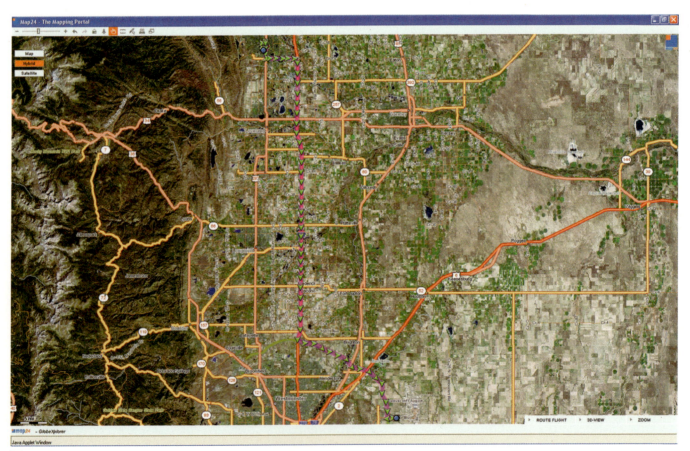

Outline

Can You Define?

chop shop
Dyer Act
motor vehicle
telematic technology
vehicle identification number (VIN)

 Do You Know?

- What a VIN is and why it is important?
- What the five major categories of motor vehicle theft are?
- What the elements of the crime of unauthorized use of a motor vehicle are?
- What types of vehicles are considered "motor vehicles"?
- What embezzlement of a motor vehicle is?
- How the Dyer Act assists in motor vehicle theft investigation?
- Why false reports of auto theft are sometimes made?
- What two agencies can help investigate motor vehicle theft?
- How to improve effectiveness in recognizing stolen vehicles?
- How to help prevent motor vehicle theft?

It is not unusual for an American family to finance or own more than $30,000 in motor vehicles. Yet the motor vehicle, even though highly vulnerable, is the least protected of all property subject to theft. The vehicle, its accessories and the property inside are all targets for thieves.

Most people use motor vehicles to travel to work and for pleasure. Thousands of recreational vehicles are also targets for theft and burglary. Aircraft and watercraft thefts add to the problems facing police investigators.

According to the FBI Crime Clock, a car is stolen every 39.7 seconds in the United States ("Crime Clock Statistics," 2010). In 2009, 794,616 motor vehicles were reported stolen nationwide, at a theft rate of about 258.8 motor vehicles stolen for every 100,000 inhabitants (*Crime in the United States, 2009*, 2010). Motor vehicle theft is on a downward trend, decreasing by 17.1 percent from 2008. According to preliminary data, auto theft in 2009 has declined for the sixth consecutive year, down 35.7 percent from 2005 data and 31.5 percent from 2000 data (*Crime in the United States, 2009*, 2010). The estimated cost of motor vehicle theft in 2009 was $5.2 billion, with the average value of a stolen vehicle placed at $6,505. Automobiles represented 72.1 percent of all motor vehicles stolen. Only 12.4 percent of thefts were cleared by arrest, with 30 percent of the vehicles never recovered. Table 15.1 lists the most commonly stolen vehicles in the United States.

According to the Rocky Mountain Insurance Information Association (RMIIA), the top 10 hot spot states ranked by number of auto thefts are (1) California, (2) Texas, (3) Florida, (4) Arizona, (5) Michigan, (6) Washington, (7) Georgia, (8) Illinois, (9) Ohio and (10) New York ("National and Rocky Mountain Region," 2008). The RMIIA also ranked the top 10 metro areas with the highest auto theft rates in 2007: (1) Modesto, California; (2) Las Vegas/Paradise, Nevada; (3) San Diego/Carlsbad/San Marcos, California; (4) Stockton, California; (5) San Francisco/Oakland/Fremont, California; (6) Laredo, Texas; (7) Albuquerque, New Mexico; (8) Phoenix/Mesa/Scottsdale, Arizona; (9) Yakima, Washington; and (10) Tucson, Arizona.

Researchers Walsh and Taylor (2007, p.64) studied motor vehicle theft and community demographics and noted that motor vehicle theft rates went up in communities more racially mixed and in those surrounded by initially higher motor vehicle theft rates, suggesting extant community structure and surrounding crime generate higher motor vehicle theft rates. Walsh and Taylor's work also suggested the presence of young males is a contributing factor in motor vehicle theft (p.80).

TABLE 15.1 National Insurance Crime Bureau's (NICB) Top 10 Stolen Autos in the United States, 2010

Rank	Vehicle	Model Year Stolen
1	Honda Accord	1994
2	Honda Civic	1995
3	Toyota Camry	1991
4	Chevrolet Pickup (full size)	1999
5	Ford F150 Series/Pickup	1997
6	Dodge Ram	2004
7	Dodge Caravan	2000
8	Acura Integra	1994
9	Ford Explorer	2002
10	Ford Taurus	1999

Source: National Insurance Crime Bureau. "Hot Wheels: Vehicle Thefts Post Sixth Consecutive Yearly Decline." September 20, 2010. https://www.nicb.org/newsroom/nicb_campaigns/hot%E2%80%93wheels

MOTOR VEHICLE IDENTIFICATION

Given the millions of motor vehicles operating on our roads, an identification system is imperative. The most important means of vehicle identification is the **vehicle identification number (VIN)**.

> The VIN is the primary nonduplicated, serialized number assigned by a manufacturer to each vehicle made. This number—critical in motor vehicle theft investigation—identifies the specific vehicle in question.

VINs for vehicles manufactured between 1958 and 1970 may have 11 numbers and letters or fewer, whereas all automobiles manufactured in North America since 1971 contain a series of 17 numbers and letters (Steck-Flynn, 2008, p.92).

The Motor Vehicle Theft Law Enforcement Act of 1984 requires manufacturers to place the 17-digit VIN on 14 specified component parts including the engine, the transmission, both front fenders, the hood, both front doors, both bumpers, both rear quarter panels, both rear doors and the deck, lid, tailgate or hatchback. In most late-model cars, the VIN is located on the left instrumentation or dash plate by the window, on the driver's door or post or on the firewall.

A fictional example of a VIN would be "1F1CY62X1YK555888," where

    1 = nation of origin (1, 4, 5 = United States;
        2 = Canada; 3 = Mexico; and J = Japan)
    F = manufacturer symbol (A = Audi, B = BMW,
        H = Honda, etc.)
    1 = make
    C = restraint
    Y = car line
    62 = body type
    X = engine symbol
    1 = check digit
    Y = model year
    K = assembly plant
    555888 = sequential production number

The VIN of a vehicle is the automotive equivalent of human DNA; no two VINs are identical. The VIN allows investigators to trace a vehicle from the factory to the scrap

A section of the front subframe of the truck that was used in the bombing of the U.S. Embassy in Dar Es Salaam, Tanzania. This critical piece of evidence was used in the trial against the suspected terrorists—the number stamped in the metal is the vehicle identification number, which was instrumental in tracking down the suspects. This embassy and another in Nairobi, Kenya, were bombed almost simultaneously on August 7, 1998.
© Robert Mecea/Newsmakers/Getty Images

yard. Some manufacturers position the label in plain view; others hide it. Car thieves frequently attempt to change or replace VINs to conceal vehicles' true identities. Decoding VINs can aid in investigating auto theft, cloning and chop shop operations, to be discussed shortly.

Manufacturers also use numbers to identify engines and various vehicle components.

CLASSIFICATION OF MOTOR VEHICLE THEFT

Motor vehicle thefts are often classified by the thief's motive or purpose, but it may be impossible to determine the motive for thefts that end in the vehicle's being abandoned.

> Classifications of motor vehicle theft based on the offenders' motive include
> - Joyriding.
> - Transportation.
> - Commission of another crime.
> - Gang initiation.
> - Stripping for parts and accessories.
> - Reselling for profit.

Joyriding

The joyrider and the person stealing for transportation are sometimes grouped together, but there is an important distinction between them. The joyrider is generally a younger person who steals for thrills and excitement.

Joyriders look for cars with keys in the ignition that can be started and driven away rapidly. The vehicle is taken for a comparatively short time and then abandoned near the location of the theft or near the joyrider's destination. A vehicle taken to another community is generally left there, and another vehicle is then stolen for the return trip.

Stolen vehicles are often found where young people congregate: fast-food places, malls and athletic events. Several vehicle thefts within a short time may follow a pattern, providing clues for investigators. For example, most cars stolen by the same individual or group in a short period are the same make, entered in the same manner and stolen and dropped off in the same general area. Juvenile informants can be extremely helpful in investigating such auto thefts.

Motor vehicle thefts by juveniles are often not regarded seriously by the courts, even though they account for most vehicle thefts and can cause injury or death to others. It is not unusual for juveniles to be involved in as many as a hundred car thefts before apprehension.

Vehicle theft by juveniles is a serious problem, and in some states joyriding is a separate offense.

Transportation

Theft of a motor vehicle for transportation can involve a joyrider but is more apt to involve a transient, a hitchhiker or a runaway. The objective is to travel from one point to another at no cost. These offenders are generally older than joyriders. Late fall and winter are peak periods for this type of theft.

A vehicle stolen for transportation is kept longer than one stolen for joyriding. Frequently it is operated until it runs out of gas or stops running. It is then abandoned (often to avoid suspicion) and another vehicle is stolen. The license plates may be changed, or a plate may be stolen and put on the rear of the vehicle.

Commission of Another Crime

Automobiles are used in most serious crimes. Robberies of banks, bank messengers, payroll offices, businesses and service stations, as well as criminal escapes, almost always involve a getaway in a stolen vehicle. Vehicles provide both rapid transportation and a means to transport the loot. Other crimes frequently committed while using stolen vehicles include rapes, kidnappings, burglaries, larcenies to obtain gas and assaults of police officers attempting to apprehend a suspect. Records indicate that many habitual criminals have stolen at least one car in their criminal careers. Some began as car thieves.

Stolen cars are used in committing other crimes to escape detection at the crime scene and to avoid being identified by witnesses. Therefore, the criminal normally uses the stolen vehicle only briefly. In fact, a stolen vehicle report may not yet have been made when the crime is committed. Stolen plates are often used to cause confusion in identification. The vehicle used in committing the crime—the "hot" car—is usually soon abandoned for a "cold" car—a vehicle used to escape from the crime scene vicinity.

Stolen vehicles played a major role in the search for serial killer Andrew Cunanan. Authorities were able to recreate the route taken by Cunanan in his cross-country killing spree by locating one victim's vehicle in the vicinity of the next victim's body. Cunanan's homicidal rampage began in late April 1997 in Minnesota with the killing of two men. Cunanan then stole the Jeep Grand Cherokee of one of the victims, and police later discovered this vehicle near the home of a third victim in Chicago. The Chicago victim's Lexus was reported missing and was later found in New Jersey at the murder scene of Cunanan's fourth victim. In continuing the pattern, the fourth victim's pickup truck was stolen and later turned up in a Miami Beach parking ramp, several blocks from where fashion designer Gianni Versace was murdered in front of his home by Cunanan, who then killed himself.

A stolen motor vehicle driven by a criminal is 150 to 200 times more likely to be in an accident than is a vehicle driven by a noncriminal; therefore, regard as suspicious any damaged abandoned vehicles you observe. Conditions contributing to this high accident rate include operating the vehicle on unfamiliar streets and roads, driving at high speeds in an attempt to escape police pursuit, testing the vehicle's speed, unfamiliarity with the vehicle and use of drugs.

A criminal apprehended with a stolen vehicle after committing another crime is usually prosecuted for only the major crime, not the auto theft.

Gang Initiation

Occasionally a vehicle is stolen as part of a gang initiation or "putting in work" for the gang. As noted in the unpublished court transcript of *The People v. Gregory Shelton* (2011): "[A gang expert] explained that 'to put in work for the gang' means doing something for the benefit of the gang. The gang would consider itself benefited if a gang member shoots or kills a member of another gang or if a gang member commits a robbery, by way of an example. It is very important 'to put in work for the gang' because this is what makes a gang's reputation."

Stripping for Parts and Accessories

Many vehicles are stolen by juveniles and young adults who strip them for parts and accessories to sell: transmissions, rear ends, motors and wheels. Batteries, radiators and heaters are sold to wrecking yards, used car lots and auto repair shops. Expensive accessories such as car phones, stereo tape decks, radios, citizens' band (CB) radios and compact disc (CD) players also are removed for resale. The stripped vehicle is often crushed for scrap metal. The profit is extremely high.

Sometimes thieves steal specific items for friends, other vehicle owners or themselves. These are often parts that are impossible to buy or are very expensive.

Catalytic converter thefts have been on the rise. Metals such as platinum, palladium and rhodium are found inside catalytic converters and, as precious metals rise in value, so do the converters. Scrap yards buy these converters, which are relatively easy for thieves to cut out of vehicles, for approximately $100 to $150.

Airbag Theft. The National Insurance Crime Bureau (NICB) reports that airbags are a primary accessory on the black market for stolen vehicle parts. A new airbag retails for approximately $1,000. Unscrupulous collision repair shops may replace a deployed airbag with a stolen one and charge the customer or the customer's insurer the full price (which constitutes insurance fraud). Insurance statistics show that approximately 50,000 airbags are stolen each year, resulting in an annual loss of more than $50 million to vehicle owners and their insurers ("Airbag Theft and Fraud," n.d.).

Stealing for Chop Shops. A **chop shop** is a business, usually a body shop, that disassembles stolen autos and sells the parts. The chop shop deals with car thieves who steal the cars specifically for them, often on demand, stealing the exact make, model and color. The vehicle may triple in value when sold for parts. There is no waiting period and no tax to the customer. The cars are dismantled, and the parts are cataloged. In some cities, this business is so big that organized crime has been heavily involved and network organizations dispose of the stolen parts. Auto parts are also sought outside the United States.

The chop shop may also deal directly with the owner of a vehicle who wants to dispose of it for insurance purposes because of dissatisfaction with its performance. The owner leaves the vehicle registration with the chop shop. The shop returns the registration to the owner after the vehicle is dismantled and crushed. The insurance company has no chance of recovery.

Reselling

Auto thefts are also committed by professional thieves who take an unattended vehicle, with or without the keys, and simply drive it away. Or they may go to a used car lot, posing as a buyer, and drive the vehicle away on a no-return test drive. Another method is to answer an ad in the

This vehicle was taken by car thieves, who stripped it for parts and then dumped it in a remote rural area.
© Malcom Fife/zefa/CORBIS

paper for a particular car, try it out and then never return it. This gives the thief time to escape because the owner gave permission to take the vehicle—which makes the case one of embezzlement. Cars are also stolen by using bad checks. Recovering a vehicle stolen by professionals requires a specialized knowledge of investigative techniques and often depends on a reliable informant to get started. Moreover, such thieves are difficult to detect and prosecute. As specialists in automobiles, the thieves know how to steal cars and how to alter them or the documents needed to make them eligible for resale. The professional is rarely the actual thief; rather, the professional hires others to steal cars and bring them to a specified location, usually a garage, for making the necessary alterations.

Alterations include repainting, changing seat covers, repairing existing damage and altering the engine number. The car is also completely searched to eliminate any items that connect it with the former owner. The VIN is almost always altered or replaced. The most common method of changing the VIN is to buy a similar vehicle from a salvage lot and then remove and replace the entire dash, making the change undetectable. If the VIN is not located on the dash, the car thief has a much more difficult time. In some cases, the VIN plate itself is removed and carefully altered, or the car thief can make embossed tape with a handheld tape-numbering device and place it over the regular VIN plate. Unless the inside of the car is investigated, a false VIN plate is not usually detected.

After all number changes on the motor and the VIN plate are completed, the vehicle is prepared for resale with stolen or forged titles, fictitious bills of sale or titles received with salvage vehicles bought by the thieves. When the mechanical alterations and paperwork are completed, the vehicle is registered through the department of motor vehicles (DMV) and resold, usually at a public car auction, to a used car dealer or a private individual.

Many stolen cars are exported for resale in other countries, the most common destinations being Central and South America. Hundreds of thousands of vehicles are estimated to be illegally exported each year. One international car theft ring was indicted by a federal grand jury for illegally obtaining vehicles from Reno, Nevada, car dealers and transporting them to the Port of Long Beach in California, where the cars were loaded onto freighters and shipped to China to be sold at three to four times their original price. The ring members then reported the cars stolen to police and insurance companies for reimbursement of their losses. Charges against ring members included making false statements on loan and credit applications, mail fraud, interstate and foreign transportation of stolen property, aiding and abetting and attempting to evade financial reporting requirements. The FBI estimated that the scheme involved total losses of as much as $6 million.

ELEMENTS OF THE CRIME

Unauthorized Use of a Motor Vehicle

Most car thieves are prosecuted for unauthorized use of a motor vehicle rather than for auto theft. Prosecution for auto theft requires proof that the thief intended to permanently deprive the owner of the vehicle, which is often difficult or impossible to establish.

> The elements of the crime of unauthorized use of a motor vehicle are
> ■ Intentionally taking or driving
> ■ a motor vehicle
> ■ without the consent of the owner or the owner's authorized agent.

Intentionally Taking or Driving. *Intent* is often described in state laws as "with intent to permanently or temporarily deprive the owner of title or possession" or "with intent to steal." Intent can be inferred from the act of taking or driving, being observed taking or driving or being apprehended while taking or driving. Laws often include as culpable any person who voluntarily rides in a vehicle knowing it is stolen.

A Motor Vehicle. Motor vehicle is not restricted to automobiles. It includes any self-propelled device for moving people or property or pulling implements, whether operated on land, on water or in the air.

> Motor vehicles include automobiles, trucks, buses, motorcycles, motor scooters, mopeds, snowmobiles, vans, self-propelled watercraft and aircraft.

Homemade motor vehicles are also included.

Without the Consent of the Owner or the Owner's Authorized Agent. Legitimate ownership of motor vehicles exists when the vehicle is in the factory being manufactured, when it is being sold by an authorized dealership or when it is owned by a private person, company or corporation. *Owner* and *true owner* are not necessarily the same. For example, the true owner can be a lending agency that retains title until the loan is paid.

Usually the owner or the owner's authorized agent reports the theft. Thus, it can be determined immediately whether consent was given. Previous consent is not a defense, although it may be considered.

If you stop a suspicious vehicle and the driver does not have proof of ownership, check the registration with the state DMV to determine who the legal owner is. If that person is not the driver, check with the legal owner to determine whether the driver has permission to use the vehicle.

Interstate Transportation

In 1919 the need for federal control of motor vehicle theft was recognized, and Congress approved the National Motor Vehicle Theft Act, commonly known as the *Dyer Act*.

> The **Dyer Act** made interstate transportation of a stolen motor vehicle a federal crime and allowed for federal help in prosecuting such cases.

The act was amended in 1945 to include aircraft and is now called the *Interstate Transportation of Stolen Motor Vehicles Act*. Since the Dyer Act was passed, more than 300,000 vehicles have been recovered and more than 100,000 criminals have been convicted in interstate car theft cases.

The elements of the crime of interstate transportation of a motor vehicle are

- The motor vehicle was stolen.
- It was transported in interstate or foreign commerce.
- The person transporting or causing it to be transported knew it was stolen.
- The person receiving, concealing, selling or bartering it knew it was stolen.

The vehicle thief may be prosecuted in any state through which the stolen vehicle passed. Prosecution is normally in the state in which the vehicle was stolen, but sometimes it is in the state in which the person was arrested.

Intent is not required. The stolen vehicle could accidentally be driven over the state line or forced to detour into another state. If the vehicle is transported by train or truck through another state, prosecution is also possible.

The Anti-Car Theft Act of 1992 provides tougher legislation against auto theft, previously a low-profile crime. The penalty for importing or exporting stolen vehicles was increased from 5 to 10 years, as was the penalty for interstate transportation of stolen vehicles. The act empowers U.S. Customs with new authority to check for stolen vehicles and provides funds to states that participate in the National Motor Vehicle Title Information System. The act also made armed carjacking a federal offense.

MOTOR VEHICLE EMBEZZLEMENT

This most frequently occurs when a new or used-car agency permits a prospective buyer to try out a vehicle for a specific time. The person decides to convert the vehicle to personal use and does not return it. This is fraudulent appropriation of property. Motor vehicle embezzlement can also occur under rental or lease agreements or when private persons let someone test-drive a vehicle that is for sale.

> Motor vehicle embezzlement exists if the person who took the vehicle initially had consent and then exceeded the terms of that consent.

THE PRELIMINARY INVESTIGATION

When a motor vehicle theft is reported, initial information obtained by police includes the time, date and location of the theft; the make, model and color of the vehicle; the state of issue of the license plate; license plate number; direction of travel; description of any suspect; and the complainant's present location.

The complainant is asked to remain at his or her present location, and a police officer is dispatched to obtain further information and to complete the proper complaint form.

> False motor vehicle theft reports are often filed when a car has been taken by a family member or misplaced in a parking lot, when the driver wants to cover up an accident or crime committed with the vehicle or when the driver wants to provide an alibi for being late for some commitment.

It is also possible that the vehicle has been re-claimed by a loan company—a civil matter. Another civil matter is a situation in which someone lends a vehicle to another person and then the borrower fails to return the vehicle when the owner wants it back. This does not necessarily constitute a theft of motor vehicle; depending on the circumstances, such a scenario is often a civil matter.

A preliminary description is provided to patrol officers, who are told that the theft has not been verified; therefore, no all-points bulletin is issued. During this time, patrol officers are alerted, but they make no move if they see the stolen vehicle because the report has not been validated. The officer in the field obtains information to determine the validity of the theft charge: the circumstances surrounding the alleged theft, identification of characteristics of the stolen vehicle, any details of items in the car and any possible suspects. Interviews with witnesses are another crucial aspect of the preliminary investigation. Frequent false reports impair cooperation from other agencies, especially when the errors should have been detected by the investigating officers.

Recovered vehicles must be examined for usable latent prints and other physical evidence. If a vehicle is found with accident damage, it is necessary to determine whether the damage occurred before or after the report. Vehicles involved in a hit-and-run incident are sometimes abandoned by the driver and then reported as stolen. Drunk drivers may also report their cars stolen if they crash while driving under the influence and then leave the scene of the crash. Younger people sometimes report a car stolen if they crash and are afraid to tell their parents.

Computerized police files can assist in searching for suspects. Investigators can enter data concerning past suspects and other individuals in vehicles, types of vehicles stolen, the manner in which vehicles were entered or stolen, the types of locations from which they were stolen (apartment complexes, private residences or commercial parking lots, for example), where vehicles were abandoned and where vehicles were if the suspects were arrested in them.

Investigators must be familiar with the tools and methods commonly used to commit vehicle theft, including car openers, rake and pick guns, tryout keys, impact tools, keyway decoders, modified vise grips, tubular pick locks, modified screwdrivers and hot wiring. Be familiar with these items and techniques and know what evidence to collect to prove their use.

INSURANCE FRAUD

Vehicle insurance fraud is a major economic crime that affects every premium payer through increased insurance rates. Many police departments facilitate insurance fraud by allowing car theft reports to be phoned in or by taking them "over the counter" at the police station and then never investigating the reports. The primary reason the auto theft is reported is often for insurance purposes. To avoid this situation law enforcement agencies should investigate all auto theft reports and should not discount the possibility that the "victim" is actually committing insurance fraud.

For example, a luxury car stolen from a suburban mall parking lot was found four days later on fire on a rural road. The case seemed routine until a detective began an investigation to eliminate the car's reported owner. The detective found that there were three pending lawsuits against the "victim,"

who had filed for bankruptcy shortly after the lawsuits and months before the car was stolen. He had filed an affidavit claiming he no longer owned the car because he had sold it six months before. Investigation revealed that the buyer was a friend who let the car be transferred into his name so it would not be involved in the bankruptcy proceedings.

This was a clear case of filing false information with the police. Further, after a fire investigator and a mechanic inspected the car, they reported that the lab tests showed ongoing engine failure. The victim wanted the insurance company to pay for a replacement vehicle—an obvious case of fraud.

VEHICLE CLONING

The NICB describes vehicle cloning as a crime in which stolen vehicles assume the identity of legally owned, or "nonstolen," vehicles of a similar make and model. Criminals apply counterfeit labels, plates, stickers and titles to these stolen cars, making them appear legitimate. The nonstolen vehicles can be actively registered or titled in another state or country, resulting in multiple vehicles having the same VIN being simultaneously registered or titled—but, of course, only the nonstolen vehicles are legitimate. The rest are fakes, or clones.

The first step in the cloning process is to copy a VIN from a legally owned car. Then the criminal steals a vehicle similar to the one from which the VIN had been lifted. The stolen vehicle's legitimate VIN is replaced with a counterfeit one, making the stolen vehicle a clone of the legally owned original vehicle. The criminal then creates counterfeit ownership documents and sells the stolen vehicle to an innocent buyer ("It's Not a Feat," n.d.).

High-end luxury cars are the usual targets of cloning. Cadillac Escalades, Lexus RX 300s and BMW 5 Series are among the models most widely reported by local detectives ("Vehicle Identification Cloning," 2008). Table 15.2 lists the most popular cloned vehicles uncovered during recent NICB investigations.

The NICB notes, "Vehicle cloning is a relatively easy crime to commit, especially by organized rings of professional

TABLE 15.2 2007 Top Five Cloned Vehicles	
1.	Cadillac Escalade
2.	Ford F Series Pickup
3.	GMC Yukon
4.	Chevrolet Tahoe
5.	(GM) Hummer H2

Source: National Insurance Crime Bureau Agent Recoveries

vehicle thieves and fraud artists enticed by its allure of huge profits" (*Doing a Double-Take*, 2004, p.2). According to this source, conservative vehicle cloning profits in the United States are estimated to exceed $12 million annually, with an average net of $30,000 per cloned vehicle (p.2).

Compounding the cloning problem is that many cloned vehicles are used for illegal operations: "Savvy criminals are using some of the country's most credible logos, including FedEx, Walmart, Direct TV and the U.S. Border Patrol to create fake trucks for smuggling drugs, money, and illegal aliens" (Ross, 2008). In one instance, a routine traffic stop by the Texas Department of Public Safety of a Walmart truck, driven by a man in a Walmart uniform, was found to be carrying 3,058 pounds of marijuana and 204 kilograms of cocaine in a fake truck trailer. In another case, a U.S. Border Patrol van was found to be carrying 31 illegal aliens in Casa Grande, Arizona (Ross, 2008).

COOPERATING AGENCIES IN MOTOR VEHICLE THEFT

Police most frequently use state DMVs to check owners' registrations. They also use them to compare the driver of a vehicle with the registered owner. When vehicle registration and driver's registration checks are completed, further checks can be made in the FBI's National Crime Information Center (NCIC) files to determine whether the vehicle is stolen and whether the driver has a criminal record.

> The FBI and the NICB provide valuable help in investigating motor vehicle thefts.

The FBI

The FBI assists local and state authorities who notify the bureau that a stolen motor vehicle or aircraft has been transported interstate—which places it within the provisions of the Interstate Transportation of Stolen Motor Vehicles Act. The FBI works with local authorities to find the vehicle and the person who stole it. The FBI can also examine suspicious documents relating to false sales or registrations. The bureau's NCIC contains information on stolen vehicles and stolen auto accessories.

The National Insurance Crime Bureau

In 1992 the National Auto Theft Bureau was incorporated into the NICB, a nonprofit organization supported and maintained by hundreds of automobile insurance companies. The organization helps law enforcement agencies reduce and prevent auto thefts and investigate questionable or fraudulent vehicle fires and thefts.

The NICB also disseminates reports on stolen vehicles to law enforcement agencies and serves as a clearinghouse for information on stolen vehicles. Computer files are maintained for several million wanted or stolen cars, listed by make, engine number, VIN and component part number. This information is available free upon request to law enforcement agencies. The NICB can also trace cars from the factory to the owner. Its staff of specialists and technicians are experts in identifying stolen cars and restoring mutilated, changed or defaced numbers. They also restore altered or obliterated VINs.

The NICB publishes and distributes to police agencies an annual *Passenger Vehicle Identification Manual*. This publication describes the location of identifying numbers, gives license plate reproductions and provides a short legal digest of each state's motor vehicle laws.

Also of assistance is the National Vehicle Identification Program (NVIP). This program promotes use of vehicle identification technology and provides a $1,000 reward for information leading to recovery of an NVIP-registered vehicle and the arrest and conviction of the auto thief.

RECOGNIZING A STOLEN MOTOR VEHICLE OR AN UNAUTHORIZED DRIVER

"Alert patrol officers can help recover stolen vehicles and take dirtbag thieves off the streets" (Scoville, 2007, p.26). As with other crimes, a suspicious nature and an alert mind help an officer detect motor vehicle thefts. Detection is sometimes improved by an instinct developed through training, observation and experience. Police officers develop individual techniques for recognizing stolen cars. No absolute, single peculiarity identifies a stolen car or its driver, but either one can draw the attention of an observant officer.

> To improve your ability to recognize stolen vehicles,
> - Keep a list of stolen vehicles, or a "hot sheet," in your car.
> - Develop a checking system for rapidly determining whether a suspicious vehicle is stolen.
> - Learn the common characteristics of stolen vehicles and car thieves.
> - Take time to check suspicious persons and vehicles.
> - Learn how to question suspicious drivers and occupants.

A *potential car thief on foot* usually appears nervous. He or she may be looking into cars on the street or in parking lots, trying door handles and carrying some sort of entry tool. Observe such an individual from a distance until an overt act is committed.

Characteristics of a driver of a stolen vehicle include making sudden jerks or stops, driving without lights or excessively fast or slow, wearing gloves in hot weather and attempting to avoid or outrun a squad car. Any unusual or inappropriate driving behavior may be suspicious. In addition, "Car theft has become a gateway crime, the point where juvenile delinquents graduate from Hot Wheels to hot cars. Juveniles account for some 16 percent of stolen vehicles, so it makes sense to take a second glance at stature and youthful appearances of drivers" (Scoville, 2007, p.27).

Characteristics of a stolen vehicle include having one license plate when two are required, two when one is required or no plates displayed at all. Double or triple plates with one on top of the other can indicate lack of time to take off the original plates. A set of old plates with new screws, wired-on plates, altered numbers, dirty plates on a clean car or clean plates on a dirty car, differing front and rear plate numbers, plates bent to conceal a number, upside-down or hanging plates and homemade cardboard plates are all suspicious. Expired registration tabs are worth a closer look. Observe whether the trunk lid has been pried or whether side windows or door locks are broken. Look for evidence of a broken steering column or of tampering with the ignition switch. Abandoned vehicles are also suspicious.

When *questioning drivers and any occupants of cars* you have stopped on suspicion of motor vehicle theft, observe their behavior. Watch for signs of nervousness, hesitancy in answers, over-politeness and indications that the driver does not know the vehicle. Request the driver's license and the vehicle registration papers for identification. Examine the driver's license and ask for the driver's birth date. The driver will probably not know the correct date unless it is his or her license. Compare the description on the license with the person. Compare the state of issuance of the license with the car's license plates. Ask the driver to sign his or her name and compare the signature with that on the driver's license.

Ask the driver the year, make and model of the car and compare the answers with the registration papers. Ask the mileage. The driver of a stolen car rarely knows the mileage, whereas the owner or regular driver knows within a reasonable number of miles. Ask the driver to describe the contents of the car's trunk and glove compartment.

Check inside the vehicle for an extra set of license plates, bullet holes or other damage, bloodstains and service stickers showing where and when the car was last serviced. Inspect the VIN plate for alterations. A roll of adhesive tape can indicate it was used to tape windows before breaking them. Wire or coat hangers bent straight to open doors, rubber gloves, jumper cables or tools for breaking into a car are also alerting signals.

Parked cars may have been stolen if debris under the car indicates it has been in the same place for a long time. Check with neighbors to determine how long the vehicle has been parked there. The neighborhood canvass is one of the most effective techniques in investigating abandoned cars. Check for illegal entrance, for open car windows in inclement weather and for dirty vehicles indicating lack of care. A citation under the wiper can indicate when the car was abandoned. Keys left in the ignition and lack of license plates are also grounds for checking.

A warm or running motor and firearms or valuables left in the car may indicate that the thief has temporarily parked the car and intends to return. Stake out stolen vehicles (identified by license number or description) because the thief may return. Consider partially immobilizing the vehicle to prevent an attempted escape.

Scoville (2007, p.28) offers one last consideration: "Fridays and Saturdays are hands down the busiest car theft days, giving 'weekend getaway' a whole new meaning."

RECOVERING AN ABANDONED OR STOLEN MOTOR VEHICLE

Most motor vehicle thefts are local problems involving locally stolen and recovered vehicles. The majority of stolen vehicles are recovered, most of them within 48 hours, especially those stolen by juveniles. Stolen vehicles are recovered when patrol officers observe a vehicle that is listed on a hot sheet, a suspicious vehicle or driver or an apparently abandoned vehicle or when private citizens report an abandoned vehicle.

Although patrol units are responsible for most of the stolen vehicles recovered, investigative personnel play a major role in furnishing information to the uniformed patrol in all areas of motor vehicle theft.

The initial patrol officer at the scene examines recovered and abandoned vehicles unless there is reason to believe the vehicle was involved in a serious crime. Investigators assigned to such a crime may want to look for specific items in the vehicle that might not be known to the patrol officers. In these cases, the vehicle is protected until the specialists arrive.

Once recovery and impound reports have been completed, the car is removed from the hot sheet and the owner is notified of the recovery. A vehicle recovery report should be completed and filed.

If a crime has recently been committed in the area or if the vehicle's position and location suggest that the suspect may return, drive by and arrange for a stakeout. If the car is locked and the keys are gone, if heavy rain or fog exists and the windshield-wiper marks indicate they were recently used or if no dry spot appears under the car, the vehicle was probably used recently and the driver may return. Round rain spots on the vehicle mean that it has been parked for a longer period than if there are elongated raindrops, which indicate recent movement. A quick check of heat remaining on the hood, radiator or exhaust pipe also indicates whether the car was recently parked. Consider attempting to apprehend the criminal on return to the vehicle.

However, if a car has a flat tire or is up on blocks, it is probably abandoned and can be immediately processed at the scene, the police station or a storage location. Consider the possibility that the vehicle was used in committing another crime such as robbery, burglary, murder, hijacking or abduction or kidnapping. Search the vehicle's exterior first and then the interior as described in Chapter 4. Many car thieves have been located through items left in a vehicle.

If you suspect the vehicle was used in another crime, have it impounded to be processed (it should not be driven until processing is complete). After processing, notify the rightful owner.

Technology is facilitating the recovery of stolen vehicles. LoJack, a Massachusetts company, has developed a system that places a homing device in an obscure place on a vehicle. If the vehicle is reported stolen, the device is activated and a tracker picks up a signal that is displayed on a lighted compass. An illuminated strength meter tells operators when they are nearing the stolen vehicle. The display also shows the model and color of the car. The LoJack Web site reports that the radio frequency–based system is used in more than 30 countries, has been installed in more than 8 million vehicles worldwide and has helped track and recover more than 800,000 vehicles around the world—assets worth nearly $4 billion, of which, nearly $2 billion were located within the United States. Furthermore, the tracking technology has shown a consistently high 90 percent recovery rate.

The system is not without its drawbacks, however. First, the lag time between a car theft and its report may be hours or even days. Second, there are some dead spots—locations where transmitted radio signals will not be detected. Third, some departments hesitate to become a partner with a private company. Finally, some departments worry that the public will perceive them to be focused on preventing car theft from the more affluent members of the community—those who can afford the $600 auto recovery system.

Other systems also are available, some of which activate automatically. If someone drives off in the car without deactivating the system, an alarm is sent to the tracking center. Such systems might, however, result in false alarms and pose as great a problem as false burglar alarms. Other systems provide a personal alert service that allows motorists to signal authorities in case of emergencies. One system allows controllers to shut off a stolen car's engine by remote control if police tracking the car believe it would be safe to do so.

COMBATING MOTOR VEHICLE THEFT

Police departments are using several strategies to combat rising auto theft levels:

- Setting up sting operations—for example, a body shop that buys stolen vehicles—and using bait cars
- Providing officers with auto theft training
- Coordinating efforts across jurisdictional lines
- Instituting anti–car theft campaigns
- Increasing penalties for stealing vehicles

To combat auto theft in Atlanta, the Auto Theft Task Force (ATTF) was initiated to target high-risk areas at high-risk times. The approach involved high-visibility uniformed patrol, members' making frequent traffic stops and heavy reliance on field investigative interviews. The efforts of the task force paid off, with the seven ATTF officers making 2,500 arrests in the first year and recovering more than 400 vehicles.

To combat the rising auto theft rate at Newark International Airport in New Jersey, airport police took several steps, including

- Increasing the candlepower of parking lot lights.
- Conducting weekly inspections of the lot perimeter to locate access points for thieves (e.g., broken or cut fences).
- Offering monetary rewards to the public for information leading to the arrest of car thieves.
- Securing unused remote entrances.
- Touring the lots with marked and unmarked patrol cars.

In areas where police have made special efforts to educate the public and to assign extra squads to patrol high-auto-theft areas, auto theft has significantly decreased.

New York City has instituted the Combat Auto Theft (CAT) program, which has been highly successful. Participating car owners sign a form indicating that they do not normally operate their automobiles between 1 A.M. and 5 A.M., the peak auto-theft hours. They also sign a consent form that authorizes the police to stop their vehicle during these hours without probable cause. Owners are given a CAT program decal to affix prominently on the inside of the car's rear window. Officers may stop any car having the decal, without probable cause, if they see it traveling on city streets between 1 A.M. and 5 A.M.

Minnesota's Help Eliminate Auto Theft (HEAT) program offers as much as $5,000 for information leading to the arrest and trial of suspected auto-theft-ring members or chop shop operators. The program's toll-free number is answered by the Minnesota Highway Patrol.

The increased use of alarms and protective devices may partly account for the rise in armed carjackings, as explained in Chapter 12. Unwilling to give up their lucrative "trade," car thieves may use force against a vehicle operator to gain control of the vehicle rather than risk being thwarted by antitheft devices. Whereas carjacking is treated as quite a severe crime, regular unarmed auto theft remains a relatively minor offense and, from a criminal perspective, a safe crime to commit.

License Plates

Something as low-tech as a license plate can often be used to identify and capture auto thieves. Automatic license plate recognition (ALPR) is being used in patrol cars across the country, with one of the leaders in ALPR being PlateScan (Molnar, 2007, p.20).

Technology Innovations

PlateScan is unique in that it uses technology known as neural networks, which basically means it uses sophisticated algorithms to identify characteristics on plates. As the system reads a license plate, it compares the plate to the database. If it makes a hit, it alerts the operator. If not, it stores the plate information in the computer, as well as the time and location of the read via GPS integration. According to PlateScan, testing of its systems indicated an accuracy rate of approximately 95.8 percent.

Interestingly, PlateScan can also generate hits off of partial plates.... Using the system, 170,000 stored plates were analyzed in approximately five minutes time, with an analysis of possible plate matches based on characters, time stamps, and GPS. The result? Six images in full color of a vehicle suspected in or involvement in [a series of rapes].... The addition of a separate color camera allows the capture of vehicle description, make, model, color, damage, unique characteristics, etc. to the database. In other words, you get a complete picture of the vehicle, not just the plate. The PlateScan system can read and process four cameras simultaneously, which allows for multi-directional, real-time analysis.

Routine Activities and Motor Vehicle Theft

The routine activity approach to crime suggests that the daily, routine activities of populations influence the availability of targets of crime. The existence of potential offenders, suitable targets and lack of guardianship explains variation in the rate of motor vehicle theft. Research indicates that city blocks with bars have almost twice as many auto thefts as do city blocks without bars and that blocks adjacent to high schools have higher levels of auto theft than do blocks that are not near high schools. In addition, parking lots with attendants have lower rates of auto theft than do similar lots with no attendants on duty. Such findings might be used in designing auto theft prevention programs such as using bait cars.

Bait Cars. The basic idea of a bait car is simple. A model of vehicle with a high theft rate is selected and placed in a high crime area. Officers then simply sit back and wait for the vehicle to be stolen.

The Los Angeles Sheriff's Department's Taskforce for Regional Autotheft Prevention (TRAP) uses a traditional, watch-and-wait method of bait vehicles. In Modesto, California, the nation's "car-theft capital," bait cars are used extensively. In California, car theft is classified as a nonviolent felony, typically earning the perpetrator just 120 to 150 days in jail, and it isn't subject to California's three-strikes rule. Most of the offenders arrested have prior histories and consider jail time to be like going away to school to catch up on the latest techniques from colleagues.

Bait cars can be enhanced using **telematic technology**, which transfers data between a remote vehicle and a host computer. The data are transferred using the Internet and wireless technology as well as a global positioning system (GPS). A small radio transceiver called a vehicle locator unit (VLU) is hidden in the bait vehicle. The VLU transmits a silent homing signal, revealing the vehicle's location to an officer's remote control unit (RCU), a handheld two-way radio equipped with a keypad from which commands are entered, activating the tracking transmitter and controlling the bait vehicle's engine, door locks, flashers and horn. The car is tracked by satellite and located. Mapping software can display the location, direction and speed of the vehicle. When an officer catches up with the thief, he or she can remotely kill the stolen car's engine and lock the car's door.

Border Area Auto Theft

According to the NICB, many of the top metropolitan areas for vehicle theft are in or near ports or the Mexican or Canadian borders. Actually, there is no international border for this highly mobile crime. Particularly hard hit by auto theft are California, Nevada, Texas, New Mexico, Arizona and Washington, which the NICB ranks as the leading car theft states in the nation.

The Arizona law enforcement community has created programs to encourage binational cooperation. At the center of this effort is Policia Internacional Sonora y Arizona (PISA), a cross-border networking group that began more than 20 years ago when a few Arizona and Sonora (Mexico) officers gathered informally over breakfast. The group now has hundreds of members throughout the border region. Relationships established at these conferences create personal connections that could not be made any other way.

In 2003, Arizona established a Border Auto Theft Information Center (BATIC), a toll-free, long-distance telephone line that Sonoran police can use to seek and share information about vehicles recovered in or stolen from Mexico. The program averages about 50 calls a day from Mexican law enforcement officers.

Theft of Patrol Cars

Police vehicles are also vulnerable to thieves. Just as border area auto theft presents unique challenges, so does the theft of police vehicles. About the only police vehicle that appears to be immune from theft is a K-9 vehicle. A stolen unit driven by a fleeing felon might run down civilians, practically guaranteeing that the department will be sued. In addition, police cars grant the drivers access to high-security areas, so terrorists would jump at the chance to obtain one.

Most reports of stolen police vehicles involve suspects who get into a unit an officer has left unattended, usually to take a report or chase a suspect. Many officers need to keep their vehicles running almost nonstop through a shift. Turning the engine off drains the car's battery quickly because of the power demands of emergency lights, communications systems, laptops and other devices. Turning off the engine also powers down those instruments, requiring inconvenient rebooting.

Technology offers some answers here. One solution is a brake-light kill switch. With the brake lights cut off, the car will not come out of park even when running. This solution works only with later-model vehicles that require the driver to step on the brake before the transmission can shift out of park.

Another solution is a secure-idle system in which an officer presses a button, places the transmission in park, turns the key to the normal off position and removes the key. The engine keeps running and all accessories remain on. However, any unauthorized attempt to step on the

brake or move the shift lever out of park cuts all electrical power. It can also trigger an optional alarm. The system is deactivated by putting the key back into the ignition and turning it to the on position.

PREVENTING AUTO THEFT

Effective preventive measures could eliminate many motor vehicle thefts. Vehicle theft requires both desire and opportunity, and it is often difficult to know which comes first. An unlocked automobile with keys in the ignition is a temptation. A parked vehicle with the motor running is also extremely inviting. Many juveniles take cars under such conditions and then boast of their ability to steal.

 Numerous motor vehicle thefts can be prevented by effective educational campaigns and by installing antitheft devices in vehicles during manufacture.

Educate motor vehicle owners about the importance of removing their keys from the ignition and locking their vehicles when parked. Public education campaigns might include distributing dashboard stickers with the reminder "Have you removed your keys from the ignition?" or "Don't forget to take your keys and lock your car."

To deter theft, some automakers have developed ignition systems and keys that use microchips with electronic codes embedded in them. However, car thieves have

A car jack club immobilizes the steering wheel and deters thieves.
© Thomas Sztanek/ Shutterstock

been able to duplicate these antitheft keys by using code grabbers similar to the devices used to duplicate codes that open garage doors. In response, as with garage door makers, some auto manufacturers are now using rolling codes and encrypted systems that use randomly generated codes to defeat thieves. They have also developed a buzzer system that warns the driver that the keys are still in the vehicle. Keyless entry and ignition systems are additional technologies designed to make it harder for thieves to break into vehicles to steal them. Immobilizer systems, in which the engine recognizes only the preprogrammed key(s) assigned to the car, are a further safety device to prevent auto theft.

The NICB Web site suggests a four-layered approach to combat auto theft ("Vehicle Theft," n.d.):

1. *Common sense.* Remove keys, close windows and lock doors. Park in well-lit areas. Do not leave the car running and unattended, especially with small children inside.
2. *Visible and audible warning devices.* Use steering wheel locks, wheel locks, theft deterrent decals, identification markers such as the VIN etched in the window and audible alarms.
3. *Immobilizing devices.* Use cut-off switches, kill switches, smart keys and fuel disablers.
4. *Tracing devices.* Give police the vehicle location.

THEFTS OF TRUCKS, CONSTRUCTION VEHICLES, AIRCRAFT AND OTHER MOTORIZED VEHICLES

Investigating thefts of trucks and trailers, construction vehicles and equipment, recreational vehicles, motorized boats, snowmobiles, motorcycles, motor scooters, mopeds and aircraft is similar to investigating auto thefts.

Trucks and Trailers

Usually trucks and trailers are stolen by professional thieves, although they are also stolen for parts. A "fingerman" often provides information to the thief. In most cases, the fingerman is an employee of the company that owns the truck. A "spotter" locates the truck after getting information from the fingerman and then follows the truck to the point where it is to be stolen. A driver experienced in operating the targeted vehicle then commits the actual theft.

Truck trailers are usually stolen by simply backing up a tractor to the trailer and hauling it away. The trailer's cargo is generally the target.

Stolen trucks and trailers are identified much as passenger vehicles are—by the manufacturer or through the *Commercial Vehicle Identification Manual* published by the NICB.

Construction Vehicles and Equipment

The NICB notes that heavy equipment theft is a growing problem, with approximately 13,452 heavy equipment thefts reported in 2009, including backhoes, bulldozers and dump trucks. Most of the thefts were committed by organized crime rings, which often had targeted equipment shopping lists. Many of the rings are international, filling equipment needs in underdeveloped countries ("ISO and NICB Release," 2010).

National surveys suggest that the total cost of heavy equipment theft could be as much as $1 billion each year in the United States alone. More worrisome is that less than 20 percent of stolen heavy equipment is ever recovered; the recovery rate in 2009 was only 18 percent. Adding to the problem is that product identification numbers (PINs) are nonstandard, vary dramatically in format among manufacturers and may be located in numerous, often hard-to-find locations.

The NICB Web site notes that rubber-tired equipment is most likely to be stolen because it can be driven away under its own power. The most popular targets are skid steers, backhoes and dump trucks. Most vulnerable are less-secure construction sites on weekends. The stolen vehicles usually stay intact.

In 2002 the National Equipment Register (NER) was launched, a significant step toward reducing this ongoing problem. According to the NER, heavy equipment is often stolen by organized crime rings and has a high benefit-to-risk ratio. Heavy equipment has little physical machine or site security, is valuable and easy to sell and is often transported to a port or across the border before the theft is even discovered and reported ("Heavy Equipment Is a Tempting Target," n.d.).

The NER has registered more than 70,000 theft reports and provides access to more than 12 million equipment ownership records. The NER provides law enforcement officers with expert, free assistance in investigating and prosecuting equipment theft, including

■ 24/7 access to specialist NER operators who will offer expert advice on equipment identification, PIN locations and other identification techniques.

■ 24/7 searches of the NER database online via a toll-free number (866-FIND-PIN).

- 24/7 access to millions of ownership records through NER operators.

- Additional online investigation tools such as PIN location information.

- Local and national training programs.

Many construction companies have formed protection programs, have identified their equipment with special markings and have offered rewards for information about thefts. Local construction firms can also provide information about possible outlets for stolen parts.

The NER recommends that site security be enhanced by posting "no trespassing" signs and using fencing, gates, locks and good lighting. Vehicle security can be enhanced by marking, anchoring and immobilizing equipment. Equipment not being used should be arranged in a way so that a missing unit would be obvious. Equipment should not be left on a trailer unattended.

The NER has a pocket-sized reference, *Law Enforcement Identification Guide for Construction and Agricultural Equipment*, which includes theft indicators, commonly stolen equipment, location of PIN numbers and other useful items for investigators. The NER offers the following "red flags" as theft indicators, cautioning that legitimate explanations might exist for any of the indicators.

Transport

- Equipment being transported late at night or on weekends or holidays. Equipment theft most often happens at those times.

- Hauled equipment that is being moved in a hurry and therefore lacks the proper tie-downs, over-width/over-weight signs or lights.

- Equipment being hauled on trucks not designed to haul such equipment.

- Equipment being hauled with buckets in the up position or booms not lowered.

- New equipment on old transport.

- The labels/markings on a piece of equipment do not match those of the unit carrying or hauling it.

Use and Location

- Equipment in an unsecured location that has not been moved for some time—either by repeat observation or the age of the tracks leading to the equipment.

- The type of equipment does not suit the location or use—such as construction equipment on a farm or in a residential area with no building activity.

Equipment and Markings

- Equipment with missing PIN plates. Manufacturers generally use mounting techniques that make it unlikely for a PIN plate to fall off during normal use.

- Equipment that has been entirely repainted or that has decals removed or painted over.

- Manufacturer decals or model number stickers do not match the piece of equipment to which they are affixed.

- A commercially manufactured trailer with registration plates reflecting a homemade trailer (certain states only).

Price

- Equipment that is being offered, or has been purchased, at a price well below market value.

When looking for "red flags," focus on the 10 most commonly stolen pieces of equipment, which account for 90 percent of all stolen equipment reported to the NER.

Recreational Vehicles

More than 450 makes and models of recreational vehicles (RVs) are marketed in the United States. Because there are so many makes and models, contact the manufacturer for any special numbers not readily visible. Recreational vehicles are also targets for vehicle burglaries because many contain CB radios, televisions, DVDs and appliances. Many false theft claims are made because of the high cost of operating these vehicles.

Motorized Boats and Jet Skis

Since 1972 many states have required licensing boats, including an identification number on the boat's hull. Most such identification numbers are 10 to 13 digits. The first several digits are the manufacturer's number. This is followed by 4 or 5 identification digits and several certification digits.

To prevent boat theft, mark the vessel by etching your driver's license number in several inconspicuous places and affixing a Boat Watch USA decal in a prominent location. Record the specifics and effects of the boat by inventorying all electronics and other gear, as well as the boat and trailer. Photograph the boat. Secure it using the best locks you can buy (Eskew, n.d.). Other options include arming the vessel with an alarm system and insuring it. The same precautions apply to Jet Skis.

Because boats also are the objects of many fraudulent insurance claims, investigators should determine whether the theft claim is legitimate.

Snowmobiles

Snowmobiles are easy to steal because they can be transported inside vans and trucks. Most major snowmobile manufacturers use chassis and engine numbers that aid in identification.

A popular snowmobile resort in Lanaudière, Quebec, reduced snowmobile theft by more than 50 percent through the joint efforts of tourism operators and law enforcement. Tourism operators invested heavily in video surveillance and alarm equipment at restaurants, lodges, hotels, motels and other tourist-oriented businesses. Police involvement was stepped up as well, with local law enforcement waging a deliberate war on snowmobile thieves, making the region known as a bad place to steal snowmobiles, trucks and trailers.

Motorcycles, Motor Scooters and Mopeds

Many motorcycles cost $20,000 or more. In 2009, 56,093 motorcycles were reported stolen to law enforcement ("Motorcycle Thefts Down," 2010). Motorcycles, motor scooters and mopeds are easy to steal because they lack security devices and are often left unprotected. The lock number is easily identified, and substitute keys can be made. These cycles can be driven away or loaded onto trailers or into vans and transported, perhaps several at a time. A professional thief takes only 20 seconds to steal a motorcycle.

Identifying motorcycles is difficult because of the many types and the fact that parts are not readily identifiable. However, identification numbers can often be obtained through the NICB, local dealers and manufacturers. Even so, the recovery rate of 25 to 30 percent for motorcycles is significantly lower than that for vehicles ("Motorcycles Offer a Tempting Target," n.d.).

The NICB offers the following prevention suggestions: lock your motorcycle, even when it is stored in a garage; be wary of used cycles titled or registered as an "assembled vehicle"; be wary of cloned motorcycles; and obtain an expert appraisal or insurance policy pre-inspection before purchasing and insuring a used cycle.

Aircraft

Yet another area of motor vehicle theft that may be investigated, although relatively rare, is theft of aircraft: "Thefts of single-engine propeller-driven planes are rare; typically fewer than ten occur each year" (Straw, 2007, p.30). Aircraft theft, although infrequent, is a high-value theft. Such thefts are jointly investigated by the FBI and the Federal Aviation Administration (FAA). Many stolen aircraft are used in narcotics smuggling, so that the plane can be sacrificed at no cost if there is danger of apprehension.

Aircraft identification consists of a highly visible *N* identification number painted on the fuselage. Many aircraft parts, including the engine, radio equipment, landing gear and tires, also have individual serial numbers. Aircraft identification can be verified through the manufacturer.

After the September 11, 2001, attacks on the World Trade Center and the Pentagon, security of aircraft has become more of a priority. However, a security brief by the Aircraft Owners and Pilots Association (AOPA) stressed, "General aviation (GA) aircraft do not pose a significant terrorist threat to the United States. In fact, there has been no terrorist attack anywhere in the world using a general aviation aircraft ("General Aviation," n.d.). According to the brief, GA aircraft are incapable of causing significant damage. The typical GA aircraft—for example, a Cessna 172—weighs less than a Honda Civic and carries even less cargo.

The AOPA sponsors an Airport Watch, similar to a community's Neighborhood Watch, with America's pilots and aircraft owners banding together to protect our small airports. Everyone is encouraged to get to know one another and to report anything that appears to be suspicious. Greet strangers. Have a cell phone, a camera or pen and paper handy to record any suspicious activity, including

- Pilots who appear under the control of someone else.

- Anyone trying to access an aircraft through force.

- Anyone who seems unfamiliar with aviation procedures.

- Anyone who misuses aviation lingo—or seems too eager to use the lingo.

- People or groups who seem determined to keep to themselves.

- Anyone who appears to be just loitering.

- Any out-of-the-ordinary videotaping of aircraft or hangars.

- Dangerous cargo or loads.

- Anything that strikes you as wrong.

The AOPA urges its members to use common sense. Any of the preceding could have a logical explanation. However, when in doubt it should be checked out ("AOPA's Airport Watch," n.d., p.11). Chapter 20 discusses in depth the investigation of terrorist activity.

Summary

Motor vehicle thefts take much investigative time, but they can provide important information on other crimes under investigation. The VIN is the primary nonduplicated, serialized number assigned by a manufacturer to each vehicle made. This number—critical in motor vehicle theft investigation—identifies the specific vehicle in question.

Classifications of motor vehicle theft based on the offender's motive include (1) joyriding, (2) transportation, (3) commission of another crime, (4) gang initiation, (5) stripping for parts and accessories and (6) reselling for profit.

Although referred to as "motor vehicle theft," most of these crimes are prosecuted as "unauthorized use of a motor vehicle" because a charge of theft requires proof that the thief intended to deprive the owner of the vehicle permanently, which is often difficult or impossible to establish.

The elements of the crime of unauthorized use of a motor vehicle are (1) intentionally taking or driving (2) a motor vehicle (3) without the consent of the owner or the owner's authorized agent. Motor vehicles include automobiles, trucks, buses, motorcycles, motor scooters, mopeds, snowmobiles, vans, self-propelled watercraft and aircraft. Motor vehicle embezzlement exists if the person who took the vehicle initially had consent and then exceeded the terms of that consent.

The Dyer Act made interstate transportation of a stolen motor vehicle a federal crime and allowed for federal help in prosecuting such cases. False motor vehicle theft reports are often filed when a car has been taken by a family member or misplaced in a parking lot, when the driver wants to cover up an accident or crime committed with the vehicle or when the driver wants to provide an alibi for being late to some commitment. The FBI and the NICB provide valuable help in investigating motor vehicle thefts.

To improve your ability to recognize stolen vehicles, keep list of stolen vehicles, or a "hot sheet," in your car, develop a checking system for rapidly determining whether a suspicious vehicle is stolen, learn the common characteristics of stolen vehicles and car thieves, take time to check suspicious persons and vehicles and learn how to question suspicious drivers and occupants.

Numerous motor vehicle thefts can be prevented by effective educational campaigns and by installing anti-theft devices in vehicles during manufacture.

Checklist

Motor Vehicle Theft

- Description of vehicle: year, make, color, body type?
- Anything unusual about the vehicle, such as color combination or damage?
- Identification of vehicle: VIN, engine number, license number by state and year, registered owner and legal owner, address, telephone number?
- What were the circumstances of the theft: date and time reported stolen, location of theft? Were doors locked? Was the key in the ignition?
- Was the vehicle insured and by whom?
- Was the vehicle mortgaged and by whom? Are payments current?
- Did anyone have permission to use the vehicle? Have they been contacted?
- Was the owner arrested for another crime or suspected in a crime?
- Does the owner have any motive to falsely report the vehicle stolen?
- Was the owner involved in a hit-and-run incident or driving while intoxicated?
- Did the spouse report the vehicle missing?
- What method was used to take the vehicle?
- Has the vehicle been recovered? Where?
- Were crimes committed in the area where the vehicle was stolen or recovered?
- Was anybody seen near where the vehicle was stolen or found? When? How were they dressed? Approximate age?
- Was the vehicle seen on the street with suspects in it? Description of the suspects? Does the owner have any suspects?
- Were police field interrogation cards checked for the day of the theft and the days after to determine whether the vehicle had been stopped by police for other reasons?
- Were pawnshops checked for items that were in the vehicle?
- If the vehicle was a motorcycle, were motorcycle shops checked?
- If the vehicle was a truck, have there been other truck thefts in the area or labor problems?

■ Is the vehicle suspected of going interstate? Was the FBI notified?

■ Has a check been made with the National Insurance Crime Bureau?

■ Have junkyards been checked?

■ Have known auto thieves been checked to determine whether they were in the area at the time of the theft?

■ Was a check made with the DMV to determine the registered owner?

Applications

A. On July 2, an internist finished his shift at a Veterans Administration hospital and went to the hospital parking lot to find that his Triumph TR4A was missing. He called the local police, but they refused to come, saying that because the theft occurred on federal property, it was the FBI's problem. The doctor called the FBI, which first said it would not investigate a car theft unless the car was transported out of the state. The doctor's insurance company finally convinced the FBI to investigate the theft, which it did. Two days later, local police in a town 529 miles away discovered the TR4A abandoned in the parking lot at a racetrack. Because the car had been hot-wired, they assumed it was stolen and made inquiries to the state DMV about its ownership. The car was towed to a local storage garage. When it was learned who owned the TR4A, local police contacted the police in the doctor's city.

Because that police department had no record of a stolen TR4A, officers there assumed that the message was in error. It was a holiday weekend, they were busy and the matter was dropped. Eight months later, the storage garage called the doctor to ask him when he was coming to get his car.

Questions

1. What mistakes were made in this incident?

2. Who is primarily to blame for the eight-month delay in returning the car to the owner?

B. Samuel Paris parked his 1999 Corvette in front of his home shortly after midnight when he and his wife returned from a party. He locked the car and took the keys with him. He discovered the vehicle missing the following morning at about 7:45 when he was leaving for work. He immediately called the police to report an auto theft.

Questions

1. Were his actions correct?

2. What should the police department do upon receiving the call?

3. What should the officer who is assigned to the case do?

Discussion Questions

1. How do you identify a stolen vehicle so you can prove in court it was in fact stolen?

2. What evidence do you need to charge a suspect with unauthorized use of a motor vehicle? Embezzlement of a vehicle?

3. Where would you start looking for a stolen vehicle used in a crime? For joyriding? For transportation? For stripping and sale of parts?

4. How large a problem is auto theft in your community? Are such thefts thoroughly investigated?

5. What agencies besides local police are involved in investigating auto thefts, and under what circumstances can their services be requested? Who would be contacted in your area? What services can they perform?

6. How do juvenile and professional auto thieves differ with regard to motive and type of vehicle stolen? Are there different methods for locating each?

7. At what point might a report of a stolen motor vehicle become a civil matter instead of a criminal one?

8. Does the value of the stolen vehicle affect the charge made? The punishment?

9. What other crimes are frequently committed along with motor vehicle theft?

10. What measures does your community take to prevent motor vehicle theft? What else might it do?

Media Explorations

Internet

Select one of the following assignments to complete.

■ Go to the FBI Web site at www.fbi.gov. Click on "library and reference." Select "Uniform Crime Reports" and outline what the report says about motor vehicle theft.

■ Select one of the following key terms: *auto theft, motor vehicle theft, motor vehicle theft prevention, vehicle identification number*. Find one article relevant to motor vehicle theft investigations to outline and share with the class.

Gale Criminal Justice Database Assignments

The following assignments require access to Gale's Custom Journals Database for Emergency Services and Criminal Justice. Check with your instructor if you have questions about this.

■ Find the article "Car Thieves Smell a RATT" on the Gale Emergency Services Database. Read the article and outline the problem and response. Be prepared to share your findings in class.

■ Find the article "Labeling Automobile Parts to Combat Theft" on the Gale Emergency Services Database. Read the article and write a one-page paper on the topic.

References

"Airbag Theft and Fraud: Deflating a Growing Crime Trend." National Insurance Crime Bureau fact sheet, no date. Accessed July 14, 2011. https://www.nicb.org/theft_and_fraud_awareness/fact_sheets

"AOPA's Airport Watch." Aircraft Owners and Pilots Association Web site, no date. Accessed July 14, 2011. http://www.aopa.org/airportwatch/brochure.pdf

"Crime Clock Statistics." In *Crime in the United States, 2009.* Washington, DC: Federal Bureau of Investigation, September 2010. Accessed May 27, 2011. http://www.fbi.gov/ucr/cius2009/about/crime_clock.html

Crime in the United States, 2009. Washington, DC: Federal Bureau of Investigation, September 2010. Accessed May 27, 2011. http://www.fbi.gov/ucr/cius2009/index.html

Doing a Double-Take: Vehicle Clones Are a Street-Level Problem for Insurers. Washington, DC: National Insurance Crime Bureau, Strategic Analysis Report, October 10, 2004. Accessed October 7, 2008. http://www.nicbtraining.org/Vehicle_Cloning.pdf

Eskew, Marc. "5 Steps to Crime Prevention at Your Marina," no date. Accessed July 14, 2011. http://www.friendsofvista.org/articles/article33728.html

"General Aviation and Homeland Security." American Owners and Pilots Association, no date. Accessed July 15, 2011. http://www.aopa.org/whatsnew/newsitems/2002/020621_homeland_security.html

"Heavy Equipment Is a Tempting Target for Thieves." National Insurance Crime Bureau fact sheet, no date. Accessed July 14, 2011. https://www.nicb.org/theft_and_fraud_awareness/fact_sheets

"Hot Wheels: Vehicle Thefts Post Sixth Consecutive Yearly Decline." September 20, 2010. National Insurance Crime Bureau. Accessed July 14, 2011. https://www.nicb.org/newsroom/nicb_campaigns/hot%E2%80%93wheels

"ISO and NICB Release 2009 Heavy-Equipment Theft Report." National Insurance Crime Bureau. June 1, 2010. Accessed July 14, 2011. https://www.nicb.org/newsroom/news-releases/nicb-ner-2009-heavy-equipment-report

"It's Not a Feat of Science: Cloned Vehicles Are a Crime." National Insurance Crime Bureau. fact sheet, no date. Accessed July 14, 2011. http://www.ojp.usdoj.gov/BJA/pdf/NICB_Cloned_Vehicles.pdf

Molnar, J. P. "Automatic License Plate Recognition." *Law Officer Magazine,* March 2007, pp.20–24.

"Motorcycles Offer a Tempting Target for Criminals." National Insurance Crime Bureau fact sheet, no date. Accessed July 14, 2011. https://www.nicb.org/theft_and_fraud_awareness/fact_sheets

"Motorcycle Thefts Down 13 Percent in 2009." National Insurance Crime Bureau, April 13, 2010. Accessed July 14, 2011. https://www.nicb.org/newsroom/news-releases/motorcycle-thefts-and-recoveries-in-the-u-s-

"National and Rocky Mountain Region Auto Theft Statistics." Rocky Mountain Insurance Information Association. Accessed June 11, 2008. http://www.rmiia.org/Auto/Auto_theft/Statistics.htm

Ross, Brian. "Fake FedEx Trucks: When the Drugs Absolutely Have to Get There." *ABC News,* January 18, 2008.

Scoville, Dean. "How to Spot Stolen Cars." *Police,* May 2007, pp.26–29.

Steck-Flynn, Kathy. "What's in a VIN?" *Law Enforcement Technology,* June 2008, pp.90–96.

Straw, Joseph. "Very Light Jets: A Very Real Threat?" *Security Management,* March 2007, pp.28–30.

"Vehicle Identification Cloning Makes Stealing Your Car Easy." *Road and Travel Magazine,* 2008.

"Vehicle Theft." NICB brochure. https://www.nicb.org/theft_and_fraud_awareness/brochures

Walsh, Jeffrey A., and Taylor, Ralph B. "Predicting Decade-Long Changes in Community Motor Vehicle Theft Rates: Impacts of Structure and Surround." *Journal of Research in Crime and Delinquency,* February 2007, pp.64–90.

Case Cited

The People v. Gregory Shelton, No. B332259, Court of Appeals of California, Second District, Division Eight, Filed April 6, 2011.

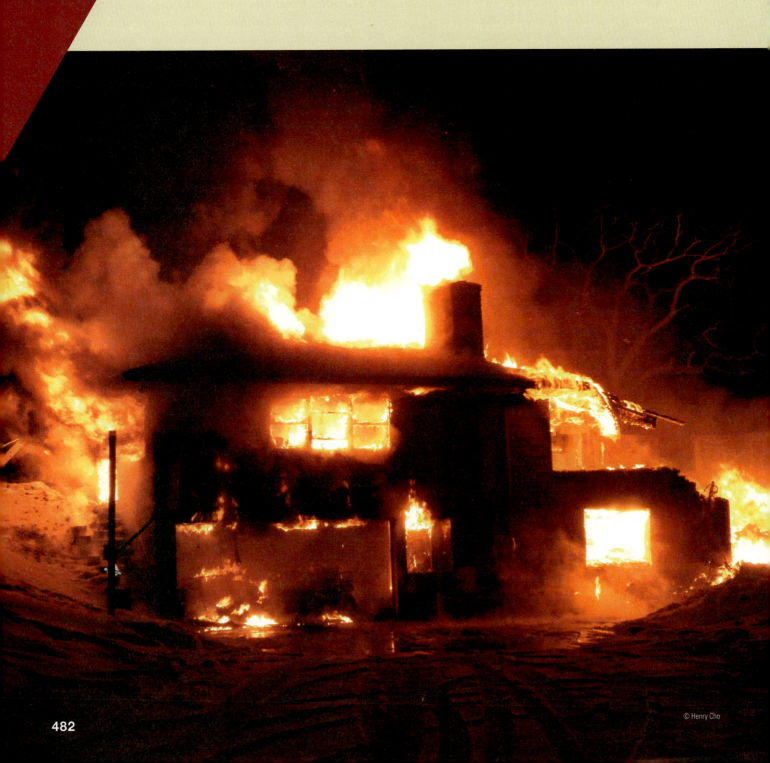

CHAPTER 16
Arson, Bombs and Explosives

Outline

Can You Define?

accelerants
administrative warrant
aggravated arson
alligatoring
arson
burn indicators
crazing
depth of char

disrupters
fire triangle
igniters
line of demarcation
simple arson
spalling
strikers
trailer

 ## Do You Know?

- How fires are classified?
- What presumption is made when investigating fires?
- What the elements of arson are?
- What constitutes aggravated arson? Simple arson?
- What degrees of arson the Model Arson Law establishes?
- Who is responsible for detecting arson? Investigating arson?
- What special challenges exist in investigating arson?
- What the fire triangle is and why it is important in arson investigations?
- What accelerants are and which are most commonly used in arson?
- What common igniters are used in arson?
- What common burn indicators are?
- How to determine a fire's point of origin?
- How fires normally burn?
- What factors indicate the likelihood of arson?
- When an administrative warrant is issued? A criminal warrant?
- When a warrant is needed for investigating a fire scene and what the precedent case is?
- What to check when investigating suspected arson of a vehicle?
- What to pay special attention to when investigating explosions and bombings?

Arson, the malicious, willful burning of a building or property, is one of the oldest crimes known. It has probably been practiced since soon after fire was discovered. Arson is a combination crime against persons and property, threatening life and causing immense property losses. In October 1978 Congress mandated that the Federal Bureau of Investigation (FBI) reclassify arson as a Part One Index crime in its Uniform Crime Reporting Program, effective March 1979.

Arson is difficult to prove because in many fires the evidence is consumed and there are few witnesses. Few police officers or investigators have extensive training in investigating arson, and they are often confused by the complications involved in securing evidence and cooperating with other agencies. Because proper arson investigation typically requires knowledge of both fire and law enforcement fields, some agencies have police investigators partner with fire investigators to handle these crimes. Other agencies staff fire marshals, who also have law enforcement powers for fire related incidents, investigate these crimes.

Many sources gather statistics on fires, including the FBI, the National Fire Protection Association (NFPA), insurance companies, state fire marshal's offices, state crime bureaus, sheriff's offices and local police and fire departments. The FBI's Uniform Crime Reports (UCR) show 58,571 arson offenses were reported in 2009, with an average damage of $17,411 (*Crime in the United States, 2009*, 2010). Of these arson offenses, 44.5 percent were structure fires, 28.4 percent were mobile properties and 27.1 percent accounted for other properties. Arson of structures had the highest average of damage, valued at approximately $93,287.

The NFPA presents somewhat different statistics, describing all fires reported during 2009, many of which needed to be investigated to rule out arson (Karter, 2010). Some 1,348,500 fires were reported, down 7 percent from 2008, with 3,010 civilian fire deaths, 17,050 civilian fire injuries, $12.5 billion in property damage and 82 firefighter deaths (not necessarily restricted to fires). Of all fires reported in 2009, 480,500 were structure fires, down 7 percent from 2008, with 2,695 civilian fire deaths, 14,740 civilian fire injuries and $10.8 billion in property damage. Vehicle fires numbered 219,000, down 7 percent from 2008, with 280 civilian fire deaths, 1,610 civilian fire injuries and $1.4 billion in property damage (Karter, 2010).

The NFPA "Fire Loss Clock" reports that in 2010, fire departments responded to a fire every 24 seconds, one structure fire was reported every 65 seconds, one home structure fire was reported every 85 seconds, one vehicle fire was reported every 146 seconds, one civilian fire injury was reported every 30 minutes and one civilian fire death occurred every 2 hours and 49 minutes (Karter, 2010).

CLASSIFICATION OF FIRES

The NFPA has developed *NFPA 921* (2011) as the definitive national guide for fire and explosives investigations, in which four classifications of fire cause are identified and defined.

> Fires are classified as natural, accidental, incendiary (arson) or of undetermined origin.

A *natural fire* is one caused without direct human action or intervention, such as fires caused by lightning, earthquakes and other natural events. This category may also include fires set intentionally to destroy refuse, weeds or waste products in industrial processes or to provide warmth. It is easy to determine that such fires are natural.

An *accidental fire*, as the name implies, is not intentional. Fires can be accidentally ignited by faulty wiring, leaking gas, a carelessly tossed cigarette, overheated Christmas tree lights, children playing with matches and many other causes. Arsonists usually try to make their fires appear accidental.

An *incendiary fire* (arson) is ignited intentionally and maliciously under circumstances in which the person knows that the fire should not be set. Such fires are often started to destroy property or buildings. Proof must be obtained that the fire was not natural or accidental.

A fire of *undetermined origin* is one in which there is no evidence to indicate whether the fire was natural, accidental or incendiary. The cause simply cannot be proven to an acceptable level of certainty.

> Fires are presumed natural or accidental unless proven otherwise.

The prosecution has the burden of proving that a fire is not accidental or natural. Because arson cases are hard to prove and require a great deal of work, they are unattractive to prosecutors. Moreover, a prosecutor may feel uneasy with the large amount of expert scientific testimony required.

Exercise caution in investigating fires. Most are not the result of arson. Do not unduly suspect property owners who have already been subjected to fire losses.

ELEMENTS OF THE CRIME: ARSON

Under common law, the *crime of arson* was defined as the malicious, willful burning of another's house or outbuilding. It was considered such a serious offense that the penalty was death. Laws have now extended arson to cover other buildings, personal property, crops and the burning of one's own property. As in other crimes, arson laws vary from state to state but share some common elements.

> The elements of the crime of arson include
> - Willful, malicious burning of a building or property,
> - of another or of one's own to defraud,
> - or causing to be burned, or aiding, counseling or procuring such burning.

Attempted arson is also a crime in most states.

Willful, Malicious Burning of a Building or Property

Willful means "intentional." If a motive is determined, intent can be proven; therefore, when possible, show motive even if it is not required by law. Merchandise or household goods moved in or out immediately before the fire help to establish motive and intent.

Malicious denotes a "spiteful, vindictive desire to harm others." Malice is shown by circumstantial evidence such as statements of ill will, threats against persons or property, a recent increase in insurance coverage or past property burned.

Burning is the prime element in the corpus delicti. There must be more than an exposure to heat, although flames need not have been visible nor the property destroyed. Heating to the ignition point is sufficient even if the fire extinguishes itself.

Of Another or of One's Own to Defraud

The motive for burning another's property can range from revenge to economic gain. The burning of one's own property, however, is almost always to defraud. Prove that the property was insured and show a motive for desiring the insurance money. Copies of the insurance policies obtained from the victim after serving proper notice show whether an excessive amount of insurance was taken out, whether recent additions or changes were made in the policy or whether the insurance was soon to expire. Businesses are sometimes burned because they are failing financially, which can be established by business records or employee statements.

Causing to Be Burned, or Aiding, Counseling or Procuring the Burning

A person who hires a professional (a "torch") to commit arson is also guilty of the crime. Seek evidence connecting this person with the actual arsonist.

CLASSIFICATION OF ARSON

States vary in how they classify arson and related crimes.

Aggravated and Simple Arson

Some laws categorize arson as either aggravated or simple.

> **Aggravated arson** is intentionally destroying or damaging a dwelling or other property by means of fire or explosives or other infernal device—creating an imminent danger to life or great bodily harm, which risk was known or reasonably foreseeable to the suspect. **Simple arson** is an intentional destruction by fire or explosives that does not create imminent danger to life or risk of great bodily harm.

Fire does not require visible burning or an actual flame, but it must involve some extent of burning. *Explosives* include any device, apparatus or equipment that causes damage by combustion or explosion, such as time bombs, Molotov cocktails, missiles, plastic explosives, grenades and dynamite. *Destruction or damage* does not require total destruction or consummation. Damage that affects the value or usefulness of the property is sufficient.

Creating an imminent danger to life or risk of great bodily harm is assumed whenever the burned structure is a dwelling or is likely to have people within it. People need not be there at the time. *If the danger or risk was known or reasonably foreseeable* means that even if the suspect did not intend to harm anyone, the risk should have been known or reasonably anticipated. If a person dies in a fire set by an arsonist, the death is first-degree murder, an additional offense to be prosecuted.

Attempted Arson

The elements of attempted arson are the intent to set a fire and some preparation to commit the crime. The intent is normally specific, and the act must be overt. It must be shown that the fire would have occurred except for some intervention. Attempted arson also includes placing any combustible or explosive material or device in or near any property with the intent to set fire, to destroy or to otherwise damage property. Putting materials together at a location where they could not cause a fire does not constitute attempted arson.

Setting Negligent Fires

Setting a negligent fire is defined as causing a fire to burn or to get out of control through culpable negligence, creating an unreasonable risk and the likelihood of damage or injury to persons or property. This charge is often brought against people who leave smoldering campfires that cause forest fires.

The Model Arson Law

The Model Arson Law was written and promoted in the 1920s by the NFPA. Many states do not classify fires as aggravated or simple but instead have adopted the Model Arson Law, which specifies four degrees of arson.

The Model Arson Law divides arson into the following degrees:

- *First-degree:* burning of dwellings
- *Second-degree:* burning of buildings other than dwellings
- *Third-degree:* burning of other property
- *Fourth-degree:* attempting to burn buildings or property

The Model Arson Law includes within each degree the actual act and anyone who aids, counsels or procures the act.

THE ARSONIST

According to the FBI's UCR, most of those arrested for arson are white males and more than half are under age 18, a higher rate of juvenile involvement than any other Index crime. The typical adult male arsonist has been reared in a broken or unstable home, has an extensive criminal history, is below average intelligence, lacks marital ties, is socially maladjusted or a loner, is unemployed or working in an unskilled position and is intoxicated at the time he sets the fire.

Female arsonists usually burn their own property, rarely that of an employer, neighbor or associate. They are often self-destructive, mentally defective, older, lonely and unhappy and often have some psychotic problems, primarily schizophrenia.

Juvenile Firesetting

Juvenile firesetting can have tragic, costly consequences: "In a typical year, fires set by children and youths claim the lives of approximately 300 people and destroy more than $300 million worth of property. Children are the predominant victims of these fires, accounting for 85 of every 100 lives lost" (Putnam and Kirkpatrick, 2005, p.1). A review of the literature reveals a distinction between fireplay and firesetting behavior. Fireplay conveys a low level of intent to inflict harm and an absence of malice; rather, it involves curiosity and fascination. Firesetting is "decidedly different" and involves malice and intent to inflict harm (Putnam and Kirkpatrick).

Juvenile firesetters are often divided into four categories: curiosity/experimental, troubled/crisis, delinquent/criminal and pathological/emotionally disturbed (*Juvenile Firesetting*, 2006, p.1). The curiosity firesetters are mainly children between ages 2 and 10 who experiment with or cause accidental fires. The troubled/crisis firesetters are mostly boys of any age whose firesetting represents "underlying psychosocial conflicts." Delinquent/criminal firesetters are adolescents between ages 13 and 18 with a long history of undetected firesetting who start fires as acts of vandalism or malicious mischief, but always with an intent to destroy. Pathological/emotionally disturbed firesetters' actions result from psychosocial conflict and may be random, ritualized or with specific intent to destroy property. These firesetters can be boys or girls of any age and typically display a chronic history of behavioral and social problems.

In arson, unlike other crimes, the victim is often the prime suspect. Motivation, although it need not be proved, has great significance in arson investigations.

Motivation

Common motives include revenge, spite or jealousy; vandalism and malicious mischief; crime concealment and diversionary tactics; profit and insurance fraud; intimidation, extortion and sabotage; and psychiatric afflictions, pyromania, alcoholism and mental retardation.

Revenge, spite and jealousy motivate jilted lovers, feuding neighbors, disgruntled employees, quarreling spouses, people who feel cheated or abused and those who feel racial or religious hostility. In rural areas, disagreements often result in the burning of homes or barns.

Vandalism and malicious mischief are frequent motives for juveniles who burn property merely to relieve boredom or as a general protest against authority. Many fires in schools, abandoned autos, vacant buildings and trash containers are caused by this type of arsonist.

Crime concealment and diversionary tactics motivate criminals to set fires to destroy evidence of a crime or evidence connecting them to the crime. In murder cases arson can be used to attempt to make it impossible to identify a victim. In other cases, people set fires to destroy records containing evidence of embezzlement, forgery or fraud. Arson is also used to divert attention while criminals commit another crime or cover their escape.

Profit and insurance fraud are frequent motives for arson. A businessperson may wind up in financial straits and decide that the easiest way out is to burn the business and collect the insurance. Some people over-insure property and then burn it, collecting far more than the property was worth. For example, a St. Louis property owner received more than $415,000 in insurance payments for 54 fires occurring within a 2-year period. In large cities, professional arson rings defraud insurance companies of millions of dollars.

Other methods of obtaining profit have used arson to stimulate business, to eliminate business rivals or to secure employment—for example, a security guard, firefighter or police officer might set fires to obtain a job. In South Carolina, five firefighters were charged with arson believed to be motivated not by profit but by a desire to practice fighting fires. In other cases, firefighters have set fires and then responded to the alarm, receiving attention and praise at having "played the hero." These "vanity" arsonists are called **strikers**.

Firefighters aren't the only ones who seek to become heroes. In December 1999, a male nurse set a fire that killed billionaire banker Edmond Safra, stating he hoped to emerge as the hero who saved his employer's life. Safra was terrified that assailants were after him and locked himself in his Monaco penthouse bathroom, refusing to leave even when police and firefighters arrived. He died of asphyxiation.

Intimidation, extortion and sabotage are motives of striking workers and employers to apply pressure during a strike. Criminals, especially mobsters, use arson to intimidate witnesses and to extort money. Protesters have also used arson as a way of sending a message. For example, an environmental group claimed responsibility for a series of fires that caused $12 million in damage in protest of Vail Associates moving forward with its controversial 885-acre ski resort expansion.

Psychiatric afflictions, pyromania, alcoholism and mental retardation account for many other fires. Pyromaniacs start fires because of an irresistible urge or passion for fire. Some derive sexual satisfaction from watching fires. Others become arsonists to show power over their environment or because they believe they are acting with divine guidance.

Several studies reveal revenge as the most common motive. Nonetheless, many arson investigators believe that insurance fraud is the most prevalent motive for arson. It may be that arson intended to defraud is often hired out to a professional who is less likely to get caught and, if apprehended, is more likely to have better legal counsel.

The professional torch—the arsonist for hire—is extremely difficult to identify because such individuals have no apparent link to the fire. However, the victim is also under suspicion in many instances. A guilty victim typically has an ironclad alibi. Also to be considered is the unintentional firesetter, that is, the individual who accidentally sets a fire and then is too embarrassed to admit it or who fears that insurance may not cover the loss if the accident is made known.

Computer software can play a pivotal role in identifying serial arsonists by allowing investigators to efficiently organize and manage tips, evidence and other information about related fires. Such case management can shorten investigations by months.

POLICE AND FIRE DEPARTMENT COOPERATION

Arson is investigated by many agencies with joint jurisdiction: state fire marshals, state police, county sheriffs and local police and fire departments. In addition, insurance investigators often become involved. Utility companies may also send investigators to the scene if there is concern that malfunctioning electrical or gas equipment caused the fire.

Lack of trained personnel to investigate arson is a major problem in both police and fire departments, except in large cities that have their own arson investigation squads. Although arson is a crime, police tend to give it low priority, believing that the fire department should investigate. However, many firefighters are volunteers who are not trained in arson investigation. Many full-time fire departments do not train their personnel to investigate arson. Rural areas and cities of as many as 75,000 in population rely heavily on the state fire marshal's office, which usually does not have enough staff to conduct full investigations throughout the state. State fire marshal's offices can help local police and fire agencies by providing advice, coordinating activities and supplying information on suspect profiles. They cannot, however, assume full responsibility for the investigation. Even fire departments that provide training in arson detection seldom include training on the criminal procedures followed in prosecuting arson.

Attitudes about the responsibility for investigating arson vary. Some fire departments feel that arson investigation and prosecution are their responsibility; others feel just as strongly that arson is a police matter.

> Logic suggests that the fire department should work to detect arson and determine the fire's point of origin and probable cause, whereas the police department should investigate arson and prepare the case for prosecution.

Fire Department Expertise

Recognizing factors concerning smoke and fire conditions, detecting arson evidence and determining the origin and cause (O&C) of a fire are specific areas of expertise for the fire department, which investigates many accidental and natural fires. To delegate this responsibility to the police department would be an unnecessary duplication of skill, especially because only a small number of fires are the result of arson.

Trained fire personnel know about buildings, how fires are started and the various components necessary for ignition. Fire marshals also have extralegal powers to summon witnesses, subpoena records and take statements under oath that police officers do not have.

Moreover, fire personnel may enter buildings after a fire without a warrant, a benefit to criminal investigations. They also work closely with insurance companies and are apt to recognize people frequently present at fires.

The fire department's basic role is fire investigation and arson detection, rather than arson investigation. Once the cause of the fire is determined to be arson, the police are notified and the process becomes a joint investigation, with the police taking the lead on the associated criminal investigation.

Police Department Expertise

Police on patrol duty and investigators, through intelligence files, are likely to know possible arson suspects. Field-interview cards can include names of people present in an area where arson fires are being set. Specialized techniques such as interviewing witnesses and interrogating suspects are normal police operations. Moreover, police have contacts with informants and arrest power.

Coordinating Efforts

Regardless of the actual agency assigned to an arson investigation, someone must coordinate the efforts of everyone involved. A full-time arson squad has the potential for conducting the best arson investigation. The next best arrangement is to have a well-trained arson investigator from local jurisdictions or the state fire marshal's office. However, police personnel trained in criminal investigation working with fire personnel trained in arson detection can do an effective job if they mutually agree about

Law enforcement and fire department personnel must collaborate to solve cases of arson.
© 911 Pictures

who is in charge. Cross-training is one way to help police and firefighters understand each other's roles.

OTHER SOURCES OF ASSISTANCE IN INVESTIGATING ARSON

Other sources of assistance in investigating arson are the Bureau of Alcohol, Tobacco, Firearms and Explosives (ATF), the news media, insurance companies and arson task forces.

The Bureau of Alcohol, Tobacco, Firearms and Explosives

On January 24, 2003 the Bureau of Alcohol, Tobacco and Firearms became part of the Department of Justice under the Homeland Security bill and had its name expanded to the Bureau of Alcohol, Tobacco, Firearms and Explosives to reflect the new focus on explosives-related crime and terrorism. The ATF has extensive resources for investigating arsons, including the ATF National Response Team, ready to investigate within 24 hours of receiving a call. For example, in January 2007, the team was called in to assist in the investigation of the fatal fire at the landmark Mizpah residential hotel at the request of the Reno (Nevada) Fire and Police Departments, the 620th activation since the program began ("ATF National Response Team Activated in Mizpah," 2007). In May 2008 the team joined with special agents from the Los Angeles Field Division to help the Los Angeles Fire Department investigate the Basque Night Club fire in Hollywood because of the size and complexity of the fire scene and the historical significance of the structure ("ATF National Response Team Joins Hollywood," 2008). In June 2008 the team was called in to help the Texas State Fire Marshals Office and the Texas Department of Public Safety investigate a fire that occurred at the Texas State Governor's Mansion ("ATF National Response Team Activated to Texas," 2008).

Other ATF resources include arson profilers; national laboratories in Georgia, Maryland and California; the Explosives Incidents Systems (EXIS) database, an intelligence division; financial auditors; accelerant-detecting canines; photograph examiners; and Certified Fire Investigators.

News Media

One source of assistance frequently overlooked is the news media, which can publish profiles of arsonists and seek the public's help in identifying them. Media may also have photographs or videotapes of in-progress fires that can be extremely useful in investigations.

Insurance Companies

Insurance companies can be very helpful in an arson investigation, but police must keep some things in mind: "Often, insurance adjustors or private investigators may arrive at the scene to do their own investigation and analysis on behalf of their organization or employer.... Insurance company fire investigators often bring a vast amount of experience, knowledge, and specific training. They will often agree to pay for lab analysis at an agreed-upon neutral third party laboratory.... Just keep in mind that they work for someone who stands to potentially lose a lot of money" (Smith and Gipson, 2008, p.58).

Many insurance companies have full-time fire loss investigators, which can be of tremendous benefit to those fire and police agencies do not. The objective is the same for both—obtaining the truth. For fire and police authorities, the goal is to locate the suspect. If the suspect in a fire-for-profit act is arrested, fire loss problems for the insurance company are resolved.

The property owner must work with the fire and police departments and insurance company to collect the insurance money. Consequently, interviewing and interrogating efforts are much enhanced. In addition, insurance companies usually request the insured to sign a release authorizing the company to obtain private records such as income tax returns, financial audits, bank accounts, credit reports, telephone records and utility company records. Without this release, obtaining such records is a long, complex process.

Insurance investigators have the additional advantage of being able to enter the fire scene without a warrant in their efforts to examine the damage and to determine the cause of the fire. However, as with any criminal investigation, even insurance loss investigators must be denied access to the area until the preliminary investigation has been conducted and the crime scene thoroughly processed (Smith and Gipson, 2008).

Several index bureaus gather insurance-claim information in attempting to determine whether the same claim is being made to more than one company or whether a pattern of claims exists. Law enforcement investigators can benefit from information gathered by these bureaus as well. Most states provide limited civil immunity to insurance companies that provide information to law enforcement agencies in their investigations.

Arson Task Forces

To coordinate existing forces and create new sources for combating arson and related problems in any community, county or state, arson task forces should be developed comprising fire and police department personnel; community leaders; insurance representatives; city, county and district attorneys; federal agency personnel;

and others. Arson has the lowest clearance by arrest of the major crimes, primarily because of inadequate training of fire and police department personnel, the difficulty of locating and preserving evidence and a lack of coordination of personnel of the various organizations involved.

The Web site of the Office of the Illinois State Fire Marshal describes its Juvenile Firesetters Task Force (www .state.il.us/osfm/jfs/jfs.htm), whose goal is "to develop and coordinate a comprehensive statewide program to identify, intervene with and counsel juveniles." The goal of the task force is, "To develop and coordinate a comprehensive statewide program to identify, intervene with, and counsel juveniles to reduce fire deaths, injuries, and property damage from criminal and non-criminal fires."

Other task force approaches can accomplish at least three goals:

1. Detecting arson, including seeking ways to improve detection of, as well as to properly investigate and successfully prosecute the crime.

2. Reducing the number of arsons and deliberately set fires, in turn reducing property damage, physical injuries and deaths.

3. Developing a preventive program aimed at educating and developing a working relationship with the people the task force serves.

The Importance of the Dispatcher

Local emergency dispatchers can play an important role in arson cases: "Today's highly trained emergency dispatchers … are often a fire investigator's first link to solving what may turn out to be a difficult fire investigation. Often and without realizing it, the person answering the 9-1-1 call for help may be speaking to the person responsible for starting the fire. At the very least, persons dialing 9-1-1 are early witnesses to the fire and may hold valuable information that no one else has" (Acker, 2007, p.22).

SPECIAL CHALLENGES IN INVESTIGATION

Special challenges in investigating arson include
- Coordinating efforts with the fire department and others.
- Determining whether a crime has been committed.
- Finding physical evidence, most of which is destroyed by the fire.
- Finding witnesses.
- Determining whether the victim is a suspect.

Investigating arson often requires even more persistence, thoroughness and attention to minute details than do other crimes. Arson is a difficult crime to investigate because there are seldom witnesses and the evidence needed to prove that a crime has been committed is usually consumed in the fire. Moreover, arson is an easy crime to write off without being publicly criticized because the victim and the suspect are often the same person. However, the innocent victim of arson is frequently frustrated by the lack of evidence and witnesses and by the police's inability to prove that a crime was committed.

RESPONDING TO THE SCENE

While approaching a fire scene, first responders should observe, mentally note and, when time permits, record in notes (*Fire and Arson*, 2000, pp.13–14):

- The presence, location and conditions of victims and witnesses.
- Vehicles leaving the scene, bystanders or unusual activities near the scene.
- Flame and smoke conditions (e.g., the volume of flames and smoke; the color, height and location of flames; the direction in which the flames and smoke are moving).
- The type of occupancy, use and condition of the structure.
- Conditions surrounding the scene.
- Weather conditions.
- Fire-suppression techniques used, including ventilation, forcible entry and utility shutoff measures.
- Status of fire alarms, security alarms and sprinklers.

THE PRELIMINARY INVESTIGATION

The fire department usually receives the initial fire call unless the departments have a joint dispatcher or are merged into a public safety department. Fire personnel make out the reports and forward them to the state fire marshal. Insurance companies are also represented, and their efforts are coordinated with those of fire and police personnel.

The scene of a fire is dirty, messy and complicated, making it difficult to obtain evidence of possible arson. An arson scene may be the most contaminated crime scene you will ever encounter. Piles of smoldering, blackened debris, often coated in foam or soaked with water, are difficult environments in which to locate evidence. In addition, structural damage caused by the fire may make searching for such evidence even more hazardous.

Although the fire department is responsible for establishing that arson has occurred, investigators must verify those findings by understanding what distinguishes an accidental fire from arson and by knowing what evidence and information are available for proving the elements of the crime.

The Fire Triangle

The fire triangle is a basic concept critical to an arson investigation.

> The **fire triangle** consists of three elements necessary for a substance to burn: air, fuel and heat. In arson, one or more of these elements is usually present in abnormal amounts for the structure.

Extra amounts of *air* or oxygen can result from opened windows or doors, pried-open vents or holes knocked in walls. Because firefighters often chop holes in structures, determine whether any such openings were made by the firefighters or by someone else. *Fuel* can be added by piling up newspapers, excelsior or other combustible materials found at or brought to the scene. Gasoline, kerosene and other accelerants add sufficient *heat* to the fire to cause the desired destruction after it has been ignited.

Arson Indicators

Several factors can alert investigators that the fire was probably the result of arson.

Accelerants.

> Evidence of **accelerants**, substances that promote combustion, especially gasoline, is a primary form of physical evidence at an arson scene.

Most arson cases involve a flammable liquid, and in 80 percent of these cases, it is gasoline. Perhaps this is because gasoline is easily obtained and widely known to arsonists or because gasoline's familiar odor makes it easier for investigators to detect. Other common accelerants are kerosene, charcoal lighter, paint thinner and lacquer solvent.

Look for residues of liquid fire accelerants on floors, carpets and soil because the liquid accelerants run to the lowest level. In addition, these areas often have the lowest temperatures during the fire and may not have enough oxygen to support complete combustion of the accelerant. Accelerants may seep through porous or cracked floors to underlying soil that has excellent retention properties for flammable liquids. Accelerants can also be found on the clothes and shoes of the suspect if apprehended. You can also identify fire accelerants at the scene either by your own sense of smell or by using portable equipment that detects residues of flammable liquids.

Olfactory detection, the sensitivity of the human nose to gasoline vapor, is ineffective if the odor is masked by another strong odor, such as that of burned debris. Moreover, it is often inconvenient or impossible to sniff for accelerant odors along floors or in recessed areas.

Catalytic combustion detectors are the most common type of flammable vapor detector used by arson investigators. Commonly known as a *sniffer,* a *combustible gas indicator,* an *explosimeter* or a *vapor detector,* this detector is portable, moderately priced and fairly simple to operate. Basically, vapor samples are pumped over a heated, platinum-plated wire coil that causes any combustible gas present to oxidize. The heat from the oxidation raises the coil's electrical resistance, and this change is measured electrically.

Although fire accelerants are the most frequent type of evidence submitted to laboratories for analysis (80 percent), explosives (13 percent) and incendiary devices (4 percent) are also frequently submitted.

Igniters. Igniters are substances or devices used to start fires. The most common igniters are matches. To be carrying matches is not damaging evidence unless some have been removed from the book or box and those found at an arson scene match those found in the suspect's possession.

> Common igniters include matches; candles; cigars; cigarettes; cigarette lighters; electrical, mechanical and chemical devices; and explosives.

Electrical devices left on, kerosene-soaked papers in waste baskets, time fuses, shorted light switches, magnifying glasses, matches tied around a lighted cigarette and numerous other igniters have been used to commit arson.

Candles are often used in arsons because they give the suspect time to leave the scene. The average candle burns about 30 to 45 minutes per inch, depending on its size, shape, composition and the amount of air in the room. Tapered candles burn faster at the top and slower toward the base. The arsonist may control the length of time by cutting off part of the candle before lighting it. The candle can be set in a material that will ignite once the candle burns down or the hot wax may be allowed to drip onto a surface to start a fire. The candle's flame can also be used to ignite other materials in the room.

Regardless of whether arsonists use direct or delayed ignition, they usually plan for the fire to consume the igniter; however, this often does not happen. Moreover,

Varying degrees of alligatoring and charring are observed on the floor joists of this single-family home that burned in Pacifica, California. This photo depicts intense heat from left to right and at the base of the flooring.
© Robert Pinto

in their haste to leave the scene, arsonists may drop parts of the igniter in an area unaffected by the fire. Any igniter not normally present at the location is evidence.

Burn Indicators. **Burn indicators** are visible evidence of the effects of heating or partial burning. They indicate various aspects of a fire such as rate of development, temperature, duration, time of occurrence, presence of flammable liquids and points of origin. Interpreting burn indicators is a primary means of determining the causes of fires.

 Common burn indicators include alligatoring, crazing, the depth of char, lines of demarcation, sagged furniture springs and spalling.

Alligatoring is the checking of charred wood that gives it the appearance of alligator skin. Large, rolling blisters indicate rapid, intense heat. Small, flat alligatoring indicates slow, less intense heat.

Crazing is the formation of irregular cracks in glass caused by rapid, intense heat, possibly caused by a fire accelerant.

The **depth of char**, or how deeply wood is burned, indicates the length of burn and the fire's point of origin. Use a ruler to measure depth of char.

A **line of demarcation** is a boundary between charred and uncharred material. A puddle-shaped line of demarcation on floors or rugs can indicate use of a liquid fire accelerant. In a cross section of wood, a sharp, distinct line of demarcation indicates a rapid, intense fire.

A photograph of a line of demarcation, seen in this carpet, is important evidence in an arson investigation. A puddle-shaped line of demarcation on floors or rugs can indicate the use of a liquid fire accelerant.
© James Shaffer

Sagged furniture springs usually occur when a fire originates inside the cushions of upholstered furniture (as from a lighted cigarette rolling behind a cushion) or when a fire is intensified by an accelerant.

Spalling is the breaking off of surface pieces of concrete or brick because of intense heat. Brown stains around the spall indicate use of an accelerant.

Point of Origin. Knowing the fire's point of origin helps to establish how the fire spread and whether it followed a normal burning pattern. The more extensive the destruction, the more difficult it is to determine the fire's point of origin.

The point of origin is established by finding the area with the deepest char, alligatoring and usually the greatest destruction. More than one point of origin indicates arson.

Incendiary (igniter) evidence might be discovered at the point of origin. In addition, information from witnesses who saw the fire can establish where the flames began.

Burning Pattern.

Fires normally burn upward, not outward. They are drawn toward ventilation and follow fuel paths.

Given adequate ventilation, a fire will burn upward. If a door or window is open, it will be drawn toward that opening.

If the arsonist places a path of flammable liquid, the fire will follow that path, known as a **trailer**. Trailers can be made of paper, hay, flammable compounds or any substance that burns readily, and they result in an abnormal pattern. The char marks will follow the trailer's path.

Areas of uneven burning can also indicate the presence of an incendiary or that a great amount of flammable material was already at the scene.

Appearance of Collapsed Walls. Notice how walls seem to have collapsed, especially if you smell gas. Lighter gases tend to explode walls out from the top of the room; heavier gases explode walls out from the bottom of the room. Fast-exploding gases such as hydrogen, acetylene or butane give the appearance of the walls caving in. If odors or the walls' appearance suggests gas as the igniter or accelerator, determine whether the gas is normally on the premises.

Smoke Color. Generally, blue smoke results from burning alcohol; white smoke from burning vegetable compounds, hay or phosphorous; yellow or brownish yellow smoke from film, nitric acid, sulfur, hydrochloric acid or smokeless gunpowder; and black smoke from petroleum or petroleum products.

Notice the smoke's color if the fire is still in progress. If it has been put out when you arrive, ask the firefighters or witnesses what color the smoke was. Determine whether substances likely to produce smoke of that color were on the premises before the fire.

Summary of Arson Indicators

Arson is likely in fires that
■ Have more than one point of origin.
■ Deviate from normal burning patterns.
■ Show evidence of trailers.
■ Show evidence of having been accelerated.
■ Produce odors or smoke of a color associated with substances not normally present at the scene.
■ Indicate that an abnormal amount of air, fuel or heat was present.
■ Reveal evidence of incendiary igniters at the point of origin.

The black smoke in this fire indicates the involvement of petroleum or petroleum products. If these are not normally on the premises, arson is probable.
© 911 Pictures

Professional arsonists use a variety of methods to ignite fires, including

- Connecting magnesium rods to timed detonators and placing them in a building's electrical system. The rods burn with extreme intensity and cause a fire that looks as though it was caused by faulty wiring.
- Connecting a timed explosive charge on one or more barrels of gasoline or other highly flammable liquid. This method is often used when large areas such as warehouses are to be burned.
- Pouring acid on key support points in steel-structured buildings to make certain the building will collapse during the fire.

Photographing and Videotaping an Arson Fire

Pictures of a fire in progress show the smoke's color and its origination as well as the size of the fire at different points and times. Pictures are especially useful if there appears to be acceleration of the fire at a specific time that would indicate arson or the presence of highly combustible substances. Many fire departments take such in-progress photographs. Smaller departments may seek help from television or newspaper photographers who may take pictures that can be of immense help. Photographs or videotapes of the fire scene are also ideal to show the judge and jury.

Pictures taken of people at the fire scene might reveal the presence of a known arsonist or show a person who repeatedly appears in photos taken at fires and is therefore an arson suspect.

After the fire, take enough pictures to show the entire scene in detail. Start with the outside of the structure, showing all entries and exits. Also show any obstructions that were placed in front of windows to prevent seeing inside the building. People familiar with the structure can review the pictures for anything out of the ordinary.

Take inside pictures to show the extent of burning. These will prove the corpus delicti. Take close-up pictures of extra papers, rags, gas cans or other suspicious substances, as well as examples of alligatoring and deep charring. Take pictures at each stage of the search to show the point of origin, the nature of the burning and the direction and speed of the fire's spread.

Physical Evidence

Preserving evidence is a major problem because much of the evidence is very fragile. Follow carefully the procedures described in Chapter 5. Use disposable cellulose sponges to sop up accelerants for transfer to a container. Use hypodermic or cooking syringes to suck up accelerants between boards or crevices. Sift ashes to detect small objects such as the timing device from an igniter.

Incendiary evidence at the point of origin can be part of a candle, an empty flammable liquid container, excessive amounts of unburned newspaper folded together or a number of unburned matches.

Paper exposed to high temperatures and sufficient air burns with little ash to examine. However, with a limited supply of air, only partial combustion occurs, leaving charred paper evidence that can be collected for laboratory examination. Paper in a fireplace or stove may be only partially burned, even if the building was totally consumed. These papers may provide a motive for the arson. If the paper is not destroyed, a laboratory may be able to recover any messages on it.

Do not overlook computer data, even if the computer has been involved in an intense fire. The hard drive may survive extreme heat and sometimes even direct flames. It may also survive the water and steam encountered during suppression efforts.

An important step in an arson investigation is identifying potential accelerants at a fire scene. The accepted method is to use gas chromatography with a flame ionization detector (GC-FID), which can make identification in 95 percent of the cases.

Using K-9s in Arson Investigations

Dogs can be of great assistance in arson investigation. Connecticut's K-9 accelerant-detection program, for example, is the result of collaboration among the ATF, the New Haven County state's attorney's office, the State Police Science Laboratory, the Emergency Services Division Canine Unit and the Bureau of the State Fire Marshal. Their first dog, Mattie, was trained to detect extremely small quantities of highly diluted flammable and combustible liquids, including paint remover and thinner, lacquer thinner, charcoal lighter fluid, kerosene, naphtha, acetone, dry gas, heptone, gasoline, number 2 fuel, diesel fuel, gum turpentine, Heritage lamp oil, transmission fluid, octane and Jet-A-Fuel.

A lab-certified accelerant-detection canine can detect accelerants at fire scenes and can also search a crowd for possible suspects, search a suspect's clothing and vehicle for the presence of accelerants and search areas for accelerant containers.

Evidence on a Suspect, at a Residence or in a Vehicle

If you have a suspect, look for any burns he or she may have received while setting the fire. The suspects may have scorched hair, torn clothing, soot on their skin, stains, cuts and other injuries or their clothing or shoes may have traces of accelerants or charred soot. Be alert to the presence of unique odors such as gasoline or other chemicals, either on the suspect or in his or her vehicle. The suspect's residence or vehicle may contain clothes noticed at the fire

Cars burn during a massive wildfire October 22, 2007, in Poway, California. The Witch Fire, which started outside of Ramona, California, burned hundreds of structures and forced thousands of evacuations as fires burned across Southern California. Although such wildfires may be caused by natural forces such as lightning storms, others have been the result of arson.
© Sandy Huffaker/Getty Images

by a witness, objects removed from the scene of the fire or incendiary devices. You may also find insurance documents or business or financial records that provide a motive.

Observing Unusual Circumstances

Suspicious circumstances implying arson include suddenly emptied premises, the presence of materials not normally part of the business, holes in wall plaster or drywall that expose the wood, disconnected sprinkler systems, blocked-open interior doors, nailed-open fire doors and other alterations that would provide more air, heat or fuel to the area.

Interviewing the Owner/Victim, Witnesses and Firefighters

One of the most basic and valuable investigative techniques is the interview, and fire investigations are no exception. Ask questions such as, How was the fire discovered? Who discovered it? Who were witnesses? What did they see? Who owns the property and where are they? Is there anyone else who occupies or has access to the property? What color was the smoke, and where was it coming from? What direction was the wind? Did the fire appear to suddenly accelerate? Did anything out of the ordinary occur before the fire? Were there unusual odors? Were the shades up or down? Did obstructions prevent seeing into the building? Were suspicious persons or vehicles observed at the scene before, during or after the fire?

Also try to learn who had an opportunity to set the fire and who might benefit from it. Determine who had keys and how the property was normally guarded or protected. Check the victim's financial status and find out how much insurance was carried on the property. Make note of whether the owner is cooperative with the investigators.

Document the names and badge numbers of the "first in" firefighters. Interview this crew and record their observations while suppressing the fire, including the methods used and steps taken to fight the fire (Smith and Gipson, 2008). Finally, "It is imperative that when you are interviewing people at the incident such as the owner, witnesses, bystanders watching or photographing the fire, and transients that you don't forget to interview the person who called 9-1-1 to report the fire. Chances are, he or she saw the fire in its beginning stages and may have seen other things relevant to the investigation" (Smith and Gipson, 2008, p.55).

SEARCH WARRANTS AND FIRE INVESTIGATIONS

The U.S. Supreme Court requires a two-step warrant process for investigating fires involving crimes. The initial search may require an **administrative warrant** for searching the premises for cause of fire and origin determination *and* a criminal warrant when evidence of a crime is discovered. Both require probable cause for issuance.

An administrative warrant is issued when it is necessary for a government agent to search the premises to determine the fire's cause and origin. A criminal warrant is issued on probable cause when the premises yield evidence of a crime.

Both require an affidavit in support of the warrant that states the location and legal description of the property, the purpose (to determine the fire's cause and origin), the area and time of the search, the use of the building and the measures taken to secure the structure or area of the fire. Searches are limited to the items specified in the warrant. Found evidence may be seized, but once the officers leave after finding the evidence, they must have a criminal warrant to return to the premises for a further search.

Administrative warrants allow civil inspections of private property to determine compliance with city ordinances such as fire codes. The Supreme Court has established guidelines for arson investigators. In *Michigan v. Clifford* (1984), the Court held, "If a warrant is necessary, the object of the search determines the type of warrant required. If the primary object is to determine the cause and origin of a fire, an administrative warrant will suffice … and if the primary object is to gather evidence of criminal activity, a criminal search warrant may be obtained only on a showing of probable cause to believe that relevant evidence will be found in the place to be searched."

In *Coolidge v. New Hampshire* (1971), the Court held that evidence of criminal activity discovered during a search with a valid administrative warrant may be seized under the plain view doctrine. Any evidence so seized may be used to establish the probable cause needed to obtain a criminal search warrant.

> Entry to fight a fire requires no warrant. Once in the building, fire officials may remain a reasonable time to investigate the cause of the blaze. After this time, an administrative warrant is needed, as established in *Michigan v. Tyler* (1978).

Guidelines on the current legal status of searches conducted during fire investigations include:

■ Warrants are not required when an authorized individual consents to the search. The consent must be written and must specify the areas to be searched and the purpose of the search. This consent can be revoked at any time.

■ Warrants are not required when investigators enter under "exigent circumstances," that is, if investigators enter the premises while firefighters are extinguishing the blaze or conducting overhaul. The scope of the search must be limited to determining the cause and origin. If evidence of a crime is discovered, a criminal warrant is required to continue the search.

■ Without consent or an exigency, warrants are required if the premises are subject to a "reasonable expectation of privacy." This includes commercial businesses as well as private residences. Exceptions would be premises that are so utterly devastated by the fire that no expectation of privacy is reasonable and property that has been abandoned.

■ Evidence of a crime discovered during an administrative search may be seized if in plain view.

■ Once evidence of arson is discovered, the fire's cause and origin are assumed to be known. The scope of the administrative warrant has been exhausted. A criminal warrant is required to continue the search.

When in doubt, obtain a warrant: "At the scene of the fire, a firefighter or ranking fire official may request to take you on a 'walk-through' of the scene to explain his or her observations that led to the conclusion that the fire was arson. Before you go on that walk-through, remember that law enforcement officers must have the legal authority to enter and investigate the scene after the fire is out" (Smith and Gipson, 2008, pp.55–56).

FINAL SAFETY AND LEGAL CONSIDERATIONS

Entering a burned-out building can be a dangerous endeavor, from both a safety perspective and a legal standpoint, and requires some advanced preparation (Smith and Gipson, 2010). These are some final tips to remember before entering fire damaged property:

■ Obtain either consent from the legal owner or a search warrant.

■ Turn off utilities.

■ Have the structure inspected and ventilated.

■ Bring a partner.

■ Put on safety boots, protective eyewear and a hard hat.

■ Wash your boots with detergent to eliminate cross contamination. (Smith and Gipson, 2008, p.55)

INVESTIGATING VEHICLE ARSON

Although vehicle fires can be caused by accident, vehicles usually do not burn readily. Accelerants are used on many vehicles to accomplish arson. A quart to a half-gallon of flammable liquid is required to cause a major vehicle fire.

> When investigating vehicle fires, look for evidence of accelerants and determine whether the vehicle was insured. It is seldom arson if there was no insurance.

Motives for vehicle arson include the desire to collect insurance, inability to make needed repairs after an unreported accident, desire to eliminate a loan on the vehicle, desire to cover up another crime committed in or with the vehicle, general dissatisfaction with the vehicle's performance and desire to resolve arguments over the vehicle's use.

A close correlation exists between insurance coverage and vehicle arson. Obtain proof that the vehicle was insured against fire, that the fire was willfully set, that damage resulted and that there was intent to defraud.

PROSECUTING ARSONISTS

Some studies indicate that considerably more than 90 percent of arsonists go unpunished, probably because arson is most often committed without the benefit of witnesses. According to the International Association of Arson Investigators, approximately 25 percent of all fires in the United States—about 500,000 per year—result from arson, but only about 2 percent of all arsonists are ever arrested and convicted for their crimes.

The difficulty of investigating arson has been discussed, as has the need for cooperation between law enforcement investigators and firefighters. Equally difficult is prosecution. There is a big difference between proving a fire as arson and proving arson in court. Cooperative investigation and prosecution are required if the losses from arson are to be stemmed.

Many prosecutors fail to bring charges because all they have is circumstantial evidence. However, circumstantial evidence can be used to successfully prosecute a case. Look for evidence of planning, such as increasing insurance coverage, removing items or making offhand remarks or unusual changes. Also look for evidence of disabled or turned-off alarms or sprinkler systems and doors left open. Finally, look for evidence of motive.

PREVENTING ARSON

To prevent arson, various properties at risk of being set on fire might be identified by computer mapping. In some instances, crime analysis has determined that most properties that had experienced arson were either abandoned or vacant properties located near or adjacent to notably high crime locations. In one instance, six key factors were merged into one master map: (1) abandoned properties, (2) negative-equity properties, (3) properties whose gas or electric utilities were shut off, (4) sites of prior-year fires, (5) gang locales and (6) known drug hot spot locations. With accurate predictions, officers can be stationed close to and be more observant of targeted zones.

BOMBINGS AND EXPLOSIONS

It seems hardly a week passes when the media doesn't report a bombing incident having occurred somewhere around the globe, often with significant casualties. Bombs have become a high-profile, almost routine, weapon of mass destruction. Bombs generate substantial media attention and provide an impersonal means of causing considerable damage, while either allowing bombers to be a safe distance away when detonation occurs or enabling suicide bombers to achieve martyrdom and incite other holy warriors to follow in their path. As noted, this emphasis on explosives was reflected in the addition of "and explosives" to the ATF name in 2003.

Most explosive incidents in this country fall into one of five classes (Laska, 2008, p.40):

1. Juvenile/experimentation
2. Recovered military ordnance or commercial explosives
3. Emotionally disturbed persons
4. Criminal actions
5. Terrorist or extremist activity

Motives for bombings include vandalism, revenge and protest. Bombs are relatively easy to build from directions that can be found on the Internet. The following are common types of improvised explosive devices (IEDs) or homemade bombs:

■ *Dry ice.* Combines dry ice and some water in a 2-liter plastic soda bottle. Depending on the condition of the bottle, the amount of ice and the weather, the device will explode in 3 to 7 minutes, causing a dangerous, loud explosion.

■ *Mailbox bomb.* Combines a bit of sugar and some water in a 2-liter bottle of chlorine. The explosion can launch an average mailbox 20 feet into the air.

■ *Car bomb.* A fuse is wrapped around a car's exhaust manifold. The fuse is ignited by the heat of the manifold, detonating the explosion.

■ *Nail bomb.* An explosive device packed with nails to increase destructive power when detonated in crowded places. The July 7, 2005, explosion in London atop a double-decker bus near Shoreditch was thought to be this type of bomb.

■ *Pipe bomb.* Consists of pipe, end caps and smokeless powder, detonated by a spark or some heat source. Common containers are pipes, bottles, cans, boxes, pressurized cartridges and grenade hulls. A pipe bomb laced with nails and other hardware to increase fragmentation caused two deaths in Atlanta's Centennial Park bombing.

Terrorists have long used cellular phones to trigger IEDs because they have adequate power, time synchronization capabilities and alarm clock function; allow for worldwide usage; and are extremely difficult if not impossible to track, especially if they're disposable.

A homemade explosive known as "TATP"—triacetone triperoxide—is the explosive that Richard Reid, the "shoe bomber," carried aboard American Airlines Flight 63 from Paris to Miami in 2001. TATP is composed of acetone, hydrogen peroxide and an acid, even a can of Coke. The ingredients can easily be bought for about $17 at any hardware or home improvement store or online. The explosive concoction is virtually undetectable and quite easy to get past security, although new restrictions on carry-on liquids may make it more difficult to get the requisite materials through security checkpoints (Moore, 2007, p.210).

The threat of liquid explosives is of great concern, especially to airlines, as the aircraft environment requires very little explosive force because of the already pressurized cabin. Thus, law enforcement should be familiar with several types of liquid and gel explosives, some of which are very volatile (Morgenstern, 2007). Even picking up a bottle of nitroglycerine and shaking it could cause an explosion.

Bombers sometimes take their explosives one step further, creating a weapon known as the vehicle-borne improvised explosive device (VBIED), or the "car bomb": "Bad guys have transformed all types of wheeled conveyances from pushcarts and bicycles to cement trucks and tractor-trailers, into bombs" (Gundy and Linett, 2007, p.38). Furthermore, "There has been a distinct increase in the use of creative and sophisticated attack methods, such as multiple VBIEDs, combined attacks (assault teams used in conjunction with VBIEDs), secondary devices, and deceptive delivery tactics" (p.40).

Numerous Web sites give detailed instructions about how to make bombs, especially pipe bombs. For example, the Linkbase Web site offers the following links: homemade explosives, high explosives, how to make a detonator, how to make a pipe bomb, how to make a smoke bomb, how to make a grenade, how to make a time bomb and the like. The instructions are only two pages long, and all the materials needed are readily available.

Bombs, more than any other weapon, make people feel vulnerable. Unlike a gun, a bomb does not have to be aimed. Unlike poison, it does not have to be administered. Bombs are weapons of chance. Victims are simply in the wrong place at the wrong time. For example, the 1993 World Trade Center bombing in New York resulted in six dead, more than a thousand injured and millions of dollars in property damage. The 1995 bombing at the Murrah Federal Building in Oklahoma City claimed 169 lives, caused nearly 500 injuries and resulted in losses of $651 million. Bomber Timothy McVeigh was found guilty of the crime and executed. And, the explosions in 2001 at the World Trade Center and the Pentagon resulted in thousands of deaths. Terrorist acts are discussed in Chapter 20.

National attention also focused on the Unabomber case. Theodore Kaczynski, a Montana hermit who hated our technological society, expressed his social criticism through a campaign of bombing between 1978 and 1995. During this interval, his 16 separate bombs killed 3 people and injured 23 others. After 18 years of investigation, Kaczynski was arrested, found guilty and sentenced to life in prison without possibility of release. Evidence found in Kaczynski's cabin included scrap metal and wood, batteries and electric wire, 10 three-ring binders filled with writings and diagrams about constructing and concealing explosive devices and two manual typewriters that investigators believe Kaczynski used to type his "Unabomber Manifesto."

In the late 1990s Eric Rudolph used nail-laden bombs during the Atlanta Summer Olympics as well as at abortion clinics and at nightclubs catering to a mostly gay and lesbian clientele. His 11-page statement was devoid of remorse but rife with anti-abortion and anti-gay rhetoric. The attack at the Olympics was meant to embarrass the government for legalizing abortion.

In 2002 Luke Helder, age 21 at the time, left a trail of 18 pipe bombs in rural mailboxes in Illinois, Iowa, Nebraska, Texas and Colorado. The bombs were accompanied by typewritten notes in clear plastic bags indicating the bomber wanted to get people's attention. Six of the bombs exploded, injuring four letter carriers and two residents, but no one was killed. Law enforcement pulled Helder over three times during the course of his 1,500-mile journey in which he attempted to create a "smiley face" pattern of mailbox bombings. He was stopped in Nebraska and given a speeding ticket. He was stopped in Oklahoma for driving without a seatbelt. And he was stopped in Colorado for speeding. Within 48 hours of these three encounters, Helder was arrested on bombing charges after his cell phone calls were traced. The FBI was the lead agency in investigating these bombings and in apprehending Helder.

RESPONDING TO A BOMB THREAT

Too often officers respond to a bomb threat call with a blasé approach. As with any other aspect of policing, a nonchalant attitude could prove fatal. Special safety precautions must be taken when responding to a bomb threat. The International Association of Chiefs of Police

BOMB THREAT INSTRUCTIONS

Place this card under your telephone.

Questions to ask:

1. *When is bomb going to explode?*
2. *Where is it right now?*
3. *What does it look like?*
4. *What kind of bomb is it?*
5. *What will cause it to explode?*
6. *Did you place the bomb?*
7. *Why?*
8. *What is your address?*
9. *What is your name?*

Exact wording of the threat:

_____
_____
_____
_____
_____
_____

Sex of caller: _____ *Race:* _____
Age: _____ *Length of call:* _____

Additional information on reverse.

Number at which call is received:
_____
Time: _____ Date:___/___/___
Caller's Voice:
☐ Loud   ☐ Soft   ☐ High   ☐ Deep
☐ Intoxicated ☐ Disguised ☐ Calm ☐ Angry
☐ Fast   ☐ Slow   ☐ Stutter ☐ Nasal
☐ Distinct ☐ Slurred ☐ Accent (*Type:* ____)
Other Characteristics: _____
_____
If voice is familiar, who did it sound like? _____

Background Sounds:
☐ Voices   ☐ Quiet   ☐ Animals
☐ Street Traffic ☐ Office Machinery ☐ Airplanes
☐ Trains   ☐ Factory Machinery ☐ Music
Other: _____

Threat Language:
☐ Foul   ☐ Well-spoken (*educated*)
☐ Taped   ☐ Message read by threat-maker
☐ Irrational ☐ Incoherent
Remarks: _____
_____
_____

Report call immediately to: _____
Phone Number: _____

Date:___/___/___
Name: _____
Position: _____
Phone Number: _____

FIGURE 16.1
Bomb threat instructions.

Source: Reprinted from *Project Response: The Oklahoma City Tragedy,* p.12, April 24, 2002. Copyright held by the International Association of Chiefs of Police, 515 North Washington Street, Alexandria, VA 22314 USA. Further reproduction without express written permission from IACP is strictly prohibited.

(IACP) has developed detailed bomb threat instructions to be kept near telephones where such a threat might be received (Figure 16.1).

Management should assist first responders in devising a thorough search of the building using employees to help in the search because employees will know if anything is out of place and "doesn't fit." Management will also decide if the building is to be evacuated after the search.

Searchers pay attention to unattended bags, boxes or briefcases as well as areas with suspended ceilings with panels that are easily pushed up to hide an IED. Other items to pay attention to are trash cans, ashtrays and flowerpots. In addition, any incoming mail or packages should be carefully screened.

Once responding officers establish that a suspicious package could be a threat or potential bomb, they must contact a specially trained bomb squad to handle the situation from that point. Other than the initial call, responding patrol officers do not deal with explosives. If the agency does not have a local explosives unit, the agency typically requests mutual aid assistance from the closest agency with a bomb squad.

If a bomb is found, the most important rule in handling suspect packages is to NOT TOUCH the package. The area should be cleared to a 300-foot radius. Emergency personnel (fire and emergency medical personnel) should be alerted. All radios should be turned off.

Methods of Explosives Detection

Often, additional tools are needed to help responding officers determine if an explosive threat truly exists. Some of the methods are low-tech, such as using dogs to sniff out compounds used to build bombs. Other techniques employ highly advanced equipment and technology to detect explosive material.

Using K-9s in Detecting Explosives. As with arson investigations, dogs have become increasingly useful in bomb detection and in searches for evidence following explosions: "Field deployable electronic sensors or instruments can't top dogs, which have been increasingly in demand since 9/11. Canines are still our best detection technology" (Kanable, 2007, p.68). Following the precaution of not handling the explosive, bomb dogs are trained to alert the handler by sitting near a suspect package without touching it.

Using Stationary Technology in Detecting Explosives. Airports and cargo terminals use X-ray and computed axial tomography (CAT) equipment to scan large numbers of items and people. Such methods require highly trained operators, are stationary and cannot readily be used on vehicles or individuals or to investigate where bomb-making activities are ongoing or have taken place. Because of this, law enforcement must rely on what is referred to as

A detective with the New York City Counter Terrorism Unit uses a device to inspect a truck for radiation at a checkpoint near the Holland tunnel on June 5, 2007. Police officials believe that roving check points could thwart potential plots, including those involving fertilizer-based truck bombs like the ones used in the attacks on the World Trade Center in 1993 and a federal building in Oklahoma City in 1995.
© AP/Wide World Photos

"sniffer" technology: "A sniffer detection device is an instrument that takes in a sample of air, processes it through a detector and then identifies and calculates the approximate quantities of explosive material in the air sample" (Hanson, 2005).

Using Robots in a Bomb Threat Response.

Bomb squads in larger departments are using robots to approach and detonate suspected packages. Robots can be equipped with **disrupters**, devices that use gunpowder to fire a jet of water or a projectile at a particular component of an explosive to make it safe (Cox, 2004). Other features of bomb robots include portable X-ray machines and devices to remotely cut open a car door.

THE BOMB SCENE INVESTIGATION

If there has been an explosion, investigators should

- Ensure that a search for secondary explosive devices has been conducted.

- Ensure that the scene has been secured, that a perimeter and staging areas for the investigation have been established and that all personnel have been advised of the need to prevent contaminating the scene.

- Ensure that the chain of custody is initiated for evidence that may have been previously collected.

- Establish procedures to document personnel entering and exiting the scene.

- Establish and document procedures for evidence collection, control and chain of custody. Throughout

the investigation, safety should be of prime concern. (*A Guide for Explosion,* 2000, pp.19–21)

 When investigating explosions and bombings, pay special attention to fragments of the explosive device as well as to powder present at the scene. Determine motive.

Bomb-scene investigations must progress logically. The first step is to determine the scene's parameters. In general, once the farthest piece of recognizable evidence is located, a radius 50 percent wider is established. For example, in the Oklahoma City bombing, the rear axle of the truck carrying the explosives was located three blocks from the blast site, so the scene parameters were approximately four and a half blocks in all directions.

Raising Awareness

Awareness training programs should teach employees to notice individuals wearing clothes unsuitable for the time of year, people trying to blend into a group that he or she clearly doesn't belong to or an object protruding from a person's clothing. Other behaviors to watch for are people acting very nervous or perspiring profusely, someone obviously staying clear of security personnel, a person walking slowly while constantly glancing back or a person running suspiciously.

Importance of the Team Approach

The teamwork of field investigators and laboratory specialists in investigating bombings is critical. Such teamwork followed a California pipe-bombing incident

Technology Innovations

Researchers at the Oak Ridge National Laboratory have been working to develop miniature sensors that detect explosives based on the physical properties of their vapors (Page, 2010, pp.59–60):

"Our technology shows that different explosives have unique thermal characteristics that can be used for identification," says Thomas Thundat, a scientist with Oak Ridge National Labs and the University of Tennessee.

Current miniature sensors have a chemical layer attached to their surface designed to bind specifically to explosives, but they are often unable to discriminate between chemicals of similar nature, one of which may be dangerous and the other benign. This tends to create false positives.

"They may detect a trace amount of TNT, for instance, but they may not be able to distinguish that from a trace amount of gasoline," Thundat says.

Instead, the Oak Ridge sensor uses a micromechanical concept called a microfabricated bridge that can be electronically heated from room temperature to 500 degrees Celsius in 50 milliseconds. During this heating process, absorbed explosive molecules are burned, melted and evaporated.

"The process creates a signature that is unique to explosives," Thundat says.

The Oak Ridge method is therefore capable not only of differentiating individual explosive vapors such as trinitrotoluene (TNT), pentaerythritol tetranitrate (PETN) and cyclotrimethylenetrinitramine (RDX), but also of differentiating explosive vapors from non-explosives. Ergo, fewer false positives.

Eventually, the homeland security benefit of cheap, tiny sensors is that they can be deployed almost anywhere. Presumably, they could be networked and GPS-located. Homeland protection authorities could sprinkle them liberally in and around strategic buildings, ports and other critical infrastructure components. Transportation Security Administration (TSA) officials could finally saturate airport luggage and cargo handling areas, as well as passenger lounges and parking garages with explosive detection sensors.

Technology Innovations

Ashley (2008, p.32) describes the latest generation of robots being used by law enforcement:

The basic idea of a robot is to use a piece of technology—an automated capability—in an arena that might be dangerous or inhospitable to a person. Enhanced surveillance capability is yet another service robots can provide, particularly in areas that are unsafe or difficult to reach. Through the use of cameras and microphones, as well as wireless communications, critical intelligence can be gathered without exposing officers.

Another robot, the Negotiator Tactical Surveillance Robot, can be controlled wirelessly or by tether (Kozlowski, 2007, pp.124–129).

The plug-and-play architecture connects virtually any peripheral device (sensors, detectors, external devices, etc.) through a port located in the robot's cargo area, then transmits that peripheral's data to the operator control unit (OCU). The 8-pound, handheld OCU can be substituted for a wearable heads-up-display (HUD). With the HUD, the operator is able to view what the Negotiator's cameras see through a goggled view instead of on the OCU's screen.

The Negotiator robot's single joystick and push-button operation is another intuitive aspect of the package. The Negotiator's controlling joystick is directionally related to the direction of the robot. The robot's speed is directly proportional in that the throw of the joystick determines how fast or slow the robot will move.

Using a remote-controlled robot to approach and analyze suspected bombs has the advantage of not risking lives.
© 911 Pictures

that killed the driver of a vehicle to which a bomb had been attached. The Rialto Police Department, the San Bernardino Sheriff's Office and the ATF combined their efforts. They investigated and forwarded evidence from the scene to the ATF laboratory for examination. Chemists identified the type and brand of powder used in the bomb by examining intact powder particles found in the bomb's end caps. A subsequent search at the suspect's home uncovered a can of smokeless powder identical to the identified powder. Additional evidence obtained during the search provided further links between the suspect and the bombing. The suspect was arrested and charged with murder.

Investigators with technical questions about commercial explosives can receive assistance from the Institute of Makers of Explosives (IME) in Washington, DC. This nonprofit safety organization has 31 member companies and more than 80 subsidiaries and affiliates, which together produce more than 85 percent of the commercial explosives used in the United States. Also of help is the ATF National Response Team (NRT), which can be deployed in the most urgent, difficult bomb cases.

Summary

Fires are classified as natural, accidental, incendiary (arson) or of undetermined origin. They are presumed to be natural or accidental unless proven otherwise.

The elements of the crime of arson include (1) the willful, malicious burning of a building or property (2) of another or of one's own to defraud (3) or causing to be burned, or aiding, counseling or procuring such burning. Attempted arson is also a crime. Some states categorize arson as either aggravated or simple. Aggravated arson is intentionally destroying or damaging a dwelling or other property by means of fire or explosives or other infernal device, creating an imminent danger to life or great bodily harm, which risk was known or reasonably foreseeable to the suspect.

Simple arson is intentional destruction by fire or explosives that does not create imminent danger to life or risk of great bodily harm. Other states use the Model Arson Law, which divides arson into four degrees: first-degree involves the burning of dwellings; second-degree involves the burning of buildings other than dwellings; third-degree involves the burning of other property; and fourth-degree involves attempts to burn buildings or property.

Logic suggests that the fire department should work to detect arson and determine the fire's point of origin and probable cause, whereas the police department should investigate arson and prepare the case for prosecution.

Special challenges in investigating arson include coordinating efforts with the fire department and others, determining whether a crime has been committed, finding physical evidence, most of which is destroyed by the fire, and finding witnesses and determining whether the victim is a suspect.

The fire triangle consists of three elements necessary for a substance to burn: air, fuel and heat. In arson, at least one of these elements is usually present in abnormal amounts for the structure. Evidence of accelerants, substances that promote combustion, especially gasoline, is a primary form of physical evidence at an arson scene. Also important as evidence are igniters, which include matches, candles, cigars, cigarettes, cigarette lighters, electrical, mechanical and chemical devices, and explosives.

Common burn indicators include alligatoring, crazing, the depth of char, lines of demarcation, sagged furniture springs and spalling. The point of origin is established by finding the area with the deepest char, alligatoring and (usually) the greatest destruction. More than one point of origin indicates arson. Fires normally burn upward, not outward. They are drawn toward ventilation and follow fuel paths. Arson is likely in fires that

- Have more than one point of origin.
- Deviate from normal burning patterns.
- Show evidence of trailers.
- Show evidence of having been accelerated.
- Produce odors or smoke of a color associated with substances not normally present at the scene.
- Indicate that an abnormal amount of air, fuel or heat was present.
- Reveal evidence of incendiary igniters at the point of origin.

An administrative warrant is issued when it is necessary for a government agent to search the premises to determine the fire's cause and origin. A criminal warrant is issued on probable cause when the premises yield evidence of a crime. Entry to fight a fire requires no warrant. Once in the building, fire officials may remain a reasonable time to investigate the cause of the blaze. After this time, an administrative warrant is needed, as established in *Michigan v. Tyler* (1978).

When investigating vehicle fires, look for evidence of accelerants and determine whether the vehicle was insured. It is seldom arson if there is no insurance. When investigating explosions and bombings, pay special attention to fragments of the explosive device as well as to powder present at the scene. Determine motive.

Checklist

Arson

- Who first noticed the fire?

- Who notified authorities?

- Who responded from the fire department?

- Did the fire department record the color of the smoke? The color of the flame?

- What was the fire's point of origin? Was there more than one point of origin?

- What material was used to ignite the fire?

- Was there an explosion before the fire? During the fire? After the fire?

- How did the building explode: inward or outward?

- Was the fire's burn time normal? Did it appear to be accelerated?

- Were any accelerants (newspapers, rags or gasoline) found at the scene?

- What was the weather: dry, windy, snowy?

- What property was destroyed that was unusual for the premises?

- Were there any unusual circumstances?

- Was anyone injured or killed? Was an autopsy done to determine whether there were other causes for death than fire? Were carbon monoxide tests made of the victim to determine when death occurred—whether before or during the fire?

- Were regular informants checked to determine possible suspects?

- Who had access to the building?

- What appeared to be the motive for the fire? Who would benefit?

- Who owns the property destroyed? For how long?

- Was there insurance and, if so, how much?

- Who was the insurance payable to?

- What is the name of the insurance company? Has a copy of the company's report been obtained?

- Does the owner have any record of other property destroyed by fire?

- Does the owner have a criminal record for this or other types of crimes?

- Were any suspicious people or vehicles observed at the scene before, during or after the fire?

- Was the state fire marshal's office notified? Did it send an investigator? If so, obtain a copy of the investigator's report.

- Were photographs or videos taken? Are they available?

Applications

A. It is mid-afternoon on a Sunday. The fire department has just received a call to proceed to the Methodist Church on St. Anthony Boulevard. Smoke has been reported coming out of the church's windows by a nearby resident. When the fire department arrives, the church is engulfed in flames. By the time the fire is brought under control, the church is gutted, with damage estimated at $320,000. Suspecting arson, the fire department asks for help from the local police department.

Questions

1. Was the request for assistance justified at this point?

2. What are the responsibilities of the investigator assigned to respond to the call?

B. Investigators Ron McNeil and Brett Joyce worked together as part of Boston's special arson task force. Just before midnight, they received a call from the dispatcher and were told to proceed to a certain address. They arrived minutes later at a small, one-story frame house and pulled in behind the first fire rig. Orange flames were shooting from every window of the house.

While the firefighters fought the blaze, McNeil and Joyce walked among the bystanders, asking if anyone had seen anything suspicious before the fire, but no one had. When the fire was out and the smoke cleared, floodlights illuminated the house and McNeil and Joyce started their investigation. Beginning in the small front room, they noticed extensive burning and windows totally blackened from the fire. They proceeded through a small alcove, where the top portion had been destroyed, and then entered the kitchen. The glass in a window over the kitchen sink had broken and melted, with a series of intricate cracks running through each fragment. After shoveling out layers of debris and dragging in a fire hose to wash the floor, McNeil and Joyce noticed that the floor was deeply charred and spongy with water. Inspection of the wooden cabinets around the sink revealed large, rolling blisters. The investigators also discovered that the electricity to the structure had been disconnected. Then they began to photograph the fire scene.

Shortly afterward, the owner and his wife arrived. The owner calmly answered questions, informing the investigators that he had been letting a carpenter live in the house in exchange for fixing up the place. But when the tenant failed to make the repairs and instead stole the construction materials, much of the furniture and many appliances, the owner kicked him out. The carpenter threatened to "make him sorry." The owner had no fire insurance because he had intended not to live in the house but to use it as an investment property.

After filing their report, McNeil and Joyce returned to the property at 4 A.M. A heavy rain the day before had soaked the ground, and the mud in the backyard was crisscrossed with footprints. Joyce noticed some boot prints leading from the back door and took a plaster cast of them. Just then, a neighbor stopped over to say he had seen a green pickup parked behind the house with the motor running just before the fire. McNeil photographed all the tire tracks in the dirt alley where the pickup was reportedly parked. The next morning the investigators learned that the carpenter, now their prime suspect, had been in jail when the fire broke out. The green pickup was registered to a friend of his, a man who had been previously arrested for arson.

They obtained a search warrant and executed it later that morning. The tires of the carpenter's friend's truck and his boot soles resembled the impressions found at the fire scene, but the impressions were so spongy that it was difficult to match them exactly. The investigators found no further evidence linking the man to the fire. (Adapted from Kevin Krajick's "Seattle: Sifting through the Ashes." *Police Magazine*, July 1979, pp.10–11.)

Questions

1. Where did the fire probably originate? What factors indicate this?

2. What indicated that the fire was probably arson?

3. Did the investigators have probable cause to arrest the carpenter's friend? Would the owner also be a possible suspect? Why or why not?

4. What aspects of this case illustrate an effective arson investigation?

Discussion Questions

1. Do you agree that investigating arson cases is the joint responsibility of police and fire departments? Which department should be in charge?

2. What are the respective roles of the police and fire departments in your community during an arson investigation?

3. Arson has a low conviction rate. What factors make an arson investigation difficult? What factors make prosecution difficult?

4. Imagine you are called to the scene of a fire to determine whether it was accidental or of criminal origin. What initial steps would you take in making this determination?

5. What types of evidence are material to the crime of arson? Where do you find such evidence at a fire scene? How do you collect it? Where do you send it for examination in your area?

6. What are common motives for arson? How do these motives help an investigator locate suspects?

7. How does a street patrol officer respond to a bomb threat or suspicious package? Are there any specialized units within law enforcement to deal with these situations?

8. What agencies outside the police and fire departments can assist in an arson investigation? Who would you contact? What services could they provide?

9. What other types of crimes might be involved along with arson?

10. Organized crime has used arson to bring pressure on uncooperative people and businesses. Why is arson effective for this purpose? Why is it difficult to prosecute such cases?

Media Explorations

Internet

Select one of the following assignments to complete.

■ Search for the key phrase *National Institute of Justice* (NIJ). Click on "NCJRS" (National Criminal Justice Research Service). Click on "law enforcement." Click on "sort by Doc#." Search for one of the NCJ reference numbers from the list of References at the end of this chapter. Outline the selection to share with the class.

■ Go to the FBI Web site at www.fbi.gov. Click on "library and reference." Select "Uniform Crime Reports" and outline what the report says about arson.

■ Select one of the following key terms: *administrative warrant, arson, arsonists, bombs, burn indicators, explosives, fire triangle, pyromaniac.* Find one article relevant to arson or bombing investigations to outline and share with the class.

ONLINE Database
Gale Criminal Justice Database Assignments

The following assignments require access to Gale's Custom Journals Database for Emergency Services and Criminal Justice. Check with your instructor if you have questions about this.

■ Find the article "Arson Investigation" on the Gale Emergency Services Database. Read the article and outline for in-class discussion. Research who investigates arson in your community and be prepared to share your findings.

■ Find the article "BATS Sparks Arson Investigation Expansion: Arson and Explosives Investigators Share Information Nationwide" on the Gale Emergency Services Database. Read the article and identify what the BATS system is and how it benefits arson investigations.

■ Find the article "High-Profile Arson Cases Point to Need for Tougher Laws" on the Gale Emergency Services Database. Read the article and be prepared to discuss the case in class. Also research for discussion what arson laws your state has.

References

Acker, Jim. "Arson Investigation and the Dispatch Center." *9-1-1 Magazine*, June 2007, pp.22–24,52.

Ashley, Steve. "High-Tech Tin Soldiers." *Police*, March 2008, pp.32–40.

"ATF National Response Team Activated in Mizpah Fire Investigation." RGJ.com, January 18, 2007. Accessed June 19, 2008. http://news.rgj.com/apps/pbcs.dll/article?AID=/20061102/NEWS18/101190019/0/NEWS

"ATF National Response Team Activated to Texas Governor's Mansion Fire." Washington, DC: Bureau of Alcohol, Tobacco, Firearms and Explosives, June 9, 2008.

"The ATF National Response Team Joins Hollywood Fire Investigation." *LAFD News and Information*, May 3, 2008.

Cox, Jennifer. "Recoilless Disrupter Enhances EOD Technology." *Law Enforcement Technology*, February 2004, pp.106–109.

Crime in the United States, 2009. Washington, DC: U.S. Department of Justice, Federal Bureau of Investigation, September 2010. Accessed May 27, 2011. http://www2.fbi .gov/ucr/cius2009/index.html

Fire and Arson Scene Evidence: A Guide for Public Safety Personnel. Washington, DC: National Institute of Justice, June 2000. (NCJ 181584). Accessed July 17, 2011. http:// www.ojp.usdoj.gov/nij/pubs-sum/181584.htm

A Guide for Explosion and Bombing Scene Investigation. Washington, DC: National Institute of Justice, June 2000. (NCJ 181869). Accessed June 18, 2008. https://www.ncjrs .gov/pdffiles1/nij/181869.pdf

Gundy, Craig, and Linett, Howard. "Car Bombings." *Police*, September 2007, pp.38–43.

Hanson, Doug. "Sniffing Out Explosives: Explosives Detection Devices Come in a Variety of Shapes and Sizes, Utilizing an Array of Analysis Detection Methods." *Law Enforcement Technology*, February 1, 2005. Online: http://www.highbeam .com/doc/1G1-130466118.html Retrieved December 30, 2011.

Juvenile Firesetting: A Growing Concern. Emmitsburg, MD: U.S. Fire Administration, July 2006 (FA-307). Accessed July 19, 2011. http://www.usfa.dhs.gov/downloads/pdf/ publications/fa_307.pdf

Kanable, Rebecca. "The Best from Man's Best Friend." *Law Enforcement Technology*, September 2007, pp.68–77.

Karter, Michael J., Jr. *Fire Loss in the United States during 2010.* Quincy, MA: National Fire Protection Association, September 2011. Accessed November 2, 2011 http://www .nfpa.org/assets/files/PDF/OS.fireloss.pdf

Kozlowski, Jonathan. "The Robotic Effect: Saving Time, Money and Lives." *Law Enforcement Technology*, May 2007, pp.124–129.

Laska, Paul R. "Bombs and the Street Cop." *Law Officer Magazine*, February 2008, pp.40–43.

Moore, Carole. "Improvised Explosives." *Law Enforcement Technology*, October 2007, p.210.

Morgenstern, Henry. "Simple Plot." *Law Enforcement Technology*, January 2007, pp.8–16.

National Fire Protection Association. *NFPA 921*, 2011 Edition. Quincy, MA: National Fire Protection Association, 2011.

Page, Douglas. "Let Us Spray: Low-Cost Explosive Sensor." *Law Enforcement Technology*, February 2010, pp.56, 58–61.

Putnam, Charles T., and Kirkpatrick, John T. *Juvenile Firesetting: A Research Overview.* Washington, DC: OJJDP Juvenile Justice Bulletin, May 2005.

Smith, Matt, and Gipson, Justin. "Don't Get Burned." *Police*, November 2008, pp.54–59.

Smith, Matt, and Gipson, Justin. "Inner-Agency Cooperation for Fire Investigation." *Law and Order*, June 2010, pp.32–34.

Cases Cited

Coolidge v. New Hampshire, 403 U.S. 443 (1971)

Michigan v. Clifford, 464 U.S. 287 (1984)

Michigan v. Tyler, 436 U.S. 499 (1978)

SECTION 5
OTHER CHALLENGES TO THE CRIMINAL INVESTIGATOR

The two preceding sections discussed investigating violent crimes and crimes against property. Many crimes do not fall neatly into one of the eight Index crimes reported in the Federal Bureau of Investigation's Uniform Crime Reports (UCR) but involve a combination of illegal acts related to both people and property. Unique investigative challenges are presented by investigating computers and cybercrime (Chapter 17), drug-related and organized crime (Chapter 18), the criminal activities of gangs and other dangerous groups (Chapter 19) and the war against terrorism and fight for homeland security (Chapter 20). Investigating the illegal activities related to these groups is more difficult because the elements of the crimes are not neatly spelled out and statistics are not available as they are for the UCR crimes. A final and critical challenge is preparing for and presenting cases in court (Chapter 21).

Cybercrime is relatively new, but organized crime, drug- and gang-related crime, bias and hate crime and ritualistic crime have existed in one form or another for centuries. Not until recently, however, have they had such an impact on law enforcement, straining already limited resources. A further complication is that the areas commonly overlap; people involved in organized crime, drugs and gangs are often the same people—but not necessarily. Terrorists fund their activities through drug sales and various

types of fraud, including cybertheft. Although each type of crime is discussed separately, always keep this overlap in mind. Furthermore, moral and ethical issues are raised by the activities of these organizations that are not raised by the activities of, say, bank robbers, rapists and murderers. Stealing, raping and murdering are clearly wrong in our society. This is not necessarily true for gambling, worshiping Satan or smoking pot.

Among the greatest challenges are the "wars" America finds itself in, against drugs and now against terrorism. Homeland defense has become a priority for law enforcement agencies at all levels. Other great challenges for investigators are preparing final reports the prosecutor can use to bring criminal cases to trial and presenting effective testimony to bring these cases to successful resolution. Without these skills, the best investigations are futile.

CHAPTER 17
Computer Crime

Outline

Can You Define?

adware
computer crime
computer virus
cracker
cybercrime
cyberterrorism
data remanence
denial of service
domain name
dynamic IP address
e-crime
encryption
firewall
hacker
hacktivism
hardware disabler
imaging
Internet Protocol (IP) address
ISP

keystroke logging
logic bomb
malware
pharming
phishing
phreaking
piracy
port scanning
script kiddie
skimming
sniffing
spam
spoofing
spyware
static IP address
steganography
Trojan horse
URL
worm
zombie

Do You Know?

- What two key characteristics of computer crime are?
- How computer crime can be categorized?
- What special challenges are presented by computer-related crimes?
- What a common protocol for processing a crime scene involving electronic evidence is?
- What a basic tenet is for first responders at a computer crime scene?
- How an investigator with a search warrant should execute it in a computer crime investigation?
- What form electronic evidence and other computer crime evidence may take?
- What precautions to take when handling PC media?
- How electronic evidence should be stored?
- Whether "deleted" data are really deleted?
- Whether most cybercrimes against businesses are committed by insiders or outsiders?
- How cybercriminals may be categorized?
- What motivates the different types of cybercriminals?
- What approach is often required in investigating computer crime?
- How computer crimes can be prevented?

Two computer programmers at an oil company plant who were responsible for the company's purchasing files created a fictitious supply company. They altered the company's computer database so that the oil company bought its supplies twice: once from the real supplier and once from the fictitious supply company, resulting in an embezzlement of several million dollars over two years. The crime was discovered during a surprise audit, but the company declined to prosecute, not wanting to publicize how vulnerable its database was or how long it took to discover the embezzlement. Ironically, rather than being dismissed, the two embezzlers were promoted and placed in charge of computer security.

In another instance, a New York bank hired an outside consultant to work with its computer technicians on transferring funds electronically. During his work, the consultant observed the access code being used to transfer the funds. He later used this access code to transfer a large sum of money to his own bank account. When the loss was finally discovered, management insisted that everyone in the section take a polygraph test, including the consultant. All except the consultant complied, and all passed. Although management was convinced the consultant had stolen the money, they did not prosecute. They simply changed their access code.

These cases illustrate two key characteristics of computer crimes.

- Computer crimes are relatively easy to commit and difficult to detect.
- Most computer crimes are not prosecuted.

Computers and other wireless devices are pervasive in the home, workplace and school. At the end of 2010, CTIA–The Wireless Association reported 302.9 million wireless subscriber connections in the United States, with a wireless penetration equivalent to 96 percent of the total U.S. population ("Wireless Quick Facts," n.d.). Before the mid-1990s, computer crime was almost nonexistent. Computer crime typically involved actions performed on a single machine or on a small self-contained network of machines, such as stealing data off a hard drive or planting a malicious

code within the software of a company's internal computer network. Whatever the specifics of the crime, the criminal had to come in close physical contact with the computer(s) and the crime scene.

In the last decade, however, crimes involving computers have become much more sophisticated and investigating such crimes considerably more complicated. What makes cybercrime the tremendous problem it is today is that most computers on the planet are connected via the Internet, allowing a criminal thousands of miles away from a crime scene—whether at a computer in a private residence or at an extensive database within a major corporation's mainframe—to carry out theft, fraud, vandalism or any other number of crimes without ever setting foot in the same city, state, country or even continent as the victim. This medium also provides a higher level of anonymity to the offender, making identification of the perpetrator very challenging for investigators. The Internet also provides a medium through which pedophiles access and exchange child pornography, stalkers harass and threaten their targets and terrorists around the globe communicate with each other. Keeping up with these techno-savvy criminals has pushed law enforcement to develop a new breed of detective—the cybercrime investigator.

Dan Clements, CEO of Cardcops.com, a company that monitors Internet chat rooms and other hacker communications for stolen credit card numbers, then notifies merchants and consumers to block bad purchases.
© AP/Wide World Photos

THE SCOPE AND COST OF THE PROBLEM

The current hot crime tool is a personal computer linked to the Internet. This *online element* has led to a fundamental change in how many law enforcement agencies refer to such offenses—from *computer crime* to *cybercrime*. It should come as no surprise that criminals are capitalizing on this technology. Numerous online communication options are available, such as e-mail, chat rooms and Web pages.

The Internet's capacity for global interconnectivity has made the scope of the cybercrime problem transnational, the extent of which, confess most experts, is not yet fully understood. Adding to the uncertainty of the extent of the problem is that a large percentage of police departments do not yet know how to address this threat and do not keep accurate records involving such incidents. What is known, however, is that cybercrime has touched countless individuals and businesses throughout the United States and has the potential to cause a national disaster: "Cybercrime has significant economic impacts and threatens U.S. national security interests. Various studies and experts estimate the direct economic impact from cybercrime to be in the billions of dollars annually" ("Cybercrime," 2007).

Individuals can be victimized by a variety of different cybercrimes. For example, data from the Federal Trade Commission (FTC) show that each year nearly 9 million people are victims of identity theft, many of whom had information stolen from cyberspace. Internet scams continue to strip unsuspecting consumers of millions of dollars every year, along with their faith in the security of doing business online. Three other sources of information

on the scope and cost of computer crime are the Internet Crime Complaint Center, the E-Crime Watch Survey and the CSI Computer Crime and Security Survey.

The IC3 2010 Internet Crime Report

The Internet Crime Complaint Center (IC3), formerly called the Internet Fraud Complaint Center, is a partnership between the Federal Bureau of Investigation (FBI) and the National White Collar Crime Center (NW3C) designed to serve as a clearinghouse for cybercrime data for law enforcement and regulatory agencies at the federal, state and local levels and to provide cybercrime investigation training. The IC3 receives a broad spectrum of complaints including online fraud, computer intrusions (hacking), breaches of intellectual property rights (IPR), online extortion, international money laundering, economic espionage (theft of trade secrets) and, of course, identity theft. The proliferation of child pornography on the Internet has also become a serious concern, as thousands of young individuals are victimized every year by this type of exploitation.

According to the *2010 Internet Crime Report* (2011), the IC3 received 303,809 complaints in 2010, of which 121,710 were referred to law enforcement. Of the top 10 complaint categories in 2010, nondelivery of payment or merchandise was the most reported offense, composing 14.4 percent of referred crime complaints, followed by scams in which the perpetrator impersonated the FBI (13.2 percent of reports) and identity theft (9.8 percent of reports). Computer crimes (9.1 percent), miscellaneous fraud (8.6 percent), advanced fee fraud (7.6 percent), spam (6.9 percent), auction fraud (5.9 percent), credit card fraud (5.3 percent) and overpayment fraud (5.3 percent) rounded out the top 10 complaint categories.

Although auction fraud has historically topped the list of consumer complaints, reaching a high of 71.2 percent of all referrals in 2004, the steady decline in the number of reports of auction fraud and the concurrent rise and expansion of complaints in other categories indicates the growing diversification of crimes related to the Internet.

Of the top 10 countries reporting cybercrime victimization, the United States ranked first at 91.2 percent, followed by Canada (1.5 percent) and the United Kingdom (1.0 percent). Within the United States, California reported the greatest number of individual complaints (13.7 percent of the total), followed by Florida (7.9 percent), Texas (7.3 percent) and New York (5.8 percent). In cases where perpetrator information was available, nearly 75 percent of offenders were male, and the state in which the highest number of individual perpetrators resided was California (15.8 percent). The highest numbers of perpetrators outside the United States were from the

United Kingdom (10.4 percent), Nigeria (5.8 percent) and China (3.1 percent).

The 2010 CyberSecurity Watch Survey

The 2010 CyberSecurity Watch Survey was conducted jointly by *CSO Magazine*, the U.S. Secret Service, Carnegie Mellon University's Software Engineering Institute CERT® Program and Deloitte. Of the organizations responding to the survey, 37 reported an increase in cyber security events during the previous 12 months, 14 percent reported a decrease, 34 percent experienced no change and 16 percent were unsure of whether cyber security events increased or decreased. Fifty-five percent of participants reported they were more concerned about cyber security threats posed to their organization during the past 12 months compared with the prior 12 months, and 58 percent responded that they felt more prepared to deal with cyber security threats currently than they had been 12 months before.

The survey found that the technologies considered most effective at detecting or countering cyber security events were stateful firewalls (86 percent), electronic access control systems (82 percent), traditional access controls (80 percent), password complexity (79 percent) and encryption (76 percent). The least effective technologies were keystroke monitoring, biometrics and anomaly detection systems. Table 17.1 lists the types of

TABLE 17.1 Types of Cyber Security Events Committed, 2010

2010	Committed (net)	Insider	Outsider	Source Unknown	Not Applicable	Don't Know
Virus, worms or other malicious code	53%	14%	41%	19%	13%	15%
Unauthorized access to/use of information, systems or networks	35%	23%	13%	6%	36%	23%
Illegal generation of spam e-mail	32%	7%	26%	9%	37%	21%
Spyware (not including adware)	41%	15%	28%	13%	23%	23%
Denial of service attacks	27%	5%	23%	11%	41%	21%
Financial fraud (credit card fraud, etc.)	42%	11%	16%	4%	46%	24%
Phishing (someone posing as your company online in an attempt to gain personal data from your customers or employees)	38%	5%	33%	11%	31%	21%
Theft of other (proprietary) info including customer records, financial records, etc.	21%	15%	5%	4%	51%	25%
Theft of intellectual property	22%	16%	6%	4%	48%	26%
Intentional exposure of private or sensitive information	16%	11%	6%	4%	56%	23%
Sabotage: deliberate disruption, deletion or destruction of information, systems or networks	19%	10%	10%	5%	55%	21%
Zombie machines on organization's network/bots/use of network by BotNets	22%	7%	17%	8%	47%	23%
Web site defacement	14%	2%	12%	3%	61%	22%
Extortion	5%	1%	3%	1%	72%	23%
Other	4%	2%	2%	2%	56%	39%
None of the above		5%				
Theft of personally identifiable information (PII)	20%	10%	11%	4%	51%	26%
Unintentional exposure of private or sensitive information	34%	29%	3%	5%	40%	22%

Source: *2010 CyberSecurity Watch Survey—Survey Results.* Conducted by *CSO Magazine* in cooperation with the U.S. Secret Service, Software Engineering Institute CERT® Program at Carnegie Mellon University and Deloitte.

Available online: http://www.csoonline.com/documents/pdfs/2010CyberSecurityResults.pdf, p.9.

cyber security events reported in the *2010 CyberSecurity Watch Survey*.

The 2010/2011 CSI Computer Crime and Security Survey

Since 1995, the Computer Security Institute (CSI), with the help of the FBI, has conducted annual surveys of computer security practitioners in corporations, financial and medical institutions, universities and government agencies throughout the nation to analyze and assess the current state of computer network security. Richardson (2011, p.40) notes,

> CSI survey results from the past several years show plenty of good news. The percentage of respondents who have seen various kinds of attacks has generally dropped over time. Half of respondents this year said they'd suffered no security incidents. And not withstanding all the discussion and news regarding targeted attacks, most respondents have seen no evidence of "advanced persistent threat" attacks.
>
> This year and last, however, responses to open-ended questions we asked about what respondents either saw as growing concerns or desired as improved tools made it clear that what is needed is better visibility into networks, Web applications, and endpoints (particularly as those endpoints become increasingly mobile).
>
> Among current attacks, there are a growing number of highly sophisticated attacks (sophisticated at least in comparison with the attacks of, say, five years ago…). The attacks are also more malign. More money is lost when an attack is successful. More records are breached.

Key findings of the 2010/2011 survey include (p.2)

■ Malware infection continued to be the most commonly seen attack, with 67.1 percent of respondents reporting it.

■ Respondents reported markedly fewer financial fraud incidents than in previous years, with only 8.7 percent saying they'd seen this type of incident during the covered period.

■ Of the approximately half of respondents who experienced at least one security incident last year, fully 45.6 percent of them reported they'd been the subject of at least one targeted attack.

■ Fewer respondents than ever are willing to share specific information about dollar losses they incurred. Given this result, the report this year does not share specific dollar figures concerning average losses per

respondent. It would appear, however, that average losses are very likely down from prior years.

■ Respondents said that regulatory compliance efforts have had a positive effect on their security programs.

■ By and large, respondents did not believe that the activities of malicious insiders accounted for much of their losses because of cybercrime; 59.1 percent believe that no such losses resulted from malicious insiders. Only 39.5 percent could say that none of their losses resulted from non-malicious insider actions.

■ Slightly over half (51.1 percent) of the group said that their organizations do not use cloud computing. Ten percent, however, say their organizations use cloud computing and have deployed cloud-specific security tools.

To fully understand and effectively investigate computer crime, officers need a working knowledge of relevant terminology, how documents are stored and retrieved and how access to the Internet (and others' files) is obtained.

TERMINOLOGY AND DEFINITIONS

The FBI previously defined **computer crime** as "that which involves the addition, deletion, change or theft of information." However, as the Internet has become an increasingly common element among crimes committed via the computer, the FBI has refocused its efforts and created the Cyber Investigations unit. Cybercrime, as part of the larger category of computer crime, has been a challenge to define. Many crimes that *involve* computers could just as easily be committed using other methods.

During the past decade, refinements have occurred in how **cybercrime** is defined. Although a single definition has yet to be agreed on, an acceptable definition is that cybercrime is part of the larger category of computer crime, a criminal act that is carried out using *cybertechnology* (the spectrum of computing and information/communication technologies, from individual computers to computer networks to the Internet) and takes place in *cyberspace* (an intangible, virtual world existing in the network connections between two or more computers). Cybercrime has also been referred to as *electronic crime*, or **e-crime**, in describing any criminal violation in which a computer or electronic form of media is used.

Regardless of whether an agency calls such offenses computer crimes, cybercrimes or e-crimes, the effective investigator must be familiar with basic computer terminology as well as with terms specifically related to computer crime (additional terms are defined throughout this chapter):

■ **Adware**. A type of spyware used by advertisers to gather consumer and marketing information.

■ Browser. A computer program that accesses and displays data from the World Wide Web, such as Internet Explorer.

■ Byte. The amount of space needed to store one character of information.

■ Digital evidence. Information stored or transmitted in binary form that may be relied on in court.

■ Disk drive. A device that reads, writes and stores data that are accessed via computer (personal computers [PCs] generally have one or more internal disk drives and external or portable disk drives are commonly used to supplement storage needs, back up PCs and transport or share data between PCs).

■ Electronic device. A device that operates on principles governing the behavior of electrons.

■ Electronic evidence. Information and data of investigative value that are stored in or transmitted by an electronic device.

■ Encryption. Any procedure used in cryptography to convert plain text into cipher-text to prevent anyone but the intended recipient from reading the data.

■ **Firewall**. A software or hardware protective measure that blocks ports of access to a computer or network to prevent unauthorized access and stop malicious programs from entering.

■ Gigabyte (GB). One billion bytes. A gigabyte can hold the equivalent of 10 yards of books on a shelf. A 16GB memory card or flash drive will hold approximately 2000 high-resolution photos from a 12 megapixel digital camera.

■ **Hacktivism**. Using cyberspace to harass or sabotage sites that conduct activities or advocate philosophies that "hacktivists" find unacceptable.

■ **Imaging**. Making a byte-by-byte copy of everything on the hard drive.

■ **Keystroke logging**. A diagnostic technique that captures a user's keystrokes. Used in espionage to bypass security measures and obtain passwords or encryption keys. Also called *keylogging*.

■ Kilobyte (KB). One thousand bytes.

■ **Logic bomb**. Secretly attaches to another program in a company's computer system. The attached program monitors the input data and waits for an error to occur. When this happens, the new program exploits the weakness to steal money or company secrets or to sabotage the system. For example, if a specific name fails to appear in the payroll system, the logic bomb would delete the entire payroll database.

■ **Malware**. A contraction of "malicious software." Software developed to cause harm.

■ Megabyte (MB). One million bytes.

■ Network. A group of computers connected to one another to share information and resources.

■ **Phreaking**. Exploiting the telephone system's vulnerabilities to acquire free access and usage in a dial-up Internet provider system. Considered a type of electronic hacking.

■ **Piracy**. Copying and using computer programs in violation of copyrights and trade secret laws.

■ **Port scanning**. Looking for access (open "doors") into a computer.

■ Removable media. Flash drives, thumb drives, pen drives or other portable devices for storing electronic data, including rewriteable CD-ROMs and DVDs.

■ Script. A text file containing a sequence of computer commands.

■ **Skimming**. A method in which a device is placed in a card reader, such as that found at an automated teller machine (ATM), to record sensitive information, such as bank account numbers, credit cards numbers and passwords.

■ **Sniffing**. Monitoring data traveling along a network.

■ **Spyware**. Malicious, covert (difficult to detect) software that infects a computer in a manner similar to viruses, collecting information or executing other programs without the user's knowledge. Some programs can track which Web sites a user visits; some can track and capture personal user information.

■ Terabyte (TB). One thousand gigabytes, a common hard drive size for new PCs.

■ **Trojan horse**. A malicious program hidden inside an apparently harmless, legitimate program, intended to carry out unauthorized or illegal functions. For example, a program controlling a computer log-on process could log on a user (legitimate) but also record the user's password (unauthorized, illegal).

■ **URL**. Universal Resource Locator. A string of characters representing an Internet resource.

- Virtual reality. An artificial, interactive world created by computer technology (usually involving some kind of immersion system, such as a headset).
- **Zombie**. A computer that has been taken over by another computer, typically through infection with hidden software (virus) that allows the zombie machine to be accessed and controlled remotely, often with the intention of perpetrating attacks on other computers.

The Net versus the Web

Confusion exists among many computer users regarding the differences between the Internet (aka "the Net") and the World Wide Web (aka "the Web"). Tim Berners-Lee (n.d.), creator of the Web, explains,

> The Internet ('Net) is a network of networks. Basically it is made from computers and cables.... [It] sends around little "packets" of information....A packet is a bit like a postcard with a simple address on it. If you put the right address on a packet, and gave it to any computer which is connected as part of the Net, each computer would figure out which cable to send it down next so that it would get to its destination. That's what the Internet does. It delivers packets—anywhere in the world, normally well under a second....
>
> The Web is an abstract (imaginary) space of information. On the Net, you find computers—on the Web, you find document, sounds, videos…information. On the Net, the connections are cables between computers; on the Web, connections are hypertext links. The Web exists because of programs which communicate between computers on the Net. The Web could not be without the Net. The Web made the Net useful because people are really interested in information (not to mention knowledge and wisdom!) and don't really want to…know about computers and cables.

A basic understanding of the Internet helps investigators trace suspected criminal activity and its perpetrators. To access the Internet, a user must have an **Internet Protocol (IP) address**, which is a unique number, analogous to a phone number (see Figure 17.1). Typically, there is only one IP address per network connection: "Just as every house has an address, every computer connected to the Internet has an address" (*Investigations Involving the Internet*, 2007, p.5). A common analogy is to compare an IP address to an apartment address. IP addressing uses four decimal-separated numbers.

IP addresses can be static or dynamic. A **static IP address** does not change. A **dynamic IP address**, in contrast, fluctuates and is, thus, more secure because it is

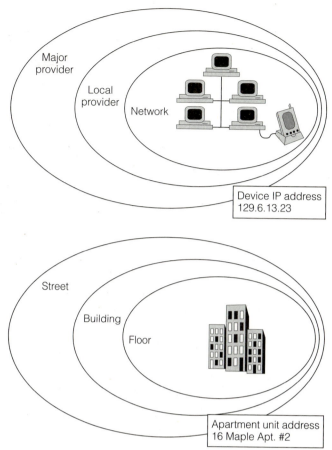

FIGURE 17.1
IP address and apartment address.
© Cengage Learning, 2013

changed frequently. The IP address is commonly issued by a user's Internet service provider (**ISP**), a company that offers access to the Internet for a fee, such as America Online (AOL), EarthLink and NetZero. The details of IP address distribution and registration are complex and not necessary to go into for a general understanding of cybercrime investigation. The importance lies in recognizing that an IP address and ISP, if known, can lead to a specific computer and, by extension, a specific user.

Deciphering E-mail and Web Addresses. It is useful for investigators to understand the parts of an e-mail or Web address and to accurately refer to the individual elements of each. E-mail addresses typically have two parts: the e-mail name or identification (ID) and the e-mail domain, separated by @ (for example, janedoe@abc123.com). Be aware that it is relatively easy and common for cyber criminals to spoof or create fake e-mail accounts to misrepresent themselves while attempting to commit fraud via the Internet.

A **domain name** is the unique name of a computer system on the Internet that distinguishes it from all other online systems. It is associated with a specific IP address and is easier to remember than a string of numbers. A domain name is not the same as a Web address, although many people incorrectly refer to it as such. A Web address, or URL, has several more elements. For example,

> URL: http://www.amz456.com
>
> Scheme name: http (https typically denotes a secure Web site)—this part simply means an http request is being made to the host server
>
> Domain name: amz456.com
>
> Subdomain: www
>
> Domain: amz456
>
> Top level domain: com
>
> Common top-level domains include the following:

.com	Commercial
.edu	Educational
.gov	U.S. government
.mil	U.S. Department of Defense
.net	Networks
.int	international organizations

Social Networking, Live Chat and Instant Messaging

The world of social networking has opened a new forum in which people can interact and communicate. Many ISPs provide chat rooms and offer instant messaging (IM) to their subscribers, features that allow two or more people to "talk" online in real time. Such conversations can involve criminal activity, including child pornography. Some of the bigger providers, such as Facebook, Yahoo, MSN, and AOL all engage in some policing of subscriber activity to reduce undesirable or illegal activity. The Internet Relay Chat (IRC) environment is similar to other chat and messaging but offers worldwide communication and is not as closely monitored; therefore, it is common to see names such as #teensex or #newidentities (all IRC channel names begin with #). Twitter is often compared to an IRC client. All chat services allow "chatters" to leave a group room and have a private conversation over a more secure connection using Direct Channel Chat (DCC).

CLASSIFICATION AND TYPES OF COMPUTER CRIMES

Investigators should also be familiar with the types of crimes that may involve computers. The crimes committed with computers range from students changing school records and grades to thieves embezzling millions of dollars from large corporations to pedophiles luring unsuspecting children into child pornography: "Computers and other electronic media can be used to commit crimes, store evidence of crimes and provide information on suspects and victims" (*Best Practices*, 2010, p.7).

The U.S. Secret Service's Electronic Crimes Branch (ECB) of its Financial Crimes Division has investigated

The Internet and World Wide Web have spread across the globe during the past two decades. The proliferation of wireless services has brought with it a host of security implications and has increased the vulnerability of data stored on or sent via personal laptops and other wireless devices.

© Bill Bachmann/Alamy

matters involving credit card fraud, unauthorized computer access, cellular and landline telephone service tampering, the production of false identification, counterfeit currency, threats made against the president, narcotics, illegal firearms trafficking and even homicides. Some even contend there will come a point when cybercrime laws become unnecessary because most crimes will involve computers in some way.

As computer crime evolves and specific offenses emerge, different categories are being identified. The U.S. Department of Justice has delineated three basic ways computers are being used criminally:

1. *Computer as target.* A computer or network's confidentiality, integrity or availability is attacked, resulting in the theft of services or information or the damaging of victim computers. Denial of service (DoS) attacks and the release of malware (viruses and worms) are examples of this type of computer crime.

2. *Computer as tool.* Includes crimes that have migrated from the physical world into cyberspace, such as child pornography, fraud, intellectual property violations, gambling, harassment and the online sale of illegal substances and goods.

3. *Computer as incidental to an offense.* Significant for law enforcement because of the role the computer played in facilitating or executing a crime. For example, computers may be used by pedophiles to store child pornography, by drug traffickers to store business contact information and by prostitution rings to manage payroll and customer accounts.

> Computer-related crimes may be categorized as computer as target, computer as tool or computer as incidental to the offense.

However one chooses to categorize the various types of computer-related crimes, investigators should be aware of the ever-expanding ways in which computers are used for criminal endeavors.

The Computer as Target

Some cybercrimes involve the infection or infiltration of a computer system's software by a malware that, when executed, removes a degree of control of the machine from the authorized user and places it in the hands of an outsider. These crimes can involve viruses, worms and DoS attacks and almost invariably involve hacking.

Hacking. The terms *hacking* and *cracking* are alternately used by law enforcement agencies to refer to the act of gaining unauthorized access to a computer system. However, among the people who perform these actions, a clear distinction is made between those who intrude for the challenge and status (hackers) and those who intrude to commit a crime (crackers). A **hacker** is not necessarily a negative term. A **cracker**, on the other hand, is a hacker in the negative sense, someone who cracks software protection and removes it. Crackers deliberately, maliciously intrude into a computer or network to cause damage. A **script kiddie**, or skiddie, is a derogatory term used to describe a less talented hacker who must use script or programs (scripts) created by others to carry out a cyber attack. Many investigative agencies refer to these people simply as "intruders" or "attackers" instead of hackers or crackers.

Viruses. A **computer virus** is a program that attacks, attaches itself to and becomes part of another executable program. The purpose may be to replace or destroy data on the computer's hard drive or to simply leave a back door open for later entry.

Hacking has evolved significantly during the past three decades and is often, although not necessarily, a negative term used to refer to cybercriminals. Credited as the original hacker, John Draper (aka "Captain Crunch") is the creator of the infamous Blue Box, a device that hacked telephone systems in the early 1970s by mimicking the tones that control phone switches, allowing hackers to make free long-distance calls, bill calls to someone else's phone number, and so forth.

With this first form of hacking, coined "phone phreaking" by Draper, began the custom of "ph" spellings used in many hacker pseudonyms and organizations.

Phishing, first referenced in hacker literature in 1996, was a term given to the act of "fishing" in the sea of Internet users for sensitive information (passwords, financial data, etc.) hackers could use for personal benefit. First applied to stealing AOL user information, phishing has become increasingly widespread and malicious, targeting major financial institutions and e-commerce sites.

© Getty Images

Viruses can be transmitted through communication lines or by an infected disk or other removable media and can infect any PC. Just as human viruses are spread from one person to another, so computer viruses are spread from program to program. Viruses can be accidentally introduced into a system by infected media carried between home and work or passed among students or colleagues (Figure 17.2). The publicity surrounding recent mass virus attacks has raised the public's and corporate America's awareness of their computer systems' vulnerabilities and led many to install protective devices, such as antivirus or virus detection programs, downloadable software patches and firewalls. Nonetheless, vast numbers of machines remain unprotected, and many consumers neglect to keep their virus detection subscriptions current.

Worms. Although the general computing public fears exposure to computer viruses, many are unaware that worms are actually more powerful and destructive. A **worm** is a self-contained program that travels from machine to machine across network connections, often clogging networks and information systems as it spreads. Whereas viruses require some action by the computer user (clicking or downloading), worms do not. They simply come in through an "open door" or unprotected port on a machine connected to the Internet. And, unlike a virus, a worm need not become part of another program to propagate itself.

Denial-of-Service Attacks. A **denial of service** (DoS) attack disrupts or degrades a computer or network's Internet connection or e-mail service, thus interrupting the regular flow of data. Using multiple agents to

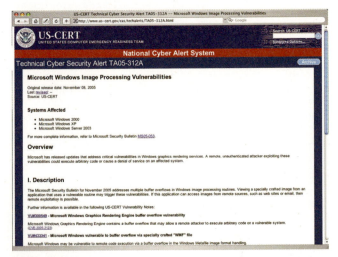

FIGURE 17.2

Established in 2003 to protect the nation's Internet infrastructure, US-CERT coordinates defense against and responses to cyberattacks across the nation.

Source: http://www.us-cert.gov/cas/techalerts/

create a widespread interruption is a *distributed DoS*, or DDoS. When a target company's Web site is flooded with requests for information or by some other onslaught of incoming data, the system is eventually overloaded and the site shuts down. At this time the company's cost clock starts ticking: either the company submits to extortion by its attackers or it is forced to incur millions of dollars in lost revenue as a result of its Web site being down.

Extortion. Cybercriminals may attempt to extort thousands, even millions, of dollars from companies by threatening to or actually damaging the company's computers, network or Web presence. Extortion can be achieved via DoS attacks or threats to expose a company's Web vulnerabilities, making the offense fit both categories of computer as *target* and as *tool*.

The Computer as Tool

A computer connected to the Internet has become the tool of choice for many criminals because they have taken the traditional methods of committing their illegalities and elevated them to high-tech levels. Many of the theft offenses described later overlap or are commonly committed together and thus may be investigated from a variety of angles and prosecuted under numerous laws.

Fraud. Internet fraud can involve several other offenses singled out in this section, such as phishing, spamming and identity theft. The types of fraud committed online span a wide range of businesses and topics. **Phishing**, first discussed in Chapter 14, is a method in which criminals misrepresent themselves as a trustworthy source to get victims to disclose personal, sensitive information, such as passwords, bank account numbers and the like, which is then used by the criminals to commit fraud or other crimes.

Reshipper Schemes. In this age of telecommuting and rising gas prices, the appeal of working from home has never been greater. Preying on this interest are scam artists who lure unsuspecting job seekers into reshipping schemes, transforming these citizens into "mules" who unwittingly help their "employers" commit international crime. To top it off, prospective employees must usually complete an application, on which they disclose such information as their birth date and social security number—harmless enough in the hands of a legitimate employer, but money in the pocket for identity thieves and others with a criminal bent.

Victims are attracted to the scheme through ads posted on popular employment Web sites seeking "correspondence managers," "freight-forwarding coordinators" or other respectable-sounding titles and are guaranteed to earn money by working from home without even quitting their current jobs. After applicants are informed they have been hired—and nearly everyone who applies is hired—they begin receiving parcels at home with instructions on how to forward this merchandise to the company's home office abroad. The reshippers are compensated well, with one correspondence manager earning $24 for every package he reshipped. Thus, employee complaints, at this stage, are few. What employees do not know, however, is that the products they are reshipping are actually goods ordered online, purchased with fraudulent credit cards and sent overseas to be sold on the black market, or that they (the mules) have become part of a high-end fencing operation that converts stolen personal and financial data into tangible goods and cash.

Offenders also lure victims into their scheme by establishing relationships with them in online chat rooms. Over time, offenders weave a tale of how, because of various legal restrictions, they are unable to direct business shipments from the United States into their home countries. They play up the injustice of these laws and how their government uses such restrictions to keep its citizens in poverty. Eventually, the scam artist gains the victim's trust, through either befriending or seduction. Offenders may even send small gifts to their victims as tokens of their affection. Whatever ploy is used, victims ultimately agree to have packages sent to their home, which they will then reship to their "friend" in another country.

The FBI, through IC3, has investigated numerous reshipper schemes throughout the United States and abroad. IC3 has also formed a public-private alliance with the Merchants Risk Council (MRC) in an effort to shut down such Internet fraud through use of real-time data sharing between law enforcement and private industry.

Spam.
Spam is unsolicited bulk e-mail messages, similar to junk mail and commonly commercial. Lesser known by its formal designation as unsolicited commercial e-mail (UCE), spam is most often perceived by recipients as an annoyance and nothing more. Granted, it is a widespread, persistent annoyance. Chain letter spam is an example of the type of unsolicited e-mail that clogs the Internet and fills people's inboxes but falls well short of criminal conduct. Sometimes, however, spam is distributed on such a massive scale, with such malicious or contentious content or with intent to defraud, that the spamming becomes criminal. For example, chain letters calling for a payment to participate may be construed as pyramid schemes, which are illegal in most states. Investment or business opportunity spam, which entices people with the promise of effortless income and financial

freedom for the small price of an upfront "investment," commonly results in only the spammer getting rich, and victims file complaints alleging theft or online fraud.

Spam that leaves no question as to its illegality is that intended to phish, commit identity theft or otherwise extract sensitive information from a computer user with the ultimate goal of using such information to engage in criminal activity. Identity theft and phishing were discussed in Chapter 14.

Spoofing.
Spoofing, often considered synonymous with phishing, is acquiring unauthorized access to a computer or network through a message using an IP address that appears to be from a trusted host, in an attempt to commit identity theft.

Pharming.
Pharming is a cybercrime that is catching even the most cautious, experienced Internet users off guard. Pharming involves hijacking a domain name to redirect online traffic away from a legitimate Web site toward a fake site, such as a bogus bank Web site. Cybercriminals have become very skilled at making their fraudulent sites appear quite similar to the legitimate site, so that unsuspecting victims are often unaware they are being led into a trap to steal information. Even if a computer user types in the correct domain name of a legitimate site, if that site has been pharmed, the user will be unknowingly taken to the fraudulent site, where they may unwittingly reveal account numbers, passwords and other sensitive personal information that can be used for identity theft or other criminal endeavors.

Theft of Intellectual Property.
This offense involves the pirating of proprietary information and copyrighted material. Illegal online piracy is rampant, with criminals around the globe cashing in on the lucrative black market of illegally copied and distributed software, movies, music and video and computer games. These offenses typically take place in un-policed peer-to-peer networks or forums where is it easy to exploit media-related intellectual property.

Because successful criminal prosecution of intellectual property theft requires reliable investigative resources, the FBI's Cyber Division and Intellectual Property Rights Division were created to investigate intellectual property theft and fraud.

Online Child Pornography and Child Sexual Abuse.
An increasingly persistent, pervasive cyber problem for law enforcement is the flow of child pornography. Pedophiles and other sex offenders around the world have discovered how quickly and surreptitiously they can exchange illegal images online. The Internet also provides a forum in which pedophiles can "meet"

potential victims, in hopes of arranging a face-to-face meeting at some point. In one case involving a missing child, detectives asked the family about the child's hobbies and were told he spent a great deal of time on the computer. By examining the computer files, detectives learned that the child had been contacted by a pedophile and had unwittingly arranged a meeting. When investigators went to the meeting site, they found the child with the pedophile.

The development of software now enables more computer-savvy pornographers to create virtual child pornography in which an image of an actual child is manipulated, or "morphed," into an image no longer identifiable as that particular child. Some programs allow entirely computer-generated children to be depicted in a variety of sexual situations. As these programs become more refined, it is getting more difficult to distinguish between real children and virtual children. Such software presents considerable legal implications and challenges involving how a jurisdiction defines child pornography and how investigators proceed with child pornography cases.

Investigating crimes against children was discussed in Chapter 11.

Cyberterrorism.
Terrorism—traditionally defined as the actual or threatened use of force or violence, motivated by political or religious ideals or grievances and exacted for the purposes of intimidation, coercion or ransom—has evolved into cyberterrorism courtesy of the Internet. **Cyberterrorism** is the premeditated, politically motivated attack against information, computer systems, computer programs and data that results in violence against noncombatant targets by subnational groups or clandestine agents. It also refers to using a computer system as a conduit for causing terror. Terrorists use this global interconnectivity to communicate with each other and to commit crimes to fund their other nefarious activities.

Cyberterrorism, however, does not merely equate to terrorists communicating through cyberspace. It is the actual use of computers and Internet technology to cause intimidation and destruction. Cyberterrorists can target a specific business or industry, or they can wreak electronic havoc indiscriminately across giant segments of the Internet. In recent years, intense concern has developed about the threat of a possible terrorist attack on the computer networks that link to critical parts of the U.S. infrastructure, such as those dedicated to public health and the distribution of emergency services, government and defense operations, energy and utility services and elements that keep our economy in motion, such as shipping and cargo distribution. Terrorism is the focus of Chapter 20.

SPECIAL CHALLENGES IN INVESTIGATION

Any type of criminal investigation carries potential challenges, and those involving computer crime are no exception.

> Special challenges in investigating computer crime include victims' reluctance or failure to report such crimes, the investigator's lack of training and the lack of understanding of computer crimes by others within the justice system, the need for specialists and teamwork, the fragility of the evidence and jurisdictional issues.

Other major challenges in investigating computer crimes include determining the exact nature of the crime and gathering evidence in a way that does not disrupt an organization's regular operation.

Nonreporting of Computer Crimes

For the police to deter cybercrimes, the crimes must be reported, thoroughly investigated and, when the evidence is sufficient, prosecuted. Law enforcement's ability to identify coordinated threats is directly tied to the amount of reporting that takes place. Too often, however, victims of computer-related crimes either are unaware that a crime has been committed or have a reason for not reporting the crime to authorities. The *2010 CyberSecurity Watch Survey* found that most e-crimes committed by insiders are handled internally without involving legal action or law enforcement (72 percent). When asked why they had not referred these e-crimes for legal action, respondents stated that either the damage level was insufficient to warrant prosecution (37 percent), there was a lack of evidence or not enough information to prosecute (35 percent) or they could not identify the individuals responsible (29 percent). The *CSI Survey* (Richardson, 2011) reports that the most common reason for not reporting e-crimes to the police was a belief that law enforcement would be unable to help in the matter, followed by the belief that the incident(s) were too small or insignificant to report.

To help companies more effectively address cyberthreats and cybercrimes, the FBI, Secret Service and *CIO Magazine* have collaborated to create a Cyberthreat Report form outlining the basic information needed by law enforcement when responding to an initial call of a suspected computer crime (Figure 17.3).

Welcome to the US-CERT Incident Reporting System

What is an incident?

A good but fairly general definition of an incident is *The act of violating an explicit or implied security policy*. Unfortunately, this definition relies on the existence of a security policy that, while generally understood, varies among organizations.

For the federal government, an incident, defined by NIST Special Publication 800-61, is a violation or imminent threat of violation of computer security policies, acceptable use policies, or standard computer security practices. Federal incident reporting guidelines, including definitions and reporting timeframes can be found at http://www.us-cert.gov/federal/reportingRequirements.html.

In general, types of activity that are commonly recognized as being in violation of a typical security policy include but are not limited to

- attempts (either failed or successful) to gain unauthorized access to a system or its data, including PII related incidents (link to the below description)
- unwanted disruption or denial of service
- the unauthorized use of a system for processing or storing data
- changes to system hardware, firmware, or software characteristics without the owner's knowledge, instruction, or consent

We encourage you to report any activities that you feel meet the criteria for an incident. Note that our policy is to keep any information specific to your site confidential unless we receive your permission to release that information.

Using the US-CERT Incident Reporting System

In order for us to respond appropriately, please answer the questions as completely and accurately as possible. Questions that must be answered are labeled "Required". As always, we will protect your sensitive information. This web site uses Secure Sockets Layer (SSL) to provide secure communications. Your browser must allow at least 40-bit encryption. This method of communication is much more secure than unencrypted email.

Section: Reporter's Contact Information

First Name *(Required)*

Last Name *(Required)*

Email Address *(Required)*

Telephone number *(Required)*

Are you reporting as part of an Information Sharing and Analysis Center (ISAC)? | No, this is not an ISAC report

What type of organization is reporting this incident? *(Required)* | Please select

What is the impact to the reporting organization? *(Required)* | Please select

What type of followup action are you requesting at this time? *(Required)* | Please select

Describe the current status or resolution of this incident. *(Required)* | Please select

From what time zone are you making this report? *(Required)* | Please select a time zone

What is the approx time the incident started? (localtime) | November 05, 2008 : 18 : 01

When was this incident detected? (localtime) | November 05, 2008 : 18 : 01

Section: Incident Details

Please provide a short description of the incident and impact *(Required)*

How many systems are impacted by this incident? (Leave blank if Unknown)

How many sites are impacted by this incident? (Leave blank if Unknown)

Was the data involved in this incident encrypted? | N/A

Was critical infrastructure impacted by this incident? | N/A

What was the primary method used to identify the incident | Unknown

If available, please include 5-10 lines of time-stamped logs in plain ASCII text.(e.g.,CSV).

FIGURE 17.3
CIO Cyberthreat report form.

Source: Adapted from https://forms.us-cert.gov/report

Lack of Investigator Training

Another challenge facing investigators assigned to computer crimes is that often they have not been adequately trained or equipped to investigate these felonies. Cybercriminals are usually more technologically sophisticated and have more resources, more access to the newest technology and more time to devote than do the investigators assigned to the cases. The technological disadvantage of many law enforcement agencies is painfully obvious.

Law enforcement at all levels needs additional training in the following areas: the unique requirements of computer crimes; digital evidence; identifying, marking and storing this evidence; the capabilities of present private and state agencies to analyze this evidence; and the procedures for developing teams to conduct investigations of computer-related crimes.

Need for Specialists and Teamwork

Computer-related crimes may be relatively low tech, but for cybercrimes of a highly technical nature in which fragile digital evidence must be extracted from extensive database systems with equipment that is unfamiliar to police officers, the proactive law enforcement department has already devised a response protocol and assembled an investigative team of qualified specialists.

When forming a cybercrime unit, the areas to focus on are selecting the right personnel, establishing a specific protocol to guide investigators, providing the proper training for team members and acquiring the necessary tools and equipment to do the job. Enlisting the aid of specialists is extremely critical considering the fragile nature of much computer crime evidence. Specialized cybercrime investigative teams are examined later in the chapter.

Fragility and Sensitivity of Evidence in Computer Crime

The biggest difference between traditional evidence and computer evidence is the fragility of the latter: "Digital evidence, by its very nature, is fragile and can be altered, damaged, or destroyed by improper handling or examination. For these reasons special precautions should be taken to preserve this type of evidence. Failure to do so may render it unusable or lead to an inaccurate conclusion" (*Forensic Examination of Digital Evidence*, 2004, p.11). Much the same way an officer responding to a more traditional crime may contaminate the scene by inadvertently altering the environment, an officer responding to a computer crime may destroy digital evidence simply by turning a computer or other device on or off at the wrong time. Recommended techniques and processes for collecting computer evidence are presented shortly.

Jurisdictional Issues

The global reach of the Internet poses another challenge in computer crime cases by introducing jurisdictional complications on top of an already complex area of criminal investigation. Difficulties exist in determining jurisdiction when the equipment being employed criminally is located in one community and the computer that is illegally entered electronically is in another state or even another country. For example, a 28-year-old in St. Petersburg, Russia, hacked into Citibank's cash-management system in New York City and stole millions of dollars. Where did the crime take place—St. Petersburg or New York City? Who has jurisdiction?

The traditional concept of jurisdiction focuses almost exclusively on the territorial aspect of "where did the act take place?" However, traditional territorial boundaries are often complicated in cybercrime cases because the location of the acts must account for the location of the defendant and where the material originated (was uploaded from), any servers this information passed through, the location of computers where material was downloaded and the location of any effects this material may have set in motion.

In cases of international scope, it is necessary to determine whether the act is illegal in all of the countries involved. For example, the Love Bug virus that spread across the globe in two hours in May 2000, affecting more than 45 million users in more than 20 countries, was developed in and distributed from the Philippines, where the act of virus dissemination was not illegal at the time. The location of the defendant in such a country meant he could not be extradited to the United States, where his acts were considered illegal, because of a treaty-established requirement of double criminality in cases involving international jurisdiction, meaning the act would have needed to be criminal in both countries. This requirement of double criminality presents numerous problems for law enforcement and prosecutors trying to stem the rising tide of international cybercrime. For example, in cases of child pornography,

- The age of majority (or consent) varies from country to country.
- In some countries, such as Germany, the age of consent is as low as 14.
- Virtual child pornography is legal in some countries and illegal in others.

Virtual child pornography, illegal in Canada and the European Union, was also declared illegal in the United States under the Child Pornography Prevention Act (CPPA) of 1996. However, the Supreme Court ruled in *Ashcroft v. Free Speech Coalition* (2002) that the portion of the CPPA prohibiting the production or distribution of such virtual pornography was overly broad and an unconstitutional infringement on the First Amendment right to freedom of speech.

Recognizing the need for a more unified global approach to handling cybercrime, the Council of Europe formed a Convention on Cybercrime on November 23, 2001, in Budapest. The convention set forth a framework for investigating and prosecuting cybercrimes and required that signers pass laws in their countries making specific acts, such as hacking, copyright infringement and child pornography, illegal.

A computer crime investigation may also involve domestic jurisdictional issues, between state and federal levels of jurisdiction as well as between states. Complicating the matter is that states, like nations, have varying definitions of cybercrime. Some states take a very broad approach to the issue, relying on statutes defining general criminal jurisdiction to establish jurisdiction in cybercrime cases, but other states have more specific statutes delineating the elements constituting the crime and its accompanying jurisdiction.

Another piece of the jurisdiction puzzle—one the courts have yet to reach consensus on—centers on whether cybercrime necessarily falls under federal jurisdiction because of the commerce clause and what is commonly referred to as the *nexus requirement*. Disagreement exists between the various courts regarding when a nexus, or link, exists regarding the interstate commerce clause to justify federal jurisdiction. Some courts have ruled that cybercrime automatically comes under federal jurisdiction because the Internet falls under the commerce clause as an instrumentality of interstate commerce, just as do common carriers, phone services and so forth (*United States v. Sutcliffe*, 2007). Other courts, however, have held that digital content does not automatically come under federal jurisdiction simply because it was transmitted across the Internet and that judicial notice is required, similar to showing that a gun traveled in interstate commerce, for the case to elevate to federal jurisdiction (*United States v. Schaefer*, 2007).

In the Comprehensive Crime Control Act of 1984, Congress enacted a single new statute to address federal computer-related offenses—18 U.S.C. §1030—and in 1986, following a series of hearings on potential computer crime bills, Congress enacted the Computer Fraud and Abuse Act (CFAA) to amend 18 U.S.C. §1030: "As computer crimes continued to grow in sophistication and as prosecutors gained experience with the CFAA, the CFAA required further amending, which Congress did in 1988, 1989, 1990, 1994, 1996, 2001, 2002, and 2008" (*Prosecuting Computer Crimes*, 2010, p.2).

This area of law is still suffering from growing pains, as courts struggle to define jurisdiction with regard to computer crime. For this reason, we suggest investigators keep close dialogue with prosecutors on the evolving nature of jurisdiction in cybercrime cases. A valuable resource for the status of laws at the federal level; recent cases involving cybercrime; and information on computer crime, intellectual property, electronic evidence and other high tech legal issues is www.cybercrime.gov, the home page for the U.S. Department of Justice's Computer Crime and Intellectual Property Section.

As with any other crime, once a report of a cybercrime or cyberthreat has been received, the department generally conducts a preliminary investigation.

THE PRELIMINARY INVESTIGATION

Cybercrime investigations share many of the same characteristics of other felony cases, including adherence to a consistent and documented investigative methodology. However, because of the highly technical nature of computer crimes and the fragile nature of the evidence, officers must receive "first responder" training and have extensive knowledge of computers or seek the assistance of a computer expert. The U.S. Secret Service's *Best Practices for Seizing Electronic Evidence: A Pocket Guide for First Responders* (Version 3, 2010) is a valuable resource for investigators undertaking such endeavors.

When a police department receives a report of a possible computer crime, the departmental report procedure is followed for the initial information. The officer assigned to the case interviews the reporting person to obtain the information necessary to determine whether a crime has been committed.

This first responder has a critical role in preserving the crime scene to protect the integrity of the evidence because this is the point where such digital evidence is most vulnerable.

A common protocol for processing a crime scene involving electronic evidence is as follows:

- Secure and evaluate the crime scene
- Obtain a search warrant
- Recognize and identify the evidence
- Document the crime scene
- Collect and preserve evidence
- Package, transport and store evidence
- Submit digital evidence (such as hard drives) for analysis and data recovery.
- Document the investigation in an incident report.

Securing and Evaluating the Scene

As with any other crime scene, the first responder's initial priority is to ensure the safety of everyone at the scene and to protect the integrity of evidence, both conventional (physical) and electronic. Next, the responding officer should restrict access to any digital evidence, including computers, storage media, personal digital assistants (PDAs), cell phones, digital cameras and iPads; *visually* identify potential evidence (do not touch anything yet); determine whether such evidence is perishable; and formulate a search plan. When securing and evaluating the crime scene, it is recommended that the first responder (*Electronic Crime Scene Investigation*, 2008, pp.15–16):

- Follow departmental policy for securing crime scenes.

- Immediately secure all electronic devices, including personal or portable devices.

- Ensure that no unauthorized person has access to any electronic devices at the crime scene.

- Refuse offers of help or technical assistance from any unauthorized persons.

- Remove all persons from the crime scene or the immediate area from which evidence is to be collected.

- Ensure that the condition of any electronic device is not altered.

- Leave a computer or electronic device off if it is already turned off.

First responders should protect perishable data on pagers, caller ID boxes, cell phones and so on, physically and electronically, always keeping in mind that devices containing perishable data should be immediately secured and documented (photographed). Identify any communications lines (telephone, LAN/Ethernet connections) attached to devices such as modems and caller ID boxes. Document, label and disconnect each line from the wall rather than the device, if possible. Communication via such lines must be severed to prevent remote access to data on the computers. *Do not touch* the keyboard, mouse, CDs, DVDs or any other computer equipment or electronic devices (evidence) at this stage (*Electronic Crime Scene Investigation*, 2008). Figure 17.4 presents a flow chart for the process of collecting digital evidence.

A basic tenet for first responders at computer crime scenes is to observe the ON/OFF rule: If it's on, leave it on. If it's off, leave it off.

Before any evidence is touched, it must be properly documented (a later stage, discussed shortly). However, before identifying and documenting evidence, preliminary interviews must be conducted.

Preliminary Interviews. If a crime is suspected or determined, further interviewing of the complainant and witnesses should continue. Information must be obtained as soon as possible because evidence is easily destroyed. Preliminary interviews are conducted before collecting evidence because these interviews help determine the nature of the crime and develop suspects. If the crime involves a computer user in a private residence or other type of singular victim, ask how the user became aware of the crime and who his or her ISP is. The victim will need to provide his or her username(s) and password(s) because such information is typically required to access the system. Ask about security devices or programs installed on the machine and obtain as much documentation as possible regarding the victim computer's hardware and software configurations.

If the victim is a business or other organization, interview employees and staff because they are a good source of information unless they are suspected of collusion. Internal reporting of this type of crime is the same as for any other crime within an organization, normally beginning at the lowest level and reporting upward to the supervisor and then to management. However, supervisory or management personnel are conceivably part of the collusion, so care must be used in the initial stages to eliminate those capable of being involved. Those with security clearance to access sensitive data or areas within a company's network must also be interviewed and evaluated as possible suspects. If a computer has been stolen, determine if it is protected by CompuTrace, computer security and tracking software that helps deter theft and recover stolen machines.

The National Institute of Justice (NIJ) (*Electronic Crime Scene Investigation*, 2008, pp.17–18) recommends the following information be obtained in the preliminary interviews:

- Names of all users of the computers and devices
- All computer and Internet user information
- All log-in names and user account names
- Purpose and uses of computers and devices
- All passwords
- Any automated applications in use
- Types of Internet access
- Any offsite storage

- Internet service provider
- Installed software documentation
- All e-mail accounts
- Security provisions in use
- Web mail account information
- Data access restrictions in place

- All instant message screen names
- All destructive devices or software in use
- MySpace, Facebook or other online social networking Web site account information

Also during this time, the investigator should attempt to assess the skill levels of the computer users involved because proficient users may conceal or destroy evidence

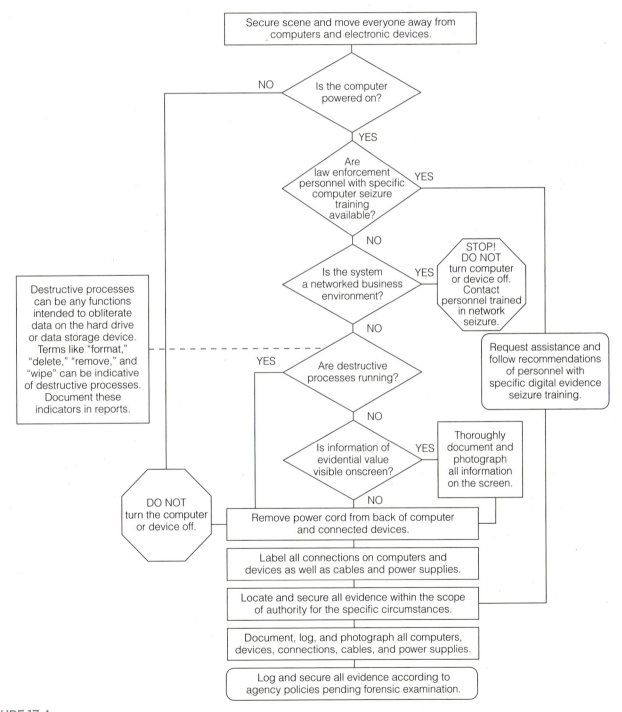

FIGURE 17.4
Collecting digital evidence flow chart.

Source: *Electronic Crime Scene Investigation: A Guide for First Responders*, 2nd ed. Washington, DC: U.S. Department of Justice, National Institute of Justice, April 2008, p.29. (NIJ 187736)

by employing sophisticated techniques such as **encryption**, which puts information in code and thus obscures a normally comprehensible message, or **steganography**, which is Greek for "hidden writing" and aims to keep everyone except the intended recipient of a message oblivious to its very existence (*Forensic Examination*, 2004, p.8). A steganographic message often appears as some type of "cover" message—a shopping list, a picture and so forth. Steganography should not be confused with *stenography* (shorthand).

Before evidence can be collected, it must be recognized and documented. First, however, it may be necessary to obtain a warrant because having a search warrant generally decreases the amount of resistance investigators face at the scene and increases the odds of successful prosecution should the case go to court (*Best Practices*, 2010).

Obtaining a Search Warrant

Searches may be conducted by consent. However, if the suspect is unknown, this is not desirable because it could alert the person who committed the crime. In such cases, a search warrant must be obtained.

Privacy issues surrounding some or all the information contained in the digital evidence desired may pose a legal technicality. If the organization involved is the victim of the crime, its management normally grants permission. If it is not the victim, it may be necessary to obtain permission from individuals named in the evidentiary file, which could be an enormous task. It may be better to take the evidence to a court and obtain court permission if possible.

Investigators may have both a consent search form and a search warrant, thus avoiding the possibility of destruction of evidence. Consent is better than a search warrant in that it avoids the usual attack by the defense in search warrant cases. However, consent may be revoked by the owner at any time during the search. Thus, a warrant provides authority to continue with a search in the absence or revocation of consent.

> **Request the consent initially, and if that fails, use the search warrant.**

If the order is reversed, the consent is bastardized because the search warrant was used as a threat in obtaining voluntary consent. The areas of search and the sought items must be specified in the warrant. Determine the computer system used and the types of physical evidence available from this system. Include this information in the search warrant application. A person connected with the computer operation in question should assist with the search warrant to provide information to the investigators, and this person should accompany the investigators with the affidavit for warrant in case the judge requires technical explanations that the investigators cannot provide regarding the equipment and the evidence desired.

Recognizing Evidence—Traditional and Digital

Computer crimes commonly involve both conventional evidence (fingerprints, documents, computer hard drive, etc.) and digital evidence (electronic computer files, e-mails, etc.). For physical evidence, search techniques and patterns described in Chapter 4 apply. Seal the area and search it according to the type and location of the evidence necessary for prosecution. Avoid pressures to speed up the search because of a desire for continued use of the system, but return the equipment as soon as possible and be sensitive to the company's need to get back to "business as usual" as quickly as possible.

The NIJ has defined electronic evidence as "information and data that is of value to an investigation that is stored on, received or transmitted by an electronic device" (*Electronic Crime Scene Investigation*, 2008, p.ix). The NIJ also explains that electronic evidence

- Is latent like fingerprints or DNA evidence.
- Crosses jurisdictional borders quickly and easily.
- Is easily altered, damaged or destroyed.
- Can be time sensitive.

It is usually not difficult for an investigator to recognize obvious evidence such as a computer, keyboard or mouse, but digital evidence may also exist among a host of other electronic devices too often overlooked. Some of these devices contain perishable data and thus must be immediately secured and documented. Remember: Do not alter a device's condition at this point. If it is off, leave it off. Electronic devices, components and peripherals that first responders may need to collect as digital evidence include (*Electronic Crime Scene Investigation*, 2008, pp.27–28):

- Answering machines—voice messages and other recordings
- Audio recorders
- Cables
- Caller ID boxes
- Cell phones

■ Computer chips—when found in quantity may indicate chip theft

■ Copy machines—usage logs, time and date stamps

■ Cordless landline telephones

■ Fax machines

■ Hard drive duplicators

■ Laptop power supplies and accessories

■ Multifunction machines (printer, scanner, copier and fax)

■ Pagers

■ PDAs

■ Personal computer memory card international association (PCMCIA) cards

■ Printers

■ Scanners

■ Smart cards

■ Videocassette recorders (VCRs)

■ Wireless access points

For certain crimes—such as child pornography, identity theft and computer attacks—CDs, DVDs, flash drives and external hard drives are likely to hold an abundance of evidence. Because criminals often keep "trophies" or collections to document their activities, investigators should search the work area around computers as well as CD and DVD storage units throughout the premises. Some wily offenders try to hide incriminating CDs and DVDs among legitimate ones or insert illicit data into a disk that contains otherwise aboveboard content. Table 17.2 lists the types of digital evidence commonly encountered during a computer crime scene search as they relate to specific crimes.

Investigators should remember that digital evidence may also contain physical evidence such as DNA, fingerprints or serology.

Documenting Digital Evidence

As with other crime scenes, thorough notes, sketches and photographs are necessary to create a permanent record of the scene. The NIJ (*Forensic Examination*, 2004, pp.19–20) suggests these steps:

■ Observe and document the physical scene, such as the position of the mouse and location of components relative to each other (e.g., a mouse to the left of the keyboard may indicate a left-handed user).

■ Document the condition and location of the computer system, noting the computer's power status (on, off,

sleep mode). Check the power status light if no other obvious indication exists. An "off" machine that still feels warm was most likely just recently turned off.

■ Identify and document related electronic components that will not be collected.

■ Photograph the entire scene with 360-degree coverage, if possible.

■ Photograph the front and back of the computer, the monitor screen and other peripheral components connected to the computer. An active program may require videotaping or more extensive documentation of screen activity.

The preceding guidelines are generally sufficient for most stand-alone computers. However, in a business environment, multiple computers may be connected to each other or to a central server: "Securing and processing a crime scene where the computer systems are networked poses special problems, as improper shutdown may destroy data. This can result in loss of evidence and potential severe civil liability" (*Electronic Crime Scene Investigation*, 2008, p.32). Indicators of a computer network include

■ The presence of multiple computer systems.

■ The presence of cables and connectors running between computers or central devices such as hubs.

■ Information provided by those on the scene or by informants.

Collecting Physical and Digital Evidence

Investigators assigned to cybercrimes or other computer-related crimes must have ready certain tools and equipment commonly required in cases involving electronic evidence:

In most cases, items or devices containing digital evidence can be collected using standard seizure tools and materials. First responders must…avoid using any tools or materials that may produce or emit static electricity or a magnetic field as they may damage or destroy the evidence.…

In addition to tools for processing crime scenes in general, first responders should have the following items in their digital evidence collection toolkit: cameras (photo and video); cardboard boxes; notepads; gloves; evidence inventory logs; evidence tape; paper evidence bags; evidence stickers, labels or tags; crime scene tape; antistatic bags, permanent markers and nonmagnetic tools.

TABLE 17.2 Crimes and Digital Evidence

Computer Fraud Investigations:

- Account data from online auctions
- Accounting software and files
- Address books
- Calendar
- Chat logs
- Credit card data
- Customer information
- Databases
- Digital camera software
- E-mail, notes and letters
- Financial and asset records

Child Abuse and Pornography Investigations:

- Chat logs
- Digital camera software
- E-mail, notes and letters
- Games
- Graphic editing and viewing software
- Images
- Internet activity logs
- Movie files
- User-created directory and file names which classify images

Network Intrusion Investigations:

- Address books
- Configuration files
- E-mail, notes and letters
- Executable programs
- Internet activity logs
- Internet protocol address and usernames
- Internet relay chat logs
- Source code
- Text files and documents with usernames and passwords

Homicide Investigations:

- Address books
- Diaries
- E-mail, notes and letters
- Financial asset records
- Internet activity logs
- Legal documents and wills
- Maps
- Medical records
- Photos of victim/suspect
- Telephone records
- Trophy photos

Domestic Violence Investigations:

- Address books
- Diaries
- E-mail, notes and letters
- Financial asset records
- Telephone records

Financial Fraud and Counterfeiting Investigations:

- Address books
- Bank logs
- Calendar
- Check and money order images
- Counterfeit currency images
- Credit card numbers
- Currency images
- Customer information
- Databases
- E-mail, notes and letters
- False identification
- Financial asset records
- Images of signatures
- Internet activity logs
- Online banking software

E-Mail Threats, Harassment and Stalking Investigations:

- Address books
- Diaries
- E-mail, notes and letters
- Financial asset records
- Images
- Internet activity logs
- Legal documents
- Maps to victim locations
- Telephone records
- Victim background research

Narcotics Investigations:

- Address books
- Calendar
- Databases
- Drug recipes
- E-mail, notes and letters
- False ID
- Financial asset records
- Internet activity logs
- Prescription form images

TABLE 17.2 (*continued*)

Software Piracy Investigations:	Identity Theft Investigations, continued:

■ Chat logs
■ E-mail, notes and letters
■ Image files of software certificates
■ Internet activity logs
■ Software serial numbers
■ Software cracking utilities
■ User-created directories and file names which classify copyrighted software
	■ Identification Templates
	  • Birth certificates
	  • Check cashing cards
	  • Counterfeit insurance documents
	  • Counterfeit vehicle registrations
	  • Digital photo images
	  • Driver's licenses
	  • Electronic signatures
	  • Social security cards
	■ Internet Activity Related to ID Theft:
	  • Deleted documents
	  • E-mail and newsgroup postings
	  • Internet activity logs
	  • Online orders
	  • Online trading information
	■ Negotiable Instruments
	  • Business checks
	  • Cashier's checks
	  • Counterfeit court documents
	  • Counterfeit gift certificates
	  • Counterfeit loan documents
	  • Counterfeit sales receipts
	  • Credit card numbers
	  • Money orders
	  • Personal checks

Telecommunication Fraud Investigations:	
■ Cloning software ■ Customer database records ■ Electronic serial numbers ■ E-mail, notes and letters ■ Financial asset records ■ Internet activity logs ■ Mobile identification numbers	
Identity Theft Investigations:	

■ Hardware and Software Tools
  • Backdrops
  • Credit card reader/writer
  • Digital camera software
  • Scanner software	

Source: *Best Practices for Seizing Electronic Evidence: A Pocket Guide for First Responders*, Version 3.0. Washington, DC: U.S. Department of Homeland Security, U.S. Secret Service, March 7, 2010, pp.12–14.

First responders should also have radio frequency-shielding material such as faraday isolation bags or aluminum foil to wrap cell phones, smart phones, and other mobile communication devices after they have been seized. [This]… prevents the phones from receiving a call, text message or other communications signal that may alter the evidence. (*Electronic Crime Scene Investigation*, 2008, pp.13–14)

Digital evidence can be altered, damaged or destroyed simply by turning the computer on or off at the wrong time. The NIJ (*Electronic Crime Scene Investigation*, 2008, p.6) strongly cautions, "Without having the necessary skills and training, no responder should attempt to explore the contents or recover data from a computer (e.g., do not touch the keyboard or click the mouse) or other electronic device other than to record what is visible on its display." First responders and investigators must be aware that destruction of the program or of information files may be programmed in so that any attempt to access the information or to print it will cause it to self-destruct. Check for a **hardware disabler**, a device designed to ensure a self-destruct sequence of any potential evidence. It may be present on or around a computer, with a remote power switch being the most prevalent of the disabler hardware devices. If found, a disabler switch should be taped in the position in which it was found.

Evidence in computer cases is also unique in that it is not as readily discernible as is evidence in most other criminal cases. Computer disks, for example, although visible in the physical sense, contain "invisible" information.

 Digital evidence is often contained on disks, CDs or hard drives, or on any number of peripheral electronic devices; is not readily discernible; and is highly susceptible to destruction. Other computer crime evidence may exist in the form of data reports, logs, programming or other printed information run from information in the computer. Latent prints may be found on the keyboard, mouse, power button or any other peripheral equipment near the computer.

Because chemicals used in processing fingerprints can damage electronic equipment and data, latent prints should be collected after electronic evidence recovery is complete.

A backup of the hard disk contents should be made as quickly as possible. A portable hard drive duplication tool is available that lets investigators quickly create a mirror image of one or more hard drives in the field without removing the original to a remote site.

Investigators must reproduce the material within the rules of evidence. Identification should include the case number, date, time and initials of the person taking the evidence into custody. To mark a metal container, use a carbide metal scribe such as that used in marking items in the Operation Identification program. Use a permanent black-ink marker or felt-tip pen to identify disks. If the evidence is in a container, both the container and the inside disks should be identified in the same way. Marking both identically avoids interchangeability and retains the credibility of the item as evidence. Use normal evidence tape to mark containers and to seal them.

> Avoid contact with the recording surfaces of computer tapes and disks. Never write on disk labels with a ballpoint pen or pencil or use paper clips or rubber bands with disks. To do so may destroy the data they contain.

Usually printouts must be made of data contained on computer disks or CDs. These printouts should be clearly identified and matched with the software they represent.

In more complex cases, the volume of evidence is significant because large amounts of information can be stored on a single disk, CD or DVD. In most felony investigations, the amount of evidence is not a major problem, but in the case of computer crimes, the evidence may involve hundreds of disks, CDs or DVDs. Copying this amount of evidence can be costly and time-consuming. In addition, taking equipment into evidence can be a major problem because some equipment is heavy and bulky.

In a very few cases, the evidence is the computer equipment. Also, it may be necessary to keep the equipment operating to continue business. Investigators must work with management to determine how to best accomplish this. If the evidence cannot be moved from the premises, management may have to provide on-premises security with their own guards or with temporarily hired security until the evidence can be copied or otherwise secured by court order or by police security.

Other nonelectronic evidence that may prove valuable to the investigation includes material found in the vicinity of the suspect computer system, such as handwritten notes, Post-It notes with passwords written on them, blank pads of paper with the indentations from previous pages torn off, hardware and software manuals, calendars and photographs.

Any evidence collected and removed from the premises must be entered onto an evidence log, thus creating a chain of custody that must be maintained from this point forward throughout the investigation. Two chains of custody are involved in digital evidence: the physical items themselves and their associated data (*Digital Evidence in the Courtroom*, 2007). Investigators should be aware that the chain-of-custody issues regarding data are additional to the chain-of-custody issues regarding the physical item.

Collecting Evidence from Cyberspace.

Most, if not all, cybercrimes leave some type of cyber trail or "e-print" as evidence because ISPs maintain records of everything a subscriber does online, at least for a while. If an investigator knows a suspect user's screen name, it can be linked to an identifiable IP address: "All communications on the Internet and across networks rely on an IP address to reach their destination. The key to investigating crimes relating to the Internet and networks is to identify the originating IP address and trace it to a source" (*Investigations Involving the Internet*, 2007, p.15). The IP address(es) associated with suspect pieces of data transmitted via the Internet will help track down the user's ISP. However, no law yet requires maintaining online activity data, and the storage policies of ISPs can vary tremendously. For example, large ISPs commonly maintain data for as long as 30 days, whereas others dump these records every 30 minutes. Data storage is a major expense for ISPs, and many try to save money by purging their files fairly quickly. Therefore, if a crime has involved Internet use, investigators should proceed quickly to subpoena the ISP for stored records. If the subpoena will take several days or longer to obtain, send a letter to the ISP requesting that they preserve the data until a subpoena, warrant or court order can be obtained. An example of an administrative subpoena can be found on CourseMate.

These records, once obtained, will provide such information as the suspect's billing address and log-in records, which can in turn lead to the location of the computer used, such as in a private residence, a public library or an Internet café. Although the billing information and credit card numbers associated with a user's account can be falsified, this information may still be of value to the investigation. Once the suspect's location is known, the investigation typically expands to involve another jurisdiction because the perpetrators of cybercrimes can be thousands of miles away from their victims and the investigation's point of origin.

After the desired target information is culled from the general ISP data records, the investigator needs a search warrant to delve further into a particular user's account information. These files are likely to include e-mails, Web site data, images, spreadsheets and other digital log files that can help assess what activity the account is being used for.

Other tools available to cybersleuths are the Internet pen register and Internet Title III Intercept, the use of which requires court approval. Internet pen registers track transactions originating at the target's computer and can reveal Web surfing habits and sites commonly visited, the types of applications being used and the e-mail addresses of those being communicated with. Title III Intercepts are similar in function to the Internet pen but trap more comprehensive data, allowing investigators to see where the target is surfing, with whom the target communicates and what the target sees, as well as to read the content of the target's e-mail and chat messages.

Understanding how to decipher e-mail headers is a necessary skill for cyber investigators. When an Internet e-mail message is sent, the user typically controls only the recipient line(s) (To, Cc and Bcc) and the subject line; mail software adds the rest of the header information during processing: "The journey of the message can usually be reconstructed by reading the e-mail header from bottom to top. As the message passes through additional mail servers, the mail server will add its information above the previous information in the header. One of the most important pieces of information for the investigator to obtain from the detailed header is the originating IP address" (*Investigations Involving the Internet*, 2007, p.19). The following guidelines are provided for tracing an Internet e-mail (*Investigations Involving the Internet*, 2007, pp.20–22):

12. **X-Message-Info: JGTYoYF78jEv6iDU7aTDV/ xX2xdjzKcH**

X-headers are nonstandard headers and are not essential for the delivery of mail. The usefulness of the X-header needs to be explored with the Internet Service Provider (ISP).

11. **Received: from web11603.mail.yahoo.com ([216.136.172.55]) by mc4-f4 with Microsoft SMTPSVC(5.0.2195.5600); Mon, 8 Sep 2003 18:53:07-0700**

Received:

This "Received" line is the last stamp that was placed in the header. It is placed there by the last

mail server to receive the message and will identify the mail server from which it was received. Note that the date and time stamp is generated by the receiving mail server and indicates its offset from **UTC** (-0700). In this example, the mail server's name is indicated. This can be accomplished by either the receiving server resolving the IP address of the last mail server or the prior mail server broadcasting its name.

10. **Message-ID: 20030909015303.27404.qmail@ web11603.mail.yahoo.com**

Message-ID:

A unique identifier assigned to each message. It is usually assigned by the first e-mail server and is a key piece of information for the investigator. Unlike the originating IP address (below), which can give subscriber information, the message-id can link the message to the sender if appropriate logs are kept.

9. **Received: from [165.247.94.223] by web11603.mail.yahoo.com via HTTP; Mon, 08 Sep 2003 18:53:03 PDT**

Received:

The bottom "Received" line identifies the IP address of the originating mail server. It could indicate the name of the server, the protocol used, and the date and time settings of the server. Note the time zone information that is reported.

CAUTION: If the date and time associated with the e-mail are important to the investigation, consider that this "Received" time recorded in the e-mail header comes from the e-mail server and may not be accurate.

8. **Date: Mon, 8 Sep 2003 18:53:03-0700 (PDT)**

Date:

This date is assigned by the sender's machine and it may not agree with the e-mail server's date and time stamp. If the creation date and time of the e-mail are important to the investigation, consider that the time recorded in the e-mail header comes from the sender's machine and may not be accurate.

7. **From: John Sender <sendersname2003 @yahoo.com>**

From:

This is information usually configured in the e-mail client by the user and may not be reliable.

6. **Subject:The Plan!**

Subject: [ ]

This is information entered by the user.

5. **To: RecipientName_1@hotmail.com**

To: [ ]

This is information entered by the user.

4. **MIME-Version: 1.0 Content-Type: multipart/mixed; boundary="0-2041413029-1063072383=:26811"**

The purpose of these two lines is to give the recipient's e-mail client information on how to interpret the content of the message.

3. **Return-Path: sendersname2003@yahoo.com**

Return-Path: [ ]

This is information usually configured in the e-mail client by the user and may not be reliable.

2. **X-OriginalArrivalTime: 09 Sep 2003 01:53:07.0873 (UTC) FILETIME=[1DBDB910:01C37675]**

X-headers are nonstandard headers and are not essential for the delivery of mail.

The usefulness of the X-header needs to be explored with the Provider ISP.

1. **–0-2041413029-1063072383=:26811**

E-mail client information; not relevant to the investigation.

Mobile Evidence. The electronic memory devices within cell phones that store digital data have become an important source of evidence for criminal investigators. Cell phone use may factor into an investigation involving any of the crimes discussed in this text.

Evidence on a mobile or cell phone system may be found on the communication equipment (the phone itself), the subscriber identity module (SIM), a fixed base station, switching network, the operation and maintenance system for the network and the customer management system. It may also be possible to retrieve deleted items. Call data records (CDRs) obtained from the network service provider are also very valuable as evidence, for they can reveal the location of the mobile phone user every time a call is sent or received.

The following guidelines are offered for the proper seizure and preservation of mobile devices such as personal digital assistants (PDAs), cell phones and digital cameras and associated removable media (*Best Practices*, 2010, pp.5–6):

■ If the device is "off," do not turn "on."

■ With PDAs or cell phones, if device is on, leave on. Powering down device could enable a password, thus preventing access to evidence.

■ Photograph the device and screen display (if available).

■ Label and collect all cables (to include power supply) and transport with device.

■ Keep the device charged.

■ If the device cannot be kept charged, analysis by a specialist must be completed before battery discharge or data may be lost.

■ Seize additional storage media (memory sticks, compact flash, etc):

■ Collect instruction manuals, documentation and notes associated with storage media.

■ Keep away from magnets, radio transmitters and other potentially damaging devices.

■ Document all steps involved in seizure of device and components.

Packaging, Transporting and Storing Digital and Other Computer Crime Evidence

Computer evidence—electronic devices and the data contained within them—is fragile and sensitive to temperature, humidity, physical shock, static electricity and magnetic sources. Thus, investigators must use due diligence when packaging, transporting and storing the evidence. Furthermore, documenting these procedures is necessary for maintaining the chain of custody.

Before electronic evidence is packaged, it must be properly documented, labeled, marked, photographed, video recorded or sketched and inventoried. All connections and connected devices should be labeled for easy reconfiguration of the system later. All digital evidence should be packed in antistatic packaging and in a way that will prevent it from being bent, scratched or otherwise deformed. Only paper bags and envelopes, cardboard boxes and antistatic containers should be used. Plastic materials should not be used because plastic can produce or convey static electricity and allow humidity and condensation to develop, which may damage or destroy the evidence. All containers should be clearly labeled. Cellular, mobile or smart phone(s) should be left in the power state (on or off) in which they were found.

When transporting computer evidence, investigators should keep digital evidence away from magnetic fields such as those produced by radio transmitters, speaker magnets and magnetic mount emergency lights. Store disks in the manufacturers' containers, and store all computer evidence in areas away from strong sources of light.

> Store electronic evidence in a secure area away from temperature and humidity extremes and protected from magnetic sources, moisture, dust and other harmful particles or contaminants. Do not use plastic bags.

Also be aware of the time-sensitive nature of perishable data evidence. Potential evidence such as dates, times and system configurations may be lost because of prolonged storage or the depletion of a device's battery. Therefore, when submitting such evidence for examination, notify the appropriate personnel that a device powered by batteries needs immediate attention.

Crime-Specific Investigations

Several NIJ documents provide in-depth coverage of specific computer crime investigations. *Investigations Involving the Internet and Computer Networks* (2007) provides in-depth explanations of investigations involving e-mail; Web sites; instant message services and chat rooms; file sharing networks, network intrusion or denial of service; and bulletin boards, message boards and newsgroups. *Electronic Crime Scene Investigation* (2008) contains detailed discussions of electronic crime and digital evidence considerations by crime category: child abuse or exploitation; computer intrusion; counterfeiting; death investigation; domestic violence, threats and extortion; e-mail threats, harassment and stalking; gaming; identity theft; narcotics; online or economic fraud; prostitution; software piracy or telecommunication fraud; and terrorism. For those interested in these in-depth discussions, search the Internet by their titles.

FORENSIC EXAMINATION OF COMPUTER EVIDENCE

Computer forensics carries the potential to benefit nearly every type of criminal investigation: "In the last decade, computer forensics has quietly resolved cases that would otherwise have gone unsolved. Considering that computers and digital devices capable of retaining data are ubiquitous in modern society and that criminals are using these devices with greater frequency, it shouldn't be a surprise that computer forensics is being used in more investigations. Computer forensics can provide evidence of motivation, a chronology of events, insight into an offender's interests and activities and links among multiple offenders" (Olien, 2007, p.24).

Crime laboratories, either public or private, have much of the equipment necessary to examine computer evidence. Computer hardware has individual characteristics, much the same as other items of evidence, such as tools. The hardware might also contain fingerprints, but frequently the perpetrator's fingerprints are not unusual because he or she has legal access to the hardware. Printers also have individual characteristics, much the same as typewriters. Document examinations of printouts can be made, and these printouts can be analyzed for fingerprints. Fragments of software may be compared. And, as discussed, the entire file content of a computer's hard drive may be analyzed for incriminating text or images.

Because the skills required for some of today's complex digital and electronic forensic evidence examination are very technical and usually fall outside the realm of what is expected of the typical criminal investigator, this discussion will not delve too deeply into specific techniques required during such examinations but, rather, presents an overview of what happens to evidence once it is submitted to the lab.

Data Analysis and Recovery

In an ideal case, digital data on a seized computer's hard drive or contained on other media such as diskettes, CDs or tapes is intact, unencrypted and has not been "deleted." In these scenarios, the digital forensic examiner can simply retrieve the data and print it. Another place to look for evidence is in the computer's recycle bin, as some less computer-savvy criminals might equate putting a file in "the trash" with deleting it. In many cases, however, the suspect has taken steps to hide evidence of criminal activity, such as through data encryption or steganography, installing booby traps or other destructive programs to keep outsiders from gaining access or by deleting files. Sometimes computer evidence is damaged through exposure to fire, water or physical impact.

Data recovery is a computer forensic technique that requires an extensive knowledge of computer technology and storage devices and an understanding of the laws of search and seizure and the rules of evidence, to be discussed shortly. Software programs can help investigators restore data on damaged hard drives or other computer media or recover information that has been deleted, or so the suspect thought.

Modern operating systems often leave copies of "deleted" files scattered about, in temporary directories, unallocated sectors and swap files.

> Although deleted files remain on the hard drive in a nonviewable format, their existence hidden from most computer users, the computer forensic expert knows where to look and how to make such files viewable again.

Data remanence refers to the residual physical representation of data that have been erased. In addition to recovering deleted material, a qualified computer forensic analyst may be able to recover evidence of the copying of documents, whether to another computer on the network or to some removable storage device such as a flash drive; the printing of documents; the dates and times specific documents were created, accessed or modified; the type and amount of use a particular computer has had; Internet searches run from a computer; and more.

LEGAL CONSIDERATIONS IN COLLECTING AND ANALYZING COMPUTER EVIDENCE

Throughout the entire evidence collection and analysis processes, investigators and forensic technicians must adhere to strict standards if the evidence is to be of value in the courtroom. Individuals must testify in court to the authenticity of the disks, CDs or printouts. The materials must be proven to be either the originals or valid substitutes in accordance with the best-evidence rule. This evidence must be tied to its source by a person qualified to testify about it.

Besides adhering to authenticity standards, investigators must be alert to situations where the Privacy Protection Act (PPA) of 1980 may be implicated. Under this act, with certain exceptions, it is considered unlawful for a government agent to search for or seize materials possessed by a person reasonably believed to have a legitimate purpose for disseminating information to the public. For example, seizure of First Amendment materials such as drafts of newsletters or Web pages may implicate the PPA (*Electronic Crime Scene Investigation*, 2008). The PPA prohibition on use of a search warrant does not apply in the following circumstances (*Investigations Involving the Internet*, 2007):

■ Materials searched for or seized are contraband, fruits or instrumentalities of the crime.

■ There is reason to believe that the immediate seizure of such materials is necessary to prevent death or serious bodily injury.

■ Probable cause exists to believe that the person possessing the materials has committed or is committing a criminal offense to which the materials relate.

The NIJ also cautions first responders seizing electronic devices that improper access of data stored within may violate provisions of certain federal laws, including the Electronic Communications Privacy Act of 1986. The recommended course of action, should this be a concern, is to consult the local prosecutor before accessing stored data on an electronic device (*Electronic Crime Scene Investigation*, 2008, p.7).

An evolving area of legal wrangling concerns copyright laws and investigative agencies that seize computers that have an operating system installed on them, as most do. Operating systems, which are copyright protected, may not be copied without the author's, or in this case the software company's, expressed permission.

FOLLOW-UP INVESTIGATION

Once the initial report has been completed and the general information has been obtained, a plan is made for the remaining investigation. The plan should identify the problem and the crime or crimes committed. A suspect must be developed, as must other peripheral parties to the crime. Determine the areas involved in the crime, equipment used, internal and external staffing needs, approximate length of time required for the investigation, a method of handling and storing evidence and the assignment of personnel. When developing a suspect, ascertain motive, opportunity, means of commission, the type of security system bypassed and known bypass techniques. It may be necessary to conduct covert operations as part of the investigation. In such cases, an officer with expert-level knowledge in cybercrime is a critical factor in achieving a successful resolution. It is also necessary to determine which federal, state or local laws apply to the specific type of computer crime committed.

Developing Suspects

A few decades ago, computer crime was the exclusive domain of a relatively small group of electronic geniuses whose incredibly specialized knowledge and programming skills afforded them unique opportunities to pry into individuals' and corporations' computers and steal money, trade secrets or other information of value. Today, however, cybercrooks are not such an elite bunch. Today's global population of twenty-somethings and younger are often as proficient on the computer as they are with using a TV or cell phone.

A significant change from previous editions of this text is in the number of crimes committed by insiders versus outsiders. It used to be that most computer-related crimes against businesses and other organizations were committed by insiders because these people had the best access to the devices. With the expansion of the Internet, however, outsiders have gained increasing levels of access, to the extent that today most (80 percent) of electronic crimes are perpetrated by outsiders.

> Most cybercrimes against businesses are committed by "outsiders."

The *2010 CyberSecurity Watch Survey* reports that of the 53 percent of businesses that were victims of virus, worms or other malicious code, 41 percent were infiltrated by outsiders compared with 14 percent victimized by insiders (in the remaining cases, the source of the attack was reported as unknown). Of the 32 percent of businesses victimized by illegal generation of spam, 26 percent of the cases were committed by outsiders compared with 7 percent by insiders (in the remaining cases, the source

WikiLeaks founder Julian Assange speaks about the United States and human rights during a press conference in Geneva, Switzerland, in November 2010. WikiLeaks was created as a whistleblower Web site to bring government transparency to the people and, in 2010, published several classified documents about U.S. involvement in the Iraq and Afghan wars. Some call Assange a glorified hacker and threat to national and international security, but others herald the Internet activist as a champion for human rights and freedom of speech.
© AP Photo/Keystone, Martial Rezzini

of the attack was reported as unknown). Of the 41 percent of businesses victimized by spyware, 28 percent of the cases were committed by outsiders compared with 15 percent by insiders (in the remaining cases, the source of the attack was reported as unknown). The crimes committed more frequently by insiders than by outsiders were unauthorized access to or use of information, systems or networks; theft of proprietary information including customer records, financial records and so forth; theft of intellectual property; and both intentional and unintentional exposure of private or sensitive information.

Although anyone with the requisite know-how can take up a life of cybercrime, the FBI and other organizations that have been compiling records on the perpetrators of cybercrime have developed a sort of cybercriminal profile of characteristics these individuals are likely to exhibit:

■ A cybercriminal will likely fall into one of three categories:
  ■ Crackers (hackers): motivated by achieving prohibited access; inspired by boredom and the desire for intellectual challenge; no real damage done
  ■ Vandals: motivated to cause damage and as much harm as possible; are often disgruntled, either with their employer or with life and society in general
  ■ Criminals: motivated by economic gain; use espionage and fraud, among other tactics, to accomplish their goals
■ Cybercriminals can generally be classified by organization level:
  ■ Most computer criminals, although commonly active in a social underground, commit their criminal acts alone.
  ■ A smaller percentage of cybercriminals will exist in organized groups, such as corporate spies and organized crime groups.

> Three general categories of cybercriminals are crackers, vandals and criminals. Motivations vary, from the cracker's need for an intellectual challenge, to the vandal's urge to cause damage, to the criminal's desire for financial or other personal gain.

The *2010 Internet Crime Report* (2011) found that perpetrators were predominantly male (approximately 75 percent) and more than half resided in one of the following states: California, Florida, New York, Texas and the District of Columbia. Most reported perpetrators were from the United States. However, a significant number of perpetrators also were located in the United Kingdom, Nigeria and Canada. Most perpetrators were in contact with the complainant through either e-mail or via the Web. These statistics highlight the anonymous nature of the Internet.

Normal or special audit procedures may have brought a computer crime to the attention of the proper persons, as in embezzlement cases. Because computer operations require contact with other employees in collecting computer-input information, suspicion develops when employees appear to withdraw from other normal relationships.

Overloading of the computer system or a lack of accessibility to records that the system was designed for may indicate illegal use of the computer, a crime that occurs more frequently in small computer operations, where greater opportunity exists. However, this makes an investigator's task easier because the number of suspects is reduced.

The suspect may act alone or in collusion in committing the crime. In cases of internal abuse, commission normally occurs during authorized use or during periods of overtime when the employee is working alone. Developing a suspect's work history assists in locating past opportunities for committing the offense. The suspect's training will provide information about his or her knowledge of computers and computer languages. Comparisons of these factors with the equipment at the crime scene will help determine whether the suspect was capable of the crime.

A complete review of everyone within the organization who has access, their type of access and their technical capability or opportunity greatly assists the investigation if the crime is internal. Check for employees who have a history of computer crimes.

Investigators will often find that computer-related thefts originate from agencies that already have highly trained computer personnel on staff. If the theft is internal, the investigator may confidentially involve personnel of that agency who are not suspect. In internal crimes of this nature, the number of suspects will necessarily be limited, compared with a crime such as a residential burglary, in which the suspect could be a local or an outsider. In computer theft crimes, supervisory and management personnel may use computers to hide their offenses and then misdirect the investigative team toward subordinate staff who have committed relatively minor transgressions.

Internal auditing procedures are normally started with the security director involved. If an employee is suspected at this point, management must decide whether to handle the matter internally or proceed with prosecution. If the decision is to handle the matter internally, then the

case is closed. If not, the investigation continues, often involving state or private investigators. Such individuals may have the expertise and anonymity not available to local police departments.

Organized Cybercrime Groups

Most cybercriminals work alone. However, on occasion these individuals may come together for a common criminal endeavor. They generally are not Mafia-style organizations and usually lack any real loyalty to one another. The transitional nature of these cybercrime rings makes prosecution an effective tool against such groups and sends a message of deterrence to other online criminals, who, because of the anonymity involved with Internet communications, often do not know who they are really dealing with.

Although cybercriminal rings have not historically been formally structured like traditional organized crime, a few hacker groups have been observed to have a Mafia-like hierarchy, with virtual godfathers mapping strategy, capos issuing orders and soldiers carrying out the dirty work. Some cybergangs have evolved into highly organized criminal enterprises whose membership and illegal activities span the globe. Particularly challenging are cases involving cybergangs that operate in countries with weak hacking laws and lax enforcement, such as Russia, Eastern European countries and China.

An effective tactic being used to apprehend organized cybercrime networks is undercover investigation and surveillance.

Undercover Investigation and Surveillance

Sometimes it is necessary to develop an undercover operation to further the investigation. This operation must be headed by a computer expert and coordinated with the non-suspects. Lists must be prepared of all individuals to be used in the case and the evidence to be obtained. Undercover work can be used in nearly every aspect of cybercrime. As with undercover work in the real world, investigators must be sensitive to entrapment issues and to undercover involvement with criminal activity.

Covert investigation including ongoing surveillance operations is a method being used to gather evidence against cybercrime gangs. Undercover tactics are also commonly used in cases of online child pornography and sexual exploitation. An officer will go online, undercover, into predicted locations and, using a fictitious screen name and profile, pose as a child or teenager and engage in real-time chat or e-mail conversations with subjects to obtain evidence of criminal activity. Investigations of specific Internet locations can be initiated through a citizen complaint; a complaint by an ISP; a referral from another law enforcement agency; or the name of an online location, such as a chat room, which can suggest illicit activity ("Innocent Images," n.d.).

SECURITY OF THE POLICE DEPARTMENT'S COMPUTERS

When considering computer crime, law enforcement officers should not overlook the possibility that their own computers may be accessed by criminals. Any computer attached to a phone line is accessible by unauthorized people outside the department, even thousands of miles away on a different continent. Considering the critical nature of law enforcement data and communications, such as systems that control computer-aided dispatch, records management applications and offender databases, ensuring the security of an agency's network should be a top priority. Law enforcement departments cannot afford to have their evidence logs hacked or have reports and other valuable data hijacked in a system takeover following a virus attack.

LEGISLATION

With the proliferation of online child pornography, phishing and other crimes involving the computer, legislation has necessarily been developed to address the problem. For example, in 1986, President Ronald Reagan signed a bill to modernize the federal wiretap law to protect the privacy of high-tech communications. This bill makes it illegal to eavesdrop on electronic mail, video conference calls, conversations on cellular car phones and computer-to-computer transmissions.

However, following the September 11, 2001, tragedy and the realization that the terrorists had used the Internet and other electronic means to communicate and coordinate their plans, the government took measures to allow law enforcement greater latitude in its surveilling of electronic communication if there is a reasonable suspicion that such activity involves terrorism. On October 26, 2001 President George W. Bush signed the USA PATRIOT Act (Uniting and Strengthening America by Providing Appropriate Tools Required to Intercept and Obstruct Terrorism), a major piece of legislation consisting of more than 150 sections, many of which pertain to electronic communications and other areas of cybercrime investigation.

The act made several amendments to the Foreign Intelligence Surveillance Act (FISA) of 1978, such as granting "roving" authority to FBI and other law enforcement agents to more efficiently serve orders on communications carriers and thus meet the challenges posed by individuals who rapidly switch telephone carriers, cell phones or Internet accounts as a way of evading detection and thwarting surveillance.

The PATRIOT Act also changed key features of existing National Security Letter (NSL) protocol. NSLs are a type of subpoena issued in foreign counterintelligence and international terrorism investigations to obtain records under the statutory authority of the Electronic Communications Privacy Act (telephone and ISP records), the Right to Financial Privacy Act of 1978 (financial institution records) and the Fair Credit Reporting Act of 1970 (records from credit bureaus). The PATRIOT Act expanded signature authority for NSLs to increase the efficiency and effectiveness of processing such subpoenas. Recently, the "Emergency Disclosure of E-Mail and Records by ISPs" provision of the act helped law enforcement to quickly track down and restore an abducted 14-year-old girl to her family. The PATRIOT Act received a four-year extension in May 2011.

Other federal statutes relevant to computer-related crimes include patent laws, espionage and sabotage laws, trade secret laws, the Copyright Act of 1976 and the Financial Privacy Act of 1978. In 1998, the Child Protection and Sexual Predator Punishment Act was passed after members of Congress cited horror stories involving sexual predators making initial contact with young children through the Internet.

In the past decade, all 50 states have enacted tough computer crime control laws. States address computer crime either by modifying existing statutes such as those pertaining to theft or by adding computer crime chapters to their criminal codes. For example, to address the growing problem of cyberstalking, some states have amended their traditional stalking laws to include threats transmitted via the Internet. Phishing schemes are likely to violate various existing state statutes on fraud and identity theft and several federal criminal laws. Those who phish may be committing identity theft (18 U.S.C. §1028(a)(7)), wire fraud (18 U.S.C. §1343), credit card or "access-device" fraud (18 U.S.C. §1029), bank fraud (18 U.S.C. §1344), computer fraud (18 U.S.C. §1030(a)(4)) and the newly enacted criminal offenses delineated in the Controlling the Assault of Non-Solicited Pornography and Marketing (CAN-SPAM) Act (18 U.S.C. §1037). Transmission of computer viruses and worms may be prosecuted under the federal provisions of the computer fraud and abuse statute relating to damage to computer systems and files (18 U.S.C. §1028(a) (5)). These federal criminal offenses can carry substantial penalties and fines, with convictions for wire fraud and bank fraud earning the offender as many as 30 years in prison and the possibility of fines as high as $250,000, plus forfeiture of the defendant's property.

Well-defined statutes are critical to investigating and prosecuting computer crimes successfully, and the area of cyber law is rapidly evolving. Lawmakers are challenged, however, by the complex nature of the technology and nontraditional jurisdictional concerns, elements that complicate the effort to define cybercrime and cyber-crooks. Through it all, cybercrime investigators must stay on top of the ever-changing body of state and federal law regarding electronic crimes.

THE INVESTIGATIVE TEAM

Criminals around the world have their sticky fingers poised at the keyboard, prepared to click their way into places they don't belong and steal. The rising tide of Internet activity has washed ashore an increasing variety of old crimes in new bottles and shows no signs of ebbing. To handle this challenge, many departments have formed cybercrime investigative teams comprising various specialists, similar to the approach taken in cases involving complex art thefts, bank embezzlements, narcotics trafficking or other types of crime in which a generalist investigator has little expertise.

> Investigating computer crime often requires a team approach.

The investigative team is responsible for assigning all team personnel according to their specialties, including securing outside specialists if necessary; securing the crime scene area; obtaining search warrant applications; determining the specific hardware and software involved; searching for, obtaining, marking, preserving and storing evidence; obtaining necessary disks, printouts and other records; and preparing information for investigative reports. In most computer-related crimes, investigators seek assistance from the victim who owns the equipment, database processing technicians, auditors, highly trained computer experts or programmers and others. If necessary, the team should contact the manufacturer of the equipment, the consulting services of a private computer crime investigative agency or the technology resources found at local universities and other institutions of higher learning.

An article by the New York State Police (2007, p.54) provides an example of how investigators from the computer crime unit found digital evidence in a felony investigation that seemingly had nothing to do with computers:

> Local police investigating a homicide in Upstate New York during 2005 found a weird combination of evidence in the home of the chief suspect: an old, war-relic hatchet, a note written in Italian, and a personal computer. Investigators from the New York State Police (NYSP) Computer Crimes Unit (CCU) were called in to see if they could shed any light on the puzzle. Their analysis of the PC showed the online search engines Google and Ask had been used to research methods of committing a homicide. A review of the Web sites the suspect had visited disclosed several that featured Italian-Mafia axe murders with letters left behind. Combining this information and a timeline of the searches, CCU members were able to provide evidence supporting premeditation, invalidating several spurious defense theories, and leading to a conviction for second-degree murder.

The Illinois State Police's Internet Crimes Unit (ICU) has helped address the growing need for law enforcement to effectively respond to and investigate computer crime: "Anyone in the law enforcement field knows how difficult it can be to investigate these crimes, not to mention the additional resources and personnel needed. To address these needs, the Illinois State Police established one of the nation's largest state teams dedicated to Internet crime. The unit consists of 10 officers, eight crime analysts, and seven computer forensic investigators" (Gordon, 2008, p.89). Gordon adds, "Contrary to typical crimes where jurisdictions are usually clear, online investigations could have more than one ongoing investigation with each agency unaware of the other. The ICU will not be reactive in nature, but will actively search the Web for criminal activity. The unit will also perform the needed forensics to assist in the successful prosecution of Internet crimes, from identity theft, to fraud, to exploitation from sexual predators and everything in between."

To assist in combating increasing computer crimes, government and private businesses are developing computer crime teams similar to the FBI's kidnapping crime teams and the arson investigation specialist teams of the Bureau of Alcohol, Tobacco, Firearms and Explosives (ATF). The FBI's Computer Analysis Response Team (CART) helps state and local law enforcement as well as federal agents. CART helps write and execute search warrants, seize and catalog evidence and perform routine examinations of digital evidence.

In addition to CART, investigators working cybercrime cases may seek assistance from a growing pool of resources, both domestic and international.

RESOURCES AVAILABLE

Police agencies in many states are forming cooperative groups and providing training seminars on investigating computer crimes. Such groups are especially helpful for small departments, which are less likely to have the needed expertise in-house. For example, Florida's law enforcement agencies can submit computer evidence to the Computer Evidence Recovery (CER) program, which also trains the state's law enforcement agencies to prepare warrants to search computers and to follow specific procedures when seizing computer crime evidence.

Training in computer crimes investigation is also available from other sources. Working in partnership with state, local, federal and international law enforcement agencies, the U.S. Department of Justice (DOJ) has developed the National Cybercrime Training Partnership (NCTP) to develop and promote a long-range strategy for high-tech police work, including interagency and interjurisdictional cooperation, information networking and technical training; to garner public and political understanding of the problem and generate support for solutions; and to serve as a proactive force to focus the momentum of the entire law enforcement community to ensure that proposed solutions are fully implemented. The NCTP is open to any law enforcement agency involved in electronic crime investigation, prosecution or training.

Another resource to help law enforcement handle computer crimes is the IC3. The IC3 provides to cybercrime victims a convenient, user-friendly reporting mechanism that notifies authorities of suspected violations.

One mandate of the USA PATRIOT Act was that the Secret Service establish a nationwide network of Electronic Crimes Task Forces (ECTFs). The ECTF network brings together federal, state and local law enforcement, as well as prosecutors, private industry and academia. The common purpose is the prevention, detection, mitigation and aggressive investigation of attacks on the nation's financial and critical infrastructures (U.S. Secret Service, n.d.). The U.S. Secret Service offers numerous services to its field agents, including technical assistance in developing cybercrime cases, help in preparing search warrants involving electronic storage devices, laboratory analysis of and courtroom testimony regarding the evidentiary contents of electronic storage devices and educational seminars for law enforcement officers nationwide.

The Computer Crime and Intellectual Property Section of the DOJ maintains a Web resource for law enforcement (www.cybercrime.gov) and is a one-stop resource for everything related to computer crime. The site offers a collection of documents and links to other sites and agencies that may help prevent, detect, investigate and prosecute cybercrime.

Other resources include the Computer Crime Research Center and the Electronic Evidence Information Center.

Perverted Justice is an Internet-based organization whose volunteers pose as young kids, then trawl the Internet for predators (Garrett, 2007, p.12). Founded in 2002 by Xavier Von Erck, Perverted Justice has the resources to spend hundreds of hours on a single case, with volunteers able to chat all hours of the day and night. Volunteers undergo an in-depth background check and are extensively trained in setting up a profile, charting online steganography, Web cam transmission and documentation, sending audio files, building evidence packets, submitting evidence to law enforcement, audio authentication, making police statements and the like. Perverted Justice volunteers have worked with police to collar more than 157 criminals (Garrett, p.17).

Technology Innovations

The National Center for Missing and Exploited Children, the Internet Crimes against Children Task Force and the Boys and Girls Clubs of America have created an Internet safety and awareness program called NetSmartz:

The concept was developed to help parents, educators, and law enforcement officers teach children from an early age how to avoid dangers online. The NetSmartz program strongly advocates open communication and sharing in the family setting while providing an understanding of potential troubles that exist in the online world. The NetSmartz program consists of four PowerPoint presentations that have been created as educational tools for law enforcement and educators. Substantial research and testing went into development to ensure they are all age appropriate. The program uses a multimedia approach combining talking points and videos of real-life children sharing stories of the situations they found themselves in as a result of risky online activity....

To complement its presentations, the NetSmartzkids.org Web site has been developed for the youngest Internet users. It's a safe Web site for kids to play and learn on. NetSmartzkids.org features games, puzzles, songs, activity cards, and videos designed to teach kids how to be safer online. The children absorb the message while having fun.

In addition to the NetSmartzkids.org Web site, there is another site, NetSmartz.org for teens, parents, educators, and law enforcement. All of the NetSmartz resources are available free to the public. (Kerlikowske and Wilson, 2007, p.52)

PREVENTING COMPUTER CRIME

Although computers and related technologies have added immeasurable benefits and value to our quality of life, this technology has opened new avenues of crime and exploitation. One reason computer crime has proliferated among businesses in the private sector is that many managers are unprepared to deal with it. They may be ignorant, indifferent or both. They also frequently lack control over their information. Without standards to violate, there is no violation.

> Computer crimes can be prevented by educating top management and employees and by instituting internal security precautions. Top management must make a commitment to defend against computer crime.

Management must institute organization-wide policies to safeguard its databases and must educate employees in these policies and any security measures implemented. Management should also take internal security precautions: firewalls and virus protection are two safeguards for computers. Data disks and removable storage media should have backup copies and be kept in locked files. The FBI's National Computer Crime Squad suggests the following procedures for computer users to institute, both before becoming a computer crime victim and after a violation has occurred:

- Place a log-in banner to ensure that unauthorized users are warned that they may be subject to monitoring.
- Turn audit trails on.
- Consider keystroke-level monitoring if an adequate banner is displayed.
- Request trap and tracing from your local telephone company.
- Consider installing caller identification.
- Make backups of damaged or altered files.
- Maintain old backups to show the status of the original.
- Designate one person to secure potential evidence.
- Evidence can consist of tape backups and printouts. These should be initialed by the person obtaining the evidence. Evidence should be retained in a locked cabinet with access limited to one person.
- Keep a record of resources used to reestablish the system and locate the perpetrator.

One of the most important, yet most frequently overlooked, security measures is to use a paper shredder for all sensitive documents once they are no longer needed. Another technique gaining momentum in the effort to increase computer security is biometrics, using physical characteristics the user cannot lose or give away, including facial, voice and fingerprint recognition.

Computer crimes also plague and persist among private American citizens because, like corporate managers, they remain uninformed about how to protect themselves. One of the most common ways home users become victims of cybercrime is through phishing or other scams devised to get computer users to relinquish sensitive information.

Businesses also need to become more proactive. *CIO Magazine*, the FBI and the U.S. Secret Service have collaborated to produce guidelines for how businesses should plan for and respond to attacks on information systems, including viruses, hacks and other breaches. The guidelines suggest that chief information officers (CIOs) and business leaders establish a relationship with law enforcement now, before the next attack occurs.

Finally, the U.S. Secret Service contends that law enforcement must take a proactive approach to cyberthreats and that prevention coupled with aggressive proactive investigations deliver the best outcome in the fight against cybercrime. The Cyber Incident Detection and Data Analysis Center (CIDDAC) is one initiative helping law enforcement protect the private-sector networks that control 85 percent of the country's technological infrastructure. CIDDAC uses real-time cyberattack detection sensors, or RCADs, to prevent outside attackers from penetrating a system's perimeter defenses and reaching a target's internal database. If a hack is detected, CIDDAC is notified immediately and begins analyzing the incident. They can track the origin of the attack and notify the target, in real time, that an intrusion is being attempted.

Besides individuals and companies, the entire U.S. population faces risk of victimization by cybercriminals because of our increasing reliance on information technology and the role computers play in many aspects of our daily lives: "The United States is increasingly vulnerable to cyberattacks that could have catastrophic effects on critical physical infrastructure, and severely damage the country's economic, military, and strategic interests" (Bain, 2008). In fact,

> Our nation's critical infrastructures are composed of public and private institutions in the sectors of agriculture, food, water, public health, emergency services, government, defense industrial base, information and telecommunications, energy,

transportation, banking and finance, chemicals and hazardous materials, and postal and shipping. Cyberspace is their nervous system—the control system of our country. Cyberspace is composed of hundreds of thousands of interconnected computers, servers, routers, switches, and fiber optic cables that allow the critical infrastructures to work. Thus the healthy functioning of cyberspace is essential to the United States economy and national security. (*National Strategy*, 2003)

Cyberattacks on any part of this infrastructure could lead to tremendous loss of revenue and intellectual property and to loss of life. For these reasons, the scope of cybercrime, even if undetermined, has the potential to cause extreme damage.

Summary

Computer crimes are relatively easy to commit and difficult to detect, and most are not prosecuted. Computer-related crimes may be categorized as computer as target, computer as tool or computer as incidental to the offense.

Special challenges in investigating computer crime include victims' reluctance or failure to report such crimes, the investigator's lack of training and the lack of understanding of computer crimes by others within the justice system, the need for specialists and teamwork, the fragility of the evidence and jurisdictional questions.

A common protocol for processing a crime scene involving electronic evidence is:

1. Secure and evaluate the crime scene.
2. Obtain a search warrant.
3. Recognize and identify the evidence.
4. Document the crime scene.
5. Collect and preserve evidence.
6. Package, transport and store evidence.
7. Submit digital evidence (such as hard drives) for analysis and data recovery.
8. Document the investigation in an incident report.

A basic tenet for first responders at computer crime scenes is to observe the ON/OFF rule: If it's on, leave it on. If it's off, leave it off. Request the consent initially, and if that fails, use the search warrant.

Digital evidence is often contained on disks, CDs or hard drives, or on any number of peripheral electronic devices; is not readily discernible; and is highly susceptible to destruction. Other computer crime evidence may exist in the form of data reports, logs, programming or other printed information run from information in the computer. Latent prints may be found on the keyboard, mouse, power button or any other peripheral equipment near the computer.

Avoid contact with the recording surfaces of computer tapes and disks. Never write on disk labels with a ballpoint pen or pencil or use paper clips or rubber bands with disks. To do so may destroy the data they contain. Store electronic evidence in a secure area away from temperature and humidity extremes and protected from magnetic sources, moisture, dust and other harmful particles or contaminants. Do not use plastic bags.

Although deleted files remain on the hard drive in a nonviewable format, their existence hidden from most computer users, the computer forensic expert knows where to look and how to make such files viewable again.

Most cybercrimes against businesses are committed by "outsiders." Three general categories of cybercriminals are crackers, vandals and criminals. Motivations vary, from the cracker's need for an intellectual challenge, to the vandal's urge to cause damage, to the criminal's desire for financial or other personal gain.

Investigating such crimes often requires a team approach. Computer crimes can be prevented by educating top management and employees and by instituting internal security precautions. Top management must make a commitment to defend against computer crime.

Checklist
Cybercrime

- Who is the complainant?
- Has a crime been committed?
- What is the specific nature of the crime reported to the police?
- What statutes are applicable? Can the required elements of the crime be proven?
- Has the crime been terminated, or is it continuing?
- Is the origin of the crime internal or external?
- Does the reported crime appear to be a cover-up for a larger crime?
- What barriers exist to investigating the crime?

- What are the make, model and identification numbers of the equipment involved? The hardware? The software?

- Is the equipment individually or company owned?

- Is an operations manual available for the hardware?

- Is a flowchart of computer operations available? Is a computer configuration chart available?

- Is documentation for the software available?

- What computer language is involved? What computer programs are involved?

- What is the degree of technicality involved? Simple or complex?

- What are the input and output codes?

- What accounting procedures were used?

- What is the database system? What are the system's main vulnerabilities?

- Is there a built-in security system? What is it? How was it bypassed?

- What are the present security procedures? How were they bypassed?

- Can the equipment be shut down during the search and investigation or for a sufficient time to investigate the portion essential to obtaining evidence?

- Can the computer records be "dumped" without interfering with the ongoing operations, or must the system be closed down and secured?

- Does the equipment need to be operational to conduct the investigation?

- Does the reporting person desire prosecution or only disciplinary action?

- Are there any suspects? Internal or external?

- If internal, are they presently employed by the reporting organization or person?

- Is a list of current employees and their work histories available? Are all current computer-related job descriptions available?

- What level of employees is involved? Is an organizational table available?

- How can the investigation be carried out without the knowledge of the suspect?

- What is the motive for the crime?

- What competitors might be suspect?

- What types of evidence are needed or likely to be present?

- What external experts are needed as part of the search team?

- Does the available evidence meet the best-evidence requirement?

- What are the main barriers to the continued investigation? How can they be overcome?

Application

A. (From "Marijuana Buyers Club Sets Up Site on Internet," *Las Vegas Review Journal*, November 14, 1996, p.14E.)

After voters in one state approved a proposition legalizing marijuana use "for medicinal purposes," an Internet site began offering marijuana to severely ill or disabled people who need it, requiring proof of a doctor's recommendation to use marijuana. The site's director states, "I don't want people trying to order marijuana without the proper authorization. I'm really trying to do this in keeping with the proper spirit of [the proposition]."

A police sergeant from the jurisdiction from which the marijuana is being shipped contends the operation is clearly illegal. "Along with supplying and selling marijuana, which are felonies, I imagine you could cook up something extra for using the Internet," he said. The site is receiving orders from all over the state, as well as from people outside the state who are using in-state mailing addresses.

Questions

1. What crime is being committed, if any?
2. Who has jurisdiction?
3. What steps would you take to conduct this investigation?
4. How would you prepare a search warrant?
5. What types of evidence would you look for?

B. A local firm contacts your police department concerning theft of customer credit card and Social Security numbers from their computer records. This operation and theft are suspected to be internal, so present and past employees are the prime suspects.

Questions

1. How would you plan to initiate the investigation?
2. What statements would you obtain?
3. Would you use internal or external assistance?
4. What types of evidence would you need?

Discussion Questions

1. What do you perceive to be the differences between investigating computer crime and investigating other felonies?

2. What are the differences in interviewing and interrogating individuals involved in computer crime?

3. What are the legal differences between a computer crime investigation and other felony investigations?

4. If you were in charge of a computer crime investigation team, what would you include in your plan?

5. Do you have a computer crime law in your municipality? In your state?

6. Is anyone in your police department trained specifically in computer crime investigation? If so, where was this training obtained?

7. Do you have a computer? If so, how do you store your information?

8. Do you think that today's police officer should have a standard of computer knowledge? What are the benefits and drawbacks to having a computer skill standard for employment?

9. Of all the various types of computer crime, which do you think is the most serious?

10. What do you consider the greatest challenge in investigating computer crimes?

Media Explorations

Internet

Select one of the following assignments to complete.

■ Go to the International Association of Chiefs of Police Web site to find and outline *Best Practices for Seizing Electronic Evidence*.

■ Search for the key phrase *National Institute of Justice*. Click on "NCJRS" (National Criminal Justice Research Service). Click on "law enforcement." Click on "sort by Doc#." Search for one of the NCJ reference numbers cited in the References for this chapter. Outline the selection to share with the class.

■ Go to the FBI Web site. Click on "library and reference." Select "Uniform Crime Reports" and outline what the report says about computer crime.

■ Select one of the following key terms: *computer crime, computer crime prevention, hacker, logic bomb*. Find one article relevant to computer crime investigations to outline and share with the class.

 ## Gale Criminal Justice Database Assignments

The following assignments require access to Gale's Custom Journals Database for Emergency Services and Criminal Justice. Check with your instructor if you have questions about this.

■ Find the article "The Computer as a Significant Other" on the Gale Emergency Services Database. Read and outline the article for in-class discussion.

■ Find the article "Making Computer Crime Count" on the Gale Emergency Services Database. Read and complete a one-page paper on this subject using information from this article.

■ Find the article "The Angels of Cyber Space: The Cyber Angels Cyber Crime Unit Is Watching over Victims of Internet Crimes" on the Gale Emergency Services Database. Read and identify the purpose of this unit. Establish the benefits and the drawbacks of this unit, and be prepared to discuss your thoughts with the class.

■ Find the article "Computer Intrusion Investigation Guidelines" on the Gale Emergency Services Database. Read and summarize the investigative steps that this article identifies and be prepared to discuss this process with the class.

References

Bain, Ben. "Critical Infrastructure Central to Cyber Threat." *Federal Computer Week*, April 24, 2008.

Berners-Lee, Tim. "Frequently Asked Questions," no date. Accessed August 11, 2011. http://www.w3.org/People/Berners-Lee/FAQ.html#InternetWeb

Best Practices for Seizing Electronic Evidence: A Pocket Guide for First Responders, Version 3.0. Washington, DC: U.S. Department of Homeland Security, U.S. Secret Service, March 7, 2010.

"Cybercrime: Addressing Cyber Threats, Report." *Tech News*, July 24, 2007.

Digital Evidence in the Courtroom: A Guide for Law Enforcement and Prosecutors. Washington, DC: National Institute of Justice, January 2007. (NCJ 211314). Accessed August 11, 2011. https://www.ncjrs.gov/pdffiles1/nij/211314.pdf

Electronic Crime Scene Investigation: A Guide for First Responders, 2nd ed. Washington, DC: National Institute of Justice, 2008. (NCJ 219941). Accessed August 11, 2011. https://www.ncjrs.gov/pdffiles1/nij/219941.pdf

Forensic Examination of Digital Evidence: A Guide for Law Enforcement. Washington, DC: National Institute of Justice, April 2004. (NCJ 199408). Accessed August 11, 2011. https://www.ncjrs.gov/pdffiles1/nij/199408.pdf

Garrett, Ronnie. "Internet Watchdogs." *Law Enforcement Technology*, March 2007, pp.10–22.

Gordon, Kevin. "Illinois State Police Internet Crimes Unit." *Law and Order*, July 2008, pp.89–90.

"Innocent Images National Initiative: Online Child Pornography/Child Sexual Exploitation Investigations." Washington, DC: Federal Bureau of Investigation, no date. Accessed August 11, 2011. http://www.fbi.gov/stats-services/publications/innocent-images-1

Investigations Involving the Internet and Computer Networks. Washington, DC: National Institute of Justice, January 2007. (NCJ 210798). Accessed August 11, 2011. https://www.ncjrs.gov/pdffiles1/nij/210798.pdf

Kerlikowske, R. Gil, and Wilson, Malinda. "NetSmartz: A Comprehensive Approach to Internet Safety and Awareness." *The Police Chief*, April 2007, pp.45–54.

The National Strategy to Secure Cyberspace. Washington, DC: The White House, 2003. Accessed August 11, 2011. http://www.dhs.gov/xlibrary/assets/National_Cyberspace_Strategy.pdf

New York State Police. "NYSP Computer Crimes Unit: A Full-Service Approach to Fighting Crime." *The Police Chief*, January 2007, pp.54–57.

Olien, Charles L. "The Growing Challenge of Computer Forensics." *The Police Chief*, March 2007, pp.24–29.

Prosecuting Computer Crimes, 2nd edition. Edited by Scott Eltringham, Computer Crime and Intellectual Property Section, Department of Justice. Washington, DC: Office of Legal Education, Executive Office for United States Attorneys, 2010. Accessed August 11, 2011. http://www.cybercrime.gov/ccmanual/ccmanual.pdf

Richardson, Robert. *2010/2011 CSI Computer Crime and Security Survey.* New York: Computer Security Institute, 2011.

2010 CyberSecurity Watch Survey—Survey Results. Conducted by *CSO Magazine* in cooperation with the U.S. Secret Service, Software Engineering Institute CERT® Program at Carnegie Mellon University and Deloitte. Accessed August 3, 2011. http://www.csoonline.com/documents/pdfs/2010CyberSecurityResults.pdf

2010 Internet Crime Report. Washington, DC: The National White Collar Crime Center, 2011.

U.S. Secret Service. "Electronic Crimes Task Forces and Working Groups," no date. Accessed June 30, 2008. http://www.secretservice.gov/ectf.shtml

"Wireless Quick Facts." CTIA—The Wireless Association. Accessed August 2, 2011. http://ctia.org/media/industry_info/index.cfm/AID/10323

Cases Cited

Ashcroft v. Free Speech Coalition, 535 U.S. 234 (2002)

United States v. Schaefer, 501 F.3d 1197, 1206–07 (10th Cir. 2007)

United States v. Sutcliffe, 505 F.3d 944 (9th Cir. 2007)

CHAPTER 18
A Dual Threat: Drug-Related Crime and Organized Crime

Can You Define?

analogs

body packing

bookmaking

capital flight

club drugs

cook

crack

crank

criminal enterprise

depressant

designer drugs

drug addict

Ecstasy

excited delirium

flashroll

hallucinogen

loan-sharking

MDMA

mules

narcotic

organized crime

OTC drugs

pharming

raves

reverse buy

robotripping

sinsemilla

skittling

sting

tweaker

victimless crime

Do You Know?

- What act made it illegal to sell or use certain narcotics and dangerous drugs?
- When it is illegal to use or sell narcotics or dangerous drugs?
- How drugs are commonly classified?
- What drugs are most commonly observed on the street, in the possession of users and seized in drug raids, and what the most frequent drug arrest is?
- What the major legal evidence in prosecuting drug use and possession is?
- What the major legal evidence in prosecuting drug sale and distribution is?
- When an on-sight arrest can be made for a drug buy?
- What precautions to take in undercover drug buys and how to avoid a charge of entrapment?
- What hazards exist in raiding a clandestine drug laboratory?
- What agency provides unified leadership in combating illegal drug activities and what its primary emphasis is?
- What the key to reducing our nation's drug problem is?
- What the distinctive characteristics of organized crime are? Its major activities?
- What organized crime activities are specifically made crimes by law?
- What crimes organized crime is typically involved in?
- What the investigator's primary role in dealing with the organized crime problem is?
- What agencies cooperate in investigating organized crime?

The violence inspired by drug-related and organized crime activities translates into murders, arsons, drive-by shootings, car bombs and other acts that threaten and terrorize communities across the country. Drug gangs have turned many communities into virtual war zones. Sometimes these acts are gang reprisals or witness intimidation; others are designed simply to frighten innocent citizens enough to ensure that they refrain from calling the police. Similarly, organized crime groups have infiltrated some communities to the point where the people looked upon as leaders and role models, or as guardians of the law, have become corrupt themselves.

Organized crime is heavily involved in the drug trade, and many drug cartels, particularly Latino ones, are structured and operated much like other crime syndicates. Thus, these two investigative challenges are discussed in this chapter. Keep in mind, however, that the two topics, while overlapping, are also separate. Organized crime is involved in many more activities than just drug trafficking, and drug-related crimes, though sometimes linked to organized crime, are usually committed by other groups and individuals with no mob associations. Another facet of these two crime problems to be aware of is the response and involvement of different jurisdictional levels. Federal law enforcement has devoted substantial investigative resources to both the illegal drug trade and organized crime. In most cases, however, local law enforcement first detects these problems and opens the cases.

THE THREAT OF DRUGS

American history is filled with drug use, including alcohol and tobacco. As the early settlers moved west, one of the first buildings in each frontier town was a saloon. Cocaine use was also common by the 1880s. At the beginning of the 20th century, cocaine was the drug of choice, said to cure everything from indigestion to toothaches. It was added to flavor soft drinks such as Coca-Cola.

In 1909 a presidential commission reported to President Theodore Roosevelt that cocaine was a hazard, leading to loss of livelihoods and lives. As the public became increasingly aware of the hazards posed by cocaine and other drugs, it pressed for legislation against use of such drugs.

> In 1914, the federal government passed the Harrison Narcotics Act, which made the sale or use of certain drugs illegal.

In 1920, every state required its students to learn about narcotics' effects. In 1937, under President Franklin Delano Roosevelt, marijuana became the last drug to be banned. For a quarter of a century, the drug problem lay dormant.

Then came the 1960s, a time of youthful rebellion, of Haight Ashbury and the flower children, a time to protest the Vietnam War. A whole culture had as its theme, tune in, turn on and drop out—often through marijuana and LSD. By the 1970s, marijuana had been tried by an estimated 40 percent of 18- to 21-year-olds and was being used by many soldiers fighting in Vietnam. Many other soldiers turned to heroin. At the same time, an estimated half million Americans began using heroin back in the States.

The United States became the most drug-pervaded nation in the world, with marijuana leading the way. The 1980s saw a turnaround in drug use, with celebrities advocating, "It's not cool to do drugs" and "Just say no to drugs." At the same time, however, other advertisements suggested that alcohol and smoking are where the "fun is."

SERIOUSNESS AND EXTENT OF THE DRUG PROBLEM

An estimated 14.2 percent of Americans age 12 years and older have used illicit drugs during the past year. Drug addiction and the crime it engenders weigh heavily on American society and pose a formidable challenge for law enforcement. The Drug Enforcement Administration (DEA) reports that more young Americans die from drugs than from firearms, suicide or school violence; the use of illicit drugs and the abuse of prescription medication directly led to the deaths of 38,000 Americans in 2006;

substance abuse is the single largest contributor to crime in the United States; and the most recent data estimates that drug abuse imposes a direct cost of $52 billion a year on our nation, with indirect costs of $128 billion (*Drugs of Abuse*, 2011).

An increasing threat is posed by drug trafficking organizations (DTOs), complex entities with highly defined command-and-control structures that produce, transport and distribute large quantities of one or more illicit drugs: "Wholesale-level DTOs, especially Mexican DTOs, constitute the greatest drug trafficking threat to the United States. These organizations derive tens of billions of dollars annually from the trafficking and abuse of illicit drugs and associated activities. All of the adverse societal impact resulting from the illicit drug trade begins with the criminal acts of DTOs that produce, transport, and distribute the drugs" (*National Drug Threat Assessment*, 2010, p.9). Other findings reported in the *National Drug Threat Assessment* include

- The influence of Mexican DTOs, already the dominant wholesale drug traffickers in the United States, is still expanding, primarily in areas where the direct influence of Colombian DTOs is diminishing. (p.9)

- Asian DTOs have expanded their influence nationally in recent years by trafficking MDMA [3,4-Methylenedioxymethylamphetamine] and high-potency marijuana—drugs that do not put them in direct competition with Mexican, Colombian or Dominican DTOs. (p.10)

- Cuban DTOs and criminal groups are slowly expanding their drug trafficking activities beyond the Florida/Caribbean region, in part by partnering with Mexican DTOs. (p.11)

Especially disturbing is the violence connected with the Mexican drug cartels, with drug violence from Mexico spilling into the United States and creating formidable problems for law enforcement on both sides of the border. Conflict between rival cartels and the Mexican government led to the murders of 6,500 to 8,000 individuals in 2009, according to unofficial estimates (*National Drug Threat Assessment*, 2010). Although the majority of violence has been confined to Mexico, some has occurred in the United States: "Violence in the United States . . . has been limited primarily to attacks against alien smuggling organization (ASO) members and their families—some of whom have sought refuge from the violence in Mexico by moving to U.S. border communities such as Phoenix. For example, in recent years, kidnappings in Phoenix have numbered in the hundreds, with 260 in 2007, 299 in 2008, and 267 in 2009" (*National Drug Threat Assessment*, 2010, p.15).

The drug problem remains a serious issue, as evidenced by data presented in *Monitoring the Future 2010* (MTF), a report by the University of Michigan's Institute for Social Research that summarizes the findings of annual surveys of 8th-, 10th- and 12th-grade students, college students and adults ages 19 to 50 throughout the United States: "Despite the substantial improvement in this country's drug situation in the 1980s and early 1990s, and then some further improvement beginning in the late 1990s, American secondary school students and young adults show a level of involvement with *illicit drugs* that is among the highest in the world's industrialized nations. Even by longer-term historical standards in the U.S. these rates remain extremely high, though in general they are not as high as in the peak years of the epidemic in the late 1970s. *Heavy drinking* also remains widespread and troublesome, though it has been declining gradually" (Johnston et al., 2011, p.41). According to MTF (Johnston et al., pp.36–37),

- Among 8th graders in 2010, 36% report having tried *alcohol* (more than just a few sips), and nearly one in six (16%) say they have already been *drunk* at least once.

- One 8th grader in seven (15%) reported using *inhalants*, and 1 in 28 (3.6%) reported inhalant use in just the month prior to the 2010 survey. This is the only class of drugs for which use is substantially higher in 8th grade than in 10th or 12th grade.

- *Marijuana* has been tried by one in every six 8th graders (17%) and has been used in the prior month by about 1 in every 13 (8.0%). Some 1.2% actively use it on a daily or near daily basis in 8th grade.

- A surprisingly large number of 8th graders (5.7%) say they have tried prescription-type *amphetamines* without medical instruction; 1.8% say they have used them in the prior 30 days.

- In total, 29% of all 8th graders in 2010 have tried some *illicit drug* (including inhalants), while 11%, or one in nine, have tried *some illicit drug other than marijuana or inhalants*. Put another way, in an average 30-student classroom of 8th graders, about nine have used some illicit drug other than marijuana including inhalants, and about three have used some illicit drug other than marijuana or inhalants.

- The very large number of 8th graders who have already begun using the so-called "gateway drugs" (*tobacco, alcohol, inhalants* and *marijuana*) suggests that a substantial number are also at risk of proceeding further to such drugs as LSD, cocaine, amphetamines and heroin.

LEGAL DEFINITIONS

Most narcotics laws prohibit possessing, transporting, selling, furnishing or giving away narcotics. Possession of controlled substances is probably the most frequent charge in narcotics arrests. Actual or constructive possession and knowledge by a suspect that a drug was illegal must be shown. If the evidence is not on the person, it must be shown to be under the suspect's control.

The legal definitions of *narcotics* and *controlled substances* as stated in local, state and federal laws are lengthy and technical. The laws define the terms that describe the drugs, the various categories and the agencies responsible for enforcement.

Laws generally categorize drugs into five schedules of controlled substances, arranged by the degree of danger associated with the drug, with Schedule I drugs being the most dangerous (see Table 18.1). The five schedules contain the official, common, usual, trade and chemical names of the drugs. The laws also establish prohibited acts concerning the controlled substances and assign penalties in ratio to the drug's danger. Basically, these laws state that no person, firm or corporation may manufacture, sell, give away, barter or deliver, exchange, distribute or possess these substances with intent to do any of the prohibited acts.

It is illegal to possess or use narcotics or dangerous drugs without a prescription and to sell or distribute them without a license.

Specific laws vary by state. For example, possessing a small amount of marijuana is a felony in some states, a misdemeanor in others and not a crime at all in a few

TABLE 18.1 Five Federal Schedules of Controlled Substances

	Abuse Tendency	Accepted Medical Use of Any Kind in the U.S.	Available by Physician Prescription?	Do Pharmacies Stock/Sell?	Other Comments	Examples
Schedule I	High	None	No	No	There is a lack of accepted safety for use of the drug under medical supervision	Marijuana Heroin Ecstasy LSD GHB
Schedule II	High	Some	Yes	Some do; even with valid prescription, some will not fill Rx	Abuse of the drug may lead to severe psychological or physical dependence	Cocaine Morphine Opium
Schedule III	Low	Yes	Yes	Not all	Abuse of the drug may lead to moderate or low physical dependence or high psychological dependence	Anabolic steroids Codeine Ketamine
Schedule IV	Very low, with low chance of addiction	Yes	Yes	Not all	Abuse of the drug may lead to limited physical dependence or psychological dependence relative to the drugs in Schedule III	Valium Xanax Rohypnol
Schedule V	Very low, with very low chance of addiction	Yes	No Rx needed	Yes, very commonly, although such sales have become restricted by stores to limited quantities purchased by adults only	Abuse of the drug may lead to limited physical dependence or psychological dependence relative to the drugs in Schedule IV	Cough suppressants with codeine

For a more comprehensive list of drugs and their assigned schedules, refer to 21 U.S.C. Sec. 812 (revised 01/03/07): U.S. Code Title 21—Food and Drugs, Chapter 13—Drug Abuse Prevention and Control, Subchapter I—Control and Enforcement, Part B—Authority To Control; Standards and Schedules. Accessed from http://www.deadiversion.usdoj.gov/21cfr/21usc/812.htm

states. Laws also define the type of activity drug traffickers are involved in and can be used to impose criminal sanctions even when the intended act is unsuccessful.

IDENTIFICATION AND CLASSIFICATION OF CONTROLLED DRUGS

The sale of prescription drugs, the fastest-growing category of drugs being abused, has skyrocketed since 1990. Consequently, a major challenge for law enforcement officers is to recognize and identify drugs found in a suspect's possession. Because of the countless different types, colors, sizes, trade names and strengths of commercial drugs, many officers rely on a pharmaceutical reference book, the *Physicians' Desk Reference* (PDR; 2007), used widely by health care providers. It is the basis for mobile PDR™ software installed on handheld devices. These portable tools provide instant access to concise monographs about thousands of commonly prescribed drugs.

A reference considered by many in law enforcement to be easier and faster to use than the PDR is the *Drug Identification Bible* (2007). The revised, expanded 2004/2005 edition contains more than 1,100 full-color actual-size photos of prescription drugs scheduled by the DEA; tablet and capsule imprints for more than 14,000 prescription and over-the-counter (OTC) drugs; hundreds of photos of drug packaging and paraphernalia; sources, methods of use, purity levels and street prices for all major illicit drugs; and updated street slang to help officers understand the language of the drug culture. For example, "A" is a street name for LSD. "Abe" means $5 worth of a drug.

Web-based pill identifiers such as those provided on drugs.com or rxlist.com are commonly used by patrol officers in the field because of their ease of use and accessibility. These resources can be accessed on the squad car mobile data terminal (MDT) through a wireless Internet connection to quickly identify pills encountered out in the field.

In the absence of a printed field guide or reference book, street drugs can be identified with a narcotic field-test kit. Identification via field testing, however, can be tricky: "Most of [these drugs] are pills or powders that could be pure, uncut dope or baking soda, marijuana or oregano, and the people that market them aren't widely known for their reverence of truth in labeling" (Dees, 2008, p.74). Several brands of self-contained, single-use test kits are available that reduce the likelihood of user error and require very small samples: "Between the variations of similar-looking drugs and the quantity of fake or 'bunk' drugs found by street officers, it's unwise to rely solely on

appearance or packaging to form probable cause for an arrest. These tests are reliable and inexpensive" (Dees, p.79). Officers must understand, however, that field testing cannot be used to *establish* probable cause, only *confirm* it. Probable cause, through observation and evaluation of other factors, must already exist before a substance can be field-tested. For example, an undercover officer who buys a small bag of white powder from a suspected cocaine dealer has established probable cause and may run a substance-specific field test for cocaine. Officers must be properly trained in how to use these field-testing kits to ensure accurate results and to avoid sample contamination or waste and reduce liability concerns associated with false arrests based on faulty testing procedures.

Knowing the street terms for various drugs, drug paraphernalia and drug-related activity is also beneficial to the drug investigator. The Office of National Drug Control Policy (ONDCP) maintains a street-term database with more than 2,300 entries referencing current street slang for drug types, the drug trade, drug cost and quantities and drug use.

Drugs are commonly classified as belonging in one of these groups:

■ Central nervous system depressants (alcohol, barbiturates, tranquilizers)

■ Central nervous system stimulants (cocaine, amphetamines, methamphetamine)

■ Narcotic analgesics (heroin, codeine, methadone, meperidine [Demerol], OxyContin)

■ Hallucinogens (LSD, phencyclidine or PCP [angel dust], peyote, psilocybin, mescaline, dimethyltryptamine or DMT, alpha-methyltryptamine or AMT, dextromethorphan or DXM and Foxy)

■ Cannabis (marijuana, hashish, hash oil)

■ Inhalants (hobby model glue, cleaning solvents, lighter fluid, aerosols)

> **Drugs can be classified as depressants, stimulants, narcotics, hallucinogens, cannabis or inhalants.**

Stimulants and depressants are controlled under the Drug Abuse Control Amendments to the Federal Food, Drug, and Cosmetic Act (U.S. Code Title 21).

> **The most commonly observed drugs on the street, in possession of users and seized in drug raids are cocaine, codeine, crack, heroin, marijuana, morphine and opium. Arrest for possession or use of marijuana is the most frequent drug arrest.**

Figure 18.1 provides a threat matrix for five commonly encountered drugs including the source and transit countries, primary entry points into the United States and domestic wholesale and retail price ranges.

Powder Cocaine and Crack

Cocaine and its derivative, crack, are major problems for law enforcement officers, with crack consistently being ranked as the drug with the most serious consequences. **Crack**, also called *rock* or *crack rock*, is produced by mixing cocaine with baking soda and water, heating the solution in a pan and then drying and splitting the substance into pellet-size bits or chunks. Crack is generally less expensive than powder cocaine.

Crack is most often smoked in a glass pipe and has ten times the impact of cocaine. It is described as "cocaine intensified or amplified" in its effects on the human body. The intense high produced by crack is usually followed by a severe depression, or "crash," and a deep craving for more of the drug. It is more addictive than cocaine, at a much earlier stage of use, sometimes after the first use. Some users "space-base" the drug; that is, they lace it with PCP or other drugs. PCP causes out-of-control behavior, an added hazard to the already dangerous effects of crack itself.

The U.S.–Mexico border is the primary point of entry for cocaine into the United States, with an estimated 77 percent of the national supply arriving via the Mexico–Central America corridor. However, "Cocaine availability has decreased sharply in the United States since 2006. Every national-level cocaine availability data indicator (seizures, price, purity, workplace drug tests, and [emergency department] ED data) points to significantly less availability in 2009 than in 2006" (*National Drug Threat Assessment*, 2010, p.27). Despite the drop in availability, concern is rising over indications that Colombian cocaine producers are increasing their use of a harmful cutting agent, levamisole, a pharmaceutical compound typically used to deworm livestock:

According to Drug Enforcement Administration (DEA) Cocaine Signature Program data, before 2008, less than 10 percent of the tested wholesale-level cocaine samples contained levamisole. By 2009 approximately 71 percent of the tested cocaine samples contained levamisole. Because levamisole is being found in kilogram quantities of cocaine, investigators are confident that Colombian traffickers are adding it as part of the production process, possibly to enhance the effects of the cocaine. However, levamisole can be hazardous to humans, especially those with weakened immune systems. Ingesting levamisole can

cause a person to develop agranulocytosis, a serious, sometimes fatal, blood disorder. At least 20 confirmed and probable cases of agranulocytosis, including two deaths, have been associated with cocaine adulterated with levamisole. The consequences of abusing levamisole are serious enough that in September 2009, the Substance Abuse and Mental Health Services Administration (SAMHSA) issued a nationwide public alert on its effects. (*National Drug Threat Assessment*, 2010, p.4)

Heroin

Heroin, a commonly abused narcotic, is synthesized from morphine and is as much as 10 times more powerful in its effects. It is physically addictive and relatively inexpensive. Heroin can be injected, smoked or snorted,

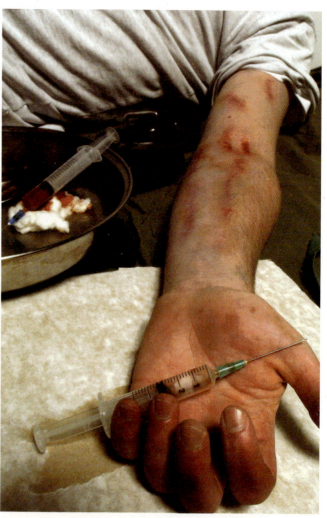

Once a person is addicted, it can be extremely difficult for him or her to quit using drugs without special intervention and treatment. Here, a heroin addict suffers an overdose after getting his fix through a hypodermic needle.
© Arthur Turner/Alamy

National Drug Threat Assessment 2005: Threat Matrix

Overall Key Findings

• Mexican criminal groups exert more influence over drug trafficking in the United States than any other group. Mexican criminal groups smuggle most of the cocaine available in domestic drug markets into the country. Moreover, Mexican criminal groups produce and subsequently smuggle into the country much of the heroin, marijuana, and methamphetamine available in the U.S. drug markets.

• Mexican drug trafficking organizations (DTOs) appear to be gaining control of a larger percentage of the cocaine smuggled into the United States. The estimated percentage of cocaine smuggled into the United States via the Mexico–Central America corridor increased sharply from 72 percent in 2002 to 77 percent in 2003, and preliminary data indicate that the percentage may be higher than 90 percent for 2004.

• Domestic drug markets appear to be increasingly supplied with methamphetamine produced in methamphetamine superlabs in Mexico.

• Production and distribution of ice methamphetamine—a higher purity, more addictive form of methamphetamine—by Mexican criminal groups has increased sharply over the past 2 years in many drug markets.

• Colombian DTOs are increasingly relying on Mexican DTOs and criminal groups to transport South American heroin to the United States much as they rely on Mexican DTOs to transport cocaine.

• The threat posed to the United States by the illegal diversion and abuse of prescription drugs has increased sharply since the mid-1990s and is now among the leading drug threats to the country.

• Law enforcement reporting indicates that transportation of bulk currency out of the United States—primarily overland across the U.S.–Mexico border—is the principal form of money laundering by DTOs.

February 2005

Illicit Drug	Key Findings	Source Locations	Seized En Route/Within U.S. in 2003	Transit Countries	Primary Entry Points Into U.S.
Cocaine	• Powder cocaine use by adolescents decreased since 1999 while cocaine use among adults increased slightly. • Cocaine production declined from 700 metric tons in 2001 to 460 metric tons in 2003. • Increased seizures in Texas indicate it is the state through which most cocaine enters the U.S.	**Foreign:** Colombia, Bolivia, Peru **Domestic:** None	116,898 kg (233,000 kg reportedly available to U.S. markets)	Mexico, Central American countries, Caribbean island nations	Southwest Border (SWB) states (Texas, California, Arizona, New Mexico); Miami/S Florida; New York City (NYC)
Methamphetamine	• Increasing methamphetamine availability in the Northeast region. • Ice availability has increased sharply since 2002. • Production of methamphetamine in Mexico is increasing. • Sharp increase in methamphetamine seizures at and between Arizona ports of entry (POEs).	**Foreign:** Mexico and, to a much lesser extent, Southeast Asia **Domestic:** California	3,845 kg	**Mexican:** Direct from source **SE Asian:** Direct from source	**Mexican:** SWB states (California, Texas, Arizona, and New Mexico) **SE Asian:** California, Hawaii
Marijuana	• Since 1994, marijuana emergency department (ED) mentions and treatment admissions increased. • U.S. marijuana production increasing partly because of increased involvement by U.S.-based Mexican DTOs. • Size of marijuana shipments from Canada increased.	**Foreign:** Mexico, Colombia, Canada, Jamaica **Domestic:** California, Appalachia (Tennessee, Kentucky), Hawaii, Pacific Northwest (Washington, Oregon)	1,225,000 kg (seizures in Texas, Arizona, California, and New Mexico account for 1,139,000 kg)	**Mexican:** Direct from source **Colombian:** Mexico, Caribbean island nations **Canadian:** Direct from source **Jamaican:** Caribbean island nations	**Mexican:** SWB states (primarily Texas and Arizona followed by California and New Mexico) **Colombian:** Miami/S Florida, SWB states, New York City **Canadian:** Northern Border states **Jamaican:** Miami/S Florida, New York City
Heroin	• Heroin treatment admissions increased each year since 1992. • Potential worldwide heroin production increased in 2002, 2003, and 2004 primarily because of increased production in Afghanistan. • Sharp increase in South American heroin seizures along Southwest Border.	Mexico, Colombia, Southeast Asia (Burma, Laos, Thailand); Southwest Asia (Afghanistan, Pakistan)	2,361.8 kg	**Mexican (MX):** Direct from source **South American (SA):** Direct from source, Central/South American countries, Caribbean island nations, Mexico **Southeast Asian (SEA):** China, SE Asian countries, Taiwan, Hong Kong, Canada **Southwest Asian (SWA):** European and Central Asian countries, Canada	**MX:** SWB states (primarily California and Texas followed by Arizona and New Mexico) **SA:** Miami/S Florida, NYC, Newark, SWB states (primarily Texas) **SEA:** NYC, Los Angeles, Northern Border states (Washington, Michigan, New York) **SWA:** NYC, Chicago, Detroit, Atlanta, Washington, D.C.
MDMA	• MDMA availability has decreased since 2001. • More adolescents perceive risk in using MDMA. • Decrease in MDMA smuggled directly to the U.S. from source areas. Asian DTOs increasingly are involved in MDMA trafficking and may become the primary domestic suppliers.	**Foreign:** Netherlands, Belgium (also Poland, Germany, Canada, Latin America) **Domestic:** Limited	1,319,492 du	Western European countries, Canada, Mexico, Dominican Republic	New York City, Newark, Miami, Los Angeles (via international airports); Northern Border states (New York, Washington), Texas

FIGURE 18.1

(continued)

Threat matrix for cocaine, methamphetamine, marijuana, heroin and MDMA.

Source: *National Drug Threat Assessment 2005: Threat Matrix.* Washington, DC: National Drug Intelligence Center, February 2005b. (Product No 2005-Q0317-006)

Primary Markets and Principal Suppliers	Wholesale Price Range in the U.S.	Principal Retailers	Retail Price Range in the U.S.	Projections
Atlanta: Mexican, Colombian, Dominican **Chicago:** Mexican, Colombian **Houston:** Mexican, Colombian, Dominican, Jamaican **Los Angeles:** Mexican **Miami:** Colombian, Haitian **New York:** Colombian, Dominican, Mexican	$13,000-$30,000 per kg (powder)	African American, Hispanic street gangs; African American, Caucasian, Cuban, Dominican, Haitian, and Puerto Rican independent dealers and criminal groups	$25-$110 per gram (powder) $10-$100 per rock (crack)	• Rates of cocaine use among adolescents likely will continue to decline. • Continued reduction of cocaine production in Colombia and interdiction of cocaine shipments in the transit zone may result in worldwide reductions of retail cocaine availability.
Los Angeles: Mexican, outlaw motorcycle gangs (OMGs) **Phoenix:** Mexican **San Diego:** Mexican **San Francisco:** Mexican (Hawaiian, Filipino, and Asian DTOs distribute ice)	$3,500-$99,000 per kg* (powder); $13,200-$154,000 per kg* (ice) *normally sold in pound quantities: $1,600-$45,000 per pound (powder); $6,000-$70,000 per lb (ice)	Mexican, Caucasian, and Asian criminal groups; Caucasian independent dealers; Asian and Hispanic street gangs; OMGs	$20-$300 per gram (powder) $60-$700 per gram (ice)	• Increases in foreign and domestic production should raise domestic methamphetamine availability. • Production and distribution of ice by Mexican criminal groups is likely to increase.
Chicago: Mexican **Dallas/Houston:** Mexican **Los Angeles/San Diego:** Mexican, Jamaican; street gangs **Miami:** Hispanic, Haitian, African American **New York:** Jamaican, Mexican **Phoenix/Tucson:** Mexican, Jamaican **Seattle:** Caucasian, Hispanic, Vietnamese, OMGs	$770-$4,400 per kg* (commercial-grade); $1,980-$13,200 per kg* (sinsemilla) *normally sold in pound quantities: $350-$2,000 per lb (commercial-grade); $900-$6,000 per lb (sinsemilla)	Caucasian, Jamaican, African American, Hispanic, Asian, and Native American local independent dealers; African American and Hispanic street gangs; Jamaican, Mexican, and Asian criminal groups; OMGs; prison gangs	$5-$50 per gram $2-$10 per joint	• As DTOs continue to expand large-scale domestic cultivation operations, overall marijuana production in the U.S. will increase. • Expansion of cannabis cultivation on public lands may increase the threat of violence against unsuspecting passersby.
Chicago: Colombian (SA), Mexican (MX), Nigerian (SEA, SWA) **Los Angeles:** Mexican **New York:** Colombian, Dominican, Mexican, Chinese, Nigerian, Pakistani	**MX:** $18,000-$50,000 per kg **SA:** $52,000-$90,000 per kg **SEA:** $40,000-$80,000 per kg **SWA:** $60,000-$70,000 per kg	African American (MX, SA), Asian (SEA, SWA), Caucasian (SA), Colombian (SA), Dominican (SA), Guatemalan (MX), Honduran (MX), Mexican (MX), Puerto Rican (SA) criminal groups; African American (MX, SA, SEA, SWA), Hispanic (MX, SA, SEA, SWA) street gangs	$10 per dose (approximately 50-100 mg)	• Demand for heroin will remain lower than for other major drugs. • The increase in worldwide heroin production is unlikely to cause an increase in heroin availability in the U.S. because the increase is mostly attributed to Southwest Asian heroin, which is typically destined for Asian and European drug markets.
Los Angeles: Israeli, Russian, Asian **Miami:** Russian, Israeli, Eastern European, Dominican (also Colombian, Caucasian) **New York:** Israeli, Russian, (also Asian, Eastern European, Dominican, Colombian, OMGs, Traditional Organized Crime [TOC] groups)	$4-$20 per du (1,000 du lots)	Caucasian independent dealers; African American, Asian, and Hispanic street gangs; OMGs; prison gangs	$6-$50 per du	• MDMA abuse likely to continue declining among all age groups. • MDMA smuggling across the Northern Border may increase as MDMA trafficking organizations avoid transporting the MDMA directly to the U.S. by first transporting the drug to Canada.

FIGURE 18.1 (*continued*)

with intravenous injection producing the greatest intensity and most rapid onset of euphoria, usually within 7 or 8 seconds. Heroin that is sniffed or smoked takes longer to enter the bloodstream (10 to 15 minutes), but these methods have increased in popularity because of the availability of high-purity heroin and the growing fear of sharing needles. According to the *National Drug Threat Assessment* (2010, p.30), "Law enforcement reporting indicates that heroin remains widely available and that availability is increasing in some areas, as evidenced by high wholesale purity, low prices, increased levels of abuse,

and elevated numbers of heroin-related overdoses and overdose deaths."

Marijuana

Marijuana is made from a plant in the genus *Cannabis* and is the most widely available and most commonly used illicit drug in the United States, with 25.8 million individuals age 12 and older (10.3 percent of the national population) reporting past year use, a rate that remained stable from previous years (*National Drug Threat Assessment*, 2010).

Marijuana is variously classified as a **narcotic**,[1] a **depressant**,[2] and a **hallucinogen**,[3] and street names include *grass, pot, dope, joint, herb, Mary Jane, mj, reefer* and *weed*. The federal Marihuana Tax Act of 1937 outlawed its use.

Marijuana is the most controversial of the illicit drugs, and a wide spectrum of opinion exists regarding its harmfulness. Some feel it should be legalized; others think it is a very dangerous drug. Many opponents of legalizing marijuana contend that it is a "gateway" drug, exposing new and curious experimenters to a fairly benign drug that will eventually lead them to explore other, "harder" chemical substances. Whether marijuana users progress to hard narcotics or other controlled substances has not been thoroughly researched. Most hard-narcotics users once used marijuana, but how many marijuana users proceed to hard drugs is unknown.

In the never-ending quest to enhance their high, some users lace marijuana with other substances, including PCP, cocaine and even embalming fluid, or formaldehyde, stolen from funeral homes or university labs. Marijuana laced with PCP or embalming fluid, called "wet" marijuana, will likely cause hallucinations, euphoria and, sometimes, panic or violence.

Mexican commercial-grade marijuana is the most common variety, but "BC Bud," marijuana from British Columbia, generally has a higher concentration of the active substance tetrahydrocannabinol (THC), and thus greater potency. According to the *National Drug Threat Assessment* (2010, p.36), "The amount of marijuana produced in Mexico has increased an estimated 59 percent overall since 2003. . . . Contributing to the increased production in Mexico is a decrease in cannabis eradication. . . , which has resulted in significantly more marijuana being smuggled into the United States from Mexico, as evidenced by a sharp rise in border seizures."

Although the quantity of marijuana produced domestically is unknown, law enforcement reporting and eradication data suggest the amount is very high: "Marijuana is produced in the United States by various DTOs and criminal groups, including Caucasian, Asian, and Mexican groups, but Caucasian independents and criminal groups are well established in every region of the country and very likely produce the most marijuana domestically overall. Mexican, Asian, and Cuban criminal groups and DTOs, in particular, pose an increasing threat in regard to domestic cultivation, since their cultivation activities often involve illegal immigrants and large-scale growing operations ranging from 100 to more than 1,000 plants

per site. In addition, these groups appear to be expanding and shifting operations within the United States" (*National Drug Threat Assessment*, 2010, p.36).

Large quantities of marijuana are being grown hydroponically indoors, often in abandoned barns or other buildings in rural areas. Such controlled cultivation increases marijuana potency by 3 to 10 times, which increases its value and thus the growers' profits. Known as **sinsemilla**, homegrown marijuana has become extremely popular, and indoor marijuana-growing operations have proliferated, domestically and abroad.

A new type of synthetic marijuana cropping up across the country is K2 or "spice," a mixture of herbs and spices typically sprayed with a synthetic compound chemically similar to THC, the psychoactive ingredients in marijuana. K2 is often marketed as incense or "fake weed" and, until recently, was legal to buy and commonly sold at many tobacco and drug paraphernalia storefronts (head shops). Effective March 1, 2011, however, this synthetic drug was placed into Schedule I of the Controlled Substances Act (CSA) as a necessary measure to protect the public safety. Classification of K2 as a Schedule I substance means it is subject to the same criminal, civil and administrative penalties, sanctions and regulatory controls that are imposed on the manufacture, distribution, possession, importation and exportation of other Schedule I drugs such as marijuana, heroin and Ecstasy ("K2 or Spice," 2011, pp.24–25).

Methamphetamine

Methamphetamine (meth) is now firmly entrenched as a major U.S. drug problem that is only getting bigger. Meth is a highly addictive synthetic stimulant that looks like cocaine but is made from toxic chemicals, such as drain cleaner, paint thinner and other easily obtained OTC products, including cold medications containing pseudoephedrine.

Concocting **crank**, a street name for methamphetamine, is relatively simple and inexpensive. Typical meth users are high school and college students and working-class white men and women. A **tweaker** is a methamphetamine addict; a meth **cook** is someone who produces the drug.

The most common form is powder meth, which is usually injected or snorted but can also be ingested orally or smoked. Other forms include ice meth—which resembles shards of ice, is usually smoked and is highly pure and very addictive—and methamphetamine tablets, commonly the size of a pencil eraser, which are typically ingested orally or smoked, but can also be crushed and snorted or mixed with water and injected.

Many sources report the particularly devastating effect meth is having on America's rural communities, where much of the production and abuse occurs and where law

---

[1]Narcotic: a drug that is physically and psychologically addicting; examples include heroin, morphine, codeine and cocaine.

[2]Depressant: a drug that reduces restlessness and emotional tension and induces sleep; most common are the barbiturates.

[3]Hallucinogen: a drug that induces hallucinations or perceptual distortions of reality.

enforcement and public health officials lack adequate resources to effectively address the growing problems.

Because of the growing popularity of meth, the proliferation of extremely dangerous clandestine labs and the recognition that one of the main ingredients in the production of meth is pseudoephedrine, a powerful stimulant found in many OTC decongestant and allergy medications as well as in energy boosting pills, the U.S. Congress passed the Combat Methamphetamine Epidemic Act of 2005 (aka CMEA) as an amendment to the renewal of the USA PATRIOT Act. President George W. Bush signed the amendment into law on March 6, 2006, amending 21 U.S.C. § 830 regarding the sale of products containing pseudoephedrine. The law encompasses new purchasing restrictions and standards along with new standards for storage, employee training and record keeping.

Forty-one states have additional laws and restrictions regarding the sale and regulation of pseudoephedrine. Private U.S.-based companies such as Target, CVS, Walgreens and Winn-Dixie have created their own company policies in addition to mandated laws on the sale of pseudoephedrine as well.

A chemical additive, GloTell, can identify those who handle anhydrous ammonia fertilizer, a common ingredient in producing methamphetamine. GloTell leaves bright pink stains on the skin and clothes of anyone who comes in contact with the fertilizer and is detectable with black light as long as 72 hours after exposure. The additive also impedes the production process of meth by making the drug very difficult to dry.

Club Drugs

Club drugs are those drugs commonly found at **raves**, dance parties that feature fast-paced, repetitive electronic music and light shows. Rave culture also uses a range of licit and illicit drugs. Although tobacco and alcohol are the most common substances found at the club scene, other substances such as Ecstasy, Rohypnol, GHB and LSD have gained popularity with young people. Methamphetamine has also been increasingly used at raves.

Ecstasy. 3,4-Methylenedioxymethylamphetamine (**MDMA**), known more commonly as **Ecstasy** or XTC, is a powerful stimulant derivative of amphetamine, or speed. MDMA is considered a moderate threat in the United States, with reported levels of availability and abuse trending downward. Mixing drugs such as MDMA along with prescription drugs has also gained popularity in the club scene. For example, consuming both Ecstasy and Viagra is known as "Sextacy," which has been reported to produce a unique high that combines the effects of both drugs. Increased interdiction efforts and the dismantling of large MDMA trafficking organizations are credited as the major reasons for decreased use and availability.

Rohypnol. A second club drug that has made news in the past is the "date-rape" drug, Rohypnol, also known as "roofies." Available by prescription outside the United States, Rohypnol is a central nervous system depressant 10 times more potent than Valium. The drug by itself can

Two jars of methamphetamine in the beginning stages of production. The jar with the cloudy solution has not been treated with GloTell. The pink one has been treated with GloTell, a compound that renders the finished product known as meth into a gooey unusable substance.

Courtesy Gathering of Warriors Min. in Houston, TX

This image shows how the treated methamphetamine glows pink under a black light, revealing why GloTell is so named. Anyone or anything that has come in contact with the GloTell-treated meth will also glow pink when exposed to black light.

Courtesy Gathering of Warriors Min. in Houston, TX

produce extreme lethargy and significant reduction in the brain's recall ability. Combined with alcohol, it causes memory loss, blackouts and disinhibition. Because Rohypnol was originally colorless, odorless and tasteless, it became used as a way to facilitate sexual assault, hence the tag "date-rape drug." Once it was learned that Rohypnol was being slipped into unwary victims' drinks as an aid for committing sexual assault, the manufacturer of the drug reformulated it to increase its detectability in clear fluid and to retard its dissolution rate.

GHB. Another drug used to commit sexual assault is gamma-hydroxybutyric acid, or GHB, a colorless, odorless, slightly salty liquid or white powder. It is taken orally and costs $5 to $20 per dose (capful or ounce). Investigating cases involving GHB may be very challenging, and investigators have started referring to it as a "stealth drug" because of the difficulty in detecting its use. Because GHB causes unconsciousness, victims may be unable to provide much useful information to investigators regarding any attack that may have occurred following ingestion of the drug.

Ketamine. A prescription general anesthetic primarily marketed for veterinary use, ketamine or "special K," is sold as both a liquid and a powder. In humans, it causes some physical effects similar to PCP and visual or hallucinogenic effects such as LSD. At low dosage, ketamine impairs attention, learning ability and memory. At higher doses, it can produce delirium, impaired motor function, high blood pressure, depression and potentially fatal respiratory problems. Ketamine may also cause agitation, unconsciousness and amnesia ("Ketamine," 2011, pp.26–27). Its amnesiac effects have reportedly led to its use as a date-rape drug.

LSD. LSD (lysergic acid diethylamide), a Schedule I Controlled Substance with severe penalties for possession and use, is a potent hallucinogen derived from lysergic acid, a fungus that grows on rye and other grains. Often referred to as *acid* on the club scene, it is clandestinely manufactured in relatively professional laboratory settings because some chemistry background and a working knowledge of laboratory control are generally necessary to safely and successfully synthesize the drug. The initial synthesis produces a crystalline powder, which is then reduced to a liquid and placed onto blotting paper. LSD can also be sold in tablet or capsule form.

Prescription Drugs

Prescription drug abuse has become a nationwide epidemic. Pain relievers such as Vicodin, Percodan, Percocet and OxyContin top the list of abused prescription drugs. Other commonly abused prescription drugs include tranquilizers such as Xanax and Valium, stimulants and Viagra. Marijuana, the illicit drug which has previously and pervasively been the most popular drug with teens, has lately taken a backseat to the nonmedical use of pain relievers, with surveys showing more initiates (first-time users) in recent years of these pain relievers than of marijuana (Wethal, 2008, p.88).

Prescription drug diversion occurs by faking, forging or altering a prescription; obtaining bogus prescriptions from criminal medical practitioners; or buying drugs diverted from health care facilities by personnel. Pharmacy thefts are increasing nationwide to feed the growing demand for prescription drugs. The rising cost of prescription drugs has also enticed senior citizens to join in the diversion and sell their prescriptions. Prescription drugs are also obtained through a practice called *doctor shopping*. A doctor shopper will visit multiple health care providers as a "new patient" or "visiting from out of town," and will exaggerate or feign medical problems to obtain prescriptive medications.

Frequently involved in prescription fraud are narcotics, stimulants, barbiturates, benzodiazepines, tranquilizers and other psychoactive substances manufactured for use in legitimate medical treatment. Law enforcement officers spend a significant amount of time investigating cases involving prescription fraud, many of which also involve insurance, Medicare or Medicaid fraud.

OxyContin. OxyContin is a pain medication derived from opium with heroin-like effects and is used in treating pain related to cancer and other debilitating diseases. OxyContin is intended to be swallowed whole, providing a long-acting, time-release formula for pain relief, the subtlety of which is not popular among abusers. Instead, abusers chew it, melt it to inject intravenously or crush the tablet and snort it.

Inhalants

Although many drugs have shown steady or declining numbers of users during the past few years, inhalant use has increased. More than 1,000 household and commercial products can be inhaled to produce a high: adhesives, aerosols, anesthetics, cleaning agents, gases and solvents. Methods used to inhale include sniffing or snorting the inhalant directly from the container, *huffing* the chemical from a saturated piece of cloth held firmly to the nose and mouth and *bagging* the inhalant by spraying or pouring it into a plastic or paper bag and holding the opening over the nose and mouth.

Khat

Khat (pronounced "cot"), a natural narcotic whose primary psychoactive ingredients are chemically similar to amphetamines, is a relative newcomer to the U.S. drug scene but is well known in eastern African and southern Middle Eastern countries, where its use is culturally acceptable and a part of many traditional social situations ("Khat," 2011, p.28). The drug is harvested from the leaves of the khat tree. Users either chew the leaves or smoke the powder obtained from dried leaves. Cathinone, one of the main chemicals in khat, is a Schedule I narcotic in the United States and is regulated by law. The rising use of khat in the United States appears to coincide with the increased numbers of immigrants coming from eastern African and Middle Eastern countries where the substance is legal, and many immigrants may be unaware of khat's illegal status in this country.

Over-the-Counter (OTC) Drugs

Some teens are turning to legal **OTC drugs** for their highs, mistakenly assuming that if something is legal and readily available, it can't be dangerous, or at least not deadly. Youths have their own language to describe the methods used to get these "legal highs." Drinking bottles of cough syrup, such as Robitussin DM, to get high is called **robotripping. Skittling**, so named because the pills resemble small, red pieces of Skittles candy, is ingesting high doses of Coricidin Cough and Cold ("Triple C") tablets. Perhaps the riskiest and most hazardous practice of all is **pharming**—rifling through the family medicine cabinet for pills, both OTC and prescription, combining everything in a bowl, scooping out and ingesting a handful and waiting to see what happens. When groups of youth get together and combine their respective medicinal booty, it is called a *pharm party*.

OTC drugs taken in excessive quantities for their psychoactive effects fall into three general categories: uppers, downers and all-arounders. The most popular upper is pseudoephedrine, a main ingredient in nasal decongestants such as Sudafed. Benadryl Allergy formula is the top downer choice. The biggest all-arounder is dextromethorphan, also called DXM or Dex, a primary ingredient in cough and cold medicines. DXM, often purchased over the Internet, has been linked to numerous overdose deaths.

Because these drugs are legal, law enforcement requires a more proactive approach to the problem, such as educating youths and their parents and networking with professional organizations such as the American Pharmacists Association, public health departments and school administrations.

Other Narcotics and Drugs

Designer drugs are created by adding to or omitting something from an existing drug. In many instances, the primary drug is not illegal. The illicit drugs are called **analogs** of the drug from which they are created—for example, meperidine analog or mescaline analog. These drugs may cause the muscles to stiffen and give the appearance of someone suffering from Parkinson's disease. Because designer drugs are difficult for amateurs to manufacture, they are high-profit drugs for dealers. Because of their complex natures, these drugs must be submitted to a laboratory for analysis.

Table 18.2 summarizes the various narcotics and dangerous drugs. Pay special attention to each drug's effects. This information is important in investigating the sale and use of drugs.

TABLE 18.2 Summary of Controlled Substances

Drug	Trade or Other Names	Usual Methods of Administration	Possible Effects	Effects of Overdose	Withdrawal Syndrome
Narcotics					
Opium	Dover's powder, paregoric, Parepectolin	Oral, smoked	Euphoria, drowsiness, respiratory depression, constricted pupils, nausea	Slow and shallow breathing, clammy skin, convulsions, coma, possible death	Watery eyes, runny nose, yawning, loss of appetite, irritability, tremors, panic, chills and sweating, cramps, nausea
Morphine	Morphine, pectoral syrup	Oral, smoked, injected			
Codeine	Tylenol with Codeine, Empirin Compound with Codeine, Robitussin A-C	Oral, injected			

TABLE 18.2 *(continued)*

Drug	Trade or Other Names	Usual Methods of Administration	Possible Effects	Effects of Overdose	Withdrawal Syndrome
Heroin	Diacetylmorphine, horse, smack	Injected, sniffed, smoked			
Hydromorphone	Dilaudid	Oral, injected			
Meperidine (pethidine)	Demerol, Merpergan	Oral, injected			
Methadone	Dolophine, methadone, Methadose	Oral, injected			
Other narcotics	LAAM, Leritine, Numorphan, Percodan, Tussionex, Fentanyl, Darvon, Talwin, Lomotil*	Oral, injected			
Depressants					
Chloral hydrate	Noctec, Somnos	Oral	Slurred speech, disorientation, drunken behavior without odor of alcohol	Shallow respiration, clammy skin, dilated pupils, weak and rapid pulse, coma, possible death	Anxiety, insomnia, tremors, delirium, convulsions, possible death
Barbiturates	Phenobarbital, Tuinal, Amytal, Nembutal, Seconal, Lotusate	Oral			
Benzodiazepines	Ativan, Azene, Clonopin, Dalmane, diazepam, Librium, Xanax, Serax, Tranxene, Valium, Verstran, Halcion, Paxipam, Restoril	Oral			
Methaqualone	Quaalude	Oral			
Gluethimide	Doriden	Oral			
Other depressants	Equanil, Miltown, Noludar, Placidyl, Valmid	Oral			
Stimulants					
Cocaine*	Coke, flake, snow	Sniffed, smoked, injected	Increased alertness, excitation, euphoria, increased pulse rate and blood pressure, insomnia, loss of appetite	Agitation, increase in body temperature, hallucinations, convulsions, possible death	Apathy, long periods of sleep, irritability, depression, disorientation

(continued)

TABLE 18.2 *(continued)*

Drug	Trade or Other Names	Usual Methods of Administration	Possible Effects	Effects of Overdose	Withdrawal Syndrome
Amphetamines	Biphetamine, Delcobese, Desoxyn, Dexedrine, Mediatric	Oral, injected			
Methylphenidate	Ritalin	Oral, injected			
Other stimulants	Adipex, Bacarate, Cylert, Didrex, Ionamin, Plegine, Pre-Sate, Sanorex, Tenuate, Tepanil, Voranil	Oral, injected			.
Hallucinogens					
LSD	Acid, microdot	Oral	Illusions and hallucinations, poor perception of time and distance	Longer, more-intense "trip" episodes, psychosis, possible death	Withdrawal syndrome not reported
Mescaline and peyote	Mesc, buttons, cactus	Oral			
Amphetamine variants	2,5-DMA, PMA, STP, MDA, MDMA, TMA, DOM, DOB	Oral, injected			
Phencyclidine	PCP, angel dust, hog	Smoked, oral, injected			
Phencyclidine analogs	PCE, PCP, TCP	Smoked, oral, injected			
Other hallucinogens	Bufotenine, Ibogaine, DMT, DET, psilocybin, Psilocyn	Oral, injected, smoked, sniffed			
Cannabis					
Marijuana	Pot, Acapulco gold, grass, reefer, sinsemilla, Thai sticks	Smoked, oral	Euphoria, relaxed inhibitions, increased appetite, disoriented behavior	Fatigue, paranoia, possible psychosis	Insomnia, hyperactivity and decreased appetite occasionally reported
Tetrahydrocannabinol	THC	Smoked, oral			
Hashish	Hash	Smoked, oral			
Hashish oil	Hash oil	Smoked, oral			

*Designated a narcotic under the Controlled Substance Act (CSA).

© Cengage Learning, 2013

INVESTIGATING ILLEGAL POSSESSION OR USE OF CONTROLLED SUBSTANCES

If you observe someone using a narcotic or other dangerous drug, you may arrest the person and seize the drugs as evidence. The arrested person may be searched incidental to the arrest. If a vehicle is involved but the suspect was not in the vehicle, post a guard at the vehicle or impound it. Drugs found on a person during a legally conducted search for other crimes may also be seized, and additional charges may be made.

Take the suspect into custody quickly. Then make sure the suspect does not dispose of the drugs by swallowing them, putting them between car seat cushions or placing them in other convenient hiding places. Suspects who are high can be extremely dangerous and difficult for officers to control. Also, while in custody, the suspect may experience withdrawal pains and other bodily ills that can create special problems for the arresting officers.

In drug crimes, the victims are implicated; thus, they usually avoid contact with the police, conspiring with the sellers to remain undetected. If apprehended and faced with charges, however, the drug addict may be willing to work with the police. In exchange for a reduced punishment or monetary compensation, such informants or confidential informants (CIs) will provide information to the police information about drug sellers. Therefore, many drug investigations involve identifying those who buy drugs illegally and who can thus provide information about sources of supply.

Recognizing the Drug Addict: Drug-Recognition Experts

Congress has defined a **drug addict** as "any person who habitually uses any habit-forming narcotic drug so as to endanger the public morals, health, safety or welfare, or who is or has been so far addicted to the use of habit-forming narcotic drugs as to have lost the power of self-control with reference to the addiction" (42 U.S.C. §201). Drug addiction is a progressive disease. The victim uses increased amounts of the same drug or harder drugs. Each increase in habit has a corresponding cost increase—thus the frequent necessity for committing crime. In addition, as the addiction increases, the ability to control the habit decreases. Drug addicts become unfit for employment as their mental, emotional and physical condition deteriorates. Because addicts often help each other obtain drugs, exercise extreme caution when addicts are in jail, to prevent visitors from getting drugs to them.

Police officers are adept at recognizing and legally charging individuals who are under the influence of alcohol, especially if they are driving. They are not always so able to recognize drug-impaired individuals. However, drug evaluation classification (DEC) programs, more commonly known as drug recognition expert (DRE) programs, have demonstrated international success in detecting and deterring drug-impaired driving. The International Association of Chiefs of Police (IACP) sets DRE program guidelines, and the National Highway Traffic Safety Administration (NHTSA) supports the program's operation.

If an officer suspects a driver is impaired, the officer begins his or her assessment by using the standard field sobriety tests. If impairment is noticeable, the subject is given a breath test. If the blood alcohol reading is inconsistent with the perceived impairment, a DRE evaluates the individual's appearance, performance on psychological tests, eyes and vital signs using additional tests that go beyond the scope of a standard field sobriety test.

The initial interview includes questions about the subject's behavior; response to being stopped; attitude and demeanor; speech patterns; and possible injury, sickness or physical problems. Physical evidence such as smoking paraphernalia, injection-related material and needle marks on the subject is sought.

The physical examination includes an eye examination, an improved walk-and-turn test, the Rhomberg Standing Balance test and the one-leg stand test, as well as the finger-to-nose test. Also tested are vital signs (blood pressure, pulse rate and temperature), reaction time and muscle rigidity. If warranted, a toxicological examination is also conducted. However, toxicology results typically take a few days to weeks to come back; thus, in the case of a driving while intoxicated (DWI) stop, the suspect may be released pending the results of the toxicology text and then charged formally at a later time if the results come back positive.

A pupilometer allows officers to inexpensively conduct sobriety checks in the field. This lightweight, handheld binocular-type instrument measures absolute pupil dynamics to presumptively detect alcohol, drugs, inhalants or fatigue in a suspect. If the pass/fail indicators show green, the person is not under the influence of any substances. Yellow suggests the person may be under the influence and that further testing is warranted. Red indicates the person is definitely under the influence. The name of the potential substance appears next to the pass/fail indicator along with the percentage probability level.

Physical Evidence of Possession or Use of Controlled Substances

The suspect's clothing may conceal drugs, which have been found in neckties, shirt collars, coat and pants linings and seams, shoe tongues, soles of shoes or slippers, hat or cap bands and, naturally, pockets. Drugs can also be hidden in the hair, behind the ears, and between the toes and attached to other body parts with tape. A strip-search is usually conducted because drugs can be concealed in any body opening including the rectum or vagina—a method known as **body packing**. Some criminals smuggle drugs by body packing animal couriers. In addition to insertion into body orifices, contraband may be ingested or surgically implanted for concealment in an effort to evade detection by authorities. These methods have been used to smuggle drugs into prisons as well as to transport drugs internationally. More recently it has been reported that there is a possible terrorist application of implanting explosives for use in suicide missions.

Objects in the suspect's possession can also contain drugs, depending on the suspect's ingenuity. Cigarette cases, lighters, holders and packages, as well as chewing-gum wrappers, fountain pens, jewelry, eyeglass cases, lockets, pencil erasers and many other objects can conceal illegal drugs.

Vehicles have innumerable hiding places, including under seat covers; behind cushions or seats; in heater pipes, hubcaps or glove compartments; under floor mats; in false auto batteries and oil filters; and in secret compartments devised for great amounts of smuggled drugs. Put the vehicle on a hoist and examine the undercarriage.

In a residence or building, do not give the suspect a chance to flush the toilet or turn on the water in a sink to destroy evidence. Look for drugs in drawer bottoms, in fuse boxes, in bedposts, behind pictures, in tissue boxes, in overhead light fixtures, under rugs and carpets, in and under furniture and in holes in walls. If you find evidence, attempt to locate the property owner and inform him or her of the arrest. Gather all correspondence addressed to the person arrested if it is not in a mailbox. Obtain rent receipts, utility bills and other evidence that establishes that the suspect resides at that location.

One initial problem is identifying the suspected substance. As noted earlier, pharmaceutical manuals and physicians' desk manuals provide information needed to identify various drugs. Field tests can be conducted to serve as the basis for a search warrant, but such tests must always be verified by laboratory examination. A residue-detection swab can be used to test surfaces for traces of cocaine. Investigators simply wipe the swab across the area to be tested, and if cocaine residue is present, the swab instantly turns color. Individually wrapped in foil packaging, these swabs are easy to carry and to use and have a relatively long shelf life.

If evidence of narcotics or other dangerous drugs is found on an arrested suspect, as a result of a search of the premises or even by accident, immediately place it in a container, label it and send it to a laboratory. If it is already in a container, leave it there and process the container for fingerprints. Package uncontained drug evidence carefully to avoid a challenge to its integrity as evidence. Use special precautions to avoid contaminating or altering the drugs by exposure to humidity, light or chemicals.

> Physical evidence of possession or use of controlled substances includes the actual drugs, apparatus associated with their use, the suspect's appearance and behavior and urine and blood tests.

Often found along with drugs are various types of pipes, syringes, grinders, cotton, spoons, medicine droppers, safety pins, razor blades, hypodermic needles and other drug paraphernalia.

A suspect's general appearance and signs such as dilated pupils, needle marks or razor cuts in the veins, confusion, aggressiveness, watery eyes, runny nose and profuse perspiration provide additional evidence of drug use. Table 18.3 lists abuse indicators of various drugs.

To establish that an arrested person is under the influence of drugs, urine and blood tests, a medical examination and a report of personal observations are used along with an alcoholic or drug-influence test form and an admission form signed by the subject.

In-Custody Deaths

Hundreds of people die each year in the United States while in police custody, often without any obvious reason or explanation. Sometimes the cause is a medical condition; other times, it is a consequence of drug use. Most of the time, it is a combination of factors.

One serious problem that may be encountered in dealing with drug users is **excited delirium**, which may occur in people under the influence of an illicit stimulant substance such as cocaine or in people with a history of mental illness who are not taking their medications. The person may exhibit extremely agitated and noncoherent behavior, elevated temperature and excessive endurance without fatigue. People in this mental state do not perceive or respond to the brain's signals to calm down before the body collapses. They continue to push past the point of exhaustion by running, fighting with officers or

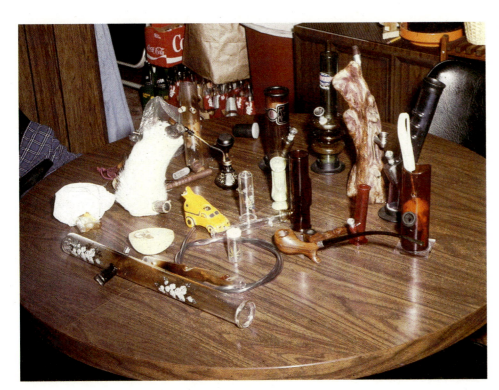

A collection of drug paraphernalia.
© James Shaffer

TABLE 18.3 Indicators of Drug Abuse		
Drug	**Physical Evidence**	**Observable Conditions**
Morphine	Burning spoon, candle, hypodermic needle, actual substance	Needle marks, euphoria
Heroin	Burning spoon, candle, hypodermic needle, razor blade, eyedropper, actual substance	Needle marks or razor cuts, euphoria, starry look, constricted pupils, profuse perspiration
Cocaine	White or colorless crystalline powder, hypodermic needle, pipe	Needle marks, dilated pupils, increased heart rate, convulsing
Crack	Pellets, glass pipes, plastic bottle	Depression, euphoria, convulsions
Stimulants	Pills of various shapes and sizes	Restlessness, nervousness, hand tremor, dilated pupils, dry mouth, excessive perspiration
Depressants	Pills of various shapes and sizes	Symptoms resemble those of drunkenness: slurred, indistinct speech and loss of physical coordination
Hallucinogens	Hypodermic needle, eyedropper, spoon, bottle caps, tourniquets, cotton balls, actual substances	Needle marks on inner elbow, extreme emotionalism, noticeable dilation of pupils, often causing persons to wear dark glasses even at night
Marijuana	Roach holder, pipe with a fine screen placed halfway down the bowl, actual substance	Sweet smoke odor; symptoms resemble those of mild intoxication: staring off into space, glassy eyes, semiconsciousness, drowsiness
Methamphetamine	Makeshift laboratory with ingredients present	Violent behavior, paranoia, other psychotic episodes

resisting against restraints, until their body reaches a potentially fatal medical condition called metabolic acidosis, which can lead to shock, cardiac arrest and sudden in-custody death in a matter of minutes.

Occasionally, a suspect in a drug case will attempt to hide or destroy evidence by ingesting it, which could lead to an in-custody overdose death. In an effort to avoid arrest, subjects have also been known to swallow entire packages or bags containing drugs, which results in their suffocating or choking to death. Using restrictive restraint devices and procedures, such as handcuffing subjects behind their back and placing them facedown, can lead to positional asphyxia. According to one study, 53 percent of the people who die suddenly while in police custody have used illicit substances proximal to their collapse.

INVESTIGATING ILLEGAL SALE AND DISTRIBUTION OF CONTROLLED SUBSTANCES

Because addiction depends on drug availability, drug control must be directed toward the supplier. This is often a joint effort among law enforcement agencies at all levels. Drug users and sellers know the local police, so it is difficult to mount undercover or surveillance operations locally. Outsiders are frequently brought in by the police to make buys and arrests, and drug task forces comprised of law enforcement personnel from multiple agencies and jurisdictions have become an increasingly popular and valuable option for such endeavors. However, local patrol officers are still responsible for investigating drug offenses because they see the users and sometimes observe drug sales. Actions these officers take against users can put pressure on sellers because their market is hurt when users are arrested and jailed.

Drug users often become sellers to support their habits. Many such individuals, called **mules**, sell or transport drugs for a regular dealer in return for being assured of a personal drug supply. Whereas some remain in small operations sufficient to support their needs, others see the profit they can make in large operations and go into business on a larger scale. Further, many drug pushers become users—an occupational hazard. This sometimes occurs accidentally as the result of testing the quality of the merchandise over an extended period.

Investigating the illegal sale and distribution of drugs requires all the basic techniques used for other crimes, plus special investigative skills related to the behavior of drug users and sellers, both of whom can be dangerous and unpredictable. An increasing challenge to narcotics

investigators is the evolving use of technology by drug traffickers and street dealers. Law enforcement agencies have encountered all types of devices used by drug sellers, ranging from two-way radios and cellular phones to robot planes. One seller of two-way radios stated that drug dealers were his biggest customers. If a radio was confiscated in an arrest, another was immediately purchased. Drug dealers use personal computers, sophisticated encryption systems that even federal agencies have difficulty deciphering, night-vision equipment, police frequency jamming equipment, scanners and networking systems. The main advantages drug dealers have over government in using technology are the availability of almost unlimited funds and a lack of bureaucratic approval systems.

Other challenges concern the wide variety of drugs, the difficulty faced when trying to identify them under street conditions and the special types of searches often required to locate minute amounts of drugs that may be hidden ingeniously. Investigators also encounter special problems in finding drugs smuggled across national borders in a variety of ways and in identifying those who transport and distribute them. It takes much time and expense to develop informants and to make a purchase or otherwise discover and confiscate drugs while ensuring that the evidence will stand up in court. In the past few years, international drug lords have benefited from lowered political and economic barriers as well as easy access to sophisticated communications technology that can be frequently changed to evade law enforcement.

 The actual transfer of drugs from the seller to the buyer is the major legal evidence in prosecuting drug-sale cases.

A patrol officer may see a drug transfer by chance or observe it after long surveillance or when an undercover officer makes a planned buy. Some transfers are quite intricate. In one case, a drug seller put drugs on a dog's back, and the dog brought them to the buyer and then returned to the seller with the payment. Even though the seller did not personally hand the drugs to the seller, there was a sale. In other cases, the seller leaves drugs at a predetermined location and picks up payment at another location. Such subterfuge is countered by personal testimony.

If either the buyer or seller throws the drugs away to avoid being caught with them in possession, the drugs can be recovered as abandoned property and taken into custody. If the suspect was seen discarding the drugs, they can be used as evidence.

Narcotics cases begin with a report of suspicious drug activity, a search warrant obtained on information from a

reliable informant or an on-sight observation of a drug buy. Undercover officers and informants then become central figures in obtaining evidence: "Confidential informants are crucial to many law enforcement investigations and are especially essential in the field of narcotics investigations. Informants can provide specific information that is simply not available from other sources. However, the informants are often criminals themselves; if not properly managed, they can render a law enforcement investigation useless, destroy an agency's credibility and even endanger officers' lives" (Lieberman, 2007, p.62). Informants are often vital to making on-sight arrests.

On-Sight Arrests

Patrol officers witnessing a suspected drug buy should obtain as complete a description as possible of the persons and vehicles involved. There is usually no urgency in making a drug arrest because the seller and buyer continue to meet over time.

> If you observe what appears to be a drug buy, you can make a warrantless arrest if you have probable cause. Often, however, it is better to simply observe and gather information.

Probable cause is established through knowledge of the suspect's criminal record, by observing other people making contact with the suspect and finding drugs on them, by knowing of the suspect's past relationships with other drug users or sellers and through observing actions of the suspect that indicate a drug buy. The courts usually give weight to officers' experience and to their information about the suspect and the circumstances of the arrest, including actions by the suspect before the arrest commonly associated with drug selling.

If probable cause is based on information supplied by an informant, check the information for accuracy against intelligence files. If no prior intelligence information exists, add the facts provided to the file. Check the informant's reliability by asking about other suspects in drug cases. Are these suspects already in the files? Has the informant helped before? How many arrests or convictions were based on the information? You might ask the informant to obtain a small amount of the drug if possible.

Surveillance

Neighborhood residents often know where the drug dealers live or which houses are the crack houses. They are, however, usually reluctant to provide such information to police for fear of retributive consequences. Therefore, it may be necessary to surveil a property to develop evidence of drug dealing activity. Some common indicators of residential drug trafficking are

■ A high volume of foot or vehicle traffic to and from a residence at late or unusual hours.

■ Periodic visitors who stay at the residence for very brief periods.

■ Altered property to maximize privacy.

It is frequently best simply to watch and obtain information if you witness a drug buy. The suspected seller or the location of the buy can then be put under surveillance, an especially important technique in narcotics investigations. Surveillance can provide protection for planned buys, protect the buy money, provide credibility for the buyer, provide information regarding the seller's contacts and provide information to establish probable

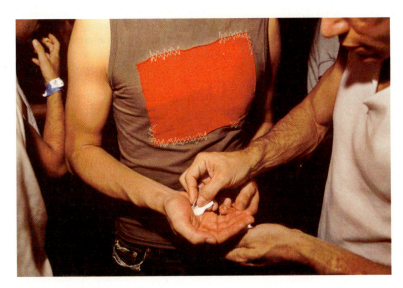

Drugs are commonly bought and sold at raves and other events where young people congregate.
© Debbie Bragg/Everynight Images/Alamy

cause for an arrest or search warrant. It is not necessary to make an arrest on the first surveillance. Actually, it is generally advisable to make several surveillances to gather evidence. Surveillance officers must have patience because many planned drug buys necessitate a long period of surveillance before the actual sale, or bust, is made.

Undercover Assignments

According to Logue (2008, pp.94–95), "U/C [undercover work] has changed dramatically over the past 10 to 20 years. The days of the Lone Ranger going out with a pocketful of money and being a bad guy are over for the most part. Advances in technology, increased liability and budget constraints have caused many smaller agencies to steer away from U/C operations and, in turn, these causes have put a once common practice on the endangered species list. . . . The old Playstation II slogan 'Live in your world, play in ours' adequately sums up the life of the U/C operative. It is American policing at its best but no one ever said being the best would be easy."

Undercover investigations are used more routinely in drug cases than perhaps any other type of criminal investigation. The downside to this common tactic is that drug dealers also know it is routinely used, and they have become fairly adept at sniffing out a "narc." Street dealers are also aware of the restrictions imposed on undercover agents, such as the fact that law enforcement cannot smoke marijuana legally. As a result, undercover narcotics officers have had to develop more convincing ways to fit into the drug culture.

An undercover agent might dress a certain way, use certain slang and talk with an accent or even gargle with beer or hard liquor just before meeting with a dealer. But several new products by Narc-Scent Incorporated are helping undercover officers gain street credibility by giving them the right smell. For example, an incense stick that produces a similar odor to that of smoked marijuana can be burned inside an officer's vehicle. The scent can also permeate the undercover operative's clothing, leading the dealer to believe the buyer is a doper. A loose weed version of the stick can be rolled into an imitation marijuana cigarette and used as if it were real marijuana.

Undercover officers often have permission to consume small amounts of alcohol so they do not look out of place or suspicious. In addition, if placed in a situation where officers fear for their own safety if they do not participate in drug activity, they can. If this occurs, there are generally procedures in place where officers must report the incident and go through proper treatment if it is needed.

Planned Buys. Planned buys usually involve working an undercover agent into a group selling or buying drugs or having an informant make the buy. Before using an informant to buy drugs, determine why the person is involved and keep a strict log of his or her activities. Use care in working with drug users as buyers because they are known by the courts to be chronic liars.

The enormous number of drug buys by undercover agents and informants have made drug sellers wary of new customers. Informants typically introduce the undercover officer. Informants are often involved in criminal narcotics as users or sellers and are "turned" by the police for providing information in exchange for lesser charges. The prosecutor's office usually makes the decision to use an informant in this way. Most people arrested for dealing drugs who are given the option of either going to jail or becoming an informant choose the latter. Police departments should have written policies on using informants.

Undercover agents are usually police officers of the investigating agency (in large cities) or of cooperative agencies on the same level of government in an exchange operation or a mutual-aid agreement that provides an exchange of narcotics officers.

If working undercover, be thoroughly conversant with the language of the user and the seller, know the street prices of drugs and have a tight cover. Talk little and listen much. Observe without being noticed. Also devise an excuse to avoid using the drugs. Work within the seller's system. Drug pushers, like other criminals, tend to develop certain methods for making their sales. Asking them to change their method can cause suspicion, whereas going along with the system establishes your credibility for subsequent buys. Avoid dangerous situations by insisting you do not want to get into a situation where you could be ripped off, injured or killed.

> **Undercover drug buys are carefully planned, witnessed and conducted so that no charge of entrapment can be made.**

Make careful plans before a drug buy. Select a surveillance group and fully brief group members on the signals to use and their specific assignments. Small transmitters are important communications devices for surveillance team members. Have alternative plans in case the original plan fails.

Careful preparation includes searching the buyer immediately before the transaction to avoid the defense that drugs were planted on the suspect. Any items on the buyer other than the money are retained at the police station or with other police officers until after the buy.

Prepare the buy money in advance. It must be marked, identified, counted and recorded by serial number, date, time and denomination. Have this procedure witnessed by one or more people. The money is not given to the buyer until immediately before the buy. Fluorescent powders can be used, but some drug sellers check money for these powders before making a transaction. All buys should be observed from a location where the movements of both the seller and buyer can be seen by the surveillance team.

At the meeting, record the seller's description, the vehicles used, telephone numbers called to set up the buy and observations about the seller's personal statements and habits. If the informant and the undercover officer are both present, the officer makes the buy to protect the informant's identity if an arrest is planned. If no arrest is planned, both the undercover officer and the informant make buys, providing additional evidence.

If several buys are made from the same seller over a period, the seller may relax security and include others higher in the organization. Even if this is not the case, the seller usually visits his or her drug source frequently. The route to or the actual location of the supplier can then be put under surveillance. Such an opportunity seldom arises on the first contact because sellers usually devise very clever ruses to cover their tracks.

The three things valued by dealers are the drugs, the money the drugs can bring and their freedom to do business. In the middle of the triangle is the officer. When both the money—that is, the **flashroll**—and the drugs are present at the same time, the undercover officer faces the greatest danger.

The ability to negotiate is essential for an undercover officer. Almost everything is negotiable in a drug deal. Remaining cool and collected during the actual buy is absolutely necessary. If the situation does not look right or appears to be too dangerous, walk away from the deal; there is always another time and place. Because of the prevalence of weapons in drug trafficking, undercover officers can be in extreme danger, especially because they are usually alone.

If the buy is successful, an arrest can be made immediately, or a search warrant can be obtained based on the buyer's observation of other drugs on the premises. After the buy, the buyer is searched again and the exact amount of money and drugs on the buyer recorded.

> Make two or more buys to avoid the charge of entrapment.

Although police are responsible for investigating narcotics offenses and arresting violators, they are equally responsible for making every reasonable effort to avoid arresting an innocent person. The illegal act involved in the sale should be voluntary, without special urging or persuasion. An agent who knows that a seller is in business and merely asks for, pays for and receives drugs is not using entrapment. But continued requests for drugs from a person who does not ordinarily sell them *is* entrapment. If there has been more than one voluntary drug transaction, no basis for a defense of entrapment exists.

Stings. A **sting**, or **reverse buy**, is a complex operation organized and implemented by undercover agents to apprehend drug dealers and buyers and to deter other users from making drug purchases at a certain location. As with other planned buys, reverse buys are labor intensive, complex and require officers to be well trained. In a typical reverse buy, a team of officers conducts a street sweep to clear an area of drug dealers, and a second undercover team moves in posing as dealers. A third group of officers is stationed nearby conducting surveillance on the operation, videotaping transactions and providing backup should a deal go awry. A fourth group of uniformed officers waits just outside the perimeter of the reverse buy, to arrest those who have just purchased drugs.

Narcotics Raids

Raids are another method used to apprehend narcotics dealers. Surveillance frequently provides enough information for obtaining a no-knock search or arrest warrant. Successful narcotics raids are rarely spontaneous; they are planned on the basis of information obtained during an extended period. They can be designed to occur in two, three or more places simultaneously, not only in the same community but also in other communities and even in other states. The raid itself must be carried out forcefully and swiftly because drugs can easily be destroyed in seconds.

Narcotics raids are often dangerous; therefore, before the raid, gather information about the people involved and the premises where the drugs are located. Also determine how many officers are needed, the types of weapons needed and the location of evidence, as discussed in Chapter 7.

Drug Paraphernalia Stores

Another avenue available to investigators concerns paraphernalia shops and their clientele. Such stores fall into two broad categories. "Head shops" sell products that help the end user ingest drugs, such as pipes, syringes and so on. "Cut or vial stores," in contrast, sell adulterants, diluents and other "office supplies" used by drug organizations in measuring, separating, chemically altering and packaging mass quantities of drugs. The trail of drug paraphernalia may help investigators track down drug gangs and other major drug distributors.

Online Drug Dealers

One challenge for 21st-century narcotics investigators involves a move from the street corner into cyberspace. Club drugs, prescription narcotics and ultra-pure forms of DXM, an ingredient found in OTC cough medication, can all be purchased online and shipped directly to the user's home—transactions that are extremely difficult for law enforcement to detect. Online drug dealers commonly try to disguise their activities by posting their available products as some type of legitimate substance.

CLANDESTINE DRUG LABORATORIES

An increase in clandestine drug laboratories has occurred as more emphasis has been placed on reducing illegal foreign drug imports into the United States. For example, the number of clandestine methamphetamine labs seized nationwide by the DEA increased by more than 500 percent from 1994 to 2000, and the figures continued to rise in 2011. These laboratories pose serious hazards to law enforcement agencies conducting raids on the premises, including booby traps and assaults from attack dogs or violent drug "cooks" under the influence of their products. In addition, many of the substances, often unidentified or misidentified, are explosive and extremely flammable. Irritants and corrosives, asphyxiants and nerve toxins also may be encountered. Figure 18.2 lists the toxic, explosive and hazardous chemicals commonly found in clandestine drug labs.

> Clandestine drug laboratories present physical, chemical and toxic hazards to law enforcement officers engaged in raids on the premises.

Most clandestine labs produce one or more types of amphetamine, but a few produce club drugs such as Ecstasy and LSD. The most serious challenge is posed by covert drug labs involved in the manufacture of methamphetamine, the most widely used and clandestinely produced synthetic drug in the United States. Meth labs are found across the country, in cities and rural areas and have been found in private residences, motel rooms, storage units, garages, barns and vehicles.

The production of meth involves a variety of hazardous ingredients, including strong acids and bases, flammable solvents and highly explosive and toxic chemicals. Because of their volatility, these labs present a significant threat to public safety. An estimated 20 percent of meth labs come to the attention of law enforcement because of fire or explosion. Meth labs run out of homes can have a particularly devastating impact on the health of children living there.

Identifying a Clandestine Lab

Drug labs can be set up almost anywhere. Smaller operations are more portable and easily moved, making detection more difficult. Clandestine or "clan" labs tend to share some common characteristics, however, and knowing what to watch for can help investigators uncover these dangerous, unlawful operations. From the outside of a structure, investigators may observe blacked out or boarded up windows, hoses sticking out through windows and doors, dead vegetation from dumped chemical wastes and strong chemical odors, all of which may indicate a clan lab is operating inside. Inside a structure, indicators of a clan lab include coffee grinders with white residue; coffee filters with red stains; large quantities of acetone, antifreeze, camping fuel, drain cleaner, lithium batteries, matches, plastic baggies, cold tablets or cough syrup containing the ingredient pseudoephedrine; an abundance of mixing containers such as Pyrex glassware, crock pots and other large pots; strips of bed linen or cloth for filtering liquid drug mixtures; and general clutter, disarray and filthy living conditions (Hanson, 2005, pp.10–14).

Because hotel rooms are commonly used for those setting up "clan" labs, some law enforcement agencies are training hotel managers and employees on the dangers such labs pose and ways to identify suspected "meth cooks." DEA agents profile a typical meth cook as White, trashy looking, with rotting teeth (the meth cook look) and poor-quality tattoos and with a local address on his identification. Because the chemicals, such as Drano, used in the production are corrosive and the cooks usually do not get all of them out before using the drug, they suffer corrosion on their teeth and skin.

Entering a Clandestine Drug Lab

When encountering a drug lab or its components, do not use matches, lighters or items that could ignite fumes. Do not turn switches on or off, because the electric connection could produce sparks and cause an explosion. Do not taste, smell or touch any substance, and do check for booby traps before moving or touching containers.

Typical Chemicals Found in Lab Sites	Common Legitimate Uses	Poison	Flammable	Toxic Vapors	Explosive	Corrosive	Skin Absorption	Common Health Hazards
Acetone	Fingernail polish remover, solvents	X	X	X				Reproductive disorders
Methanol	Brake cleaner fluid, fuel	X	X	X				Blindness, eye damage
Ammonia	Disinfectants	X		X		X	X	Blistering, lung damage
Benzene	Dye, varnishes, lacquers	X	X		X	X	X	Carcinogen, leukemia
Ether	Starter fluid, anesthetic	X	X		X			Respiratory disorders
Freon	Refrigerant, propellants	X		X		X	X	Frostbite, lung damage
Hydriodic acid	Driveway cleaner	X		X		X	X	Burns, thyroid damage
Hydrochloric acid (HCl gas)	Iron ore processing, mining	X		X		X	X	Respiratory, liver damage
Iodine crystals	Antiseptic, catalyst	X	X		X	X		Birth defects, kidney failure
Lithium metal	Lithium batteries	X				X	X	Burns, pulmonary edema
Muriatic acid	Swimming pool cleaners	X		X		X		Burns, toxic vapors
Phosphine gas	Pesticides	X		X			X	Respiratory failure
Pseudoephedrine	Cold medicines	X						Abuse: health damage
Red phosphorus	Matches, fireworks	X	X	X	X			Unstable, flammable
Sodium hydroxide	Drain cleaners, lye	X		X		X	X	Burns, skin ulcers
Sulfuric acid	Battery acid	X		X		X	X	Burns, thyroid damage
Toulene	Paint thinners, solvents	X	X	X	X		X	Fetal damage, pneumonia
Liquid lab waste	None	X	X	X	X	X	X	Unknown long-term effects

FIGURE 18.2

Toxic, explosive and hazardous chemicals found in clandestine drug labs.

Source: *Law Enforcement Technology*, May 2005, p.10. Courtesy of the Clandestine Drug Lab Program of the Division of Environmental Health in the Washington State Department of Health.

The various health and safety hazards encountered at a clandestine drug lab necessitate that only properly trained and equipped personnel proceed onto the site. A safety program developed by the DEA and the California Bureau of Narcotics Enforcement following recommendations by the Occupational Safety and Health Administration and the National Institute for Occupational Safety and Health has four basic elements: policies and procedures, equipment and protective clothing, training and medical monitoring.

Policies and procedures are aimed at ensuring officer safety through a certification process. Only certified individuals are allowed to seize, process and dispose of clandestine laboratories. Their procedure for conducting a raid has five stages: planning, entry, assessment, processing and exit.

During the planning stage, certified agents and chemists identify the chemicals that may be present and arrange for the proper safety equipment and protective clothing. Entry has the most potential for danger. The entry team faces the possibility of armed resistance by owners and operators, booby traps and exposure to hazardous chemicals. Still, the entry team wears the least protection because the gear limits mobility, dexterity, vision and voice communications.

Once entry has been successful, the assessment team—an agent and a chemist—enter the site to deal with immediate hazards, to ventilate the site and to segregate incompatible chemicals to halt reactions. Assessment team members wear fire-protective, chemical-resistant suits, gloves and boots. They also use self-contained breathing devices for respiratory protection. This team determines what safety equipment and clothing the processing team will need. The processing team then enters and identifies and collects evidence. They photograph and videotape the site and collect samples of the various chemicals. The final step involves removing and disposing of hazardous materials and decontaminating and posting the site.

Training involves 40 hours of classroom instruction followed by a 24-hour in-service training course at the

field level. Medical monitoring has two stages: medical screening of potential team members and annual monitoring to learn whether any team members have developed adverse health effects as a result of working with hazardous chemicals. Guidelines and training for clandestine drug laboratory investigations are available through the National Sheriffs' Association.

Clan labs pose a danger to officers and the public, as well as generating an enormous amount of waste, and can be very expensive to clean up.

Technology Innovations

Weiss (2007, pp.66–73) describes how autonomous robotics can enhance officers' safety in investigating a suspected meth lab and be an important force multiplier.

Imagine if "thinking" robots made the first entry into these hazardous surroundings [meth labs], while responding officers watched their activities from a safe distance away.

By using autonomous robots, law enforcement could gather intelligence in a stakeout and have the robots enter the area before sending in a SWAT team. . . .

As robots enter a lab's vicinity, they use sensor arrays to determine if any humans are present, and whether the individuals are armed or extremely agitated, and potentially dangerous. The robots also can determine whether chemical or dry cooking is taking place, and if poisonous gases are present in the air. The robots use efficient algorithms to search each room—having a plan for every type of contingency. In some situations they would be programmed to alert and acquire the assistance of officers. . . .

Arming autonomous robots with lethal or less-lethal weapons, allowing them to use force or be allowed to move at-will could help protect the officer.

Assessment team members investigating clandestine drug laboratories wear fire- and chemical-resistant suits, gloves, and boots and use self-contained breathing devices for protection. The team determines what safety equipment and clothing the processing team (who will identify and collect evidence) will need. Here, a member of the Southwest Virginia Clandestine Lab Team piles up methamphetamine-making ingredients and cooking devices on the lawn of a Damascus, Virginia, home.

© AP Images/Washington County Times, Rain Smith

Processing of Clandestine Drug Labs

Proper processing of a clandestine drug lab requires taking photographs with identifying labels, completing a thorough inventory, collecting evidentiary samples and preparing chemicals and equipment for disposal. The DEA stresses, "No material or apparatus are moved until the agent has inspected and inventoried each piece of evidence. The certified chemist or agent takes samples as needed for evidence. . . . Except for evidence, absolutely

TABLE 18.4 Information to Be Collected during Laboratory Processing—Drawings, Photographs, Inventory and Samples

- Drawing of clandestine drug laboratory site
- Photographs
  - Photograph everything in place
    - General overviews
    - Close-ups
    - Specific items during inventory
    - Evidentiary samples and original containers
    - Visible contamination
    - Photograph site after removal of bulk materials
- Inventory
  - Inventory all equipment and paraphernalia present in terms of quantity, size, manufacturer's serial number, condition and location
  - Inventory all chemicals present for type, concentration and quantity
  - Describe unknown or unlabeled materials in terms of phase (solid, liquid or gas), color, volume/mass and appearance
  - Describe the type, size, condition and labeling of all containers
    - Plastic, glass, metal
    - Five-gallon, 2-ounce, etc.
    - Punctured, rusty, leaking, corroded, damaged, uncapped, bulging
    - Label, markings, etc.
  - Identify the location of leaking or broken containers
    - Describe spilled solids or liquids, specifying odor, color, appearance, location, size of spill, etc.
  - Identify the leaking compressed-gas cylinders
  - Identify unstable container storage
  - Identify other concerns
- Samples
  - Take samples of appropriate items for evidence
  - One-ounce sample size is usually sufficient
  - Photograph samples and original containers with identifying labels
  - Maintain chain of custody

Source: *Drugs of Abuse, 2011 Edition: A DEA Resource Guide.* Washington, DC: Drug Enforcement Administration, 2011, p.24.

no waste, glassware or equipment should be moved from the site or retained by law enforcement personnel" (*Drugs of Abuse*, 2011, p.24). Table 18.4 lists information to collect and steps to take when processing a clandestine drug laboratory.

Cleanup of Clandestine Drug Labs

Estimates suggest that for every pound of meth produced, as much as five pounds of waste are created, including empty chemical containers, contaminated cooking equipment and other items that have become hazardous through exposure to the vapors produced during the drug manufacturing process. Such trash requires special handling and disposal, often at great expense. The Comprehensive Methamphetamine Control Act (MCA) of 1996 allows the courts to order a defendant convicted of manufacturing methamphetamine to pay the cost of cleanup of the lab site. Despite efforts to detect and shut them down, however, clan labs continue to proliferate.

INDOOR MARIJUANA GROWING OPERATIONS

Another type of clandestinely produced drug is sinsemilla, a potent form of marijuana cultivated indoors. One good indication of indoor marijuana growing operations is excessive use of electricity needed to run the lighting system, and a residence that pulls a great deal more electricity than the average home in a particular location may warrant a closer look. If such a residence is identified, police may observe the type and amount of traffic to and from the house and, based on the combination of information involving electricity use and traffic, obtain a search warrant. This approach has been used many times to break up large marijuana-growing operations.

Many grow operations steal electricity by diverting power from a main supply line. In addition to tampered-with electric meters and supply lines, other signs of an indoor grow operation include water lines or electrical cords running to a basement or outbuilding, an outbuilding with air conditioners, an unusual number of roof vents, excessive condensation around windows and unusual security measures.

Inherent dangers associated with the high-energy needs of these indoor grow operations include the risk of electrocution from exposing and tampering with high-wattage wires, explosion and fire risks because of the presence and prevalence of chemicals stored inside and upper respiratory infections caused by mold that thrives in these high-humidity environments.

INVESTIGATIVE AIDS

One tool to help federal, state and local law enforcement agencies investigate drug trafficking is the DEA's National Drug Pointer Index (NDPIX), a nationwide database that became operational across the United States in 1997. The NDPIX is intended to enhance agent and officer safety, eliminate duplication, increase information sharing and coordination and minimize costs by using existing technology and 24-hour access to information through an effective, secure law enforcement telecommunications system.

Some investigative aids are not so high-tech. For example, using dogs to detect drugs has been common for decades because their keen sense of smell enables them to detect minute traces of illicit drugs. Law enforcement agencies depend on their K-9s and handlers for many tasks essential to police work, with drug detection topping the list—90 percent of surveyed agencies reported they use dogs for this purpose ("Almost 50% of Agencies," 2008, p.14). For example, in one investigation, the Middlesex (Massachusetts) Sheriff's Department's K-9 unit seized 8,000 grams of cocaine, 2,000 grams of heroin, 80 pounds of marijuana and $2.5 million in drug-smeared cash (Redmond, 2008). The Supreme Court has ruled that a canine sniff in a public area or during a lawful traffic stop is not a Fourth Amendment "search." However, use of a narcotics-detection dog to sniff at the door of an apartment or a home has been ruled a search within the meaning of the Fourth Amendment and therefore requires a warrant.

Another assist for investigators is a special high-accuracy laser rangefinder developed for the U.S. Customs Service that can find secret compartments that might contain drugs. Investigators use the unit to measure the interior dimensions of cargo containers in their search for hidden compartments in which drugs may be smuggled. The small laser beam allows measurements of loaded containers in which physical access to the rear wall is limited. The handheld, battery-operated laser rangefinder measures distances from 6 to 85 feet with an accuracy of 1 inch.

Technology Innovations

Flying drones are being used by the U.S. Forest Service to battle pot growers operating in remote California woodlands. The pilotless, camera-equipped aircraft allows law enforcement to pinpoint marijuana fields and size up potential dangers before agents attempt arrests. The SkySeer drones are lighter than most other drones, less than five pounds, and can fly for only about an hour. The battery-powered SkySeer can fly at nearly 30 miles per hour, has a two-mile range and is operated by a two-person crew on the ground. More than 2.3 million marijuana plants were eradicated from Forest Service lands nationwide in 2007. In California's 18 national forests, an estimated 6 million plants have been removed since 2000 (Brown, 2008).

AGENCY COOPERATION

Investigating illegal drug activities requires the cooperation of all law enforcement agencies, including the exchange of suspect car lists and descriptions of sellers and buyers. Local police assist state and federal narcotics investigators by sharing their knowledge of drug users and sellers in their community. In addition, many narcotics officers exchange vehicles and personnel with other agencies to have less identifiable operators and equipment.

The federal government has mobilized an all-out attack on illegal drug activities. Before 1973, several federal agencies separately investigated illegal drug activities. In 1973 these agencies were merged into the DEA.

> The federal Drug Enforcement Administration (DEA) provides unified leadership in attacking narcotics trafficking and drug abuse. The DEA's emphasis is on the source and distribution of illicit drugs rather than on arresting abusers.

The DEA emphasis is on stopping the flow of drugs at their foreign sources, disrupting illicit domestic commerce at the highest levels of distribution and helping state and local police prevent the entry of illegal drugs into their communities. The DEA's Mobile Enforcement Team (MET), established in 1995, consists of more than 200 agents deployed across the nation to help fight the drug war. The National Drug Intelligence Center (NDIC) also plays a vital role in providing police administrators and officers with the latest information on drug distribution patterns.

U.S. agencies must cooperate with law enforcement in other countries because much of the U.S. domestic drug problem originates across national borders. To overcome interjurisdictional competition and minimize duplication of effort, multijurisdictional drug task forces have been implemented across the country. Sometimes task forces and programs are created because of a need to eliminate dissention, rather than from a desire to cooperate. One benefit of working with a task force is shared forfeiture revenues.

DRUG ASSET FORFEITURES

Asset forfeiture is a tool that allows agencies investigating various types of crimes, including drug trafficking, to seize items used in or acquired through committing that crime. The federal Comprehensive Crime Control Act of 1984 initiated procedures for asset forfeitures as a result of drug arrests. The U.S. Congress gave final approval to the Civil Asset Forfeiture Reform Act of 2000, which lowered the burden of proof from "clear and convincing" to "a preponderance of the evidence." The act also reduced the statute of limitations from 11 years to 5 years for a property owner to make a claim on the property.

Confiscating drug dealers' cash and property has been effective in reducing drug trafficking and is providing local, state and federal law enforcement agencies with assets they need for their fight against drugs. Asset forfeiture laws provide for the confiscation of cash and other property in possession of a drug dealer at the time of the arrest. Seized vehicles, boats or airplanes may be used directly by the agency or sold at auction to generate funds. Monetary assets may be used to purchase police equipment, to hire additional law enforcement personnel or to provide training in drug investigation.

Currency seizures pose special challenges to law enforcement because there is no law against possessing a large quantity of cash, and many currency seizures occur in the absence of narcotics, making it difficult to link the money to criminal activity. The investigator must establish the ownership of the currency (Was it inherited? Was it won at the track? What does the person do for a living?), the origin of the currency and the packaging and transportation methods used with the currency. An attempt to disguise or otherwise hide the currency suggests criminal involvement.

Precise recording of all proceedings is necessary to avoid allegations of abuse or misuse of these funds. Because of the required legal and judicial proceedings regarding these confiscations, often six months or more often pass after an arrest before the assets are available for police agency use.

A common defense to asset seizure is the *innocent owner defense*. If an owner can prove that he or she had no knowledge of the prohibited activity, the property is not subject to forfeiture.

The forfeiture program has not been without problems and misunderstandings. The confiscated funds may be used only for police department efforts to increase their fight against drugs. Police budgets cannot be reduced because of the availability of the asset-forfeiture funds.

PREVENTING PROBLEMS WITH ILLEGAL DRUGS: COMMUNITY PARTNERSHIPS

Tremendous national, state and local efforts are being directed to meeting the challenges of drug use and abuse in the United States. A national drug czar serves at the direction of the president, and many states appoint people to

similar positions to direct state and local efforts. Federal funding is available through state agencies. Federal, state and local agencies with roles in the drug war coordinate their efforts. Any successful effort to address drug-related crime and drug addiction must also necessarily involve partnerships with the community. Businesses, schools, public health departments and individual citizens are invaluable components of an effective response.

Thousands of volunteers, groups and agencies have joined the fight against illegal drugs. For example, Operation Weed and Seed is a national initiative for marshaling the resources of a number of federal agencies to strengthen law enforcement and revitalize communities. It is a comprehensive, coordinated approach to controlling drugs and crime in targeted high-crime neighborhoods. The Weed and Seed program links community policing and concentrated law enforcement efforts to identify, arrest and prosecute violent offenders, drug traffickers and other criminals (weeding) with human services such as after-school, weekend and summer youth activities; adult literacy classes; parental counseling; and neighborhood revitalization efforts to prevent and deter further crime (seeding).

But crime control is only one of several drug-control strategies that individual communities and the nation as a whole have available. Figure 18.3 depicts the multi-faceted drug-control strategies competing for funds and support.

Some communities are developing specific programs to address the drug problem and are recognizing the need for innovative approaches. For example, in jurisdictions facing high incidence of youths abusing OTC drugs, law enforcement can take steps to educate business owners and operators who sell these products about the risks involved. Clerks can be trained to recognize common signs of drug abuse and to understand why they should not sell a dozen packages of Coricidin Cough and Cold medicine to a group of teenagers. Some businesses may voluntarily move the drugs behind the counter, limit the number of packages a customer may purchase at one time or require customers to be over age 18. Law enforcement cannot force retailers to restrict OTC drugs. States have passed legislation banning OTC sales of certain products deemed threats to public safety.

A summary of the findings from all rigorous academic studies evaluating a range of street-level drug law enforcement interventions found that strategic crime-control partnerships with a range of third parties are more effective at disrupting drug problems than are law enforcement-only approaches (Mazerolle et al., 2007). Addressing the drug problem has been a priority for the past quarter century.

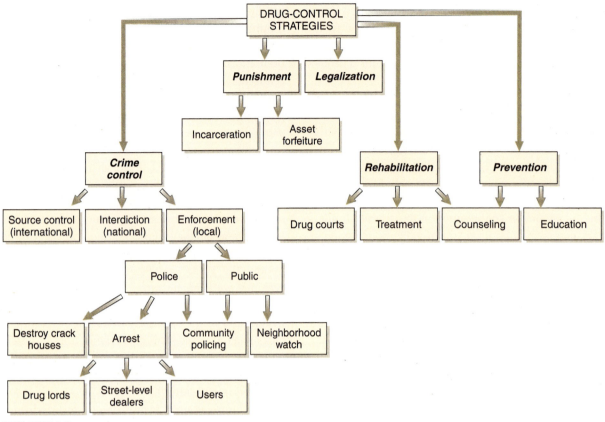

FIGURE 18.3
Overview of drug-control strategies.

Source: From HESS. *Introduction to Law Enforcement and Criminal Justice*, 9E. © 2009 Wadsworth, a part of Cengage Learning, Inc. Reproduced by permission www.cengage.com/permissions

THE NATIONAL DRUG CONTROL STRATEGY

In 1973 President Richard M. Nixon declared "war" on drugs. Since then, federal spending on this war against drug smugglers, users and sellers has increased 35-fold—from $420 million in 1973 to more than $15 billion in 2010 (*National Drug Control Strategy*, 2010). Drug arrests have nearly tripled since 1980, when the federal drug policy shifted to arresting and incarcerating users. In 2009 approximately 1.7 million state and local arrests were made for drug-related offenses, more than 50 percent of which involved the sale, distribution or possession of marijuana (*Crime in the United States, 2009*, 2010).

In the 2010 *National Drug Control Strategy*, the annual blueprint published by the Office of National Drug Control Policy (ONDCP), President Barack Obama pledged (p.iii), "While I remain steadfast in my commitment to continue our strong enforcement efforts, especially along the southwest border, I directed the Office of National Drug Control Policy to reengage in efforts to prevent drug use and addiction and to make treatment available for those who seek recovery This new, balanced approach

will expand efforts for the three critical ways that we can address the drug problem: prevention, treatment, and law enforcement."

The key to addressing our nation's drug problem is a three-pronged approach including prevention, treatment and law enforcement.

In addition to presenting a major challenge to law enforcement in itself, the illegal drug trade is an essential source of revenue for organized crime.

ORGANIZED CRIME: AN OVERVIEW

Organized crime is a global scourge, entangling communities around the world in its web of corruption and violence. Organized crime undermines legitimate commerce, manipulates stock markets, steals merchandise, distributes drugs, controls labor unions and enslaves innocent women and children. These criminal enterprises have developed an online presence, with organized crime groups actively and increasingly engaged in Internet fraud and identity theft. Bratton (2007, p.22) describes the evolution of organized crime:

> In the "old days," organized crime was exclusively synonymous with La Cosa Nostra, and organized-crime figures focused their energies on prostitution and gambling. Back then, violence was present but predictable, and narcotics trafficking was frowned upon as "bad business" because of the great risks and potential penalties involved. At some point between the old days and today, organized criminal groups entered the illicit drug-trafficking trade. Today, however, through advances in technology the illicit trade market has grown exponentially—not only geographically due to decreasing transportation costs, but also in terms of diversification, by making illicit trade possible in a wide range of goods, beyond drugs, that ever existed before. With the dismantling of Communism and the globalization of the world's economies as a result of technology and trade agreements between nations, a new and challenging concern for the world's law enforcement community has evolved. . . .

> Today, organized-crime entities have morphed from the traditional fixed hierarchies with controlling leaders or families to more decentralized, loosely linked, multiple networks that come together and cooperate only on an opportunistic basis and then separate. . . .

The FBI defines **organized crime** as any group having some manner of a formalized structure and whose primary objective is to obtain money through illegal activities. Organized crime groups achieve and retain their status through the use of actual or threatened violence, corruption of public officials and other coercive tactics. A **criminal enterprise**, by FBI definition, is a group of individuals with an identified hierarchy, or comparable structure, engaged in significant criminal activity. Although *organized crime* and *criminal enterprise* are often equated and used interchangeably, several federal statutes specifically delineate the elements of an *enterprise* that must be proven to convict individuals or groups under those statutes. For example, the Racketeering Influenced and Corrupt Organizations (RICO) Act, or Title 18 U.S.C. 1961(4), passed in 1970, defines an enterprise as "any individual, partnership, corporation, association, or other legal entity, and any union or group of individuals associated in fact although not a legal entity."

Albanese (2008, pp.263–264) provides a definition based on the consensus of a review of definitions of organized crime in the literature: "Organized crime is a continuing criminal enterprise that rationally works to profit from illegal activities that are often in great public demand. Its continuing existence is maintained through the use of force, threats, monopoly control, and/or the corruption of public officials."

Several characteristics distinguish organized crime from crimes committed by individuals or unorganized groups.

> **Distinctive characteristics of organized crime include**
> - Definite organization and control.
> - High-profit and continued-profit crimes.
> - Singular control through force and threats.
> - Protection through corruption.

Other characteristics not as frequently mentioned in definitions of organized crime include restricted membership, being nonideological, specialization and a code of secrecy.

The *organization* provides direct *control*, leadership and discipline. The leaders are isolated from the general operations through field or area leaders, who in turn control the everyday activities that bring in the profits. Organized crime deals primarily in *high-profit* crimes that are susceptible to organizational control and that can be developed into larger operations that provide the continued profit necessary for future existence.

Organized crime functions through many forms of corruption and intimidation to create a *singular control* over specific goods and services that ultimately results in a monopoly. Monopoly provides the opportunity to set higher prices and profits for that product or service.

Organized crime flourishes most where *protection* from interference and prosecution exist. The first line of immunity is the indifference of the general public and their knowing or unknowing use of the services or purchase of the goods offered by organized crime. Through such activities, citizens provide the financial power that gives organized crime immunity from legal authorities. Moreover, organized crime uses enforcement tactics to ensure compliance with its decrees. Members or paid enforcers intimidate, brutalize and even murder those who fail to obey the dictates of organized crime bosses.

In the early 1960s, Joseph Valachi became the first member of the Mafia to publicly acknowledge its existence when he testified before a Senate subcommittee about the nature of organized crime and dispelled many misconceptions about it. First, organized crime is not a single entity controlled by one superpower. Although a large share of organized crime is controlled by the Italian Mafia, other organizations throughout the United States have sprung up. As America has become more diverse, so too have the organized crime groups operating within it. Asian and Russian/Eurasian criminal groups, for example, have been spreading across the country in recent years.

Second, organized crime does not exist only in metropolitan areas. Although organized crime operates primarily in larger metropolitan areas, it has associate operations in many smaller cities, towns and rural areas.

Third, organized crime does not involve only activities such as narcotics, prostitution, racketeering and gambling. Rather, organized crime is involved in virtually every area where profits are to be made, including legitimate businesses.

Fourth, citizens are not isolated from organized crime. They are directly affected by it through increased prices of consumer goods controlled by behind-the-scenes activities of organized crime. In addition, citizens who buy items on the black market, solicit prostitutes, purchase pornography, bet through a bookie, take chances on punch boards or participate in other innocent betting operations directly contribute to the financial success of organized crime. Millions of citizens support organized crime by knowingly or unknowingly taking advantage of the goods and services it provides.

APPLICABLE LAWS AGAINST ORGANIZED CRIME

In addition to various state laws, two other distinct groups of laws seek to control organized crime: criminal laws that attack the criminal act itself and laws that make violations a criminal conspiracy. Charges have also been brought against some types of organized crime through prosecution under the Internal Revenue laws and initiation of civil lawsuits.

The major federal acts specifically directed against organized crime are the 1946 Hobbs Anti-Racketeering Act, the 1968 Omnibus Crime Control and Safe Streets Act, the RICO Act of 1970 and the Organized Crime Control Act of 1970. These acts make it permissible to use circumstantial rather than direct evidence to enforce conspiracy violations. These acts also prohibit the use of funds derived from illegal sources to enter into legitimate enterprises (commonly known as *laundering* money). Title 18 U.S. Code, Section 1962, defines three areas that can be prosecuted.

It is a prosecutable conspiracy to
- Acquire any enterprise with money obtained from illegal activity.
- Acquire, maintain or control any enterprise by illegal means.
- Use any enterprise to conduct illegal activity.

MAJOR ACTIVITIES OF ORGANIZED CRIME

Organized crime is involved in almost every legal and illegal activity that makes large sums of money with little risk.

Organized crime is heavily involved in the so-called victimless crimes of gambling, drugs, pornography and prostitution, as well as fraud, loan-sharking, money laundering and infiltration of legitimate businesses.

Federal crimes prosecutable under the RICO statute include bribery, sports bribery, counterfeiting, embezzlement of union funds, mail fraud, wire fraud, money laundering, obstruction of justice, murder for hire, drug trafficking, prostitution, sexual exploitation of children, alien smuggling, trafficking in counterfeit goods, theft from interstate shipment and interstate transportation of stolen property. State crimes chargeable under RICO include murder, kidnapping, gambling, arson, robbery, bribery, extortion and drug offenses. Thus, investigating organized crime effectively means investigating any of these other types of criminal activity in which the organization is involved.

Although the history of organized crime is filled with bloodshed, violence and corruption, organized crime bosses no longer wield power through a Thompson submachine gun. They manipulate the business economy to their benefit. Such crimes as labor racketeering, unwelcome infiltration of unions, fencing stolen property, gambling, loan-sharking, drug trafficking, employment of illegal aliens and white-collar crimes of all types can signal syndicate involvement.

Victimless Crimes

A **victimless crime** is an illegal activity in which all involved are willing participants. Among the crimes categorized as "victimless" are gambling, drug use, pornography and prostitution. Because there is no complainant, these crimes are difficult to investigate and to prosecute.

Arguments for legalizing so-called victimless crimes have been made periodically over the years but without success. Proponents argue that it is not the government's function to regulate morality, that the laws are ineffective as well as hypocritical and unenforceable. Further, the laws have created a whole class of "criminals" who would not otherwise be considered such. Perhaps most important, the laws create the conditions under which organized crime can thrive.

Opponents of legalizing these activities argue that it *is* the government's proper function to regulate morality and to protect individuals from themselves. As long as the activities are illegal, law enforcement is obligated to enforce the laws. Among the most difficult laws to enforce are those making gambling illegal *in some instances.*

Gambling is regarded by some as a vice, a sinful activity that corrupts society; others see gambling as simply a harmless form of entertainment. Within the gambling industry, the term *gambling* is being replaced with the term *gaming,* giving it the appearance of respectability. Legal "gaming" has greatly expanded throughout the country in the form of state lotteries, pari-mutuel betting on horses and greyhounds, bingo, slot machines and casinos. The Internet has hundreds of gambling-related sites, many of which have set up operations offshore. Some contend that when casino gambling comes to a city, robberies, check and credit card fraud, property crimes, domestic abuse and alcohol-related violations increase.

In addition to the problems associated with legal gambling, most reports on organized crime indicate that illegal gambling is the backbone of its activities and its largest source of income. **Bookmaking**—soliciting and accepting bets on any type of sporting event—is the most prevalent gambling operation. Furthermore, various forms of numbers/policy and other lottery games net substantial portions of the financial gain to organized crime from gambling.

Loan-Sharking

Loan-sharking—lending money at exorbitant interest rates—is supported initially by the profits from gambling operations. The upper hierarchy lends money to lower-echelon members of the organization, charging them 1 to 2 percent interest on large sums. These members in turn lend the money to customers at rates of 20 to 30 percent or more. The most likely customers are people who cannot obtain loans through legitimate sources, often to pay off illegal gambling debts.

Money Laundering and the Infiltration of Legitimate Business

In recent years, organized crime has become increasingly involved in legitimate business. The vast profits from illegal activities are given legitimacy by being invested in legal business. This is another way of turning dirty money into clean money, or "laundering" it. (Money laundering was discussed in depth in Chapter 14.) For example, a medium-sized company experiences a lack of business and is unable to get credit. Convinced that an infusion of capital will turn the business around, the president turns to a loan shark and borrows at an interest rate of 50 percent per week. Within months, organized crime has taken over the company. The crime boss keeps the president as a figurehead and uses his reputation to order goods worth thousands of dollars, never intending to pay for them. After a few months, the company files for bankruptcy.

Investigators must be aware that some criminal groups are more involved than others are in particular activities. Familiarity with a crime group's "specialties" or crimes of preference will greatly assist in investigations and will help identify the presence of new organized crime factions.

THE THREAT OF SPECIFIC ORGANIZED CRIME GROUPS

Whereas Italian crime syndicates such as La Cosa Nostra (LCN) may have predominated in the early days of organized crime in the United States, groups from other parts of the world are now cashing in on America's reputation as the "land of opportunity." The rise of Asian, Latino, African and Russian gangs requires the government to redesign the fight against organized crime. Nonetheless, Italian criminal groups persist as the stereotypical organized crime threat to American society and are indeed the most *organized* criminal presence in America.

Italian Organized Crime

Although most Americans lump all organized crime figures of Italian descent into one general group called *the Mafia,* Italian organized crime in the United States actually comprises four separate groups: the Sicilian Mafia; the Neapolitan Camorra; the 'Ndrangheta, or Calabrian Mafia; and Sacra Corona Unita, or "United Sacred Crown." These four groups have thousands of members and affiliates throughout the United States, but the largest percentage of them operate out of New

York, New Jersey and Philadelphia. Italian organized crime groups are heavily involved in drug trafficking and money laundering, as well as illegal gambling, political corruption, extortion, fraud, counterfeiting, weapons trafficking, infiltration of legitimate businesses, bombings, kidnappings and murders.

LCN is a nationwide alliance of criminals with both familial and conspiratorial connections. Although rooted in Italian organized crime, LCN is an Americanized version of the "old school" mafias from Italy, separate and distinct from the other Italian organized crime groups. LCN is, in fact, what most people are referring to when they speak of the Mafia. LCN is involved in many of the same activities as other Italian organized crime groups, as well as labor racketeering, prostitution, pornography, tax fraud schemes and stock manipulation schemes. One distinguishing feature of LCN, compared with all other criminal organizations in the United States, is how it has operated as a bridge between the upperworld and the underworld (Finckenauer, n.d., p.1).

The estimated membership of the LCN is 1,100 nationwide, with the vast majority (roughly 80 percent) operating in the New York metropolitan area. Finckenauer (n.d., p.1) explains, "Becoming a made member of LCN requires serving an apprenticeship and then being proposed by a Boss. This is followed by gaining approval for membership from all the other families. Once approved, there is a secret, ritualized induction ceremony. Made membership means both honor and increased income."

Five crime families make up New York City's LCN: the Bonanno, Colombo, Genovese, Gambino and Lucchese families. Beside the made members, roughly 10,000 associate members work for the families. Each family has roughly the same organizational structure. The boss controls the family and makes executive decisions. The underboss is second in command, and the consigliere serves as a senior adviser or counselor. Surrounding the boss are captains ("capos") who supervise crews of "soldiers." The soldiers and their associates carry out the actual crimes, the proceeds from which go to the capos and those of higher rank. LCN was originally grounded on standards of conduct borrowed from southern Italian tradition, particularly loyalty to the family. In the Mafia, however, this meant that loyalty to the crime family took precedence over loyalty to one's own blood family. This loyalty began to unravel with the 1992 testimony of an underboss, Salvatore "Sammy the Bull" Gravano, of the Gambino family, against his boss, John Gotti, which sent Gotti to prison for life and set the precedent for other turncoat mobsters to inform on their crime bosses in exchange for reduced prison sentences.

Asian Organized Crime

Asian organized crime groups, referred to as Asian criminal enterprises by the FBI, are involved in murder, kidnapping, extortion, prostitution, pornography, loan-sharking, gambling, money laundering, alien smuggling, trafficking in heroin and methamphetamine, counterfeiting of computer and clothing products and various protection schemes. Asian organized crime is often well run and hard to crack, using very fluid, mobile global networks of criminal associates. Asian criminal enterprises are classified as either traditional, such as the Yakuza and Triads, or nontraditional, such as ethnic Asian street gangs.

Japanese organized crime is sometimes known as Boryokudan but is more commonly known as the Yakuza. A gyangu (Japanese gangster) is a member of the Yakuza (organized crime family) and is affiliated with the Yamaguchi-gumi (Japan's largest organized crime family) as a boryokudan (used primarily for muscle). Triads are the oldest of the Chinese organized crime groups. The Triads engage in a wide range of criminal activities, including money laundering, drug trafficking, gambling, extortion, prostitution, loan-sharking, pornography, alien smuggling and numerous protection schemes.

Vietnamese organized crime is generally one of two kinds: roving or local. As the name suggests, roving bands travel from community to community, have a propensity for violence and have no permanent leaders or group loyalty. They lack language and job skills and have no family in the United States. Local groups, in contrast, tend to band together in a certain area of a specific community and have a charismatic leader. They also have a propensity for violence and tend to engage in extortion, illegal gambling and robbery.

Asian organized crime investigations present some unique challenges, primarily because of cultural and social differences. Many Asians are suspicious of the police and the U.S. criminal justice system. Asian criminals exploit this distrust by preying on other Asians, secure in the knowledge that their crimes will most likely go unreported. Another challenge is that many Asian groups are very mobile and have associates or family scattered throughout the United States.

Latino Organized Crime

Latino organized crime groups within the United States include Cubans, Colombians, Mexicans, Dominicans and El Salvadorians. These criminal enterprises are heavily involved in drug trafficking, typically bringing their criminal organization into this country along with the drugs they sell. For example, most of the world's cocaine market

Former Asian Boyz gang member Marvin Mercado, shown in court with his attorney, was sentenced in March 2011 to eight consecutive life prison terms without the possibility of parole for his role in eight Los Angeles-area killings. Along with the eight consecutive life terms without parole, additional time was added for other charges.

© AP Images/Nick Ut

is controlled by Colombian cartels. In the United States, cartel representatives serve as brokers to coordinate cocaine deliveries to various drug networks.

Because of Mexico's proximity to the United States, its organized crime groups are becoming an increasing threat to the United States and are among the fastest growing gangs in the country. Mexican drug trafficking has had an enormous impact on the United States, as organizations smuggle heroin, cocaine, marijuana and, most recently, meth. The Mexican Mafia is a prison-based gang that has been growing within the U.S. correctional system for nearly 50 years and is found in several state prison systems. The Mexican Mafia also has links to Hispanic street gangs and controls, to varying degrees, their drug trafficking activities.

African Organized Crime

African criminal enterprises, an emerging criminal threat facing law enforcement agencies worldwide and known to be operating in at least 80 other countries, have proliferated in the United States since the 1980s. Although some groups comprise members originating in Ghana, Liberia and Somalia, by far the predominant nationality in African organized crime is Nigerian. According to the FBI, Nigerian criminal enterprises in the United States are most prevalent in Atlanta; Baltimore; Washington, DC; Chicago; Milwaukee; Dallas; Houston; New York; and Newark, New Jersey. Financial frauds and advance

fee schemes, often perpetrated over the Internet, are common methods used by Nigerian organized crime groups. Known as "4-1-9 scams," after Section 4-1-9 of the Nigerian Penal Code relating to fraudulent schemes, these scams prey on victims' sympathy, naïveté and, often, greed, promising a handsome monetary reward in exchange for help making a financial transaction. Usually received via e-mail or fax, these frauds are often riddled with misspellings, improper grammar and other potential "tip-offs" that the correspondence is less than legitimate.

Russian Organized Crime

Russia has a 400-year history of dealing with organized crime groups, which for the most part kept their illegal activities inside the border. However, following the collapse of the Soviet Union, Russian organized crime has gone international and poses a great threat to and challenge for U.S. justice. The FBI refers to these groups as Eurasian Organized Crime (EOC). Former FBI director Louis Freeh has called the Russian Mafia the fastest-growing criminal organization in the United States.

Unlike members of organized crime groups originating from economically and educationally disadvantaged areas, EOC members tend to be well educated. EOC has had little to no involvement in some of the more traditional organized crime activities, such as drug trafficking, loan-sharking and gambling, choosing instead to focus on a wide range of frauds and scams, including insurance scams, securities and investment fraud and fuel oil scams. In the United States, EOC has become the primary purveyor of credit card scams. Contract murders, kidnappings and business arson are also common. In addition to transnational money laundering, Russian organized crime is known to traffic in women and children.

EOC members also traffic in such hazardous commodities as weapons and nuclear material smuggled out of their homeland. This removal of otherwise legal raw materials is a major concern to the Russian government because it deprives the country of export income and diminishes the global market value of these goods. The large-scale removal of funds or capital from a country is called **capital flight**. Do not confuse *money laundering* and *capital flight*, which are not interchangeable terms. Money laundering is capital flight, but not all capital flight is money laundering. Money laundering is illegal; capital flight is not.

U.S. money laundering laws recognize only three offenses committed outside the United States as predicate for a charge of money laundering: drug violations, terrorism and bank fraud. Any funds resulting from a theft from the Russian government, evasion of Russian taxes or bribes received by Russian officials can legally be processed through U.S. banks. Such activities do not qualify as money laundering.

Investigating Russian organized crime is challenged by several factors. First, the EOC consists of hundreds of groups, all acting independently. Russian crime groups in the United States are loosely structured, lacking any formal hierarchy. They tend to be fluid with membership fluctuating between 5 and 20 people, depending on the operation. Most members are already hardened criminals, have military experience and are highly educated. As with cases involving other immigrant organized crime groups, language barriers present a challenge to investigators. Another problem lies in the cooperation among and pooling of resources between Russian and other organized crime groups.

ORGANIZED CRIME AND CORRUPTION

One of the greatest threats posed by organized crime is the corruption it engenders throughout the entire legal system. Although the police are interested in any corruption by public officials, they are especially concerned about corruption in their own department. Bribes of police officers can take many forms: outright offers of money, taking care of medical bills or providing free merchandise or free vacations. Any police officer who is offered a bribe must report it immediately to a superior and then attempt to make an arrest that will involve the person making the offer as well as those responsible higher in the organization.

Some officials repay organized crime figures by providing inside information that can be used to manipulate securities or to purchase real estate in areas of future development that can be sold for a much higher price.

THE POLICE RESPONSE

It is frequently difficult for local law enforcement officers to understand their role in investigating or controlling organized crime. But there is a direct relationship between what officers do on assignment and investigation of organized crime activities. Local law enforcement officers are the first line of defense in controlling all crime, and

organized crime is no exception. Because of the highly structured nature of many organized crime groups, law enforcement officers can seldom break into these hierarchies, but they can remain the "eyes" and "ears" of the information and intelligence system essential to combat organized crime.

The daily observations of local law enforcement officers provide vital information for investigating organized crime. Report all suspicious activities and persons possibly associated with organized crime to the appropriate person or agency.

Because organized crime is involved in a great number of activities, information can arise from many sources. Thus, your street-level observations can be critical. Every day you observe many conditions related to crime and deal with individuals who are part of the community's activities. Seemingly unimportant details can fit into an overall picture that an intelligence unit is putting together (Figure 18.4).

Ways to become aware of people and conditions that suggest organized crime activity are provided by the International Association of Chiefs of Police:

A retail establishment seems to be doing a brisk business—many customers coming and going. But the customers do not remain in the store very long and do not leave with packages or other evidence that purchases were made. The store may have a meager selection of merchandise, which raises the question of how it can attract so many customers day after day. This could indicate the presence of a policy operation at the writer level or the place of business of a bookmaker's commission man.

At about the same time each day, a package is delivered to a newsstand, bar, or other location. Later the package is picked up by another individual. The location could be a policy drop—the place to which a policy writer sends his slips and/or day's receipts.

You are called to investigate a beating in a bar or at a location near a factory or other place of employment. The incident may occur on a payday or within a couple of days thereafter. The beating may have resulted from the impatience of a loan shark who has not been paid on schedule.

Merchants complain about another price rise by the cartage company that removes their garbage or trash. They also mention that there is either no competitor to deal with or if there is one, it will not

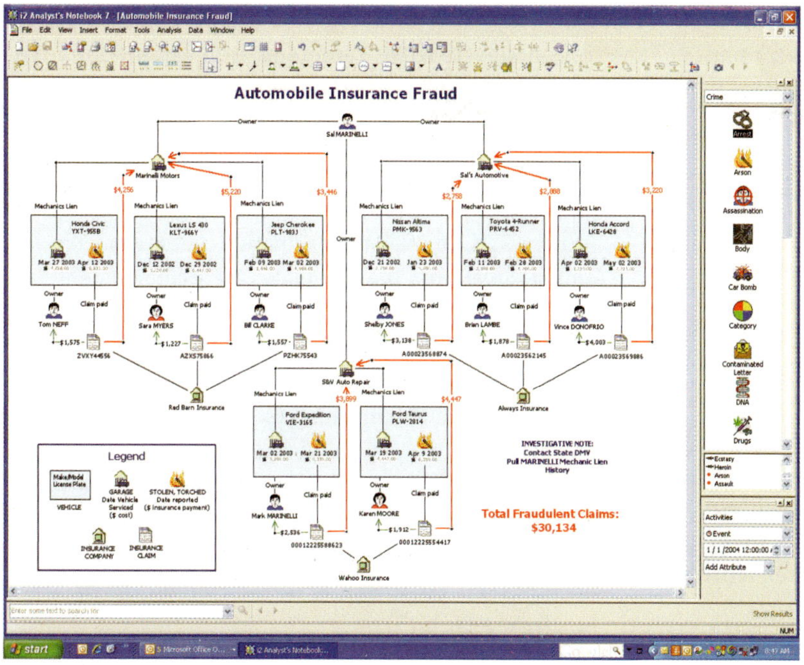

FIGURE 18.4

The progress and details of an organized crime investigation may make perfect sense to those who have spent months putting it together, but bringing others up to date can be challenging and time consuming. Analytical charts like this—made with i2 Analyst's Notebook—can quickly uncover key relationships, identify patterns/trends and focus on important leads and clues among suspects, witnesses, vehicles and events. This brings into focus individuals at the center of organized crime and fraud, allowing analysts and investigators to pinpoint the most significant areas of interest in an investigation and aid decision makers in targeting their resources.

© i2 Inc.

accept their business. Frequently, this indicates that an organized crime group is trying to monopolize the cartage business or limit competition through territorial agreements.

A rash of vandalism strikes a number of establishments engaged in the same type of business—such as dry cleaning. Racketeers may be trying to coerce reluctant owners into joining an association or into doing business with mob-controlled vendors. (Reprinted from *Criminal Intelligence,* Training Key #223, with permission of the International Association of Chiefs of Police)

Make a habit of checking out new businesses in your area. If the enterprise requires a license, such as a bar, ask to see the license if for no other reason than to observe who the owners are, ascertain the identity of the company that distributes or services the jukeboxes and so forth. If, for example, the jukebox or vending machine distributor is a company controlled by the organized underworld, so also might be the bar in which the equipment is located.

Report in writing all information pertaining to such activities, either immediately, if the activity involves an imminent meeting, or when time permits. Report as nearly as possible exact conversations with assault victims suspected of associating with organized crime members. These conversations can include names of people or organizations responsible for violence and crime in the community.

AGENCIES COOPERATING IN INVESTIGATING ORGANIZED CRIME

Under the authority of the 1968 Omnibus Crime Control and Safe Streets Act and the Organized Crime Control Act of 1970, the U.S. Justice Department established the Organized Crime and Racketeering Unit. Organized crime strike forces were formed throughout the country, mostly in major cities.

> Organized-crime strike forces coordinate all federal organized crime investigation activities and work closely with state, county and municipal law enforcement agencies.

Other agencies that play important roles in investigating organized crime are the FBI, which often has a member on the strike forces; the Postal Inspection Service, which is in charge of mail fraud, embezzlements and other crimes involving material distributed through the mails; the U.S. Secret Service, which investigates government checks and bonds as well as foreign securities; the Department of Labor, which investigates organized crime activities related to labor practices and pension funds; the Securities and Exchange Commission, which investigates organized crime activities in the purchase of securities; and the

Internal Revenue Service, which investigates violations of income tax laws. Other agencies committed to sustained cooperation in investigating organized crime include U.S. Immigration and Customs Enforcement (ICE); the DEA; the Bureau of Alcohol, Tobacco, Firearms and Explosives; the Bureau of Diplomatic Security; the Department of Labor/Office of the Inspector General; and components of the State Department, the Treasury Department and the intelligence community. In addition to these agencies, the state attorney general's office and the district attorney's office can assist police in building a case against organized crime figures who violate local and state laws.

Organized crime investigations in the United States increasingly involve agencies from other countries, as such criminal organizations rarely restrict their illegal activities to the jurisdiction of one nation. Thus, many current discussions of these criminal enterprises refer, instead, to international organized crime (IOC):

> In today's world of international crime fighting, the categories of 'domestic' or 'foreign' law enforcement cases are almost archaic. International organized criminals simply do not operate within the confines of national borders and geographic law enforcement jurisdictions. Yet, all too often our criminal laws and operational procedures do not sufficiently equip us to address the modern realities and needs of international crime fighting. United States law enforcement and our foreign counterparts are joined in a global offensive against organized crime. We must consider this problem in that broad context and amend relevant laws to enable us to effectively fight international organized crime domestically and in cooperation with our foreign partners. (*Overview of the Law Enforcement Strategy*, 2008, p.14)

METHODS TO COMBAT ORGANIZED CRIME

Because organized crime groups often have abundant resources and international connections to help protect their interests, law enforcement must deploy a wide variety of tactics to conquer the threat. Proactive community policing and problem-solving approaches hold much promise in combating organized crime. Intra-agency cooperation is also needed because most organized crime activities cross jurisdictions. Surveillance and undercover operations are also sometimes indicated.

One strategy that is essential to combating IOC is the formation of interagency analytical teams to systematically collect, synthesize and disseminate intelligence information on selected IOC targets as well as emerging IOC threats and trends:

> The ability of U.S. law enforcement to successfully investigate and prosecute targeted international organized crime figures or organizations will depend heavily on the quality of information that is available on the targets and the capability of law enforcement personnel to systematically collect, synthesize, and analyze that information. As international organized criminals cross borders to conduct their illicit operations, U.S. law enforcement must closely coordinate and communicate across agencies and jurisdictions to identify and exchange the best information available on IOC targets so that quick and decisive action can be taken against the targeted individuals or organizations. (*Overview of the Law Enforcement Strategy*, 2008, p.13)

Another resource for combating organized crime is the local citizenry. However, victims, witnesses and others with knowledge about organized crime activities are usually, and understandably, reluctant to come forth with information. Consequently, the government is often prepared to provide federal protection to those whose testimony is deemed crucial in building a case against organized crime.

The enterprise theory of investigation (ETI) is a combined organized crime and drug strategy the FBI uses to focus investigations and prosecutions on entire criminal enterprises rather than on individuals. ETI is a proactive approach to attack a criminal organization's structure and, when combined with appropriate federal and state laws, can enable law enforcement to effectively target and terminate a criminal enterprise with a single criminal indictment. ETI, as with other FBI initiatives, focuses on major regional, national and international crime groups that control large segments of organized crime's illegal activities.

Investigative Aids

Electronic surveillance of suspects is essential in investigating organized crime. Organized crime leaders often avoid direct involvement in criminal acts by planning and coordinating criminal activity over the phone or the Internet. Consequently, electronic surveillance can be used to build an effective case based on a criminal's own words while avoiding the risks associated with using informants or undercover agents.

Pen registers also are important in investigating sophisticated criminal networks. Pen registers record the

International arms dealer Viktor Bout arrives in New York, flanked by DEA agents, to stand trial on terrorism charges. Arrested in Bangkok in 2008 during a foreign sting operation, it took more than two years of legal proceedings to get Bout extradited to the United States. In November 2011 he was convicted of conspiring to kill American citizens, officers and employees by agreeing to sell weapons to drug enforcement informants whom he believed to be members of the Revolutionary Armed Forces of Colombia, a terrorist organization known as FARC. Bout was also found guilty of conspiring to acquire and export surface-to-air antiaircraft missiles and of conspiring to provide material support or resources in the form of weapons to a foreign terrorist organization.
Source: DEA Photo

numbers dialed from a telephone by monitoring the electrical impulses of the numbers dialed. In *Smith v. Maryland* (1979), the Supreme Court held that using a pen register does not constitute a search within the meaning of the Fourth Amendment, so neither probable cause nor a warrant is required to use the device. Several state courts, however, have held that using a pen register *is* a search under the respective state statutes and that a warrant supported by probable cause *is* needed. Investigators must be familiar with their state's statutes in this area. The same situation exists for trap-and-trace devices, which reveal the telephone number of the source of all *incoming* calls to a particular number. Their use may or may not require a warrant, depending on the specific state. Caller ID and phone numbers stored in speed dialers, fax machines and computer files can also be of assistance, as discussed in Chapter 17.

The Regional Information Sharing System (RISS), a multijurisdictional intelligence sharing system comprising nearly 5,000 local, state and federal agencies, is another tool to help investigators identify, target and remove criminal conspiracies and activities that reach across jurisdictional boundaries.

Asset Forfeiture

An effective weapon against organized crime, as with drug crimes, is the asset-forfeiture program, which allows law enforcement agencies to seize funds and property associated with criminal activity and effectively subjects

criminals to 100 percent tax on their earnings. Asset forfeiture was presented in detail earlier in the section on drug-related criminal investigations.

THE DECLINE OF ORGANIZED CRIME?

Certainly one hopes that tougher legislation, improved investigative techniques and increased use of tools such as asset forfeiture have brought about a decline in organized crime. Although perhaps these measures have forced a decline in the threat of *traditional* organized crime, the vacancies left by recent LCN associates and Gambino crime family members will easily be filled by any number of new criminal enterprises finding their way onto American soil.

Furthermore, in the wake of the September 11, 2001, terrorist attacks, many of the law enforcement resources previously allocated to organized crime investigations have been redirected toward counterterrorism efforts, allowing a resurgence in organized crime activity throughout the country.

It is sometimes difficult to determine whether criminal events are the work of organized crime or of gangs. Many defining characteristics of organized crime groups are strikingly similar to those of better-organized gangs, and prison gangs often have direct ties to organized crime groups. Gangs are the focus of Chapter 19.

Summary

In 1914, the federal government passed the Harrison Narcotics Act, which made the sale or use of certain drugs illegal. It is illegal to possess or use narcotics or other dangerous drugs without a prescription and to sell or distribute them without a license. Drugs can be classified as depressants, stimulants, narcotics, hallucinogens, cannabis or inhalants. The most commonly observed drugs on the street, in possession of users and seized in drug raids are cocaine, codeine, crack, heroin, marijuana, morphine and opium. Arrest for possession or use of marijuana is the most frequent drug arrest.

Physical evidence of possession or use of controlled substances includes the actual drugs, apparatus associated with their use, the suspect's appearance and behavior and urine and blood tests. The actual transfer of drugs from the seller to the buyer is the major legal evidence in prosecuting drug-sale cases. If you observe what appears to be a drug buy, you can make a warrantless arrest if you have probable cause. Often, however, it is better simply to observe and gather information. Undercover drug buys are carefully planned, witnessed and conducted so that no charge of entrapment can be made. Make two or more buys to avoid the charge of entrapment. Clandestine drug laboratories present physical, chemical and toxic hazards to law enforcement officers engaged in raids on the premises.

The federal Drug Enforcement Administration (DEA) provides unified leadership in attacking narcotics trafficking and drug abuse. The DEA's emphasis is on the source and distribution of illicit drugs rather than on arresting abusers. The key to reducing our nation's drug problem is a three-pronged approaching including prevention, treatment and law enforcement.

Distinctive characteristics of organized crime include definite organization and control, high-profit and continued-profit crimes, singular control through force and threats and protection through corruption. It is a prosecutable conspiracy to acquire any enterprise with money obtained from illegal activity; to acquire, maintain or control any enterprise by illegal means; or to use any enterprise to conduct illegal activity.

Organized crime is heavily involved in the so-called victimless crimes of gambling, drugs, pornography and prostitution, as well as fraud, loan-sharking, money laundering and infiltration of legitimate businesses. The daily observations of local law enforcement officers provide vital information for investigating organized crime. Report all suspicious activities and persons possibly associated with organized crime to the appropriate person or agency. Organized crime strike forces coordinate all federal organized crime activities and work closely with state, county and municipal law enforcement agencies.

Checklists

Drugs and Controlled Substances

- How did the complaint originate? From police? Victim? Informant? Neighbor?

- What is the specific nature of the complaint? Selling? Using? Possessing? Overdose? Are all required elements present?

- What type of narcotics are suspect?

- Is there enough evidence of sale to justify planning a buy?

- Were obtained drugs tested with a department drug-detection kit?

- Has the evidence been properly collected, identified and preserved?

- Has the evidence been sent to a laboratory for examination?

- Has the drug been determined to be a controlled substance?

- Has everyone involved been interviewed or interrogated?

- Do those involved have prior arrests for similar offenses?

- Is surveillance necessary to obtain evidence for an arrest or a search warrant?

- Is a raid called for? (If so, review the checklist for raids in Chapter 7.)

- Have cooperating agencies been alerted?

Organized Crime

- Have people recently moved into the city and purchased businesses that obviously could not support their standard of living?

- Do any public officials appear to live beyond their means?

- Does a public official continuously vote in favor of a business that is suspected of being connected with organized crime?

- Have business owners complained of pressure to use a specific service or of threats to close the business if they do not hire certain people?

- Does a business have high-level executives with police records?

- Have there been complaints of someone on the premises operating as a bookie?

- Have families complained about loss of wages paid to a loan shark?

- Have union officials suddenly been replaced by new, nonlocal persons?

- Has there been damage or injury to property during union problems?

- Are goods being received at a store that do not fit with merchandise sold there?

- Has a discount store suddenly appeared without a clear indication of true ownership?

- Has arson suddenly increased?

- Do non-employees hang around manufacturing plants or non-students hang around a school? (This could indicate a bookie operation or drug sales.)

- Is the same person using a pay telephone at the same time each day?

- Is evidence of betting operations being left in public wastebaskets or trash containers on the streets?

- When assaults occur, what are the motives? Could they be a result of gambling debts owed to a loan shark?

- Are people seen going into and out of certain businesses with which they are not ordinarily associated?

- Are known gamblers or persons with other criminal records repeatedly seen in a specific location?

Application

The Stakeout (adapted from an account of an actual narcotics investigation written by David Peterson): It is dark as the five men emerge from the plane. They haul out their luggage and walk to the parking lot of the tiny, one-strip airport. The pilot enters a white shack that is trimmed in red. When the pilot leaves, the others gather around a young man who has driven out to meet them. His name is Bruce Preece, and he looks like an outdoorsman. Bearded, he wears a suede hat and red plaid jacket.

Moments later, a camper occupied by two more men pulls into the parking lot, and most of the group pile into the back. Seated along foam-rubber benches, they are dim in the shadows as the camper moves through the empty town.

"That guy sure was an inquisitive one," the pilot remarks, referring to the man in the shack. "He knew we were here last week, and he wanted to know what we were up to."

"Tourists," someone else replies, his head silhouetted against a window. Everyone looks like a visitor—a hunter, perhaps, or a fisherman. They carry small bags and wear down jackets and jeans. The clothing is deceptive.

Four narcotics agents, or *narcs*, and four agents from the federal Drug Enforcement Administration are staked out in a camper outside the home of a man who works for a chemical firm. They suspect that at home he is manufacturing illegal drugs in a clandestine laboratory. The agents call him "No. 1."

They suspect that another man is getting illegal drugs and distributing them in nearby towns. They call him "No. 2."

No. 1 came under suspicion when a chemical supply company in Connecticut notified the feds that someone in this little town was ordering chemicals often used to make illegal substances. No. 2 came under suspicion when he told a local deputy sheriff he would be paid $2,000 if he notified him of any narcotics investigations.

The two men have been under surveillance for several weeks. One agent has even been inside the house by taking a shipment of chemicals from the Connecticut firm and making a "controlled delivery"—that is, he pretended to be the mailman and hauled the heavy boxes inside the house.

The agents have noticed a pattern. On Wednesdays, No. 1's wife goes into town and No. 2 stops by. It is Wednesday night. The plan is to watch No. 2 enter and leave the house and arrest him before he reaches his car. Assuming he is carrying illegal drugs, the agents will arrest No. 1 as well, search his home and seize the contents of the lab. Both men are known to be armed.

By 7 P.M., surveillance has begun in earnest. The eight agents are waiting for something to happen. Two agents sit in an unmarked car along the highway leading to the house. Two others are in the woods, within view of the house. The other four are in the camper, parked just off the highway. Even from inside, the camper looks normal. But its cabinets contain an array of radios, cameras, lenses, firearms and other gear. From the camper's bathroom, one agent takes out a telephoto lens the size of a small wastebasket and attaches it to a "night scope."

At about 7:15, the woman leaves.

Each of the three groups of agents has a radio. However, No. 1 is believed to have a police scanner, which would allow him to monitor their conversation. So they speak in a rough sort of code, as though they were squad cars checking for speeders. "401," for example, will mean that No. 2 has arrived.

Hours pass. None of the agents has eaten since noon. They pass around a bag of Halloween-sized Snickers bars and start telling narc stories.

At 10 P.M., a sober, low voice over the radio says, "You may have three visitors shortly." A few minutes later, three agents climb into the camper, shivering. One agent, who has been watching No. 1 through his kitchen window with binoculars, says, "He's busy in there. He's pouring stuff, and he's running something, like a tableting machine."

The agents know that if they could just bust into that house, they'd find a guilty man surrounded by evidence. No. 2 doesn't show. Another night wasted?

Questions

1. Do the agents have probable cause to conduct a raid at this time?
2. Could they seize the materials No. 1 is working with as plain-view evidence? Why or why not?
3. What aspects of the surveillance illustrate effective investigation?
4. Have the agents made any mistakes?
5. What should their next step be?
6. Is there likely to be a link between the suspects and organized crime? Why or why not?

Discussion Questions

1. How serious do you feel the drug problem is nationally? Statewide? Locally?
2. Would legalizing drugs be a feasible solution to the problem?
3. Why should alcohol abuse be considered an illness and drug abuse a crime?
4. What do you think law enforcement can do to reduce drug use and drug-related crimes?
5. What types of drugs have you been exposed to in your community? Is it difficult or easy to obtain these drugs?
6. Should the penalty for use of marijuana be reduced to a misdemeanor as it has been in some states? Should it be legalized, or should it remain a felony? In what amounts should the determination be made?
7. Most experts believe that organized crime can flourish only in areas where it has corrupted local officials. Do you agree?
8. What is your perception of the prevalence of organized crime in your community? Your state? The country?
9. Has organized crime become more or less of a problem for police in the past decade?
10. Have you participated in any victimless crimes—for example, gambling? Do you feel that victimless crimes should be legalized?

Media Explorations

Internet

Select one of the following assignments to complete.

■ Go to www.whitehousedrugpolicy.gov and outline the *President's Drug Policy* to share with the class.

■ Search for the key phrase *National Institute of Justice*. Click on "NCJRS" (National Criminal Justice Research Service). Click on "law enforcement." Click on "sort by Doc#." Search for one of the NCJ reference numbers from the list of References for this chapter. Outline the selection to share with the class.

■ Select one of the following key terms: *capital flight, gambling, loan-sharking, money laundering, organized crime, organized crime prevention, victimless crimes.* Find one article relevant to organized crime to outline and share with the class.

Gale Criminal Justice Database Assignments

The following assignments require access to Gale's custom Journal Database for Emergency Services and Criminal Justice. Check with your instructor if you have questions about this.

■ Find the article "Drug Detection Dogs Legal Considerations" on the Gale Emergency Services Database. Read the article and outline it for an in-class discussion.

■ Find the article "Part I: Pill Pushers on the 'Net; Taking on Online Prescription Drug Diversion" on the Gale Emergency Services Database. Read the article and write a one-page paper on why this is a growing problem.

■ Find the article "A Model for Success in the Drug War" on the Gale Emergency Services Database. Read the article and be prepared to discuss the suggested approaches in class. Be prepared to debate your position on whether you agree or disagree with this model, and why you agree or disagree.

References

Albanese, Jay S. "Risk Assessment in Organized Crime." *Journal of Contemporary Criminal Justice*, August 2008, pp.263–273.

"Almost 50% of Agencies Routinely Use K-9s." *Police*, March 2008, p.14.

Bratton, William F. "The Mutation of the Illicit Trade Market." *The Police Chief*, May 2007, pp.22–24.

Brown, Matthew. "Flying Drones to Battle Pot Growers." *Police One.com News*, April 4, 2008.

Crime in the United States, 2009. Washington, DC: Federal Bureau of Investigation, September 2010.

Criminal Intelligence. Training Key #223. Alexandria, VA: International Association of Chiefs of Police, no date.

Dees, Tim. "Field Narcotics Testing." *Law Officer Magazine*, June 2008, pp.74–79.

Drug Identification Bible. Grand Junction, CO: Amera-Chem, Inc., 2007.

Drugs of Abuse, 2011 Edition: A DEA Resource Guide. Washington, DC: Drug Enforcement Administration, 2011.

Finckenauer, James O. *La Cosa Nostra in the United States*. Washington, DC: National Institute of Justice, International Center, no date.

Hanson, Doug. "Clandestine Drug Labs Right in Your Backyard." *Law Enforcement Technology*, May 2005, pp.8–16.

Johnston, Lloyd D.; O'Malley, Patrick M.; Bachman, Jerald G.; and Schulenberg, John E. *Monitoring the Future—National Survey Results on Drug Use, 1975–2010: Volume I, Secondary School Students*. Ann Arbor: Institute for Social Research, The University of Michigan, 2011.

"K2 or Spice." Washington, DC: Drug Enforcement Administration, Drug Fact Sheets, 2011, pp.24–25. Accessed August 15, 2011. http://www.justice.gov/dea/pubs/1107_all_fact_sheets.pdf

"Ketamine." Washington, DC: Drug Enforcement Administration, Drug Fact Sheets, 2011, pp.26–27. Accessed August 15, 2011. http://www.justice.gov/dea/pubs/1107_all_fact_sheets.pdf

"Khat." Washington, DC: Drug Enforcement Administration, Drug Fact Sheets, 2011, p.28. Retrieved August 15, 2011. http://www.justice.gov/dea/pubs/1107_all_fact_sheets.pdf

Lieberman, Brian. "Ethical Issues in the Use of Confidential Informants for Narcotic Operations." *The Police Chief*, June 2007, pp.62–66.

Logue, Darin. "The Hidden Badge: The Undercover Narcotics Operation." *Law Enforcement Technology*, February 2008, pp.94–100.

Mazerolle, Lorraine; Soole, David W.; and Rombouts, Sacha. *Crime Prevention Research Reviews No. 1: Disrupting Street-Level Drug Markets*. Washington, DC: Office of Community Oriented Policing Services, July 22, 2007.

National Drug Control Strategy—2010. Washington, DC: The White House, 2010.

National Drug Threat Assessment 2010. Washington, DC: National Drug Intelligence Center, October 2010.

Overview of the Law Enforcement Strategy to Combat International Organized Crime. Washington, DC: U.S. Department of Justice, April 2008.

Physicians' Desk Reference 2008, 62nd ed. Montvale, NJ: Thomson PDR, 2007.

Redmond, Lisa. "'Sophisticated' K-9 Units Help Mass. Cops." *The Lowell Sun*, June 23, 2008.

Weiss, Joseph. "Autonomous Robotics for Law Enforcement." *Law Enforcement Technology*, February 2007, pp.66–73.

Wethal, Tabatha. "Idle Hands." *Law Enforcement Technology*, July 2008, pp.86–94.

Case Cited

Smith v. Maryland, 442 U.S. 735 (1979)

CHAPTER 19
Criminal Activities of Gangs and Other Dangerous Groups

Outline

Can You Define?

Antichrist
Beelzebub
bias crime
Black Mass
coven
cult
flash mob
gang
graffiti
Hand of Glory
hate crime
hate incidents
incantation
magick
moniker
occult
ritual
ritualistic crime
sabbat
street gang
turf

Do You Know?

- Whether the gang problem is increasing or decreasing?
- How gangs may be classified?
- What types of crimes gangs typically engage in?
- What the first step in dealing with a gang problem is?
- How to identify gang members?
- What kinds of records to keep on gangs?
- What special challenges are involved in investigating illegal activities of gangs?
- What strategies have been used to combat a gang problem?
- What two defense strategies are commonly used by gang members' lawyers in court?
- What the primary motivation for bias or hate crimes is and who is most frequently targeted?
- What a cult is? How better to refer to cults?
- What a ritualistic crime is?
- What may be involved in ritualistic crime?
- What are indicators of ritualistic crimes?
- What special challenges are involved in investigating ritualistic crimes?

In Minneapolis, a 12-year-old boy and an 18-year-old man, both with ties to a local gang, are shot to death while sitting in a car parked behind an apartment building, allegedly by a reputed member of a rival gang. In Denver, a 16-year-old girl tries to break free from gang life and is stabbed to death a month later by a rival gang member.

In Jasper, Texas, a Black man is chained by his ankles to a pickup truck and dragged to his death, his head and arm ripped from his body during the incident. In Laramie, Wyoming, a gay college student is beaten, tied to a fence and left to die alone.

On a lonely rural road in Wisconsin, a pharmacist who was a member of a voodoo cult arranges to have himself shot and killed by two friends, also cult members. In Rancho Santa Fe, California, 39 members of a high-tech cult pack their bags and commit mass suicide, believing that in death they will rendezvous with a UFO that was trailing the Hale-Bopp comet. In Tavares, Florida, members of a teenage "vampire clan" use cigarettes to burn a "V" onto the body of a man they had just bludgeoned to death.

These are actual events that have occurred across the country and reflect the everyday reality of gangs, hate crime and ritualistic crime in the United States.

THE THREAT OF GANGS: AN OVERVIEW

Gangs have been of interest and concern for centuries. Street gangs have existed in the United States for most of the country's history and have been studied since the 1920s. The 1900s saw street gangs flourishing, influenced by such mobsters as Al Capone. And gangs continue to pose a problem for law enforcement in the 21st century.

Belonging to a gang is *not* illegal in this country; however, many activities that gangs engage in are illegal. Gangs traffic in drugs; commit shootings, assaults, robbery, extortion and other felonies; and terrorize neighborhoods. Previously loose-knit groups of juveniles and young adults who engaged in petty crimes have, over time, become powerful, organized gangs, representing a form of domestic terrorism. Gang wars, drive-by shootings and disregard for innocent bystanders have a chilling effect. Gangs now exist in almost every community.

To investigate gang-related crimes effectively, law enforcement personnel must understand the makeup of these organizations, what types of crimes to expect, how to identify their members and how to deal with the special challenges of investigating such crimes.

GANGS DEFINED

Although most people are easily able to form an image in their mind when they think of a gang, defining a gang is a bit more difficult, and no single, agreed-upon definition exists. Actually, "One of the greatest impediments to the collection of accurate gang-related data is the lack of a national, uniform definition of a gang used by all federal, state, and local law enforcement agencies" (*National Youth Gang Assessment*, 2009, p.3). Some definitions emphasize criminal activity whereas others stress territoriality. One commonly accepted definition is that a *gang* is a group of individuals with a recognized name and symbol that forms an allegiance for a common purpose and to engage in continuous unlawful activity. The National Alliance of Gang Investigators' Associations (NAGIA) defines a **gang** as "a group or association of three or more persons with a common identifying sign, symbol, or name who individually or collectively engage in criminal activity that creates an atmosphere of fear and intimidation" (*National Youth Gang Assessment*, 2009, p.3). The current federal law (18 U.S.C. § 521 (a)) defines a gang as "an ongoing group, club, organization, or association of five or more persons: (A) that has as one of its primary purposes the commission of one or more of the criminal offenses described in subsection (c); (B) the members of which engage, or have engaged within the past five years, in a continuing series of offenses described in subsection (c); and (C) the activities of which affect interstate or foreign commerce" (*Brief Review of Federal and State Definitions*, 2009, p.1).

Gang investigators must be aware, however, that many states have legislatively enacted their own definitions of a *gang* that all local and state law enforcement agencies are mandated to follow. A state-by-state list of criteria used to define gangs and gang members may be found online at the National Gang Center's government Web site.

EXTENT OF GANGS

The last quarter of the 20th century saw significant growth in gang problems across the country. In the 1970s, less than half the states reported youth gang problems, but by the late 1990s, every state and the District of Columbia reported gang activity. During that same period, the number of cities reporting youth gang problems mushroomed nearly tenfold.

Gangs range in size from small groups of three to five to as many as several thousand. Nationally known gangs such as the Crips number around 50,000 and the Bloods number about 20,000 to 30,000. Large gangs are normally broken down into smaller groups but are known collectively under one name. More than 90 percent of gangs have between 3 and 100 members, and only 4 percent have more than 100 members. The number of gangs in large cities ranges from 1,200 to 1,500.

Different sources vary in their estimates of the number of gangs and gang members currently active within the United States. The *2009 National Gang Threat Assessment*, published by the National Gang Intelligence Center, reports that at year-end 2008, an estimated 1 million gang members and more than 20,000 gangs were criminally active in the United States. According to the *National Youth Gang Survey* (NYGS), published by the Office of Juvenile Justice and Delinquency Prevention (OJJDP), an estimated 731,000 gang members belonging to 28,100 gangs were in existence across the nation during 2009 (Egley and Howell, 2011). One explanation for the discrepancy could be the inconsistency in how various jurisdictions define a gang. Regardless of which data set one looks at, however, it is clear that gangs and gang-related crime are a serious threat to communities throughout the country.

Analysis of past estimates reveals three general trends in the national extent of gangs and gang activity: "a sharp decline throughout the late 1990s, a sudden upturn beginning in 2001 and continuing until 2005, and a relative leveling off thereafter" (Egley and Howell, 2011, p.1).

> The number of gangs and gang members has remained relatively stable over the last few years, but gang-related crime is still a serious concern for law enforcement.

Gang violence has become increasingly lethal, as gang members have evolved from carrying knives and chains to wielding handguns and, for some of the hardcore gang members, high-powered semi-automatic and fully automatic weapons (Eggers, 2009). Another reason gangs pose such a serious threat to communities is that gang violence is increasingly likely to touch non-gang-involved citizens: "In previous generations, if there was violence, it was primarily directed at other gang members or targeted victims. Certainly, there were times when innocent bystanders got hurt, but there wasn't the

random violence that's seen on the streets today. Today's gang members will shoot into a crowd with wanton disregard for life, as if they're playing a video game" (Eggers, 2009, p.17).

According to the NYGS, the three factors, as reported by law enforcement, that most influence local gang violence are drug-related factors (73 percent of respondents identified this factor as one influencing gang violence), intergang conflict (61 percent) and a return of gang members to society from secure confinement, such as prison (50 percent) (Egley and Howell, 2011). Factors that were reported less frequently as contributing to gang violence were gang-member migration within the United States (42 percent), emergence of new gangs (36 percent), intragang conflict (32 percent) and gang-member migration from outside the United States (23 percent).

The gang problem is not restricted to metropolitan areas. As society in general has become more mobile, gangs and gang members have also increased their mobility, contributing to gang migration: "Like a cancer, gangs are spreading to communities across America. Gang violence has become a part of the daily lives of teachers and taxi drivers, police officers and pastors, parents and children" (Pistole, 2008). Whereas early gangs tended to exist primarily in large cities near the country's borders (Los Angeles, New York, Miami, Chicago), gangs are now sending members across the country and into the nation's heartland to take advantage of new territory, diminished competition from other gangs and law enforcement agencies with less experience in dealing with gang activity: "Gang migration from larger cities to suburban and rural areas is an ongoing concern for law enforcement.…the percentage of law enforcement agencies in the United States reporting gang activity in their jurisdictions increased from 45 percent in 2004 to 58 percent in 2008" (*National Gang Threat Assessment*, 2009, p.5).

WHY PEOPLE JOIN GANGS

Gangs provide protection to youth from violent peers. Gangs offer a sense of acceptance, belonging and importance to their members that society and family may not provide. Gang membership may be seen as a way to obtain money, power and drugs. And some people join gangs because they come from a gang-involved family and it is simply what they are expected to do. Recent research has revealed three common themes regarding why males and females join gangs:

■ Neighborhood disadvantage

■ Having gang-involved family and friends

■ Parent-child relationship problems, such as neglect, lack of supervision and substance abuse and addiction (Bell, 2009).

A lack of parental attachment is an important risk factor in adolescent gang membership, with the results of several studies suggesting that "adolescents, particularly females, join gangs to find 'familial' and emotionally fulfilling relationships that they do not find in other areas of their lives" (Bell, 2009, p.380).

TYPES OF GANGS

Gangs can be differentiated in many ways, such as by age (e.g., youth gangs), race or ethnicity (e.g., Hispanic gangs, Native American gangs), gender composition (e.g., female gangs), setting (e.g., street or prison gangs), type of activity (e.g., drug gangs) and so on. The *National Gang Threat Assessment* (2009, p.6) reports: "Gangs vary extensively regarding membership, structure, age, and ethnicity. However, three basic types of gangs have been identified by gang investigators: street gangs, prison gangs, and outlaw motorcycle gangs (OMGs)."

> The National Gang Intelligence Center has identified three general types of gangs: street gangs, prison gangs and outlaw motorcycle gangs (OMGs).

Street Gangs

A broadly applicable definition of street gangs has evolved from several years' worth of intense discussions among working groups of American and European gang researchers in an assembly that has come to be known as the *Eurogang program*. The Eurogang consensus nominal definition of a **street gang** is "any durable, street-oriented youth group whose own identity includes involvement in illegal activity" (Klein, 2007, p.18). In identifying five general types of street gangs, Klein (2007, pp.54–55) notes,

> There is no *one* form of street gang. Gangs can be large or small, long term or short term, more or less territorial, more or less criminally involved, and so on. If one treats all gangs as being the same, then the treatment will often be wrong, perhaps even making things worse....It is the fact of gang diversity itself that should make us cautious about generalizing too quickly about their nature.
>
> We have shown "traditional" and "nontraditional" gangs to be the largest, longest-enduring, and most

crime-producing gangs. They are not the most common form, but they best fit the media stereotype of large inner-city gangs with strong intergang rivalries and violent tendencies.

"Compressed" gangs, primarily adolescent groups of 50 to 100 members and less then ten years' duration, are the most common, found in both large and small cities. Least common are "collective" gangs, rather amorphous, but large collections with little internal structure, sometimes held together by loose neighborhood ties and extensive drug dealing. The smallest in size of our five types, but the most tightly structured, is the "specialty" gang, which is not versatile like the other four types, but rather manifests a narrow pattern of criminal behavior. Drug gangs, robbery or burglary gangs, car theft gangs and skinheads are common examples.

Within the street gang category, groups are classified as national-level, regional-level and local- or neighborhood-level (*National Gang Threat Assessment*, 2009, pp.6–7):

■ *National-level street gangs* are highly organized and typically have several hundred to several thousand members nationwide who operate in multiple regions. These gangs may have cells in foreign countries with members who assist the U.S.-based gangs, further developing associations with drug trafficking organizations (DTOs) and other criminal organizations in those countries. Currently, 11 national-level street gangs have been identified in the United States.

■ *Regional-level street gangs* are typically organized with several hundred to several thousand members. Regional-level street gangs may have some members in foreign countries and maintain ties to DTOs and other criminal groups operating in the United States. These gangs increasingly distribute drugs at the wholesale level. At least five street gangs (Florencia 13, Fresno Bulldogs, Latin Disciples, Tango Blast and United Blood Nation) have been identified as operating at a regional level.

■ *Local- or neighborhood-level street gangs* mostly operate in a single location and usually range in membership from three to several hundred members. Most of these gangs engage in violence in conjunction with a variety of crimes, including retail-level drug distribution. These neighborhood-based groups pose a considerable challenge to local law enforcement and are a concern for federal law enforcement. Law enforcement officials in communities along the U.S.–Mexico border have noted an increase in the number of local gang members establishing dual membership with their counterpart gangs in Mexico.

Street gangs are very often organized by ethnicity. Among the most well-known ethnic street gangs are African American gangs (Bloods, Crips, Vice Lords), Hispanic gangs (Latin Kings and Mara Salvatrucha 13 [MS-13]), Asian gangs (Chinese, Filipino, Vietnamese, Hmong) and Indian Country gangs.

The literature on ethnic gangs is abundant, and Howell and Moore's *History of Street Gangs in the United States* (2010) is an informative read for those seeking a more comprehensive understanding of how various gangs evolved throughout our country.

A new breed of increasingly violent street gangs appearing throughout the country is hybrid gangs, in which several small groups, some of them rivals, band together into one larger gang (Ortega and Calderoni, 2007). Members of hybrid gangs are generally young and particularly profit driven. They thrive in areas with relatively new gang problems and often include gangbangers who have migrated from larger cities. These gangs represent a "sea of change in gang culture" and bear little resemblance to traditional gangs. Unlike older gangs based on race or neighborhood loyalty, this new generation is singularly focused on making money from drugs, robbery and prostitution.

Prison Gangs

Although prison gangs would seem to be more of a problem for corrections, the reality is that most incarcerated gang members will one day be released to the streets. In fact, "many of the most notorious and violent street gangs we now see across the nation had their beginnings in our nation's prisons and jails" (Dawe, 2009, p.16). According to the most recently available data, 11.7 percent of federal inmates, 13.4 percent of state inmates and 15.6 percent of county inmates belong to gangs (*2005 National Gang Threat Assessment*). Examining why gangs seem to thrive in prisons, Fine (2009, p.17) asserts: "Membership is often the only way for young offenders to survive in an atmosphere where life is ruled by sheer physical power. . . . In some cases, gang activity is tacitly encouraged [by prison officials] since it makes inmates easier to handle and a certain order rules the prison population."

Iron bars and razor-wire-topped walls cannot contain the impact prison gangs can have on free society:

> Prison gangs pose a serious domestic threat, particularly national-level prison gangs that affiliate with Mexican DTOs and maintain substantial influence over street gangs in the communities in which they operate. Prison gangs are highly structured criminal networks that operate within the federal and state prison system. Furthermore, these gangs operate in local communities through members who have been

released from prison. Released members typically return to their home communities and resume their former street gang affiliations, acting as representatives of their prison gang to recruit street gang members who perform criminal acts on behalf of the prison gang.

> Prison gangs often control drug distribution within correctional facilities and heavily influence street-level distribution in some communities. (*National Gang Threat Assessment*, 2009, p.7)

Outlaw Motorcycle Gangs

The major OMGs are the Hell's Angels, Bandidos, Outlaws, Mongols and Pagans. "OMG-related criminal activity poses a threat to public safety in local communities in which these gangs operate because of their wide-ranging criminal activity, propensity to use violence, and ability to counter law enforcement efforts" (*National Gang Threat Assessment*, 2009, p.8). These gangs' primary source of income is drug trafficking, but they are also involved in murder, assault, kidnapping, prostitution, money laundering, weapons trafficking, intimidation, extortion, arson and smuggling. At midyear 2008, law enforcement intelligence estimated there were more than 20,000 validated OMGs members belonging to as many as 520 OMGs (*National Gang Threat Assessment*, 2009).

Female Gang Involvement

Although gangs are still primarily male-dominated, female gang membership is increasing and, as females grow more independent from their male counterparts, females are assuming greater responsibility in gang activities (*National Gang Threat Assessment*, 2009). Although they do exist, all-female gangs are rare and are not often the focus of the criminal justice system: "Traditionally, female gangs have received less attention from researchers and law enforcement, and most efforts have focused on intervention programs designed to provide an alternative refuge for girls attempting to escape abusive environments. Furthermore, law enforcement officials are less likely to recognize or stop female gang members, and they have experienced difficulty in identifying female involvement in gang-related activity" (*National Gang Threat Assessment*, 2009, p.12).

The National Youth Gang Center reports that, during its most recent survey, a large percentage of law enforcement agencies were unable to provide quantitative data regarding female gang membership, which suggests that the issue of girls in gangs is "of lesser significance for law enforcement" (*National Youth Gang Survey Analysis*, 2009). Of those law enforcement agencies that did provide

Members from the Culver City Boyz gang flash their signs at North Hollywood Park in Hollywood, California.
© A. Ramey/PhotoEdit

data to the survey, proportionately few reported that the gangs active in their jurisdiction had no female members, while approximately 15 percent of larger cities, 18 percent of smaller cities, 13 percent of suburban counties and 12 percent of rural counties reported that at least half of the gangs in their jurisdictions included female members. Data from the NYGS also shows that the gender proportion of gang members nationally has changed very little from 1998 to 2007, with the ratio of male to female gang members being a fairly consistent 93:7.

Gang Members in the Military

Military bases are not immune to the influence of gangs: "Members of nearly every major street gang as well as some prison gangs and OMGs have been identified on both domestic and international military installations. Deployments . . . and military transfers have resulted in gang members, both service members and dependents/relatives, moving to new areas and establishing a gang presence" (*National Gang Threat Assessment*, 2009, p.10). The specialized military skills these gang members possess, such as those involving weapons, tactics and attack planning, pose a unique threat to law enforcement personnel.

GANG CULTURE, MEMBERSHIP AND ORGANIZATION

Some gang experts talk about the three Rs of the gang culture: reputation, respect and revenge. Reputation is of prime concern to gang members, both individually and collectively. They expect, indeed demand, respect. And

they are required to show disrespect for rival gang members, called a "diss" in gang slang. Disrespect inevitably leads to the third R—revenge. Every challenge must be answered, often in the form of a drive-by shooting.

Most gangs are of limited numbers sufficient for the entire group to meet and discuss things in person. Incidents that happen to them or that are expressly initiated by them cause them to identify as a group. Sometimes gang members are multigenerational—that is, father and son may have been members of the same gang. Most gang members are unemployed or work at part-time jobs. Many are most active at night and sleep during the day. Some stay with their gangs into adulthood, and others may go back to school or gain full-time employment, usually in jobs with very low pay.

Most gang members are weak academically because they lack good study habits, although they are mentally capable. This is an important factor because gangs are essentially self-operated and self-governed. Some operate by consensus, but most have leaders and a subgoverning structure. Leadership may be single or dual. Status is generally obtained by joining the gang, but equal status within the gang once joined is not automatically guaranteed.

Gang members have differing levels of commitment and involvement in gang activities. Most gang members are either hard-core, associate or peripheral members. The hard-core members are those most dedicated to the gang. Knowing how a gang is organized and what level of involvement a member has can be of great assistance to investigators. The hard-core member is least likely to cooperate with the police; the peripheral members are most likely to be cooperative.

A gang's degree of organization influences the behavior observed among its members, with even low levels of organization having important implications regarding criminality: "Indeed, even incremental increases in gang organization are related to increased involvement in offending and victimization" (Decker et al., 2008, p.153).

Symbols

Gang *symbols* are common. Clothing, hand signals, graffiti and tattoos are all used as symbolic representations of a person's affiliation with a specific gang. Clothing can distinguish a particular gang. Sometimes "colors" are used to distinguish a gang, and the most well-known symbol of street gangs in the United States is a displayed colored rag or bandana. Gang members also use jerseys, T-shirts and jackets with emblems, athletic team logos or designer crests. However, some gangs, such as Asian gangs, don't have a particular dress code, making identification difficult. Another form of symbolic communication typical of gang members is hand signals. Certain signs are flashed to indicate membership in a specific gang. Symbols are often displayed in graffiti to mark a gang's turf.

Turf and Graffiti

Many gangs establish a **turf**, the *geographic* area of domination that gang members will defend to the death. The turf includes the schools, businesses, residential areas, streets and alleys in the area, all controlled through fear, intimidation and violence. In the past, turf wars took the form of gang fights. Today, however, they often take the form of drive-by shootings from a moving vehicle, many of which have killed innocent citizens as well as rival gang members.

Gangs identify their turf through **graffiti**. Other gangs may challenge the turf claim by writing over or crossing out the graffiti and replacing it with their own. Such cross-outs are usually found at the edge of a gang's territory and are a sign of intentional disrespect, meant to elicit a response from a gang's rivals. Gang members caught in the act of crossing out graffiti in a rival's territory may be killed, or a turf war can result. Gang graffiti is a source of frustration and expense to property owners and local governments.

In Wilson and Kelling's classic Broken Windows crime model, graffiti is a foothold crime leading to a neighborhood's decay: "Neighborhoods plagued with graffiti often become breeding grounds for loitering, littering, loud music, and public urination. . . . As 'good' citizens begin to avoid 'that side of town,' the criminal element becomes more comfortable and these small public disorder crimes snowball into more serious criminal behaviors. When these more serious crimes flourish, it becomes difficult to assess the true cost of the graffiti offense: expenses mount in terms of prevention, arrests, incarceration, and lost revenue" (Petrocelli, 2008, p.18).

Police officers who deal with gangs can learn much by understanding wall graffiti. The center of a gang's turf will have the most graffiti. It may name members of the gang, often in order of authority, listed in neat rows under the gang's logo. Reading graffiti is discussed later in the chapter. Unchallenged graffiti affirms the gang's control. With the increasing mobility of society, graffiti no longer has to necessarily remain within a gang's turf.

Hispanic graffiti is highly artistic and very detailed. It frequently refers to group or gang power. In contrast, graffiti of Black gangs shows less flair and attention to detail and often is filled with profanity as well as expressions of individual power. The symbolism is more obvious and often includes weapons. Investigators should be aware that some urban artists unaffiliated with gangs have begun replicating graffiti as one type of artistic expression; mistakenly identifying such "art" as gang-affiliated graffiti

can complicate or obstruct a jurisdiction's efforts to get a handle on its gang crime. Figure 19.1 shows some typical symbols used by various gangs in their graffiti.

Tattoos

Tattoos are also used by some gangs, particularly OMGs and Hispanic gangs. Gang tattoos are meant to intimidate, show gang affiliation and indicate rank, and they are a gang member's permanent record, telling who he is, what he believes, what he's done, where he's been, where he did time and for how many years and how many people he's killed. An officer trained to read gang tattoos can discern a suspect's history.

GANG ACTIVITIES

Many gang activities are similar to those of other segments of society and are *not* illegal. Gangs gather informally on streets and street corners, in parks, homes, abandoned buildings, vehicles, vacant lots or recreational areas and buildings. Indeed, many of the defining characteristics of a gang could apply to any other organization in society, with the exception of the purpose, which is to engage in antisocial or criminal behavior.

Gangs and Crime

Street gang members engage in a wide variety of illegal activities. The *National Gang Threat Assessment* (2009, p.iii) reports, "Criminal gangs commit as much as 80 percent of the crime in many communities, according to law enforcement officials throughout the nation. Typical gang-related crimes include alien smuggling, armed robbery, assault, auto theft, drug trafficking, extortion, fraud, home invasions, identity theft, murder, and weapons trafficking." And although most gang crime consists of relatively minor offenses, such as property damage, theft and the like, the more serious, albeit infrequent, crimes, such as robbery, assault and murder, garner more publicity: "It is these more serious offenses that capture media attention, create fear in some communities, and end up receiving the most concentrated attention of the police and the courts" (Klein, 2007, p.37).

Gangs, particularly those at the national and regional levels, are increasingly associating with organized crime entities, such as Mexican DTOs, Asian criminal groups and Russian organized crime groups. These organized crime groups often turn to gangs to conduct low-level criminal activity, protect territories and facilitate drug-trafficking activities. The primary goal of any association between these groups is financial gain. Table 19.1 summarizes the main types of criminal organizations

M.O.B. Member of Bloods

C̶K Crip Killa

Dog paw made up of three dots

The number **5** and five-point star signify alliance with People Nation

Refer to each other as "dawgs" and "Crip Killers"

Bloods

B̶K Blood Killer

The number **6** and six-point star signify alliance with Folk Nation

Refer to each other as "cuz" (cousin) and "Blood Killers"

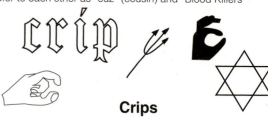

Crips

Set of People Nation, allied with Bloods

The number **5** and five-point star signify alliance with Bloods

Vice Lords (People Nation)

GD Gangster Disciples, set of Folk Nation, allied with Crips

The number **74** signifying **G**, the 7th letter of the alphabet, **D** the 4th.

Gangster Disciples (Folk Nation)

13 means *Sureño*

Three- or five-point crown signifies Latin Kings

ADR *Amor de Rey* (Love of the King)

Mi Vida Loca (My Crazy Life)

Three- or five-point crown signifies Latin Kings

Latino Gangs: Latin Kings, Sureños 13, MS-13

Tien	Money
Tinh	Love
Tu	Prison
Toi	Crime
Thu	Revenge

Asian Gangs

Aryan Brotherhood

G27

Group 27

Mexican Mafia

Nuestra Familia

Prison

Nickname

Position

Outlaw patch

Top rocker (gang/club)

Logo

Bottom rocker (city/state)

B = Bandidos = **2**

O = Outlaws = **15**

P = Pagans = **16**

HA = Hell's Angels = **81**

Outlaw Motorcycle

FIGURE 19.1

A sampling of gang symbols, including graffiti and hand signs.

© Cengage Learning, 2013

TABLE 19.1 Criminal Organizations			
Type of Group	**Subtype of Group**	**Specific Groups and Distinct Gangs**	**Criminal Activity**
Asian gangs	Chinese street gangs, Triads, Tongs	Flying Dragons, Fuk Ching, Ghost Shadows, Ping On, Taiwan Brotherhood, United Bamboo, Wah Ching, White Tigers	Extortion of Chinese businesses, gambling, heroin distribution, exploitation of recent immigrants, smuggling of humans
	Japanese gangs (Boryokudan or Yakuza)	Kumlai, Sumiyoshi Rengo, Yamaguchi Gumi	Gambling, prostitution and sex trade, money laundering, trafficking in weapons and drugs
	Korean gangs	AB (American Burger), Flying Dragons, Junior Korean Power, KK (Korean Killers), Korean Power	Prostitution, massage parlors; gambling; loan-sharking; extortion of Korean businesses (particularly produce markets and restaurants)
	Laotian/ Cambodian/ Vietnamese gangs	Born to Kill (BTK), Laotian Bloods (LBs), Richtown Crips, Tiny Oriental Crips, Tiny Rascal Gang (TRG[1])	Strong-arm and violent crimes related to business extortion; home invasion for theft of gold, jewelry and money coupled with rape to deter reporting; street crimes; prostitution; drug trafficking; assault; murder
	Hmong gangs	Cobra gang, Menace of Destruction (MOD), Oriental Ruthless Boys, Totally Gangster Crips, Totally Mafia Crips, True Asian Crips, True Crip Gangster, True Lady Crips (female Hmongs), True Local Crips, Westside Crips, White Tigers	Gang rape, prostitution, burglary, auto theft, vandalism, home invasion, street crimes, strong-arm robbery of businesses, drug trafficking, assault, murder
Latin American gangs	Mexican	18th Street gang, Sureños-Mexican Mafia, Norteños-Nuestra Family, Tijuana Cartel-Arellano Felix organization, Colima Cartel-Amazcua Contreras brothers, Juarez Cartel-Amado Carillo Fuentes group, Sonora Cartel-Miguel Caro Quintero organization, Sinaloa Cartel-Guzman/Leora Organization, Guadalajara Cartel-Rafael Caro Quintero/Miguel Angel Felix Gallardo, Gulf Cartel	Drug trafficking (cocaine, crack, heroin, marijuana), counterfeiting, pickpocketing, money laundering, murder
	Cuban	Cuban Mafia	Drug trafficking (cocaine, crack, heroin, marijuana), counterfeiting, pickpocketing, money laundering, murder
	Puerto Rican	Latin Kings, Puerto Rican Stones	Street crimes, drug trafficking, burglary, assault, rape, murder
	Columbian gangs and cartels	Cali cartel, Medellin cartel, Norte Del Valle Cartel, North Coast Cartel, Bogota Cartel, Santander DeQuilichao Cartel, Black Eagles, AUC, ELN, FARC	Drug trafficking (cocaine, crack, heroin, marijuana), counterfeiting, pickpocketing, money laundering, murder
	El Salvadoran gangs	Mara Salvatrucha 13 (MS-13)	Street crimes, strong-arming businesses, assault, drug trafficking, rape, murder
	Peruvian gangs	Shining Path—guerilla organization with a mission for Maoist government	Vandalism and other property damage, assault, rape, murder

(continued)

TABLE 19.1 (*continued*)

Type of Group	Subtype of Group	Specific Groups and Distinct Gangs	Criminal Activity
Jamaican posses		Shower posse, Spangler posse	Drug trafficking (cocaine, crack, marijuana), weapons trafficking, trafficking green cards
Native American gangs		Native Mob	Retail-level distribution of illicit drugs (primarily marijuana and meth), auto theft, assault, carjacking, drive-by shootings, extortion, robbery, murder
Nigerian gangs		NCE (Nigerian Criminal Enterprise)	Heroin smuggling (via mules) and heroin dealing; credit card fraud, infiltration of private security, planned bankruptcy of companies, exploitation of other Africans
Somali gangs		Somali Outlaws, Somalian Hot Boys, Murda Gang, Somali Mafia, Ma Thug Boys, Ruff Tuff Somali Crips[2]	Street crimes, strong-arming businesses, drug trafficking, assault, rape, murder
Russian (or Soviet) gangs		Evangelical Russian Mafia, Malina/Organizatsiya, Odessa Mafia, Gypsy gangs	Theft (diamonds, furs, gold) and fencing stolen goods, export and sale of stolen Russian religious art and gold; extortion, insurance fraud, money laundering, counterfeiting, daisy chain tax evasion schemes, credit card scams and fraud; smuggling illegal immigrants; drug trafficking
Street gangs	African American, Caucasian, Hispanic and others	Disciples, Latin Kings, Vice Lords, Dog Pound and many others, including variants of Bloods/Crips (e.g., Westside Crips or Rolling Crips)	Motor vehicle theft, drug sales (especially crack and marijuana), weapons trafficking, assaults, drive-by shootings, robbery; burglary, theft and fencing stolen goods, vandalism, graffiti
Drug-trafficking gangs	Traditional street gangs	Bloods, Crips, Gangster Disciples, Latin Kings and many others	Trafficking of heroin, cocaine, crack and other drugs; violence; arson; indirect prostitution; vandalism, property crime; strong-arm robbery; African American gangs known for crack; Chicano gangs known for heroin and crack
	International drug cartels	Medellin cartel, Cali cartel	Drug trafficking (cocaine, crack, heroin, marijuana)
Graffiti or tagger crews (also tagger posses, mobs, tribes and piecers)		Known by three-letter monikers such as NBT (Nothing But Trouble) or ETC (Elite Tagger Crew)	Graffiti vandalism, tag-banging accompanied by violence
Prison gangs		Aryan Brotherhood, Barrio Azteca, Black Guerilla Family, Consolidated Crip Organization, Mexican Mafia, Mexikanemi, Ñeta, Nuestra Familia, Texas Syndicate	Drug trafficking; prostitution; extortion; protection, murder for hire
Outlaw motorcycle gangs (OMGs)		Hell's Angels, Outlaws, Mongols, Pagans, Bandidos, Sons of Silence	Drug trafficking (methamphetamine/crank, speed, ice, PCP, LSD, angel dust), weapons trafficking, chop shops, massage parlors, strip bars, prostitution, arson

TABLE 19.1 *(continued)*

Type of Group	Subtype of Group	Specific Groups and Distinct Gangs	Criminal Activity
Hate groups (including militia and terrorist groups, which also share a focus on ideology)		Aryan Nation, Ku Klux Klan, skinheads (White Aryan Resistance), American Nazi Party, Christian Defense League	Bombings; counterfeiting; loan fraud; armored car and bank robberies; theft rings
La Cosa Nostra (aka the Mafia)		Families such as Bonnano, Columbo, Gambino, Genovese and Lucchese	Gambling; loan-sharking; corruption of public officials/institutions; extortion; money laundering; theft of precious metals, food and clothing; fencing stolen property; labor racketeering; stock manipulation; securities fraud; weapons trafficking; drug trafficking (particularly heroin distribution); systemic use of violence as a tool in business transactions; murder

Note: Although nationality and ethnicity are often unifying characteristics of criminal organizations and used to identify them, this view is overly narrow and promotes ethnic stereotypes. The organization of criminal groups by nationality and ethnicity in this table is not intended to suggest that criminal behavior is characteristic of any group; ethnicity, however, is often a marker to police.

[1]TRGs originated as a Cambodian gang but now allow Laotian members.

[2]Somali gangs often change their name, colors and signs every few months. For example, the Somali Outlaws, Hot Boys and Murda Gang are all one gang that has changed its identity. Somali Mafia and Ma Thugs are break-offs of these gangs.

Source: Adapted in part from Deborah Lamm Weisel. "Criminal Investigation." In *Local Government Police Management*, edited by William A. Geller and Darrel W. Stephens. 2003, p.270. Washington, DC: International City/County Management Association. Adapted with permission of the International city/county Management Association, 777 North Capital Street, NE, Suite 500, Washington, DC 20002. All rights reserved.

existing within the United States, most of which are gangs, listing specific group names and the types of criminal activities they engage in.

Although gang crime often involves only a few members at a time, occasionally the entire gang, or a large portion of it, participates in the illegal activity. For example, a surveillance video from a Las Vegas mini-market showed more than 40 teenagers flooding into the tiny store. Three youths jumped the counter and robbed the cashier at gunpoint while the others flocked to coolers. Teens clogged the doorways as they rushed out, carrying cases of beer and handfuls of food. The whole incident took less than 90 seconds. Such an incident is referred to as a **flash mob** or mob rob. Some police call this technique *swarming*.

In addition to drug dealing, gang members often engage in vandalism, arson, auto theft, shoplifting, shootings, stabbings, intimidation and other forms of violence.

The nexus between gangs and crime has been well studied, with nearly a century's worth of criminological research supporting the association between the two: "Gang members have higher offending rates than non-gang members in survey and official records data" (Gibson et al., 2009, p.626). However, identification of causal factors has been more elusive, and questions still exist about which way, if any, the influence flows: does gang involvement lead to higher criminal activity or, in contrast, are those individuals who are already predisposed to antisocial or criminal behavior more likely to join a gang? The competing hypotheses currently circulating to explain the relationship between gangs and crime, including involvement in drug use/sales and violence, are these (Bjerregaard, 2010):

■ The facilitation model: Gang membership facilitates or promotes drug involvement, which, in turn, facilitates or increases violence.

■ The selection model: Gangs attract members who are already delinquent or criminally involved and antisocial behaviors precede joining the gang.

■ The enhancement model: Gangs attract those who are already delinquent or criminally involved, and membership in the gang further facilitates or enhances their preexisting antisocial behavior.

Research efforts to disentangle the forces at work have led to some interesting conclusions. For example, increases in a gang's organization have been correlated with elevated levels of criminal involvement and victimization (Decker et al., 2008). Another study has found that increases in neighborhood disadvantage, as measured by socioeconomic conditions and indices, intensify the influence that gang membership and drug sales have on violence (Bellair and McNulty, 2009).

Gangs and Drugs

Until the early 1980s, when crack, or rock cocaine, hit the market, gangs engaged primarily in burglary, robbery, extortion and car theft. Although drug trafficking existed, it was nowhere near current levels. The reason: enormous profit. Economic gain is often the reason youths join gangs. It is hard to convince a youth that $7.50 an hour for busing tables is preferable to making $600 for 2 hours' work as a drug courier. Thus, today, gangs remain the primary retail-level distributors of most drugs throughout the United States: "Drug distribution by gang members poses a growing concern in suburban and rural communities; gang members are the primary retail-level drug distributors and are increasing their wholesale-level drug distribution in most urban and suburban communities. According to the NDTS [National Drug Threat Survey] 2008, 58 percent of law enforcement agencies in the United States report that gangs are involved in drug distribution, compared with 45 percent in 2004; much of this increase occurred in suburban and rural areas" (*National Gang Threat Assessment*, 2009, p.9).

Some caution that drug trafficking by gangs is not as rampant as others might claim. Results of one study found that gang membership is only weakly associated with drug use and distribution (Bjerregaard, 2010). However, the results of this study also provided empirical support for the concept that gang membership facilitates drug use, not vice versa, and promotes drug sales among the juveniles examined in the study (Bjerregaard, 2010). Furthermore, this research revealed that among youth who use and sell drugs, distinct differences exist between gang and nongang members, with gang members who use drugs doing so at higher rates than nongang members (Bjerregaard, 2010).

Aside from some expert opinions that most gangs lack the discipline, leadership and crime skills necessary to sustain a successful drug operation, those gangs that are successful—particularly those who align with DTOs and other criminal organizations—are serious forces to be reckoned with.

Gangs and Violence

Gangs rely on intimidation, force and violence to attain and maintain power and control over a territory. The nexus between gang membership, drug involvement and violence has been a subject of research interest for many years, with recent results providing empirical support for several conclusions. Research by Bellair and McNulty (2009, pp.661–662) found drug distribution to be a major facilitator of violence: "Gang members who report selling drugs engage in violence at a significantly higher rate than non-selling gang members and non-gang drug sellers. [Furthermore]…gang members who sell drugs are by far most violent when they reside in highly disadvantaged locales. These findings support…our conceptualization that gang membership and drug selling fill the vacuity of economic opportunity and isolation from mainstream society within disadvantaged neighborhood environments. The findings clearly contradict prior research suggesting that gang member involvement in drug sales does not necessarily increase the frequency of violent behavior." The influence of neighborhood disadvantage on violence among drug sellers who are not in gangs, gang members who do not sell drugs and gang members who do sell drugs is illustrated very simply in Figure 19.2.

Another study found that although drug involvement, even among gang members, was not related to assaults, it was associated with gun-carrying behaviors, which does not necessarily correlate to actual violence but certainly increases the potential for violence (Bjerregaard, 2010).

RECOGNIZING A GANG PROBLEM

Failure to recognize or acknowledge the existence of gang activity, whether willingly or through the lack of gang identification training, dramatically increases a gang's ability to thrive and develop a power base. Many communities begin to address gang issues only after a high-profile gang-related incident occurs.

 The first step in dealing with a gang problem is to recognize it.

Recognizing a gang can be challenging, but law enforcement, schools and communities can be aware of warning signs such as graffiti, obvious colors of clothing, tattoos, initiations, hand signals or handshakes,

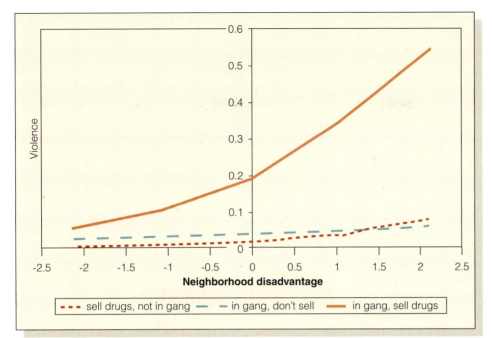

FIGURE 19.2
Simple slope of gang membership and drug selling on violence by neighborhood disadvantage.

Source: "Gang Membership, Drug Selling, and Violence in Neighborhood Context" by Paul E. Bellair and Thomas L. McNulty. *Justice Quarterly*, Vol. 26, (4), December 2009. © Academy of Criminal Justice Sciences, reprinted by permission of Taylor & Francis Ltd, www.tandfonline.com on behalf of Academy of Criminal Justice Sciences.

TABLE 19.2 Definitional Characteristics of Gangs

Definitional Characteristics	Average Rank (1 = Least Important, 6 = Most Important)			
	Larger Cities	Suburban Counties	Smaller Cities	Rural Counties
Commits Crimes Together	4.8	4.9	4.7	4.5
Has a Name	3.9	3.7	3.3	3.5
Displays Colors or Other Symbols	3.3	3.2	3.3	3.2
Hangs Out Together	3.1	3.0	3.6	3.3
Claims Turf or Territory	3.3	3.1	3.0	2.9
Has a Leader(s)	2.6	3.1	3.0	3.5

Source: "Defining Gangs and Designating Gang Membership." In *National Youth Gang Survey Analysis*. National Gang Center, 2009. Accessed August 28, 2011. http://www.nationalgangcenter.gov/Survey-Analysis/Defining-Gangs

uncommon terms or phrases and a sudden change in behavior. Communities and law enforcement may not know when a group of misbehaving youths crosses the line into becoming a bona fide gang. To answer the question, "Does our community have a gang problem?" or "Is there gang activity occurring in our jurisdiction?" agencies may use a list of criteria. Table 19.2 lists the definitional criteria used by law enforcement agencies to identify gangs, by average rank of importance. In general, law enforcement agencies regard group criminality as the most important criteria and the presence of leadership as the least important criteria in defining a gang.

After a gang problem has been recognized, the next step is to identify the gang members.

IDENTIFYING GANG MEMBERS

Just as variation exists in how gangs as groups are defined, there is no consistent national criteria used to identify individual gang members. The Violent Gang and Terrorist Organizations File (VGTOF), contained within the FBI's National Crime Information Center (NCIC), defines a gang member as one who admits gang membership or meets any two of the following criteria (*Brief Review of Federal and State Definitions*, 2009, p.4):

■ Has been identified as a gang member by an individual of proven reliability

- Has been identified as a gang member by an individual of unknown reliability, and that information has been corroborated in significant respects
- Has been observed by law enforcement members to frequent a known gang's area, associate with known gang members or affect that gang's style of dress, tattoos, hand signals or symbols
- Has been arrested on more than one occasion with known gang members consistent with gang activity
- Has admitted membership in a gang at any time other than at the time of current arrest/incarceration

A list of criteria used by individual states to identify gang members is available online at the National Gang Center's government Web site. According to the *National Youth Gang Survey Analysis*, an individual's claim to belong to a gang is met with different levels of credibility and importance, depending on the size of the jurisdiction involved (Table 19.3): "For larger and smaller cities and suburban counties, a clear majority of agencies emphasize the use of the self-nomination technique compared with other criteria (e.g., arrested or associates with known gang members; tattoos, colors, or other symbols; identified by a reliable source) in identifying and documenting individuals as gang members in their jurisdictions" ("Defining Gangs and Designating Gang Membership," 2009).

> Gang members may be identified by their names, symbols (clothing and tattoos) and communication styles, including graffiti and sign language.

The Crips, for example, are associated with blue or purple bandannas, scarves or rags. The Bloods are identified by red or green colors. Mexican gangs often wear brown bandannas as a symbol of ethnic pride. Some gangs wear jackets and caps identified with professional sports teams, posing a problem for those youths who wear them because of actual loyalty to the particular team. Gang members may also be identified by the hand signals they use. Tattoos (sometimes called body art) are another means of identifying gang members. The most respected tattoos are those earned by serving a prison sentence.

Often, the stylized dress and haircuts, tattoos, graffiti, slang, hand signs and jewelry used by other street gangs are also used by Southeast Asian gangs. Another characteristic of Southeast Asian street gangs is that they do not claim turf but, rather, are very mobile, with informal networks throughout the United States.

Table 19.4 summarizes warning signs that an individual may be involved in a gang.

RECORDS TO KEEP

The most common way to gather information about gangs is internal contacts with patrol officers and detectives, followed by internal departmental records and computerized files and then by review of offense reports: "Patrol officers are an essential source of gang information and

TABLE 19.3 Designating Gang Membership				
Individual Claims Membership	**Larger Cities**	**Suburban Counties**	**Smaller Cities**	**Rural Counties**
Frequently Used	78.7%	69.3%	67.8%	47.8%
Infrequently Used	21.3%	30.7%	32.2%	52.2%

Source: "Defining Gangs and Designating Gang Membership." In *National Youth Gang Survey Analysis*. National Gang Center, 2009. Access August 28, 2011. http://www.nationalgangcenter.gov/Survey-Analysis/Defining-Gangs

TABLE 19.4 Warning Signs That a Youth May Be Involved with a Gang
Admits to "hanging out" with kids in gangs
Shows an unusual interest in one or two particular colors of clothing or a particular logo
Has an unusual interest in gangster-influenced music, videos, movies or Web sites
Uses unusual hand signals to communicate with friends
Has specific drawings of gang symbols on schoolbooks, clothes, walls or tattoos
Has unexplained physical injuries (fighting-related bruises, injuries to hands/knuckles)
Has unexplained cash or goods, such as clothing or jewelry
Carries a weapon
Has been in trouble with the police
Exhibits negative change in behavior such as ■ Withdrawing from family ■ Declining school attendance, performance, behavior ■ Staying out late without reason ■ Displaying an unusual desire for secrecy ■ Exhibiting signs of drug use ■ Breaking rules consistently ■ Speaking in gang-style slang

Source: Washington, DC Office of Community Oriented Policing Services. Accessed August 28, 2011. http://www.cops.usdoj.gov/files/RIC/Publications/GangsCard_FBI.pdf

usually make up the front line defense against gangs. Through field contacts and observations, they can supply confirmation of an individual's gang membership" (O'Deane and Murphy, 2010, p.54).

Information is an essential tool for law enforcement, and an effective records system is critical in dealing with any gang problem. A gang file should be maintained with the following information: type of gang (street, motorcycle, etc.), ethnic composition, number of active and associate members, territory, hideouts, types of crimes usually committed, method of operation, choice of targets or victims, leadership and members known to be violent. Included within the record system should be a *gang member pointer file* that cross-references the names of suspected gang members with the gang file. This may be a card or computerized file.

A *moniker file* connects suspected gang members' street names with their legal names. A **moniker**, or nickname, is the name gang members use among their peers and often during the commission of crimes. Although no two members of the same gang will have the same moniker, several gangs may have members with the same moniker. Therefore, one card should have on it the moniker and all gang members who use it.

A *photograph file* is of great help in conducting photographic identification sessions. A *gang vehicle file* can be maintained, arranged alphabetically by vehicle make. Include color, year, body type, license number, distinguishing features, known drivers and usual parking spots. An *illegal activities file* can also be maintained, arranged alphabetically, listing the gangs known to engage in the activities.

 Maintain records on gangs, gang members, monikers, photographs, vehicles and illegal activities. Cross-reference the records.

Departments can use improving technology by combining the efforts of sworn officers and the capabilities of the information technology (IT) staff with its computer-aided dispatch (CAD) and records management system (RMS) to deliver accurate, timely information on gang activity directly to patrol officers who need it, thus maximizing their effectiveness when dealing with known gang members (Posey, 2008, p.39).

INVESTIGATING ILLEGAL GANG ACTIVITY

Illegal activities of gangs usually involve multiple suspects, which makes investigation much more difficult. Evidence may link only a few of the suspects with the crime, and,

as with organized crime figures, gang members maintain fierce loyalty to each other and are often unwilling to "rat."

Most often the witnesses to gang-related crimes are gang members themselves or people who at least sympathize with the gang, which presents a challenge to investigators trying to extract credible information from such individuals as these witnesses may deliberately lie to mislead investigators and protect the suspects. Other witnesses who are not gang-involved may be too afraid to provide any information. Because they live in the neighborhood with the gang and may fear for their lives, they may provide information and then later deny it. For this reason, tape-record or videotape all such interviews.

 Special challenges in investigating the illegal activities of gangs include the multitude of suspects and the unreliability or fear of witnesses.

Gang investigations should proceed like most other criminal investigations. Uniformed officers should establish personal contacts with the gangs in the community and become familiar with their size, the names and monikers of as many members as possible and each gang's identifying symbols, colors and graffiti.

Some disenchanted gang members may become police informants. Children know what is going on among their peers even though they may not be gang members themselves. Teachers and school counselors are other sources of information on acceptable and unacceptable youth activities. In addition, recreation department personnel know what is going on in the youth community and are therefore good sources of information. Valdemar (2007, pp.52–53) points out, "Anyone can be an 'unofficial informant' and 'cooperative witness.' Every person you contact is a potential gang informant. Kids, moms, girlfriends, the local letter carrier and especially the nosy old lady down the street have all witnessed gang crimes in progress. They hold the solution to many crimes. Treat them that way. But whatever you do, don't ask them for information about gangs in public. Protect their identities, protect their lives. And above all, always keep your word." Indeed, as Morley (2008, p.53) advises, "Wise investigators make an effort to provide for the safety of witnesses, especially witnesses who have information on gang crimes. And that includes gang members."

The immediate area in which a crime occurs may yield much information. Any graffiti present indicates which gang controls the territory. Keep in mind that gang members do not like to be on foot in a strange area, especially one dominated by their enemies; therefore, commando-type raids on foot are very rare.

If a neighborhood canvass is conducted and information is received, it is important that the canvass not stop at that point. This would implicate the house or business at which the canvass was terminated as the source of information. In addition, more information might be available from a source not yet contacted during the canvass.

Field interviews (FI) are considered "the bread and butter of any gang investigator," and properly filled out FI cards can be an important part of a gang-related crime investigation (O'Deane and Murphy, 2010, p.54). Certain field interview techniques are more likely to yield results than others. For instance (O'Deane and Murphy, 2010),

■ When dealing with gang members, address their expectation of respect (whether it is deserved or not) by maintaining a firm but fair attitude. This will get an investigator farther in extracting useful information from the individual.

■ When talking to a gang member about a significant matter, such as a crime or another gang member, hold your conversation where other gang members can neither see nor hear you. This will encourage subject cooperation.

■ Isolate gang members suspected of a crime immediately so that they cannot collaborate on their "story." This technique is similar to any police response in which multiple suspects are apprehended at the crime scene.

■ Keep in mind that gang members will often attempt to discard any contraband they are carrying, such as weapons or drugs, when they see an officer approaching. Therefore, it is important to check the area surrounding the location of contact.

Crime scenes that involve gangs are unique. Often the crime scene is part of a chain of events. When a gang assault occurs, for example, often a chase precedes and follows the assault, considerably widening the crime scene. If vehicles are involved, the assault is probably by a rival gang. If no vehicles appear to have been involved, the suspects are probably local, perhaps even members of the same gang as the victim. This frequently occurs when narcotics, girlfriends or family disputes are involved.

Evidence obtained in gang-related criminal investigations is processed in the same way as evidence related to any other crime. Photograph graffiti for later identification. File FI cards on members, vehicles, territory, locations, crimes committed, drug activities and any other information. Gang members may usually be located within their territory even after they commit a crime—because this is their "home."

A helpful source of information on gangs is the Internet. Thousands of gang-related sites have been posted.

In addition, investigators can learn much about gangs in their jurisdiction by paying attention to graffiti.

Gangs use graffiti to send the following types of messages:

■ To mark the gang's turf (territory)
■ To disrespect a rival gang or gang member
■ To memorialize a deceased gang member
■ To make a statement

Technology Innovations

Gang members can be very prolific with their graffiti, presenting a challenge to law enforcement in trying to keep track of the myriad tags scrawled throughout their jurisdictions. A specialized free-to-law-enforcement database called Tracking Automated Graffiti Reporting System (TAGRS) is now helping gang investigators track, store and analyze graffiti incidents (Miller, 2010). Anyone can submit data online to TAGRS. Government employees—such as public transportation workers, public works employees and law enforcement officers—can take a photo of graffiti using a smartphone, digital camera or personal digital assistant (PDA) and upload the images to TAGRS along with information such as the address or location of the graffiti, the date and time it was discovered and the amount of damaged estimated. Anonymous tips can be submitted via a public Internet portal. Once data is entered into TAGRS, information is relayed to the jurisdiction's designated graffiti offense investigator or analyst, a measure that ensures consistency:

> In the case of a crime report, the designated officer may be responsible for filling in information such as damage amount, the tagger's moniker and gang name, and other information including known associates, personal images, address, vehicle description and phone number. . . .

> Not only does TAGRS provide reports on individuals; it also reports on cost analysis and graffiti trends. A reporting feature includes GIS mapping, which uses GPS coordinates to generate a map of the incident area so investigators and shift commanders can see hotspots (Miller, 2010, p.43).

Some gang investigators have reported that using TAGRS has cut in half the amount of time spent analyzing graffiti to successfully conclude a case and refer it to prosecution.

- To send a message
- To conduct business

    To document graffiti evidence, take the following steps:

- Photograph it whole and in sections.
- Analyze it while it is intact.
- Remove it (paint over it, sandblast it, etc.).
- Archive the photo.
- Record the colors used.
- Record the gang "tag" names.
- Record indicators of "beef" or violence.
- Create an anti-graffiti program to cover over all graffiti.

APPROACHES TO THE GANG PROBLEM

A straightforward three-pronged approach to addressing the gang problem is to apply a balance of prevention, intervention and suppression strategies, an approach identified as either the Comprehensive Community-Wide Gang Program Model or, more simply, the Spergel Model (Howell, 2010; Villanueva, 2009).

A three-pronged approach to address the gang problem uses a balance of prevention, intervention and suppression strategies.

The first strategy—prevention—aims at keeping youths from becoming gang members in the first place and is divided into two tiers: primary prevention, directed at all youths living in communities where gangs are present, and secondary prevention, targeting at-risk youths. Primary prevention efforts include after-school activities, truancy and dropout prevention programs and job programs—strategies that disrupt gang recruiting efforts by keeping kids in pro-social activities and away from unstructured social environments (*Best Practices*, 2010). Secondary prevention identifies children ages 7 to 14 at high risk, who have already displayed early signs of delinquency, and intervenes with appropriate school, community and faith-based services before their problem behaviors can evolve into serious delinquency and gang involvement (*Best Practices*, 2010).

According to some gang experts, prevention is the weakest link in the effort to stop gang crime. One retired gang investigator puts it this way: "The biggest cause of gangs is we do nothing for the 90 percent who aren't gang members. If all the attention and respect goes to the gang members, then what happens to the kids who aren't getting the attention and are getting beaten up by gang members?" (Basich, 2009, p.21).

In certain parts of the country, such as Southern California, prevention efforts are particularly crucial and can pay big dividends:

> According to various studies, less than 10 percent of kids in a neighborhood are gang members. That leaves 90% potential members who are at risk, but might be savable. These kids often seek the protection of the gangs because they live in rough neighborhoods and are frequently accosted by rival gangs. But with effective programs, they can be turned away from membership. "It's a tough choice for a young man, particularly in Los Angeles, in making a decision on how to survive," [one detective and leading gang expert] said. (Eggers, 2009, pp.14,16)

The second strategy—intervention—is directed at youths already involved in gangs, either as active members or close associates, and provides sanctions and services designed to push these juveniles out of and away from gangs. This strategy "involves aggressive outreach and recruitment activity. Support services for gang-involved youths and their families help youth make positive choices" (*Best Practices*, 2010). This group of gang-involved youths make up a relatively large share of the population, typically range in age from 12 to 24 and are involved in significant levels of illegal activity but are not necessarily considered the more serious or chronic offenders.

The third strategy—suppression—targets serious and chronic offenders, those hard-core members most embedded in the gang culture, who comprise a relatively small proportion of the population but who commit a disproportionately large share of crime and violence (Howell, 2010). Suppression involves both formal and informal social control procedures, such as "close supervision and monitoring of gang-involved youth by agencies of the juvenile/criminal justice system and also by community-based agencies, schools, and grassroots groups" (*Best Practices*, 2010, p.4). Furthermore, members of this group "are candidates for targeted enforcement and prosecution because of their high level of involvement in crime and violent gangs and the small probability that other strategies will reduce their criminal behavior" (Howell, 2010, p.12).

Civil gang injunctions (CGIs) and ordinances are legal tools used with urban gangs that focus on individuals and the locations of their routine activities. These neighborhood-level intervention strategies target specific individuals who intimidate residents and cause other public nuisance issues and restricts these gang members' activities within a specific geographic area.

However, injunctions and ordinances may be challenged as unconstitutional violations of the freedom of speech, the right of association and due process rights if they do not clearly delineate how officers may apply such orders. For example, Chicago passed a gang congregation ordinance to combat the problems created by the city's street gangs. During the three years following passage of the ordinance, Chicago police officers issued more than 89,000 dispersal orders and arrested more than 42,000 people. But in *Chicago v. Morales* (1999), the Supreme Court struck down the ordinance as unconstitutional because its vague wording failed to provide adequate standards to guide police discretion. The lesson here is that any civil injunctions a city passes must be clear in what officers can and cannot do when they observe what they believe to be gang members congregating in public places.

Another gang ordinance passed in Sunnyside, Washington, allows police to aggressively pursue individuals who engage in peripheral gang activities. The ordinance makes joining a gang illegal and prohibits hand signals, wearing gang-related clothes and other typical gang activities. This ordinance, however, is being opposed by the Washington American Civil Liberties Union (ACLU), which claims that it could lead to racial profiling, a finding many gang experts find "baffling" given that race is paramount in gang activity (Moore, 2007a, p.98).

Tougher legislation is also being used as a gang control approach. Because some gangs use their younger members to commit serious crimes, relying on the more lenient juvenile sentencing laws, some jurisdictions have allowed courts to raise the penalties for teenagers convicted of gang-related offenses.

COLLABORATIVE EFFORTS: GANG TASK FORCES

Collaboration among law enforcement agencies can greatly enhance efforts to cope with the gang problem: "Fighting gang-related crime with traditional methods is a lot like putting out a forest fire with a measuring cup—something's being done, but in the long run it's a futile gesture" (Moore, 2007b, p.52). Multiagency task forces bring together differing perspectives and focus human labor efforts and resources on a common goal, providing a more effective response to the issue of gangs (*2005 National Gang Threat Assessment*, p.v). Even though law

enforcement unquestionably plays a major role in effectively combating the gang problem, partnerships with the community, parents and schools significantly increase the likelihood of a successful response.

The OJJDP's Comprehensive Gang Model for a gang reduction program (GRP) is based on years of experimentation and research on gang prevention. The model's key distinguishing feature is a strategic planning process that empowers communities to assess their own gang problems and fashion a complement of antigang strategies and program activities. The report, *Best Practices to Address Community Gang Problems* (2010), presents the best practices for the Comprehensive Gang Model and highlights results of the National Youth Gang Center Survey and a meeting of practitioners regarding their experiences in implementing the model. Another valuable resource available to all communities is the National Gang Crime Research Center Web site (http://www.ngcrc.com).

PROSECUTING GANG-RELATED CRIMES

Valdemar (2010, p.43) stresses, "The gang investigator should form a close partnership with the gang prosecutor and each must be available to the other 24/7. This ensures critical input in the early stages of the case and the swift reaction to witness intimidation later." One valuable and effective tactic in prosecuting gang-related crimes is to make use of conspiracy laws such as the federal Racketeering Influenced and Corrupt Organizations Act (RICO) statutes commonly used with organized crime cases. As many of the gang members ("aiders and abettors") as possible should be charged and prosecuted: "Charging and trying the defendants jointly strengthens the overall case" (Valdemar, 2010, p.43).

Some jurisdictions are seeing positive results by escalating the level of prosecution, particularly for higher level gang members: "One of the best tools small town law enforcement can wield against gangs is to build a federal case against them. 'Some of the career offenders are looking at serious crime without parole when we make federal cases. They are scared of federal charges,' [one detective] says. The fear of federal time can be used to get even hardcore gangsters who say they will never snitch to rollover on their homies" (Griffith, 2008, pp.52–53).

San Diego Police Chief William Lansdowne explains why the threat of federal prison is an important deterrent and valuable strategy for law enforcement: "It's nothing for a gang member to go to prison in California. They know they are going to be able to keep those gang connections.

But if you send a gang member from California to a federal prison in Connecticut, they lose their local gang connections. They are no longer connected to their gang, and they don't have that safety net. Gang members do everything they can not to be sent to federal prison. That's why we turn over information to federal prosecutors when we really want to go after a gang leader" ("PERF Report Describes Changes," 2010, p.7).

Throughout the investigation of illegal gang activities, be aware of the most common defenses gang members use in court.

> The two most often used defense strategies are pleas of diminished capacity and self-defense.

Although some states have eliminated "diminished capacity" as a defense, many have not. Therefore, *document* whether the suspect was under the influence of alcohol or other drugs at the time of the crime. Likewise, *document* whether the suspect was threatened by the victim and could possibly have been acting in self-defense.

FEDERAL EFFORTS TO COMBAT THE GANG PROBLEM

Several entities exist to combat the nation's gang problem. The National Gang Intelligence Center (NGIC) is one such collaborative effort:

> The NGIC is a multiagency effort that integrates the gang intelligence assets of federal, state, and local law enforcement entities to serve as a centralized intelligence resource for gang information and analytical support. The mission of the NGIC is to support law enforcement agencies through timely and accurate information sharing and strategic/tactical analysis of federal, state, and local law enforcement intelligence focusing on the growth, migration, criminal activity, and association of gangs that pose a significant threat to communities throughout the United States. The NGIC concentrates on gangs operating on a national level that demonstrate criminal connectivity between sets and common identifiers and goals. Because many violent gangs do not operate on a national level, the NGIC also focuses on regional-level gangs. NGIC is staffed and supported by a number of partnering agencies, including the Bureau of Alcohol, Tobacco, Firearms, and Explosives (ATF), Bureau of Prisons (BOP), Department of Justice (DOJ), Department

of Homeland Security (DHS), Customs and Border Protection (CBP), Drug Enforcement Administration (DEA), Federal Bureau of Investigation (FBI), Immigration and Customs Enforcement (ICE), NDIC, and United States Marshals Service (USMS). The NGIC produces intelligence assessments, intelligence bulletins, joint agency intelligence products, and other nonstandard intelligence products for customers. (*National Gang Threat Assessment*, 2009, p.2)

Another multiagency effort is the National Gang Targeting, Enforcement and Coordination Center (Gang-TECC), created in 2006 to serve as a "one-stop shop" for local, state and federal gang investigators and prosecutors. The mission of GangTECC is "to help disrupt and dismantle the most significant and violent gangs in the United States" (*National Gang Threat Assessment*, 2009, p.2). GangTECC investigators are federal agents from the ATF, BOP, DEA, FBI, USMS and ICE at the Department of Homeland Security who work closely with the Gang Squad prosecutors in the Criminal Division of the Department of Justice and with the analysts and others at the NGIC.

Previous editions of this text also discussed the National Youth Gang Center (NYGC), which was established in 1995 and funded by the OJJDP, as another "one-stop shop for information about gangs and effective responses to them." In October 2009 the NYGC merged with the National Gang Center (NGC), which was established in 2003 and funded by the Bureau of Justice Assistance, to create a new consolidated National Gang Center. The current NGC provides a plethora of published research about gangs; descriptions of evidence-based, anti-gang programs; and links to tools, databases and other resources to assist in developing and implementing effective community-based gang prevention, intervention and suppression strategies. The center also offers a variety of anti-gang training courses and provides an online database of gang-related state legislation and municipal codes; a list of newspaper articles on nationwide gang activity that is updated daily; and GANGINFO, an electronic mailing list for professionals working with gangs.

BIAS AND HATE CRIME: AN OVERVIEW

In addition to youth and street gangs, law enforcement is often confronted with the criminal activities of hate groups. Hate is a complex subject that can be divided into two general categories: rational and irrational. Unjust acts inspire rational hate. Hatred of a person based on race, religion, sexual orientation, ethnicity or national origin constitutes irrational hate. Generically, a **bias crime** or a **hate crime** is a traditional criminal act, such as murder, arson or vandalism with the added element of bias—it is committed because of someone's actual or perceived membership in a particular group. For the purposes of data collection, Congress has defined a hate crime as a "criminal offense against a person or property motivated in whole or in part by an offender's bias against a race, religion, disability, ethnic origin or sexual orientation." Hate itself is not a crime; the freedom to feel hatred is a protected civil liberty. However, when that feeling is translated into action, it becomes a criminal offense. Crimes range from verbal intimidation and harassment to destruction of property, physical violence and murder.

Hate crime is not a new development in our country. It has probably existed in America for more than 300 years; however, only recently has it become recognized as a violation of the law. The Southern Poverty Law Center (SPLC), which monitors hate groups and other extremists throughout the United States, reports that since 2000 the number of hate groups organized in the United States has increased by 54 percent, a surge fueled by fears of Latino immigration and, more recently, by the election of the country's first African American president and the economic crisis. The SPLC estimates there are currently 1,002 known groups operating across the country, up from an estimated 888 groups in 2007. These groups include Klansmen, neo-Nazis, racist skinheads, White nationalists, Black separatists, neo-Confederates, border vigilantes and others ("Hate and Extremism," 2011).

The FBI's Uniform Crime Report for 2009 indicates there were 6,604 hate crime incidents reported that year involving 7,789 offenses. Further breakdown of incidents revealed that there were 6,598 single-bias incidents involving 7,776 offenses, 8,322 victims and 6,219 offenders. Six multiple-bias incidents were reported in 2009 involving 14 offenses, 14 victims and 6 offenders (*Crime in the United States*, 2009).

MOTIVATION FOR HATE CRIME

According to the FBI, of the 6,598 single-bias hate incidents reported in 2009,

- 48.5 percent of hate incidents were motivated by a bias against a race.

- 19.7 percent were motivated by a bias against a religious belief.

- 18.5 percent were motivated by a bias against a particular sexual orientation.

- 11.8 percent were motivated by a bias against an ethnicity/national origin.

- 1.5 percent were motivated by a bias against a disability (*Hate Crime Statistics*, 2010).

Figure 19.3 illustrates the distribution of hate incidents by bias type.

> Bias or hate crimes are motivated by bigotry and hatred against a specific group of people. Race is usually the primary motivation for hate crimes, and African Americans are most often the victims.

The groups most likely to be victims of hate crime are (in alphabetical order) African Americans, Arabs, Asians, gay males, Jews, Latinos, lesbians, Native Americans and White women in interracial relationships. Given the events of September 11, 2001, concern has arisen over an increase of hate crimes against young men of Middle Eastern descent. In addition, FBI statistics suggest a 35 percent rise in hate crimes against Latinos between 2003 and 2006, with experts believing such crimes are typically carried out by those who think they are attacking immigrants.

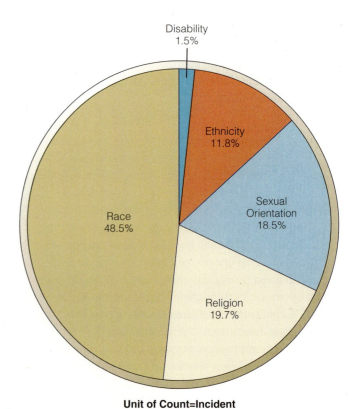

Unit of Count=Incident

FIGURE 19.3

Distribution of hate incidents by bias type, 2009.

Source: Adapted from *Hate Crime Statistics*, 2009

TABLE 19.5 Non–Hate-Based Crime Versus Hate-Based Crime

Characteristics	Non–Hate-Based Incidents	Hate-Based Incidents
Relationship of victim to perpetrator	Most assaults involve two people who know each other	Assaults tend to be "stranger" crimes
Number of perpetrators	Most assaults have one perpetrator and one victim	Involve an average of four assailants for each victim
Nature of the conflict	Tend to be even	Tend to be uneven—hate crime perpetrators often attack younger or weaker victims or arm themselves and attack unarmed victims
Amount of physical damage inflicted	Not typically "excessive"	Extremely violent, with victims being three times more likely to require hospitalization than "normal" assault victims
Treatment of property	In most property crimes, something of value is taken	More likely that valuable property will be damaged or destroyed
Perpetrator's personal gain	Attacker settles a score or profits from the crime	In most, no personal score is settled and no profit is made
Location of crime	No place with any symbolic significance	Frequently occur in churches, synagogues, mosques, cemeteries, monuments, schools, camps and in or around the victim's home

Source: Adapted from Christina Bodinger-deUriarte. "Hate Crime: The Rise of Hate Crime on School Campuses." Research Bulletin No.10 of Phi Delta Kappa, Center for Evaluation, Development, and Research, December 1991, p.2. Reprinted by permission of Phi Delta Kappa International. All rights reserved.

A group often overlooked in discussions of hate crime is the homeless. Homeless people have been run over; hit with stun guns, pellet guns, paint guns and pepper balls; set on fire; beaten; robbed; raped; and firebombed. Some characteristics typical of hate-motivated violence are relatively rare in other crimes of violence, as shown in Table 19.5.

Offenses

Of the 7,789 hate crimes reported to law enforcement in 2009, 4,793 (61.5 percent) were crimes against persons: 45.0 percent of these were intimidation; 35.3 percent, simple assault; 19.1 percent, aggravated assault; 0.4 percent were the violent crimes of murder (8 offenses) and forcible rape (9 offenses); and 0.3 percent involved the offense category "other," which is collected only in the National Incident-Based Reporting System (NIBRS) (*Hate Crime Statistics*, 2010). Of the 2,970 hate crimes (38.1 percent) committed against property, 83.0 percent were acts of destruction, damage or vandalism. The remaining 17.0 percent of crimes against property consisted of robbery, burglary, larceny-theft, motor vehicle theft, arson and other crimes (*Hate Crime Statistics*, 2010). A total of 26 offenses defined as crimes against society (e.g., drug or narcotic offenses or prostitution) were reported in 2009 (*Hate Crime Statistics*, 2010).

Offenders

Of the 6,225 known offenders involved in hate crimes during 2009, 62.4 percent were White, 18.5 percent were Black, 7.3 percent were groups made up of individuals of various races, 1.0 percent were American Indian/Alaskan Native, 0.7 percent were Asian/Pacific Islander and 10.2 percent were of unknown race (*Hate Crime Statistics*, 2010).

HATE GROUPS

The main hate groups in the United States are "skinheads," Christian Identity groups, the Ku Klux Klan (KKK), Black separatists, White supremacists and neo-Nazis. Such hate crime groups terrorize innocent civilians and spread fear throughout communities nationwide: "From a law enforcement and safety standpoint, these are people who are on the most violent edge of the extreme right, people whose culture is a violent culture" (Phillips, 2007, p.64).

Several watchdog organizations such as the SPLC and the Anti-Defamation League track the size and activities of racist groups and are good resources for law enforcement.

THE POLICE RESPONSE

Respond promptly to reports of hate crime, attempt to reduce the victims' fears and determine the exact type of prejudice involved. Investigators should ask the following questions to determine whether an incident was hate or bias motivated:

▪ Was the victim a member of a targeted class and outnumbered?

▪ Were the offenders from a different racial or ethnic group than the victim(s)?

▪ Did the offender use biased language?

Always provide follow-up information to the victims. Include in the report the exact words or language used reflecting racial, religious, ethnic or sexual orientation bias; the perpetrators' actions, symbols, colors and dress; or any other identifying characteristics or actions.

The International Association of Chiefs of Police (IACP) has outlined key indicators that a hate crime may have been committed (Turner, 1999, p.7):

▪ Perception of the victim(s) and witnesses about the crime

▪ The perpetrators' comments, gestures or written statements that reflect bias, including graffiti or other symbols

▪ Any differences between perpetrator and victim, whether actual or perceived by the perpetrator

▪ Similar incidents in the same location or neighborhood to determine whether a pattern exists

▪ Whether the victim was engaged in activities promoting his or her group or community—for example, by clothing or conduct

▪ Whether the incident coincided with a holiday or date of particular significance

▪ Involvement of organized hate groups or their members

▪ Absence of any other motive such as economic gain

Symbols commonly associated with extremist or hate groups are shown in Figure 19.4.

Officers must differentiate between hate crimes and hate incidents: "**Hate incidents** involve behaviors that, though motivated by bias against a victim's race, religion, ethnic/national origin, gender, age, disability or sexual orientation, are *not* criminal acts. Hostile or hateful speech or other disrespectful/discriminatory behavior may be motivated by bias but is not illegal" (Turner, 1999, p.4).

The passage of the Hate Crime Statistics Act of 1990 requires the attorney general to collect data "about crimes that manifest evidence of prejudice based on race, religion, sexual orientation, or ethnicity." The responsibility for developing the procedures for implementing, collecting and managing hate crime data was delegated to the director of the FBI, who in turn assigned the tasks to the Uniform Crime Reporting (UCR) Program. In 2009 Congress further amended the Hate Crime Statistics Act with the passage of the Matthew Shepard and James Byrd, Jr. Hate Crime Prevention Act. This amendment includes the collection of data for crimes motivated by bias against a particular gender and gender identity, as well as for crimes committed by, and crimes directed against, juveniles. As this text goes to press, the FBI is still planning how to implement changes to collect these data.

In 2009 the law enforcement agencies that participated in the hate crime program represented nearly 279 million inhabitants, or 90.9 percent of the nation's population, and their jurisdictions covered 49 states, the District of Columbia and outlying areas (Guam). Appendix F contains a form for collecting data for a bias offense report. Such forms can help ensure quality field reports properly identifying the crime, the elements of the offense and the evidence clearly demonstrating that a hate crime was committed.

The FBI has also published manuals concerning the types of statistics needed and has established training programs in major cities. Nonetheless, it is difficult to establish hate crime records because some hate crimes involve groups rather than individuals. Table 19.6 summarizes the variables that may encourage or discourage an agency from reporting hate crimes.

EFFORTS TO COMBAT BIAS AND HATE CRIMES

Garrett (2008, p.27) stresses the importance of celebrating diversity and not tolerating bigotry and suggests that an ideal place to start is within the police department itself as well as on college campuses across the country: "At the end of the day, actions speak louder than words. If you are simply saying all the right things, but it's just lip service, your efforts will be undermined. Removing the tarnish of bigotry doesn't happen overnight, but through hard work agencies can shine the spotlight on tolerance and diversity before it spins into hate."

Regardless of how an agency or individual officer views hate crime, it remains a criminal offense that requires a law enforcement response. Two responses have been taken: legislation to expand the scope of the law and increase the severity of punishment for hate crimes and

American Front

American Nazi Party

Aryan Nation

Ku Klux Klan

New Black Panther Party

National Socialist Movement

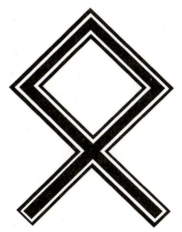

Odin Rune

Posse Comitatus

Storm Front

Nationalist Movement

Triskele

Volksfront

FIGURE 19.4

A sampling of extremist group symbols. Their origins and meanings may be found online at the Anti-Defamation League's Web site.

Source: www.adl.org/hate_symbols/default_graphics.asp

TABLE 19.6 **Variables That Affect Whether Agencies Report Hate Crimes**

Agency Encouragers	Agency Discouragers
Ability to assess intergroup tensions in community	Not deemed important by department
Desire to give support to communities	Perception on part of police that no problem exists
Belief that hate crime reporting will improve police/community relations	Insufficient support staff to process, record and submit hate crime data
Belief that police help set level of acceptable behavior	Perceived as not being real police work in the community
Understanding that community wants police to report	A belief that reporting hate crimes will make things worse for hate violence victim
Need to know extent of problem as first step to developing solutions	A belief that reporting hate crimes will make things worse for communities
Lets community know that department takes hate crimes seriously	Perception that some minority groups complain unnecessarily
A belief that victims will get help	Not a priority of local government
Will help diffuse racial tensions within the police department	A belief that identifying a crime as a hate crime will have no effect on the outcome
The right thing to do politically	A belief that it is wrong to make these types of crimes special
The right thing to do morally	A belief that hate crime reporting will result in negative publicity for the community
Will help maintain department's good relationship with diverse groups	A belief that hate crime reporting supports the political agendas of gay and minority groups (which is seen as a negative outcome)
Consistent with values of department	It creates too much additional work
A belief that identifying problem will keep others safe	Hate crimes are not as serious as other crimes (i.e., lower priority)
Citizens appreciate the hate crime reporting efforts of police	Agency does not have the adequate technological resources

Source: James J. Nolan and Yoshio Akiyama. "An Analysis of Factors that Affect Law Enforcement Participation in Hate Crime Reporting," *Journal of Contemporary Criminal Justice*, 15:1. p.118. © 1999 by Sage Publications. Reprinted by permission of Sage Publications.

Graves scribbled with swastikas and other anti-Semitic graffiti in a Jewish cemetery. One of the results of increased awareness of hate crimes is the creation of laws that exact higher penalties from convicted hate-crime offenders.

© Vincent Kessler/Reuters/CORBIS

more police focus on and fully investigating such crimes. Other efforts include community-based programs to increase awareness of and offer solutions to the problem of hate crime.

No national consensus exists about whether hate crimes should be a separate crime, and those supporting hate crime statutes disagree about what should be included. States vary greatly in legislation related to hate crimes. The most common elements of hate crime legislation include

■ Enhanced penalties.

■ Criminal penalties for vandalism of religious institutions.

■ Collection of data.

Legislation must also keep up with the technology used to spread messages of hate. Despite such legislation, those who propagate messages of bigotry, intolerance and hatred claim they have a constitutionally protected right to do so, citing free speech, due process and equal protection challenges. And although state courts have repeatedly upheld the constitutionality of legislation that enhances penalties for hate-motivated violence, the U.S. Supreme Court struck down a Virginia law banning cross burning in 2003, saying the statute violated the First Amendment (*Virginia v. Black*).

Furthermore, research has found minimal public support for harsher penalties for offenders who commit hate crimes than for offenders who commit identical crimes with no biased motivation.

Sometimes, the hideous nature of hate crimes leaves investigators wondering whether the offense is truly based on bias or whether some type of ritualistic torture was involved.

RITUALISTIC CRIME: AN OVERVIEW

Ritualistic crimes are most often associated with cults or occult groups.

> A **cult** is a system of religious beliefs and rituals. It also refers to those who practice such beliefs.

One informal definition of a *cult* is "any religion other than your own." The term is often applied to religious or mystical groups that society does not understand. Most cults involve some form of worship and followers dedicated to the concepts promoted by the leader.

Cults range in size from a few followers to worldwide organizations directed by a complex chain of command. According to some estimates, 3,000 cults exist throughout the world, claiming a total estimated membership of more than 3 million people, mostly young adults.

One cult in the late 1970s was the People's Temple, led by Jim Jones, a Protestant clergyman. Hundreds of his followers moved into Jonestown, a rural commune in Guyana, South America, and lived under his absolute rule. In 1978 cult leaders killed a U.S. congressman and three journalists investigating activities in Jonestown. Jones then ordered his followers to commit suicide, resulting in the deaths of more than 900 people.

Another well-known group regarded as a cult is the International Society for Krishna Consciousness, better known as the Hare Krishna movement. This cult came from India in 1954. Most members wear orange robes, and the men shave their heads.

Some scholars refer to cults as "new religious movements," or NRMs, because most cults are young religious movements still in their first generation. As such, these authors stress, most NRMs are law abiding. For example, the neo-pagan Wicca movement, although it may have aspects of a cult, continually disclaims association with witchcraft and insists on its status as a religion.

Moreover, the pervasive effect of mass media has elevated some superficial characteristics of cults—such as goth/vampire makeup and clothing—to an almost pop-culture status; consequently, the display of such trappings may not be indicative of serious involvement.

> A less negative term than *cult* is *new religious movement* (NRM).

Normally, NRMs have a charismatic leader who develops an idea that attracts people looking for fulfillment. The leader is usually self-appointed and claims the right of rule because of a supernatural power of appointment. NRM membership may include males and females, and there is normally no room for democratic participation. Leadership is most often exerted through fear and mysticism. Charles Manson and Jim Jones are examples of such leaders.

An NRM in Waco, Texas, the "Branch Davidians" headed by David Koresh, clashed with federal agents attempting a raid in February 1993. The raid turned into a gun battle in which four federal agents and at least two Branch Davidian members were killed. Sixteen agents were wounded. Weapons inside the compound included at least one tripod-mounted .50-caliber machine gun and many semiautomatic weapons. A child released from the compound who had lived there for 4 years said she had been taught to put a gun into her mouth and told how to commit suicide by taking cyanide.

A 51-day standoff between the federal government and Koresh's armed followers ended in April 1993, when fire engulfed the compound. The FBI had sent an armored combat vehicle to ram holes into the buildings and pump tear gas into them. The FBI asserted that Davidians started the blaze, an apparent mass suicide that killed at least 70, including women and children.

Survivors of the fire, however, insisted that it was caused by the tank's hitting a barrel of propane and tipping over lit camping lanterns. The FBI has been cleared of wrongdoing in this incident.

TERMINOLOGY AND SYMBOLS OF CULTS

Over the years, a number of terms have been associated with cults. Among the terms law enforcement officers should be familiar with are:

■ **Antichrist**—the son of Satan

■ **Beelzebub**—a powerful demon, directly under Satan

■ **Coven**—a group of witches or Satanists

■ **Hand of Glory**—the left hand of a person who has died

■ **Incantation**—verbal spell

■ **Magick**—the "glue" that binds occult groups, a supernatural act or force that causes a change in the environment

■ **Occult**—secret knowledge of supernormal powers

■ **Ritual**—prescribed form of religious or mystical ceremony

■ **Sabbat**—a gathering of witches

Among the satanic and occult symbols are the circle, which symbolizes totality and wholeness and within which ceremonies are often performed; the *inverted cross*, which mocks the Christian cross; the *goat's head*, symbolizing the devil; the *heart*, symbolizing the center of life; the hexagram (six-pointed star), purported to protect and control demons; the *pentagram* (five-pointed star), representing the four elements of the earth surmounted by "the Spirit"; and the *horned hand*, a hand signal of recognition used between those members. This is similar to the hand signals used by street gangs. Figure 19.5 illustrates symbols commonly associated with satanic and occult groups.

Colors also have significance to many cults:

■ Black—darkness, night, sorrow, evil, the devil

■ Blue—water, tears, sadness

■ Green—vegetation, nature, restfulness

■ Red—blood, physical life, energy, sexuality

■ White—cleanliness, purity, innocence, virginity

■ Yellow—perfection, wealth, glory, power

THE NATURE OF RITUALISTIC CRIMES

Cults and the occult have created great interest because of recurring stories from children and adults in different areas of the United States concerning bizarre satanic rituals and behaviors. Although some may be fantasies, there appears to be some truth, especially regarding the danger to children of the members of satanic groups.

A **ritualistic crime** is an unlawful act committed within the context of a ceremony. Investigate the crime, not the belief system.

Like gangs, occult groups have three levels of activity: dabbling, serious involvement and criminal involvement.

Ritualistic crimes include vandalism, destruction or theft of religious artifacts; desecration of cemeteries; the maiming, torturing or killing of animals and people; and the sexual abuse of children.

The "Black Masses" of Satanism often incorporate religious articles stolen from churches. A **Black Mass** mocks the Christian ritual of communion by substituting blood and urine for the wine and feces for the bread. The cross is usually inverted, and candles and cups may be used in sexual acts. "Hymns" either obscene or praising Satan may be sung, and heavy-metal music may be played.

The Black Mass frequently involves animal mutilation and sacrifice and sometimes torture and sacrifice of humans, often babies or virgins. The sacrifice often incorporates ritualistic incantations. Victims, animal or human, are tortured and mutilated because it is believed that while the victim struggles, the life forces given off can be captured and stored for later use. Such sacrifices may be followed by a dance and an orgy.

"Stoner" gangs consist of middle-class youths involved in drugs, alcohol and often Satanism. Although stoners are not as apt to engage in the violent crimes associated with other street gangs, they may mutilate animals, rob graves and desecrate churches and human

FIGURE 19.5
Common satanic and occult symbols.
© Cengage Learning, 2013

remains. Their graffiti frequently depicts satanic symbolism such as inverted crosses and the number 666.

WHO COMMITS RITUALISTIC CRIME?

A psychological profile of males and females involved in the occult reveals that they tend to be creative, imaginative, curious, daring and thus intelligent and well educated, yet are frequently underachievers. Although they are egocentric, they also have low self-esteem and have suffered peer rejection or persecution. They come from various social and economic backgrounds, can be any age (although the age range of 13 to 24 is the most common), and are of a variety of races, nationalities and religions. Interestingly, few Jews are involved in Satanism, because Judaism does not emphasize the devil.

A number of factors may lead an individual to occult involvement, including family alienation, insecurity and a quest for personal power, unfulfilled ambitions, a spiritual search for answers, idealism, nonconformity, adolescent rebellion, a desire for adventure and excitement, a need for attention and recognition and a need to escape reality or the circumstances of his or her own birth.

Although the personal appearance of those involved in occult activity is often quite normal, some adopt a less mainstream look. For example, they may dress entirely in black or other dark clothing; pierce various parts of their bodies; grow their hair long and dye it; wear chains as implements of confinement; wear heavy eye shadow and white makeup to appear more ashen or deathlike; wear heavy boots; display tattoos depicting serpents, skulls or other occult symbols; and have scars indicating cuttings, burnings or whippings.

Perlmutter (2003/2004) categorizes perpetrators of ritualistic crime as dabblers, true believers and "true criminals" and asserts that knowledge of how these various groups approach their crimes can help investigators focus their efforts in locating suspects and solving cases. Dabblers are intermittently involved in the occult and have a strong, curious interest in supernatural belief systems: "Such perpetrators most often act alone or in small, loosely organized groups. Dabblers usually make up their own belief system based upon some occult ideology and perpetrate criminal activity that conforms to that ideology" (Perlmutter). The crime scene of a dabbler is generally disorderly and considered by experts to be "sloppy."

True believers are committed to their religion and commit ritualistic crimes because the acts are required by their belief system. According to Perlmutter, true believers "do not consider their actions criminal although they do understand them to be illegal. For [these perpetrators], the violent act is a necessary religious ritual." Conversely, true criminals use the occult as an excuse to justify or rationalize their crimes: "They are committed not to the belief system but to the criminal action" (Perlmutter, 2003/2004). A well-known example of a true criminal was Richard Ramirez, also known as the Night Stalker:

> Self-styled Satanists such as Ramirez are not viewed as true believers since their primary interest is usually the acquisition of personal power, material gain, or gratification through criminal activity rather than spiritual Satanic worship. This does not mean that Richard Ramirez was not conducting ritualistic crimes; his crimes involved obvious ritual activities and contained Satanic symbolism, and he clearly identifies himself as a Satanist. Although dabblers, true criminals, and true believers can all be identified as Satanists, the differences in motivation significantly affect the types of rituals they conduct—hence the investigation and the evidence sought at the crime scene. For example, true criminals are not as concerned about the accurate symbolism, place, date,

> or victim of the rituals and are not connected to any organized group or specific Satanic tradition; consequently the symbolic evidence will be unique to that person. Dabblers most often are true believers who are emulating a particular tradition or theology but are not yet experienced enough to accurately conduct the ritual. Occasionally dabblers are true criminals who use the occult as a method to gain followers; in either case, the crime scene reflects a lack of knowledge or skill in sacred rites. (Perlmutter, 2003/2004)

INVESTIGATING RITUALISTIC CRIMES

Occult reports and activities are investigated in much the same way as any other crime. Interview the people who report these incidents, and prepare reports concerning witnesses or alleged victims of criminal activity. Take photos, sketch symbols, describe colors found and measure objects. Preserve all objects at the scene as evidence. Work from the outside perimeter to the center or the focus point of the site.

Numerous books on the beliefs and rituals of various cults are available. The background contained in such books is beyond the scope of this book, but investigators should be alert to signs that criminal activity may be cult related.

One challenge in investigating ritualistic crime is determining that an act is, in fact, motivated by a religious belief system, rather than by hate or bias. Some crimes, such as arson or vandalism, may not initially present clearly as one type of crime or the other, particularly when the victim or target has some religious component, such as a church or cemetery. Understanding the motivations behind these crimes will help investigators distinguish whether an act is rooted in hate or ritualism. Most of the signs, symbols and other indicators of ritualistic crime discussed next are rarely found at the scene of a hate crime, whereas derogatory or hate-filled verbalizations, graffiti or other written evidence are often present in bias crimes. Victim statements, if available, can provide valuable information regarding possible offender motivations. For example, did the offender(s) use racially charged language or other words indicating a hatred for the victim or others in the victim's perceived group (homosexuals, immigrants, religious groups, etc.), or did the offender's words and actions convey more of a ceremonial tone, mentioning sacrifices or other ritualistic purposes, including prayers or incantations? Did the offenders wear ceremonial-looking clothing or use any type of ceremonial or symbolic item, or were they brandishing baseball bats and other nonsymbolic weapons? These elements help investigators distinguish between hate crimes and ritualistic crimes.

Signs of Cult-Related Activity

The following items may be important indicators of satanic or cult activity. If you suspect ritualistic crime, list these items in any search warrant sought:

- Altars (stone or metal) or a wooden stand for an altar
- Animal parts (anus, heart, tongue, ears, front teeth, front legs, genitals), cages
- Ashes or bowls with powder, colored salt, drugs or herbs
- Bells, gongs, drums
- Blood, bottles containing blood (may be in a refrigerator), hypodermic needles (for removing blood)
- Body paint, painted rocks
- Body parts (may be in a freezer), skulls and bones, perhaps taken from graves (femur, fibula, index finger, skull and other large bones; the upper right leg and joints of the right-hand fingers are valued)
- Booby traps
- Books on Satanism (especially *Book of Shadows*)
- Bullwhips, cat-o'-nine-tails
- Candles, candle holders, candle drippings, incense
- Cauldron for a fire
- Chalices
- Circle with a 9-foot diameter (may contain a pentagram)
- Coffins
- Cords (colored and knotted) and ligatures
- Crystals
- Daggers, knives, swords (particularly double-edged short swords), martial arts weaponry and clothing
- Effigy-like clay figures or voodoo dolls stuck with pins or otherwise mutilated
- Flash powder, smoke bombs
- Hoods, robes (especially red, white or black), hats, helmets, gloves (black satin or velvet) for the right hand, masks
- Inverted crosses, vandalized Christian artifacts
- Jewelry such as amulets or medallions with satanic symbols

- Nondiscernible alphabet, satanic symbols painted on rocks or trees, unusual drawings or symbols on walls or floors (hexagrams, pentagrams, horns of death, etc.)
- Occult games, Ouija boards, tarot cards
- Parchment (for making contracts)
- Pillows
- Rooms draped in black or red (or nail holes in walls and ceiling indicating that such drapes may have been used)

Scott Dyleski, 16 at the time of this photo, appears behind a protective glass barrier in Judge David Flinn's courtroom in Martinez, California, Thursday, October 27, 2005. Dyleski was convicted of first-degree murder as an adult in the death of Pamela Vitale, the wife of prominent defense attorney and television commentator Daniel Horowitz. The 16-year-old suspect was reported to have been involved in some kind of self-styled Satanism, including the reading of Anton LeVay's Satanic Bible and use of occult symbols at the crime scene. Vitale was killed October 15, 2005, having been hit 39 times with a piece of crown molding and stabbed in the abdomen. A Lorraine Cross (a cross with two horizontal lines, the lower one larger than the upper one, which is associated with Satanism and suggests fire and brimstone) was carved into her back.

Dyleski was a juvenile at the time of the murder and, as such, was not eligible for the death penalty. Shortly after his 18th birthday on October 30, 2006, he was transferred from the juvenile facility where he was being held to a state prison, where he will serve his sentence of life without parole.

Indicators of Ritualistic Crimes

> Indicators that criminal activity may be cult related include symbols, candles, makeshift altars, bones, cult-related books, swords, daggers and chalices.

If evidence is found to support the commission of a crime, submit the case to the prosecuting attorney's office, as with other crimes. Also as with other crimes, if illegal acts are being committed in the presence of an officer who arrives at the scene, an immediate arrest may be executed. However, many authorities on cult activity warn that no one, including a police officer, should ever approach or try to stop an occult ritual alone because the officer would likely be dealing with mentally deranged people high on drugs.

Investigating Animal Deaths

Unusual circumstances surrounding animal deaths may be important indicators of satanic or cult activity. The following circumstances connected with dead animals should be noted:

■ No blood (the blood has been drained from the animal)

■ An inverted cross carved on the animal's chest

■ Surgically removed head

■ Intestines or other body organs removed

If a rash of missing-animal reports occurs, gather information on the kind of animals they are, when they disappeared and from what area. Look for patterns, and coordinate efforts with the local humane society, American Society for the Prevention of Cruelty to Animals (ASPCA) and veterinarians.

Investigating Homicides

According to Perlmutter (2003/2004), "Ritual homicides committed by true believers reflect a serious knowledge of the particular theology, a high level of skill, and meticulous attention to detail.…The perpetrator considers the murder to be a sacred act and the crime scene will reflect this." At the scene of a homicide investigation, the following may suggest a ritualistic death:

■ Missing body parts—heart, genitals, left hand, tongue, index finger

■ Scarring between index finger and thumb or inside the wrist from past rituals involving members' blood

■ Blood drained from body

■ Ritualistic symbols such as a pentagram associated with satanic worshipers carved on the body or surrounding area

■ Tattoos on armpits or the bottom of feet

■ Wax drippings, oils, incense or powders of ritual on the body

■ Urine or human or animal feces smeared on body or found in body cavities

■ Semen inside, on or near body cavities or smeared on the body

■ Victim undressed

■ Body painted or tied up

■ Neck wounds, branding-iron marks or burn marks on body

■ Colored strings near the body

Occult murders are usually stabbings or cuttings—seldom are they gunshot wounds—and many victims are cult members or former members. The murderer is typically a White male from a middle- to upper-class family with above-average intelligence and using some form of drug. Perlmutter asserts, "It takes a high level of experience to remove blood from a person or animal without soiling the scene; a juvenile dabbler will not be able to remove blood in the same manner as an experienced high priest, who could have the skills of a surgeon.… The role of the sacrificer is an honored and privileged position and will most likely be given to the leader of the group."

Guard against reacting emotionally when confronted with ritualistic crimes, for they tend to be emotionally and spiritually repulsive. Also bear in mind that unusual crimes are also committed by individuals with mental problems who are not connected with cults.

During postmortem examination, the stomach contents can be of great importance in determining what occurred just before death. In many ritualistic homicides, the body is not available because it has been burned, leaving no evidence. Further, most juries disbelieve seemingly outlandish charges of Satanism and human sacrifice, and most judges do not regard Satanism as a real problem. Hence, most cases are dismissed.

Investigating Satanic Serial Killings

Serial killings may be linked to satanic-like rituals in the murder act itself as well as in the killer's behavior following the murder. Serial killings frequently linked to Satanism include:

■ Charles Manson had links with the Process, a satanic group. Many of the murders committed by Manson and his followers had ritualistic overtones.

- The "Son of Sam" murders involving David Berkowitz are claimed by author Maury Terry in *The Ultimate Evil* to have been a conspiracy among satanic cult members of the Process group.

- Some brutal, vicious serial killers find Satanism a justification for their bizarre antisocial behavior.

- "Night Stalker" Richard Ramirez had a pentagram on the palm of his hand, wrote satanic graffiti on the walls of some of his victims' homes and was obsessed with AC/DC's *Highway to Hell* album featuring the song "Night Stalker." Ramirez shouted "Hail, Satan" as he left the courtroom.

SPECIAL CHALLENGES IN RITUALISTIC CRIME INVESTIGATIONS

Just as law enforcement officers may have difficulty relating to gang members and not reacting with scorn toward them because of their gang associations, they will almost certainly have difficulty relating to those who engage in ritualistic activity. This is also true of the general public and the media, which frequently sensationalize cases involving ritualistic or cult-related crimes, particularly sexual abuse of children and homicides.

> Special challenges involved in investigating ritualistic or cult-related crimes include separating the belief system from the illegal acts, the sensationalism that frequently accompanies such crimes and the "abnormal" personalities of some victims and suspects.

Frequently, the victims of cult-related crimes are former cult participants. Many have been or are currently undergoing psychological counseling, which makes their testimony less than credible to some people. Likewise, many suspects, the leaders in particular, are beyond the pale of what most people would consider to be normal and consequently may be treated differently because of how they look and what they believe rather than because of their actions.

Summary

Belonging to a gang is not illegal in this country; however, the activities of gang members frequently *are* illegal. The number of gangs and gang members has remained relatively stable over the last few years, but gang-related crime is still a serious concern for law enforcement. The National Gang Intelligence Center has identified three general types of gangs: street gangs, prison gangs and outlaw motorcycle gangs (OMGs).

In addition to drug dealing, gang members often engage in vandalism, arson, auto theft, shoplifting, shootings, stabbings, intimidation and other forms of violence. The first step in dealing with a gang problem is to recognize it. Gang members may be identified by their names, symbols (clothing and tattoos) and communication styles, including graffiti and sign language. Maintain records on gangs, gang members, monikers, photographs, vehicles and illegal activities. Cross-reference the records.

Special challenges in investigating the illegal activities of gangs include the multitude of suspects and the unreliability or fear of witnesses. A three-pronged approach to address the gang problem uses a balance of prevention, intervention and suppression strategies. The two most often used defense strategies in gang-related crime prosecutions are pleas of diminished capacity and of self-defense.

Other challenges are investigating bias or hate crimes and ritualistic crimes. Bias or hate crimes are acts motivated by bigotry and hatred against a specific group of people. Race is usually the primary motivation for bias and hate crime, and African Americans are often the victims.

Ritualistic crimes are often associated with the occult. A *cult* is a system of religious beliefs and rituals. It also refers to those who practice such beliefs. A less negative term than *cult* is a *new religious movement* (NRM). A ritualistic crime is an unlawful act committed within the context of a ceremony. Investigate the crime, not the belief system.

Ritualistic crimes include vandalism, destruction or theft of religious artifacts; desecration of cemeteries; the maiming, torturing or killing of animals and people; and the sexual abuse of children. Indicators that criminal activity may be cult related include symbols, candles,

■ Find the article "Understanding and Tackling Gang Violence" on the Gale Emergency Services Database. Read the article and outline it for in-class discussion.

■ Find the article "Gangs inside Prison Walls around the World" on the Gale Emergency Services Database. Read the article; compare and contrast the differences between prison gangs and non-prison gangs for in-class discussion.

References

Basich, Melanie. "Are Gang Members Hopeless Cases?" *Police*, May 2009, p.21.

Bell, Kerryn E. "Gender and Gangs: A Quantitative Comparison." *Crime & Delinquency*, Vol.55, No.3, July 2009, pp.363–387.

Bellair, Paul E., and McNulty, Thomas L. "Gang Membership, Drug Selling, and Violence in Neighborhood Context." *Justice Quarterly*, Vol.26, No.4, December 2009, pp.644–669.

Best Practices to Address Community Gang Problems, 2nd ed. Washington, DC: National Gang Center, October 2010.

Bjerregaard, Beth. "Gang Membership and Drug Involvement: Untangling the Complex Relationship." *Crime & Delinquency*, Vol.56, No.1, January 2010, pp.3–34.

Brief Review of Federal and State Definitions of the Terms "Gang," "Gang Crime," and "Gang Member." Washington DC: National Gang Center, 2009. Accessed August 28, 2011. http://www.nationalgangcenter.gov/Content/Documents/Definitions.pdf

Crime in the United States 2009. Washington, DC: Federal Bureau of Investigation, 2009.

Dawe, Brian. "Prison Gangs: An Overview." *American Cop Magazine*, November/December 2009, pp.16–17.

Decker, Scott H.; Katz, Charles M.; and Webb, Vincent J. "Understanding the Black Box of Gang Organization." *Crime & Delinquency*, January 2008, Vol.54, No.1, pp.153–172.

"Defining Gangs and Designating Gang Membership." In *National Youth Gang Survey Analysis*. National Gang Center, 2009. Accessed August 28, 2011. http://www.national gangcenter.gov/Survey-Analysis/Defining-Gangs

Eggers, Ron. "The Gang Problem: Difficult to Define and Even More Difficult to Solve. Part 1 of 3." *9-1-1 Magazine*, August–September–October 2009, pp.12–20.

Egley, Arlen, Jr., and Howell, James C. *Highlights of the 2009 National Youth Gang Survey*. Washington, DC: Office of Juvenile Justice Delinquency Prevention, June 2011. (NCJ 233581)

Fine, John Christopher. "Street Gangs on the East Coast." *9-1-1 Magazine*, November–December 2009, pp.16–22.

Garrett, Ronnie. "Loosening the Noose on Bigotry." *Law Enforcement Technology*, June 2008, pp.20–27.

Gibson, Chris L.; Miller, J. Mitchell; Jennings, Wesley G.; Swatt, Marc; and Gover, Angela. "Using Propensity Score Matching to Understand the Relationship between Gang Membership and Violent Victimization: A Research Note." *Justice Quarterly*, Vol.26, No.4, December 2009, pp.625–643.

Griffith, David. "Gangster Nation." *Police*, November 2008, pp.46–53.

"Hate and Extremism." Southern Poverty Law Center, 2011. Accessed August 28, 2011. http://splcenter.org/what-we-do/hate-and-extremism

Hate Crime Statistics, 2009. Washington, DC: Federal Bureau of Investigation, Uniform Crime Report, November 2010. Accessed August 28, 2011. http://www2.fbi.gov/ucr/hc2009/index.html

Howell, James C. *Gang Prevention: An Overview of Research and Programs*. Washington, DC: Office of Juvenile Justice and Delinquency Prevention, Juvenile Justice Bulletin, December 2010. (NCJ 231116)

Howell, James C., and Moore, John P. *History of Street Gangs in the United States*. Washington, DC: National Gang Center, Bulletin No.4, May 2010.

Klein, Malcolm W. *Chasing after Street Gangs: A Forty-Year Journey*. Upper Saddle River, NJ: Pearson/Prentice Hall, 2007.

Miller, Christa. "Vandalists Were Here." *Law Enforcement Technology*, September 2010, pp.40–45.

Moore, Carole. "The ACLU Plays 'Go Fish.'" *Law Enforcement Technology*, November 2007a, p.98.

Moore, Carole. "Street Gangs." *Law Enforcement Technology*, January 2007b, pp.52–57.

Morley, Patrick J. "Eyes on the Street." *Police*, October 2008, pp.52–54.

National Gang Threat Assessment, 2009. Washington, DC: National Gang Intelligence Center, 2009.

National Youth Gang Survey Analysis. Washington, DC: National Youth Gang Center, 2009. Accessed August 23, 2011. http://www.nationalgangcenter.gov/Survey-Analysis

O'Deane, Matthew, and Murphy, William Patrick. "Identifying and Documenting Gang Members." *Police*, September 2010, pp.52–61.

Ortega, Francisca, and Calderoni, Valeria. "Gangs Unite as 'Hybrids,' Increasing Violence." *Police One*, October 1, 2007.

"PERF Report Describes Changes in Gang Dynamics." *Subject to Debate*, Vol.24, No.2, February 2010, pp.1, 7

Perlmutter, Dawn. "The Forensics of Sacrifice: A Symbolic Analysis of Ritualistic Crime." *Anthropoetics*, Fall 2003/Winter 2004. Accessed September 2, 2008. http://www.anthropoetics.ucla.edu/ap0902/sacrifice.htm

Petrocelli, Joseph. "Graffiti." *Police*, March 2008, pp.18–19.

Phillips, Amanda. "Skinheads in America." *Law Enforcement Technology*, October 2007, pp.64–71.

Pistole, John S. "Major Executive Speeches." Washington, DC: Federal Bureau of Investigation, March 3, 2008.

Posey, Ed. "Using Existing Records to Keep a Closer Eye on Sex Offenders and Gang Members in the Community." *The Police Chief*, June 2008, pp.38–47.

Turner, Nancy. *Responding to Hate Crimes: A Police Officer's Guide to Investigation and Prevention*. Alexandria, VA: International Association of Chiefs of Police, 1999. Accessed October 19, 2005. Available through the IACP Web site, http://www.theiacp.org

2005 National Gang Threat Assessment. Washington, DC: Bureau of Justice Statistics, 2005.

Valdemar, Richard. "Investigating Gangs Outside the Gang Squad." *Police*, July 2007, pp.48–53.

Valdemar, Richard." Investigating Gang Homicides." *Police*, October 2010, pp.36–43.

Villanueva, Alexandro. "Ends-Based Model of Multi-Dimensional Policing." *Law and Order*, July 2009, pp.70–74.

Cases Cited

Chicago v. Morales, 527 U.S. 41 (1999)

Virginia v. Black, 538 U.S. 343 (2003)

CHAPTER 20
Terrorism and Homeland Security

Outline

Can You Define?

asymmetric warfare

bioterrorism

contagion effect

cyberterrorism

deconfliction

ecoterrorism

fusion center

hawala

intifada

jihad

sleeper cell

technological terrorism

terrorism

Do You Know?

- What most definitions of terrorism have in common?
- What motivates most terrorist attacks?
- How the FBI classifies terrorist acts?
- What groups are commonly identified as Islamic terrorist organizations?
- What domestic terrorist groups exist in the United States?
- What methods terrorists may use?
- What federal office was established as a result of 9/11?
- What the two lead agencies in combating terrorism are?
- How the USA PATRIOT Act enhances counterterrorism efforts by the United States?
- What the first line of defense against terrorism in the United States is?
- What the three-tiered model of al-Qaeda terrorist attacks consists of?
- What a key to successfully combating terrorism is?
- What the Law Enforcement Officers Safety Act authorizes?
- What two concerns related to the war on terrorism are?
- What balance must be maintained in investigating terrorism?

The terrorist attacks of September 11, 2001, sounded a wake-up call to Americans. And although the 9/11 attacks were a shock, they should not have been a surprise. Islamist extremists had given ample warning that they meant to kill Americans. The critical failures were not believing the gravity of the threat or piecing together quickly enough the intelligence that had been gathered about the impending attack. However, in his speech before Congress, the country and the world on September 20, 2001, President George W. Bush stated, "Tonight we are a country awakened to danger and called to defend freedom. Our grief has turned to anger, and anger to resolution."

In addition to galvanizing the nation, the events of that tragic day had other ramifications, such as changing how our nation views its security, with law

The terrorist attacks of September 11, 2001, rocked the entire nation. First responders to the World Trade Center crime scene, including law enforcement officers and firefighters, were invaluable in saving countless lives but were also among the many casualties of the horrific event. A positive consequence of this tragedy was the galvanization of American patriotism and a resolve of citizens to join law enforcement in the daily efforts to protect our freedoms and valued way of life.
Left: A police officer lowers his face mask and signals to someone near the site of the World Trade Center, Wednesday, September 12, 2001, in New York.
© AP Images/Virgil Case
Right: Firemen, police officers and workers lock arms while observing a moment of prayer during a short interfaith memorial service held at the World Trade Center disaster site, Thursday morning, October 11, 2001, in New York.
© AP Images/Gary Friedman, Pool

enforcement working to redefine its role as traditional crime fighters while taking on tremendous new counterterrorism activities. But the threat remains. The Justice Department's top priority is to support law enforcement and intelligence agencies in the fight against terrorism. Stockton (2008, p.8) notes,

After Sept. 11, our country entered a new era of policing. Departments around the country looked at their mission differently. Think back on some of the major changes:

- Federal agencies were reorganized.

- Entirely new agencies were established, including the Transportation Security Administration and the Department of Homeland Security.

- Billions of dollars have been spent in an effort to better equip and prepare agencies to respond to both natural and humanmade disasters.

- Interoperability in communications and data sharing has not only become a priority but is also the norm in some parts of the country.

Burruss et al. (2010, p.78) note, "During the past 10 years, many agencies have enhanced emergency preparedness through a variety of measures including, but not limited to, completing risk assessments, gathering and/or disseminating terrorism-related intelligence, updating or entering into mutual aid agreements, participating in joint-training activities, and developing formal written response plans for terrorist incidents."

Despite the necessity to ramp up our strategy to address the threat of terrorism, we cannot afford to neglect the attention and resources devoted to traditional crimes. Many have voiced concern over the increased attention and funding given to terrorism: "The Department of Homeland Security announced $1.9 billion in anti-terrorism grants yesterday, stirring a growing debate among state and local officials nationwide over whether such funds are coming at the expense of other law enforcement priorities that some say are more urgent, such as fighting drugs, gangs, and violent crime" (Hsu, 2008, p.A02). The increase in violent crime in recent years has led some to dub homeland security "the monster that ate criminal justice" and resulted in louder warnings that local police departments cannot be effective homeland security partners if they are overwhelmed by the responsibilities of their core mission (Garrett, 2007, p.10). The need for balancing crime fighting efforts with counterterrorism efforts should be kept in mind while reading this chapter, for as Kelling et al. (2007) point out, "For cops crime fighting and counterterrorism go hand in hand."

TERRORISM: AN OVERVIEW

The United States has not been immune from terrorist attacks from within and without. Consider, for example, the raids of the Ku Klux Klan, the mail bombings of the Unabomber, the 1993 attack on the World Trade Center and the 1995 bombing of the Alfred P. Murrah Building in Oklahoma City. Most terrorist acts result from dissatisfaction with a religious, political or social system or policy and an inability to change it through acceptable, nonviolent means.

The United States paid lip service to fighting terrorism in 1995 when the Federal Bureau of Investigation (FBI) established a Counterterrorism Center. In 1996 the Antiterrorism and Effective Death Penalty Act was passed, enhancing the federal government's powers to deny visas to individuals belonging to terrorist groups and simplifying the process for deporting aliens convicted of crimes. On February 23, 1998, Osama bin Laden called for **jihad**, a holy war, on the United States, calling on every Muslim to comply with God's order to kill Americans and plunder their money wherever and whenever they find it.

In 1999 FBI Director Louis Freeh announced, "Our number-one priority is the prevention of terrorism." But it took the horrendous attacks of September 11, 2001, to truly get our attention. Those attacks were criminal. It is up to law enforcement throughout the country to investigate possible terrorist activities. To do so, it is important to "know the enemy" and to understand terrorism and those who engage in it.

Terrorism Defined

Terrorism is difficult to define because, as the saying goes, "One man's terrorist is another man's freedom fighter." The FBI defines **terrorism** as "the unlawful use of force or violence against persons or property to intimidate or coerce a government, the civilian population, or any segment thereof, in furtherance of political or social objectives" (28 *Code of Federal Regulations* Section 0.85). The U.S. Code, Title 22, defines terrorism as the "premeditated, politically motivated violence perpetrated against noncombatant targets by subnational groups or clandestine agents" (22 U.S.C. § 2656f(d)(2)).

> Most definitions of terrorism have common elements, including the systematic use of physical violence, either actual or threatened, against noncombatants to create a climate of fear to cause some religious, political or social change.

Motivations for Terrorism

> Most terrorist acts result from dissatisfaction with a religious, political or social system or policy and frustration resulting from an inability to change it through acceptable, nonviolent means.

Al-Qaeda. A very different terrorist group, and perhaps the greatest threat to the United States, is al-Qaeda, meaning "the base." Founded in the late 1980s by now-deceased bin Laden, al-Qaeda is a broad-based Islamic militant organization that began as a logistical network to support Muslims fighting against the Soviet Union during the Afghan War. When the Soviets withdrew from Afghanistan in 1989, the organization dispersed but continued to oppose what its leaders considered corrupt Islamic regimes and foreign presence in Islamic lands. The group eventually reestablished its headquarters in Afghanistan under the patronage of the Taliban militia.

Al-Qaeda merged with other Islamic extremist organizations, and long before the events of 9/11, its leaders openly declared jihad on the United States. Tens of thousands of Muslim militants throughout the world were trained in military skills, and its agents have engaged in numerous terrorist attacks, including the 1998 bombings of the U.S. embassies in Dar es Salaam, Tanzania, and Nairobi, Kenya—attacks that killed more than 200 people. Bin Laden was indicted for his role in planning the attacks and added to the FBI's Ten Most Wanted Fugitives list in 1999. After 9/11, when intelligence agencies learned that the attacks were carried out by bin Laden's terrorist organization, his name was added to the U.S. Department of State's Most Wanted Terrorists List and a nearly decade-long global search for bin Laden began.

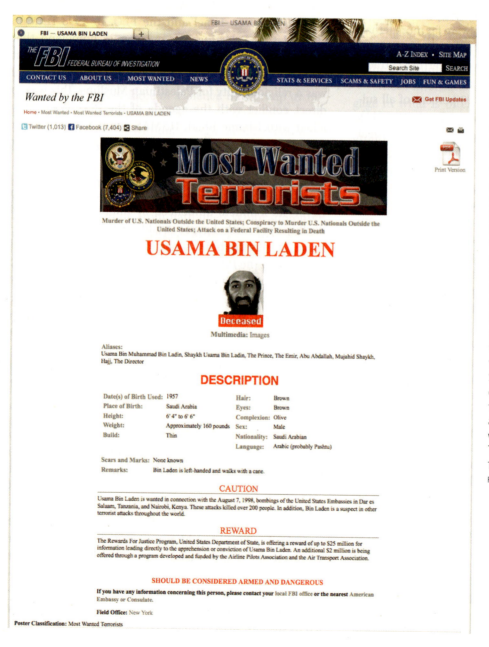

Long before the tragic events of September 11, 2001, al Qaeda leader, Osama bin Laden, had openly declared jihad on the United States and was determined to kill as many Americans as possible. Bin Laden was on both the FBI's Ten Most Wanted Fugitives list and the U.S. Department of State's Most Wanted Terrorists list.

The FBI's "Ten Most Wanted Fugitives" list began in March 1950, when a reporter for the International News Service (the predecessor to United Press International) asked the FBI for the names and descriptions of the "toughest guys" the Bureau would like to capture. The overwhelming publicity generated by the story prompted then-FBI Director J. Edgar Hoover to create the "Ten Most Wanted Fugitives" program. The first person placed on the list was Thomas James Holden, wanted for the murder of his wife, her brother, and her stepbrother. Since its inception, 494 fugitives (8 of whom were women) have been on the "Top Ten" list, and 465 have been apprehended or located. Bin Laden was the 456th person placed on the Top Ten Fugitives list, added on June 7, 1999 and removed on May 1, 2011.
FBI photo

By August 2010, intelligence had developed to a point where there existed a "high probability" that bin Laden was hiding at a compound deep inside Pakistan. For the next eight months, intelligence and counterterrorism agencies worked tirelessly to confirm the data, while special forces trained for their anticipated mission involving a "high value target." On May 1, 2011, President Barack Obama authorized U.S. special forces to raid the compound in Abbottabad, Pakistan, where bin Laden was located and executed. His body was removed from the compound by the highly classified and now infamous Seal Team 6, his identity was verified and he was then immediately buried at sea. In August 2011 al-Qaeda suffered another major blow when its second-in-command, Atiyah Abd al-Rahman, was killed in Pakistan. There are reports that al-Qaeda is currently planning to produce Disney-like animated cartoons aimed at recruiting young children into the terror network, a tactic that may indicate they are having difficulty recruiting older members in more traditional ways.

The Threat and Reality of Terrorism

The events of 9/11 turned the threat of terrorism into a reality for U.S. citizens. Just how real this threat is has been examined in *National Intelligence Estimate: The Terrorist Threat to the U.S. Homeland* (2007), a report that uses *estimative language*, that is, language based on analytical assessments and judgments rather than on facts or hard evidence. The report uses terms such as *we assess* and *we judge* synonymously and outlines several key judgments (pp.6–7):

> We judge the U.S. Homeland will face a persistent and evolving terrorist threat over the next three years. The main threat comes from Islamic terrorist groups and cells, especially al-Qa'ida, driven by their undiminished intent to attack the Homeland and a continued effort by these terrorist groups to adapt and improve their capabilities.
>
> We assess that greatly increased worldwide counterterrorism efforts over the past five years have constrained the ability of al-Qa'ida to attack the U.S. Homeland again and have led terrorist groups to perceive the Homeland as a harder target to strike than on 9/11. These measures have helped disrupt known plots against the United States since 9/11.
>
> We are concerned, however, that this level of international cooperation may wane as 9/11 becomes a more distant memory and perceptions of the threat diverge.
>
> Al-Qa'ida is and will remain the most serious terrorist threat to the Homeland, as its central leadership continues to plan high-impact plots, while pushing

> others in extremist Sunni communities to mimic its efforts and to supplement its capabilities. . . . We judge that the United States currently is in a heightened threat environment.
>
> We assess that al-Qa'ida will continue to enhance its capabilities to attack the Homeland through greater cooperation with regional terrorist groups. . . .
>
> We assess that al-Qa'ida's Homeland plotting is likely to continue to focus on prominent political, economic and infrastructure targets with the goal of producing mass casualties, visually dramatic destruction, significant economic aftershocks, and/or fear among the U.S. population. The group is proficient with conventional small arms and improvised explosive devices, and is innovative in creating new capabilities and overcoming security obstacles.
>
> We assess that al-Qa'ida will continue to try to acquire and employ chemical, biological, radiological or nuclear material in attacks and would not hesitate to use them if it develops what it deems is sufficient capability. . . .
>
> We assess that other, non-Muslim terrorist groups—often referred to as "single-issue" groups by the FBI—probably will conduct attacks over the next three years given their violent histories, but we assess this violence is likely to be on a small scale.

DeYoung (2007, p.A01) is one of many who believe the next terrorist assault on the United States is likely to consist of relatively unsophisticated, near simultaneous attacks similar to those attempted in Britain in June, 2007, intended to cause widespread fear and panic rather than to cause major losses. Counterterrorism officials say the attacks in England and Scotland coincide with U.S. intelligence indicating increased movement of money and people from al-Qaeda camps in the ungoverned tribal areas of Pakistan near the Afghan border (DeYoung).

The Dual Threat

While the United States seeks to protect itself from international terrorist groups such as al-Qaeda, it must also protect its citizens from those among us who would like nothing better than to tear the country apart and recast it in their own image. America's police officers are on the front lines of both battles.

TERRORIST GROUPS IN THE UNITED STATES

Several groups on the left and right, including environmentalist groups, pose specific challenges and threats to law enforcement.

> Domestic terrorist groups within the United States include White supremacists, Black supremacists, militia groups, other right-wing extremists, left-wing extremists, pro-life extremists, animal rights extremists and environmental extremists.

Many of these groups were discussed in Chapter 19 as hate groups or cults.

White Supremacists

The Ku Klux Klan (KKK) is one of America's original terrorist organizations. Founded by gifted Confederate cavalry commander Nathan Bedford Forrest, the Klan's original purpose was to create an anti-unionist organization to preserve Southern culture and tradition and exert political influence over the Reconstruction south. When the newly formed Klan became violent toward freed slaves, Forrest tried unsuccessfully to disband the group. But the momentum was too strong, and the KKK became a campaign of hate (White, 2012). The strength and organization of the Klan has waxed and waned over the years, and the modern Klan is fragmented and decentralized, yet still dominated by hate-filled rhetoric aimed at racial minorities. Neo-Nazi groups also espouse White supremacy, as do "skinheads."

Black Supremacists

The Black Panther Party for Self-Defense was established in 1966 during a time of racial turmoil: "Today, a newly reconstituted Black Panther Party for Self-Defense has been organized, and it qualifies as a hate group. These contemporary Panthers are heavily armed, advocate violence against Whites and, like their 1960s predecessors, see cops as the enemy" (Scoville, 2003, p.46).

The Militia Movement

Most militia groups are heavily armed and place great emphasis on practicing sharpshooting skills. Militia members are commonly frustrated, overwhelmed and socially unable to cope with the rapid pace of change in the modern world. Many militia groups provide the rhetoric for violence (White, 2012).

Other Right-Wing Extremists

The preceding groups might also be described as right-wing extremists. Three issues that rejuvenated the extreme right during the 1980s and have kept it active since then are the Brady Bill and the Ruby Ridge and Waco incidents (White, 2012). The Brady Bill caused militia groups to fear federal gun control legislation. The Ruby Ridge incident involved an attempt to arrest Randy Weaver, a White supremacist charged with selling illegal firearms to undercover agents of the Bureau of Alcohol, Tobacco and Firearms (ATF). A shootout ensued, resulting in the death of a U.S. marshal and Weaver's young son. The FBI laid siege to Weaver's Ruby Ridge cabin and killed his pregnant wife before Weaver surrendered.

The third galvanizing incident occurred in 1993 with the federal siege of the Branch Davidian compound near Waco, Texas, which began when ATF agents attempted to serve a search warrant on the compound and were met with a hail of gunfire. Four federal agents were killed in the exchange, and several others were wounded. After a three-month siege, FBI agents moved in with tear gas, unaware that the compound had been laced with gasoline. Rather than surrender to the FBI, the Branch Davidians set fire to their compound, killing more than 70 people inside, including several young children. Claims by compound survivors that government tanks started the fire have been unfounded.

Left-Wing Extremists

Left-wing extremists believe in a Pro-Marxist stance that the rich must be brought down and the poor elevated. Presently, the largest groups of supporters for this cause are Anarchists.

Pro-Life Extremists

Although many pro-life, antiabortion advocates stay within the law in promoting their beliefs, some groups do not. One such group is an active terrorist organization called the Army of God: "Abortion clinics and their staffs are common Army of God targets, with zealots committing crimes ranging from arson to assault to assassination" (Scoville, 2003, p.48).

Animal Rights Extremists

The Animal Liberation Front (ALF), a clandestine, decentralized group, is one of the most active domestic terrorist assemblages, its objective being to eliminate animal euthanasia and prevent the use of animals in scientific lab testing by "liberating" such caged animals. Their acts of arson, vandalism and other crimes targeted at research labs, meat packing plants and furriers "often do not rise to the level of a federal violation—placing them directly in the wheelhouse of local law enforcement agencies" (Downing, 2009, p.35). ALF members also commit petty theft and robbery to sustain themselves and their criminal enterprise. Some elements of this group have become increasingly violent in recent years (Downing, 2009).

Environmental Extremists

Environmental extremists are often referred to as "ecoterrorists," with *eco* being derived from *ecology*—the study of the interrelationships of organisms and their environment. **Ecoterrorism** seeks to inflict economic damage on those who profit from the destruction of the natural environment. The term *ecoterrorism* in conjunction with saving the environment is controversial because few people want to harm animals, and even fewer want to harm the planet. However, some cross the line from rhetoric to terror. When they cross this line, their violent actions are criminal.

One such group is the Earth Liberation Front (ELF), which often works with the ALF. Arson is a favorite weapon, responsible for tens of millions of dollars of property damage, including a U.S. Department of Agriculture building, a U.S. Forest Service ranger station and a Colorado ski resort. The group has claimed responsibility for releasing 5,000 mink from a Michigan fur farm, releasing 600 wild horses from an Oregon corral and burning the Michigan State University's genetic engineering research offices.

TERRORISTS AS CRIMINALS

Law enforcement agencies and officers who have been trained and equipped to deal with traditional crimes are now focusing on apprehending individuals operating with different motivations, different objectives and much deadlier weapons than traditional criminals use. Whereas conventional criminals generally seek personal financial or material gain and an escape route, terrorists seek to cause wide-scale damage and inflict fear and may be less concerned with escape—suicide bombers being the extreme type of terrorism willing to sacrifice their lives for their cause. Furthermore, "Research has shown that traditional criminals are spontaneous, but terrorists seem to go to great lengths preparing for their attacks—and may commit other crimes while doing so" (Smith, 2008, p.2). A critical difference in approach exists between dealing with a terrorist and a street criminal: when fighting terrorists, it's kill or be killed, not capture and convict.

METHODS USED BY TERRORISTS

Terrorists have employed a variety of techniques in furtherance of their cause. Figure 20.1 illustrates the primary attack types used by terrorists in 2010.

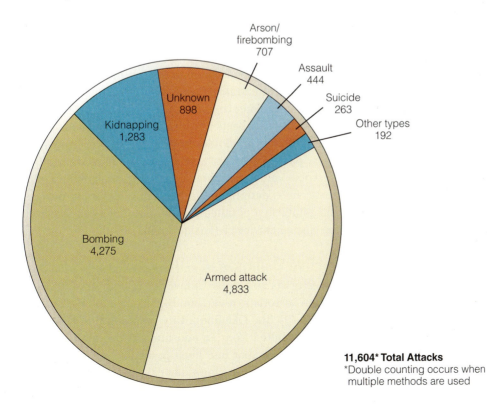

FIGURE 20.1
Primary attack types.
Source: http://www.nctc.gov/witsbanner/docs/2010

Arson/firebombing 707
Assault 444
Suicide 263
Other types 192
Unknown 898
Kidnapping 1,283
Bombing 4,275
Armed attack 4,833

11,604* Total Attacks
*Double counting occurs when multiple methods are used

> In addition to armed attacks, terrorists use arson, explosives and bombs; weapons of mass destruction (biological, chemical or nuclear agents); or technology.

Law enforcement agencies use the term *CBR* to include all potential terrorist threats that can have consequences for the health of large numbers of people. These threats include chemical agents (C), biological agents (B) and radiation exposure (R). Figure 20.2 presents the most likely to least likely terrorist threats; Figure 20.3 illustrates the relative level of impact by weapon used. Although explosives are considered the most likely to be used by terrorists, they also carry the least amount of impact relative to the other threats.

Explosives and Bombs

Directions for making pipe bombs and other incendiary devices can be found easily on the Internet, and the use of improvised explosive devices (IEDs) by terrorists and conventional criminals is recognized as the most dangerous emerging threat to our homeland defense: "Cheap, lethal, and low-tech, the IED has been the weapon of choice for foreign terrorists since the first World Trade Center attack in 1993 and for domestic terrorists since the Oklahoma City bombing in 1995. From Madrid to London, Bali to Mumbai, and Baghdad to Kabul, the IED is a global tactical and strategic threat to Americans and our allies" (Corderre and Register, 2009, p.38).

An estimated 2,600 to 3,000 explosive incidents occur in the United States every year (Galvin, 2010). Incendiary devices and explosives are commonly used because they are easy to make. Bombing does require a certain level of organization, equipment, materials and a place to put the bomb together, all aspects that an investigator's knowledge can help detect, helping prevent these crimes. Furthermore, to be a good bomber, one must have practice: "Well-educated people do not necessarily make good terrorists. The medical doctors behind the failed 2007 car bombings in London and Glasgow, Scotland, lacked the bomb making skills of the petty criminals who killed 56 people in the London Tube and bus bombings two years before" (Kenney, 2010, p.18). Successful bombers must hone their skills through practical application and detonation of their work, which necessarily exposes them to detection and apprehension by authorities: "Lack of practice leads to mistakes that alert law enforcement officers can detect" (Kenney, 2010, p.20).

Investigating bombings was discussed in Chapter 16. The following discussion is intended to provide supplemental information within the context of investigating terrorist activities.

Most Likely

Explosives
Toxic Industrial Chemicals
Radiological Dispersal Devices
Biological Agents/Weapons
Nuclear Weapons

Least Likely

FIGURE 20.2
Terrorist threats from most likely to least likely.
Source: Melissa Reuland and Heather J. Davis. *Protecting Your Community form Terrorism: Strategies for Local Law Enforcement, Vol. 3: Preparing for and Responding to Bioterrorism.* Washington, DC: Community Oriented Policing Services Office and the Police Executive Research Forum, September 2004, p.7, Reprinted by permission of the Police Executive Research Forum.

Greatest Impact

Biological Agents/Weapons
Nuclear Weapons
Toxic Industrial Chemicals
Radiological Dispersal Devices
Explosives

Least Impact

FIGURE 20.3
Level of impact by weapon used.
Source: Melissa Reuland and Heather J. Davis. *Protecting Your Community form Terrorism: Strategies for Local Law Enforcement, Vol. 3: Preparing for and Responding to Bioterrorism.* Washington, DC: Community Oriented Policing Services Office and the Police Executive Research Forum, September 2004, p.8, Reprinted by permission of the Police Executive Research Forum.

Suspicious Packages. Security officers dispatched to a suspicious package, unattended bag or other such items must be extremely cautious: "Once any item is considered suspicious, treat it as a bomb" (Laska, 2008, p.41). If an officer suspects the involved device is an actual bomb, the officer should move to hard cover away from glass, parked vehicles and secondary hazards such as electricity and gas; secure all radios and cell phones until the scene is determined to be clear of explosive devices; and establish a perimeter a minimum of 1,000 feet from the suspicious device (Laska, 2008).

Vehicle Bombs. Cars and large vehicles are also used by terrorists as bombs: "A favorite of both domestic and foreign terrorists, a car bomb packs a punch" (Griffith, 2010, p.49). The Oklahoma City bombing that killed 168 people resulted from an enormous bomb ignited inside a rental truck that had been parked in a drop-off zone underneath the building's day care center. The 2010 attempted bombing in Times Square involved a parked vehicle, from which smoke was coming. Two street vendors reported the suspicious vehicle to police before any damage occurred. Griffith (2010, p.49) offers two pieces of advice: "The first thing you need to remember is that a simple parking violation could be a car bomb. . . .The second thing that you need to remember is that the first explosion may not be the primary attack. Terrorists can be very cunning. They know that a bomb attack is going to draw a lot of attention. And to their point of view, all those responders, all those firefighters, cops, and EMTs [emergency medical technicians], are a juicy target."

Suicide Bombers. With regard to bombs, "The suicide bomber has emerged internationally as a most serious threat" (Laska, 2008, p.42). Suicide terrorists intentionally kill themselves as a means of killing as many bystanders as possible, and they do so in the name of their political or ideological beliefs. Whereas a typical criminal will very rarely look to lay down his life for the sake of crime, suicide bombers go to their targets knowing that they will die there. Most believe the act makes them martyrs and ensures them a place in their version of heaven. Their families are usually held in reverence and taken care of.

Wexler (2007, p.i) suggests, "The 9/11 hijackers were the ultimate suicide bombers. They used commercial aircraft as bombs rather than devices that fit inside a backpack. But at their core, their motivations were the same—they believed that political or religious ideology justified murdering innocent bystanders and killing themselves in the process." Wexler reports that when experts were asked which two types of terrorist attacks are most likely, the most common response was "suicide bombing attacks" closely followed by "attack on major infrastructure."

The notion of a suicide bomber as a young male, fundamentalist fanatic is dangerously narrow-minded. Potential suicide terrorists may come from different backgrounds and different age groups, and be male or female, educated or uneducated, upstanding citizen or deviant. Among the warning signs revealing a suicide bomber are unseasonable garb; profuse sweating; obvious disguises (such as a police uniform with a security badge); and a well-dressed, perfumed appearance and demeanor fitting for one who is going to meet his maker.

Priem et al. (2007, p.35) explain the typical phases in a suicide bombing attack:

> The operational cycle for suicide bombing attacks can be viewed as a nine-phase process that begins with identification and recruitment of bombers; continues through their training, target selection, purchase of components, fabrication of devices, final preparation, and movement to the target; and ends with the detonation of the device. . . .

Interdiction during the last two phases is extremely difficult. Law enforcement agencies must be proactive, taking advantage of opportunities for detection and effective interdiction during the initial seven stages. . . .

There is evidence to suggest that recruiting initiatives may be under way in U.S. prison populations and among radicalized extremists—including U.S. citizens in a number of U.S. communities. . . .

Perhaps the best opportunities for detection and successful interdiction occur when terrorist organizations are selecting targets and conducting reconnaissance against them as well as when they are purchasing explosives components and fabricating explosive devices.

Agencies are strongly encouraged to develop suicide bomb response protocols, with principles consistent with the agency's use of force policies, procedures and training (Spahr et al., 2007, p.13). The Police Executive Research Forum (PERF) has developed guidelines for a patrol-level response to a suicide bomb threat, stressing that any protocol should be consistent with the agency's policies and procedures for use of force, active shooter situations and bomb threats.

Weapons of Mass Destruction (WMDs)

Much concern centers around potential use of nuclear, biological and chemical agents, also referred to as NBC agents. Because such agents carry the potential to cause widespread devastation, they are also referred to as weapons of mass destruction (WMDs). Biological WMDs have actually been in use since the 1300s. The 20th century brought the first use of artificially produced WMDs—or chemical agents—during World War I. Today, the means for developing nuclear, radiological, biological and chemical weapons are well known.

Some experts suggest that, of these three NBC means, bioterrorism is the least likely to occur whereas chemical attacks are the most likely because the raw materials are easy to get and the devices are simple to assemble and use.

Biological Agents. Bioterrorism involves dissemination of anthrax, botulism and smallpox as WMDs, and is a potential reality following the anthrax scare of 2001 on the heels of the 9/11 attacks. Especially susceptible to bioterrorism are the nation's food and water supplies, which might also be attacked using chemical agents.

Chemical Agents. The attention of security experts was riveted on the potential for chemical terrorism in 1995 when members of Aum Shinrikyu, a new-age cult, released deadly sarin gas into the Tokyo subway system, killing 12 and sending 5,000 to the hospital. It was what many considered their worst nightmare. Unfortunately, anyone with Internet access and a Web browser can, in less than 40 minutes, obtain the chemical formula for the invisible, odorless and highly toxic sarin gas.

One chemical agent receiving increased attention in security periodicals is chlorine gas. Although a chlorine gas attack requires perfect conditions and a poor emergency response to cause heavy casualties, "if properly released in a well-populated area, chlorine gas has the potential to cause tens of thousands of casualties" (Harwood, 2007, p.18).

The four common types of chemical weapons are nerve agents, blood agents, choking agents and blistering agents. One agent, ricin toxin, is both a biological and a chemical weapon. Ricin is more than 1,000 times more poisonous than cyanide and in its purest form, a grain of ricin no bigger than a grain of table salt can kill an adult.

The Department of Homeland Security (DHS) has released interim rules to streamline federal security regulations for high-risk chemical facilities nationwide (Edwards, 2007, p.1). The DHS will screen more than 15,000 chemical facilities and require those with certain quantities of specified chemicals complete an assessment to determine a risk level. A company found to pose greater risk will be required to conduct a vulnerability assessment and submit site security plans that meet the DHS performance standards (Daniels, 2007, p.8). Failure to comply could result in penalties as high as $25,000 per day and an order to cease operations.

Nuclear Terrorism.
A survey conducted for the Sage Foundation found that the top fear of Americans is nuclear terrorism; 74 percent of Americans believe that a successful terrorist attack on U.S. soil is likely to happen, with almost half (49 percent) believing an attack will include some sort of nuclear device ("Survey: Nuclear Terrorism," 2008). Goodwyn (2008, p.48) notes, "Terrorists' attraction to nuclear weapons is due to the destructive capability of the weapons, the horrific effects it would have on life and property, and also the economic impact on all U.S. citizens as well as the entire world."

The U.S. Nuclear Regulatory Commission (NRC) estimates that an average of 375 devices of all kinds containing radioactive material are reported lost or stolen each year. Such devices are also called "dirty bombs." Although this may seem another horrific addition to a terrorist arsenal as a weapon of choice, the most destruction and disruption from a dirty bomb detonation will be caused by public panic, not radiation.

Detecting Radiation and Other Bioterrorism Agents.
Dosimeters are small, lightweight devices that use silicon diode technology to instantaneously detect and display the accumulated exposure dose and dose rate. They can identify the specific radionuclide(s) involved and let investigators calculate how long they can safely remain on the scene.

Another advance in detecting hazardous agents is the *electronic nose*. Already used to select fragrant wines and diagnose diseases, electronic noses are now "sniffing" their way into the market for detecting hazardous agents. Electronic nose technology is designed to detect all chemicals within an aroma or fragrance and miss nothing. Some electronic noses already use wireless technology, allowing an investigator more than a mile away from the device to use a computer to monitor the vapors, smells, odors and chemistry of the air remotely.

Robotic detection and identification technology can warn responders of NBC agents' presence and strength. Global positioning systems (GPS) can be applied to determine the coordinates of an NBC release relative to the position of responders, residential or other civilian centers or other critical location information. GPS can also track vehicles charged with transporting NBC materials to and from the site. Finally, weather data, such as wind direction and speed, barometric pressure, relative humidity and so on, is critical to responders at NBC scenes.

A WMD Team.
Law enforcement agencies should select and train officers to form a WMD team to be ready if needed. Members of the team must have adequate personal protective equipment (PPE). Implementing a PPE program protects first responders and eliminates "blue canaries." (Police officers who walk into hazardous situations and die are sometimes described as blue canaries from the practice of coal miners releasing a canary into a mine shaft to see whether the shaft was safe for breathing—if the canary died, more ventilation was needed). Table 20.1 outlines the level of protection, description, type of protection afforded and circumstance for use of each level of equipment.

Technological Terrorism

Technological terrorism includes attacks *on* our technology as well as *by* technology. We rely on energy to drive our technology. An attack on the U.S. energy supply could be devastating. Likewise, an attack on the computer systems and networks critical to the functioning of businesses, health care facilities, educational institutions, the military and all governmental agencies would be catastrophic. **Cyberterrorism** is defined by the FBI

TABLE 20.1 Personal Protective Equipment

Level	Description	Protection	Circumstance
D	Work uniform	Provides no respiratory protection and minimal skin protection	Should not be worn on any site where respiratory or skin hazards exist
C	Full facepiece, air-purifying, canister-equipped respirator and chemical-resistant clothing	Same skin protection as level B, but a lower level respirator	Worn when airborne substance is known, concentration is measured, criteria for using air-purifying respirators are met and skin and eye exposures are unlikely
B	Chemical-resistant clothing (overalls and long sleeves) and self-contained breathing apparatus (SCBA)	Provides splash protection	When the highest level of respiratory protection is needed but a lesser level of skin and eye protection is sufficient
A	Fully encapsulating chemical-resistant suit and SCBA can be worn for only 15 to 30 minutes due to overheating; special training is required	Provides full protection	When the highest level of respiratory, skin, eye and mucous membrane protection is needed

Source: Melissa Reuland and Heather J. Davies. *Protecting Your Community from Terrorism: Strategies for Local Law Enforcement, Vol. 3: Preparing for and Responding to Bioterrorism.* Washington, DC: Community Oriented Policing Services and the Police Executive Research Forum, September 2004.

as "terrorism that initiates, or threatens to initiate, the exploitation of or attack on information systems."

Damage to our critical computer systems can put our safety and our national security in jeopardy. Each of the preceding types of terrorism poses a threat to our national security.

FUNDING TERRORISM

It takes money for both weapons and general operating expenses to carry out terrorism. Terrorist groups commonly collaborate with organized criminal groups to deal drugs, arms and, in some instances, people. The concept of *narcoterrorism* refers to the use of terrorist tactics to support drug operations or the use of drug trade profits to finance terrorism (White, 2012). To finance their operations, terrorist groups smuggle stolen goods and contraband, forge documents, profit from the diamond trade and engage in extortion and protection rackets.

Many terrorist operations are financed by charitable groups and wealthy Arabs sympathetic to the group's cause. To investigate local charities, any interested individual can access the information by contacting the Better Business Bureau or the Wise Giving Alliance.

Fraud has become increasingly common among terrorists—as a way to generate revenue and as a way to gain access to their targets. Fraudulently obtained driver's licenses, passports and other identification documents are often found among terrorists' belongings. No matter how terrorist groups are financed, they usually need to hide where the money came from.

Money laundering was discussed in Chapter 14. However, one tactic is especially important in hiding the money trail of terrorist financing—*hawala*. **Hawala** is an informal banking system based on trust and often bartering, common throughout the Middle East and used to transfer billions of dollars every year. No tax records or paper trails exist. This practice has been used for many years to move terrorist money without a trace of banking records or currency transaction reports (CTR). Hawala allows money launderers to secretly hide and send money out of the country without detection.

THE FEDERAL RESPONSE TO TERRORISM

On October 19, 1984, President Ronald Reagan signed into law the Act to Combat International Terrorism (ACIT), which established a monetary reward program for information involving terrorism. In 1996, the FBI established the National Counterterrorism Center. Also in 1996 the Antiterrorism and Effective Death Penalty Act was passed, including several specific measures aimed at terrorism. It enhanced the federal government's power to deny visas to individuals belonging to terrorist groups and simplified the process for deporting aliens convicted of crimes.

Having announced in 1999 that preventing terrorism was its top priority, the FBI added a new Counterterrorism Division with four subunits: the International Terrorism Section, the Domestic Terrorism Section, the National Infrastructure Protection Center and the National Domestic Preparedness Office. But this was not enough to avert the tragic events of 9/11. It took a disaster of that magnitude to make the war on terrorism truly the number-one priority of the United States. One of the first initiatives was establishing a new federal agency at the cabinet level.

The Department of Homeland Security

On October 8, 2001, President George W. Bush signed Executive Order 13228 establishing the Department of Homeland Security (DHS) to be headed by Tom Ridge, who resigned as governor of Pennsylvania to take the post.

The Department of Homeland Security was established as a result of 9/11, reorganizing the departments of the federal government.

Homeland security is "a concerted effort to prevent terrorist attacks within the United States, reduce America's vulnerability to terrorism and minimize the damage and recover from attacks that do occur." The mission of the DHS is "to develop and coordinate the implementation of a comprehensive national strategy to secure the United States from terrorist threats or attacks." Figure 20.4 shows the organization of the DHS.

Also in September 2001 Attorney General John Ashcroft announced that all U.S. attorneys were establishing antiterrorism task forces to serve as conduits for information about suspected terrorists between federal and local agencies.

At the federal level, the FBI is the lead agency for responding to acts of domestic terrorism. The Federal Emergency Management Agency (FEMA) is the lead agency for consequence management (after an attack).

The DHS serves in a broad capacity, facilitating collaboration between local and federal law enforcement

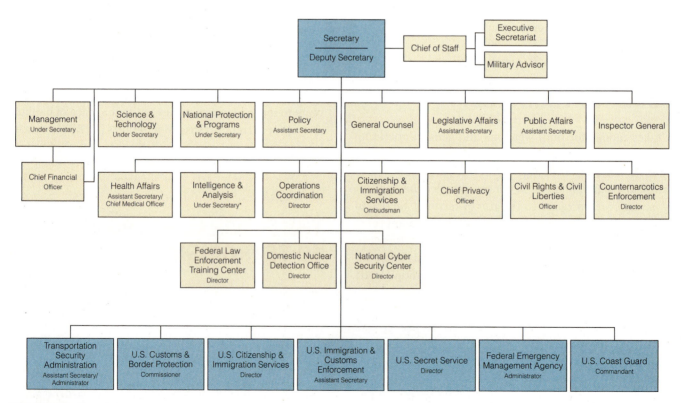

FIGURE 20.4
Organization of the Department of Homeland Security.

*Under Secretary for Intelligence & Analysis title created by Public Law 110-53, August 3, 2007. Approved 3/20/2008.

© Cengage Learning, 2013.

to develop a national strategy to detect, prepare for, prevent, protect against, respond to and recover from terrorist attacks within the United States. In April 2011 DHS Secretary Janet Napolitano announced that the five-tiered color-coded security advisory system that had been used since 2002 would be replaced by a two-level threat advisory:

■ Elevated Threat: warns of a credible terrorist threat against the United States

■ Imminent Threat: warns of a credible, specific and impending terrorist threat against the United States

The basic difference between the two levels is that "elevated" applies when "we have no specific information about the timing or location" of a credible threat. "Imminent" applies when "we believe the threat is impending or very soon" (*National Terrorism Advisory System*, 2011, p.4).

Michael Chertoff, U.S. Secretary of Homeland Security, described five goals he saw as priorities for the DHS ("An Interview," 2007, pp.16–18):

1. Increase our ability to keep bad people out of the country

2. Keep bad things out of the country, increasing port security

3. Protect our infrastructure better

4. Continue to build a response capability with modern computer tools

5. Promote intelligence sharing, horizontally across the federal government and vertically with the local government

The USA PATRIOT Act

On October 26, 2001, President Bush signed into law the Uniting and Strengthening America by Providing Appropriate Tools Required to Intercept and Obstruct Terrorism (USA PATRIOT) Act, giving police unprecedented ability to search, seize, detain and eavesdrop in their pursuit of possible terrorists. The law expands the FBI's wiretapping and electronic surveillance authority and allows nationwide jurisdiction for search warrants and electronic surveillance devices, including legal expansion of those devices to e-mail and the Internet. The act includes money laundering provisions, sets strong penalties for anyone who harbors or finances terrorists and establishes new punishments for possessing biological weapons. Further, it makes it a federal crime to commit an act of terrorism against a mass transit system.

The USA PATRIOT Act significantly improves the nation's counterterrorism efforts by

■ Allowing investigators to use the tools already available to investigate organized crime and drug trafficking.

■ Facilitating information sharing and cooperation among government agencies so they can better "connect the dots."

■ Updating the law to reflect new technologies and new threats.

■ Increasing the penalties for those who commit or support terrorist crimes.

President Obama signed a 4-year extension of the USA PATRIOT Act on May 26, 2011, which includes three key provisions related to roving wiretaps, surveillance and searches of business records.

The PATRIOT Act has come under attack from groups across the political spectrum. Some members of Congress and civil liberties groups say the act has given federal agents too much power to pursue suspected terrorists, threatening the civil rights and privacy of Americans.

The intent of the PATRIOT Act when passed in 2001 as a response to the 9/11 attacks was to provide *federal* law enforcement with better means to defend against terrorism. Several other federal initiatives are aimed at preventing terrorist attacks or at least mitigating their effects.

The National Infrastructure Protection Plan (NIPP)

The *National Infrastructure Protection Plan (NIPP)* (2009) is a comprehensive risk management framework defining critical infrastructure protection roles and responsibilities of federal, state, local, tribal and private security partners. The goal of the NIPP is to "Build a safer, more secure, and more resilient America by preventing, deterring, neutralizing, or mitigating the effects of deliberate efforts by terrorists to destroy, incapacitate, or exploit elements of our Nation's CIKR [critical infrastructure and key resources] and to strengthen national preparedness, timely response, and rapid recovery of CIKR in the event of an attack, natural disaster or other emergency" (2009, p.1). The cornerstone of the NIPP is the risk management framework, shown in Figure 20.5. This framework establishes the process for combining consequence, vulnerability and threat information to produce a comprehensive, systematic and rational assessment or national or sector-specific risk that drives CIKR-protection activities.

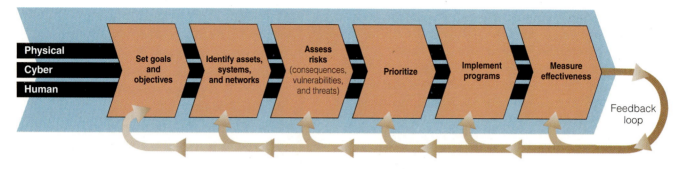

Continuous improvement to enhance protection of CIKR

FIGURE 20.5
Risk management framework.
Source: http://www.dhs.gov/xlibrary/assets/NIPP_Plan.pdf (Figure S-2 on p.4)

The 17 specific sectors included in the plan include agriculture and food; banking and finance; chemical; commercial facilities; communications; dams; defense industrial base; drinking water and water treatment systems; emergency services; energy; government facilities; information technology; national monuments and icons; nuclear reactors, materials and waste; postal and shipping; public health and healthcare; and transportation.

Fusion Centers

An initiative aimed at promoting and facilitating information and intelligence sharing among federal and local law enforcement agencies is the development of fusion centers throughout the country. Straw (2008, p.68) notes, "While government is notoriously slow to implement change, one post–9/11 reform has bucked the trend: the rapidly growing national network of state, regional and urban intelligence fusion centers. At the centers, teams of analysts crunch data and produce refined intelligence to help stakeholders address all hazards and all crimes."

A **fusion center** is a "collaborative effort of two or more agencies that provide resources, expertise, and information to the center with the goal of maximizing their ability to detect, prevent, investigate, and respond to criminal and terrorist activity" (*Fusion Center Guidelines*, 2006, p.3). Fusion centers enhance and enable the exchange of critical information and intelligence between law enforcement and public safety agencies at the local, state and federal levels (Lambert, 2010). There are 72 recognized fusion centers operating throughout the country (Colwell and Kelly, 2010). However, general assessment of the centers is that they are a costly but largely ineffective weapon against terrorism (Hall, 2007). DHS has given states $380 million to set up the centers, but they tend to gravitate to an "all-crimes and even broader all-hazards approach" rather than focusing on recognizing suspicious activity, patterns and people and using the information to prevent terrorist attacks.

HOMETOWN SECURITY AND HOMELAND SECURITY

The criticality of local law enforcement has been recognized ever since homeland security became a focus. Law enforcement personnel have realized that, in our post–9/11 society, their duties have expanded considerably, and they are no longer looking to federal agencies and the military as the source of our county's protection: "With past terrorist assaults and the threat of more to come, keeping the (bigger) bad guy at bay is no longer the sole domain of the FBI" (Schreiber, 2008, p.49). Lovette (2008, p.34) echoes, "On 9/11 cops became a vital component of the homeland security mission. And the majority of the responsibility for this additional requirement came to rest squarely on the shoulders of the uniformed patrol officer, America's first line of defense in the war on crime, the war on drugs, the war on gangs, and now, the war on terror."

The International Association of Chiefs of Police (IACP) report *From Hometown Security to Homeland Security* (2005, p.2), from its "Taking Command" project, suggests that our nation's current homeland security strategy "is handicapped by a fundamental flaw. It does not sufficiently incorporate the advice, expertise or consent of public safety organizations at state, tribal or local levels." The IACP has identified five key principles that should form the basis for a national homeland security strategy:

1. All terrorism is local.
2. Prevention is paramount.
3. Hometown security is homeland security.

4. Homeland security strategies must be coordinated nationally, not federally.

5. Bottom-up engineering is important, involving the diversity of the state, tribal and local public safety communities in noncompetitive collaboration.

The 17,500 state and local law enforcement agencies in the United States employ more than 750,000 officers who patrol the city streets daily and know their communities intimately. As Kelling and Bratton (2006, p.2) contend, "The counterterrorist potential of local police is partly a function of numbers. More than 700,000 local law enforcement officers work in the continental U.S. compared with just 12,000 FBI agents. Based on numbers alone, local law enforcement personnel are much more likely than feds to cross paths with terrorists." Myers (2006, p.3) advocates putting the "home" back in homeland security, asserting, "Neighborhood-by-neighborhood, our people expect us to be the front line of keeping them safe and secure. . . . Under our American tradition, the absence of a national police force means that the response of better funding and coordination between local, regional, state and federal resources holds the most hope."

The first line of defense against terrorism is the patrol officer in the field.

Any law enforcement officer can potentially come in contact with a terrorist at any time, whether investigating an unrelated crime, conducting routine duties or backing up another officer. Many of the 9/11 hijackers had prior contact with law enforcement officers in various parts of the country. For example, on September 9, 2001, Ziad Jarrah, hijacker of the plane that crashed in Shanksville, Pennsylvania, was stopped by police in Maryland for driving 90 mph in a 65 mph zone. Jarrah was issued a ticket and released. Similarly, in August 2001, Hani Hanjour, hijack pilot of the plane that crashed into the Pentagon and killed 289 persons, was stopped for speeding by police in Arlington, Virginia, was issued a ticket and released. Hanjour paid the ticket to avoid having to show up in court.

INVESTIGATING POSSIBLE TERRORIST ACTIVITIES

Investigating possible terrorist activities is facilitated by the fact that terrorists also often engage in other criminal activities: "A growing body of literature supports the hypothesis of a crime–terror nexus, especially as a result of

the post–9/11 alarm on terrorism financing (Belli, 2011, p.12). One way to address terrorism is to modify laws that deal with white-collar crimes, traditionally nonviolent and involving some form of fraud to achieve financial gain. These crimes include credit card fraud, insurance fraud, identity theft, money laundering, immigration fraud and tax evasion.

This approach rests on the assumption that terrorist activities require funding for weaponry, training, travel and living expenses. In addition, terrorists create and use false identifications to enter the country, gain employment, acquire equipment and accumulate money. Cases involving money laundering should be looked at as a white-collar crime but also as potentially linked to terrorism. The investigative techniques described in Chapter 18 would be applicable in this counterterrorism strategy.

Some differences have been observed to exist in the types of crimes terrorists use to fund their operations. For example, in the United States, right-wing terrorists are more likely to engage in mail fraud, racketeering and other financial crimes than are international jihad groups (Belli, 2011, p.13). Furthermore, crimes such as credit card theft and fraud appear popular among jihad groups such as al-Qaeda, HAMAS and Hezbollah, presumably because these crimes require minimal expertise, are low cost and present few barriers to accomplish (Shapiro, 2007). Other crimes engaged in by terrorists have included drug trafficking, money laundering, extortion and insurance fraud.

A major challenge in the war on terrorism is ensuring that individual officers remain vigilant and cognizant of their critical role in homeland security. Law enforcement officers should be aware of terrorist *indicators* such as negative rhetoric, excessive physical training, anti-American literature or a disregard for U.S. laws. Terrorists and their supporters tend to act alike because many have trained in the same camps and share the same negative beliefs. In addition: "Most terrorists live close to their selected targets, and they engage in a great deal of preparation—some over the course of months or even years—that has the potential of coming to the attention of local law enforcement" (Smith, 2008, p.3).

Investigators should also be knowledgeable of vulnerable, valuable targets for a terrorist attack, such as any high-occupancy structure or any site where a significant number of lives are affected; a structure containing dangerous substances or articles; any vital, high-use structure composing an infrastructure; a site of significant historical, symbolic, strategic, defensive or functional value to the nation, including structures holding highly sensitive, rare, historical or irreplaceable artifacts, documents or other such content.

Although focusing on logical targets for terrorist attacks, "soft" targets—that is, those that are relatively unguarded or difficult to guard—should not be overlooked, including shopping malls, subways, trains, sporting stadiums, theaters, schools, hospitals, restaurants, entertainment parks, compressed gas and oil storage areas, chemical plants, pharmaceutical companies and many others.

The Typical Stages in a Terrorist Attack

Terrorist attacks typically have three stages. The first stage is research, including surveillance, stakeouts and local inquiries. Local law enforcement officers can best serve the counterterrorism effort at this stage because the terrorists are out in public, watching us, studying our habits, discovering our vulnerabilities and reporting back to their handlers with prospective targeting data to begin the planning stage. Interestingly, a study of terrorist attack sites found that nearly half of the attackers lived within 30 miles of their selected target (Smith, 2008).

The second stage is planning, usually conducted behind closed doors. The average planning cycle for international terrorists is 92 days, compared with 14 days for environmental terrorists (Smith, 2008). The third stage is execution, the actual attack and possible escape. Often these attacks are carried out by a **sleeper cell**, a group of terrorists who blend into a community.

> The three-tiered model of al-Qaeda terrorist attacks consists of sleeper cells attacking in conjunction with the group's leaders in Afghanistan, sleeper cells attacking on their own apart from centralized command and individuals attacking with support from small cells.

It is crucial that investigators identify members of sleeper cells within their community. Profiling, a useful tool in law enforcement for decades, is equally useful in these antiterrorism efforts in that the "typical" al-Qaeda terrorist is a young (20 to 30) Middle Eastern–appearing male of average height and weight with prominent facial hair and a foreign accent. However, the profile does not always fit, as many cell members are now being instructed to westernize their appearance by dressing to fit into mainstream American society, shave their beards or otherwise disguise or downplay physical traits that may betray their true identity.

Another approach to identifying potential terrorists is to use behavior pattern recognition (BPR), observing irregular behaviors for the environment as well as targeted conversations with suspects. The Transportation Security Administration (TSA) has trained 600 screeners who patrol the three airports in the Washington area and look for signs of stress, fear and deception among airline passengers (Wilber and Nakashima, 2007, p.D01). These screeners have referred more than 40,000 people for extra screening since January 2006. Of those passengers, nearly 300 were arrested on charges including carrying concealed weapons and drug trafficking.

The New York City Police Department is using a different tactic, having detectives visit scuba shops and hardware stores, talk to parking garage attendants and plastic surgeons, hotel managers and tool rental companies, bulk fuel dealers and trade schools. Although admittedly somewhat of a "needle-in-a-haystack approach," the program, called Operation Nexus, has the potential to identify terrorists. Information from an al-Qaeda manual for terrorist operatives and debriefings of some of the group's leaders and foot soldiers suggest that al-Qaeda has considered using scuba divers to blow up bridges, riding in tourist helicopters for surveillance, turning trucks and limousines into rolling bombs and using special torches to cut the cables of the Brooklyn Bridge.

Terrorists might be hunted down using confidential informant reward programs established by the 1984 ACIT. The PATRIOT Act amended the reward program by increasing the amount offered to an informant to $250,000.

Surveillance Cameras as Investigative Tools

When terrorists attacked London's transit system in 2005, four homemade bombs stuffed into backpacks failed to fully explode. Only one person was injured. A day later, photographs of four suspects captured on surveillance cameras near the sites of the attempted attacks were broadcast on television. The remarkable speed of that investigation was repeated on July 7, 2007, following another attack. British investigators, aided by surveillance cameras, tracked the suspects to Glasgow, Scotland, and arrested several individuals: "Police officials credited the 'Ring of Steel'—a network of thousands of surveillance cameras that line London's intersections and neighborhoods—for providing license plate numbers, suspects' image and other important clues" (Tanneeru, 2007). New York City has implemented the Lower Manhattan Security Initiative in a similar attempt to monitor what is "arguably one of the most valuable and sensitive pieces of real estate in the world" (Tanneeru).

Community policing efforts can do much to overcome these obstacles.

Closely related concerns are the rights of citizens detained as enemy combatants and the rights of detained foreign nationals. In *Hamdi v. Rumsfeld* (2004) the Supreme Court ruled that a citizen detained in the United States as an enemy combatant must be afforded the opportunity to rebut such a designation. Petitioner Hamdi was captured in an active combat zone in Afghanistan following the September 11, 2001, attacks on the United States and surrendered an assault rifle. The U.S. District Court found that the declaration from the Defense Department did not support Hamdi's detention and ordered the government to turn over numerous materials for review. The U.S. Court of Appeals for the Fourth Circuit reversed the decision, stressing that because it was undisputed that Hamdi was captured in an active combat zone, no factual inquiry or evidentiary hearing allowing Hamdi to rebut the government's assertions was necessary. The U.S. Supreme Court voted 6 to 3 to vacate and remand, concluding that Hamdi should have a meaningful opportunity to offer evidence that he was not an enemy combatant.

In *Rasul v. Bush* (2004), the Supreme Court ruled that U.S. courts have jurisdiction to consider challenges to the legality of the detention of foreign nationals captured in Afghanistan in a military campaign against al-Qaeda and the Taliban regime that supported it. The petitioners, 2 Australians and 12 Kuwaitis, were being held at Guantánamo Bay, Cuba, without charges. These and other legal issues regarding civil rights will be debated as the country seeks to balance the need for security with civil rights.

INFORMATION GATHERING AND INTELLIGENCE SHARING

An important distinction differentiates information and intelligence, with intelligence broadening to become organized information: "Intelligence has come to mean information that has not only been selected and collected, but also analyzed, evaluated and distributed to meet the unique policymaking needs of one particular enterprise" (Loyka et al., 2005, p.7). One way to conceptualize the difference is to think of information as raw data; once that data has been placed through various filters, sieves and other analytical processes, the more meaningful or useful bits of data that are extracted are referred to as *intelligence*. The process of extracting intelligence from raw data is referred to as the *intelligence cycle* (Figure 20.6).

The cycle begins with knowing the *intelligence requirements* needed for an investigation. What do investigators need to know to effectively safeguard the nation? These requirements are established by the director of National Intelligence under the guidance of the president and the national and homeland security advisors and are based on critical information necessary for homeland security. The second step—*planning and direction*—is a function of the FBI and is led by the executive assistant director of the National Security Branch.

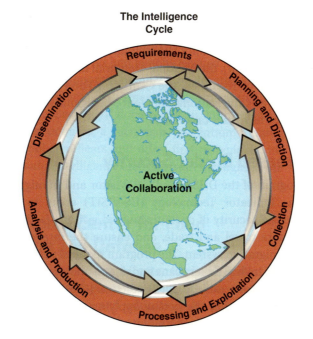

FIGURE 20.6
The intelligence cycle.
Source: http://www.fbi.gov/about-us/intelligence/intelligence-cycle/

The third step is *collecting raw information* from local, state and federal investigations. Such information may come from interviews, technical and physical surveillance, searches, human source operations and liaison relationships. Fourth is *processing and exploiting* the raw information into a form usable by analysts. Fifth is *analysis and production*, which converts the raw information into intelligence. The final step is *dissemination* of intelligence to consumers, who make decisions based on the intelligence. These decisions may levy further requirements, thus continuing the intelligence cycle.

Local and state law enforcement agencies are critical to the third step in the intelligence cycle and benefit from the sixth step as well. Many day-to-day duties of local law enforcement officers bring them into proximity with sources of information about terrorism. Patrol operations, especially traffic officers, properly trained in what to look for and what questions to ask when interacting with citizens, can be a tremendous source of intelligence for their state and federal homeland security counterparts as well as for local investigators.

The difficult tasks of counterterrorism and antiterrorism are made even harder by the operational style that pervades law enforcement—that of withholding, rather than sharing, intelligence. States lack a single point of contact for both receiving "downstream" information needs and pushing intelligence and other information "upstream." Gorman (2007) reports that state and local officials are protesting efforts by the Department of Homeland Security to exclude them from a new unit designed to share information about possible terrorist threats to the country. According to Gorman, DHS officials are opposed to letting representatives of state and local government serve on the unit that would send out the information because they believe it would confuse the process: "It is the latest example of the government's failure to heed one of the most critical lessons of the Sept. 11 attacks: the inability or unwillingness of federal officials to share information with those at the state and local level who might be in a position to help stave off a terrorist attack." The director of national intelligence (DNI), John Michael "Mike" McConnell, has criticized the DHS approach, saying the culture of intelligence agencies must change to appreciate the needs of police chiefs and their colleagues around the country: "This is a different age and a different time. . . . There has to be a leap of faith to trust local officials with sensitive information" (Gorman, p.1A). A major step in improving the sharing of information is the appointment of a new assistant secretary in DHS to serve as a liaison between state and local law enforcement and DHS policymakers —an important position in the policy directorate (Bain, 2008).

CONCERNS RELATED TO THE WAR ON TERRORISM

> Two pressing concerns related to the "war on terrorism" are that civil liberties may be jeopardized and that people of Middle Eastern descent may be discriminated against or become victims of hate crimes.

These two concerns were explored by Getlin (2005), who found that some of those he interviewed saw the searches at New York City's Penn Station as an intrusion on personal freedom, whereas other people wanted police to be able to openly focus on Muslim commuters. One city council member noted, "There is a particular group who engages in these [terrorist] activities. They're not skinny balding Italian Americans from Staten Island."

The first guiding principle of the DHS is to protect civil rights and civil liberties: "We will defend America while protecting the freedoms that define America. Our strategies and actions will be consistent with the individual rights and liberties enshrined by our Constitution and the Rule of Law. While we seek to improve the way we collect and share information about terrorists, we will nevertheless be vigilant in respecting the confidentiality and protecting the privacy of our citizens. We are committed to securing our nation while protecting civil rights and civil liberties" (*Securing Our Homeland*, n.d., p.6).

Concern for Civil Rights

Civil libertarians are concerned that valued American freedoms will be sacrificed in the interest of national safety. For example, the Justice Department has issued a new regulation giving itself the authority to monitor inmate-attorney communications if "reasonable suspicion" exists that inmates are using such communications to further or facilitate acts of terrorism. However, criminal defense lawyers and members of the American Civil Liberties Union (ACLU) have protested the regulation, saying that it effectively eliminates the Sixth Amendment right to counsel because, under codes of professional responsibility, attorneys cannot communicate with clients if confidentiality is not ensured. The ACLU has vowed to monitor police actions closely to see that freedoms protected under the Constitution are not jeopardized.

The government must preserve the rights and freedoms guaranteed by America's democracy, but, at the same time, ensure that the fight against terrorism is vigorous and effective.

A d
and
to r

Retali
People

Another
against i
of whom
uralized
significa
lice and

- Distru
  law er
- Lack
  office
- Lang
- Conce

New
a ran
© Paul J

---

4. Emphasize the importance of reporting information without making assumptions about a person's guilt.

It is far preferable to be proactive and interfere with an attack in the preparation stage than to be reactive and respond to an attack after the fact: "Because they know when something is amiss in the neighborhood, local law enforcement officers play a critical role in counterterrorism. . . . Officers must be able to recognize the warning signs of terrorism-related surveillance and other preparatory acts, such as building explosives. Dead flowers outside the covered window of an inner-city apartment, the gradual lightening of a young man's hair color or apartment trash littered with empty containers of hydrogen peroxide are subtle signals. . . . Law enforcement officers who can recognize and act on these warning signs will make a valuable contribution to counterterrorism in the months and years ahead" (Kenney, 2010, p.21). Officers must keep their ears to the ground and establish a rapport with the various sources of information in their community, including storage facilities, religious groups, real estate agents, hotels and motels, colleges and universities, transportation centers and tourist attractions.

Summary

The threat of terrorism has become a reality in America. Most definitions of terrorism have common elements, including the systematic use of physical violence, either actual or threatened, against noncombatants to create a climate of fear to cause some religious, political or social change. Most terrorist acts result from dissatisfaction with a religious, political or social system or policy and frustration resulting from an inability to change it through acceptable, nonviolent means.

The FBI classifies terrorist acts as either domestic or international. Islamic terrorist groups include Hezbollah, HAMAS, Palestinian Islamic Jihad (PIJ), the al-Aqsa Martyrs Brigades and al-Qaeda. Domestic terrorist groups within the United States include White supremacists, Black supremacists, militia groups, other right-wing extremists, left-wing extremists, pro-life extremists, animal rights extremists and environmental extremists. In addition to armed attacks, terrorists use arson, explosives and bombs; weapons of mass destruction (biological, chemical or nuclear agents); or technology.

The Department of Homeland Security was established as a result of 9/11, reorganizing the departments of the federal government. At the federal level, the FBI is the lead agency for responding to domestic terrorism. The Federal Emergency Management Agency (FEMA) is the lead agency for consequence management (after an attack).

The USA PATRIOT Act significantly improves the nation's counterterrorism efforts by

- Allowing investigators to use the tools already available to investigate organized crime and drug trafficking.

- Facilitating information sharing and cooperation among government agencies so they can better "connect the dots."

- Updating the law to reflect new technologies and new threats.

- Increasing the penalties for those who commit or support terrorist crimes.

The first line of defense against terrorism is the patrol officer in the field.

The three-tiered model of al-Qaeda terrorist attacks consists of sleeper cells attacking in conjunction with the group's leaders in Afghanistan, sleeper cells attacking on their own apart from centralized command and individuals attacking with support from small cells. A key to combating terrorism lies with the local police and the intelligence they can provide to federal authorities. The Law Enforcement Officers Safety Act of 2004 gives qualified active duty as well as qualified retired police officers the right to carry their firearms concealed in all 50 states.

Two pressing concerns related to the "war on terrorism" are that civil liberties may be jeopardized and that people of Middle Eastern descent may be discriminated against or become victims of hate crimes. A difficult challenge facing law enforcement is balancing the need to enhance security with the need to maintain freedom.

Checklist
Terrorism

- What method of attack was used?
- What was the target of the attack?
- Who had access to the location?
- What was the likely motivation?
- Has any group claimed responsibility?
- What was the damage?
- Were there injuries? Fatalities?

- Who notified authorities?
- Who responded first?
- Were there any witnesses?
- Were any suspicious individuals or vehicles observed at the location before the attack? During the attack? After the attack?
- Was the scene photographed or videotaped?
- What evidence was found at the scene?
- Were there any unusual circumstances?
- Was a canvass of the area conducted?

Application

Detective Smith has had a young Middle Eastern–appearing male under surveillance as a suspected terrorist. She has followed him for several days and has observed him buy a newspaper from a machine every morning, walk to the state capitol building several times each day and take pictures from various angles, enter the building and come out shortly. He then returns to an inexpensive motel on the edge of town. He has visits from other Middle Eastern–appearing young males who bring him packages. He does not appear to be employed but wears expensive clothing and eats at expensive restaurants.

On this particular day, she sees that the suspect is carrying a briefcase, something he has not done before. He goes directly to the state capitol building and enters. Approximately one hour later, he comes out, but without the briefcase.

Questions

1. Does Detective Smith have reasonable suspicion to stop the suspect and question him?
2. If so, based on what?
3. What should be the next step?

Discussion Questions

1. Which is the greater threat—domestic or international terrorism? Why?
2. Does your police department have a counterterrorism strategy in place? If so, what?
3. What type of terrorist attack would you fear most? Why?
4. Do you feel Americans have become complacent about terrorism?
5. What provisions of the PATRIOT Act do you think are most important?

6. What barriers to sharing information among the various local, state and federal agencies do you think are most problematic?
7. Does media coverage of terrorist acts lead to more terrorism? That is, do you think the contagion effect is in operation?
8. Should Americans expect to give up some civil liberties to allow law enforcement officers to pursue terrorists?
9. Do you think a terrorist sleeper cell could operate in your community? What signs might indicate that such a cell exists?
10. What means might terrorists use to attack the United States in the future? Are we more vulnerable at home or at our interests abroad?

Media Explorations

Internet

Select one of the following assignments to complete.

- Go to the Web sites of the Drug Enforcement Administration (www.dea.gov), the FBI (www.fbi.gov), the Department of Justice (www.usdoj.gov) and the Department of the Treasury (www.ustreas.gov) and note how the different agencies are addressing the issue of terrorism. How do their focuses differ? Be prepared to share your findings with the class.

- Search for *USA PATRIOT Act* (2001). List specific applications of the act to law enforcement practices and explain how they might differ from conventional practices. Do you believe the phrase "extraordinary times demand extraordinary measures" and that it justifies bending the rules, so to speak, in the war on terrorism? In other words, do the ends justify the means? Should law enforcement be permitted to use roving wiretaps and breach privileged inmate-attorney communications in the name of national security, or is this the beginning of the end of our civil liberties? Be prepared to discuss your answers with the class.

- Go to the Department of Justice Web site devoted to the PATRIOT Act and list the myths the site dispels.

- Go to www.policeforum.org and find "Local Law Enforcement's Role in Preventing and Responding to Terrorism." Read and outline the article. Be prepared to share your outline with the class.

- To learn what the U.S. Department of Homeland Security is doing to keep America safe, go to www.ready.gov.

■ Go to the Counterterrorism Training and Resources Web site at www.counterterrorismtraining.gov and outline what resources are available for local police departments.

■ Search for the key phrase *National Institute of Justice.* Click on "NCJRS" (National Criminal Justice Research Service). Click on "law enforcement." Click on "sort by Doc#." Search for one of the NCJ reference numbers from the list of References for this chapter. Outline the selection to share with the class.

ONLINE Database

Gale Criminal Justice Database Assignments

The following assignment requires access to Gale's Custom Journals Database for Emergency Services and Criminal Justice. Check with your instructor if you have questions about this.

Choose one of the following articles to read and find it on the Gale Emergency Services Database. Write a 2- to 3-page paper summarizing the major points of the article and be prepared to share your summary with the class.

■ "Be Prepared for Terrorists Both Foreign and Domestic: Managing Terrorism Impact Risk"

■ "DHS Discontinues Color Coded Alert System"

■ "'Confronting' Foreign Intelligence: Crawford Roadblocks to Domestic Terrorism Trials"

■ "Valuable Lessons Learned at an International Counterterrorism Forum"

■ "State and Local Law Enforcement: Contributions to Terrorism Prevention"

■ "Foreign Intelligence Surveillance Act: Before and After the USA PATRIOT Act"

References

Bain, Ben. "DHS Creates Exec-Level Liaison to Law Enforcement Agencies." *Federal Computer Week*, January 17, 2008.

Belli, Roberta. *Where Political Extremists and Greedy Criminals Meet: A Comparative Study of Financial Crimes and Criminal Networks in the United States.* Unpublished doctoral dissertation, 2011. Accessed September 3, 2011. https://www .ncjrs.gov/pdffiles1/nij/grants/234524.pdf

Burruss, George W.; Giblin, Matthew J.; and Schafer, Joseph A. "Threatened Globally, Acting Locally: Modeling Law Enforcement Homeland Security Practices." *Justice Quarterly*, Vol.27, No.1, February 2010, pp.77–101.

Colwell, Lee, and Kelly, Dennis. "Engaging Untapped Local Law Enforcement and Private Industry Capabilities to Fight Crime and Terrorism." *The Police Chief*, February 2010, pp.64–74.

Corderre, Michael, and Register, Michael. "Fighting Back against IEDs." *Police*, September 2009, pp.38–41.

Daniels, Rhianna. "Chemical Facilities Secure DHS Standards." *Security Director News*, February 2007, p.8.

DeYoung, Karen. "Attempts Seen as Model for New Attacks on U.S. Soil." *Washington Post*, July 3, 2007, p.A01.

"DHS Secretary Ridge Approves National Incident Management System (NIMS)." *NCJA Justice Bulletin*, March 2004, pp.14–16.

"Domestic Terrorism in the Post-9/11 Era." Washington, DC: Federal Bureau of Investigation, September 7, 2009. Accessed September 2, 2011. http://www.fbi.gov/news/ stories/2009/september/domterror_090709

Downing, Michael P. "Policing Terrorism in the United States: The Los Angeles Police Department's Convergence Strategy." *The Police Chief*, February 2009, pp.28–43.

Edwards, Al. "DHS Reveals Chemical Guidelines." *Security Director News*, May 2007, p.1.

From Hometown Security to Homeland Security: IACP's Principles for a Locally Designed and Nationally Coordinated Homeland Security Strategy. Alexandria, VA: International Association of Chiefs of Police, May 17, 2005.

Fusion Center Guidelines: Developing and Sharing Information and Intelligence in a New Era. Washington, DC: Department of Justice, April 2006.

Galvin, Robert. "Bomb Reconstruction Training: Post-Blast Practice." *Law Enforcement Technology*, August 2010, pp.52–59.

Garrett, Ronnie. "A Storm Is Brewing. . . . " *Law Enforcement Technology*, October 2007, p.10.

Getlin, Josh. "Profiling Fears Surface in Subway." *Los Angeles Times*, August 8, 2005.

Goodwyn, Al. "Minimizing the Nuclear Threat: A Local Law Enforcement Strategy." *The Police Chief*, February 2008, pp.45–59.

Gorman, Siobhan. "Out of the Loop on Terror Threats: Homeland Security Excludes State, Local Officials from Group that Shares Data." *Baltimore Sun*, February 2, 2007, p.1A.

Griffith, David. "Global Terror, Local Targets." *Police*, September 2010, pp.48–51.

Hall, Mimi. "State-Run Sites Not Effective vs. Terror." *USA Today*, July 23, 2007.

Harwood, Matthew. "Assessing Chlorine Gas Bombs." *Security Management*, June 2007, pp.18–19.

Henderson, Nicole J.; Ortiz, Christopher W.; Sugie, Naomi F.; and Miller, Joel. *Policing in Arab-American Communities.* Washington, DC: National Institute of Justice, July 2008. (NCJ 221706)

Hsu, Spencer S. "Anti-Terror Funds Questioned." *Washington Post*, July 26, 2008, p.A02.

"An Interview with Homeland Security Secretary Michael Chertoff." *The Police Chief*, February 2007, pp.14–18.

Kelling, George L., and Bratton, William J. "Policing Terrorism." *Manhattan Institute Civic Bulletin*, September 2006.

Kelling, George L.; Eddy, R. P.; and Bratton, William J. "The Blue Front Line in the War on Terror." *City Journal*, September 20, 2007. Accessed September 4, 2011. http://www.city-journal .org/html/eon2007-09-20.html

Kenney, Michael. "Organizational Learning and Islamic Militancy." *NIJ Journal*, No.265, April 2010, pp.18–21.

Lambert, David. "Intelligence-Led Policing in a Fusion Center." *FBI Law Enforcement Bulletin*, December 2010, pp.1–6.

Laska, Paul R. "Bombs and the Street Cop." *Law Officer Magazine*, February 2008, pp.40–43.

Lovette, Ed. "Anti-Terrorism Intel for the Patrol Officer." *Police*, February 2008, pp.32–37.

Loyka, Stephan A.; Faggiani, Donald A.; and Karchmer, Clifford. *Protecting Your Community from Terrorism: Strategies for Local Law Enforcement, Vol. 4: The Production and Sharing of Intelligence*. Washington, DC: Community Oriented Policing Services and the Police Executive Research Forum, February 2005.

Myers, Rick. "Putting the 'Home' Back in Homeland Security." *Subject to Debate*, October 2006, pp.2–3.

National Center for Food Protection and Defense Web site, no date. Accessed September 4, 2011. www.ncfpd.umn.edu/

National Infrastructure Protection Plan. Washington, DC: Department of Homeland Security, 2009.

National Intelligence Estimate: The Terrorist Threat to the U.S. Homeland. Washington, DC: National Intelligence Council, July 2007.

National Terrorism Advisory System Public Guide. Washington, DC: Department of Homeland Security, April 2011.

Priem, Richard G.; Hunter, Dennis M.; and Polisar, Joseph M. "Terrorists and Suicide Tactics: Preparing for the Challenge." *The Police Chief*, September 2007, pp.32–36.

Scheider, Matthew C.; Chapman, Robert E.; and Seelman, Michael E. "Connecting the Dots for a Proactive Approach." *BTS (Border and Transportation Security) America*, no date, pp.158–162.

Schreiber, Sara. "Your Role in Terror Preparedness." *Law Enforcement Technology*, June 2008, pp.48–54.

Scoville, Dean. "The Enemies Within." *Police*, September 2003, pp.44–50.

Securing Our Homeland. Washington, DC: U.S. Department of Homeland Security, no date.

Shapiro, Jacob N. "Terrorists' Organizations' Vulnerabilities and Inefficiencies: A Rational Choice Perspective." In *Terrorism Financing and State Responses: A Comparative Perspective*, edited by Jeanne K. Giraldo and Harold A. Trinkunas. Stanford, CA: Stanford University Press, 2007, pp.56–71.

Smith, Brent. "A Look at Terrorist Behavior: How They Prepare, Where They Strike." *NIJ Journal*, July 2008, pp.2–7.

Spahr, Lisa L.; Ederheimer, Joshua; and Bilson, David. *Patrol-Level Response to a Suicide Bomb Threat: Guidelines for Consideration*. Washington, DC: Police Executive Research Forum, April 2007.

Stockton, Dale. "The End of the Beginning." *Law Officer Magazine*, January 2008, p.8.

Straw, Joseph. "Smashing Intelligence Stovepipes." *Security Management*, March 2008, pp.68–74.

"Survey: Nuclear Terror Is Top Fear of Americans." 1105 Media, Inc., January 3, 2008.

Tanneeru, Manav. "'Ring of Steel' Coming to New York." *CNN*, August 1, 2007.

2010 NCTC Report on Terrorism. Washington, DC: Office of the Director of National Intelligence, National Counterterrorism Center, April 30, 2011.

Vernon, Bob. "Reliable Sources: The Right Way to Mobilize Your Community to Increase Security." *Law Officer Magazine*, June 2008, pp.56–57.

Wexler, Chuck. "Foreword." In *Patrol-Level Response to a Suicide Bomb Threat: Guidelines for Consideration*, by Lisa L. Spahr, Joshua Ederheimer and David Bilson. Washington, DC: Police Executive Research Forum, April 2007.

White, Jonathan R. *Terrorism and Homeland Security*, 7th ed. Belmont, CA: Wadsworth Publishing Company, 2012.

Wilber, Del Quentin, and Nakashima, Ellen. "Searching Passengers' Faces for Subtle Cues to Terror." *Washington Post*, September 19, 2007, p.D01.

Cases Cited

Hamdi v. Rumsfeld, 542 U.S. 507 (2004)

Rasul v. Bush, 542 U.S. 466 (2004)

Useful Resources

- The Counterterrorism Training and Resources Web site: www.counterterrorismtraining.gov

- U.S. Department of Homeland Security: www.ready.gov

- Federal Emergency Management Agency: www.fema .gov/areyouready

- Federal Bureau of Investigation: www.fbi.gov

- Centers for Disease Control and Prevention: www.cdc.gov

The most important rule to eradicate fear of testifying in court is to always tell the truth.

THE FINAL REPORT

The effectiveness of the final report is often the determining factor in whether a case is prosecuted: "It's not just skillful investigation that brings the bad guy to justice. . . . It's the investigator's ability to prepare a report that can withstand minute scrutiny by judges, prosecutors, defense counsel, citizens and the media. The report's ability to hold up under scrutiny may determine whether the guilty go free or justice is rendered to the victim" (Jetmore, 2008, p.26). The recommendations and guidelines presented in Chapter 3 apply to the final report as well. Therefore, you might review that chapter.

The final report presents the facts of the case, a criminal history of the person charged, the types of evidence available and the names of those who can support such evidence by testimony in court, names of people the prosecutor can talk to for further information and a chronological account of the crime and subsequent investigation.

The final report contains (1) the complaint; (2) the preliminary investigation report; (3) all follow-up, supplemental and progress reports; (4) statements, admissions and confessions; (5) laboratory reports; (6) photographs, sketches and drawings; and (7) a summary of all negative (exculpatory) evidence. The quality of the content and writing of the report influences its credibility.

Prepare the report after a careful review of all information. Organize the facts logically.

The Complaint

Include a copy of the original complaint received by the police dispatcher and complaint desk. This should include the date and time of the complaint, location of the incident, brief details, times when officers were dispatched and the names of the officers assigned to the initial call.

The Preliminary Investigation Report

The report of the officer's initial investigation at the crime scene provides essential information about the time of arrival, lighting and weather conditions, observations at the scene and immediate and subsequent actions taken by officers responding to the call.

Follow-Up Reports

Assemble each contact and follow-up report in chronological order, presenting the sequence of the investigation and the pattern used to follow leads. These reports contain the essential information gathered in proving the elements of the crime and in linking the crime to the suspect. The reports can be in the form of progress notes.

Statements, Admissions and Confessions

Include the statements of all witnesses interviewed during the investigation, as discussed in Chapter 6. If written statements were not obtained, report the results of oral interviews with witnesses. Assemble all statements, admissions or confessions by suspects in a separate part of the report. Include the reports of all polygraphs or other examinations used to determine the truth of statements, admissions or confessions.

Laboratory Reports

Assemble laboratory results in one segment of the final report. Make recommendations regarding how these results relate to other areas of the report.

Photographs, Sketches and Drawings

Include photographs, sketches and drawings of the crime scene to show conditions when officers arrived and the available evidence, as discussed in Chapter 2.

Summary of Negative Evidence

Include a summary of all negative or exculpatory evidence developed during the investigation. Statements of witnesses who claim the suspect was elsewhere at the time of the crime are sometimes proved false, but the prosecution must consider such statements and develop a defense. If information exists that the suspect committed the crime but did so in self-defense or accidentally, state this in the report. Include all recognizable weaknesses in proving the corpus delicti or the offender's identity.

Write the report clearly and accurately, following the guidelines presented in Chapter 3. The quality of the final report influences its credibility. Arrange the material in a logical sequence and a convenient format. A binder or loose-leaf notebook works well for this because it allows the various units of information to be separated, with a labeled, tabbed divider for each unit. Although the prosecutor may have been consulted at various stages of the investigation, at this point the prosecutor might offer a plea bargain to the defendant based on the strength of the case and of the final report. It has been said that some cases are, in effect, trial by report.

THE ROLE OF THE PROSECUTOR

The prosecutor is the gatekeeper of the court system, determining which cases are prosecuted and which are not: "The prosecutor is of critical importance because of the office's central position in the criminal justice system. Whereas police, defense attorneys, judges and probation officers specialize in specific phases of the criminal justice process, the duties of the prosecutor bridge all of these areas. This means that on a daily basis the prosecutor is the only official who works with all actors of the criminal justice system. As Justice Robert Jackson once remarked, 'The prosecutor has more control over life, liberty and reputation than any other person in America'" (Neubauer and Fradella, 2011, p.138).

 The prosecutor is the most powerful official in the court system.

At the county level, the prosecutor, or district attorney (DA), is the chief law enforcement official. DAs may be appointed or elected and are responsible for prosecuting felonies and serious misdemeanors in the trial courts of general jurisdiction. At the federal level, the prosecutor is called the U.S. attorney, a position appointed by the president, approved by Congress and confirmed by the Senate. Although prosecutors' offices at the local level generally do not have in-house investigators, federal prosecutors' offices commonly have staff investigators and are in frequent contact with other federal investigative agencies, such as the Federal Bureau of Investigation (FBI), Drug Enforcement Administration (DEA), Bureau of Alcohol, Tobacco, Firearms and Explosives (ATF) and U.S. Secret Service. Also, unlike local prosecutors, federal prosecutors are typically those who initiate a federal criminal investigation, whereas by the time a case comes to a local prosecutor or DA, the investigation has already been completed by local law enforcement.

The ability to wield broad discretion is a key characteristic of prosecutors in our justice system, and the various actors in a trial often have conflicting views about how this discretion should be used: "The police push for harsher penalties; defense attorneys, for giving their clients a break; and judges, to clear the docket" (Neubauer and Fradella, 2011, p.138). In addition, although the prosecutor tries cases in the court, the office is part of the executive branch of government, independent from the judiciary. This independence is crucial for the adversary system to function because prosecutors often challenge judicial decisions. The adversary system is discussed later in the chapter.

Tensions and conflicts sometimes exist between investigators and prosecutors. An investigator may feel a case is strong and the suspect should be brought to trial, but the prosecutor may disagree. In these cases, officers must remain cognizant of the varying standards of proof at work when considering legal arrests and prosecutable offenses. Crime-charging gaps may occur when the prosecutor thinks a reduced charge is more likely to obtain a conviction than is the charge the defendant was originally arrested on. Although officers can arrest based on probable cause, prosecutors are held to a much higher standard—proof *beyond a reasonable doubt*—in the courtroom: "Unless it appears that this higher burden of proof can be met, criminal proceedings cannot ethically be commenced. Sometimes, therefore the charging gaps result from the simple fact that the quantity and quality of evidence that may be more than enough to constitute probable cause nevertheless falls short of what would be needed to establish guilt at trial" (Rutledge, 2008, p.70). However, this burden of proof is often misunderstood. Many cases are won on circumstantial evidence alone. There is a significant difference between *reasonable doubt* and *reason to doubt*. Many defense lawyers exploit that reason to doubt, which is very easy to do in most cases.

One of the facets of prosecution that frustrates law enforcement is the fact that the chief prosecutor holds a political position, whether appointed or elected, and is expected to have a successful track record of charged cases that win. Because of this, prosecutors can be very selective and conservative on cases they decide to pursue, not wanting to take chances on cases that they are not certain can be won. Regardless of the politics, the prosecutor is an investigator's legal adviser throughout the process—during the investigation, the pretrial conference and the court presentation. It is ultimately the prosecutor's decision. Investigators should follow prosecutors' advice even if they disagree, for it is best to work out the issues of cases together. Investigators should listen to and learn from prosecutors. There may be valid reasons for not prosecuting a case.

For many reasons, most criminal cases are resolved without a trial. An excellent investigation and report may cause the defendant to plead guilty, the defendant may desire to plead guilty without going through a trial, or the plea-bargaining process may bring about a satisfactory resolution.

Cases are not prosecuted if
- The complaint is invalid.
- The prosecutor declines after reviewing the case.
- The complainant refuses to prosecute.
- The offender dies.
- The offender is in prison or out of the country and cannot be returned.
- No evidence or leads exist.

Administrative policy sometimes closes cases to further investigation. Specific criteria are established for these decisions. The caseload of investigative personnel has grown so large that cases with little probability of successful prosecution must be closed as a matter of maintaining priorities.

Many police departments have incorporated such criteria into their crime report forms. If enough criteria are met, the department closes the case to further investigation and notifies the complainant. This often happens when complainants file reports only because their insurance companies require them to report the loss to police. The loss may have occurred many days before the report, or there may be no leads. In some cases, there are insufficient facts to support the complaint, but the victim insists on filing a complaint and has the right to do so.

In other cases, the report is valid but investigation reveals that witnesses have left the area or that no physical evidence remains at the crime scene. Without physical evidence, witnesses, identifiable leads or information to follow up, it is unwise to pursue the case when more pressing cases abound. Such a case is placed in an inactive file and is reopened only if time is available or new information is received. Occasionally, such cases are cleared by the admission or confession of a suspect arrested for another crime. Cases are **exceptionally cleared** when circumstances outside the investigation result in no charges being filed—for example, the suspect dies.

A motion is a request to the court for a decision on a specific legal issue. A motion can lead to a hearing, an appearance before the court to resolve the issue raised in the motion. Hearings are typically less formal and shorter than a full trial. Motions can be filed before, during or after trial, but one type of pretrial motion investigators should be aware of is the *motion to suppress*. If the defense files such a motion, claiming that evidence was illegally obtained or a confession unconstitutionally extracted, and an evidentiary hearing is granted by the court, the possibility exists for the case to fold before ever going to trial, effectively resulting in non-prosecution. If the court ruling is favorable to the defense and the evidence is excluded from trial, the prosecution has the option to appeal the court's decision, generally the only point in the judicial process when such an appeal by the state is allowed.

If no motions have been submitted to court and the prosecutor decides to bring the case to trial, the investigator must thoroughly prepare for testifying in court.

PREPARING A CASE FOR PROSECUTION

Once the decision is made to prosecute a case, more than "probable cause" is required. The prosecution must prove the case *beyond a reasonable doubt*—the degree of proof necessary to obtain a conviction. To do so, the prosecution must know what evidence it can introduce, what witnesses will testify, the strengths and weaknesses of the case and the type of testimony police investigators can supply.

To prepare a case for court,
- Review and evaluate all evidence, positive and negative, and the chain of custody.
- Review all reports on the case, including transcripts of any depositions you have given.
- Prepare witnesses.
- Hold a pretrial conference with the prosecutor.

Review and Evaluate Evidence

Each crime consists of one or more elements that must be proven. The statutes and ordinances of the particular jurisdiction define these elements.

Concentrate on proving the elements of the crime and establishing the offender's identity.

Review physical evidence to ensure that it has been properly gathered, identified, transported and safeguarded between the time it was obtained and the time of the trial. Make sure the evidence is available for the trial and is taken to the courtroom and turned over to the prosecuting attorney. Arrange for trained laboratory technicians' testimony if necessary. As discussed in detail in Chapter 5, select evidence that is material, relevant and competent and that helps establish the corpus delicti: what happened and who is responsible. How evidence is moved along in the system is shown in Figure 21.1.

The pretrial **discovery process** requires the prosecution and defense to disclose to each other certain evidence they intend to use at trial, thus avoiding surprises. There is no general constitutional right to discovery in criminal trials (*Weatherford v. Bursey,* 1977). Courts have expressed concern that requiring too much prosecutorial disclosure might put the prosecution at a disadvantage or that witnesses for the defense might be intimidated (Neubauer and Fradella, 2011). The type of information that is discoverable varies greatly from state to state, with some states allowing only limited discovery, others taking a middle ground and yet others adopting liberal discovery rules.

The landmark Supreme Court case in the discovery process is *Brady v. Maryland* (1963), in which the Court held, "The suppression by the prosecution of evidence favorable to the accused upon request violates due process where the evidence is material either to guilt or to punishment, irrespective of the good faith or bad faith of the prosecution." As Gardner and Anderson (2010, p.36) noted, "Although an accused does not have a right to all information available to the prosecutor, he does have the right to information as provided by the statutes of the state and to information required under the **Brady rule**." As discussed in Chapter 1, exculpatory evidence, that is, evidence that tends to show innocence of the accused, must be disclosed. Investigators who are aware of such evidence are obligated to bring it to the prosecutor's attention. When officers intentionally withhold exculpatory material from the prosecution, they leave themselves open to personal liability for violating a defendant's due process rights.

In most states, "missing" evidence or failing to turn over evidence violates the Brady rule only if it can be shown it was done in bad faith; that is, it was known the evidence was exculpatory and was intentionally withheld (Gardner and Anderson, 2010). The defense must prove a "conscious effort" to suppress exculpatory evidence.

The Supreme Court has held that due process requires the government to disclose information regarding witness credibility before trial, extending *Brady* to impeachment material in *Giglio v. United States* (1972). Defense attorneys will try to **impeach** the testimony of prosecution witnesses; that is, they will try to discredit the testimony, to challenge the truth or accuracy of what

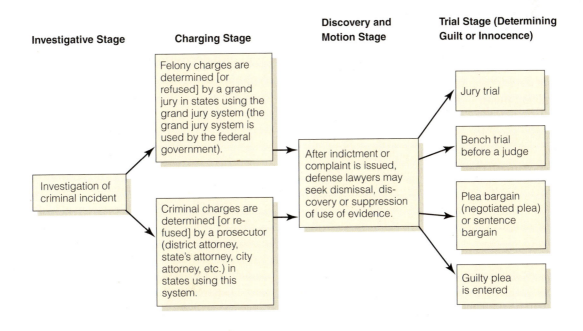

FIGURE 21.1

The use of evidence in the stages of the criminal justice process.

From GARDNER/ANDERSON. *Criminal Evidence,* 7E © 2010 Wadsworth, a part of Cengage Learning, Inc. Reproduced by permission. www.cengage.com/permissions

a prosecution witness testified to under direct examination. This applies to police officers and investigators who testify.

In 1996 the U.S. Department of Justice (DOJ) issued a policy for all DOJ investigative agencies obligating each of their *employees* to inform prosecutors of potential impeachment material as early as possible before providing a sworn statement or testimony in any criminal investigation. The DOJ guidelines suggest that the following must be disclosed: substantiated allegations; pending investigations or allegations; and criminal charges, past or pending.

There are limits on what the defense is entitled to learn about law enforcement witnesses. In *Pennsylvania v. Ritchie* (1987), the Supreme Court held, "Evidence is material only if there is a reasonable probability that had the evidence been disclosed to the defense, the result of the proceeding would have been different. . . . The government has the obligation to turn over evidence in its possession that is both favorable to the accused and *material* to guilt or punishment." The issue of credibility also applies to witnesses other than those of law enforcement who may testify for the prosecution.

Review and evaluate witnesses' statements for credibility. If a witness claims to have seen a specific act, determine whether the light was sufficient and whether the witness has good eyesight and was in a position to see the act clearly. Also assess the witness's relationship to the suspect and the victim.

Establish the suspect's identity by eyewitness testimony, transfer evidence and supporting evidence such as motive, prior knowledge, opportunity and known modus operandi.

Videotapes are being used increasingly in court, especially in child abuse and sex crime cases. Expert witnesses with heavy time commitments may be allowed to testify by videotape, saving the time and expense of a trip to the city where the trial is taking place. Videotapes have also been made of witnesses who are severely injured and cannot appear in court. In addition, videotapes of suspects' confessions and of crime scenes are invaluable.

Reviewing every aspect of the case before entering the courtroom is excellent preparation for testifying. Do not memorize answers to imagined questions, but be prepared.

Depositions. In many states, officers must provide a deposition before trial as part of the discovery. Testifying at a "depo" can be particularly stressful for the unprepared officer and, consequently, quite damaging to the prosecution: "In some ways depositions are more critical than the actual trial. Plaintiff's counsel will try to lock you into your version of the facts via transcript and under oath well before you get to trial" (Grossi, 2007, p.32). Referring to depositions as "fishing expeditions," Grossi (p.32) cautions that the rules of deposition differ from those of trials: "Put simply, you must answer just about every question asked of you, regardless of how probing, embarrassing or insignificant it may seem." The defense counsel will likely dig deep into your professional background and work history, including formal education and law enforcement training, and may venture into your personal life. In addition to assessing the content of your responses, the plaintiff's attorney is seeking to evaluate what type of witness you'll be if the case goes to trial: "Do you have a tendency to become argumentative? Are you quick to anger? What's your demeanor? Do you have any quirks that might cause a jury to question your truthfulness? Do you sweat profusely? . . . If you come across during the deposition as a strong, believable and credible witness, they'll probably get you on and off the witness stand as quickly as possible. On the other hand, if your weaknesses outweigh your strengths as a witness, expect to be 'in the box' a long time" (Grossi, p.34).

Review Reports

Review written reports of everything done during the investigation. This includes the preliminary report, memorandums, summary reports, progress reports, evidence records and receipts, photographs and sketches, medical examiner's reports, emergency squad records, laboratory test reports on evidence, statements of witnesses (positive and negative) and any other reports on actions taken during the investigation. This also includes the transcript of your own deposition:

> The deposition gets typed up and, if you're like most cops, you never read it, though you are entitled to. You can bet your next paycheck that the defense attorney has not only read it, but has gone through it with a fine-tooth comb, compared it to your report, to witness statements, to other officers' reports, and to case evidence to try to find inconsistencies.
>
> The defense attorney will no doubt have his copy all marked up and ready for attack at the table for trial. He's banking on the high probability that you still haven't sufficiently studied the deposition and that you'll say something contrary to what you said before, which can sometimes be a year or more ago. Do yourself and the prosecution a favor by making sure to review the deposition so you don't make any unintentional missteps during the trial. (Nyberg, 2006, p.20)

Prepare Witnesses

Reinterview witnesses to refresh their memories. Read their previous statements to them and ask if this is the evidence they will present in court. Such a review also helps allay any fears witnesses have about testifying. Describe trial procedures to witnesses so they understand what will occur. Explain that they can testify only to facts from their own personal knowledge or from common knowledge. Emphasize that they must tell the truth and present the facts as they know them. Explain the importance of remaining calm; having a neat, clean appearance; and remaining impartial.

By experience, police officers know of the many delays in court proceedings and of the waits in the courtroom or in the hall outside before they can testify. This should also be explained to witnesses who may be testifying for the first time so they can make flexible arrangements for the day. In addition, complainants should be prepared for the possible delays and continuances that may be part of the defense's strategy to wear them down so they will drop the charges.

Pretrial Conference

Before testifying in court and after you have made the final case preparation, arrange for a pretrial conference with the prosecuting attorney. Organize the facts and evidence and prepare a summary of the investigation. Include in this summary the focal points and main issues of the case, an envelope containing copies of all reports and all other relevant documents.

> At the pretrial conference with the prosecutor,
> - Review all the evidence.
> - Discuss the strengths and weaknesses of the case.
> - Discuss the probable line of questioning by the prosecutor and the defense.

An important step in preparing a case for prosecution is to reinterview witnesses to refresh their memories. Officers should read the witnesses' previous statements to them and ask if this is the evidence they will present in court. This review helps alleviate fears witnesses have about testifying in court.

Victims and witnesses may also have the opportunity to speak to the court during the sentencing phase of a trial, should a conviction occur. Statements made during this stage are often emotionally charged and intended to provide the court with insight about the impact of the crime on the victim(s) or witness(es). Preparation is also important in making the most of these "statement of opinion" opportunities.

Brendan Costin, shown here speaking at the sentencing trial of Thomas Junta, the man found guilty of beating Brendan's father to death at the boy's hockey practice, is noticeably choked up as he states, "I can still remember being hysterical, trying to wake him up as the blood streamed down his face. Rushed to the hospital in the ambulance, my father had stopped breathing and had no pulse and his heart stopped beating. After two days in the hospital I realized I had just witnessed my dad literally getting beaten to death."

The 6-foot-1, 270-pound Junta was convicted of involuntary manslaughter for beating 160-pound Michael Costin to death at a Reading, Massachusetts, ice rink in 2000, after Junta got angry over rough play on the ice. Junta testified that he struck Costin only in self-defense. Others said Junta was red-faced with rage. After hearing both sides, the judge determined there were aggravating circumstances surrounding Costin's death, including the fact that the beating took place in front of children.
© Reuters/CORBIS

Discuss complicated or detailed information fully to avoid misunderstanding. Discuss any legal questions concerning admissibility of evidence or testimony. The prosecutor may be able to offer insights into the style of the defense attorney as well as the judge hearing the case.

Sometimes witnesses are included in the pretrial conference. If so, listen carefully to what each witness says to the prosecuting attorney and to what the prosecuting attorney says in response. During the trial, the judge may exclude all witnesses from the courtroom except the person testifying, a practice called *sequestering*. Therefore, you may have no opportunity to hear the testimony of other witnesses or the approach used by the prosecuting attorney.

It is also a good idea to review the case with other officers who are going to testify. You may not hear their actual testimony, and it will help you if you know in advance what they are going to say.

Final Preparations

Shortly before the trial, again review your notes and your final report. Take with you only those notes you want to use in testifying. Be certain the physical evidence is being taken to the courtroom and will be available for the prosecuting attorney when needed. Also make sure that laboratory technicians are available to appear when necessary. Find out which courtroom you will be testifying in and look it over before the trial.

If you are asked to bring physical evidence with you to the trial, use an appropriate container to prevent passersby from seeing it: "If you have a bloody shirt or a sawed-off shotgun across your lap in the waiting area or the courthouse snack shop, potential jurors might be exposed to it before it's introduced in evidence (And if the judge excludes the evidence, the prejudice has already been created)" (Rutledge, 2004, p.71).

Know What Is Expected and the Rules of the Court.

When an officer receives a **subpoena**, an order to appear before the court, it may not indicate what kind of hearing it is. It might be a grand jury or a preliminary hearing or a criminal trial. The rules of evidence are different, as is the burden of proof required. If the subpoena does not specify the type of hearing, call the prosecutor or the attorney who sent the subpoena to determine the nature of the hearing.

The subpoena will also usually indicate whether the officer is to make a personal appearance or be on call, meaning the officer need not appear personally unless called by the prosecution. On-call officers should provide the prosecutor or county clerk with a phone or pager number where they can be reached and should be available to receive the call and respond within a relatively short time.

Witnesses usually are excluded from the courtroom during a trial to prevent one witness from hearing another witness's testimony. This is known as the **rule on witnesses** or **witness sequestration rule**. Find out before going into the courtroom whether witnesses have been excluded. If they have and an investigator goes into the courtroom and sits, the investigator may be severely reprimanded or, worse, be the cause for a mistrial.

Be familiar with any pretrial rulings a judge has issued. In some instances, a judge may have issued a **motion in limine**, a motion requesting the judge to issue a protective order against prejudicial questions or statements. For example, a defense attorney may ask a judge to restrict any reference to his client's criminal record during the trial. An investigator who is unaware of this motion and violates it may cause the judge to order a mistrial.

Dress Appropriately.

Most police departments have regulations regarding attire when officers appear in court. Some departments specify that officers should appear in uniform. A weapon may not be worn into the courtroom without special permission. If one is worn, it should not be visible. Do not wear dark or deeply tinted glasses. If you wear street clothes, dress conservatively. Avoid bright colors and large plaids. Do not overdo on accessories, and avoid bizarre haircuts. Your personal appearance reflects your attitude and your professionalism and will have a definite effect on the jury.

Be on Time.

If you are delayed for any reason, phone the prosecutor or the court clerk, explain the reason and give an approximate time when you can be expected to appear.

THE TRIAL

Trials occur within a construct called the **adversary system**, which establishes clearly defined roles for both the prosecution and the defense and sets the judge as the neutral party. This has important implications for the investigator, who is on the "side" of the prosecutor in the proceeding, as will be discussed shortly. The main participants in a trial are the judge, jury, attorneys, defendant and witnesses (Figure 21.2).

The *judge*, or *magistrate*, presides over the trial; determines whether a witness is qualified and competent; addresses questions of law, including motions, objections and procedures; rules on the admissibility of evidence; keeps order; interprets the law for the jurors; and passes sentence if the defendant is found guilty.

The *jurors* hear and evaluate the testimony of all witnesses. Called *fact finders*, jurors consider many factors other than the words spoken. The attitude and behavior of witnesses, suspects and attorneys are constantly under the jury's scrutiny. Jurors notice how witnesses respond to questions and their attitudes toward the prosecution and the defense. Jurors reach their verdict based on what they see, hear and feel during the trial. Typical jurors will have had limited or no experience with the criminal justice system outside of what they have read in the newspaper and seen on television.

Legal counsel presents the prosecution and defense evidence before the court and jury. Lawyers act as checks against each other and present the case as required by court procedure and the rulings of the presiding judge.

Defendants may or may not take the witness stand. The Fifth Amendment protects defendants against self-incrimination. If a defendant chooses not to testify, this fact cannot be used against him or her. However, if a defendant

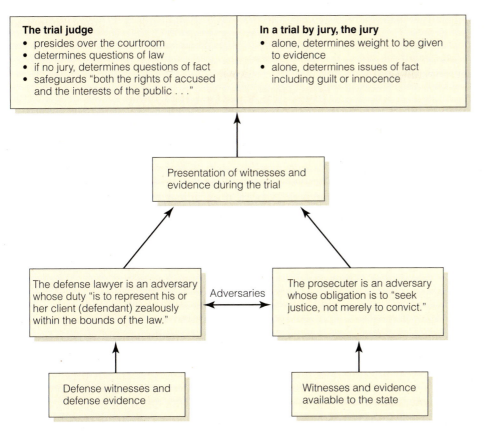

FIGURE 21.2
The American adversary system.

From GARDNER/ANDERSON. Criminal Evidence, 7E © 2010 Wadsworth, a part of Cengage Learning, Inc. Reproduced by permission. www.cengage.com/permissions

does choose to testify, waiving the privilege against self-incrimination, that defendant cannot tell only a part of the story. If a defendant testifies, the state can ask questions about all the facts surrounding the event testified to. In addition, once the defendant takes the stand, the state can impeach the defendant's credibility by introducing any prior felony convictions: "The defense attorney must make the difficult decision whether to arouse the jury's suspicion by not letting the accused testify or [let] the defendant testify and be subjected to possibly damaging cross-examination" (Neubauer and Fradella, 2011, p.357).

Witnesses present the facts as they know them: "To qualify as a witness, a person must have relevant information, must be competent and must declare that he or she will testify truthfully. To be competent, a witness must be able to remember and tell what happened, must be able to distinguish fact from fantasy and must know that he or she must tell the truth. . . . Anglo-Saxon law seeks to keep witnesses honest by having them testify under oath or affirmation in the presence of the fact finder and the accused, subject to cross-examination and subject to possible perjury charges for failure to tell the truth" (Gardner and Anderson, 2010, p.107).

Police officers are witnesses for the prosecution. Law enforcement witnesses present a challenge to the prosecution's case because the prosecuting attorney must establish the burden of proof beyond a reasonable doubt.

SEQUENCE OF A CRIMINAL TRIAL

A trial begins with a case being called from the court docket. If both the prosecution and the defense are ready, the case is presented before the court.

The sequence in a criminal trial is as follows:

- Jury selection
- Opening statements by the prosecution and the defense
- Presentation of the prosecution's case; cross-examination by the defense
- Presentation of the defense's case; cross-examination by the prosecution
- Rebuttal and surrebuttal testimony
- Closing statements by the prosecution and the defense
- Instructions to the jury
- Jury deliberation to reach a verdict
- Reading of the verdict
- Acquittal or passing of sentence

If the trial is before a judge *without a jury*, called a **bench trial**, the prosecution and the defense make their opening statements directly to the judge. The opening statements are brief summaries of both the prosecution and defense attorneys' plans. In a *jury trial*, the jury is selected and then both counsels make their opening statements before the judge and jury.

The prosecution presents its case first. Witnesses for the prosecution are sworn in, and the prosecuting attorney asks them questions. Then the defense attorney may cross-examine the witnesses. After this cross-examination, the prosecuting attorney may redirect-examine, and then the defense attorney may re-cross-examine.

Direct examination is the initial questioning of a witness or defendant by the lawyer who is using the person's testimony to further his or her case. **Cross-examination** is questioning by the opposing side to assess the validity of the testimony.

After the prosecutor has completed direct examination of all prosecution witnesses, the defense presents its case. After the direct examination of each defense witness, the prosecutor may cross-examine, the defense counsel may redirect-examine and the prosecutor may re-cross-examine.

After each side has presented its regular witnesses, both sides may present *rebuttal* and *surrebuttal* witnesses. The prosecution can call **rebuttal** witnesses to contradict the testimony (or evidence) presented by the defense. The defense, in turn, can call **surrebuttal** witnesses to contradict the testimony (or evidence) presented by the prosecution. When the entire case has been presented, prosecution and defense counsel present their closing arguments. In these arguments, the lawyers review the trial evidence of both sides and tell the jury why the defendant should be convicted or acquitted. Sometimes the lawyers also make recommendations for penalty.

The judge instructs the jury on the laws applicable to the case and on how they are to arrive at a decision. The jury then retires to the jury room to deliberate and arrive at a verdict. When the jury reaches a verdict, court is reconvened and the verdict is read. If the verdict is for acquittal, the defendant is released. If the verdict is guilty, the judge passes sentence or sets a time and date for sentencing.

WHILE WAITING TO TESTIFY

Do not discuss the case while waiting in the hallway to testify. If a juror or another witness hears your statements, you may have created grounds for a mistrial. Although it may be impractical or impossible to avoid all contact with jurors, such as chance encounters in a crowded elevator or passing each other in the hallway, **de minimus communication**, that is, a simple hello

or giving of directions, is allowable. It is important not to appear aloof or unfriendly.

TESTIFYING UNDER DIRECT EXAMINATION

Rutledge (2000, p.15) asserts, "No matter how brilliant the investigation, how careful the arrest, and how thorough the report, if an officer isn't just as competent on the stand as he is in the field, he is just processing bodies." He (p.12) stresses, "You are on trial, too—your credibility, your professionalism, your knowledge, your competence, your judgment, your conduct in the field, your use of force, your adherence to official policies, your observance of the defendant's rights—they're all on trial."

As you enter the courtroom, keep in mind your goal, which is similar to that sought on the street—to win. However, this does not mean winning the case but, instead, winning the trust of the court and the jury: "The 'win' for every honest officer in every courtroom confrontation is as simple as it is difficult: at the end of their testimony, when the last question has been answered, the jury must find them *credible*. Credibility is the degree to which the jury believes a witness. That's it. That's the only goal, the only win, the only job for the testifying officer—to be believed by the jury" (Van Brocklin, 2005, p.44).

> The "win" for an investigator who testifies is to have established credibility.

First impressions are critical. Know what you are doing when you enter the courtroom. When your name is called, answer "Here" or "Present" and move directly to the front of the courtroom. Do not walk between the prosecutor and the judge; go behind the attorneys. Never walk in front of the judge or between the judge and the attorneys' tables. This area, called **the well**, is off-limits and is to be entered only if the judge so directs or permission is granted. Traditionally, the area is a sword's length and was intended for the judge's protection.

Walk confidently; the jurors are there to hear the facts from you. If your investigation has been thorough and properly conducted, the jury will give a great deal of weight to your testimony.

If you have notes or a report, carry them in a clean manila file folder in your left hand so your right hand is free for taking the oath. Taking the oath in court is basically the same as taking your oath of office. Stand straight and face the clerk of the court, holding the palm of your hand toward the clerk. Use a clear, firm voice to answer "I do" to the question "Do you promise to tell the truth, the whole truth, and nothing but the truth, so help you God?" Do not look at the judge, either legal counsel or the jury.

Sit with your back straight but in a comfortable position, usually with your hands folded in your lap or held on the arms of the chair. Do not move the chair around or fidget because this is distracting. Hold notes and other reports in your lap. If the reports are bulky, many experts on testifying recommend placing them under the chair until needed.

The witness chair in all courtrooms is positioned so you can face the judge, legal counsel, jury or the audience, depending on to whom your answers are directed. In most instances, if the judge asks you a question, look directly at the judge to answer. If either the prosecutor or defense counsel asks you a question, look directly at the jury to give your answer. The prosecutor will ask you to state your name, department and position. As you respond, keep in mind the types of statements that are not admissible.

> **Inadmissible statements include**
> - Opinions and conclusions (unless the witness is qualified as an expert).
> - Hearsay.
> - Privileged communication.
> - Statements about character and reputation, including the defendant's criminal record.

Testify only to what you actually saw, heard or did, not what you believe, heard from others or were told about. You can testify to what a defendant told you directly, but any other statements must be testified to by the person making them.

Preparation is the key to being a good witness. After a review of your personal notes and all relevant reports, you will be familiar with the case and can "tell it like it is." This will come across well to the jury and establish your credibility.

> **Guidelines for effective testimony are**
> - Speak clearly, firmly and with expression.
> - Answer questions directly. Do *not* volunteer information.
> - Pause briefly before answering.
> - Refer to your notes if you do not recall exact details.
> - Admit calmly when you do not know an answer.
> - Admit any mistakes you make in testifying.
> - Avoid police jargon, sarcasm and humor.
> - Tell the complete truth as you know it.

How you speak is often as important as what you say. Talk slowly, deliberately and loudly enough to be heard by everyone. Never use obscenity or vulgarity unless the court requests a suspect's or victim's exact words. In such cases, inform the court before you answer that the answer requested includes obscenity or vulgarity.

Ignore the courtroom's atmosphere. Devote your entire attention to giving truthful answers to questions. Answer all questions directly and politely with "yes" or "no" unless asked to relate an action taken, an observation made or information told to you directly by the defendant. Refer to the judge as "Your Honor" and to the defendant as "the defendant." Do not volunteer information. Instead, let the prosecution decide whether to pursue a particular line of questioning.

Take a few seconds after hearing the question to form your answer. If the counsel or the court objects to a question, wait until instructed to proceed. If it takes some time for the judge to rule on an objection, ask to have the question repeated.

Reviewing the case thoroughly before your courtroom appearance does not mean that you should memorize specific dates, addresses or spellings of names and places. Memorization can lead to confusion. Instead, use notes to help avoid contradictions and inconsistencies. An extemporaneous answer is better received by the judge and jury than one that sounds rehearsed.

> **Refer to your notes if you are uncertain of specific facts, but do not rely on them excessively.**

Using notes too much detracts from your testimony, weakens your presentation and gives the impression you have not adequately prepared for the case. It can also lead to having your notes introduced into the record. If, as you refer to your notes, you discover you have given erroneous testimony such as an incorrect date or time, notify the court immediately. Do not try to cover up the discrepancy. Everyone makes mistakes. If you admit them in a professional manner, little harm results. Do not hesitate to admit that you do not know the answer to a question or that you do not understand a question. Never bluff or attempt to fake your way through an answer.

In addition, be aware of certain phrases that may leave a negative impression on the jury. Phrases such as "I believe" or "to the best of my recollection" will not impress a jury. Do not argue or use sarcasm, witticisms or "smart" answers. Be direct, firm and positive. Be courteous, whether in response to a question from the prosecutor or an objection from the defense or the judge. Do not hesitate to give information favorable to the defendant. Your primary responsibility is to state what you know about the case.

If asked to identify evidence with your personal mark, take time to examine the item thoroughly. Make sure that all marks are accounted for and that your mark has not been altered. A rapid identification may make a bad impression on the jury and may lead you into an erroneous identification.

Nonverbal Factors

Do not underestimate the power of nonverbal factors as you testify. More than 25 years ago, Dr. Albert Mehrabian (1981) conducted his famous, often-cited study at the University of California, Los Angeles (UCLA) and concluded that communication is made up of several components:

■ *What* is said—the actual words spoken (7 percent of the total message communicated)

■ *How* it is said—tone of voice, pitch, modulation and the like (38 percent of the message)

■ *Nonverbal factors*—body language, gestures, demeanor (55 percent)

Thus, the bulk of a message is conveyed not through which words are used but in how they are delivered. Never overlook the importance of how you present information and nonverbal factors when testifying.

> Important nonverbal elements include dress, eye contact, posture, gestures, mannerisms, rate of speech, tone of voice and facial expressions.

Make eye contact with the jury often while testifying. Be aware of facial expressions that might indicate indifference, disgust, displeasure or arrogance. Avoid actions associated with deception such as putting a hand over your mouth, rubbing your nose, straightening your hair, buttoning your coat, picking lint off your clothing or tugging at your shirt or a pant leg.

Strategies for Excelling as a Witness

> To excel as a witness, (1) set yourself up, (2) provoke the defense into giving you a chance to explain, (3) be unconditional and (4) do not stall.

Rutledge (2000) suggests several basic points to enhance the chance of success, some of which have been discussed:

Testifying in court is part of working in law enforcement. Officers must never underestimate the power of nonverbal communication when they testify. Although what is being said (the "facts" to which the officer is testifying) is certainly important, the way these facts are presented can speak just as loudly, if not more loudly, to the judge and jury. Important nonverbal elements include dress, eye contact, posture, gestures, mannerisms, rate of speech and tone of voice. These factors can provide far more insight and depth into an officer's statement of fact and experience, particularly as pertains to a brutal or otherwise horrific crime scene, than can mere words recorded onto the court transcript.

Consider the expression of Montgomery County police officer Cynthia Martin, the first officer on the scene of the shooting of sniper shooting victim Sarah Ramos, as she testifies during the trial of Washington area sniper suspect John Allen Muhammad.
© Adrin Snider-Pool/Getty Images

■ Get into the habit of thinking ahead to the trial while you are still out in the field. Ask yourself, "What if they ask me this in court?" (p.20).

■ Be unconditional. Some police officers seem to like the sound of the conditional word *would*. When I am prosecuting a case, I cringe at the sound of it because it is too indefinite.

EXAMPLE:

Q: Who was your partner?

A: That would be Officer Hill. (p.72)

■ Do not stall. Do not repeat the attorney's question.

EXAMPLE:

Q: Were you holding a flashlight?

A: Was I holding a flashlight? Yes, I was. (p.75)

In some instances, officers may qualify to testify as *expert witnesses.* In such cases, the restrictions on testimony are somewhat more relaxed.

Expert Testimony

Rule 702 of the Federal Rules of Evidence states, "If scientific, technical or other specialized knowledge will assist the trier of fact to understand the evidence or to determine a fact in issue, a witness qualified as an expert by knowledge, skill, experience, training or education, may testify thereto in the form of an opinion or otherwise, if (1) the testimony is based upon sufficient facts of data, (2) the testimony is the product of reliable principles and methods and (3) the witness has applied the principles and methods reliably to the facts of the case."

An **expert witness** is a person who has had special training, education or experience: "Expert testimony is testimony that seeks to explain matters beyond the usual comprehension or knowledge of a typical jury. It is based on specialized knowledge, training, experience or skills, the application of which will help the jury understand the evidence" (Kruger, 2005, p.11).

Daubert v. Merrell Dow Pharmaceuticals, Inc. (1993) established standards for the admission of expert testimony in federal courts. Under *Daubert*, an expert's testimony must be specialized and relate directly to some fact at issue in the case: "Expert testimony which does not relate to any issue in the case is not relevant and, ergo, non-helpful." The Supreme Court noted that expert testimony must fit the case. Fitness is determined by examining how helpful the testimony is. This "helpfulness" standard requires a valid connection between the expert testimony and the inquiry.

Officers who qualify as experts in an area are allowed to give opinions and conclusions, but the prosecution must qualify the officer as an expert on the stand. The prosecution must establish that the person has special knowledge that others of moderate education or experience in the same field do not possess. To qualify as an expert witness, one must have as many of the following as possible:

■ Present or prior employment in the specific field

■ Active membership in a professional group in the field

■ Research work in the field

■ An educational degree directly related to the field

■ Direct experience with the subject if not employed in the field

■ Papers, treatises or books published on the subject or teaching experience in it

Police officers can become experts on sounds, firearms, distances, lengths of time, speed, visibility problems and so on simply by years of experience in police work. Other areas, such as firearms identification, fingerprint classification and handwriting analysis, require specialized training. Just who qualifies as an expert is not always clear, and different qualifications may exist for scientific and nonscientific evidence.

It is strongly recommended that officers document their training, studies and experience in a format such as that shown in Figure 21.3. Take this record to court to establish yourself as an expert witness.

TESTIFYING UNDER CROSS-EXAMINATION

Recall the earlier description of the adversary system. It is understandable that an investigator would consider the defense attorney's cross-examination as an attack on the prosecution's case. However, also recall that investigators' *attitudes* determine their testimony style and their body language. During cross-examination, while the defense attorney attempts to impeach your testimony or at least undermine your credibility, posttrial interviews of jurors reveal other body language or behaviors that can weaken a witness's credibility (Van Brocklin, 2005, p.48):

■ Uses a defensive or evasive tone of voice

■ Appears ill at ease or nervous

■ Avoids eye contact

■ Crosses arms defensively across chest

■ Quibbles over common terms

■ Sits stiffly

■ Looks to attorney for assistance during cross-examination

■ Cracks jokes inappropriately

■ Uses lots of "ah's" or "uh's"

In contrast, jurors have noted that several behaviors enhance credibility:

■ Displays an even temperament on direct and cross

■ Doesn't become angry or defensive when pressed

■ Appears relaxed and at ease

■ Is likeable and polite

IN-SERVICE TRAINING

	Date	Place	Subject	# of Hours
Basic Academy				
Advanced Academy				
Special Schools				
Roll-Call Training				

SPECIAL STUDIES/EXPERIMENTS

Dates	Place	Subject	Description

COLLEGE, UNIVERSITY, TECH SCHOOL

Dates	Place	Subject	Description

READINGS

Dates	Title	Subject	Description

PROFESSIONAL ASSOCIATIONS

OJT
Supervised Training

Dates	Supervisor	Subject	# of Hrs or Cases

INVESTIGATIONS, ARRESTS, EVALUATIONS, ETC.
Approximate Number

Narc.	Prints	T/A	Bkmkg	Ballis.	DWI	Handwriting	Poly.

FIGURE 21.3

Record of training, studies and experience.

PRIOR EXPERT TESTIMONY (Number)								
Court	Narc.	Prints	T/A	Bkmkg	Ballis.	DWI	Handwriting	Poly.
Justice								
Municipal								
Superior								
Supreme								
Federal								
Other States								
OTHER QUALIFICATION(S)								

FIGURE 21.3
(continued)

■ Maintains eye contact with attorney and jury

■ Is not affected by interruptions or objections

Rutledge (2000, p.60) notes, "You're not an advocate—you're a witness. Don't try to help the prosecutor. Don't try to thwart the defense lawyer." Cross-examination is usually the most difficult part of testifying. "The defense lawyer's most important task is to destroy your credibility—to make you look like you're either a . . . bungler, a liar, or both. How does he do that? He attacks you. He tricks you. He outsmarts you. He confuses you. He frustrates you. He annoys you. He probes for your most vulnerable characteristics" (Rutledge, p.118). How does this make officers feel?

One testimony expert noted that when officers were given a word-association test and the words *defense attorney* were given, exclamations flew: "*Snake, shark, weasel, slime, dishonest, deceptive, liar,* and several that need not be printed" (Van Brocklin, 2005, pp.46–47). This negative attitude explains why an officer can do a competent job in the investigation, be truthful and still not be believed by the jury. If jurors perceive that an investigator is acting defensively, they may think the investigator is not testifying truthfully, as it is often presumed that only someone with something to hide acts defensively. The key is to recognize this tendency and remain professional and objective.

The defense attorney will attempt to cast doubt on your direct testimony in an effort to win an acquittal for the defendant. Know the methods of attack for cross-examination to avoid being trapped.

During cross-examination the defense attorney may

■ Be disarmingly friendly or intimidatingly rude.

■ Attack your credibility and impartiality.

■ Attack your investigative skill.

■ Attempt to force contradictions or inconsistencies.

■ Ask leading questions or deliberately misquote you.

■ Ask for a simple answer to a complex question.

■ Use rapid-fire questioning.

■ Use the silent treatment.

The defense attorney can be extremely friendly, hoping to put you off guard by making the questioning appear to be just a friendly chat. The attorney may praise your skill in investigation and lead you into boasting or a show of self-glorification that will leave a very bad impression on the jury. The "friendly" defense attorney may also try to lead you into testifying about evidence of which you have no personal knowledge. This error will be immediately exposed and your testimony tainted, if not completely discredited.

At the opposite extreme is the defense attorney who appears outraged by statements you make and goes on the attack immediately. This kind of attorney appears very excited and outraged, as though the trial is a travesty of justice. A natural reaction to such an approach is to exaggerate your testimony or lose your temper, which is exactly what the defense attorney wants. If you show anger, the jury may believe you are more interested in obtaining a conviction than determining the truth. It is often hard for a jury to believe that the well-dressed, meek-appearing defendant in court is the person who, armed with a gun, robbed a store and assaulted several bystanders. Maintain your dignity and impartiality, and show concern for only the facts.

The credibility of your testimony can be undermined in many ways. The defense may attempt to show that you are prejudiced, have poor character or are interested only in seeing your arrest "stick." If asked, "Do you want to see the defendant convicted?" reply that you are there to present the facts you know and that you will abide by the court's decision. No contemporary case demonstrated these cross-examination attacks on police credibility more effectively than the O. J. Simpson murder trial. The defense was successful in shifting the focus away from the issue of the defendant's guilt and putting it directly on the incompetence of the police investigators.

The defense may also try to show that your testimony itself is erroneous because you are incompetent, lack information, are confused, have forgotten facts or could not have had personal knowledge of the facts you have testified to. Do not respond to such criticism. Let your testimony speak for itself. If the defense criticizes your reference to notes, state that you simply want to be completely accurate. Be patient. If the defense counsel becomes excessively offensive, the prosecutor will intervene. Alternatively, the prosecutor may see that the defense is hurting its own case by such behavior and will allow the defense attorney to continue.

The defense attorney may further try to force contradictions or inconsistencies by incessantly repeating questions using slightly different wording. Repeat your previous answer. If the defense claims that your testimony does not agree with that of other officers, do not change your testimony. Whether your testimony is like theirs or different is irrelevant. The defense will attack it either way. If it is exactly alike, the defense will allege collusion. If it is slightly different, the defense will exaggerate this to convince the jury that the differences are so great that the officers are not even testifying about the same circumstances.

A common tactic of defense lawyers to destroy credibility is to try to get you to commit yourself to something and then later have to admit you could be wrong about it. Rutledge (2000, p.77) suggests that if either attorney asks for any kind of *measurement* you did not personally make, including distance, time, height, weight, speed,

age and the like, allow yourself some leeway. Either give an *approximation*—for example, "he was approximately 45 feet away"—or put your answer in brackets. **Brackets** provide a range—for example, "he was 40 to 50 feet away." Nyberg (2006, p.22) states, "You might get a question like, 'How many times did you ask my client if he knew where his wife was?' The temptation is to come up with a number, to make it sound impressive. Don't get snared into answering something like this. The best answer is, 'I have no idea. I've never even considered counting how many times I've asked someone something. During an interview, I am more tuned in to what the other person is saying.' Show the jury that you are a professional and that your goal is to get to the truth."

Another defense tactic is to use an accusatory tone in asking whether you talked with others about the case and what they told you about how to testify. Such accusations may make inexperienced officers feel guilty because they know they have talked about the case with many people. Because the accusing tone implies that this was legally incorrect, the officers may reply that they talked to no one. Such a response is a mistake because you may certainly discuss the case before testifying. Simply state that you have discussed the case with several people in an official capacity, but that none of them told you how to testify.

If defense counsel asks whether you have refreshed your memory before testifying, do not hesitate to say "yes." You would be a poor witness if you had not done so. Discussions with the prosecution, officers and witnesses and a review of notes and reports are entirely proper. They help you tell the truth, the main purpose of testimony.

Leading questions are another defense tactic. For example, defense counsel may ask, "When did you first strike the defendant?" This implies that you did in fact strike the defendant. Defense attorneys also like to ask questions that presume you have already testified to something when in fact you may not have done so. If you are misquoted, call it to the counsel's attention and then repeat the facts you testified to. If you do not remember your exact testimony, have it read from the court record.

In addition, defense counsel may ask complicated questions and then say, "Please answer 'yes' or 'no.'" Obviously, some questions cannot be answered that simply. Ask to have the question broken down. No rule requires a specific answer. If the court does not grant your request, answer the question as directed and let the prosecutor bring out the information through redirect examination.

Rapid-fire questioning is yet another tactic that defense attorneys use to provoke unconsidered answers. Do not let the attorney's pace rush you. Take time to consider your responses.

Do not be taken in by the "silent treatment." The defense attorney may remain silent for what seems like many seconds after you answer a question. If you have given a complete answer, wait patiently. Do *not* attempt to fill the silence by saying things such as, "At least that's how I remember it" or "It was something very close to that."

Another tactic frequently used by defense attorneys is to mispronounce officers' names intentionally or address them by the wrong rank. This is an attempt to distract the officer.

Regardless of how your testimony is attacked, treat the defense counsel as respectfully as you do the prosecutor. Do not regard the defense counsel as your enemy. You are in court to state the facts and tell the truth. Your testimony should exhibit no personal prejudice or animosity, and you should not become excited or provoked at defense counsel. Be professional.

Few officers are prepared for the rigor of testifying in court, even if they have received training in this area. Until officers have actually testified in court, they cannot understand how difficult it is. Because police officers are usually the primary and most damaging witnesses in a criminal case, defense attorneys know they must attempt to confuse, discredit or destroy the officers' testimony. The best testimony is accurate, truthful and in accordance with the facts. Every word an officer says is recorded and may be played back or used by the defense.

> A key to testifying during cross-examination is to NEVER volunteer any information.

During cross-examination, the defense attorney can ask questions about only subjects raised by the prosecution during direct examination. If an investigator volunteers additional information, he or she may open up areas the prosecution did not intend to present and may not be prepared for.

HANDLING OBJECTIONS

Three general types of objections common during trials are

- Objections to the *form of the question*, arguing the question, as asked, is leading, speculative, argumentative, misstates facts in evidence, assumes facts not in evidence, is vague and ambiguous, repetitive or cumulative or is misleading.
- Objections to the *substance of the question*, arguing that the question is irrelevant, immaterial, incompetent, calls for hearsay, has insufficient foundation, calls

for inadmissible opinion or is beyond the scope of the direct examination.
- Objections to the *answer* in that it is either unresponsive, an inadmissible opinion or an inadmissible hearsay statement.

Rutledge (2000, pp.97–115) gives the following suggestions for handling objections (reprinted by permission of the publisher):

> There are at least 44 standard trial objections in most states. We're only going to talk about the two that account for upwards of 90 percent of the problems a testifying officer will have: that your answer is a conclusion, or that it is nonresponsive.
>
> - How to avoid conclusions. One way is to listen to the form of the question. You know the attorney is asking you to speculate when he starts his questions with these loaded phrases:
>
>   Would you assume . . . ?
>
>   Do you suppose . . . ?
>
>   Don't you think that . . . ?
>
>   Couldn't it be that . . . ?
>
>   Do you imagine . . . ?
>
>   Wouldn't it be fair to presume . . . ?
>
>   Isn't it strange that . . . ?
>
>   And the one you're likely to hear most often:
>
>   Isn't it possible that . . . ?
>
> - Another major area of conclusionary testimony is what I call mind reading. You can't get inside someone else's brain. That means you don't know for a fact—so you can't testify—as to what someone else sees, hears, feels, thinks or wants; and you don't know for a fact what somebody is trying to do, or is able to do, or whether he is nervous, excited, angry, scared, happy, upset, disturbed, or in any of the other emotional states that can only be labeled with a conclusion.
> - How to give "responsive" answers. You have to answer just the question you're asked—no more, no less. That means you have to pay attention to how the question is framed. You answer a yes-or-no question with a "yes" or "no."
>
>   **Q:** Did he perform the alphabet test?
>
>   **A:** Yes, twice—but he only went to "G."
>
>   Everything after the "yes" is nonresponsive. The officer anticipated the next three questions and

volunteered the answers. He should have limited each answer to one question:

Q: Did he perform the alphabet test?

A: Yes.

Q: How many times?

A: Twice.

Q: How far did he go correctly the first time?

A: To the letter "G."

To avoid objections to your testimony, avoid conclusions and nonresponsive answers. Answer yes-or-no questions with "yes" or "no."

CONCLUDING YOUR TESTIMONY

Do not leave the stand until instructed to do so by counsel or the court. As you leave the stand, do not pay special attention to the prosecution, defense counsel, defendant or jury. Return immediately to your seat in the courtroom or leave the room if you have been sequestered. If you are told you may be needed for further testimony, remain available. If told you are no longer needed, leave the courtroom and resume your normal activities. To remain gives the impression that you have a special interest in the case.

If you are in the courtroom at the time of the verdict, show neither approval nor disapproval at the outcome. If you have been a credible witness and told the truth, win or lose in court, you have done your job and should not take the outcome personally.

The complainant should be notified of the disposition of the case. A form such as the one shown in Figure 21.4 is frequently used.

ADVICE ON TESTIFYING FROM A SEASONED, "OFFICER OF THE YEAR" INVESTIGATOR

You were introduced to Detective Richard Gautsch at the beginning of the text. He returns to furnish the book's conclusion, emphasizing the areas to focus on when giving courtroom testimony and providing examples of some of his experiences testifying.

Although everything in this chapter is important, Gautsch emphasizes three major areas:

1. *Preparation.* While testifying, an investigator should not use his or her report as a crutch or a script. It should be a safety net—seldom used. Constantly referring to a report gives the jury the impression that you do not know the case. Officers should *study* their reports and the reports of fellow officers before testifying.

2. *Communication.* Understand that words are a small part of communicating. Expressions, demeanor, personality, appearance and more are what jurors use to form an opinion. If you remind them of the obstinate cop who wrote them a ticket for going two miles over the speed limit, they're going to sympathize with the defendant.

3. *Credibility.* If jurors question your credibility, the case is in big trouble. If you are caught in a lie, an embellishment or an obvious omission, why should a juror believe anything you say? In the O. J. Simpson murder trial, a detective lied about whether he had ever used racial slurs. Even though it had nothing to do with the evidence he was presenting, once he lost his credibility, his testimony lost its value and, indeed, severely damaged the prosecution's case.

Detective Gautsch was nervous the night before his first major trial, his mind filled with stories of defense attorneys ripping cops to shreds during cross-examination—stories artfully embellished by fellow cops—and the knowledge that a bad day testifying can lose a case. He had good reason to be nervous, as the defense attorney assigned to the case was infamous for picking apart police reports. He studied his reports as if he were taking a final exam and rehearsed responses to every dirty trick a defense attorney could throw at him. He wasn't going to be some ill-prepared cop referring to his report for the suspect's name or the location of an arrest.

He took the stand, scanned the packed courtroom and hoped his voice would not crack. The direct testimony went smoothly, but he knew what was coming. The defense attorney smiled and greeted him. His voice was calm and reassuring. He knew all about the detective's background and that he had reached the rank of detective at a very young age. The attorney's tone was complimentary, and Gautsch's fear of being ripped to shreds was replaced with a sense of importance. He began to enjoy the cross-examination.

Most of the initial questions were general and easy to answer. The defense attorney asked several questions about the defendant's level of cooperation. He cited things that his client had done at their request, including having

FIGURE 21.4
Case disposition notice.
© Cengage Learning, 2013

CASE DISPOSITION REPORT

Date Disposition Made: __4-25-20__   D.R. #: __97-1002__
Date of Incident: __2-10-20__   Type of Incident: __Burglary__

DISPOSITION:
(X) Case Clearance
(X) Property Recovered
( ) Disposition of Property: (X) Owner ( ) Police Evidence
( ) Other
If <u>Other</u>, specify type:_____

VICTIM: (If Runaway Juvenile or Missing Adult, disregard this section)
Name __Jerome Slater__   Address __3041 Harding St., Edina, Minn.__

SUSPECT(S):
NO. 1: __John Toben__   Arrested? __Yes__   BCPD I.D. # __20146__
NO. 2: __William Moss__   Arrested? __Yes__   BCPD I.D. # __20147__
NO. 3: _____   Arrested? _____   BCPD I.D. # _____

PROPERTY RECOVERED:
Item No. 1: __One car radio, Sears__   Value __$87.00__
Item No. 2: __One car battery, Sears__   Value __$60.00__
Item No. 3: __Microwave oven, GE__   Value __$250.00__
Item No. 4: __One 17" TV, Sears Solid State__   Value __$350.00__
Recovering Agency: __Edina Police Department__   Total Value Recovered Property: __$747.00__

CANCELLATIONS: (Specify date, time, agency and officer receiving cancellation and officer making cancellation)

NCIC: _____
Other Agencies: __Hennepin County Sheriff's Office__
Other Agencies: _____

OFFICER MAKING DISPOSITION: _____
SUPERVISOR APPROVING: _____
DETAILS: __Full recovery of property__

---

his hands swabbed for gunpowder residue. Gautsch acknowledged that the defendant had been cooperative. The defense attorney asked if his client had refused any of their requests. Gautsch paused to think, and the defense attorney quickly added, "Did you ask him to do anything else?"

It seemed to Gautsch that the defense attorney was helping him remember something in his report without making him look stupid. Then Gautsch remembered, "Oh, yes. He agreed to take a polygraph test." The defense attorney thanked Gautsch and sat down. The prosecutor slowly slumped in his chair. Gautsch had been tricked into telling the jury that the defendant was willing to take a lie-detector test—something that wasn't admissible and

that the defense could not have presented without the detective's help. In fact, the defendant offered to take the test, but later refused—something the jury would never hear. His mistake left the jury with the impression that the defendant had passed a polygraph test. The jury returned a guilty verdict for a lesser charge and left Gautsch wondering what role his mistake on the stand had played in its decision.

Another defense attorney taught Detective Gautsch a more positive lesson during his first murder trial—a case described at the beginning of the text. Two men robbed and murdered a teenage boy working as an attendant at a gas station. They netted less than $50, but decided the boy had to be killed because he had seen their faces. They forced him into their car, bound his hands and drove him to secluded woods. They shot him nine times and left him to bleed to death. The boy was missing for a week before his body was found. During that week, Detective Gautsch got to know the boy's family as wonderful people. He fought back tears when he brought them the news of their son's death.

Experienced detectives do not allow their emotions to influence their professionalism. At age 24, Gautsch was inexperienced and emotional. The scene was chaotic as the team of detectives raided a house where one of the suspects was living. Cops rushed in to secure the scene and control a group of suspects. Gautsch grabbed the first person he could get his hands on and forced him against a wall. He recognized him as one of the murderers. As Gautsch held him against the wall, he felt the suspect tremble. Gautsch asked why he was shaking, and the suspect said they had scared him. Gautsch asked how scared the boy had been when they had marched him into the woods. The suspect smirked and laughed nervously. At that instant Gautsch made a stupid, unprofessional mistake—he punched the smirk off the suspect's face, satisfying his need for retribution, but jeopardizing the entire case.

Seasoned detectives interviewed the suspect for several hours. He denied any involvement in the murder. During a break in the questioning, the suspect and Detective Gautsch were left alone in the interview room. They were the same age, and the suspect felt more comfortable talking to Gautsch. Eventually he confessed to the murder.

Gautsch did not include the striking incident in his report, but it was ever-present in his mind. He was the key witness at the trial, and the confession was the most important evidence. The defense attorney was one of the very best. He methodically questioned the detective about various aspects of the investigation, then paused and switched legal pads. "Detective, did you punch my client before he confessed to you?"

Gautsch's heart pounded so loudly he was sure everyone could hear it. The confession, the case and his job were all about to be lost. The murdering little creep was going to get off because of Gautsch's stupidity. The courtroom was silent. The jury, the prosecutor, the judge, the press and the victim's family all stared at him, waiting for his answer. For the sake of justice, Gautsch wondered if one lie would really hurt. He looked squarely into the defense attorney's eyes and responded, "Yes sir, I did."

For a moment the defense attorney looked perplexed. He asked a few more questions and sat down. The prosecutor was furious that Gautsch had neglected to share that damaging information with him. Fortunately, the defendants were found guilty and sentenced to life in prison. After the trial, the defense attorney asked to meet with Gautsch in the prosecutor's office. Gautsch arrived expecting some type of sanctions. Instead, the defense attorney extended his hand and commended Gautsch for telling the truth on the stand. The attorney said he had hoped Gautsch would deny hitting his client. If he had, the attorney was prepared to show that the detective was lying and ruin his credibility with the jury. When Gautsch told the truth, the attorney's strategy failed, and the detective's credibility with the jury was actually enhanced.

The lesson to be learned is never lie, exaggerate or embellish your testimony. It is more obvious to a jury than you may realize. Once you lose your credibility, it is nearly impossible to recover it. The truth can only strengthen a good case.

Summary

The most important rule to eradicate fear of testifying in court is to always tell the truth.

Before testifying, the final report must be written and presented to the prosecutor. The final report contains (1) the complaint; (2) the preliminary investigation report; (3) all follow-up, supplemental and progress reports; (4) statements, admissions and confessions; (5) laboratory reports; (6) photographs, sketches and drawings; and (7) a summary of all negative (exculpatory) evidence. The quality of the content and writing of the report influences its credibility.

The prosecutor is the most powerful official in the court system. Some cases are never prosecuted because the complaint is invalid, the prosecutor declines after reviewing the case, the complainant refuses to prosecute, the offender dies, the offender is in prison or out of the country and cannot be returned or no evidence or leads exist. If the decision is made to prosecute, thorough preparation is required. To prepare a case for court, (1) review and evaluate all evidence, positive and negative, and the chain of custody; (2) review all reports on the case, including transcripts of any depositions you have given; (3) prepare witnesses; and (4) hold a pretrial conference with the prosecutor. Concentrate on proving the elements of the crime and establishing the offender's identity.

At the pretrial conference with the prosecutor, review all the evidence, discuss the strengths and weaknesses of the case and discuss the probable line of questioning by the prosecutor and the defense.

The sequence in a criminal trial is jury selection, opening statements by the prosecution and the defense, presentation of the prosecution's case and cross-examination by the defense, presentation of the defense's case and cross-examination by the prosecution, rebuttal and surrebuttal testimony, closing statements by the prosecution and the defense, the judge instructs the jury, jury deliberation to reach a verdict, reading of the verdict and acquittal or passing of sentence.

The "win" for an investigator who testifies is to have established credibility. Inadmissible statements include opinions and conclusions (unless the witness is qualified as an expert), hearsay, privileged communications and statements about the defendant's character and reputation, including the defendant's criminal record. To present testimony effectively, speak clearly, firmly and with expression; answer questions directly, and do *not* volunteer information; pause briefly before answering; refer to your notes if you do not recall exact details; admit calmly when you do not know an answer; admit any mistakes you make in testifying; avoid police jargon, sarcasm and humor; and tell the complete truth as you know it. Refer to your notes if you are uncertain of specific facts, but do not rely on them excessively. Important nonverbal elements include dress, eye contact, posture, gestures, mannerisms, rate of speech, tone of voice and facial expressions.

To excel as a witness, (1) set yourself up, (2) provoke the defense into giving you a chance to explain, (3) be unconditional and (4) do not stall. During cross-examination the defense attorney may be disarmingly friendly or intimidatingly rude, attack your credibility and impartiality, attack your investigative skill, attempt to force contradictions or inconsistencies, ask leading questions or deliberately misquote you, ask for a simple answer to a complex question, use rapid-fire questioning or use the "silent treatment." A key to testifying during cross-examination is to NEVER volunteer any information. To avoid objections to your testimony, avoid conclusions and nonresponsive answers. Answer yes-or-no questions with "yes" or "no."

Checklists

Final Report

- Have I met all the criteria for an effective report? (See Chapter 3)
- Have I included all relevant information?
- Have I included headings?
- Have I proofread the paper to spot content and composition errors?

Preparing to Testify

- Have all reports been reviewed?
- Have all reports been organized for presentation to the prosecutor?
- Has all evidence been located and made available for court presentation?
- Has all evidence been examined by competent laboratories and the results obtained? Are copies of the reports available?
- Have all known leads been developed?
- Have both negative and positive information been submitted to the prosecuting attorney?
- Has all arrest information been submitted?
- Has a list of witnesses been prepared? Addresses? Telephone numbers?
- Has the final report been assembled? Does it contain copies of investigators' reports? Photographs? Sketches? Evidence? Lab reports? Medical examiner's reports? Statements? Confessions? Maps? All other pertinent information?
- Has the deposition transcript been reviewed?
- Has a pretrial conference been held with the prosecutor's office?
- Have all witnesses been reinterviewed? Notified of the date and time of the trial?
- Have all expert witnesses been notified of the date and time of the trial?
- Has someone been designated to take the evidence to court?
- Have notes needed for testimony been removed from your notebook?
- Is your personal appearance professional?

Discussion Questions

1. Plea bargaining has become very controversial in many states, and some states have eliminated it as a part of the prosecution process. Is plea bargaining good or bad?
2. The news media can affect jury and court decisions by publicizing information about a criminal case before it goes to trial. May police refuse to give information to the press if doing so might jeopardize the case in court? How significantly does such publicity affect the trial?

3. Should criminal trials be televised? What are the advantages and disadvantages?

4. What is the investigator's role in preparing a case for court? How does the investigator cooperate with the prosecutor to enhance the courtroom presentation?

5. Imagine that you are preparing a final report for the prosecutor. What materials should you include? How should you organize them to show the continuity of your investigation and the way you gathered evidence related to the elements of the offense charged?

6. If you were accused of a crime, would you prefer a trial with or without a jury?

7. Why would a defendant choose a jury over a bench trial, or vice versa?

8. Does an acquittal mean that the investigator failed?

9. How prevalent do you believe "testilying" (not telling the truth) is by law enforcement officers?

10. If you were to testify in a major case, what would you wear?

Media Explorations

 ### Internet

Select one of the following key terms: *expert witness, report writing in law enforcement, testifying.* Find one article relevant to writing offense reports and testifying in court to outline and share with the class.

ONLINE Database ### Gale Criminal Justice Database Assignments

The following assignment requires access to Gale's Custom Journals Database for Emergency Services and Criminal Justice. Check with your instructor if you have questions about this.

■ Find the article "Getting It Write Right: Convictions Require Good Report Writing " on the Gale Emergency Services Database. Read the article and outline it. Be prepared to discuss your outline in class.

■ Find the article "Taking the Stand: Preparing Officers for the Trying Task of Testifying in Court" on the Gale Emergency Services Database. Read the article and outline it. Be prepared to discuss your outline in class.

References

Gardner, Thomas J., and Anderson, Terry M. *Criminal Evidence: Principles and Cases*, 7th ed. Belmont, CA: Wadsworth Publishing Company, 2010.

Grossi, Dave. "Tactics for Testimony: Surviving the Witness Stand." *Law Officer Magazine*, August 2007, pp.32–36.

Jetmore, Larry F. "Investigative Report Writing." *Law Officer Magazine*, February 2008, pp.26–30.

Kruger, Karen J. "The Police Officer as Expert Witness," *The Police Chief*, June 2005, pp.10–11.

Mehrabian, Albert. *Silent Messages: Implicit Communication of Emotions and Attitudes*. Belmont, CA: Wadsworth, 1981.

Neubauer, David W., and Fradella, Henry F. *America's Courts and the Criminal Justice System*, 10th ed. Belmont, CA: Wadsworth Publishing Company, 2011.

Nyberg, Ramesh. "How to Testify in Court." *Police*, April 2006, pp.18–22.

Rutledge, Devallis. *Courtroom Survival: The Officer's Guide to Better Testimony.* Belmont, CA: Wadsworth Publishing Company, 2000.

Rutledge, Devallis. "Courthouse Conduct," *Police*, June 2004, pp.70–72.

Rutledge, Devallis. "The Crime-Charging Gap." *Police*, April 2008, pp.70–71.

Van Brocklin, Valerie. "Winning Courtroom Confrontations: A New Approach to Training," *The Law Enforcement Trainer*, April/May/June 2005, pp.44–49.

Cases Cited

Brady v. Maryland, 373 U.S. 83 (1963)

Daubert v. Merrell Dow Pharmaceuticals, Inc., 509 U.S. 579 (1993)

Giglio v. United States, 405 U.S. 150 (1972)

Pennsylvania v. Ritchie, 480 U.S. 39 (1987)

Weatherford v. Bursey, 429 U.S. 545 (1977)

Patrol Crime Scene Management Checklist

Because there's so much to do as a crime scene first responder, a checklist can help you ensure that all necessary steps have been taken. The following checklist is presented as a guideline only. Each agency should develop a list that's geared to its specific requirements.

ARRIVAL AND ASSESSMENT

- Establish perimeter and secure area.
- Render aid to victims and ensure scene is safe for medical personnel.
- Coordinate arriving units.
- Record names and unit numbers of fire/rescue, medical personnel and LEOs on scene.
- Remove unnecessary personnel from scene as soon as possible.
- Assign officer to escort or ride with victim to hospital.
  - Secure clothing and evidence.
  - Obtain tape-recorded statement, if possible.
- Initial assessment. Does this appear to be a crime? If so, what type of crime?
- Assign officer to suspect.
  - Assess need for immediate suspect arrest. Does probable cause exist?
  - Is evidence present on the suspect? Collect perishable evidence from suspect if exigency exists.
  - Is it necessary to bag hands, etc?

ESTABLISHING COMMAND

- Designate command. Who's in charge?
- Designate common radio channel for all arriving personnel.

STABILIZE AND SECURE SCENE

- Clear crime scene and establish clearly delineated perimeter with crime scene tape.
  - Record time.
  - Make scene bigger than it needs to be.
  - Create one entry/exit point in scene to reduce contamination.
- Assign crime scene security personnel and start detailed crime scene access log.
- Begin initial areas canvass. Assign officers to locate witnesses, separate witnesses and obtain initial statements from witnesses.
- If required, assign personnel to search immediate area for additional evidence or crime scenes.
- Establish a command post and staging area.
  - Incident command vehicle available?
  - Building or home nearby?
  - Secure area for equipment and evidence?
  - Bathroom facilities?
- Obtain case number. Have number broadcast by communications/dispatch.

Source: David Spraggs. "Crime Scene Response for the Patrol Officer." *Police*, January 2006, p.42.

NOTIFICATIONS

- Detective supervisor paged.
- Coroner paged.
- Public information officer/media relations paged.
- Management staff paged.
- Victim Services paged.

MAINTENANCE

- Key witnesses separated, officer assigned, witnesses secured or transported to police department.
- Obtain voluntary written statements.
- Suspect(s) secured, transported.
- Given *Miranda* warning?
- Record any spontaneous statements/utterances made by suspect—tape record if possible.
- Perishable evidence protected from elements or tampering.
- Photograph overall area of scene.
- Create staging and briefing area for media.

TRANSFER OF COMMAND

- Meet and brief detective supervisor and other personnel.
- Help determine need for warrant.
- Help prepare initial statement for press release.
- Direct all patrol personnel to complete detailed reports as soon as possible.
- Logistics covered.
  - Do you need more equipment, personnel, etc., to respond?
- Meet with crime scene investigators to discuss scene and evidence.
- Transfer command to detective supervisor.

HELP YOUR INVESTIGATORS

In preparation for writing this article, I polled about one hundred detectives from various law enforcement agencies in my county. The following summarizes the responses I received regarding what to do and what not to do as a crime scene first responder:

WHAT NOT TO DO

- Don't smoke in or near the scene. Besides potentially contaminating other physical evidence, it can ruin a K-9's chance of tracking a suspect or locating additional evidence through scent.
- Don't eat or drink in a scene. If you need to eat or drink, do it in your patrol car, in the incident command vehicle or at some other location outside of the scene.
- Don't use the bathroom at a crime scene. I've collected toilet paper, fecal material, condoms and swabs from toilets. They can provide useful physical evidence in certain cases.
- Don't allow command staff or other nonessential personnel to walk through the scene. This is not appropriate before the scene is processed. It's useful for first responders to snap digital pictures of the scene that can be viewed by other nonessential personnel.
- Don't laugh or look like you're having too much fun at a scene. It just looks unprofessional.
- Don't forget to think about secondary scenes.
- Don't prematurely handle evidence within the scene—wait for crime scene personnel.
- Don't replace evidence if it's been moved. For example, if medical personnel had to move a table, don't move the table back into position. Simply note that the table was moved and leave it alone.
- Don't use the phone within the scene.
- Don't use the trash can in the scene as a trash receptacle for your garbage. Trash cans often hold physical evidence.

PRESERVE THE SCENE

Make the scene much bigger than you think you have to. Remember, you can always shrink a scene but you can never make it bigger.

- Establish one point of entry and exit into the scene to minimize contamination.
- Limit access to nonessential personnel.
- Keep an accurate and detailed record of your actions and observations.
- Write a detailed report including accurate times.
- Protect perishable evidence by any means necessary. For example, cover a footwear impression with a plastic container if it starts to rain or snow.

APPENDIX B

Washington, DC, Metropolitan Police Department Homicide Case Review Solvability Chart

SUSPECT COMMENTS

☐   Arrested but released   _____

☐   Named, no arrest   _____

☐   Incarcerated/other charge   _____

☐   Under investigation/other charge   _____

☐   Deceased   _____

☐   Seen but unidentified   _____

☐   No suspects   _____

WITNESS

☐   Witness under investigation/trial   _____

☐   Witness incarcerated   _____

☐   Multiple eyewitnesses   _____

☐   Other   _____

FIREARM EVIDENCE

☐   Shell casings recovered   _____

☐   Slugs recovered   _____

☐   Linked to another crime   _____

☐   No firearm evidence recovered   _____

FINGERPRINT EVIDENCE

☐   Unidentified prints recovered   _____

☐   No fingerprint evidence recovered   _____

DNA EVIDENCE

☐   Potential suspect DNA recovered   _____

☐   Potential probative victim DNA   _____

☐   No DNA evidence recovered   _____

OTHER CRIMES

☐   Potential link to another crime   _____

MISCELLANEOUS SOLVABILITY FACTORS

☐   _____

☐   _____

Source: Promoting Effective Homicide Investigations by James M. Cronin, Gerard R. Murphy, Lisa L. Spahr, Jessica I. Toliver, and Richard E. Weger. Published by the Police Executive Research Forum. Washington, DC: U.S. Department of Justice, August 2007, pp.173–174. "http://www.policeforum.org/upload/homicide_759980432_1282008145753.pdf"

Sudden In-Custody Death: An Investigator's Checklist

The following checklists are designed to help investigators organize the collection of evidence suggested by this protocol—especially transient evidence, which can become altered within a few minutes—during the first few minutes after a subject dies in custody.

Subject's History

❑ Residential ❑ Educational ❑ Family ❑ Medical ❑ Behavioral
❑ Employment ❑ Financial History ❑ Police Contact ❑ Nutritional ❑ Substance Abuse
❑ The Common Link

The Incident

❑ Duration of unusual behavior prior to police contact? _____

_____

❑ Detailed history of behavior immediately before police intervention? _____

_____

❑ Subject utterances _____

_____

❑ Subject actions, activities _____

_____

❑ Hyperventilation ❑ Shouting ❑ Other _____
❑ Running ❑ Pacing furiously

❑ Type of resistance _____
❑ Duration of resistance _____
❑ Length of time taken to subdue subject _____
❑ Number of officers involved _____

❑ Method of subject transport _____

❑ Time transport begins _____ ❑ Time transport ends _____

❑ Struggle against restraints during transport? _____

❑ Describe struggle _____

_____

_____

_____

_____

_____

❑ Describe breathing pattern _____

_____

_____

_____

_____

❑ Shouting? _____

_____

_____

_____

_____

❑ Presence or absence of sweating by the subject? _____

❑ Pulse rate during incident _____

❑ Strength during incident _____

❑ Determined by _____

❑ Time _____

❑ Name _____

❑ Presence or absence of sweating by persons involved with subject? _____

_____

_____

_____

_____

_____

The Scene

❑ Air temperature _____

❑ Relative humidity _____

❑ Determined by _____

❑ Time _____

❑ Name _____

❑ Transport vehicle interior temperature _____

❑ Climate control settings _____

❑ Functional? _____

❑ Used _____

❑ Determined by _____

❑ Time _____

❑ Name _____

❑ Treatment facility temperature _____

❑ Relative humidity _____

❑ Climate control settings _____

❑ Functional? _____

❑ Used _____

❑ Determined by _____

❑ Time _____

❑ Name _____

❑ Describe surface where subject was restrained _____

_____

_____

_____

_____

_____

_____

❑ Surface temperature _____

❑ Determined by _____

❑ Time _____

❑ Name _____

Resuscitation Efforts

❑ Describe _____

_____

_____

_____

_____

_____

❑ **Subject's core temperatures**	**Before**	**Upon death**	**PM**
Time	_____	_____	_____
Determined by	_____	_____	_____
Name	Name _____	Name _____	Name _____

Thyroid/cricoid pressure (pressure over the front of the windpipe used) _____

Number of times the attempt was made _____

ID of person making efforts _____

_____

_____

Environmental Factors

❑ External air temperature _____ ❑ Humidity _____

❑ Humidex _____ ❑ Wind chill _____

❑ Wind speed _____ ❑ Direction _____

❑ Determined by _____

❑ Time _____

❑ Name _____

❑ Weather trend _____

❑ Surface temperature of the ground _____

❑ Determined by _____

❑ Time _____

❑ Name _____

❑ Duration of contact with ground _____

❑ Position _____

❑ Other _____

_____

_____

_____

_____

_____

_____

_____

_____

APPENDIX D

Death Scene Checklist

This form is to be used as a supplementary source sheet for readily available information and is not intended to replace conventional reports. Copies should be distributed to investigating officers and medical examiners.

Name of deceased:

First   Middle   Last

Address:

Age: **Race:**   White   Black   Hispanic   Asian   Native   American   Unknown

Sex: Male   Female

Telephone number:

Marital status: S   M   W   D   Separated   Unknown

Next-of-kin:

Name:

Address:

Telephone number:

Policy notified by:

Date: Time:

Name:

Address:

Telephone number:

Relationship to deceased:

Source: James C. Beger, M.D., and William F. Enos, M.D. *FBI Law Enforcement Bulletin.* August 1981, pp.16–18. Reprinted by permission of the FBI.

Deceased found:

Date: Time:

Address: (if different from above)

Location: Apartment   House   Townhouse   Other (describe)

Entrance by: Key   Cutting chain   Forcing door   Other (describe)

Type of lock on door:

Condition of other doors and windows: Open   Closed   Locked   Unlocked

Body found:

Living Room   Dining Room   Bedroom   Kitchen   Attic   Basement   Other (describe)

Location in room:

Position of body: On back   Face down   Other:

Condition of body:

Fully clothed   Partially clothed   Unclothed

Preservation: Well preserved   Decomposed

Estimated Rigor: Complete   Head   Arms   Legs

Livor: Front   Back   Localized

Color:

Blood: Absent   Present   Location

Ligatures: Yes   No

Apparent wounds: None   Gunshot   Stab   Blunt force

Number:

Location: Head   Neck   Chest   Abdomen   Extremities

Hanging: Yes   No   Means:

Weapon(s) present: Gun (estimate caliber)

Type:

Knife:

Other (describe)

Condition of surroundings: Orderly   Untidy   Disarray

Odors: Decomposition   Other

Evidence of last food preparation:

Where:

Type:

Dated material:

Mail:

Newspapers:

TV guide:

Liquor bottles:

Last contact with deceased:

Date:

Type of contact:

Name of contact:

Evidence of robbery: Yes   No   Not determined

Identification of deceased: Yes   No

If yes, how accomplished:

If no, how is it to be accomplished:

Evidence of drug use: (prescription and nonprescription)   Yes   No

If drugs present, collect them and send with body.

Evidence of drug paraphernalia: Yes   No

Type:

Evidence of sexually deviant practices: Yes   No

Type: (collect and send with body)

Name and telephone number of investigating officer:

Las Vegas Metropolitan
Police Department
Cold Case Solvability Criteria

LEVEL 1

- Named suspect
- Forensic evidence (DNA, latent prints [AFIS], firearms)
- Witness identification of suspect
- Physical evidence that connects suspect to the victim (photographs, writing, fibers, etc.)

LEVEL 2

- Unknown suspect
- Forensic evidence (DNA, latent prints [AFIS], firearms)
- Witness identification of suspect
- Physical evidence that connects suspect to the victim

LEVEL 3

- Unknown suspect
- Forensic evidence (DNA, latent prints [AFIS], firearms)
- Physical evidence
- Witnesses unable to identify

LEVEL 4

- Unknown suspect
- Physical evidence
- Witnesses unable to identify
- Unidentified victim

LEVEL 5

- Unknown suspect
- Little or no physical evidence
- No witnesses
- Unidentified victim

Source: *Promoting Effective Homicide Investigations* by James M. Cronin, Gerard R. Murphy, Lisa L. Spahr, Jessica I. Toliver, Richard E. Weger. Published by the Police Executive Research Forum. Washington, DC: U.S. Department of Justice, August 2007, pp.171–172. http://www.policeforum.org/upload/homicide_759980432_1282008145753.pdf

BIAS OFFENSE REPORT

AGENCY IDENTIFIER (ORI)_____

MONTH AND YEAR_____   AGENCY NAME_____

This form is to be used to report any bias motivated crimes in violation of Minnesota State Statute 626.5531. The chief law enforcement officer for an agency must complete form and return to the Department of Public Safety, Office of Information Systems Management, 314 Transportation Building, 395 John Ireland Blvd., St. Paul, Minnesota 55155 within 30 days (Laws of Minnesota, 1996, Chapter 643).

A. GENERAL OFFENSE INFORMATION

1) Agency Case Number: _____   2) Date of Offense: _____
3) Bias offense base on: ❑ Officer's belief   ❑ Victim's belief
4) *Description of Offense: _____   5) *Disposition: _____
6) *Type of Bias and Description: _____ / _____
                                Type Code   Description Code or Literal
7) *Target: _____   8) Place of Occurrence: _____

B. VICTIM/OFFENDER INFORMATION

9) VICTIMS				10) OFFENDERS			11) *RELATIONSHIP TO VICTIM	12) AFFILIATION (if any)
#	Age	Sex	Race	Age	Sex	Race		
1								
2								
3								
4								
5								
6								
7								
8								
9								
10								
11								
12								
13								
14								
15								

COMMENTS: _____
_____
_____
_____

*Use code tables on reverse.

Return to: DPS/OISM
              314 DOT Building
              395 John Ireland Blvd.
              St. Paul, MN 55155

Source: Minnesota Bureau of Criminal Apprehension.

CODE TABLES

4) *DESCRIPTION of OFFENSE:*
To be used in further identifying offense
01-Cross Burning
02-Swastika
03-Bombing
04-Hanging in Effigy
05-Disturbing Public Meeting
06-Graffiti
07-Spitting
08-Letter
09-Verbal Abuse (Person to Person)
10-Telephone
11-Homicide
12-Criminal Sexual Conduct
13-Robbery
14-Burglary
15-Aggravated Assault
16-Arson
17-Larceny Theft
18-Disturbing the Peace
19-Property Damage
20-Simple Assault
00-Other (Describe)

5) *DISPOSITION:* Based on CJRS Reporting
    System—Major Offenses
A-Arrest of Adult and/or Adult & Juvenile
J-Arrest of Juvenile
E-Exceptionally Cleared
U-Unfounded
P-Pending

6) *TYPE of BIAS and DESCRIPTION:*

Type	Description
01-Racial	W-White
	H-White/Hispanic Origin
	N-Negro/Black
	B-Black/Hispanic Origin
	I-Indian or Alaskan Native
	M-Indian w/Hispanic Origin
	O-Asian or Pacific Islander
	A-Asian or Pacific Islander w/Hispanic Origin
02-Religious	01-Catholic
	02-Hindu/Buddhist
	03-Islamic/Moslem
	04-Jewish
	05-Protestant
	06-Fundamentalist
	07-Other (Describe)
03-National Origin	Specify
04-Sex	M-Male
	F-Female

05-Age — Specify age(s)
06-Disability — Specify disability
07-Sexual Orientation — 01-Homosexual Male
02-Homosexual Female
03-Heterosexual Male
04-Heterosexual Female

7) *TARGET CODES:*
01-Person
02-Private Property
03-Public Property

8) *PLACE of OCCURRENCE:*
01-Residence
02-Hotel, Motel or Other Commercial Short-Term
    Residence
03-Parking Lot Areas
04-Business
05-Vehicle
06-Street/Sidewalk
07-Highway/Freeway
08-Park/School Ground
09-Vacant Lot
10-Jail
11-Rural Area/Country Road
12-Cemetery
13-Religious Building
14-Government Building
15-School Building
16-Private Club
17-Other (Describe)

11) *RELATIONSHIP of OFFENDER to VICTIM:*
01-Family Member
02-Neighbor
03-Acquaintance
04-Boyfriend/Ex-Boyfriend
05-Girlfriend/Ex-Girlfriend
06-Ex-Husband
07-Ex-Wife
08-Employee
09-Employer
10-Friend
11-Homosexual Relation
12-Other-Known to Victim
13-Stranger
14-Gang Member
15-Peace Officer Related
16-Unknown
17-Other (Describe)

Glossary

Number in parentheses is the chapter in which the term is discussed.

A

accelerants substances that cause fires to burn faster and hotter. (16)

active voice in which the subject performs the action of the sentence; contrasts with passive voice. (3)

adipocere soapy appearance of a dead body left for weeks in a hot, moist location. (8)

administrative warrant official permission to inspect a given property to determine compliance with city regulations; for example, compliance with fire codes. (16)

admission statement containing some information concerning the elements of a crime, but falling short of a full confession. (6)

adoptive admission occurs when someone else makes a statement in a person's presence and under circumstances where it would be logical to expect the person to make a denial if the statement falsely implicated him or her, but the person does not deny the allegations. (6)

Advanced Fingerprint Information Technology (AFIT) an integrated system, the precursor to which was the FBI's AFIS, that can also incorporate additional biometric data such as latent palmprints and facial recognition technology. (5)

adversary system justice system used in the United States; establishes clearly defined roles for both the prosecution and the defense and sets the judge as the neutral party. (21)

adware type of spyware used by advertisers to gather consumer and marketing information. (17)

aggravated arson intentionally destroying or damaging a dwelling or other property, real or personal, by means of fire or explosives, creating an imminent danger to life or great bodily harm, which risk was known or reasonably foreseeable to the suspect. (16)

aggravated assault (felonious assault) unlawful attack by one person on another to inflict severe bodily injury. (9)

algor mortis postmortem cooling process of the body. (8)

alligatoring the checking of charred wood giving the appearance of alligator skin; large, rolling blisters indicate rapid, intense heat; small, flat blisters indicate slow, less intense heat. (16)

analogs drugs created by adding to or omitting something from an existing drug. (18)

Antichrist son of Satan. (19)

anticipatory warrant one based upon prior knowledge or an affidavit showing probable cause that at some future time (but not presently) certain evidence of crime will be located at a specified place; such warrants are constitutional if a proper showing is made that contraband or evidence will likely be found at the target location at a given time, or when a specific triggering event occurs. (4)

arrest taking a person into custody in the manner authorized by law to present that person before a magistrate to answer for the commission of a crime. (7)

arson malicious, willful burning of a building or property; *see also* **aggravated arson**. (16)

asphyxiation death or unconsciousness resulting from insufficient oxygen to support the red blood cells reaching the body tissues and the brain. (8)

assault unlawfully threatening to harm another person, actually harming another person or attempting unsuccessfully to do so; formerly referred to threats of or attempts to cause bodily harm, but now usually includes *battery*. (9)

associative evidence links a suspect with a crime. (5)

asymmetric warfare combat in which a weaker group attacks a superior group not head-on but by targeting areas where the adversary least expects to be hit, causing great psychological shock, along with loss of life among random victims. (20)

autoerotic asphyxiation accidental death from suffocation, strangulation or chemical asphyxia resulting from a combination of ritualistic behavior, oxygen deprivation, danger and fantasy for sexual gratification. (8)

B

backing marking photographs on their back with a felt-tip pen or label to indicate the photographer's initials, date photo was taken, a brief description of what it depicts and the direction of north; evidence can be circled on the back of the photo in the same way. (2)

bait money currency for which serial numbers are recorded and that is placed so it can be added to any robbery loot. (12)

ballistics the study of the dynamics of projectiles, from propulsion through flight to impact; a narrower definition is the study of the functioning of firearms. (5)

baseline (plotting) method establishes a straight line from one fixed point to another, from which measurements are taken at right angles. (2)

battery actually hitting or striking someone. (9)

beachheading interrogation technique where an officer questions a custodial suspect without giving the *Miranda* warnings and obtains incriminating statements; the officer then gives the warning, gets a waiver and repeats the interrogation to obtain the same statement. (6)

Beelzebub powerful demon, subordinate only to Satan, according to Satanists. (19)

bench trial a trial before a judge without a jury. (21)

best evidence original object, or the highest available degree of proof that can be produced. (5)

bias crime motivated by bigotry and hatred against a specific group of people. (19)

bigamy marrying another person when one or both of the parties are already married. (10)

biometrics statistical study of biological data and a means to positively identify an individual by measuring that person's unique physical or behavioral characteristics such as fingerprints. (5)

bioterrorism involves dissemination of such biological weapons of mass destruction (WMDs) as anthrax, botulism and smallpox. (20)

Black Mass diabolical communion ritual performed by Satanists that mocks and desecrates the Christian mass. (19)

blind reporting allows sexual assault victims to retain their anonymity and confidentiality while sharing critical information with law enforcement; also permits victims to gather legal information from law enforcement without having to commit immediately to an investigation. (10)

blowing (a safe) opening a safe using cotton, primer cap, copper wire and nitroglycerin. (13)

body packing a method of smuggling or otherwise concealing drugs inside a body opening, including the rectum or vagina. (18)

bookmaking soliciting and accepting bets on any type of sporting event. (18)

bore inside portion of a weapon's barrel, which is surrounded by raised ridges called *lands* and recessed areas called *grooves*. (5)

brackets testimony tactic that allows the witness some leeway and helps him or her retain credibility; provides a range, for example, "He was 40 to 50 feet away." (21)

Brady rule entitles the accused to information as provided by the statutes of the state and disclosure of exculpatory evidence. (21)

bugging using a machine to record conversations within a room without the consent of those involved. (7)

Buie sweep the authorized search by police of areas immediately adjoining the place of arrest, justified when reasonable suspicion exists that another person might be present who poses a danger to the arresting officers; held constitutional in *Maryland v. Buie* (1990); synonymous with *protective sweep*. (4)

burglary unlawful entry of a structure to commit a felony or theft. (13)

burn indicators visible evidence of the effects of heating or partial burning. (16)

burning (a safe) opening a safe using a burn bar or other safecracking device to burn a hole into the safe to gain entry. (13)

C

caliber diameter of a weapon's bore as measured between lands, as well as the size of bullet intended for use with a specific weapon. (5)

capital flight large-scale removal of funds or capital from a country; not to be confused with money laundering. (18)

carjacking taking of a motor vehicle from a person by force or the threat of force. (12)

Carroll decision established that vehicles may be searched without a warrant if there is probable cause for the search and if the vehicle would be gone before a search warrant could be obtained. (4)

cast to make an impression using plaster of Paris or a similar substance; also, the physical reproduction of such an impression. (5)

chain of custody *see* **chain of evidence**. (5)

chain of evidence documentation of what has happened to evidence from the time it was discovered until it is needed in court, including every person who has had custody of the evidence and why. (5)

chicken hawk an adult who has either heterosexual or homosexual preferences for young boys or girls of a specific, limited age range; used synonymously with *pedophile*. (11)

child molestation violation of a child by lewd or lascivious acts, indecent exposure, incest or statutory rape; usually a felony. (10)

Chimel decision established that in a search incidental to a lawful arrest, the search must be made simultaneously with the arrest and must be confined to the area within the suspect's immediate control. (4)

chopping (a safe) opening a safe by chopping a hole in the bottom of the safe large enough to remove the contents. (13)

chop shop a business, usually an auto body shop, that disassembles stolen vehicles and sells the parts. (15)

chronological order in time sequence. (3)

circle search (pattern) begins at the center of the crime scene and then spreads out in ever-widening concentric circles. (4)

circumstantial evidence evidence from which inferences are drawn; fact or event that tends to incriminate a person in a crime; for example, being seen running from a crime scene; also called *indirect evidence*. (5)

civil liability person's degree of risk of being sued; any person acting under the authority of law who violates another person's constitutional rights can be sued. (1)

class characteristics features that place an item into a specific category; for example, the size and shape of a tool. (5)

clearance rate the ratio of crimes resolved to the number of crimes reported. (8)

closed-ended question requires only a "yes" or "no," or other short, simple answer and should be avoided during interviews; not to be confused with a direct question. (6)

close tail used when it is important not to lose the subject; staying within a few steps of the subject or keeping the subject in sight; also called a *tight tail*. (7)

club drugs commonly found at raves (dance parties). (18)

cognitive interview interviewing technique that helps victims or witnesses put themselves mentally at the scene of the crime. (6)

commercial burglary one that involves churches, schools, barns, public buildings, shops, offices, stores, factories, warehouses, stables, ships or railroad cars. (13)

community policing philosophy that the police must work with the community through partnerships and problem solving to address problems of crime and disorder; a belief that by working together, the police and the community can accomplish what neither can accomplish alone. (1)

compass-point (plotting) method uses a protractor to measure the angle formed by two lines. (2)

competent evidence has been properly collected, identified, filed and continuously secured. (5)

competent photograph accurately represents what it purports to represent, is properly identified and is properly placed in the chain of evidence and secured until court presentation. (2)

complainant person who requests an investigation or that action be taken; is often the victim of a crime. (6)

computer crime that which involves the addition, deletion, change or theft of information. (17)

computer virus program created specifically to "infect" other programs with copies of itself; it attacks, attaches itself to and becomes part of another executable program. (17)

concise avoiding wordiness; making every word count without leaving out important facts. (3)

conclusionary language nonfactual; drawing inferences; for example, "The man was nervous"; to be avoided in police reports. (3)

confession information supporting the elements of a crime that is provided and attested to by any person involved in committing the crime; can be oral or written and must be voluntary and not given in response to threats, promises or rewards. (6)

confidence game obtains money or property by a trick, device or swindle that takes advantage of a victim's trust in the swindler; the confidence game offers a get-rich-quick scheme. (14)

connotative adjective describing words that have an emotional effect, with meanings that impart either positive or negative overtones. (3)

contagion effect phenomenon in which media publicity of an act or event inspires more such acts or events; for example, the belief that coverage of terrorism inspires more terrorism. (20)

contamination post-crime transfer of material to or from evidence. (5)

content what is said in a narrative; as opposed to form, which is *how* a narrative is written; the content of an effective report is factual, accurate, objective and complete. (3)

cook (meth) someone who produces methamphetamine. (18)

corporate crime *see* **white-collar crime**. (14)

corpus delicti "body of the crime"; elements of a specific crime; evidence establishing that a specific crime has been committed. (5)

corpus delicti evidence establishes that a crime was committed. (5)

coven group of witches or Satanists. (19)

cover assumed identity used while on an undercover assignment. (7)

crack cocaine mixed with baking soda and water, heated in a pan and then dried and split into pellet-size bits or chunks, which are smoked to produce effects reportedly 10 times greater than powder cocaine at a fraction of the cost. (18)

cracker computer hacker in the negative sense; someone who cracks software protection and removes it, deliberately and maliciously intruding into a computer or network to cause damage. (17)

cramming billing consumers for unauthorized, misleading or deceptive charges, such as a personal 800 number, paging and voice mail. (14)

crank street name for methamphetamine, not to be confused with crack. (18)

crazing formation of irregular cracks in glass caused by rapid, intense heat; can indicate arson or the use of an accelerant. (16)

crime act or omission forbidden by law and punishable by a fine, imprisonment or even death; crimes and their penalties are established and defined by state and federal statutes and local ordinances. (1)

crime mapping focuses on the location of crimes—the hot spots where most crimes occur—rather than on the criminal. (1)

crime prevention through environmental design (CPTED) altering physical characteristics of a property to make it less attractive to criminals—for example, removing dense shrubbery next to windows and doors, improving lighting and closing garage doors; also called *target hardening*. (13)

criminal enterprise by FBI definition, a group of individuals with an identified hierarchy, or comparable structure, engaged in significant criminal activity; although *organized crime* and *criminal enterprise* are often equated and used interchangeably, several federal statutes specifically delineate the elements of an *enterprise* that must be proven to convict individuals or groups under those statutes. (18)

criminal homicide includes murder and manslaughter and is a felony. (8)

criminal intent performing an unlawful act on purpose, knowing the act to be illegal. (1)

criminal investigation the process of discovering, collecting, preparing, identifying and presenting evidence to determine what happened and who is responsible. (1)

criminalist a person who searches for, collects and preserves physical evidence in the investigations of crime and suspected criminals; also called a *crime scene technician, examiner* or *investigator*. (1)

criminalistics specialists trained in recording, identifying and interpreting the *minutiae* (minute details) of physical evidence. (1)

criminal negligence acts of commission or omission creating situations resulting in unreasonable risk of death or great bodily harm. (8)

criminal profiling method of suspect identification that attempts to identify the individual's mental, emotional and psychological characteristics; also called *psychological profiling*. (7)

criminal statute legislative act relating to crime and its punishment. (1)

cross-contamination allowing items of evidence to touch one another and thus exchange matter. (5)

cross-examination questioning by the opposite side in a trial that attempts to assess the validity of testimony given under direct examination. (21)

cross-projection sketch presents the floor and walls of a room as though they were on the same surface. (2)

cult system of religious beliefs and rituals and its body of adherents also called *New Religious Movement (NRM)*. (19)

culturally adroit skilled in interacting across gender, ethnic, generational, social and political group lines. (1)

cunnilingus sexual activity involving oral contact with the female genitals. (10)

curtilage portion of the residence that is not open to the public and is reserved for private owner or family use, in contrast to sidewalks and alleys, which are used by the public and which hold no reasonable expectation of privacy. (4)

custodial arrest *see* **in custody**. (6)

custodial interrogation questioning by law enforcement officers after a person has been taken into custody or otherwise deprived of freedom in a significant way; requires that the *Miranda* warning be given. (6)

cybercrime part of the larger category of *computer crime*, a criminal act that is carried out using cybertechnology and that takes place in cyberspace. (17)

cyberstalking repeated use of the Internet, e-mail or other digital electronic communications devices to stalk another person. (9)

cyberterrorism premeditated, politically motivated attack against information, computer systems, computer programs and data that results in harm to noncombatant targets by subnational groups or clandestine agents; also refers to the use of a computer system as a conduit for causing terror. (17,20)

D

data mining process that uses powerful analytical tools to quickly and thoroughly explore mountains of data to discover new patterns or confirm suspected patterns or trends. (1)

data remanence refers to the residual physical representation of data that have been erased from a computer's hard drive. (17)

date rape type of sexual assault where the victim knows the suspect. (10)

***Daubert* standard** two-pronged requirement that an expert's testimony be both reliable and relevant. (5)

deconfliction protocol or guidelines to avoid conflict; can be applied to declassified and confidential investigations. (20)

deductive reasoning a logical process in which a conclusion follows from specific facts; a reconstructive process based on specific pieces of evidence to establish proof that a suspect is guilty of an offense. (1)

***de facto* arrest** functional equivalent of an arrest; illegally bringing someone in for questioning without probable cause; any evidence obtained through this method is inadmissible in court. (7)

defense wounds nonfatal wounds—cuts on the hands, arms and legs—incurred by victims as they attempt to ward off attackers; indicative of murder. (8)

de minimus communication allowed or acceptable contact between a witness and juror, such as exchanging a simple hello or giving directions. (21)

denial-of-service (DoS) attack disruption or degradation of a computer or network's Internet connection or e-mail service that interrupts the regular flow of data; using multiple agents to create a widespread interruption is a distributed DoS, or DDoS. (17)

denotative adjective describing words that have little emotional effect and are objective in their meaning. (3)

depressant drug that reduces restlessness and emotional tension and induces sleep; most common are the barbiturates. (18)

depth of char how deeply wood is burned; indicates the length of burn and the fire's point of origin. (16)

designer drugs substances created by adding to or taking something away from an existing drug. (18)

digital penetration the act of using fingers (digits) to penetrate or manipulate sexual organs that include the penis, vagina and anus. (10)

direct evidence establishes proof of a fact without any other evidence. (5)

direct examination initial questioning of a witness or defendant during a trial by the lawyer who is using the person's testimony to further his or her case. (21)

direct question is to the point with little chance of misinterpretation; for example, "What time did you leave?" (6)

discovery process pretrial disclosure between prosecution and defense about the evidence they intend to use at trial, thus avoiding "trial by surprise." (21)

disposition how a case is disposed of—for example, referred, closed (inactive), open (active), dismissed, pending further information and so on. (3)

disrupters devices that use gunpowder to fire a jet of water or a projectile at a particular component of an explosive to make it safe. (16)

DNA (deoxyribonucleic acid) organic substance found in the nucleus of living cells that provides the genetic code determining a person's individual characteristics. (5)

DNA profiling forensic analysis of blood, hair, saliva, semen or cells from almost any part of the body to ascertain a positive identity or match. (5)

domain name unique name of a computer system on the Internet that distinguishes it from all other online systems; associated with a specific IP address and easier to remember than a string of numbers; not the same as a Web address. (17)

domestic violence pattern of behaviors involving physical, sexual, economic and emotional abuse, alone or in combination, often by an intimate partner and often for the purpose of establishing and maintaining power and control over the other partner. (9)

dragging (a safe) *see* **pulling**. (13)

drug addict person who habitually uses habit-forming narcotic drugs and thus endangers the public morals, health, safety or welfare, or who is or has been so far addicted to habit-forming narcotic drugs as to have lost self-control. (18)

dye pack bundle of currency containing a colored dye and tear gas; taken during a robbery, it is activated when the robber crosses an electromagnetic field at the facility's exit, staining the money with brightly colored dye and emitting a cloud of colored smoke. (12)

Dyer Act made interstate transportation of a stolen motor vehicle a federal crime and allowed for federal assistance in prosecuting such cases. (15)

dying declaration a statement that can provide valuable information to investigators and usually qualifies as a hearsay exception, making it admissible as evidence. (6)

dynamic IP address an IP address that fluctuates and is, thus, more secure because it is changed frequently. (17)

E

economic crime *see* **white-collar crime**. (14)

ecoterrorism seeks to inflict economic damage to those who profit from the destruction of the natural environment. (20)

e-crime electronic crime; any criminal violation in which a computer or electronic media is used in the commission of that crime; also called *cybercrime*. (17)

Ecstasy (MDMA) derivative of amphetamine or speed, a powerful stimulant; an increasingly popular club drug. (18)

elder abuse physical or mental mistreatment, financial exploitation and general neglect of the elderly; may include fraud as well as assault, battery and even murder. (9)

elements of the crime specific conditions that must occur for an act to be called a specific kind of crime. (1)

"elephant in a matchbox" doctrine requires that searchers consider the probable size and shape of evidence they seek because, for example, large objects cannot be concealed in tiny areas. (4)

elimination prints fingerprints taken of every individual whose prints are likely to be found at the crime scene but who are not suspects. (5)

embezzlement fraudulent appropriation of property by a person to whom it has been entrusted. (14)

emotional abuse causing fear or feelings of unworthiness in others; with children, this occurs by such means as locking them in closets, ignoring them or constantly belittling them. (11)

encryption technique that puts information in code and thus obscures a normally comprehensible message. (17)

entrapment tricking someone into committing a crime that he or she would not normally commit. (7)

equivocal death situations that are open to interpretation in investigations; the case may present as homicide, suicide or accidental death depending on the circumstances. (8)

evidence data on which a judgment or conclusion may be based; used for determining the facts in a case, for later laboratory examination and for direct presentation in court. (5)

exceptionally cleared disposition of a case when circumstances outside the investigation result in no charges being filed (e.g., if the suspect dies). (21)

excessive force more than ordinary force, justified only when exceptional resistance occurs and there is no other way to make the arrest. (7)

excited delirium describes the manifestations of extreme drug abuse; may occur in people under the influence of an illicit stimulant substance such as cocaine or in people with a history of mental illness who are not taking their medications. (18)

exclusionary rule established that the courts cannot accept evidence obtained by unreasonable searches and seizures, regardless of its relevance to the case (*Weeks v. United States; Mapp v. Ohio*). (4)

exculpatory evidence evidence favorable to the accused that would clear the accused of blame; for example, having a blood type different from that found at a homicide. (1)

excusable homicide unintentional, truly accidental killing of another person. (8)

exhibitionists people who gain sexual satisfaction by exposing themselves. (10)

exigent circumstances emergency situations; they do not require a warrant. (4)

expert witness person who has had special training, education or experience. (21)

exploitation taking unfair advantage of children or using them illegally. (11)

expressive violence stems from hurt feelings, anger or rage, in contrast to instrumental violence, which is goal-directed predatory behavior used to exert control. (8)

F

fellatio sexual activity involving oral contact with the male genitals. (10)

felonious assault *see* **aggravated assault**. (9)

felony serious crime such as homicide, aggravated assault or robbery; generally punishable by death or imprisonment of more than one year in a penitentiary . (1)

femicide murder of a woman. (9)

fence go-between who receives stolen goods for resale. (13)

field identification on-the-scene identification of a suspect by the victim of or witnesses to a crime, conducted within a short time after the crime was committed; also called *show-up identification*. (7)

field interview when questioning occurs spontaneously at the scene. (6)

finished scale drawing done in ink on a good grade of paper and drawn to scale, using exact measurements. (2)

fire triangle three elements necessary for a substance to burn: heat, fuel and air. (16)

firewall software or hardware protective measure that blocks ports of access to a computer or network to prevent unauthorized access and stop malicious programs from entering. (17)

first-degree murder premeditated killing of another person or killing someone while committing or attempting to commit a felony. (8)

first person use of *I, me, we* and *us* in speaking and writing; in contrast to the second person (*you*) and the third person (*he* or *this officer*). (3)

fixed surveillance observing a location from a fixed location; also called *plant* and *stakeout*. (7)

flaggers thieves who go around neighborhoods targeting mailboxes with their flags up, searching for envelopes containing checks and other forms of payment. (14)

flash mob theft technique where a mass of individuals rapidly enter, steal from and exit an establishment, overwhelming employees' capabilities to do anything about the situation; also called a *mob rob* or *swarming*. (19)

flashroll money used in an undercover drug buy. (18)

flipping *see* **property flipping**. (14)

floor-release limit maximum dollar amount that may be paid with a check or credit card without authorization from the central office unless the business assumes liability for any loss. (14)

fluffing increasing telephone rates without notification. (14)

force the amount of physical influence required to control a person's behavior under police authority. (7)

forcible rape sexual intercourse against a person's will by use or threat of force. (10)

forensic photogrammetry technique of extrapolating 3-D measurements directly from two-dimensional photographs. (2)

forensic science application of the physical sciences and their technology to examining physical evidence of crimes; includes the branch of criminalistics. (1,5)

forgery signing someone else's name to a document or altering the name or amount on a check or document with the intent to defraud. (14)

form *how* a narrative is written; in contrast to content, which is what is said in a narrative; the form of a well-written report is concise, clear, grammatically and mechanically correct and written in Standard English. (3)

fraud intentional deception to cause a person to give up property or some lawful right. (14)

frisk external search of an individual's clothing; also called a *patdown*. (4)

fruit-of-the-poisonous-tree doctrine established that evidence obtained as a result of an earlier illegality must be excluded from trial. (4)

full faith and credit legal status wherein a document, contract, license or court order issued anywhere in the country is legally binding and enforceable nationwide. (9)

fusion center a repository of intelligence and information, where analysts crunch data to produce actionable knowledge; a national network of such centers promotes and facilitates information and intelligence sharing among local, state and federal law enforcement agencies in an effort to fight crime and terrorism. (20)

G

gang a group of people who form an allegiance for a common purpose and engage in unlawful or criminal activity. (19)

geographic profiling uses the fact that everyone has a pattern to their lives, particularly in relation to the geographical areas they frequent, to help identify suspects who commit multiple crimes (serial criminals). (7)

good-faith doctrine established that illegally obtained evidence may be admissible if the police were truly not aware that they were violating the suspect's Fourth Amendment rights. (4)

goods property, including anything that is tangible and has value; for example, gas, clothing, money, food and animals. (14)

gouging charging undisclosed fees when calls are made from pay phones or hotel rooms. (14)

graffiti wall writing; sometimes called the "newspaper of the street." (19)

grand larceny felony based on the substantial value of the property stolen. (14)

H

hacker computer buff; one who intrudes into another's computer or network for the challenge and status; not necessarily a negative term; in contrast to a *cracker*, who is someone who intrudes to commit a crime. (17)

hacktivism using cyberspace to harass or sabotage sites that conduct activities or advocate philosophies that hacktivists find unacceptable. (17)

hallucinogen a drug that induces hallucinations or perceptual distortions of reality; e.g., LSD, DMT and PCP or angel dust. (18)

Hand of Glory left hand of a person who has died. (19)

hardware disabler device designed to ensure a self-destruct sequence of any potential evidence; it may be present on or around a computer, with a remote power switch being the most prevalent of the disabler hardware devices. (17)

hate crime in which the defendant intentionally selects a victim, or in the case of a property crime, the property that is the object of the crime, because of the actual or perceived race, color, national origin, ethnicity, gender, disability or sexual orientation of any person; also called *bias crime*. (19)

hate incidents behaviors that, though motivated by bias against a victim's race, religion, ethnic/national origin, gender, age, disability or sexual orientation, are *not* criminal acts; for example, hostile or hateful speech, or other disrespectful or discriminatory behavior motivated by bias. (19)

hawala informal banking system based on trust and often bartering, common throughout the Middle East and used to transfer billions of dollars every year. (20)

heat of passion extremely volatile emotional condition. (8)

hebephile person who selects high school–age youths as sex victims. (11)

hesitation wounds less severe cutting marks caused by an individual's attempts to build up nerve before making a fatal cutting wound; indicates suicide. (8)

hit-and-run burglary theft in which a window is smashed to steal merchandise; also called *smash and grab*. (13)

holder person to whom a credit or debit card is issued and who agrees to pay obligations arising from its use. (14)

homicide killing of one person by another. (8)

hot spots geographic areas with a higher incidence rate of criminal activity. (1)

I

identity theft criminal act of assuming someone else's identity for some type of gain, normally financial. (14)

igniters substances or devices used to start a fire. (16)

imaging making a byte-by-byte copy of everything on the hard drive. (17)

immediate control within a person's reach. (4)

immersive imaging 360-degree photographic view of a crime scene that allows viewers to virtually "walk through it" as though they were there. (2)

impeach to discredit testimony; to challenge the truth or accuracy of what a prosecution witness testified to under direct examination. (21)

incantation verbal spell, ritualistic prayer. (19)

incest sexual intercourse between family members or close relatives, including children related by adoption. (10)

in custody (custodial arrest) that point at which an officer has decided a suspect is not free to leave, there has been considerable deprivation of the suspect's liberty or the officer has arrested the suspect. (6)

indecent exposure revealing one's genitals to another person to such an extent as to shock the other's sense of decency. (10)

indicator crimes offenses that, in situations involving the same victim and suspect, can establish a pattern of events indicative of an abusive relationship; can range from harassing phone calls to hit-and-run. (9)

indirect evidence evidence from which inferences are drawn; fact or event that tends to incriminate a person in a crime; for example, being seen running from a crime scene; also called *circumstantial evidence*. (5)

indirect question skirts the issue; for example, "How do you and the victim get along?"; should be used sparingly, if at all. (6)

individual characteristics features that distinguish one item from others of the same type; also called *identifying characteristics*. (5)

inductive reasoning going from the generalization and establishing it by gathering specific facts. (1)

inevitable-discovery doctrine established that if illegally obtained evidence would in all likelihood eventually have been discovered legally, it may be used. (4)

informant any individual who can provide information related to a case but who is not a complainant, witness, victim or suspect. (6)

information age period driven by information rather than by agriculture or industry as in the past. (6)

inkless fingerprint digital, live-scan capture of a fingerprint that can be stored in a database for rapid retrieval. (5)

in loco parentis having the authority to take the place of the parent; teachers usually have this right. (9)

instrumental violence goal-directed predatory behavior used to exert control, in contrast to expressive violence, which stems from hurt feelings, anger or rage. (8)

integration third and final step in the money laundering cycle, where criminals repatriate their money through seemingly legitimate business transactions. (14)

integrity of evidence referring to the requirement that any item introduced in court must be in the same condition as when it was found at the crime scene. (5)

Internet Protocol (IP) address unique number, analogous to a phone number, needed to access the Internet; commonly issued by a user's Internet service provider (ISP). (17)

interrogation questioning people suspected of direct or indirect involvement in the crime being investigated. (6)

interview questioning people not suspected of being involved in a crime but who know something about the crime or the individuals involved in it. (6)

intifada armed uprising of Palestinians against Israel's occupation of the West Bank and the Gaza strip. (20)

intimate parts usually refers to the primary genital areas, groin, inner thighs, buttocks and breasts. (10)

intuition a "sudden knowing" without any conscious reasoning or apparent logic; based on knowledge and experience or what is commonly called *street sense*; a "gut feeling" developed by experience. (1)

investigate to observe or study closely; to inquire into something systematically in a search for truthful information. (1)

involuntary manslaughter accidental homicide that results from extreme (culpable) negligence. (8)

ISP Internet service provider; a company that offers access to the Internet for a fee. (17)

J

jamming setting up roadblocks to make it difficult to switch in-state long-distance service. (14)

jihad holy war. (20)

justifiable homicide killing another person under authorization of the law. (8)

K

keystroke logging diagnostic technique that captures a user's keystrokes; used in espionage to bypass security measures and obtain passwords or encryption keys; also called *keylogging*. (17)

kidnapping taking a person to another location by force, often for ransom. (11)

L

lane-search pattern partitions a crime scene into lanes, or narrow strips, by using stakes and strings or by having officers walk shoulder to shoulder or at arm's length. (4)

larceny/theft unlawful taking, carrying, leading or driving away of property from another's possession. (14)

laser-beam photography an imaging process that reveals evidence indiscernible to the naked eye, such as the outline of a footprint in a carpet, even though the fibers have returned to normal position. (2)

latent fingerprints print impressions transferred to a surface, either by sweat on the ridges of the fingers or because the fingers carry residue of oil, dirt, blood or other substances. (5)

layering second step in the money laundering process, where the money is "cleaned" by moving it around through a series of elaborate transactions, often involving offshore bank accounts and international business companies (IBCs). (14)

leading question prompts or leads a person to a specific response and often implies an answer; a useful interrogation technique. (6)

leads avenues bearing clues or potential sources of information relevant to solving a crime. (1)

leakage the illegal or unauthorized removal of cargo from the supply chain; a concept similar to that of *shrinkage*. (14)

legend that part of a crime scene sketch containing the case number, type of crime, name of victim or complainant, location, date, time, investigator, anyone assisting, scale of the sketch, direction of north and name of the person making the sketch. (2)

lewdness (with a minor) touching a minor to arouse, appeal to or gratify the perpetrator's sexual desires; the touching may be done by the perpetrator or by the minor under the perpetrator's direction. (11)

line of demarcation (fire) boundary between charred and uncharred material. (16)

livor mortis *see* **postmortem lividity**. (8)

loan-sharking lending money at exorbitant rates. (18)

Locard's principle of exchange basic forensic theory that objects that come in contact with each other always transfer material, however minute, to each other. (1)

logic bomb secretly attaches another program to a company's computer system; the attached program monitors the input data and waits for some type of error to occur; when this happens, the new program exploits the weakness to steal money or company secrets or to sabotage the system. (17)

long-con games schemes in which the victims are strung along and allowed to win several small stakes before being convinced to place the "big bet," in which they inevitably lose far more than they had won previously. (14)

loose tail moving surveillance in which it is more important to remain undetected than to keep the subject under constant observation. (7)

lust murder sex-related homicide involving a sadistic, deviant assault, where the killer depersonalizes the victim, sexually mutilates the body and may displace body parts. (8)

M

macrophotography photographic enlargement of a subject to show details of evidence such as fingerprints or tool marks. (2)

magick glue that binds occult groups; the supernatural act or force that causes a change in the environment. (19)

malicious intent (malice) element of first- and second-degree murder; implies ill will, wickedness, cruelty or recklessness. (8)

maltreatment includes neglect, medical neglect, physical abuse, sexual abuse and psychological maltreatment. (11)

malware contraction of "malicious software"; software developed to cause harm. (17)

mandated reporters certain individuals—including teachers, school authorities, child care personnel, camp personnel, clergy, physicians, dentists, chiropractors, nurses, psychologists, medical assistants, attorneys and social workers—who work with or treat children and are required by law to report cases of suspected neglect or abuse. (11)

manslaughter unlawful killing of another person with no prior malice; can be voluntary or involuntary. (8)

marker (photographic) item included in a photograph to show accurate or relative size. (2)

mass murder when multiple victims are killed in a single incident by one or a few suspects. (8)

material evidence that which is relevant to the specific case and forms a substantive part of the case presented or that has a legitimate and effective influence on the decision of the case. (5)

material photograph image that relates to the specific case and the subject being discussed. (2)

MDMA 3,4-Methylenedioxymethylamphetamine, known more commonly as *Ecstasy*; a powerful stimulant derivative of amphetamine or speed. (18)

mechanics use of spelling, capitalization and punctuation in written communication. (3)

megapixel pixels are the dots making up a digital image; one megapixel is about a million dots. (2)

microphotography taking pictures through a microscope to help identify minute particles of evidence (e.g., hair or fiber). (2)

minor person under the legal age for becoming an adult, the most common being under the age of 16 or 18, depending on the state. (11)

Miranda warning informs suspects of their right to remain silent, to have counsel present and to have the state appoint and pay counsel if they cannot afford one; it also warns suspects that anything they say can be used against them in court. (6)

misdemeanor crime or offense that is less serious than a felony and is punishable by a fine or imprisonment of as long as one year in an institution other than a penitentiary. (1)

misoped person who hates children, has sex with them and then brutally murders them. (11)

modus operandi (MO) characteristic way a criminal commits a specific type of crime. (1)

molestation (sexual) acts motivated by unnatural or abnormal sexual interest in minors that would reasonably be expected to disturb, irritate or offend the victim; no touching of the victim is necessary. (11)

money laundering converting illegally earned (dirty) cash to one or more alternative forms (clean) to conceal its illegal origin and true ownership. (14)

moniker gang member's street name; nickname. (19)

motion in limine request for the judge to issue a protective order against prejudicial questions or statements. (21)

motor vehicle any self-propelled device for moving persons or property or pulling implements, whether operated on land, on water or in the air; includes automobiles, trucks, buses, motorcycles, motor scooters, mopeds, snowmobiles, vans, self-propelled watercraft and aircraft. (15)

mug shots photographs of those who have been taken into custody and booked. (2)

mules individuals who sell or transport drugs for a regular dealer in return for being assured of a personal drug supply. (18)

mummification complete dehydration of all body tissues that occurs when a cadaver is left in an extremely dry, hot area. (8)

Munchausen syndrome involves self-induced or self-inflicted injuries. (11)

Munchausen by proxy syndrome (MBPS) a form of child abuse in which the parent or adult caregiver deliberately stimulates or causes medical distress in a child. (11)

murder see **first-**, **second-** and **third-degree murder.** (8)

N

narcotic drug that is physically and psychologically addicting; examples include heroin, morphine, codeine and cocaine. (18)

narrative technical report structured in chronological order describing a sequence of investigative events. (3)

neglect failure to meet a child's basic needs, including housing, food, clothing, education and access to medical care. (11)

network relationships, links between people and between people and their beliefs; two or more computers connected for the purpose of sharing data and resources. (6)

nightcapped provision court-approved stipulation that an arrest or search warrant may be carried out at night. (4)

no-knock warrant search warrant that contains a special provision permitting officers to execute the warrant without first announcing themselves. (4)

noncriminal homicide includes excusable and justifiable homicide. (8)

nonverbal communication messages conveyed by dress, eye contact, posture, gestures, distance, mannerisms, rate of speech and tone of voice. (6)

O

objective non-opinionated, fair and impartial. (3)

occult secret knowledge of supernormal powers; many cults claim to have such knowledge. (19)

open-ended question gives the victim, witness or suspect the opportunity to provide a much fuller response, allowing the investigator greater insight into the person's knowledge and feelings; often begins with "Why," "How" or "Tell me about"; should be asked liberally during interrogation. (6)

open tail no extraordinary means are used to remain undetected; also called a *rough tail*. (7)

oral copulation act of joining the mouth of one person with the sexual organ of another person; *see* **cunnilingus** and **fellatio**. (10)

ordinance act of the legislative body of a municipality or county relating to all the rules governing the municipality or county, including misdemeanor crimes. (1)

organized crime any group having some manner of a formalized structure and whose primary objective is to obtain money through illegal activities. (18)

osteogenesis imperfecta (OI) genetic disorder characterized by bones that break easily, often from little or no apparent cause; also called *brittle bone disease*. (11)

OTC drugs over-the-counter drugs, no prescription required. (18)

overlapping photographic technique whereby the entire scene is photographed in a clockwise direction so that a specific object is on the right side of the first photograph, on the next photo the same object is on the left side of the photo and so on until the entire scene is photographed. (2)

P

parallel proceedings pursing civil and criminal sanctions at the same time. (14)

particularity requirement dictates that a search conducted with a warrant must be limited to the specific area and specific items named in the warrant, as held in *Stanford v. Texas* (1965). (4)

past tense use of verbs that indicate that events have already occurred; for example, *lived* rather than *lives*. (3)

patdown *see* **frisk**. (4)

pedophile person who is sexually attracted to young children. (10, 11)

peeling (a safe) opening a safe by drilling a hole in a corner of the safe and then making the hole successively larger by using other drills until the narrow end of a jimmy can be inserted in the hole to pry the door partially open. (13)

penetration *see* **sexual penetration**. (10)

petty (petit) larceny a misdemeanor based on the value of the property stolen. (14)

pharming a cybercrime that involves the hijacking of a domain name for the purpose of redirecting online traffic away from a legitimate Web site toward a fake site, such as a bogus bank Web site; also refers to the dangerous act of rifling through the family medicine cabinet for pills, both OTC and prescription, combining everything in a bowl, scooping out and ingesting a handful and waiting to see what happens. (17,18)

phishing a method in which criminals misrepresent themselves as a trustworthy source to get victims to disclose personal, sensitive information, such as passwords, bank account numbers and the like, which is then used by the criminals to commit fraud or other crimes. (17)

phreaking exploiting the telephone system's vulnerabilities to acquire free access and usage; considered a type of electronic hacking. (17)

physical abuse beating, whipping, burning or otherwise inflicting physical harm upon a child. (11)

physical evidence anything real—that has substance—and helps establish the facts of a case. (5)

Pictometry® unique, patented computer technology that integrates various aerial shots of a land-based artifact taken straight down (orthogonal) and from numerous angles (oblique); the result is a high-resolution 3-D image of the object. (2)

piracy copying and using computer programs in violation of copyrights and trade secret laws. (17)

pixel smallest unit of a digital image, also referred to as a *dot*. (2)

placement first step in the process of laundering money that inserts the ill-gotten funds into the legitimate U.S. market; common methods include *smurfing* (technically known as *structuring*) whereby large amounts of cash are broken into increments less than $10,000 to avoid federal reporting requirements and then deposited into various bank accounts. (14)

plain feel/touch evidence object discovered by a police officer who is lawfully patting down a suspect's outer clothing and that is *immediately* identified, by touch, as contraband; a warrantless seizure is justified because there is no invasion of the suspect's privacy beyond that already authorized by the officer's search for weapons (*Minnesota v. Dickerson*, 1993). (4)

plain-view evidence unconcealed evidence that is seen by an officer engaged in a lawful activity. (4)

plant observing a location from a fixed location; also called *fixed surveillance* and *stakeout*. (7)

plastic fingerprints impressions left in soft substances such as putty, grease, tar, butter or soft soap. *See also* **visible prints**. (5)

poaching illegally taking or possessing fish, game or other wildlife, including deer, elk, bear, pheasant, ducks, wild turkeys and grouse. (14)

polygraph scientifically measures respiration and depth of breathing, changes in the skin's electrical resistance and blood pressure and pulse; also called *lie detector*. (6)

Ponzi scheme pyramid-type fraud scheme, named after Charles Ponzi, that involves using capital from new investors to pay off earlier investors, requiring an ever-expanding base of new investors to support the financial obligations to the existing "higher ups," which, eventually and inevitably, will collapse. (14)

port scanning looking for access (open "doors") into a computer. (17)

postmortem artifact an injury occurring after death from another source that can look like it was related to the homicide when it actually occurred from an outside source after death. (8)

postmortem lividity dark blue or purple discoloration of the body where blood has drained to the lowest level after death; also called *livor mortis* or simply *lividity*. (8)

PPI pixels per inch. (2)

premeditation considering, planning or preparing for an act, no matter how briefly, before committing it. (8)

presumptive evidence provides a reasonable basis for belief. (13)

pretextual traffic stops stops of vehicles when an officer's intent (pretext) was not the real reason for the stop; presence of an ulterior motive by an officer for the stop. (7)

prima facie evidence established by law; for example, the blood alcohol level for intoxication; also called *direct evidence*. (5)

probable cause what would lead a person of "reasonable caution" to believe that something connected with a crime is on the premises or person to be searched. (4)

probative evidence tends to prove or actually proves guilt or innocence; vital for the investigation or prosecution of a case. (5)

profiling *see* **psychological profiling**. (7)

property all forms of tangible property, real and personal, including valuable documents, electricity, gas, water, heat and animals. (14)

property flipping practice whereby an offender buys a property near its estimated market value, artificially inflates the property value through a false appraisal and then resells (flips) the property, often within days of the original purchase, for a greatly increased price; although flipping per se is not illegal, it often involves mortgage fraud, which is illegal. (14)

prostitution soliciting sexual intercourse for pay. (10)

protective sweep the authorized search by police of areas immediately adjoining the place of arrest, justified when reasonable suspicion exists that another person might be present who poses a danger to the arresting officers; held constitutional in *Maryland v. Buie* (1990); also called a *Buie sweep*. (4)

proxy data remnants of an interaction, transfer or exchange of material between two items (*see Locard's exchange principle*); the evidence analyzed by forensic scientists to uncover the relationships between people, places and objects. (5)

psychological profiling attempts to identify an individual's mental, emotional and psychological characteristics to provide investigators with corroborative information about a known suspect or possible leads to an unknown suspect; also called simply *profiling*. (7)

public safety exception ruling that police may interrogate a suspect without first giving the *Miranda* warning if a public threat exists that might be removed by having the suspect talk. (6)

pulling (dragging) a safe opening a safe by inserting a V plate behind the dial and tightening screw bolts on the edges of the V plate until the dial and the spindle are pulled out; this method, the opposite of punching, works on many older safes, but not on newer ones. (13)

punching (a safe) opening a safe by shearing the dial from the safe door by a downward blow with a sledge or by holding a chisel to the dial and using a sledge to knock it off, exposing the safe mechanism spindle. (13)

R

racial profiling occurs when an officer focuses on an individual as a suspect based solely on that person's race, excluding legitimate factors such as behavior; this is unconstitutional. (7)

raid a planned, organized invasion that uses the element of surprise to recover stolen property, seize evidence or arrest a suspect. (7)

rape having sexual intercourse with a person against his or her will. (10)

rapport understanding between individuals created by genuine interest and concern. (6)

raves dance parties that feature fast-paced, repetitive electronic music and accompanying light shows and usually entail the use of alcohol, tobacco and drugs. (18)

reasonable force amount of force a prudent person would use in similar circumstances. (7)

rebuttal testimony by a witness for the prosecution given to contradict the testimony (or evidence) presented by the defense. (21)

rectangular-coordinate (plotting) method uses two adjacent walls of a room as fixed points from which distances are measured at right angles from each wall. (2)

relevant evidence applies to the matter in question. (5)

relevant photograph image that assists or explains. (2)

***res gestae* statements** spontaneous statements made at the time a crime is committed and closely related to actions involved in the crime; considered more truthful than later, planned responses. (1)

residential burglary occurs in buildings, structures or attachments that are used as or are suitable for dwellings, even though they may be unoccupied at the time of the burglary. (13)

resolution fineness of image detail either captured with a camera, displayed on a monitor or printed on paper, commonly quantified by pixels. (2)

reverse buy labor-intensive, logistically complex narcotics investigation tactic; also called a *sting*. (18)

rifling lands and grooves inside a weapon, which grip and spin the bullet as it passes through the bore, providing greater projectile control and accuracy. (5)

rigor mortis stiffening of the joints of the body after death because of partial skeletal muscle contraction. (8)

ritual prescribed form of religious or mystical ceremony. (19)

ritualistic crime unlawful act committed within the context of a ceremony. (19)

robbery felonious taking of another's property, either directly from the person or in the person's presence, through force or intimidation. (12)

robotripping slang for the act of drinking bottles of cough syrup, such as Robitussin DM, to get high. (18)

rogues' gallery mug shots gathered in files and displayed in groups. (2)

Rohypnol the "date rape drug," a sedative that dissolves rapidly when placed in a carbonated drink and acts quickly (20 to 30 minutes) to produce physical as well as mental incapacitation after ingestion. (10)

rough sketch first, pencil-drawn outline of the crime scene, which shows the location of objects and evidence within this outline. (2)

rough tail moving surveillance in which it does not matter if the surveillant is detected; also called an *open tail*. (7)

routine activity theory crime results from the convergence of three elements in time and space: the presence of likely or motivated offenders; the presence of suitable targets; and an absence of guardians to prevent the criminal act. (13)

rule on witnesses common exclusion of witnesses from the courtroom during a trial, in an effort to keep witnesses from hearing each other's testimony; also called the *witness sequestration rule*. (21)

S

sabbat gathering of witches. (19)

sadist person who receives sexual gratification from causing pain to others, often through mutilation. (10)

sadomasochistic abuse fettering, binding or otherwise physically restraining, whipping or torturing for sexual gratification. (10)

safe semiportable strongbox with a combination lock. (13)

scale used in sketching, determined by taking the longest measurement at the scene and dividing it by the longest measurement of the paper used for sketching. (2)

script kiddie a derogatory term used to describe a less talented hacker who must use script or programs (scripts) created by others to carry out a cyber attack; also called a *skiddie*. (17)

second-degree murder intent to cause the death of another, but without premeditation. (8)

sector (search pattern) *see* **zone search pattern**. (4)

serial murder killing of three or more victims with emotional time breaks between the killings. (8)

sexting a category of child pornography involving the sending or posting of a nude picture of oneself to another person or on the Internet, using a cell phone to transmit the image. (11)

sexual abuse includes sexually molesting a child, performing sexual acts with a child and statutory rape and seduction. (11)

sexual contact (illegal) any sexual act committed without the complainant's consent for the suspect's sexual or aggressive satisfaction. (10)

sexual exploitation (of a minor) to employ, use, persuade, induce, entice or coerce a minor to engage or assist in engaging in any sexually explicit conduct; for example, prostitution and pornography. (11)

sexually explicit conduct any type of sexual intercourse between persons of the same or opposite sex, bestiality, sadomasochistic abuse, lewd exhibition or masturbation. (10)

sexual penetration includes sexual intercourse, cunnilingus, fellatio, anal intercourse or any other intrusion, no matter how slight, into the victim's genital, oral or anal openings by the suspect's body or by an object; an emission of semen is not required. (10)

sexual seduction (of a minor) ordinary sexual intercourse, anal intercourse, cunnilingus or fellatio committed by a nonminor with a consenting minor. (11)

short-con games schemes in which victims are taken for whatever money they have on their person at the time of the swindle. (14)

show-up identification on-the-scene identification of a suspect by a victim of or witness to a crime; also called *field identification*. (7)

shrinkage unexplained or unauthorized reduction of inventory, merchandise, cash or any other asset from a retail establishment. (14)

simple arson intentional destruction by fire or explosives that does not create imminent danger to life or risk of great bodily harm. (16)

simple assault intentionally causing another person to fear immediate bodily harm or death or intentionally inflicting or attempting to inflict bodily harm on another; usually a misdemeanor. (9)

sinsemilla homegrown marijuana. (18)

sketch drawing (noun), or to create a drawing (verb); may be a rough or a finished sketch; accurately portrays the physical facts, relates to the sequence of events at the scene, establishes the precise location and relationship of objects and evidence at the scene, helps create a mental picture of the scene for those not present, is a permanent record of the scene and is usually admissible in court. (2)

skimming electronic crime method in which a device is placed in a card reader, such as that found at an ATM, to record sensitive information, such as bank account numbers, credit cards numbers and passwords. (17)

skittling ingesting high doses of Coricidin Cough and Cold ("Triple C") tablets to get high. (18)

slamming the unauthorized switch of a long-distance carrier. (14)

slanting including only one side of a story or only facts that tend to prove or support one side's theory; result of a lack of objectivity. (3)

sleeper cell a group of terrorists who blend into a community. (20)

sliding occurs when an unauthorized carrier switches a specific call from the long-distance carrier. (14)

smash and grab in burglary, breaking a window and taking items from the window display. (13)

smurfing more technically known as *structuring*; a method of money laundering whereby large amounts of cash are broken into increments less than $10,000 to avoid federal reporting requirements and deposited into various bank accounts. (14)

sniffing monitoring data traveling along a network. (17)

sodomy any form of anal or oral copulation. (10)

solvability factors those crucial to resolving criminal investigations. (7)

sources-of-information file contains the name and location of persons, organizations and records that can assist in a criminal investigation. (6)

spalling breaking off of surface pieces of concrete, cement or brick because of intense heat. (16)

spam unsolicited bulk e-mail messages, similar in concept to junk mail and commonly commercial in nature; less commonly known by its formal designation as *unsolicited commercial email* (UCE). (17)

spoofing acquiring unauthorized access to a computer or network through a message using an IP address that appears to be from a trusted host; often considered synonymous with *phishing*. (17)

spyware malicious, covert (difficult to detect) software that infects a computer in a manner similar to viruses, collecting information or executing other programs without the user's knowledge; some programs can track which Web sites a user visits and some can track and capture personal user information. (17)

stake in conformity constellation of variables that, in effect, influence someone to take a particular course of action; for offenders, it constitutes what they stand to lose if convicted, such as marital status, residential stability or employment. (9)

stakeout observing a location from a fixed location; also called *fixed surveillance* and *plant*. (7)

stalking the willful or intentional commission of a series of acts that would cause a reasonable person to fear death or serious bodily injury and that, in fact, does place the victim in fear of death or serious bodily injury. (9)

standard of comparison object, measure or model with which evidence is compared to determine whether both originated from the same source. (5)

statement legal narrative description of events related to a crime. (6)

static IP address an IP address that does not change. (17)

statutory rape sexual intercourse with a minor, with or without consent. (10)

steganography Greek for "hidden writing"; aims to keep everyone except the intended recipient of a message oblivious to its very existence by making the message appear as some type of "cover" message—a shopping list, a picture, etc. (17)

sting complex operation organized and implemented by undercover agents to apprehend criminals, especially drug dealers; also called a *reverse buy*. (18)

Stockholm syndrome psychological phenomenon where hostages bear no ill feelings toward the hostage takers and fear the police more than their captors. (12)

street gang a group of individuals who form a social allegiance and engage in unlawful or criminal activity. (19)

striations highly individualized and characteristic scratches made on a projectile (bullet) as it passes through a weapon's rifling; provide valuable comparison evidence on recovered bullets. (5)

strikers firefighters who set fires to become heroes in putting them out. (16)

strip-search pattern adaptation of the lane search pattern that is used when only one officer is available to search. (4)

structuring common method of money laundering whereby large amounts of cash are broken into increments less than $10,000 to avoid federal reporting requirements and deposited into various bank accounts; also called *smurfing*. (14)

subject what is observed during surveillance; for example, a person, place, property, vehicle, group of people, organization or object. (7)

subpoena written order to appear before the court. (21)

sudden infant death syndrome (SIDS) tragic condition, whose cause is uncertain, that takes the lives of young victims and for which parents may become suspected of child abuse. (11)

suicide intentionally taking one's own life. (8)

suicide by police situation where a person decides he or she wants to die but doesn't want to pull the trigger and so, therefore, creates a situation where police are forced to shoot. (8)

surrebuttal testimony by a witness for the defense given to contradict the testimony (or evidence) presented by the prosecution. (21)

surveillance covert, discreet observation of people or places. (7)

surveillant plainclothes investigator assigned to surveillance. (7)

T

tail following people or vehicles on foot or in a vehicle to observe their actions or destinations. (7)

target hardening altering physical characteristics of a property to make it less attractive to criminals; also called *crime prevention through environmental design (CPTED)*. (13)

technological terrorism includes attacks on technology as well as by technology. (20)

telematic technology transfers data between a remote vehicle and a host computer, such as with bait cars. (15)

temporary custody without hearing removing a child from the custody of parents or guardians for a brief period, usually 48 hours. (11)

terrorism unlawful use of force or violence against persons or property to intimidate or coerce a government, the civilian population or any segment thereof, in furtherance of political or social objectives. (20)

***Terry* stop** detaining, questioning and possible frisking of an individual based on an officer's *reasonable suspicion* of that individual's involvement in criminal activity. (4)

testimonial hearsay prior testimony or statements made as a result of police interrogation; a witness's statement obtained through "structured questioning" by police officers that is inadmissible in a criminal trial unless the witness is unavailable to testify and was previously cross-examined by the defendant. (6)

theft *see* **larceny**. (14)

the well area within the courtroom that exists in front of the judge and between the judge and the attorneys' tables; normally off-limits and to be entered only if the judge so directs or permission is granted; traditionally, the area is a sword's length and was intended for the judge's protection. (21)

third degree use of physical force, threats of force or other physical, mental or psychological abuse to induce a suspect to confess. (6)

third-degree murder death that results from an imminently dangerous act but does not involve premeditation or intent. (8)

tight tail *see* **close tail**. (7)

tool mark impression left by a tool on a surface. (5)

totality-of-the-circumstances test principle upon which a number of legal assessments are made; refers to the sum total of factors leading a reasonable person to a course of action. (4)

toxicology study of poisons; toxicologists are consulted if food or drink poisoning is suspected. (8)

trace evidence extremely small physical matter. (5)

trailer path, consisting of paper, hay, flammable compounds or any other substance that burns, that is set down for a fire to follow; indicates arson. (16)

trap photography photos that prove an incident occurred; can assist in identifying suspects and the weapons used; can also corroborate witness testimony and identification; also called *surveillance photography*. (2)

triangulation (plotting method) uses straight-line measurements from two fixed objects to the evidence to create a triangle with the evidence in the angle formed by the two straight lines; the degree of the angle formed at the location of the object or evidence can then be measured with a protractor. (2)

Trojan horse malicious program hidden inside an apparently harmless, legitimate program and intended to carry out unauthorized or illegal functions. (17)

true (uncontaminated) scene crime scene where no evidence has been introduced or removed except by the person(s) committing the crime. (4)

turf geographic area claimed by a gang; often marked by graffiti. (19)

tweaker methamphetamine addict. (18)

U

ultraviolet-light photography uses the low end of the color spectrum, which is invisible to human sight, to make visible impressions of bruises and injuries long after their occurrence; the type of weapon used can often be determined by examining its impression, developed using ultraviolet light. (2)

uncontaminated scene *see* **true scene**. (4)

undercover using an assumed identity to obtain information or evidence. (7)

URL Uniform Resource Locator; a string of characters representing an Internet resource. (17)

V

vault stationary security chamber of reinforced concrete, often steel-lined, with a combination lock. (13)

vehicle identification number *see* **VIN**. (15)

verified response policy procedure implemented by some law enforcement agencies, whereby they will not respond to a burglary alarm unless criminal activity is first confirmed through either an onsite security officer or some method of electronic surveillance, such as CCTV. (13)

victimless crime illegal activity in which the victim is a willing participant; for example, a person who bets. (18)

VIN (vehicle identification number) primary nonduplicated, serialized number assigned by the manufacturer to each vehicle manufactured; this number—critical in motor vehicle theft investigations—identifies the specific vehicle in question. (15)

visible fingerprints prints made when fingers are dirty or stained and leave their impression on a glossy or light-colored surface and can be dusted and lifted. (5)

voiceprint graphic record of an individual's voice characteristics made by a sound spectrograph of the energy patterns emitted by speech. (5)

voluntary manslaughter intentionally causing the death of another person in the heat of passion. (8)

voyeurism the act of gaining sexual pleasure from watching others when they are naked or engaged in sexual activity; a voyeur is often called a peeping Tom. (10)

W

waiver giving up of certain rights. (6)

white-collar crime business-related or occupational crime that involves illegal acts characterized by fraud, concealment or a violation of trust and does not depend on the actual or threatened use of physical force or violence; for example, embezzlement, computer crimes, bribery, pilferage; also called *corporate crime* or *economic crime*. (14)

wiretapping intercepting and recording telephone conversations by a mechanical device without the consent of either party in the conversation. (7)

witness sequestration rule common practice of excluding witnesses from the courtroom during a trial to prevent one witness from hearing another witness's testimony; also called the *rule on witnesses*. (21)

worm (computer) self-contained program that travels from machine to machine across network connections, often clogging networks and information systems as it spreads; need not become part of another program to propagate itself. (17)

Z

zero floor release requirement that all transactions by credit card be authorized. (14)

zombie computer that has been taken over by another computer, typically through infection with hidden software (virus) that allows the zombie machine to be accessed and controlled remotely, often with the intention of perpetrating attacks on other computers. (17)

zone (search pattern) search pattern in which an area is divided into equal squares and numbered and then each square is searched individually; also called *sector search pattern*. (4)

Author Index

Subject Index

S